Quantum Information Theory

Developing many of the major, exciting pre- and post-millennium developments from the ground up, this book is an ideal entry point for graduate students into quantum information theory. Significant attention is given to quantum mechanics for quantum information theory, and careful studies of the important protocols of teleportation, super-dense coding, and entanglement distribution are presented.

In this new edition, readers can expect to find over 100 pages of new material, including detailed discussions of Bell's theorem, the CHSH game, Tsirelson's theorem, the axiomatic approach to quantum channels, the definition of the diamond norm and its interpretation, and a proof of the Choi–Kraus theorem. Discussion of the importance of the quantum dynamic capacity formula has been completely revised, and many new exercises and references have been added. This new edition will be warmly welcomed by the upcoming generation of quantum information theorists and the already-established community of classical information theorists.

MARK M. WILDE is an Assistant Professor in the Department of Physics and Astronomy, and in the Center for Computation and Technology, at Louisiana State University in Baton Rouge, Louisiana. He is the recipient of a National Science Foundation Career Development Award and the APS-IUSSTF Professorship Award in Physics. He is also a Senior Member of the IEEE, and is currently serving as Associate Editor for Quantum Information Theory for the leading journal, *IEEE Transactions on Information Theory*. His current research interests are in quantum Shannon theory, quantum optical communication, quantum computational complexity theory, and quantum error correction.

Quantum Information Theory

Second Edition

MARK M. WILDE
Louisiana State University

CAMBRIDGE
UNIVERSITY PRESS

University Printing House, Cambridge CB2 8BS, United Kingdom

One Liberty Plaza, 20th Floor, New York, NY 10006, USA

477 Williamstown Road, Port Melbourne, VIC 3207, Australia

314-321, 3rd Floor, Plot 3, Splendor Forum, Jasola District Centre, New Delhi - 110025, India

79 Anson Road, #06-04/06, Singapore 079906

Cambridge University Press is part of the University of Cambridge.

It furthers the University's mission by disseminating knowledge in the pursuit of education, learning and research at the highest international levels of excellence.

www.cambridge.org
Information on this title: www.cambridge.org/9781107176164

First published 2013
Second edition 2017

A catalogue record for this publication is available from the British Library

ISBN 978-1-107-17616-4 Hardback

Cambridge University Press has no responsibility for the persistence or accuracy of URLs for external or third-party internet websites referred to in this publication, and does not guarantee that any content on such websites is, or will remain, accurate or appropriate.

Contents

Preface to the Second Edition

It has now been some years since I completed the first draft of the first edition of this book. In this time, I have learned much from many collaborators and I am grateful to them. During the past few years, Mario Berta, Nilanjana Datta, Saikat Guha, and Andreas Winter have strongly shaped my thinking about quantum information theory, and Mario and Nilanjana in particular have influenced my technical writing style, which is reflected in the new edition of the book. Also, the chance to work with them and others has led me to new research directions in quantum information theory that I never would have imagined on my own.

I am also thankful to Todd Brun, Paul Cuff, Ludovico Lami, Ciara Morgan, and Giannicola Scarpa for using the book as the main text in their graduate courses on quantum information theory and for feedback. One can try as much as possible to avoid typos in a book, but inevitably, they seem to show up in unexpected places. I am grateful to many people for pointing out typos or errors and for suggesting how to fix them, including Todd Brun, Giulio Chiribella, Paul Cuff, Dawei (David) Ding, Will Matthews, Milan Mosonyi, David Reeb, and Marco Tomamichel. I also thank Corsin Pfister for helpful discussions about unique linear extensions of quantum physical evolutions. I am grateful to David Tranah and the editorial staff at Cambridge University Press for their help with publishing the second edition.

So what's new in the second edition? Suffice it to say that every page of the book has been rewritten and there are over 100 pages of new material! I formulated many thoughts about the revision during fall 2013 while teaching a graduate course on quantum information at LSU, and I then formulated many more thoughts and made the actual changes during fall 2015 (when teaching it again). In that regard, I am thankful to both the Department of Physics and Astronomy and the Center for Computation and Technology at LSU for providing a great environment and support. I also thank the graduate students at LSU who gave feedback during and after lectures. There are many little changes throughout that will probably go unnoticed. For example, I have come to prefer writing a quantum state shared between Alice and Bob as ρ_{AB} rather than ρ^{AB} (i.e., with system labels as subscripts rather than superscripts). Admittedly, several collaborators influenced me here, but there are a few good reasons for this convention: the phrase "state of a quantum system" suggests that the state ρ should be "resting on" the systems AB, the often-used partial trace $\text{Tr}_A\{\rho_{AB}\}$ looks better than $\text{Tr}_A\{\rho^{AB}\}$, and the notation ρ_{AB} is more consistent with the standard notation p_X for a probability distribution corresponding to a random variable X. OK, that's perhaps minor. Major changes include the addition of many new exercises, a detailed discussion of Bell's theorem, the CHSH game, and Tsirelson's theorem, the axiomatic approach to quantum channels, a proof of the Choi–Kraus theorem, a definition of unital and adjoint maps, a discussion of states, channels, and measurements all as quantum channels, the equivalence of purifications, the adjoint map in terms of isometric extension, the definition of the diamond norm and its interpretation, how a measurement achieves the fidelity, how the Hilbert–Schmidt distance is not monotone with respect to channels, more detailed definitions of classical and quantum relative entropies, new continuity bounds for classical and quantum entropies, refinements of classical entropy inequalities, streamlined proofs of data processing inequalities using relative entropy, the equivalence of quantum entropy inequalities like strong subadditivity and monotonicity of relative entropy, Chapter 12 on recoverability, modified proofs of additivity of channel information quantities, sequential decoding for classical communication, simpler proofs of the Schumacher compression theorem, a complete rewrite of Chapter 19, alternate proofs for the achievability part of the HSW theorem, a proof for the classical capacity of the erasure channel, simpler converse proofs for the entanglement-assisted capacity theorem, a revised proof of the trade-off coding resource inequality, a revised proof of the hashing bound, a simplified converse proof of the quantum dynamic capacity theorem, a completely revised discussion of the importance of the quantum dynamic capacity formula, and the addition of many new references that have been influential in recent years. Minor changes include improved presentations of many theorems and definitions throughout.

I am most grateful to my family for all of their support and encouragement throughout my life, including my mother, father, sister, and brother and all of my surrounding family members. I am still indebted to my wife Christabelle and her family for warmth and love. Christabelle has been an unending source of support and love for me. I dedicate this second edition to my nephews David and Matthew.

Preface to the First Edition

I began working on this book in the summer of 2008 in Los Angeles, with much time to spare in the final months of dissertation writing. I had a strong determination to review quantum Shannon theory, a beautiful area of quantum information science that Igor Devetak had taught me three years earlier at USC in fall 2005. I was carefully studying a manuscript entitled "Principles of Quantum Information Theory," a text that Igor had initiated in collaboration with Patrick Hayden and Andreas Winter. I read this manuscript many times, and many parts of it I understood well, though other parts I did not.

After a few weeks of reading and rereading, I decided "if I can write it out myself from scratch, perhaps I would then understand it!", and thus began the writing of the chapters on the packing lemma, the covering lemma, and quantum typicality. I knew that Igor's (now former) students Min-Hsiu Hsieh and Zhicheng Luo knew the topic well because they had already written several quality research papers with him, so I requested if they could meet with me weekly for an hour to review the fundamentals. They kindly agreed and helped me quite a bit in understanding the packing and covering techniques.

After graduating, I began collaborating with Min-Hsiu on a research project that Igor had suggested to the both of us: "find the triple trade-off capacity formulas of a quantum channel." This was perhaps the best starting point for me to learn quantum Shannon theory because proving this theorem required an understanding of most everything that had already been accomplished in the area. After a month of effort, I continued to work with Min-Hsiu on this project while joining Andreas Winter's Singapore group for a two-month visit. As I learned more, I added more to the notes, and they continued to grow.

After landing a job in the DC area for January 2009, I realized that I had almost enough material for teaching a course, and so I contacted local universities in the area to see if they would be interested. Can Korman, formerly chair of the Electrical Engineering Department at George Washington University, was excited about the possibility. His enthusiasm was enough to keep me going on the notes, and so I continued to refine and add to them in my spare time in preparing for teaching. Unfortunately (or perhaps fortunately?), the course ended up being canceled. This was disheartening to me, but in the mean time, I had contacted Patrick Hayden to see if he would be interested in having me join his group at

McGill University. Patrick Hayden and David Avis then offered me a postdoctoral fellowship, and I moved to Montréal in October 2009. After joining, I learned a lot by collaborating and discussing with Patrick and his group members. Patrick offered me the opportunity to teach his graduate class on quantum Shannon theory while he was away on sabbatical, and this encouraged me further to persist with the notes.

I am grateful to everyone mentioned above for encouraging and supporting me during this project, and I am also grateful to everyone who provided feedback during the course of writing up. In this regard, I am especially grateful to Dave Touchette for detailed feedback on all of the chapters in the book. Dave's careful reading and spotting of errors has immensely improved the quality of the book. I am grateful to my father, Gregory E. Wilde, Sr., for feedback on earlier chapters and for advice and love throughout. I thank Ivan Savov for encouraging me, for feedback, and for believing that this is an important scholarly work. I also thank Constance Caramanolis, Raza-Ali Kazmi, John M. Schanck, Bilal Shaw, and Anna Vershynina for valuable feedback. I am grateful to Min-Hsiu Hsieh for the many research topics we have worked on together that have enhanced my knowledge of quantum Shannon theory. I thank Michael Nielsen and Victor Shoup for advice on Creative Commons licensing and Kurt Jacobs for advice on book publishing. I am grateful to Sarah Payne and David Tranah of Cambridge University Press for their extensive feedback on the manuscript and their outstanding support throughout the publication process. I acknowledge funding from the MDEIE (Quebec) PSR-SIIRI grant.

I am indebted to my mentors who took me on as a student. Todd Brun was a wonderful PhD supervisor—helpful, friendly, and encouraging of creativity and original pursuit. Igor Devetak taught me quantum Shannon theory in fall 2005 and helped me once per week during his office hours. He also invited me to join Todd's and his group, and more recently, Igor provided much encouragement and "big-picture" feedback during the writing of this book. Bart Kosko shaped me as a scholar during my early years at USC and provided helpful advice regarding the book project. Patrick Hayden has been an immense bedrock of support at McGill. His knowledge of quantum information and many other areas is unsurpassed, and he has been kind, inviting, and helpful during my time at McGill. I am also grateful to Patrick for giving me the opportunity to teach at McGill and for advice throughout the development of this book.

I thank my mother, father, sister, and brother and all of my surrounding family members for being a source of love and support. Finally, I am indebted to my wife Christabelle and her family for warmth and love. I dedicate this book to the memory of my grandparents Joseph and Rose McMahon, and Norbert Jay and Mary Wilde. *Lux aeterna luceat eis, Domine.*

How To Use This Book

For Students

Prerequisites for understanding the content in this book are a solid background in probability theory and linear algebra. If you are new to information theory, then there should be enough background in this book to get you up to speed (Chapters 2, 10, 13, and 14). However, classics on information theory such as Cover & Thomas (2006) and MacKay (2003) could be helpful as a reference. If you are new to quantum mechanics, then there should be enough material in this book (Part II) to give you the background necessary for understanding quantum Shannon theory. The book of Nielsen & Chuang (2000), sometimes affectionately known as "Mike and Ike", has become the standard starting point for students in quantum information science and might be helpful as well. Some of the content of that book is available in the dissertation of Nielsen (1998). If you are familiar with Shannon's information theory (at the level of Cover & Thomas, 2006, for example), then the present book should be a helpful entry point into the field of quantum Shannon theory. We build on intuition developed classically to help in establishing schemes for communication over quantum channels. If you are familiar with quantum mechanics, it might still be worthwhile to review Part II because some content there might not be part of a standard course on quantum mechanics.

The aim of this book is to develop "from the ground up" many of the major, exciting pre- and post-millennium developments in the general area of study known as quantum Shannon theory. As such, we spend a significant amount of time on quantum mechanics for quantum information theory (Part II), we give a careful study of the important unit protocols of teleportation, super-dense coding, and entanglement distribution (Part III), and we develop many of the tools necessary for understanding information transmission or compression (Part IV). Parts V and VI are the culmination of this book, where all of the tools developed come into play for understanding many of the important results in quantum Shannon theory.

For Instructors

This book could be useful for self-learning or as a reference, but one of the main goals is for it to be employed as an instructional aid for the classroom.

To aid instructors in designing a course to suit their own needs, a draft, pre-publication copy of this book is available under a Creative Commons Attribution-NonCommercial-ShareAlike license. This means that you can modify and redistribute this draft, pre-publication copy as you wish, as long as you attribute the author, you do not use it for commercial purposes, and you share a modification or derivative work under the same license (for a readable summary of the terms of the license, see `http://creativecommons.org/licenses/by-nc-sa/3.0/`). These requirements can be waived if you obtain permission directly from the author. By releasing the draft, pre-publication copy of the book under this license, I expect and encourage instructors to modify it for their own needs. This will allow for the addition of new exercises, new developments in the theory, and the latest open problems. It might also be a helpful starting point for a book on a related topic, such as network quantum Shannon theory.

I used an earlier version of this book in a one-semester course on quantum Shannon theory at McGill University during the winter semester 2011 (in many parts of the USA, this semester is typically called "spring semester"). We almost went through the entire book, but it might also be possible to spread the content over two semesters instead. Here is the order in which we proceeded:

1. Introduction in Part I.
2. Quantum mechanics in Part II.
3. Unit protocols in Part III.
4. Chapter 9 on distance measures, Chapter 10 on classical information and entropy, and Chapter 11 on quantum information and entropy.
5. The first part of Chapter 14 on classical typicality and Shannon compression.
6. The first part of Chapter 15 on quantum typicality.
7. Chapter 18 on Schumacher compression.
8. Back to Chapters 14 and 15 for the method of types.
9. Chapter 19 on entanglement concentration.
10. Chapter 20 on classical communication.
11. Chapter 21 on entanglement-assisted classical communication.
12. The final explosion of results in Chapter 22 (one of which is a route to proving the achievability part of the quantum capacity theorem).

The above order is just a particular order that suited the needs for the class at McGill, but other orders are of course possible. One could sacrifice the last part of Part III on the unit resource capacity region if there is no desire to cover the quantum dynamic capacity theorem. One could also focus on going from classical communication to private classical communication to quantum communication in order to develop some more intuition behind the quantum capacity theorem. I later did this when teaching the course at LSU in fall 2013. But just recently in fall 2015, I went back to the ordering above while including lectures devoted to the CHSH game and the new results in Chapter 12.

Other Sources

There are many other sources to obtain a background in quantum Shannon theory. The standard reference has become the book of Nielsen & Chuang (2000), but it does not feature any of the post-millennium results in quantum Shannon theory. Other excellent books that cover some aspects of quantum Shannon theory are (Hayashi, 2006, Holevo, 2002a, Holevo, 2012, Watrous, 2015). Patrick Hayden has had a significant hand as a collaborative guide for many PhD and Masters' theses in quantum Shannon theory, during his time as a postdoctoral fellow at the California Institute of Technology and as a professor at McGill University. These include the theses of Yard (2005), Abeyesinghe (2006), Savov (2008), Savov (2012), Dupuis (2010), and Dutil (2011). All of these theses are excellent references. Hayden also had a strong influence over the present author during the development of the first edition of this book.

Part I

Introduction

1 Concepts in Quantum Shannon Theory

In these first few chapters, our aim is to establish a firm grounding so that we can address some fundamental questions regarding information transmission over quantum channels. This area of study has become known as "quantum Shannon theory" in the broader quantum information community, in order to distinguish this topic from other areas of study in quantum information science. In this text, we will use the terms "quantum Shannon theory" and "quantum information theory" somewhat interchangeably. We will begin by briefly overviewing several fundamental aspects of the quantum theory. Our study of the quantum theory, in this chapter and future ones, will be at an abstract level, without giving preference to any particular physical system such as a spin-$1/2$ particle or a photon. This approach will be more beneficial for the purposes of our study, but, here and there, we will make some reference to actual physical systems to ground us in reality.

You may be wondering, what is *quantum Shannon theory* and why do we name this area of study as such? In short, quantum Shannon theory is the study of the ultimate capability of noisy physical systems, governed by the laws of quantum mechanics, to preserve information and correlations. Quantum information theorists have chosen the name *quantum Shannon theory* to honor Claude Shannon, who single-handedly founded the field of classical information theory with a groundbreaking paper (Shannon, 1948). In particular, the name refers to the asymptotic theory of quantum information, which is the main topic of study in this book. Information theorists since Shannon have dubbed him the "Einstein of the information age."[1] The name *quantum Shannon theory* is fit to capture this area of study because we often use quantum versions of Shannon's ideas to prove some of the main theorems in quantum Shannon theory.

We prefer the name "quantum Shannon theory" over such names as "quantum information science" or just "quantum information." These other names are too broad, encompassing subjects as diverse as quantum computation, quantum algorithms, quantum complexity theory, quantum communication complexity, entanglement theory, quantum key distribution, quantum error correction, and

---

[1] It is worthwhile to look up "Claude Shannon—Father of the Information Age" on YouTube and watch several renowned information theorists speak with awe about "the founding father" of information theory.

even the experimental implementation of quantum protocols. Quantum Shannon theory does overlap with some of the aforementioned subjects, such as quantum computation, entanglement theory, quantum key distribution, and quantum error correction, but the name "quantum Shannon theory" should evoke a certain paradigm for quantum communication with which the reader will become intimately familiar after some exposure to the topics in this book. For example, it is necessary for us to discuss *quantum gates* (a topic in quantum computing) because quantum Shannon-theoretic protocols exploit them to achieve certain information-processing tasks. Also, in Chapter 23, we are interested in the ultimate limitation on the ability of a noisy quantum communication channel to transmit private information (information that is secret from any third party besides the intended receiver). This topic connects quantum Shannon theory with quantum key distribution because the private information capacity of a noisy quantum channel is strongly related to the task of using the quantum channel to distribute a secret key. As a final connection, one of the most important theorems of quantum Shannon theory is the *quantum capacity theorem*. This theorem determines the ultimate rate at which a sender can reliably transmit quantum information over a quantum channel to a receiver. The result provided by the quantum capacity theorem is closely related to the theory of quantum error correction, but the mathematical techniques used in quantum Shannon theory and in quantum error correction are so different that these subjects merit different courses of study.

Quantum Shannon theory intersects two of the great sciences of the twentieth century: the quantum theory and information theory. It was really only a matter of time before physicists, mathematicians, computer scientists, and engineers began to consider the convergence of the two subjects because the quantum theory was essentially established by 1926 and information theory by 1948. This convergence has sparked what we may call the "quantum information revolution" or what some refer to as the "second quantum revolution" (Dowling & Milburn, 2003, with the first revolution being the discovery of the quantum theory).

The fundamental components of the quantum theory are a set of postulates that govern phenomena on the scale of atoms. Uncertainty is at the heart of the quantum theory—"quantum uncertainty" or "Heisenberg uncertainty" is not due to our lack or loss of information or due to imprecise measurement capability, but rather, it is a fundamental uncertainty inherent in nature itself. The discovery of the quantum theory came about as a total shock to the physics community, shaking the foundations of scientific knowledge. Perhaps it is for this reason that every introductory quantum mechanics course delves into its history in detail and celebrates the founding fathers of the quantum theory. In this book, we do not discuss the history of the quantum theory in much detail but instead refer to several great introductory books for these details (Bohm, 1989; Sakurai, 1994; Griffiths, 1995; Feynman, 1998). Physicists such as Planck, Einstein, Bohr, de Broglie, Born, Heisenberg, Schrödinger, Pauli, Dirac, and von Neumann contributed to the foundations of the quantum theory in the 1920s and 1930s. We introduce the quantum theory by *briefly* commenting on its history and major underlying concepts.

Information theory is the second great foundational science for quantum Shannon theory. In some sense, it could be viewed as merely an application of probability theory. Its aim is to quantify the ultimate compressibility of information and the ultimate ability for a sender to transmit information reliably to a receiver. It relies upon probability theory because "classical" uncertainty, arising from our lack of total information about any given scenario, is ubiquitous throughout all information-processing tasks. The uncertainty in classical information theory is the kind that is present in the flipping of a coin or the shuffle of a deck of cards: the uncertainty due to imprecise knowledge. "Quantum" uncertainty is inherent in nature itself and is perhaps not as intuitive as the uncertainty that classical information theory measures. We later expand further on these differing kinds of uncertainty, and Chapter 4 shows how a theory of quantum information captures both kinds of uncertainty within one formalism.[2]

The history of classical information theory began with Claude Shannon. Shannon's contribution is heralded as one of the single greatest contributions to modern science because he established the field in his seminal paper (Shannon, 1948). In this paper, he coined the essential terminology, and he stated and justified the main mathematical definitions and the two fundamental theorems of information theory. Many successors have contributed to information theory, but most, if not all, of the follow-up contributions employ Shannon's line of thinking in some form. In quantum Shannon theory, we will notice that many of Shannon's original ideas are present, though they take a particular "quantum" form.

One of the major assumptions in both classical information theory and quantum Shannon theory is that local computation is free but communication is expensive. In particular, for the classical case, we assume that each party has unbounded computation available. For the quantum case, we assume that each party has a fault-tolerant quantum computer available at his or her local station and the power of each quantum computer is unbounded. We also assume that both communication and a shared resource are expensive, and for this reason, we keep track of these resources in a *resource count*. Sometimes, however, we might say that classical communication is free in order to simplify a scenario. A simplification like this one can lead to greater insights that might not be possible without making such an assumption.

We should first study and understand the postulates of the quantum theory in order to study quantum Shannon theory properly. Your heart may sink when you learn that the Nobel Prize-winning physicist Richard Feynman is famously quoted as saying, "I think I can safely say that nobody understands quantum

---

[2] Von Neumann established the density operator formalism in his 1932 book on the quantum theory. This mathematical framework captures both kinds of uncertainty (von Neumann, 1996).

mechanics." We should take the liberty of clarifying Feynman's statement. Of course, Feynman does not intend to suggest that no one knows how to work with the quantum theory. Many well-abled physicists are employed to spend their days exploiting the laws of the quantum theory to do fantastic things, such as the trapping of ions in a vacuum or applying the quantum tunneling effect in a transistor to process a single electron. I am hoping that you will give me the license to interpret Feynman's statement. I think he means that it is very difficult for us to understand the quantum theory intuitively because we do not experience the phenomena that it predicts. If we were the size of atoms and we experienced the laws of quantum theory on a daily basis, then perhaps the quantum theory would be as intuitive to us as Newton's law of universal gravitation.[3] Thus, in this sense, I would agree with Feynman—nobody can really understand the quantum theory because it is not part of our everyday experiences. Nevertheless, our aim in this book is to work with the laws of quantum theory so that we may begin to gather insights about what the theory predicts. Only by exposure to and practice with its postulates can we really gain an intuition for its predictions. It is best to imagine that the world in our everyday life does incorporate the postulates of quantum mechanics, because, indeed, as many, many experiments have confirmed, it does!

We delve into the history of the convergence of the quantum theory and information theory in some detail in this introductory chapter because this convergence does have an interesting history and is relevant to the topic of this book. The purpose of this historical review is not only to become familiar with the field itself but also to glimpse into the minds of the founders of the field so that we may see the types of questions that are important to think about when tackling new, unsolved problems.[4] Many of the most important results come about from asking simple, yet profound, questions and exploring the possibilities.

We first briefly review the history and the fundamental concepts of the quantum theory before delving into the convergence of the quantum theory and information theory. We build on these discussions by introducing some of the initial fundamental contributions to quantum Shannon theory. The final part of this chapter ends by posing some of the questions to which quantum Shannon theory provides answers.

---

[3] Of course, Newton's law of universal gravitation was a revolutionary breakthrough because the phenomenon of gravity is not entirely intuitive when a student first learns it. But we do experience the gravitational law in our daily lives, and I would argue that this phenomenon is much more intuitive than, say, the phenomenon of quantum entanglement.

[4] Another way to discover good questions is to attend parties that well-established professors hold. The story goes that Oxford physicist David Deutsch attended a 1981 party at the Austin, Texas house of reknowned physicist John Archibald Wheeler, in which many attendees discussed the foundations of computing (Mullins, 2001). Deutsch claims that he could immediately see that the quantum theory would give an improvement for computation. A few years later, in 1985, he published an algorithm that was the first instance of a quantum speed-up over the fastest classical algorithm (Deutsch, 1985).

1.1   Overview of the Quantum Theory

1.1.1   Brief History of the Quantum Theory

A physicist living around 1890 would have been well pleased with the progress of physics, but perhaps frustrated at the seeming lack of open research problems. It seemed as though the Newtonian laws of mechanics, Maxwell's theory of electromagnetism, and Boltzmann's theory of statistical mechanics explained most natural phenomena. In fact, Max Planck, one of the founding fathers of the quantum theory, was searching for an area of study in 1874 and his advisor gave him the following guidance:

"In this field [of physics], almost everything is already discovered, and all that remains is to fill a few holes."

Two Clouds

Fortunately, Planck did not heed this advice and instead began his physics studies. Not everyone agreed with Planck's former advisor. Lord Kelvin stated in his famous April 1900 lecture that "two clouds" surrounded the "beauty and clearness of theory" (Kelvin, 1901). The first cloud was the failure of Michelson and Morley to detect a change in the speed of light as predicted by an "ether theory," and the second cloud was the ultraviolet catastrophe, the classical prediction that a blackbody emits radiation with an infinite intensity at high ultraviolet frequencies. Also in 1900, Planck started the quantum revolution that began to clear the second cloud. He assumed that light comes in discrete bundles of energy and used this idea to produce a formula that correctly predicts the spectrum of blackbody radiation (Planck, 1901). A great cartoon lampoon of the ultraviolet catastrophe shows Planck calmly sitting fireside with a classical physicist whose face is burning to bits because of the intense ultraviolet radiation that his classical theory predicts the fire is emitting (McEvoy & Zarate, 2004). A few years later, Einstein (1905) contributed a paper that helped to further clear the second cloud (he also cleared the first cloud with his other 1905 paper on special relativity). He assumed that Planck was right and showed that the postulate that light arrives in "quanta" (now known as the photon theory) provides a simple explanation for the photoelectric effect, the phenomenon in which electromagnetic radiation beyond a certain threshold frequency impinging on a metallic surface induces a current in that metal.

These two explanations of Planck and Einstein fueled a theoretical revolution in physics that some now call the first quantum revolution (Dowling & Milburn, 2003). Some years later, de Broglie (1924) postulated that every element of matter, whether an atom, electron, or photon, has both particle-like behavior and wave-like behavior. Just two years later, Schrödinger (1926) used the de Broglie idea to formulate a wave equation, now known as Schrödinger's equation, that governs the evolution of a closed quantum-mechanical system. His formalism later became known as wave mechanics and was popular among physicists because it appealed to notions with which they were already familiar. Meanwhile, Heisenberg (1925) formulated an "alternate" quantum theory called matrix mechanics. His theory used matrices and linear algebra, mathematics with which many physicists at the time were not readily familiar. For this reason, Schrödinger's wave mechanics was more popular than Heisenberg's matrix mechanics. In 1930, Paul Dirac published a textbook (now in its fourth edition and reprinted 16 times) that unified the formalisms of Schrödinger and Heisenberg, showing that they were actually equivalent (Dirac, 1982). In a later edition, he introduced the now ubiquitous "Dirac notation" for quantum theory that we will employ in this book.

After the publication of Dirac's textbook, the quantum theory then stood on firm mathematical grounding and the basic theory had been established. We thus end our historical overview at this point and move on to the fundamental concepts of the quantum theory.

1.1.2   Fundamental Concepts of the Quantum Theory

Quantum theory, as applied in quantum information theory, really has only a few important concepts. We review each of these aspects of quantum theory briefly in this section. Some of these phenomena are uniquely "quantum" but others do occur in the classical theory. In short, these concepts are as follows:[5]

1. indeterminism;
2. interference;
3. uncertainty;
4. superposition;
5. entanglement.

The quantum theory is *indeterministic* because the theory makes predictions about probabilities of events only. This aspect of quantum theory is in contrast with a deterministic classical theory such as that predicted by the Newtonian laws. In the Newtonian system, it is possible to predict, with certainty, the trajectories of all objects involved in an interaction if one knows only the initial positions and velocities of all the objects. This deterministic view of reality even led some to believe in determinism from a philosophical point of view. For instance, the mathematician Pierre-Simon Laplace once stated that a supreme intellect, colloquially known as "Laplace's demon," could predict all future events from present and past events:

"We may regard the present state of the universe as the effect of its past and the cause of its future. An intellect which at a certain moment would know all forces that set nature in motion, and all positions of all items of which nature is composed, if this intellect were also vast enough to submit these data to analysis, it would embrace in a single formula the movements of the greatest bodies of the universe and those of the tiniest atom; for such an intellect nothing would be uncertain and the future just like the past would be present before its eyes."

[5] I have used Todd A. Brun's list from his lecture notes (Brun, n.d.).

The application of Laplace's statement to atoms is fundamentally incorrect, but we can forgive him because the quantum theory had not yet been established in his time. Many have extrapolated from Laplace's statement to argue the invalidity of human free will. We leave such debates to philosophers.[6]

In reality, we never can possess full information about the positions and velocities of every object in any given physical system. Incorporating probability theory then allows us to make predictions about the probabilities of events and, with some modifications, the classical theory becomes an indeterministic theory. Thus, indeterminism is not a unique aspect of the quantum theory but merely a feature of it. But this feature is so crucial to the quantum theory that we list it among the fundamental concepts.

Interference is another feature of the quantum theory. It is also present in any classical wave theory—constructive interference occurs when the crest of one wave meets the crest of another, producing a stronger wave, while destructive interference occurs when the crest of one wave meets the trough of another, canceling out each other. In any classical wave theory, a wave occurs as a result of many particles in a particular medium coherently displacing one another, as in an ocean surface wave or a sound pressure wave, or as a result of coherent oscillating electric and magnetic fields, as in an electromagnetic wave. The strange aspect of interference in the quantum theory is that even a single "particle" such as an electron can exhibit wavelike features, as in the famous double slit experiment (see, e.g., Greene, 1999, for a history of these experiments). This quantum interference is what contributes wave–particle duality to every fundamental component of matter.

Uncertainty is at the heart of the quantum theory. Uncertainty in the quantum theory is fundamentally different from uncertainty in the classical theory (discussed in the former paragraph about an indeterministic classical theory). The archetypal example of uncertainty in the quantum theory occurs for a single particle. This particle has two complementary variables: its position and its momentum. The uncertainty principle states that it is impossible to know both the particle's position and momentum to arbitrary accuracy. This principle even calls into question the meaning of the word "know" in the previous sentence in the context of quantum theory. We might say that we can only know that which we measure, and thus, we can only know the position of a particle after performing a precise measurement that determines it. If we follow with a precise measurement of its momentum, we lose all information about the position of the particle after learning its momentum. In quantum information science, the BB84 protocol for quantum key distribution exploits the uncertainty principle and statistical analysis to determine the presence of an eavesdropper on a quantum communication channel by encoding information into two complementary variables (Bennett & Brassard, 1984).

---

[6] John Archibald Wheeler may disagree with this approach. He once said, "Philosophy is too important to be left to the philosophers" (Misner et al., 2009).

The *superposition* principle states that a quantum particle can be in a linear combination state, or *superposed state*, of any two other allowable states. This principle is a result of the linearity of quantum theory. Schrodinger's wave equation is a linear differential equation, meaning that the linear combination $\alpha\psi + \beta\phi$ is a solution of the equation if ψ and ϕ are both solutions of the equation. We say that the solution $\alpha\psi + \beta\phi$ is a coherent superposition of the two solutions. The superposition principle has dramatic consequences for the interpretation of the quantum theory—it gives rise to the notion that a particle can somehow "be in one location and another" at the same time. There are different interpretations of the meaning of the superposition principle, but we do not highlight them here. We merely choose to use the technical language that the particle is in a superposition of both locations. The loss of a superposition can occur through the interaction of a particle with its environment. Maintaining an arbitrary superposition of quantum states is one of the central goals of a quantum communication protocol.

The last, and perhaps most striking, quantum feature that we highlight here is *entanglement*. There is no true classical analog of entanglement. The closest analog of entanglement might be a secret key that two parties possess, but even this analogy does not come close. Entanglement refers to the strong quantum correlations that two or more quantum particles can possess. The correlations in quantum entanglement are stronger than any classical correlations in a precise, technical sense. Schrödinger (1935) first coined the term "entanglement" after observing some of its strange properties and consequences. Einstein, Podolsky, and Rosen then presented an apparent paradox involving entanglement that raised concerns over the completeness of the quantum theory (Einstein et al., 1935). That is, they suggested that the seemingly strange properties of entanglement called the uncertainty principle into question (and thus the completeness of the quantum theory) and furthermore suggested that there might be some "local hidden-variable" theory that could explain the results of experiments. It took about 30 years to resolve this paradox, but John Bell did so by presenting a simple inequality, now known as a Bell inequality (Bell, 1964). He showed that any two-particle classical correlations that satisfy the assumptions of the "local hidden-variable theory" of Einstein, Podolsky, and Rosen must be less than a certain amount. He then showed how the correlations of two entangled quantum particles can violate this inequality, and thus, entanglement has no explanation in terms of classical correlations but is instead a uniquely quantum phenomenon. Experimentalists later verified that two entangled quantum particles can violate Bell's inequality (Aspect et al., 1981).

In quantum information science, the non-classical correlations in entanglement play a fundamental role in many protocols. For example, entanglement is the enabling resource in teleportation, a protocol that disembodies a quantum state in one location and reproduces it in another. We will see many other examples of entanglement throughout this book.

Entanglement theory concerns methods for quantifying the amount of entanglement present not only in a two-particle state but also in a multiparticle state. A large body of literature exists that investigates entanglement theory (Horodecki et al., 2009), but we only address aspects of it that are relevant in our study of quantum Shannon theory.

The above five features capture the essence of the quantum theory, but we will see more aspects of it as we progress through our overview in Chapters 3, 4, and 5.

1.2 The Emergence of Quantum Shannon Theory

In the previous section, we discussed several unique quantum phenomena such as superposition and entanglement, but it is not clear what kind of information these unique quantum phenomena represent. Is it possible to find a convergence of the quantum theory and Shannon's information theory, and if so, what is the convergence?

1.2.1 The Shannon Information Bit

A fundamental contribution of Shannon is the notion of a *bit* as a measure of information. Typically, when we think of a bit, we think of a two-valued quantity that can be in the state "off" or the state "on." We represent this bit with a binary number that can be "0" or "1." We also associate a physical representation with a bit—this physical representation can be whether a light switch is off or on, whether a transistor allows current to flow or not, whether a large number of magnetic spins point in one direction or another, the list going on and on. These are all physical notions of a bit.

Shannon's notion of a bit is quite different from these physical notions, and we motivate his notion with the example of a fair coin. Without flipping the coin, we have no idea what the result of a coin flip will be—our best guess at the result is to guess randomly. If someone else learns the result of a random coin flip, we can ask this person the question: What was the result? We then learn *one bit of information.*

Though it may seem obvious, it is important to stress that we do not learn any (or not as much) information if we do not ask the right question. This point becomes even more important in the quantum case. Suppose that the coin is not fair—without loss of generality, suppose the probability of "heads" is greater than the probability of "tails." In this case, we would not be as surprised to learn that the result of a coin flip is "heads." We may say in this case that we would learn less than one bit of information if we were to ask someone the result of the coin flip.

The Shannon binary entropy is a measure of information. Given a probability distribution $(p, 1 - p)$ for a binary random variable, its Shannon binary entropy is

$$h_2(p) \equiv -p \log p - (1 - p) \log(1 - p), \tag{1.1}$$

where (here and throughout the book, unless stated explicitly otherwise) the logarithm is taken base two. The Shannon binary entropy measures information in units of bits. We will discuss it in more detail in the next chapter and in Chapter 10.

The Shannon bit, or Shannon binary entropy, is a measure of the surprise upon learning the outcome of a random binary experiment. Thus, the Shannon bit has a completely different interpretation from that of the physical bit. The outcome of the coin flip resides in a physical bit, but it is the information associated with the random nature of the physical bit that we would like to measure. It is this notion of a bit that is important in information theory.

1.2.2   A Measure of Quantum Information

The above section discusses Shannon's notion of a bit as a measure of information. A natural question is whether there is an analogous measure of quantum information, but before we can even ask that question, we might first wonder: What is *quantum information*? As in the classical case, there is a *physical* notion of quantum information. A quantum state always resides "in" a physical system. Perhaps another way of stating this idea is that every physical system is in some quantum state. The physical notion of a quantum bit, or qubit for short (pronounced "cue · bit"), is a two-level quantum system. Examples of two-level quantum systems are the spin of the electron, the polarization of a photon, or an atom with a ground state and an excited state. The physical notion of a qubit is straightforward to understand once we have a grasp of the quantum theory.

A more pressing question for us in this book is to understand an *informational* notion of a qubit, as in the Shannon sense. In the classical case, we quantify information by the amount of knowledge we gain after learning the answer to a probabilistic question. In the quantum world, what knowledge can we have of a quantum state?

Sometimes we may know the exact quantum state of a physical system because we prepared the quantum system in a certain way. For example, we may prepare an electron in its "spin-up in the z direction" state, where $|\uparrow_z\rangle$ denotes this state. If we prepare the state in this way, we know for certain that the state is indeed $|\uparrow_z\rangle$ and no other state. Thus, we do not gain any information, or equivalently, there is no removal of uncertainty if someone else tells us that the state is $|\uparrow_z\rangle$. We may say that this state has zero qubits of quantum information, where the term "qubit" now refers to a measure of the quantum information of a state.

In the quantum world, we also have the option of measuring this state in the x direction. The postulates of quantum theory, given in Chapter 3, predict that the state will then be $|\uparrow_x\rangle$ or $|\downarrow_x\rangle$ with equal probability after measuring in the

x direction. One interpretation of this aspect of quantum theory is that the system does not have any definite state in the x direction: in fact there is maximal uncertainty about its x direction, if we know that the physical system has a definite z direction. This behavior is one manifestation of the Heisenberg uncertainty principle. So before performing the measurement, we have no knowledge of the resulting state and we gain one Shannon bit of information after learning the result of the measurement. If we use Shannon's notion of entropy and perform an x measurement, this classical measure loses some of its capability here to capture our knowledge of the state of the system. It is inadequate to capture our knowledge of the state because we actually prepared it ourselves and know with certainty that it is in the state $|\uparrow_z\rangle$. With these different notions of information gain, which one is the most appropriate for the quantum case?

It turns out that the first way of thinking is the one that is most useful for quantifying quantum information. If someone tells us the definite quantum state of a particular physical system, and this state is indeed the true state, then we have complete knowledge of the state and thus do not learn more "qubits" of quantum information from this point onward. This line of thinking is perhaps similar in one sense to the classical world, but different from the classical world, in the sense of the case presented in the previous paragraph.

Now suppose that a friend (let us call him "Bob") randomly prepares quantum states as a probabilistic ensemble. Suppose Bob prepares $|\uparrow_z\rangle$ or $|\downarrow_z\rangle$ with equal probability. With only this probabilistic knowledge, we acquire one bit of information if Bob reveals which state he prepared. We could also perform a quantum measurement on the system to determine what state Bob prepared (we discuss quantum measurements in detail in Chapter 3). One reasonable measurement to perform is a measurement in the z direction. The result of the measurement determines which state Bob actually prepared because both states in the ensembles are states with definite z direction. The result of this measurement thus gives us one bit of information—the same amount that we would learn if Bob informed us which state he prepared. It seems that most of this logic is similar to the classical case—i.e., the result of the measurement only gave us one Shannon bit of information.

Another measurement to perform is a measurement in the x direction. If the actual state prepared is $|\uparrow_z\rangle$, then the quantum theory predicts that the state becomes $|\uparrow_x\rangle$ or $|\downarrow_x\rangle$ with equal probability. Similarly, if the actual state prepared is $|\downarrow_z\rangle$, then the quantum theory predicts that the state again becomes $|\uparrow_x\rangle$ or $|\downarrow_x\rangle$ with equal probability. Calculating probabilities, the resulting state is $|\uparrow_x\rangle$ with probability $1/2$ and $|\downarrow_x\rangle$ with probability $1/2$. So the Shannon bit content of learning the result is again one bit, but we arrived at this conclusion in a much different fashion from the scenario in which we measured in the z direction. How can we quantify the *quantum information* of this ensemble? We claim for now that this ensemble contains one *qubit* of quantum information and this result derives from either the measurement in the z direction or the measurement in the x direction for this particular ensemble.

Let us consider one final example that perhaps gives more insight into how we might quantify quantum information. Suppose Bob prepares $|\uparrow_z\rangle$ or $|\uparrow_x\rangle$ with equal probability. The first state is spin-up in the z direction and the second is spin-up in the x direction. If Bob reveals which state he prepared, then we learn one Shannon bit of information. But suppose now that we would like to learn the prepared state on our own, without the help of our friend Bob. One possibility is to perform a measurement in the z direction. If the state prepared is $|\uparrow_z\rangle$, then we learn this result with probability $1/2$. But if the state prepared is $|\uparrow_x\rangle$, then the quantum theory predicts that the state becomes $|\uparrow_z\rangle$ or $|\downarrow_z\rangle$ with equal probability (while we learn what the new state is). Thus, quantum theory predicts that the act of measuring this ensemble inevitably disturbs the state some of the time. Also, there is no way that we can learn with certainty whether the prepared state is $|\uparrow_z\rangle$ or $|\uparrow_x\rangle$. Using a measurement in the z direction, the resulting state is $|\uparrow_z\rangle$ with probability $3/4$ and $|\downarrow_z\rangle$ with probability $1/4$. We learn less than one Shannon bit of information from this ensemble because the probability distribution becomes skewed when we perform this particular measurement.

The probabilities resulting from the measurement in the z direction are the same that would result from an ensemble where Bob prepares $|\uparrow_z\rangle$ with probability $3/4$ and $|\downarrow_z\rangle$ with probability $1/4$ and we perform a measurement in the z direction. The actual Shannon entropy of the distribution $(3/4, 1/4)$ is about 0.81 bits, confirming our intuition that we learn approximately less than one bit. A similar, symmetric analysis holds to show that we gain 0.81 bits of information when we perform a measurement in the x direction.

We have more knowledge of the system in question if we gain less information from performing measurements on it. In the quantum theory, we learn less about a system if we perform a measurement on it that does not disturb it too much. Is there a measurement that we can perform in which we learn the least amount of information? Recall that learning the least amount of information is ideal because it has the interpretation that we require fewer questions on average to learn the result of a random experiment. Indeed, it turns out that a measurement in the $x + z$ direction reveals the least amount of information. Avoiding details for now, this measurement returns a state that we label $|\uparrow_{x+z}\rangle$ with probability $\cos^2(\pi/8)$ and a state $|\downarrow_{x+z}\rangle$ with probability $\sin^2(\pi/8)$. This measurement has the desirable effect that it causes the least amount of disturbance to the original states in the ensemble. The entropy of the distribution resulting from the measurement is about 0.6 bits and is less than the one bit that we learn if Bob reveals the state. The entropy ≈ 0.6 is also the least amount of information among all possible sharp measurements that we may perform on the ensemble. We claim that this ensemble contains ≈ 0.6 *qubits* of quantum information.

We can determine the ultimate compressibility of classical data with Shannon's source coding theorem (we overview this technique in the next chapter). Is there a similar way that we can determine the ultimate compressibility of quantum information? This question was one of the early and profitable ones for quantum Shannon theory and the answer is affirmative. The technique for quantum compression is called Schumacher compression, named after Benjamin Schumacher. Schumacher used ideas similar to that of Shannon— he created the notion of a quantum information source that emits random physical qubits, and he invoked the law of large numbers to show that there is a so-called *typical subspace* where most of the quantum information really resides. This line of thought is similar to that which we will discuss in the overview of data compression in the next chapter. The size of the typical subspace for most quantum information sources is exponentially smaller than the size of the space in which the emitted physical qubits resides. Thus, one can "quantum compress" the quantum information to this subspace without losing much. Schumacher's quantum source coding theorem then quantifies, in an operational sense, the amount of actual quantum information that the ensemble contains. The amount of actual quantum information corresponds to the number of qubits, in the informational sense, that the ensemble contains. It is this measure that is equivalent to the "optimal measurement" one that we suggested in the previous paragraph. We will study this idea in more detail later when we introduce the quantum theory and a rigorous notion of a quantum information source.

Some of the techniques of quantum Shannon theory are the direct *quantum* analog of the techniques from classical information theory. We use the law of large numbers and the notion of the typical subspace, but we require generalizations of measures from the classical world to determine how "close" two different quantum states are. One measure, the *fidelity*, has the operational interpretation that it gives the probability that one quantum state would pass a test for being another. The *trace distance* is another distance measure that is perhaps more similar to a classical distance measure—its classical analog is a measure of the closeness of two probability distributions. The techniques in quantum Shannon theory also reside firmly in the quantum theory and have no true classical analog for some cases. Some of the techniques will seem similar to those in the classical world, but the answer to some of the fundamental questions in quantum Shannon theory are rather different from some of the answers in the classical world. It is the purpose of this book to explore the answers to the fundamental questions of quantum Shannon theory, and we now begin to ask what kinds of tasks we can perform.

1.2.3 Operational Tasks in Quantum Shannon Theory

Quantum Shannon theory has several resources that two parties can exploit in a quantum information-processing task. Perhaps the most natural quantum resource is a *noiseless qubit channel*. We can think of this resource as some medium through which a physical qubit can travel without being affected by any noise. One example of a noiseless qubit channel could be the free space through which a photon travels, where it ideally does not interact with any other particles along the way to its destination.[7]

A *noiseless classical bit channel* is a special case of a noiseless qubit channel because we can always encode classical information into quantum states. For the example of a photon, we can say that horizontal polarization corresponds to a "0" and vertical polarization corresponds to a "1." We refer to the dynamic resource of a noiseless classical bit channel as a *cbit*, in order to distinguish it from the noiseless qubit channel.

Perhaps the most intriguing resource that two parties can share is noiseless entanglement. Any entanglement resource is a *static resource* because it is one that they share. Examples of static resources in the classical world are an information source that we would like to compress or a common secret key that two parties may possess. We actually have a way of measuring entanglement that we discuss later on, and for this reason, we can say that a sender and receiver have bits of entanglement or *ebits*.

Entanglement turns out to be a useful resource in many quantum communication tasks. One example where it is useful is in the teleportation protocol, where a sender and receiver use one ebit and two classical bits to transmit one qubit faithfully. This protocol is an example of the extraordinary power of noiseless entanglement. The name "teleportation" is really appropriate for this protocol because the physical qubit vanishes from the sender's station and appears at the receiver's station after the receiver obtains the two transmitted classical bits. We will see later on that a noiseless qubit channel can generate the other two noiseless resources, but it is impossible for each of the other two noiseless resources to generate the noiseless qubit channel. In this sense, the noiseless qubit channel is the strongest of the three unit resources.

The first quantum information-processing task that we have discussed is Schumacher compression. The goal of this task is to use as few noiseless qubit channels as possible in order to transmit the output of a quantum information source reliably. After we understand Schumacher compression in a technical sense, the main focus of this book is to determine what quantum information-processing tasks a sender and receiver can accomplish with the use of a noisy quantum channel. The first and perhaps simplest task is to determine how much classical information a sender can transmit reliably to a receiver, by using a noisy quantum channel a large number of times. This task is known as HSW coding, named after its discoverers Holevo, Schumacher, and Westmoreland. The HSW coding theorem is one quantum generalization of Shannon's channel coding theorem (the latter overviewed in the next chapter). We can also assume that a sender and receiver share some amount of noiseless entanglement prior to communication. They can then use this noiseless entanglement in addition to a large number of uses of a noisy quantum channel. This task is known as *entanglement-assisted classical*

---

[7] We should be careful to note here that this is not actually a perfect channel because even empty space can be noisy in quantum mechanics, but nevertheless, it is a simple physical example to imagine.

communication over a noisy quantum channel. The capacity theorem corresponding to this task again highlights one of the marvelous features of entanglement. It shows that entanglement gives a boost to the amount of noiseless classical communication we can generate using a noisy quantum channel—the classical capacity is generally higher with entanglement assistance than without it.

One of the most important theorems for quantum Shannon theory is the *quantum channel capacity theorem*. Any proof of a capacity theorem consists of two parts: one part establishes a lower bound on the capacity and the other part establishes an upper bound. If the two bounds coincide, then we have a characterization of the capacity in terms of these bounds. The lower bound on the quantum capacity is colloquially known as the LSD coding theorem,[8] and it gives a characterization of the highest rate at which a sender can transmit quantum information reliably over a noisy quantum channel so that a receiver can recover it perfectly. The rate is generally lower than the classical capacity because it is more difficult to keep quantum information intact. As we have said before, it is possible to encode classical information into quantum states, but this classical encoding is only a special case of a quantum state. In order to preserve quantum information, we have to be able to preserve arbitrary quantum states, not merely a classical encoding within a quantum state.

The pinnacle of this book is in Chapter 24, where we finally reach our study of the quantum capacity theorem. All efforts and technical developments in preceding chapters have this goal in mind.[9] Our first coding theorem in the dynamic setting is the HSW coding theorem. A rigorous study of this coding theorem lays an important foundation—an understanding of the structure of a code for reliable communication over a noisy quantum channel. The method for the HSW coding theorem applies to the "entanglement-assisted classical capacity theorem," which is one building block for other protocols in quantum Shannon theory. We then develop a more complex coding structure for sending private classical information over a noisy quantum channel. In *private coding*, we are concerned with coding in such a way that the intended receiver can learn the transmitted message perfectly, but a third-party eavesdropper cannot learn anything about what the sender transmits to the intended receiver. This study of the private classical capacity may seem like a detour at first, but it is closely linked with our ultimate aim. The coding structure developed for sending private information proves to be indispensable for understanding the structure of a quantum code. There are strong connections between the goals of keeping classical information private and keeping quantum information coherent. In the private coding scenario, the goal is to avoid leaking any information to an eavesdropper so that she cannot

---

[8] The LSD coding theorem does not refer to the synthetic crystalline compound, lysergic acid diethylamide (which one may potentially use as a hallucinogenic drug), but refers rather to Lloyd (1997), Shor (2002b), and Devetak (2005), all of whom gave separate proofs of the lower bound on the quantum capacity with increasing standards of rigor.

[9] One goal of this book is to unravel the mathematical machinery behind Devetak's proof of the quantum channel coding theorem (Devetak, 2005).

learn anything about the transmission. In the quantum coding scenario, we can think of quantum noise as resulting from the environment learning about the transmitted quantum information and this act of learning disturbs the quantum information. This effect is related to the information–disturbance trade-off that is fundamental in quantum information theory. If the environment learns something about the state being transmitted, there is inevitably some sort of noisy disturbance that affects the quantum state. Thus, we can see a correspondence between private coding and quantum coding. In quantum coding, the goal is to avoid leaking any information to the environment because the avoidance of such a leak implies that there is no disturbance to the transmitted state. So the role of the environment in quantum coding is similar to the role of the eavesdropper in private coding, and the goal in both scenarios is to decouple either the environment or eavesdropper from the picture. It is then no coincidence that private codes and quantum codes have a similar structure. In fact, we can say that the quantum code inherits its structure from that of the private code.[10]

We also consider "trade-off" problems in addition to discussing the quantum capacity theorem. Chapter 22 is another high point of the book, featuring a whole host of results that emerge by combining several of the ideas from previous chapters. The most appealing aspect of this chapter is that we can construct virtually all of the protocols in quantum Shannon theory from just one idea in Chapter 21. Also, Chapter 22 provides partial answers to many practical questions concerning information transmission over noisy quantum channels. Some example questions are as follows:

- How much quantum and classical information can a noisy quantum channel transmit?
- An entanglement-assisted noisy quantum channel can transmit more classical information than an unassisted one, but how much entanglement is really necessary?
- Does noiseless classical communication help in transmitting quantum information reliably over a noisy quantum channel?
- How much entanglement can a noisy quantum channel generate when aided by classical communication?
- How much quantum information can a noisy quantum channel communicate when aided by entanglement?

These are examples of trade-off problems because they involve a noisy quantum channel and either the consumption or generation of a noiseless resource. For every combination of the generation or consumption of a noiseless resource, there is a corresponding coding theorem that states what rates are achievable (and, in

---

[10] There are other methods of formulating quantum codes using random subspaces (Shor, 2002b; Hayden, Horodecki, Winter & Yard, 2008; Hayden, Shor & Winter, 2008; Klesse, 2008), but we prefer the approach of Devetak because we learn about other aspects of quantum Shannon theory, such as the private capacity, along the way to proving the quantum capacity theorem.

some cases, optimal). Some of these trade-off questions admit interesting answers, but some of them do not. Our final aim in these trade-off questions is to determine the full triple trade-off solution where we study the optimal ways of combining all three unit resources (classical communication, quantum communication, and entanglement) with a noisy quantum channel.

The coding theorems for a noisy quantum channel are just as important as (if not more important than) Shannon's classical coding theorems because they determine the ultimate capabilities of information processing in a world where the postulates of quantum theory apply. It is thought that quantum theory is the ultimate theory underpinning all physical phenomena, and any theory of gravity will have to incorporate the quantum theory in some fashion. Thus, it is reasonable that we should be focusing our efforts now on a full Shannon theory of quantum information processing in order to determine the tasks that these systems can accomplish. In many physical situations, some of the assumptions of quantum Shannon theory may not be justified (such as an independent and identically distributed quantum channel), but nevertheless, it provides an ideal setting in which we can determine the capabilities of these physical systems.

1.2.4   History of Quantum Shannon Theory

We conclude this introductory chapter by giving a brief overview of the problems that researchers were thinking about that ultimately led to the development of quantum Shannon theory.

The 1970s—The first researchers in quantum information theory were concerned with transmitting classical data by optical means. They were ultimately led to a quantum formulation because they wanted to transmit classical information by means of a coherent laser. *Coherent states* are special quantum states that a coherent laser ideally emits. Glauber provided a full quantum-mechanical theory of coherent states in two seminal papers (Glauber, 1963b; Glauber, 1963a), for which he shared the Nobel Prize in 2005 (Glauber, 2005). The first researchers of quantum information theory were Helstrom, Gordon, Stratonovich, and Holevo. Gordon (1964) first conjectured an important bound for our ability to access classical information from a quantum system and Levitin (1969) stated it without proof. (Holevo 1973a; see also Holevo, 1973b) later provided a proof that the bound holds. This important bound is now known as the Holevo bound, and it is useful in proving converse theorems (theorems concerning optimality) in quantum Shannon theory. The simplest (yet rough) statement of the Holevo bound states that it is not possible to transmit more than one classical bit of information using a noiseless qubit channel, while at the same time being able to decode it reliably—i.e., we get *one cbit per qubit*. Helstrom (1976) developed a full theory of quantum detection and quantum estimation and published a textbook that discusses this theory. Fannes (1973) contributed a useful continuity property of the entropy that is also useful in proving converse theorems in quantum Shannon theory. Wiesner also used the uncertainty principle to devise a notion of "quantum money" in 1970, but unfortunately, his work was not accepted upon its initial submission. This work was *way* ahead of its time, and it was only until much later that it was accepted (Wiesner, 1983). Wiesner's ideas paved the way for the BB84 protocol for quantum key distribution. Fundamental entropy inequalities, such as the strong subadditivity of quantum entropy (Lieb & Ruskai, 1973b; Lieb & Ruskai, 1973a) and the monotonicity of quantum relative entropy (Lindblad, 1975), were proved during this time as well. These entropy inequalities generalize the Holevo bound and are foundational for establishing optimality theorems in quantum Shannon theory.

The 1980s—The 1980s witnessed only a few advances in quantum information theory because just a handful of researchers thought about the possibilities of linking quantum theory with information-theoretic ideas. The Nobel Prize-winning physicist Richard Feynman published an interesting 1982 article that was one of the first to discuss computing with quantum-mechanical systems (Feynman, 1982). His interest was in using a quantum computer to simulate quantum-mechanical systems—he figured there should be a speed-up over a classical simulation if we instead use one quantum system to simulate another. This work is less quantum Shannon theory than it is quantum computing, but it is still a landmark because Feynman began to think about exploiting the actual quantum information in a physical system, rather than just using quantum systems to process classical information as the researchers in the 1970s suggested.

Wootters & Zurek (1982) produced one of the simplest, yet most profound, results that is crucial to quantum information science (Dieks, 1982, also proved this result in the same year). They proved the *no-cloning theorem*, showing that the postulates of the quantum theory imply the impossibility of universally cloning quantum states. Given an arbitrary unknown quantum state, it is impossible to build a device that can copy this state. This result has deep implications for the processing of quantum information and shows a strong divide between information processing in the quantum world and that in the classical world. We will prove this theorem in Chapter 3 and use it time and again in our reasoning. The history of the no-cloning theorem is one of the more interesting "sociology of science" stories that you may come across. The story goes that Nick Herbert submitted a paper to *Foundations of Physics* with a proposal for faster-than-light communication using entanglement. Asher Peres was the referee (Peres, 2002), and he knew that something had to be wrong with the proposal because it allowed for superluminal communication, yet he could not put his finger on what the problem might be (he also figured that Herbert knew his proposal was flawed). Nevertheless, Peres recommended the paper for publication (Herbert, 1982) because he figured it would stimulate wide interest in the topic. Not much later, Wootters and Zurek published their paper, and since then, there have been thousands of follow-up results on the no-cloning theorem (Scarani et al., 2005).

The work of Wiesner on conjugate coding inspired an IBM physicist named Charles Bennett. Bennett & Brassard (1984) published a groundbreaking paper that detailed the first quantum communication protocol: the BB84 protocol. This protocol shows how a sender and a receiver can exploit a quantum channel to establish a secret key. The security of this protocol, roughly speaking, relies on the uncertainty principle. If any eavesdropper tries to learn about the random quantum data that they use to establish the secret key, this act of learning inevitably disturbs the transmitted quantum data and the two parties can discover this disturbance by noticing the change in the statistics of random sample data. The secret key generation capacity of a noisy quantum channel is inextricably linked to the BB84 protocol, and we study this capacity problem in detail when we study the ability of quantum channels to communicate private information. Interestingly, the physics community largely ignored the BB84 paper when Bennett and Brassard first published it, likely because they presented it at an engineering conference and the merging of physics and information had not yet taken effect.

The 1990s—The 1990s was a time of much increased activity in quantum information science: perhaps some of the most exciting years, with many seminal results. One of the first major results was from Ekert. He published a different way of performing quantum key distribution, this time relying on the strong correlations of entanglement (Ekert, 1991). He was unaware of the BB84 protocol when he was working on his entanglement-based quantum key distribution. The physics community embraced this result, and a short time later, Ekert, Bennett, and Brassard became aware of each other's respective works (Bennett, Brassard & Ekert, 1992). Bennett, Brassard, and Mermin later showed a sense in which these two seemingly different schemes are equivalent (Bennett, Brassard & Mermin, 1992). Bennett later developed the B92 protocol for quantum key distribution using any two non-orthogonal quantum states (Bennett, 1992).

Two of the most profound results that later impacted quantum Shannon theory appeared in the early 1990s. First, Bennett & Wiesner (1992) devised the super-dense coding protocol. This protocol consumes one noiseless ebit of entanglement and one noiseless qubit channel to simulate two noiseless classical bit channels. Let us compare this result to that of Holevo. Holevo's bound states that we can reliably send only one classical bit per qubit, but the super-dense coding protocol states that we can double this rate if we consume entanglement as well. Thus, entanglement is the enabler in this protocol that boosts the classical rate beyond that possible with a noiseless qubit channel alone. The next year, Bennett and some other coauthors reversed the operations in the super-dense coding protocol to devise a protocol that has more profound implications. They devised the *teleportation protocol* (Bennett et al., 1993)—this protocol consumes two classical bit channels and one ebit to transmit a qubit from a sender to a receiver. Right now, without any technical development yet, it may be unclear how the qubit gets from the sender to the receiver. The original authors described it as the "disembodied transport of a quantum state." Suffice it for now to say that it is the unique properties of entanglement (in particular, the ebit) that enable this disembodied transport to occur. Yet again, it is entanglement that is the resource that enables this protocol, but let us be careful not to overstate the role of entanglement. Entanglement alone does not suffice for implementing quantum teleportation. These protocols show that it is the unique combination of entanglement and quantum communication or entanglement and classical communication that yields these results. These two noiseless protocols are cornerstones of quantum Shannon theory, originally suggesting that there are interesting ways of combining the resources of classical communication, quantum communication, and entanglement to formulate uniquely quantum protocols and leading the way to more exotic protocols that combine the different noiseless resources with noisy resources. Simple questions concerning these protocols lead to quantum Shannon-theoretic protocols. In super-dense coding, how much classical information can Alice send if the quantum channel becomes noisy? What if the entanglement is noisy? In teleportation, how much quantum information can Alice send if the classical channel is noisy? What if the entanglement is noisy? Researchers addressed these questions quite a bit after the original super-dense coding and teleportation protocols were available, and we discuss these important questions in this book.

The year 1994 was a landmark for quantum information science. Shor (1994) published his algorithm that factors a number in polynomial time—this algorithm gives an exponential speed-up over the best known classical algorithm. We cannot overstate the importance of this algorithm for the field. Its major application is to break RSA encryption (Rivest et al., 1978) because the security of that encryption algorithm relies on the computational difficulty of factoring a large number. This breakthrough generated wide interest in the idea of a quantum computer and started the quest to build one and study its capabilities.

Initially, much skepticism met the idea of building a practical quantum computer (Landauer, 1995; Unruh, 1995). Some experts thought that it would be impossible to overcome errors that inevitably occur during quantum interactions, due to the coupling of a quantum system with its environment. Shor met this challenge by devising the first quantum error-correcting code (Shor, 1995) and a scheme for fault-tolerant quantum computation (Shor, 1996). His paper on quantum error correction is the one most relevant for quantum Shannon theory. At the end of this paper, he posed the idea of the quantum capacity of a noisy quantum channel as the highest rate at which a sender and receiver can maintain the fidelity of a quantum state when it is sent over a large number of uses of the noisy channel. This open problem set the main task for researchers interested in quantum Shannon theory. A flurry of theoretical activity then ensued in quantum error correction (Calderbank & Shor, 1996; Steane, 1996; Laflamme et al., 1996; Gottesman, 1996; Gottesman, 1997; Calderbank et al., 1997; Calderbank et al., 1998) and fault-tolerant quantum computation (Aharonov & Ben-Or, 1997; Kitaev, 1997; Preskill, 1998; Knill et al., 1998). These two areas are now important subfields within quantum information science, but we do not focus on them in any detail in this book.

Schumacher published a critical paper in 1995 as well (Schumacher, 1995; we discussed some of his contributions in the previous section). This paper gave the first informational notion of a qubit, and it even established the now ubiquitous term "qubit." He proved the quantum analog of Shannon's source coding theorem, giving the ultimate compressibility of quantum information. He used the notion of a typical subspace as an analogy of Shannon's typical set. This notion of a typical subspace proves to be one of the most crucial ideas for constructing codes in quantum Shannon theory, just as the notion of a typical set is so crucial for Shannon's information theory.

Not much later, several researchers began investigating the capacity of a noisy quantum channel for sending classical information (Hausladen et al., 1996). Holevo (1998) and Schumacher & Westmoreland (1997) independently proved that the Holevo information of a quantum channel is an achievable rate for classical communication over it. They appealed to Schumacher's notion of a typical subspace and constructed channel codes for sending classical information. The proof looks somewhat similar to the proof of Shannon's channel coding theorem (discussed in the next chapter) after taking a few steps away from it. The proof of the converse theorem proceeds somewhat analogously to that of Shannon's theorem, with the exception that one of the steps uses Holevo's bound from 1973. In hindsight, it is perhaps somewhat surprising that it took over 20 years between the appearance of the proof of Holevo's bound (the main step in the converse proof) and the appearance of a direct coding theorem for sending classical information.

The quantum capacity theorem is perhaps one of the most fundamental theorems of quantum Shannon theory. Initial work by several researchers provided some insight into the quantum capacity theorem (Bennett, Brassard, Popescu, Schumacher, Smolin & Wootters, 1996; Bennett, DiVincenzo, Smolin & Wootters, 1996; Bennett et al., 1997; Schumacher & Westmoreland, 1998), and a series of papers established an upper bound on the quantum capacity (Schumacher, 1996; Schumacher & Nielsen, 1996; Barnum et al., 1998; Barnum et al., 2000). For the lower bound, Lloyd (1997) was the first to construct an idea for a proof, but it turns out that his proof was more of a heuristic argument. Shor (2002b) then followed with another proof of the lower bound, and some of Shor's ideas appeared much later in a full publication (Hayden, Shor & Winter, 2008). Devetak (2005) and Cai, Winter & Yeung (2004) independently solved the private capacity theorem at approximately the same time (with the publication of the CWY paper appearing a year after Devetak's arXiv post). Devetak took the proof of the private capacity theorem a step further and showed how to apply its techniques to construct a quantum code that achieves a good lower bound on the quantum capacity, while also providing an alternate, cleaner proof of the converse theorem (Devetak, 2005). It is Devetak's technique that we mainly explore in this book because it provides some insight into the coding structure (however, we also explore a different technique via the entanglement-assisted classical capacity theorem).

The 2000s—In recent years, we have had many advancements in quantum Shannon theory (technically, some of the above contributions were in the 2000s, but we did not want to break the continuity of the history of the quantum capacity theorem). One major result was the proof of the entanglement-assisted classical capacity theorem—it is the noisy version of the super-dense coding protocol where the quantum channel is noisy (Bennett et al., 1999; Bennett et al., 2002; Holevo, 2002b). This theorem assumes that Alice and Bob share unlimited entanglement and they exploit the entanglement and the noisy quantum channel to send classical information.

A few fantastic results have arisen in recent years. Horodecki, Oppenheim, and Winter showed the existence of a state-merging protocol (Horodecki et al., 2005; Horodecki et al., 2007). This protocol gives the minimum rate at which Alice and Bob consume noiseless qubit channels in order for Alice to send her share of a quantum state to Bob. This rate is the conditional quantum entropy—the protocol thus gives an operational interpretation to this entropic quantity. What was most fascinating about this result is that the conditional quantum entropy can be negative in quantum Shannon theory. Prior to their work, no one really understood what it meant for the conditional quantum entropy to become negative (Wehrl, 1978; Horodecki & Horodecki, 1994; Cerf & Adami, 1997), but this state-merging result gave a compelling operational interpretation. A negative rate implies that Alice and Bob gain the ability for future quantum communication, instead of consuming quantum communication as when the rate is positive.

Another fantastic result came from Smith & Yard (2008). Suppose we have two noisy quantum channels and each of them individually has zero capacity to transmit quantum information. One would expect intuitively that the "joint quantum capacity" (when using them together) would also have zero ability to transmit quantum information. But this result is not generally the case in the quantum world. It is possible for some particular noisy quantum channels with no individual quantum capacity to have a non-zero joint quantum capacity. It is not clear yet how we might practically take advantage of such a "superactivation" effect, but the result is nonetheless fascinating, counterintuitive, and not yet fully understood.

The latter part of the 2000s saw the unification of quantum Shannon theory. The resource inequality framework was the first step because it unified many previously known results into one formalism (Devetak et al., 2004; Devetak et al., 2008). Devetak, Harrow, and Winter provided a family tree for quantum Shannon theory and showed how to relate the different protocols in the tree to one another. We will go into the theory of resource inequalities in some detail throughout this book because it provides a tremendous conceptual simplification when considering coding theorems in quantum Shannon theory. In fact, the last chapter of this book contains a concise summary of many of the major quantum Shannon-theoretic protocols in the language of resource inequalities. Abeyesinghe, Devetak, Hayden & Winter (2009) published a work showing a sense in which the mother protocol of the family tree can generate the father protocol. We have seen unification efforts in the form of triple trade-off coding theorems (Abeyesinghe & Hayden, 2003; Hsieh & Wilde, 2010a; Hsieh & Wilde, 2010b). These theorems give the optimal combination of classical communication, quantum communication, entanglement, and an asymptotic noisy resource for achieving a variety of quantum information-processing tasks.

We have also witnessed the emergence of a study of network quantum Shannon theory. Some authors have tackled the quantum broadcasting paradigm (Guha & Shapiro, 2007; Guha et al., 2007; Dupuis et al., 2010; Yard et al., 2011), where one sender transmits to multiple receivers. A multiple-access quantum channel has many senders and one receiver. Some of the same authors (and others) have tackled multiple-access communication (Winter, 2001; Yard, 2005; Yen & Shapiro, 2005; Yard et al., 2005; Yard et al., 2008; Hsieh, Devetak & Winter, 2008; Czekaj & Horodecki, 2009). This network quantum Shannon theory should become increasingly important as we get closer to the ultimate goal of a quantum Internet.

Quantum Shannon theory has now established itself as an important and distinct field of study. The next few chapters discuss the concepts that will prepare us for tackling some of the major results in quantum Shannon theory.

2   Classical Shannon Theory

We cannot overstate the importance of Shannon's contribution to modern science. His introduction of the field of information theory and his solutions to its two main theorems demonstrate that his ideas on communication were far beyond the other prevailing ideas in this domain around 1948.

In this chapter, our aim is to discuss Shannon's two main contributions in a descriptive fashion. The goal of this high-level discussion is to build up the intuition for the problem domain of information theory and to understand the main concepts before we delve into the analogous quantum information-theoretic ideas. We avoid going into deep technical detail in this chapter, leaving such details for later chapters where we formally prove both classical and quantum Shannon-theoretic coding theorems. We do use some mathematics from probability theory (namely, the law of large numbers).

We will be delving into the technical details of this chapter's material in later chapters (specifically, Chapters 10, 13, and 14). Once you have reached later chapters that develop some more technical details, it might be helpful to turn back to this chapter to get an overall flavor for the motivation of the development.

2.1   Data Compression

We first discuss the problem of data compression. Those who are familiar with the Internet have used several popular data formats such as JPEG, MPEG, ZIP, GIF, etc. All of these file formats have corresponding algorithms for compressing the output of an information source. A first glance at the compression problem might lead one to believe that it is not possible to compress the output of the information source to an arbitrarily small size, and Shannon proved that this is the case. This result is the content of Shannon's first noiseless coding theorem.

2.1.1   An Example of Data Compression

We begin with a simple example that illustrates the concept of an information source. We then develop a scheme for coding this source so that it requires fewer bits to represent its output faithfully.

Suppose that Alice is a sender and Bob is a receiver. Suppose further that a noiseless bit channel connects Alice to Bob—a noiseless bit channel is one that transmits information perfectly from sender to receiver, e.g., Bob receives "0" if Alice transmits "0" and Bob receives "1" if Alice transmits "1." Alice and Bob would like to minimize the number of times that they use this noiseless channel because it is expensive to use it.

Alice would like to use the noiseless channel to communicate information to Bob. Suppose that an information source randomly chooses from four symbols $\{a, b, c, d\}$ and selects them with a skewed probability distribution:

$$\Pr\{a\} = 1/2, \tag{2.1}$$
$$\Pr\{b\} = 1/8, \tag{2.2}$$
$$\Pr\{c\} = 1/4, \tag{2.3}$$
$$\Pr\{d\} = 1/8. \tag{2.4}$$

So it is clear that the symbol a is the most likely one, c the next likely, and both b and d are least likely. We make the additional assumption that the information source chooses each symbol independently of all previous ones and chooses each with the same probability distribution above. After the information source makes a selection, it gives the symbol to Alice for coding.

A noiseless bit channel accepts only bits as input—it does not accept the symbols a, b, c, d as input. So, Alice has to encode her information into bits. Alice could use the following coding scheme:

$$a \to 00, \quad b \to 01, \quad c \to 10, \quad d \to 11, \tag{2.5}$$

where each binary representation of a letter is a *codeword*. How do we measure the performance of a particular coding scheme? The expected length of a codeword is one way to measure performance. For the above example, the expected length is equal to two bits. This measure reveals a problem with the above scheme—the scheme does not take advantage of the skewed nature of the distribution of the information source because each codeword has the same length.

One might instead consider a scheme that uses shorter codewords for symbols that are more likely and longer codewords for symbols that are less likely.[1] Then the expected length of a codeword with such a scheme should be shorter than that in the former scheme. The following coding scheme gives an improvement in the expected length of a codeword:

$$a \to 0, \quad b \to 110, \quad c \to 10, \quad d \to 111. \tag{2.6}$$

---

[1] Such coding schemes are common. Samuel F. B. Morse employed this idea in his popular Morse code. Also, in the movie *The Diving Bell and the Butterfly*, a writer becomes paralyzed with "locked-in" syndrome so that he can only blink his left eye. An assistant then develops a "blinking code" where she reads a list of letters in French, beginning with the most commonly used letter and ending with the least commonly used letter. The writer blinks when she says the letter he wishes and they finish an entire book using this coding scheme.

This scheme has the advantage that any coded sequence is uniquely decodable. For example, suppose that Bob obtains the following sequence:

$$0011010111010100010. \tag{2.7}$$

Bob can parse the above sequence as

$$0\ 0\ 110\ 10\ 111\ 0\ 10\ 10\ 0\ 0\ 10, \tag{2.8}$$

and determine that Alice transmitted the message

$$aabcdaccaac. \tag{2.9}$$

We can calculate the expected length of this coding scheme as follows:

$$\frac{1}{2}(1) + \frac{1}{8}(3) + \frac{1}{4}(2) + \frac{1}{8}(3) = \frac{7}{4}. \tag{2.10}$$

This scheme is thus more efficient because its expected length is 7/4 bits as opposed to two bits. It is a *variable-length* code because the number of bits in each codeword depends on the source symbol.

2.1.2   A Measure of Information

The above scheme suggests a way to measure information. Consider the probability distribution in (2.1)–(2.4). Would we be more surprised to learn that the information source produced the symbol a or to learn that it produced the symbol d? The answer is d because the source is less likely to produce it. Let X denote a random variable with distribution given in (2.1)–(2.4). One measure of the surprise of symbol $x \in \{a, b, c, d\}$ is

$$i(x) \equiv \log\left(\frac{1}{p_X(x)}\right) = -\log\left(p_X(x)\right), \tag{2.11}$$

where the logarithm is base two—this convention implies the units of this measure are bits. This measure of surprise has the desirable property that it is higher for lower probability events and lower for higher probability events. Here, we take after Shannon, and we name $i(x)$ the *information content* or *surprisal* of the symbol x. Observe that the length of each codeword in the coding scheme in (2.6) is equal to the information content of its corresponding symbol.

The information content has another desirable property called *additivity*. Suppose that the information source produces two symbols, x_1 and x_2, with corresponding random variables X_1 and X_2. The probability for this event is $p_{X_1 X_2}(x_1, x_2)$ and the joint distribution factors as $p_{X_1}(x_1)p_{X_2}(x_2)$ if we assume the source is *memoryless*—that it produces each symbol independently. The information content of the two symbols x_1 and x_2 is additive because

$$i(x_1, x_2) = -\log\left(p_{X_1 X_2}(x_1, x_2)\right) \tag{2.12}$$
$$= -\log\left(p_{X_1}(x_1)p_{X_2}(x_2)\right) \tag{2.13}$$

$$= -\log\left(p_{X_1}(x_1)\right) - \log\left(p_{X_2}(x_2)\right) \qquad (2.14)$$

$$= i(x_1) + i(x_2). \qquad (2.15)$$

In general, additivity is a desirable property for any information measure. We will return to the issue of additivity in many different contexts in this book (especially in Chapter 13).

The expected information content of the information source is

$$\sum_x p_X(x) i(x) = -\sum_x p_X(x) \log\left(p_X(x)\right). \qquad (2.16)$$

The above quantity is so important in information theory that we give it a name: the *entropy* of the information source. The reason for its importance is that the entropy and variations of it appear as the answer to many questions in information theory. For example, in the above coding scheme, the expected length of a codeword is the entropy of the information source because

$$-\frac{1}{2}\log\frac{1}{2} - \frac{1}{8}\log\frac{1}{8} - \frac{1}{4}\log\frac{1}{4} - \frac{1}{8}\log\frac{1}{8}$$

$$= \frac{1}{2}(1) + \frac{1}{8}(3) + \frac{1}{4}(2) + \frac{1}{8}(3) \qquad (2.17)$$

$$= \frac{7}{4}. \qquad (2.18)$$

It is no coincidence that we chose the particular coding scheme in (2.6). The effectiveness of the scheme in this example is related to the structure of the information source—the number of symbols is a power of two and the probability of each symbol is the reciprocal of a power of two.

2.1.3   Shannon's Source Coding Theorem

The next question to ask is whether there is any other scheme that can achieve a better compression rate than the scheme in (2.6). This question is the one that Shannon asked in his first coding theorem. To answer this question, we consider a more general information source and introduce a notion of Shannon, the idea of the *set of typical sequences*.

We can represent a more general information source with a random variable X whose realizations x are *letters* in an *alphabet* $\mathcal{X}$. Let $p_X(x)$ be the probability mass function associated with random variable X, so that the probability of realization x is $p_X(x)$. Let $H(X)$ denote the entropy of the information source:

$$H(X) \equiv -\sum_{x \in \mathcal{X}} p_X(x) \log\left(p_X(x)\right). \qquad (2.19)$$

The entropy $H(X)$ is also the entropy of the random variable X. Another way of writing it is $H(p)$, but we use the more common notation $H(X)$ throughout this book.

The information content $i(X)$ of random variable X is

$$i(X) \equiv -\log\left(p_X(X)\right), \qquad (2.20)$$

and is itself a random variable. There is nothing wrong mathematically here with having random variable X as the argument to the density function p_X, though this expression may seem self-referential at a first glance. This way of thinking turns out to be useful later. Again, the expected information content of X is equal to the entropy:

$$\mathbb{E}_X \left\{ -\log\left(p_X(X)\right) \right\} = H(X). \tag{2.21}$$

EXERCISE 2.1.1   Show that the entropy of a uniform random variable is equal to $\log|\mathcal{X}|$, where $|\mathcal{X}|$ is the size of the variable's alphabet.

We now turn to source coding the above information source. We *could* associate a binary codeword for each symbol x as we did in the scheme in (2.6). But this scheme may lose some efficiency if the size of our alphabet is not a power of two or if the probabilities are not a reciprocal of a power of two as they are in our nice example. Shannon's breakthrough idea was to let the source emit a large number of realizations and then code the emitted data as a large block, instead of coding each symbol as the above example does. This technique is called *block coding*. Shannon's other insight was to allow for a slight error in the compression scheme, but to show that this error vanishes as the block size becomes arbitrarily large. To make the block coding scheme more clear, Shannon suggests to let the source emit the following sequence:

$$x^n \equiv x_1 x_2 \cdots x_n, \tag{2.22}$$

where n is a large number that denotes the size of the block of emitted data and x_i, for all $i = 1, \ldots, n$, denotes the ith emitted symbol. Let X^n denote the random variable associated with the sequence x^n, and let X_i be the random variable for the ith symbol x_i. Figure 2.1 depicts Shannon's idea for a classical source code.

An important assumption regarding this information source is that it is independent and identically distributed (i.i.d.). The i.i.d. assumption means that each random variable X_i has the same distribution as random variable X, and we use the index i merely to track to which symbol x_i the random variable X_i corresponds. Under the i.i.d. assumption, the probability of any given emitted sequence x^n factors as

$$p_{X^n}(x^n) = p_{X_1,X_2,\ldots,X_n}(x_1, x_2, \ldots, x_n) \tag{2.23}$$
$$= p_{X_1}(x_1)p_{X_2}(x_2)\cdots p_{X_n}(x_n) \tag{2.24}$$
$$= p_X(x_1)p_X(x_2)\cdots p_X(x_n) \tag{2.25}$$
$$= \prod_{i=1}^{n} p_X(x_i). \tag{2.26}$$

The above rule from probability theory results in a remarkable simplification of the mathematics. Suppose that we now label the letters in the alphabet $\mathcal{X}$ as a_1, $\ldots$, $a_{|\mathcal{X}|}$ in order to distinguish the letters from the realizations. Let $N(a_i|x^n)$

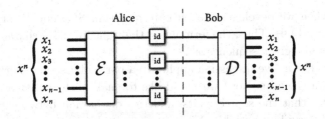

Figure 2.1 This figure depicts Shannon's idea for a classical source code. The information source emits a long sequence x^n to Alice. She encodes this sequence as a block with an encoder $\mathcal{E}$ and produces a codeword whose length is less than that of the original sequence x^n (indicated by fewer lines coming out of the encoder $\mathcal{E}$). She transmits the codeword over noiseless bit channels (each indicated by "id" which stands for the identity bit channel) and Bob receives it. Bob decodes the transmitted codeword with a decoder $\mathcal{D}$ and produces the original sequence that Alice transmitted, only if their chosen code is good, in the sense that the code has a small probability of error.

denote the number of occurrences of the letter a_i in the sequence x^n (where $i = 1, \ldots, |\mathcal{X}|$). As an example, consider the sequence in (2.9). The quantities $N(a_i|x^n)$ for this example are

$$N(a|x^n) = 5, \tag{2.27}$$
$$N(b|x^n) = 1, \tag{2.28}$$
$$N(c|x^n) = 4, \tag{2.29}$$
$$N(d|x^n) = 1. \tag{2.30}$$

We can rewrite the result in (2.26) as

$$p_{X^n}(x^n) = \prod_{i=1}^{n} p_X(x_i) = \prod_{i=1}^{|\mathcal{X}|} p_X(a_i)^{N(a_i|x^n)}. \tag{2.31}$$

Keep in mind that we are allowing the length n of the emitted sequence to be extremely large, so that it is much larger than the alphabet size $|\mathcal{X}|$:

$$n \gg |\mathcal{X}|. \tag{2.32}$$

The formula on the right in (2.31) is much simpler than the formula in (2.26) because it has fewer iterations of multiplications. There is a sense in which the i.i.d. assumption allows us to permute the sequence x^n as

$$x^n \rightarrow \underbrace{a_1 \cdots a_1}_{N(a_1|x^n)} \underbrace{a_2 \cdots a_2}_{N(a_2|x^n)} \cdots \underbrace{a_{|\mathcal{X}|} \cdots a_{|\mathcal{X}|}}_{N(a_{|\mathcal{X}|}|x^n)}, \tag{2.33}$$

because the probability calculation is invariant under this permutation. We introduce the above way of thinking right now because it turns out to be useful later when we develop some ideas in quantum Shannon theory (specifically in Section 14.9). Thus, the formula on the right in (2.31) characterizes the probability of any given sequence x^n.

The above discussion applies to a particular sequence x^n that the information source emits. Now, we would like to analyze the behavior of a *random sequence* X^n that the source emits, and this distinction between the realization x^n and the random variable X^n is important. In particular, let us consider the sample average of the information content of the random sequence X^n (divide the information content of X^n by n to get the sample average):

$$-\frac{1}{n} \log \left(p_{X^n}(X^n)\right). \tag{2.34}$$

It may seem strange at first glance that X^n, the argument of the probability mass function p_{X^n} is itself a random variable, but this type of expression is perfectly well defined mathematically. (This self-referencing type of expression is similar to (2.20), which we used to calculate the entropy.) For reasons that will become clear shortly, we call the above quantity the *sample entropy* of the random sequence X^n.

Suppose now that we use the function $N(a_i|\bullet)$ to calculate the number of appearances of the letter a_i in the random sequence X^n. We write the desired quantity as $N(a_i|X^n)$ and note that it is also a random variable, whose random nature derives from that of X^n. We can reduce the expression in (2.34) to the following one with some algebra and the result in (2.31):

$$-\frac{1}{n} \log \left(p_{X^n}(X^n)\right) = -\frac{1}{n} \log \left(\prod_{i=1}^{|\mathcal{X}|} p_X(a_i)^{N(a_i|X^n)} \right) \tag{2.35}$$

$$= -\frac{1}{n} \sum_{i=1}^{|\mathcal{X}|} \log \left(p_X(a_i)^{N(a_i|X^n)} \right) \tag{2.36}$$

$$= -\sum_{i=1}^{|\mathcal{X}|} \frac{N(a_i|X^n)}{n} \log \left(p_X(a_i) \right). \tag{2.37}$$

We stress again that the above quantity is random.

Is there any way that we can determine the behavior of the above sample entropy when n becomes large? Probability theory gives us a way. The expression $N(a_i|X^n)/n$ represents an empirical distribution for the letters a_i in the alphabet $\mathcal{X}$. As n becomes large, one form of the law of large numbers states that it is overwhelmingly likely that a random sequence has its empirical distribution $N(a_i|X^n)/n$ close to the true distribution $p_X(a_i)$, and conversely, it is highly unlikely that a random sequence does not satisfy this property. Thus, a random emitted sequence X^n is highly likely to satisfy the following condition for all $\delta > 0$ as n becomes large:

$$\lim_{n \to \infty} \Pr \left\{ \left| -\frac{1}{n} \log \left(p_{X^n}(X^n) \right) - \sum_{i=1}^{|\mathcal{X}|} p_X(a_i) \log \left(\frac{1}{p_X(a_i)} \right) \right| \leq \delta \right\} = 1. \quad (2.38)$$

The quantity $-\sum_{i=1}^{|\mathcal{X}|} p_X(a_i) \log \left(p_X(a_i) \right)$ is none other than the entropy $H(X)$, so that the above expression is equivalent to the following one for all $\delta > 0$:

$$\lim_{n \to \infty} \Pr \left\{ \left| -\frac{1}{n} \log \left(p_{X^n}(X^n) \right) - H(X) \right| \leq \delta \right\} = 1. \quad (2.39)$$

Another way of stating this property is as follows:

It is highly likely that the information source emits a sequence whose sample entropy is close to the true entropy, and conversely, it is highly unlikely that the information source emits a sequence that does not satisfy this property.[2]

Now we consider a particular realization x^n of the random sequence X^n. We name a particular sequence x^n a *typical sequence* if its sample entropy is close to the true entropy $H(X)$ and the set of all typical sequences is the *typical set*. Fortunately for data compression, the set of typical sequences is not too large. In Chapter 14 on typical sequences, we prove that the size of this set is much smaller than the set of all sequences. We accept for now (and prove later) that the size of the typical set is $\approx 2^{nH(X)}$, whereas the size of the set of all sequences is equal to $|\mathcal{X}|^n$. We can rewrite the size of the set of all sequences as

$$|\mathcal{X}|^n = 2^{n \log |\mathcal{X}|}. \quad (2.40)$$

Comparing the size of the typical set to the size of the set of all sequences, the typical set is exponentially smaller than the set of all sequences whenever the random variable is not equal to the uniform random variable. Figure 2.2 illustrates this concept. We summarize these two crucial properties of the typical set and give another that we prove later:

PROPERTY 2.1.1 (Unit Probability)   The probability that an emitted sequence is typical approaches one as n becomes large. Another way of stating this property is that the typical set has almost all of the probability.

PROPERTY 2.1.2 (Exponentially Smaller Cardinality)   The size of the typical set is $\approx 2^{nH(X)}$ and is exponentially smaller than the size $2^{n \log |\mathcal{X}|}$ of the set of all sequences whenever random variable X is not uniform.

PROPERTY 2.1.3 (Equipartition)   The probability of a particular typical sequence is roughly uniform $\approx 2^{-nH(X)}$. (The probability $2^{-nH(X)}$ is easy to

---

[2] Do not fall into the trap of thinking, "the possible sequences that the source emits are typical sequences." That line of reasoning is quantitatively far from the truth. In fact, what we can show is much different because the set of typical sequences is much smaller than the set of all possible sequences.

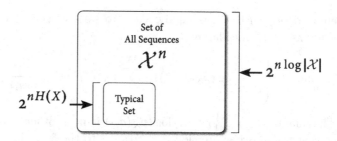

Figure 2.2 This figure indicates that the typical set is much smaller (exponentially smaller) than the set of all sequences. The typical set is roughly the same size as the set of all sequences only when the entropy $H(X)$ of the random variable X is equal to $\log|\mathcal{X}|$—implying that the distribution of random variable X is uniform.

calculate if we accept that the typical set has all of the probability, its size is $2^{nH(X)}$, and the distribution over typical sequences is uniform.)

These three properties together are collectively known as the *asymptotic equipartition theorem*. The word "asymptotic" applies because the theorem exploits the asymptotic limit when n is large and the word "equipartition" refers to the third property above.

With the above notions of a typical set under our belt, a strategy for compressing information should now be clear. The strategy is to compress only the typical sequences that the source emits. We simply need to establish a one-to-one encoding function that maps from the set of typical sequences (size $2^{nH(X)}$) to the set of all binary strings of length $nH(X)$ (this set also has size $2^{nH(X)}$). If the source emits an atypical sequence, we declare an error. This coding scheme is reliable in the asymptotic limit because the probability of an error event vanishes as n becomes large, due to the unit probability property in the asymptotic equipartition theorem. We measure the rate of this block coding scheme as follows:

$$\text{compression rate} \equiv \frac{\#\text{ of noiseless channel bits}}{\#\text{ of source symbols}}. \tag{2.41}$$

For the case of Shannon compression, the number of noiseless channel bits is equal to $nH(X)$ and the number of source symbols is equal to n. Thus, the compression rate is equal to the entropy $H(X)$.

One may then wonder whether this rate of data compression is the best that we can do—whether this rate is optimal (we could achieve a lower rate of compression if it were not optimal). In fact, the above rate is the optimal rate at which we can compress information, and this is the content of Shannon's data compression theorem. We hold off on a formal proof of optimality for now and delay it until we reach Chapter 18. We just mention for now that this data compression protocol gives an *operational interpretation* to the Shannon entropy $H(X)$ because it appears as the optimal rate of data compression.

The above discussion highlights the common approach in information theory for establishing a coding theorem. Proving a coding theorem has two parts—traditionally called the *direct coding theorem* and the *converse theorem*. First, we give a coding scheme that can achieve a given rate for an information-processing task. This first part includes a direct construction of a coding scheme, hence the name *direct coding theorem*. The statement of the direct coding theorem for the above task is as follows:

If the rate of compression is greater than the entropy of the source, then there exists a coding scheme that can achieve lossless data compression in the sense that it is possible to make the probability of error for incorrectly decoding arbitrarily small.

The second task is to prove that the rate from the direct coding theorem is optimal—that we cannot do any better than the suggested rate. We traditionally call this part the converse theorem because it corresponds to the converse of the above statement:

If there exists a coding scheme that can achieve lossless data compression with arbitrarily small probability of decoding error, then the rate of compression is greater than the entropy of the source.

The techniques used in proving each part of the coding theorem are completely different. For most coding theorems in information theory, we can prove the direct coding theorem by appealing to the ideas of typical sequences and large block sizes. That this technique gives a good coding scheme is directly related to the asymptotic equipartition properties that govern the behavior of random sequences of data as the length of the sequence becomes large. The proof of a converse theorem relies on information inequalities that give tight bounds on the entropic quantities appearing in the coding constructions. We spend some time with information inequalities in Chapter 10 to build up our ability to prove converse theorems.

Sometimes, in the course of proving a direct coding theorem, one may think to have found the optimal rate for a given information-processing task. Without a matching converse theorem, it is not generally clear that the suggested rate is optimal. So, always prove converse theorems!

2.2   Channel Capacity

The next issue that we overview is the transmission of information over a noisy classical channel. We begin with a standard example—transmitting a single bit of information over a noisy bit-flip channel.

2.2.1   An Example of an Error Correction Code

We again have our protagonists, Alice and Bob, as respective sender and receiver. This time, however, we assume that a noisy classical channel connects them, so that information transfer is not reliable. Alice and Bob realize that a noisy channel is not as expensive as a noiseless one, but it still is expensive for them to use. For this reason, they would like to maximize the amount of information that Alice can communicate reliably to Bob, where reliable communication implies that there is a negligible probability of error when transmitting this information.

The simplest example of a noisy classical channel is a bit-flip channel, with the technical name *binary symmetric channel*. This channel flips the input bit with probability p and leaves it unchanged with probability $1 - p$. Figure 2.3 depicts the action of the bit-flip channel. Alice and Bob are allowed to use the channel multiple times, and in so doing, we assume that the channel behaves independently from one use to the next and behaves in the same random way as described above. For this reason, we describe the multiple uses of the channel as i.i.d. channels. This assumption will be helpful when we go to the asymptotic regime of a large number of uses of the channel.

Suppose that Alice and Bob just use the channel as is—Alice just sends plain bits to Bob. This scheme works reliably only if the probability of bit-flip error vanishes. So, Alice and Bob could invest their best efforts into engineering the physical channel to make it reliable. But, generally, it is not possible to engineer a classical channel this way for physical or logistical reasons. For example, Alice and Bob may only have local computers at their ends and may not have access to the physical channel because the telephone company may control the channel.

Alice and Bob can employ a "systems engineering" solution to this problem rather than an engineering of the physical channel. They can redundantly encode information in a way such that Bob can have a higher probability of determining what Alice is sending, effectively reducing the level of noise on the channel. A simple example of this systems engineering solution is the three-bit majority vote code. Alice and Bob employ the following encoding:

$$0 \rightarrow 000, \qquad 1 \rightarrow 111, \tag{2.42}$$

where both "000" and "111" are *codewords*. Alice transmits the codeword "000" with three independent uses of the noisy channel if she really wants to communicate a "0" to Bob and she transmits the codeword "111" if she wants to send a "1" to him. The *physical* or *channel* bits are the actual bits that she transmits over the noisy channel, and the *logical* or *information* bits are those that

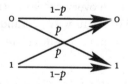

Figure 2.3 This figure depicts the action of the bit-flip channel. It preserves the input bit with probability $1 - p$ and flips it with probability p.

Table 2.1 The first column gives the eight possible outputs of the noisy bit-flip channel when Alice encodes a "0" with the majority vote code. The second column gives the corresponding probability of Bob receiving the particular outputs.

Channel Output	Probability
000	$(1-p)^3$
001, 010, 100	$p(1-p)^2$
011, 110, 101	$p^2(1-p)$
111	p^3

she intends for Bob to receive. In our example, "0" is a logical bit and "000" corresponds to the physical bits.

The rate of this scheme is 1/3 because it encodes one information bit. The term "rate" is perhaps a misnomer for coding scenarios that do not involve sending bits in a time sequence over a channel. We may just as well use the majority vote code to store one bit in a memory device that may be unreliable. Perhaps a more universal term is *efficiency*. Nevertheless, we follow convention and use the term *rate* throughout this book.

Of course, the noisy bit-flip channel does not always transmit these codewords without error. So how does Bob decode in the case of error? He simply takes a *majority vote* to determine the transmitted message—he decodes as "0" if the number of zeros in the codeword he receives is greater than the number of ones.

We now analyze the performance of this simple "systems engineering" solution. Table 2.1 enumerates the probability of receiving every possible sequence of three bits, assuming that Alice transmits a "0" by encoding it as "000." The probability of no error is $(1-p)^3$, the probability of a single-bit error is $3p(1-p)^2$, the probability of a double-bit error is $3p^2(1-p)$, and the probability of a total failure is p^3. The majority vote solution can "correct" for no error and it corrects for all single-bit errors, but it has no ability to correct for double-bit and triple-bit errors. In fact, it actually incorrectly decodes these latter two scenarios by "correcting" "011", "110", or "101" to "111" and decoding "111" as a "1." Thus, these latter two outcomes are errors because the code has no ability to correct them. We can employ similar arguments as above to the case in which Alice transmits a "1" to Bob using the majority vote code.

When does this majority vote scheme perform better than no coding at all? It is exactly when the probability of error with the majority vote code is less than p, the probability of error with no coding. Letting e denote the event that an error occurs, the probability of error is equal to the following quantity:

$$\Pr\{e\} = \Pr\{e|0\}\Pr\{0\} + \Pr\{e|1\}\Pr\{1\}. \qquad (2.43)$$

Our analysis above suggests that the conditional probabilities $\Pr\{e|0\}$ and $\Pr\{e|1\}$ are equal for the majority vote code because of the symmetry in the noisy bit-flip channel. This result implies that the probability of error is

$$\Pr\{e\} = 3p^2(1-p) + p^3 \tag{2.44}$$
$$= 3p^2 - 2p^3, \tag{2.45}$$

because $\Pr\{0\} + \Pr\{1\} = 1$. We consider the following inequality to determine if the majority vote code reduces the probability of error:

$$3p^2 - 2p^3 < p. \tag{2.46}$$

This inequality simplifies as

$$0 < 2p^3 - 3p^2 + p \tag{2.47}$$
$$\therefore 0 < p\,(2p-1)\,(p-1). \tag{2.48}$$

The only values of p that satisfy the above inequality are $0 < p < 1/2$. Thus, the majority vote code reduces the probability of error only when $0 < p < 1/2$, i.e., when the noise on the channel is not too much. Too much noise has the effect of causing the codewords to flip too often, throwing off Bob's decoder.

The majority vote code gives a way for Alice and Bob to reduce the probability of error during their communication, but unfortunately, there is still a non-zero probability for the noisy channel to disrupt their communication. Is there any way that they can achieve reliable communication by reducing the probability of error to zero?

One simple approach to achieve this goal is to exploit the majority vote idea a second time. They can *concatenate* two instances of the majority vote code to produce a code with a larger number of physical bits. Concatenation consists of using one code as an "inner" code and another as an "outer" code. There is no real need for us to distinguish between the inner and outer code in this case because we use the same code for both the inner and outer code. The concatenation scheme for our case first encodes the message i, where $i \in \{0,1\}$, using the majority vote code. Let us label the codewords as follows:

$$\bar{0} \equiv 000, \qquad \bar{1} \equiv 111. \tag{2.49}$$

For the second layer of the concatenation, we encode $\bar{0}$ and $\bar{1}$ with the majority vote code again:

$$\bar{0} \rightarrow \bar{0}\bar{0}\bar{0}, \qquad \bar{1} \rightarrow \bar{1}\bar{1}\bar{1}. \tag{2.50}$$

Thus, the overall encoding of the concatenated scheme is as follows:

$$0 \rightarrow 000\ 000\ 000, \qquad 1 \rightarrow 111\ 111\ 111. \tag{2.51}$$

The rate of the concatenated code is $1/9$ and smaller than the original rate of $1/3$. A simple application of the above performance analysis for the majority vote code shows that this concatenation scheme reduces the probability of error as follows:

$$3[\Pr\{e\}]^2 - 2[\Pr\{e\}]^3 = O(p^4). \qquad (2.52)$$

The error probability $\Pr\{e\}$ is in (2.45) and $O(p^4)$ indicates that the leading order term of the left-hand side is the fourth power in p.

The concatenated scheme achieves a lower probability of error at the cost of using more physical bits in the code. Recall that our goal is to achieve reliable communication, where there is no probability of error. A first guess for achieving reliable communication is to continue concatenating. If we concatenate again, the probability of error reduces to $O(p^6)$, and the rate drops to $1/27$. We can continue indefinitely with concatenating to make the probability of error arbitrarily small and achieve reliable communication, but the problem is that the rate approaches zero as the probability of error becomes arbitrarily small.

The above example seems to show that there is a trade-off between the rate of the encoding scheme and the desired order of error probability. Is there a way that we can code information for a noisy channel while maintaining a good rate of communication?

2.2.2 Shannon's Channel Coding Theorem

Shannon's second breakthrough coding theorem provides an affirmative answer to the above question. This answer came as a complete shock to communication researchers in 1948. Furthermore, the techniques that Shannon used in demonstrating this fact were rarely used by engineers at the time. We give a broad overview of Shannon's main idea and techniques that he used to prove his second important theorem—the noisy channel coding theorem.

2.2.3 General Model for a Channel Code

We first generalize some of the ideas in the above example. We still have Alice trying to communicate with Bob, but this time, she wants to be able to transmit a larger set of messages with asymptotically perfect reliability, rather than merely sending "0" or "1." Suppose that she selects messages from a message set $[M]$ that consists of M messages:

$$[M] \equiv \{1, \ldots, M\}. \qquad (2.53)$$

Suppose furthermore that Alice chooses a particular message m with uniform probability from the set $[M]$. This assumption of a uniform distribution for Alice's messages indicates that we do not really care much about the content of the actual message that she is transmitting. We just assume total ignorance of her message because we only really care about her ability to send any message reliably. The message set $[M]$ requires $\log(M)$ bits to represent it, where the logarithm is again base two. This number becomes important when we calculate the rate of a channel code.

The next aspect of the model that we need to generalize is the noisy channel that connects Alice to Bob. We used the bit-flip channel before, but this channel is not general enough for our purposes. A simple way to extend the channel model is to represent it as a conditional probability distribution involving an input random variable X and an output random variable Y:

$$\mathcal{N}: \qquad p_{Y|X}(y|x). \tag{2.54}$$

We use the symbol $\mathcal{N}$ to represent this more general channel model. One assumption that we make about random variables X and Y is that they are discrete, but the respective sizes of their outcome sets do not have to match. The other assumption that we make concerning the noisy channel is that it is i.i.d. Let $X^n \equiv X_1 X_2 \cdots X_n$ and $Y^n \equiv Y_1 Y_2 \cdots Y_n$ be the random variables associated with respective sequences $x^n \equiv x_1 x_2 \cdots x_n$ and $y^n \equiv y_1 y_2 \cdots y_n$. If Alice inputs the sequence x^n to the n inputs of n respective uses of the noisy channel, a possible output sequence may be y^n. The i.i.d. assumption allows us to factor the conditional probability of the output sequence y^n:

$$p_{Y^n|X^n}(y^n|x^n) = p_{Y_1|X_1}(y_1|x_1)p_{Y_2|X_2}(y_2|x_2) \cdots p_{Y_n|X_n}(y_n|x_n) \tag{2.55}$$

$$= p_{Y|X}(y_1|x_1)p_{Y|X}(y_2|x_2) \cdots p_{Y|X}(y_n|x_n) \tag{2.56}$$

$$= \prod_{i=1}^{n} p_{Y|X}(y_i|x_i). \tag{2.57}$$

The technical name of this more general channel model is a *discrete memoryless channel*.

A coding scheme or *code* translates all of Alice's messages into codewords that can be input to n i.i.d. uses of the noisy channel. For example, suppose that Alice selects a message m to encode. We can write the codeword corresponding to message m as $x^n(m)$ because the input to the channel is some codeword that depends on m.

The last part of the model involves Bob receiving the corrupted codeword y^n over the channel and determining a potential codeword x^n with which it should be associated. We do not get into any details just yet for this last decoding part— imagine for now that it operates similarly to the majority vote code example. Figure 2.4 displays Shannon's model of communication that we have described.

We calculate the *rate* of a given coding scheme as follows:

$$\text{rate} \equiv \frac{\text{\# of message bits}}{\text{\# of channel uses}}. \tag{2.58}$$

In our model, the rate of a given coding scheme is

$$R = \frac{1}{n} \log(M), \tag{2.59}$$

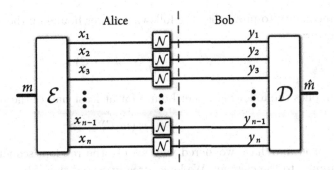

Figure 2.4 This figure depicts Shannon's idea for a classical channel code. Alice chooses a message m from a message set $[M] \equiv \{1, \ldots, M\}$. She encodes the message m with an encoding operation $\mathcal{E}$. This encoding operation assigns a codeword x^n to the message m and inputs the codeword x^n to a large number of i.i.d. uses of a noisy channel $\mathcal{N}$. The noisy channel randomly corrupts the codeword x^n to a sequence y^n. Bob receives the corrupted sequence y^n and performs a decoding operation $\mathcal{D}$ to estimate the codeword x^n. This estimate of the codeword x^n then produces an estimate $\hat{m}$ of the message that Alice transmitted. A reliable code has the property that Bob can decode each message $m \in [M]$ with a vanishing probability of error when the block length n becomes large.

where $\log(M)$ is the number of bits needed to represent any message in the message set $[M]$ and n is the number of channel uses. The *capacity* of a noisy channel is the highest rate at which it can communicate information reliably.

We also need a way to determine the performance of any given code. Here, we list several measures of performance. Let $\mathcal{C} \equiv \{x^n(m)\}_{m \in [M]}$ represent a code that Alice and Bob choose, where $x^n(m)$ denotes each codeword corresponding to the message m. Let $p_e(m, \mathcal{C})$ denote the probability of error when Alice transmits a message $m \in [M]$ using the code $\mathcal{C}$. We denote the average probability of error as

$$\bar{p}_e(\mathcal{C}) \equiv \frac{1}{M} \sum_{m=1}^{M} p_e(m, \mathcal{C}). \tag{2.60}$$

The maximal probability of error is

$$p_e^*(\mathcal{C}) \equiv \max_{m \in [M]} p_e(m, \mathcal{C}). \tag{2.61}$$

Our ultimate aim is to make the maximal probability of error $p_e^*(\mathcal{C})$ arbitrarily small, but the average probability of error $\bar{p}_e(\mathcal{C})$ is important in the analysis. These two performance measures are related—the average probability of error is small if the maximal probability of error is. Perhaps surprisingly, the maximal probability is small for at least half of the messages if the average probability of error is. We make this statement more quantitative in the following exercise.

EXERCISE 2.2.1   Let $\varepsilon \in [0, 1/2]$ and let $p_e(m, \mathcal{C})$ denote the probability of error when Alice transmits a message $m \in [M]$ using the code $\mathcal{C}$. Use Markov's inequality to prove that the following upper bound on the average probability of error:

$$\frac{1}{M} \sum_m p_e(m, \mathcal{C}) \leq \varepsilon \tag{2.62}$$

implies the following upper bound for at least half of the messages m:

$$p_e(m, \mathcal{C}) \leq 2\varepsilon. \tag{2.63}$$

You may have wondered why we use the random sequence X^n to model the inputs to the channel. We have already stated that Alice's message is a uniform random variable, and the codewords in any coding scheme directly depend on the message to be sent. For example, in the majority vote code, the channel inputs are always "000" whenever the intended message is "0" and similarly for the channel inputs "111" and the message "1". So why is there a need to overcomplicate things by modeling the channel inputs as the random variable X^n when it seems like each codeword is a deterministic function of the intended message? We are not yet ready to answer this question but will return to it shortly.

We should also stress an important point before proceeding with Shannon's ingenious scheme for proving the existence of reliable codes for a noisy channel. In the above model, we described essentially two "layers of randomness":

1. The first layer of randomness is the uniform random variable associated with Alice's choice of a message.
2. The second layer of randomness is the noisy channel. The output of the channel is a random variable because we cannot always predict the output of the channel with certainty.

It is not possible to "play around" with these two layers of randomness. The random variable associated with Alice's message is fixed as a uniform random variable because we assume ignorance of Alice's message. The conditional probability distribution of the noisy channel is also fixed. We are assuming that Alice and Bob can learn the conditional probability distribution associated with the noisy channel by estimating it. Alternatively, we may assume that a third party has knowledge of the conditional probability distribution and informs Alice and Bob of it in some way. Regardless of how they obtain the knowledge of the distribution, we assume that they both know it and that it is fixed.

2.2.4 Proof Sketch of Shannon's Channel Coding Theorem

We are now ready to present an overview of Shannon's technique for proving the existence of a code that can achieve the capacity of a given noisy channel. Some of the methods that Shannon uses in his outline of a proof are similar to those in the first coding theorem. We again use the channel a large number of times so that the law of large numbers from probability theory comes into play and allow for a small probability of error that vanishes as the number of channel uses becomes large. If the notion of typical sequences is so important in the first coding theorem, we might suspect that it should be important in the noisy channel coding theorem as well. The typical set captures a certain notion of efficiency because it is a small set when compared to the set of all sequences, but it is the set that has almost all of the probability. Thus, we should expect this efficiency to come into play somehow in the channel coding theorem.

The aspect of Shannon's technique for proving the noisy channel coding theorem that is different from the other ideas in the first theorem is the idea of *random coding*. Shannon's technique adds a *third* layer of randomness to the model given above (recall that the first two are Alice's random message and the random nature of the noisy channel).

The third layer of randomness is to choose the codewords themselves in a random fashion according to a random variable X, where we choose each letter x_i of a given codeword x^n independently according to the distribution $p_X(x_i)$. It is for this reason that we model the channel inputs as a random variable. We can then write each codeword as a random variable $X^n(m)$. The probability distribution for choosing a particular codeword $x^n(m)$ is

$$\Pr\{X^n(m) = x^n(m)\} = p_{X_1,X_2,\ldots,X_n}(x_1(m), x_2(m), \ldots, x_n(m)) \tag{2.64}$$

$$= p_X(x_1(m))p_X(x_2(m))\cdots p_X(x_n(m)) \tag{2.65}$$

$$= \prod_{i=1}^{n} p_X(x_i(m)). \tag{2.66}$$

The important result to notice is that the probability for a given codeword factors because we choose the code in an i.i.d. fashion, and, perhaps more importantly, the distribution of each codeword has no explicit dependence on the message m with which it is associated. That is, the probability distribution of the first codeword is exactly the same as the probability distribution of all of the other codewords. The code $\mathcal{C}$ itself becomes a random variable in this scheme for choosing a code randomly. We now let $\mathcal{C}$ refer to the random variable that represents a random code, and we let $\mathcal{C}_0$ represent any particular deterministic code. The probability of choosing a particular code $\mathcal{C}_0 = \{x^n(m)\}_{m \in [M]}$ is

$$p_{\mathcal{C}}(\mathcal{C}_0) = \prod_{m=1}^{M} \prod_{i=1}^{n} p_X(x_i(m)), \tag{2.67}$$

and this probability distribution again has no explicit dependence on each message m in the code $\mathcal{C}_0$.

Choosing the codewords in a random way allows for a dramatic simplification in the mathematical analysis of the probability of error. One of Shannon's breakthrough ideas was to analyze the *expectation* of the average probability of error, where the expectation is with respect to the random code $\mathcal{C}$, rather than analyzing the average probability of error itself. The expectation of the average probability of error is

$$\mathbb{E}_{\mathcal{C}}\left\{\bar{p}_e(\mathcal{C})\right\}. \tag{2.68}$$

This expectation is much simpler to analyze because of the random way that we choose the code. Consider that

$$\mathbb{E}_{\mathcal{C}}\left\{\bar{p}_e(\mathcal{C})\right\} = \mathbb{E}_{\mathcal{C}}\left\{\frac{1}{M}\sum_{m=1}^{M}p_e(m,\mathcal{C})\right\}. \tag{2.69}$$

Using linearity of the expectation, we can exchange the expectation with the sum so that

$$\mathbb{E}_{\mathcal{C}}\left\{\bar{p}_e(\mathcal{C})\right\} = \frac{1}{M}\sum_{m=1}^{M}\mathbb{E}_{\mathcal{C}}\left\{p_e(m,\mathcal{C})\right\}. \tag{2.70}$$

Now, the expectation of the probability of error for a particular message m does not actually depend on the message m because the distribution of each random codeword $X^n(m)$ does not explicitly depend on m. This line of reasoning leads to the dramatic simplification because $\mathbb{E}_{\mathcal{C}}\left\{p_e(m,\mathcal{C})\right\}$ is then the same for all messages. So we can then say that

$$\mathbb{E}_{\mathcal{C}}\left\{p_e(m,\mathcal{C})\right\} = \mathbb{E}_{\mathcal{C}}\left\{p_e(1,\mathcal{C})\right\}. \tag{2.71}$$

(We could have equivalently chosen any message instead of the first.) We then have that

$$\mathbb{E}_{\mathcal{C}}\left\{\bar{p}_e(\mathcal{C})\right\} = \frac{1}{M}\sum_{m=1}^{M}\mathbb{E}_{\mathcal{C}}\left\{p_e(1,\mathcal{C})\right\} \tag{2.72}$$

$$= \mathbb{E}_{\mathcal{C}}\left\{p_e(1,\mathcal{C})\right\}, \tag{2.73}$$

where the last step follows because the quantity $\mathbb{E}_{\mathcal{C}}\left\{p_e(1,\mathcal{C})\right\}$ has no dependence on m. We now only have to determine the expectation of the probability of error for *one message* instead of determining the expectation of the average error probability of the whole set. This simplification follows because random coding results in the equality of these two quantities.

Shannon then determined a way to obtain a bound on the expectation of the average probability of error (we soon discuss this technique briefly) so that

$$\mathbb{E}_{\mathcal{C}}\left\{\bar{p}_e(\mathcal{C})\right\} \leq \varepsilon, \tag{2.74}$$

where ε is some number $\in (0,1)$ that we can make arbitrarily small by letting the block size n become arbitrarily large. If it is possible to obtain a bound on the expectation of the average probability of error, then surely there exists some deterministic code $\mathcal{C}_0$ whose average probability of error meets this same bound:

$$\bar{p}_e(\mathcal{C}_0) \leq \varepsilon. \tag{2.75}$$

If it were not so, then the original bound on the expectation would not be possible. This step is the *derandomization* step of Shannon's proof. Ultimately, we require a deterministic code with a high rate and arbitrarily small probability of error and this step shows the *existence* of such a code. The random coding technique is only useful for simplifying the mathematics of the proof.

The last step of the proof is the *expurgation* step. It is an application of the result of Exercise 2.2.1. Recall that our goal is to show the existence of a high-rate code that has low maximal probability of error. But so far we only have a bound on the average probability of error. In the expurgation step, we simply throw out the half of the codewords with the worst probability of error. Throwing out the worse half of the codewords reduces the number of messages by a factor of two, but only has a negligible impact on the rate of the code. Consider that the number of messages is 2^{nR} where R is the rate of the code. Thus, the number of messages is $2^{n\left(R-\frac{1}{n}\right)}$ after throwing out the worse half of the codewords, and the rate $R - \frac{1}{n}$ is asymptotically equal to the rate R. After throwing out the worse half of the codewords, the result of Exercise 2.2.1 shows that the following bound then applies to the maximal probability of error:

$$p_e^*(\mathcal{C}_0) \leq 2\varepsilon. \tag{2.76}$$

This last expurgation step ends the analysis of the probability of error.

We now discuss the size of the code that Alice and Bob employ. Recall that the rate of the code is $R = \log(M)/n$. It is convenient to define the size M of the message set $[M]$ in terms of the rate R. When we do so, the size of the message set is

$$M = 2^{nR}. \tag{2.77}$$

What is peculiar about the message set size when defined this way is that it grows exponentially with the number of channel uses. But recall that any given code exploits n channel uses to send M messages. So when we take the limit as the number of channel uses tends to infinity, we are implying that there exists a sequence of codes whose message set size is $M = 2^{nR}$ and number of channel uses is n. We are focused on keeping the rate of the code constant and use the limit $n \to \infty$ to make the probability of error vanish for a certain fixed rate R.

What is the maximal rate at which Alice can communicate to Bob reliably? We need to determine the number of distinguishable messages that Alice can reliably send to Bob, and we require the notion of *conditional typicality* to do so. Consider that Alice chooses codewords randomly according to random variable X with probability distribution $p_X(x)$. By the asymptotic equipartition theorem, it is highly likely that each of the codewords that Alice chooses is a typical sequence with sample entropy close to $H(X)$. In the coding scheme, Alice transmits a particular codeword x^n over the noisy channel and Bob receives a random sequence Y^n. The random sequence Y^n is a random variable that depends on x^n through the conditional probability distribution $p_{Y|X}(y|x)$. We would like a way to determine the number of possible output sequences that are likely to correspond to a particular input sequence x^n. A useful entropic quantity for this situation is the conditional entropy $H(Y|X)$, the technical details of which we leave for Chapter 10. For now, just think of this conditional entropy as measuring the uncertainty of a random variable Y when one already knows the value of the random variable X. The conditional entropy $H(Y|X)$ is always less than the entropy $H(Y)$ unless X and Y are independent. This inequality holds because knowledge of a correlated random variable X does not increase the uncertainty about Y. It turns out that there is a notion of conditional typicality (depicted in Figure 2.5), similar to the notion of typicality, and a similar asymptotic equipartition theorem holds for conditionally typical sequences (more details in Section 14.9). This theorem also has three important properties. For each input sequence x^n, there is a corresponding conditionally typical set with the following properties:

1. It has almost all of the probability—it is highly likely that a random channel output sequence is conditionally typical given a particular input sequence.
2. Its size is $\approx 2^{nH(Y|X)}$.
3. The probability of each conditionally typical sequence y^n, given knowledge of the input sequence x^n, is $\approx 2^{-nH(Y|X)}$.

If we disregard knowledge of the input sequence used to generate an output sequence, the probability distribution that generates the output sequences is

$$p_Y(y) = \sum_x p_{Y|X}(y|x)p_X(x). \tag{2.78}$$

We can think that this probability distribution is the one that generates all the possible output sequences. The likely output sequences are in an output typical set of size $2^{nH(Y)}$.

We are now in a position to describe the structure of a random code and the size of the message set. Alice generates 2^{nR} codewords according to the distribution $p_X(x)$ and suppose for now that Bob has knowledge of the code after Alice generates it. Suppose Alice sends one of the codewords over the channel. Bob is ignorant of the transmitted codeword, so from his point of view, the

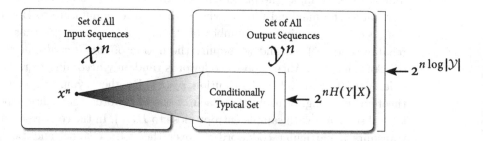

Figure 2.5 This figure depicts the notion of a conditionally typical set. Associated to every input sequence x^n is a conditionally typical set consisting of the likely output sequences. The size of this conditionally typical set is $\approx 2^{nH(Y|X)}$. It is exponentially smaller than the set of all output sequences whenever the conditional random variable is not uniform.

output sequences are generated according to the distribution $p_Y(y)$. Bob then employs typical sequence decoding. He first determines if the output sequence y^n is in the typical output set of size $2^{nH(Y)}$. If not, he declares an error. The probability of this type of error is small by the asymptotic equipartition theorem. If the output sequence y^n is in the output typical set, he uses his knowledge of the code to determine a conditionally typical set of size $2^{nH(Y|X)}$ to which the output sequence belongs. If he decodes an output sequence y^n to the wrong conditionally typical set, then an error occurs. This last type of error suggests how they might structure the code in order to prevent this type of error from happening. If they structure the code so that the output conditionally typical sets do not overlap too much, then Bob should be able to decode each output sequence y^n to a unique input sequence x^n with high probability. This line of reasoning suggests that they should divide the set of output typical sequences into M sets of conditionally typical output sets, each of size $2^{nH(Y|X)}$. Thus, if they set the number of messages $M = 2^{nR}$ as follows:

$$2^{nR} \approx \frac{2^{nH(Y)}}{2^{nH(Y|X)}} = 2^{n(H(Y)-H(Y|X))}, \tag{2.79}$$

then our intuition is that Bob should be able to decode correctly with high probability. Such an argument is a "packing" argument because it shows how to pack information into the space of all output sequences. Figure 2.6 gives a visual depiction of the packing argument. It turns out that this intuition is correct— Alice can reliably send information to Bob if the quantity $H(Y)-H(Y|X)$ bounds the rate R:

$$R < H(Y) - H(Y|X). \tag{2.80}$$

A rate less than $H(Y) - H(Y|X)$ ensures that we can make the expectation of the average probability of error as small as we would like. We then employ the derandomization and expurgation steps, discussed before, in order to show that there exists a code whose maximal probability of error vanishes as the number n of channel uses tends to infinity.

The entropic quantity $H(Y) - H(Y|X)$ deserves special attention because it is another important entropic quantity in information theory. It is the *mutual information* between random variables X and Y and we denote it as

$$I(X;Y) \equiv H(Y) - H(Y|X). \tag{2.81}$$

It is important because it arises as the limiting rate of reliable communication. We will discuss its properties in more detail throughout this book.

There is one final step that we can take to strengthen the above coding scheme. We mentioned before that there are three layers of randomness in the coding construction: Alice's uniform choice of a message, the noisy channel, and Shannon's random coding scheme. The first two layers of randomness we do not have control over. But we actually do have control over the last layer of randomness. Alice chooses the code according to the distribution $p_X(x)$. She can choose the code

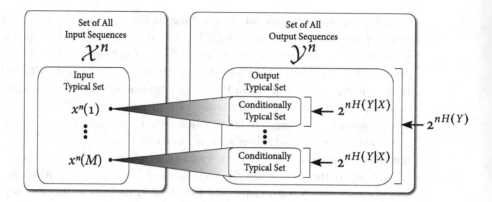

Figure 2.6 This figure depicts the packing argument that Shannon used. The channel induces a conditionally typical set corresponding to each codeword $x^n(i)$ where $i \in \{1, \ldots, M\}$. The size of each conditionally typical output set is $2^{nH(Y|X)}$. The size of the typical set of all output sequences is $2^{nH(Y)}$. These sizes suggest that we can divide the output typical set into M conditionally typical sets and be able to distinguish $M \approx 2^{nH(Y)}/2^{nH(Y|X)}$ messages without error.

according to any distribution that she would like. If she chooses it according to $p_X(x)$, the resulting rate of the code is the mutual information $I(X;Y)$. We will prove later on that the mutual information $I(X;Y)$ is a concave function of the distribution $p_X(x)$ when the conditional distribution $p_{Y|X}(y|x)$ is fixed. Concavity implies that there is a distribution $p_X^*(x)$ that maximizes the mutual information. Thus, Alice should choose an optimal distribution $p_X^*(x)$ when she randomly generates the code, and this choice gives the largest possible rate of communication that they could have. This largest possible rate is the *capacity* of the channel and we denote it as

$$C(\mathcal{N}) \equiv \max_{p_X(x)} I(X;Y). \tag{2.82}$$

Our discussion here is just an overview of Shannon's channel capacity theorem. In Section 14.10, we give a full proof of this theorem after having developed some technical tools needed for a formal proof.

We clarify one more point. In the discussion of the operation of the code, we mentioned that Alice and Bob both have knowledge of the code. Well, how can Bob know the code if a noisy channel connects Alice to Bob? One solution to this problem is to assume that Alice and Bob have unbounded computation on their local ends. Thus, for a given code that uses the channel n times, they can both compute the above optimization problem and generate "test" codes randomly until they determine the best possible code to employ for n channel uses. They then both end up with the unique, best possible code for n uses of the given channel. This scheme might be impractical, but nevertheless, it provides a justification for both of them to have knowledge of the code that they use.

Another solution to this problem is simply to allow them to meet before going their separate ways in order to coordinate on the choice of code.

We have said before that the capacity $C(\mathcal{N})$ is the maximal rate at which Alice and Bob can communicate. But in our discussion above, we did not prove optimality—we only proved a direct coding theorem for the channel capacity theorem. It took quite some time and effort to develop this elaborate coding procedure—along the way, we repeatedly invoked one of the powerful tools from probability theory, the law of large numbers. It perhaps seems intuitive that typical sequence coding and decoding should lead to optimal code constructions. Typical sequences exhibit some kind of asymptotic efficiency by being the most likely to occur, but in the general case, their cardinality is exponentially smaller than the set of all sequences. But is this intuition about typical sequence coding correct? Is it possible that some other scheme for coding might beat this elaborate scheme that Shannon devised? *Without a converse theorem that proves optimality, we would never know!* If you recall from our previous discussion in Section 2.1.3 about coding theorems, we stressed how important it is to prove a converse theorem that matches the rate that the direct coding theorem suggests is optimal. For now, we delay the proof of the converse theorem because the tools for proving it are much different from the tools we described in this section. For now, accept that the formula in (2.82) is indeed the optimal rate at which two parties can communicate and we will prove this result in a later chapter.

We end the description of Shannon's channel coding theorem by summarizing the statements of the direct coding theorem and the converse theorem. The statement of the direct coding theorem is as follows:

If the rate of communication is less than the channel capacity, then it is possible for Alice to communicate reliably to Bob, in the sense that a sequence of codes exists whose maximal probability of error vanishes as the number of channel uses tends to infinity.

The statement of the converse theorem is as follows:

If a reliable sequence of codes exists, then the rate of this sequence of codes is less than the channel capacity.

Another way of stating the converse proves to be useful later on:

If the rate of a coding scheme is greater than the channel capacity, then a reliable code does not exist, in the sense that the error probability of the coding scheme is bounded away from zero.

2.3   Summary

A general communication scenario involves one sender and one receiver. In the classical setting, we discussed two information-processing tasks that they can perform. The first task was data compression or source coding, and we assumed that the sender and receiver are linked together by a noiseless classical bit channel that they can use a large number of times. We can think of this noiseless classical bit channel as a *noiseless dynamic resource* that the two parties share. The resource is dynamic because we assume that there is some physical medium through which the physical carrier of information travels in order to get from the sender to the receiver. It was our aim to count the number of times they would have to use the noiseless resource in order to send information reliably. The result of Shannon's source coding theorem is that the entropy gives the minimum rate at which they have to use the noiseless resource. The second task we discussed was channel coding and we assumed that the sender and receiver are linked together by a noisy classical channel that they can use a large number of times. This noisy classical channel is a *noisy dynamic resource* that they share. We can think of this information-processing task as a *simulation task*, where the goal is to simulate a noiseless dynamic resource by using a noisy dynamic resource in a redundant way. This redundancy is what allows Alice to communicate reliably to Bob, and reliable communication implies that they have effectively simulated a noiseless resource. We again had a resource count for this case, where we counted n as the number of times they use the noisy resource and nC is the number of noiseless bit channels they simulate (where C is the capacity of the channel). This notion of resource counting may not seem so important for the classical case, but it becomes much more important for the quantum case.

We now conclude our overview of Shannon's information theory. The main points to take home from this overview are the ideas that Shannon employed for constructing source and channel codes. We let the information source emit a large sequence of data, or similarly, we use the channel a large number of times so that we can invoke the law of large numbers from probability theory. The result is that we can show vanishing error for both schemes by taking a limit. In Chapter 14, we develop the theory of typical sequences in detail, proving many of the results taken for granted in this overview.

In hindsight, Shannon's methods for proving the two coding theorems are merely a *tour de force* for one idea from probability theory: the law of large numbers. Perhaps this viewpoint undermines the contribution of Shannon, until we recall that no one else had even come close to devising these methods for data compression and channel coding. The theoretical development of Shannon is one of the most important contributions to modern science because his theorems determine the ultimate rate at which we can compress and communicate classical information.

Part II

The Quantum Theory

3   The Noiseless Quantum Theory

The simplest quantum system is the physical quantum bit or *qubit*. The qubit is a two-level quantum system—example qubit systems are the spin of an electron, the polarization of a photon, or a two-level atom with a ground state and an excited state. We do not worry too much about physical implementations in this chapter, but instead focus on the mathematical postulates of the quantum theory and operations that we can perform on qubits. From qubits we progress to a study of physical *qudits*. Qudits are quantum systems that have d levels and are an important generalization of qubits. Again, we do not discuss physical realizations of qudits.

Noise can affect quantum systems, and we must understand methods of modeling noise in the quantum theory because our ultimate aim is to construct schemes for protecting quantum systems against the detrimental effects of noise. In Chapter 1, we remarked on the different types of noise that occur in nature. The first, and perhaps more easily comprehensible type of noise, is that which is due to our lack of information about a given scenario. We observe this type of noise in a casino, with every shuffle of cards or toss of dice. These events are random, and the random variables of probability theory model them because the outcomes are unpredictable. This noise is the same as that in all classical information-processing systems.

On the other hand, the quantum theory features a fundamentally different type of noise. Quantum noise is inherent in nature and is not due to our lack of information, but is due rather to nature itself. An example of this type of noise is the "Heisenberg noise" that results from the uncertainty principle. If we know the momentum of a given particle from performing a precise measurement of it, then we know absolutely nothing about its position—a measurement of its position gives a random result. Similarly, if we know the rectilinear polarization of a photon by precisely measuring it, then a future measurement of its diagonal polarization will give a random result. It is important to keep the distinction clear between these two types of noise.

We explore the postulates of the quantum theory in this chapter, by paying particular attention to qubits. These postulates apply to a closed quantum system that is isolated from everything else in the universe. We label this first chapter "The Noiseless Quantum Theory" because closed quantum systems do not interact with their surroundings and are thus not subject to corruption and information loss. Interaction with surrounding systems can lead to loss of information in the sense of the classical noise that we described above. Closed quantum systems do undergo a certain type of quantum noise, such as that from the uncertainty principle and the act of measurement, because they are subject to the postulates of the quantum theory. The name "noiseless quantum theory" thus indicates the closed, ideal nature of the quantum systems discussed.

This chapter introduces the four postulates of the quantum theory. The mathematical tools of the quantum theory rely on the fundamentals of linear algebra—vectors and matrices of complex numbers. It may seem strange at first that we need to incorporate the machinery of linear algebra in order to describe a physical system in the quantum theory, but it turns out that this description uses the simplest set of mathematical tools to predict the phenomena that a quantum system exhibits. A hallmark of the quantum theory is that certain operations do not commute with one another, and matrices are the simplest mathematical objects that capture this idea of non-commutativity.

3.1   Overview

We first briefly overview how information is processed with quantum systems. This usually consists of three steps: state preparation, quantum operations, and measurement. State preparation is the initialization of a quantum system to some beginning state, depending on what operation we would like a quantum system to execute. There could be some classical control device that initializes the state of the quantum system. Observe that the input system for this step is a classical system, and the output system is quantum. After initializing the state of the quantum system, we perform some quantum operations that evolve its state. This stage is where we can take advantage of quantum effects for enhanced information-processing abilities. Both the input and output systems of this step are quantum. Finally, we need some way of reading out the result of the computation, and we can do so with a measurement. The input system for this step is quantum, and the output is classical. Figure 3.1 depicts all of these steps. In a quantum communication protocol, spatially separated parties may execute different parts of these steps, and we are interested in keeping track of the non-local resources needed to implement a communication protocol. Section 3.2 describes quantum states (and thus state preparation), Section 3.3 describes the noiseless evolution of quantum states, and Section 3.4 describes "read out" or measurement. For now, we assume that we can perform all of these steps perfectly and later chapters discuss how to incorporate the effects of noise.

3.2   Quantum Bits

The simplest quantum system is a two-state system: a physical qubit. Let $|0\rangle$ denote one possible state of the system. The left vertical bar and the right angle

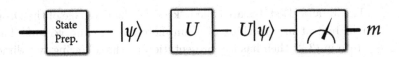

Figure 3.1 All of the steps in a typical noiseless quantum information processing protocol. A classical control (depicted by the thick black line on the left) initializes the state of a quantum system. The quantum system then evolves according to some unitary operation (described in Section 3.3). The final step is a measurement that reads out some classical data m from the quantum system.

bracket indicate that we are using the Dirac notation to represent this state. The Dirac notation has some advantages for performing calculations in the quantum theory, and we highlight some of these advantages as we progress through our development. Let $|1\rangle$ denote another possible state of the qubit. We can encode a classical bit or *cbit* into a qubit with the following mapping:

$$0 \to |0\rangle, \qquad 1 \to |1\rangle. \qquad (3.1)$$

So far, nothing in our description above distinguishes a classical bit from a qubit, except for the funny vertical bar and angle bracket that we place around the bit values. However, the quantum theory predicts that the above states are not the only possible states of a qubit. Arbitrary *superpositions* (linear combinations) of the above two states are possible as well because the quantum theory is a linear theory. Suffice it to say that the linearity of the quantum theory results from the linearity of Schrödinger's equation that governs the evolution of quantum systems.[1] A general noiseless qubit can be in the following state:

$$|\psi\rangle \equiv \alpha|0\rangle + \beta|1\rangle, \qquad (3.2)$$

where the coefficients α and β are arbitrary complex numbers with unit norm: $|\alpha|^2 + |\beta|^2 = 1$. The coefficients α and β are *probability amplitudes*—they are not probabilities themselves, but they do allow us to calculate probabilities. The unit-norm constraint leads to the *Born rule* (the probabilistic interpretation) of the quantum theory, and we speak more on this constraint and probability amplitudes when we introduce the measurement postulate.

The possibility of superposition states indicates that we cannot represent the states $|0\rangle$ and $|1\rangle$ with the Boolean algebra of the respective classical bits 0 and 1 because Boolean algebra does not allow for superposition states. We instead require the mathematics of *linear algebra* to describe these states. It is beneficial at first to define a vector representation of the states $|0\rangle$ and $|1\rangle$:

$$|0\rangle \equiv \begin{bmatrix} 1 \\ 0 \end{bmatrix}, \qquad |1\rangle \equiv \begin{bmatrix} 0 \\ 1 \end{bmatrix}. \qquad (3.3)$$

---

[1] We will not present Schrödinger's equation in this book, but instead focus on a "quantum information" presentation of the quantum theory. Griffith's book on quantum mechanics introduces the quantum theory from the Schrödinger equation if you are interested (Griffiths, 1995).

The $|0\rangle$ and $|1\rangle$ states are called "kets" in the language of the Dirac notation, and it is best at first to think of them merely as column vectors. The superposition state in (3.2) then has a representation as the following two-dimensional vector:

$$|\psi\rangle = \alpha|0\rangle + \beta|1\rangle = \begin{bmatrix} \alpha \\ \beta \end{bmatrix}. \tag{3.4}$$

The representation of quantum states with vectors is helpful in understanding some of the mathematics that underpins the theory, but it turns out to be much more useful for our purposes to work directly with the Dirac notation. We give the vector representation for now, but later on, we will exclusively employ the Dirac notation.

The *Bloch sphere*, depicted in Figure 3.2, gives a valuable way to visualize a qubit. Consider any two qubits that are equivalent up to a differing global phase. For example, these two qubits could be

$$|\psi_0\rangle \equiv |\psi\rangle, \qquad |\psi_1\rangle \equiv e^{i\chi}|\psi\rangle, \tag{3.5}$$

where $0 \le \chi < 2\pi$. These two qubits are physically equivalent because they give the same physical results when we measure them (more on this point when we introduce the measurement postulate in Section 3.4). Suppose that the probability amplitudes α and β have the following representations as complex numbers:

$$\alpha = r_0 e^{i\varphi_0}, \qquad \beta = r_1 e^{i\varphi_1}. \tag{3.6}$$

We can factor out the phase $e^{i\varphi_0}$ from both coefficients α and β, and we still have a state that is physically equivalent to the state in (3.2):

$$|\psi\rangle \equiv r_0|0\rangle + r_1 e^{i(\varphi_1 - \varphi_0)}|1\rangle, \tag{3.7}$$

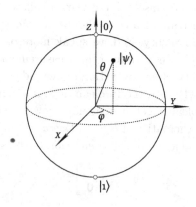

Figure 3.2 The Bloch sphere representation of a qubit. Any qubit $|\psi\rangle$ admits a representation in terms of two angles θ and φ where $0 \le \theta \le \pi$ and $0 \le \varphi < 2\pi$. The state of any qubit in terms of these angles is $|\psi\rangle = \cos(\theta/2)|0\rangle + e^{i\varphi}\sin(\theta/2)|1\rangle$.

where we redefine $|\psi\rangle$ to represent the state because of the equivalence mentioned in (3.5). Let $\varphi \equiv \varphi_1 - \varphi_0$, where $0 \leq \varphi < 2\pi$. Recall that the unit-norm constraint requires $|r_0|^2 + |r_1|^2 = 1$. We can thus parametrize the values of r_0 and r_1 in terms of one parameter θ so that

$$r_0 = \cos(\theta/2), \qquad r_1 = \sin(\theta/2). \tag{3.8}$$

The parameter θ varies between 0 and π. This range of θ and the factor of two give a unique representation of the qubit. One may think to have θ vary between 0 and 2π and omit the factor of two, but this parametrization would not uniquely characterize the qubit in terms of the parameters θ and φ. The parametrization in terms of θ and φ gives the Bloch sphere representation of the qubit in (3.2):

$$|\psi\rangle \equiv \cos(\theta/2)|0\rangle + \sin(\theta/2)e^{i\varphi}|1\rangle. \tag{3.9}$$

In linear algebra, column vectors are not the only type of vectors—row vectors are useful as well. Is there an equivalent of a row vector in Dirac notation? The Dirac notation provides an entity called a "bra," that has a representation as a row vector. The bras corresponding to the kets $|0\rangle$ and $|1\rangle$ are as follows:

$$\langle 0| \equiv \begin{bmatrix} 1 & 0 \end{bmatrix}, \qquad \langle 1| \equiv \begin{bmatrix} 0 & 1 \end{bmatrix}, \tag{3.10}$$

and are the matrix conjugate transpose of the kets $|0\rangle$ and $|1\rangle$:

$$\langle 0| = (|0\rangle)^\dagger, \qquad \langle 1| = (|1\rangle)^\dagger. \tag{3.11}$$

We require the conjugate transpose operation (as opposed to just the transpose) because the mathematical representation of a general quantum state can have complex entries.

The bras do not represent quantum states, but are helpful in calculating probability amplitudes. For our example qubit in (3.2), suppose that we would like to determine the probability amplitude that the state is $|0\rangle$. We can combine the state in (3.2) with the bra $\langle 0|$ as follows:

$$\langle 0||\psi\rangle = \langle 0| \left(\alpha|0\rangle + \beta|1\rangle \right) \tag{3.12}$$

$$= \alpha\langle 0||0\rangle + \beta\langle 0||1\rangle \tag{3.13}$$

$$= \alpha \begin{bmatrix} 1 & 0 \end{bmatrix} \begin{bmatrix} 1 \\ 0 \end{bmatrix} + \beta \begin{bmatrix} 1 & 0 \end{bmatrix} \begin{bmatrix} 0 \\ 1 \end{bmatrix} \tag{3.14}$$

$$= \alpha \cdot 1 + \beta \cdot 0 \tag{3.15}$$

$$= \alpha. \tag{3.16}$$

The above calculation may seem as if it is merely an exercise in linear algebra, with a "glorified" Dirac notation, but it is a standard calculation in the quantum theory. A quantity like $\langle 0||\psi\rangle$ occurs so often in the quantum theory that we abbreviate it as

$$\langle 0|\psi\rangle \equiv \langle 0||\psi\rangle, \tag{3.17}$$

and the above notation is known as a "braket."[2] The physical interpretation of the quantity $\langle 0|\psi\rangle$ is that it is the probability amplitude for being in the state $|0\rangle$, and likewise, the quantity $\langle 1|\psi\rangle$ is the probability amplitude for being in the state $|1\rangle$. We can also determine that the amplitude $\langle 1|0\rangle$ (for the state $|0\rangle$ to be in the state $|1\rangle$) and the amplitude $\langle 0|1\rangle$ are both equal to zero. These two states are *orthogonal states* because they have no overlap. The amplitudes $\langle 0|0\rangle$ and $\langle 1|1\rangle$ are both equal to one by following a similar calculation.

Our next task may seem like a frivolous exercise, but we would like to determine the amplitude for any state $|\psi\rangle$ to be in the state $|\psi\rangle$, i.e., to be itself. Following the above method, this amplitude is $\langle\psi|\psi\rangle$ and we calculate it as

$$\langle\psi|\psi\rangle = ((\langle 0|\alpha^* + \langle 1|\beta^*)(\alpha|0\rangle + \beta|1\rangle)) \tag{3.18}$$

$$= \alpha^*\alpha\,\langle 0|0\rangle + \beta^*\alpha\,\langle 1|0\rangle + \alpha^*\beta\,\langle 0|1\rangle + \beta^*\beta\,\langle 1|1\rangle \tag{3.19}$$

$$= |\alpha|^2 + |\beta|^2 \tag{3.20}$$

$$= 1, \tag{3.21}$$

where we have used the orthogonality relations of $\langle 0|0\rangle$, $\langle 1|0\rangle$, $\langle 0|1\rangle$, and $\langle 1|1\rangle$, and the unit-norm constraint. We also write this in terms of the Euclidean norm of $|\psi\rangle$ as

$$\||\psi\rangle\|_2 \equiv \sqrt{\langle\psi|\psi\rangle} = 1. \tag{3.22}$$

We come back to the unit-norm constraint in our discussion of quantum measurement, but for now, we have shown that any quantum state has a unit amplitude for being itself.

The states $|0\rangle$ and $|1\rangle$ are a particular basis for a qubit that we call the *computational basis*. The computational basis is the standard basis that we employ in quantum computation and communication, but other bases are important as well. Consider that the following two vectors form an orthonormal basis:

$$\frac{1}{\sqrt{2}}\begin{bmatrix} 1 \\ 1 \end{bmatrix}, \qquad \frac{1}{\sqrt{2}}\begin{bmatrix} 1 \\ -1 \end{bmatrix}. \tag{3.23}$$

The above alternate basis is so important in quantum information theory that we define a Dirac notation shorthand for it, and we can also define the basis in terms of the computational basis:

$$|+\rangle \equiv \frac{|0\rangle + |1\rangle}{\sqrt{2}}, \qquad |-\rangle \equiv \frac{|0\rangle - |1\rangle}{\sqrt{2}}. \tag{3.24}$$

The common names for this alternate basis are the "+/−" basis, the Hadamard basis, or the diagonal basis. It is preferable for us to use the Dirac notation, but we are using the vector representation as an aid for now.

---

[2] It is for this (somewhat silly) reason that Dirac decided to use the names "bra" and "ket," because putting them together gives a "braket." The names in the notation may be silly, but the notation itself has persisted over time because this way of representing quantum states turns out to be useful. We will avoid the use of the terms "bra" and "ket" as much as we can, only resorting to these terms if necessary.

EXERCISE 3.2.1 Determine the Bloch sphere angles θ and φ for the states $|+\rangle$ and $|-\rangle$.

What is the amplitude that the state in (3.2) is in the state $|+\rangle$? What is the amplitude that it is in the state $|-\rangle$? These are questions to which the quantum theory provides simple answers. We employ the bra $\langle+|$ and calculate the amplitude $\langle+|\psi\rangle$ as

$$\langle+|\psi\rangle = \langle+|(\alpha|0\rangle + \beta|1\rangle) \tag{3.25}$$
$$= \alpha\langle+|0\rangle + \beta\langle+|1\rangle \tag{3.26}$$
$$= \frac{\alpha+\beta}{\sqrt{2}}. \tag{3.27}$$

The result follows by employing the definition in (3.24) and doing similar linear algebraic calculations as the example in (3.16). We can also calculate the amplitude $\langle-|\psi\rangle$ as

$$\langle-|\psi\rangle = \frac{\alpha-\beta}{\sqrt{2}}. \tag{3.28}$$

The above calculation follows from similar manipulations.

The $+/-$ basis is a *complete* orthonormal basis, meaning that we can represent any qubit state in terms of the two basis states $|+\rangle$ and $|-\rangle$. Indeed, the above probability amplitude calculations and the fact that the $+/-$ basis is complete imply that we can represent the qubit in (3.2) as the following superposition state:

$$|\psi\rangle = \left(\frac{\alpha+\beta}{\sqrt{2}}\right)|+\rangle + \left(\frac{\alpha-\beta}{\sqrt{2}}\right)|-\rangle. \tag{3.29}$$

The above representation is an alternate one if we would like to "see" the qubit state represented in the $+/-$ basis. We can substitute the equalities in (3.27) and (3.28) to represent the state $|\psi\rangle$ as

$$|\psi\rangle = \langle+|\psi\rangle|+\rangle + \langle-|\psi\rangle|-\rangle. \tag{3.30}$$

The amplitudes $\langle+|\psi\rangle$ and $\langle-|\psi\rangle$ are both scalar quantities so that the above quantity is equal to the following one:

$$|\psi\rangle = |+\rangle\langle+|\psi\rangle + |-\rangle\langle-|\psi\rangle. \tag{3.31}$$

The order of the multiplication in the terms $|+\rangle\langle+|\psi\rangle$ and $|-\rangle\langle-|\psi\rangle$ does not matter, i.e., the following equality holds:

$$|+\rangle\left(\langle+|\psi\rangle\right) = \left(|+\rangle\langle+|\right)|\psi\rangle, \tag{3.32}$$

and the same for $|-\rangle\langle-|\psi\rangle$. The quantity on the left is a ket multiplied by an amplitude, whereas the quantity on the right is a linear operator multiplying a ket, but linear algebra tells us that these two quantities are equal. The operators $|+\rangle\langle+|$ and $|-\rangle\langle-|$ are special operators—they are rank-one projection operators, meaning that they project onto a one-dimensional subspace. Using linearity, we have the following equality:

$$|\psi\rangle = (|+\rangle\langle+| + |-\rangle\langle-|) |\psi\rangle. \tag{3.33}$$

The above equation indicates a seemingly trivial, but important point—the operator $|+\rangle\langle+| + |-\rangle\langle-|$ is equal to the identity operator and we can write

$$I = |+\rangle\langle+| + |-\rangle\langle-|, \tag{3.34}$$

where I stands for the identity operator. This relation is known as the *completeness relation* or the *resolution of the identity*. Given any orthonormal basis, we can always construct a resolution of the identity by summing over the rank-one projection operators formed from each of the orthonormal basis states. For example, the computational basis states give another way to form a resolution of the identity operator:

$$I = |0\rangle\langle0| + |1\rangle\langle1|. \tag{3.35}$$

This simple trick provides a way to find the representation of a quantum state in any basis.

3.3   Reversible Evolution

Physical systems evolve as time progresses. The application of a magnetic field to an electron can change its spin and pulsing an atom with a laser can excite one of its electrons from a ground state to an excited state. These are only a couple of ways in which physical systems can change.

The Schrödinger equation governs the evolution of a closed quantum system. In this book, we will not even state the Schrödinger equation, but we will instead focus on an important implication of it. *The evolution of a closed quantum system is reversible if we do not learn anything about the state of the system (that is, if we do not measure it).* Reversibility implies that we can determine the input state of an evolution given the output state and knowledge of the evolution. An example of a single-qubit reversible operation is a NOT gate:

$$|0\rangle \to |1\rangle, \qquad |1\rangle \to |0\rangle. \tag{3.36}$$

In the classical world, we would say that the NOT gate merely flips the value of the input classical bit. In the quantum world, the NOT gate flips the basis states $|0\rangle$ and $|1\rangle$. The NOT gate is reversible because we can simply apply the NOT gate again to recover the original input state—the NOT gate is its own inverse.

In general, a closed quantum system evolves according to a unitary operator U. Unitary evolution implies reversibility because a unitary operator always possesses an inverse—its inverse is merely $U^\dagger$, the conjugate transpose. This property gives the relations:

$$U^\dagger U = U U^\dagger = I. \tag{3.37}$$

The unitary property also ensures that evolution preserves the unit-norm constraint (an important requirement for a physical state that we discuss in Section 3.4). Consider applying the unitary operator U to the example qubit state in (3.2): $U|\psi\rangle$. Figure 3.3 depicts a quantum circuit diagram for unitary evolution.

The bra that is dual to the above state is $\langle\psi|U^\dagger$ (we again apply the conjugate transpose operation to get the bra). We showed in (3.18)–(3.21) that every quantum state should have a unit amplitude for being itself. This relation holds for the state $U|\psi\rangle$ because the operator U is unitary:

$$\langle\psi|U^\dagger U|\psi\rangle = \langle\psi|I|\psi\rangle = \langle\psi|\psi\rangle = 1. \tag{3.38}$$

The assumption that a vector always has a unit amplitude for being itself is one of the crucial assumptions of the quantum theory, and the above reasoning demonstrates that unitary evolution complements this assumption.

EXERCISE 3.3.1 A linear operator T is norm preserving if $\|T|\psi\rangle\|_2 = \||\psi\rangle\|_2$ holds for all quantum states $|\psi\rangle$ (unit vectors), where the Euclidean norm is defined in (3.22). Prove that an operator T is unitary if and only if it is norm preserving. *Hint: For showing the "only-if" part, consider using the polarization identity:*

$$4\langle\psi|\phi\rangle = \||\psi\rangle + |\phi\rangle\|_2^2 - \||\psi\rangle - |\phi\rangle\|_2^2 + i\||\psi\rangle + i|\phi\rangle\|_2^2 - i\||\psi\rangle - i|\phi\rangle\|_2^2. \tag{3.39}$$

3.3.1 Matrix Representations of Operators

We now explore some properties of the NOT gate. Let X denote the operator corresponding to a NOT gate. The action of X on the computational basis states is as follows:

$$X|i\rangle = |i \oplus 1\rangle, \tag{3.40}$$

where $i = \{0,1\}$ and $\oplus$ denotes binary addition. Suppose the NOT gate acts on a superposition state:

$$X\left(\alpha|0\rangle + \beta|1\rangle\right). \tag{3.41}$$

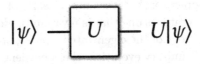

Figure 3.3 A quantum circuit diagram that depicts the evolution of a quantum state $|\psi\rangle$ according to a unitary operator U.

By linearity of the quantum theory, the X operator distributes so that the above expression is equal to the following one:

$$\alpha X|0\rangle + \beta X|1\rangle = \alpha|1\rangle + \beta|0\rangle. \tag{3.42}$$

Indeed, the NOT gate X merely flips the basis states of any quantum state when represented in the computational basis.

We can determine a *matrix representation* for the operator X by using the bras $\langle 0|$ and $\langle 1|$. Consider the relations in (3.40). Let us combine the relations with the bra $\langle 0|$:

$$\langle 0|X|0\rangle = \langle 0|1\rangle = 0, \qquad \langle 0|X|1\rangle = \langle 0|0\rangle = 1. \tag{3.43}$$

Likewise, we can combine with the bra $\langle 1|$:

$$\langle 1|X|0\rangle = \langle 1|1\rangle = 1, \qquad \langle 1|X|1\rangle = \langle 1|0\rangle = 0. \tag{3.44}$$

We can place these entries in a matrix to give a matrix representation of the operator X:

$$\begin{bmatrix} \langle 0|X|0\rangle & \langle 0|X|1\rangle \\ \langle 1|X|0\rangle & \langle 1|X|1\rangle \end{bmatrix}, \tag{3.45}$$

where we order the rows according to the bras and order the columns according to the kets. We then say that

$$X = \begin{bmatrix} 0 & 1 \\ 1 & 0 \end{bmatrix}, \tag{3.46}$$

and adopt the convention that the symbol X refers to both the operator X and its matrix representation (this is an abuse of notation, but it should be clear from the context when X refers to an operator and when it refers to the matrix representation of the operator).

Let us now observe some uniquely quantum behavior. We would like to consider the action of the NOT operator X on the $+/-$ basis. First, let us consider what happens if we operate on the $|+\rangle$ state with the X operator. Recall that the state $|+\rangle = (|0\rangle + |1\rangle)/\sqrt{2}$ so that

$$X|+\rangle = X\left(\frac{|0\rangle + |1\rangle}{\sqrt{2}}\right) = \frac{X|0\rangle + X|1\rangle}{\sqrt{2}} = \frac{|1\rangle + |0\rangle}{\sqrt{2}} = |+\rangle. \tag{3.47}$$

The above development shows that the state $|+\rangle$ is a special state with respect to the NOT operator X—it is an *eigenstate* of X with *eigenvalue* one. An eigenstate of an operator is one that is invariant under the action of the operator. The coefficient in front of the eigenstate is the *eigenvalue* corresponding to the eigenstate. Under a unitary evolution, the coefficient in front of the eigenstate is just a complex phase, but this global phase has no effect on the observations resulting from a measurement of the state because two quantum states are equivalent up to a differing global phase.

Now, let us consider the action of the NOT operator X on the state $|-\rangle$. Recall that $|-\rangle = (|0\rangle - |1\rangle)/\sqrt{2}$. Calculating similarly, we get that

$$X|-\rangle = X\left(\frac{|0\rangle - |1\rangle}{\sqrt{2}}\right) = \frac{X|0\rangle - X|1\rangle}{\sqrt{2}} = \frac{|1\rangle - |0\rangle}{\sqrt{2}} = -|-\rangle. \quad (3.48)$$

So the state $|-\rangle$ is also an eigenstate of the operator X, but its eigenvalue is -1.

We can find a matrix representation of the X operator in the $+/-$ basis as well:

$$\left[\begin{array}{cc} \langle+|X|+\rangle & \langle+|X|-\rangle \\ \langle-|X|+\rangle & \langle-|X|-\rangle \end{array}\right] = \left[\begin{array}{cc} 1 & 0 \\ 0 & -1 \end{array}\right]. \quad (3.49)$$

This representation demonstrates that the X operator is diagonal with respect to the $+/-$ basis, and therefore, the $+/-$ basis is an *eigenbasis* for the X operator. It is always handy to know the eigenbasis of a unitary operator U because this eigenbasis gives the states that are invariant under an evolution according to U.

Let Z denote the operator that flips states in the $+/-$ basis:

$$Z|+\rangle \to |-\rangle, \qquad Z|-\rangle \to |+\rangle. \quad (3.50)$$

Using an analysis similar to that which we did for the X operator, we can find a matrix representation of the Z operator in the $+/-$ basis:

$$\left[\begin{array}{cc} \langle+|Z|+\rangle & \langle+|Z|-\rangle \\ \langle-|Z|+\rangle & \langle-|Z|-\rangle \end{array}\right] = \left[\begin{array}{cc} 0 & 1 \\ 1 & 0 \end{array}\right]. \quad (3.51)$$

Interestingly, the matrix representation for the Z operator in the $+/-$ basis is the same as that for the X operator in the computational basis. For this reason, we call the Z operator the *phase-flip* operator.[3]

We expect the following steps to hold because the quantum theory is a linear theory:

$$Z\left(\frac{|+\rangle + |-\rangle}{\sqrt{2}}\right) = \frac{Z|+\rangle + Z|-\rangle}{\sqrt{2}} = \frac{|-\rangle + |+\rangle}{\sqrt{2}} = \frac{|+\rangle + |-\rangle}{\sqrt{2}}, \quad (3.52)$$

$$Z\left(\frac{|+\rangle - |-\rangle}{\sqrt{2}}\right) = \frac{Z|+\rangle - Z|-\rangle}{\sqrt{2}} = \frac{|-\rangle - |+\rangle}{\sqrt{2}} = -\left(\frac{|+\rangle - |-\rangle}{\sqrt{2}}\right). \quad (3.53)$$

The above steps demonstrate that the states $(|+\rangle + |-\rangle)/\sqrt{2}$ and $(|+\rangle - |-\rangle)/\sqrt{2}$ are both eigenstates of the Z operators. These states are none other than the respective computational basis states $|0\rangle$ and $|1\rangle$, by inspecting the definitions in (3.24). Thus, a matrix representation of the Z operator in the computational basis is

$$\left[\begin{array}{cc} \langle0|Z|0\rangle & \langle0|Z|1\rangle \\ \langle1|Z|0\rangle & \langle1|Z|1\rangle \end{array}\right] = \left[\begin{array}{cc} 1 & 0 \\ 0 & -1 \end{array}\right], \quad (3.54)$$

---

[3] A more appropriate name might be the "bit flip in the $+/-$ basis operator," but this name is too long, so we stick with the term "phase flip."

and is a diagonalization of the operator Z. So, the behavior of the Z operator in the computational basis is the same as the behavior of the X operator in the $+/-$ basis.

3.3.2   Commutators and Anticommutators

The *commutator* $[A, B]$ of two operators A and B is as follows:

$$[A, B] \equiv AB - BA. \tag{3.55}$$

Two operators commute if and only if their commutator is equal to zero.

The *anticommutator* $\{A, B\}$ of two operators A and B is as follows:

$$\{A, B\} \equiv AB + BA. \tag{3.56}$$

We say that two operators *anticommute* if their anticommutator is equal to zero.

EXERCISE 3.3.2   Find a matrix representation for $[X, Z]$ in the basis $\{|0\rangle, |1\rangle\}$.

3.3.3   The Pauli Matrices

The convention in quantum theory is to take the computational basis as the *standard basis* for representing physical qubits. The standard matrix representation for the above two operators is as follows when we choose the computational basis as the standard basis:

$$X \equiv \begin{bmatrix} 0 & 1 \\ 1 & 0 \end{bmatrix}, \quad Z \equiv \begin{bmatrix} 1 & 0 \\ 0 & -1 \end{bmatrix}. \tag{3.57}$$

The identity operator I has the following representation in any basis:

$$I \equiv \begin{bmatrix} 1 & 0 \\ 0 & 1 \end{bmatrix}. \tag{3.58}$$

Another operator, the Y operator, is a useful one to consider as well. The Y operator has the following matrix representation in the computational basis:

$$Y \equiv \begin{bmatrix} 0 & -i \\ i & 0 \end{bmatrix}. \tag{3.59}$$

It is easy to check that $Y = iXZ$, and for this reason, we can think of the Y operator as a combined bit and phase flip. The four matrices I, X, Y, and Z are special for the manipulation of physical qubits and are known as the *Pauli matrices*.

EXERCISE 3.3.3   Show that the Pauli matrices are all Hermitian, unitary, they square to the identity, and their eigenvalues are ± 1.

EXERCISE 3.3.4   Represent the eigenstates of the Y operator in the computational basis.

EXERCISE 3.3.5   Show that the Pauli matrices either commute or anticommute.

EXERCISE 3.3.6   Let us label the Pauli matrices as $\sigma_0 \equiv I$, $\sigma_1 \equiv X$, $\sigma_2 \equiv Y$, and $\sigma_3 \equiv Z$. Show that $\text{Tr} \{\sigma_i \sigma_j\} = 2\delta_{ij}$ for all $i, j \in \{0, \ldots, 3\}$, where Tr denotes the trace of a matrix, defined as the sum of the entries along the diagonal (see also Definition 4.1.1).

3.3.4   Hadamard Gate

Another important unitary operator is the transformation that takes the computational basis to the $+/-$ basis. This transformation is the Hadamard transformation:

$$|0\rangle \rightarrow |+\rangle, \qquad |1\rangle \rightarrow |-\rangle. \tag{3.60}$$

Using the above relations, we can represent the Hadamard transformation as the following operator:

$$H \equiv |+\rangle\langle 0| + |-\rangle\langle 1|. \tag{3.61}$$

It is straightforward to check that the above operator implements the transformation in (3.60).

Now consider a generalization of the above construction. Suppose that one orthonormal basis is $\{|\psi_i\rangle\}_{i\in\{0,1\}}$ and another is $\{|\phi_i\rangle\}_{i\in\{0,1\}}$ where the index i merely indexes the states in each orthonormal basis. Then the unitary operator that takes states in the first basis to states in the second basis is

$$\sum_{i=0,1} |\phi_i\rangle\langle\psi_i|. \tag{3.62}$$

EXERCISE 3.3.7   Show that the Hadamard operator H has the following matrix representation in the computational basis:

$$H = \frac{1}{\sqrt{2}} \begin{bmatrix} 1 & 1 \\ 1 & -1 \end{bmatrix}. \tag{3.63}$$

EXERCISE 3.3.8   Show that the Hadamard operator is its own inverse by employing the above matrix representation and by using its operator form in (3.61).

EXERCISE 3.3.9   If the Hadamard gate is its own inverse, then it takes the states $|+\rangle$ and $|-\rangle$ to the respective states $|0\rangle$ and $|1\rangle$ and we can represent it as the following operator: $H = |0\rangle\langle+| + |1\rangle\langle-|$. Show that $|0\rangle\langle+| + |1\rangle\langle-| = |+\rangle\langle0| + |-\rangle\langle1|$.

EXERCISE 3.3.10   Show that $HXH = Z$ and that $HZH = X$.

3.3.5   Rotation Operators

We end this section on the evolution of quantum states by discussing "rotation evolutions" and by giving a more complete picture of the Bloch sphere. The rotation operators $R_X(\phi)$, $R_Y(\phi)$, $R_Z(\phi)$ are functions of the respective Pauli operators X, Y, Z where

$$R_X(\phi) \equiv \exp\{iX\phi/2\}, \quad R_Y(\phi) \equiv \exp\{iY\phi/2\}, \quad R_Z(\phi) \equiv \exp\{iZ\phi/2\}, \tag{3.64}$$

and ϕ is some angle such that $0 \leq \phi < 2\pi$. How do we determine a function of an operator? The standard way is to represent the operator in its diagonal basis and apply the function to the non-zero eigenvalues of the operator. For example, the diagonal representation of the X operator is

$$X = |+\rangle\langle+| - |-\rangle\langle-|. \tag{3.65}$$

Applying the function $\exp\{iX\phi/2\}$ to the non-zero eigenvalues of X gives

$$R_X(\phi) = \exp\{i\phi/2\}|+\rangle\langle+| + \exp\{-i\phi/2\}|-\rangle\langle-|. \tag{3.66}$$

This is a special case of the following more general convention that we follow throughout this book:

DEFINITION 3.3.1 (Function of a Hermitian Operator)   Suppose that a Hermitian operator A has a spectral decomposition $A = \sum_{i:a_i \neq 0} a_i |i\rangle\langle i|$ for some orthonormal basis $\{|i\rangle\}$. Then the operator $f(A)$ for some function f is defined as follows:

$$f(A) \equiv \sum_{i:a_i \neq 0} f(a_i)|i\rangle\langle i|. \tag{3.67}$$

EXERCISE 3.3.11   Show that the rotation operators $R_X(\phi)$, $R_Y(\phi)$, $R_Z(\phi)$ are equal to the following expressions:

$$R_X(\phi) = \cos(\phi/2)I + i\sin(\phi/2)X, \tag{3.68}$$
$$R_Y(\phi) = \cos(\phi/2)I + i\sin(\phi/2)Y, \tag{3.69}$$
$$R_Z(\phi) = \cos(\phi/2)I + i\sin(\phi/2)Z, \tag{3.70}$$

by using the facts that $\cos(\phi/2) = (e^{i\phi/2} + e^{-i\phi/2})/2$ and $\sin(\phi/2) = (e^{i\phi/2} - e^{-i\phi/2})/2i$.

Figure 3.4 provides a more detailed picture of the Bloch sphere since we have now established the Pauli operators and their eigenstates. The computational basis states are the eigenstates of the Z operator and are the north and south poles on the Bloch sphere. The $+/-$ basis states are the eigenstates of the X operator and the calculation from Exercise 3.2.1 shows that they are the "east and west poles" of the Bloch sphere. We leave it as another exercise to show that the Y eigenstates are the other poles along the equator of the Bloch sphere.

EXERCISE 3.3.12   Determine the Bloch sphere angles θ and φ for the eigenstates of the Pauli Y operator.

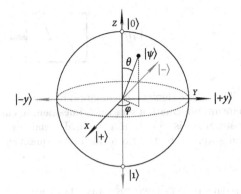

Figure 3.4 This figure provides more labels for states on the Bloch sphere. The Z axis has its points on the sphere as eigenstates of the Pauli Z operator, the X axis has eigenstates of the Pauli X operator, and the Y axis has eigenstates of the Pauli Y operator. The rotation operators $R_X(\phi)$, $R_Y(\phi)$, and $R_Z(\phi)$ rotate a state on the sphere by an angle ϕ about the respective X, Y, and Z axis.

3.4 Measurement

Measurement is another type of evolution that a quantum system can undergo. It is an evolution that allows us to retrieve classical information from a quantum state and thus is the way that we can "read out" information. Suppose that we would like to learn something about the quantum state $|\psi\rangle$ in (3.2). Nature prevents us from learning anything about the probability amplitudes α and β if we have only one quantum measurement that we can perform on one copy of the state. Nature only allows us to measure *observables*. Observables are physical variables such as the position or momentum of a particle. In the quantum theory, we represent observables as Hermitian operators in part because their eigenvalues are real numbers and every measuring device outputs a real number. Examples of qubit observables that we can measure are the Pauli operators X, Y, and Z.

Suppose that we measure the Z operator. This measurement is called a "measurement in the computational basis" or a "measurement of the Z observable" because we are measuring the eigenvalues of the Z operator. The measurement postulate of the quantum theory, also known as the *Born rule*, states that the system reduces to the state $|0\rangle$ with probability $|\alpha|^2$ and reduces to the state $|1\rangle$ with probability $|\beta|^2$. That is, the resulting probabilities are the squares of the probability amplitudes. After the measurement, our measuring apparatus tells us whether the state reduced to $|0\rangle$ or $|1\rangle$—it returns $+1$ if the resulting state is $|0\rangle$ and returns -1 if the resulting state is $|1\rangle$. These returned values are the eigenvalues of the Z operator. The measurement postulate is the aspect of the quantum theory that makes it probabilistic or "jumpy" and is part of the "strangeness" of the quantum theory. Figure 3.5 depicts the notation for a measurement that we will use in diagrams throughout this book.

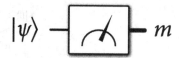

Figure 3.5 This figure depicts our diagram of a quantum measurement. Thin lines denote quantum information and thick lines denote classical information. The result of the measurement is to output a classical variable m according to a probability distribution governed by the Born rule of the quantum theory.

What is the result if we measure the state $|\psi\rangle$ in the $+/-$ basis? Consider that we can represent $|\psi\rangle$ as a superposition of the $|+\rangle$ and $|-\rangle$ states, as given in (3.29). The measurement postulate then states that a measurement of the X operator gives the state $|+\rangle$ with probability $|\alpha + \beta|^2/2$ and the state $|-\rangle$ with probability $|\alpha - \beta|^2/2$. Quantum interference is now coming into play because the amplitudes α and β interfere with each other. So this effect plays an important role in quantum information theory.

In some cases, the basis states $|0\rangle$ and $|1\rangle$ may not represent the spin states of an electron, but may represent the *location* of an electron. So, a way to interpret this measurement postulate is that the electron "jumps into" one location or another depending on the outcome of the measurement. But what is the state of the electron before the measurement? We will just say in this book that it is in a superposed, indefinite, or unsharp state, rather than trying to pin down a philosophical interpretation. Some might say that the electron is in "two different locations at the same time."

Also, we should stress that we cannot interpret the measurement postulate as meaning that the state is in $|0\rangle$ or $|1\rangle$ with respective probabilities $|\alpha|^2$ and $|\beta|^2$ before the measurement occurs, because this latter interpretation is physically different from what we described above and is also completely classical. The superposition state $\alpha|0\rangle + \beta|1\rangle$ gives fundamentally different behavior from the probabilistic description of a state that is in $|0\rangle$ or $|1\rangle$ with respective probabilities $|\alpha|^2$ and $|\beta|^2$. Suppose that we have the two different descriptions of a state (superposition and probabilistic) and measure the Z operator. We get the same result for both cases—the resulting state is $|0\rangle$ or $|1\rangle$ with respective probabilities $|\alpha|^2$ and $|\beta|^2$.

But now suppose that we measure the X operator. The superposed state gives the result from before—we get the state $|+\rangle$ with probability $|\alpha + \beta|^2/2$ and the state $|-\rangle$ with probability $|\alpha - \beta|^2/2$. The probabilistic description gives a much different result. Suppose that the state is $|0\rangle$. We know that $|0\rangle$ is a uniform superposition of $|+\rangle$ and $|-\rangle$:

$$|0\rangle = \frac{|+\rangle + |-\rangle}{\sqrt{2}}. \tag{3.71}$$

Table 3.1 This table summarizes the differences in probabilities for a quantum state in a superposition $\alpha|0\rangle + \beta|1\rangle$ and a classical state that is a probabilistic mixture of $|0\rangle$ and $|1\rangle$.

Quantum State	Probability of $|+\rangle$	Probability of $|-\rangle$
Superposition state	$|\alpha + \beta|^2/2$	$|\alpha - \beta|^2/2$
Probabilistic description	$1/2$	$1/2$

So the state collapses to $|+\rangle$ or $|-\rangle$ with equal probability in this case. If the state is $|1\rangle$, then it collapses again to $|+\rangle$ or $|-\rangle$ with equal probabilities. Summing up these probabilities, it follows that a measurement of the X operator gives the state $|+\rangle$ with probability $\left(|\alpha|^2 + |\beta|^2\right)/2 = 1/2$ and gives the state $|-\rangle$ with the same probability. These results are fundamentally different from those in which the state is the superposition state $|\psi\rangle$, and experiment after experiment has supported the predictions of the quantum theory. Table 3.1 summarizes the results that we just discussed.

Now we consider a "Stern–Gerlach"-like argument to illustrate another example of fundamental quantum behavior (Gerlach & Stern, 1922). The Stern–Gerlach experiment was a crucial one for determining the "strange" behavior of quantum spin states. Suppose that we prepare the state $|0\rangle$. If we measure this state in the Z basis, the result is that we always obtain the state $|0\rangle$ because the prepared state is a definite Z eigenstate. Suppose now that we measure the X operator. The state $|0\rangle$ is equal to a uniform superposition of $|+\rangle$ and $|-\rangle$. The measurement postulate then states that we get the state $|+\rangle$ or $|-\rangle$ with equal probability after performing this measurement. If we then measure the Z operator again, the result is completely random. The Z measurement result is $|0\rangle$ or $|1\rangle$ with equal probability if the result of the X measurement is $|+\rangle$ and the same outcome occurs if the result of the X measurement is $|-\rangle$. This argument demonstrates that the measurement of the X operator "throws off" the measurement of the Z operator. The Stern–Gerlach experiment was one of the earliest to validate the predictions of the quantum theory.

3.4.1 Probability, Expectation, and Variance of an Operator

We have an alternate, more formal way of stating the measurement postulate that turns out to be more useful for a general quantum system. Suppose that we are measuring the Z operator. The diagonal representation of this operator is

$$Z = |0\rangle\langle 0| - |1\rangle\langle 1|. \tag{3.72}$$

Consider the Hermitian operator

$$\Pi_0 \equiv |0\rangle\langle 0|. \tag{3.73}$$

It is a projection operator because applying it twice has the same effect as applying it once: $\Pi_0^2 = \Pi_0$. It projects onto the subspace spanned by the single vector $|0\rangle$. A similar line of analysis applies to the projection operator

$$\Pi_1 \equiv |1\rangle\langle 1|. \tag{3.74}$$

So we can represent the Z operator as $\Pi_0 - \Pi_1$. Performing a measurement of the Z operator is equivalent to asking the question: Is the state $|0\rangle$ or $|1\rangle$? Consider the quantity $\langle \psi | \Pi_0 | \psi \rangle$:

$$\langle \psi | \Pi_0 | \psi \rangle = \langle \psi | 0 \rangle \langle 0 | \psi \rangle = \alpha^* \alpha = |\alpha|^2. \tag{3.75}$$

A similar analysis demonstrates that

$$\langle \psi | \Pi_1 | \psi \rangle = |\beta|^2. \tag{3.76}$$

These two quantities then give the probability that the state reduces to $|0\rangle$ or $|1\rangle$.

A more general way of expressing a measurement of the Z basis is to say that we have a set $\{\Pi_i\}_{i \in \{0,1\}}$ of measurement operators that determine the outcome probabilities. These measurement operators also determine the state that results after the measurement. If the measurement result is $+1$, then the resulting state is

$$\frac{\Pi_0 | \psi \rangle}{\sqrt{\langle \psi | \Pi_0 | \psi \rangle}} = |0\rangle, \tag{3.77}$$

where we implicitly ignore the irrelevant global phase factor $\frac{\alpha}{|\alpha|}$. If the measurement result is -1, then the resulting state is

$$\frac{\Pi_1 | \psi \rangle}{\sqrt{\langle \psi | \Pi_1 | \psi \rangle}} = |1\rangle, \tag{3.78}$$

where we again implicitly ignore the irrelevant global phase factor $\frac{\beta}{|\beta|}$. Dividing by $\sqrt{\langle \psi | \Pi_i | \psi \rangle}$ for $i = 0, 1$ ensures that the state resulting after measurement corresponds to a physical state (a unit vector).

We can also measure any orthonormal basis in this way this type of projective measurement is called a *von Neumann measurement*. For any orthonormal basis $\{|\phi_i\rangle\}_{i \in \{0,1\}}$, the measurement operators are $\{|\phi_i\rangle\langle\phi_i|\}_{i \in \{0,1\}}$, and the state reduces to $|\phi_i\rangle\langle\phi_i|\psi\rangle / |\langle\phi_i|\psi\rangle|$ with probability $\langle\psi|\phi_i\rangle\langle\phi_i|\psi\rangle = |\langle\phi_i|\psi\rangle|^2$.

EXERCISE 3.4.1 Determine the set of measurement operators corresponding to a measurement of the X observable.

We might want to determine the expectation of the measurement result when measuring the Z operator. The probability of getting the $+1$ value corresponding to the $|0\rangle$ state is $|\alpha|^2$ and the probability of getting the -1 value corresponding to the -1 eigenstate is $|\beta|^2$. Standard probability theory then gives us a way to calculate the expected value of a measurement of the Z operator when the state is $|\psi\rangle$:

$$\mathbb{E}[Z] = |\alpha|^2 (1) + |\beta|^2 (-1) = |\alpha|^2 - |\beta|^2. \qquad (3.79)$$

We can formulate an alternate way to write this expectation, by making use of the Dirac notation:

$$\mathbb{E}[Z] = |\alpha|^2 (1) + |\beta|^2 (-1) \qquad (3.80)$$
$$= \langle\psi|\Pi_0|\psi\rangle + \langle\psi|\Pi_1|\psi\rangle (-1) \qquad (3.81)$$
$$= \langle\psi|\Pi_0 - \Pi_1|\psi\rangle \qquad (3.82)$$
$$= \langle\psi|Z|\psi\rangle. \qquad (3.83)$$

It is common for physicists to denote the expectation as

$$\langle Z \rangle \equiv \langle\psi|Z|\psi\rangle, \qquad (3.84)$$

when it is understood that the expectation is with respect to the state $|\psi\rangle$. This type of expression is a general one and the next exercise asks you to show that it works for the X and Y operators as well.

EXERCISE 3.4.2   Show that the expressions $\langle\psi|X|\psi\rangle$ and $\langle\psi|Y|\psi\rangle$ give the respective expectations $\mathbb{E}[X]$ and $\mathbb{E}[Y]$ when measuring the state $|\psi\rangle$ in the respective X and Y basis.

We also might want to determine the variance of the measurement of the Z operator. Standard probability theory again gives that

$$\mathrm{Var}[Z] = \mathbb{E}[Z^2] - \mathbb{E}[Z]^2. \qquad (3.85)$$

Physicists denote the standard deviation of the measurement of the Z operator as

$$\Delta Z \equiv \left\langle (Z - \langle Z\rangle)^2 \right\rangle^{1/2}, \qquad (3.86)$$

and thus the variance is equal to $(\Delta Z)^2$. Physicists often refer to ΔZ as the uncertainty of the observable Z when the state is $|\psi\rangle$.

In order to calculate the variance $\mathrm{Var}[Z]$, we really just need the second moment $\mathbb{E}[Z^2]$ because we already have the expectation $\mathbb{E}[Z]$:

$$\mathbb{E}[Z^2] = |\alpha|^2 (1)^2 + |\beta|^2 (-1)^2 = |\alpha|^2 + |\beta|^2. \qquad (3.87)$$

We can again calculate this quantity with the Dirac notation. The quantity $\langle\psi|Z^2|\psi\rangle$ is the same as $\mathbb{E}[Z^2]$ and the next exercise asks you for a proof.

EXERCISE 3.4.3   Show that $\mathbb{E}[X^2] = \langle\psi|X^2|\psi\rangle$, $\mathbb{E}[Y^2] = \langle\psi|Y^2|\psi\rangle$, and $\mathbb{E}[Z^2] = \langle\psi|Z^2|\psi\rangle$.

3.4.2   The Uncertainty Principle

The uncertainty principle is a fundamental feature of the quantum theory. In the case of qubits, one instance of the uncertainty principle gives a lower bound on the product of the uncertainty of the Z operator and the uncertainty of the X operator:

$$\Delta Z \Delta X \geq \frac{1}{2} |\langle \psi | [Z, X] | \psi \rangle|. \tag{3.88}$$

We can prove this principle using the postulates of the quantum theory. Let us define the operators $Z_0 \equiv Z - \langle Z \rangle$ and $X_0 \equiv X - \langle X \rangle$. First, consider that

$$\Delta Z \Delta X = \langle \psi | Z_0^2 | \psi \rangle^{1/2} \langle \psi | X_0^2 | \psi \rangle^{1/2} \geq |\langle \psi | Z_0 X_0 | \psi \rangle|. \tag{3.89}$$

The above step follows by applying the Cauchy–Schwarz inequality to the vectors $X_0 | \psi \rangle$ and $Z_0 | \psi \rangle$. For any operator A, we define its real part Re $\{A\}$ as Re $\{A\} \equiv (A + A^\dagger)/2$, and its imaginary part Im $\{A\}$ as Im $\{A\} \equiv (A - A^\dagger)/2i$, so that $A = \text{Re}\,\{A\} + i \,\text{Im}\,\{A\}$. So the real and imaginary parts of the operator $Z_0 X_0$ are

$$\text{Re}\,\{Z_0 X_0\} = \frac{Z_0 X_0 + X_0 Z_0}{2} \equiv \frac{\{Z_0, X_0\}}{2}, \tag{3.90}$$

$$\text{Im}\,\{Z_0 X_0\} = \frac{Z_0 X_0 - X_0 Z_0}{2i} \equiv \frac{[Z_0, X_0]}{2i}, \tag{3.91}$$

where $\{Z_0, X_0\}$ is the anticommutator of Z_0 and X_0 and $[Z_0, X_0]$ is the commutator of the two operators. We can then express the quantity $|\langle \psi | Z_0 X_0 | \psi \rangle|$ in terms of the real and imaginary parts of $Z_0 X_0$:

$$|\langle \psi | Z_0 X_0 | \psi \rangle| = |\langle \psi | \text{Re}\,\{Z_0 X_0\} | \psi \rangle + i \langle \psi | \text{Im}\,\{Z_0 X_0\} | \psi \rangle| \tag{3.92}$$

$$\geq |\langle \psi | \text{Im}\,\{Z_0 X_0\} | \psi \rangle| \tag{3.93}$$

$$= |\langle \psi | [Z_0, X_0] | \psi \rangle| / 2 \tag{3.94}$$

$$= |\langle \psi | [Z, X] | \psi \rangle| / 2. \tag{3.95}$$

The first equality follows by substitution. The first inequality follows because the magnitude of any complex number is greater than the magnitude of its imaginary part. The second equality follows by substitution with (3.91). Finally, the third equality follows from the result of Exercise 3.4.4 below. We worked out the above derivation for particular observables acting on qubit states, but note that it holds for general observables and quantum states.

The commutator of the operators Z and X arises in the lower bound, and thus, the non-commutativity of the operators Z and X is the fundamental reason that there is an uncertainty principle for them. Also, there is no uncertainty principle for any two operators that commute with each other.

It is worthwhile to interpret the uncertainty principle in (3.88), which really receives an interpretation after conducting a large number of independent experiments of two different kinds. In the first kind of experiment, one prepares the state $|\psi\rangle$ and measures the Z observable. After repeating this experiment independently many times, one can calculate an estimate of the standard deviation ΔZ, which becomes closer and closer to the true standard deviation ΔZ as the number of independent experiments becomes large. In the second kind of experiment, one prepares the state $|\psi\rangle$ and measures the X observable. After repeating many times, one can calculate an estimate of ΔX. The uncertainty principle then states that the product of the estimates (for a large number of independent experiments) is bounded from below by the expectation of the commutator: $\frac{1}{2}|\langle\psi|[X,Z]|\psi\rangle|$.

EXERCISE 3.4.4   Show that $[Z_0, X_0] = [Z, X]$ and that $[Z, X] = -2iY$.

EXERCISE 3.4.5   The uncertainty principle in (3.88) has the property that the lower bound has a dependence on the state $|\psi\rangle$. Find a state $|\psi\rangle$ for which the lower bound on the uncertainty product $\Delta X \Delta Z$ vanishes.[4]

3.5   Composite Quantum Systems

A single physical qubit is an interesting physical system that exhibits uniquely quantum phenomena, but it is not particularly useful on its own (just as a single classical bit is not particularly useful for classical communication or computation). We can only perform interesting quantum information-processing tasks when we combine qubits together. Therefore, we should have a way to describe their behavior when they combine to form a composite quantum system.

Consider two classical bits c_0 and c_1. In order to describe bit operations on the pair of cbits, we write them as an ordered pair (c_1, c_0). The space of all possible bit values is the Cartesian product $\mathbb{Z}_2 \times \mathbb{Z}_2$ of two copies of the set $\mathbb{Z}_2 \equiv \{0, 1\}$:

$$\mathbb{Z}_2 \times \mathbb{Z}_2 \equiv \{(0,0), (0,1), (1,0), (1,1)\}. \tag{3.96}$$

Typically, we make the abbreviation $c_1 c_0 \equiv (c_1, c_0)$ when representing cbit states.

We can represent the state of two cbits with particular states of qubits. For example, we can represent the two-cbit state 00 using the following mapping:

$$00 \rightarrow |0\rangle|0\rangle. \tag{3.97}$$

Many times, we make the abbreviation $|00\rangle \equiv |0\rangle|0\rangle$ when representing two-cbit states with qubits. Any two-cbit state $c_1 c_0$ has the following representation as a two-qubit state:

$$c_1 c_0 \rightarrow |c_1 c_0\rangle. \tag{3.98}$$

---

[4] Do not be alarmed by the result of this exercise! The usual formulation of the uncertainty principle only gives a lower bound on the uncertainty product. This lower bound never vanishes for the case of position and momentum observables because the commutator of these two observables is equal to the identity operator multiplied by i, but it can vanish for the operators given in the exercise.

The above qubit states are not the only possible states that can occur in the quantum theory. By the superposition principle, any possible linear combination of the set of two-cbit states is a possible two-qubit state:

$$|\xi\rangle \equiv \alpha|00\rangle + \beta|01\rangle + \gamma|10\rangle + \delta|11\rangle. \tag{3.99}$$

The unit-norm condition $|\alpha|^2 + |\beta|^2 + |\gamma|^2 + |\delta|^2 = 1$ again must hold for the two-qubit state to correspond to a physical quantum state. It is now clear that the Cartesian product is not sufficient for representing two-qubit quantum states because it does not allow for linear combinations of states (just as the mathematics of Boolean algebra is not sufficient to represent single-qubit states).

We again turn to linear algebra to determine a representation that suffices. The *tensor product* is a mathematical operation that suffices to give a representation of two-qubit quantum states. Suppose we have two two-dimensional vectors:

$$\begin{bmatrix} a_1 \\ b_1 \end{bmatrix}, \quad \begin{bmatrix} a_2 \\ b_2 \end{bmatrix}. \tag{3.100}$$

The tensor product of these two vectors is

$$\begin{bmatrix} a_1 \\ b_1 \end{bmatrix} \otimes \begin{bmatrix} a_2 \\ b_2 \end{bmatrix} \equiv \begin{bmatrix} a_1 \begin{bmatrix} a_2 \\ b_2 \end{bmatrix} \\ b_1 \begin{bmatrix} a_2 \\ b_2 \end{bmatrix} \end{bmatrix} = \begin{bmatrix} a_1 a_2 \\ a_1 b_2 \\ b_1 a_2 \\ b_1 b_2 \end{bmatrix}. \tag{3.101}$$

One can understand this operation as taking the vector on the right and stacking two copies of it together, while multiplying each copy by the corresponding number in the first vector.

Recall, from (3.3), the vector representation of the single-qubit states $|0\rangle$ and $|1\rangle$. Using these vector representations and the above definition of the tensor product, the two-qubit basis states have the following vector representations:

$$|00\rangle = \begin{bmatrix} 1 \\ 0 \\ 0 \\ 0 \end{bmatrix}, \quad |01\rangle = \begin{bmatrix} 0 \\ 1 \\ 0 \\ 0 \end{bmatrix}, \quad |10\rangle = \begin{bmatrix} 0 \\ 0 \\ 1 \\ 0 \end{bmatrix}, \quad |11\rangle = \begin{bmatrix} 0 \\ 0 \\ 0 \\ 1 \end{bmatrix}. \tag{3.102}$$

A simple way to remember these representations is that the bits inside the ket index the element equal to one in the vector. For example, the vector representation of $|01\rangle$ has a one as its second element because 01 is the second index for the two-bit strings. The vector representation of the superposition state in (3.99) is

$$\begin{bmatrix} \alpha \\ \beta \\ \gamma \\ \delta \end{bmatrix}. \tag{3.103}$$

There are actually many different ways that we can write two-qubit states, and we list all of these right now. Physicists have developed many shorthands, and it is important to know each of them because they often appear in the literature (this book even uses different notations depending on the context). We may use any of the following two-qubit notations if the two qubits are local to one party and only one party is involved in a protocol:

$$\alpha|0\rangle \otimes |0\rangle + \beta|0\rangle \otimes |1\rangle + \gamma|1\rangle \otimes |0\rangle + \delta|1\rangle \otimes |1\rangle, \tag{3.104}$$

$$\alpha|0\rangle|0\rangle + \beta|0\rangle|1\rangle + \gamma|1\rangle|0\rangle + \delta|1\rangle|1\rangle, \tag{3.105}$$

$$\alpha|00\rangle + \beta|01\rangle + \gamma|10\rangle + \delta|11\rangle. \tag{3.106}$$

We can put labels on the qubits if two or more parties, such as A and B, are involved

$$\alpha|0\rangle_A \otimes |0\rangle_B + \beta|0\rangle_A \otimes |1\rangle_B + \gamma|1\rangle_A \otimes |0\rangle_B + \delta|1\rangle_A \otimes |1\rangle_B, \tag{3.107}$$

$$\alpha|0\rangle_A|0\rangle_B + \beta|0\rangle_A|1\rangle_B + \gamma|1\rangle_A|0\rangle_B + \delta|1\rangle_A|1\rangle_B, \tag{3.108}$$

$$\alpha|00\rangle_{AB} + \beta|01\rangle_{AB} + \gamma|10\rangle_{AB} + \delta|11\rangle_{AB}. \tag{3.109}$$

This second scenario is different from the first scenario because two spatially separated parties share the two-qubit state. If the state has quantum correlations, then it can be valuable as a communication resource. We go into more detail on this topic in Section 3.6, which discusses *entanglement*.

3.5.1 Evolution of Composite Systems

The postulate on unitary evolution extends to the two-qubit scenario as well. First, let us establish that the tensor product $A \otimes B$ of two operators A and B is

$$A \otimes B \equiv \begin{bmatrix} a_{11} & a_{12} \\ a_{21} & a_{22} \end{bmatrix} \otimes \begin{bmatrix} b_{11} & b_{12} \\ b_{21} & b_{22} \end{bmatrix} \tag{3.110}$$

$$\equiv \begin{bmatrix} a_{11} \begin{bmatrix} b_{11} & b_{12} \\ b_{21} & b_{22} \end{bmatrix} & a_{12} \begin{bmatrix} b_{11} & b_{12} \\ b_{21} & b_{22} \end{bmatrix} \\ a_{21} \begin{bmatrix} b_{11} & b_{12} \\ b_{21} & b_{22} \end{bmatrix} & a_{22} \begin{bmatrix} b_{11} & b_{12} \\ b_{21} & b_{22} \end{bmatrix} \end{bmatrix} \tag{3.111}$$

$$= \begin{bmatrix} a_{11}b_{11} & a_{11}b_{12} & a_{12}b_{11} & a_{12}b_{12} \\ a_{11}b_{21} & a_{11}b_{22} & a_{12}b_{21} & a_{12}b_{22} \\ a_{21}b_{11} & a_{21}b_{12} & a_{22}b_{11} & a_{22}b_{12} \\ a_{21}b_{21} & a_{21}b_{22} & a_{22}b_{21} & a_{22}b_{22} \end{bmatrix}. \tag{3.112}$$

The tensor-product operation for matrices is similar to what we did for vectors, but now we are stacking copies of the matrix on the right both vertically and horizontally, and multiplying each copy by the corresponding number in the first matrix.

Consider the two-qubit state in (3.99). We can perform a NOT gate on the first qubit so that it changes to $\alpha|10\rangle + \beta|11\rangle + \gamma|00\rangle + \delta|01\rangle$. We can alternatively flip its second qubit: $\alpha|01\rangle + \beta|00\rangle + \gamma|11\rangle + \delta|10\rangle$, or flip both at the same time: $\alpha|11\rangle + \beta|10\rangle + \gamma|01\rangle + \delta|00\rangle$. Figure 3.6 depicts quantum circuit representations

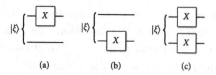

Figure 3.6 This figure depicts circuits for the example two-qubit unitaries $X_1 I_2$, $I_1 X_2$, and $X_1 X_2$.

of these operations. These are all reversible operations because applying them again gives the original state in (3.99). In the first case, we did nothing to the second qubit, and in the second case, we did nothing to the first qubit. The identity operator acts on the qubits that have nothing happen to them.

Let us label the first qubit as "1" and the second qubit as "2." We can then label the operator for the first operation as $X_1 I_2$ because this operator flips the first qubit and does nothing (applies the identity) to the second qubit. We can also label the operators for the second and third operations respectively as $I_1 X_2$ and $X_1 X_2$. The matrix representation of the operator $X_1 I_2$ is the tensor product of the matrix representation of X with the matrix representation of I—this relation similarly holds for the operators $I_1 X_2$ and $X_1 X_2$. We show that it holds for the operator $X_1 I_2$ and ask you to verify the other two cases. We can use the two-qubit computational basis to get a matrix representation for the two-qubit operator $X_1 I_2$:

$$
\begin{bmatrix}
\langle 00|X_1 I_2|00\rangle & \langle 00|X_1 I_2|01\rangle & \langle 00|X_1 I_2|10\rangle & \langle 00|X_1 I_2|11\rangle \\
\langle 01|X_1 I_2|00\rangle & \langle 01|X_1 I_2|01\rangle & \langle 01|X_1 I_2|10\rangle & \langle 01|X_1 I_2|11\rangle \\
\langle 10|X_1 I_2|00\rangle & \langle 10|X_1 I_2|01\rangle & \langle 10|X_1 I_2|10\rangle & \langle 10|X_1 I_2|11\rangle \\
\langle 11|X_1 I_2|00\rangle & \langle 11|X_1 I_2|01\rangle & \langle 11|X_1 I_2|10\rangle & \langle 11|X_1 I_2|11\rangle
\end{bmatrix}
$$

$$
=
\begin{bmatrix}
\langle 00|10\rangle & \langle 00|11\rangle & \langle 00|00\rangle & \langle 00|01\rangle \\
\langle 01|10\rangle & \langle 01|11\rangle & \langle 01|00\rangle & \langle 01|01\rangle \\
\langle 10|10\rangle & \langle 10|11\rangle & \langle 10|00\rangle & \langle 10|01\rangle \\
\langle 11|10\rangle & \langle 11|11\rangle & \langle 11|00\rangle & \langle 11|01\rangle
\end{bmatrix}
=
\begin{bmatrix}
0 & 0 & 1 & 0 \\
0 & 0 & 0 & 1 \\
1 & 0 & 0 & 0 \\
0 & 1 & 0 & 0
\end{bmatrix}. \quad (3.113)
$$

This last matrix is equal to the tensor product $X \otimes I$ by inspecting the definition of the tensor product for matrices in (3.110).

EXERCISE 3.5.1   Show that the matrix representation of the operator $I_1 X_2$ is equal to the tensor product $I \otimes X$. Show the same for $X_1 X_2$ and $X \otimes X$.

3.5.2   Probability Amplitudes for Composite Systems

We relied on the orthogonality of the two-qubit computational basis states for evaluating amplitudes such as $\langle 00|10\rangle$ or $\langle 00|00\rangle$ in the above matrix representation. It turns out that there is another way to evaluate these amplitudes that relies only on the orthogonality of the single-qubit computational basis states.

Suppose that we have four single-qubit states $|\phi_0\rangle$, $|\phi_1\rangle$, $|\psi_0\rangle$, $|\psi_1\rangle$, and we make the following two-qubit states from them:

$$|\phi_0\rangle \otimes |\psi_0\rangle, \qquad |\phi_1\rangle \otimes |\psi_1\rangle. \tag{3.114}$$

We may represent these states equally well as follows:

$$|\phi_0, \psi_0\rangle, \qquad |\phi_1, \psi_1\rangle, \tag{3.115}$$

because the Dirac notation is versatile (virtually anything can go inside a ket as long as its meaning is not ambiguous). The bra $\langle\phi_1, \psi_1|$ is dual to the ket $|\phi_1, \psi_1\rangle$, and we can use it to calculate the following amplitude:

$$\langle\phi_1, \psi_1|\phi_0, \psi_0\rangle. \tag{3.116}$$

This amplitude is equal to the multiplication of the single-qubit amplitudes:

$$\langle\phi_1, \psi_1|\phi_0, \psi_0\rangle = \langle\phi_1|\phi_0\rangle \langle\psi_1|\psi_0\rangle. \tag{3.117}$$

EXERCISE 3.5.2 Verify that the amplitudes $\{\langle ij|kl\rangle\}_{i,j,k,l\in\{0,1\}}$ are respectively equal to the amplitudes $\{\langle i|k\rangle \langle j|l\rangle\}_{i,j,k,l\in\{0,1\}}$. By linearity, this exercise justifies the relation in (3.117) (at least for two-qubit states).

3.5.3 Controlled Gates

An important two-qubit unitary evolution is the controlled-NOT (CNOT) gate. We consider its classical version first. The classical gate acts on two cbits. It does nothing if the first bit is equal to zero, and flips the second bit if the first bit is equal to one:

$$00 \rightarrow 00, \quad 01 \rightarrow 01, \quad 10 \rightarrow 11, \quad 11 \rightarrow 10. \tag{3.118}$$

We turn this gate into a quantum gate[5] by demanding that it act in the same way on the two-qubit computational basis states:

$$|00\rangle \rightarrow |00\rangle, \quad |01\rangle \rightarrow |01\rangle, \quad |10\rangle \rightarrow |11\rangle, \quad |11\rangle \rightarrow |10\rangle. \tag{3.119}$$

By linearity, this behavior carries over to superposition states as well:

$$\alpha|00\rangle + \beta|01\rangle + \gamma|10\rangle + \delta|11\rangle \quad \underrightarrow{\text{CNOT}} \quad \alpha|00\rangle + \beta|01\rangle + \gamma|11\rangle + \delta|10\rangle. \tag{3.120}$$

A useful operator representation of the CNOT gate is

$$\text{CNOT} \equiv |0\rangle\langle 0| \otimes I + |1\rangle\langle 1| \otimes X. \tag{3.121}$$

The above representation truly captures the coherent quantum nature of the CNOT gate. In the classical CNOT gate, we can say that it is a conditional gate, in the sense that the gate applies to the second bit conditioned on the value of the

---

[5] There are other terms for the action of turning a classical operation into a quantum one. Some examples are "making it coherent," "coherifying," or the quantum gate is a "coherification" of the classical one. The term "coherify" is not a proper English word, but we will use it regardless at certain points.

first bit. In the quantum CNOT gate, the second operation is *controlled* on the basis state of the first qubit (hence the choice of the name "controlled-NOT"). That is, the gate acts on superpositions of quantum states and maintains these superpositions, shuffling the probability amplitudes around while it does so. The one case in which the gate has no effect is when the first qubit is prepared in the state $|0\rangle$ and the state of the second qubit is arbitrary.

A controlled-U gate is similar to the CNOT gate in (3.121). It simply applies the unitary U (assumed to be a single-qubit unitary) to the second qubit, controlled on the first qubit:

$$\text{controlled-}U \equiv |0\rangle\langle 0| \otimes I + |1\rangle\langle 1| \otimes U. \tag{3.122}$$

The control qubit could alternatively be controlled with respect to any orthonormal basis $\{|\phi_0\rangle, |\phi_1\rangle\}$:

$$|\phi_0\rangle\langle\phi_0| \otimes I + |\phi_1\rangle\langle\phi_1| \otimes U. \tag{3.123}$$

Figure 3.7 depicts the circuit diagrams for a controlled-NOT and controlled-U operation.

EXERCISE 3.5.3   Verify that the matrix representation of the CNOT gate in the computational basis is

$$\begin{bmatrix} 1 & 0 & 0 & 0 \\ 0 & 1 & 0 & 0 \\ 0 & 0 & 0 & 1 \\ 0 & 0 & 1 & 0 \end{bmatrix}. \tag{3.124}$$

EXERCISE 3.5.4   Consider applying Hadamards to the first and second qubits before and after a CNOT acts on them. Show that this gate is equivalent to a CNOT in the $+/-$ basis (recall that the Z operator flips the $+/-$ basis):

$$H_1 H_2 \text{ CNOT } H_1 H_2 = |+\rangle\langle +| \otimes I + |-\rangle\langle -| \otimes Z. \tag{3.125}$$

EXERCISE 3.5.5   Show that two CNOT gates with the same control qubit commute.

EXERCISE 3.5.6   Show that two CNOT gates with the same target qubit commute.

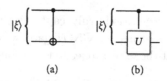

(a)   (b)

Figure 3.7 Circuit diagrams that we use for (a) a CNOT gate and (b) a controlled-U gate.

3.5.4   The No-Cloning Theorem

The no-cloning theorem is one of the simplest results in the quantum theory, yet it has some of the most profound consequences. It states that it is impossible to build a *universal copier* of quantum states. A universal copier would be a device that could copy any arbitrary quantum state that is input to it. It may be surprising at first to hear that copying quantum information is impossible because copying classical information is ubiquitous.

We now give a simple proof of the no-cloning theorem. Suppose for a contradiction that there is a two-qubit unitary operator U acting as a universal copier of quantum information. That is, if we input an arbitrary state $|\psi\rangle = \alpha|0\rangle + \beta|1\rangle$ as the first qubit and input an ancilla qubit $|0\rangle$ as the second qubit, such a device should "write" the first qubit to the second qubit slot as follows:

$$U|\psi\rangle|0\rangle = |\psi\rangle|\psi\rangle \tag{3.126}$$
$$= (\alpha|0\rangle + \beta|1\rangle)(\alpha|0\rangle + \beta|1\rangle) \tag{3.127}$$
$$= \alpha^2|0\rangle|0\rangle + \alpha\beta|0\rangle|1\rangle + \alpha\beta|1\rangle|0\rangle + \beta^2|1\rangle|1\rangle. \tag{3.128}$$

The copier is universal, meaning that it copies an arbitrary state. In particular, it also copies the states $|0\rangle$ and $|1\rangle$:

$$U|0\rangle|0\rangle = |0\rangle|0\rangle, \qquad U|1\rangle|0\rangle = |1\rangle|1\rangle. \tag{3.129}$$

Linearity of the quantum theory then implies that the unitary operator acts on a superposition $\alpha|0\rangle + \beta|1\rangle$ as follows:

$$U(\alpha|0\rangle + \beta|1\rangle)|0\rangle = \alpha|0\rangle|0\rangle + \beta|1\rangle|1\rangle. \tag{3.130}$$

However, the consequence in (3.128) contradicts the consequence in (3.130) because these two expressions do not have to be equal for all α and β:

$$\exists \alpha, \beta : \alpha^2|0\rangle|0\rangle + \alpha\beta|0\rangle|1\rangle + \alpha\beta|1\rangle|0\rangle + \beta^2|1\rangle|1\rangle \neq \alpha|0\rangle|0\rangle + \beta|1\rangle|1\rangle. \tag{3.131}$$

Thus, linearity of the quantum theory contradicts the existence of a universal quantum copier.

We would like to stress that this proof does not mean that it is impossible to copy certain quantum states—it only implies the impossibility of a *universal copier*. Observe that (3.131) is satisfied for $\alpha = 1, \beta = 0$ or $\alpha = 0, \beta = 1$, so that we can copy unknown classical states prepared in the basis $|0\rangle, |1\rangle$ (or any other orthonormal basis for that matter).

Another proof of the no-cloning theorem arrives at a contradiction by exploiting unitarity of quantum evolutions. Let us again suppose that a universal copier U exists. Consider two arbitrary states $|\psi\rangle$ and $|\phi\rangle$. If a universal copier U exists, then it performs the following copying operation for both states:

$$U|\psi\rangle|0\rangle = |\psi\rangle|\psi\rangle, \qquad U|\phi\rangle|0\rangle = |\phi\rangle|\phi\rangle. \tag{3.132}$$

Consider the probability amplitude $\langle\psi|\langle\psi||\phi\rangle|\phi\rangle$:

$$\langle\psi|\langle\psi||\phi\rangle|\phi\rangle = \langle\psi|\phi\rangle\langle\psi|\phi\rangle = \langle\psi|\phi\rangle^2. \tag{3.133}$$

The following relation for $\langle\psi|\langle\psi||\phi\rangle|\phi\rangle$ holds as well by using the results in (3.132) and the unitarity property $U^\dagger U = I$:

$$\langle\psi|\langle\psi||\phi\rangle|\phi\rangle = \langle\psi|\langle 0|U^\dagger U|\phi\rangle|0\rangle \tag{3.134}$$

$$= \langle\psi|\langle 0||\phi\rangle|0\rangle \tag{3.135}$$

$$= \langle\psi|\phi\rangle\,\langle 0|0\rangle \tag{3.136}$$

$$= \langle\psi|\phi\rangle. \tag{3.137}$$

As a consequence, we find that

$$\langle\psi|\langle\psi||\phi\rangle|\phi\rangle = \langle\psi|\phi\rangle^2 = \langle\psi|\phi\rangle, \tag{3.138}$$

by employing the above two results. The equality $\langle\psi|\phi\rangle^2 = \langle\psi|\phi\rangle$ holds for exactly two cases, $\langle\psi|\phi\rangle = 1$ and $\langle\psi|\phi\rangle = 0$. The first case holds only when the two states are the same state and the second case holds when the two states are orthogonal to each other. Thus, it is impossible to copy quantum information in any other case because we would contradict unitarity.

The no-cloning theorem has several applications in quantum information processing. First, it underlies the security of the quantum key distribution protocol because it ensures that an attacker cannot copy the quantum states that two parties use to establish a secret key. It finds application in quantum Shannon theory because we can use it to reason about the quantum capacity of a certain quantum channel known as the erasure channel. We will return to this point in Chapter 24.

EXERCISE 3.5.7   Suppose that two states $|\psi\rangle$ and $|\psi^\perp\rangle$ are orthogonal: $\langle\psi|\psi^\perp\rangle = 0$. Construct a two-qubit unitary that can copy the states, i.e., find a unitary U that acts as follows: $U|\psi\rangle|0\rangle = |\psi\rangle|\psi\rangle$, $U|\psi^\perp\rangle|0\rangle = |\psi^\perp\rangle|\psi^\perp\rangle$.

EXERCISE 3.5.8 (No-Deletion Theorem)   Somewhat related to the no-cloning theorem, there is a no-deletion theorem. Suppose that two copies of a quantum state $|\psi\rangle$ are available, and the goal is to delete one of these states by a unitary interaction. That is, there should exist a universal quantum deleter U that has the following action on the two copies of $|\psi\rangle$ and an ancilla state $|A\rangle$, regardless of the input state $|\psi\rangle$:

$$U|\psi\rangle|\psi\rangle|A\rangle = |\psi\rangle|0\rangle|A'\rangle, \tag{3.139}$$

where $|A'\rangle$ is another state. Show that this is impossible.

3.5.5   Measurement of Composite Systems

The measurement postulate also extends to composite quantum systems. Suppose again that we have the two-qubit quantum state in (3.99). By a straightforward analogy with the single-qubit case, we can determine the following probability amplitudes:

$$\langle 00|\xi\rangle = \alpha, \quad \langle 01|\xi\rangle = \beta, \quad \langle 10|\xi\rangle = \gamma, \quad \langle 11|\xi\rangle = \delta. \tag{3.140}$$

We can also define the following projection operators:

$$\Pi_{00} \equiv |00\rangle\langle 00|, \quad \Pi_{01} \equiv |01\rangle\langle 01|, \quad \Pi_{10} \equiv |10\rangle\langle 10|, \quad \Pi_{11} \equiv |11\rangle\langle 11|, \quad (3.141)$$

and apply the Born rule to determine the probabilities for each result:

$$\langle\xi|\,\Pi_{00}\,|\xi\rangle = |\alpha|^2, \quad \langle\xi|\,\Pi_{01}\,|\xi\rangle = |\beta|^2, \quad \langle\xi|\,\Pi_{10}\,|\xi\rangle = |\gamma|^2, \quad \langle\xi|\,\Pi_{11}\,|\xi\rangle = |\delta|^2.$$
$$(3.142)$$

Suppose that we wish to perform a measurement of the Z operator on the first qubit only. What is the set of projection operators that describes this measurement? The answer is similar to what we found for the evolution of a composite system. We apply the identity operator to the second qubit because no measurement occurs on it. Thus, the set of measurement operators is

$$\{\Pi_0 \otimes I, \Pi_1 \otimes I\}, \quad (3.143)$$

where the definition of Π_0 and Π_1 is in (3.73)–(3.74). The state reduces to

$$\frac{(\Pi_0 \otimes I)\,|\xi\rangle}{\sqrt{\langle\xi|\,(\Pi_0 \otimes I)\,|\xi\rangle}} = \frac{\alpha|00\rangle + \beta|01\rangle}{\sqrt{|\alpha|^2 + |\beta|^2}}, \quad (3.144)$$

with probability $\langle\xi|\,(\Pi_0 \otimes I)\,|\xi\rangle = |\alpha|^2 + |\beta|^2$, and reduces to

$$\frac{(\Pi_1 \otimes I)\,|\xi\rangle}{\sqrt{\langle\xi|\,(\Pi_1 \otimes I)\,|\xi\rangle}} = \frac{\gamma|10\rangle + \delta|11\rangle}{\sqrt{|\gamma|^2 + |\delta|^2}}, \quad (3.145)$$

with probability $\langle\xi|\,(\Pi_1 \otimes I)\,|\xi\rangle = |\gamma|^2 + |\delta|^2$. Normalizing by $\sqrt{\langle\xi|\,(\Pi_0 \otimes I)\,|\xi\rangle}$ and $\sqrt{\langle\xi|\,(\Pi_1 \otimes I)\,|\xi\rangle}$ again ensures that the resulting vector corresponds to a physical state.

3.6   Entanglement

Composite quantum systems give rise to a uniquely quantum phenomenon: *entanglement*. Schrödinger first observed that two or more quantum systems can be entangled and coined the term after noticing some of the bizarre consequences of this phenomenon.[6]

We first consider a simple, unentangled state that two parties, Alice and Bob, may share, in order to see how an unentangled state contrasts with an entangled state. Suppose that they share the state

$$|0\rangle_A|0\rangle_B, \quad (3.146)$$

---

[6] Schrödinger actually used the German word "Verschränkung" to describe the phenomenon, which literally translates as "little parts that, though far from one another, always keep the exact same distance from each other." The one-word English translation is "entanglement." Einstein described the "Verschränkung" as a "spukhafte Fernwirkung," most closely translated as "long-distance ghostly effect" or the more commonly stated "spooky action at a distance."

where Alice has the qubit in system A and Bob has the qubit in system B. Alice can definitely say that her qubit is in the state $|0\rangle_A$ and Bob can definitely say that his qubit is in the state $|0\rangle_B$. There is nothing really too strange about this scenario.

Now, consider the composite quantum state $|\Phi^+\rangle_{AB}$:

$$|\Phi^+\rangle_{AB} \equiv \frac{1}{\sqrt{2}} \left(|0\rangle_A |0\rangle_B + |1\rangle_A |1\rangle_B \right). \qquad (3.147)$$

Alice again has possession of the first qubit in system A and Bob has possession of the second qubit in system B. But now, it is not clear from the above description how to determine the individual state of Alice or the individual state of Bob. The above state is really a uniform superposition of the joint state $|0\rangle_A|0\rangle_B$ and the joint state $|1\rangle_A|1\rangle_B$, and it is not possible to describe either Alice's or Bob's individual state in the noiseless quantum theory. We also cannot describe the entangled state $|\Phi^+\rangle_{AB}$ as a product state of the form $|\phi\rangle_A|\psi\rangle_B$, for any states $|\phi\rangle_A$ or $|\psi\rangle_B$. This leads to the following general definition:

DEFINITION 3.6.1 (Pure-State Entanglement)   A pure bipartite state $|\psi\rangle_{AB}$ is entangled if it cannot be written as a product state $|\phi\rangle_A \otimes |\varphi\rangle_B$ for any choices of states $|\phi\rangle_A$ and $|\varphi\rangle_B$.

EXERCISE 3.6.1   Show that the entangled state $|\Phi^+\rangle_{AB}$ has the following representation in the $+/-$ basis:

$$|\Phi^+\rangle_{AB} = \frac{1}{\sqrt{2}} \left(|+\rangle_A |+\rangle_B + |-\rangle_A |-\rangle_B \right). \qquad (3.148)$$

Figure 3.8 gives a graphical depiction of entanglement. We use this depiction often throughout this book. Alice and Bob must receive the entanglement in some way, and the diagram indicates that some source distributes the entangled pair to them. It indicates that Alice and Bob are spatially separated and they possess the entangled state after some time. If they share the entangled state in (3.147), we say that they share one bit of entanglement, or one *ebit*. The term "ebit" implies that there is some way to quantify entanglement and we will make this notion clear in Chapter 19.

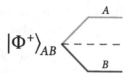

Figure 3.8 We use the above diagram to depict entanglement shared between two parties A and B. The diagram indicates that a source location creates the entanglement and distributes one system to A and the other system to B. The standard unit of entanglement is the ebit $|\Phi^+\rangle_{AB} \equiv (|00\rangle_{AB} + |11\rangle_{AB})/\sqrt{2}$.

3.6.1   Entanglement as a Resource

In this book, we are interested in the use of entanglement as a resource. Much of this book concerns the theory of quantum information-processing resources, and we have a standard notation for the theory of resources. Let us represent the resource of a shared ebit as

$$[qq], \tag{3.149}$$

meaning that the ebit is a noiseless, quantum resource shared between two parties. Square brackets indicate a noiseless resource, the letter q indicates a quantum resource, and the two copies of the letter q indicate a two-party resource.

Our first example of the use of entanglement is its role in generating *shared randomness*. We define one bit of shared randomness as the following probability distribution for two binary random variables X_A and X_B:

$$p_{X_A, X_B}(x_A, x_B) = \frac{1}{2}\delta(x_A, x_B), \tag{3.150}$$

where δ is the Kronecker delta function. Suppose Alice possesses random variable X_A and Bob possesses random variable X_B. Thus, with probability 1/2, they either both have a zero or they both have a one. We represent the resource of one bit of shared randomness as

$$[cc], \tag{3.151}$$

indicating that a bit of shared randomness is a noiseless, classical resource shared between two parties.

Now suppose that Alice and Bob share an ebit and they decide that they will each measure their qubits in the computational basis. Without loss of generality, suppose that Alice performs a measurement first. Thus, Alice performs a measurement of the Z_A operator, meaning that she measures $Z_A \otimes I_B$ (she cannot perform anything on Bob's qubit because they are spatially separated). The projection operators for this measurement are given in (3.143), and they project the joint state. Just before Alice looks at her measurement result, she does not know the outcome, and we can describe the system as being in the following ensemble of states:

$$|0\rangle_A |0\rangle_B \text{ with probability } \frac{1}{2}, \tag{3.152}$$

$$|1\rangle_A |1\rangle_B \text{ with probability } \frac{1}{2}. \tag{3.153}$$

The interesting thing about the above ensemble is that Bob's result is already determined even before he measures, just after Alice's measurement occurs. Suppose that Alice knows the result of her measurement is $|0\rangle_A$. When Bob measures his system, he obtains the state $|0\rangle_B$ with probability one and *Alice knows that he has measured this result*. Additionally, Bob knows that Alice's state is $|0\rangle_A$ if he obtains $|0\rangle_B$. The same results hold if Alice knows that the result of her measurement is $|1\rangle_A$. Thus, this protocol is a method for them to generate one bit of shared randomness as defined in (3.150).

We can phrase the above protocol as the following *resource inequality*:

$$[qq] \geq [cc].\qquad(3.154)$$

The interpretation of the above resource inequality is *that there exists a protocol which generates the resource on the right by consuming the resource on the left and using only local operations*, and for this reason, the resource on the left is a stronger resource than the one on the right. The theory of resource inequalities plays a prominent role in this book and is a useful shorthand for expressing quantum protocols.

A natural question is to wonder if there exists a protocol to generate entanglement exclusively from shared randomness. It is not possible to do so, and one reason justifying this inequivalence of resources is another type of inequality (different from the resource inequality mentioned above), called a Bell's inequality. In short, Bell's theorem places an upper bound on the correlations present in any two classical systems. Entanglement violates this inequality, showing that it has no known classical equivalent. Thus, entanglement is a strictly stronger resource than shared randomness and the resource inequality in (3.154) only holds in the given direction.

Shared randomness is a resource in classical information theory, and may be useful in some scenarios, but it is actually a rather weak resource. Surely, generating shared randomness is not the only use of entanglement. It turns out that we can construct far more exotic protocols such as the teleportation protocol or the super-dense coding protocol by combining the resource of entanglement with other resources. We discuss these protocols in Chapter 6.

EXERCISE 3.6.2   Use the representation of the ebit in Exercise 3.6.1 to show that Alice and Bob can measure the X operator to generate shared randomness. This ability to obtain shared randomness by both parties measuring in either the Z or X basis is the foundation for an entanglement-based secret key distribution protocol.

EXERCISE 3.6.3 (Cloning Implies Signaling)   Prove that if a universal quantum cloner were to exist, then it would be possible for Alice to signal to Bob faster than the speed of light by exploiting only the ebit state $|\Phi^+\rangle_{AB}$ shared between them and no communication. That is, show the existence of a protocol that would allow for this. (Hint: One possibility is for Alice to measure the X or Z Pauli operator locally on her share of the ebit, and then for Bob to exploit the universal quantum cloner. Consider the representation of the ebit in (3.147) and (3.148). Note that there could be a variety of answers to this question because quantum theory becomes effectively nonlinear if we assume the existence of a cloner!)

3.6.2 Entanglement in the CHSH Game

One of the simplest means for demonstrating the power of entanglement is with a two-player game known as the CHSH game (after Clauser, Horne, Shimony, and Holt), which is a particular variation of the original setup in Bell's theorem. We first present the rules of the game, and then we find an upper bound on the probability that players operating according to a classical strategy can win. We finally leave it as an exercise to show that players sharing a maximally entangled Bell state $|\Phi^+\rangle$ can have an approximately 10% higher chance of winning the game using a quantum strategy. This result, known as *Bell's theorem*, represents one of the most striking separations between classical and quantum physics.

The players of the game are Alice and Bob, who are spatially separated from each other from the time that the game starts until it is over. The game begins with a referee selecting two bits x and y uniformly at random. The referee then sends x to Alice and y to Bob. Alice and Bob are not allowed to communicate with each other in any way at this point. Alice sends back to the referee a bit a, and Bob sends back a bit b. Since they are spatially separated, Alice's response bit a cannot depend on Bob's input bit y, and similarly, Bob's response bit b cannot depend on Alice's input bit x. After receiving the response bits a and b, the referee determines if the AND of x and y is equal to the exclusive OR of a and b. If so, then Alice and Bob win the game. That is, the winning condition is

$$x \wedge y = a \oplus b. \tag{3.155}$$

Figure 3.9 depicts the CHSH game.

We need to figure out an expression for the winning probability of the CHSH game. Let $V(x, y, a, b)$ denote the following indicator function for whether they win in a particular instance of the game:

$$V(x, y, a, b) = \begin{cases} 1 & \text{if } x \wedge y = a \oplus b \\ 0 & \text{else} \end{cases}. \tag{3.156}$$

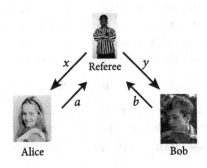

Figure 3.9 A depiction of the CHSH game. The referee distributes the bits x and y to Alice and Bob in the first round. In the second round, Alice and Bob return the bits a and b to the referee.

There is a conditional probability distribution $p_{AB|XY}(a,b|x,y)$, which corresponds to the particular strategy that Alice and Bob employ. Since the inputs x and y are chosen uniformly at random and each take on two possible values, the distribution $p_{XY}(x,y)$ for x and y is as follows:

$$p_{XY}(x,y) = 1/4. \tag{3.157}$$

So an expression for the winning probability of the CHSH game is

$$\frac{1}{4} \sum_{a,b,x,y} V(x,y,a,b) p_{AB|XY}(a,b|x,y). \tag{3.158}$$

In order to calculate this winning probability for a classical or quantum strategy, we need to understand the distribution $p_{AB|XY}(a,b|x,y)$ further. In order to do so, we need a way for describing the strategy that Alice and Bob employ. For this purpose, we will assume that there is a random variable Λ taking values λ, which describes either a classical or quantum strategy, and its values could be all of the entries in a matrix and even taking on continuous values. Using the law of total probability, we can expand the conditional probability $p_{AB|XY}(a,b|x,y)$ as follows:

$$p_{AB|XY}(a,b|x,y) = \int d\lambda \; p_{AB|\Lambda XY}(a,b|\lambda,x,y) \; p_{\Lambda|XY}(\lambda|x,y), \tag{3.159}$$

where $p_{\Lambda|XY}(\lambda|x,y)$ is a conditional probability distribution. Decomposing the distribution $p_{AB|XY}(a,b|x,y)$ in this way leads to the depiction of their strategy given in Figure 3.10(i).

Classical Strategies

Let us suppose that they act according to a classical strategy. What is the most general form of such a strategy? Looking at the picture in Figure 3.10(i), there are a few aspects of it which are not consistent with our understanding of how the game works.

In a classical strategy, the random variable Λ corresponds to classical correlations that Alice and Bob can share *before the game begins*. They could meet beforehand and select a value λ of Λ at random. According to the specification of the game, the input bits x and y for Alice and Bob are chosen independently at random, and so the random variable Λ cannot depend on the bits x and y. So the conditional distribution $p_{\Lambda|XY}(\lambda|x,y)$ simplifies as follows:

$$p_{\Lambda|XY}(\lambda|x,y) = p_{\Lambda}(\lambda), \tag{3.160}$$

and Figure 3.10(ii) reflects this constraint.

Next, Alice and Bob are spatially separated and acting independently, so that the distribution $p_{AB|\Lambda XY}(a,b|\lambda,x,y)$ factors as follows:

$$p_{AB|\Lambda XY}(a,b|\lambda,x,y) = p_{A|\Lambda XY}(a|\lambda,x,y) \, p_{B|\Lambda XY}(b|\lambda,x,y). \tag{3.161}$$

But we also said that Alice's strategy cannot depend on Bob's input bit y and neither can Bob's strategy depend on Alice's input x, because they are spatially

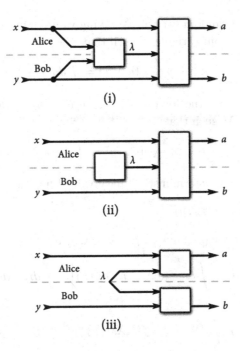

Figure 3.10 Various reductions of a classical strategy in the CHSH game: (i) an unconstrained strategy, (ii) strategy resulting from demanding that the parameter λ is independent of the input bits x and y, and (iii) further demanding that Alice and Bob's actions are independent and that they do not have access to each other's input bits.

separated. However, their strategies could depend on the random variable Λ, which they are allowed to share before the game begins. All of this implies that the conditional distribution describing their strategy should factor as follows:

$$p_{AB|\Lambda XY}(a, b|\lambda, x, y) = p_{A|\Lambda X}(a|\lambda, x) \, p_{B|\Lambda Y}(b|\lambda, y), \qquad (3.162)$$

and Figure 3.10(iii) reflects this change. Now Figure 3.10(iii) depicts the most general classical strategy that Alice and Bob could employ if Λ corresponds to a random variable that Alice and Bob are both allowed to access before the game begins.

Putting everything together, the conditional distribution $p_{AB|XY}(a, b|x, y)$ for a classical strategy takes the following form:

$$p_{AB|XY}(a, b|x, y) = \int d\lambda \, p_{A|\Lambda X}(a|\lambda, x) \, p_{B|\Lambda Y}(b|\lambda, y) \, p_{\Lambda}(\lambda), \qquad (3.163)$$

and we can now consider optimizing the winning probability in (3.158) with respect to all classical strategies. Consider that any stochastic map $p_{A|\Lambda X}(a|\lambda, x)$ can be simulated by applying a deterministic binary-valued function $f(a|\lambda, x, n)$

to a local random variable N taking values labeled by n. That is, we can always find a random variable N such that

$$p_{A|\Lambda X}(a|\lambda, x) = \int dn \; f(a|\lambda, x, n) \; p_N(n). \tag{3.164}$$

The same is true for the stochastic map $p_{B|\Lambda Y}(b|\lambda, y)$; i.e., there is a random variable M such that

$$p_{B|\Lambda Y}(b|\lambda, y) = \int dm \; g(b|\lambda, y, m) \; p_M(m), \tag{3.165}$$

where g is a deterministic binary-valued function. So this implies that

$$p_{AB|XY}(a, b|x, y)$$

$$= \int d\lambda \; p_{A|\Lambda X}(a|\lambda, x) \; p_{B|\Lambda Y}(b|\lambda, y) \; p_\Lambda(\lambda) \tag{3.166}$$

$$= \int d\lambda \left[\int dn \; f(a|\lambda, x, n) \; p_N(n) \right] \left[\int dm \; g(b|\lambda, y, m) \; p_M(m) \right] p_\Lambda(\lambda) \tag{3.167}$$

$$= \int \int \int d\lambda \, dn \, dm \; f(a|\lambda, x, n) \; g(b|\lambda, y, m) \; p_\Lambda(\lambda) \, p_N(n) \, p_M(m). \tag{3.168}$$

By inspecting the last line above, it is clear that we could then have the shared random variable Λ subsume the local random variables N and M, allowing us to write any conditional distribution $p_{AB|XY}(a, b|x, y)$ for a classical strategy as follows:

$$p_{AB|XY}(a, b|x, y) = \int d\lambda \; f'(a|\lambda, x) \; g'(b|\lambda, y) \; p_\Lambda(\lambda), \tag{3.169}$$

where f' and g' are deterministic binary-valued functions (related to f and g). Substituting this expression into the winning probability expression in (3.158), we find that

$$\frac{1}{4} \sum_{a,b,x,y} V(x, y, a, b) p_{AB|XY}(a, b|x, y)$$

$$= \frac{1}{4} \sum_{a,b,x,y} V(x, y, a, b) \int d\lambda \; f'(a|\lambda, x) \; g'(b|\lambda, y) \; p_\Lambda(\lambda) \tag{3.170}$$

$$= \int d\lambda \, p_\Lambda(\lambda) \left[\frac{1}{4} \sum_{a,b,x,y} V(x, y, a, b) \; f'(a|\lambda, x) \; g'(b|\lambda, y) \right] \tag{3.171}$$

$$\leq \frac{1}{4} \sum_{a,b,x,y} V(x, y, a, b) \; f'(a|\lambda^*, x) \; g'(b|\lambda^*, y). \tag{3.172}$$

In the second equality, we just exchanged the integral over λ with the sum. In the inequality in the last step, we used the fact that the average is always less than the maximum. That is, there is always a particular value λ^* that leads to the same or a higher winning probability than when averaging over all values of

λ. As a consequence of the above development, we see that it suffices to consider deterministic strategies of Alice and Bob when analyzing the winning probability.

Since we now know that deterministic strategies are optimal among all classical strategies, let us focus on these. A deterministic strategy would have Alice select a bit a_x conditioned on the bit x that she receives, and similarly, Bob would select a bit b_y conditioned on y. The following table presents the winning conditions for the four different values of x and y with this deterministic strategy:

$$
\begin{array}{cccc}
x & y & x \wedge y & = a_x \oplus b_y \\
\hline
0 & 0 & 0 & = a_0 \oplus b_0 \\
0 & 1 & 0 & = a_0 \oplus b_1 \\
1 & 0 & 0 & = a_1 \oplus b_0 \\
1 & 1 & 1 & = a_1 \oplus b_1
\end{array}
\qquad (3.173)
$$

However, we can observe that it is impossible for them to always win. If we add the entries in the column $x \wedge y$, the binary sum is equal to one, while if we add the entries in the column $= a_x \oplus b_y$, the binary sum is equal to zero. Thus, it is impossible for all of these equations to be satisfied. At most, only three out of four of them can be satisfied, so that the maximal winning probability with a classical deterministic strategy $p_{AB|XY}(a,b|x,y)$ is at most $3/4$:

$$
\frac{1}{4} \sum_{a,b,x,y} V(x,y,a,b) p_{AB|XY}(a,b|x,y) \le \frac{3}{4}. \qquad (3.174)
$$

We can then see that a strategy for them to achieve this upper bound is for Alice and Bob always to return $a = 0$ and $b = 0$ no matter the values of x and y.

Quantum Strategies

What does a quantum strategy of Alice and Bob look like? Here the parameter λ can correspond to a shared quantum $|\phi\rangle_{AB}$. Alice and Bob perform local measurements depending on the values of the inputs x and y that they receive. We can write Alice's x-dependent measurement as $\{\Pi_a^{(x)}\}$ where for each x, $\Pi_a^{(x)}$ is a projector and $\sum_a \Pi_a^{(x)} = I$. Similarly, we can write Bob's y-dependent measurement as $\{\Pi_b^{(y)}\}$. Then we instead employ the Born rule to determine the conditional probability distribution $p_{AB|XY}(a,b|x,y)$:

$$
p_{AB|XY}(a,b|x,y) = \langle\phi|_{AB}\Pi_a^{(x)} \otimes \Pi_b^{(y)}|\phi\rangle_{AB}, \qquad (3.175)
$$

so that the winning probability with a particular quantum strategy is as follows:

$$
\frac{1}{4} \sum_{a,b,x,y} V(x,y,a,b)\langle\phi|_{AB}\Pi_a^{(x)} \otimes \Pi_b^{(y)}|\phi\rangle_{AB}. \qquad (3.176)
$$

Interestingly, if Alice and Bob share a maximally entangled state, they can achieve a higher winning probability than if they share classical correlations only. This is one demonstration of the power of entanglement, and we leave it as an exercise to prove that the following quantum strategy achieves a winning probability of $\cos^2(\pi/8) \approx 0.85$ in the CHSH game.

EXERCISE 3.6.4   Suppose that Alice and Bob share a maximally entangled state $|\Phi^+\rangle$. Show that the following strategy has a winning probability of $\cos^2(\pi/8)$. If Alice receives $x = 0$ from the referee, then she performs a measurement of Pauli Z on her system and returns the measurement outcome as "a" after identifying $a = 0$ with the measurement outcome $+1$ and $a = 1$ with the measurement outcome -1. (The same convention is applied to the following scenarios.) If she receives $x = 1$, then she performs a measurement of Pauli X and returns the outcome as "a." If Bob receives $y = 0$ from the referee, then he performs a measurement of $(X + Z)/\sqrt{2}$ on his system and returns the outcome as b. If Bob receives $y = 1$ from the referee, then he performs a measurement of $(Z - X)/\sqrt{2}$ and returns the outcome as b.

Maximum Quantum Winning Probability

Given that classical strategies cannot win with probability any larger than $3/4$, it is natural to wonder if there is a bound on the winning probability of a quantum strategy. It turns out that $\cos^2(\pi/8)$ is the maximum probability with which Alice and Bob can win the CHSH game using a quantum strategy, a result known as *Tsirelson's bound*. To establish this result, let us go back to the CHSH game. Conditioned on the inputs x and y being equal to 00, 01, or 10, we know that Alice and Bob win if they report back the same results. The probability for this to happen with a given quantum strategy is

$$\langle\phi|_{AB}\Pi_0^{(x)} \otimes \Pi_0^{(y)}|\phi\rangle_{AB} + \langle\phi|_{AB}\Pi_1^{(x)} \otimes \Pi_1^{(y)}|\phi\rangle_{AB}, \qquad (3.177)$$

and the probability for it not to happen is

$$\langle\phi|_{AB}\Pi_0^{(x)} \otimes \Pi_1^{(y)}|\phi\rangle_{AB} + \langle\phi|_{AB}\Pi_1^{(x)} \otimes \Pi_0^{(y)}|\phi\rangle_{AB}. \qquad (3.178)$$

So, conditioned on x and y being equal to 00, 01, or 10, the probability of winning minus the probability of losing is

$$\langle\phi|_{AB}A^{(x)} \otimes B^{(y)}|\phi\rangle_{AB}, \qquad (3.179)$$

where we define the *observables* $A^{(x)}$ and $B^{(y)}$ as follows:

$$A^{(x)} \equiv \Pi_0^{(x)} - \Pi_1^{(x)}, \qquad (3.180)$$

$$B^{(y)} \equiv \Pi_0^{(y)} - \Pi_1^{(y)}. \qquad (3.181)$$

If x and y are both equal to one, then Alice and Bob should report back different results, and similar to the above, one can work out that the probability of winning minus the probability of losing is equal to

$$- \langle\phi|_{AB}A^{(1)} \otimes B^{(1)}|\phi\rangle_{AB}. \qquad (3.182)$$

Thus, when averaging over all values of the input bits, the probability of winning minus the probability of losing is equal to

$$\frac{1}{4} \langle \phi |_{AB} C_{AB} | \phi \rangle_{AB}, \tag{3.183}$$

where C_{AB} is the CHSH operator, defined as

$$C_{AB} \equiv A^{(0)} \otimes B^{(0)} + A^{(0)} \otimes B^{(1)} + A^{(1)} \otimes B^{(0)} - A^{(1)} \otimes B^{(1)}. \tag{3.184}$$

It is a simple exercise to check that

$$C_{AB}^2 = 4 I_{AB} - \left[A^{(0)}, A^{(1)} \right] \otimes \left[B^{(0)}, B^{(1)} \right]. \tag{3.185}$$

The infinity norm $\|R\|_\infty$ of an operator R is equal to its largest singular value. It obeys the following relations:

$$\|cR\|_\infty = |c| \, \|R\|_\infty, \tag{3.186}$$

$$\|RS\|_\infty \le \|R\|_\infty \|S\|_\infty, \tag{3.187}$$

$$\|R + S\|_\infty \le \|R\|_\infty + \|S\|_\infty, \tag{3.188}$$

where $c \in \mathbb{C}$ and S is another operator. Using these, we find that

$$\left\| C_{AB}^2 \right\|_\infty = \left\| 4 I_{AB} - \left[A^{(0)}, A^{(1)} \right] \otimes \left[B^{(0)}, B^{(1)} \right] \right\|_\infty \tag{3.189}$$

$$\le 4 \|I_{AB}\|_\infty + \left\| \left[A^{(0)}, A^{(1)} \right] \otimes \left[B^{(0)}, B^{(1)} \right] \right\|_\infty \tag{3.190}$$

$$= 4 + \left\| \left[A^{(0)}, A^{(1)} \right] \right\|_\infty \left\| \left[B^{(0)}, B^{(1)} \right] \right\|_\infty \tag{3.191}$$

$$\le 4 + 2 \cdot 2 = 8, \tag{3.192}$$

implying that

$$\|C_{AB}\|_\infty \le \sqrt{8} = 2\sqrt{2}. \tag{3.193}$$

Given this and the expression in (3.183), the probability of winning minus the probability of losing can never be larger than $\sqrt{2}/2$ for any quantum strategy. Combined with the fact that the probability of winning summed with the probability of losing is equal to one, we find that the winning probability of any quantum strategy can never be larger than $1/2 + \sqrt{2}/4 = \cos^2(\pi/8)$.

3.6.3 The Bell States

There are other useful entangled states besides the standard ebit. Suppose that Alice performs a Z_A operation on her share of the ebit $|\Phi^+\rangle_{AB}$. Then the resulting state is

$$|\Phi^-\rangle_{AB} \equiv \frac{1}{\sqrt{2}} \left(|00\rangle_{AB} - |11\rangle_{AB} \right). \tag{3.194}$$

Similarly, if Alice performs an X operator or a Y operator, the global state transforms to the following respective states (up to a global phase):

$$\left|\Psi^{+}\right\rangle_{AB} \equiv \frac{1}{\sqrt{2}}\left(\left|01\right\rangle_{AB} + \left|10\right\rangle_{AB}\right), \tag{3.195}$$

$$\left|\Psi^{-}\right\rangle_{AB} \equiv \frac{1}{\sqrt{2}}\left(\left|01\right\rangle_{AB} - \left|10\right\rangle_{AB}\right). \tag{3.196}$$

The states $\left|\Phi^{+}\right\rangle_{AB}$, $\left|\Phi^{-}\right\rangle_{AB}$, $\left|\Psi^{+}\right\rangle_{AB}$, and $\left|\Psi^{-}\right\rangle_{AB}$ are known as the *Bell states* and are the most important entangled states for a two-qubit system. They form an orthonormal basis, called the *Bell basis*, for a two-qubit space. We can also label the Bell states as

$$\left|\Phi^{zx}\right\rangle_{AB} \equiv Z_A^z X_A^x \left|\Phi^{+}\right\rangle_{AB}, \tag{3.197}$$

where the two-bit binary number zx indicates whether Alice applies I_A, Z_A, X_A, or $Z_A X_A$. Then the states $\left|\Phi^{00}\right\rangle_{AB}$, $\left|\Phi^{01}\right\rangle_{AB}$, $\left|\Phi^{10}\right\rangle_{AB}$, and $\left|\Phi^{11}\right\rangle_{AB}$ are in correspondence with the respective states $\left|\Phi^{+}\right\rangle_{AB}$, $\left|\Psi^{+}\right\rangle_{AB}$, $\left|\Phi^{-}\right\rangle_{AB}$, and $\left|\Psi^{-}\right\rangle_{AB}$.

EXERCISE 3.6.5 Show that the Bell states form an orthonormal basis:

$$\left\langle\Phi^{z_1 x_1}\middle|\Phi^{z_2 x_2}\right\rangle = \delta_{z_1, z_2}\delta_{x_1, x_2}. \tag{3.198}$$

EXERCISE 3.6.6 Show that the following identities hold:

$$\left|00\right\rangle_{AB} = \frac{1}{\sqrt{2}}\left(\left|\Phi^{+}\right\rangle_{AB} + \left|\Phi^{-}\right\rangle_{AB}\right), \tag{3.199}$$

$$\left|01\right\rangle_{AB} = \frac{1}{\sqrt{2}}\left(\left|\Psi^{+}\right\rangle_{AB} + \left|\Psi^{-}\right\rangle_{AB}\right), \tag{3.200}$$

$$\left|10\right\rangle_{AB} = \frac{1}{\sqrt{2}}\left(\left|\Psi^{+}\right\rangle_{AB} - \left|\Psi^{-}\right\rangle_{AB}\right), \tag{3.201}$$

$$\left|11\right\rangle_{AB} = \frac{1}{\sqrt{2}}\left(\left|\Phi^{+}\right\rangle_{AB} - \left|\Phi^{-}\right\rangle_{AB}\right). \tag{3.202}$$

EXERCISE 3.6.7 Show that the following identities hold by using the relation in (3.197):

$$\left|\Phi^{+}\right\rangle_{AB} = \frac{1}{\sqrt{2}}\left(\left|++\right\rangle_{AB} + \left|--\right\rangle_{AB}\right), \tag{3.203}$$

$$\left|\Phi^{-}\right\rangle_{AB} = \frac{1}{\sqrt{2}}\left(\left|-+\right\rangle_{AB} + \left|+-\right\rangle_{AB}\right), \tag{3.204}$$

$$\left|\Psi^{+}\right\rangle_{AB} = \frac{1}{\sqrt{2}}\left(\left|++\right\rangle_{AB} - \left|--\right\rangle_{AB}\right), \tag{3.205}$$

$$\left|\Psi^{-}\right\rangle_{AB} = \frac{1}{\sqrt{2}}\left(\left|-+\right\rangle_{AB} - \left|+-\right\rangle_{AB}\right). \tag{3.206}$$

Entanglement is one of the most useful resources in quantum computing, quantum communication, and in the setting of quantum Shannon theory that we explore in this book. Our goal in this book is merely to study entanglement as a resource, but there are many other aspects of entanglement that one can study, such as measures of entanglement, multiparty entanglement, and generalized Bell's inequalities (Horodecki et al., 2009).

3.7 Summary and Extensions to Qudit States

We now end our overview of the noiseless quantum theory by summarizing its main postulates in terms of quantum states that are on d-dimensional systems. Such states are called *qudit states*, in analogy with the name "qubit" for two-dimensional quantum systems.

3.7.1 Qudits

A qudit state $|\psi\rangle$ is an arbitrary superposition of some set of orthonormal basis states $\{|j\rangle\}_{j\in\{0,...,d-1\}}$ for a d-dimensional quantum system:

$$|\psi\rangle \equiv \sum_{j=0}^{d-1} \alpha_j |j\rangle. \tag{3.207}$$

The amplitudes α_j obey the normalization condition $\sum_{j=0}^{d-1} |\alpha_j|^2 = 1$.

3.7.2 Unitary Evolution

The first postulate of the quantum theory is that we can perform a unitary (reversible) evolution U on this state. The resulting state is $U|\psi\rangle$, meaning that we apply the operator U to the state $|\psi\rangle$.

One example of a unitary evolution is the cyclic shift operator $X(x)$ that acts on the orthonormal states $\{|j\rangle\}_{j\in\{0,...,d-1\}}$ as follows:

$$X(x)|j\rangle = |x \oplus j\rangle, \tag{3.208}$$

where $\oplus$ is a cyclic addition operator, meaning that the result of the addition is $(x + j) \bmod (d)$. Notice that the X Pauli operator has a similar behavior on the qubit computational basis states because

$$X|i\rangle = |i \oplus 1\rangle, \tag{3.209}$$

for $i \in \{0, 1\}$. Therefore, the operator $X(x)$ is a qudit generalization of the X Pauli operator.

EXERCISE 3.7.1 Show that the inverse of $X(x)$ is $X(-x)$.

EXERCISE 3.7.2 Show that the matrix representation $X(x)$ of the $X(x)$ operator, with respect to the standard basis $\{|j\rangle\}$, is a matrix with elements $[X(x)]_{i,j} = \delta_{i,j\oplus x}$.

Another example of a unitary evolution is the *phase operator* $Z(z)$. It applies a state-dependent phase to a basis state. It acts as follows on the qudit computational basis states $\{|j\rangle\}_{j\in\{0,\ldots,d-1\}}$:

$$Z(z)|j\rangle = \exp\{i2\pi zj/d\}\,|j\rangle. \tag{3.210}$$

This operator is the qudit analog of the Pauli Z operator. The d^2 operators $\{X(x)Z(z)\}_{x,z\in\{0,\ldots,d-1\}}$ are known as the *Heisenberg–Weyl operators*.

EXERCISE 3.7.3 Show that $Z(1)$ is equivalent to the Pauli Z operator for the case that the dimension $d = 2$.

EXERCISE 3.7.4 Show that the inverse of $Z(z)$ is $Z(-z)$.

EXERCISE 3.7.5 Show that the matrix representation of the phase operator $Z(z)$, with respect to the standard basis $\{|j\rangle\}$, is

$$[Z(z)]_{j,k} = \exp\{i2\pi zj/d\}\,\delta_{j,k}. \tag{3.211}$$

In particular, this result implies that the $Z(z)$ operator has a diagonal matrix representation with respect to the qudit computational basis states $\{|j\rangle\}_{j\in\{0,\ldots,d-1\}}$. Thus, the qudit computational basis states $\{|j\rangle\}_{j\in\{0,\ldots,d-1\}}$ are eigenstates of the phase operator $Z(z)$ (similar to the qubit computational basis states being eigenstates of the Pauli Z operator). The eigenvalue corresponding to the eigenstate $|j\rangle$ is $\exp\{i2\pi zj/d\}$.

EXERCISE 3.7.6 Show that the eigenstates $|\widetilde{l}\rangle$ of the cyclic shift operator $X(1)$ are the Fourier-transformed states $|\widetilde{l}\rangle$, where

$$|\widetilde{l}\rangle \equiv \frac{1}{\sqrt{d}}\sum_{j=0}^{d-1}\exp\{i2\pi lj/d\}\,|j\rangle, \tag{3.212}$$

and l is an integer in the set $\{0,\ldots,d-1\}$. Show that the eigenvalue corresponding to the state $|\widetilde{l}\rangle$ is $\exp\{-i2\pi l/d\}$. Conclude that these states are also eigenstates of the operator $X(x)$, but the corresponding eigenvalues are $\exp\{-i2\pi lx/d\}$.

EXERCISE 3.7.7 Show that the $+/-$ basis states are a special case of the states in (3.212) when $d = 2$.

EXERCISE 3.7.8 The Fourier transform operator F is a qudit analog of the Hadamard H. We define it to take Z eigenstates to X eigenstates: $F \equiv \sum_{j=0}^{d-1}|\widetilde{j}\rangle\langle j|$, where the states $|\widetilde{j}\rangle$ are defined in (3.212). It performs the following transformation on the qudit computational basis states:

$$|j\rangle \rightarrow \frac{1}{\sqrt{d}}\sum_{k=0}^{d-1}\exp\{i2\pi jk/d\}\,|k\rangle. \tag{3.213}$$

Show that the following relations hold for the Fourier transform operator F: $FX(x)F^\dagger = Z(x)$, $FZ(z)F^\dagger = X(-z)$.

EXERCISE 3.7.9 Show that the commutation relations of the cyclic shift operator $X(x)$ and the phase operator $Z(z)$ are as follows:

$$X(x_1)Z(z_1)X(x_2)Z(z_2) =$$
$$\exp\{2\pi i \left(z_1 x_2 - x_1 z_2\right)/d\} X(x_2)Z(z_2)X(x_1)Z(z_1). \quad (3.214)$$

You can get this result by first showing that

$$X(x)Z(z) = \exp\{-2\pi izx/d\} Z(z)X(x). \quad (3.215)$$

3.7.3 Measurement of Qudits

Measurement of qudits is similar to measurement of qubits. Suppose that we have some state $|\psi\rangle$. Suppose further that we would like to measure some Hermitian operator A with the following diagonalization:

$$A = \sum_j f(j)\Pi_j, \quad (3.216)$$

where $\Pi_j\Pi_k = \Pi_j\delta_{j,k}$, and $\sum_j \Pi_j = I$. A measurement of the operator A then returns the result j with the following probability:

$$p(j) = \langle\psi|\Pi_j|\psi\rangle, \quad (3.217)$$

and the resulting state is

$$\frac{\Pi_j|\psi\rangle}{\sqrt{p(j)}}. \quad (3.218)$$

The calculation of the expectation of the operator A is similar to how we calculate in the qubit case:

$$\mathbb{E}[A] = \sum_j f(j)\langle\psi|\Pi_j|\psi\rangle = \langle\psi|\sum_j f(j)\Pi_j|\psi\rangle = \langle\psi|A|\psi\rangle. \quad (3.219)$$

We give two quick examples of qudit operators that we might like to measure. The operators $X(1)$ and $Z(1)$ are not completely analogous to the respective Pauli X and Pauli Z operators because $X(1)$ and $Z(1)$ are not Hermitian. Thus, we cannot directly measure these operators. Instead, we construct operators that are essentially equivalent to "measuring the operators" $X(1)$ and $Z(1)$. Let us first consider the $Z(1)$ operator. Its eigenstates are the qudit computational basis states $\{|j\rangle\}_{j\in\{0,\dots,d-1\}}$. We can form the operator $M_{Z(1)}$ as

$$M_{Z(1)} \equiv \sum_{j=0}^{d-1} j|j\rangle\langle j|. \quad (3.220)$$

Measuring this operator is equivalent to measuring in the qudit computational basis. The expectation of this operator for a qudit $|\psi\rangle$ in the state in (3.207) is

$$\mathbb{E}[M_{Z(1)}] = \langle\psi|M_{Z(1)}|\psi\rangle \quad (3.221)$$

$$= \sum_{j'=0}^{d-1} \langle j'| \alpha_{j'}^* \sum_{j=0}^{d-1} j|j\rangle \langle j| \sum_{j''=0}^{d-1} \alpha_{j''} |j''\rangle \tag{3.222}$$

$$= \sum_{j',j,j''=0}^{d-1} j \alpha_{j'}^* \alpha_{j''} \langle j'|j\rangle \langle j|j''\rangle \tag{3.223}$$

$$= \sum_{j=0}^{d-1} j |\alpha_j|^2. \tag{3.224}$$

Similarly, we can construct an operator $M_{X(1)}$ for "measuring the operator $X(1)$" by using the eigenstates $|j\rangle_X$ of the $X(1)$ operator:

$$M_{X(1)} \equiv \sum_{j=0}^{d-1} j|\tilde{j}\rangle\langle\tilde{j}|. \tag{3.225}$$

We leave it as an exercise to determine the expectation when measuring the $M_{X(1)}$ operator.

EXERCISE 3.7.10   Suppose the qudit is in the state $|\psi\rangle$ in (3.207). Show that the expectation of the $M_{X(1)}$ operator is

$$\mathbb{E}\left[M_{X(1)}\right] = \frac{1}{d} \sum_{j=0}^{d-1} j \left| \sum_{j'=0}^{d-1} \alpha_{j'} \exp\left\{-i2\pi j'j/d\right\} \right|^2. \tag{3.226}$$

Hint: First show that we can represent the state $|\psi\rangle$ in the $X(1)$ eigenbasis as follows:

$$|\psi\rangle = \sum_{l=0}^{d-1} \frac{1}{\sqrt{d}} \left(\sum_{j=0}^{d-1} \alpha_j \exp\left\{-i2\pi lj/d\right\} \right) |\tilde{l}\rangle. \tag{3.227}$$

3.7.4   Composite Systems of Qudits

We can define a system of multiple qudits again by employing the tensor product. A general two-qudit state on systems A and B has the following form:

$$|\xi\rangle_{AB} \equiv \sum_{j,k=0}^{d-1} \alpha_{j,k} |j\rangle_A |k\rangle_B. \tag{3.228}$$

Evolution of two-qudit states is similar as before. Suppose Alice applies a unitary U_A to her qudit. The result is as follows:

$$(U_A \otimes I_B) |\xi\rangle_{AB} = (U_A \otimes I_B) \sum_{j,k=0}^{d-1} \alpha_{j,k} |j\rangle_A |k\rangle_B \tag{3.229}$$

$$= \sum_{j,k=0}^{d-1} \alpha_{j,k} (U_A|j\rangle_A) |k\rangle_B, \tag{3.230}$$

which follows by linearity. Bob applying a local unitary U_B has a similar form. The application of some global unitary U_{AB} results in the state

$$U_{AB} |\xi\rangle_{AB}. \tag{3.231}$$

The Qudit Bell States

Two-qudit states can be entangled as well. The maximally entangled qudit state is as follows:

$$|\Phi\rangle_{AB} \equiv \frac{1}{\sqrt{d}} \sum_{i=0}^{d-1} |i\rangle_A |i\rangle_B. \tag{3.232}$$

When Alice possesses the first qudit and Bob possesses the second qudit and they are also separated in space, the above state is a resource known as an *edit* (pronounced "ee · dit"). It is useful in the qudit versions of the teleportation protocol and the super-dense coding protocol discussed in Chapter 6. Throughout the book, we often find it convenient to make use of the unnormalized maximally entangled vector:

$$|\Gamma\rangle_{AB} \equiv \sum_{i=0}^{d-1} |i\rangle_A |i\rangle_B. \tag{3.233}$$

Consider applying the operator $X(x)Z(z)$ to Alice's share of the maximally entangled state $|\Phi\rangle_{AB}$. We use the following notation:

$$|\Phi^{x,z}\rangle_{AB} \equiv (X_A(x)Z_A(z) \otimes I_B) |\Phi\rangle_{AB}. \tag{3.234}$$

The d^2 states $\{|\Phi^{x,z}\rangle_{AB}\}_{x,z=0}^{d-1}$ are known as the qudit Bell states and are important in qudit quantum protocols and in quantum Shannon theory. Exercise 3.7.11 asks you to verify that these states form a complete, orthonormal basis. Thus, one can measure two qudits in the qudit Bell basis. Similar to the qubit case, it is straightforward to see that the qudit state can generate a *dit* of shared randomness by extending the arguments in Section 3.6.1.

EXERCISE 3.7.11   Show that the set of states $\{|\Phi^{x,z}\rangle_{AB}\}_{x,z=0}^{d-1}$ forms a complete, orthonormal basis:

$$\langle \Phi^{x_1,z_1} | \Phi^{x_2,z_2} \rangle = \delta_{x_1,x_2} \delta_{z_1,z_2}, \tag{3.235}$$

$$\sum_{x,z=0}^{d-1} |\Phi^{x,z}\rangle\langle\Phi^{x,z}|_{AB} = I_{AB}. \tag{3.236}$$

EXERCISE 3.7.12 (Transpose Trick)   Show that the following "transpose trick" or "ricochet" property holds for a maximally entangled state $|\Phi\rangle_{AB}$ (as defined in (3.232)) and any $d \times d$ matrix M:

$$(M_A \otimes I_B) |\Phi\rangle_{AB} = (I_A \otimes M_B^T) |\Phi\rangle_{AB}, \tag{3.237}$$

where M^T is the transpose of the operator M with respect to the basis $\{|i\rangle_B\}$ from (3.232). The implication is that some local action of Alice on $|\Phi\rangle_{AB}$ is equivalent to Bob performing the transpose of this action on his share of the state. Of course, the same equality is true for the unnormalized maximally entangled vector $|\Gamma\rangle_{AB}$ from (3.233):

$$(M_A \otimes I_B) |\Gamma\rangle_{AB} = (I_A \otimes M_B^T) |\Gamma\rangle_{AB}.$$

3.8   Schmidt Decomposition

The Schmidt decomposition is one of the most important tools for analyzing bipartite pure states in quantum information theory, showing that it is possible to decompose any pure bipartite state as a superposition of coordinated orthonormal states. It is a consequence of the well known singular value decomposition theorem from linear algebra. We state this result formally as the following theorem:

THEOREM 3.8.1 (Schmidt Decomposition)   Suppose that we have a bipartite pure state,

$$|\psi\rangle_{AB} \in \mathcal{H}_A \otimes \mathcal{H}_B, \qquad (3.238)$$

where $\mathcal{H}_A$ and $\mathcal{H}_B$ are finite-dimensional Hilbert spaces, not necessarily of the same dimension, and $\||\psi\rangle_{AB}\|_2 = 1$. Then it is possible to express this state as follows:

$$|\psi\rangle_{AB} \equiv \sum_{i=0}^{d-1} \lambda_i |i\rangle_A |i\rangle_B, \qquad (3.239)$$

where the amplitudes λ_i are real, strictly positive, and normalized so that $\sum_i \lambda_i^2 = 1$, the states $\{|i\rangle_A\}$ form an orthonormal basis for system A, and the states $\{|i\rangle_B\}$ form an orthonormal basis for the system B. The vector $[\lambda_i]_{i \in \{0,\dots,d-1\}}$ is called the vector of Schmidt coefficients. The Schmidt rank d of a bipartite state is equal to the number of Schmidt coefficients λ_i in its Schmidt decomposition and satisfies

$$d \leq \min\{\dim(\mathcal{H}_A), \dim(\mathcal{H}_B)\}. \qquad (3.240)$$

Proof This is essentially a restatement of the singular value decomposition of a matrix. Consider an arbitrary bipartite pure state $|\psi\rangle_{AB} \in \mathcal{H}_A \otimes \mathcal{H}_B$. Let $d_A \equiv \dim(\mathcal{H}_A)$ and $d_B \equiv \dim(\mathcal{H}_B)$. We can express $|\psi\rangle_{AB}$ as follows:

$$|\psi\rangle_{AB} = \sum_{j=0}^{d_A-1} \sum_{k=0}^{d_B-1} \alpha_{j,k} |j\rangle_A |k\rangle_B, \qquad (3.241)$$

for some amplitudes $\alpha_{j,k}$ and some orthonormal bases $\{|j\rangle_A\}$ and $\{|k\rangle_B\}$ on the respective systems A and B. Let us write the matrix formed by the coefficients $\alpha_{j,k}$ as some $d_A \times d_B$ matrix G where

$$[G]_{j,k} = \alpha_{j,k}. \qquad (3.242)$$

Since every matrix has a singular value decomposition, we can write G as

$$G = U \Lambda V, \tag{3.243}$$

where U is a $d_A \times d_A$ unitary matrix, V is a $d_B \times d_B$ unitary matrix, and Λ is a $d_A \times d_B$ matrix with d real, strictly positive numbers λ_i along the diagonal and zeros elsewhere. Let us write the matrix elements of U as $u_{j,i}$ and those of V as $v_{i,k}$. The above matrix equation is then equivalent to the following set of equations:

$$\alpha_{j,k} = \sum_{i=0}^{d-1} u_{j,i} \lambda_i v_{i,k}. \tag{3.244}$$

Let us make this substitution into the expression for the state in (3.241):

$$|\psi\rangle_{AB} = \sum_{j=0}^{d_A-1} \sum_{k=0}^{d_B-1} \left(\sum_{i=0}^{d-1} u_{j,i} \lambda_i v_{i,k} \right) |j\rangle_A |k\rangle_B. \tag{3.245}$$

Readjusting some terms by exploiting the properties of the tensor product, we find that

$$|\psi\rangle_{AB} = \sum_{i=0}^{d-1} \lambda_i \left(\sum_{j=0}^{d_A-1} u_{j,i} |j\rangle_A \right) \otimes \left(\sum_{k=0}^{d_B-1} v_{i,k} |k\rangle_B \right) \tag{3.246}$$

$$= \sum_{i=0}^{d-1} \lambda_i |i\rangle_A |i\rangle_B, \tag{3.247}$$

where we define the orthonormal basis on the A system as $|i\rangle_A \equiv \sum_j u_{j,i} |j\rangle_A$ and we define the orthonormal basis on the B system as $|i\rangle_B \equiv \sum_k v_{i,k} |k\rangle_B$. This final step completes the proof of the theorem, but Exercise 3.8.1 asks you to verify that the set of states $\{|i\rangle_A\}$ form an orthonormal basis (the proof for the set of states $\{|i\rangle_B\}$ is similar). $\qquad\square$

The statement of Theorem 3.8.1 is rather remarkable, after pausing to think about it further. For example, the Hilbert space $\mathcal{H}_A$ of Alice could be a qubit Hilbert space of dimension two, and the Hilbert space $\mathcal{H}_B$ of Bob could be of dimension one billion (or some other large number). Then, in spite of this large dimension for Bob's Hilbert space, if we know that the state of systems A and B is a pure state, then it is always possible to find a two-dimensional subspace of $\mathcal{H}_B$ which along with $\mathcal{H}_A$ suffices to represent the state. So all those extra degrees of freedom are unnecessary in this example. Often, in quantum Shannon theory, we are optimizing certain functions over pure states. In such cases, the Schmidt decomposition theorem is helpful in limiting the size of the space we have to consider in such optimization problems.

REMARK 3.8.1 The Schmidt decomposition applies not only to bipartite systems but to any number of systems where we can make a bipartite cut of the systems. For example, suppose that there is a state $|\phi\rangle_{ABCDE}$ on systems

$ABCDE$. We could say that AB are part of one system and CDE are part of another system and write a Schmidt decomposition for this state as follows:

$$|\phi\rangle_{ABCDE} = \sum_y \sqrt{p_Y(y)}|y\rangle_{AB}|y\rangle_{CDE}, \qquad (3.248)$$

where $\{|y\rangle_{AB}\}$ is an orthonormal basis for the joint system AB and $\{|y\rangle_{CDE}\}$ is an orthonormal basis for the joint system CDE.

EXERCISE 3.8.1   Verify that the set of states $\{|i\rangle_A\}$ from the proof of Theorem 3.8.1 forms an orthonormal basis by exploiting the unitarity of the matrix U.

EXERCISE 3.8.2   Prove that the Schmidt decomposition gives a way to identify if a pure state is entangled or product. In particular, prove that a pure bipartite state is entangled if and only if it has more than one Schmidt coefficient. First, suppose that a pure bipartite state $|\phi\rangle_{AB}$ has only one Schmidt coefficient. Prove that its maximum overlap with a product state is equal to one:

$$\max_{|\varphi\rangle_A, |\psi\rangle_B} |\langle\varphi|_A \otimes \langle\psi|_B|\phi\rangle_{AB}|^2 = 1. \qquad (3.249)$$

Now, suppose that there is more than one Schmidt coefficient for a state $|\phi\rangle_{AB}$. Prove that this state's maximum overlap with a product state is strictly less than one (and thus it cannot be written as a product state):

$$\max_{|\varphi\rangle_A, |\psi\rangle_B} |\langle\varphi|_A \otimes \langle\psi|_B|\phi\rangle_{AB}|^2 < 1. \qquad (3.250)$$

(Hint: Use the Schmidt! Use the Schwarz! (as in Cauchy–Schwarz...))

3.9   History and Further Reading

There are many great books on quantum mechanics that outline the mathematical background. The books of Bohm (1989), Sakurai (1994), and Nielsen & Chuang (2000) are among these. The ideas for the resource inequality formalism first appeared in the popular article by Bennett (1995) and another of Bennett's papers (Bennett, 2004). The no-deletion theorem is in Pati & Braunstein (2000). The review article of the Horodecki family is a helpful reference on the study of quantum entanglement (Horodecki et al., 2009). Our presentation of the CHSH game and its analysis follows the approach detailed in Scarani (2013). The bound on the maximum quantum winning probability of the CHSH game was established in Tsirelson (1980).

4 The Noisy Quantum Theory

In general, we may not know for certain whether we possess a particular quantum state. Instead, we may only have a probabilistic description of an ensemble of quantum states. This chapter re-establishes the foundations of the quantum theory so that they incorporate a lack of complete information about a quantum system. The density operator formalism is a powerful mathematical tool for describing this scenario. This chapter also establishes how to model the noisy evolution of a quantum system, and we explore models of noisy quantum channels that are generalizations of the noisy classical channel discussed in Section 2.2.3 of Chapter 2.

You might have noticed that the development in the previous chapter relied on the premise that the possessor of a quantum system has perfect knowledge of the state of a given system. For instance, we assumed that Alice knows that she possesses a qubit in the state $|\psi\rangle$ where

$$|\psi\rangle = \alpha|0\rangle + \beta|1\rangle, \tag{4.1}$$

for some $\alpha, \beta \in \mathbb{C}$ such that $|\alpha|^2 + |\beta|^2 = 1$. Also, in some examples, we assumed that Alice and Bob know that they share an ebit $|\Phi^+\rangle_{AB}$. We even assumed perfect knowledge of a unitary evolution or a particular measurement that a possessor of a quantum state may apply to it.

This assumption of perfect, definite knowledge of a quantum state is a difficult one to justify in practice. In reality, it is challenging to prepare, evolve, or measure a quantum state exactly as we wish. Slight errors may occur in the preparation, evolution, or measurement due to imprecise devices or to coupling with other degrees of freedom outside of the system that we are controlling. An example of such imprecision can occur in the coupling of two photons at a beamsplitter. We may not be able to tune the reflectivity of the beamsplitter exactly or may not have the timing of the arrival of the photons exactly set. The noiseless quantum theory as we presented it in the previous section cannot handle such imprecisions.

In this chapter, we relax the assumption of perfect knowledge of the preparation, evolution, or measurement of quantum states and develop a noisy quantum theory that incorporates an imprecise knowledge of these states. The noisy quantum theory fuses probability theory and the quantum theory into a single formalism.

We proceed with the development of the noisy quantum theory in the following order:

1. We first present the density operator formalism, which gives a representation for a noisy, imprecise quantum state.
2. We then discuss a general form of measurements and the effect of them on our description of a noisy quantum state.
3. We proceed to composite noisy systems, which admit a particular form, and we discuss several possible states of composite noisy systems including product states, separable states, classical–quantum states, entangled states, and arbitrary states.
4. Next, we consider the Kraus representation of a quantum channel, which gives a way to describe noisy evolution, and we discuss important examples of noisy quantum channels. We also stress how every operation we have discussed so far, including preparations and measurements, can be viewed as quantum channels.

4.1   Noisy Quantum States

We generally may not have perfect knowledge of a prepared quantum state. Suppose a third party, Bob, prepares a state for us and only gives us a probabilistic description of it. That is, we might only know that Bob selects the state $|\psi_x\rangle$ with a certain probability $p_X(x)$. Our description of the state is then as an ensemble $\mathcal{E}$ of quantum states where

$$\mathcal{E} \equiv \{p_X(x), |\psi_x\rangle\}_{x \in \mathcal{X}}. \tag{4.2}$$

In the above, X is a random variable with distribution $p_X(x)$. Each realization x of random variable X belongs to an alphabet $\mathcal{X}$. Thus, the realization x merely acts as an index, meaning that the quantum state is $|\psi_x\rangle$ with probability $p_X(x)$. We also assume that each state $|\psi_x\rangle$ is a d-dimensional qudit state.

A simple example is the following ensemble: $\{\{1/3, |1\rangle\}, \{2/3, |3\rangle\}\}$. The states $|1\rangle$ and $|3\rangle$ are in a four-dimensional space spanned by $\{|0\rangle, |1\rangle, |2\rangle, |3\rangle\}$. The interpretation of this ensemble is that the state is $|1\rangle$ with probability $1/3$ and the state is $|3\rangle$ with probability $2/3$.

4.1.1   The Density Operator

Suppose now that we have the ability to perform a perfect, projective measurement of a system with ensemble description $\mathcal{E}$ in (4.2). Let Π_j be the elements of this projective measurement so that $\sum_j \Pi_j = I$, and let J be the random variable corresponding to the measurement outcome j. Let us suppose at first, without loss of generality, that the state in the ensemble is $|\psi_x\rangle$ for some $x \in \mathcal{X}$. Then the Born rule of the noiseless quantum theory states that the conditional probability $p_{J|X}(j|x)$ of obtaining measurement result j (given that the state is $|\psi_x\rangle$) is equal to

$$p_{J|X}(j|x) = \langle\psi_x|\Pi_j|\psi_x\rangle, \tag{4.3}$$

and the post-measurement state is $\Pi_j|\psi_x\rangle/\sqrt{p_{J|X}(j|x)}$. However, we would also like to know the unconditional probability $p_J(j)$ of obtaining measurement result j for the ensemble description $\mathcal{E}$. By the *law of total probability*, the unconditional probability $p_J(j)$ is

$$p_J(j) = \sum_{x\in\mathcal{X}} p_{J|X}(j|x)p_X(x) \tag{4.4}$$

$$= \sum_{x\in\mathcal{X}} \langle\psi_x|\Pi_j|\psi_x\rangle p_X(x). \tag{4.5}$$

At this point, it is helpful for us to introduce the *trace* of a square operator, which will be used extensively throughout this book.

DEFINITION 4.1.1 (Trace)   The *trace* Tr $\{A\}$ of a square operator A acting on a Hilbert space $\mathcal{H}$ is defined as follows:

$$\text{Tr}\,\{A\} \equiv \sum_i \langle i|A|i\rangle, \tag{4.6}$$

where $\{|i\rangle\}$ is some complete, orthonormal basis for $\mathcal{H}$.

Observe that the trace operation is *linear*. It is also independent of which orthonormal basis we choose because

$$\text{Tr}\,\{A\} = \sum_i \langle i|A|i\rangle \tag{4.7}$$

$$= \sum_i \langle i|A\left(\sum_j |\phi_j\rangle\langle\phi_j|\right)|i\rangle \tag{4.8}$$

$$= \sum_{i,j} \langle i|A|\phi_j\rangle\langle\phi_j|i\rangle \tag{4.9}$$

$$= \sum_{i,j} \langle\phi_j|i\rangle\langle i|A|\phi_j\rangle \tag{4.10}$$

$$= \sum_j \langle\phi_j|\left(\sum_i |i\rangle\langle i|\right)A|\phi_j\rangle \tag{4.11}$$

$$= \sum_j \langle\phi_j|A|\phi_j\rangle. \tag{4.12}$$

In the above, $\{|\phi_j\rangle\}$ is some other orthonormal basis for $\mathcal{H}$ and we made use of the completeness relation: $I = \sum_j |\phi_j\rangle\langle\phi_j| = \sum_i |i\rangle\langle i|$.

EXERCISE 4.1.1   Prove that the trace is cyclic. That is, for three operators A, B, and C, the following relation holds Tr$\{ABC\}$ = Tr$\{CAB\}$ = Tr$\{BCA\}$.

Returning to (4.5), we can then show the following useful property:

$$\langle \psi_x | \Pi_j | \psi_x \rangle = \langle \psi_x | \left(\sum_i |i\rangle\langle i| \right) \Pi_j | \psi_x \rangle \qquad (4.13)$$

$$= \sum_i \langle \psi_x | i \rangle \langle i | \Pi_j | \psi_x \rangle \qquad (4.14)$$

$$= \sum_i \langle i | \Pi_j | \psi_x \rangle \langle \psi_x | i \rangle \qquad (4.15)$$

$$= \mathrm{Tr} \left\{ \Pi_j | \psi_x \rangle \langle \psi_x | \right\}. \qquad (4.16)$$

The first equality uses the completeness relation $\sum_i |i\rangle\langle i| = I$. Thus, we continue with the development in (4.5) and show that

$$p_J(j) = \sum_{x \in \mathcal{X}} \mathrm{Tr} \left\{ \Pi_j | \psi_x \rangle \langle \psi_x | \right\} p_X(x) \qquad (4.17)$$

$$= \mathrm{Tr} \left\{ \Pi_j \sum_{x \in \mathcal{X}} p_X(x) | \psi_x \rangle \langle \psi_x | \right\}. \qquad (4.18)$$

We can rewrite the last equation as follows:

$$p_J(j) = \mathrm{Tr} \left\{ \Pi_j \rho \right\}, \qquad (4.19)$$

introducing ρ as the *density operator* corresponding to the ensemble $\mathcal{E}$:

DEFINITION 4.1.2 (Density Operator)   The *density operator* ρ corresponding to an ensemble $\mathcal{E} \equiv \{ p_X(x), |\psi_x\rangle \}_{x \in \mathcal{X}}$ is defined as

$$\rho \equiv \sum_{x \in \mathcal{X}} p_X(x) | \psi_x \rangle \langle \psi_x |. \qquad (4.20)$$

The operator ρ as defined above is known as the *density* operator because it is the quantum generalization of a probability density function. Throughout this book, we often use the symbols ρ, σ, τ, π, and ω to denote density operators.

We sometimes refer to the density operator as the *expected density operator* because there is a sense in which we are taking the expectation over all of the states in the ensemble in order to obtain the density operator. We can equivalently write the density operator as follows:

$$\rho = \mathbb{E}_X \left\{ |\psi_X\rangle\langle\psi_X| \right\}, \qquad (4.21)$$

where the expectation is with respect to the random variable X. Note that we are careful to use the notation $|\psi_X\rangle$ instead of the notation $|\psi_x\rangle$ for the state inside of the expectation because the state $|\psi_X\rangle$ is a random quantum state, random with respect to a classical random variable X.

EXERCISE 4.1.2   Suppose the ensemble has a degenerate probability distribution, say $p_X(0) = 1$ and $p_X(x) = 0$ for all $x \neq 0$. What is the density operator of this degenerate ensemble?

EXERCISE 4.1.3 Prove the following equality:

$$\text{Tr}\{A\} = \langle\Gamma|_{RS} I_R \otimes A_S |\Gamma\rangle_{RS}, \tag{4.22}$$

where A is a square operator acting on a Hilbert space $\mathcal{H}_S$, I_R is the identity operator acting on a Hilbert space $\mathcal{H}_R$ isomorphic to $\mathcal{H}_S$ and $|\Gamma\rangle_{RS}$ is the unnormalized maximally entangled vector from (3.233). This gives an alternate formula for the trace of a square operator A.

EXERCISE 4.1.4 Prove that $\text{Tr}\{f(G^\dagger G)\} = \text{Tr}\{f(GG^\dagger)\}$, where G is **any** operator (not necessarily Hermitian) and f is any function. (Recall the convention for a function of an operator given in Definition 3.3.1.)

Properties of the Density Operator

What are the properties that a given density operator corresponding to an ensemble satisfies? Let us consider taking the trace of ρ:

$$\text{Tr}\{\rho\} = \text{Tr}\left\{\sum_{x\in\mathcal{X}} p_X(x)|\psi_x\rangle\langle\psi_x|\right\} \tag{4.23}$$

$$= \sum_{x\in\mathcal{X}} p_X(x)\,\text{Tr}\{|\psi_x\rangle\langle\psi_x|\} \tag{4.24}$$

$$= \sum_{x\in\mathcal{X}} p_X(x)\,\langle\psi_x|\psi_x\rangle \tag{4.25}$$

$$= \sum_{x\in\mathcal{X}} p_X(x) \tag{4.26}$$

$$= 1. \tag{4.27}$$

The above development shows that every density operator corresponding to an ensemble has *unit trace*.

Let us consider taking the conjugate transpose of the density operator ρ:

$$\rho^\dagger = \left(\sum_{x\in\mathcal{X}} p_X(x)|\psi_x\rangle\langle\psi_x|\right)^\dagger \tag{4.28}$$

$$= \sum_{x\in\mathcal{X}} p_X(x)\,(|\psi_x\rangle\langle\psi_x|)^\dagger \tag{4.29}$$

$$= \sum_{x\in\mathcal{X}} p_X(x)|\psi_x\rangle\langle\psi_x| \tag{4.30}$$

$$= \rho. \tag{4.31}$$

Every density operator is thus a *Hermitian* operator as well because the conjugate transpose of ρ is ρ.

Every density operator is furthermore *positive semi-definite*, meaning that

$$\langle\varphi|\rho|\varphi\rangle \geq 0 \quad \forall\,|\varphi\rangle. \tag{4.32}$$

We write $\rho \geq 0$ to indicate that an operator is positive semi-definite. A proof for non-negativity of any density operator ρ is as follows:

$$\langle \varphi | \rho | \varphi \rangle = \langle \varphi | \left(\sum_{x \in \mathcal{X}} p_X(x) |\psi_x\rangle\langle\psi_x| \right) |\varphi\rangle \tag{4.33}$$

$$= \sum_{x \in \mathcal{X}} p_X(x) \langle \varphi | \psi_x \rangle \langle \psi_x | \varphi \rangle \tag{4.34}$$

$$= \sum_{x \in \mathcal{X}} p_X(x) |\langle \varphi | \psi_x \rangle|^2 \geq 0. \tag{4.35}$$

The inequality follows because each $p_X(x)$ is a probability and is therefore non-negative.

Ensembles and the Density Operator

Every ensemble has a unique density operator, but the opposite does not necessarily hold: every density operator does not correspond to a unique ensemble and could correspond to many ensembles. However, there are restrictions on which ensembles can realize a given density operator and there is a relation between them. We return to this question in Section 5.1.2, after we have developed more tools.

EXERCISE 4.1.5   Show that the following ensembles have the same density operator: $\{\{1/2, |0\rangle\}, \{1/2, |1\rangle\}\}$ and $\{\{1/2, |+\rangle\}, \{1/2, |-\rangle\}\}$.

This last result has profound implications for the predictions of the quantum theory because it is possible for two or more completely different ensembles to have the same probabilities for measurement results. It also has important implications for quantum Shannon theory as well.

By the spectral theorem, it follows that every density operator ρ has a spectral decomposition in terms of eigenstates $\{|\phi_x\rangle\}_{x \in \{0,...,d-1\}}$ because every ρ is Hermitian:

$$\rho = \sum_{x=0}^{d-1} \lambda_x |\phi_x\rangle\langle\phi_x|, \tag{4.36}$$

where the coefficients λ_x are the eigenvalues.

EXERCISE 4.1.6   Show that the coefficients λ_x are probabilities using the facts that $\text{Tr}\{\rho\} = 1$ and $\rho \geq 0$.

Thus, given any density operator ρ, we can define a "canonical" ensemble $\{\lambda_x, |\phi_x\rangle\}$ corresponding to it. Note that this ensemble is not unique: if $\lambda_x = \lambda_{x'}$ for $x \neq x'$, then the choice of eigenvectors corresponding to these eigenvalues is not unique. The fact that an ensemble can correspond to a density operator is so important for quantum Shannon theory that we see this idea arise again and again throughout this book. Any ensemble arising from the spectral theorem is the most "efficient" ensemble, in a sense, and we will explore this idea more in Chapter 18 on quantum data compression.

Density Operator as the State

We can also refer to the density operator as the *state* of a given quantum system because it is possible to use it to calculate probabilities for any measurement performed on that system. We can make these calculations without having an ensemble description—all we need is the density operator. The noisy quantum theory also subsumes the noiseless quantum theory because any state $|\psi\rangle$ has a corresponding density operator $|\psi\rangle\langle\psi|$ in the noisy quantum theory, and all calculations with this density operator in the noisy quantum theory give the same results as using the state $|\psi\rangle$ in the noiseless quantum theory. For these reasons, we will say that the *state* of a given quantum system is a density operator.

DEFINITION 4.1.3 (Density Operator as the State) The state of a quantum system is given by a density operator ρ, which is a positive semi-definite operator with trace equal to one. Let $\mathcal{D}(\mathcal{H})$ denote the set of all density operators acting on a Hilbert space $\mathcal{H}$.

One of the most important states is the maximally mixed state π:

DEFINITION 4.1.4 (Maximally Mixed State) The maximally mixed state π is the density operator corresponding to a uniform ensemble of orthogonal states $\{\frac{1}{d}, |x\rangle\}$, where d is the dimensionality of the Hilbert space. The maximally mixed state π is then equal to

$$\pi \equiv \frac{1}{d} \sum_{x \in \mathcal{X}} |x\rangle\langle x| = \frac{I}{d}. \tag{4.37}$$

EXERCISE 4.1.7 Show that π is the density operator of the ensemble that chooses $|0\rangle$, $|1\rangle$, $|+\rangle$, $|-\rangle$ with equal probability.

EXERCISE 4.1.8 (Convexity) Show that the set of density operators acting on a given Hilbert space is a convex set. That is, if $\lambda \in [0, 1]$ and ρ and σ are density operators, then $\lambda\rho + (1 - \lambda)\sigma$ is a density operator.

DEFINITION 4.1.5 (Purity) The purity $P(\rho)$ of a density operator ρ is equal to

$$P(\rho) \equiv \text{Tr}\left\{\rho^\dagger \rho\right\} = \text{Tr}\left\{\rho^2\right\}. \tag{4.38}$$

The purity is one particular measure of the noisiness of a quantum state. The purity of a pure state is equal to one, and the purity of a mixed state is strictly less than one, as the following exercise asks you to verify.

EXERCISE 4.1.9 Prove that the purity of a density operator ρ is equal to one if and only if ρ is a pure state, such that it can be written as $\rho = |\psi\rangle\langle\psi|$ for some unit vector ψ.

The Density Operator on the Bloch Sphere

Consider that the following pure qubit state

$$|\psi\rangle \equiv \cos(\theta/2)|0\rangle + e^{i\varphi}\sin(\theta/2)|1\rangle \tag{4.39}$$

has the following density operator representation:

$$|\psi\rangle\langle\psi| = \left(\cos(\theta/2)|0\rangle + e^{i\varphi}\sin(\theta/2)|1\rangle\right)\left(\cos(\theta/2)\langle 0| + e^{-i\varphi}\sin(\theta/2)\langle 1|\right) \quad (4.40)$$
$$= \cos^2(\theta/2)|0\rangle\langle 0| + e^{-i\varphi}\sin(\theta/2)\cos(\theta/2)|0\rangle\langle 1|$$
$$+ e^{i\varphi}\sin(\theta/2)\cos(\theta/2)|1\rangle\langle 0| + \sin^2(\theta/2)|1\rangle\langle 1|. \quad (4.41)$$

The matrix representation, or *density matrix*, of this density operator with respect to the computational basis is as follows:

$$\begin{bmatrix} \cos^2(\theta/2) & e^{-i\varphi}\sin(\theta/2)\cos(\theta/2) \\ e^{i\varphi}\sin(\theta/2)\cos(\theta/2) & \sin^2(\theta/2) \end{bmatrix}. \quad (4.42)$$

Using trigonometric identities, it follows that the density matrix is equal to the following matrix:

$$\frac{1}{2}\begin{bmatrix} 1 + \cos(\theta) & \sin(\theta)\left(\cos(\varphi) - i\sin(\varphi)\right) \\ \sin(\theta)\left(\cos(\varphi) + i\sin(\varphi)\right) & 1 - \cos(\theta) \end{bmatrix}. \quad (4.43)$$

We can further exploit the Pauli matrices, defined in Section 3.3.3, to represent the density matrix as follows:

$$\frac{1}{2}\left(I + r_x X + r_y Y + r_z Z\right), \quad (4.44)$$

where $r_x = \sin(\theta)\cos(\varphi)$, $r_y = \sin(\theta)\sin(\varphi)$, and $r_z = \cos(\theta)$. The coefficients r_x, r_y, and r_z are none other than the Cartesian coordinate representation of the angles θ and φ, and they thus correspond to a unit vector.

More generally, the formula in (4.44) can represent an arbitrary qubit density operator where the coefficients r_x, r_y, and r_z do not necessarily correspond to a unit vector, but rather a vector $\mathbf{r}$ such that $\|\mathbf{r}\|_2 \leq 1$. Consider that the density matrix in (4.44) is as follows:

$$\frac{1}{2}\begin{bmatrix} 1 + r_z & r_x - ir_y \\ r_x + ir_y & 1 - r_z \end{bmatrix}. \quad (4.45)$$

The above matrix corresponds to a valid density matrix because it has unit trace, it is Hermitian, and it is non-negative (the next exercise asks you to verify these facts). This alternate representation of the density matrix as a vector in the Bloch sphere is useful for visualizing noisy qubit processes in the noisy quantum theory.

EXERCISE 4.1.10   Show that the matrix in (4.45) has unit trace, is Hermitian, and is non-negative for all $\mathbf{r}$ such that $\|\mathbf{r}\|_2 \leq 1$. It thus corresponds to any valid density matrix.

EXERCISE 4.1.11   Show that we can compute the Bloch sphere coordinates r_x, r_y, and r_z with the respective formulas $\text{Tr}\{X\rho\}$, $\text{Tr}\{Y\rho\}$, and $\text{Tr}\{Z\rho\}$ using the representation in (4.45) and the result of Exercise 3.3.6.

EXERCISE 4.1.12   Show that the eigenvalues of a general qubit density operator with density matrix representation in (4.45) are as follows: $\frac{1}{2}\left(1 \pm \|\mathbf{r}\|_2\right)$.

EXERCISE 4.1.13 Show that a mixture of pure states $|\psi_j\rangle$ each with Bloch vector $\mathbf{r}_j$ and probability $p(j)$ gives a density matrix with the Bloch vector $\mathbf{r}$ where $\mathbf{r} = \sum_j p(j)\mathbf{r}_j$.

4.1.2 An Ensemble of Ensembles

The most general ensemble that we can construct is an *ensemble of ensembles*, i.e., an ensemble $\mathcal{F}$ of density operators where

$$\mathcal{F} \equiv \{p_X(x), \rho_x\}. \tag{4.46}$$

The ensemble $\mathcal{F}$ essentially has two layers of randomization. The first layer is from the distribution $p_X(x)$. Each density operator ρ_x in $\mathcal{F}$ arises from an ensemble $\{p_{Y|X}(y|x), |\psi_{x,y}\rangle\}$. The conditional distribution $p_{Y|X}(y|x)$ represents the second layer of randomization. Each ρ_x is a density operator with respect to the above ensemble:

$$\rho_x \equiv \sum_y p_{Y|X}(y|x)|\psi_{x,y}\rangle\langle\psi_{x,y}|. \tag{4.47}$$

The ensemble $\mathcal{F}$ has its own density operator ρ where

$$\rho \equiv \sum_{x,y} p_{Y|X}(y|x)p_X(x)|\psi_{x,y}\rangle\langle\psi_{x,y}| = \sum_x p_X(x)\rho_x. \tag{4.48}$$

The density operator ρ is the density operator from the perspective of someone who does not possess x. Figure 4.1 displays the process by which we can select the ensemble $\mathcal{F}$.

4.1.3 Noiseless Evolution of an Ensemble

Quantum states can evolve in a noiseless fashion either according to a unitary operator or a measurement. In this section, we determine the noiseless evolution of an ensemble and its corresponding density operator. We also show how density operators evolve under a quantum measurement.

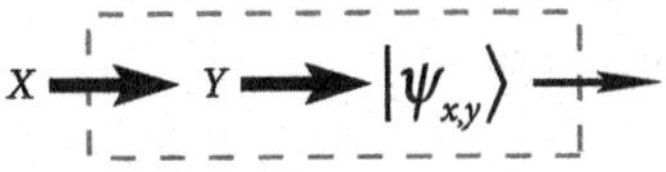

Figure 4.1 The mixing process by which we can generate an "ensemble of ensembles." First choose a realization x according to distribution $p_X(x)$. Then choose a realization y according to the conditional distribution $p_{Y|X}(y|x)$. Finally, choose a state $|\psi_{x,y}\rangle$ according to the realizations x and y. This leads to an ensemble $\{p_X(x), \rho_x\}$ where $\rho_x \equiv \sum_y p_{Y|X}(y|x)|\psi_{x,y}\rangle\langle\psi_{x,y}|$.

Noiseless Unitary Evolution of a Noisy State

We first consider noiseless evolution according to some unitary U. Suppose we have the ensemble $\mathcal{E}$ in (4.2) with density operator ρ. Suppose without loss of generality that the state is $|\psi_x\rangle$. Then the evolution postulate of the noiseless quantum theory gives that the state after the unitary evolution is as follows: $U|\psi_x\rangle$. This result implies that the evolution leads to a new ensemble

$$\mathcal{E}_U \equiv \{p_X(x), U|\psi_x\rangle\}_{x\in\mathcal{X}}. \tag{4.49}$$

The density operator of the evolved ensemble is

$$\sum_{x\in\mathcal{X}} p_X(x)U|\psi_x\rangle\langle\psi_x|U^\dagger = U\left(\sum_{x\in\mathcal{X}} p_X(x)|\psi_x\rangle\langle\psi_x|\right)U^\dagger \tag{4.50}$$

$$= U\rho U^\dagger. \tag{4.51}$$

Thus, the above relation shows that we can keep track of the evolution of the density operator ρ, rather than worrying about keeping track of the evolution of every state in the ensemble $\mathcal{E}$. It suffices to keep track of only the density operator evolution because this operator is sufficient to determine probabilities when performing any measurement on the system.

Noiseless Measurement of a Noisy State

In a similar fashion, we can analyze the result of a measurement on a system with ensemble description $\mathcal{E}$ in (4.2). Suppose that we perform a projective measurement with projection operators $\{\Pi_j\}_j$ where $\sum_j \Pi_j = I$. The main result of this section is that two things happen after a measurement occurs. First, as shown in the development preceding (4.19), we receive the outcome j with probability $p_J(j) = \text{Tr}\{\Pi_j\rho\}$. Second, if the outcome of the measurement is j, then the state evolves as follows:

$$\rho \longrightarrow \frac{\Pi_j\rho\Pi_j}{p_J(j)}. \tag{4.52}$$

To see the above, let us suppose that the state in the ensemble $\mathcal{E}$ is $|\psi_x\rangle$. Then the noiseless quantum theory predicts that the probability of obtaining outcome j conditioned on the index x is

$$p_{J|X}(j|x) = \langle\psi_x|\Pi_j|\psi_x\rangle, \tag{4.53}$$

and the resulting state is

$$\frac{\Pi_j|\psi_x\rangle}{\sqrt{p_{J|X}(j|x)}}. \tag{4.54}$$

Supposing that we receive outcome j, then we have a new ensemble:

$$\mathcal{E}_j \equiv \left\{p_{X|J}(x|j), \frac{\Pi_j|\psi_x\rangle}{\sqrt{p_{J|X}(j|x)}}\right\}_{x\in\mathcal{X}}. \tag{4.55}$$

The density operator for this ensemble is

$$\sum_{x \in \mathcal{X}} p_{X|J}(x|j) \frac{\Pi_j |\psi_x\rangle \langle \psi_x| \Pi_j}{p_{J|X}(j|x)}$$

$$= \Pi_j \left(\sum_{x \in \mathcal{X}} \frac{p_{X|J}(x|j)}{p_{J|X}(j|x)} |\psi_x\rangle \langle \psi_x| \right) \Pi_j \tag{4.56}$$

$$= \Pi_j \left(\sum_{x \in \mathcal{X}} \frac{p_{J|X}(j|x) p_X(x)}{p_{J|X}(j|x) p_J(j)} |\psi_x\rangle \langle \psi_x| \right) \Pi_j \tag{4.57}$$

$$= \frac{\Pi_j \left(\sum_{x \in \mathcal{X}} p_X(x) |\psi_x\rangle \langle \psi_x| \right) \Pi_j}{p_J(j)} \tag{4.58}$$

$$= \frac{\Pi_j \rho \Pi_j}{p_J(j)}. \tag{4.59}$$

The second equality follows from applying the Bayes rule:

$$p_{X|J}(x|j) = p_{J|X}(j|x) p_X(x) / p_J(j). \tag{4.60}$$

4.1.4   Probability Theory as a Special Case

It may help to build some intuition for the noisy quantum theory by showing how it contains probability theory as a special case. Indeed, we should expect this containment of probability theory within the noisy quantum theory to hold if the noisy quantum theory is making probabilistic predictions about the physical world.

Let us again begin with an ensemble of quantum states, but this time, let us pick the states in the ensemble to be special states, where they are all orthogonal to one another. If the states in the ensemble are all orthogonal to one another, then they are essentially classical states because there is a measurement that distinguishes them from one another. So, let us pick the ensemble to be $\{p_X(x), |x\rangle\}_{x \in \mathcal{X}}$ where the states $\{|x\rangle\}_{x \in \mathcal{X}}$ form an orthonormal basis for a Hilbert space of dimension $|\mathcal{X}|$. These states are classical because a measurement with the following projection operators can distinguish them:

$$\{|x\rangle\langle x|\}_{x \in \mathcal{X}}. \tag{4.61}$$

The generalization of a probability distribution to the quantum world is the density operator:

$$p_X(x) \leftrightarrow \rho. \tag{4.62}$$

The reason for this is that we can use the density operator to calculate expectations and moments of observables. Furthermore, a probability distribution can be encoded as a density operator that is diagonal with respect to a known orthonormal basis, as follows:

$$\sum_{x \in \mathcal{X}} p_X(x) |x\rangle \langle x|. \tag{4.63}$$

The generalization of a random variable is an observable. For example, let us consider the following observable:

$$X \equiv \sum_{x \in \mathcal{X}} x |x\rangle\langle x|, \tag{4.64}$$

analogous to the observable in (3.220). We perform the following calculation to determine the expectation of the observable X:

$$\mathbb{E}_\rho[X] = \mathrm{Tr}\{X\rho\}. \tag{4.65}$$

Explicitly calculating this quantity, we find that it is consistent with the formula for the expectation of random variable X with probability distribution $p_X(x)$:

$$\mathrm{Tr}\{X\rho\} = \mathrm{Tr}\left\{ \sum_{x \in \mathcal{X}} x |x\rangle\langle x| \sum_{x' \in \mathcal{X}} p_X(x')|x'\rangle\langle x'| \right\} \tag{4.66}$$

$$= \sum_{x, x' \in \mathcal{X}} x \, p_X(x') \, |\langle x|x'\rangle|^2 \tag{4.67}$$

$$= \sum_{x \in \mathcal{X}} x \, p_X(x). \tag{4.68}$$

Another useful notion in probability theory is the notion of an indicator random variable $I_A(X)$. We define the indicator function $I_A(x)$ for a set A as follows:

$$I_A(x) \equiv \begin{cases} 1 & : & x \in A \\ 0 & : & x \notin A \end{cases}. \tag{4.69}$$

The expectation $\mathbb{E}[I_A(X)]$ of the indicator random variable $I_A(X)$ is

$$\mathbb{E}[I_A(X)] = \sum_{x \in A} p_X(x) \equiv p_X(A), \tag{4.70}$$

where $p_X(A)$ represents the probability of the set A. In the quantum theory, we can define an indicator observable $I_A(X)$:

$$I_A(X) \equiv \sum_{x \in A} |x\rangle\langle x|. \tag{4.71}$$

It has eigenvalues equal to one for all eigenvectors with labels x in the set A, and it has zero eigenvalues for those eigenvectors with labels outside of A. It is straightforward to show that the expectation $\mathrm{Tr}\{I_A(X)\rho\}$ of the indicator observable $I_A(X)$ is $p_X(A)$.

You may have noticed that the indicator observable is also a projection operator. So, according to the postulates of the quantum theory, we can perform a measurement with elements:

$$\{I_A(X), I_{A^c}(X) \equiv I - I_A(X)\}. \tag{4.72}$$

The result of such a projective measurement is to project onto the subspace given by $I_A(X)$ with probability $p_X(A)$ and to project onto the complementary subspace given by $I_{A^c}(X)$ with probability $1 - p_X(A)$.

We highlight the connection between the noisy quantum theory and probability theory with two more examples. First, suppose that we have two *disjoint* sets A and B. Then the probability of their union is the sum of the probabilities of the individual sets:

$$\Pr\{A \cup B\} = \Pr\{A\} + \Pr\{B\}, \tag{4.73}$$

and the probability of the complementary set $(A \cup B)^c = A^c \cap B^c$ is equal to $1 - \Pr\{A\} - \Pr\{B\}$. We can perform the analogous calculation in the noisy quantum theory. Let us consider two projection operators

$$\Pi(A) \equiv \sum_{x \in A} |x\rangle\langle x|, \quad \Pi(B) \equiv \sum_{x \in B} |x\rangle\langle x|. \tag{4.74}$$

The sum of these projection operators gives a projection onto the union set $A \cup B$:

$$\Pi(A \cup B) \equiv \sum_{x \in A \cup B} |x\rangle\langle x| = \Pi(A) + \Pi(B). \tag{4.75}$$

EXERCISE 4.1.14 Show that $\text{Tr}\{\Pi(A \cup B)\rho\} = \Pr\{A\} + \Pr\{B\}$ whenever the projectors $\Pi(A)$ and $\Pi(B)$ satisfy $\Pi(A)\Pi(B) = 0$ and the density operator ρ is diagonal in the same basis as $\Pi(A)$ and $\Pi(B)$.

We can also consider intersections of sets. Suppose that we have two sets A and B. The intersection of these two sets consists of all the elements that are common to both sets. There is an associated probability $\Pr\{A \cap B\}$ with the intersection. We can again formulate this idea in the noisy quantum theory. Consider the projection operators in (4.74). The multiplication of these two projectors gives a projector onto the intersection of the two spaces:

$$\Pi(A \cap B) = \Pi(A)\Pi(B). \tag{4.76}$$

EXERCISE 4.1.15 Show that $\text{Tr}\{\Pi(A)\Pi(B)\rho\} = \Pr\{A \cap B\}$ whenever the density operator ρ is diagonal in the same basis as $\Pi(A)$ and $\Pi(B)$.

Such ideas and connections to the classical world are crucial for understanding quantum Shannon theory. Many times, we will be thinking about unions of disjoint subspaces and it is helpful to make the analogy with a union of disjoint sets. Also, in Chapter 17 on the covering lemma, we will use projection operators to remove some of the support of an operator, and this operation is analogous to taking intersections of sets.

Despite the fact that there is a strong connection for classical states, some of this intuition breaks down by considering the non-orthogonality of quantum states. For example, consider the case of the projectors $\Pi_0 \equiv |0\rangle\langle 0|$ and $\Pi_+ \equiv |+\rangle\langle +|$. The two subspaces onto which these operators project do not intersect, yet we know that the projectors have some overlap because their corresponding states are non-orthogonal. One analogy of the intersection operation is to sandwich one operator with another. For example, we can form the operators

$$\Pi_0 \Pi_+ \Pi_0, \quad \Pi_+ \Pi_0 \Pi_+. \tag{4.77}$$

If the two projectors were to commute, then this ordering would not matter, and the resulting operator would be a projector onto the intersection of the two subspaces. But this is not the case for our example here, and the resulting operators are quite different.

EXERCISE 4.1.16 (Union Bound) Prove a union bound for commuting projectors Π_1 and Π_2 where $0 \leq \Pi_1, \Pi_2 \leq I$ and for an *arbitrary* density operator ρ (not necessarily diagonal in the same basis as Π_1 and Π_2):

$$\text{Tr}\left\{(I - \Pi_1\Pi_2)\rho\right\} \leq \text{Tr}\left\{(I - \Pi_1)\rho\right\} + \text{Tr}\left\{(I - \Pi_2)\rho\right\}. \tag{4.78}$$

4.2   Measurement in the Noisy Quantum Theory

We have described measurement in the quantum theory using a set of projectors that form a resolution of the identity. For example, the set $\{\Pi_j\}_j$ of projectors that satisfy the condition $\sum_j \Pi_j = I$ form a valid projective quantum measurement.

There is an alternate description of quantum measurements that follows from allowing the system of interest to interact unitarily with a probe system that we measure after the interaction occurs. So suppose that the system of interest is in a state $|\psi\rangle_S$ and that the probe is in a state $|0\rangle_P$, so that the overall state before anything happens is as follows:

$$|\psi\rangle_S \otimes |0\rangle_P. \tag{4.79}$$

Let $\{|0\rangle_P, |1\rangle_P, \ldots, |d-1\rangle_P\}$ be an orthonormal basis for the probe system (assuming that it has dimension d). Now suppose that the system and the probe interact according to a unitary U_{SP}, and then we perform a measurement of the probe system, described by measurement operators $\{|j\rangle\langle j|_P\}$. The probability to obtain outcome j is

$$p_J(j) = \left(\langle\psi|_S \otimes \langle 0|_P U_{SP}^\dagger\right)\left(I_S \otimes |j\rangle\langle j|_P\right)\left(U_{SP}|\psi\rangle_S \otimes |0\rangle_P\right), \tag{4.80}$$

and the post-measurement state upon obtaining outcome j is

$$\frac{1}{\sqrt{p_J(j)}}\left(I_S \otimes |j\rangle\langle j|_P\right)\left(U_{SP}|\psi\rangle_S \otimes |0\rangle_P\right). \tag{4.81}$$

We can rewrite the expressions above in a different way. Let us expand the unitary operator U_{SP} in the orthonormal basis of the probe system P as follows:

$$U_{SP} = \sum_{j,k} M_S^{j,k} \otimes |j\rangle\langle k|_P, \tag{4.82}$$

where $\{M_S^{j,k}\}$ is a set of operators. Up to a permutation of the S and P systems and using the mathematics of the tensor product (described in Section 3.5.1), this is the same as writing the unitary U_{SP} as follows:

$$\begin{bmatrix} M_S^{0,0} & M_S^{0,1} & \cdots & M_S^{0,d-1} \\ M_S^{1,0} & M_S^{1,1} & \cdots & M_S^{1,d-1} \\ \vdots & \vdots & \ddots & \vdots \\ M_S^{d-1,0} & M_S^{d-1,1} & \cdots & M_S^{d-1,d-1} \end{bmatrix}. \tag{4.83}$$

This set $\{M_S^{j,k}\}$ needs to satisfy some constraints corresponding to the unitarity of U_{SP}. In particular, consider the following operator:

$$\sum_j M_S^{j,0} \otimes |j\rangle\langle 0|_P, \tag{4.84}$$

which corresponds to the first column of operator-valued entries in U_{SP}, as illustrated in (4.83). In what follows, we employ the shorthand $M_S^j \equiv M_S^{j,0}$. From the fact that $U_{SP}^\dagger U_{SP} = I_{SP} = I_S \otimes I_P$, we deduce that the following equality must hold

$$I_S \otimes |0\rangle\langle 0|_P = \left(\sum_{j'} M_S^{j'\dagger} \otimes |0\rangle\langle j'|_P \right) \left(\sum_j M_S^j \otimes |j\rangle\langle 0|_P \right) \tag{4.85}$$

$$= \sum_{j',j} M_S^{j'\dagger} M_S^j \otimes |0\rangle \langle j'|j\rangle \langle 0|_P \tag{4.86}$$

$$= \sum_j M_S^{j\dagger} M_S^j \otimes |0\rangle\langle 0|_P, \tag{4.87}$$

where the last line follows from the fact that we chose an orthonormal basis in the representation of U_{SP} in (4.82). So the above equality implies that the following condition holds

$$\sum_j M_S^{j\dagger} M_S^j = I_S. \tag{4.88}$$

Plugging (4.82) into (4.80) and (4.81), a short calculation (similar to the above one) reveals that they simplify as follows:

$$p_J(j) = \langle\psi|M_j^\dagger M_j|\psi\rangle, \tag{4.89}$$

$$\frac{1}{\sqrt{p_J(j)}} (I_S \otimes |j\rangle\langle j|_P) (U_{SP}|\psi\rangle_S \otimes |0\rangle_P) = \frac{M_j|\psi\rangle_S \otimes |j\rangle_P}{\sqrt{p_J(j)}}. \tag{4.90}$$

Since the system and the probe are in a pure product state (and thus independent of each other) after the measurement occurs, we can discard the probe system and deduce that the post-measurement state of the system S is simply $M_j|\psi\rangle_S/\sqrt{p_J(j)}$.

Motivated by the above development, we allow for an alternate notion of quantum measurement, saying that it consists of a set of measurement operators $\{M_j\}_j$ that satisfy the following completeness condition:

$$\sum_j M_j^\dagger M_j = I. \tag{4.91}$$

Observe from the above development that this is the only constraint that the operators $\{M_j\}$ need to satisfy. This constraint is a consequence of unitarity, but can be viewed as a generalization of the completeness relation for a set of projectors that constitute a projective quantum measurement. Given a set of measurement operators of the above form, the probability for obtaining outcome j when measuring a state $|\psi\rangle$ is

$$p_J(j) \equiv \langle\psi|M_j^\dagger M_j|\psi\rangle, \tag{4.92}$$

and the post-measurement state when we receive outcome j is

$$\frac{M_j|\psi\rangle}{\sqrt{p_J(j)}}. \tag{4.93}$$

Suppose that we instead have an ensemble $\{p_X(x), |\psi_x\rangle\}$ with density operator ρ. We can carry out an analysis similar to that which led to (4.59) to conclude that the probability $p_J(j)$ for obtaining outcome j is

$$p_J(j) \equiv \text{Tr}\{M_j^\dagger M_j \rho\}, \tag{4.94}$$

and the post-measurement state when we measure result j is

$$\frac{M_j \rho M_j^\dagger}{p_J(j)}. \tag{4.95}$$

The expression $p_J(j) = \text{Tr}\{M_j^\dagger M_j \rho\}$ is a reformulation of the Born rule.

4.2.1   POVM Formalism

Sometimes, we simply may not care about the post-measurement state of a quantum measurement, but instead we only care about the probability for obtaining a particular outcome. For example, this situation arises in the transmission of classical data over a quantum channel. In this situation, we are merely concerned with minimizing the error probabilities of the classical transmission. The receiver does not care about the post-measurement state because he no longer needs it in the quantum information-processing protocol. We can specify a measurement of this sort by a POVM, defined as follows:

DEFINITION 4.2.1 (POVM)   A positive operator-valued measure (POVM) is a set $\{\Lambda_j\}_j$ of operators that satisfy non-negativity and completeness:

$$\forall j : \Lambda_j \geq 0, \qquad \sum_j \Lambda_j = I. \tag{4.96}$$

The probability for obtaining outcome j is

$$\langle\psi|\Lambda_j|\psi\rangle, \tag{4.97}$$

if the state is some pure state $|\psi\rangle$. The probability for obtaining outcome j is

$$\text{Tr}\{\Lambda_j \rho\}, \tag{4.98}$$

if the state is in a mixed state described by some density operator ρ. This is another reformulation of the Born rule.

EXERCISE 4.2.1 Consider the following five "Chrysler" states:

$$|e_k\rangle \equiv \cos(2\pi k/5)|0\rangle + \sin(2\pi k/5)|1\rangle, \tag{4.99}$$

where $k \in \{0,\ldots,4\}$. These states are the "Chrysler" states because they form a pentagon on the XZ-plane of the Bloch sphere. Show that the following set of operators forms a valid POVM: $\left\{\frac{2}{5}|e_k\rangle\langle e_k|\right\}$.

EXERCISE 4.2.2 Suppose we have an ensemble $\{p_X(x), \rho_x\}$ of density operators and a POVM with elements $\{\Lambda_x\}$ that should identify the states ρ_x with high probability, i.e., we would like $\text{Tr}\{\Lambda_x \rho_x\}$ to be as high as possible. The expected success probability of the POVM is then

$$\sum_x p_X(x) \text{Tr}\{\Lambda_x \rho_x\}. \tag{4.100}$$

Suppose that there exists some operator τ such that

$$\tau \geq p_X(x)\rho_x, \tag{4.101}$$

where the condition $\tau \geq p_X(x)\rho_x$ is the same as $\tau - p_X(x)\rho_x \geq 0$ (i.e., that the operator $\tau - p_X(x)\rho_x$ is a positive semi-definite operator). Show that $\text{Tr}\{\tau\}$ is an upper bound on the expected success probability of the POVM. After doing so, consider the case of encoding n bits into a d-dimensional subspace. By choosing states uniformly at random (in the case of the ensemble $\{2^{-n}, \rho_i\}_{i \in \{0,1\}^n}$), show that the expected success probability is bounded above by $d\,2^{-n}$. Thus, it is not possible to store more than n classical bits in n qubits and have a perfect success probability of retrieval.

4.3   Composite Noisy Quantum Systems

We are again interested in the behavior of two or more quantum systems when we join them together. Some of the most exotic, truly "quantum" behavior occurs in joint quantum systems, and we observe a marked departure from the classical world.

4.3.1   Independent Ensembles

Let us first suppose that we have two independent ensembles for quantum systems A and B. The first quantum system belongs to Alice and the second quantum system belongs to Bob, and they may or may not be spatially separated. Let $\{p_X(x), |\psi_x\rangle\}$ be the ensemble for the system A and let $\{p_Y(y), |\phi_y\rangle\}$ be the ensemble for the system B. Suppose for now that the state on system A is $|\psi_x\rangle$ for some x and the state on system B is $|\phi_y\rangle$ for some y. Then, using the composite system postulate of the noiseless quantum theory, the joint state for a given x and y is $|\psi_x\rangle \otimes |\phi_y\rangle$. The density operator for the joint quantum system is the expectation of the states $|\psi_x\rangle \otimes |\phi_y\rangle$ with respect to the random variables X and Y that describe the individual ensembles:

$$\mathbb{E}_{X,Y} \left\{ (|\psi_X\rangle \otimes |\phi_Y\rangle)(\langle\psi_X| \otimes \langle\phi_Y|) \right\}. \tag{4.102}$$

The above expression is equal to the following one:

$$\mathbb{E}_{X,Y} \left\{ |\psi_X\rangle\langle\psi_X| \otimes |\phi_Y\rangle\langle\phi_Y| \right\}, \tag{4.103}$$

because $(|\psi_x\rangle \otimes |\phi_y\rangle)(\langle\psi_x| \otimes \langle\phi_y|) = |\psi_x\rangle\langle\psi_x| \otimes |\phi_y\rangle\langle\phi_y|$. We then explicitly write out the expectation as a sum over probabilities:

$$\sum_{x,y} p_X(x)p_Y(y)|\psi_x\rangle\langle\psi_x| \otimes |\phi_y\rangle\langle\phi_y|. \tag{4.104}$$

We can distribute the probabilities and the sum because the tensor product obeys a distributive property:

$$\sum_x p_X(x)|\psi_x\rangle\langle\psi_x| \otimes \sum_y p_Y(y)|\phi_y\rangle\langle\phi_y|. \tag{4.105}$$

The density operator for this ensemble admits the following simple form:

$$\rho \otimes \sigma, \tag{4.106}$$

where $\rho = \sum_x p_X(x)|\psi_x\rangle\langle\psi_x|$ is the density operator of the X ensemble and $\sigma = \sum_y p_Y(y)|\phi_y\rangle\langle\phi_y|$ is the density operator of the Y ensemble. We can say that Alice's local density operator is ρ and Bob's local density operator is σ. The overall state is a tensor product of these two density operators.

DEFINITION 4.3.1 (Product State)   A density operator is a *product state* if it is equal to a tensor product of two or more density operators.

We should expect the density operator to factor as it does above because we assumed that the ensembles are independent. There is nothing much that distinguishes this situation from the classical world, except for the fact that the states in each respective ensemble may be non-orthogonal to other states in the same ensemble. But even here, there is some equivalent description of each ensemble in terms of an orthonormal basis so that there is really not too much difference between this description and a joint probability distribution that factors as two independent distributions.

EXERCISE 4.3.1   Show that the purity $P(\rho_A)$ is equal to the following expression:

$$P(\rho_A) = \text{Tr} \left\{ (\rho_A \otimes \rho_{A'}) F_{AA'} \right\}, \tag{4.107}$$

where system A' has a Hilbert space structure isomorphic to that of system A and $F_{AA'}$ is the swap operator that has the following action on kets in A and A':

$$\forall x, y \quad F_{AA'}|x\rangle_A|y\rangle_{A'} = |y\rangle_A|x\rangle_{A'}. \tag{4.108}$$

(One can in fact show more generally that $\mathrm{Tr}\left\{f(\rho_A)\right\} = \mathrm{Tr}\left\{(f(\rho_A) \otimes I_{A'})\, F_{AA'}\right\}$ for any function f on the operators in system A.)

4.3.2 Separable States

Let us now consider two systems A and B whose corresponding ensembles are correlated in a classical way. We describe this correlated ensemble as the joint ensemble

$$\left\{p_X(x), |\psi_x\rangle \otimes |\phi_x\rangle\right\}. \tag{4.109}$$

It is straightforward to verify that the density operator of this correlated ensemble has the following form:

$$\mathbb{E}_X\left\{(|\psi_X\rangle \otimes |\phi_X\rangle)(\langle\psi_X| \otimes \langle\phi_X|)\right\} = \sum_x p_X(x)|\psi_x\rangle\langle\psi_x| \otimes |\phi_x\rangle\langle\phi_x|. \tag{4.110}$$

By ignoring Bob's system, Alice's local density operator is of the form

$$\mathbb{E}_X\left\{|\psi_X\rangle\langle\psi_X|\right\} = \sum_x p_X(x)|\psi_x\rangle\langle\psi_x|, \tag{4.111}$$

and similarly, Bob's local density operator is

$$\mathbb{E}_X\left\{|\phi_X\rangle\langle\phi_X|\right\} = \sum_x p_X(x)|\phi_x\rangle\langle\phi_x|. \tag{4.112}$$

States of the form in (4.110) can be generated by a classical procedure. A third party generates a symbol x according to the probability distribution $p_X(x)$ and sends the symbol x to both Alice and Bob. Alice then prepares the state $|\psi_x\rangle$ and Bob prepares the state $|\phi_x\rangle$. If they then discard the symbol x, the state of their systems is given by (4.110).

We can generalize this classical preparation procedure one step further, using an idea similar to the "ensemble of ensembles" idea in Section 4.1.2. Let us suppose that we first generate a random variable Z according to some distribution $p_Z(z)$. We then generate two other ensembles, conditioned on the value of the random variable Z. Let $\{p_{X|Z}(x|z), |\psi_{x,z}\rangle\}$ be the first ensemble and let $\{p_{Y|Z}(y|z), |\phi_{y,z}\rangle\}$ be the second ensemble, where the random variables X and Y are independent when conditioned on Z. Let us label the density operators of the first and second ensembles when conditioned on a particular realization z by ρ_z and σ_z, respectively. It is then straightforward to verify that the density operator of an ensemble created from this classical preparation procedure has the following form:

$$\mathbb{E}_{X,Y,Z}\left\{(|\psi_{X,Z}\rangle \otimes |\phi_{Y,Z}\rangle)(\langle\psi_{X,Z}| \otimes \langle\phi_{Y,Z}|)\right\} = \sum_z p_Z(z)\rho_z \otimes \sigma_z. \tag{4.113}$$

EXERCISE 4.3.2 By ignoring Bob's system, we can determine Alice's local density operator. Show that

$$\mathbb{E}_{X,Y,Z}\left\{|\psi_{X,Z}\rangle\langle\psi_{X,Z}|\right\} = \sum_z p_Z(z)\rho_z, \tag{4.114}$$

so that the above expression is the density operator for Alice. It similarly follows that the local density operator for Bob is

$$\mathbb{E}_{X,Y,Z}\{|\phi_{Y,Z}\rangle\langle\phi_{Y,Z}|\} = \sum_z p_Z(z)\sigma_z. \qquad (4.115)$$

EXERCISE 4.3.3 Show that we can always write a state of the form in (4.113) as a convex combination of pure product states:

$$\sum_w p_W(w)|\phi_w\rangle\langle\phi_w| \otimes |\psi_w\rangle\langle\psi_w|, \qquad (4.116)$$

by manipulating the general form in (4.113).

As a consequence of Exercise 4.3.3, we see that any state of the form in (4.113) can be written as a convex combination of pure product states. Such states are called *separable* states, defined formally as follows:

DEFINITION 4.3.2 (Separable State) A bipartite density operator σ_{AB} is a separable state if it can be written in the following form:

$$\sigma_{AB} = \sum_x p_X(x)|\psi_x\rangle\langle\psi_x|_A \otimes |\phi_x\rangle\langle\phi_x|_B \qquad (4.117)$$

for some probability distribution $p_X(x)$ and sets $\{|\psi_x\rangle_A\}$ and $\{|\phi_x\rangle_B\}$ of pure states.

The term "separable" implies that there is no quantum entanglement in the above state, i.e., there is a completely classical procedure that prepares the above state. In fact, this leads to the definition of entanglement for a general bipartite density operator:

DEFINITION 4.3.3 (Entangled State) A bipartite density operator ρ_{AB} is entangled if it is not separable.

EXERCISE 4.3.4 (Convexity) Show that the set of separable states acting on a given tensor-product Hilbert space is a convex set. That is, if $\lambda \in [0, 1]$ and ρ_{AB} and σ_{AB} are separable states, then $\lambda\rho_{AB} + (1 - \lambda)\sigma_{AB}$ is a separable state.

Separable States and the CHSH Game

One motivation for Definitions 4.3.2 and 4.3.3 was already given above: for a separable state, there is a classical procedure that can be used to prepare it. Thus, for an entangled state, there is no such procedure. That is, a non-classical (quantum) interaction between the systems is necessary to prepare an entangled state.

Another related motivation is that separable states admit an explanation in terms of a classical strategy for the CHSH game, discussed in Section 3.6.2. Recall from (3.163) that classical strategies $p_{AB|XY}(a, b|x, y)$ are of the following form:

$$p_{AB|XY}(a, b|x, y) = \int d\lambda\, p_\Lambda(\lambda)\, p_{A|\Lambda X}(a|\lambda, x)\, p_{B|\Lambda Y}(b|\lambda, y). \qquad (4.118)$$

If we allow for a continuous index λ for a separable state, then we can write such a state as follows:

$$\sigma_{AB} = \int d\lambda \, p_\Lambda(\lambda) \, |\psi_\lambda\rangle\langle\psi_\lambda|_A \otimes |\phi_\lambda\rangle\langle\phi_\lambda|_B. \tag{4.119}$$

Recall that in a general quantum strategy, there are measurements $\{\Pi_a^{(x)}\}$ and $\{\Pi_b^{(y)}\}$, giving output bits a and b based on the input bits x and y and leading to the following strategy:

$$
\begin{aligned}
& p_{AB|XY}(a,b|x,y) \\
&= \text{Tr}\{(\Pi_a^{(x)} \otimes \Pi_b^{(y)})\sigma_{AB}\} \tag{4.120} \\
&= \text{Tr}\left\{(\Pi_a^{(x)} \otimes \Pi_b^{(y)})\left(\int d\lambda \, p_\Lambda(\lambda) \, |\psi_\lambda\rangle\langle\psi_\lambda|_A \otimes |\phi_\lambda\rangle\langle\phi_\lambda|_B\right)\right\} \tag{4.121} \\
&= \int d\lambda \, p_\Lambda(\lambda) \, \text{Tr}\left\{\Pi_a^{(x)}|\psi_\lambda\rangle\langle\psi_\lambda|_A \otimes \Pi_b^{(y)}|\phi_\lambda\rangle\langle\phi_\lambda|_B\right\} \tag{4.122} \\
&= \int d\lambda \, p_\Lambda(\lambda) \, \langle\psi_\lambda|_A\Pi_a^{(x)}|\psi_\lambda\rangle_A \, \langle\phi_\lambda|_B\Pi_b^{(y)}|\phi_\lambda\rangle_B. \tag{4.123}
\end{aligned}
$$

By picking the probability distributions $p_{A|\Lambda X}(a|\lambda, x)$ and $p_{B|\Lambda Y}(b|\lambda, y)$ in (4.118) as follows:

$$p_{A|\Lambda X}(a|\lambda, x) = \langle\psi_\lambda|_A\Pi_a^{(x)}|\psi_\lambda\rangle_A, \tag{4.124}$$

$$p_{B|\Lambda Y}(b|\lambda, y) = \langle\phi_\lambda|_B\Pi_b^{(y)}|\phi_\lambda\rangle_B, \tag{4.125}$$

we see that there is a classical strategy that can simulate any quantum strategy which uses separable states in the CHSH game. Thus, the winning probability of quantum strategies involving separable states are subject to the classical bound of $3/4$ derived in Section 3.6.2. In this sense, such strategies are effectively classical.

4.3.3 Local Density Operators and Partial Trace

A First Example

Consider the entangled Bell state $|\Phi^+\rangle_{AB}$ shared on systems A and B. In the above analyses, we determined a local density operator description for both Alice and Bob. Now, we are curious if it is possible to determine such a local density operator description for Alice and Bob with respect to the state $|\Phi^+\rangle_{AB}$ or more general ones.

As a first approach to this issue, recall that the density operator description arises from its usefulness in determining the probabilities of the outcomes of a particular measurement. We say that the density operator is "the state" of the system because it is a mathematical representation that allows us to compute the probabilities resulting from a physical measurement. So, if we would like to determine a "local density operator," such a local density operator should predict the result of a local measurement.

Let us consider a local POVM $\{\Lambda^j\}_j$ that Alice can perform on her system. The global measurement operators for this local measurement are $\{\Lambda_A^j \otimes I_B\}_j$ because nothing (the identity) happens to Bob's system. The probability of obtaining outcome j when performing this measurement on the state $|\Phi^+\rangle_{AB}$ is

$$\langle\Phi^+|_{AB}\,\Lambda_A^j \otimes I_B\,|\Phi^+\rangle_{AB} = \frac{1}{2}\sum_{k,l=0}^{1}\langle kk|_{AB}\Lambda_A^j \otimes I_B\,|ll\rangle_{AB} \tag{4.126}$$

$$= \frac{1}{2}\sum_{k,l=0}^{1}\langle k|_A\Lambda_A^j|l\rangle_A\,\langle k|l\rangle_B \tag{4.127}$$

$$= \frac{1}{2}\left(\langle 0|_A\Lambda_A^j|0\rangle_A + \langle 1|_A\Lambda_A^j|1\rangle_A\right) \tag{4.128}$$

$$= \frac{1}{2}\left(\mathrm{Tr}\left\{\Lambda_A^j|0\rangle\langle 0|_A\right\} + \mathrm{Tr}\left\{\Lambda_A^j|1\rangle\langle 1|_A\right\}\right) \tag{4.129}$$

$$= \mathrm{Tr}\left\{\Lambda_A^j\frac{1}{2}\left(|0\rangle\langle 0|_A + |1\rangle\langle 1|_A\right)\right\} \tag{4.130}$$

$$= \mathrm{Tr}\left\{\Lambda_A^j\pi_A\right\}. \tag{4.131}$$

The above steps follow by applying the rules of taking the inner product with respect to tensor product operators. The last line follows by recalling the definition of the maximally mixed state π in (4.37), where π here is a qubit maximally mixed state.

The above calculation demonstrates that we can predict the result of any local "Alice" measurement using the density operator π. Therefore, it is reasonable to say that Alice's local density operator is π, and we even go as far to say that her *local state* is π. A symmetric calculation shows that Bob's local state is also π.

This result concerning their local density operators may seem strange at first. The following global state gives equivalent predictions for local measurements:

$$\pi_A \otimes \pi_B. \tag{4.132}$$

Can we then conclude that an equivalent representation of the global state is the above state? Absolutely not. The global state $|\Phi^+\rangle_{AB}$ and the above state give drastically different predictions for global measurements. Exercise 4.3.6 below asks you to determine the probabilities for measuring the global operator $Z_A \otimes Z_B$ when the global state is $|\Phi^+\rangle_{AB}$ or $\pi_A \otimes \pi_B$, and the result is that the predictions are rather different.

EXERCISE 4.3.5   Show that the projection operators corresponding to a measurement of the observable $Z_A \otimes Z_B$ are as follows:

$$\Pi_{\text{even}} \equiv \frac{1}{2}\left(I_A \otimes I_B + Z_A \otimes Z_B\right) = |00\rangle\langle 00|_{AB} + |11\rangle\langle 11|_{AB}, \tag{4.133}$$

$$\Pi_{\text{odd}} \equiv \frac{1}{2}\left(I_A \otimes I_B - Z_A \otimes Z_B\right) = |01\rangle\langle 01|_{AB} + |10\rangle\langle 10|_{AB}. \tag{4.134}$$

This measurement is a parity measurement, where the measurement operator Π_{even} coherently measures even parity and the measurement operator Π_{odd} measures odd parity.

EXERCISE 4.3.6   Show that a parity measurement (defined in the previous exercise) of the state $|\Phi^+\rangle_{AB}$ returns an even parity result with probability one, and a parity measurement of the state $\pi_A \otimes \pi_B$ returns even or odd parity with equal probability. Thus, despite the fact that these states have the same local description, their global behavior is very different. Show that the same is true for the phase parity measurement, given by

$$\Pi^X_{\text{even}} \equiv \frac{1}{2}\left(I_A \otimes I_B + X_A \otimes X_B\right), \tag{4.135}$$

$$\Pi^X_{\text{odd}} \equiv \frac{1}{2}\left(I_A \otimes I_B - X_A \otimes X_B\right). \tag{4.136}$$

EXERCISE 4.3.7   Show that the maximally correlated state $\overline{\Phi}_{AB}$, where

$$\overline{\Phi}_{AB} = \frac{1}{2}\left(|00\rangle\langle00|_{AB} + |11\rangle\langle11|_{AB}\right), \tag{4.137}$$

gives results for local measurements that are the same as those for the maximally entangled state $|\Phi^+\rangle_{AB}$. Show that the above parity measurements can distinguish these states.

Partial Trace

In general, we would like to determine a local density operator that predicts the outcomes of all local measurements. The general method for determining a local density operator is to employ the *partial trace operation*, which we motivate and define here, as a generalization of the example discussed at the beginning of Section 4.3.3.

Suppose that Alice and Bob share a bipartite state ρ_{AB} and that Alice performs a local measurement on her system, described by a POVM $\{\Lambda_A^j\}$. Then the overall POVM on the joint system is $\{\Lambda_A^j \otimes I_B\}$ because we are assuming that Bob is not doing anything to his system. According to the Born rule, the probability for Alice to receive outcome j after performing the measurement is given by the following expression:

$$p_J(j) = \text{Tr}\{(\Lambda_A^j \otimes I_B)\rho_{AB}\}. \tag{4.138}$$

In order to evaluate the trace, we can choose any orthonormal basis that we wish (see Definition 4.1.1 and subsequent statements). Taking $\{|k\rangle_A\}$ as an orthonormal basis for Alice's Hilbert space and $\{|l\rangle_B\}$ as an orthonormal basis for Bob's Hilbert space, the set $\{|k\rangle_A \otimes |l\rangle_B\}$ constitutes an orthonormal basis for the tensor product of their Hilbert spaces. So we can evaluate (4.138) as follows:

$$\text{Tr}\{(\Lambda_A^j \otimes I_B)\rho_{AB}\}$$
$$= \sum_{k,l} \left(\langle k|_A \otimes \langle l|_B\right)\left[(\Lambda_A^j \otimes I_B)\rho_{AB}\right]\left(|k\rangle_A \otimes |l\rangle_B\right) \tag{4.139}$$

$$= \sum_{k,l} \langle k|_A \left(I_A \otimes \langle l|_B \right) \left[(\Lambda_A^j \otimes I_B)\rho_{AB} \right] \left(I_A \otimes |l\rangle_B \right) |k\rangle_A \qquad (4.140)$$

$$= \sum_{k,l} \langle k|_A \Lambda_A^j \left(I_A \otimes \langle l|_B \right) \rho_{AB} \left(I_A \otimes |l\rangle_B \right) |k\rangle_A \qquad (4.141)$$

$$= \sum_{k} \langle k|_A \Lambda_A^j \left[\sum_{l} \left(I_A \otimes \langle l|_B \right) \rho_{AB} \left(I_A \otimes |l\rangle_B \right) \right] |k\rangle_A. \qquad (4.142)$$

The first equality follows from the definition of the trace in Definition 4.1.1 and using the orthonormal basis $\{|k\rangle_A \otimes |l\rangle_B\}$. The second equality follows because

$$|k\rangle_A \otimes |l\rangle_B = \left(I_A \otimes |l\rangle_B \right) |k\rangle_A. \qquad (4.143)$$

The third equality follows because

$$\left(I_A \otimes \langle l|_B \right) \left(\Lambda_A^j \otimes I_B \right) = \Lambda_A^j \left(I_A \otimes \langle l|_B \right). \qquad (4.144)$$

The fourth equality follows by bringing the sum over l inside. Using the definition of the trace in Definition 4.1.1 and the fact that $\{|k\rangle_A\}$ is an orthonormal basis for Alice's Hilbert space, we can rewrite (4.142) as

$$\mathrm{Tr} \left\{ \Lambda_A^j \left[\sum_{l} \left(I_A \otimes \langle l|_B \right) \rho_{AB} \left(I_A \otimes |l\rangle_B \right) \right] \right\}. \qquad (4.145)$$

Our final step is to define the partial trace operation as follows:

DEFINITION 4.3.4 (Partial Trace)   Let X_{AB} be a square operator acting on a tensor product Hilbert space $\mathcal{H}_A \otimes \mathcal{H}_B$, and let $\{|l\rangle_B\}$ be an orthonormal basis for $\mathcal{H}_B$. Then the partial trace over the Hilbert space $\mathcal{H}_B$ is defined as follows:

$$\mathrm{Tr}_B\{X_{AB}\} \equiv \sum_{l} \left(I_A \otimes \langle l|_B \right) X_{AB} \left(I_A \otimes |l\rangle_B \right). \qquad (4.146)$$

For simplicity, we often suppress the identity operators I_A and write this as follows:

$$\mathrm{Tr}_B\{X_{AB}\} \equiv \sum_{l} \langle l|_B X_{AB} |l\rangle_B. \qquad (4.147)$$

For the same reason that the definition of the trace is invariant under the choice of an orthonormal basis, the same is true for the partial trace operation. We can also observe from the above definition that the partial trace is a linear operation. Continuing with our development above, we can define a local operator ρ_A, using the partial trace, as follows:

$$\rho_A = \mathrm{Tr}_B\{\rho_{AB}\}. \qquad (4.148)$$

This then allows us to arrive at a rewriting of (4.145) as $\mathrm{Tr}\{\Lambda_A^j \rho_A\}$, which allows us to conclude that

$$p_J(j) = \mathrm{Tr}\{(\Lambda_A^j \otimes I_B)\rho_{AB}\} = \mathrm{Tr}\{\Lambda_A^j \rho_A\}. \qquad (4.149)$$

Thus, from the operator ρ_A, we can predict the outcomes of local measurements that Alice performs on her system. Also important here is that the global picture, in which we have a density operator ρ_{AB} and a measurement of the form $\{\Lambda_A^j \otimes I_B\}$, is consistent with the local picture, in which the measurement is written as $\{\Lambda_A^j\}$ and the operator ρ_A is used to calculate the probabilities $p_J(j)$. The operator ρ_A is itself a density operator, called the *local* or *reduced density operator*, and the next exercise asks you to verify that it is indeed a density operator.

EXERCISE 4.3.8 (Local Density Operator) Let ρ_{AB} be a density operator acting on a bipartite Hilbert space. Prove that $\rho_A = \text{Tr}_B\{\rho_{AB}\}$ is a density operator, meaning that it is positive semi-definite and has trace equal to one.

In conclusion, given a density operator ρ_{AB} describing the joint state held by Alice and Bob, we can always calculate a local density operator ρ_A, which describes the local state of Alice if Bob's system is inaccessible to her.

There is an alternate way of describing partial trace, of which it is helpful to be aware. For a simple state of the form

$$|x\rangle\langle x|_A \otimes |y\rangle\langle y|_B, \qquad (4.150)$$

with $|x\rangle_A$ and $|y\rangle_B$ each unit vectors, the partial trace has the following action:

$$\text{Tr}_B\{|x\rangle\langle x|_A \otimes |y\rangle\langle y|_B\} = |x\rangle\langle x|_A \ \text{Tr}\{|y\rangle\langle y|_B\} = |x\rangle\langle x|_A, \qquad (4.151)$$

where we "trace out" the second system to determine the local density operator for the first. If the partial trace acts on a tensor product of rank-one operators (not necessarily corresponding to a state)

$$|x_1\rangle\langle x_2|_A \otimes |y_1\rangle\langle y_2|_B, \qquad (4.152)$$

its action is as follows:

$$\text{Tr}_B\{|x_1\rangle\langle x_2|_A \otimes |y_1\rangle\langle y_2|_B\} = |x_1\rangle\langle x_2|_A \ \text{Tr}\{|y_1\rangle\langle y_2|_B\} \qquad (4.153)$$

$$= |x_1\rangle\langle x_2|_A \ \langle y_2|y_1\rangle. \qquad (4.154)$$

In fact, an alternate way of defining the partial trace is as above and to extend it by linearity.

EXERCISE 4.3.9 Show that the two notions of the partial trace operation are consistent. That is, show that

$$\text{Tr}_B\{|x_1\rangle\langle x_2|_A \otimes |y_1\rangle\langle y_2|_B\} = \sum_i \langle i|_B \left(|x_1\rangle\langle x_2|_A \otimes |y_1\rangle\langle y_2|_B\right)|i\rangle_B \qquad (4.155)$$

$$= |x_1\rangle\langle x_2|_A \ \langle y_2|y_1\rangle, \qquad (4.156)$$

for some orthonormal basis $\{|i\rangle_B\}$ on Bob's system.

It can be helpful to see the alternate notion of partial trace worked out in detail. The most general density operator on two systems A and B is some operator ρ_{AB} that is positive semi-definite with unit trace. We can obtain the local density operator ρ_A from ρ_{AB} by tracing out the B system:

$$\rho_A = \text{Tr}_B \{\rho_{AB}\}. \tag{4.157}$$

In more detail, let us expand an arbitrary density operator ρ_{AB} with an orthonormal basis $\{|i\rangle_A \otimes |j\rangle_B\}_{i,j}$ for the bipartite (two-party) state:

$$\rho_{AB} = \sum_{i,j,k,l} \lambda_{i,j,k,l} (|i\rangle_A \otimes |j\rangle_B)(\langle k|_A \otimes \langle l|_B). \tag{4.158}$$

The coefficients $\lambda_{i,j,k,l}$ are the matrix elements of ρ_{AB} with respect to the basis $\{|i\rangle_A \otimes |j\rangle_B\}_{i,j}$, and they are subject to the constraint of non-negativity and unit trace for ρ_{AB}. We can rewrite the above operator as

$$\rho_{AB} = \sum_{i,j,k,l} \lambda_{i,j,k,l} |i\rangle\langle k|_A \otimes |j\rangle\langle l|_B. \tag{4.159}$$

We can now evaluate the partial trace:

$$\rho_A = \text{Tr}_B \left\{ \sum_{i,j,k,l} \lambda_{i,j,k,l} |i\rangle\langle k|_A \otimes |j\rangle\langle l|_B \right\} \tag{4.160}$$

$$= \sum_{i,j,k,l} \lambda_{i,j,k,l} \text{Tr}_B \{|i\rangle\langle k|_A \otimes |j\rangle\langle l|_B\} \tag{4.161}$$

$$= \sum_{i,j,k,l} \lambda_{i,j,k,l} |i\rangle\langle k|_A \text{Tr} \{|j\rangle\langle l|_B\}. \tag{4.162}$$

The second equality exploits the linearity of the partial trace operation. Continuing,

$$= \sum_{i,j,k,l} \lambda_{i,j,k,l} |i\rangle\langle k|_A \langle j|l\rangle \tag{4.163}$$

$$= \sum_{i,j,k} \lambda_{i,j,k,j} |i\rangle\langle k|_A \tag{4.164}$$

$$= \sum_{i,k} \left(\sum_j \lambda_{i,j,k,j} \right) |i\rangle\langle k|_A. \tag{4.165}$$

EXERCISE 4.3.10   Verify that the partial trace of a product state gives one of the density operators in the product state:

$$\text{Tr}_B \{\rho_A \otimes \sigma_B\} = \rho_A. \tag{4.166}$$

This result is consistent with the observation near (4.106).

EXERCISE 4.3.11   Verify that the partial trace of a separable state gives the result in (4.114):

$$\text{Tr}_B \left\{ \sum_z p_Z(z) \rho_A^z \otimes \sigma_B^z \right\} = \sum_z p_Z(z) \rho_A^z. \tag{4.167}$$

EXERCISE 4.3.12   Consider the following density operator that embeds a joint probability distribution $p_{X,Y}(x,y)$ in a bipartite quantum state:

$$\rho = \sum_{x,y} p_{X,Y}(x,y) |x\rangle\langle x| \otimes |y\rangle\langle y|, \tag{4.168}$$

where the set of states $\{|x\rangle\}_x$ and $\{|y\rangle\}_y$ each form an orthonormal basis. Show that, in this case, tracing out the second system is the same as taking the marginal distribution $p_X(x) = \sum_y p_{X,Y}(x,y)$ of the joint distribution $p_{X,Y}(x,y)$. That is, we are left with a density operator of the form

$$\sum_x p_X(x) |x\rangle\langle x|. \tag{4.169}$$

Keep in mind that the partial trace is a generalization of the marginalization because it handles more exotic quantum states besides the above "classical" state.

EXERCISE 4.3.13   Show that the two partial traces in any order on a bipartite system are equivalent to a full trace:

$$\text{Tr}\{\rho_{AB}\} = \text{Tr}_A\{\text{Tr}_B\{\rho_{AB}\}\} = \text{Tr}_B\{\text{Tr}_A\{\rho_{AB}\}\}. \tag{4.170}$$

EXERCISE 4.3.14   Verify that Alice's local density operator does not change if Bob performs a unitary operator or a measurement in which he does not inform her of the measurement result.

EXERCISE 4.3.15   Prove that the partial trace operation obeys a cyclicity relation with respect to operators that act exclusively on the system over which we trace. That is, let X_{AB} be a square operator acting on the tensor-product Hilbert space $\mathcal{H}_A \otimes \mathcal{H}_B$, and let Y_B, Z_B and W_B be square operators acting on the Hilbert space $\mathcal{H}_B$. Prove that

$$\text{Tr}_B\{X_{AB} Y_B Z_B W_B\} = \text{Tr}_B\{W_B X_{AB} Y_B Z_B\} \tag{4.171}$$

$$= \text{Tr}_B\{Z_B W_B X_{AB} Y_B\} \tag{4.172}$$

$$= \text{Tr}_B\{Y_B Z_B W_B X_{AB}\}. \tag{4.173}$$

In the above, it is implicit that $Y_B = I_A \otimes Y_B$, etc.

EXERCISE 4.3.16   Recall that the purity of a density operator ρ_A is equal to $\text{Tr}\{\rho_A^2\}$. Suppose that $\rho_A = \text{Tr}_B\{\Phi_{AB}\}$, where Φ_{AB} is a maximally entangled state. Prove that the purity is equal to the inverse of the dimension of the A system.

4.3.4   Classical–Quantum Ensemble

We end our overview of composite noisy quantum systems by discussing one last type of joint ensemble: the *classical–quantum ensemble*. This ensemble is a generalization of the "ensemble of ensembles" from before.

Let us consider the following ensemble of density operators:

$$\{p_X(x), \rho_A^x\}_{x \in \mathcal{X}}. \tag{4.174}$$

The intuition here is that Alice prepares a quantum system in the state ρ_A^x with probability $p_X(x)$. She then passes this ensemble to Bob, and it is Bob's task to learn about it. He can learn about the ensemble if Alice prepares a large number of them in the same way.

There is generally a loss of the information in the random variable X once Alice has prepared this ensemble. It is easier for Bob to learn about the distribution of the random variable X if each density operator ρ_A^x is a pure state $|x\rangle\langle x|$ where the states $\{|x\rangle\}_{x \in \mathcal{X}}$ form an orthonormal basis. The resulting density operator would be

$$\rho_A = \sum_{x \in \mathcal{X}} p_X(x) |x\rangle\langle x|_A. \tag{4.175}$$

Bob could then perform a measurement with measurement operators $\{|x\rangle\langle x|\}_{x \in \mathcal{X}}$, and learn about the distribution $p_X(x)$ with a large number of measurements.

In the general case, the density operators $\{\rho_A^x\}_{x \in \mathcal{X}}$ do not correspond to pure states, much less orthonormal ones, and it is more difficult for Bob to learn about random variable X. The density operator of the ensemble is

$$\rho_A = \sum_{x \in \mathcal{X}} p_X(x) \rho_A^x, \tag{4.176}$$

and the information about the distribution of random variable X becomes "mixed in" with the "mixedness" of the density operators ρ_x. There is then no measurement that Bob can perform on ρ that allows him to directly learn about the probability distribution of random variable X.

One solution to this issue is for Alice to prepare the following classical–quantum ensemble:

$$\{p_X(x), |x\rangle\langle x|_X \otimes \rho_A^x\}_{x \in \mathcal{X}}, \tag{4.177}$$

where we label the first system as X and the second as A. She simply correlates a state $|x\rangle$ with each density operator ρ_A^x, where the states $\{|x\rangle\}_{x \in \mathcal{X}}$ form an orthonormal basis. We call this ensemble a "classical–quantum" ensemble because the first system is classical and the second system is quantum. This then leads to the notion of a *classical–quantum state* ρ_{XA} defined as follows:

DEFINITION 4.3.5 (Classical–Quantum State) The density operator corresponding to a classical–quantum ensemble $\{p_X(x), |x\rangle\langle x|_X \otimes \rho_A^x\}_{x \in \mathcal{X}}$, as discussed above, is called a classical–quantum state and takes the following form:

$$\rho_{XA} \equiv \sum_{x \in \mathcal{X}} p_X(x) |x\rangle\langle x|_X \otimes \rho_A^x. \tag{4.178}$$

It is a particular kind of separable state of systems X and A, in which the individual states of the X system are perfectly distinguishable and thus classical.

The "enlarged" ensemble in (4.177) lets Bob easily learn about random variable X while at the same time he can learn about the ensemble that Alice prepares. Bob can learn about the distribution of random variable X by performing a local measurement of the system X. He also can learn about the states ρ_x by performing a measurement on A and combining the result of this measurement with the result of the first measurement. The next exercises ask you to verify these statements.

EXERCISE 4.3.17 Show that a local measurement of system X reproduces the probability distribution $p_X(x)$. Use local measurement operators $\{|x\rangle\langle x|\}_{x \in \mathcal{X}}$ to show that $p_X(x) = \text{Tr}\{\rho_{XA}(|x\rangle\langle x|_X \otimes I_A)\}$.

EXERCISE 4.3.18 Show that performing a measurement with measurement operators $\{\Lambda_A^j\}$ on system A is the same as performing a measurement of the ensemble in (4.174). That is, show that $\text{Tr}\{\rho_A \Lambda_A^j\} = \text{Tr}\{\rho_{XA}(I_X \otimes \Lambda_A^j)\}$, where ρ_A is defined in (4.176).

EXERCISE 4.3.19 (Lack of Convexity) Prove that the set of classical–quantum states is not a convex set. That is, show that there exists a classical–quantum state ρ_{XA} and another σ_{XA} and $\lambda \in [0,1]$, such that $\lambda \rho_{XA} + (1 - \lambda)\sigma_{XA}$ is not a classical–quantum state.

4.4   Quantum Evolutions

The evolution of a quantum state is never perfect. In this section, we begin by discussing the most general approach to understanding quantum evolutions: the *axiomatic approach*. This powerful approach starts with three physically reasonable axioms that should hold for any quantum evolution and from there we deduce a set of mathematical constraints that any quantum evolution should satisfy (this is known as the *Choi–Kraus theorem*). Throughout the book, we will refer to quantum evolutions satisfying these constraints as *quantum channels*. We then show how noise resulting from the loss of information about a quantum system or from lack of access to an environment system is equivalent to what we find from the Choi–Kraus theorem. We finally discuss how every operation we have discussed so far, including preparations and measurements, can be viewed as a quantum channel, and we follow by giving several important examples of quantum channels.

4.4.1   Axiomatic Approach to Quantum Evolutions

We now discuss a powerful approach to understanding quantum physical evolutions called the *axiomatic approach*. Here we make three physically reasonable assumptions that any quantum evolution should satisfy and then prove that these axioms imply mathematical constraints on the form of any quantum physical evolution.

All of the constraints we impose are motivated by the reasonable requirement for the output of the evolution to be a quantum state (density operator) if the input to the evolution is a quantum state (density operator). An important assumption to clarify at the outset is that we are viewing a quantum physical evolution as a "black box," meaning that Alice can prepare any state that she wishes before the evolution begins, including pure states or mixed states. Critically, we even allow her to input one share of an entangled state. This is a standard assumption in quantum information theory, but one could certainly question whether this assumption is reasonable. If we do accept this criterion as physically reasonable, then the Choi–Kraus representation theorem for quantum evolutions follows as a consequence.

NOTATION 4.4.1 (Density Operators and Linear Operators)   Let $\mathcal{D}(\mathcal{H})$ denote the space of density operators acting on a Hilbert space $\mathcal{H}$, let $\mathcal{L}(\mathcal{H})$ denote the space of square linear operators acting on $\mathcal{H}$, and let $\mathcal{L}(\mathcal{H}_A, \mathcal{H}_B)$ denote the space of linear operators taking a Hilbert space $\mathcal{H}_A$ to a Hilbert space $\mathcal{H}_B$.

Throughout this development, we let $\mathcal{N}$ denote a map which takes density operators in $\mathcal{D}(\mathcal{H}_A)$ to those in $\mathcal{D}(\mathcal{H}_B)$. In general, the respective input and output Hilbert spaces $\mathcal{H}_A$ and $\mathcal{H}_B$ need not be the same. Implicitly, we have already stated a first physically reasonable requirement that we impose on $\mathcal{N}$, namely, that $\mathcal{N}(\rho_A) \in \mathcal{D}(\mathcal{H}_B)$ if $\rho_A \in \mathcal{D}(\mathcal{H}_A)$. Extending this requirement, we demand that $\mathcal{N}$ should be *convex linear* when acting on $\mathcal{D}(\mathcal{H}_A)$:

$$\mathcal{N}(\lambda \rho_A + (1 - \lambda)\sigma_A) = \lambda \mathcal{N}(\rho_A) + (1 - \lambda)\mathcal{N}(\sigma_A), \qquad (4.179)$$

where $\rho_A, \sigma_A \in \mathcal{D}(\mathcal{H}_A)$ and $\lambda \in [0, 1]$.

The physical interpretation of this convex-linearity requirement is in terms of repeated experiments. Suppose a large number of experiments are conducted in which identical quantum systems are prepared in the state ρ_A for a fraction λ of the experiments and in the state σ_A for the other fraction $1 - \lambda$ of the experiments. Suppose further that it is not revealed which states are prepared for which experiments. Before you are allowed to perform measurements on each system, the evolution $\mathcal{N}$ is applied to each of the systems. The density operator characterizing the state of each system for these experiments is then $\mathcal{N}(\lambda \rho_A + (1 - \lambda)\sigma_A)$. You are then allowed to perform a measurement on each system, which after a large number of experiments allow you to infer that the density operator is $\mathcal{N}(\lambda\rho_A + (1-\lambda)\sigma_A)$. Now, in principle, it could have been revealed which fraction of the experiments had the state ρ_A prepared and which fraction had σ_A prepared. In this case, the density operator describing the ρ_A experiments would be $\mathcal{N}(\rho_A)$ and that describing the σ_A experiments would be $\mathcal{N}(\sigma_A)$. So, it is reasonable to expect that the statistics observed in your measurement outcomes in the first scenario would be consistent with those observed in the second scenario, and this is the physical statement that the requirement (4.179) makes.

Now, it is mathematically convenient to extend the domain and range of the quantum channel to apply not only to density operators but to all linear operators. To this end, it is possible to find a unique linear extension $\widetilde{\mathcal{N}}$ of any quantum evolution $\mathcal{N}$ defined as above (originally defined exclusively by its action on density operators and satisfying convex linearity). See Appendix B for a full development of this idea. Thus, it is reasonable to associate this unique linear extension $\widetilde{\mathcal{N}}$ to the quantum physical evolution $\mathcal{N}$ mathematically, and in what follows (and for the rest of the book), we simply identify a physical evolution $\mathcal{N}$ with its unique linear extension $\widetilde{\mathcal{N}}$, and this is what we call a *quantum channel*. For these reasons, we now impose that any quantum channel $\mathcal{N}$ is linear:

CRITERION 4.4.1 (Linearity)   A quantum channel $\mathcal{N}$ is a linear map:

$$\mathcal{N}(\alpha X_A + \beta Y_A) = \alpha\mathcal{N}(X_A) + \beta\mathcal{N}(Y_A), \tag{4.180}$$

where $X_A, Y_A \in \mathcal{L}(\mathcal{H}_A)$ and $\alpha, \beta \in \mathbb{C}$.

We have already demanded that quantum physical evolutions should take density operators to density operators. Combining with linearity (in particular, scale invariance) implies that quantum channels should preserve the class of positive semi-definite operators. That is, they should be positive maps, as defined below:

DEFINITION 4.4.1 (Positive Map)   A linear map $\mathcal{M} : \mathcal{L}(\mathcal{H}_A) \rightarrow \mathcal{L}(\mathcal{H}_B)$ is positive if $\mathcal{M}(X_A)$ is positive semi-definite for all positive semi-definite $X_A \in \mathcal{L}(\mathcal{H}_A)$.

If we were dealing with classical systems, then positivity would be sufficient to describe the class of physical evolutions. However, above we argued that we are working in the "black box" picture of quantum physical evolutions, and here, in principle, we allow for Alice to prepare the input system A to be one share of an arbitrary two-party state $\rho_{RA} \in \mathcal{D}(\mathcal{H}_R \otimes \mathcal{H}_A)$, where R is a reference system of arbitrary size. So this means that the evolution consisting of the identity acting on the reference system R and the map $\mathcal{N}$ acting on system A should take ρ_{RA} to a density operator on systems R and B. Let $\mathrm{id}_R \otimes \mathcal{N}_{A \to B}$ denote this evolution, where id_R denotes the identity superoperator acting on the system R.

How do we describe the evolution $\mathrm{id}_R \otimes \mathcal{N}_{A \to B}$ mathematically? Let X_{RA} be an arbitrary operator acting on $\mathcal{H}_R \otimes \mathcal{H}_A$, and let $\{|i\rangle_R\}$ be an orthonormal basis for $\mathcal{H}_R$. Then we can expand X_{RA} with respect to this basis as follows:

$$X_{RA} = \sum_{i,j} |i\rangle\langle j|_R \otimes X_A^{i,j}, \tag{4.181}$$

and the action of $\mathrm{id}_R \otimes \mathcal{N}_{A\to B}$ on X_{RA} (for linear $\mathcal{N}$) is defined as follows:

$$(\mathrm{id}_R \otimes \mathcal{N}_{A\to B})(X_{RA}) = (\mathrm{id}_R \otimes \mathcal{N}_{A\to B})\left(\sum_{i,j} |i\rangle\langle j|_R \otimes X_A^{i,j}\right) \tag{4.182}$$

$$= \sum_{i,j} (\mathrm{id}_R \otimes \mathcal{N}_{A\to B})\left(|i\rangle\langle j|_R \otimes X_A^{i,j}\right) \tag{4.183}$$

$$= \sum_{i,j} \mathrm{id}_R \left(|i\rangle\langle j|_R\right) \otimes \mathcal{N}_{A\to B}\left(X_A^{i,j}\right) \tag{4.184}$$

$$= \sum_{i,j} |i\rangle\langle j|_R \otimes \mathcal{N}_{A\to B}\left(X_A^{i,j}\right). \tag{4.185}$$

That is, the identity superoperator id_R has no effect on the R system. The above development leads to the notion of a linear map being *completely positive* and our next criterion for any quantum physical evolution:

DEFINITION 4.4.2 (Completely Positive Map)   A linear map $\mathcal{M} : \mathcal{L}(\mathcal{H}_A) \to \mathcal{L}(\mathcal{H}_B)$ is completely positive if $\mathrm{id}_R \otimes \mathcal{M}$ is a positive map for a reference system R of arbitrary size.

CRITERION 4.4.2 (Complete Positivity)   A quantum channel is a completely positive map.

There is one last requirement that we impose for quantum physical evolutions, known as *trace preservation*. This requirement again stems from the reasonable constraint that $\mathcal{N}$ should map density operators to density operators. That is, it should be the case that $\mathrm{Tr}\{\rho_A\} = \mathrm{Tr}\{\mathcal{N}(\rho_A)\} = 1$ for all input density operators ρ_A. However, now that we have argued for linearity of every quantum physical evolution, trace preservation on density operators combined with linearity implies that quantum channels are trace preserving on the set of all operators. This is due to the fact that there are sets of density operators that form a basis for $\mathcal{L}(\mathcal{H}_A)$. Indeed, one such basis of density operators is as follows:

$$\rho_A^{x,y} = \begin{cases} |x\rangle\langle x|_A & \text{if } x = y \\ \frac{1}{2}(|x\rangle_A + |y\rangle_A)(\langle x|_A + \langle y|_A) & \text{if } x < y \\ \frac{1}{2}(|x\rangle_A + i|y\rangle_A)(\langle x|_A - i\langle y|_A) & \text{if } x > y \end{cases} . \tag{4.186}$$

Consider that for all x, y such that $x < y$, the following holds

$$|x\rangle\langle y|_A = \left(\rho_A^{x,y} - \frac{1}{2}\rho_A^{x,x} - \frac{1}{2}\rho_A^{y,y}\right) - i\left(\rho_A^{y,x} - \frac{1}{2}\rho_A^{x,x} - \frac{1}{2}\rho_A^{y,y}\right), \tag{4.187}$$

$$|y\rangle\langle x|_A = \left(\rho_A^{x,y} - \frac{1}{2}\rho_A^{x,x} - \frac{1}{2}\rho_A^{y,y}\right) + i\left(\rho_A^{y,x} - \frac{1}{2}\rho_A^{x,x} - \frac{1}{2}\rho_A^{y,y}\right), \tag{4.188}$$

so that we can represent any operator X_A as a linear combination of density operators from the set $\{\rho_A^{x,y}\}$. This leads to our final criterion for quantum channels:

CRITERION 4.4.3 (Trace Preservation)   A quantum channel is trace preserving, in the sense that $\mathrm{Tr}\{X_A\} = \mathrm{Tr}\{\mathcal{N}(X_A)\}$ for all $X_A \in \mathcal{L}(\mathcal{H}_A)$.

DEFINITION 4.4.3 (Quantum Channel)   A quantum channel is a linear, completely positive, trace preserving map, corresponding to a quantum physical evolution.

Criteria 4.4.1, 4.4.2, and 4.4.3 detailed above lead naturally to the Choi–Kraus representation theorem, which states that a map satisfies all three criteria if and only if it takes a particular form according to a Choi–Kraus decomposition:

THEOREM 4.4.1 (Choi–Kraus)   A map $\mathcal{N} : \mathcal{L}(\mathcal{H}_A) \to \mathcal{L}(\mathcal{H}_B)$ (denoted also by $\mathcal{N}_{A \to B}$) is linear, completely positive, and trace-preserving if and only if it has a Choi–Kraus decomposition as follows:

$$\mathcal{N}_{A \to B}(X_A) = \sum_{l=0}^{d-1} V_l X_A V_l^\dagger, \tag{4.189}$$

where $X_A \in \mathcal{L}(\mathcal{H}_A)$, $V_l \in \mathcal{L}(\mathcal{H}_A, \mathcal{H}_B)$ for all $l \in \{0, \ldots, d-1\}$,

$$\sum_{l=0}^{d-1} V_l^\dagger V_l = I_A, \tag{4.190}$$

and d need not be any larger than $\dim(\mathcal{H}_A)\dim(\mathcal{H}_B)$.

Before we delve into a proof, it is helpful to give a sketch. There is an easier part and a more challenging part of the proof. For the more challenging part, a helpful tool is an operator called the Choi operator:

DEFINITION 4.4.4 (Choi Operator)   Let $\mathcal{H}_R$ and $\mathcal{H}_A$ be isomorphic Hilbert spaces, and let $\{|i\rangle_R\}$ and $\{|i\rangle_A\}$ be orthonormal bases for $\mathcal{H}_R$ and $\mathcal{H}_A$, respectively. Let $\mathcal{H}_B$ be some other Hilbert space, and let $\mathcal{N} : \mathcal{L}(\mathcal{H}_A) \to \mathcal{L}(\mathcal{H}_B)$ be a linear map (written also as $\mathcal{N}_{A \to B}$). The Choi operator corresponding to $\mathcal{N}_{A \to B}$ and the bases $\{|i\rangle_R\}$ and $\{|i\rangle_A\}$ is defined as the following operator:

$$(\mathrm{id}_R \otimes \mathcal{N}_{A \to B})(|\Gamma\rangle\langle\Gamma|_{RA}) = \sum_{i,j=0}^{d_A - 1} |i\rangle\langle j|_R \otimes \mathcal{N}_{A \to B}(|i\rangle\langle j|_A), \tag{4.191}$$

where $d_A \equiv \dim(\mathcal{H}_A)$ and $|\Gamma\rangle_{RA}$ is an unnormalized maximally entangled vector, as defined in (3.233):

$$|\Gamma\rangle_{RA} \equiv \sum_{i=0}^{d_A - 1} |i\rangle_R \otimes |i\rangle_A. \tag{4.192}$$

The rank of the Choi operator is called the Choi rank.

If $\mathcal{N}_{A \to B}$ is a completely positive map, then the Choi operator is positive semi-definite. This follows as a direct consequence of Definition 4.4.2 and the fact that $|\Gamma\rangle\langle\Gamma|_{RA}$ is positive semi-definite. The converse is true as well, and Exercise 4.4.1 asks you to verify this. The converse is in some sense a much more powerful statement. Definition 4.4.2 suggests that we would have to check a seemingly infinite number of cases in order to verify whether a given linear map is completely positive, but the converse statement establishes that we need to check only one condition: whether the Choi operator is positive semi-definite.

Why else is the Choi operator a useful tool? One other important reason is that it encodes how a quantum channel acts on any possible input operator X_A, and thus specifies the channel completely. Consider that we can expand the Choi operator as a matrix of matrices (of total size $d_A d_B \times d_A d_B$) in the following way, by exploiting properties of the tensor product:

$$
\begin{bmatrix}
\mathcal{N}(|0\rangle\langle0|) & \mathcal{N}(|0\rangle\langle1|) & \cdots & \mathcal{N}(|0\rangle\langle d_A - 1|) \\
\mathcal{N}(|1\rangle\langle0|) & \mathcal{N}(|1\rangle\langle1|) & \cdots & \mathcal{N}(|1\rangle\langle d_A - 1|) \\
\vdots & \vdots & \ddots & \vdots \\
\mathcal{N}(|d_A - 1\rangle\langle0|) & \mathcal{N}(|d_A - 1\rangle\langle1|) & \cdots & \mathcal{N}(|d_A - 1\rangle\langle d_A - 1|)
\end{bmatrix}. \tag{4.193}
$$

So if we would like to figure out how the channel $\mathcal{N}_{A \to B}$ acts on an input operator X_A, we can first expand X_A with respect to the orthonormal basis $\{|i\rangle_A\}$ as $X_A = \sum_{i,j} x^{i,j} |i\rangle\langle j|_A$ and then apply the channel, using linearity:

$$
\mathcal{N}_{A \to B}(X_A) = \mathcal{N}_{A \to B}\left(\sum_{i,j} x^{i,j} |i\rangle\langle j|_A\right) = \sum_{i,j} x^{i,j} \mathcal{N}_{A \to B}(|i\rangle\langle j|_A). \tag{4.194}
$$

So the procedure is to expand X_A as above, multiple the (i,j) coefficient $x^{i,j}$ with the (i,j) entry in the Choi operator, and then sum these operators over all indices i and j.

Proof of Theorem 4.4.1 We first prove the easier "if" part of the theorem. So let us suppose that $\mathcal{N}_{A \to B}$ has the form in (4.189) and that the condition in (4.190) holds as well. Then $\mathcal{N}_{A \to B}$ is clearly a linear map. It is completely positive because $(\mathrm{id}_R \otimes \mathcal{N}_{A \to B})(X_{RA}) \geq 0$ if $X_{RA} \geq 0$ when $\mathcal{N}_{A \to B}$ has the form in (4.189), and this holds for a reference system R of arbitrary size. That is, consider from (4.185) that $\{I_R \otimes V_l\}$ is a set of Kraus operators for the extended channel $\mathrm{id}_R \otimes \mathcal{N}_{A \to B}$ and thus

$$
(\mathrm{id}_R \otimes \mathcal{N}_{A \to B})(X_{RA}) = \sum_{l=0}^{d-1} (I_R \otimes V_l) X_{RA} (I_R \otimes V_l^\dagger). \tag{4.195}
$$

We know that $(I_R \otimes V_l) X_{RA} (I_R \otimes V_l)^\dagger \geq 0$ for all l when $X_{RA} \geq 0$, and the same is true for the sum. Trace preservation follows because

$$
\mathrm{Tr}\{\mathcal{N}_{A \to B}(X_A)\} = \mathrm{Tr}\left\{\sum_{l=0}^{d-1} V_l X_A V_l^\dagger\right\} \tag{4.196}
$$

$$= \mathrm{Tr} \left\{ \sum_{l=0}^{d-1} V_l^\dagger V_l X_A \right\} \tag{4.197}$$

$$= \mathrm{Tr} \left\{ X_A \right\}, \tag{4.198}$$

where the second line follows from linearity and cyclicity of trace and the last line follows from the condition in (4.190).

We now prove the more difficult "only-if" part. Let $d_A \equiv \dim(\mathcal{H}_A)$ and $d_B \equiv \dim(\mathcal{H}_B)$. Consider that we can diagonalize the Choi operator as given in Definition 4.4.4, because it is positive semi-definite:

$$\mathcal{N}_{A \to B} \left(|\Gamma\rangle\langle\Gamma|_{RA} \right) = \sum_{l=0}^{d-1} |\phi_l\rangle\langle\phi_l|_{RB}, \tag{4.199}$$

where $d \le d_A d_B$ is the Choi rank of the map $\mathcal{N}_{A \to B}$. (This decomposition does not necessarily have to be such that the vectors $\{|\phi_l\rangle_{RB}\}$ are orthonormal, but keep in mind that there is always a choice such that $d \le d_A d_B$.) Consider by inspecting (4.191) that

$$\left(\langle i|_R \otimes I_B \right) \left(\mathcal{N}_{A \to B} \left(|\Gamma\rangle\langle\Gamma|_{RA} \right) \right) \left(|j\rangle_R \otimes I_B \right) = \mathcal{N}_{A \to B} \left(|i\rangle\langle j| \right). \tag{4.200}$$

Now, consider that for any bipartite vector $|\phi\rangle_{RB}$, we can expand it in terms of an orthonormal basis $\{|j\rangle_B\}$ and the basis $\{|i\rangle_R\}$ given above:

$$|\phi\rangle_{RB} = \sum_{i=0}^{d_A-1} \sum_{j=0}^{d_B-1} \alpha_{ij} |i\rangle_R \otimes |j\rangle_B. \tag{4.201}$$

Let $V_{A \to B}$ denote the following linear operator:

$$V_{A \to B} \equiv \sum_{i=0}^{d_A-1} \sum_{j=0}^{d_B-1} \alpha_{i,j} |j\rangle_B \langle i|_A, \tag{4.202}$$

where $\{|i\rangle_A\}$ is the orthonormal basis given above. Then we see that

$$(I_R \otimes V_{A \to B}) |\Gamma\rangle_{RA} = \sum_{i=0}^{d_A-1} \sum_{j=0}^{d_B-1} \alpha_{i,j} |j\rangle_B \langle i|_A \sum_{k=0}^{d_A-1} |k\rangle_R \otimes |k\rangle_A \tag{4.203}$$

$$= \sum_{i=0}^{d_A-1} \sum_{j=0}^{d_B-1} \sum_{k=0}^{d_A-1} \alpha_{i,j} |k\rangle_R \otimes |j\rangle_B \langle i|k\rangle_A \tag{4.204}$$

$$= \sum_{i=0}^{d_A-1} \sum_{j=0}^{d_B-1} \alpha_{ij} |i\rangle_R \otimes |j\rangle_B \tag{4.205}$$

$$= |\phi\rangle_{RB}. \tag{4.206}$$

So this means that for all bipartite vectors $|\phi\rangle_{RB}$, we can find a linear operator $V_{A \to B}$ such that $(I_R \otimes V_{A \to B}) |\Gamma\rangle_{RA} = |\phi\rangle_{RB}$. Consider also that

$$\langle i|_R |\phi\rangle_{RB} = \langle i|_R (I_R \otimes V_{A\to B}) |\Gamma\rangle_{RA} \tag{4.207}$$

$$= V_{A\to B}|i\rangle_A. \tag{4.208}$$

Applying this to our case of interest, for each l, we can write

$$|\phi_l\rangle_{RB} = I_R \otimes (V_l)_{A\to B} |\Gamma\rangle_{RA}, \tag{4.209}$$

where $(V_l)_{A\to B}$ is some linear operator of the form in (4.202). After making this observation, we realize that it is possible to write

$$\mathcal{N}_{A\to B}(|i\rangle\langle j|) = (\langle i|_R \otimes I_B)(\mathcal{N}_{A\to B}(|\Gamma\rangle\langle\Gamma|_{RA}))(|j\rangle_R \otimes I_B) \tag{4.210}$$

$$= (\langle i|_R \otimes I_B)\sum_{l=0}^{d-1}|\phi_l\rangle\langle\phi_l|_{RB}(|j\rangle_R \otimes I_B) \tag{4.211}$$

$$= \sum_{l=0}^{d-1}[(\langle i|_R \otimes I_B)|\phi_l\rangle_{RB}][\langle\phi_l|_{RB}(|j\rangle_R \otimes I_B)] \tag{4.212}$$

$$= \sum_{l=0}^{d-1}V_l|i\rangle\langle j|_A V_l^\dagger. \tag{4.213}$$

By linearity of the map $\mathcal{N}_{A\to B}$, exploiting the above result, and the development in (4.194), it follows that the action of $\mathcal{N}_{A\to B}$ on any input operator X_A can be written as follows:

$$\mathcal{N}_{A\to B}(X_A) = \sum_{l=0}^{d-1}V_l X_A V_l^\dagger. \tag{4.214}$$

To prove the condition in (4.190), let us begin by exploiting the fact that the map $\mathcal{N}_{A\to B}$ is trace preserving, so that

$$\text{Tr}\{\mathcal{N}_{A\to B}(|i\rangle\langle j|_A)\} = \text{Tr}\{|i\rangle\langle j|_A\} = \delta_{ij}. \tag{4.215}$$

for all operators $\{|i\rangle\langle j|_A\}_{i,j}$. But consider also that

$$\text{Tr}\{\mathcal{N}_{A\to B}(|i\rangle\langle j|_A)\} = \text{Tr}\left\{\sum_l V_l(|i\rangle\langle j|_A)V_l^\dagger\right\} \tag{4.216}$$

$$= \text{Tr}\left\{\sum_l V_l^\dagger V_l(|i\rangle\langle j|_A)\right\} \tag{4.217}$$

$$= \langle j|_A \sum_l V_l^\dagger V_l|i\rangle_A. \tag{4.218}$$

Thus, in order to have consistency with (4.215), we require that $\langle j|_A \sum_l V_l^\dagger V_l|i\rangle_A = \delta_{i,j}$, or equivalently, for (4.190) to hold. $\qquad\square$

REMARK 4.4.1   If the decomposition in (4.199) is a spectral decomposition, then it follows that the Kraus operators $\{V_l\}$ are orthogonal with respect to the Hilbert–Schmidt inner product:

$$\text{Tr}\{V_l^\dagger V_k\} = \text{Tr}\{V_l^\dagger V_l\}\delta_{l,k}. \tag{4.219}$$

This follows from the fact that

$$\delta_{l,k} \langle \phi_l | \phi_l \rangle = \langle \phi_l | \phi_k \rangle \tag{4.220}$$

$$= \langle \Gamma |_{RB} \left[I_R \otimes \left(V_l^\dagger V_k \right)_B \right] |\Gamma\rangle_{RB} \tag{4.221}$$

$$= \text{Tr} \left\{ V_l^\dagger V_k \right\}, \tag{4.222}$$

where in the third line we have applied the result of Exercise 4.1.3.

EXERCISE 4.4.1   Prove that a linear map $\mathcal{N}$ is completely positive if its corresponding Choi operator, as defined in Definition 4.4.4, is a positive semi-definite operator. (Hint: Use the fact that any positive semi-definite operator can be diagonalized, the fact that $\text{id}_R \otimes \mathcal{N}$ is linear, and use something similar to (4.203)–(4.206)).

4.4.2   Unique Specification of a Quantum Channel

We emphasize again that any linear map $\mathcal{N} : \mathcal{L}(\mathcal{H}_A) \to \mathcal{L}(\mathcal{H}_B)$ is specified completely by its action $\mathcal{N}_{A\to B}(|i\rangle\langle j|_A)$ on an operator of the form $|i\rangle\langle j|_A$ where $\{|i\rangle_A\}$ is some orthonormal basis. Thus, two linear maps $\mathcal{N}_{A\to B}$ and $\mathcal{M}_{A\to B}$ are equal if they have the same effect on all operators of the form $|i\rangle\langle j|$:

$$\mathcal{N}_{A\to B} = \mathcal{M}_{A\to B} \quad \Leftrightarrow \quad \forall i,j \quad \mathcal{N}_{A\to B}\left(|i\rangle\langle j|_A\right) = \mathcal{M}_{A\to B}\left(|i\rangle\langle j|_A\right). \tag{4.223}$$

As a consequence, there is an interesting way to test whether two quantum channels are equal to each other. Let us now consider a maximally entangled qudit state $|\Phi\rangle_{RA}$ where

$$|\Phi\rangle_{RA} = \frac{1}{\sqrt{d}} \sum_{i=0}^{d-1} |i\rangle_R |i\rangle_A, \tag{4.224}$$

and d is the dimension of each system R and A. The density operator Φ_{RA} corresponding to $|\Phi\rangle_{RA}$ is as follows:

$$\Phi_{RA} = \frac{1}{d} \sum_{i,j=0}^{d-1} |i\rangle\langle j|_R \otimes |i\rangle\langle j|_A. \tag{4.225}$$

Let us now send the A system of Φ_{RA} through a quantum channel $\mathcal{N}$:

$$(\text{id}_R \otimes \mathcal{N}_{A\to B})(\Phi_{RA}) = \frac{1}{d} \sum_{i,j=0}^{d-1} |i\rangle\langle j|_R \otimes \mathcal{N}_{A\to B}(|i\rangle\langle j|_A). \tag{4.226}$$

The resulting state completely characterizes the quantum channel $\mathcal{N}$ because the following map translates between the state in (4.226) and the operators $\mathcal{N}_{A\to B}\left(|i\rangle\langle j|_A\right)$ in (4.223):

$$d\langle i|_R (\text{id}_R \otimes \mathcal{N}_{A\to B})(\Phi_{RA}) |j\rangle_R = \mathcal{N}_{A\to B}\left(|i\rangle\langle j|_A\right). \tag{4.227}$$

Thus, we can completely characterize a quantum channel by determining the quantum state resulting from sending one share of a maximally entangled state through it, and the following condition is necessary and sufficient for any two quantum channels to be equal:

$$\mathcal{N} = \mathcal{M} \quad \Leftrightarrow \quad (\mathrm{id}_R \otimes \mathcal{N}_{A \to B})(\Phi_{RA}) = (\mathrm{id}_R \otimes \mathcal{M}_{A \to B})(\Phi_{RA}). \quad (4.228)$$

It is equivalent to the condition in (4.223).

4.4.3   Serial Concatenation of Quantum Channels

A quantum state may undergo not just one type of quantum evolution—it can of course undergo one quantum channel followed by another quantum channel. Let $\mathcal{N} : \mathcal{L}(\mathcal{H}_A) \to \mathcal{L}(\mathcal{H}_B)$ denote a first quantum channel and let $\mathcal{M} : \mathcal{L}(\mathcal{H}_B) \to \mathcal{L}(\mathcal{H}_C)$ denote a second quantum channel. Suppose that the Kraus operators of $\mathcal{N}$ are $\{N_k\}$ and the Kraus operators of $\mathcal{M}$ are $\{M_k\}$. It is straightforward to define the serial concatenation $\mathcal{M}_{B \to C} \circ \mathcal{N}_{A \to B}$ of these two quantum channels. Consider that the output of the first channel is

$$\mathcal{N}_{A \to B}(\rho_A) \equiv \sum_k N_k \rho_A N_k^\dagger, \quad (4.229)$$

for some input density operator $\rho_A \in \mathcal{D}(\mathcal{H}_A)$. The output of the serially concatenated channel $\mathcal{M}_{B \to C} \circ \mathcal{N}_{A \to B}$ is then

$$(\mathcal{M}_{B \to C} \circ \mathcal{N}_{A \to B})(\rho_A) = \sum_k M_k \mathcal{N}_{A \to B}(\rho) M_k^\dagger = \sum_{k,k'} M_k N_{k'} \rho_A N_{k'}^\dagger M_k^\dagger. \quad (4.230)$$

It is clear that the Kraus operators of the serially concatenated channel $\mathcal{M}_{B \to C} \circ \mathcal{N}_{A \to B}$ are $\{M_k N_{k'}\}_{k,k'}$. Serial concatenation of channels has an obvious generalization to a serial concatenation of more than two channels.

4.4.4   Parallel Concatenation of Quantum Channels

We can also use two channels in parallel. That is, suppose that we send a system A through a channel $\mathcal{N} : \mathcal{L}(\mathcal{H}_A) \to \mathcal{L}(\mathcal{H}_C)$ and a system B through a channel $\mathcal{M} : \mathcal{L}(\mathcal{H}_B) \to \mathcal{L}(\mathcal{H}_D)$. Suppose further that the Kraus operators of $\mathcal{N}_{A \to C}$ are $\{N_k\}$ and those for $\mathcal{M}_{B \to D}$ are $\{M_{k'}\}$. Then the parallel concatenation of the two channels is equal to the following serial concatenation:

$$\mathcal{N}_{A \to C} \otimes \mathcal{M}_{B \to D} = (\mathcal{N}_{A \to C} \otimes \mathrm{id}_D)(\mathrm{id}_A \otimes \mathcal{M}_{B \to D}), \quad (4.231)$$

or equivalently

$$\mathcal{N}_{A \to C} \otimes \mathcal{M}_{B \to D} = (\mathrm{id}_C \otimes \mathcal{M}_{B \to D})(\mathcal{N}_{A \to C} \otimes \mathrm{id}_B). \quad (4.232)$$

Intuitively, if Alice is conducting a local action and Bob is as well, the order in which they conduct their actions does not matter for determining the final output state. We have already discussed that a set of Kraus operators for $\mathcal{N}_{A \to C} \otimes \mathrm{id}_D$ is

$\{N_k \otimes I_D\}$ and a set for $\mathrm{id}_A \otimes \mathcal{M}_{B \to D}$ is $\{I_A \otimes M_{k'}\}$, so that it is straightforward to verify that a set of Kraus operators for $\mathcal{N}_{A \to C} \otimes \mathcal{M}_{B \to D}$ is $\{N_k \otimes M_{k'}\}$. The parallel concatenated channel $\mathcal{N}_{A \to C} \otimes \mathcal{M}_{B \to D}$ thus has the following action on an input density operator $\rho_{AB} \in \mathcal{D}(\mathcal{H}_A \otimes \mathcal{H}_B)$:

$$(\mathcal{N}_{A \to C} \otimes \mathcal{M}_{B \to D})(\rho_{AB}) = \sum_{k,k'} (N_k \otimes M_{k'})(\rho_{AB})(N_k \otimes M_{k'})^\dagger. \tag{4.233}$$

Parallel concatenation of channels also has an obvious generalization to more than two channels.

4.4.5 Unital Maps and Adjoints of Quantum Channels

Recall that the adjoint $G^\dagger$ of a linear operator G is defined as the unique linear operator satisfying the following set of equations:

$$\langle y, Gx \rangle = \langle G^\dagger y, x \rangle, \tag{4.234}$$

for all vectors x and y, and with $\langle z, w \rangle = \sum_i z_i^* w_i$ defined as the inner product between vectors z and w.

As an extension of this idea, we can define an inner product for operators:

DEFINITION 4.4.5 (Hilbert–Schmidt Inner Product)   The Hilbert–Schmidt inner product between two operators $C, D \in \mathcal{L}(\mathcal{H})$ is defined as follows:

$$\langle C, D \rangle \equiv \mathrm{Tr}\{C^\dagger D\}. \tag{4.235}$$

This then allows us to define the adjoint $\mathcal{N}^\dagger$ of a linear map $\mathcal{N}$ in a way similar to (4.234):

DEFINITION 4.4.6 (Adjoint Map)   Let $\mathcal{N} : \mathcal{L}(\mathcal{H}_A) \to \mathcal{L}(\mathcal{H}_B)$ be a linear map. The adjoint $\mathcal{N}^\dagger : \mathcal{L}(\mathcal{H}_B) \to \mathcal{L}(\mathcal{H}_A)$ of a linear map $\mathcal{N}$ is the unique linear map satisfying the following set of equations:

$$\langle Y, \mathcal{N}(X) \rangle = \langle \mathcal{N}^\dagger(Y), X \rangle, \tag{4.236}$$

for all $X \in \mathcal{L}(\mathcal{H}_A)$ and $Y \in \mathcal{L}(\mathcal{H}_B)$.

Another important class of linear maps are unital maps, defined as follows:

DEFINITION 4.4.7 (Unital Map)   A linear map $\mathcal{N} : \mathcal{L}(\mathcal{H}_A) \to \mathcal{L}(\mathcal{H}_B)$ is unital if it preserves the identity operator, in the sense that $\mathcal{N}(I_A) = I_B$.

Given the notion of an adjoint map, it is natural to inquire what is the adjoint of a quantum channel, and furthermore, what is an interpretation of it. So let us now suppose that $\mathcal{N} : \mathcal{L}(\mathcal{H}_A) \to \mathcal{L}(\mathcal{H}_B)$ is a quantum channel with a set $\{V_l\}$ of Kraus operators satisfying $\sum_l V_l^\dagger V_l = I_A$. Then we compute

$$\langle Y, \mathcal{N}(X) \rangle = \mathrm{Tr}\left\{ Y^\dagger \sum_l V_l X V_l^\dagger \right\} = \mathrm{Tr}\left\{ \sum_l V_l^\dagger Y^\dagger V_l X \right\} \tag{4.237}$$

$$= \mathrm{Tr}\left\{\left(\sum_l V_l^\dagger Y V_l\right)^\dagger X\right\} = \left\langle \sum_l V_l^\dagger Y V_l, X \right\rangle, \qquad (4.238)$$

where the second equality is from linearity and cyclicity of trace and the last is from the definition of the Hilbert–Schmidt inner product. Thus, the adjoint $\mathcal{N}^\dagger$ of any quantum channel $\mathcal{N}$ is given by

$$\mathcal{N}^\dagger(Y) = \sum_l V_l^\dagger Y V_l. \qquad (4.239)$$

The adjoint $\mathcal{N}^\dagger$ is completely positive, as one can verify by applying Exercise 4.4.1. Furthermore, the adjoint $\mathcal{N}^\dagger$ is unital because

$$\mathcal{N}^\dagger(I_B) = \sum_l V_l^\dagger I_B V_l = \sum_l V_l^\dagger V_l = I_A. \qquad (4.240)$$

We summarize these results as follows:

PROPOSITION 4.4.1 The adjoint $\mathcal{N}^\dagger : \mathcal{L}(\mathcal{H}_B) \to \mathcal{L}(\mathcal{H}_A)$ of a quantum channel $\mathcal{N} : \mathcal{L}(\mathcal{H}_A) \to \mathcal{L}(\mathcal{H}_B)$ is a completely positive, unital map.

What is an interpretation of the adjoint of a quantum channel? It provides a connection from the Schrödinger picture of quantum physics, in which the focus is on the evolution of states, to the Heisenberg picture, in which the focus is on the evolution of observables or measurement operators. To see this, let $\{\Lambda_B^j\}$ be a POVM, ρ_A be a density operator, and $\mathcal{N} : \mathcal{L}(\mathcal{H}_A) \to \mathcal{L}(\mathcal{H}_B)$ be a quantum channel. Suppose that we prepare the state ρ_A, apply the channel $\mathcal{N}$, and then perform the measurement $\{\Lambda_B^j\}$. The probability of getting outcome j from the measurement is given by the Born rule:

$$p_J(j) = \mathrm{Tr}\{\Lambda_B^j \mathcal{N}(\rho_A)\} = \mathrm{Tr}\{\mathcal{N}^\dagger(\Lambda_B^j)\rho_A\}, \qquad (4.241)$$

where the second equality follows because $\mathcal{N}^\dagger$ is the adjoint of $\mathcal{N}$. This latter expression is what corresponds to the Heisenberg picture. Here, the interpretation is that each measurement operator Λ_B^j "evolves backwards" to become $\mathcal{N}^\dagger(\Lambda_B^j)$ and then the measurement $\{\mathcal{N}^\dagger(\Lambda_B^j)\}$ is performed on the state ρ_A. We should verify that the set $\{\mathcal{N}^\dagger(\Lambda_B^j)\}$ indeed constitutes a measurement. Consider that each $\mathcal{N}^\dagger(\Lambda_B^j)$ is positive semi-definite, given that the adjoint is a completely positive map, and that

$$\sum_j \mathcal{N}^\dagger(\Lambda_B^j) = \mathcal{N}^\dagger\left(\sum_j \Lambda_B^j\right) = \mathcal{N}^\dagger(I_B) = I_A, \qquad (4.242)$$

where the equalities are following because $\mathcal{N}^\dagger$ is linear and unital. The interpretation of the measurement $\{\mathcal{N}^\dagger(\Lambda_B^j)\}$ is that it is the physical procedure corresponding to applying the channel $\mathcal{N}$ and then performing the measurement $\{\Lambda_B^j\}$, which is of course a valid measurement procedure.

4.5 Interpretations of Quantum Channels

We now detail two interpretations of quantum channels that are consistent with the Choi–Kraus theorem (Theorem 4.4.1). The first is that we can interpret the noise occurring in a quantum channel as the loss of a measurement outcome, and the second is that we can interpret noise as being due to a unitary interaction with an environment to which we do not have access.

4.5.1 Noisy Evolution as the Loss of a Measurement Outcome

We can interpret the noise resulting from a quantum channel as arising from the loss of a measurement outcome (see Figure 4.2). Suppose that the state of a system is described by a density operator ρ and that we then perform a measurement with a set $\{M_k\}$ of measurement operators for which $\sum_k M_k^\dagger M_k = I$. The probability of obtaining outcome k from the measurement is given by the Born rule: $p_K(k) = \text{Tr}\{M_k^\dagger M_k \rho\}$, and the post-measurement state is $M_k \rho M_k^\dagger / p_K(k)$, as discussed at the end of Section 4.2. Let us now suppose that we lose track of the measurement outcome, or equivalently, someone else measures the system and does not inform us of the measurement outcome. The resulting ensemble description is then

$$\left\{ p_K(k), M_k \rho M_k^\dagger / p_K(k) \right\}_k . \tag{4.243}$$

The density operator corresponding to this ensemble is then

$$\sum_k p_K(k) \frac{M_k \rho M_k^\dagger}{p_K(k)} = \sum_k M_k \rho M_k^\dagger . \tag{4.244}$$

We can thus write this evolution as a quantum channel $\mathcal{N}(\rho)$ where $\mathcal{N}(\rho) = \sum_k M_k \rho M_k^\dagger$. The measurement operators are playing the role of Kraus operators in this evolution.

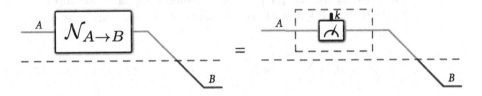

Figure 4.2 The diagram on the left depicts a quantum channel $\mathcal{N}_{A \to B}$ that takes a quantum system A to a quantum system B. This quantum channel has an interpretation in terms of the diagram on the right, in which some third party performs a measurement on the input system and does not inform the receiver of the measurement outcome.

4.5.2   Noisy Evolution from a Unitary Interaction

There is another perspective on quantum noise that is helpful to consider. It is equivalent to the perspective given in Chapter 5 when we discuss isometric evolution. Suppose that a quantum system A begins in the state ρ_A and that there is an environment system E in a pure state $|0\rangle_E$. So the initial state of the joint system AE is $\rho_A \otimes |0\rangle\langle 0|_E$. Suppose that these two systems interact according to some unitary operator U_{AE} acting on both systems A and E. If we only have access to the system A after the interaction, then we calculate the state σ_A of this system by taking the partial trace over the environment E:

$$\sigma_A = \mathrm{Tr}_E \left\{ U_{AE} \left(\rho_A \otimes |0\rangle\langle 0|_E\right) U_{AE}^\dagger \right\}. \tag{4.245}$$

This evolution is equivalent to that of a completely positive, trace-preserving map with Kraus operators $\{B_i \equiv (I_A \otimes \langle i|_E) U_{AE} (I_A \otimes |0\rangle_E)\}_i$. This follows because we can take the partial trace with respect to an orthonormal basis $\{|i\rangle_E\}$ for the environment:

$$\mathrm{Tr}_E \left\{ U_{AE} \left(\rho_A \otimes |0\rangle\langle 0|_E\right) U_{AE}^\dagger \right\}$$

$$= \sum_i (I_A \otimes \langle i|_E) U_{AE} \left(\rho_A \otimes |0\rangle\langle 0|_E\right) U_{AE}^\dagger (I_A \otimes |i\rangle_E) \tag{4.246}$$

$$= \sum_i (I_A \otimes \langle i|_E) U_{AE} (I_A \otimes |0\rangle_E) (\rho_A) (I_A \otimes \langle 0|_E) U_{AE}^\dagger (I_A \otimes |i\rangle_E) \tag{4.247}$$

$$= \sum_i B_i \rho_A B_i^\dagger. \tag{4.248}$$

The first equality follows from Definition 4.3.4 for partial trace. The second equality follows because

$$\rho_A \otimes |0\rangle\langle 0|_E = (I_A \otimes |0\rangle_E) (\rho_A) (I_A \otimes \langle 0|_E). \tag{4.249}$$

That the operators $\{B_i\}$ are a legitimate set of Kraus operators satisfying $\sum_i B_i^\dagger B_i = I_A$ follows from the unitarity of U_{AE} and the orthonormality of the basis $\{|i\rangle_E\}$:

$$\sum_i B_i^\dagger B_i = \sum_i (I_A \otimes \langle 0|_E) U_{AE}^\dagger (I_A \otimes |i\rangle_E) (I_A \otimes \langle i|_E) U_{AE} (I_A \otimes |0\rangle_E)$$

$$= (I_A \otimes \langle 0|_E) U_{AE}^\dagger \left(I_A \otimes \sum_i |i\rangle\langle i|_E\right) U_{AE} (I_A \otimes |0\rangle_E) \tag{4.250}$$

$$= (I_A \otimes \langle 0|_E) U_{AE}^\dagger U_{AE} (I_A \otimes |0\rangle_E) \tag{4.251}$$

$$= (I_A \otimes \langle 0|_E) I_A \otimes I_E (I_A \otimes |0\rangle_E) \tag{4.252}$$

$$= I_A. \tag{4.253}$$

4.6 Quantum Channels are All-Encompassing

In this section, we show how everything we have considered so far can be viewed as a quantum channel. This includes physical evolutions as we have discussed so far, but additionally (and perhaps surprisingly) density operators, discarding of systems, and quantum measurements. From this perspective, one could argue that that there really is just a single underlying postulate of quantum physics, that everything we consider in the theory is just a quantum channel of some sort.

4.6.1 Preparation and Appending Channels

The preparation of a system A in a state $\rho_A \in \mathcal{D}(\mathcal{H}_A)$ is a particular type of quantum channel, with trivial input Hilbert space $\mathbb{C}$ and output Hilbert space $\mathcal{H}_A$. Let $\rho_A = \sum_x p_X(x)|x\rangle\langle x|_A$ be a spectral decomposition of ρ_A. Then the Kraus operators of this channel are $\{N_x \equiv \sqrt{p_X(x)}|x\rangle_A\}$, and we can easily verify that these are legitimate Kraus operators by calculating

$$\sum_x N_x^\dagger N_x = \sum_x \left(\sqrt{p_X(x)}\langle x|_A\right)\left(\sqrt{p_X(x)}|x\rangle_A\right) = \sum_x p_X(x) = 1, \qquad (4.254)$$

so that the completeness relation holds, given that the number 1 is the identity for the trivial Hilbert space $\mathbb{C}$. Considering that the number 1 is also the only density operator in $\mathcal{D}(\mathbb{C})$, we can view this channel as mapping the trivial density operator 1 to a density operator $\rho_A \in \mathcal{D}(\mathcal{H}_A)$. It is thus a preparation channel.

DEFINITION 4.6.1 (Preparation Channel) A preparation channel $\mathcal{P}_A \equiv \mathcal{P}_{\mathbb{C}\to A}$ prepares a quantum system A in a given state $\rho_A \in \mathcal{D}(\mathcal{H}_A)$.

This leads to a related channel, called an appending channel:

DEFINITION 4.6.2 (Appending Channel) An appending channel is the parallel concatenation of the identity channel and a preparation channel.

Thus, an appending channel has the following action on a system B in the state σ_B:

$$(\mathcal{P}_A \otimes \text{id}_B)(\sigma_B) = \rho_A \otimes \sigma_B. \qquad (4.255)$$

The Kraus operators of such an appending channel are then $\{\sqrt{p_X(x)}|x\rangle_A \otimes I_B\}$.

4.6.2 Trace-out and Discarding Channels

In some sense, the opposite of preparation is discarding. So suppose that we completely discard the contents of a quantum system A. The channel that does so is called a *trace-out channel* Tr_A, and its action is to map any density operator $\rho_A \in \mathcal{D}(\mathcal{H}_A)$ to the trivial density operator 1. The Kraus operators of the trace-out channel are $\{N_x \equiv \langle x|_A\}$, where $\{|x\rangle_A\}$ is some orthonormal basis for the system A. These Kraus operators satisfy the completeness relation because

$$\sum_x N_x^\dagger N_x = \sum_x |x\rangle\langle x|_A = I_A. \tag{4.256}$$

This channel is in direct correspondence with the trace operation, given in Definition 4.1.1.

Now suppose that we have two systems A and B, and we would like to discard system A only. The channel that does so is a *discarding channel*, which is the parallel concatenation of the trace-out channel Tr_A and the identity channel id_B. It has the following action on a density operator $\rho_{AB} \in \mathcal{D}(\mathcal{H}_A \otimes \mathcal{H}_B)$:

$$(\mathrm{Tr}_A \otimes \mathrm{id}_B)(\rho_{AB}) = \sum_x (\langle x|_A \otimes I_B) \rho_{AB} (|x\rangle_A \otimes I_B) = \mathrm{Tr}_A\{\rho_{AB}\}, \tag{4.257}$$

where we have taken the Kraus operators of $\mathrm{Tr}_A \otimes \mathrm{id}_B$ to be $\{\langle x|_A \otimes I_B\}$. Clearly, this channel is in direct correspondence with the partial trace operation, given in Definition 4.3.4.

4.6.3 Unitary and Isometric Channels

Unitary evolution is a special kind of quantum channel in which there is a single Kraus operator $U \in \mathcal{L}(\mathcal{H})$, satisfying $UU^\dagger = U^\dagger U = I_\mathcal{H}$. Unitary channels are thus completely positive, trace-preserving, and unital. Let $\rho \in \mathcal{D}(\mathcal{H})$. Under the action of a unitary channel $\mathcal{U}$, this state evolves as

$$\mathcal{U}(\rho) = U\rho U^\dagger, \tag{4.258}$$

where $\mathcal{U}(\rho) \in \mathcal{D}(\mathcal{H})$. Our convention henceforth is to denote a unitary channel by $\mathcal{U}$ and a unitary operator by U.

There is a related, but more general kind of quantum channel called an *isometric* quantum channel. Before defining it, we need to define the notion of a linear isometry:

DEFINITION 4.6.3 (Isometry) Let $\mathcal{H}$ and $\mathcal{H}'$ be Hilbert spaces such that $\dim(\mathcal{H}) \leq \dim(\mathcal{H}')$. An isometry V is a linear map from $\mathcal{H}$ to $\mathcal{H}'$ such that $V^\dagger V = I_\mathcal{H}$. Equivalently, an isometry V is a linear, norm-preserving operator, in the sense that $\||\psi\rangle\|_2 = \|V|\psi\rangle\|_2$ for all $|\psi\rangle \in \mathcal{H}$.

An isometry is a generalization of a unitary, because it maps between spaces of different dimensions and is thus generally rectangular and need not satisfy $VV^\dagger = I_{\mathcal{H}'}$. Rather, it satisfies $VV^\dagger = \Pi_{\mathcal{H}'}$, where $\Pi_{\mathcal{H}'}$ is some projection onto $\mathcal{H}'$, because

$$(VV^\dagger)(VV^\dagger) = V(V^\dagger V)V^\dagger = VI_\mathcal{H}V^\dagger = VV^\dagger. \tag{4.259}$$

In later chapters, we repeatedly use the notion of an isometry.

We can now define an isometric channel:

DEFINITION 4.6.4 (Isometric Channel) A channel $\mathcal{V} : \mathcal{L}(\mathcal{H}) \rightarrow \mathcal{L}(\mathcal{H}')$ is an isometric channel if there exists a linear isometry $V : \mathcal{H} \rightarrow \mathcal{H}'$ such that

$$\mathcal{V}(X) = VXV^\dagger, \tag{4.260}$$

for $X \in \mathcal{L}(\mathcal{H})$.

Isometric channels are completely positive and trace-preserving. Furthermore, as in the case of unitary channels, there is just a single Kraus operator V satisfying $V^\dagger V = I_\mathcal{H}$.

Reversing Unitary and Isometric Channels

Suppose that we would like to reverse the action of a unitary channel $\mathcal{U}$. It is easy to do so: the adjoint map $\mathcal{U}^\dagger$ is a unitary channel, and by performing it after $\mathcal{U}$, we get

$$(\mathcal{U}^\dagger \circ \mathcal{U})(X) = U^\dagger U X U^\dagger U = X, \tag{4.261}$$

for $X \in \mathcal{L}(\mathcal{H})$.

If we would like to reverse the action of an isometric channel $\mathcal{V}$, we need to be a bit more careful. In this case, the adjoint map $\mathcal{V}^\dagger$ is not a channel, because it is not trace-preserving. Consider that

$$\text{Tr}\{\mathcal{V}^\dagger(Y)\} = \text{Tr}\{V^\dagger Y V\} = \text{Tr}\{VV^\dagger Y\} \tag{4.262}$$

$$= \text{Tr}\{\Pi_{\mathcal{H}'} Y\} \leq \text{Tr}\{Y\}, \tag{4.263}$$

for $Y \in \mathcal{L}(\mathcal{H}')$ and where the projection $\Pi_{\mathcal{H}'} \equiv VV^\dagger$.

However, it is possible to construct a *reversal channel* $\mathcal{R}$ for any isometric channel $\mathcal{V}$ in the following way:

$$\mathcal{R}(Y) \equiv \mathcal{V}^\dagger(Y) + \text{Tr}\{(I_{\mathcal{H}'} - \Pi_{\mathcal{H}'})Y\}\sigma, \tag{4.264}$$

where $\sigma \in \mathcal{D}(\mathcal{H})$. One can verify that the map $\mathcal{R}$ is completely positive, and it is trace-preserving because

$$\text{Tr}\{\mathcal{R}(Y)\} = \text{Tr}\{[\mathcal{V}^\dagger(Y) + \text{Tr}\{(I_{\mathcal{H}'} - \Pi_{\mathcal{H}'})Y\}\sigma]\} \tag{4.265}$$

$$= \text{Tr}\{\mathcal{V}^\dagger(Y)\} + \text{Tr}\{(I_{\mathcal{H}'} - \Pi_{\mathcal{H}'})Y\}\text{Tr}\{\sigma\} \tag{4.266}$$

$$= \text{Tr}\{\Pi_{\mathcal{H}'}Y\} + \text{Tr}\{(I_{\mathcal{H}'} - \Pi_{\mathcal{H}'})Y\} \tag{4.267}$$

$$= \text{Tr}\{Y\}. \tag{4.268}$$

Furthermore, it perfectly reverses the action of the isometric channel $\mathcal{V}$ because

$$(\mathcal{R} \circ \mathcal{V})(X) = \mathcal{V}^\dagger(\mathcal{V}(X)) + \text{Tr}\{(I_{\mathcal{H}'} - \Pi_{\mathcal{H}'})\mathcal{V}(X)\}\sigma \tag{4.269}$$

$$= V^\dagger VXV^\dagger V + \text{Tr}\{(I_{\mathcal{H}'} - VV^\dagger)VXV^\dagger\}\sigma \tag{4.270}$$

$$= X + [\text{Tr}\{VXV^\dagger\} - \text{Tr}\{VV^\dagger VXV^\dagger\}]\sigma \tag{4.271}$$

$$= X + [\text{Tr}\{V^\dagger VX\} - \text{Tr}\{V^\dagger VV^\dagger VX\}]\sigma \tag{4.272}$$

$$= X + [\text{Tr}\{X\} - \text{Tr}\{X\}]\,\sigma \qquad (4.273)$$
$$= X, \qquad (4.274)$$

for $X \in \mathcal{L}(\mathcal{H})$.

4.6.4 Classical-to-Classical Channels

It is natural to expect that classical channels are special cases of quantum channels, and indeed, this is the case. To see this, fix an input probability distribution $p_X(x)$ and a classical channel $p_{Y|X}(y|x)$. Fix an orthonormal basis $\{|x\rangle\}$ corresponding to the input letters and an orthonormal basis $\{|y\rangle\}$ corresponding to the output letters. We can then encode the input probability distribution $p_X(x)$ as a density operator ρ of the following form:

$$\rho = \sum_x p_X(x)|x\rangle\langle x|. \qquad (4.275)$$

Let $\mathcal{N}$ be a quantum channel with the following Kraus operators

$$\left\{\sqrt{p_{Y|X}(y|x)}|y\rangle\langle x|\right\}_{x,y}. \qquad (4.276)$$

(The fact that these are legitimate Kraus operators follows directly from the fact that $p_{Y|X}(y|x)$ is a conditional probability distribution.) The quantum channel then has the following action on the input ρ:

$$\mathcal{N}(\rho) = \sum_{x,y} \sqrt{p_{Y|X}(y|x)}|y\rangle\langle x| \left(\sum_{x'} p_X(x')|x'\rangle\langle x'|\right) \sqrt{p_{Y|X}(y|x)}|x\rangle\langle y| \quad (4.277)$$

$$= \sum_{x,y,x'} p_{Y|X}(y|x)p_X(x')\,|\langle x'|x\rangle|^2\,|y\rangle\langle y| \qquad (4.278)$$

$$= \sum_{x,y} p_{Y|X}(y|x)p_X(x)|y\rangle\langle y| \qquad (4.279)$$

$$= \sum_y \left(\sum_x p_{Y|X}(y|x)p_X(x)\right)|y\rangle\langle y|. \qquad (4.280)$$

Thus, the evolution is the same that a noisy classical channel $p_{Y|X}(y|x)$ would enact on a probability distribution $p_X(x)$ by taking it to

$$p_Y(y) = \sum_x p_{Y|X}(y|x)p_X(x) \qquad (4.281)$$

at the output.

Since a noiseless classical channel has $p_{Y|X}(y|x) = \delta_{x,y}$, we are led to the following definition:

Figure 4.3 This figure illustrates the internal workings of a classical–quantum channel. It first measures the input state in some basis $\{|k\rangle\}$ and outputs a quantum state σ_k conditioned on the measurement outcome.

DEFINITION 4.6.5 (Noiseless Classical Channel)   Let $\{|x\rangle\}$ be an orthonormal basis for a Hilbert space $\mathcal{H}$. A noiseless classical channel has the following action on a density operator $\rho \in \mathcal{D}(\mathcal{H})$:

$$\rho \to \sum_x |x\rangle\langle x|\rho|x\rangle\langle x|. \tag{4.282}$$

That is, it removes the off-diagonal elements of ρ when represented as a matrix with respect to the basis $\{|x\rangle\}$.

4.6.5   Classical-to-Quantum Channels

Classical-to-quantum channels, or classical–quantum channels for short, are channels which take classical systems to quantum systems. They thus go one step beyond both classical-to-classical channels and preparation channels. More generally, they make a given quantum system classical and then prepare a quantum state, as discussed in the following definition:

DEFINITION 4.6.6 (Classical–Quantum Channel)   A classical–quantum channel first measures the input state in a particular orthonormal basis and outputs a density operator conditioned on the result of the measurement. Given an orthonormal basis $\{|k\rangle_A\}$ and a set of states $\{\sigma_B^k\}$, each of which is in $\mathcal{D}(\mathcal{H}_B)$, a classical–quantum channel has the following action on an input density operator $\rho_A \in \mathcal{D}(\mathcal{H}_A)$:

$$\rho_A \to \sum_k \langle k|_A \rho_A |k\rangle_A \sigma_B^k. \tag{4.283}$$

Let us see how this comes about, using the definition above. The classical–quantum channel first measures the input state ρ_A in the basis $\{|k\rangle_A\}$. Given that the result of the measurement is k, the post measurement state is

$$\frac{|k\rangle\langle k|\rho_A|k\rangle\langle k|}{\langle k|\rho_A|k\rangle}. \tag{4.284}$$

The channel then correlates a density operator σ_B^k with the post-measurement state k:

$$\frac{|k\rangle\langle k|\rho_A|k\rangle\langle k|}{\langle k|\rho_A|k\rangle} \otimes \sigma_B^k. \tag{4.285}$$

This action leads to an ensemble:

$$\left\{ \langle k|\rho_A|k\rangle, \frac{|k\rangle\langle k|\rho_A|k\rangle\langle k|}{\langle k|\rho_A|k\rangle} \otimes \sigma_B^k \right\}, \tag{4.286}$$

and the density operator of the ensemble is

$$\sum_k \langle k|\rho_A|k\rangle \frac{|k\rangle\langle k|\rho_A|k\rangle\langle k|}{\langle k|\rho_A|k\rangle} \otimes \sigma_B^k = \sum_k |k\rangle\langle k|\rho_A|k\rangle\langle k| \otimes \sigma_B^k. \tag{4.287}$$

The channel then only outputs the system on the right (tracing out the first system) so that the resulting channel is as given in (4.283).

EXERCISE 4.6.1   What is a set of Kraus operators for a classical–quantum channel?

4.6.6   Quantum-to-Classical Channels (Measurement Channels)

Quantum-to-classical, or quantum–classical channels for short, are in some sense the opposite of classical–quantum channels. They take a quantum system to a classical one, and as such, they are in direct correspondence with measurements. So sometimes they are referred to as measurement channels. They also represent a way of generalizing classical channels different from classical–quantum channels.

DEFINITION 4.6.7 (Quantum–Classical Channels)   Let $\{|x\rangle_X\}$ be an orthonormal basis for a Hilbert space $\mathcal{H}_X$, and let $\{\Lambda_A^x\}$ be a POVM acting on the system A. A quantum–classical channel has the following action on an input density operator $\rho_A \in \mathcal{D}(\mathcal{H}_A)$:

$$\rho_A \rightarrow \sum_x \mathrm{Tr}\{\Lambda_A^x \rho_A\}|x\rangle\langle x|_X. \tag{4.288}$$

We should verify that this is indeed a quantum channel, by determining its Kraus operators. Consider that the trace operation can be written as $\mathrm{Tr}\{\cdot\} = \sum_j \langle j|_A \cdot |j\rangle_A$, where $\{|j\rangle_A\}$ is some orthonormal basis for $\mathcal{H}_A$. Then we can rewrite (4.288) as

$$\sum_x \mathrm{Tr}\{\Lambda_A^x \rho_A\}|x\rangle\langle x|_X = \sum_x \mathrm{Tr}\left\{\sqrt{\Lambda_A^x}\rho_A\sqrt{\Lambda_A^x}\right\}|x\rangle\langle x|_X \tag{4.289}$$

$$= \sum_{x,j} \langle j|_A \sqrt{\Lambda_A^x}\rho_A\sqrt{\Lambda_A^x}|j\rangle_A|x\rangle\langle x|_X \tag{4.290}$$

$$= \sum_{x,j} |x\rangle_X\langle j|_A \sqrt{\Lambda_A^x}\rho_A\sqrt{\Lambda_A^x}|j\rangle_A\langle x|_X. \tag{4.291}$$

So this development reveals that a set of Kraus operators for the channel in (4.288) is $\{N_{x,j} \equiv |x\rangle_X\langle j|_A \sqrt{\Lambda_A^x}\}$. Let us verify the completeness relation for them:

$$\sum_{x,j} N_{x,j}^\dagger N_{x,j} = \sum_{x,j} \sqrt{\Lambda_A^x}|j\rangle_A\langle x|_X|x\rangle_X\langle j|_A\sqrt{\Lambda_A^x} \tag{4.292}$$

$$= \sum_{x,j} \sqrt{\Lambda_A^x} |j\rangle_A \langle j|_A \sqrt{\Lambda_A^x} \qquad (4.293)$$

$$= \sum_x \Lambda_A^x = I_A, \qquad (4.294)$$

where the last equality follows because $\{\Lambda_A^x\}$ is a POVM.

4.6.7 Entanglement-Breaking Channels

An important class of channels is the set of entanglement-breaking channels, and we will see that both quantum–classical and classical–quantum channels are special cases of them.

DEFINITION 4.6.8 (Entanglement-Breaking Channel) An entanglement-breaking channel $\mathcal{N}^{\text{EB}} : \mathcal{L}(\mathcal{H}_A) \rightarrow \mathcal{L}(\mathcal{H}_B)$ is defined by the property that the channel $\text{id}_R \otimes \mathcal{N}^{\text{EB}}_{A \rightarrow B}$ takes any state ρ_{RA} to a separable state, where R is a reference system of arbitrary size.

Fortunately, we do not need to check this property for all possible ρ_{RA}. In fact, it suffices to check whether $(\text{id}_R \otimes \mathcal{N}^{\text{EB}}_{A \rightarrow B}) (\Phi_{RA})$ is a separable state, where Φ_{RA} is a maximally entangled state, as defined in (3.232).

EXERCISE 4.6.2 Prove that a quantum channel $\mathcal{N}_{A \rightarrow B}$ is entanglement-breaking if $(\text{id}_R \otimes \mathcal{N}_{A \rightarrow B}) (\Phi_{RA})$ is a separable state, where Φ_{RA} is a maximally entangled state. (Hint: You can use a trick similar to that which you used to solve Exercise 4.4.1. Alternatively, you can inspect the proof of Theorem 4.6.1 below.)

EXERCISE 4.6.3 Show that both a classical–quantum channel and a quantum–classical channel are entanglement-breaking—i.e., if we input the A system of a bipartite state ρ_{RA} to either of these channels, then the resulting state on systems RB is separable.

We can prove a more general structural theorem regarding entanglement-breaking channels by exploiting its definition.

THEOREM 4.6.1 A channel is entanglement-breaking if and only if it has a Kraus representation with Kraus operators that are unit rank.

Proof We first prove the "if" part of the theorem. Suppose that the Kraus operators of a quantum channel $\mathcal{N}_{A \rightarrow B}$ are

$$\{N_z \equiv |\xi_z\rangle_B \langle \varphi_z|_A\}. \qquad (4.295)$$

Without loss of generality, we can take each $|\xi_z\rangle_B$ to be a unit vector, simply by rescaling the corresponding $|\varphi_z\rangle_A$. In order for this set to be a legitimate set of Kraus operators, the following condition should hold

$$I_A = \sum_z N_z^\dagger N_z = \sum_z |\varphi_z\rangle_A \langle \xi_z|_B |\xi_z\rangle_B \langle \varphi_z|_A = \sum_z |\varphi_z\rangle \langle \varphi_z|_A. \qquad (4.296)$$

Now consider when such a channel acts on one share of a general bipartite state $\rho_{RA} \in \mathcal{D}(\mathcal{H}_A \otimes \mathcal{H}_B)$:

$$(\mathrm{id}_R \otimes \mathcal{N}_{A \to B})(\rho_{RA}) = \sum_z (I_R \otimes |\xi_z\rangle_B \langle \varphi_z|_A) \, \rho_{RA} \, (I_R \otimes |\varphi_z\rangle_A \langle \xi_z|_B) \quad (4.297)$$

$$= \sum_z \mathrm{Tr}_A \{ |\varphi_z\rangle\langle\varphi_z|_A \rho_{RA} \} \otimes |\xi_z\rangle\langle\xi_z|_B \quad (4.298)$$

$$= \sum_z p_Z(z) \rho_R^z \otimes |\xi_z\rangle\langle\xi_z|_B, \quad (4.299)$$

where in the last line we define the state $\rho_R^z \equiv \mathrm{Tr}_A \{ |\varphi_z\rangle\langle\varphi_z|_A \rho_{RA} \} / p_Z(z)$ and the probability distribution p_Z from $p_Z(z) = \mathrm{Tr} \{ |\varphi_z\rangle\langle\varphi_z|_A \rho_{RA} \}$ (the fact that p_Z is a probability distribution follows from (4.296)). Consider now that the density operator in the last line above is separable. Since ρ_{RA} is arbitrary, the "if" part of the theorem follows.

We now prove the "only-if" part. Consider that the output of an entanglement-breaking channel $\mathcal{N}^{\mathrm{EB}}$ acting on one share of a maximally entangled state Φ_{RA} is as follows:

$$\left(\mathrm{id}_R \otimes \mathcal{N}_{A \to B}^{\mathrm{EB}} \right) (\Phi_{RA}) = \sum_z p_Z(z) |\phi_z\rangle\langle\phi_z|_R \otimes |\psi_z\rangle\langle\psi_z|_B, \quad (4.300)$$

where p_Z is a probability distribution and $\{|\phi_z\rangle_R\}$ and $\{|\psi_z\rangle_B\}$ are sets of pure states. This holds because the output of a channel is a separable state (the channel "breaks" entanglement), and it is always possible to find a representation of the separable state with pure states (see Exercise 4.3.3). Now consider constructing a quantum channel $\mathcal{M}$ with the following unit-rank Kraus operators:

$$N_z \equiv \left\{ \sqrt{d \, p_Z(z)} |\psi_z\rangle_B \langle\phi_z^*|_A \right\}_z, \quad (4.301)$$

where d is the Schmidt rank of the maximally entangled state Φ_{RA} and $|\phi_z^*\rangle_A$ is the state $|\phi_z\rangle_A$ with all of its elements conjugated with respect to the bases defined from Φ_{RA}. We should first verify that these Kraus operators form a valid channel, by checking that $\sum_z N_z^\dagger N_z = I_A$:

$$\sum_z N_z^\dagger N_z = \sum_z d \, p_Z(z) |\phi_z^*\rangle_A \langle\psi_z|\psi_z\rangle_B \langle\phi_z^*|_A \quad (4.302)$$

$$= d \sum_z p_Z(z) |\phi_z^*\rangle\langle\phi_z^*|_A. \quad (4.303)$$

Consider that

$$\mathrm{Tr}_B \left\{ \left(\mathrm{id}_R \otimes \mathcal{N}_{A \to B}^{\mathrm{EB}} \right) (\Phi_{RA}) \right\} = \pi_R \quad (4.304)$$

$$= \mathrm{Tr}_B \left\{ \sum_z p_Z(z) |\phi_z\rangle\langle\phi_z|_R \otimes |\psi_z\rangle\langle\psi_z|_B \right\} \quad (4.305)$$

$$= \sum_z p_Z(z) |\phi_z\rangle\langle\phi_z|_R, \quad (4.306)$$

where π_R is the maximally mixed state. Thus, it follows that $\mathcal{M}$ is a valid quantum channel because

$$d \sum_z p_Z(z)|\phi_z\rangle\langle\phi_z|_R = d\,\pi_R = I_R = (I_A)^* \tag{4.307}$$

$$= d \sum_z p_Z(z)|\phi_z^*\rangle\langle\phi_z^*|_A = \sum_z N_z^\dagger N_z. \tag{4.308}$$

Now let us consider the action of the channel $\mathcal{M}$ on the maximally entangled state:

$$(\mathrm{id}_R \otimes \mathcal{M}_{A\to B})\,(\Phi_{RA}) \tag{4.309}$$

$$= \frac{1}{d} \sum_{z,i,j} |i\rangle\langle j|_R \otimes \sqrt{d\,p_Z(z)}|\psi_z\rangle_B\langle\phi_z^*|_A|i\rangle\langle j|_A|\phi_z^*\rangle_A\langle\psi_z|_B\sqrt{d\,p_Z(z)} \tag{4.310}$$

$$= \sum_{z,i,j} p_Z(z)\,|i\rangle\langle j|_R \otimes \langle\phi_z^*|i\rangle\,\langle j|\phi_z^*\rangle\,|\psi_z\rangle\langle\psi_z|_B \tag{4.311}$$

$$= \sum_{z,i,j} p_Z(z)\,|i\rangle\,\langle j|\phi_z^*\rangle\,\langle\phi_z^*|i\rangle\,\langle j|_R \otimes |\psi_z\rangle\langle\psi_z|_B \tag{4.312}$$

$$= \sum_z p_Z(z)\,|\phi_z\rangle\langle\phi_z|_R \otimes |\psi_z\rangle\langle\psi_z|_B. \tag{4.313}$$

The last equality follows from recognizing $\sum_{i,j} |i\rangle\langle j| \cdot |i\rangle\langle j|$ as the transpose operation (with respect to the bases from Φ_{RA}) and noting that the transpose is equivalent to conjugation for a Hermitian operator $|\phi_z\rangle\langle\phi_z|$. Finally, since the action of both $\mathcal{N}_{A\to B}^{\mathrm{EB}}$ and $\mathcal{M}_{A\to B}$ on the maximally entangled state is the same, we can conclude that the two channels are equal (see Section 4.4.2). Thus, $\mathcal{M}$ is a representation of the channel with unit-rank Kraus operators. $\square$

The proof of the above theorem leads to the following important corollary:

COROLLARY 4.6.1　An entanglement-breaking channel $\mathcal{N}_{A\to B}^{\mathrm{EB}}$ is a serial concatenation of a quantum–classical channel $\mathcal{M}_{A\to Z}$ with a classical–quantum channel $\mathcal{P}_{Z\to B}$, i.e., $\mathcal{N}_{A\to B}^{\mathrm{EB}} = \mathcal{P}_{Z\to B} \circ \mathcal{M}_{A\to Z}$. That is, every entanglement-breaking channel can be written as a measurement followed by a preparation.

Proof　Due to the above theorem, we can take the Kraus operators for an entanglement-breaking channel $\mathcal{N}_{A\to B}^{\mathrm{EB}}$ to be as in (4.295), with $\{|\xi_z\rangle_B\}$ a set of unit vectors and $\{|\varphi_z\rangle_A\}$ satisfying (4.296). Let $\{|z\rangle_Z\}$ be an orthonormal basis for a Hilbert space $\mathcal{H}_Z$. Then take the quantum–classical channel $\mathcal{M}_{A\to Z}$ to be

$$\mathcal{M}_{A\to Z}(\rho_A) = \sum_z \mathrm{Tr}\{|\varphi_z\rangle\langle\varphi_z|_A\rho_A\}|z\rangle\langle z|_Z \tag{4.314}$$

and the classical–quantum channel $\mathcal{P}_{Z\to B}$ to be

$$\mathcal{P}_{Z\to B}(\sigma_Z) = \sum_z \langle z|\sigma_Z|z\rangle_Z\,|\xi_z\rangle\langle\xi_z|_B. \tag{4.315}$$

One can then verify that $\mathcal{N}_{A\to B}^{\mathrm{EB}} = \mathcal{P}_{Z\to B} \circ \mathcal{M}_{A\to Z}$. $\square$

4.6.8 Quantum Instruments

The description of a quantum channel with Kraus operators gives the most general evolution that a quantum state can undergo. We may want to specialize this definition somewhat for another scenario. Suppose that we would like to determine the most general evolution where the input is a quantum system and the output consists of both a quantum system and a classical system. Such a scenario may arise in a case where Alice is trying to transmit both classical and quantum information, and Bob exploits a quantum instrument to decode both kinds of information. A *quantum instrument* gives such an evolution with a hybrid output.

DEFINITION 4.6.9 (Trace Non-Increasing Map) A linear map $\mathcal{M}$ is trace non-increasing if $\mathrm{Tr}\{\mathcal{M}(X)\} \leq \mathrm{Tr}\{X\}$ for all positive semi-definite $X \in \mathcal{L}(\mathcal{H})$, with $\mathcal{H}$ a Hilbert space.

DEFINITION 4.6.10 (Quantum Instrument) A quantum instrument consists of a collection $\{\mathcal{E}_j\}$ of completely positive, trace non-increasing maps such that the sum map $\sum_j \mathcal{E}_j$ is trace preserving. Let $\{|j\rangle\}$ be an orthonormal basis for a Hilbert space $\mathcal{H}_J$. The action of a quantum instrument on a density operator $\rho \in \mathcal{D}(\mathcal{H})$ is the following quantum channel, which features a quantum and classical output:

$$\rho \to \sum_j \mathcal{E}_j(\rho) \otimes |j\rangle\langle j|_J. \tag{4.316}$$

Let us see one way in which this definition comes about. Recall that we may view a noisy quantum channel as arising from the forgetting of a measurement outcome, as in (4.244). Let us now suppose that some third party performs a measurement with two outcomes j and k, but does not give us access to the measurement outcome j. Suppose that the measurement operators for this two-outcome measurement are $\{M_{j,k}\}_{j,k}$. Let us first suppose that the third party performs the measurement on a quantum system with density operator ρ and gives us both of the measurement outcomes. The post-measurement state in such a scenario is

$$\frac{M_{j,k}\rho M_{j,k}^\dagger}{p_{J,K}(j,k)}, \tag{4.317}$$

where the joint distribution of outcomes j and k is

$$p_{J,K}(j,k) = \mathrm{Tr}\{M_{j,k}^\dagger M_{j,k}\rho\}. \tag{4.318}$$

We can calculate the marginal distributions $p_J(j)$ and $p_K(k)$ according to the law of total probability:

$$p_J(j) = \sum_k p_{J,K}(j,k) = \sum_k \mathrm{Tr}\{M_{j,k}^\dagger M_{j,k}\rho\}, \tag{4.319}$$

$$p_K(k) = \sum_j p_{J,K}(j,k) = \sum_j \mathrm{Tr}\{M_{j,k}^\dagger M_{j,k}\rho\}. \tag{4.320}$$

Suppose the measuring device also places the classical outcomes in classical registers J and K, so that the post-measurement state is

$$\frac{M_{j,k}\rho M_{j,k}^{\dagger}}{p_{J,K}(j,k)} \otimes |j\rangle\langle j|_{J} \otimes |k\rangle\langle k|_{K}, \tag{4.321}$$

where the sets $\{|j\rangle\}$ and $\{|k\rangle\}$ form respective orthonormal bases. Such an operation is possible physically, and we could retrieve the classical information at some later point by performing a complete projective measurement of the registers J and K. If we would like to determine the Kraus map for the overall quantum evolution, we simply take the expectation over all measurement outcomes j and k:

$$\sum_{j,k} p_{J,K}(j,k)\left(\frac{M_{j,k}\rho M_{j,k}^{\dagger}}{p_{J,K}(j,k)}\right) \otimes |j\rangle\langle j|_{J} \otimes |k\rangle\langle k|_{K}$$

$$= \sum_{j,k} M_{j,k}\rho M_{j,k}^{\dagger} \otimes |j\rangle\langle j|_{J} \otimes |k\rangle\langle k|_{K}. \tag{4.322}$$

Let us now suppose that we do not have access to the measurement result k. This lack of access is equivalent to lacking access to classical register K. To determine the resulting state, we should trace out the classical register K. Our map then becomes

$$\sum_{j,k} M_{j,k}\rho M_{j,k}^{\dagger} \otimes |j\rangle\langle j|_{J}. \tag{4.323}$$

The above map corresponds to a quantum instrument, and is a general noisy quantum evolution that produces both a quantum output and a classical output. Figure 4.4 depicts a quantum instrument.

We can rewrite the above map more explicitly as follows:

$$\sum_{j}\left(\sum_{k} M_{j,k}\rho M_{j,k}^{\dagger}\right) \otimes |j\rangle\langle j|_{J} = \sum_{j} \mathcal{E}_{j}(\rho) \otimes |j\rangle\langle j|_{J}, \tag{4.324}$$

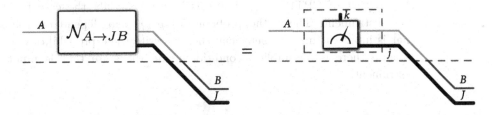

Figure 4.4 The figure on the left illustrates a quantum instrument, a general noisy evolution that produces both a quantum and classical output. The figure on the right illustrates the internal workings of a quantum instrument, showing that it results from having only partial access to a measurement outcome.

where we define

$$\mathcal{E}_j(\rho) \equiv \sum_k M_{j,k}\rho M_{j,k}^\dagger. \tag{4.325}$$

Each j-dependent map $\mathcal{E}_j(\rho)$ is a completely positive trace-non-increasing map because $\text{Tr}\{\mathcal{E}_j(\rho)\} \leq 1$. In fact, by examining the definition of $\mathcal{E}_j(\rho)$ and comparing to (4.319), it holds that

$$\text{Tr}\{\mathcal{E}_j(\rho)\} = p_J(j). \tag{4.326}$$

It is important to note that the probability $p_J(j)$ is dependent on the density operator ρ that is input to the instrument. We can determine the quantum output of the instrument by tracing over the classical register J. The resulting quantum output is then

$$\text{Tr}_J\left\{\sum_j \mathcal{E}_j(\rho) \otimes |j\rangle\langle j|_J\right\} = \sum_j \mathcal{E}_j(\rho). \tag{4.327}$$

The above "sum map" is a trace-preserving map because

$$\text{Tr}\left\{\sum_j \mathcal{E}_j(\rho)\right\} = \sum_j \text{Tr}\{\mathcal{E}_j(\rho)\} = \sum_j p_J(j) = 1, \tag{4.328}$$

where the last equality follows because the marginal probabilities $p_J(j)$ sum to one. The above points that we have mentioned are the most salient for the quantum instrument. We will exploit this type of evolution when we require a device that outputs both a classical and quantum system.

We should stress that a quantum instrument is more general than applying a mixture of CPTP maps to a quantum state. Suppose that we apply a mixture $\{\mathcal{N}_j\}$ of CPTP maps to a quantum state ρ, chosen according to a distribution $p_J(j)$. The resulting expected state is as follows:

$$\sum_j p_J(j)|j\rangle\langle j|_J \otimes \mathcal{N}_j(\rho). \tag{4.329}$$

The probabilities $p_J(j)$ here are independent of the state ρ that is input to the mixture of CPTP maps, but this is not generally the case for a quantum instrument. There, the probabilities $p_J(j)$ can depend on the state ρ that is input—it may be beneficial then to write these probabilities as $p_J(j|\rho)$ because there is an implicit conditioning on the state that is input to the instrument.

4.7   Examples of Quantum Channels

This section discusses some of the most important examples of quantum channels that we will consider in this book. Throughout, we will be considering the information-carrying ability of these various channels. They will provide some useful, "hands on" insight into quantum Shannon theory.

4.7.1 Noisy Evolution from a Random Unitary

Perhaps the simplest example of a quantum channel is the quantum bit-flip channel, which has the following action on a qubit density operator ρ:

$$pX\rho X^\dagger + (1-p)\rho. \tag{4.330}$$

The above density operator is more "mixed" than the original density operator and we will make this statement more precise in Chapter 10, when we study entropy. The evolution $\rho \to pX\rho X^\dagger + (1-p)\rho$ is clearly a legitimate quantum channel. Here the Kraus operators are $\{\sqrt{p}X, \sqrt{1-p}I\}$ and it is clear that they satisfy the completeness relation.

A generalization of the above discussion is to consider some ensemble of unitaries (a random unitary) $\{p(k), U_k\}$ that we can apply to a density operator ρ, resulting in the following output density operator:

$$\sum_k p(k)U_k\rho U_k^\dagger. \tag{4.331}$$

4.7.2 Dephasing Channels

We have already given the example of a noisy quantum bit-flip channel in Section 4.7.1. Another important example is a bit flip in the conjugate basis, or equivalently, a *phase-flip channel*. This channel acts as follows on any given density operator:

$$\rho \to (1-p)\rho + pZ\rho Z. \tag{4.332}$$

It is also known as a *dephasing channel*.

For $p = 1/2$, the action of the dephasing channel on a given quantum state is equivalent to the action of measuring the qubit in the computational basis and forgetting the result of the measurement. We make this idea more clear with an example. First, suppose that we have a qubit

$$|\psi\rangle = \alpha|0\rangle + \beta|1\rangle, \tag{4.333}$$

and we measure it in the computational basis. Then the postulates of quantum theory state that the qubit becomes $|0\rangle$ with probability $|\alpha|^2$ and it becomes $|1\rangle$ with probability $|\beta|^2$. Suppose that we forget the measurement outcome, or alternatively, that we do not have access to it. Then our best description of the qubit is with the following ensemble:

$$\left\{\left\{|\alpha|^2, |0\rangle\right\}, \left\{|\beta|^2, |1\rangle\right\}\right\}. \tag{4.334}$$

The density operator of this ensemble is

$$|\alpha|^2 |0\rangle\langle 0| + |\beta|^2 |1\rangle\langle 1|. \tag{4.335}$$

Now let us check if the dephasing channel gives the same behavior as the forgetful measurement above. We can consider the qubit as being an ensemble $\{1, |\psi\rangle\}$, i.e., the state is certain to be $|\psi\rangle$. The density operator of the ensemble is then ρ where

$$\rho = |\alpha|^2 |0\rangle\langle 0| + \alpha\beta^* |0\rangle\langle 1| + \alpha^*\beta |1\rangle\langle 0| + |\beta|^2 |1\rangle\langle 1|. \tag{4.336}$$

If we act on the density operator ρ with the dephasing channel with $p = 1/2$, then it preserves the density operator with probability $1/2$ and phase flips the qubit with probability $1/2$:

$$\frac{1}{2}\rho + \frac{1}{2}Z\rho Z$$

$$= \frac{1}{2}\left(|\alpha|^2 |0\rangle\langle 0| + \alpha\beta^* |0\rangle\langle 1| + \alpha^*\beta |1\rangle\langle 0| + |\beta|^2 |1\rangle\langle 1|\right)$$

$$+ \frac{1}{2}\left(|\alpha|^2 |0\rangle\langle 0| - \alpha\beta^* |0\rangle\langle 1| - \alpha^*\beta |1\rangle\langle 0| + |\beta|^2 |1\rangle\langle 1|\right) \tag{4.337}$$

$$= |\alpha|^2 |0\rangle\langle 0| + |\beta|^2 |1\rangle\langle 1|. \tag{4.338}$$

The dephasing channel eliminates the off-diagonal terms of the density operator when represented with respect to the computational basis. The resulting density operator description is the same as what we found for the forgetful measurement. It is also equivalent to a classical channel, as given in Definition 4.6.5.

EXERCISE 4.7.1   Verify that the action of the dephasing channel on the Bloch vector is

$$\frac{1}{2}\left(I + r_x X + r_y Y + r_z Z\right) \rightarrow$$

$$\frac{1}{2}\left(I + (1 - 2p)r_x X + (1 - 2p)r_y Y + r_z Z\right), \tag{4.339}$$

so that the channel preserves any component of the Bloch vector in the Z direction, while shrinking any component in the X or Y direction.

4.7.3   Pauli Channels

A Pauli channel is a generalization of the above dephasing channel and the bit-flip channel. It simply applies a random Pauli operator according to a probability distribution. The map for a qubit Pauli channel is

$$\rho \rightarrow \sum_{i,j=0}^{1} p(i,j) Z^i X^j \rho X^j Z^i. \tag{4.340}$$

The generalization of this channel to qudits is straightforward. We simply replace the Pauli operators with the Heisenberg–Weyl operators. The Pauli qudit channel is

$$\rho \to \sum_{i,j=0}^{d-1} p(i,j) Z(i) X(j) \rho X^\dagger(j) Z^\dagger(i). \tag{4.341}$$

These channels have been prominent in the study of quantum key distribution.

EXERCISE 4.7.2 We can write a Pauli channel as

$$\rho \to p_I \rho + p_X X \rho X + p_Y Y \rho Y + p_Z Z \rho Z. \tag{4.342}$$

Verify that the action of the Pauli channel on the Bloch vector is

$$(r_x, r_y, r_z) \to$$
$$((p_I + p_X - p_Y - p_Z) r_x, \ (p_I + p_Y - p_X - p_Z) r_y, \ (p_I + p_Z - p_X - p_Y) r_z).$$
$$\tag{4.343}$$

4.7.4 Depolarizing Channels

The depolarizing channel is a "worst-case scenario" channel. It assumes that we completely lose the input qubit with some probability, i.e., it replaces the lost qubit with the maximally mixed state. The map for the depolarizing channel is

$$\rho \to (1-p)\rho + p\pi, \tag{4.344}$$

where π is the maximally mixed state: $\pi = I/2$.

Most of the time, this channel is too pessimistic. Usually, we can learn something about the physical nature of the channel by some estimation process. We should only consider using the depolarizing channel as a model if we have little to no information about the actual physical channel.

EXERCISE 4.7.3 (Pauli Twirl) Show that randomly applying the Pauli operators I, X, Y, Z with uniform probability to any density operator gives the maximally mixed state:

$$\frac{1}{4}\rho + \frac{1}{4}X \rho X + \frac{1}{4}Y \rho Y + \frac{1}{4}Z \rho Z = \pi. \tag{4.345}$$

(Hint: Represent the density operator as $\rho = (I + r_x X + r_y Y + r_z Z)/2$ and apply the commutation rules of the Pauli operators.) This is known as the "twirling" operation.

EXERCISE 4.7.4 Show that we can rewrite the depolarizing channel as the following Pauli channel:

$$\rho \to (1 - 3p/4)\, \rho + p \left(\frac{1}{4} X \rho X + \frac{1}{4} Y \rho Y + \frac{1}{4} Z \rho Z \right). \tag{4.346}$$

EXERCISE 4.7.5 Show that the action of a depolarizing channel on the Bloch vector is

$$(r_x, r_y, r_z) \to ((1-p)r_x, \ (1-p)r_y, \ (1-p)r_z). \tag{4.347}$$

Thus, it uniformly shrinks the Bloch vector to become closer to the maximally mixed state.

The generalization of the depolarizing channel to qudits is again straightforward. It is the same as the map in (4.344), with the exception that the density operators ρ and π are qudit density operators.

EXERCISE 4.7.6 (Qudit Twirl)   Show that randomly applying the Heisenberg–Weyl operators

$$\{X(i)Z(j)\}_{i,j\in\{0,\ldots,d-1\}} \tag{4.348}$$

with uniform probability to any qudit density operator gives the maximally mixed state π:

$$\frac{1}{d^2}\sum_{i,j=0}^{d-1}X(i)Z(j)\rho Z^\dagger(j)X^\dagger(i) = \pi. \tag{4.349}$$

(Hint: You can do the full calculation, or you can decompose this channel into the composition of two completely dephasing channels where the first is a dephasing in the computational basis and the next is a dephasing in the conjugate basis).

4.7.5   Amplitude Damping Channels

The amplitude damping channel is an approximation to a noisy evolution that occurs in many physical systems ranging from optical systems to chains of spin-1/2 particles to spontaneous emission of a photon from an atom.

In order to motivate this channel, we give a physical interpretation to our computational basis states. Let us think of the $|0\rangle$ state as the ground state of a two-level atom and let us think of the state $|1\rangle$ as the excited state of the atom. Spontaneous emission is a process that tends to decay the atom from its excited state to its ground state, even if the atom is in a superposition of the ground and excited states. Let the parameter γ denote the probability of decay so that $0\leq\gamma\leq1$. One Kraus operator that captures the decaying behavior is

$$A_0 = \sqrt{\gamma}|0\rangle\langle1|. \tag{4.350}$$

The operator A_0 annihilates the ground state:

$$A_0|0\rangle\langle0|A_0^\dagger = 0, \tag{4.351}$$

and it decays the excited state to the ground state:

$$A_0|1\rangle\langle1|A_0^\dagger = \gamma|0\rangle\langle0|. \tag{4.352}$$

The Kraus operator A_0 alone does not specify a physical map because $A_0^\dagger A_0 = \gamma|1\rangle\langle1|$ (recall that the Kraus operators of any channel should satisfy the condition $\sum_k A_k^\dagger A_k = I$). We can satisfy this condition by choosing another operator A_1 such that

$$A_1^\dagger A_1 = I - A_0^\dagger A_0 = |0\rangle\langle0| + (1-\gamma)|1\rangle\langle1|. \tag{4.353}$$

The following choice of A_1 satisfies the above condition:

$$A_1 \equiv |0\rangle\langle 0| + \sqrt{1 - \gamma}|1\rangle\langle 1|. \tag{4.354}$$

Thus, the operators A_0 and A_1 are valid Kraus operators for the amplitude damping channel.

EXERCISE 4.7.7 Consider a single-qubit density operator with the following matrix representation with respect to the computational basis:

$$\rho = \begin{bmatrix} 1 - p & \eta \\ \eta^* & p \end{bmatrix}, \tag{4.355}$$

where $0 \leq p \leq 1$ and η is some complex number. Show that applying the amplitude damping channel with parameter γ to a qubit with the above density operator gives a density operator with the following matrix representation:

$$\begin{bmatrix} 1 - (1 - \gamma)\,p & \sqrt{1 - \gamma}\,\eta \\ \sqrt{1 - \gamma}\,\eta^* & (1 - \gamma)\,p \end{bmatrix}. \tag{4.356}$$

EXERCISE 4.7.8 Show that the amplitude damping channel obeys a composition rule. Consider an amplitude damping channel $\mathcal{N}_1$ with transmission parameter $(1 - \gamma_1)$ and consider another amplitude damping channel $\mathcal{N}_2$ with transmission parameter $(1 - \gamma_2)$. Show that the composition channel $\mathcal{N}_2 \circ \mathcal{N}_1$ is an amplitude damping channel with transmission parameter $(1 - \gamma_1)(1 - \gamma_2)$. (Note that the transmission parameter is equal to one minus the damping parameter.)

4.7.6 Erasure Channels

The erasure channel is another important channel in quantum Shannon theory. It admits a simple model and is amenable to relatively straightforward analysis when we later discuss its capacity. The erasure channel can serve as a simplified model of photon loss in optical systems.

We first recall the classical definition of an erasure channel. A classical erasure channel either transmits a bit with some probability $1 - \varepsilon$ or replaces it with an erasure symbol e with some probability ε. The output alphabet contains one more symbol than the input alphabet, namely, the erasure symbol e.

The generalization of the classical erasure channel to the quantum world is straightforward. It implements the following map:

$$\rho \to (1 - \varepsilon)\,\rho + \varepsilon|e\rangle\langle e|, \tag{4.357}$$

where $|e\rangle$ is some state that is not in the input Hilbert space, and thus is orthogonal to it. The output space of the erasure channel is larger than its input space by one dimension. The interpretation of the quantum erasure channel is similar to that for the classical erasure channel. It transmits a qubit with probability $1 - \varepsilon$ and "erases" it (replaces it with an orthogonal erasure state) with probability ε.

EXERCISE 4.7.9 Show that the following operators are Kraus operators for the quantum erasure channel: $\{\sqrt{1-\varepsilon}(|0\rangle_B\langle 0|_A + |1\rangle_B\langle 1|_A), \sqrt{\varepsilon}|e\rangle_B\langle 0|_A, \sqrt{\varepsilon}|e\rangle_B\langle 1|_A\}$.

At the receiving end of the channel, a simple measurement can determine whether an erasure has occurred. We perform a measurement with measurement operators $\{\Pi_{\text{in}}, |e\rangle\langle e|\}$, where Π_{in} is the projector onto the input Hilbert space. This measurement has the benefit of detecting no more information than necessary. It merely detects whether an erasure occurs, and thus preserves the quantum information at the input if an erasure does not occur.

4.7.7 Conditional Quantum Channels

We end this chapter by considering one final type of evolution. A *conditional quantum encoder* $\mathcal{E}_{MA\rightarrow B}$, or *conditional quantum channel*, is a collection $\{\mathcal{E}^m_{A\rightarrow B}\}_m$ of CPTP maps. Its inputs are a classical system M and a quantum system A and its output is a quantum system B. A conditional quantum encoder can function as an encoder of both classical and quantum information.

A classical–quantum state ρ_{MA}, where

$$\rho_{MA} \equiv \sum_m p(m)|m\rangle\langle m|_M \otimes \rho^m_A, \tag{4.358}$$

can act as an input to a conditional quantum encoder $\mathcal{E}_{MA\rightarrow B}$. The action of the conditional quantum encoder $\mathcal{E}_{MA\rightarrow B}$ on the classical–quantum state ρ_{MA} is as follows:

$$\mathcal{E}_{MA\rightarrow B}(\rho_{MA}) = \text{Tr}_M\left\{\sum_m p(m)|m\rangle\langle m|_M \otimes \mathcal{E}^m_{A\rightarrow B}(\rho^m_A)\right\}. \tag{4.359}$$

Figure 4.5 depicts the behavior of the conditional quantum encoder.

It is actually possible to write *any* quantum channel as a conditional quantum encoder when its input is a classical–quantum state. Indeed, consider any quantum channel $\mathcal{N}_{XA\rightarrow B}$ that has input systems X and A and output system B.

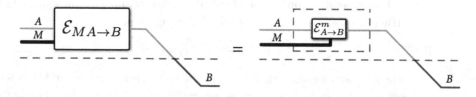

Figure 4.5 The figure on the left depicts a general operation, a conditional quantum encoder, that takes a classical system to a quantum system. The figure on the right depicts the inner workings of the conditional quantum encoder.

Suppose the Kraus decomposition of this channel is as follows:

$$\mathcal{N}_{XA \to B}(\rho) \equiv \sum_j A_j \rho A_j^\dagger. \tag{4.360}$$

Suppose now that the input to the channel is the following classical–quantum state:

$$\sigma_{XA} \equiv \sum_x p_X(x)|x\rangle\langle x|_X \otimes \rho_A^x. \tag{4.361}$$

Then the channel $\mathcal{N}_{XA \to B}$ acts as follows on the classical–quantum state σ_{XA}:

$$\mathcal{N}_{XA \to B}(\sigma_{XA}) = \sum_{j,x} A_j \left(p_X(x)|x\rangle\langle x|_X \otimes \rho_A^x\right) A_j^\dagger. \tag{4.362}$$

Consider that a classical–quantum state admits the following matrix representation by exploiting the tensor product:

$$\sum_{x \in \mathcal{X}} p_X(x)|x\rangle\langle x|_X \otimes \rho_A^x \tag{4.363}$$

$$= \begin{bmatrix} p_X(x_1)\rho_A^{x_1} & 0 & \cdots & 0 \\ 0 & p_X(x_2)\rho_A^{x_2} & & \vdots \\ \vdots & & \ddots & 0 \\ 0 & \cdots & 0 & p_X(x_{|\mathcal{X}|})\rho_A^{x_{|\mathcal{X}|}} \end{bmatrix} \tag{4.364}$$

$$= \bigoplus_{x \in \mathcal{X}} p_X(x)\rho_x. \tag{4.365}$$

It is possible to specify a matrix representation for each Kraus operator A_j in terms of $|\mathcal{X}|$ block matrices:

$$A_j = \begin{bmatrix} A_{j,1} & A_{j,2} & \cdots & A_{j,|\mathcal{X}|} \end{bmatrix}. \tag{4.366}$$

Each operator $A_j \left(p_X(x)|x\rangle\langle x|_X \otimes \rho_A^x\right) A_j^\dagger$ in the sum in (4.362) then takes the following form:

$$A_j \left(p_X(x)|x\rangle\langle x|_X \otimes \rho_A^x\right) A_j^\dagger$$

$$= \begin{bmatrix} A_{j,1} & A_{j,2} & \cdots & A_{j,|\mathcal{X}|} \end{bmatrix} \begin{bmatrix} p_X(x_1)\rho_A^{x_1} & 0 & \cdots & 0 \\ 0 & \ddots & & \vdots \\ \vdots & & \ddots & 0 \\ 0 & \cdots & 0 & p_X(x_{|\mathcal{X}|})\rho_A^{x_{|\mathcal{X}|}} \end{bmatrix} \begin{bmatrix} A_{j,1}^\dagger \\ A_{j,2}^\dagger \\ \vdots \\ A_{j,|\mathcal{X}|}^\dagger \end{bmatrix}$$

$$= \sum_{x \in |\mathcal{X}|} p_X(x) A_{j,x} \rho_A^x A_{j,x}^\dagger. \tag{4.367}$$

We can write the overall map as follows:

$$\mathcal{N}_{XA \to B}(\sigma_{XA}) = \sum_j \sum_{x \in \mathcal{X}} p_X(x) A_{j,x} \rho_A^x A_{j,x}^\dagger \tag{4.368}$$

$$= \sum_{x \in \mathcal{X}} p_X(x) \sum_j A_{j,x} \rho_A^x A_{j,x}^\dagger \tag{4.369}$$

$$= \sum_{x \in \mathcal{X}} p_X(x) \mathcal{N}_{A \to B}^x(\rho_A^x), \tag{4.370}$$

where we define each map $\mathcal{N}_{A \to B}^x$ as follows:

$$\mathcal{N}_{A \to B}^x(\rho_A^x) = \sum_j A_{j,x} \rho_A^x A_{j,x}^\dagger. \tag{4.371}$$

Thus, the action of any quantum channel on a classical–quantum state is the same as the action of the conditional quantum encoder.

EXERCISE 4.7.10   Show that the condition $\sum_j A_j^\dagger A_j = I$ implies the $|\mathcal{X}|$ conditions:

$$\forall x \in \mathcal{X} : \sum_j A_{j,x}^\dagger A_{j,x} = I. \tag{4.372}$$

4.8   Summary

We give a brief summary of the main results in this chapter. We derived all of these results from the noiseless quantum theory and an ensemble viewpoint. An alternate viewpoint is to say that the density operator is the state of the system and then give the postulates of quantum mechanics in terms of the density operator. Regardless of which viewpoint you consider as more fundamental, they are consistent with each other.

The density operator ρ for an ensemble $\{p_X(x), |\psi_x\rangle\}$ is the following expectation:

$$\rho = \sum_x p_X(x) |\psi_x\rangle\langle\psi_x|. \tag{4.373}$$

The evolution of the density operator according to a unitary operator U is

$$\rho \to U\rho U^\dagger. \tag{4.374}$$

A measurement of the state according to a measurement $\{M_j\}$ where $\sum_j M_j^\dagger M_j = I$ leads to the following post-measurement state:

$$\rho \to \frac{M_j \rho M_j^\dagger}{p_J(j)}, \tag{4.375}$$

where the probability $p_J(j)$ for obtaining outcome j is

$$p_J(j) = \text{Tr}\left\{M_j^\dagger M_j \rho\right\}. \tag{4.376}$$

The most general noisy evolution that a quantum state can undergo is according to a completely positive, trace-preserving map $\mathcal{N}(\rho)$ that we can write as follows:

$$\mathcal{N}(\rho) = \sum_j A_j \rho A_j^\dagger, \tag{4.377}$$

where $\sum_j A_j^\dagger A_j = I$. A special case of this evolution is a quantum instrument. A quantum instrument has a quantum input and a classical and quantum output. The most general way to represent a quantum instrument is as follows:

$$\rho \to \sum_j \mathcal{E}_j(\rho) \otimes |j\rangle\langle j|_J, \tag{4.378}$$

where each map $\mathcal{E}_j$ is a completely positive, trace-non-increasing map, where

$$\mathcal{E}_j(\rho) = \sum_k A_{j,k} \rho A_{j,k}^\dagger, \tag{4.379}$$

and $\sum_{j,k} A_{j,k}^\dagger A_{j,k} = I$, so that the overall map is trace-preserving.

4.9 History and Further Reading

Nielsen & Chuang (2000) have given an excellent introduction to noisy quantum channels. Werner (1989) defined what it means for a multiparty quantum state to be entangled. Horodecki et al. (2003) introduced entanglement-breaking channels and proved several properties of them (e.g., the proof of Theorem 4.6.1). Davies & Lewis (1970) introduced the quantum instrument formalism, and Ozawa (1984) developed it further. Grassl et al. (1997) introduced the quantum erasure channel and constructed some simple quantum error-correcting codes for it. A discussion of the conditional quantum channel appears in Yard (2005).

5   The Purified Quantum Theory

The final chapter of our development of the quantum theory gives perhaps the most powerful viewpoint, by providing a mathematical tool, the purification theorem, which offers a completely different way of thinking about noise in quantum systems. This theorem states that our lack of information about a set of quantum states can be thought of as arising from entanglement with another system to which we do not have access. The system to which we do not have access is known as a *purifying system*. In this purified view of the quantum theory, noisy evolution arises from the interaction of a quantum system with its environment. The interaction of a quantum system with its environment leads to correlations between the quantum system and its environment, and this interaction leads to a loss of information because we cannot access the environment. The environment is thus the purification of the output of the noisy quantum channel.

In Chapter 3, we introduced the noiseless quantum theory. The noiseless quantum theory is a useful theory to learn so that we can begin to grasp an intuition for some uniquely quantum behavior, but it is an idealized model of quantum information processing. In Chapter 4, we introduced the noisy quantum theory as a generalization of the noiseless quantum theory. The noisy quantum theory can describe the behavior of imperfect quantum systems that are subject to noise.

In this chapter, we actually show that we can view the noisy quantum theory *as a special case of the noiseless quantum theory*. This relation may seem strange at first, but the purification theorem allows us to make this connection. The quantum theory that we present in this chapter is a noiseless quantum theory, but we name it *the purified quantum theory*, in order to distinguish it from the description of the noiseless quantum theory in Chapter 3.

The purified quantum theory shows that it is possible to view noise as resulting from entanglement of a system with another system. We have actually seen a glimpse of this phenomenon in the previous chapter when we introduced the notion of the local density operator, but we did not highlight it in detail there. The example was the maximally entangled Bell state $|\Phi^+\rangle_{AB}$. This state is a pure state on the two systems A and B, but the local density operator of Alice is the maximally mixed state π_A. We saw that the local density operator is a mathematical object that allows us to make all the predictions about any local measurement or evolution. We also have seen that a density operator arises from an ensemble, but there is also the reverse interpretation, that an ensemble corresponds to a convex decomposition of any density operator. There is a sense in which we can view this local density operator as arising from an ensemble where we choose the states $|0\rangle$ and $|1\rangle$ with equal probability $1/2$. The purification idea goes as far as to say that the noisy ensemble for Alice with density operator π_A arises from the entanglement of her system with Bob's. We explore this idea in more detail in this final chapter on the quantum theory.

5.1 Purification

Suppose we are given a density operator ρ_A on a system A. Every such density operator has a *purification*, as defined below and depicted in Figure 5.1:

DEFINITION 5.1.1 (Purification) A *purification* of a density operator $\rho_A \in \mathcal{D}(\mathcal{H}_A)$ is a pure bipartite state $|\psi\rangle_{RA} \in \mathcal{H}_R \otimes \mathcal{H}_A$ on a *reference* system R and the original system A, with the property that the reduced state on system A is equal to ρ_A:

$$\rho_A = \mathrm{Tr}_R\left\{|\psi\rangle\langle\psi|_{RA}\right\}. \tag{5.1}$$

Suppose that a spectral decomposition for the density operator ρ_A is as follows:

$$\rho_A = \sum_x p_X(x)|x\rangle\langle x|_A. \tag{5.2}$$

We claim that the following state $|\psi\rangle_{RA}$ is a purification of ρ_A:

$$|\psi\rangle_{RA} \equiv \sum_x \sqrt{p_X(x)}|x\rangle_R|x\rangle_A, \tag{5.3}$$

where the set $\{|x\rangle_R\}_x$ of vectors is some set of orthonormal vectors for the reference system R. The next exercise asks you to verify this claim.

EXERCISE 5.1.1 Show that the state $|\psi\rangle_{RA}$, as defined in (5.3), is a purification of the density operator ρ_A, with a spectral decomposition as given in (5.2).

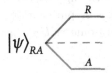

Figure 5.1 This diagram depicts a purification $|\psi\rangle_{RA}$ of a density operator ρ_A. The above diagram indicates that the reference system R is generally entangled with the system A. An interpretation of the purification theorem is that the noise inherent in a density operator ρ_A is due to entanglement with a reference system R.

EXERCISE 5.1.2 (Canonical Purification)   Let ρ_A be a density operator and let $\sqrt{\rho_A}$ be its unique positive semi-definite square root (i.e., $\rho_A = \sqrt{\rho_A}\sqrt{\rho_A}$.) We define the canonical purification of ρ_A as follows:

$$(I_R \otimes \sqrt{\rho_A}) |\Gamma\rangle_{RA}, \tag{5.4}$$

where $|\Gamma\rangle_{RA}$ is the unnormalized maximally entangled vector from (3.233). Show that (5.4) is a purification of ρ_A.

5.1.1   Interpretation of Purifications

The purification idea has an interesting physical interpretation: we can think of the noisiness inherent in a particular quantum system as being due to entanglement with some external reference system to which we do not have access. That is, we can think that the density operator ρ_A arises from the entanglement of the system A with the reference system R and from our lack of access to the system R.

Stated another way, the purification idea gives us a fundamentally different way to interpret noise. The interpretation is that any noise on a local system is due to entanglement with another system to which we do not have access. This interpretation extends to the noise from a noisy quantum channel. We can view this noise as arising from the interaction of the system that we possess with an external environment over which we have no control.

The global state $|\psi\rangle_{RA}$ is a pure state, but a reduced state ρ_A is not a pure state in general because we trace over the reference system to obtain it. A reduced state ρ_A is pure if and only if the global state $|\psi\rangle_{RA}$ is a pure product state.

5.1.2   Equivalence of Purifications

Theorem 5.1.1 below states that there is an equivalence relation between all purifications of a given density operator ρ_A. It is a consequence of the Schmidt decomposition (Theorem 3.8.1). Before stating it, recall the definition of an isometry from Definition 4.6.3.

THEOREM 5.1.1   All purifications of a density operator are related by an isometry acting on the purifying system. That is, let ρ_A be a density operator, and let $|\psi\rangle_{R_1 A}$ and $|\varphi\rangle_{R_2 A}$ be purifications of ρ_A, such that $\dim(\mathcal{H}_{R_1}) \leq \dim(\mathcal{H}_{R_2})$. Then there exists an isometry $U_{R_1 \to R_2}$ such that

$$|\varphi\rangle_{R_2 A} = (U_{R_1 \to R_2} \otimes I_A) |\psi\rangle_{R_1 A}. \tag{5.5}$$

Proof   Let us first suppose that the eigenvalues of ρ_A are distinct, so that a unique spectral decomposition of ρ_A is as follows:

$$\rho_A = \sum_x p_X(x) |x\rangle\langle x|_A. \tag{5.6}$$

Then a Schmidt decomposition of $|\varphi\rangle_{R_2 A}$ necessarily has the form

$$|\varphi\rangle_{R_2 A} = \sum_x \sqrt{p_X(x)}|\varphi_x\rangle_{R_2}|x\rangle_A, \qquad (5.7)$$

where $\{|\varphi_x\rangle_{R_2}\}$ is an orthonormal basis for the R_2 system, and similarly, the Schmidt decomposition of $|\psi\rangle_{R_1 A}$ necessarily has the form

$$|\psi\rangle_{R_1 A} = \sum_x \sqrt{p_X(x)}|\psi_x\rangle_{R_1}|x\rangle_A. \qquad (5.8)$$

(If it were not the case then we could not have $\operatorname{Tr}_{R_2}\{|\varphi\rangle\langle\varphi|_{R_2 A}\} = \operatorname{Tr}_{R_1}\{|\psi\rangle\langle\psi|_{R_1 A}\} = \rho_A$, as given in the statement of the theorem.) Given the above, we can take the isometry $U_{R_1 \to R_2}$ to be

$$U_{R_1 \to R_2} = \sum_x |\varphi_x\rangle_{R_2}\langle\psi_x|_{R_1}, \qquad (5.9)$$

which is an isometry because $U^\dagger U = I_{R_1}$. If the eigenvalues of ρ_A are not distinct, then there is more freedom in the Schmidt decompositions, but here we are free to choose them as above, and then the development is the same. $\qquad\square$

This theorem leads to a way of relating all convex decompositions of a given density operator, addressing a question raised in Section 4.1.1:

COROLLARY 5.1.1 Let two convex decompositions of a density operator ρ be as follows:

$$\rho = \sum_{x=1}^{d} p_X(x)|\psi_x\rangle\langle\psi_x| = \sum_{y=1}^{d'} p_Y(y)|\phi_y\rangle\langle\phi_y|, \qquad (5.10)$$

where $d' \leq d$. Then there exists an isometry U such that

$$\sqrt{p_X(x)}|\psi_x\rangle = \sum_y U_{x,y}\sqrt{p_Y(y)}|\phi_y\rangle. \qquad (5.11)$$

Proof Let $\{|x\rangle_R\}$ be an orthonormal basis for a purification system, with a number of states equal to $\max\{d, d'\}$. Then a purification for the first decomposition is as follows:

$$|\psi\rangle_{RA} \equiv \sum_x \sqrt{p_X(x)}|x\rangle_R \otimes |\psi_x\rangle_A, \qquad (5.12)$$

and a purification of the second decomposition is

$$|\phi\rangle_{RA} \equiv \sum_y \sqrt{p_Y(y)}|y\rangle_R \otimes |\phi_y\rangle_A. \qquad (5.13)$$

From Theorem 5.1.1, we know that there exists an isometry U_R such that $|\psi\rangle_{RA} = (U_R \otimes I_A)|\phi\rangle_{RA}$. Then consider that

$$\sqrt{p_X(x)}|\psi_x\rangle_A = \sum_{x'} \sqrt{p_X(x')}\langle x|_R|x'\rangle_R \otimes |\psi_{x'}\rangle_A = (\langle x|_R \otimes I_A)|\psi\rangle_{RA} \qquad (5.14)$$

$$= (\langle x|_R U_R \otimes I_A)|\phi\rangle_{RA} = \sum_y \sqrt{p_Y(y)}\langle x|_R U_R|y\rangle_R|\phi_y\rangle_A \qquad (5.15)$$

$$= \sum_y \sqrt{p_Y(y)} U_{x,y} |\phi_y\rangle_A, \tag{5.16}$$

where in the last step we have defined $U_{x,y} = \langle x|_R U_R |y\rangle_R$. □

EXERCISE 5.1.3   Find a purification of the following classical–quantum state:

$$\sum_x p_X(x) |x\rangle\langle x|_X \otimes \rho_A^x. \tag{5.17}$$

EXERCISE 5.1.4   Let $\{p_X(x), \rho_A^x\}$ be an ensemble of density operators. Suppose that $|\psi^x\rangle_{RA}$ is a purification of ρ_A^x. The expected density operator of the ensemble is $\rho_A \equiv \sum_x p_X(x) \rho_A^x$. Find a purification of ρ_A.

5.1.3   Extension of a Quantum State

We can also define an *extension* of a quantum state ρ_A:

DEFINITION 5.1.2 (Extension)   An extension of a density operator $\rho_A \in \mathcal{D}(\mathcal{H}_A)$ is a density operator $\Omega_{RA} \in \mathcal{D}(\mathcal{H}_R \otimes \mathcal{H}_A)$ such that $\rho_A = \mathrm{Tr}_R \{\Omega_{RA}\}$.

This notion can be useful, but keep in mind that we can always find a purification $|\psi\rangle_{R'RA}$ of the extension Ω_{RA}.

5.2   Isometric Evolution

A quantum channel admits a purification as well. We motivate this idea with a simple example.

5.2.1   Example: Isometric Extension of the Bit-Flip Channel

Consider the bit-flip channel from (4.330)—it applies the identity operator with some probability $1 - p$ and applies the bit-flip Pauli operator X with probability p. Suppose that we input a qubit system A in the state $|\psi\rangle$ to this channel. The ensemble corresponding to the state at the output has the following form:

$$\{\{1 - p, |\psi\rangle\}, \{p, X|\psi\rangle\}\}, \tag{5.18}$$

and the density operator of the resulting state is

$$(1 - p)|\psi\rangle\langle\psi| + pX|\psi\rangle\langle\psi|X. \tag{5.19}$$

The following state is a purification of the above density operator (you should quickly check that this relation holds):

$$\sqrt{1 - p}|\psi\rangle_A |0\rangle_E + \sqrt{p}X|\psi\rangle_A |1\rangle_E. \tag{5.20}$$

We label the original system as A and label the purification system as E. In this context, we can view the purification system as the environment of the channel.

There is another way for interpreting the dynamics of the above bit-flip channel. Instead of determining the ensemble for the channel and then purifying, we can say that the channel directly implements the following map from the system A to the larger joint system AE:

$$|\psi\rangle_A \to \sqrt{1-p}|\psi\rangle_A|0\rangle_E + \sqrt{p}X|\psi\rangle_A|1\rangle_E. \qquad (5.21)$$

We see that any $p \in (0,1)$, i.e., any amount of noise in the channel, can lead to entanglement of the input system with the environment E. We then obtain the noisy dynamics of the channel by discarding (tracing out) the environment system E.

EXERCISE 5.2.1   Find two input states for which the map in (5.21) does not lead to entanglement between systems A and E.

The map in (5.21) is an *isometric extension* of the bit-flip channel. Let us label it as $U_{A \to AE}$ where the notation indicates that the input system is A and the output system is AE. As discussed around Definition 4.6.3, an isometry is similar to a unitary operator but different because it maps states in one Hilbert space (for an input system) to states in a larger Hilbert space (which could be for a joint system). It generally does not admit a square matrix representation, but instead admits a rectangular matrix representation. The matrix representation of the isometric operation in (5.21) consists of the following matrix elements:

$$\begin{bmatrix} \langle 0|_A\langle 0|_E U_{A\to AE}|0\rangle_A & \langle 0|_A\langle 0|_E U_{A\to AE}|1\rangle_A \\ \langle 0|_A\langle 1|_E U_{A\to AE}|0\rangle_A & \langle 0|_A\langle 1|_E U_{A\to AE}|1\rangle_A \\ \langle 1|_A\langle 0|_E U_{A\to AE}|0\rangle_A & \langle 1|_A\langle 0|_E U_{A\to AE}|1\rangle_A \\ \langle 1|_A\langle 1|_E U_{A\to AE}|0\rangle_A & \langle 1|_A\langle 1|_E U_{A\to AE}|1\rangle_A \end{bmatrix} = \begin{bmatrix} \sqrt{1-p} & 0 \\ 0 & \sqrt{p} \\ 0 & \sqrt{1-p} \\ \sqrt{p} & 0 \end{bmatrix}. \qquad (5.22)$$

There is no reason that we have to choose the environment states as we did in (5.21). We could have chosen the environment states to be any orthonormal basis—isometric behavior only requires that the states on the environment be distinguishable. This is related to the fact that all purifications are related by an isometry acting on the purifying system (see Theorem 5.1.1).

An Isometry is Part of a Unitary on a Larger System

We can view the dynamics in (5.21) as an interaction between an initially pure environment and the qubit state $|\psi\rangle$. So, an equivalent way to implement an isometric mapping is with a two-step procedure. We first assume that the environment of the channel is in a pure state $|0\rangle_E$ before the interaction begins. The joint state of the qubit $|\psi\rangle$ and the environment is

$$|\psi\rangle_A|0\rangle_E. \qquad (5.23)$$

These two systems then interact according to a unitary operator V_{AE}. We can specify two columns of the unitary operator (we make this more clear in a bit) by means of the isometric mapping in (5.21):

$$V_{AE}|\psi\rangle_A|0\rangle_E = \sqrt{1-p}|\psi\rangle_A|0\rangle_E + \sqrt{p}X|\psi\rangle_A|1\rangle_E. \tag{5.24}$$

In order to specify the full unitary V_{AE}, we must also specify how the map behaves when the initial state of the qubit and the environment is

$$|\psi\rangle_A|1\rangle_E. \tag{5.25}$$

We choose the mapping to be as follows so that the overall interaction is unitary:

$$V_{AE}|\psi\rangle_A|1\rangle_E = \sqrt{p}|\psi\rangle_A|0\rangle_E - \sqrt{1-p}X|\psi\rangle_A|1\rangle_E. \tag{5.26}$$

EXERCISE 5.2.2   Check that the operator V_{AE}, defined by (5.24) and (5.26), is unitary by determining its action on the computational basis $\{|00\rangle_{AE}, |01\rangle_{AE}, |10\rangle_{AE}, |11\rangle_{AE}\}$ and showing that all of the outputs for each of these inputs form an orthonormal basis.

EXERCISE 5.2.3   Verify that the matrix representation of the full unitary operator V_{AE}, defined by (5.24) and (5.26), is

$$\begin{bmatrix} \sqrt{1-p} & \sqrt{p} & 0 & 0 \\ 0 & 0 & \sqrt{p} & -\sqrt{1-p} \\ 0 & 0 & \sqrt{1-p} & \sqrt{p} \\ \sqrt{p} & -\sqrt{1-p} & 0 & 0 \end{bmatrix}, \tag{5.27}$$

by considering the matrix elements $\langle i|_A \langle j|_E V|k\rangle_A |l\rangle_E$.

Complementary Channel

We may not only be interested in the receiver's output of the quantum channel. We may also be interested in determining the environment's output from the channel. This idea becomes increasingly important as we proceed in our study of quantum Shannon theory. We should consider all parties in a quantum protocol, and the purified quantum theory allows us to do so. We consider the environment as one of the parties in a quantum protocol because the environment could also be receiving some quantum information from the sender.

We can obtain the environment's output from the quantum channel simply by tracing out every system besides the environment. The map from the sender to the environment is known as a *complementary channel*. In our example of the isometric extension of the bit-flip channel in (5.21), we can check that the environment receives the following output state if the channel input is $|\psi\rangle_A$:

$$\text{Tr}_A \left\{ \left(\sqrt{1-p}|\psi\rangle_A|0\rangle_E + \sqrt{p}X|\psi\rangle_A|1\rangle_E \right) \left(\sqrt{1-p}\langle\psi|_A\langle 0|_E + \sqrt{p}\langle\psi|_A X\langle 1|_E \right) \right\}$$

$$= \text{Tr}_A \left\{ (1-p)|\psi\rangle\langle\psi|_A \otimes |0\rangle\langle 0|_E + \sqrt{p(1-p)}X|\psi\rangle\langle\psi|_A \otimes |1\rangle\langle 0|_E \right\}$$

$$+ \text{Tr}_A \left\{ \sqrt{p(1-p)}|\psi\rangle\langle\psi|_A X \otimes |0\rangle\langle 1|_E + pX|\psi\rangle\langle\psi|_A X \otimes |1\rangle\langle 1|_E \right\} \tag{5.28}$$

$$= (1-p)|0\rangle\langle 0|_E + \sqrt{p(1-p)}\langle\psi|X|\psi\rangle|1\rangle\langle 0|_E$$
$$+ \sqrt{p(1-p)}\langle\psi|X|\psi\rangle|0\rangle\langle 1|_E + p|1\rangle\langle 1|_E \qquad (5.29)$$
$$= (1-p)|0\rangle\langle 0|_E + \sqrt{p(1-p)}\langle\psi|X|\psi\rangle(|1\rangle\langle 0|_E + |0\rangle\langle 1|_E) + p|1\rangle\langle 1|_E \qquad (5.30)$$
$$= (1-p)|0\rangle\langle 0|_E + \sqrt{p(1-p)}2\operatorname{Re}\{\alpha^*\beta\}(|1\rangle\langle 0|_E + |0\rangle\langle 1|_E) + p|1\rangle\langle 1|_E, \qquad (5.31)$$

where in the last line we assume that the qubit $|\psi\rangle \equiv \alpha|0\rangle + \beta|1\rangle$.

It is helpful to examine several cases of the above example. Consider the case in which the noise parameter $p = 0$ or $p = 1$. In this case, the environment receives one of the respective states $|0\rangle$ or $|1\rangle$. Therefore, in these cases, the environment does not receive any of the quantum information about the state $|\psi\rangle$ transmitted down the channel—it does not learn anything about the probability amplitudes α or β. This viewpoint is a completely different way to see that the channel is truly noiseless in these cases. A channel is noiseless if the environment of the channel does not learn anything about the states that we transmit through it, i.e., if the channel does not leak quantum information to the environment. Now let us consider the case in which $p \in (0, 1)$. As p approaches $1/2$ from either above or below, the amplitude $\sqrt{p(1-p)}$ of the off-diagonal terms is a monotonic function that reaches its peak at $1/2$. Thus, at the peak $1/2$, the off-diagonal terms are the strongest, implying that the environment is generally "stealing" much of the coherence from the original quantum state $|\psi\rangle$.

EXERCISE 5.2.4 Show that the receiver's output density operator for a bit-flip channel with $p = 1/2$ is the same as what the environment obtains.

5.2.2 Isometric Extension of a Quantum Channel

We now give a general definition for an isometric extension of a quantum channel:

DEFINITION 5.2.1 (Isometric Extension) Let $\mathcal{H}_A$ and $\mathcal{H}_B$ be Hilbert spaces, and let $\mathcal{N} : \mathcal{L}(\mathcal{H}_A) \to \mathcal{L}(\mathcal{H}_B)$ be a quantum channel. Let $\mathcal{H}_E$ be a Hilbert space with dimension no smaller than the Choi rank of the channel $\mathcal{N}$. An isometric extension or Stinespring dilation $U : \mathcal{H}_A \to \mathcal{H}_B \otimes \mathcal{H}_E$ of the channel $\mathcal{N}$ is a linear isometry such that

$$\operatorname{Tr}_E\{UX_A U^\dagger\} = \mathcal{N}_{A\to B}(X_A), \qquad (5.32)$$

for $X_A \in \mathcal{L}(\mathcal{H}_A)$. The fact that U is an isometry is equivalent to the following conditions:

$$U^\dagger U = I_A, \qquad UU^\dagger = \Pi_{BE}, \qquad (5.33)$$

where Π_{BE} is a projection of the tensor-product Hilbert space $\mathcal{H}_B \otimes \mathcal{H}_E$.

NOTATION 5.2.1 We often write a channel $\mathcal{N} : \mathcal{L}(\mathcal{H}_A) \to \mathcal{L}(\mathcal{H}_B)$ as $\mathcal{N}_{A\to B}$ in order to indicate the input and output systems explicitly. Similarly, we often write an isometric extension $U : \mathcal{H}_A \to \mathcal{H}_B \otimes \mathcal{H}_E$ of $\mathcal{N}$ as $U^{\mathcal{N}}_{A\to BE}$ in order to indicate its association with $\mathcal{N}$ explicitly, as well the fact that it accepts an input system A and has output systems B and E. The system E is often referred to as an "environment" system. Finally, there is a quantum channel $\mathcal{U}^{\mathcal{N}}_{A \to BE}$ associated to an isometric extension $U^{\mathcal{N}}_{A \to BE}$, which is defined by

$$\mathcal{U}^{\mathcal{N}}_{A \to BE}(X_A) = U X_A U^\dagger, \tag{5.34}$$

for $X_A \in \mathcal{L}(\mathcal{H}_A)$. Note that $\mathcal{U}^{\mathcal{N}}_{A \to BE}$ is a quantum channel with a single Kraus operator U given that $U^\dagger U = I_A$.

We can think of an isometric extension of a quantum channel as a purification of that channel: the environment system E is analogous to the purification system from Section 5.1 because we trace over it to get back the original channel. An isometric extension *extends* the original channel because it produces the evolution of the quantum channel $\mathcal{N}_{A \to B}$ if we trace out the environment system E. It also behaves as an *isometry*—it is analogous to a rectangular matrix that behaves somewhat like a unitary operator. The matrix representation of an isometry is a rectangular matrix formed from selecting only a few of the columns from a unitary matrix. The property $U^\dagger U = I_A$ indicates that the isometry behaves analogously to a unitary operator, because we can determine an inverse operation simply by taking its conjugate transpose. The property $U U^\dagger = \Pi_{BE}$ distinguishes an isometric operation from a unitary one. It states that the isometry takes states in the input system A to a particular subspace of the joint system BE. The projector Π_{BE} projects onto the subspace where the isometry takes input quantum states. Figure 5.2 depicts a quantum circuit for an isometric extension.

Isometric Extension from Kraus Operators

It is possible to determine an isometric extension of a quantum channel directly from a set of Kraus operators. Consider a quantum channel $\mathcal{N}_{A \to B}$ with the following Kraus representation:

$$\mathcal{N}_{A \to B}(\rho_A) = \sum_j N_j \rho_A N_j^\dagger. \tag{5.35}$$

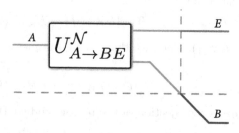

Figure 5.2 This figure depicts an isometric extension $U^{\mathcal{N}}_{A \to BE}$ of a quantum channel $\mathcal{N}_{A \to B}$. The extension $U^{\mathcal{N}}_{A \to BE}$ includes the inaccessible environment on system E as a "receiver" of quantum information. Ignoring the environment E gives the quantum channel $\mathcal{N}_{A \to B}$.

An isometric extension of the channel $\mathcal{N}_{A\to B}$ is the following linear map:

$$U^{\mathcal{N}}_{A\to BE} \equiv \sum_j N_j \otimes |j\rangle_E . \tag{5.36}$$

It is straightforward to verify that the above map is an isometry:

$$\left(U^{\mathcal{N}}\right)^\dagger U^{\mathcal{N}} = \left(\sum_k N_k^\dagger \otimes \langle k|_E\right)\left(\sum_j N_j \otimes |j\rangle_E\right) \tag{5.37}$$

$$= \sum_{k,j} N_k^\dagger N_j \langle k|j\rangle \tag{5.38}$$

$$= \sum_k N_k^\dagger N_k \tag{5.39}$$

$$= I_A. \tag{5.40}$$

The last equality follows from the completeness condition of the Kraus operators. As a consequence, we get that $U^{\mathcal{N}}\left(U^{\mathcal{N}}\right)^\dagger$ is a projector on the joint system BE, which follows by the same reasoning given in (4.259). Finally, we should verify that $U^{\mathcal{N}}$ is an extension of $\mathcal{N}$. Applying the channel $\mathcal{U}^{\mathcal{N}}_{A\to BE}$ to an arbitrary density operator ρ_A gives the following map:

$$\mathcal{U}^{\mathcal{N}}_{A\to BE}(\rho_A) \equiv U^{\mathcal{N}}\rho_A\left(U^{\mathcal{N}}\right)^\dagger \tag{5.41}$$

$$= \left(\sum_j N_j \otimes |j\rangle_E\right)\rho_A\left(\sum_k N_k^\dagger \otimes \langle k|_E\right) \tag{5.42}$$

$$= \sum_{j,k} N_j\rho_A N_k^\dagger \otimes |j\rangle\langle k|_E, \tag{5.43}$$

and tracing out the environment system gives back the original quantum channel $\mathcal{N}_{A\to B}$:

$$\text{Tr}_E\left\{\mathcal{U}^{\mathcal{N}}_{A\to BE}(\rho_A)\right\} = \sum_j N_j\rho_A N_j^\dagger = \mathcal{N}_{A\to B}(\rho_A). \tag{5.44}$$

EXERCISE 5.2.5 Show that all isometric extensions of a quantum channel are equivalent up to an isometry on the environment system (this is similar to the result of Theorem 5.1.1).

EXERCISE 5.2.6 Show that an isometric extension of the erasure channel is

$$U^{\mathcal{N}}_{A\to BE} = \sqrt{1-\varepsilon}(|0\rangle_B\langle 0|_A + |1\rangle_B\langle 1|_A) \otimes |e\rangle_E$$
$$+ \sqrt{\varepsilon}|e\rangle_B\langle 0|_A \otimes |0\rangle_E + \sqrt{\varepsilon}|e\rangle_B\langle 1|_A \otimes |1\rangle_E$$
$$= \sqrt{1-\varepsilon}I_{A\to B} \otimes |e\rangle_E + \sqrt{\varepsilon}I_{A\to E} \otimes |e\rangle_B. \tag{5.45}$$

EXERCISE 5.2.7 Determine the resulting state when Alice inputs an arbitrary pure state $|\psi\rangle$ into an isometric extension of the erasure channel. Verify that Bob and Eve receive the same ensemble (they have the same local density operator) when the erasure probability $\varepsilon = 1/2$.

EXERCISE 5.2.8   Show that the matrix representation of an isometric extension of the erasure channel is

$$
\begin{bmatrix}
\langle 0|_B\langle 0|_E U^{\mathcal{N}}_{A\to BE}|0\rangle_A & \langle 0|_B\langle 0|_E U^{\mathcal{N}}_{A\to BE}|1\rangle_A \\
\langle 0|_B\langle 1|_E U^{\mathcal{N}}_{A\to BE}|0\rangle_A & \langle 0|_B\langle 1|_E U^{\mathcal{N}}_{A\to BE}|1\rangle_A \\
\langle 0|_B\langle e|_E U^{\mathcal{N}}_{A\to BE}|0\rangle_A & \langle 0|_B\langle e|_E U^{\mathcal{N}}_{A\to BE}|1\rangle_A \\
\langle 1|_B\langle 0|_E U^{\mathcal{N}}_{A\to BE}|0\rangle_A & \langle 1|_B\langle 0|_E U^{\mathcal{N}}_{A\to BE}|1\rangle_A \\
\langle 1|_B\langle 1|_E U^{\mathcal{N}}_{A\to BE}|0\rangle_A & \langle 1|_B\langle 1|_E U^{\mathcal{N}}_{A\to BE}|1\rangle_A \\
\langle 1|_B\langle e|_E U^{\mathcal{N}}_{A\to BE}|0\rangle_A & \langle 1|_B\langle e|_E U^{\mathcal{N}}_{A\to BE}|1\rangle_A \\
\langle e|_B\langle 0|_E U^{\mathcal{N}}_{A\to BE}|0\rangle_A & \langle e|_B\langle 0|_E U^{\mathcal{N}}_{A\to BE}|1\rangle_A \\
\langle e|_B\langle 1|_E U^{\mathcal{N}}_{A\to BE}|0\rangle_A & \langle e|_B\langle 1|_E U^{\mathcal{N}}_{A\to BE}|1\rangle_A \\
\langle e|_B\langle e|_E U^{\mathcal{N}}_{A\to BE}|0\rangle_A & \langle e|_B\langle e|_E U^{\mathcal{N}}_{A\to BE}|1\rangle_A
\end{bmatrix}
=
\begin{bmatrix}
0 & 0 \\
0 & 0 \\
\sqrt{1-\varepsilon} & 0 \\
0 & 0 \\
0 & 0 \\
0 & \sqrt{1-\varepsilon} \\
\sqrt{\varepsilon} & 0 \\
0 & \sqrt{\varepsilon} \\
0 & 0
\end{bmatrix}.
$$

$$(5.46)$$

EXERCISE 5.2.9   Show that the matrix representation of an isometric extension $U^{\mathcal{N}}_{A\to BE}$ of the amplitude damping channel is

$$
\begin{bmatrix}
\langle 0|_B\langle 0|_E U^{\mathcal{N}}_{A\to BE}|0\rangle_A & \langle 0|_B\langle 0|_E U^{\mathcal{N}}_{A\to BE}|1\rangle_A \\
\langle 0|_B\langle 1|_E U^{\mathcal{N}}_{A\to BE}|0\rangle_A & \langle 0|_B\langle 1|_E U^{\mathcal{N}}_{A\to BE}|1\rangle_A \\
\langle 1|_B\langle 0|_E U^{\mathcal{N}}_{A\to BE}|0\rangle_A & \langle 1|_B\langle 0|_E U^{\mathcal{N}}_{A\to BE}|1\rangle_A \\
\langle 1|_B\langle 1|_E U^{\mathcal{N}}_{A\to BE}|0\rangle_A & \langle 1|_B\langle 1|_E U^{\mathcal{N}}_{A\to BE}|1\rangle_A
\end{bmatrix}
=
\begin{bmatrix}
0 & \sqrt{\gamma} \\
1 & 0 \\
0 & 0 \\
0 & \sqrt{1-\gamma}
\end{bmatrix}.
\quad (5.47)
$$

EXERCISE 5.2.10   Consider a full unitary $V_{AE\to BE}$ such that

$$
\mathrm{Tr}_E\left\{ V\left(\rho_A \otimes |0\rangle\langle 0|_E\right) V^\dagger\right\}
\tag{5.48}
$$

gives the amplitude damping channel. Show that a matrix representation of V is

$$
\begin{bmatrix}
\langle 0|_B\langle 0|_E V|0\rangle_A|0\rangle_E & \langle 0|_B\langle 0|_E V|0\rangle_A|1\rangle_E & \langle 0|_B\langle 0|_E V|1\rangle_A|0\rangle_E \\
\langle 0|_B\langle 1|_E V|0\rangle_A|0\rangle_E & \langle 0|_B\langle 1|_E V|0\rangle_A|1\rangle_E & \langle 0|_B\langle 1|_E V|1\rangle_A|0\rangle_E \\
\langle 1|_B\langle 0|_E V|0\rangle_A|0\rangle_E & \langle 1|_B\langle 0|_E V|0\rangle_A|1\rangle_E & \langle 1|_B\langle 0|_E V|1\rangle_A|0\rangle_E \\
\langle 1|_B\langle 1|_E V|0\rangle_A|0\rangle_E & \langle 1|_B\langle 1|_E V|0\rangle_A|1\rangle_E & \langle 1|_B\langle 1|_E V|1\rangle_A|0\rangle_E
\end{bmatrix}
$$

$$
\begin{bmatrix}
\langle 0|_B\langle 0|_E V|1\rangle_A|1\rangle_E \\
\langle 0|_B\langle 1|_E V|1\rangle_A|1\rangle_E \\
\langle 1|_B\langle 0|_E V|1\rangle_A|1\rangle_E \\
\langle 1|_B\langle 1|_E V|1\rangle_A|1\rangle_E
\end{bmatrix}
=
\begin{bmatrix}
0 & -\sqrt{1-\gamma} & \sqrt{\gamma} & 0 \\
1 & 0 & 0 & 0 \\
0 & 0 & 0 & 1 \\
0 & \sqrt{\gamma} & \sqrt{1-\gamma} & 0
\end{bmatrix}.
\tag{5.49}
$$

EXERCISE 5.2.11   Consider the full unitary operator for the amplitude damping channel from the previous exercise. Show that the density operator

$$
\mathrm{Tr}_B\left\{ V\left(\rho_A \otimes |0\rangle\langle 0|_E\right) V^\dagger\right\}
\tag{5.50}
$$

that Eve receives has the following matrix representation:

$$
\begin{bmatrix}
\gamma p & \sqrt{\gamma}\eta^* \\
\sqrt{\gamma}\eta & 1-\gamma p
\end{bmatrix}
\quad \text{if} \quad
\rho_A =
\begin{bmatrix}
1-p & \eta \\
\eta^* & p
\end{bmatrix}.
\tag{5.51}
$$

By comparing with (4.356), observe that the output to Eve is the bit flip of the output of an amplitude damping channel with damping parameter $1-\gamma$.

Complementary Channel

In the purified quantum theory, it is useful to consider all parties that are participating in a given protocol. One such party is the environment of the channel, even if it is not necessarily an active participant in a protocol. However, in a cryptographic setting, in some sense the environment is active, and we associate it with an eavesdropper, thus personifying it as "Eve."

For any quantum channel $\mathcal{N}_{A \to B}$, there exists an isometric extension $U^{\mathcal{N}}_{A \to BE}$ of that channel. The complementary channel $\mathcal{N}^c_{A \to E}$ is a quantum channel from the sender to the environment, formally defined as follows:

DEFINITION 5.2.2 (Complementary Channel)   Let $\mathcal{N} : \mathcal{L}(\mathcal{H}_A) \to \mathcal{L}(\mathcal{H}_B)$ be a quantum channel, and let $U : \mathcal{H}_A \to \mathcal{H}_B \otimes \mathcal{H}_E$ be an isometric extension of the channel $\mathcal{N}$. The complementary channel $\mathcal{N}^c : \mathcal{L}(\mathcal{H}_A) \to \mathcal{L}(\mathcal{H}_E)$ of $\mathcal{N}$, associated with U, is defined as follows:

$$\mathcal{N}^c(X_A) = \mathrm{Tr}_B \left\{ U X_A U^\dagger \right\}, \tag{5.52}$$

for $X_A \in \mathcal{L}(\mathcal{H}_A)$.

That is, we obtain a complementary channel by tracing out Bob's system B from the output of an isometric extension. It captures the noise that Eve "sees" by having her system coupled to Bob's system.

EXERCISE 5.2.12   Show that Eve's density operator (the output of a complementary channel) is of the following form:

$$\rho \to \sum_{i,j} \mathrm{Tr}\{N_i \rho N_j^\dagger\} |i\rangle\langle j|, \tag{5.53}$$

if we take an isometric extension of the channel to be of the form in (5.36).

The complementary channel is unique only up to an isometry acting on Eve's system. It inherits this property from the fact that an isometric extension of a quantum channel is unique only up to isometries acting on Eve's system. For all practical purposes, this lack of uniqueness does not affect our study of the noise that Eve sees because the measures of noise in Chapter 11 are invariant with respect to isometries acting on Eve's system.

5.2.3   Further Examples of Isometric Extensions

Generalized Dephasing Channels

A generalized dephasing channel is one that preserves states diagonal in some preferred orthonormal basis $\{|x\rangle\}$, but it can add arbitrary phases to the off-diagonal elements of a density operator represented in this basis. An isometric extension of a generalized dephasing channel acts as follows on the basis $\{|x\rangle\}$:

$$U^{\mathcal{N}_D}_{A \to BE} |x\rangle_A = |x\rangle_B |\varphi_x\rangle_E, \tag{5.54}$$

where $|\varphi_x\rangle_E$ is some state for the environment (these states need not be mutually orthogonal). Thus, we can represent the isometry as follows:

$$U^{\mathcal{N}_D}_{A \to BE} \equiv \sum_x |x\rangle_B |\varphi_x\rangle_E \langle x|_A, \tag{5.55}$$

and its action on a density operator ρ is

$$U^{\mathcal{N}_D} \rho \left(U^{\mathcal{N}_D} \right)^\dagger = \sum_{x,x'} \langle x|\rho|x'\rangle \ |x\rangle\langle x'|_B \otimes |\varphi_x\rangle\langle\varphi_{x'}|_E. \tag{5.56}$$

Tracing out the environment gives the action of the channel $\mathcal{N}_D$ to the receiver

$$\mathcal{N}_D(\rho) = \sum_{x,x'} \langle x|\rho|x'\rangle \langle\varphi_{x'}|\varphi_x\rangle \ |x\rangle\langle x'|_B, \tag{5.57}$$

where we observe that this channel preserves the diagonal components $\{|x\rangle\langle x|\}$ of ρ, but it multiplies the $d(d-1)$ off-diagonal elements of ρ by arbitrary phases, depending on the $d(d-1)$ overlaps $\langle\varphi_{x'}|\varphi_x\rangle$ of the environment states (where $x \neq x'$). Tracing out the receiver gives the action of the complementary channel $\mathcal{N}_D^c$ to the environment

$$\mathcal{N}_D^c(\rho) = \sum_x \langle x|\rho|x\rangle \ |\varphi_x\rangle\langle\varphi_x|_E. \tag{5.58}$$

Observe that the channel to the environment is entanglement-breaking. That is, the action of the channel is the same as first performing a complete projective measurement in the basis $\{|x\rangle\}$ and preparing a state $|\varphi_x\rangle_E$ conditioned on the outcome of the measurement (it is a classical–quantum channel, as discussed in Section 4.6.7). Additionally, the receiver Bob can simulate the action of this channel to the receiver by performing the same actions on the state that he receives.

EXERCISE 5.2.13   Explicitly show that the following qubit dephasing channel is a special case of a generalized dephasing channel:

$$\rho \to (1-p)\rho + pZ\rho Z. \tag{5.59}$$

Quantum Hadamard Channels

Quantum Hadamard channels are those whose complements are entanglement-breaking, and so generalized dephasing channels are a subclass of quantum Hadamard channels. We can write the output of a quantum Hadamard channel as the Hadamard product (element-wise multiplication) of a representation of the input density operator with another operator. To discuss how this comes about, suppose that the complementary channel $\mathcal{N}_{A \to E}^c$ of a channel $\mathcal{N}_{A \to B}$ is entanglement-breaking. Then, using the fact that its Kraus operators $|\xi_i\rangle_E \langle\zeta_i|_A$ are unit rank (see Theorem 4.6.1) and the construction in (5.36) for an isometric extension, we can write an isometric extension $U^{\mathcal{N}^c}$ for $\mathcal{N}^c$ as

$$U^{\mathcal{N}^c} \rho_A \left(U^{\mathcal{N}^c} \right)^\dagger = \sum_{i,j} |\xi_i\rangle_E \langle\zeta_i|_A \rho_A |\zeta_j\rangle_A \langle\xi_j|_E \otimes |i\rangle_B \langle j|_B \tag{5.60}$$

$$= \sum_{i,j} \langle\zeta_i|_A \rho_A |\zeta_j\rangle_A |\xi_i\rangle_E \langle\xi_j|_E \otimes |i\rangle_B \langle j|_B. \tag{5.61}$$

The sets $\{|\xi_i\rangle_E\}$ and $\{|\zeta_i\rangle_A\}$ each do not necessarily consist of orthonormal states, but the set $\{|i\rangle_B\}$ does because it is the environment of the complementary channel. Tracing over the system E gives the original channel from system A to B:

$$\mathcal{N}^{\mathrm{H}}_{A\to B}(\rho_A) = \sum_{i,j} \langle\zeta_i|_A \rho_A |\zeta_j\rangle_A \langle\xi_j|\xi_i\rangle_E |i\rangle_B \langle j|_B. \tag{5.62}$$

Let Σ denote the matrix with elements $[\Sigma]_{i,j} = \langle\zeta_i|_A \rho_A |\zeta_j\rangle_A$, a representation of the input state ρ, and let Γ denote the matrix with elements $[\Gamma]_{i,j} = \langle\xi_i|\xi_j\rangle_E$. Then, from (5.62), it is clear that the output of the channel is the Hadamard product $*$ of Σ and $\Gamma^\dagger$ with respect to the basis $\{|i\rangle_B\}$:

$$\mathcal{N}^{\mathrm{H}}_{A\to B}(\rho) = \Sigma * \Gamma^\dagger. \tag{5.63}$$

For this reason, such a channel is known as a Hadamard channel.

Hadamard channels are *degradable*, as introduced in the following definition:

DEFINITION 5.2.3 (Degradable Channel)   Let $\mathcal{N}_{A\to B}$ be a quantum channel, and let $\mathcal{N}^c_{A\to E}$ denote a complementary channel for $\mathcal{N}_{A\to B}$. The channel $\mathcal{N}_{A\to B}$ is degradable if there exists a degrading channel $\mathcal{D}_{B\to E}$ such that

$$\mathcal{D}_{B\to E}(\mathcal{N}_{A\to B}(X_A)) = \mathcal{N}^c_{A\to E}(X_A), \tag{5.64}$$

for all $X_A \in \mathcal{L}(\mathcal{H}_A)$.

To see that a quantum Hadamard channel is degradable, let Bob perform a complete projective measurement of his state in the basis $\{|i\rangle_B\}$ and prepare the state $|\xi_i\rangle_E$ conditioned on the outcome of the measurement. This procedure simulates the complementary channel $\mathcal{N}^c_{A\to E}$ and also implies that the degrading channel $\mathcal{D}_{B\to E}$ is entanglement-breaking. To be more precise, the Kraus operators of the degrading channel $\mathcal{D}_{B\to E}$ are $\{|\xi_i\rangle_E \langle i|_B\}$ so that

$$\mathcal{D}_{B\to E}(\mathcal{N}^{\mathrm{H}}_{A\to B}(\sigma_A)) = \sum_i |\xi_i\rangle_E \langle i|_B \mathcal{N}_{A\to B}(\sigma_A)|i\rangle_B \langle\xi_i|_E \tag{5.65}$$

$$= \sum_i \langle\zeta_i|_A \sigma_A |\zeta_i\rangle_A |\xi_i\rangle \langle\xi_i|_E, \tag{5.66}$$

demonstrating that this degrading channel simulates the complementary channel $\mathcal{N}^{\mathrm{H}}_{A\to E}$. Note that we can view this degrading channel as the composition of two channels: a first channel $\mathcal{D}^1_{B\to Y}$ performs the complete projective measurement, leading to a classical variable Y, and a second channel $\mathcal{D}^2_{Y\to E}$ performs the state preparation, conditioned on the value of the classical variable Y. We can therefore write $\mathcal{D}_{B\to E} = \mathcal{D}^2_{Y\to E} \circ \mathcal{D}^1_{B\to Y}$. This particular form of the channel has implications for its quantum capacity (see Chapter 24) and its more general capacities (see Chapter 25). Observe that a generalized dephasing channel from the previous section is a quantum Hadamard channel because the channel to its environment is entanglement-breaking.

5.2.4   Isometric Extension and Adjoint of a Quantum Channel

Recall the notion of an adjoint of a quantum channel from Section 4.4.5. Here we show an alternate way of representing an adjoint of a quantum channel using an isometric extension of it.

PROPOSITION 5.2.1   Let $\mathcal{N} : \mathcal{L}(\mathcal{H}_A) \to \mathcal{L}(\mathcal{H}_B)$ be a quantum channel and let $U : \mathcal{H}_A \to \mathcal{H}_B \otimes \mathcal{H}_E$ be an isometric extension of it. Then the adjoint map $\mathcal{N}^\dagger : \mathcal{L}(\mathcal{H}_B) \to \mathcal{L}(\mathcal{H}_A)$ can be written as follows:

$$\mathcal{N}^\dagger(Y_B) = U^\dagger(Y_B \otimes I_E)U, \tag{5.67}$$

for $Y_B \in \mathcal{L}(\mathcal{H}_B)$.

Proof   We can see this by using the definition of the adjoint map (Definition 4.4.6), the definition of an isometric extension (Definition 5.2.1), and the definition of partial trace (Definition 4.3.4). Consider from the definition of the adjoint map that $\mathcal{N}^\dagger$ is such that

$$\langle Y_B, \mathcal{N}(X_A)\rangle = \langle \mathcal{N}^\dagger(Y_B), X_A\rangle, \tag{5.68}$$

for all $X_A \in \mathcal{L}(\mathcal{H}_A)$ and $Y_B \in \mathcal{L}(\mathcal{H}_B)$. Then

$$\langle Y_B, \mathcal{N}(X_A)\rangle = \text{Tr}\{Y_B^\dagger \mathcal{N}(X_A)\} \tag{5.69}$$

$$= \text{Tr}\{Y_B^\dagger \, \text{Tr}_E\{U X_A U^\dagger\}\} \tag{5.70}$$

$$= \text{Tr}\{(Y_B^\dagger \otimes I_E)U X_A U^\dagger\} \tag{5.71}$$

$$= \text{Tr}\{U^\dagger(Y_B^\dagger \otimes I_E)U X_A\} \tag{5.72}$$

$$= \text{Tr}\{[U^\dagger(Y_B \otimes I_E)U]^\dagger X_A\} \tag{5.73}$$

$$= \langle U^\dagger(Y_B \otimes I_E)U, X_A\rangle. \tag{5.74}$$

The second equality is from the definition of an isometric extension. The third equality follows by applying the definition of partial trace. The fourth uses cyclicity of trace. Since we have shown that $\langle Y_B, \mathcal{N}(X_A)\rangle = \langle U^\dagger(Y_B \otimes I_E)U, X_A\rangle$ for all $X_A \in \mathcal{L}(\mathcal{H}_A)$ and $Y_B \in \mathcal{L}(\mathcal{H}_B)$, the statement in (5.67) follows.   □

We can verify the formula in (5.67) in a different way. Suppose that we have a Kraus representation of the channel $\mathcal{N}$ as follows:

$$\mathcal{N}(X_A) = \sum_l V_l X_A V_l^\dagger, \tag{5.75}$$

where $V_l \in \mathcal{L}(\mathcal{H}_A, \mathcal{H}_B)$ for all l and $\sum_l V_l^\dagger V_l = I_A$. An isometric extension U for this channel is then as given in (5.36):

$$U = \sum_l V_l \otimes |l\rangle_E, \tag{5.76}$$

where $\{|l\rangle_E\}$ is some orthonormal basis. We can then explicitly compute the formula in (5.67) as follows:

$$U^\dagger(Y_B \otimes I_E)U = \left(\sum_l V_l^\dagger \otimes \langle l|_E\right)(Y_B \otimes I_E)\left(\sum_{l'} V_{l'} \otimes |l'\rangle_E\right) \tag{5.77}$$

$$= \sum_{l,l'} V_l^\dagger Y_B V_{l'} \langle l|l'\rangle_E = \sum_l V_l^\dagger Y_B V_l = \mathcal{N}^\dagger(Y_B), \tag{5.78}$$

where the last equality follows from what we calculated before in (4.239).

5.3   Coherent Quantum Instrument

It is useful to consider an isometric extension of a quantum instrument (we discussed quantum instruments in Section 4.6.8). This viewpoint is important when we recall that a quantum instrument is the most general map from a quantum system to a quantum system and a classical system.

Recall from Section 4.6.8 that a quantum instrument acts as follows on an input $\rho_A \in \mathcal{D}(\mathcal{H}_A)$:

$$\rho_A \to \sum_j \mathcal{E}_{A\to B}^j(\rho_A) \otimes |j\rangle\langle j|_J, \tag{5.79}$$

where each $\mathcal{E}_{A\to B}^j$ is a completely positive trace-non-increasing (CPTNI) map that has the following form:

$$\mathcal{E}_{A\to B}^j(\rho_A) = \sum_k M_{j,k}\rho_A M_{j,k}^\dagger, \tag{5.80}$$

such that $\sum_k M_{j,k}^\dagger M_{j,k} \leq I$ for all j.

We now describe a particular coherent evolution that implements the above transformation when we trace over certain degrees of freedom. A pure extension of each CPTNI map $\mathcal{E}_j$ is as follows:

$$U_{A\to BE}^{\mathcal{E}_j} \equiv \sum_k M_{j,k} \otimes |k\rangle_E, \tag{5.81}$$

where the operator $M_{j,k}$ acts on the input system A and the environment system E is large enough to accomodate all of the CPTNI maps $\mathcal{E}_j$. That is, if the first map $\mathcal{E}_1$ has states $\{|1\rangle_E, \ldots, |d_1\rangle_E\}$, then the second map $\mathcal{E}_2$ has states $\{|d_1 + 1\rangle_E, \ldots, |d_1 + d_2\rangle_E\}$ so that the states on E are orthogonal for all the different maps $\mathcal{E}_j$ that are part of the instrument. We can embed this pure extension into the evolution in (5.79) as follows:

$$\rho_A \rightarrow \sum_j \mathcal{U}_{A \rightarrow BE}^{\mathcal{E}_j}(\rho_A) \otimes |j\rangle\langle j|_J, \tag{5.82}$$

where $\mathcal{U}_{A \rightarrow BE}^{\mathcal{E}_j}(\rho_A) = U_{A \rightarrow BE}^{\mathcal{E}_j}(\rho_A)(U_{A \rightarrow BE}^{\mathcal{E}_j})^\dagger$. This evolution is not quite fully coherent, but a simple modification of it does make it fully coherent:

$$\sum_j U_{A \rightarrow BE}^{\mathcal{E}_j} \otimes |j\rangle_J \otimes |j\rangle_{E_J}. \tag{5.83}$$

The full action of the coherent instrument is then as follows:

$$\rho_A \rightarrow \sum_{j,j'} U_{A \rightarrow BE}^{\mathcal{E}_j} \rho_A \left(U_{A \rightarrow BE}^{\mathcal{E}_{j'}} \right)^\dagger \otimes |j\rangle\langle j'|_J \otimes |j\rangle\langle j'|_{E_J} \tag{5.84}$$

$$= \sum_{j,k,j',k'} M_{j,k} \rho_A M_{j',k'}^\dagger \otimes |k\rangle\langle k'|_E \otimes |j\rangle\langle j'|_J \otimes |j\rangle\langle j'|_{E_J}. \tag{5.85}$$

One can then check that tracing over the environmental degrees of freedom E and E_J reproduces the action of the quantum instrument in (5.79).

5.4   Coherent Measurement

We end this chapter by discussing a coherent measurement. This last section, combined with the notion of an isometric extension of a quantum channel, shows that it is sufficient to describe all of the quantum theory in the so-called "traditionalist" way by using only unitary evolutions and von Neumann (complete projective) measurements.

Suppose that we have a set of measurement operators $\{M_j\}_j$ such that $\sum_j M_j^\dagger M_j = I$. In the noisy quantum theory, we found that the post-measurement state of a measurement on a quantum system S with density operator ρ is

$$\frac{M_j \rho M_j^\dagger}{p_J(j)}, \tag{5.86}$$

where the measurement outcome j occurs with probability

$$p_J(j) = \text{Tr}\left\{ M_j^\dagger M_j \rho \right\}. \tag{5.87}$$

We would like a way to perform the above measurement on system S in a *coherent* fashion. The isometry in (5.36) gives a hint for how we can structure such a coherent measurement. We can build the coherent measurement as the following isometry:

$$U_{S \rightarrow SS'} \equiv \sum_j M_S^j \otimes |j\rangle_{S'}. \tag{5.88}$$

Appying this isometry to a density operator ρ_S gives the following state:

$$\mathcal{U}_{S \to SS'}(\rho_S) = U_{S \to SS'} \rho_S (U_{S \to SS'})^\dagger \tag{5.89}$$

$$= \sum_{j,j'} M_S^j \rho_S (M_S^{j'})^\dagger \otimes |j\rangle\langle j'|_{S'}. \tag{5.90}$$

We can then apply a complete projective measurement with projection operators $\{|j\rangle\langle j|\}_j$ to the system S', which gives the following post-measurement state:

$$\frac{(I_S \otimes |j\rangle\langle j|_{S'})(\mathcal{U}_{S \to SS'}(\rho_S))(I_S \otimes |j\rangle\langle j|_{S'})}{\text{Tr}\left\{(I_S \otimes |j\rangle\langle j|_{S'})(\mathcal{U}_{S \to SS'}(\rho_S))\right\}}$$

$$= \frac{M_S^j \rho_S (M_S^j)^\dagger}{\text{Tr}\left\{(M_S^j)^\dagger M_S^j \rho_S\right\}} \otimes |j\rangle\langle j|_{S'}. \tag{5.91}$$

The result is then the same as that in (5.86). In fact, this is the same as the way in which Section 4.2 motivated an alternate description of quantum measurements.

EXERCISE 5.4.1   Suppose that there is a set of density operators ρ_S^k and a POVM $\{\Lambda_S^k\}$ that identifies these states with high probability, in the sense that

$$\forall k \quad \text{Tr}\left\{\Lambda_S^k \rho_S^k\right\} \geq 1 - \varepsilon, \tag{5.92}$$

where $\varepsilon \in (0, 1)$. Construct a coherent measurement $U_{S \to SS'}$ and show that the coherent measurement has a high probability of success in the sense that

$$|\langle \phi_k|_{RS} \langle k|_{S'} U_{S \to SS'} |\phi_k\rangle_{RS}| \geq 1 - \varepsilon, \tag{5.93}$$

where each $|\phi_k\rangle_{RS}$ is a purification of ρ_k.

5.5   History and Further Reading

The purified view of quantum mechanics has long been part of quantum information theory (e.g., see Nielsen & Chuang, 2000 or Yard, 2005). Early work of Stinespring (1955) showed that every linear CPTP map can be realized as a linear isometry with an output on a larger Hilbert space and followed by a partial trace. Giovannetti & Fazio (2005) discussed some of the observations about the amplitude damping channel that appear in our exercises. Devetak & Shor (2005) introduced generalized dephasing channels in the context of trade-off coding and they also introduced the notion of a degradable quantum channel. King et al. (2007) studied the quantum Hadamard channels. Coherent instruments and measurements appeared in Devetak & Winter (2004), Devetak (2005), and Hsieh, Devetak & Winter (2008) as part of the decoder used in several quantum coding theorems. We exploit them in Chapters 24 and 25.

Part III

Unit Quantum Protocols

6   Three Unit Quantum Protocols

This chapter begins our first exciting application of the postulates of the quantum theory to quantum communication. We study the fundamental, unit quantum communication protocols. These protocols involve a single sender Alice and a single receiver Bob. The protocols are ideal and noiseless because we assume that Alice and Bob can exploit perfect classical communication, perfect quantum communication, and perfect entanglement. At the end of this chapter, we suggest how to incorporate imperfections into these protocols for later study.

Alice and Bob may wish to perform one of several quantum information-processing tasks, such as the transmission of classical information, quantum information, or entanglement. Several fundamental protocols make use of these resources:

1. We will see that noiseless entanglement is an important resource in quantum Shannon theory because it enables Alice and Bob to perform other protocols that are not possible with classical resources only. We will present a simple, idealized protocol for generating entanglement, named *entanglement distribution.*

2. Alice may wish to communicate classical information to Bob. A trivial method, named *elementary coding*, is a simple way of doing so and we discuss it briefly.

3. A more interesting technique for transmitting classical information is *superdense coding*. It exploits a noiseless qubit channel and shared entanglement to transmit more classical information than would be possible with a noiseless qubit channel alone.

4. Finally, Alice may wish to transmit quantum information to Bob. A trivial method for her to do so is to exploit a noiseless qubit channel. However, it is useful to have other ways for transmitting quantum information because such a resource is difficult to engineer in practice. An alternative, surprising method for transmitting quantum information is *quantum teleportation.* The teleportation protocol exploits classical communication and shared entanglement to transmit quantum information.

Each of these protocols is a fundamental unit protocol and provides a foundation for asking further questions in quantum Shannon theory. In fact, the discovery of these latter two protocols was the stimulus for much of the original research in quantum Shannon theory. One could take each of these protocols and ask about its performance if one or more of the resources involved is noisy rather than noiseless. Later chapters of this book explore many of these possibilities.

This chapter introduces the technique of *resource counting*, which is of practical importance because it quantifies the communication cost of achieving a certain task. We include only non-local resources in a resource count—non-local resources include classical or quantum communication or shared entanglement.

It is important to minimize the use of certain resources, such as noiseless entanglement or a noiseless qubit channel, in a given protocol because they are expensive. Given a certain implementation of a quantum information-processing task, we may wonder if there is a way of implementing it that consumes fewer resources. A proof that a given protocol is the best that we can hope to do is an optimality proof (also known as a converse proof, as discussed in Section 2.1.3). We argue, based on good physical grounds, that the protocols in this chapter are the best implementations of the desired quantum information-processing task. Chapter 25 gives information-theoretic proofs of optimality.

6.1   Non-Local Unit Resources

We first briefly define what we mean by a noiseless qubit channel, a noiseless classical bit channel, and noiseless entanglement. Each of these resources is a *non-local, unit resource*. A resource is *non-local* if two spatially separated parties share it or if one party uses it to communicate to another. We say that a resource is *unit* if it comes in some "gold standard" form, such as qubits, classical bits, or entangled bits. It is important to establish these definitions so that we can check whether a given protocol is truly simulating one of these resources.

A noiseless qubit channel is any mechanism that implements the following map:

$$|i\rangle_A \rightarrow |i\rangle_B, \tag{6.1}$$

extended linearly to arbitrary state vectors and where $i \in \{0,1\}$, $\{|0\rangle_A, |1\rangle_A\}$ is some preferred orthonormal basis on Alice's system, and $\{|0\rangle_B, |1\rangle_B\}$ is some preferred orthonormal basis on Bob's system. The bases do not have to be the same, but it must be clear which basis each party is using. The above map is linear so that it preserves arbitrary superposition states (it preserves any qubit). For example, the map acts as follows on a superposition state:

$$\alpha|0\rangle_A + \beta|1\rangle_A \rightarrow \alpha|0\rangle_B + \beta|1\rangle_B. \tag{6.2}$$

We can also write it as the following isometry:

$$\sum_{i=0}^{1} |i\rangle_B \langle i|_A. \tag{6.3}$$

Any information-processing protocol that implements the above map simulates a noiseless qubit channel. We label the communication resource of a noiseless qubit channel as follows:

$$[q \rightarrow q], \tag{6.4}$$

where the notation indicates one forward use of a noiseless qubit channel.

A noiseless classical bit channel is any mechanism that implements the following map:

$$|i\rangle\langle i|_A \rightarrow |i\rangle\langle i|_B, \tag{6.5}$$

$$|i\rangle\langle j|_A \rightarrow 0 \quad \text{for } i \neq j, \tag{6.6}$$

extended linearly to density operators and where $i, j \in \{0, 1\}$ and the orthonormal bases are again arbitrary. This channel maintains the diagonal elements of a density operator in the basis $\{|0\rangle_A, |1\rangle_A\}$, but it eliminates the off-diagonal elements. We can write it as the following linear map acting on a density operator ρ_A:

$$\rho_A \rightarrow \sum_{i=0}^{1} |i\rangle_B \langle i|_A \rho_A |i\rangle_A \langle i|_B. \tag{6.7}$$

The form above is consistent with Definition 4.6.5 for noiseless classical channels. This resource is weaker than a noiseless qubit channel because it does not require Alice and Bob to maintain arbitrary superposition states—it merely transfers classical information. Alice can use the above channel to transmit classical information to Bob. She can prepare either of the classical states $|0\rangle\langle 0|$ or $|1\rangle\langle 1|$, send it through the classical channel, and Bob performs a computational basis measurement to determine the message Alice transmits. We denote the communication resource of a noiseless classical bit channel as follows:

$$[c \rightarrow c], \tag{6.8}$$

where the notation indicates one forward use of a noiseless classical bit channel.

We can study other ways of transmitting classical information. For example, suppose that Alice flips a fair coin that chooses the state $|0\rangle_A$ or $|1\rangle_A$ with equal probability. The resulting state is the following density operator:

$$\frac{1}{2} \left(|0\rangle\langle 0|_A + |1\rangle\langle 1|_A \right). \tag{6.9}$$

Suppose that she sends the above state through a noiseless classical channel. The resulting density operator for Bob is as follows:

$$\frac{1}{2} \left(|0\rangle\langle 0|_B + |1\rangle\langle 1|_B \right). \tag{6.10}$$

The above classical bit channel map does not preserve off-diagonal elements of a density operator. Suppose instead that Alice prepares a superposition state

$$\frac{|0\rangle_A + |1\rangle_A}{\sqrt{2}}. \tag{6.11}$$

The density operator corresponding to this state is

$$\frac{1}{2}\left(|0\rangle\langle0|_A + |0\rangle\langle1|_A + |1\rangle\langle0|_A + |1\rangle\langle1|_A\right). \tag{6.12}$$

Suppose Alice then transmits this state through the above classical channel. The classical channel eliminates all the off-diagonal elements of the density operator and the resulting state for Bob is as follows:

$$\frac{1}{2}\left(|0\rangle\langle0|_B + |1\rangle\langle1|_B\right). \tag{6.13}$$

Thus, it is impossible for a noiseless classical channel to simulate a noiseless qubit channel because it cannot maintain arbitrary superposition states. However, it is possible for a noiseless qubit channel to simulate a noiseless classical bit channel, and we denote this fact with the following *resource inequality*:

$$[q \to q] \geq [c \to c]. \tag{6.14}$$

Noiseless quantum communication is therefore a stronger resource than noiseless classical communication.

EXERCISE 6.1.1   Show that the noisy dephasing channel in (4.332) with $p = 1/2$ is equal to a noiseless classical bit channel.

The final resource that we consider is shared entanglement. The ebit is our "gold standard" resource for pure bipartite (two-party) entanglement, and we will make this point more clear operationally in Chapter 19. An ebit is the following state of two qubits:

$$|\Phi^+\rangle_{AB} \equiv \frac{1}{\sqrt{2}}\left(|00\rangle_{AB} + |11\rangle_{AB}\right), \tag{6.15}$$

where Alice possesses the first qubit and Bob possesses the second.

Below, we show how a noiseless qubit channel can generate a noiseless ebit through a simple protocol named *entanglement distribution*. However, an ebit cannot simulate a noiseless qubit channel (for reasons which we explain later). Therefore, noiseless quantum communication is the strongest of all three resources, and entanglement and classical communication are in some sense "orthogonal" to one another because neither can simulate the other.

6.2   Protocols

6.2.1   Entanglement Distribution

The entanglement distribution protocol is the most basic of the three unit protocols. It exploits one use of a noiseless qubit channel to establish one shared noiseless ebit. It consists of the following two steps:

1. Alice prepares a Bell state locally in her laboratory. She prepares two qubits in the state $|0\rangle_A|0\rangle_{A'}$, where we label the first qubit as A and the second qubit as A'. She performs a Hadamard gate on qubit A to produce the following state:

$$\left(\frac{|0\rangle_A + |1\rangle_A}{\sqrt{2}}\right)|0\rangle_{A'}. \tag{6.16}$$

She then performs a CNOT gate with qubit A as the source qubit and qubit A' as the target qubit. The state becomes the following Bell state:

$$|\Phi^+\rangle_{AA'} = \frac{|00\rangle_{AA'} + |11\rangle_{AA'}}{\sqrt{2}}. \tag{6.17}$$

2. She sends qubit A' to Bob with one use of a noiseless qubit channel. Alice and Bob then share the ebit $|\Phi^+\rangle_{AB}$.

Figure 6.1 depicts the entanglement distribution protocol.

The following resource inequality quantifies the non-local resources consumed or generated in the above protocol:

$$[q \rightarrow q] \geq [qq], \tag{6.18}$$

where $[q \rightarrow q]$ denotes one forward use of a noiseless qubit channel and $[qq]$ denotes a shared, noiseless ebit. The meaning of the resource inequality is that there exists a protocol that consumes the resource on the left in order to generate the resource on the right. The best analogy is to think of a resource inequality as a "chemical reaction"-like formula, where the protocol is like a chemical reaction that transforms one resource into another.

There are several subtleties to notice about the above protocol and its corresponding resource inequality:

1. We are careful with the language when describing the resource state. We described the state $|\Phi^+\rangle$ as a Bell state in the first step because it is a local state in Alice's laboratory. We only used the term "ebit" to describe the state

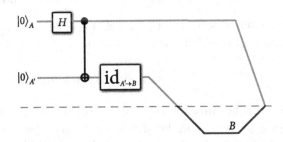

Figure 6.1 This figure depicts a protocol for entanglement distribution. Alice performs local operations (the Hadamard and CNOT) and consumes one use of a noiseless qubit channel to generate one noiseless ebit $|\Phi^+\rangle_{AB}$ shared with Bob.

after the second step, when the state becomes a non-local resource shared between Alice and Bob.

2. The resource count involves non-local resources only—we do not factor any local operations, such as the Hadamard gate or the CNOT gate, into the resource count. This line of thinking is different from the theory of computation, where it is of utmost importance to minimize the number of steps involved in a computation. In this book, we are developing a theory of quantum communication and thus count non-local resources only.

3. We are assuming that it is possible to perform all local operations perfectly. This line of thinking is another departure from practical concerns that one might have in fault-tolerant quantum computation, the study of the propagation of errors in quantum operations. Performing a CNOT gate is a highly non-trivial task at the current stage of experimental development in quantum computation, with most implementations being far from perfect. Nevertheless, we proceed forward with this communication-theoretic line of thinking.

The following exercises outline classical information-processing tasks that are analogous to the task of entanglement distribution.

EXERCISE 6.2.1   Outline a protocol for *shared randomness distribution*. Suppose that Alice and Bob have available one use of a noiseless classical bit channel. Give a method for them to implement the following resource inequality:

$$[c \to c] \geq [cc], \tag{6.19}$$

where $[c \to c]$ denotes one forward use of a noiseless classical bit channel and $[cc]$ denotes a shared, non-local bit of shared randomness.

EXERCISE 6.2.2   Consider three parties Alice, Bob, and Eve and suppose that a noiseless private channel connects Alice to Bob. Privacy here implies that Eve does not learn anything about the information that traverses the private channel—Eve's probability distribution is independent of Alice and Bob's:

$$p_{A,B,E}(a, b, e) = p_A(a)p_{B|A}(b|a)p_E(e). \tag{6.20}$$

For a noiseless private bit channel, $p_{B|A}(b|a) = \delta_{b,a}$. A noiseless secret key corresponds to the following distribution:

$$p_{A,B,E}(a, b, e) = \frac{1}{2}\delta_{b,a}p_E(e), \tag{6.21}$$

where $\frac{1}{2}$ implies that the key is equal to "0" or "1" with equal probability, $\delta_{b,a}$ implies a perfectly correlated secret key, and the factoring of the distribution $p_{A,B,E}(a, b, e)$ implies the secrecy of the key (Eve's information is independent of Alice and Bob's). The difference between a noiseless private bit channel and a noiseless secret key is that the private channel is a dynamic resource while the secret key is a shared, static resource. Show that it is possible to upgrade the protocol for shared randomness distribution to a protocol for *secret key distribution*, if Alice and Bob share a noiseless private bit channel. That is, show that they can achieve the following resource inequality:

$$[c \rightarrow c]_{\text{priv}} \geq [cc]_{\text{priv}}, \tag{6.22}$$

where $[c \rightarrow c]_{\text{priv}}$ denotes one forward use of a noiseless private bit channel and $[cc]_{\text{priv}}$ denotes one bit of shared, noiseless secret key.

Entanglement and Quantum Communication

Can entanglement enable two parties to communicate quantum information? It is natural to wonder if there is a protocol corresponding to the following resource inequality:

$$[qq] \overset{?}{\geq} [q \rightarrow q]. \tag{6.23}$$

Unfortunately, it is physically impossible to construct a protocol that implements the above resource inequality. The argument against such a protocol arises from the theory of relativity. Specifically, the theory of relativity prohibits information transfer or signaling at a speed greater than the speed of light. Suppose that two parties share noiseless entanglement over a large distance. That resource is a static resource, possessing only shared quantum correlations. If a protocol were to exist that implements the above resource inequality, it would imply that two parties could communicate quantum information faster than the speed of light, because they would be exploiting the entanglement for the instantaneous transfer of quantum information.

The entanglement distribution resource inequality is only "one-way," as in (6.18). Quantum communication is therefore strictly stronger than shared entanglement when no other non-local resources are available.

6.2.2 Elementary Coding

We can also send classical information using a noiseless qubit channel. A simple protocol for doing so is *elementary coding*. This protocol consists of the following steps:

1. Alice prepares either $|0\rangle$ or $|1\rangle$, depending on the classical bit that she would like to send.
2. She transmits this state over the noiseless qubit channel, and Bob receives the qubit.
3. Bob performs a measurement in the computational basis to determine the classical bit that Alice transmitted.

Elementary coding succeeds without error because Bob's measurement can always distinguish the classical states $|0\rangle$ and $|1\rangle$. The following resource inequality applies to elementary coding:

$$[q \rightarrow q] \geq [c \rightarrow c]. \tag{6.24}$$

Again, we are only counting non-local resources in the resource count—we do not count the state preparation at the beginning or the measurement at the end.

If no other resources are available for consumption, the above resource inequality is optimal—one cannot do better than to transmit one classical bit of information per use of a noiseless qubit channel. This result may be a bit frustrating at first, because it may seem that we could exploit the continuous degrees of freedom in the probability amplitudes of a qubit state for encoding more than one classical bit per qubit. Unfortunately, there is no way that we can access the information in the continuous degrees of freedom using any measurement scheme. The result of Exercise 4.2.2 demonstrates the optimality of the above protocol, and it holds as well by invoking the Holevo bound from Chapter 11.

6.2.3 Quantum Super-Dense Coding

We now outline a protocol named *super-dense coding*. It is named as such because it has the striking property that noiseless entanglement can double the classical communication ability of a noiseless qubit channel. It consists of three steps:

1. Suppose that Alice and Bob share an ebit $|\Phi^+\rangle_{AB}$. Alice applies one of four unitary operations $\{I, X, Z, XZ\}$ to her share of the above state. The state becomes one of the following four Bell states (up to a global phase), depending on the message that Alice chooses:

$$|\Phi^+\rangle_{AB}, \qquad |\Phi^-\rangle_{AB}, \qquad |\Psi^+\rangle_{AB}, \qquad |\Psi^-\rangle_{AB}. \qquad (6.25)$$

The definitions of these Bell states are in (3.194)–(3.196).

2. She transmits her qubit to Bob with one use of a noiseless qubit channel.

3. Bob performs a Bell measurement (a measurement in the basis $\{|\Phi^+\rangle_{AB}, |\Phi^-\rangle_{AB}, |\Psi^+\rangle_{AB}, |\Psi^-\rangle_{AB}\}$) to distinguish the four states perfectly—he can distinguish the states because they are all orthogonal to each other.

Thus, Alice can transmit two classical bits (corresponding to the four messages) if she shares a noiseless ebit with Bob and uses a noiseless qubit channel. Figure 6.2 depicts the protocol for quantum super-dense coding.

The super-dense coding protocol realizes the following resource inequality:

$$[qq] + [q \to q] \geq 2\,[c \to c]. \qquad (6.26)$$

Notice again that the resource inequality counts the use of non-local resources only—we do not count the local operations at the beginning of the protocol or the Bell measurement at the end of the protocol.

Also, notice that we could have implemented two noiseless classical bit channels with two instances of elementary coding:

$$2\,[q \to q] \geq 2\,[c \to c]. \qquad (6.27)$$

However, this method is not as powerful as the super-dense coding protocol—in super-dense coding, we consume the weaker resource of an ebit to help transmit

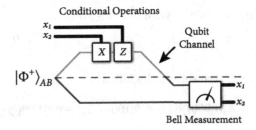

Conditional Operations

Qubit Channel

Bell Measurement

Figure 6.2 This figure depicts the dense coding protocol. Alice and Bob share an ebit before the protocol begins. Alice would like to transmit two classical bits x_1x_2 to Bob. She performs a Pauli rotation conditioned on her two classical bits and sends her share of the ebit over a noiseless qubit channel. Bob can then recover the two classical bits by performing a Bell measurement.

two classical bits, instead of consuming the stronger resource of an extra noiseless qubit channel.

The super-dense coding protocol also transmits the classical bits *privately*. Suppose a third party intercepts the qubit that Alice transmits. There is no measurement that the third party can perform to determine which message Alice transmits because the local density operator of all of the Bell states is the same and equal to the maximally mixed state π_A (the information for the eavesdropper is the same irrespective of each message that Alice transmits). The privacy of the protocol is due to Alice and Bob sharing maximal entanglement. We exploit this aspect of the super-dense coding protocol when we "make it coherent" in Chapter 7.

6.2.4   Quantum Teleportation

Perhaps the most striking protocol in noiseless quantum communication is the *quantum teleportation protocol*. The protocol destroys the quantum state of a qubit in one location and recreates it on a qubit at a distant location, with the help of shared entanglement. Thus, the name "teleportation" corresponds well to the mechanism that occurs.

The teleportation protocol is actually a flipped version of the super-dense coding protocol, in the sense that Alice and Bob merely "swap their equipment." The first step in understanding teleportation is to perform a few algebraic steps using the tricks of the tensor product and the Bell state substitutions from Exercise 3.6.6. Consider a qubit $|\psi\rangle_{A'}$ that Alice possesses, where

$$|\psi\rangle_{A'} \equiv \alpha|0\rangle_{A'} + \beta|1\rangle_{A'}. \tag{6.28}$$

Suppose she shares an ebit $|\Phi^+\rangle_{AB}$ with Bob. The joint state of the systems A', A, and B is as follows:

$$|\psi\rangle_{A'}|\Phi^+\rangle_{AB}. \tag{6.29}$$

Let us first explicitly write out this state:

$$|\psi\rangle_{A'}|\Phi^+\rangle_{AB} = (\alpha|0\rangle_{A'} + \beta|1\rangle_{A'})\left(\frac{|00\rangle_{AB} + |11\rangle_{AB}}{\sqrt{2}}\right). \tag{6.30}$$

Distributing terms gives the following equality:

$$= \frac{1}{\sqrt{2}}\left[\alpha|000\rangle_{A'AB} + \beta|100\rangle_{A'AB} + \alpha|011\rangle_{A'AB} + \beta|111\rangle_{A'AB}\right]. \tag{6.31}$$

We use the relations in Exercise 3.6.6 to rewrite the joint system $A'A$ in the Bell basis:

$$= \frac{1}{2}\left[\begin{array}{l} \alpha(|\Phi^+\rangle_{A'A} + |\Phi^-\rangle_{A'A})|0\rangle_B + \beta(|\Psi^+\rangle_{A'A} - |\Psi^-\rangle_{A'A})|0\rangle_B \\ +\alpha(|\Psi^+\rangle_{A'A} + |\Psi^-\rangle_{A'A})|1\rangle_B + \beta(|\Phi^+\rangle_{A'A} - |\Phi^-\rangle_{A'A})|1\rangle_B \end{array}\right]. \tag{6.32}$$

Simplifying gives the following equality:

$$= \frac{1}{2}\left[\begin{array}{l} |\Phi^+\rangle_{A'A}(\alpha|0\rangle_B + \beta|1\rangle_B) + |\Phi^-\rangle_{A'A}(\alpha|0\rangle_B - \beta|1\rangle_B) \\ + |\Psi^+\rangle_{A'A}(\alpha|1\rangle_B + \beta|0\rangle_B) + |\Psi^-\rangle_{A'A}(\alpha|1\rangle_B - \beta|0\rangle_B) \end{array}\right]. \tag{6.33}$$

We can finally rewrite the state as four superposed terms, with a distinct Pauli operator applied to Bob's system B for each term in the superposition:

$$= \frac{1}{2}\left[|\Phi^+\rangle_{A'A}|\psi\rangle_B + |\Phi^-\rangle_{A'A}Z|\psi\rangle_B + |\Psi^+\rangle_{A'A}X|\psi\rangle_B + |\Psi^-\rangle_{A'A}XZ|\psi\rangle_B\right]. \tag{6.34}$$

We now outline the three steps of the teleportation protocol (depicted in Figure 6.3):

1. Alice performs a Bell measurement on her systems $A'A$. The state collapses to one of the following four states with uniform probability:

$$|\Phi^+\rangle_{A'A}|\psi\rangle_B, \tag{6.35}$$

$$|\Phi^-\rangle_{A'A}Z|\psi\rangle_B, \tag{6.36}$$

$$|\Psi^+\rangle_{A'A}X|\psi\rangle_B, \tag{6.37}$$

$$|\Psi^-\rangle_{A'A}XZ|\psi\rangle_B. \tag{6.38}$$

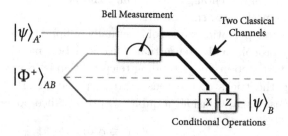

Figure 6.3 This figure depicts the teleportation protocol. Alice would like to transmit an arbitrary quantum state $|\psi\rangle_{A'}$ to Bob. Alice and Bob share an ebit before the protocol begins. Alice can "teleport" her quantum state to Bob by consuming the entanglement and two uses of a noiseless classical bit channel.

Notice that the state resulting from the measurement is a product state with respect to the cut $A'A \mid B$, regardless of the outcome of the measurement. At this point, Alice knows whether Bob's state is $|\psi\rangle_B$, $Z|\psi\rangle_B$, $X|\psi\rangle_B$, or $XZ|\psi\rangle_B$ because she knows the result of the measurement. On the other hand, Bob does not know anything about the state of his system B—Exercise 4.7.6 states that his local density operator is the maximally mixed state π_B just after Alice performs the measurement. Thus, there is no teleportation of quantum information at this point because Bob's local state is completely independent of the original state $|\psi\rangle$. In other words, teleportation cannot be instantaneous.

2. Alice transmits two classical bits to Bob that indicate which of the four measurement outcomes occurred. After Bob receives the classical information, he is immediately certain which operation he needs to perform in order to restore his state to Alice's original state $|\psi\rangle$. Notice that he does not need to have knowledge of the state in order to restore it—he only needs knowledge of the restoration operation.

3. Bob performs the restoration operation: one of the identity, a Pauli X operator, a Pauli Z operator, or the Pauli operator ZX, depending on the classical information that he receives from Alice.

Teleportation is an *oblivious* protocol because Alice and Bob do not require any knowledge of the quantum state being teleported in order to perform it. We might also say that this feature of teleportation makes it universal—it works independently of the input state.

You might think that the teleportation protocol violates the no-cloning theorem because a "copy" of the state appears on Bob's system. But this violation does not occur at any point in the protocol because the Bell measurement destroys the information about the state of Alice's original information qubit while recreating it somewhere else. Also, notice that the result of the Bell measurement is independent of the particular probability amplitudes α and β corresponding to the state Alice wishes to teleport.

The teleportation protocol is not an instantaneous teleportation, as portrayed in the television episodes of *Star Trek*. There is no transfer of quantum information instantaneously after the Bell measurement because Bob's local description of the B system is the maximally mixed state π. It is only after he receives the classical bits to "telecorrect" his state that the transfer occurs. It must be this way—otherwise, they would be able to communicate faster than the speed of light, and superluminal communication is not allowed by the theory of relativity.

Finally, we can phrase the teleportation protocol as a resource inequality:

$$[qq] + 2[c \to c] \geq [q \to q]. \tag{6.39}$$

Again, we include only non-local resources in the resource count. The above resource inequality is perhaps the most surprising of the three unit protocols we have studied so far. It combines two resources, noiseless entanglement and noiseless classical communication, that achieve noiseless quantum communication even though they are both individually weaker than it. This protocol and super-dense coding are two of the most fundamental protocols in quantum communication theory because they sparked the notion that there are clever ways of combining resources to generate other resources.

In Exercise 6.2.3 below, we discuss a variation of teleportation called *remote state preparation*, where Alice possesses a classical description of the state that she wishes to teleport. With this knowledge, it is possible to reduce the amount of classical communication necessary for teleportation.

EXERCISE 6.2.3   *Remote state preparation* is a variation of the teleportation protocol. We consider a simple example of a remote state preparation protocol. Suppose Alice possesses a classical description of a state $|\psi\rangle \equiv (|0\rangle + e^{i\phi}|1\rangle) / \sqrt{2}$ (on the equator of the Bloch sphere) and she shares an ebit $|\Phi^+\rangle_{AB}$ with Bob. Alice would like to prepare the state $|\psi\rangle$ on Bob's system. Show that Alice can prepare this state on Bob's system if she measures her system A in the $\{|\psi^*\rangle, |\psi^{\perp*}\rangle\}$ basis, transmits one classical bit, and Bob performs a recovery operation conditioned on the classical information. (Note that $|\psi^*\rangle$ is the conjugate of the vector $|\psi\rangle$).

EXERCISE 6.2.4   *Third-party controlled teleportation* is another variation on the teleportation protocol. Suppose that Alice, Bob, and Charlie possess a GHZ state:

$$|\Phi_{\text{GHZ}}\rangle \equiv \frac{|000\rangle_{ABC} + |111\rangle_{ABC}}{\sqrt{2}}. \tag{6.40}$$

Alice would like to teleport an arbitrary qubit to Bob. She performs the usual steps in the teleportation protocol. Give the final steps that Charlie should perform and the information that he should transmit to Bob in order to complete the teleportation protocol. (Hint: The resource inequality for the protocol is as follows:

$$[qqq]_{ABC} + 2\,[c \to c]_{A \to B} + [c \to c]_{C \to B} \geq [q \to q]_{A \to B}, \tag{6.41}$$

where $[qqq]_{ABC}$ represents the resource of the GHZ state shared between Alice, Bob, and Charlie, and the other resources are as before with the directionality of communication indicated by the corresponding subscript.)

EXERCISE 6.2.5   *Gate teleportation* is yet another variation of quantum teleportation that is useful in fault-tolerant quantum computation. Suppose that Alice would like to perform a single-qubit gate U on a qubit in state $|\psi\rangle$. Suppose that the gate U is difficult to perform, but that $U\sigma_i U^\dagger$, where σ_i is one of the single-qubit Pauli operators, is much less difficult to perform. A protocol for gate teleportation is as follows. Alice and Bob first prepare the ebit $U_B |\Phi^+\rangle_{AB}$. Alice performs a Bell measurement on her qubit $|\psi\rangle_{A'}$ and system A. She transmits two classical bits to Bob and Bob performs one of the four corrective operations

$U\sigma_i U^\dagger$ on his qubit. Show that this protocol works, i.e., that Bob's final state is $U|\psi\rangle$.

EXERCISE 6.2.6 Show that it is possible to simulate a dephasing qubit channel by the following technique. First, Alice prepares a maximally entangled Bell state $|\Phi^+\rangle$. She sends one share of it to Bob through a dephasing qubit channel. She and Bob perform the usual teleportation protocol. Show that this procedure gives the same result as sending a qubit through a dephasing channel. (Hint: This result holds because the dephasing channel commutes with all Pauli operators.)

EXERCISE 6.2.7 Construct an *entanglement swapping protocol* from the teleportation protocol. That is, suppose that Charlie and Alice possess a bipartite state $|\psi\rangle_{CA}$. Show that if Alice teleports her share of the state $|\psi\rangle_{CA}$ to Bob, then Charlie and Bob share the state $|\psi\rangle_{CB}$. A special case of this protocol is when the state $|\psi\rangle_{CA}$ is an ebit. Then the protocol is equivalent to an entanglement swapping protocol.

6.3 Optimality of the Three Unit Protocols

We now consider several arguments that may seem somewhat trivial at first, but they are crucial for having a good theory of quantum communication. We are always thinking about the optimality of certain protocols—if there is a better, cheaper way to perform a given protocol, then this would be advantageous. There are several questions that we can ask about the above protocols:

1. In entanglement distribution, is one ebit per qubit the best that we can do, or is it possible to generate more than one ebit with a single use of a noiseless qubit channel?
2. In super-dense coding, is it possible to generate two noiseless classical bit channels with less than one noiseless qubit channel or less than one noiseless ebit? Is it possible to generate more than two classical bit channels using the given resources?
3. In teleportation, is it possible to teleport more than one qubit using the given resources? Is it possible to teleport using less than two classical bits or less than one ebit?

In this section, we answer all of these questions in the negative—all the protocols as given are optimal protocols. Here, we begin to see the beauty of the resource inequality formalism. It allows us to chain protocols together to make new protocols. We exploit this idea in the forthcoming optimality arguments.

First, let us tackle the optimality of entanglement distribution. Is there a protocol that implements any other resource inequality such as

$$[q \to q] \geq E\,[qq]\,, \tag{6.42}$$

where the rate E of entanglement generation is greater than one?

We show that such a resource inequality can never occur, i.e., it is optimal for $E = 1$. Suppose such a resource inequality with $E > 1$ does exist. Under an assumption of free forward classical communication, we can combine the above resource inequality with teleportation to achieve the following resource inequality:

$$[q \to q] \geq E[q \to q]. \tag{6.43}$$

We could then simply keep repeating this protocol to achieve an unbounded amount of quantum communication, which is impossible. Thus, it must be that $E = 1$.

Next, we consider the optimality of super-dense coding. We again exploit a proof by contradiction argument. Let us suppose that we have an unlimited amount of entanglement available. Suppose that there exists some "super-duper"-dense coding protocol that generates an amount of classical communication greater than that which super-dense coding generates. That is, the classical communication output of super-duper-dense coding is $2C$ where $C > 1$, and its resource inequality is

$$[q \to q] + [qq] \geq 2C[c \to c]. \tag{6.44}$$

Then this super-duper-dense coding scheme (along with the infinite entanglement) gives the following resource inequality:

$$[q \to q] + \infty[qq] \geq 2C[c \to c] + \infty[qq]. \tag{6.45}$$

An infinite amount of entanglement is still available after executing the super-duper-dense coding protocol because it consumes only a finite amount of entanglement. We can then chain the above protocol with teleportation and achieve the following resource inequality:

$$2C[c \to c] + \infty[qq] \geq C[q \to q] + \infty[qq]. \tag{6.46}$$

Overall, we have then shown a scheme that achieves the following resource inequality:

$$[q \to q] + \infty[qq] \geq C[q \to q] + \infty[qq]. \tag{6.47}$$

We can continue with this protocol and perform it k times so that we implement the following resource inequality:

$$[q \to q] + \infty[qq] \geq C^k[q \to q] + \infty[qq]. \tag{6.48}$$

The result of this construction is that one noiseless qubit channel and an infinite amount of entanglement can generate an infinite amount of quantum communication. This result is impossible physically because entanglement does not boost the capacity of a noiseless qubit channel. Also, the scheme is exploiting just one noiseless qubit channel along with the entanglement to generate an unbounded amount of quantum communication—it must be signaling superluminally in order to do so. Thus, the rate of classical communication in super-dense coding is optimal.

We leave the optimality arguments for teleportation as an exercise because they are similar to those for the super-dense coding protocol. Note that it is possible to prove the optimality of these protocols without assumptions such as free classical communication (for the case of entanglement distribution), and we do so in Chapter 8.

EXERCISE 6.3.1 Show that it is impossible for $C > 1$ in the teleportation protocol where C is with respect to the following resource inequality:

$$2\,[c \to c] + [qq] \geq C\,[q \to q]\,. \tag{6.49}$$

EXERCISE 6.3.2 Show that the rates of the consumed resources in the teleportation and super-dense coding protocols are optimal.

6.4 Extensions for Quantum Shannon Theory

The previous section sparked some good questions that we might ask as a quantum Shannon theorist. We might also wonder what types of communication rates are possible if some of the consumed resources are noisy, rather than being perfect resources. We list some of these questions below.

Let us first consider entanglement distribution. Suppose that the consumed noiseless qubit channel in entanglement distribution is instead a noisy quantum channel $\mathcal{N}$. The communication task is then known as *entanglement generation*. We can rephrase the communication task as the following resource inequality:

$$\langle \mathcal{N} \rangle \geq E\,[qq]\,. \tag{6.50}$$

The meaning of the resource inequality is that we consume the resource of a noisy quantum channel $\mathcal{N}$ in order to generate entanglement between a sender and receiver at some rate E. We will make the definition of a quantum Shannon-theoretic resource inequality more precise when we begin our formal study of quantum Shannon theory, but the above definition should be sufficient for now. The optimal rate of entanglement generation with the noisy quantum channel $\mathcal{N}$ is known as the entanglement generation capacity of $\mathcal{N}$. This task is intimately related to the quantum communication capacity of $\mathcal{N}$, and we discuss the connection further in Chapter 24.

Let us now turn to super-dense coding. Suppose that the consumed noiseless qubit channel in super-dense coding is instead a noisy quantum channel $\mathcal{N}$. The name for this task is then *entanglement-assisted classical communication*. The following resource inequality captures the corresponding communication task:

$$\langle \mathcal{N} \rangle + E\,[qq] \geq C\,[c \to c]\,. \tag{6.51}$$

The meaning of the resource inequality is that we consume a noisy quantum channel $\mathcal{N}$ and noiseless entanglement at some rate E to produce noiseless classical communication at some rate C. We will study this protocol in depth in

Chapter 21. We can also consider the scenario in which the entanglement is no longer noiseless, but it is rather a general bipartite state ρ_{AB} that Alice and Bob share. The task is then known as noisy super-dense coding.[1] We study noisy super-dense coding in Chapter 22. The corresponding resource inequality is as follows (its meaning should be clear at this point):

$$\langle \rho_{AB} \rangle + Q\,[q \to q] \geq C\,[c \to c]. \tag{6.52}$$

We can ask the same questions for the teleportation protocol as well. Suppose that the entanglement resource is instead a noisy bipartite state ρ_{AB}. The task is then *noisy teleportation* and has the following resource inequality:

$$\langle \rho_{AB} \rangle + C\,[c \to c] \geq Q\,[q \to q]. \tag{6.53}$$

The questions presented in this section are some of the fundamental questions in quantum Shannon theory. We arrived at these questions simply by replacing the noiseless resources in the three fundamental noiseless protocols with noisy ones. We will spend a significant amount of effort building up our knowledge of quantum Shannon-theoretic tools that will be indispensable for answering these questions.

6.5   Three Unit Qudit Protocols

We end this chapter by studying the qudit versions of the three unit protocols. It is useful to have these versions of the protocols because we may want to process qudit systems with them.

The qudit resources are straightforward extensions of the qubit resources. A noiseless qudit channel is the following map:

$$|i\rangle_A \to |i\rangle_B, \tag{6.54}$$

where $\{|i\rangle_A\}_{i \in \{0,\dots,d-1\}}$ is some preferred orthonormal basis on Alice's system and $\{|i\rangle_B\}_{i \in \{0,\dots,d-1\}}$ is some preferred basis on Bob's system. We can also write the qudit channel map as the following isometry:

$$I_{A \to B} \equiv \sum_{i=0}^{d-1} |i\rangle_B \langle i|_A. \tag{6.55}$$

The map $I_{A \to B}$ preserves superposition states so that

$$\sum_{i=0}^{d-1} \alpha_i |i\rangle_A \to \sum_{i=0}^{d-1} \alpha_i |i\rangle_B. \tag{6.56}$$

---

[1] The name noisy super-dense coding could just as well apply to the former task of entanglement-assisted classical communication, but this terminology has "stuck" in the research literature for this specific quantum information-processing task.

A noiseless classical dit channel or *cdit* is the following map:

$$|i\rangle\langle i|_A \rightarrow |i\rangle\langle i|_B, \tag{6.57}$$

$$|i\rangle\langle j|_A \rightarrow 0 \text{ for } i \neq j. \tag{6.58}$$

A noiseless maximally entangled qudit state or an *edit* is as follows:

$$|\Phi\rangle_{AB} \equiv \frac{1}{\sqrt{d}} \sum_{i=0}^{d-1} |i\rangle_A |i\rangle_B. \tag{6.59}$$

We quantify the "dit" resources with bit measures. For example, a noiseless qudit channel is the following resource:

$$\log d \, [q \rightarrow q], \tag{6.60}$$

where the logarithm is base two. Thus, one qudit channel can transmit $\log d$ qubits of quantum information so that the qubit remains our standard unit of quantum information. We quantify the amount of information transmitted according to the dimension of the space that is transmitted. For example, suppose that a quantum system has eight levels. We can then encode three qubits of quantum information in this eight-level system.

Likewise, a classical dit channel is the following resource:

$$\log d \, [c \rightarrow c], \tag{6.61}$$

so that a classical dit channel transmits $\log d$ classical bits. The parameter d here is the number of classical messages that the channel transmits.

Finally, an edit is the following resource:

$$\log d \, [qq]. \tag{6.62}$$

We quantify the amount of entanglement in a maximally entangled state by its Schmidt rank (see Theorem 3.8.1). We measure entanglement in units of ebits (we return to this issue in Chapter 19).

6.5.1   Entanglement Distribution

The extension of the entanglement distribution protocol to the qudit case is straightforward. Alice merely prepares the state $|\Phi\rangle_{AA'}$ in her laboratory and transmits the system A' through a noiseless qudit channel. She can prepare the state $|\Phi\rangle_{AA'}$ with two gates: the qudit analog of the Hadamard gate and the CNOT gate. The qudit analog of the Hadamard gate is the Fourier gate F introduced in Exercise 3.7.8 where

$$F : |l\rangle \rightarrow \frac{1}{\sqrt{d}} \sum_{j=0}^{d-1} \exp\left\{\frac{2\pi i l j}{d}\right\} |j\rangle, \tag{6.63}$$

so that

$$F \equiv \frac{1}{\sqrt{d}} \sum_{l,j=0}^{d-1} \exp\left\{\frac{2\pi i l j}{d}\right\} |j\rangle\langle l|. \tag{6.64}$$

The qudit analog of the CNOT gate is the following controlled-shift gate:

$$\text{CNOT}_d \equiv \sum_{j=0}^{d-1} |j\rangle\langle j| \otimes X(j), \tag{6.65}$$

where $X(j)$ is the shift operator defined in (3.208).

EXERCISE 6.5.1   Verify that Alice can prepare the maximally entangled qudit state $|\Phi\rangle_{AA'}$ locally by preparing $|0\rangle_A|0\rangle_{A'}$, applying F_A and CNOT_d. Show that

$$|\Phi\rangle_{AA'} = \text{CNOT}_d \cdot F_A |0\rangle_A |0\rangle_{A'}. \tag{6.66}$$

The resource inequality for this qudit entanglement distribution protocol is as follows:

$$\log d\,[q \to q] \geq \log d\,[qq]. \tag{6.67}$$

6.5.2   Quantum Super-Dense Coding

The qudit version of the super-dense coding protocol proceeds analogously to the qudit case, with some notable exceptions. It still consists of three steps:

1. Alice and Bob begin with a maximally entangled state of the form in (6.59). Alice applies one of d^2 unitary operations in the set $\{X(x)Z(z)\}_{x,z=0}^{d-1}$ to her qudit. The shared state then becomes one of the d^2 maximally entangled qudit states in (3.234).
2. She sends her qudit to Bob with one use of a noiseless qudit channel.
3. Bob performs a measurement in the qudit Bell basis to determine the message Alice sent. The result of Exercise 3.7.11 is that these states are perfectly distinguishable with a measurement.

This qudit super-dense coding protocol realizes the following resource inequality:

$$\log d\,[qq] + \log d\,[q \to q] \geq 2\log d\,[c \to c]. \tag{6.68}$$

6.5.3   Quantum Teleportation

The operations in the qudit teleportation protocol are again similar to the qubit case. The protocol proceeds in three steps:

1. Alice possesses an arbitrary qudit $|\psi\rangle_{A'}$ where

$$|\psi\rangle_{A'} \equiv \sum_{i=0}^{d-1} \alpha_i |i\rangle_{A'}. \tag{6.69}$$

Alice and Bob share a maximally entangled qudit state $|\Phi\rangle_{AB}$ of the form in (6.59). The joint state of Alice and Bob is then $|\psi\rangle_{A'} |\Phi\rangle_{AB}$. Alice performs a measurement in the basis $\{|\Phi_{i,j}\rangle_{A'A}\}_{i,j}$.

2. She transmits the measurement result (i, j) to Bob with the use of two classical dit channels.

3. Bob then applies the unitary transformation $Z_B(j)X_B(i)$ to his state to "telecorrect" it to Alice's original qudit.

We prove that this protocol works by analyzing the probability of the measurement result and the post-measurement state on Bob's system. The techniques that we employ here are different from those for the qubit case.

First, let us suppose that Alice would like to teleport the A' system of a state $|\psi\rangle_{RA'}$ that she shares with an inaccessible reference system R. This way, our teleportation protocol encompasses the most general setting in which Alice would like to teleport a mixed state on A'. Also, Alice shares the maximally entangled edit state $|\Phi\rangle_{AB}$ with Bob. Alice first performs a measurement of the systems A' and A in the basis $\{|\Phi_{i,j}\rangle_{A'A}\}_{i,j}$ where

$$|\Phi_{i,j}\rangle_{A'A} = U_{A'}^{ij} |\Phi\rangle_{A'A}, \tag{6.70}$$

and

$$U_{A'}^{ij} \equiv Z_{A'}(j)X_{A'}(i). \tag{6.71}$$

The measurement operators are thus

$$|\Phi_{i,j}\rangle\langle\Phi_{i,j}|_{A'A}. \tag{6.72}$$

Then the unnormalized post-measurement state is

$$|\Phi_{i,j}\rangle\langle\Phi_{i,j}|_{A'A} |\psi\rangle_{RA'} |\Phi\rangle_{AB}, \tag{6.73}$$

where here and in what follows, we have taken the common practice of omitting tensor products with identity operators, instead leaving them implicit in order to reduce clutter in the notation. We can rewrite this state as follows, by exploiting the definition of $|\Phi_{i,j}\rangle_{A'A}$ in (6.70):

$$|\Phi_{i,j}\rangle\langle\Phi|_{A'A} \left(U_{A'}^{ij}\right)^{\dagger} |\psi\rangle_{RA'} |\Phi\rangle_{AB}. \tag{6.74}$$

Recall the "transpose trick" from Exercise 3.7.12 that holds for any maximally entangled state $|\Phi\rangle$. We can exploit this result to show that the action of the unitary $\left(U^{ij}\right)^{\dagger}$ on the A' system is the same as the action of the unitary $\left(U^{ij}\right)^{*}$ on the A system:

$$|\Phi_{i,j}\rangle\langle\Phi|_{A'A} \left(U_A^{ij}\right)^{*} |\psi\rangle_{RA'} |\Phi\rangle_{AB}. \tag{6.75}$$

Then the unitary $\left(U_A^{ij}\right)^{*}$ commutes with the systems R and A':

$$|\Phi_{i,j}\rangle\langle\Phi|_{A'A} |\psi\rangle_{RA'} \left(U_A^{ij}\right)^{*} |\Phi\rangle_{AB}. \tag{6.76}$$

We can again apply the transpose trick from Exercise 3.7.12 to show that the state is equal to

$$|\Phi_{i,j}\rangle\langle\Phi|_{A'A}\,|\psi\rangle_{RA'}\,\left(U_B^{ij}\right)^\dagger|\Phi\rangle_{AB}\,. \tag{6.77}$$

Then we can commute the unitary $\left(U_B^{ij}\right)^\dagger$ all the way to the left, and we can switch the order of $|\psi\rangle_{RA'}$ and $|\Phi\rangle_{AB}$ without any problem because the system labels are sufficient to track the states in these systems:

$$\left(U_B^{ij}\right)^\dagger|\Phi_{i,j}\rangle\langle\Phi|_{A'A}\,|\Phi\rangle_{AB}\,|\psi\rangle_{RA'}. \tag{6.78}$$

Now let us consider the very special overlap $\langle\Phi|_{A'A}\,|\Phi\rangle_{AB}$ of the maximally entangled edit state with itself on different systems:

$$\langle\Phi|_{A'A}\,|\Phi\rangle_{AB} = \left(\frac{1}{\sqrt{d}}\sum_{i=0}^{d-1}\langle i|_{A'}\langle i|_A\right)\left(\frac{1}{\sqrt{d}}\sum_{j=0}^{d-1}|j\rangle_A|j\rangle_B\right) \tag{6.79}$$

$$= \frac{1}{d}\sum_{i,j=0}^{d-1}\langle i|_{A'}\langle i|_A|j\rangle_A|j\rangle_B = \frac{1}{d}\sum_{i,j=0}^{d-1}\langle i|_{A'}\,\langle i|j\rangle_A\,|j\rangle_B \tag{6.80}$$

$$= \frac{1}{d}\sum_{i=0}^{d-1}\langle i|_{A'}|i\rangle_B = \frac{1}{d}\sum_{i=0}^{d-1}|i\rangle_B\langle i|_{A'} \tag{6.81}$$

$$= \frac{1}{d}I_{A'\to B}. \tag{6.82}$$

The first equality follows by definition. The second equality follows from linearity and rearranging terms in the multiplication and summation. The third and fourth equalities follow by realizing that $\langle i|_A|j\rangle_A$ is an inner product and evaluating it for the orthonormal basis $\{|i\rangle_A\}$. The fifth equality follows by rearranging the bra and the ket. The final equality is our last important realization: the operator $\sum_{i=0}^{d-1}|i\rangle_B\langle i|_{A'}$ is the noiseless qudit channel $I_{A'\to B}$ that the teleportation protocol creates from the system A' to B (see the definition of a noiseless qudit channel in (6.55)). We might refer to this as the "teleportation map."

We now apply the teleportation map to the state in (6.78):

$$\left(U_B^{ij}\right)^\dagger|\Phi_{i,j}\rangle\langle\Phi|_{A'A}\,|\Phi\rangle_{AB}\,|\psi\rangle_{RA'} = \left(U_B^{ij}\right)^\dagger|\Phi_{i,j}\rangle_{A'A}\frac{1}{d}I_{A'\to B}\,|\psi\rangle_{RA'} \tag{6.83}$$

$$= \frac{1}{d}\left(U_B^{ij}\right)^\dagger|\Phi_{i,j}\rangle_{A'A}|\psi\rangle_{RB} \tag{6.84}$$

$$= \frac{1}{d}|\Phi_{i,j}\rangle_{A'A}\left(U_B^{ij}\right)^\dagger|\psi\rangle_{RB}. \tag{6.85}$$

We can compute the probability of receiving outcome i and j from the measurement when the input state is $|\psi\rangle_{RA'}$. It is just equal to the overlap of the above vector with itself:

$$p(i,j|\psi) = \left[\frac{1}{d}\langle\Phi_{i,j}|_{A'A}\,\langle\psi|_{RB}U_B^{ij}\right]\left[\frac{1}{d}|\Phi_{i,j}\rangle_{A'A}\left(U_B^{ij}\right)^\dagger|\psi\rangle_{RB}\right] \tag{6.86}$$

$$= \frac{1}{d^2} \langle \Phi_{i,j} |_{A'A} | \Phi_{i,j} \rangle_{A'A} \ \langle \psi |_{RB} U_B^{ij} \left(U_B^{ij} \right)^\dagger | \psi \rangle_{RB} \tag{6.87}$$

$$= \frac{1}{d^2} \langle \Phi_{i,j} |_{A'A} | \Phi_{i,j} \rangle_{A'A} \ \langle \psi |_{RB} | \psi \rangle_{RB} = \frac{1}{d^2}. \tag{6.88}$$

Thus, the probability of the outcome (i, j) is completely random and independent of the input state. We would expect this to be the case for a universal teleportation protocol that operates independently of the input state. Thus, after normalization, the state on Alice and Bob's system is

$$| \Phi_{i,j} \rangle_{A'A} \left(U_B^{ij} \right)^\dagger | \psi \rangle_{RB}. \tag{6.89}$$

At this point, Bob does not know the result of the measurement. We obtain his density operator by tracing over the systems A', A, and R to which he does not have access and taking the expectation over all the measurement outcomes:

$$\mathrm{Tr}_{A'AR} \left\{ \frac{1}{d^2} \sum_{i,j=0}^{d-1} | \Phi_{i,j} \rangle \langle \Phi_{i,j} |_{A'A} \left(U_B^{ij} \right)^\dagger | \psi \rangle \langle \psi |_{RB} U_B^{ij} \right\}$$

$$= \frac{1}{d^2} \sum_{i,j=0}^{d-1} \left(U_B^{ij} \right)^\dagger \psi_B U_B^{ij} = \pi_B. \tag{6.90}$$

The first equality follows by evaluating the partial trace and by defining $\psi_B \equiv \mathrm{Tr}_R \{ | \psi \rangle \langle \psi |_{RB} \}$. The second equality follows because applying a Heisenberg–Weyl operator uniformly at random completely randomizes a quantum state to be the maximally mixed state (see Exercise 4.7.6).

Now suppose that Alice sends the measurement results i and j over two uses of a noiseless classical dit channel. Bob then knows that the state is

$$\left(U_B^{ij} \right)^\dagger | \psi \rangle_{RB}, \tag{6.91}$$

and he can apply U_B^{ij} to make the overall state become $| \psi \rangle_{RB}$. This final step completes the teleportation process. The resource inequality for the qudit teleportation protocol is as follows:

$$\log d \, [qq] + 2 \log d \, [c \to c] \geq \log d \, [q \to q]. \tag{6.92}$$

6.6 History and Further Reading

This chapter presented the three important protocols that exploit the three unit resources of classical communication, quantum communication, and entanglement. We learned, perhaps surprisingly, that it is possible to combine two resources together in interesting ways to simulate a different resource (in both super-dense coding and teleportation). These combinations of resources turn up quite a bit in quantum Shannon theory, and we see them in their most basic form in this chapter.

Bennett & Wiesner (1992) published the super-dense coding protocol, and within a year, Bennett et al. (1993) realized that Alice and Bob could teleport particles if they swap their operations with respect to the super-dense coding protocol. These two protocols were the seeds of much later work in quantum Shannon theory.

7 Coherent Protocols

We introduced three protocols in the previous chapter: entanglement distribution, teleportation, and super-dense coding. The last two of these protocols, teleportation and super-dense coding, are perhaps more interesting than entanglement distribution because they demonstrate insightful ways for combining all three unit resources to achieve an information-processing task.

It appears that teleportation and super-dense coding might be "inverse" protocols with respect to each other because teleportation arises from super-dense coding when Alice and Bob "swap their equipment." But there is a fundamental asymmetry between these protocols when we consider their respective resource inequalities. Recall that the resource inequality for teleportation is

$$2 [c \rightarrow c] + [qq] \geq [q \rightarrow q], \tag{7.1}$$

while that for super-dense coding is

$$[q \rightarrow q] + [qq] \geq 2 [c \rightarrow c]. \tag{7.2}$$

The asymmetry in these protocols is that they are not *dual under resource reversal*. Two protocols are dual under resource reversal if the resources that one consumes are the same that the other generates and vice versa. Consider that the super-dense coding resource inequality in (7.2) generates two classical bit channels. Glancing at the left-hand side of the teleportation resource inequality in (7.1), we see that two classical bit channels generated from super-dense coding are not sufficient to generate the noiseless qubit channel on the right-hand side of (7.1)—the protocol requires the consumption of noiseless entanglement in addition to the consumption of the two noiseless classical bit channels.

Is there a way for teleportation and super-dense coding to become dual under resource reversal? One way is if we assume that *entanglement is a free resource*. This assumption is strong and we may have difficulty justifying it from a practical standpoint because noiseless entanglement is extremely fragile. It is also a powerful resource, as the teleportation and super-dense coding protocols demonstrate. But in the theory of quantum communication, we often make assumptions such as this one—such assumptions tend to give a dramatic simplification of a problem. Continuing with our development, let us assume that entanglement is a free resource and that we do not have to factor it into the resource count. Under this assumption, the resource inequality for teleportation becomes

$$2\,[c \to c] \geq [q \to q]\,, \tag{7.3}$$

and that for super-dense coding becomes

$$[q \to q] \geq 2\,[c \to c]\,. \tag{7.4}$$

Teleportation and super-dense coding are then dual under resource reversal under the "free-entanglement" assumption, and we obtain the following *resource equality*:

$$[q \to q] = 2\,[c \to c]\,. \tag{7.5}$$

EXERCISE 7.0.1   Suppose that the quantum capacity of a quantum channel assisted by an unlimited amount of entanglement is equal to some number Q. What is the capacity of that entanglement-assisted channel for transmitting classical information?

EXERCISE 7.0.2   How can we obtain the following resource equality? (Hint: Assume that some resource is free.)

$$[q \to q] = [qq]\,. \tag{7.6}$$

Which noiseless protocols did you use to show the above resource equality? The above resource equality is a powerful statement: entanglement and quantum communication are equivalent under the assumption that you have found.

EXERCISE 7.0.3   Suppose that the entanglement generation capacity of a quantum channel is equal to some number E. What is the quantum capacity of that channel when assisted by free, forward classical communication?

The above assumptions are useful for finding simple ways to make protocols dual under resource reversal, and we will exploit them later in our proofs of various capacity theorems in quantum Shannon theory. But it turns out that there is a more clever way to make teleportation and super-dense coding dual under resource reversal. In this chapter, we introduce a new resource—the *noiseless coherent bit channel*. This resource produces "coherent" versions of the teleportation and super-dense coding protocols that are dual under resource reversal. The payoff of this coherent communication technique is that we can exploit it to simplify the proofs of various coding theorems of quantum Shannon theory. It also leads to a deeper understanding of the relationship between the teleportation and super-dense coding protocols from the previous chapter.

7.1   Definition of Coherent Communication

We begin by introducing the coherent bit channel as a classical channel that has "quantum feedback" (in a particular sense). Recall from Exercise 6.1.1 that a classical bit channel is equivalent to a dephasing channel that dephases in the computational basis with dephasing parameter $p = 1/2$. The CPTP map corresponding to this completely dephasing channel is as follows:

$$\mathcal{N}(\rho) = \frac{1}{2}(\rho + Z\rho Z). \tag{7.7}$$

An isometric extension $U^{\mathcal{N}}_{A \to BE}$ of the above channel then follows by applying (5.36):

$$U^{\mathcal{N}}_{A \to BE} = \frac{1}{\sqrt{2}}(I_{A \to B} \otimes |+\rangle_E + Z_{A \to B} \otimes |-\rangle_E), \tag{7.8}$$

where we choose the orthonormal basis states of the environment E to be $|+\rangle$ and $|-\rangle$ (recall that we have unitary freedom in the choice of the basis states for the environment). It is straightforward to show that the isometry $U^{\mathcal{N}}_{A \to BE}$ is as follows by expanding the operators I and Z and the states $|+\rangle$ and $|-\rangle$:

$$U^{\mathcal{N}}_{A \to BE} = |0\rangle_B \langle 0|_A \otimes |0\rangle_E + |1\rangle_B \langle 1|_A \otimes |1\rangle_E. \tag{7.9}$$

Thus, a classical bit channel is equivalent to the following map, with its action extended by linearity:

$$|i\rangle_A \to |i\rangle_B |i\rangle_E : i \in \{0, 1\}. \tag{7.10}$$

A coherent bit channel is similar to the above classical bit channel map, with the exception that we assume that Alice somehow regains control of the environment of the channel:

$$|i\rangle_A \to |i\rangle_B |i\rangle_A : i \in \{0, 1\}. \tag{7.11}$$

"Coherence" in this context is also synonymous with linearity—the maintenance and linear transformation of superposed states. The coherent bit channel is similar to classical copying because it copies the basis states while maintaining coherent superpositions. We denote the resource of a coherent bit channel as follows:

$$[q \to qq]. \tag{7.12}$$

Figure 7.1 provides a visual depiction of the coherent bit channel.

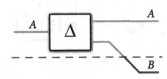

Figure 7.1 This figure depicts the operation of a coherent bit channel. It is the "coherification" of a classical bit channel in which the sender A has access to the environment's output.

EXERCISE 7.1.1   Show that the following resource inequality holds:

$$[q \to qq] \geq [c \to c].\qquad(7.13)$$

That is, devise a protocol that generates a noiseless classical bit channel with one use of a noiseless coherent bit channel.

7.2   Implementations of a Coherent Bit Channel

How might we actually implement a coherent bit channel? The simplest way to do so is with the aid of a local CNOT gate and a noiseless qubit channel. The protocol proceeds as follows (Figure 7.2 illustrates the protocol):

1. Alice possesses an information qubit in the state $|\psi\rangle_A \equiv \alpha|0\rangle_A + \beta|1\rangle_A$. She prepares an ancilla qubit in the state $|0\rangle_{A'}$.
2. Alice performs a local CNOT gate from qubit A to qubit A'. The resulting state is

$$\alpha|0\rangle_A|0\rangle_{A'} + \beta|1\rangle_A|1\rangle_{A'}.\qquad(7.14)$$

3. Alice transmits qubit A' to Bob with one use of a noiseless qubit channel $\mathrm{id}_{A'\to B}$. The resulting state is

$$\alpha|0\rangle_A|0\rangle_B + \beta|1\rangle_A|1\rangle_B,\qquad(7.15)$$

and it is now clear that Alice and Bob have implemented a noiseless coherent bit channel as defined in (7.11).

The above protocol realizes the following resource inequality:

$$[q \to q] \geq [q \to qq],\qquad(7.16)$$

demonstrating that quantum communication generates coherent communication.

EXERCISE 7.2.1   Show that the following resource inequality holds:

$$[q \to qq] \geq [qq].\qquad(7.17)$$

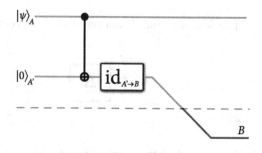

Figure 7.2 A simple protocol to implement a noiseless coherent channel with one use of a noiseless qubit channel.

That is, devise a protocol that generates a noiseless ebit with one use of a noiseless coherent bit channel.

EXERCISE 7.2.2   Show that the following two resource inequalities cannot hold:

$$[q \to qq] \geq [q \to q], \tag{7.18}$$

$$[qq] \geq [q \to qq]. \tag{7.19}$$

We now have the following chain of resource inequalities:

$$[q \to q] \geq [q \to qq] \geq [qq]. \tag{7.20}$$

Thus, the power of the coherent bit channel lies in-between that of a noiseless qubit channel and a noiseless ebit.

EXERCISE 7.2.3   Another way to implement a noiseless coherent bit channel is with a variation of teleportation that we name "coherent communication assisted by entanglement and classical communication." Suppose that Alice and Bob share an ebit $|\Phi^+\rangle_{AB}$. Alice can append an ancilla qubit $|0\rangle_{A'}$ to this state and perform a local CNOT from A to A' to give the following state:

$$|\Phi_{\text{GHZ}}\rangle_{AA'B} = \frac{1}{\sqrt{2}} \left(|000\rangle_{AA'B} + |111\rangle_{AA'B} \right). \tag{7.21}$$

Alice prepends an information qubit $|\psi\rangle_{A_1} \equiv \alpha|0\rangle_{A_1} + \beta|1\rangle_{A_1}$ to the above state so that the global state is as follows:

$$|\psi\rangle_{A_1} |\Phi_{\text{GHZ}}\rangle_{AA'B}. \tag{7.22}$$

Suppose Alice performs the usual teleportation operations on systems A_1, A, and A'. Give the steps that Alice and Bob should perform in order to generate the state $\alpha|0\rangle_{A'}|0\rangle_B + \beta|1\rangle_{A'}|1\rangle_B$, thus implementing a noiseless coherent bit channel. Hint: The resource inequality for this protocol is as follows:

$$[qq] + [c \to c] \geq [q \to qq]. \tag{7.23}$$

This should be compared with the teleportation protocol, which corresponds to $[qq] + 2[c \to c] \geq [q \to q]$.

EXERCISE 7.2.4   Determine a qudit version of coherent communication assisted by classical communication and entanglement by modifying the steps in the above protocol.

7.3   Coherent Dense Coding

In the previous section, we introduced two protocols that implement a noiseless coherent bit channel: the simple method in the previous section and coherent communication assisted by classical communication and entanglement (Exercise 7.2.3). We now introduce a different method for implementing two coherent

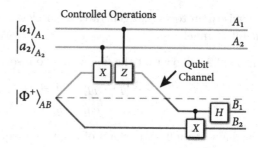

Figure 7.3 This figure depicts the protocol for coherent super-dense coding.

bit channels that makes more judicious use of available resources. We name it *coherent super-dense coding* because it is a coherent version of the super-dense coding protocol.

The protocol proceeds as follows (Figure 7.3 depicts the protocol):

1. Alice and Bob share one ebit in the state $|\Phi^+\rangle_{AB}$ before the protocol begins.
2. Alice first prepares two qubits A_1 and A_2 in the state $|a_1\rangle_{A_1}|a_2\rangle_{A_2}$ and prepends this state to the ebit. The global state is as follows:

$$|a_1\rangle_{A_1}|a_2\rangle_{A_2}|\Phi^+\rangle_{AB}, \qquad (7.24)$$

where a_1 and a_2 are binary-valued. This preparation step is reminiscent of the super-dense coding protocol (recall that, in the super-dense coding protocol, Alice has two classical bits she would like to communicate).

3. Alice performs a CNOT gate from register A_2 to register A and performs a controlled-Z gate from register A_1 to register A. The resulting state is as follows:

$$|a_1\rangle_{A_1}|a_2\rangle_{A_2} Z_A^{a_1} X_A^{a_2}|\Phi^+\rangle_{AB}. \qquad (7.25)$$

4. Alice transmits the qubit in register A to Bob. We rename this register as B_1 and Bob's other register B as B_2.
5. Bob performs a CNOT gate from his register B_1 to B_2 and performs a Hadamard gate on B_1. The final state is as follows:

$$|a_1\rangle_{A_1}|a_2\rangle_{A_2}|a_1\rangle_{B_1}|a_2\rangle_{B_2}. \qquad (7.26)$$

The above protocol implements two coherent bit channels: one from A_1 to B_1 and another from A_2 to B_2. You can check that the protocol works for arbitrary superpositions of two-qubit states on A_1 and A_2—it is for this reason that this protocol implements two coherent bit channels. The resource inequality corresponding to coherent super-dense coding is

$$[qq] + [q \to q] \geq 2[q \to qq]. \qquad (7.27)$$

EXERCISE 7.3.1 Construct a qudit version of coherent super-dense coding that implements the following resource inequality:

$$\log d \, [qq] + \log d \, [q \to q] \geq 2 \log d \, [q \to qq] \, . \tag{7.28}$$

(Hint: The qudit generalization of a controlled-NOT gate is $\sum_{i=0}^{d-1} |i\rangle\langle i| \otimes X(i)$, where X is defined in (3.208), of a controlled-Z gate is $\sum_{j=0}^{d-1} |j\rangle\langle j| \otimes Z(j)$, where Z is defined in (3.210), and of the Hadamard gate is the Fourier transform gate.)

7.4 Coherent Teleportation

We now introduce a coherent version of the teleportation protocol that we name *coherent teleportation*. Let a Z coherent bit channel Δ_Z be one that copies eigenstates of the Z operator (this is as we defined a coherent bit channel before). Let an X coherent bit channel Δ_X be one that copies eigenstates of the X operator:

$$\Delta_X : |+\rangle_A \to |+\rangle_A |+\rangle_B, \tag{7.29}$$

$$|-\rangle_A \to |-\rangle_A |-\rangle_B. \tag{7.30}$$

It does not really matter which basis we use to define a coherent bit channel—it just matters that it copies the orthogonal states of some basis.

EXERCISE 7.4.1 Show how to simulate an X coherent bit channel using a Z coherent bit channel and local operations.

The protocol proceeds as follows (Figure 7.4 depicts the protocol):

1. Alice possesses an information qubit $|\psi\rangle_A$ where

$$|\psi\rangle_A \equiv \alpha|0\rangle_A + \beta|1\rangle_A. \tag{7.31}$$

She sends her qubit through a Z coherent bit channel:

$$|\psi\rangle_A \quad \xrightarrow{\Delta_Z} \quad \alpha|0\rangle_A|0\rangle_{B_1} + \beta|1\rangle_A|1\rangle_{B_1} \equiv |\tilde{\psi}\rangle_{AB_1}. \tag{7.32}$$

Let us rewrite the above state $|\tilde{\psi}\rangle_{AB_1}$ as follows:

$$|\tilde{\psi}\rangle_{AB_1} = \alpha\left(\frac{|+\rangle_A + |-\rangle_A}{\sqrt{2}}\right)|0\rangle_{B_1} + \beta\left(\frac{|+\rangle_A - |-\rangle_A}{\sqrt{2}}\right)|1\rangle_{B_1} \tag{7.33}$$

$$= \frac{1}{\sqrt{2}}\left[|+\rangle_A \left(\alpha|0\rangle_{B_1} + \beta|1\rangle_{B_1}\right) + |-\rangle_A \left(\alpha|0\rangle_{B_1} - \beta|1\rangle_{B_1}\right)\right]. \tag{7.34}$$

2. Alice sends her qubit A through an X coherent bit channel with output systems A and B_2:

$$|\tilde{\psi}\rangle_{AB_1} \quad \xrightarrow{\Delta_X} \quad \frac{1}{\sqrt{2}}|+\rangle_A|+\rangle_{B_2} \left(\alpha|0\rangle_{B_1} + \beta|1\rangle_{B_1}\right)$$

$$+ \frac{1}{\sqrt{2}}|-\rangle_A|-\rangle_{B_2} \left(\alpha|0\rangle_{B_1} - \beta|1\rangle_{B_1}\right). \tag{7.35}$$

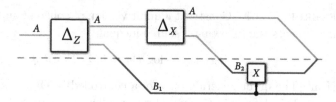

Figure 7.4 This figure depicts the protocol for coherent teleportation.

3. Bob then performs a CNOT gate from qubit B_1 to qubit B_2. Consider that the action of the CNOT gate with the source qubit in the computational basis and the target qubit in the $+/-$ basis is as follows:

$$|0\rangle|+\rangle \rightarrow |0\rangle|+\rangle, \qquad (7.36)$$

$$|0\rangle|-\rangle \rightarrow |0\rangle|-\rangle, \qquad (7.37)$$

$$|1\rangle|+\rangle \rightarrow |1\rangle|+\rangle, \qquad (7.38)$$

$$|1\rangle|-\rangle \rightarrow -|1\rangle|-\rangle, \qquad (7.39)$$

so that the last entry catches a phase of π ($e^{i\pi} = -1$). Then this CNOT gate brings the overall state to

$$\frac{1}{\sqrt{2}}\left[|+\rangle_A|+\rangle_{B_2}\left(\alpha|0\rangle_{B_1} + \beta|1\rangle_{B_1}\right) + |-\rangle_A|-\rangle_{B_2}\left(\alpha|0\rangle_{B_1} + \beta|1\rangle_{B_1}\right)\right]$$

$$= \frac{1}{\sqrt{2}}\left[|+\rangle_A|+\rangle_{B_2}|\psi\rangle_{B_1} + |-\rangle_A|-\rangle_{B_2}|\psi\rangle_{B_1}\right] \qquad (7.40)$$

$$= \frac{1}{\sqrt{2}}\left[|+\rangle_A|+\rangle_{B_2} + |-\rangle_A|-\rangle_{B_2}\right]|\psi\rangle_{B_1} \qquad (7.41)$$

$$= |\Phi^+\rangle_{AB_2}|\psi\rangle_{B_1}. \qquad (7.42)$$

Thus, Alice teleports her information qubit to Bob, and both Alice and Bob possess one ebit at the end of the protocol.

The resource inequality for coherent teleportation is as follows:

$$2[q \rightarrow qq] \geq [qq] + [q \rightarrow q]. \qquad (7.43)$$

EXERCISE 7.4.2 Show how a cobit channel and an ebit can generate a GHZ state. That is, demonstrate a protocol that realizes the following resource inequality:

$$[qq]_{AB} + [q \rightarrow qq]_{BC} \geq [qqq]_{ABC}. \qquad (7.44)$$

EXERCISE 7.4.3 Outline the qudit version of the above coherent teleportation protocol. The protocol should realize the following resource inequality:

$$2\log d[q \rightarrow qq] \geq \log d[qq] + \log d[q \rightarrow q]. \qquad (7.45)$$

EXERCISE 7.4.4   Outline a catalytic version of the coherent teleportation protocol by modifying the original teleportation protocol. Let Alice possess an information qubit $|\psi\rangle_{A'}$ and let Alice and Bob share an ebit $|\Phi^+\rangle_{AB}$. Replace the Bell measurement with a controlled-NOT and Hadamard gate, replace the classical bit channels with coherent bit channels, and replace Bob's conditional unitary operations with controlled unitary operations. The resulting resource inequality should be of the form:

$$2\,[q \to qq] + [qq] \geq [q \to q] + 2\,[qq]. \tag{7.46}$$

This protocol is catalytic in the sense that it gives the resource inequality in (7.43) when we cancel one ebit from each side.

7.5   Coherent Communication Identity

The fundamental result of this chapter is the *coherent communication identity*:

$$2[q \to qq] = [qq] + [q \to q]. \tag{7.47}$$

We obtain this identity by combining the resource inequality for coherent super-dense coding in (7.27) and the resource inequality for coherent teleportation in (7.43). The coherent communication identity demonstrates that coherent super-dense coding and coherent teleportation are dual under resource reversal—the resources that coherent teleportation consumes are the same as those that coherent super-dense coding generates and vice versa.

The major application of the coherent communication identity is in noisy quantum Shannon theory. We will find later that its application is in the "upgrading" of protocols that output private classical information. Suppose that a protocol outputs private classical bits. The super-dense coding protocol is one such example, as the last paragraph of Section 6.2.3 argues. Then it is possible to upgrade the protocol by making it coherent, similar to the way in which we made super-dense coding coherent by replacing conditional unitary operations with controlled unitary operations.

We make this idea more precise with an example. The resource inequality for entanglement-assisted classical coding (discussed in more detail in Chapter 21) has the following form:

$$\langle \mathcal{N} \rangle + E\,[qq] \geq C\,[c \to c], \tag{7.48}$$

where $\mathcal{N}$ is a noisy quantum channel that connects Alice to Bob, E is some rate of entanglement consumption, and C is some rate of classical communication. It is possible to upgrade the generated classical bits to coherent bits, for reasons that are similar to those that we used in the upgrading of super-dense coding. The resulting resource inequality has the following form:

$$\langle \mathcal{N} \rangle + E\,[qq] \geq C\,[q \to qq]. \tag{7.49}$$

We can now employ the coherent communication identity in (7.47) and argue that any protocol that realizes the above resource inequality can realize the following one:

$$\langle \mathcal{N} \rangle + E\,[qq] \geq \frac{C}{2}\,[q \to q] + \frac{C}{2}\,[qq]\,, \tag{7.50}$$

merely by using the generated coherent bits in a coherent super-dense coding protocol. We can then make a "catalytic argument" to cancel the ebits on both sides of the resource inequality. The final resource inequality is as follows:

$$\langle \mathcal{N} \rangle + \left(E - \frac{C}{2} \right)[qq] \geq \frac{C}{2}\,[q \to q]\,. \tag{7.51}$$

The above resource inequality corresponds to a protocol for *entanglement-assisted quantum communication*, and it turns out to be optimal for some channels as this protocol's converse theorem shows. This optimality is due to the efficient translation of classical bits to coherent bits and the application of the coherent communication identity.

7.6   History and Further Reading

Harrow (2004) introduced the idea of coherent communication. Later, the idea of the coherent bit channel was generalized to the continuous-variable case by Wilde et al., 2007. Coherent communication has many applications in quantum Shannon theory which we will study in later chapters.

8 Unit Resource Capacity Region

In Chapter 6, we presented the three unit protocols of teleportation, super-dense coding, and entanglement distribution. We argued in Section 6.3 that each of these protocols are individually optimal. For example, recall that the entanglement distribution protocol is optimal because two parties cannot generate more than one ebit from the use of one noiseless qubit channel.

In this chapter, we show that these three protocols are actually the most important protocols—we do not need to consider any other protocols when the noiseless resources of classical communication, quantum communication, and entanglement are available. Combining these three protocols together is the best that one can do with the unit resources.

In this sense, this chapter gives a good example of a converse proof of a capacity theorem. We construct a three-dimensional region, known as the unit resource achievable region, that the three unit protocols fill out. The converse proof of this chapter employs physical arguments to show that the unit resource achievable region is optimal, and we can then refer to it as the unit resource capacity region. We later exploit the development here when we get to the study of trade-off capacities (see Chapter 25).

8.1 The Unit Resource Achievable Region

Let us first recall the resource inequalities for the three unit protocols. The resource inequality for teleportation is

$$2[c \rightarrow c] + [qq] \geq [q \rightarrow q], \tag{8.1}$$

while that for super-dense coding is

$$[q \rightarrow q] + [qq] \geq 2[c \rightarrow c], \tag{8.2}$$

and that for entanglement distribution is as follows:

$$[q \rightarrow q] \geq [qq]. \tag{8.3}$$

Each of the resources $[q \rightarrow q]$, $[qq]$, $[c \rightarrow c]$ is a *unit resource*.

The above three unit protocols are sufficient to recover all other unit protocols. For example, we can combine super-dense coding and entanglement distribution to produce the following resource inequality:

$$2[q \to q] + [qq] \geq 2[c \to c] + [qq]. \tag{8.4}$$

The above resource inequality is equivalent to the following one:

$$[q \to q] \geq [c \to c], \tag{8.5}$$

after removing the entanglement from both sides and scaling by $1/2$ (we can remove the entanglement here because it acts as a catalytic resource).

We can justify this scaling by considering a scenario in which we use the above protocol N times. For the first run of the protocol, we require one ebit to get it started, but then every other run both consumes and generates one ebit, giving

$$2N[q \to q] + [qq] \geq 2N[c \to c] + [qq]. \tag{8.6}$$

Dividing by N gives the rate of the task, and as N becomes large, the use of the initial ebit is negligible. We refer to (8.5) as "classical coding over a noiseless qubit channel."

We can think of the above resource inequalities in a different way. Let us consider a three-dimensional space with points of the form (C, Q, E), where C corresponds to noiseless classical communication, Q corresponds to noiseless quantum communication, and E corresponds to noiseless entanglement. Each point in this space corresponds to a protocol involving the unit resources. A coordinate of a point is negative if the point's corresponding resource inequality consumes that coordinate's corresponding resource, and a coordinate of a point is positive if the point's corresponding resource inequality generates that coordinate's corresponding resource.

For example, the point corresponding to the teleportation protocol is

$$x_{\text{TP}} \equiv (-2, 1, -1), \tag{8.7}$$

because teleportation consumes two noiseless classical bit channels and one ebit to generate one noiseless qubit channel. For similar reasons, the respective points corresponding to super-dense coding and entanglement distribution are as follows:

$$x_{\text{SD}} \equiv (2, -1, -1), \quad x_{\text{ED}} \equiv (0, -1, 1). \tag{8.8}$$

Figure 8.1 plots these three points in the three-dimensional space of classical communication, quantum communication, and entanglement.

We can execute any of the three unit protocols just one time, or we can execute any one of them m times where m is some positive integer. Executing a protocol m times then gives other points in the three-dimensional space. That is, we can also achieve the points $m x_{\text{TP}}$, $m x_{\text{SD}}$, and $m x_{\text{ED}}$ for any

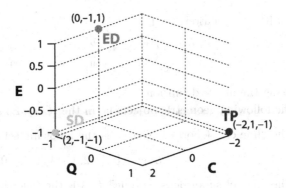

Figure 8.1 The three points corresponding to the three respective unit protocols of entanglement distribution (ED), teleportation (TP), and super-dense coding (SD).

positive m. This method allows us to fill up a certain portion of the three-dimensional space and provides an interpretation for resource inequalities with rational coefficients. Since the rational numbers are dense in the real numbers, we can also allow for real number coefficients. This becomes important later on when we consider combining the three unit protocols in order to achieve certain rates of transmission (a communication rate can be any real number). Thus, we can combine the protocols together to achieve any point of the following form:

$$\alpha x_{\text{TP}} + \beta x_{\text{SD}} + \gamma x_{\text{ED}}, \tag{8.9}$$

where $\alpha, \beta, \gamma \geq 0$.

Let us further establish some notation. Let L denote a line, Q a quadrant, and O an octant in the three-dimensional space (it should be clear from the context whether Q refers to quantum communication or "quadrant"). For example, L^{-00} denotes a line going in the direction of negative classical communication:

$$L^{-00} \equiv \{\alpha(-1, 0, 0) : \alpha \geq 0\}. \tag{8.10}$$

Q^{0+-} denotes the quadrant where there is zero classical communication, generation of quantum communication, and consumption of entanglement:

$$Q^{0+-} \equiv \{\alpha(0, 1, 0) + \beta(0, 0, -1) : \alpha, \beta \geq 0\}. \tag{8.11}$$

O^{+-+} denotes the octant where there is generation of classical communication, consumption of quantum communication, and generation of entanglement:

$$O^{+-+} \equiv \left\{ \begin{array}{c} \alpha(1, 0, 0) + \beta(0, -1, 0) + \gamma(0, 0, 1) \\ : \alpha, \beta, \gamma \geq 0 \end{array} \right\}. \tag{8.12}$$

It proves useful to have a "set addition" operation between two regions A and B (known as the Minkowski sum):

$$A + B \equiv \{a + b : a \in A, b \in B\}. \tag{8.13}$$

The following relations hold

$$Q^{0+-} = L^{0+0} + L^{00-},$$ (8.14)

$$O^{+-+} = L^{+00} + L^{0-0} + L^{00+},$$ (8.15)

by using the above definition.

The following geometric objects lie in the (C, Q, E) space:

1. The "line of teleportation" L_{TP} is the following set of points:

$$L_{\text{TP}} \equiv \{\alpha(-2, 1, -1) : \alpha \geq 0\}.$$ (8.16)

2. The "line of super-dense coding" L_{SD} is the following set of points:

$$L_{\text{SD}} \equiv \{\beta(2, -1, -1) : \beta \geq 0\}.$$ (8.17)

3. The "line of entanglement distribution" L_{ED} is the following set of points:

$$L_{\text{ED}} \equiv \{\gamma(0, -1, 1) : \gamma \geq 0\}.$$ (8.18)

DEFINITION 8.1.1 Let $\tilde{C}_{\text{U}}$ denote the unit resource achievable region. It consists of all linear combinations of the above protocols:

$$\tilde{C}_{\text{U}} \equiv L_{\text{TP}} + L_{\text{SD}} + L_{\text{ED}}.$$ (8.19)

The following matrix equation gives all achievable triples (C, Q, E) in $\tilde{C}_{\text{U}}$:

$$\begin{bmatrix} C \\ Q \\ E \end{bmatrix} = \begin{bmatrix} -2 & 2 & 0 \\ 1 & -1 & -1 \\ -1 & -1 & 1 \end{bmatrix} \begin{bmatrix} \alpha \\ \beta \\ \gamma \end{bmatrix},$$ (8.20)

where $\alpha, \beta, \gamma \geq 0$. We can rewrite the above equation using the matrix inverse:

$$\begin{bmatrix} \alpha \\ \beta \\ \gamma \end{bmatrix} = \begin{bmatrix} -1/2 & -1/2 & -1/2 \\ 0 & -1/2 & -1/2 \\ -1/2 & -1 & 0 \end{bmatrix} \begin{bmatrix} C \\ Q \\ E \end{bmatrix},$$ (8.21)

in order to express the coefficients α, β, and γ as a function of the rate triples (C, Q, E). The restriction of non-negativity of α, β, and γ gives the following restriction on the achievable rate triples (C, Q, E):

$$C + Q + E \leq 0,$$ (8.22)

$$Q + E \leq 0,$$ (8.23)

$$C + 2Q \leq 0.$$ (8.24)

The above result implies that the achievable region $\tilde{C}_{\text{U}}$ in (8.19) is equivalent to all rate triples satisfying (8.22)–(8.24). Figure 8.2 displays the full unit resource achievable region.

DEFINITION 8.1.2 The unit resource capacity region C_{U} is the closure of the set of all points (C, Q, E) in the C, Q, E space, satisfying the following resource inequality:

$$0 \geq C[c \to c] + Q[q \to q] + E[qq].$$ (8.25)

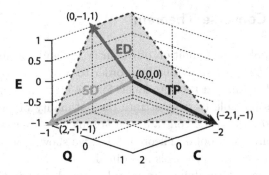

Figure 8.2 This figure depicts the unit resource achievable region $\widetilde{C}_U$.

The definition states that the unit resource capacity region consists of all those points (C, Q, E) that have corresponding protocols that can implement them. The notation in the above definition may seem slightly confusing at first glance until we recall that a resource with a negative rate implicitly belongs on the left-hand side of the resource inequality.

Theorem 8.1.1 below gives the optimal three-dimensional capacity region for the three unit resources.

THEOREM 8.1.1   The unit resource capacity region C_U is equal to the unit resource achievable region $\widetilde{C}_U$:

$$C_U = \widetilde{C}_U. \tag{8.26}$$

Proving the above theorem involves two steps: the *direct coding theorem* and the *converse theorem*. For this case, the *direct coding theorem* establishes that the achievable region $\widetilde{C}_U$ is in the capacity region C_U:

$$\widetilde{C}_U \subseteq C_U. \tag{8.27}$$

The *converse theorem*, on the other hand, establishes optimality of $\widetilde{C}_U$:

$$C_U \subseteq \widetilde{C}_U. \tag{8.28}$$

8.2   The Direct Coding Theorem

The result of the direct coding theorem, that $\widetilde{C}_U \subseteq C_U$, is immediate from the definition in (8.19) of the unit resource achievable region $\widetilde{C}_U$, the definition in (8.25) of the unit resource capacity region C_U, and the theory of resource inequalities. We can achieve points in the unit resource capacity region simply by considering positive linear combinations of the three unit protocols. The next section shows that the unit resource capacity region consists of all and only those points in the unit resource achievable region.

8.3   The Converse Theorem

We employ the definition of $\widetilde{C}_{\mathrm{U}}$ in (8.19) and consider the eight octants of the (C, Q, E) space individually in order to prove the converse theorem (that $C_{\mathrm{U}} \subseteq \widetilde{C}_{\mathrm{U}}$). Let $(\pm, \pm, \pm)$ denote labels for the eight different octants.

It is possible to demonstrate the optimality of each of these three protocols individually with a contradiction argument as we saw in Chapter 6. However, in the converse proof of Theorem 8.1.1, we show that a mixed strategy combining these three unit protocols is optimal.

We accept the following postulates and exploit them in order to prove the converse:

1. Entanglement alone cannot generate classical communication or quantum communication or both.
2. Classical communication alone cannot generate entanglement or quantum communication or both.
3. Holevo bound: One cannot generate more than one classical bit of communication per use of a noiseless qubit channel alone.

$(+, +, +)$. This octant of C_{U} is empty because a sender and receiver require some resources to implement classical communication, quantum communication, and entanglement. (They cannot generate a unit resource from nothing!)

$(+, +, -)$. This octant of C_{U} is empty because entanglement alone cannot generate either classical communication or quantum communication or both.

$(+, -, +)$. The task for this octant is to generate a noiseless classical channel of C bits and E ebits of entanglement by consuming $|Q|$ qubits of quantum communication. We thus consider all points of the form (C, Q, E) where $C \geq 0$, $Q \leq 0$, and $E \geq 0$. It suffices to prove the following inequality:

$$C + E \leq |Q|, \tag{8.29}$$

because combining (8.29) with $C \geq 0$ and $E \geq 0$ implies (8.22)–(8.24). The achievability of $(C, -|Q|, E)$ implies the achievability of the point $(C+2E, -|Q|-E, 0)$, because we can consume all of the entanglement with super-dense coding (8.2):

$$(C + 2E, -|Q| - E, 0) = (C, -|Q|, E) + (2E, -E, -E). \tag{8.30}$$

This new point implies that there is a protocol that consumes $|Q| + E$ noiseless qubit channels to send $C + 2E$ classical bits. The following bound then applies

$$C + 2E \leq |Q| + E, \tag{8.31}$$

because the Holevo bound (Exercise 4.2.2 gives a simpler statement of this bound) states that we can send only one classical bit per qubit. The bound in (8.29) then follows.

$(+, -, -)$. The task for this octant is to simulate a classical channel of size C bits using $|Q|$ qubits of quantum communication and $|E|$ ebits of entanglement.

We consider all points of the form (C, Q, E) where $C \geq 0$, $Q \leq 0$, and $E \leq 0$. It suffices to prove the following inequalities:

$$C \leq 2|Q|, \tag{8.32}$$

$$C \leq |Q| + |E|, \tag{8.33}$$

because combining (8.32)–(8.33) with $C \geq 0$ implies (8.22)–(8.24). The achievability of $(C, -|Q|, -|E|)$ implies the achievability of $(0, -|Q|+C/2, -|E|-C/2)$, because we can consume all of the classical communication with teleportation (8.1):

$$(0, -|Q| + C/2, -|E| - C/2) = (C, -|Q|, -|E|) + (-C, C/2, -C/2). \tag{8.34}$$

The following bound applies (quantum communication cannot be positive):

$$-|Q| + C/2 \leq 0, \tag{8.35}$$

because entanglement alone cannot generate quantum communication. The bound in (8.32) then follows from the above bound. The achievability of $(C, -|Q|, -|E|)$ implies the achievability of $(C, -|Q| - |E|, 0)$ because we can consume an extra $|E|$ qubit channels with entanglement distribution (8.3):

$$(C, -|Q| - |E|, 0) = (C, -|Q|, -|E|) + (0, -|E|, |E|). \tag{8.36}$$

The bound in (8.33) then applies by the same Holevo bound argument as in the previous octant.

$(-, +, +)$. This octant of C_U is empty because classical communication alone cannot generate either quantum communication or entanglement or both.

$(-, +, -)$. The task for this octant is to simulate a quantum channel of size Q qubits using $|E|$ ebits of entanglement and $|C|$ bits of classical communication. We consider all points of the form (C, Q, E) where $C \leq 0$, $Q \geq 0$, and $E \leq 0$. It suffices to prove the following inequalities:

$$Q \leq |E|, \tag{8.37}$$

$$2Q \leq |C|, \tag{8.38}$$

because combining them with $C \leq 0$ implies (8.22)–(8.24). The achievability of the point $(-|C|, Q, -|E|)$ implies the achievability of the point $(-|C|, 0, Q - |E|)$, because we can consume all of the quantum communication for entanglement distribution (8.3):

$$(-|C|, 0, Q - |E|) = (-|C|, Q, -|E|) + (0, -Q, Q). \tag{8.39}$$

The following bound applies (entanglement cannot be positive):

$$Q - |E| \leq 0, \tag{8.40}$$

because classical communication alone cannot generate entanglement. The bound in (8.37) follows from the above bound. The achievability of the point $(-|C|, Q, -|E|)$ implies the achievability of the point $(-|C| + 2Q, 0, -Q - |E|)$, because we can consume all of the quantum communication for super-dense coding (8.2):

$$(-|C| + 2Q, 0, -Q - |E|) = (-|C|, Q, -|E|) + (2Q, -Q, -Q). \quad (8.41)$$

The following bound applies (classical communication cannot be positive):

$$-|C| + 2Q \leq 0, \quad (8.42)$$

because entanglement alone cannot create classical communication. The bound in (8.38) follows from the above bound.

$(-, -, +)$. The task for this octant is to create E ebits of entanglement using $|Q|$ qubits of quantum communication and $|C|$ bits of classical communication. We consider all points of the form (C, Q, E) where $C \leq 0$, $Q \leq 0$, and $E \geq 0$. It suffices to prove the following inequality:

$$E \leq |Q|, \quad (8.43)$$

because combining it with $Q \leq 0$ and $C \leq 0$ implies (8.22)–(8.24). The achievability of $(-|C|, -|Q|, E)$ implies the achievability of $(-|C| - 2E, -|Q| + E, 0)$, because we can consume all of the entanglement with teleportation (8.1):

$$(-|C| - 2E, -|Q| + E, 0) = (-|C|, -|Q|, E) + (-2E, E, -E). \quad (8.44)$$

The following bound applies (quantum communication cannot be positive):

$$-|Q| + E \leq 0, \quad (8.45)$$

because classical communication alone cannot generate quantum communication. The bound in (8.43) follows from the above bound.

$(-, -, -)$. $\tilde{C}_U$ completely contains this octant.

We have now proved that the set of inequalities in (8.22)–(8.24) holds for all octants of the (C, Q, E) space. The next exercises ask you to consider similar unit resource achievable regions.

EXERCISE 8.3.1 Consider the resources of public classical communication:

$$[c \to c]_{\text{pub}}, \quad (8.46)$$

private classical communication:

$$[c \to c]_{\text{priv}}, \quad (8.47)$$

and shared secret key:

$$[cc]_{\text{priv}}. \quad (8.48)$$

Public classical communication is equivalent to the following channel:

$$\rho \to \sum_i \langle i|\rho|i\rangle \, |i\rangle\langle i|_B \otimes \sigma_E^i, \quad (8.49)$$

so that an eavesdropper Eve obtains some correlations with the transmitted state ρ. Private classical communication is equivalent to the following channel:

$$\rho \rightarrow \sum_i \langle i|\rho|i\rangle \, |i\rangle\langle i|_B \otimes \sigma_E, \tag{8.50}$$

so that Eve's state is independent of the information that Bob receives. Finally, a secret key is a state of the following form:

$$\overline{\Phi}_{AB} \otimes \sigma_E \equiv \left(\frac{1}{d} \sum_i |i\rangle\langle i|_A \otimes |i\rangle\langle i|_B \right) \otimes \sigma_E, \tag{8.51}$$

so that Alice and Bob share maximal classical correlation and Eve's state is independent of it. There are three protocols that relate these three classical resources. Secret key distribution is a protocol that consumes a noiseless private channel to generate a noiseless secret key. It has the following resource inequality:

$$[c \rightarrow c]_{\text{priv}} \geq [cc]_{\text{priv}} . \tag{8.52}$$

The one-time pad protocol exploits a shared secret key and a noiseless public channel to generate a noiseless private channel (it simply XORs a bit of secret key with the bit that the sender wants to transmit and this protocol is provably unbreakable if the secret key is perfectly secret). It has the following resource inequality:

$$[c \rightarrow c]_{\text{pub}} + [cc]_{\text{priv}} \geq [c \rightarrow c]_{\text{priv}} . \tag{8.53}$$

Finally, private classical communication can simulate public classical communication if we assume that Bob has a local register where he can place information and he then gives this to Eve. It has the following resource inequality:

$$[c \rightarrow c]_{\text{priv}} \geq [c \rightarrow c]_{\text{pub}} . \tag{8.54}$$

Show that these three protocols fill out an optimal achievable region in the space of public classical communication, private classical communication, and secret key. Use the following three postulates to prove optimality: (1) public classical communication alone cannot generate secret key or private classical communication, (2) private key alone cannot generate public or private classical communication, and (3) the net amount of public bit channel uses and secret key bits generated cannot exceed the number of private bit channel uses consumed.

EXERCISE 8.3.2   Consider the resource of coherent communication from Chapter 7:

$$[q \rightarrow qq] . \tag{8.55}$$

Recall the coherent communication identity in (7.47):

$$2 [q \rightarrow qq] = [q \rightarrow q] + [qq] . \tag{8.56}$$

Recall the other resource inequalities for coherent communication:

$$[q \rightarrow q] \geq [q \rightarrow qq] \geq [qq] . \tag{8.57}$$

Consider a space of points (C, Q, E) where C corresponds to coherent communication, Q to quantum communication, and E to entanglement. Determine the achievable region one obtains with the above resource inequalities and another trivial resource inequality:

$$[qq] \geq 0. \tag{8.58}$$

We interpret the above resource inequality as "entanglement consumption," where Alice simply throws away entanglement.

8.4   History and Further Reading

The unit resource capacity region first appeared in Hsieh & Wilde (2010b) in the context of trade-off coding. The private unit resource capacity region later appeared in Wilde & Hsieh (2012a).

Part IV

Tools of Quantum Shannon Theory

9 Distance Measures

We discussed the major noiseless quantum communication protocols such as teleportation, super-dense coding, their coherent versions, and entanglement distribution in detail in Chapters 6, 7, and 8. Each of these protocols relies on the assumption that noiseless resources are available. For example, the entanglement distribution protocol assumes that a noiseless qubit channel is available to generate a noiseless ebit. This idealization allowed us to develop the main principles of the protocols without having to think about more complicated issues, but in practice, the protocols do not work as expected in the presence of noise.

Given that quantum systems suffer noise in practice, we would like to have a way to determine how well a protocol is performing. The simplest way to do so is to compare the output of an ideal protocol to the output of the actual protocol using a *distance measure* of the two respective output quantum states. That is, suppose that a quantum information-processing protocol should ideally output some quantum state $|\psi\rangle$, but the actual output of the protocol is a quantum state with density operator ρ. Then a performance measure $P(\psi, \rho)$ should indicate how close the ideal output is to the actual output. Figure 9.1 depicts the comparison of an ideal protocol with another protocol that is noisy.

This chapter introduces two distance measures that allow us to determine how close two quantum states are to each other. The first distance measure that we discuss is the *trace distance* and the second is the *fidelity*. (However, note that the fidelity is not a distance measure in the strict mathematical sense—nevertheless, we exploit it as a "closeness" measure of quantum states because it admits an intuitive operational interpretation.) These two measures are mostly interchangeable, but we introduce both because it is often times more convenient in a given situation to use one or the other.

Distance measures are particularly important in quantum Shannon theory because they provide a way for us to determine how well a protocol is performing. Recall that Shannon's method (outlined in Chapter 2) for both the noiseless and noisy coding theorem is to allow for a slight error in a protocol, but to show that this error vanishes in the limit of large block length. In later chapters where we prove quantum coding theorems, we borrow this technique of demonstrating asymptotically small error, with either the trace distance or the fidelity as the measure of performance.

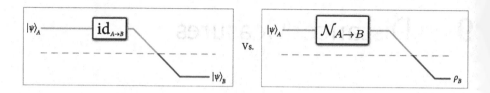

Figure 9.1 A distance measure quantifies how far the output of a given ideal protocol (depicted on the left) is from an actual protocol that exploits a noisy resource (depicted as the noisy quantum channel $\mathcal{N}_{A \to B}$ on the right).

9.1   Trace Distance

We first introduce the trace distance. Our presentation is somewhat mathematical because we exploit norms on linear operators in order to define it. Despite this mathematical flavor, this section offers an intuitive operational interpretation of the trace distance.

9.1.1   Trace Norm

DEFINITION 9.1.1 (Trace Norm)   The *trace norm* or *Schatten 1-norm* $\|M\|_1$ of an operator $M \in \mathcal{L}(\mathcal{H}, \mathcal{H}')$ is defined as

$$\|M\|_1 \equiv \mathrm{Tr}\left\{|M|\right\}, \tag{9.1}$$

where $|M| \equiv \sqrt{M^\dagger M}$.

PROPOSITION 9.1.1   The trace norm of an operator $M \in \mathcal{L}(\mathcal{H}, \mathcal{H}')$ is equal to the sum of its singular values.

Proof   Recall from Definition 3.3.1 that any function f applied to a Hermitian operator A is as follows:

$$f(A) \equiv \sum_{i:\alpha_i \neq 0} f(\alpha_i)|i\rangle\langle i|, \tag{9.2}$$

where $\sum_{i:\alpha_i \neq 0} \alpha_i |i\rangle\langle i|$ is a spectral decomposition of A. With these two definitions, it is straightforward to show that the trace norm of M is equal to the sum of its singular values. Indeed, let $M = U \Sigma V$ be the singular value decomposition of M, where U and V are unitary matrices and Σ is a rectangular matrix with the non-negative singular values along the diagonal. Then we can write

$$M = \sum_{i=0}^{d-1} \sigma_i |u_i\rangle\langle v_i|, \tag{9.3}$$

where d is the rank of M, $\{\sigma_i\}$ are the strictly positive singular values of M, $\{|u_i\rangle\}$ are the orthonormal columns of U in correspondence with the set $\{\sigma_i\}$, and $\{|v_i\rangle\}$ are the orthonormal rows of V in correspondence with the set $\{\sigma_i\}$. Then

$$M^\dagger M = \left[\sum_{j=0}^{d-1} \sigma_j |v_j\rangle\langle u_j|\right]\left[\sum_{i=0}^{d-1} \sigma_i |u_i\rangle\langle v_i|\right] \tag{9.4}$$

$$= \sum_{i,j=0}^{d-1} \sigma_j \sigma_i |v_j\rangle\langle u_j||u_i\rangle\langle v_i| \tag{9.5}$$

$$= \sum_{i=0}^{d-1} \sigma_i^2 |v_i\rangle\langle v_i|, \tag{9.6}$$

so that

$$\sqrt{M^\dagger M} = \sum_{i=0}^{d-1} \sqrt{\sigma_i^2}|v_i\rangle\langle v_i| = \sum_{i=0}^{d-1} \sigma_i |v_i\rangle\langle v_i|, \tag{9.7}$$

finally implying that

$$\mathrm{Tr}\,\{|M|\} = \sum_{i=0}^{d-1} \sigma_i. \tag{9.8}$$

This means also that

$$\|M\|_1 = \mathrm{Tr}\{\sqrt{MM^\dagger}\}, \tag{9.9}$$

because the singular values of $MM^\dagger$ and $M^\dagger M$ are the same (this is the key to Exercise 4.1.4). One can also easily show that the trace norm of a Hermitian operator is equal to the absolute sum of its eigenvalues.   □

The trace norm is indeed a *norm* because it satisfies the following three properties: non-negative definiteness, homogeneity, and the triangle inequality.

PROPERTY 9.1.1 (Non-Negative Definiteness)   The trace norm of an operator M is non-negative definite:

$$\|M\|_1 \geq 0. \tag{9.10}$$

The trace norm is equal to zero if and only if the operator M is the zero operator:

$$\|M\|_1 = 0 \quad \Leftrightarrow \quad M = 0. \tag{9.11}$$

PROPERTY 9.1.2 (Homogeneity)   For any constant $c \in \mathbb{C}$,

$$\|cM\|_1 = |c|\,\|M\|_1\,. \tag{9.12}$$

PROPERTY 9.1.3 (Triangle Inequality)   For any two operators $M, N \in \mathcal{L}(\mathcal{H}, \mathcal{H}')$, the following triangle inequality holds:

$$\|M + N\|_1 \leq \|M\|_1 + \|N\|_1\,. \tag{9.13}$$

Non-negative definiteness follows because the sum of the singular values of an operator is non-negative, and the singular values are all equal to zero (and thus the operator is equal to zero) if and only if the sum of the singular values is equal to zero. Homogeneity follows directly from the fact that $|cM| = |c|\|M\|$. We later give a proof of the triangle inequality (however, for a special case only). Exercise 9.1.1 below asks you to prove it for square operators.

Three other important properties of the trace norm are its invariance under isometries, convexity, and a variational characterization. Each of the properties below often arise as useful tools in quantum Shannon theory.

PROPERTY 9.1.4 (Isometric Invariance)   The trace norm is invariant under multiplication by isometries U and V:

$$\left\|UMV^\dagger\right\|_1 = \|M\|_1 . \tag{9.14}$$

PROPERTY 9.1.5 (Convexity)   For any two operators $M, N \in \mathcal{L}(\mathcal{H}, \mathcal{H}')$ and $\lambda \in [0, 1]$, the following inequality holds

$$\|\lambda M + (1 - \lambda)N\|_1 \leq \lambda \|M\|_1 + (1 - \lambda) \|N\|_1 . \tag{9.15}$$

Isometric invariance holds because M and $UMV^\dagger$ have the same singular values. Convexity follows directly from the triangle inequality and homogeneity (thus, any norm is convex in this sense).

PROPERTY 9.1.6 (Variational Characterization)   For a square operator $M \in \mathcal{L}(\mathcal{H})$, the following variational characterization of the trace norm holds

$$\|M\|_1 = \max_U |\mathrm{Tr}\,\{MU\}| , \tag{9.16}$$

where the optimization is with respect to all unitary operators.

Proof   The above characterization follows by taking a singular value decomposition of M as $M = WDV$, with W and V unitaries and D a diagonal matrix of singular values. Applying the Cauchy–Schwarz inequality gives

$$|\mathrm{Tr}\,\{MU\}| = |\mathrm{Tr}\,\{WDVU\}| = \left|\mathrm{Tr}\left\{\sqrt{D}\sqrt{D}VUW\right\}\right| \tag{9.17}$$

$$\leq \sqrt{\mathrm{Tr}\left\{\sqrt{D}\sqrt{D}\right\}}\sqrt{\mathrm{Tr}\left\{\left(\sqrt{D}VUW\right)^\dagger \sqrt{D}VUW\right\}} \tag{9.18}$$

$$= \mathrm{Tr}\,\{D\} = \|M\|_1 . \tag{9.19}$$

The inequality is a consequence of the Cauchy–Schwarz inequality for the Hilbert–Schmidt inner product:

$$|\mathrm{Tr}\,\{A^\dagger B\}| \leq \sqrt{\mathrm{Tr}\,\{A^\dagger A\}}\sqrt{\mathrm{Tr}\,\{B^\dagger B\}}. \tag{9.20}$$

Equality holds by picking $U = V^\dagger W^\dagger$, from which we recover (9.16).   □

EXERCISE 9.1.1   Prove that the triangle inequality (Property 9.1.3) holds for square operators $M, N \in \mathcal{L}(\mathcal{H})$. (Hint: Use the characterization in Property 9.1.6.)

9.1.2   Trace Distance from the Trace Norm

The trace norm induces a natural distance measure, called the *trace distance*.

DEFINITION 9.1.2 (Trace Distance)   Given any two operators $M, N \in \mathcal{L}(\mathcal{H}, \mathcal{H}')$, the trace distance between them is as follows:

$$\|M - N\|_1. \tag{9.21}$$

The trace distance is especially useful as a measure of the distinguishability of two quantum states with respective density operators ρ and σ. The following bounds apply to the trace distance between any two density operators ρ and σ:

$$0 \leq \|\rho - \sigma\|_1 \leq 2. \tag{9.22}$$

Sometimes it is useful to employ the *normalized* trace distance $\frac{1}{2}\|\rho - \sigma\|_1$, so that $\frac{1}{2}\|\rho - \sigma\|_1 \in [0, 1]$. The lower bound in (9.22) applies when two quantum states are equal—quantum states ρ and σ are equal to each other if and only if their trace distance is zero. The physical implication of the trace distance being equal to zero is that no measurement can distinguish ρ from σ. The upper bound in (9.22) follows from the triangle inequality:

$$\|\rho - \sigma\|_1 \leq \|\rho\|_1 + \|\sigma\|_1 = 2. \tag{9.23}$$

The trace distance is maximum when ρ and σ have support on orthogonal subspaces. Later, we will prove that this is the only case in which this happens, after introducing the fidelity. The physical implication of maximal trace distance is that there exists a measurement that can perfectly distinguish ρ from σ. We discuss these operational interpretations of the trace distance in more detail in Section 9.1.4.

EXERCISE 9.1.2   Show that the trace distance between two qubit density operators ρ and σ is equal to the Euclidean distance between their respective Bloch vectors $\vec{r}$ and $\vec{s}$, where

$$\rho = \frac{1}{2}\left(I + \vec{r} \cdot \vec{\sigma}\right), \qquad \sigma = \frac{1}{2}\left(I + \vec{s} \cdot \vec{\sigma}\right). \tag{9.24}$$

That is, show that $\|\rho - \sigma\|_1 = \|\vec{r} - \vec{s}\|_2$.

EXERCISE 9.1.3   Show that the trace distance obeys a telescoping property:

$$\|\rho_1 \otimes \rho_2 - \sigma_1 \otimes \sigma_2\|_1 \leq \|\rho_1 - \sigma_1\|_1 + \|\rho_2 - \sigma_2\|_1, \tag{9.25}$$

for any density operators ρ_1, ρ_2, σ_1, σ_2. (Hint: First prove that $\|\rho \otimes \omega - \sigma \otimes \omega\|_1 = \|\rho - \sigma\|_1$, for any density operators ρ, σ, ω.)

EXERCISE 9.1.4   Show that the trace distance is invariant with respect to an isometric quantum channel, in the following sense:

$$\|\rho - \sigma\|_1 = \|U\rho U^\dagger - U\sigma U^\dagger\|_1, \tag{9.26}$$

where U is an isometry. The physical implication of (9.26) is that an isometric quantum channel applied to both states does not increase or decrease the distinguishability of the two states.

9.1.3   Trace Distance as a Probability Difference

We now state and prove an important lemma that gives an alternative and useful way for characterizing the trace distance. This particular characterization finds application in many proofs of the lemmas that follow concerning trace distance.

LEMMA 9.1.1   The normalized trace distance $\frac{1}{2}\|\rho - \sigma\|_1$ between quantum states $\rho, \sigma \in \mathcal{D}(\mathcal{H})$ is equal to the largest probability difference that two states ρ and σ could give to the same measurement outcome Λ:

$$\frac{1}{2}\|\rho - \sigma\|_1 = \max_{0 \leq \Lambda \leq I} \operatorname{Tr}\left\{\Lambda\left(\rho - \sigma\right)\right\}. \tag{9.27}$$

The above maximization is with respect to all positive semi-definite operators $\Lambda \in \mathcal{L}(\mathcal{H})$ that have their eigenvalues bounded from above by one.

Proof Consider that the difference operator $\rho - \sigma$ is Hermitian and so we can diagonalize it as follows:

$$\rho - \sigma = \sum_i \lambda_i |i\rangle\langle i|,$$

where $\{|i\rangle\}$ is an orthonormal basis of eigenvectors and $\{\lambda_i\}$ is a set of real eigenvalues. Let us define

$$P \equiv \sum_{i:\lambda_i \geq 0} \lambda_i |i\rangle\langle i|, \qquad Q \equiv \sum_{i:\lambda_i < 0} |\lambda_i|\, |i\rangle\langle i|, \tag{9.28}$$

which implies that P and Q are positive semi-definite and that

$$\rho - \sigma = P - Q. \tag{9.29}$$

Consider also that $PQ = 0$, and let Π_P and Π_Q denote the projections onto the supports of P and Q, respectively:

$$\Pi_P \equiv \sum_{i:\lambda_i \geq 0} |i\rangle\langle i|, \qquad \Pi_Q \equiv \sum_{i:\lambda_i < 0} |i\rangle\langle i|. \tag{9.30}$$

Then it follows that

$$\Pi_P P \Pi_P = P, \qquad \Pi_Q Q \Pi_Q = Q, \tag{9.31}$$
$$\Pi_P Q \Pi_P = 0, \qquad \Pi_Q P \Pi_Q = 0. \tag{9.32}$$

The following property holds as well:

$$|\rho - \sigma| = |P - Q| = P + Q \tag{9.33}$$

because the supports of P and Q are orthogonal and the absolute value of the operator $P - Q$ takes the absolute value of its eigenvalues. Therefore,

$$\|\rho - \sigma\|_1 = \text{Tr}\{|\rho - \sigma|\} = \text{Tr}\{P + Q\} = \text{Tr}\{P\} + \text{Tr}\{Q\}. \tag{9.34}$$

But

$$\text{Tr}\{P\} - \text{Tr}\{Q\} = \text{Tr}\{P - Q\} = \text{Tr}\{\rho - \sigma\} \tag{9.35}$$

$$= \text{Tr}\{\rho\} - \text{Tr}\{\sigma\} = 0 \tag{9.36}$$

where the last equality follows because both quantum states have unit trace. Therefore, $\text{Tr}\{P\} = \text{Tr}\{Q\}$ and

$$\|\rho - \sigma\|_1 = 2 \cdot \text{Tr}\{P\}. \tag{9.37}$$

Consider then that

$$\text{Tr}\{\Pi_P (\rho - \sigma)\} = \text{Tr}\{\Pi_P (P - Q)\} = \text{Tr}\{\Pi_P P\} \tag{9.38}$$

$$= \text{Tr}\{P\} = \frac{1}{2}\|\rho - \sigma\|_1. \tag{9.39}$$

Now we prove that the operator Π_P is the maximizing one. Let Λ be any positive semi-definite operator with spectrum bounded above by one. Then

$$\text{Tr}\{\Lambda (\rho - \sigma)\} = \text{Tr}\{\Lambda (P - Q)\} \leq \text{Tr}\{\Lambda P\} \tag{9.40}$$

$$\leq \text{Tr}\{P\} = \frac{1}{2}\|\rho - \sigma\|_1. \tag{9.41}$$

The first inequality follows because Λ and Q are non-negative and so $\text{Tr}\{\Lambda Q\}$ is non-negative. The second inequality holds because $\Lambda \leq I$. The final equality follows from (9.37). $\qquad\square$

EXERCISE 9.1.5   Let $\rho = |0\rangle\langle 0|$ and $\sigma = |+\rangle\langle +|$. Compute P, Q, Π_P, and Π_Q, as defined in (9.28) and (9.30), for this choice of ρ and σ. Compute the trace distance $\|\rho - \sigma\|_1$.

EXERCISE 9.1.6   Show that the trace norm of any Hermitian operator ω is given by the following optimization:

$$\|\omega\|_1 = \max_{-I \leq \Lambda \leq I} \text{Tr}\{\Lambda \omega\}. \tag{9.42}$$

9.1.4   Operational Interpretation of the Trace Distance

We now provide an operational interpretation of the trace distance as the distinguishability of two quantum states. The interpretation results from a hypothesis-testing scenario. Suppose that Bob prepares one of two quantum states ρ_0 or ρ_1 for Alice to distinguish. Suppose further that it is equally likely a priori for him to prepare either ρ_0 or ρ_1. Let X denote the Bernoulli random variable assigned to the prior probabilities so that $p_X(0) = p_X(1) = 1/2$. Alice can perform a binary POVM with elements $\Lambda \equiv \{\Lambda_0, \Lambda_1\}$ to distinguish the two states. That is, Alice guesses the state in question is ρ_0 if she receives outcome "0" from the measurement or she guesses the state in question is ρ_1 if she receives outcome "1" from the measurement. Let Y denote the Bernoulli random variable assigned to the classical outcomes of her measurement. The success probability $p_{\text{succ}}(\Lambda)$ for this hypothesis testing scenario is the sum of the probability of detecting "0" when the state is ρ_0 and the probability of detecting "1" when the state is ρ_1:

$$p_{\text{succ}}(\Lambda) = p_{Y|X}(0|0)p_X(0) + p_{Y|X}(1|1)p_X(1) \tag{9.43}$$

$$= \text{Tr}\{\Lambda_0\rho_0\}\frac{1}{2} + \text{Tr}\{\Lambda_1\rho_1\}\frac{1}{2}. \tag{9.44}$$

We can simplify this expression using the completeness relation $\Lambda_0 + \Lambda_1 = I$:

$$p_{\text{succ}}(\Lambda) = \frac{1}{2}\left(\text{Tr}\{\Lambda_0\rho_0\} + \text{Tr}\{(I - \Lambda_0)\rho_1\}\right) \tag{9.45}$$

$$= \frac{1}{2}\left(\text{Tr}\{\Lambda_0\rho_0\} + \text{Tr}\{\rho_1\} - \text{Tr}\{\Lambda_0\rho_1\}\right) \tag{9.46}$$

$$= \frac{1}{2}\left(\text{Tr}\{\Lambda_0\rho_0\} + 1 - \text{Tr}\{\Lambda_0\rho_1\}\right) \tag{9.47}$$

$$= \frac{1}{2}\left(1 + \text{Tr}\{\Lambda_0(\rho_0 - \rho_1)\}\right). \tag{9.48}$$

Now Alice has freedom in choosing the POVM $\Lambda = \{\Lambda_0, \Lambda_1\}$ to distinguish the states ρ_0 and ρ_1, and she would like to choose one that maximizes the success probability $p_{\text{succ}}(\Lambda)$. Thus, we can define the success probability with respect to all measurements as follows:

$$p_{\text{succ}} \equiv \max_\Lambda p_{\text{succ}}(\Lambda) = \max_\Lambda \frac{1}{2}\left(1 + \text{Tr}\{\Lambda_0(\rho_0 - \rho_1)\}\right). \tag{9.49}$$

We can rewrite the above quantity in terms of the trace distance using its characterization in Lemma 9.1.1 because the expression inside of the maximization involves only the operator Λ_0:

$$p_{\text{succ}} = \frac{1}{2}\left(1 + \frac{1}{2}\|\rho_0 - \rho_1\|_1\right). \tag{9.50}$$

Thus, the normalized trace distance has an operational interpretation that it is linearly related to the maximum success probability in distinguishing two quantum states ρ_0 and ρ_1 in a quantum hypothesis testing experiment. From the above expression for the success probability, it is clear that the states are indistinguishable when $\|\rho_0 - \rho_1\|_1$ is equal to zero. That is, it is just as good for Alice to guess randomly what the state might be, and in this case, she can do no better than to have $1/2$ probability of being correct. On the other hand, the states are perfectly distinguishable when $\|\rho_0 - \rho_1\|_1$ is maximal and the measurement that distinguishes them consists of two projectors: one projects onto the non-negative eigenspace of $\rho_0 - \rho_1$ and the other projects onto the negative eigenspace of $\rho_0 - \rho_1$. In this sense, we can say that the normalized trace distance is the bias away from random guessing in a hypothesis testing experiment.

EXERCISE 9.1.7 Suppose that the prior probabilities in the above hypothesis-testing scenario are not uniform but are rather equal to p_0 and p_1. Show that the success probability is instead given by

$$p_{\text{succ}} = \frac{1}{2} \left(1 + \| p_0 \rho_0 - p_1 \rho_1 \|_1 \right). \tag{9.51}$$

9.1.5 Trace Distance Lemmas

We present several useful corollaries of Lemma 9.1.1 and their corresponding proofs. These corollaries include the triangle inequality, measurement on close states, and monotonicity of trace distance. Each of these corollaries finds application in many proofs in quantum Shannon theory.

LEMMA 9.1.2 (Triangle Inequality) The trace distance obeys a triangle inequality. For any three quantum states ρ, σ, $\tau \in \mathcal{D}(\mathcal{H})$, the following inequality holds:

$$\| \rho - \sigma \|_1 \leq \| \rho - \tau \|_1 + \| \tau - \sigma \|_1 . \tag{9.52}$$

Proof Pick Π as the maximizing operator for $\| \rho - \sigma \|_1$ (according to Lemma 9.1.1) so that

$$\| \rho - \sigma \|_1 = 2 \cdot \text{Tr} \left\{ \Pi \left(\rho - \sigma \right) \right\} \tag{9.53}$$

$$= 2 \cdot \text{Tr} \left\{ \Pi \left(\rho - \tau \right) \right\} + 2 \cdot \text{Tr} \left\{ \Pi \left(\tau - \sigma \right) \right\} \tag{9.54}$$

$$\leq \| \rho - \tau \|_1 + \| \tau - \sigma \|_1 . \tag{9.55}$$

The last inequality follows because the operator Π maximizing $\| \rho - \sigma \|_1$ in general is not the same operator that maximizes both $\| \rho - \tau \|_1$ and $\| \tau - \sigma \|_1$. $\square$

COROLLARY 9.1.1 (Measurement on Close States) Suppose we have two quantum states $\rho, \sigma \in \mathcal{D}(\mathcal{H})$ and an operator $\Pi \in \mathcal{L}(\mathcal{H})$ such that $0 \leq \Pi \leq I$. Then

$$\text{Tr} \left\{ \Pi \rho \right\} \geq \text{Tr} \left\{ \Pi \sigma \right\} - \frac{1}{2} \| \rho - \sigma \|_1 \tag{9.56}$$

$$\geq \text{Tr} \left\{ \Pi \sigma \right\} - \| \rho - \sigma \|_1 . \tag{9.57}$$

Proof Consider the following arguments:

$$\frac{1}{2} \| \rho - \sigma \|_1 = \max_{0 \leq \Lambda \leq I} \left\{ \text{Tr} \left\{ \Lambda \left(\sigma - \rho \right) \right\} \right\} \tag{9.58}$$

$$\geq \text{Tr} \left\{ \Pi \left(\sigma - \rho \right) \right\} \tag{9.59}$$

$$= \text{Tr} \left\{ \Pi \sigma \right\} - \text{Tr} \left\{ \Pi \rho \right\} . \tag{9.60}$$

The first equality follows from Lemma 9.1.1. The first inequality follows because Λ is the maximizing operator and can only lead to a probability difference greater than that for another operator Π such that $0 \leq \Pi \leq I$. $\square$

The most common way that we employ Corollary 9.1.1 in quantum Shannon theory is in the following scenario. Suppose that a measurement with operator Π succeeds with high probability on a quantum state σ:

$$\text{Tr}\{\Pi\sigma\} \geq 1 - \varepsilon, \tag{9.61}$$

where ε is some small positive number. Suppose further that another quantum state ρ is ε-close in trace distance to σ:

$$\|\rho - \sigma\|_1 \leq \varepsilon. \tag{9.62}$$

Then Corollary 9.1.1 gives the intuitive result that the measurement succeeds with high probability on the state ρ that is close to σ:

$$\text{Tr}\{\Pi\rho\} \geq 1 - 2\varepsilon, \tag{9.63}$$

by plugging (9.61) and (9.62) into (9.57).

EXERCISE 9.1.8 Prove that (9.57) holds for arbitrary Hermitian operators ρ and σ by exploiting the result of Exercise 9.1.6.

We next turn to the monotonicity of trace distance under the discarding of a system. The interpretation of this corollary is that discarding of a system does not increase distinguishability of two quantum states. That is, a global measurement on the larger system might be able to distinguish the two states better than a local measurement on an individual subsystem could. In fact, the proof of monotonicity follows this intuition exactly, and Figure 9.2 depicts the intuition behind it.

COROLLARY 9.1.2 (Monotonicity of Trace Distance) Let $\rho_{AB}, \sigma_{AB} \in \mathcal{D}(\mathcal{H}_A \otimes \mathcal{H}_B)$. The trace distance is monotone with respect to discarding of subsystems:

$$\|\rho_A - \sigma_A\|_1 \leq \|\rho_{AB} - \sigma_{AB}\|_1. \tag{9.64}$$

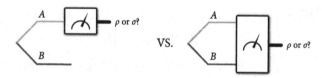

Figure 9.2 The task in this figure is for Bob to distinguish the state ρ_{AB} from the state σ_{AB} using a binary-valued measurement. Bob could perform an optimal measurement on system A alone if he does not have access to system B. If he has access to system B as well, then he can perform an optimal joint measurement on systems A and B. We would expect that he can distinguish the states more reliably if he performs a joint measurement because there could be more information about the state available in the other system B. Since the trace distance is a measure of distinguishability, we would expect it to obey the following inequality:
$\|\rho_A - \sigma_A\|_1 \leq \|\rho_{AB} - \sigma_{AB}\|_1$ (the states are less distinguishable if fewer systems are available to be part of the distinguishability test).

Proof Consider that

$$\|\rho_A - \sigma_A\|_1 = 2 \cdot \mathrm{Tr}\left\{\Lambda_A \left(\rho_A - \sigma_A\right)\right\}, \qquad (9.65)$$

for some positive semi-definite operator $\Lambda_A \leq I_A$. Then

$$2 \cdot \mathrm{Tr}\left\{\Lambda_A \left(\rho_A - \sigma_A\right)\right\} = 2 \cdot \mathrm{Tr}\left\{\left(\Lambda_A \otimes I_B\right)\left(\rho_{AB} - \sigma_{AB}\right)\right\} \qquad (9.66)$$

$$\leq 2 \cdot \max_{0 \leq \Lambda_{AB} \leq I} \mathrm{Tr}\left\{\Lambda_{AB}\left(\rho_{AB} - \sigma_{AB}\right)\right\} \qquad (9.67)$$

$$= \|\rho_{AB} - \sigma_{AB}\|_1. \qquad (9.68)$$

The first equality follows because local predictions of the quantum theory should coincide with its global predictions (as discussed in Section 4.3.3). The inequality follows because the local operator Λ_A never gives a higher probability difference than a maximization over all global operators. The last equality follows from the characterization of the trace distance in Lemma 9.1.1. □

EXERCISE 9.1.9 (Monotonicity of Trace Distance) Let $\rho, \sigma \in \mathcal{D}(\mathcal{H}_A)$ and $\mathcal{N} : \mathcal{L}(\mathcal{H}_A) \to \mathcal{L}(\mathcal{H}_B)$ be a quantum channel. Show that the trace distance is monotone with respect to the action of the channel $\mathcal{N}$:

$$\|\mathcal{N}(\rho) - \mathcal{N}(\sigma)\|_1 \leq \|\rho - \sigma\|_1. \qquad (9.69)$$

(Hint: Use the result of Corollary 9.1.2 and Exercise 9.1.4.)

The result of the previous exercise deserves an interpretation. It states that a quantum channel $\mathcal{N}$ makes two quantum states ρ and σ less distinguishable from each other. That is, a noisy channel tends to "blur" two states to make them appear as if they are more similar to each other than they are before the quantum channel acts.

EXERCISE 9.1.10 Prove that a measurement achieves the trace distance, in the following sense:

$$\|\rho - \sigma\|_1 = \max_{\{\Lambda_x\}} \sum_x \left|\mathrm{Tr}\{\Lambda_x \rho\} - \mathrm{Tr}\{\Lambda_x \sigma\}\right|, \qquad (9.70)$$

where $\rho, \sigma \in \mathcal{D}(\mathcal{H})$ and the optimization is with respect to all POVMs $\{\Lambda_x\}$. Hint: Use the result of Exercise 9.1.9 to show the following bound for any choice of POVM:

$$\|\rho - \sigma\|_1 \geq \sum_x \left|\mathrm{Tr}\{\Lambda_x \rho\} - \mathrm{Tr}\{\Lambda_x \sigma\}\right|. \qquad (9.71)$$

Next, use the developments in the proof of Lemma 9.1.1 to construct an optimal measurement that saturates this bound. (Further hint: Consider the measurement $\{\Pi_P, \Pi_Q\}$.)

EXERCISE 9.1.11 Show that the trace distance is *strongly convex*. That is, for two ensembles $\{p_{X_1}(x), \rho_x\}$ and $\{p_{X_2}(x), \sigma_x\}$ such that $\rho_x, \sigma_x \in \mathcal{D}(\mathcal{H})$ for all x, the following inequality holds

$$\left\|\sum_x p_{X_1}(x)\rho_x - \sum_x p_{X_2}(x)\sigma_x\right\|_1$$

$$\leq \sum_x |p_{X_1}(x) - p_{X_2}(x)| + \sum_x p_{X_1}(x)\|\rho_x - \sigma_x\|_1. \quad (9.72)$$

9.1.6   Channel Distinguishability and the Diamond Norm

Given the operational interpretation of trace distance in terms of the discrimination of quantum states (from Section 9.1.4), a next natural question is to understand how we can distinguish one quantum channel from another. That is, we would like to understand how close two quantum channels are to each other in an operational sense. For this purpose, there is a hypothesis testing scenario which extends that from Section 9.1.4. In the protocol for state discrimination from Section 9.1.4, there were really just two steps: Bob prepares one of two states at random and sends the state to Alice, who then performs a measurement in an attempt to figure out which one Bob prepared.

When distinguishing channels, there is an extra degree of freedom: the channel accepts an input quantum state which then gets transformed to an output quantum state. This suggests that we should allow for an extra step in a channel distinguishability scenario, in which Alice prepares a quantum state. Let $\mathcal{N}, \mathcal{M} : \mathcal{L}(\mathcal{H}_A) \to \mathcal{L}(\mathcal{H}_B)$ be quantum channels. The augmented hypothesis testing scenario consists of the following steps:

1. Alice prepares a state ρ_A and sends it to Bob.
2. Bob flips a fair coin and based on the outcome, he acts on ρ_A with either $\mathcal{N}$ or $\mathcal{M}$. Bob sends the output of the channel to Alice.
3. Alice then performs a measurement to figure out which channel Bob applied.

From our development in the previous section, we can immediately conclude that the success probability in distinguishing the channels using such a protocol is equal to

$$\frac{1}{2}\left(1 + \frac{1}{2}\|\mathcal{N}_{A\to B}(\rho_A) - \mathcal{M}_{A\to B}(\rho_A)\|_1\right). \quad (9.73)$$

However, it is clear that Alice could potentially increase the success probability by maximizing this quantity with respect to her choice of the input state. This leads to the following expression for the success probability:

$$\frac{1}{2}\left(1 + \frac{1}{2}\max_{\rho_A \in \mathcal{D}(\mathcal{H}_A)} \|\mathcal{N}_{A\to B}(\rho_A) - \mathcal{M}_{A\to B}(\rho_A)\|_1\right). \quad (9.74)$$

This suggests that we should consider the quantity

$$\max_{\rho_A \in \mathcal{D}(\mathcal{H}_A)} \|\mathcal{N}_{A\to B}(\rho_A) - \mathcal{M}_{A\to B}(\rho_A)\|_1 \quad (9.75)$$

to be our measure of distinguishability between channels $\mathcal{N}$ and $\mathcal{M}$. However, there is still a problem because the protocol for distinguishing the channels is not as general as it could be. That is, it excludes the possibility of Alice preparing an entangled state to distinguish the channels. The most general protocol for distinguishing the channels consists of the following steps (depicted in Figure 9.3):

1. Alice prepares a state ρ_{RA} on systems R and A and sends system A to Bob. The reference system R can have an arbitrarily large dimension.
2. Bob flips a fair coin and based on the outcome, he acts on the A system with either $\mathcal{N}$ or $\mathcal{M}$, which produces an output system B. Bob sends the system B to Alice.
3. Alice then performs a measurement on systems R and B to figure out which channel Bob applied.

In such a protocol, we allow for the possibility of Alice preparing an entangled state. It turns out that there can sometimes be a huge difference in Alice's ability to figure out which channel was applied, if we allow or do not allow for entangled states to be prepared (this depends on the channels).

By the same reasoning as before and allowing for an optimization over all possible input states that Alice could prepare, Alice's success probability in distinguishing the channels is as follows:

$$\frac{1}{2}\left(1 + \frac{1}{2}\sup_{n}\max_{\rho_{R_n A}}\left\|\left(\mathrm{id}_{R_n}\otimes\mathcal{N}_{A\to B}\right)\left(\rho_{R_n A}\right) - \left(\mathrm{id}_{R_n}\otimes\mathcal{M}_{A\to B}\right)\left(\rho_{R_n A}\right)\right\|_1\right),$$
$$(9.76)$$

where $\rho_{R_n A} \in \mathcal{D}(\mathcal{H}_{R_n} \otimes \mathcal{H}_A)$. In the above formula, n is a positive integer corresponding to the dimension of the reference system R_n. A priori, we require a supremum over this dimension size since we have not yet placed a bound on the dimension needed for a reference system. The channel distance measure appearing in the above formula is known as the diamond-norm distance between the channels:

DEFINITION 9.1.3 (Diamond-Norm Distance)   Let $\mathcal{N}, \mathcal{M} : \mathcal{L}(\mathcal{H}_A) \to \mathcal{L}(\mathcal{H}_B)$ be quantum channels. The diamond-norm distance is defined as

$$\|\mathcal{N} - \mathcal{M}\|_\diamond \equiv \sup_{n}\max_{\rho_{R_n A}}\left\|\left(\mathrm{id}_{R_n}\otimes\mathcal{N}_{A\to B}\right)\left(\rho_{R_n A}\right) - \left(\mathrm{id}_{R_n}\otimes\mathcal{M}_{A\to B}\right)\left(\rho_{R_n A}\right)\right\|_1,$$
$$(9.77)$$

where $\rho_{R_n A} \in \mathcal{D}(\mathcal{H}_{R_n} \otimes \mathcal{H}_A)$.

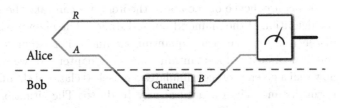

Figure 9.3 Protocol for Alice to distinguish one channel from another (described in main text).

Given the above definition, a natural question is whether we can place a bound on the dimension of the reference system required. Indeed, this is possible, as the following theorem states:

THEOREM 9.1.1 Let $\mathcal{N}, \mathcal{M} : \mathcal{L}(\mathcal{H}_A) \to \mathcal{L}(\mathcal{H}_B)$ be quantum channels. Then

$$\|\mathcal{N} - \mathcal{M}\|_\diamond =$$
$$\max_{|\psi\rangle_{RA}} \|(\mathrm{id}_R \otimes \mathcal{N}_{A\to B})(|\psi\rangle\langle\psi|_{RA}) - (\mathrm{id}_R \otimes \mathcal{M}_{A\to B})(|\psi\rangle\langle\psi|_{RA})\|_1, \quad (9.78)$$

where the optimization is with respect to all $|\psi\rangle_{RA} \in \mathcal{H}_R \otimes \mathcal{H}_A$ such that $\||\psi\rangle_{RA}\|_2 = 1$, with $\dim(\mathcal{H}_R) = \dim(\mathcal{H}_A)$.

Proof This theorem follows as a consequence of the convexity of the trace norm and the Schmidt decomposition. Indeed, let $\rho_{R_n A}$ be any density operator for systems R_n and A. Let $\sum_x p_X(x)|\psi^x\rangle\langle\psi^x|_{R_n A}$ be a spectral decomposition of $\rho_{R_n A}$. From the convexity of the trace norm, we find that

$$\|(\mathrm{id}_{R_n} \otimes \mathcal{N}_{A\to B})(\rho_{R_n A}) - (\mathrm{id}_{R_n} \otimes \mathcal{M}_{A\to B})(\rho_{R_n A})\|_1$$
$$= \left\| \sum_x p_X(x) \left[(\mathrm{id}_{R_n} \otimes \mathcal{N}_{A\to B})(|\psi^x\rangle\langle\psi^x|_{R_n A}) \right. \right.$$
$$\left. \left. - (\mathrm{id}_{R_n} \otimes \mathcal{M}_{A\to B})(|\psi^x\rangle\langle\psi^x|_{R_n A})\right] \right\|_1 \qquad (9.79)$$
$$\leq \sum_x p_X(x) \|[(\mathrm{id}_{R_n} \otimes \mathcal{N}_{A\to B})(|\psi^x\rangle\langle\psi^x|_{R_n A})$$
$$- (\mathrm{id}_{R_n} \otimes \mathcal{M}_{A\to B})(|\psi^x\rangle\langle\psi^x|_{R_n A})]\|_1 \qquad (9.80)$$
$$\leq \|[(\mathrm{id}_{R_n} \otimes \mathcal{N}_{A\to B})(|\psi^x_*\rangle\langle\psi^x_*|_{R_n A}) - (\mathrm{id}_{R_n} \otimes \mathcal{M}_{A\to B})(|\psi^x_*\rangle\langle\psi^x_*|_{R_n A})]\|_1, \qquad (9.81)$$

where the last inequality follows because the average value is never larger than the maximum value and we let $|\psi^x_*\rangle_{R_n A}$ denote the state vector giving the maximum value. From the Schmidt decomposition theorem (Theorem 3.8.1), the Schmidt rank of $|\psi^x_*\rangle_{R_n A}$ is no larger than $\dim(\mathcal{H}_A)$, implying that $|\psi^x_*\rangle_{R_n A}$ can be embedded in a tensor-product Hilbert space $\mathcal{H}_R \otimes \mathcal{H}_A$ such that $\dim(\mathcal{H}_R) = \dim(\mathcal{H}_A)$. Since this bound holds for any density operator $\rho_{R_n A}$, the statement of the theorem follows. $\square$

As a consequence of the above theorem, we can take the result in (9.78) to be the definition of the diamond-norm distance. The main use of the diamond-norm distance is for comparing quantum channels. For example, when studying the classical capacity of a quantum channel (Chapter 20), we would like to compare how well a given protocol simulates a noiseless classical channel, and the diamond-norm distance gives a natural way to do so. The situation is similar with the quantum capacity theorem (Chapter 24): here we would like to compare how well a protocol simulates a noiseless quantum channel, and we can quantify the performance using the diamond-norm distance.

EXERCISE 9.1.12 Suppose that Alice is restricted to use separable states on systems R_n and A to distinguish two quantum channels $\mathcal{N}$ and $\mathcal{M}$. Show that the success probability in doing so is given by

$$\frac{1}{2}\left(1 + \frac{1}{2}\max_{|\psi\rangle_A} \|\mathcal{N}_{A\to B}(|\psi\rangle\langle\psi|_A) - \mathcal{M}_{A\to B}(|\psi\rangle\langle\psi|_A)\|_1\right), \qquad (9.82)$$

where $|\psi\rangle\langle\psi|_A \in \mathcal{D}(\mathcal{H}_A)$.

EXERCISE 9.1.13 Suppose that channels $\mathcal{N}$ and $\mathcal{M}$ are defined as follows:

$$\mathcal{N}(X_A) = \text{Tr}\{X_A\}\rho_B, \qquad \mathcal{M}(X_A) = \text{Tr}\{X_A\}\sigma_B, \qquad (9.83)$$

where $X_A \in \mathcal{L}(\mathcal{H}_A)$ and $\rho_B, \sigma_B \in \mathcal{D}(\mathcal{H}_B)$. Show that

$$\|\mathcal{N} - \mathcal{M}\|_\diamond = \|\rho_B - \sigma_B\|_1. \qquad (9.84)$$

9.2 Fidelity

9.2.1 Pure-State Fidelity

An alternate measure of the closeness of two quantum states is the *fidelity*. We introduce its most simple form first. Suppose that we input a particular pure state $|\psi\rangle$ to a quantum information-processing protocol. Ideally, we may want the protocol to output the same state that is input, but suppose that it instead outputs a pure state $|\phi\rangle$. The pure-state fidelity $F(\psi, \phi)$ is a measure of how close the output state is to the input state.

DEFINITION 9.2.1 (Pure-State Fidelity) Let $|\psi\rangle, |\phi\rangle \in \mathcal{H}$ be pure states. The pure-state fidelity is the squared overlap of the states $|\psi\rangle$ and $|\phi\rangle$:

$$F(\psi, \phi) \equiv |\langle\psi|\phi\rangle|^2. \qquad (9.85)$$

The pure-state fidelity has the operational interpretation as the probability that the output state $|\phi\rangle$ would pass a test for being the same as the input state $|\psi\rangle$, conducted by someone who knows the input state (see Exercise 9.2.2).

The pure-state fidelity is symmetric $F(\psi, \phi) = F(\phi, \psi)$, and it obeys the following bounds:

$$0 \leq F(\psi, \phi) \leq 1. \qquad (9.86)$$

It is equal to one if and only if the two states are the same, and it is equal to zero if and only if the two states are orthogonal to each other. The fidelity measure is *not* a distance measure in the strict mathematical sense because it is equal to one when two states are equal, whereas a distance measure should be equal to zero when two states are equal.

EXERCISE 9.2.1 Suppose that two pure quantum states $|\psi\rangle, |\phi\rangle \in \mathcal{H}$ are as follows:

$$|\psi\rangle \equiv \sum_x \sqrt{p(x)}|x\rangle, \qquad |\phi\rangle \equiv \sum_x \sqrt{q(x)}|x\rangle, \qquad (9.87)$$

where $\{|x\rangle\}$ is some orthonormal basis for $\mathcal{H}$. Show that the fidelity $F(\psi, \phi)$ between these two states is equivalent to the *Bhattacharyya overlap* (classical fidelity) between the distributions $p(x)$ and $q(x)$:

$$F(\psi, \phi) = \left[\sum_x \sqrt{p(x)q(x)} \right]^2 . \tag{9.88}$$

9.2.2   Expected Fidelity

Now let us suppose that the output of a given protocol is not a pure state, but it is rather a mixed state with density operator ρ. In general, a quantum information-processing protocol could be noisy and map the pure input state $|\psi\rangle$ to a mixed state. We would like a way to compare these two states.

DEFINITION 9.2.2 (Expected Fidelity)   The expected fidelity $F(\psi, \rho)$ between a pure state $|\psi\rangle \in \mathcal{H}$ and a mixed state $\rho \in \mathcal{D}(\mathcal{H})$ is

$$F(\psi, \rho) \equiv \langle \psi | \rho | \psi \rangle. \tag{9.89}$$

We now justify the above definition of fidelity. Let us decompose ρ according to a spectral decomposition $\rho = \sum_x p_X(x)|\phi_x\rangle\langle\phi_x|$. Recall that we can think of this output density operator as arising from the ensemble $\{p_X(x), |\phi_x\rangle\}$. We generalize the pure-state fidelity from the previous paragraph by defining it as the expected pure-state fidelity, where the expectation is with respect to states in the ensemble:

$$F(\psi, \rho) \equiv \mathbb{E}_X \left[|\langle \psi | \phi_X \rangle|^2 \right] \tag{9.90}$$

$$= \sum_x p_X(x) |\langle \psi | \phi_x \rangle|^2 \tag{9.91}$$

$$= \sum_x p_X(x) \langle \psi | \phi_x \rangle \langle \phi_x | \psi \rangle \tag{9.92}$$

$$= \langle \psi | \left(\sum_x p_X(x) |\phi_x\rangle\langle\phi_x| \right) |\psi\rangle \tag{9.93}$$

$$= \langle \psi | \rho | \psi \rangle. \tag{9.94}$$

The compact formula $F(\psi, \rho) = \langle \psi | \rho | \psi \rangle$ is a good way to characterize the fidelity when the input state is pure and the output state is mixed. We can see that the above fidelity measure is a generalization of the pure-state fidelity in (9.85). It obeys the same bounds:

$$0 \le F(\psi, \rho) \le 1, \tag{9.95}$$

being equal to one if and only if the state ρ is equal to $|\psi\rangle\langle\psi|$ and equal to zero if and only if the support of ρ is orthogonal to $|\psi\rangle\langle\psi|$.

EXERCISE 9.2.2   Given a state $\sigma \in \mathcal{D}(\mathcal{H})$, we would like to see if it would pass a test for being close to a pure state $|\varphi\rangle \in \mathcal{H}$. We can measure the POVM

$\{|\varphi\rangle\langle\varphi|, I - |\varphi\rangle\langle\varphi|\}$ with result φ corresponding to a "pass" and the result $I - \varphi$ corresponding to a "fail." Show that the fidelity is then equal to $\Pr\{\text{"pass"}\}$.

EXERCISE 9.2.3   Using the result of Corollary 9.1.1, show that the following inequality holds for a pure state $|\phi\rangle \in \mathcal{H}$ and mixed states $\rho, \sigma \in \mathcal{D}(\mathcal{H})$:

$$F(\phi, \rho) \leq F(\phi, \sigma) + \tfrac{1}{2} \|\rho - \sigma\|_1. \tag{9.96}$$

9.2.3   Uhlmann Fidelity

What is the most general form of the fidelity when both quantum states are mixed? We can borrow the above idea of the pure-state fidelity that exploits the overlap between two pure states. Suppose that we would like to determine the fidelity between two mixed states ρ_A and σ_A that represent different states of some quantum system A. Let $|\phi^\rho\rangle_{RA}$ and $|\phi^\sigma\rangle_{RA}$ denote particular respective purifications of the mixed states to some reference system R (where for now we assume that the reference system has the same dimension as the system A). We can define the Uhlmann fidelity $F(\rho_A, \sigma_A)$ between two mixed states ρ_A and σ_A as the maximum overlap between their respective purifications, where the maximization is with respect to all purifications $|\phi^\rho\rangle_{RA}$ and $|\phi^\sigma\rangle_{RA}$ of the respective states ρ_A and σ_A:

$$F(\rho_A, \sigma_A) \equiv \max_{|\phi^\rho\rangle_{RA}, \, |\phi^\sigma\rangle_{RA}} |\langle \phi^\rho | \phi^\sigma \rangle_{RA}|^2. \tag{9.97}$$

We can express the fidelity as a maximization over unitaries instead (recall the result of Theorem 5.1.1 that all purifications are equivalent up to unitaries on the reference system):

$$F(\rho_A, \sigma_A) = \max_{U^\rho, U^\sigma} \left| \langle \phi^\rho |_{RA} \left((U_R^\rho)^\dagger \otimes I_A \right) (U_R^\sigma \otimes I_A) |\phi^\sigma\rangle_{RA} \right|^2 \tag{9.98}$$

$$= \max_{U^\rho, U^\sigma} \left| \langle \phi^\rho |_{RA} (U_R^\rho)^\dagger U_R^\sigma \otimes I_A |\phi^\sigma\rangle_{RA} \right|^2. \tag{9.99}$$

It is unnecessary to maximize over two sets of unitaries because the product $(U_R^\rho)^\dagger U_R^\sigma$ represents only a single unitary. The final expression for the fidelity between two mixed states is then defined as the Uhlmann fidelity.

DEFINITION 9.2.3   (Uhlmann Fidelity)   The Uhlmann fidelity $F(\rho_A, \sigma_A)$ between two mixed states ρ_A and σ_A is the maximum overlap between their respective purifications, where the maximization is with respect to all unitaries U acting on the purification system R:

$$F(\rho_A, \sigma_A) = \max_U |\langle \phi^\rho |_{RA} U_R \otimes I_A |\phi^\sigma\rangle_{RA}|^2. \tag{9.100}$$

We will find that this notion of fidelity generalizes both the pure-state fidelity in (9.85) and the expected fidelity in (9.94). This holds because the following formula for the fidelity of two mixed states, characterized in terms of the Schatten 1-norm, is equivalent to the above Uhlmann characterization:

$$F(\rho_A, \sigma_A) = \left\| \sqrt{\rho_A} \sqrt{\sigma_A} \right\|_1^2. \tag{9.101}$$

We state this result as Uhlmann's theorem.

THEOREM 9.2.1 (Uhlmann's Theorem)　The following two expressions for fidelity are equal:

$$F(\rho_A, \sigma_A) = \max_U \left| \langle \phi^\rho |_{RA} U_R \otimes I_A | \phi^\sigma \rangle_{RA} \right|^2 = \left\| \sqrt{\rho_A} \sqrt{\sigma_A} \right\|_1^2. \tag{9.102}$$

Proof　Let $|\phi^\rho\rangle_{RA}$ denote the canonical purification of ρ_A (see Exercise 5.1.2):

$$|\phi^\rho\rangle_{RA} \equiv (I_R \otimes \sqrt{\rho_A}) |\Gamma\rangle_{RA}, \tag{9.103}$$

where $|\Gamma\rangle_{RA}$ is the unnormalized maximally entangled vector:

$$|\Gamma\rangle_{RA} \equiv \sum_i |i\rangle_R |i\rangle_A. \tag{9.104}$$

Therefore, the state $|\phi^\rho\rangle_{RA}$ is a particular purification of ρ. Let $|\phi^\sigma\rangle_{RA}$ denote the canonical purification of σ_A:

$$|\phi^\sigma\rangle_{RA} \equiv (I_R \otimes \sqrt{\sigma_A}) |\Gamma\rangle_{RA}. \tag{9.105}$$

Consider that the overlap $\left| \langle \phi^\rho | U_R \otimes I_A | \phi^\sigma \rangle \right|^2$ is as follows:

$$\left| \langle \phi^\rho | U_R \otimes I_A | \phi^\sigma \rangle \right|^2 = \left| \langle \Gamma |_{RA} (U_R \otimes \sqrt{\rho_A}) (I_R \otimes \sqrt{\sigma_A}) |\Gamma\rangle_{RA} \right|^2 \tag{9.106}$$

$$= \left| \langle \Gamma |_{RA} (U_R \otimes \sqrt{\rho_A} \sqrt{\sigma_A}) |\Gamma\rangle_{RA} \right|^2 \tag{9.107}$$

$$= \left| \langle \Gamma |_{RA} (I_R \otimes \sqrt{\rho_A} \sqrt{\sigma_A} U_A^T) |\Gamma\rangle_{RA} \right|^2 \tag{9.108}$$

$$= \left| \text{Tr} \left\{ \sqrt{\rho_A} \sqrt{\sigma_A} U_A^T \right\} \right|^2. \tag{9.109}$$

The first equality follows by plugging in (9.103) and (9.105). The third equality follows from Exercise 3.7.12. The last equality follows from Exercise 4.1.3. We can finally invoke Property 9.1.6 to establish that

$$\max_{U_A} \left| \text{Tr} \left\{ \sqrt{\rho_A} \sqrt{\sigma_A} U_A^T \right\} \right|^2 = \left\| \sqrt{\rho_A} \sqrt{\sigma_A} \right\|_1^2, \tag{9.110}$$

from which (9.102) follows.　□

EXERCISE 9.2.4　Use the expression $\left\| \sqrt{\rho_A} \sqrt{\sigma_A} \right\|_1^2$ for the fidelity and the Cauchy–Schwarz inequality for the Hilbert–Schmidt inner product (from (9.20)) to prove that the quantum fidelity between two density operators never exceeds one.

REMARK 9.2.1　Note that we can define the fidelity function more generally for any two positive semi-definite operators, which can sometimes be useful. That is, let P and Q be positive semi-definite operators acting on the same Hilbert space. Then we define

$$F(P, Q) \equiv \left\| \sqrt{P} \sqrt{Q} \right\|_1^2. \tag{9.111}$$

By applying the Cauchy–Schwarz inequality for the Hilbert–Schmidt inner product (see (9.20)) and the characterization of the trace norm in Property 9.1.6, we find that

$$F(P, Q) \leq \text{Tr}\{P\} \text{Tr}\{Q\}. \tag{9.112}$$

REMARK 9.2.2   Note that in the development above, we assumed that the dimension of the reference system R is equal to that of the system A. However, this is the not the most general definition that we could have taken. We could have defined fidelity as

$$F(\rho_A, \sigma_A) = \sup_{\dim(\mathcal{H}_R)} \max_{|\phi^\rho\rangle_{RA}, |\phi^\sigma\rangle_{RA}} |\langle \phi^\rho|_{RA} |\phi^\sigma\rangle_{RA}|^2, \tag{9.113}$$

in which there is an extra optimization over the dimension of the reference system R in addition to the optimization over the purifications. However, repeating an analysis similar to the above one would lead us to the conclusion that

$$F(\rho_A, \sigma_A) = \|\sqrt{\rho_A}\sqrt{\sigma_A}\|_1^2 \tag{9.114}$$

for this definition as well. Indeed, we have that

$$|\langle \phi^\rho|_{RA} |\phi^\sigma\rangle_{RA}|^2 = \left| \left[\langle \Gamma|_{R'A}\sqrt{\rho_A}\, (V_{R'\to R})^\dagger \right] [U_{R'\to R}\sqrt{\sigma_A} |\Gamma\rangle_{R'A}] \right|^2, \tag{9.115}$$

where R' is a reference system with dimension equal to $\dim(\mathcal{H}_A)$ and $U_{R'\to R}$ and $V_{R'\to R}$ are some isometries, given that all purifications are related by an isometry acting on the reference system (Theorem 5.1.1). Carrying through the same analysis along with the characterization of the trace norm in Exercise 9.1.6 then gives that $|\langle \phi^\rho|_{RA} |\phi^\sigma\rangle_{RA}| \leq \|\sqrt{\rho_A}\sqrt{\sigma_A}\|_1$, so that having an arbitrarily large reference system does not help.

9.2.4   Properties of Fidelity

We discuss some further properties of the fidelity that often prove useful. Some of these properties are the counterpart of similar properties of the trace distance. From the characterization of fidelity in (9.102), we observe that it is symmetric in its arguments:

$$F(\rho, \sigma) = F(\sigma, \rho). \tag{9.116}$$

It obeys the following bounds:

$$0 \leq F(\rho, \sigma) \leq 1. \tag{9.117}$$

The lower bound applies if and only if the respective supports of the two states ρ and σ are orthogonal. To see this, suppose that the supports of ρ and σ are orthogonal. This implies that $\sqrt{\rho}\sqrt{\sigma} = 0$, so that $F(\rho, \sigma) = \|\sqrt{\rho}\sqrt{\sigma}\|_1^2 = 0$. On the other hand, suppose that $F(\rho, \sigma) = 0$. Then by definition, this means that $\|\sqrt{\rho}\sqrt{\sigma}\|_1^2 = 0$, and from non-negative definiteness of the trace norm, we find that $\sqrt{\rho}\sqrt{\sigma} = 0$. This then implies that the supports of ρ and σ are orthogonal.

The upper bound in (9.117) applies if and only if the two states ρ and σ are equal to each other.

EXERCISE 9.2.5 Show that the definition of fidelity in (9.101) reduces to (9.85) when the two states are pure and to (9.89) when one state is pure and the other is mixed.

PROPERTY 9.2.1 (Multiplicativity) Let $\rho_1, \sigma_1 \in \mathcal{D}(\mathcal{H}_1)$ and $\rho_2, \sigma_2 \in \mathcal{D}(\mathcal{H}_2)$. The fidelity is multiplicative with respect to tensor products:

$$F(\rho_1 \otimes \rho_2, \sigma_1 \otimes \sigma_2) = F(\rho_1, \sigma_1) F(\rho_2, \sigma_2). \tag{9.118}$$

This result holds by employing the definition of the fidelity in (9.101).

The following monotonicity lemma is similar to the monotonicity lemma for trace distance (Lemma 9.1.2) and also bears the similar interpretation that quantum states become more similar (less distinguishable) under the discarding of subsystems.

LEMMA 9.2.1 (Monotonicity) Let $\rho_{AB}, \sigma_{AB} \in \mathcal{D}(\mathcal{H}_A \otimes \mathcal{H}_B)$. The fidelity is non-decreasing with respect to partial trace:

$$F(\rho_{AB}, \sigma_{AB}) \leq F(\rho_A, \sigma_A), \tag{9.119}$$

where

$$\rho_A = \text{Tr}_B\{\rho_{AB}\}, \qquad \sigma_A = \text{Tr}_B\{\sigma_{AB}\}. \tag{9.120}$$

Proof Consider a fixed purification $|\psi\rangle_{RAB}$ of ρ_A and ρ_{AB} and a fixed purification $|\phi\rangle_{RAB}$ of σ_A and σ_{AB}. Then

$$|\langle\psi|_{RAB} U_R \otimes I_A \otimes I_B |\phi\rangle_{RAB}|^2 \leq \max_{U_{RB}} |\langle\psi|_{RAB} U_{RB} \otimes I_A |\phi\rangle_{RAB}|^2 \tag{9.121}$$

$$= F(\rho_A, \sigma_A), \tag{9.122}$$

where the first inequality follows because the maximization over unitaries U_{RB} includes $U_R \otimes I_A$ and the equality is a consequence of Uhlmann's theorem. Given that the inequality holds for all unitaries U_R, we can conclude that

$$F(\rho_{AB}, \sigma_{AB}) = \max_{U_R} |\langle\psi|_{RAB} U_R \otimes I_A \otimes I_B |\phi\rangle_{RAB}|^2 \leq F(\rho_A, \sigma_A), \tag{9.123}$$

where the equality is again a consequence of Uhlmann's theorem. □

PROPERTY 9.2.2 (Joint Concavity) Let $\rho_x, \sigma_x \in \mathcal{D}(\mathcal{H})$ for all x and let p_X be a probability distribution. The root fidelity is jointly concave with respect to its input arguments:

$$\sqrt{F}\left(\sum_x p_X(x)\rho_x, \sum_x p_X(x)\sigma_x\right) \geq \sum_x p_X(x)\sqrt{F}(\rho_x, \sigma_x). \tag{9.124}$$

Proof We prove joint concavity by exploiting the result of Exercise 5.1.4. Suppose $|\phi^{\rho_x}\rangle_{RA}$ and $|\phi^{\sigma_x}\rangle_{RA}$ are respective Uhlmann purifications of ρ_x and σ_x (these are purifications that maximize the Uhlmann fidelity). Then

$$F(\phi_{RA}^{\rho_x}, \phi_{RA}^{\sigma_x}) = F(\rho_x, \sigma_x). \tag{9.125}$$

Choose some orthonormal basis $\{|x\rangle_X\}$. Then

$$|\phi^\rho\rangle \equiv \sum_x \sqrt{p_X(x)}|\phi^{\rho_x}\rangle_{RA}|x\rangle_X, \qquad |\phi^\sigma\rangle \equiv \sum_x \sqrt{p_X(x)}|\phi^{\sigma_x}\rangle_{RA}|x\rangle_X \tag{9.126}$$

are respective purifications of $\sum_x p_X(x)\rho_x$ and $\sum_x p_X(x)\sigma_x$. The first inequality below holds by Uhlmann's theorem:

$$\sqrt{F}\left(\sum_x p_X(x)\rho_x, \sum_x p_X(x)\sigma_x\right) \geq |\langle\phi^\rho|\phi^\sigma\rangle| \tag{9.127}$$

$$= \left|\sum_x p_X(x)\langle\phi^{\rho_x}|\phi^{\sigma_x}\rangle\right| \tag{9.128}$$

$$\geq \sum_x p_X(x)|\langle\phi^{\rho_x}|\phi^{\sigma_x}\rangle| \tag{9.129}$$

$$= \sum_x p_X(x)\sqrt{F}(\rho_x, \sigma_x), \tag{9.130}$$

concluding the proof. $\qquad\qquad\qquad\qquad\qquad\qquad\qquad\qquad\qquad\qquad\square$

PROPERTY 9.2.3 (Concavity)   Let $\rho, \sigma, \tau \in \mathcal{D}(\mathcal{H})$ and $\lambda \in [0,1]$. The fidelity is concave with respect to one of its arguments:

$$F(\lambda\rho + (1-\lambda)\tau, \sigma) \geq \lambda F(\rho, \sigma) + (1-\lambda)F(\tau, \sigma). \tag{9.131}$$

Proof Let $|\psi^\sigma\rangle_{RS}$ be a fixed purification of σ_S. Let $|\psi^\rho\rangle_{RS}$ be a purification of ρ_S such that

$$|\langle\psi^\sigma|\psi^\rho\rangle|^2 = F(\rho, \sigma). \tag{9.132}$$

Similarly, let $|\psi^\tau\rangle_{RS}$ be a purification of τ_S such that

$$|\langle\psi^\sigma|\psi^\tau\rangle|^2 = F(\tau, \sigma). \tag{9.133}$$

Then consider that

$$\lambda F(\rho, \sigma) + (1-\lambda)F(\tau, \sigma)$$

$$= \lambda|\langle\psi^\sigma|\psi^\rho\rangle|^2 + (1-\lambda)|\langle\psi^\sigma|\psi^\tau\rangle|^2 \tag{9.134}$$

$$= \lambda\langle\psi^\sigma|\psi^\rho\rangle\langle\psi^\rho|\psi^\sigma\rangle + (1-\lambda)\langle\psi^\sigma|\psi^\tau\rangle\langle\psi^\tau|\psi^\sigma\rangle \tag{9.135}$$

$$= \langle\psi^\sigma|_{RS}(\lambda|\psi^\rho\rangle\langle\psi^\rho|_{RS} + (1-\lambda)|\psi^\tau\rangle\langle\psi^\tau|_{RS})|\psi^\sigma\rangle_{RS} \tag{9.136}$$

$$= F(|\psi^\sigma\rangle\langle\psi^\sigma|_{RS}, \lambda|\psi^\rho\rangle\langle\psi^\rho|_{RS} + (1-\lambda)|\psi^\tau\rangle\langle\psi^\tau|_{RS}) \tag{9.137}$$

$$\leq F(\psi_S^\sigma, \lambda\psi_S^\rho + (1-\lambda)\psi_S^\tau) \tag{9.138}$$

$$= F(\lambda\rho + (1-\lambda)\tau, \sigma). \tag{9.139}$$

The first step is a rewriting using (9.132) and (9.133). The fourth equality is a consequence of Exercise 9.2.5. The inequality follows from monotonicity of the fidelity with respect to partial trace (Lemma 9.2.1). □

EXERCISE 9.2.6   Let $\rho, \sigma \in \mathcal{D}(\mathcal{H})$. Show that we can express the root fidelity as

$$\sqrt{F}(\rho, \sigma) = \mathrm{Tr}\left\{\sqrt{\rho^{1/2}\sigma\rho^{1/2}}\right\} = \mathrm{Tr}\left\{\sqrt{\sigma^{1/2}\rho\sigma^{1/2}}\right\}, \qquad (9.140)$$

using the definition in (9.101).

EXERCISE 9.2.7   Let $\rho, \sigma \in \mathcal{D}(\mathcal{H})$. Show that the fidelity is invariant with respect to an isometry $U \in \mathcal{L}(\mathcal{H}, \mathcal{H}')$:

$$F(\rho, \sigma) = F(U\rho U^{\dagger}, U\sigma U^{\dagger}). \qquad (9.141)$$

EXERCISE 9.2.8   Let $\rho, \sigma \in \mathcal{D}(\mathcal{H}_A)$ and let $\mathcal{N} : \mathcal{L}(\mathcal{H}_A) \to \mathcal{L}(\mathcal{H}_B)$ be a quantum channel. Show that the fidelity is monotone with respect to the channel $\mathcal{N}$:

$$F(\rho, \sigma) \leq F(\mathcal{N}(\rho), \mathcal{N}(\sigma)). \qquad (9.142)$$

EXERCISE 9.2.9   Suppose that Alice uses a noisy quantum channel and a sequence of quantum channels to generate the following state, shared with Bob and Eve:

$$\frac{1}{\sqrt{M}} \sum_m |m\rangle_A |m\rangle_{B_1} |\phi_m\rangle_{B_2 E}, \qquad (9.143)$$

where $\{|m\rangle_A\}$ and $\{|m\rangle_{B_1}\}$ are orthonormal bases and $\{|\phi_m\rangle_{B_2 E}\}$ is a set of states. Alice possesses the system A, Bob possesses systems B_1 and B_2, and Eve possesses the system E. Let ϕ_E^m denote the partial trace of $|\phi_m\rangle_{B_2 E}$ over Bob's system B_2 so that

$$\phi_E^m \equiv \mathrm{Tr}_{B_2}\left\{|\phi_m\rangle\langle\phi_m|_{B_2 E}\right\}. \qquad (9.144)$$

Suppose further that $F(\phi_E^m, \theta_E) = 1$, where θ_E is some *constant* density operator (independent of m) for Eve's system E. Determine a unitary that Bob can perform on his systems B_1 and B_2 so that he *decouples* Eve's system E, in the sense that the state after the decoupling unitary is as follows:

$$\left(\frac{1}{\sqrt{M}} \sum_m |m\rangle_A |m\rangle_{B_1}\right) \otimes |\phi_\theta\rangle_{B_2 E}, \qquad (9.145)$$

where $|\phi_\theta\rangle_{B_2 E}$ is a purification of the state θ_E. The result is that Alice and Bob share maximal entanglement between the respective systems A and B_1 after Bob performs the decoupling unitary. Figure 9.4 displays the protocol.

EXERCISE 9.2.10 (Fidelity for Classical–Quantum States)   Show that the root fidelity possesses the following property:

$$\sqrt{F}\left(\omega_{XB}, \tau_{XB}\right) = \sum_x \sqrt{p(x)q(x)} \sqrt{F}\left(\omega_x, \tau_x\right), \qquad (9.146)$$

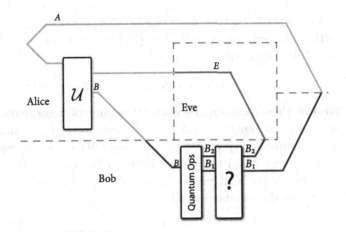

Figure 9.4 This figure depicts the protocol relevant to Exercise 9.2.9. Alice transmits one share of an entangled state through a quantum channel with isometric extension channel $\mathcal{U}$. Bob and Eve receive quantum systems as the output of the isometry. Bob performs some quantum operations so that Alice, Bob, and Eve share the state in (9.143). Exercise 9.2.9 asks you to determine a decoupling unitary that Bob can perform to decouple his system B_1 from Eve.

where

$$\omega_{XB} \equiv \sum_x p(x)|x\rangle\langle x|_X \otimes \omega_x, \qquad \tau_{XB} \equiv \sum_x q(x)|x\rangle\langle x|_X \otimes \tau_x, \qquad (9.147)$$

p and q are probability distributions, $\{|x\rangle\}$ is some orthonormal basis, and $\omega_x, \tau_x \in \mathcal{D}(\mathcal{H})$ for all x.

9.2.5 A Measurement Achieves the Fidelity

There is a classical notion of fidelity for probability distributions, which is sometimes called the classical fidelity or Bhattacharyya overlap. It is defined as follows:

DEFINITION 9.2.4 (Classical Fidelity) Let p and q be probability distributions defined over a finite alphabet $\mathcal{X}$. The classical fidelity $F(p, q)$ is defined as follows:

$$F(p, q) \equiv \left[\sum_{x \in \mathcal{X}} \sqrt{p(x)q(x)} \right]^2 . \qquad (9.148)$$

EXERCISE 9.2.11   Verify that the classical fidelity is a special case of the quantum fidelity. That is, let p and q be probability distributions defined over a finite alphabet $\mathcal{X}$, and then place the entries of these distributions along the diagonal of commuting matrices ρ and σ, respectively. Show that $F(p, q) = F(\rho, \sigma)$.

Now suppose that we have two density operators $\rho, \sigma \in \mathcal{D}(\mathcal{H})$, and suppose further that we perform a POVM $\{\Lambda_x\}$ on these states, leading to the following probability distributions:

$$p(x) = \text{Tr}\{\Lambda_x \rho\}, \qquad q(x) = \text{Tr}\{\Lambda_x \sigma\}. \tag{9.149}$$

We can then compute the classical fidelity of the distributions for the measurement outcomes by using the formula in (9.148), and this is a measure of distinguishability of the two quantum states, with respect to a particular measurement. From the monotonicity of the quantum fidelity with respect to quantum channels (Exercise 9.2.8), it follows that the quantum fidelity $F(\rho, \sigma)$ never exceeds this classical fidelity:

$$F(\rho, \sigma) \leq \left[\sum_{x \in \mathcal{X}} \sqrt{\text{Tr}\{\Lambda_x \rho\} \text{Tr}\{\Lambda_x \sigma\}} \right]^2. \tag{9.150}$$

In particular, this bound follows from Exercise 9.2.8, where the channel here is understood to be a measurement channel of the form $\omega \to \sum_x \text{Tr}\{\Lambda_x \omega\} |x\rangle\langle x|$ and then we apply the result of Exercise 9.2.11. What is perhaps surprising is that there always exists a measurement that saturates the bound above, leading to the following alternate characterization of fidelity:

THEOREM 9.2.2 (Measurement Achieves Fidelity)   Let $\rho, \sigma \in \mathcal{D}(\mathcal{H})$. Then

$$F(\rho, \sigma) = \min_{\{\Lambda_x\}} \left[\sum_{x \in \mathcal{X}} \sqrt{\text{Tr}\{\Lambda_x \rho\} \text{Tr}\{\Lambda_x \sigma\}} \right]^2, \tag{9.151}$$

where the minimization is with respect to all POVMs.

Proof   As justified before the statement of the theorem, the bound in (9.150) holds for any POVM. So here we construct a specific POVM (known as the Fuchs-Caves measurement) that saturates the bound. First consider the case in which σ is positive definite (and thus invertible). Consider the following operator (known as an operator geometric mean of ρ and σ^{-1}):

$$M = \sigma^{-1/2} \left[\sigma^{1/2} \rho \sigma^{1/2} \right]^{1/2} \sigma^{-1/2}. \tag{9.152}$$

The operator M is positive semi-definite, and thus has a spectral decomposition:

$$M = \sum_y \lambda_y |y\rangle\langle y|, \tag{9.153}$$

with $\{\lambda_y\}$ a set of non-negative eigenvalues and $\{|y\rangle\}$ a corresponding set of eigenvectors.

We will prove that the optimal measurement in (9.151) is $\{|y\rangle\langle y|\}$. We begin by noting that a simple calculation gives

$$M \sigma M = \rho. \tag{9.154}$$

So now consider the classical fidelity of the measurement $\{|y\rangle\langle y|\}$:

$$\sum_y \sqrt{\text{Tr}\{|y\rangle\langle y|\rho\}\,\text{Tr}\{|y\rangle\langle y|\sigma\}} = \sum_y \sqrt{\langle y|\rho|y\rangle\,\langle y|\sigma|y\rangle} \tag{9.155}$$

$$= \sum_y \sqrt{\langle y|M\sigma M|y\rangle\,\langle y|\sigma|y\rangle} \tag{9.156}$$

$$= \sum_y \sqrt{\langle y|\lambda_y\sigma\lambda_y|y\rangle\,\langle y|\sigma|y\rangle} \tag{9.157}$$

$$= \sum_y \lambda_y\langle y|\sigma|y\rangle. \tag{9.158}$$

The second equality follows from (9.154). The third equality follows because $M|y\rangle = \lambda_y|y\rangle$. Continuing, the last line above is equal to

$$\text{Tr}\left\{\sum_y \lambda_y|y\rangle\langle y|\sigma\right\} = \text{Tr}\{M\sigma\} = \text{Tr}\left\{\left[\sigma^{1/2}\rho\sigma^{1/2}\right]^{1/2}\right\} = \sqrt{F(\rho,\sigma)}. \tag{9.159}$$

The last equality follows from Exercise 9.2.6.

For the case in which σ is not invertible, we repeat the above analysis, replacing ρ with $\Pi_\sigma\rho\Pi_\sigma$, where Π_σ is the projection onto the support of σ. In this case, the geometric mean operator M has its support contained in the support of σ, and one can find a spectral decomposition of M as in (9.153) so that

$$\sqrt{F(\Pi_\sigma\rho\Pi_\sigma,\sigma)} = \sum_y \sqrt{\text{Tr}\{|y\rangle\langle y|\Pi_\sigma\rho\Pi_\sigma\}\,\text{Tr}\{|y\rangle\langle y|\sigma\}}. \tag{9.160}$$

Since the eigenvectors $\{|y\rangle\}$ do not necessarily span the whole space, we can add additional orthonormal vectors all orthogonal to those in $\{|y\rangle\}$, such that all of them taken together form a legitimate measurement. Since both $\Pi_\sigma\rho\Pi_\sigma$ and σ are orthogonal to all of the new vectors, the probabilities for these measurement outcomes are all equal to zero and thus they do not contribute anything to the sum in (9.160). Finally, we have that

$$F(\Pi_\sigma\rho\Pi_\sigma,\sigma) = F(\rho,\sigma) \tag{9.161}$$

because $\sigma^{1/2} = \Pi_\sigma\sigma^{1/2} = \sigma^{1/2}\Pi_\sigma$, so that

$$\sqrt{F(\rho,\sigma)} = \text{Tr}\left\{\sqrt{\sigma^{1/2}\rho\sigma^{1/2}}\right\}$$

$$= \text{Tr}\left\{\sqrt{\sigma^{1/2}\Pi_\sigma\rho\Pi_\sigma\sigma^{1/2}}\right\} = \sqrt{F(\Pi_\sigma\rho\Pi_\sigma,\sigma)}, \tag{9.162}$$

concluding the proof. $\qquad\square$

9.3 Relations between Trace Distance and Fidelity

In quantum Shannon theory, we are interested in showing that a given quantum information-processing protocol approximates an ideal protocol. We might do so by showing that the quantum output of the ideal protocol, say ρ, is close to the quantum output of the actual protocol, say σ. For example, we may be able to show that the fidelity between ρ and σ is high:

$$F(\rho, \sigma) \geq 1 - \varepsilon, \tag{9.163}$$

where ε is a small, positive real number that determines how well ρ approximates σ according to the above fidelity criterion. Typically, in a quantum Shannon-theoretic argument, we will take a limit to show that it is possible to make ε as small as we would like. As the performance parameter ε becomes vanishingly small, we expect that ρ and σ are becoming approximately equal so that they are identically equal when ε vanishes in some limit.

We would naturally think that the trace distance should be small if the fidelity is high because the trace distance vanishes when the fidelity is one and vice versa (recall the conditions for saturation of the bounds in (9.22) and (9.117)). The next theorem makes this intuition precise by establishing several relationships between the trace distance and fidelity.

THEOREM 9.3.1 (Relations Between Fidelity and Trace Distance) The following bound applies to the trace distance and the fidelity between two quantum states $\rho, \sigma \in \mathcal{D}(\mathcal{H})$:

$$1 - \sqrt{F(\rho, \sigma)} \leq \frac{1}{2} \|\rho - \sigma\|_1 \leq \sqrt{1 - F(\rho, \sigma)}. \tag{9.164}$$

Proof We first show that there is an exact relationship between fidelity and trace distance for pure states. Let us pick two arbitrary pure states $|\psi\rangle, |\phi\rangle \in \mathcal{H}$. We can write the state $|\phi\rangle$ in terms of the state $|\psi\rangle$ and a vector $|\psi^\perp\rangle$ orthogonal to $|\psi\rangle$:

$$|\phi\rangle = \cos(\theta)|\psi\rangle + \sin(\theta)|\psi^\perp\rangle. \tag{9.165}$$

First, the fidelity between these two pure states is

$$F(\psi, \phi) = |\langle \phi | \psi \rangle|^2 = \cos^2(\theta). \tag{9.166}$$

Now let us determine the trace distance. The density operator $|\phi\rangle\langle\phi|$ is as follows:

$$|\phi\rangle\langle\phi| = \left(\cos(\theta)|\psi\rangle + \sin(\theta)|\psi^\perp\rangle\right)\left(\cos(\theta)\langle\psi| + \sin(\theta)\langle\psi^\perp|\right) \tag{9.167}$$

$$= \cos^2(\theta)|\psi\rangle\langle\psi| + \sin(\theta)\cos(\theta)|\psi^\perp\rangle\langle\psi|$$
$$+ \cos(\theta)\sin(\theta)|\psi\rangle\langle\psi^\perp| + \sin^2(\theta)|\psi^\perp\rangle\langle\psi^\perp|. \tag{9.168}$$

The matrix representation of the operator $|\psi\rangle\langle\psi| - |\phi\rangle\langle\phi|$ with respect to the basis $\{|\psi\rangle, |\psi^\perp\rangle\}$ is

$$\begin{bmatrix} 1 - \cos^2(\theta) & -\sin(\theta)\cos(\theta) \\ -\sin(\theta)\cos(\theta) & -\sin^2(\theta) \end{bmatrix}. \tag{9.169}$$

It is straightforward to show that the eigenvalues of the above matrix are $|\sin(\theta)|$ and $-|\sin(\theta)|$ and it then follows that the trace distance between $|\psi\rangle$ and $|\phi\rangle$ is the absolute sum of the eigenvalues:

$$\||\psi\rangle\langle\psi| - |\phi\rangle\langle\phi|\|_1 = 2\,|\sin(\theta)|. \tag{9.170}$$

Consider the following trigonometric relationship:

$$\left(\frac{2\,|\sin(\theta)|}{2}\right)^2 \cdot = 1 - \cos^2(\theta). \tag{9.171}$$

Applying it gives the following relation between the fidelity and trace distance for pure states:

$$\left(\frac{1}{2}\||\psi\rangle\langle\psi| - |\phi\rangle\langle\phi|\|_1\right)^2 = 1 - F(\psi,\phi), \tag{9.172}$$

by plugging (9.166) into the right-hand side of (9.171) and (9.170) into the left-hand side of (9.171). Thus,

$$\frac{1}{2}\||\psi\rangle\langle\psi| - |\phi\rangle\langle\phi|\|_1 = \sqrt{1 - F(\psi,\phi)}. \tag{9.173}$$

To prove the upper bound for mixed states ρ_A and σ_A, choose purifications $|\phi^\rho\rangle_{RA}$ and $|\phi^\sigma\rangle_{RA}$ of respective states ρ_A and σ_A such that

$$F(\rho_A,\sigma_A) = |\langle\phi^\sigma|\phi^\rho\rangle|^2 = F(\phi_{RA}^\rho, \phi_{RA}^\sigma). \tag{9.174}$$

(Recall that these purifications exist by Uhlmann's theorem.) Then

$$\frac{1}{2}\|\rho_A - \sigma_A\|_1 \le \frac{1}{2}\|\phi_{RA}^\rho - \phi_{RA}^\sigma\|_1 \tag{9.175}$$

$$= \sqrt{1 - F(\phi_{RA}^\rho, \phi_{RA}^\sigma)} \tag{9.176}$$

$$= \sqrt{1 - F(\rho_A,\sigma_A)}, \tag{9.177}$$

where the first inequality follows by the monotonicity of the trace distance under the discarding of systems (Lemma 9.1.2).

To prove the lower bound for mixed states ρ and σ, recall Exercise 9.1.10 and Theorem 9.2.2. Exercise 9.1.10 states that the trace distance is the maximum classical trace distance between two probability distributions resulting from a POVM $\{\Lambda_m\}$ acting on the states ρ and σ:

$$\|\rho - \sigma\|_1 = \max_{\{\Lambda_m\}} \sum_m |p_m - q_m|, \tag{9.178}$$

where

$$p_m \equiv \operatorname{Tr}\{\Lambda_m\rho\}, \qquad q_m \equiv \operatorname{Tr}\{\Lambda_m\sigma\}. \tag{9.179}$$

Furthermore, Theorem 9.2.2 states that the quantum fidelity is the minimum classical fidelity between two probability distributions p'_m and q'_m resulting from a measurement $\{\Gamma_m\}$ of the states ρ and σ:

$$F(\rho, \sigma) = \min_{\{\Gamma_m\}} \left(\sum_m \sqrt{p'_m q'_m} \right)^2, \qquad (9.180)$$

where

$$p'_m \equiv \mathrm{Tr}\{\Gamma_m \rho\}, \qquad q'_m \equiv \mathrm{Tr}\{\Gamma_m \sigma\}. \qquad (9.181)$$

We return to the proof. Suppose that the POVM $\{\Gamma_m\}$ achieves the minimum classical fidelity and results in probability distributions p'_m and q'_m, so that

$$F(\rho, \sigma) = \left(\sum_m \sqrt{p'_m q'_m} \right)^2. \qquad (9.182)$$

Consider that

$$\sum_m \left(\sqrt{p'_m} - \sqrt{q'_m} \right)^2 = \sum_m p'_m + q'_m - 2\sqrt{p'_m q'_m} \qquad (9.183)$$

$$= 2 - 2\sqrt{F(\rho, \sigma)}. \qquad (9.184)$$

It also follows that

$$\sum_m \left(\sqrt{p'_m} - \sqrt{q'_m} \right)^2 \leq \sum_m \left| \sqrt{p'_m} - \sqrt{q'_m} \right| \left| \sqrt{p'_m} + \sqrt{q'_m} \right| \qquad (9.185)$$

$$= \sum_m |p'_m - q'_m| \qquad (9.186)$$

$$\leq \sum_m |p_m - q_m| \qquad (9.187)$$

$$= \|\rho - \sigma\|_1. \qquad (9.188)$$

The first inequality holds because $\left| \sqrt{p'_m} - \sqrt{q'_m} \right| \leq \left| \sqrt{p'_m} + \sqrt{q'_m} \right|$. The second inequality holds because the distributions p'_m and q'_m minimizing the classical fidelity in general have classical trace distance less than the distributions p_m and q_m that maximize the classical trace distance. Thus, the following inequality results

$$2 - 2\sqrt{F(\rho, \sigma)} \leq \|\rho - \sigma\|_1, \qquad (9.189)$$

and the lower bound in the statement of the theorem follows.   □

Theorem 9.3.1 allows us to complete our understanding of the extreme values of trace distance and fidelity. We have already argued that two states $\rho, \sigma \in \mathcal{D}(\mathcal{H})$ have trace distance equal to zero if and only if $\rho = \sigma$. Theorem 9.3.1 allows us to conclude that $F(\rho, \sigma) = 1$ if and only if $\rho = \sigma$. Similarly, we have argued already that $F(\rho, \sigma) = 0$ if and only if the support of ρ is orthogonal to that of σ. Theorem 9.3.1 allows us to conclude that $\|\rho - \sigma\|_1 = 2$ if and only if the support of ρ is orthogonal to that of σ.

The following two corollaries are simple consequences of Theorem 9.3.1.

COROLLARY 9.3.1   Let $\rho, \sigma \in \mathcal{D}(\mathcal{H})$ and fix $\varepsilon \in [0, 1]$. Suppose that ρ is ε-close to σ in trace distance:

$$\|\rho - \sigma\|_1 \leq \varepsilon. \tag{9.190}$$

Then the fidelity between ρ and σ is greater than $1 - \varepsilon$:

$$F(\rho, \sigma) \geq 1 - \varepsilon. \tag{9.191}$$

COROLLARY 9.3.2   Let $\rho, \sigma \in \mathcal{D}(\mathcal{H})$ and fix $\varepsilon \in [0, 1]$. Suppose the fidelity between ρ and σ is greater than $1 - \varepsilon$:

$$F(\rho, \sigma) \geq 1 - \varepsilon. \tag{9.192}$$

Then ρ is $2\sqrt{\varepsilon}$-close to σ in trace distance:

$$\|\rho - \sigma\|_1 \leq 2\sqrt{\varepsilon}. \tag{9.193}$$

EXERCISE 9.3.1   Let $\rho, \sigma \in \mathcal{D}(\mathcal{H})$. Prove the following lower bound on the probability of error p_e in a quantum hypothesis test to distinguish ρ from σ:

$$p_e \geq \frac{1}{2}\left(1 - \sqrt{1 - F(\rho, \sigma)}\right). \tag{9.194}$$

(Hint: Recall the development in Section 9.1.4.)

9.4   Gentle Measurement

The gentle measurement and gentle operator lemmas are particular applications of Theorem 9.3.1, and they concern the disturbance of quantum states. We generally expect in quantum theory that certain measurements might disturb the state which we are measuring. For example, suppose a qubit is in the state $|0\rangle$. A measurement along the X direction gives $+1$ and -1 with equal probability while drastically disturbing the state to become either $|+\rangle$ or $|-\rangle$, respectively. On the other hand, we might expect that the measurement does not disturb the state by very much if one outcome is highly likely. For example, suppose that we instead measure the qubit along the Z direction. The measurement returns $+1$ with unit probability while causing no disturbance to the qubit. The "gentle measurement lemma" below quantitatively addresses the disturbance of quantum states by demonstrating that a measurement with one outcome that is highly likely causes only a little disturbance to the quantum state that we measure (hence, the measurement is "gentle" or "tender").

LEMMA 9.4.1 (Gentle Measurement)   Consider a density operator ρ and a measurement operator Λ where $0 \leq \Lambda \leq I$. The measurement operator could be an element of a POVM. Suppose that the measurement operator Λ has a high probability of detecting state ρ:

$$\text{Tr}\,\{\Lambda\rho\} \geq 1 - \varepsilon, \tag{9.195}$$

where $\varepsilon \in [0,1]$ (the probability of detection is high if ε is close to zero). Then the post-measurement state

$$\rho' \equiv \frac{\sqrt{\Lambda}\rho\sqrt{\Lambda}}{\mathrm{Tr}\{\Lambda\rho\}} \tag{9.196}$$

is $2\sqrt{\varepsilon}$-close to the original state ρ in trace distance:

$$\|\rho - \rho'\|_1 \leq 2\sqrt{\varepsilon}. \tag{9.197}$$

Thus, the measurement does not disturb the state ρ by much if ε is small.

Proof Suppose first that ρ is a pure state $|\psi\rangle\langle\psi|$. The post-measurement state is then

$$\frac{\sqrt{\Lambda}|\psi\rangle\langle\psi|\sqrt{\Lambda}}{\langle\psi|\Lambda|\psi\rangle}. \tag{9.198}$$

The fidelity between the original state $|\psi\rangle$ and the post-measurement state above is as follows:

$$\langle\psi|\left(\frac{\sqrt{\Lambda}|\psi\rangle\langle\psi|\sqrt{\Lambda}}{\langle\psi|\Lambda|\psi\rangle}\right)|\psi\rangle = \frac{\left|\langle\psi|\sqrt{\Lambda}|\psi\rangle\right|^2}{\langle\psi|\Lambda|\psi\rangle} \geq \frac{|\langle\psi|\Lambda|\psi\rangle|^2}{\langle\psi|\Lambda|\psi\rangle} \tag{9.199}$$

$$= \langle\psi|\Lambda|\psi\rangle \geq 1 - \varepsilon. \tag{9.200}$$

The first inequality follows because $\sqrt{\Lambda} \geq \Lambda$ when $\Lambda \leq I$. The second inequality follows from the hypothesis of the lemma. Now let us consider when we have mixed states ρ_A and ρ'_A. Suppose $|\psi\rangle_{RA}$ and $|\psi'\rangle_{RA}$ are respective purifications of ρ_A and ρ'_A, where

$$|\psi'\rangle_{RA} \equiv \frac{I_R \otimes \sqrt{\Lambda_A}|\psi\rangle_{RA}}{\sqrt{\langle\psi|I_R \otimes \Lambda_A|\psi\rangle_{RA}}}. \tag{9.201}$$

Then we can apply monotonicity of fidelity (Lemma 9.2.1) and the above result for pure states to show that

$$F(\rho_A, \rho'_A) \geq F(\psi_{RA}, \psi'_{RA}) \geq 1 - \varepsilon. \tag{9.202}$$

We obtain the bound on the trace distance $\|\rho_A - \rho'_A\|_1$ by exploiting Corollary 9.3.2. $\qquad\square$

The following is a variation on the gentle measurement lemma:

LEMMA 9.4.2 (Gentle Operator) Consider a density operator ρ and a measurement operator Λ where $0 \leq \Lambda \leq I$. The measurement operator could be an element of a POVM. Suppose that the measurement operator Λ has a high probability of detecting state ρ:

$$\mathrm{Tr}\{\Lambda\rho\} \geq 1 - \varepsilon, \tag{9.203}$$

where $\varepsilon \in [0,1]$ (the probability is high if ε is close to zero). Then $\sqrt{\Lambda}\rho\sqrt{\Lambda}$ is $2\sqrt{\varepsilon}$-close to the original state ρ in trace distance:

$$\left\|\rho - \sqrt{\Lambda}\rho\sqrt{\Lambda}\right\|_1 \leq 2\sqrt{\varepsilon}. \tag{9.204}$$

Proof Consider the following chain of inequalities:

$$\left\|\rho - \sqrt{\Lambda}\rho\sqrt{\Lambda}\right\|_1$$

$$= \left\|\left(I - \sqrt{\Lambda} + \sqrt{\Lambda}\right)\rho - \sqrt{\Lambda}\rho\sqrt{\Lambda}\right\|_1 \tag{9.205}$$

$$\leq \left\|\left(I - \sqrt{\Lambda}\right)\rho\right\|_1 + \left\|\sqrt{\Lambda}\rho\left(I - \sqrt{\Lambda}\right)\right\|_1 \tag{9.206}$$

$$= \mathrm{Tr}\left|\left(I - \sqrt{\Lambda}\right)\sqrt{\rho} \cdot \sqrt{\rho}\right| + \mathrm{Tr}\left|\sqrt{\Lambda}\sqrt{\rho} \cdot \sqrt{\rho}\left(I - \sqrt{\Lambda}\right)\right| \tag{9.207}$$

$$\leq \sqrt{\mathrm{Tr}\left\{\left(I - \sqrt{\Lambda}\right)^2 \rho\right\}\mathrm{Tr}\left\{\rho\right\}} + \sqrt{\mathrm{Tr}\left\{\Lambda\rho\right\}\mathrm{Tr}\left\{\rho\left(I - \sqrt{\Lambda}\right)^2\right\}} \tag{9.208}$$

$$\leq \sqrt{\mathrm{Tr}\left\{(I - \Lambda)\rho\right\}} + \sqrt{\mathrm{Tr}\left\{\rho(I - \Lambda)\right\}} \tag{9.209}$$

$$= 2\sqrt{\mathrm{Tr}\left\{(I - \Lambda)\rho\right\}} \leq 2\sqrt{\varepsilon}. \tag{9.210}$$

The first inequality is a consequence of the triangle inequality. The second equality follows from the definition of the trace norm and the fact that ρ is a positive semi-definite operator. The second inequality follows from the Cauchy–Schwarz inequality for the Hilbert–Schmidt inner product; see (9.20). The third inequality follows because $(1 - \sqrt{x})^2 \leq 1 - x$ for $0 \leq x \leq 1$, $\mathrm{Tr}\left\{\rho\right\} = 1$, and $\mathrm{Tr}\left\{\Lambda\rho\right\} \leq 1$. The final inequality follows from applying (9.203) and because the square root function is monotone increasing. □

EXERCISE 9.4.1 Show that the gentle operator lemma holds for subnormalized positive semi-definite operators ρ (operators ρ such that $\mathrm{Tr}\left\{\rho\right\} \leq 1$).

Below is another variation on the gentle measurement lemma that applies to ensembles of quantum states.

LEMMA 9.4.3 (Gentle Measurement for Ensembles) Let $\{p_X(x), \rho_x\}$ be an ensemble with average density operator $\bar{\rho} \equiv \sum_x p_X(x)\rho_x$. Given a positive semi-definite operator Λ with $\Lambda \leq I$ and $\mathrm{Tr}\left\{\bar{\rho}\Lambda\right\} \geq 1 - \varepsilon$ where $\varepsilon \in [0,1]$, then

$$\sum_x p_X(x)\left\|\rho_x - \sqrt{\Lambda}\rho_x\sqrt{\Lambda}\right\|_1 \leq 2\sqrt{\varepsilon}. \tag{9.211}$$

Proof We can apply the same steps in the proof of the gentle operator lemma to get the following inequality, holding for all x:

$$\left\|\rho_x - \sqrt{\Lambda}\rho_x\sqrt{\Lambda}\right\|_1^2 \leq 4\left(1 - \mathrm{Tr}\left\{\Lambda\rho_x\right\}\right). \tag{9.212}$$

Taking the expectation over both sides produces the following inequality:

$$\sum_x p_X(x)\left\|\rho_x - \sqrt{\Lambda}\rho_x\sqrt{\Lambda}\right\|_1^2 \leq 4\left(1 - \mathrm{Tr}\left\{\Lambda\rho\right\}\right) \leq 4\varepsilon. \tag{9.213}$$

Taking the square root of the above inequality gives the following one:

$$\sqrt{\sum_x p_X(x) \left\| \rho_x - \sqrt{\Lambda} \rho_x \sqrt{\Lambda} \right\|_1^2} \leq 2\sqrt{\varepsilon}. \tag{9.214}$$

Concavity of the square root then implies that

$$\sum_x p_X(x) \sqrt{\left\| \rho_x - \sqrt{\Lambda} \rho_x \sqrt{\Lambda} \right\|_1^2} \leq 2\sqrt{\varepsilon}, \tag{9.215}$$

concluding the proof. □

EXERCISE 9.4.2 (Coherent Gentle Measurement) Let $\{\rho_A^k\}$ be a collection of density operators and $\{\Lambda_A^k\}$ be a POVM such that for all k:

$$\operatorname{Tr}\left\{\Lambda_A^k \rho_A^k\right\} \geq 1 - \varepsilon. \tag{9.216}$$

Let $|\phi^k\rangle_{RA}$ be a purification of ρ_A^k. Show that there exists a coherent gentle measurement $\mathcal{D}_{A \to AK}$ in the sense of Section 5.4 such that

$$\left\| \mathcal{D}_{A \to AK}(\phi_{RA}^k) - \phi_{RA}^k \otimes |k\rangle\langle k|_K \right\|_1 \leq 2\sqrt{\varepsilon(2 - \varepsilon)}. \tag{9.217}$$

(Hint: Use the result of Exercise 5.4.1.)

9.5 Fidelity of a Quantum Channel

It is useful to have measures that determine how well a quantum channel $\mathcal{N}$ preserves quantum information. We developed static distance measures, such as the trace distance and the fidelity, in the previous sections of this chapter. We would now like to exploit those measures in order to define dynamic measures.

A "first guess" measure of this sort is the minimum fidelity $F_{\min}(\mathcal{N})$, where

$$F_{\min}(\mathcal{N}) \equiv \min_{|\psi\rangle} F(\psi, \mathcal{N}(\psi)). \tag{9.218}$$

This measure seems like it may be a good one because we generally do not know the state that Alice inputs to a noisy channel before transmitting to Bob.

It may seem somewhat strange that we chose to minimize over pure states in the definition of the minimum fidelity. Are not mixed states the most general states that occur in the quantum theory? It turns out that joint concavity of the root fidelity (Property 9.2.2) and monotonicity of the square function implies that we do not have to consider mixed states for the minimum fidelity. Consider the following sequence of inequalities:

$$\sqrt{F}(\rho, \mathcal{N}(\rho)) = \sqrt{F}\left(\sum_x p_X(x)|x\rangle\langle x|, \mathcal{N}\left(\sum_x p_X(x)|x\rangle\langle x|\right)\right) \tag{9.219}$$

$$= \sqrt{F}\left(\sum_x p_X(x)|x\rangle\langle x|, \sum_x p_X(x)\mathcal{N}(|x\rangle\langle x|)\right) \tag{9.220}$$

$$\geq \sum_x p_X(x) \sqrt{F}(|x\rangle\langle x|, \mathcal{N}(|x\rangle\langle x|)) \tag{9.221}$$

$$\geq \sqrt{F}(|x_{\min}\rangle\langle x_{\min}|, \mathcal{N}(|x_{\min}\rangle\langle x_{\min}|)). \tag{9.222}$$

The first equality follows by expanding the density operator ρ with a spectral decomposition. The second equality follows from linearity of the quantum operation $\mathcal{N}$. The first inequality follows from joint concavity of the root fidelity (Property 9.2.2), and the last inequality follows because there exists some pure state $|x_{\min}\rangle$ (one of the eigenstates of ρ) with fidelity never larger than the expected fidelity in the previous line.

9.5.1   Expected Fidelity of a Quantum Channel

In general, the minimum fidelity is less useful than other measures of quantum information preservation over a quantum channel. The difficulty with the minimum fidelity is that it requires an optimization over the potentially large space of input states. Since it could be somewhat difficult to manipulate and compute in general, we introduce other ways to determine the performance of a quantum channel.

We can simplify our notion of fidelity by instead restricting the states that Alice sends and averaging the fidelity with respect to this set of states. That is, suppose that Alice is transmitting states from an ensemble $\{p_X(x), \rho_x\}$ and we would like to determine how well a quantum channel $\mathcal{N}$ is preserving this source of quantum information. Sending a particular state ρ_x through a quantum channel $\mathcal{N}$ produces the state $\mathcal{N}(\rho_x)$. The fidelity between the transmitted state ρ_x and the received state $\mathcal{N}(\rho_x)$ is $F(\rho_x, \mathcal{N}(\rho_x))$ as defined before. We define the *expected fidelity* of the ensemble as follows:

$$\overline{F}(\mathcal{N}) \equiv \mathbb{E}_X\left[F(\rho_X, \mathcal{N}(\rho_X))\right] = \sum_x p_X(x) F(\rho_x, \mathcal{N}(\rho_x)). \tag{9.223}$$

The expected fidelity indicates how well Alice is able to transmit the ensemble on average to Bob. It again lies between zero and one, just as the usual fidelity does.

A more general form of the expected fidelity is to consider the expected performance for any quantum state instead of restricting ourselves to an ensemble. That is, let us fix some quantum state $|\psi\rangle$ and apply a random unitary U to it, where we select the unitary according to the Haar measure (this is the uniform distribution on unitaries). The state $U|\psi\rangle$ represents a random quantum state and we can take the expectation with respect to it in order to define the following more general notion of expected fidelity:

$$\overline{F}(\mathcal{N}) \equiv \mathbb{E}_U\left[F(U|\psi\rangle\langle\psi|U^\dagger, \mathcal{N}(U|\psi\rangle\langle\psi|U^\dagger))\right]. \tag{9.224}$$

The above formula for the expected fidelity then becomes the following integral over the Haar measure:

$$\overline{F}(\mathcal{N}) = \int \langle\psi|U^\dagger\mathcal{N}(U|\psi\rangle\langle\psi|U^\dagger)U|\psi\rangle \, dU. \tag{9.225}$$

9.5.2   Entanglement Fidelity

We now consider a different measure of the ability of a quantum channel to preserve quantum information. Suppose that Alice would like to transmit a quantum state with density operator ρ_A. It admits a purification $|\psi\rangle_{RA}$ to a reference system R. Sending the A system of $|\psi\rangle_{RA}$ through the identity channel id_A gives back $|\psi\rangle_{RA}$. Sending the A system of $|\psi\rangle_{RA}$ through a quantum channel $\mathcal{N} : \mathcal{L}(\mathcal{H}_A) \to \mathcal{L}(\mathcal{H}_A)$ gives the state $\sigma_{RA} \equiv (\text{id}_R \otimes \mathcal{N}_A)(\psi_{RA})$. The entanglement fidelity is defined as follows:

DEFINITION 9.5.1 (Entanglement Fidelity)   For ρ, $\mathcal{N}$, σ, and $|\psi\rangle$ as defined above, the entanglement fidelity is given by $F_e(\rho, \mathcal{N}) \equiv \langle\psi|\sigma|\psi\rangle$.

It is a measure of how well the quantum channel $\mathcal{N}$ preserves entanglement with another system. Figure 9.5 visually depicts the two states that the entanglement fidelity compares.

The entanglement fidelity is invariant with respect to which purification of the input that we pick. This follows simply because all purifications are related by an isometry acting on the purifying system. That is, let $|\psi\rangle_{R_1A}$ be one purification of ρ_A, let $|\varphi\rangle_{R_2A}$ be a different one, and let $U_{R_1\to R_2}$ be an isometry that relates them via $|\varphi\rangle_{R_2A} = U_{R_1\to R_2}|\psi\rangle_{R_1A}$. Then

$$\langle\varphi|_{R_2A}(\text{id}_{R_2} \otimes \mathcal{N}_A)(\varphi_{R_2A})|\varphi\rangle_{R_2A}$$

$$= \langle\psi|_{R_1A}U^\dagger_{R_1\to R_2}\left[(\text{id}_{R_2} \otimes \mathcal{N}_A)\left(U_{R_1\to R_2}\psi_{R_1A}U^\dagger_{R_1\to R_2}\right)\right]U_{R_1\to R_2}|\psi\rangle_{R_1A} \tag{9.226}$$

$$= \langle\psi|_{R_1A}U^\dagger_{R_1\to R_2}U_{R_1\to R_2}[(\text{id}_{R_1} \otimes \mathcal{N}_A)(\psi_{R_1A})]U^\dagger_{R_1\to R_2}U_{R_1\to R_2}|\psi\rangle_{R_1A} \tag{9.227}$$

$$= \langle\psi|_{R_1A}[(\text{id}_{R_1} \otimes \mathcal{N}_A)(\psi_{R_1A})]|\psi\rangle_{R_1A}, \tag{9.228}$$

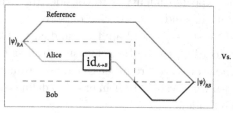 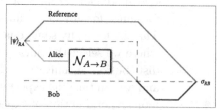

Figure 9.5 The entanglement fidelity compares the output of the ideal scenario (depicted on the left) and the output of the noisy scenario (depicted on the right).

where the second equality follows because the isometry commutes with the identity map id_{R_2} and the last follows because $U_{R_1 \to R_2}$ is an isometry so that $U^\dagger_{R_1 \to R_2} U_{R_1 \to R_2} = I_{R_1}$.

One of the benefits of considering the task of entanglement preservation is that it implies the task of quantum communication. That is, if Alice can devise a protocol that preserves the entanglement with another system, then this same protocol will also be able to preserve quantum information that she transmits.

The following theorem gives a simple way to represent the entanglement fidelity in terms of the Kraus operators of a given noisy quantum channel.

THEOREM 9.5.1 Let $\rho_A \in \mathcal{D}(\mathcal{H}_A)$ and let $\mathcal{N} : \mathcal{L}(\mathcal{H}_A) \to \mathcal{L}(\mathcal{H}_A)$ be a quantum channel. Suppose that $\{K^m\}$ is a set of Kraus operators for $\mathcal{N}$. Then the entanglement fidelity $F_e(\rho, \mathcal{N})$ is equal to the following expression:

$$F_e(\rho, \mathcal{N}) = \sum_m |\text{Tr}\{\rho_A K^m\}|^2 . \tag{9.229}$$

Proof Given that the entanglement fidelity is invariant with respect to the choice of purification, we can simply use the canonical purification $|\psi\rangle_{RA}$ of ρ_A, i.e.,

$$|\psi\rangle_{RA} = (I_R \otimes \sqrt{\rho_A}) |\Gamma\rangle_{RA} , \tag{9.230}$$

where $|\Gamma\rangle_{RA}$ is the unnormalized maximally entangled vector from (3.233). We then find that

$$\langle \psi|_{RA} (\text{id}_R \otimes \mathcal{N}_A) (\psi_{RA}) |\psi\rangle_{RA}$$

$$= \langle \psi|_{RA} \sum_m (I_R \otimes K_A^m) |\psi\rangle \langle \psi|_{RA} \left(I_R \otimes (K_A^m)^\dagger \right) |\psi\rangle_{RA} \tag{9.231}$$

$$= \sum_m \langle \psi|_{RA} (I_R \otimes K_A^m) |\psi\rangle \langle \psi|_{RA} \left(I_R \otimes (K_A^m)^\dagger \right) |\psi\rangle_{RA} \tag{9.232}$$

$$= \sum_m |\langle \psi|_{RA} (I_R \otimes K_A^m) |\psi\rangle_{RA}|^2 . \tag{9.233}$$

Then consider that

$$\langle \psi|_{RA} (I_R \otimes K_A^m) |\psi\rangle_{RA}$$

$$= \langle \Gamma|_{RA} (I_R \otimes \sqrt{\rho_A}) (I_R \otimes K_A^m) (I_R \otimes \sqrt{\rho_A}) |\Gamma\rangle_{RA} \tag{9.234}$$

$$= \langle \Gamma|_{RA} (I_R \otimes \sqrt{\rho_A} K_A^m \sqrt{\rho_A}) |\Gamma\rangle_{RA} \tag{9.235}$$

$$= \text{Tr}\{\sqrt{\rho_A} K_A^m \sqrt{\rho_A}\} \tag{9.236}$$

$$= \text{Tr}\{\rho_A K_A^m\} , \tag{9.237}$$

where we have used Exercise 4.1.3 to establish the third equality. So we find that

$$\langle \psi|_{RA} (\text{id}_R \otimes \mathcal{N}_A) (\psi_{RA}) |\psi\rangle_{RA} = \sum_m |\text{Tr}\{\rho_A K^m\}|^2 , \tag{9.238}$$

concluding the proof. $\square$

EXERCISE 9.5.1   Let $\rho_1, \rho_2 \in \mathcal{D}(\mathcal{H})$ and let $\mathcal{N} : \mathcal{L}(\mathcal{H}) \to \mathcal{L}(\mathcal{H})$ be a quantum channel. Fix $\lambda \in [0, 1]$. Show that the entanglement fidelity is convex in the input state:

$$F_e(\lambda \rho_1 + (1 - \lambda) \rho_2, \mathcal{N}) \leq \lambda F_e(\rho_1, \mathcal{N}) + (1 - \lambda) F_e(\rho_2, \mathcal{N}). \tag{9.239}$$

(Hint: The result of Theorem 9.5.1 is useful here.)

EXERCISE 9.5.2   Prove that the entanglement fidelity does not depend upon the particular choice of Kraus operators for a given channel. (Hint: Recall that there always exists an isometry that relates two different Kraus representations of a quantum channel, i.e., for a set $\{K^m\}$ of Kraus operators and another set $\{L^n\}$, we have that

$$K^m = \sum_n u_{mn} L^n, \tag{9.240}$$

where u_{mn} are the entries of a unitary matrix.)

9.5.3   Expected Fidelity and Entanglement Fidelity

The entanglement fidelity and the expected fidelity provide seemingly different methods for quantifying the ability of a noisy quantum channel to preserve quantum information. Is there any way that we can show how they are related?

It turns out that they are indeed related. First, consider that the entanglement fidelity is a lower bound on the channel's fidelity for preserving the state ρ:

$$F_e(\rho, \mathcal{N}) \leq F(\rho, \mathcal{N}(\rho)). \tag{9.241}$$

The above result follows simply from the monotonicity of fidelity under partial trace (Lemma 9.2.1). We can show that the entanglement fidelity is always less than the expected fidelity in (9.223) by combining convexity of entanglement fidelity (Exercise 9.5.1) and the bound in (9.241):

$$F_e\left(\sum_x p_X(x)\rho_x, \mathcal{N}\right) \leq \sum_x p_X(x) F_e(\rho_x, \mathcal{N}) \tag{9.242}$$

$$\leq \sum_x p_X(x) F(\rho_x, \mathcal{N}(\rho_x)) \tag{9.243}$$

$$= \overline{F}(\mathcal{N}). \tag{9.244}$$

Thus, any channel that preserves entanglement with some reference system preserves the expected fidelity of an ensemble. In most cases, we only consider the entanglement fidelity as the defining measure of performance of a noisy quantum channel.

The relationship between entanglement fidelity and expected fidelity becomes more exact (and more beautiful) in the case where we select a random quantum state according to the Haar measure. It is possible to show that the expected fidelity in (9.224) relates to the entanglement fidelity as follows:

$$\overline{F}(\mathcal{N}) = \frac{dF_e(\pi,\mathcal{N}) + 1}{d + 1},$$ (9.245)

where d is the dimension of the input system and π is the maximally mixed state with purification to the maximally entangled state.

EXERCISE 9.5.3   Prove that the relation in (9.245) holds for a quantum depolarizing channel.

9.6   The Hilbert–Schmidt Distance Measure

One final distance measure that we develop is the Hilbert–Schmidt distance measure. It is most similar to the familiar Euclidean distance measure of vectors because an ℓ_2-norm induces it. This distance measure does not have an appealing operational interpretation like the trace distance and fidelity do. Furthermore, it is neither generally increasing or decreasing with respect to the action of quantum channels, and so one *should not* employ it as a distinguishability measure of quantum states. Nevertheless, it can sometimes be helpful in calculations to exploit this distance measure and to relate it to the trace distance via the bound in Exercise 9.6.1 below.

Let us define the Hilbert–Schmidt norm of an operator $M \in \mathcal{L}(\mathcal{H},\mathcal{H}')$ as follows:

$$\|M\|_2 \equiv \sqrt{\operatorname{Tr}\{M^\dagger M\}}.$$ (9.246)

It is straightforward to show that the above norm meets the three requirements of a norm: non-negativity, homogeneity, and the triangle inequality. One can compute this norm simply by summing the squares of the singular values of the operator M and taking the square root. The reasoning for this is the same as that in the proof of Proposition 9.1.1.

The Hilbert–Schmidt norm induces the following Hilbert–Schmidt distance measure:

$$\|M - N\|_2,$$ (9.247)

where $M, N \in \mathcal{L}(\mathcal{H},\mathcal{H}')$. We can then apply this distance measure to quantum states ρ and σ simply by plugging ρ and σ into the above formula in place of M and N.

The Hilbert–Schmidt distance measure sometimes finds use in the proofs of coding theorems in quantum Shannon theory because it is often easier to find good bounds on it rather than on the trace distance. In some cases, we might be taking expectations over ensembles of density operators and this expectation often reduces to computing variances or covariances.

EXERCISE 9.6.1 Show that the following inequality holds for any operator X

$$\|X\|_1^2 \le d \|X\|_2^2, \tag{9.248}$$

where d is the rank of X. (Hint: Use the Cauchy–Schwarz inequality for the Hilbert–Schmidt inner product.)

EXERCISE 9.6.2 There are explicit counterexamples to the monotonicity of the Hilbert–Schmidt distance. Let $A = |01\rangle\langle00| + |11\rangle\langle10|$ and $B = |01\rangle\langle01| + |11\rangle\langle11|$ be Kraus operators for a channel $\mathcal{N}(\omega) = A\omega A^\dagger + B\omega B^\dagger$, and consider the states $\rho = |0\rangle\langle0| \otimes \pi$ and $\sigma = |1\rangle\langle1| \otimes \pi$, where $\pi = I/2$. First verify that $\mathcal{N}$ is a quantum channel and then show by explicit calculation that $\|\rho - \sigma\|_2 < \|\mathcal{N}(\rho) - \mathcal{N}(\sigma)\|_2$ for this example. On the other hand, let $\rho = |0\rangle\langle0|$, $\sigma = |1\rangle\langle1|$, and $\mathcal{N}(\omega) = \frac{1}{2}(\omega + X\omega X)$. Show that $\|\rho - \sigma\|_2 > \|\mathcal{N}(\rho) - \mathcal{N}(\sigma)\|_2$ for this other example. Message: Do not use the Hilbert–Schmidt distance as a measure of distinguishability!

9.7 History and Further Reading

Fuchs (1996) and Fuchs & van de Graaf (1998) are a good starting point for learning more regarding trace distance and fidelity. Other notable sources are Nielsen & Chuang (2000), Yard (2005), and von Kretschmann (2007). Helstrom (1969; see also Helstrom, 1976) demonstrated the operational interpretation of the trace distance in the context of quantum hypothesis testing. Uhlmann (1976) first proved the theorem bearing his name, and Jozsa (1994) later presented a proof of this theorem for the case of finite-dimensional quantum systems. Theorem 9.2.2 is due to Fuchs & Caves (1995). Schumacher (1996) introduced the entanglement fidelity, and Barnum et al. (2000) made further observations regarding it. Nielsen (2002) provided a simple proof of the exact relation between entanglement fidelity and expected fidelity.

Winter (1999a; see also Winter, 1999b) originally proved the "gentle measurement" lemma. There, he used it to obtain a variation of the direct part of the HSW coding theorem. Later, he used it to prove achievable rates for the quantum multiple access channel (Winter, 2001). Ogawa & Nagaoka (2007) subsequently improved this bound to $2\sqrt{\varepsilon}$.

The counterexample to the monotonicity of the Hilbert–Schmidt distance is due to Ozawa (2000).

10 Classical Information and Entropy

All physical systems register bits of information, whether it be an atom, an electrical current, the location of a billiard ball, or a switch. Information can be classical, quantum, or a hybrid of both, depending on the system. For example, an atom or an electron or a superconducting system can register *quantum* information because the quantum theory applies to each of these systems, but we can safely argue that the location of a billiard ball registers classical information only. These atoms or electrons or superconducting systems can also register classical bits because it is always possible for a quantum system to register classical bits.

The term *information*, in the context of information theory, has a precise meaning that is somewhat different from our prior "everyday" experience with it. Recall that the notion of the physical bit refers to the physical representation of a bit, and the information bit is a measure of how much we learn from the outcome of a random experiment. Perhaps the word "surprise" better captures the notion of information as it applies in the context of information theory.

This chapter begins our formal study of classical information. Recall that Chapter 2 reviewed some of the major operational tasks in classical information theory. Here, our approach is somewhat different because our aim is to provide an intuitive understanding of information measures, in terms of the parties who have access to the classical systems. We define precise mathematical formulas that measure the amount of information encoded in a single physical system or in multiple physical systems. The advantage of developing this theory is that we can study information in its own right without having to consider the details of the physical system that registers it.

We first introduce the entropy in Section 10.1 as the expected surprise of a random variable. We extend this basic notion of entropy to develop other measures of information in Sections 10.2–10.6 that prove useful as intuitive informational measures, but also, and perhaps more importantly, these measures are the answers to operational tasks that one might wish to perform using noisy resources. While introducing these quantities, we discuss and prove several mathematical results concerning them that are important tools for the practicing information theorist. These tools are useful both for proving results and for increasing our understanding of the nature of information. Section 10.7 introduces entropy inequalities that help us to understand the limits on our ability to process information, and Section 10.8 gives several refinements of these entropy inequalities. Section 10.9 ends the chapter by applying the classical informational measures developed in the forthcoming sections to the classical information that one can extract from a quantum system.

10.1   Entropy of a Random Variable

Consider a random variable X. Suppose that each realization x of random variable X belongs to an alphabet $\mathcal{X}$. Let $p_X(x)$ denote the probability density function of X so that $p_X(x)$ is the probability that realization x occurs. The information content $i(x)$ of a particular realization x is a measure of the surprise that one has upon learning the outcome of a random experiment:

$$i(x) \equiv -\log\left(p_X(x)\right). \tag{10.1}$$

The logarithm is base two and this choice implies that we measure surprise or information in units of bits.

Figure 10.1 plots the information content for values in the unit interval. This measure of surprise behaves as we would hope—it is higher for lower-probability events that surprise us more, and it is lower for higher-probability events that do not surprise us as much. Inspection of the figure reveals that the information content is non-negative for any realization x.

The information content is also additive, due to the choice of the logarithm function. Given two independent random experiments involving random variable X with respective realizations x_1 and x_2, we have that

$$i(x_1, x_2) = -\log\left(p_{X,X}(x_1, x_2)\right) = -\log\left(p_X(x_1)p_X(x_2)\right) = i(x_1) + i(x_2). \tag{10.2}$$

Additivity is a property that we look for in measures of information (so much so that we dedicate the whole of Chapter 13 to this issue for more general measures of information).

The information content is a useful measure of surprise for particular realizations of random variable X, but it does not capture a general notion of the amount of surprise that a given random variable X possesses. The entropy $H(X)$ captures this general notion of the surprise of a random variable X—it is the expected information content of random variable X:

$$H(X) \equiv \mathbb{E}_X\left\{i(X)\right\}. \tag{10.3}$$

At a first glance, the above definition may seem strangely self-referential because the argument of the probability density function $p_X(x)$ is itself the random variable X, but this is well-defined mathematically. Evaluating the above formula gives an expression which we take as the definition for the entropy $H(X)$:

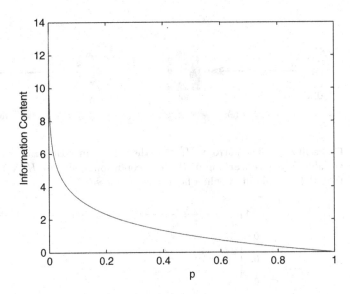

Figure 10.1 The information content or "surprise" in (10.1) as a function of a probability p ranging from 0 to 1. An event has a lower surprise if it is more likely to occur and it has a higher surprise if it less likely to occur.

DEFINITION 10.1.1 (Entropy)   The entropy of a discrete random variable X with probability distribution $p_X(x)$ is

$$H(X) \equiv - \sum_x p_X(x) \log (p_X(x)).$$ (10.4)

We adopt the convention that $0 \cdot \log(0) = 0$ for realizations with zero probability. The fact that $\lim_{\varepsilon \to 0} \varepsilon \cdot \log(1/\varepsilon) = 0$ intuitively justifies this latter convention. (We can interpret this convention as saying that the fact that the event has probability zero is more important than or outweighs the fact that you would be infinitely surprised if such an event would occur.)

The entropy admits an intuitive interpretation. Suppose that Alice performs a random experiment in her lab that selects a realization x according to the density $p_X(x)$ of random variable X. Suppose further that Bob has not yet learned the outcome of the experiment. The interpretation of the entropy $H(X)$ is that it quantifies Bob's uncertainty about X before learning it—his expected information gain is $H(X)$ bits upon learning the outcome of the random experiment. Shannon's noiseless coding theorem, described in Chapter 2, makes this interpretation precise by proving that Alice needs to send Bob bits at a rate $H(X)$ in order for him to be able to decode a compressed message. Figure 10.2(a) depicts the interpretation of the entropy $H(X)$, along with a similar interpretation for the conditional entropy that we introduce in Section 10.2.

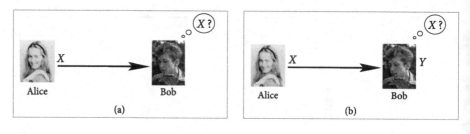

Figure 10.2 (a) The entropy $H(X)$ is the uncertainty that Bob has about random variable X before learning it. (b) The conditional entropy $H(X|Y)$ is the uncertainty that Bob has about X when he already possesses Y.

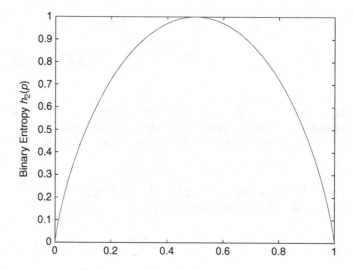

Figure 10.3 The binary entropy function $h_2(p)$ displayed as a function of the parameter p.

10.1.1   The Binary Entropy Function

A special case of the entropy occurs when the random variable X is a Bernoulli random variable with probability density $p_X(0) = p$ and $p_X(1) = 1 - p$. This Bernoulli random variable could correspond to the outcome of a random coin flip. The entropy in this case is known as the *binary entropy function*:

DEFINITION 10.1.2 (Binary Entropy)   The binary entropy of $p \in [0, 1]$ is

$$h_2(p) \equiv -p \log p - (1 - p) \log (1 - p). \tag{10.5}$$

The binary entropy quantifies the number of bits that we learn from the outcome of the coin flip. If the coin is unbiased ($p = 1/2$), then we learn a maximum of one bit ($h_2(p) = 1$). If the coin is deterministic ($p = 0$ or $p = 1$), then we do not learn anything from the outcome ($h_2(p) = 0$). Figure 10.3 displays a plot of the binary entropy function. The figure reveals that the binary entropy function $h_2(p)$ is a concave function of the parameter p and has its peak at $p = 1/2$.

10.1.2 Mathematical Properties of Entropy

We now discuss five important mathematical properties of the entropy $H(X)$.

PROPERTY 10.1.1 (Non-Negativity) The entropy $H(X)$ is non-negative for any discrete random variable X with probability density $p_X(x)$:

$$H(X) \geq 0. \tag{10.6}$$

Proof Non-negativity follows because entropy is the expected information content of $i(X)$, and the information content itself is non-negative. It is perhaps intuitive that the entropy should be non-negative because non-negativity implies that we always learn some number of bits upon learning random variable X (if we already know beforehand what the outcome of a random experiment will be, then we learn zero bits of information once we perform it). In a classical sense, we can never learn a negative amount of information! □

PROPERTY 10.1.2 (Concavity) The entropy $H(X)$ is concave in the probability density $p_X(x)$.

Proof We justify this result with a heuristic "mixing" argument for now, and provide a formal proof in Section 10.7.1. Consider two random variables X_1 and X_2 with two respective probability density functions $p_{X_1}(x)$ and $p_{X_2}(x)$ whose realizations belong to the same alphabet. Consider a Bernoulli random variable B with probabilities $q \in [0, 1]$ and $1 - q$ corresponding to its two respective realizations $b = 1$ and $b = 2$. Suppose that we first generate a realization b of random variable B and then generate a realization x of random variable X_b. Random variable X_B then denotes a mixed version of the two random variables X_1 and X_2. The probability density of X_B is $p_{X_B}(x) = qp_{X_1}(x) + (1 - q)p_{X_2}(x)$. Concavity of entropy is the following inequality:

$$H(X_B) \geq qH(X_1) + (1 - q)H(X_2). \tag{10.7}$$

Our heuristic argument is that this mixing process leads to more uncertainty for the mixed random variable X_B than the expected uncertainty over the two individual random variables. We can think of this result as a physical situation involving two gases. Two gases each have their own entropy, but the entropy increases when we mix the two gases together. We later give a more formal argument to justify concavity. □

PROPERTY 10.1.3 (Permutation Invariance) The entropy is invariant with respect to permutations of the realizations of random variable X.

Proof That is, suppose that we apply some permutation π to realizations x_1, x_2, ..., $x_{|\mathcal{X}|}$ so that they respectively become $\pi(x_1)$, $\pi(x_2)$, ..., $\pi(x_{|\mathcal{X}|})$. Then the entropy is invariant under this shuffling because it depends only on the probabilities of the realizations, not the values of the realizations.   □

PROPERTY 10.1.4 (Minimum Value)   The entropy $H(X)$ vanishes if and only if X is a deterministic variable.

Proof We would expect that the entropy of a *deterministic* variable should vanish, given the interpretation of entropy as the uncertainty of a random experiment. This intuition holds true and it is the degenerate probability density $p_X(x) = \delta_{x,x_0}$, where the realization x_0 has all the probability and other realizations have vanishing probability, that gives the minimum value of the entropy: $H(X) = 0$ when X has a degenerate density. If $H(X) = 0$, then this means that $p_X(x) \log[1/p_X(x)] = 0$ for all $x \in \mathcal{X}$, which in turn implies that either $p_X(x) = 0$ or $p_X(x) = 1$ for all $x \in \mathcal{X}$. Since p_X is required to be a probability distribution, we can have that $p_X(x) = 1$ for just one realization and $p_X(x) = 0$ for all others, so that X is a deterministic random variable.   □

Sometimes, we may not have any prior information about the possible values of a variable in a system, and we may decide that it is most appropriate to describe them with a probability density function. How should we assign this probability density if we do not have any prior information about the values? Theorists and experimentalists often resort to a "principle of maximum entropy" or a "principle of maximal ignorance"—we should assign the probability density to be the one that maximizes the entropy.

PROPERTY 10.1.5 (Maximum Value)   The maximum value of the entropy $H(X)$ for a random variable X taking values in an alphabet $\mathcal{X}$ is $\log|\mathcal{X}|$:

$$H(X) \leq \log|\mathcal{X}|. \tag{10.8}$$

The inequality is saturated if and only if X is a uniform random variable on $\mathcal{X}$.

Proof First, note that the result of Exercise 2.1.1 is that $\log|\mathcal{X}|$ is the entropy of the uniform random variable on $\mathcal{X}$. Next, we can prove the above inequality with a simple Lagrangian optimization by solving for the density $p_X(x)$ that maximizes the entropy. Lagrangian optimization is well suited for this task because the entropy is concave in the probability density, and thus any local maximum will be a global maximum. The Lagrangian $\mathcal{L}$ is as follows:

$$\mathcal{L} \equiv H(X) + \lambda \left(\sum_x p_X(x) - 1 \right), \tag{10.9}$$

where $H(X)$ is the quantity that we are maximizing, subject to the constraint that the probability density $p_X(x)$ sums to one. The partial derivative $\frac{\partial \mathcal{L}}{\partial p_X(x)}$ is as follows:

$$\frac{\partial \mathcal{L}}{\partial p_X(x)} = -\log(p_X(x)) - 1 + \lambda. \tag{10.10}$$

We set the partial derivative $\frac{\partial \mathcal{L}}{\partial p_X(x)}$ equal to zero to find the probability density that maximizes $\mathcal{L}$:

$$0 = -\log\left(p_X(x)\right) - 1 + \lambda \tag{10.11}$$

$$\Rightarrow p_X(x) = 2^{\lambda - 1}. \tag{10.12}$$

The resulting probability density $p_X(x)$ depends only on a constant λ, implying that it must be uniform $p_X(x) = 1/|\mathcal{X}|$. Thus, the uniform distribution maximizes the entropy $H(X)$ when random variable X is finite. $\qquad\square$

10.2 Conditional Entropy

Let us now suppose that Alice possesses random variable X and Bob possesses some other random variable Y. Random variables X and Y share correlations if they are not statistically independent, and Bob then possesses "side information" about X in the form of Y. Let $i(x|y)$ denote the conditional information content:

$$i(x|y) \equiv -\log\left(p_{X|Y}(x|y)\right). \tag{10.13}$$

The entropy $H(X|Y = y)$ of random variable X conditioned on a particular realization y of random variable Y is the expected conditional information content, where the expectation is with respect to $X|Y = y$:

$$H(X|Y = y) \equiv \mathbb{E}_{X|Y=y}\left\{i(X|y)\right\} \tag{10.14}$$

$$= -\sum_x p_{X|Y}(x|y)\log\left(p_{X|Y}(x|y)\right). \tag{10.15}$$

The relevant entropy that applies to the scenario where Bob possesses side information is the conditional entropy $H(X|Y)$, defined as follows:

DEFINITION 10.2.1 (Conditional Entropy) Let X and Y be discrete random variables with joint probability distribution $p_{X,Y}(x, y)$. The conditional entropy $H(X|Y)$ is the expected conditional information content, where the expectation is with respect to both X and Y:

$$H(X|Y) \equiv \mathbb{E}_{X,Y}\left\{i(X|Y)\right\} \tag{10.16}$$

$$= \sum_y p_Y(y)H(X|Y = y) \tag{10.17}$$

$$= -\sum_y p_Y(y)\sum_x p_{X|Y}(x|y)\log(p_{X|Y}(x|y)) \tag{10.18}$$

$$= -\sum_{x,y} p_{X,Y}(x, y)\log(p_{X|Y}(x|y)). \tag{10.19}$$

The conditional entropy $H(X|Y)$ as well deserves an interpretation. Suppose that Alice possesses random variable X and Bob possesses random variable Y. The conditional entropy $H(X|Y)$ is the amount of uncertainty that Bob has about X given that he already possesses Y. Figure 10.2(b) depicts this interpretation.

The above interpretation of the conditional entropy $H(X|Y)$ immediately suggests that it should be less than or equal to the entropy $H(X)$. That is, having access to a side variable Y should only decrease our uncertainty about another variable. We state this idea as the following theorem and give a formal proof in Section 10.7.1.

THEOREM 10.2.1 (Conditioning Does Not Increase Entropy) The entropy $H(X)$ is greater than or equal to the conditional entropy $H(X|Y)$:

$$H(X) \geq H(X|Y), \tag{10.20}$$

and equality occurs if and only if X and Y are independent random variables. As a consequence of the fact that $H(X|Y) = \sum_y p_Y(y) H(X|Y = y)$, we see that the entropy is concave.

Non-negativity of conditional entropy follows from non-negativity of entropy because conditional entropy is the expectation of the entropy $H(X|Y = y)$ with respect to the density $p_Y(y)$. It is again intuitive that conditional entropy should be non-negative. Even if we have access to some side information Y, we always learn some number of bits of information upon learning the outcome of a random experiment involving X. Perhaps strangely, we will see that *quantum* conditional entropy can become negative, defying our intuition of information in the classical sense given here.

10.3 Joint Entropy

What if Bob knows neither X nor Y? The natural entropic quantity that describes his uncertainty is the joint entropy $H(X, Y)$. The joint entropy is merely the entropy of the joint random variable (X, Y):

DEFINITION 10.3.1 (Joint Entropy) Let X and Y be discrete random variables with joint probability distribution $p_{X,Y}(x, y)$. The joint entropy $H(X, Y)$ is defined as

$$H(X, Y) \equiv \mathbb{E}_{X,Y} \{i(X, Y)\} \tag{10.21}$$

$$= -\sum_{x,y} p_{X,Y}(x, y) \log(p_{X,Y}(x, y)). \tag{10.22}$$

The following exercise asks you to explore the relation between joint entropy $H(X, Y)$, conditional entropy $H(Y|X)$, and marginal entropy $H(X)$. Its proof follows by considering that the multiplicative probability relation $p_{X,Y}(x, y) = p_{Y|X}(y|x) p_X(x)$ of joint probability, conditional probability, and marginal entropy becomes an additive relation under the logarithms of the entropic definitions.

EXERCISE 10.3.1 Verify that $H(X,Y) = H(X) + H(Y|X) = H(Y) + H(X|Y)$.

EXERCISE 10.3.2 Extend the result of Exercise 10.3.1 to prove the following chain rule for entropy:

$$H(X_1, \ldots, X_n) = H(X_1) + H(X_2|X_1) + \cdots + H(X_n|X_{n-1}, \ldots, X_1). \quad (10.23)$$

EXERCISE 10.3.3 Prove that entropy is *subadditive*:

$$H(X_1, \ldots, X_n) \leq \sum_{i=1}^{n} H(X_i), \quad (10.24)$$

by exploiting Theorem 10.2.1 and the entropy chain rule in Exercise 10.3.2.

EXERCISE 10.3.4 Prove that entropy is additive when the random variables $X_1, \ldots, X_n$ are independent:

$$H(X_1, \ldots, X_n) = \sum_{i=1}^{n} H(X_i). \quad (10.25)$$

10.4 Mutual Information

We now introduce an entropic measure of the common or mutual information that two parties possess. Suppose that Alice possesses random variable X and Bob possesses random variable Y.

DEFINITION 10.4.1 (Mutual Information) Let X and Y be discrete random variables with joint probability distribution $p_{X,Y}(x,y)$. The mutual information $I(X;Y)$ is the marginal entropy $H(X)$ less the conditional entropy $H(X|Y)$:

$$I(X;Y) \equiv H(X) - H(X|Y). \quad (10.26)$$

The mutual information quantifies the dependence or correlations of the two random variables X and Y. It measures how much knowing one random variable reduces the uncertainty about the other random variable. In this sense, it is the common information between the two random variables. Bob possesses Y and thus has an uncertainty $H(X|Y)$ about Alice's variable X. Knowledge of Y gives an information gain of $H(X|Y)$ bits about X and then reduces the overall uncertainty $H(X)$ about X, the uncertainty were he not to have any side information at all about X.

EXERCISE 10.4.1 Show that the mutual information is symmetric in its inputs:

$$I(X;Y) = I(Y;X), \quad (10.27)$$

implying additionally that

$$I(X;Y) = H(Y) - H(Y|X). \quad (10.28)$$

We can also express the mutual information $I(X;Y)$ in terms of the respective joint and marginal probability density functions $p_{X,Y}(x,y)$ and $p_X(x)$ and $p_Y(y)$:

$$I(X;Y) = \sum_{x,y} p_{X,Y}(x,y) \log\left(\frac{p_{X,Y}(x,y)}{p_X(x)p_Y(y)}\right). \tag{10.29}$$

The above expression leads to two insights regarding the mutual information $I(X;Y)$. Two random variables X and Y possess zero bits of mutual information if they are statistically independent (recall that the joint density factors as $p_{X,Y}(x,y) = p_X(x)p_Y(y)$ when X and Y are independent). That is, knowledge of Y does not give any information about X when the random variables are statistically independent. Later, we show that the converse statement is true as well. Also, two random variables possess $H(X)$ bits of mutual information if they are perfectly correlated in the sense that $Y = X$.

Theorem 10.4.1 below states that the mutual information $I(X;Y)$ is non-negative for any random variables X and Y—we provide a formal proof in Section 10.7.1. However, this follows naturally from the definition of mutual information in (10.26) and "conditioning does not increase entropy" (Theorem 10.2.1).

THEOREM 10.4.1   The mutual information $I(X;Y)$ is non-negative for any random variables X and Y:

$$I(X;Y) \geq 0, \tag{10.30}$$

and $I(X;Y) = 0$ if and only if X and Y are independent random variables (i.e., if $p_{X,Y}(x,y) = p_X(x)p_Y(y)$).

10.5   Relative Entropy

The relative entropy is another important entropic quantity that quantifies how "far" one probability density function $p(x)$ is from another probability density function $q(x)$. It can be helpful to have a more general definition in which we allow $q(x)$ to be a function taking non-negative values. Before defining the relative entropy, we need the notion of the support of a function.

DEFINITION 10.5.1 (Support)   Let $\mathcal{X}$ denote a finite set. The support of a function $f : \mathcal{X} \to \mathbb{R}$ is equal to the subset of $\mathcal{X}$ that takes non-zero values under f:

$$\text{supp}(f) \equiv \{x : f(x) \neq 0\}. \tag{10.31}$$

DEFINITION 10.5.2 (Relative Entropy)   Let p be a probability distribution defined on the alphabet $\mathcal{X}$, and let $q : \mathcal{X} \to [0, \infty)$. The relative entropy $D(p\|q)$ is defined as follows:

$$D(p\|q) \equiv \begin{cases} \sum_x p(x) \log\left(p(x)/q(x)\right) & \text{if } \text{supp}(p) \subseteq \text{supp}(q) \\ +\infty & \text{else} \end{cases}. \tag{10.32}$$

According to the above definition, the relative entropy is equal to the following expected log-likelihood ratio:

$$D(p\|q) = \mathbb{E}_X \left\{ \log \left(\frac{p(X)}{q(X)} \right) \right\}, \tag{10.33}$$

where X is a random variable distributed according to p.

The above definition implies that the relative entropy is not symmetric under interchange of $p(x)$ and $q(x)$. Thus, the relative entropy is not a distance measure in the strict mathematical sense because it is not symmetric (nor does it satisfy a triangle inequality).

The relative entropy has an interpretation in source coding, if we let $q(x)$ be a probability distribution. Suppose that an information source generates a random variable X according to the density $p(x)$. Suppose further that Alice (the compressor) mistakenly assumes that the probability density of the information source is instead $q(x)$ and codes according to this density. Then the relative entropy quantifies the inefficiency that Alice incurs when she codes according to the mistaken probability density—Alice requires $H(X) + D(p\|q)$ bits on average to code (whereas she would only require $H(X)$ bits on average to code if she used the true density $p(x)$).

We might also see now that the mutual information $I(X;Y)$ is equal to the relative entropy $D(p_{X,Y}\|p_X \otimes p_Y)$ by comparing the definition of relative entropy in (10.32) and the expression for the mutual information in (10.29) (by $p_X \otimes p_Y$ we mean the product of the marginal distributions). In this sense, the mutual information quantifies how far the two random variables X and Y are from being independent because it calculates the "distance" of the joint density $p_{X,Y}$ to the product $p_X \otimes p_Y$ of the marginals.

Let p_{X_1} and p_{X_2} be two probability distributions defined over the same alphabet. The relative entropy $D(p_{X_1}\|p_{X_2})$ admits a pathological property. It can become infinite if the distribution $p_{X_1}(x_1)$ does not have all of its support contained in the support of $p_{X_2}(x_2)$ (i.e., if there is some realization x for which $p_{X_1}(x) \neq 0$ but $p_{X_2}(x) = 0$). This can be somewhat bothersome if we like the interpretation of relative entropy as a notion of distance. In an extreme case, we would think that the distance between a deterministic binary random variable X_2 where $\Pr\{X_2 = 1\} = 1$ and one with probabilities $\Pr\{X_1 = 0\} = \varepsilon$ and $\Pr\{X_1 = 1\} = 1 - \varepsilon$ should be on the order of ε (this is true for the classical trace distance). However, the relative entropy $D(p_{X_1}\|p_{X_2})$ in this case is infinite, in spite of our intuition that these distributions are close. The interpretation in lossless source coding is that it would require an infinite number of bits to code a distribution p_{X_1} losslessly if Alice mistakes it as p_{X_2}. Alice thinks that the symbol $X_2 = 0$ never occurs, and in fact, she thinks that the typical set consists of just one sequence of all ones and every other sequence is atypical. But in reality, the typical set is quite a bit larger than this, and it is only in the limit of an infinite number of bits that we can say her compression is truly lossless.

EXERCISE 10.5.1   Verify that the definition of relative entropy in Definition 10.5.2 is consistent with the following limit:

$$D(p\|q) = \lim_{\varepsilon \searrow 0} D(p\|q + \varepsilon 1), \qquad (10.34)$$

where 1 denotes a vector of ones, so that the elements of $q + \varepsilon 1$ are $q(x) + \varepsilon$.

10.6   Conditional Mutual Information

What is the common information between two random variables X and Y when we have some side information embodied in a random variable Z? The entropic quantity that quantifies this common information is the conditional mutual information.

DEFINITION 10.6.1 (Conditional Mutual Information)   Let X, Y, and Z be discrete random variables. The conditional mutual information is defined as follows:

$$I(X;Y|Z) \equiv H(Y|Z) - H(Y|X,Z) \qquad (10.35)$$
$$= H(X|Z) - H(X|Y,Z) \qquad (10.36)$$
$$= H(X|Z) + H(Y|Z) - H(X,Y|Z). \qquad (10.37)$$

THEOREM 10.6.1 (Strong Subadditivity)   The conditional mutual information $I(X;Y|Z)$ is non-negative:

$$I(X;Y|Z) \geq 0, \qquad (10.38)$$

and the inequality is saturated if and only if $X - Z - Y$ is a Markov chain (i.e., if $p_{X,Y|Z}(x,y|z) = p_{X|Z}(x|z)p_{Y|Z}(y|z)$).

Proof   The proof of the above theorem is a straightforward consequence of the non-negativity of mutual information (Theorem 10.4.1). Consider the following equality:

$$I(X;Y|Z) = \sum_z p_Z(z)I(X;Y|Z = z), \qquad (10.39)$$

where $I(X;Y|Z = z)$ is a mutual information with respect to the joint density $p_{X,Y|Z}(x,y|z)$ and the marginal densities $p_{X|Z}(x|z)$ and $p_{Y|Z}(y|z)$. Non-negativity of $I(X;Y|Z)$ then follows from non-negativity of $p_Z(z)$ and $I(X;Y|Z = z)$. The saturation conditions then follow immediately from those for mutual information given in Theorem 10.4.1 (considering that the conditional mutual information is a convex combination of mutual informations).   □

The proof of the above classical version of strong subadditivity is perhaps trivial in hindsight (it requires only a few arguments). The proof of the quantum version of strong subaddivity is highly non-trivial on the other hand. We discuss strong subadditivity of quantum entropy in the next chapter.

EXERCISE 10.6.1   The expression in (10.38) represents the most compact way to express the strong subadditivity of entropy. Show that the following inequalities are equivalent ways of representing strong subadditivity:

$$H(XY|Z) \leq H(X|Z) + H(Y|Z), \tag{10.40}$$

$$H(XYZ) + H(Z) \leq H(XZ) + H(YZ), \tag{10.41}$$

$$H(X|YZ) \leq H(X|Z). \tag{10.42}$$

EXERCISE 10.6.2   Prove the following chain rule for mutual information:

$$I(X_1, \ldots, X_n; Y)$$
$$= I(X_1; Y) + I(X_2; Y|X_1) + \cdots + I(X_n; Y|X_1, \ldots, X_{n-1}). \tag{10.43}$$

The interpretation of the chain rule is that we can build up the correlations between $X_1, \ldots, X_n$ and Y in n steps: in a first step, we build up the correlations between X_1 and Y, and now that X_1 is available (and thus conditioned on), we build up the correlations between X_2 and Y, etc.

10.7   Entropy Inequalities

The entropic quantities introduced in the previous sections each have bounds associated with them. These bounds are fundamental limits on our ability to process and store information. We introduce several bounds in this section: the non-negativity of relative entropy, two data-processing inequalities, Fano's inequality, and a uniform bound for continuity of entropy. Each of these inequalities plays an important role in information theory, and we describe these roles in more detail in the forthcoming subsections.

10.7.1   Non-Negativity of Relative Entropy

The relative entropy is always non-negative. This seemingly innocuous result has several important implications—namely, the maximal value of entropy, conditioning does not increase entropy (Theorem 10.2.1), non-negativity of mutual information (Theorem 10.4.1), and strong subadditivity (Theorem 10.6.1) are straightforward corollaries of it. A proof of this entropy inequality follows from the application of a simple inequality: $\ln x \leq x - 1$.

THEOREM 10.7.1 (Non-Negativity of Relative Entropy)   Let $p(x)$ be a probability distribution over the alphabet $\mathcal{X}$ and let $q : \mathcal{X} \to [0, 1]$ be a function such that $\sum_x q(x) \leq 1$. Then the relative entropy $D(p\|q)$ is non-negative:

$$D(p\|q) \geq 0, \tag{10.44}$$

and $D(p\|q) = 0$ if and only if $p = q$.

Proof First, suppose that $\text{supp}(p) \not\subseteq \text{supp}(q)$. Then the relative entropy $D(p\|q) = +\infty$ and the inequality is trivially satisfied.

Now, suppose that $\text{supp}(p) \subseteq \text{supp}(q)$. A proof relies on the inequality $\ln x \leq x - 1$ that holds for all $x \geq 0$ and saturates for this range if and only if $x = 1$. (Brief justification: Let $f(x) = x - 1 - \ln x$. Observe that $f(1) = 0$, $f'(1) = 0$, $f'(x) > 0$ for $x > 1$ and $f'(x) < 0$ for $x < 1$. So $f(x)$ has a minimum at $x = 1$ and is strictly increasing when $x > 1$ and strictly decreasing when $x < 1$. For the saturation condition: Suppose that $f(x) = 0$. Then $x = 1$ is a solution of the equation. Since the function is strictly decreasing when $x < 1$ and strictly increasing when $x > 1$, $x = 1$ is the only solution to $f(x) = 0$.) Figure 10.4 plots the functions $\ln x$ and $x - 1$ to compare them.

We first prove the inequality in (10.44). Consider the following chain of inequalities:

$$D(p\|q) = \sum_x p(x) \log \left(\frac{p(x)}{q(x)} \right) \tag{10.45}$$

$$= -\frac{1}{\ln 2} \sum_x p(x) \ln \left(\frac{q(x)}{p(x)} \right) \tag{10.46}$$

$$\geq \frac{1}{\ln 2} \sum_x p(x) \left(1 - \frac{q(x)}{p(x)} \right) \tag{10.47}$$

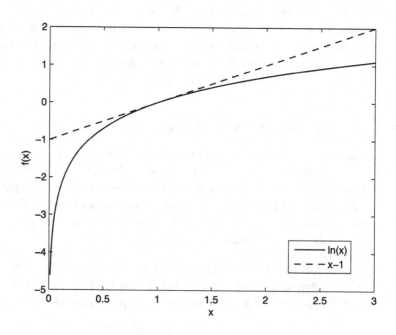

Figure 10.4 A plot that compares the functions $\ln x$ and $x - 1$, showing that $\ln x \leq x - 1$ for all positive x.

$$= \frac{1}{\ln 2} \left(\sum_x p(x) - \sum_x q(x) \right) \tag{10.48}$$

$$\geq 0. \tag{10.49}$$

The sole inequality follows because $- \ln x \geq 1 - x$ (a simple rearrangement of $\ln x \leq x - 1$). The last inequality is a consequence of the assumption that $\sum_x q(x) \leq 1$.

Now suppose that $p = q$. It is then clear that $D(p\|q) = 0$. Finally, suppose that $D(p\|q) = 0$. Then we necessarily have $\mathrm{supp}(p) \subseteq \mathrm{supp}(q)$, and the condition $D(p\|q) = 0$ implies that both inequalities above are saturated. So, first we can deduce that q is a probability distribution since we assumed that $\sum_x q(x) \leq 1$ and the last inequality above is saturated. Next, the inequality in the third line above is saturated, which implies that $\ln (q(x)/p(x)) = 1 - q(x)/p(x)$ for all x for which $p(x) > 0$. But this happens only when $q(x)/p(x) = 1$ for all x for which $p(x) > 0$, which allows us to conclude that $p = q$.   □

We can now quickly prove several corollaries of the above theorem.

Proofs of Property 10.1.5, Theorem 10.4.1, Theorem 10.2.1 Recall in Section 10.1.2 that we proved that the entropy $H(X)$ takes the maximal value $\log |\mathcal{X}|$, where $|\mathcal{X}|$ is the size of the alphabet of X. The proof method involved Lagrange multipliers. Here, we can prove this result simply by computing the relative entropy $D(p_X \| \{1/|\mathcal{X}|\})$, where p_X is the probability density of X and $\{1/|\mathcal{X}|\}$ is the uniform density, and applying the non-negativity of relative entropy:

$$0 \leq D(p_X \| \{1/|\mathcal{X}|\}) \tag{10.50}$$

$$= \sum_x p_X(x) \log \left(\frac{p_X(x)}{\frac{1}{|\mathcal{X}|}} \right) \tag{10.51}$$

$$= -H(X) + \sum_x p_X(x) \log |\mathcal{X}| \tag{10.52}$$

$$= -H(X) + \log |\mathcal{X}|. \tag{10.53}$$

It then follows that $H(X) \leq \log |\mathcal{X}|$ by combining the first line with the last. Non-negativity of mutual information (Theorem 10.4.1) follows by recalling that $I(X;Y) = D(p_{X,Y} \| p_X \otimes p_Y)$ and applying the non-negativity of relative entropy. The equality conditions follow from those for equality of $D(p\|q) = 0$. Conditioning does not increase entropy (Theorem 10.2.1) follows by noting that $I(X;Y) = H(X) - H(X|Y)$ and applying Theorem 10.4.1.   □

10.7.2   Data-Processing Inequality

Another important inequality in classical information theory is the *data-processing inequality*. There are at least two variations of it. The first one states that correlations between random variables can only decrease after we process one variable according to some stochastic function that depends only on that variable. The next one states that the relative entropy cannot increase if a channel is applied to both of its arguments. These data-processing inequalities find application in the converse proof of a coding theorem (the proof of the optimality of a communication rate).

Mutual Information Data-Processing Inequality

We detail the scenario that applies for the first data-processing inequality. Suppose that we initially have two random variables X and Y. We might say that random variable Y arises from random variable X by processing X according to a stochastic map $\mathcal{N}_1 \equiv p_{Y|X}(y|x)$. That is, the two random variables arise by first picking X according to the density $p_X(x)$ and then processing X according to the stochastic map $\mathcal{N}_1$. The mutual information $I(X;Y)$ quantifies the correlations between these two random variables. Suppose then that we process Y according to some other stochastic map $\mathcal{N}_2 \equiv p_{Z|Y}(z|y)$ to produce a random variable Z (note that the map can also be deterministic because the set of stochastic maps subsumes the set of deterministic maps). Then the first data-processing inequality states that the correlations between X and Z must be less than the correlations between X and Y:

$$I(X;Y) \geq I(X;Z), \tag{10.54}$$

because data processing according to any stochastic map $\mathcal{N}_2$ cannot increase correlations. Figure 10.5(a) depicts the scenario described above. Figure 10.5(b) depicts a slightly different scenario for data processing that helps build intuition for the forthcoming notion of quantum data-processing in Section 11.9.2 of the next chapter. Theorem 10.7.2 below states the classical data-processing inequality.

The scenario described in the above paragraph contains a major assumption: the stochastic map $p_{Z|Y}(z|y)$ that produces random variable Z depends on random variable Y only—it has no dependence on X, meaning that

$$p_{Z|Y,X}(z|y,x) = p_{Z|Y}(z|y). \tag{10.55}$$

This assumption is called the Markovian assumption and is the crucial assumption in the proof of the data-processing inequality. We say that the three random variables X, Y, and Z form a *Markov chain* and use the notation $X \to Y \to Z$ to indicate this stochastic relationship.

THEOREM 10.7.2 (Data-Processing Inequality)   Suppose three random variables X, Y, and Z form a Markov chain: $X \to Y \to Z$. Then the following data-processing inequality holds

$$I(X;Y) \geq I(X;Z). \tag{10.56}$$

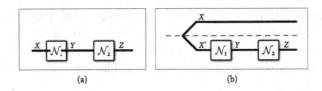

(a)   (b)

Figure 10.5 Two slightly different depictions of the scenario in the data-processing inequality. (a) The map $\mathcal{N}_1$ processes random variable X to produce some random variable Y, and the map $\mathcal{N}_2$ processes the random variable Y to produce the random variable Z. The inequality $I(X;Y) \geq I(X;Z)$ applies here because correlations can only decrease after data processing. (b) This depiction of data processing helps us to build intuition for data processing in the quantum world. The protocol begins with two perfectly correlated random variables X and X'—perfect correlation implies that $p_{X,X'}(x, x') = p_X(x)\delta_{x,x'}$ and further that $H(X) = I(X;X')$. We process random variable X' with a stochastic map $\mathcal{N}_1$ to produce a random variable Y, and then further process Y according to the stochastic map $\mathcal{N}_2$ to produce random variable Z. By the data-processing inequality, the following chain of inequalities holds: $I(X;X') \geq I(X;Y) \geq I(X;Z)$.

Proof The Markov condition $X \to Y \to Z$ implies that random variables X and Z are conditionally independent through Y because

$$p_{X,Z|Y}(x, z|y) = p_{Z|Y,X}(z|y, x)p_{X|Y}(x|y) \tag{10.57}$$

$$= p_{Z|Y}(z|y)p_{X|Y}(x|y). \tag{10.58}$$

We prove the data-processing inequality by manipulating the mutual information $I(X;YZ)$. Consider the following equalities:

$$I(X;YZ) = I(X;Y) + I(X;Z|Y) = I(X;Y). \tag{10.59}$$

The first equality follows from the chain rule for mutual information (Exercise 10.6.2). The second equality follows because the conditional mutual information $I(X;Z|Y)$ vanishes for a Markov chain $X \to Y \to Z$—i.e., X and Z are conditionally independent through Y (recall Theorem 10.6.1). We can also expand the mutual information $I(X;YZ)$ in another way to obtain

$$I(X;YZ) = I(X;Z) + I(X;Y|Z). \tag{10.60}$$

Then the following equality holds for a Markov chain $X \to Y \to Z$ by exploiting (10.59):

$$I(X;Y) = I(X;Z) + I(X;Y|Z). \tag{10.61}$$

The inequality in Theorem 10.7.2 follows because $I(X;Y|Z)$ is non-negative for any random variables X, Y, and Z (recall Theorem 10.6.1). $\qquad \square$

By inspecting the above proof, we find the following:

COROLLARY 10.7.1 The following inequality holds for a Markov chain $X \to Y \to Z$:

$$I(X;Y) \geq I(X;Y|Z). \tag{10.62}$$

Relative Entropy Data-Processing Inequality

Another kind of data-processing inequality holds for the relative entropy, known as monotonicity of relative entropy. This also is a consequence of the non-negativity of relative entropy in Theorem 10.7.1.

COROLLARY 10.7.2 (Monotonicity of Relative Entropy) Let p be a probability distribution on an alphabet $\mathcal{X}$ and let $q : \mathcal{X} \to [0, \infty)$. Let $N(y|x)$ be a conditional probability distribution (i.e., a classical channel). Then the relative entropy does not increase after the channel $N(y|x)$ acts on p and q:

$$D(p\|q) \geq D(Np\|Nq), \tag{10.63}$$

where Np is a probability distribution with elements $(Np)(y) \equiv \sum_x N(y|x)p(x)$ and Nq is a vector with elements $(Nq)(y) = \sum_x N(y|x)q(x)$. Let R be the channel defined by the following set of equations:

$$R(x|y)(Nq)(y) = N(y|x)q(x). \tag{10.64}$$

The inequality in (10.63) is saturated (i.e., $D(p\|q) = D(Np\|Nq)$) if and only if $RNp = p$, where RNp is a probability distribution with elements $(RNp)(x) = \sum_{y,x'} R(x|y)N(y|x')p(x')$.

Proof First, if p and q are such that $\text{supp}(p) \not\subseteq \text{supp}(q)$, then the inequality is trivially true because $D(p\|q) = +\infty$ in this case. So let us suppose that $\text{supp}(p) \subseteq \text{supp}(q)$, which implies that $\text{supp}(Np) \subseteq \text{supp}(Nq)$. Our first step is to rewrite the terms in the inequality. To this end, consider the following algebraic manipulations:

$$D(Np\|Nq) = \sum_y (Np)(y) \log\left(\frac{(Np)(y)}{(Nq)(y)}\right) \tag{10.65}$$

$$= \sum_{y,x} N(y|x)p(x) \log\left(\frac{(Np)(y)}{(Nq)(y)}\right) \tag{10.66}$$

$$= \sum_x p(x) \left[\sum_y N(y|x) \log\left(\frac{(Np)(y)}{(Nq)(y)}\right)\right] \tag{10.67}$$

$$= \sum_x p(x) \log \exp\left[\sum_y N(y|x) \log\left(\frac{(Np)(y)}{(Nq)(y)}\right)\right]. \tag{10.68}$$

This implies that

$$D(p\|q) - D(Np\|Nq) = D(p\|r), \tag{10.69}$$

where

$$r(x) \equiv q(x) \exp\left[\sum_y N(y|x) \log\left(\frac{(Np)(y)}{(Nq)(y)}\right)\right]. \tag{10.70}$$

Now consider that

$$\sum_x r(x) = \sum_x q(x) \exp\left[\sum_y N(y|x) \log\left(\frac{(Np)(y)}{(Nq)(y)}\right)\right] \tag{10.71}$$

$$\leq \sum_x q(x) \sum_y N(y|x) \exp\left[\log\left(\frac{(Np)(y)}{(Nq)(y)}\right)\right] \tag{10.72}$$

$$= \sum_x q(x) \sum_y N(y|x) \left(\frac{(Np)(y)}{(Nq)(y)}\right) \tag{10.73}$$

$$= \sum_y \left[\sum_x q(x)N(y|x)\right] \frac{(Np)(y)}{(Nq)(y)} \tag{10.74}$$

$$= \sum_y (Np)(y) = 1. \tag{10.75}$$

The inequality in the second line follows from convexity of the exponential function. Since r is a vector such that $\sum_x r(x) \leq 1$, we can conclude from Theorem 10.7.1 that $D(p\|r) \geq 0$, which by (10.69) is the same as (10.63).

We now comment on the saturation conditions. First, suppose that $RNp = p$. By monotonicity of relative entropy (what was just proved) under the application of the channel R, we find that

$$D(Np\|Nq) \geq D(RNp\|RNq) = D(p\|q), \tag{10.76}$$

where the equality follows from the assumption that $RNp = p$, and the fact that $RNq = q$. This last statement follows because

$$(RNq)(x) = \sum_y R(x|y)(Nq)(y) = \sum_y N(y|x)q(x) = q(x). \tag{10.77}$$

The other implication $D(p\|q) = D(Np\|Nq) \Rightarrow RNp = p$ is a consequence of a later development, Theorem 10.8.4. □

10.7.3 Fano's Inequality

Another entropy inequality that we consider is Fano's inequality. This inequality also finds application in the converse proof of a coding theorem.

Fano's inequality applies to a general classical communication scenario. Suppose Alice possesses some random variable X that she transmits to Bob over a noisy communication channel. Let $p_{Y|X}(y|x)$ denote the stochastic map corresponding to the noisy communication channel. Bob receives a random variable Y from the channel and processes it in some way to produce his best estimate $\hat{X}$ of the original random variable X. Figure 10.6 depicts this scenario.

The natural performance metric of this communication scenario is the probability of error $p_e \equiv \Pr\{\hat{X} \neq X\}$—a low probability of error corresponds to good performance. On the other hand, consider the conditional entropy $H(X|Y)$. We interpreted it before as the uncertainty about X from the perspective of someone

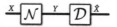

Figure 10.6 The classical communication scenario relevant in Fano's inequality. Alice transmits a random variable X over a noisy channel $\mathcal{N}$, producing a random variable Y. Bob receives Y and processes it according to some decoding map $\mathcal{D}$ to produce his best estimate $\hat{X}$ of Y.

who already knows Y. If the channel is noiseless $(p_{Y|X}(y|x) = \delta_{y,x})$, then there is no uncertainty about X because Y is identical to X:

$$H(X|Y) = 0. \tag{10.78}$$

As the channel becomes noisier, the conditional entropy $H(X|Y)$ increases away from zero. In this sense, the conditional entropy $H(X|Y)$ quantifies the information about X that is lost in the channel noise. We then might naturally expect there to be a relationship between the probability of error p_e and the conditional entropy $H(X|Y)$: the amount of information lost in the channel should be low if the probability of error is low. Fano's inequality provides a quantitative bound corresponding to this idea.

THEOREM 10.7.3 (Fano's Inequality)   Suppose that Alice sends a random variable X through a noisy channel to produce random variable Y and further processing of Y gives an estimate $\hat{X}$ of X. Thus, $X \to Y \to \hat{X}$ forms a Markov chain. Let $p_e \equiv \Pr\{\hat{X} \neq X\}$ denote the probability of error. Then the following function of the error probability p_e bounds the information lost in the channel noise:

$$H(X|Y) \leq H(X|\hat{X}) \leq h_2(p_e) + p_e \log(|\mathcal{X}| - 1), \tag{10.79}$$

where $h_2(p_e)$ is the binary entropy function. In particular, note that

$$\lim_{p_e \to 0} h_2(p_e) + p_e \log(|\mathcal{X}| - 1) = 0. \tag{10.80}$$

The bound is sharp in the sense that there is a choice of random variables X and Y that saturates it.

Proof Let E denote an indicator random variable that indicates whether an error occurs:

$$E = \begin{cases} 0 & : & X = \hat{X} \\ 1 & : & X \neq \hat{X} \end{cases}. \tag{10.81}$$

Consider the entropy

$$H(EX|\hat{X}) = H(X|\hat{X}) + H(E|X\hat{X}). \tag{10.82}$$

The entropy $H(E|X\hat{X})$ on the right-hand side vanishes because there is no uncertainty about the indicator random variable E if we know both X and $\hat{X}$. Thus,

$$H(EX|\hat{X}) = H(X|\hat{X}). \tag{10.83}$$

Also, the data-processing inequality applies to the Markov chain $X \to Y \to \hat{X}$:

$$I(X;Y) \geq I(X;\hat{X}), \tag{10.84}$$

and implies the following inequality:

$$H(X|\hat{X}) \geq H(X|Y). \tag{10.85}$$

Consider the following chain of inequalities:

$$H(EX|\hat{X}) = H(E|\hat{X}) + H(X|E\hat{X}) \tag{10.86}$$
$$\leq H(E) + H(X|E\hat{X}) \tag{10.87}$$
$$= h_2(p_e) + p_e H(X|\hat{X}, E = 1)$$
$$+ (1 - p_e) H(X|\hat{X}, E = 0) \tag{10.88}$$
$$\leq h_2(p_e) + p_e \log(|\mathcal{X}| - 1). \tag{10.89}$$

The first equality follows by expanding the entropy $H(EX|\hat{X})$. The first inequality follows because conditioning reduces entropy. The second equality follows by explicitly expanding the conditional entropy $H(X|E\hat{X})$ in terms of the two possibilities of the error random variable E. The last inequality follows from two facts: there is no uncertainty about X when there is no error (when $E = 0$) and $\hat{X}$ is available, and the uncertainty about X when there is an error (when $E = 1$) and $\hat{X}$ is available is less than the uncertainty of a uniform distribution $\frac{1}{|\mathcal{X}|-1}$ for all of the other possibilities. Fano's inequality follows from putting together (10.85), (10.83), and (10.89):

$$H(X|Y) \leq H(X|\hat{X}) = H(EX|\hat{X}) \leq h_2(p_e) + p_e \log(|\mathcal{X}| - 1). \tag{10.90}$$

To establish the statement of saturation, let X be a uniform random variable and let X' be a copy of it (so that the joint distribution is $p_{X,X'}(x, x') = \delta_{x,x'}/|\mathcal{X}|$ where $\mathcal{X}$ is the alphabet). Let $p_{Y|X'}$ denote a symmetric channel such that the input x' is transmitted faithfully with probability $1 - \varepsilon$ and becomes one of the other $|\mathcal{X}| - 1$ letters with probability $\varepsilon/(|\mathcal{X}| - 1)$, where $\varepsilon \in [0,1]$. Observe that Y is a uniform random variable, given that $p_{Y|X'}$ is a symmetric channel. Then $\Pr\{X \neq Y\} = \varepsilon$, and we find that

$$H(X|Y) = H(Y|X) + H(X) - H(Y) = H(Y|X) = h_2(\varepsilon) + \varepsilon \log(|\mathcal{X}| - 1), \tag{10.91}$$

concluding the proof. □

10.7.4 Continuity of Entropy

That the entropy is a continuous function follows from the fact that the function $-x \log x$ is continuous. However, it can be useful in applications to have explicit continuity bounds. Before we give such bounds, we should establish how we measure distance between probability distributions. A natural way for doing so is to use the classical trace distance, defined as follows:

DEFINITION 10.7.1 (Classical Trace Distance)   Let $p, q : \mathcal{X} \to \mathbb{R}$, where $\mathcal{X}$ is a finite alphabet. The classical trace distance between p and q is then

$$\|p - q\|_1 \equiv \sum_x |p(x) - q(x)|. \tag{10.92}$$

The classical trace distance is a special case of the trace distance from Definition 9.1.2, in which we place the entries of p and q along the diagonal of some square matrices. If p and q are probability distributions, then the operational meaning of the classical trace distance is the same as it was in the fully quantum case: it is the bias in the probability with which one could successfully distinguish p and q by means of any binary hypothesis test. The optimal test is given in the following lemma:

LEMMA 10.7.1   Let p and q be probability distributions on a finite alphabet $\mathcal{X}$. Let $A \equiv \{x : p(x) \geq q(x)\}$. Then

$$\frac{1}{2} \|p - q\|_1 = p(A) - q(A), \tag{10.93}$$

where $p(A) \equiv \sum_{x \in A} p(x)$ and $q(A) \equiv \sum_{x \in A} q(x)$.

Proof   A proof for this lemma is very similar to that for Lemma 9.1.1. It is brief and so we provide it here. Consider that

$$0 = \sum_x [p(x) - q(x)] \tag{10.94}$$

$$= \sum_{x \in A} [p(x) - q(x)] + \sum_{x \in A^c} [p(x) - q(x)], \tag{10.95}$$

which implies that

$$\sum_{x \in A} [p(x) - q(x)] = \sum_{x \in A^c} [q(x) - p(x)]. \tag{10.96}$$

Now consider that

$$\|p - q\|_1 = \sum_x |p(x) - q(x)| \tag{10.97}$$

$$= \sum_{x \in A} [p(x) - q(x)] + \sum_{x \in A^c} [q(x) - p(x)] \tag{10.98}$$

$$= 2 \sum_{x \in A} [p(x) - q(x)], \tag{10.99}$$

where the last line follows from (10.96).   □

One can interpret the set A and its complement A^c as a binary hypothesis test that one could perform after receiving a sample x from either the distribution p or q (without knowing which distribution was used to generate the sample). If the sample x is in A, then we would decide that p generated x, and otherwise, we would decide that q generated x. The success probability for distinguishing p from q is then

$$\frac{1}{2}\left[\sum_{x\in A} p(x) + \sum_{x\in A^c} q(x)\right] = \frac{1}{2}\left[1 + \sum_{x\in A}[p(x) - q(x)]\right] \tag{10.100}$$

$$= \frac{1}{2}\left[1 + \frac{1}{2}\|p - q\|_1\right]. \tag{10.101}$$

It turns out that this test is the optimal test, which follows from the same reasoning given in Section 9.1.4. Thus, we can interpret the classical trace distance as an important measure of distinguishability between probability distributions, with an operational interpretation as given above.

We can now state an important entropy continuity bound.

THEOREM 10.7.4 (Zhang–Audenaert)   Let X and Y be discrete random variables taking values in a finite alphabet $\mathcal{A}$. Let p_X and p_Y denote their distributions, respectively. Then the following bound holds

$$|H(X) - H(Y)| \le T \log(|\mathcal{A}| - 1) + h_2(T), \tag{10.102}$$

where $T \equiv \frac{1}{2}\|p_X - p_Y\|_1$. Furthermore, this bound is optimal, meaning that there exists a pair of random variables saturating the bound for every $T \in [0,1]$ and alphabet size $|\mathcal{A}|$.

In order to prove this theorem, we need to establish the notion of a maximal coupling of two random variables.

DEFINITION 10.7.2 (Coupling)   A coupling of a pair (X, Y) of two random variables is a pair $(\hat{X}, \hat{Y})$ of two other random variables that have the same marginal distributions as those of X and Y.

DEFINITION 10.7.3 (Maximal Coupling)   A coupling $(\hat{X}, \hat{Y})$ of a pair of two random variables (X, Y) is maximal if $\Pr\{\hat{X} = \hat{Y}\}$ takes on its maximum value, with respect to all couplings of X and Y.

We can now relate the classical trace distance to a maximal coupling:

LEMMA 10.7.2   Let X and Y be discrete random variables taking values in a finite alphabet $\mathcal{A}$. Let p_X and p_Y denote their distributions, respectively. If $(\hat{X}, \hat{Y})$ is a maximal coupling of X and Y, then the following equalities hold

$$\Pr\{\hat{X} = \hat{Y}\} = \sum_{u\in\mathcal{A}} \min\{p_X(u), p_Y(u)\}, \tag{10.103}$$

$$\Pr\{\hat{X} \ne \hat{Y}\} = \frac{1}{2}\|p_X - p_Y\|_1. \tag{10.104}$$

Proof Let $\mathcal{B} = \{u \in \mathcal{A} : p_X(u) < p_Y(u)\}$. Let $\mathcal{B}^c = \mathcal{A}\backslash\mathcal{B}$. Then for every coupling $(\hat{X}, \hat{Y})$ of (X, Y), the following holds

$$\Pr\{\hat{X} = \hat{Y}\} = \Pr\{\hat{X} = \hat{Y} \wedge \hat{Y} \in \mathcal{B}\} + \Pr\{\hat{X} = \hat{Y} \wedge \hat{Y} \in \mathcal{B}^c\} \tag{10.105}$$

$$\leq \Pr\{\hat{X} \in \mathcal{B}\} + \Pr\{\hat{Y} \in \mathcal{B}^c\} \tag{10.106}$$

$$= \Pr\{X \in \mathcal{B}\} + \Pr\{Y \in \mathcal{B}^c\} \tag{10.107}$$

$$= \sum_{u \in \mathcal{B}} p_X(u) + \sum_{u \in \mathcal{B}^c} p_Y(u) \tag{10.108}$$

$$= \sum_{u \in \mathcal{B}} \min\{p_X(u), p_Y(u)\} + \sum_{u \in \mathcal{B}^c} \min\{p_X(u), p_Y(u)\} \tag{10.109}$$

$$= \sum_{u \in \mathcal{A}} \min\{p_X(u), p_Y(u)\}. \tag{10.110}$$

We now establish a construction of a coupling that achieves the bound above, so that it is maximal. Let $q \equiv \sum_{u \in \mathcal{A}} \min\{p_X(u), p_Y(u)\}$. Let U, V, W, and J be independent discrete random variables, with $p_J(0) = 1 - q$ and $p_J(1) = q$. Let U, V, and W have the following probability distributions:

$$p_U(u) = \frac{1}{q} \left[\min\{p_X(u), p_Y(u)\} \right], \tag{10.111}$$

$$p_V(v) = \frac{1}{1-q} \left[p_X(v) - \min\{p_X(v), p_Y(v)\} \right], \tag{10.112}$$

$$p_W(w) = \frac{1}{1-q} \left[p_Y(w) - \min\{p_X(w), p_Y(w)\} \right], \tag{10.113}$$

where $u, v, w \in \mathcal{A}$. If $J = 1$, then let $\hat{X} = \hat{Y} = U$, and if $J = 0$, then let $\hat{X} = V$ and $\hat{Y} = W$. So we find that for all $x, y \in \mathcal{A}$

$$p_{\hat{X}}(x) = q \, p_{X|J}(x|1) + (1 - q) \, p_{X|J}(x|0) \tag{10.114}$$

$$= q \, p_U(x) + (1 - q) \, p_V(x) \tag{10.115}$$

$$= p_X(x). \tag{10.116}$$

By similar reasoning, it follows that $p_{\hat{Y}}(y) = p_Y(y)$, so that we can conclude that the constructed $(\hat{X}, \hat{Y})$ is a coupling of (X, Y). It is maximal because

$$\Pr\{\hat{X} = \hat{Y}\} \geq \Pr\{J = 1\} = q, \tag{10.117}$$

and we can conclude from (10.110) that $\Pr\{\hat{X} = \hat{Y}\} = q$. The equality in (10.104) follows from (10.103) and the following equality $\min\{a, b\} = \frac{1}{2}[a + b - |a - b|]$, which holds for all $a, b \in \mathbb{R}$.   □

We can finally give a proof of Theorem 10.7.4, by invoking the above results and Fano's inequality (Theorem 10.7.3).

Proof of Theorem 10.7.4   Let $(\hat{X}, \hat{Y})$ be a maximal coupling of (X, Y). Then

$$|H(X) - H(Y)| = \left| H(\hat{X}) - H(\hat{Y}) \right| \tag{10.118}$$

$$= \left| H(\hat{X}) - H(\hat{X}\hat{Y}) + H(\hat{X}\hat{Y}) - H(\hat{Y}) \right| \tag{10.119}$$

$$= \left| H(\hat{X}|\hat{Y}) - H(\hat{Y}|\hat{X}) \right| \tag{10.120}$$

$$\leq \max \left\{ H(\hat{X}|\hat{Y}), H(\hat{Y}|\hat{X}) \right\} \tag{10.121}$$

$$\leq \Pr\{\hat{X} \neq \hat{Y}\} \log\left(|\mathcal{A}| - 1\right) + h_2(\Pr\{\hat{X} \neq \hat{Y}\}) \tag{10.122}$$

$$= T \log\left(|\mathcal{A}| - 1\right) + h_2(T). \tag{10.123}$$

The first equality follows because $(\hat{X}, \hat{Y})$ is a maximal coupling of (X, Y). The second inequality is an application of Fano's inequality (Theorem 10.7.3). The last equality follows from (10.104).

The bound given in the statement of the theorem is optimal. An example of a pair of probability distributions p_X and p_Y saturating the bound is

$$p_X = \begin{bmatrix} 1 & 0 & \cdots & 0 \end{bmatrix}, \tag{10.124}$$

$$p_Y = \begin{bmatrix} 1 - \varepsilon & \varepsilon/\left(|\mathcal{A}| - 1\right) & \cdots & \varepsilon/\left(|\mathcal{A}| - 1\right) \end{bmatrix}, \tag{10.125}$$

where $\varepsilon \in [0, 1]$. The normalized classical trace distance between p_X and p_Y is $\frac{1}{2} \|p_X - p_Y\|_1 = \varepsilon$, while an explicit calculation reveals that

$$|H(X) - H(Y)| = H(Y) = \varepsilon \log\left(|\mathcal{A}| - 1\right) + h_2(\varepsilon), \tag{10.126}$$

concluding the proof. $\square$

10.8 Near Saturation of Entropy Inequalities

The entropy inequalities discussed in the previous section are foundational in classical information theory. In fact, one can prove the converse parts of many classical capacity theorems by making use of these entropy inequalities. Thus, it seems worthwhile to study them in more detail and to explore the possibility of more refined statements. For example, in each of these entropy inequalities, there is a condition for when it is saturated: the non-negativity of relative entropy is saturated if and only if $p = q$ and the non-negativity of mutual information is saturated if and only if random variables X and Y are independent. It is thus a natural question to consider what kind of statement we can make when these entropy inequalities are nearly saturated.

10.8.1 Pinsker Inequality

One of the main tools for refining entropy inequalities in the classical case is the Pinsker inequality, which provides a relation between the relative entropy and the classical trace distance.

THEOREM 10.8.1 (Pinsker Inequality)   Let p be a probability distribution on a finite alphabet $\mathcal{X}$ and let $q : \mathcal{X} \to [0, 1]$ be such that $\sum_x q(x) \leq 1$. Then

$$D(p\|q) \geq \frac{1}{2\ln 2} \|p - q\|_1^2. \tag{10.127}$$

The utility of the Pinsker inequality is that it relates one measure of distinguishability to another, and thus allows us to make precise statements about the near saturation of an entropy inequality. For example, Theorem 10.7.1 states that $D(p\|q) \geq 0$ for p and q as given above. The Pinsker inequality is a strong refinement of this entropy inequality: it says more than just $D(p\|q) \geq 0$, considering that $\|p - q\|_1 \geq 0$. Letting q be subnormalized as above gives us a little more flexibility when applying the Pinsker inequality.

Before proving it, we establish the following lemma:

LEMMA 10.8.1   Let $a, b \in [0, 1]$. Then $a \ln \left(\frac{a}{b}\right) + (1 - a) \ln \left(\frac{1-a}{1-b}\right) \geq 2 (a - b)^2$.

Proof   This bound follows by elementary calculus. First, if $b = 0$ or $b = 1$, then the bound holds trivially. So suppose that $b \in (0, 1)$. Let us suppose furthermore (for now) that $a \geq b$. Consider the following function:

$$g(a, b) \equiv a \ln \left(\frac{a}{b}\right) + (1 - a) \ln \left(\frac{1 - a}{1 - b}\right) - 2 (a - b)^2, \tag{10.128}$$

so that $g(a, b)$ corresponds to the difference of the left-hand side and the right-hand side in the statement of the lemma. Then

$$\frac{\partial g(a, b)}{\partial b} = -\frac{a}{b} + \frac{1 - a}{1 - b} - 4 (b - a) \tag{10.129}$$

$$= -\frac{a (1 - b)}{b (1 - b)} + \frac{b (1 - a)}{b (1 - b)} - 4 (b - a) \tag{10.130}$$

$$= \frac{b - a}{b (1 - b)} - 4 (b - a). \tag{10.131}$$

Continuing,

$$= \frac{(b - a) \left(4b^2 - 4b + 1\right)}{b (1 - b)} \tag{10.132}$$

$$= \frac{(b - a) (2b - 1)^2}{b (1 - b)} \tag{10.133}$$

$$\leq 0. \tag{10.134}$$

The last step follows from the assumption that $a \geq b$ and $b \in (0, 1)$. Also, observe that both $\partial g(a, b)/\partial b = 0$ and $g(a, b) = 0$ when $a = b$. Thus, the function $g(a, b)$ is decreasing in b for every a whenever $b \leq a$ and reaches a minimum when $b = a$. So $g(a, b) \geq 0$ whenever $a \geq b$. The lemma holds in general by applying it to $a' \equiv 1 - a$ and $b' \equiv 1 - b$ so that $b' \geq a'$.   □

Proof of Pinsker's inequality (Theorem 10.8.1)   The main idea is to exploit the monotonicity of relative entropy and the lemma above. First let us suppose that q is a probability distribution. Let $\mathcal{A}$ denote a classical "coarse-graining" channel that outputs 1 if $x \in A$ and 0 if $x \in A^c$, where A is the set defined in Lemma 10.7.1 (i.e., $A \equiv \{x : p(x) \geq q(x)\}$). Then

$$D(p\|q) \geq D(\mathcal{A}(p)\|\mathcal{A}(q)) \tag{10.135}$$

$$= p(A) \log \left(\frac{p(A)}{q(A)}\right) + (1 - p(A)) \log \left(\frac{1 - p(A)}{1 - q(A)}\right) \tag{10.136}$$

$$\geq \frac{2}{\ln 2} \left(p(A) - q(A) \right)^2 \tag{10.137}$$

$$= \frac{2}{\ln 2} \left(\frac{1}{2} \| p - q \|_1 \right)^2 \tag{10.138}$$

$$= \frac{1}{2 \ln 2} \| p - q \|_1^2 . \tag{10.139}$$

The first inequality follows from monotonicity of the relative entropy (Corollary 10.7.2), with the quantities $p(A)$ and $q(A)$ defined in Lemma 10.7.1. The second inequality is an application of Lemma 10.8.1, where we gain the factor $\ln 2$ by converting from natural logarithm to binary logarithm. The second equality follows from Lemma 10.7.1.

If q is not a probability distribution (so that $\sum_x q(x) < 1$), then we can add an extra letter to $\mathcal{X}$ to make q a probability distribution. That is, we define a probability distribution q' to have its first $|\mathcal{X}|$ entries to be those from q and its last entry to be $1 - \sum_x q(x)$. We also define an augmented distribution p' to have its first $|\mathcal{X}|$ entries to be those from p and its last entry to be 0. Then $0 \cdot \log \left(0 / \left[1 - \sum_x q(x) \right] \right) = 0$, so that

$$D(p\|q) = D(p'\|q') \tag{10.140}$$

$$\geq \frac{1}{2 \ln 2} \| p' - q' \|_1^2 \tag{10.141}$$

$$= \frac{1}{2 \ln 2} \left(\| p - q \|_1 + \left[1 - \sum_x q(x) \right] \right)^2 \tag{10.142}$$

$$\geq \frac{1}{2 \ln 2} \| p - q \|_1^2 , \tag{10.143}$$

concluding the proof. □

10.8.2 Refinements of Entropy Inequalities

The first refinement of an entropy inequality that we give is regarding the non-negativity of mutual information and its maximal value:

THEOREM 10.8.2 Let X and Y be discrete random variables taking values in alphabets $\mathcal{X}$ and $\mathcal{Y}$, respectively, let p_{XY} denote their joint distribution, and let $p_X \otimes p_Y$ denote the product of their marginal distributions. Then

$$I(X;Y) \geq \frac{2}{\ln 2} \Delta^2, \tag{10.144}$$

and

$$I(X;Y) \leq \Delta \log(\min\{|\mathcal{X}|, |\mathcal{Y}|\} - 1) + h_2(\Delta), \tag{10.145}$$

where $\Delta = \frac{1}{2} \| p_{XY} - p_X \otimes p_Y \|_1$.

Proof The first inequality is a direct application of the Pinsker inequality (Theorem 10.8.1), noting that

$$I(X;Y) = D(p_{XY} \| p_X \otimes p_Y).$$ (10.146)

To prove the second inequality, let $\hat{X}$ and $\hat{Y}$ denote a pair of random variables with joint distribution $p_X \otimes p_Y$. Then

$$I(X;Y) = \left| I(X;Y) - I(\hat{X};\hat{Y}) \right|$$ (10.147)

$$= \left| H(X|Y) - H(\hat{X}|\hat{Y}) \right|$$ (10.148)

$$= \left| \sum_y p_Y(y) \left[H(X|Y=y) - H(\hat{X}|\hat{Y}=y) \right] \right|.$$ (10.149)

The first equality follows because $I(\hat{X};\hat{Y}) = 0$. The second equality follows because $I(X;Y) = H(X) - H(X|Y)$, $I(\hat{X};\hat{Y}) = H(\hat{X}) - H(\hat{X}|\hat{Y})$, and $H(X) = H(\hat{X})$. The third equality follows from the definition of conditional entropy. Continuing,

$$\leq \sum_y p_Y(y) \left| H(X|Y=y) - H(\hat{X}|\hat{Y}=y) \right|$$ (10.150)

$$\leq \sum_y p_Y(y) \left[\Delta(y) \log(|\mathcal{X}|-1) + h_2(\Delta(y)) \right]$$ (10.151)

$$\leq \Delta \log(|\mathcal{X}|-1) + h_2(\Delta).$$ (10.152)

The first inequality is a consequence of the triangle inequality. The second inequality follows from an application of Theorem 10.7.4, and from defining

$$\Delta(y) = \frac{1}{2} \sum_x \left| p_{X|Y}(x|y) - p_X(x) \right|.$$ (10.153)

The final inequality follows because

$$\Delta = \frac{1}{2} \sum_{x,y} |p_{XY}(x,y) - p_X(x)p_Y(y)|$$ (10.154)

$$= \sum_y p_Y(y) \left[\frac{1}{2} \sum_x |p_{X|Y}(x|y) - p_X(x)| \right]$$ (10.155)

$$= \sum_y p_Y(y) \Delta(y),$$ (10.156)

and from the fact that the binary entropy is concave. We obtain the other bound

$$I(X;Y) \leq \Delta \log(|\mathcal{Y}|-1) + h_2(\Delta),$$ (10.157)

by expanding the mutual information as $I(X;Y) = |I(X;Y) - I(\hat{X};\hat{Y})| = |H(Y|X) - H(\hat{Y}|\hat{X})|$ and proceeding in a similar fashion. $\square$

We can make a similar kind of statement for the conditional mutual information:

THEOREM 10.8.3 Let X, Y, and Z be discrete random variables taking values in alphabets $\mathcal{X}$, $\mathcal{Y}$, and $\mathcal{Z}$, respectively, let p_{XYZ} denote their joint distribution, and let $p_{X|Z}p_{Y|Z}p_Z$ denote another distribution which corresponds to the Markov chain $X - Z - Y$. Then

$$I(X;Y|Z) \geq \frac{2}{\ln 2}\Delta^2, \tag{10.158}$$

and

$$I(X;Y|Z) \leq \Delta \log(\min\{|\mathcal{X}|, |\mathcal{Y}|\} - 1) + h_2(\Delta), \tag{10.159}$$

where $\Delta = \frac{1}{2}\left\|p_{XYZ} - p_{X|Z}p_{Y|Z}p_Z\right\|_1$.

Proof A proof for the first inequality is similar to the proof of (10.144). One can write $I(X;Y|Z) = \sum_z p_Z(z)I(X;Y|Z=z)$, apply the Pinsker inequality (Theorem 10.8.1), and then convexity of the square function and the trace norm. Alternatively, one can directly compute that $I(X;Y|Z) = D(p_{XYZ}\|p_{X|Z}p_{Y|Z}p_Z)$ and then apply the Pinsker inequality (Theorem 10.8.1).

A proof for the second inequality is similar to that for (10.145). Let $\hat{X}$, $\hat{Y}$, and $\hat{Z}$ denote a triple of random variables with joint distribution $p_{X|Z}p_{Y|Z}p_Z$. Then

$$I(X;Y|Z) = \left|I(X;Y|Z) - I(\hat{X};\hat{Y}|\hat{Z})\right| \tag{10.160}$$

$$= \left|H(Y|Z) - H(Y|XZ) - \left[H(\hat{Y}|\hat{Z}) - H(\hat{Y}|\hat{X}\hat{Z})\right]\right| \tag{10.161}$$

$$= \left|H(\hat{Y}|\hat{X}\hat{Z}) - H(Y|XZ)\right|, \tag{10.162}$$

where the first equality follows because $I(\hat{X};\hat{Y}|\hat{Z}) = 0$, the second by expanding the conditional mutual informations, and the third because $H(Y|Z) = H(\hat{Y}|\hat{Z})$. The rest of the steps proceed as in the proof of (10.145), and we end up with

$$I(X;Y|Z) \leq \Delta \log(|\mathcal{Y}| - 1) + h_2(\Delta). \tag{10.163}$$

A proof for $I(X;Y|Z) \leq \Delta \log(|\mathcal{X}| - 1) + h_2(\Delta)$ follows by expanding the conditional mutual information $I(X;Y|Z)$ in the other way, as $I(X;Y|Z) = H(X|Z) - H(X|YZ)$. $\qquad\square$

Finally, the following theorem gives a strong refinement of the monotonicity of relative entropy (Corollary 10.7.2). An important implication is that if the relative entropy decrease $D(p\|q) - D(Np\|Nq)$ is not too large under the action of a classical channel N, then one can perform a recovery channel R, satisfying (10.165), such that the recovered distribution RNp is close to the original distribution p.

THEOREM 10.8.4 (Refined Monotonicity of Relative Entropy) Let p be a probability distribution on a finite alphabet $\mathcal{X}$ and let $q : \mathcal{X} \to [0, \infty)$ be a function such that $\text{supp}(p) \subseteq \text{supp}(q)$. Let $N(y|x)$ be a conditional probability distribution (classical channel). Then the following refinement of the monotonicity of relative entropy holds:

$$D(p\|q) - D(Np\|Nq) \geq D(p\|RNp) \tag{10.164}$$

where Np is a probability distribution with elements $(Np)(y) \equiv \sum_x N(y|x)p(x)$, Nq is a vector with elements $(Nq)(y) = \sum_x N(y|x)q(x)$, and the recovery channel $R(x|y)$ (a conditional probability distribution) is defined by the following set of equations:

$$R(x|y)(Nq)(y) = N(y|x)q(x), \tag{10.165}$$

which correspond to the Bayes theorem if q is a probability distribution. Also, RNp is a probability distribution with elements $(RNp)(x) = \sum_{y,x'} R(x|y)N(y|x')p(x')$.

Proof Consider that

$$(RNp)(x) = \sum_y \frac{N(y|x)q(x)}{(Nq)(y)} [(Np)(y)] \tag{10.166}$$

$$= q(x) \sum_y \frac{N(y|x)(Np)(y)}{(Nq)(y)}. \tag{10.167}$$

Thus,

$$D(p\|RNp) = \sum_x p(x) \log\left(\frac{p(x)}{q(x)\sum_y \frac{N(y|x)(Np)(y)}{(Nq)(y)}}\right),$$

and by definition we have that

$$D(p\|q) = \sum_x p(x) \log\left(\frac{p(x)}{q(x)}\right), \tag{10.168}$$

$$D(Np\|Nq) = \sum_y (Np)(y) \log\left(\frac{(Np)(y)}{(Nq)(y)}\right). \tag{10.169}$$

Then

$$D(p\|q) - D(p\|RNp) = \sum_x p(x) \log\left(\sum_y \frac{N(y|x)(Np)(y)}{(Nq)(y)}\right) \tag{10.170}$$

$$\geq \sum_x p(x) \sum_y N(y|x) \log\left(\frac{(Np)(y)}{(Nq)(y)}\right) \tag{10.171}$$

$$= \sum_y \left[\sum_x N(y|x)p(x)\right] \log\left(\frac{(Np)(y)}{(Nq)(y)}\right) \tag{10.172}$$

$$= \sum_y (Np)(y) \log\left(\frac{(Np)(y)}{(Nq)(y)}\right) \tag{10.173}$$

$$= D(Np\|Nq). \tag{10.174}$$

The sole inequality is a consequence of concavity of the logarithm. $\square$

10.9   Classical Information from Quantum Systems

We can always process classical information by employing a quantum system as the carrier of information. The inputs and the outputs to a quantum protocol can both be classical. For example, we can prepare a quantum state according to some random variable X—the ensemble $\{p_X(x), \rho_x\}$ captures this idea. We can retrieve classical information from a quantum state in the form of some random variable Y by performing a measurement—the POVM $\{\Lambda_y\}$ captures this notion (recall that we employ the POVM formalism from Section 4.2.1 if we do not care about the state after the measurement). Suppose that Alice prepares a quantum state according to the ensemble $\{p_X(x), \rho_x\}$ and Bob measures the state according to the POVM $\{\Lambda_y\}$. Recall that the following formula gives the conditional probability $p_{Y|X}(y|x)$:

$$p_{Y|X}(y|x) = \text{Tr}\{\Lambda_y \rho_x\}. \tag{10.175}$$

Is there any benefit to processing classical information using quantum systems? Later, in Chapter 20, we see that there indeed is an enhanced performance because we can achieve higher communication rates in general by processing classical data using quantum resources. For now, we extend our notions of entropy in a straightforward way to include the above ideas.

10.9.1   Shannon Entropy of a POVM

The first notion that we can extend is the Shannon entropy, by determining the Shannon entropy of a POVM. Suppose that Alice prepares a quantum state ρ (there is no classical index here). Bob can then perform a particular POVM $\{\Lambda_x\}$ to learn about the quantum system. Let X denote the random variable corresponding to the classical output of the POVM. The probability density function $p_X(x)$ of random variable X is then

$$p_X(x) = \text{Tr}\{\Lambda_x \rho\}. \tag{10.176}$$

The Shannon entropy $H(X)$ of the POVM $\{\Lambda_x\}$ is

$$H(X) = -\sum_x p_X(x) \log(p_X(x)) \tag{10.177}$$

$$= -\sum_x \text{Tr}\{\Lambda_x \rho\} \log(\text{Tr}\{\Lambda_x \rho\}). \tag{10.178}$$

In the next chapter, we prove that the minimum Shannon entropy with respect to all rank-one POVMs is equal to a quantity known as the quantum entropy of the density operator ρ.

10.9.2   Accessible Information

Let us consider the scenario introduced at the beginning of this section, in which Alice prepares an ensemble $\mathcal{E} \equiv \{p_X(x), \rho_x\}$ and Bob performs a POVM $\{\Lambda_y\}$.

Suppose now that Bob is actually trying to retrieve as much information as possible about the random variable X. The quantity that governs how much information he can learn about random variable X if he possesses random variable Y is the mutual information $I(X;Y)$. But here, Bob can actually choose which measurement he would like to perform, and it would be good for him to perform the measurement that maximizes his information about X. The resulting quantity is known as the accessible information $I_{\text{acc}}(\mathcal{E})$ of the ensemble $\mathcal{E}$ (because it is the information that Bob can access about random variable X):

$$I_{\text{acc}}(\mathcal{E}) \equiv \max_{\{\Lambda_y\}} I(X;Y), \tag{10.179}$$

where the marginal density $p_X(x)$ is that from the ensemble and the conditional density $p_{Y|X}(y|x)$ is given in (10.175). In the next chapter, we show how to obtain a natural bound on this quantity, called the *Holevo bound*. The bound arises from a quantum generalization of the data-processing inequality.

10.9.3   Classical Mutual Information of a Bipartite State

A final quantity that we introduce is the classical mutual information $I_c(\rho_{AB})$ of a bipartite state ρ_{AB}. Suppose that Alice and Bob possess some bipartite state ρ_{AB} and would like to extract maximal classical correlation from it. That is, they each retrieve a random variable by performing respective local POVMs $\{\Lambda_A^x\}$ and $\{\Lambda_B^y\}$ on their shares of the bipartite state ρ_{AB}. These measurements produce respective random variables X and Y, and they would like X and Y to be as correlated as possible. A good measure of their resulting classical correlations obtainable from local quantum information processing is as follows:

$$I_c(\rho_{AB}) \equiv \max_{\{\Lambda_A^x\},\{\Lambda_B^y\}} I(X;Y), \tag{10.180}$$

where the joint distribution

$$p_{X,Y}(x,y) \equiv \text{Tr}\left\{(\Lambda_A^x \otimes \Lambda_B^y)\rho_{AB}\right\}. \tag{10.181}$$

Suppose that the state ρ_{AB} is classical, that is, it has the form

$$\rho_{AB} = \sum_{x,y} p_{X,Y}(x,y)|x\rangle\langle x|_A \otimes |y\rangle\langle y|_B, \tag{10.182}$$

where the states $|x\rangle_A$ form an orthonormal basis and so do the states $|y\rangle_B$. Then, the optimal measurement in this case is for Alice to perform a complete projective measurement in the basis $|x\rangle_A$ and inform Bob to perform a similar measurement in the basis $|y\rangle_B$. The amount of correlation they extract is then equal to $I(X;Y)$.

EXERCISE 10.9.1   Prove that it suffices to consider maximizing with respect to rank-one POVMs when computing (10.180). (Hint: Consider refining the POVM $\{\Lambda_x\}$ as the rank-one POVM $\{|\phi_{x,z}\rangle\langle\phi_{x,z}|\}$, where we spectrally decompose Λ_x as $\sum_z |\phi_{x,z}\rangle\langle\phi_{x,z}|$, and then exploit the data-processing inequality.)

10.10   History and Further Reading

Cover & Thomas (2006) have given an excellent introduction to entropy and information theory (some of the material in this chapter is similar to material appearing in that book). MacKay (2003) also gives a good introduction. E. T. Jaynes was an advocate of the principle of maximum entropy, proclaiming its utility in several sources (Jaynes, 1957a; Jaynes, 1957b; Jaynes, 2003). A good exposition of Fano's inequality appears on Scholarpedia (Fano, 2008). Theorem 10.7.4 (continuity of entropy bound) is due to Zhang (2007) and Audenaert (2007). The particular proof that we give in this chapter is Zhang's (2007), but we used the presentation of Sason (2013). The Pinsker inequality was first proved by Pinsker (1960), with subsequent enhancements by Csiszar (1967), Kemperman (1969), and Kullback (1967). Theorem 10.8.2 was realized in private communication with Andreas Winter (August 2015). The refinement of the monotonicity of relative entropy in Theorem 10.8.4 was established by Li & Winter (2014).

11 Quantum Information and Entropy

In this chapter, we discuss several information measures that are important for quantifying the amount of information and correlations that are present in quantum systems. The first fundamental measure that we introduce is the von Neumann entropy (or simply *quantum entropy*). It is the quantum generalization of the Shannon entropy, but it captures both classical and quantum uncertainty in a quantum state.[1] The quantum entropy gives meaning to the notion of an *information qubit*. This notion is different from that of the physical qubit, which is the description of a quantum state of an electron or a photon. The information qubit is the fundamental quantum informational unit of measure, determining how much quantum information is present in a quantum system.

The initial definitions here are analogous to the classical definitions of entropy, but we soon discover a radical departure from the intuitive classical notions from the previous chapter: the conditional quantum entropy can be negative for certain quantum states. In the classical world, this negativity simply does not occur, but it takes on a special meaning in quantum information theory. Pure quantum states that are entangled have stronger-than-classical correlations and are examples of states that have negative conditional entropy. The negative of the conditional quantum entropy is so important in quantum information theory that we even have a special name for it: the coherent information. We discover that the coherent information obeys a quantum data-processing inequality, placing it on a firm footing as a particular informational measure of quantum correlations.

We then define several other quantum information measures, such as quantum mutual information, that bear similar definitions as in the classical world, but with Shannon entropies replaced with quantum entropies. This replacement

---

[1] We should point out the irony in the historical development of classical and quantum entropy. The von Neumann entropy has seen much widespread use in modern quantum information theory, and perhaps this would make one think that von Neumann discovered this quantity much after Shannon. But in fact, the reverse is true. Von Neumann first discovered what is now known as the von Neumann entropy and applied it to questions in statistical physics. Much later, Shannon determined an information-theoretic formula and asked von Neumann what he should call it. Von Neumann told him to call it the entropy for two reasons: 1) it was a special case of the von Neumann entropy and 2) he would always have the advantage in a debate because von Neumann claimed that no one at the time really understood entropy.

may seem to make quantum entropy somewhat trivial on the surface, but a simple calculation reveals that a maximally entangled state on two qubits registers *two bits* of quantum mutual information (recall that the largest the mutual information can be in the classical world is *one bit* for the case of two maximally correlated bits). We then discuss several entropy inequalities that play an important role in quantum information processing: the monotonicity of quantum relative entropy, strong subadditivity, the quantum data-processing inequalities, and continuity of quantum entropy.

11.1   Quantum Entropy

We might expect a measure of the entropy of a quantum system to be vastly different from the classical measure of entropy from the previous chapter because a quantum system possesses not only classical uncertainty but also quantum uncertainty that arises from the uncertainty principle. But recall that the density operator captures both types of uncertainty and allows us to determine probabilities for the outcomes of any measurement on a given system. Thus, a quantum measure of uncertainty should be a direct function of the density operator, just as the classical measure of uncertainty is a direct function of a probability density function. It turns out that this function has a strikingly similar form to the classical entropy, as we see below.

DEFINITION 11.1.1 (Quantum Entropy) Suppose that Alice prepares some quantum system A in a state $\rho_A \in \mathcal{D}(\mathcal{H}_A)$. Then the entropy $H(A)_\rho$ of the state is defined as follows:

$$H(A)_\rho \equiv - \operatorname{Tr}\{\rho_A \log \rho_A\}. \tag{11.1}$$

The entropy of a quantum system is also known as the *von Neumann entropy* or the *quantum entropy* but we often simply refer to it as the *entropy*. We can denote it by $H(A)_\rho$ or $H(\rho_A)$ to show the explicit dependence on the density operator ρ_A. The quantum entropy has a special relation to the eigenvalues of the density operator, as the following exercise asks you to verify.

EXERCISE 11.1.1 Consider a density operator ρ_A with the following spectral decomposition:

$$\rho_A = \sum_x p_X(x)|x\rangle\langle x|_A. \tag{11.2}$$

Show that the quantum entropy $H(A)_\rho$ is the same as the Shannon entropy $H(X)$ of a random variable X with probability distribution $p_X(x)$.

In our definition of quantum entropy, we use the same notation H as in the classical case to denote the entropy of a quantum system. It should be clear from the context whether we are referring to the entropy of a quantum or classical system.

The quantum entropy admits an intuitive interpretation. Suppose that Alice generates a quantum state $|\psi_y\rangle$ in her lab according to some probability density $p_Y(y)$, corresponding to a random variable Y. Suppose further that Bob has not yet received the state from Alice and does not know which one she sent. The expected density operator from Bob's point of view is then

$$\sigma = \mathbb{E}_Y\{|\psi_Y\rangle\langle\psi_Y|\} = \sum_y p_Y(y)|\psi_y\rangle\langle\psi_y|. \qquad (11.3)$$

The interpretation of the entropy $H(\sigma)$ is that it quantifies Bob's uncertainty about the state Alice sent—his expected information gain is $H(\sigma)$ qubits upon receiving and measuring the state that Alice sends. Schumacher's noiseless quantum coding theorem, described in Chapter 18, gives an alternative operational interpretation of the quantum entropy by proving that Alice needs to send Bob qubits at a rate $H(\sigma)$ in order for him to be able to decode a compressed quantum state.

The above interpretation of quantum entropy seems qualitatively similar to the interpretation of classical entropy. However, there is a significant quantitative difference that illuminates the difference between Shannon entropy and quantum entropy. Let us consider an example. Suppose that Alice generates a sequence $|\psi_1\rangle|\psi_2\rangle\cdots|\psi_n\rangle$ of quantum states according to the following "BB84" ensemble:

$$\{\{1/4,|0\rangle\},\{1/4,|1\rangle\},\{1/4,|+\rangle\},\{1/4,|-\rangle\}\}. \qquad (11.4)$$

Suppose that Alice and Bob share a noiseless classical channel. If she employs Shannon's classical noiseless coding protocol, she should transmit classical data to Bob at a rate of two classical channel uses per source state $|\psi_i\rangle$ in order for him to reliably recover the classical data needed to reproduce the sequence of states that Alice transmitted (the Shannon entropy of the uniform distribution $1/4$ is 2 bits).

Now let us consider computing the quantum entropy of the above ensemble. First, we determine the expected density operator of Alice's ensemble:

$$\frac{1}{4}\left(|0\rangle\langle0| + |1\rangle\langle1| + |+\rangle\langle+| + |-\rangle\langle-|\right) = \pi, \qquad (11.5)$$

where π is the maximally mixed state. The quantum entropy of the above density operator is one qubit because the eigenvalues of π are both equal to $1/2$. Suppose now that a noiseless quantum channel connects Alice to Bob—this is a channel that can preserve quantum coherence without any interaction with an environment. Then Alice only needs to send qubits at a rate of one channel use per source symbol if she employs a protocol known as Schumacher compression (we discuss this protocol in detail in Chapter 18). Bob can then reliably decode the qubits that Alice sent. The protocol also causes a slight disturbance to the state, which however vanishes in the limit of many invocations of the source. The above departure from classical information theory holds in general—Exercise 11.9.3 of this chapter asks you to prove that the Shannon entropy of any ensemble is never less than the quantum entropy of its expected density operator.

11.1.1 Mathematical Properties of Quantum Entropy

We now discuss several mathematical properties of the quantum entropy: non-negativity, its minimum value, its maximum value, its invariance with respect to isometries, and concavity. The first three of these properties follow from the analogous properties in the classical world because the quantum entropy of a density operator is the Shannon entropy of its eigenvalues (see Exercise 11.1.1). We state them formally below:

PROPERTY 11.1.1 (Non-Negativity) The quantum entropy $H(\rho)$ is non-negative for any density operator ρ:

$$H(\rho) \geq 0. \tag{11.6}$$

Proof This follows from non-negativity of Shannon entropy. □

PROPERTY 11.1.2 (Minimum Value) The minimum value of the quantum entropy is zero, and it occurs when the density operator is a pure state.

Proof The minimum value occurs when the eigenvalues of a density operator are distributed with all the probability mass on one eigenvector and zero on the others, so that the density operator is rank one and corresponds to a pure state. □

Why should the entropy of a pure quantum state vanish? It seems that there is quantum uncertainty inherent in the state itself and that a measure of quantum uncertainty should capture this fact. This last observation only makes sense if we do not know anything about the state that is prepared. But if we know exactly how it is prepared, we can perform a special quantum measurement to verify this, and we do not learn anything from this measurement because the outcome of it is always certain. For example, suppose that Alice prepares the state $|\phi\rangle$ and Bob knows that she does so. He can then perform the following measurement $\{|\phi\rangle\langle\phi|, I - |\phi\rangle\langle\phi|\}$ to verify that she prepared this state. He always receives the first outcome from the measurement and thus never gains any information from it. Thus, in this sense it is reasonable that the entropy of a pure state vanishes.

PROPERTY 11.1.3 (Maximum Value) The maximum value of the quantum entropy is $\log d$ where d is the dimension of the system, and it occurs for the maximally mixed state.

Proof A proof of the above property is the same as that for the classical case. □

PROPERTY 11.1.4 (Concavity) Let $\rho_x \in \mathcal{D}(\mathcal{H})$ and let $p_X(x)$ be a probability distribution. The entropy is concave in the density operator:

$$H(\rho) \geq \sum_x p_X(x) H(\rho_x), \tag{11.7}$$

where $\rho \equiv \sum_x p_X(x)\rho_x$.

The physical interpretation of concavity is as before for classical entropy: entropy can never decrease under a mixing operation. This inequality is a fundamental property of the entropy, and we prove it after developing some important entropic tools (see Exercise 11.6.10).

PROPERTY 11.1.5 (Isometric Invariance)   Let $\rho \in \mathcal{D}(\mathcal{H})$ and $U : \mathcal{H} \rightarrow \mathcal{H}'$ be an isometry. The entropy of a density operator is invariant with respect to isometries, in the following sense:

$$H(\rho) = H(U\rho U^{\dagger}). \tag{11.8}$$

Proof Isometric invariance of entropy follows by observing that the eigenvalues of a density operator are invariant with respect to an isometry:

$$U\rho U^{\dagger} = U \sum_x p_X(x)|x\rangle\langle x|U^{\dagger} \tag{11.9}$$

$$= \sum_x p_X(x)|\phi_x\rangle\langle\phi_x|, \tag{11.10}$$

where $\{|\phi_x\rangle\}$ is some orthonormal basis such that $U|x\rangle = |\phi_x\rangle$. The above property follows because the entropy is a function of the eigenvalues of a density operator. □

A unitary or isometric operator is a quantum generalization of a permutation in this context (recall Property 10.1.3 of the classical entropy).

11.1.2   Alternate Characterization of Quantum Entropy

There is an interesting alternate characterization of the quantum entropy of a state ρ as the minimum Shannon entropy when a rank-one POVM is performed on it (we discussed this briefly in Section 10.9.1). In this sense, there is some optimal measurement to perform on ρ such that its entropy is equal to the quantum entropy, and this optimal measurement is the "right question to ask" (as we discussed very early on in Section 1.2.2).

THEOREM 11.1.1   Let $\rho \in \mathcal{D}(\mathcal{H})$. The quantum entropy $H(\rho)$ has the following characterization:

$$H(\rho) = \min_{\{\Lambda_y\}} \left[-\sum_y \text{Tr}\{\Lambda_y\rho\} \log\left(\text{Tr}\{\Lambda_y\rho\}\right) \right], \tag{11.11}$$

where the minimum is restricted to be with respect to rank-one POVMs (those with $\Lambda_y = |\phi_y\rangle\langle\phi_y|$ for some vectors $|\phi_y\rangle$ such that $\text{Tr}\{|\phi_y\rangle\langle\phi_y|\} \leq 1$ and $\sum_y |\phi_y\rangle\langle\phi_y| = I$).

Proof In order to prove the above result, we should first realize that a complete projective measurement in the eigenbasis of ρ should achieve the minimum. That is, if $\rho = \sum_x p_X(x)|x\rangle\langle x|$, we should expect that the measurement $\{|x\rangle\langle x|$

achieves the minimum. In this case, the Shannon entropy of the measurement is equal to the Shannon entropy of $p_X(x)$, as discussed in Exercise 11.1.1.

We now prove that any other rank-one POVM has a higher entropy than that given by this measurement. Consider that the distribution of the measurement outcomes for $\{|\phi_y\rangle\langle\phi_y|\}$ is equal to

$$\text{Tr}\{|\phi_y\rangle\langle\phi_y|\rho\} = \sum_x |\langle\phi_y|x\rangle|^2 p_X(x), \tag{11.12}$$

so that we can think of $|\langle\phi_y|x\rangle|^2$ as a conditional probability distribution. Introducing $\eta(p) \equiv -p \log p$, which is a concave function, we can write the quantum entropy as

$$H(\rho) = \sum_x \eta(p_X(x)) \tag{11.13}$$

$$= \sum_x \eta(p_X(x)) + \eta(p_X(x_0)), \tag{11.14}$$

where x_0 is a symbol added to the alphabet of x such that $p_X(x_0) = 0$. Let us denote the enlarged alphabet with the symbols x' so that $H(\rho) = \sum_{x'} \eta(p_X(x'))$. We know that $\sum_y |\langle\phi_y|x\rangle|^2 = 1$ from the fact that the set $\{|\phi_y\rangle\langle\phi_y|\}$ forms a POVM and $|x\rangle$ is a normalized state. We also know that $\sum_x |\langle\phi_y|x\rangle|^2 \leq 1$ because $\text{Tr}\{|\phi_y\rangle\langle\phi_y|\} \leq 1$ for a rank-one POVM. Thinking of $|\langle\phi_y|x\rangle|^2$ as a distribution over x, we can add a symbol x_0 with probability $1 - \langle\phi_y|\phi_y\rangle$ so that it makes a normalized distribution. Let us call this distribution $p(x'|y)$. We then have that

$$H(\rho) = \sum_x \eta(p_X(x)) \tag{11.15}$$

$$= \sum_{x,y} |\langle\phi_y|x\rangle|^2 \eta(p_X(x)) \tag{11.16}$$

$$= \sum_{x',y} p(x'|y)\eta(p_X(x')) \tag{11.17}$$

$$= \sum_y \left(\sum_{x'} p(x'|y)\eta(p_X(x')) \right) \tag{11.18}$$

$$\leq \sum_y \eta\left(\sum_{x'} p(x'|y)p_X(x') \right) \tag{11.19}$$

$$= \sum_y \eta\left(\text{Tr}\{|\phi_y\rangle\langle\phi_y|\rho\} \right). \tag{11.20}$$

The third equality follows from the fact that $p_X(x_0) = 0$ for the added symbol x_0. The only inequality follows from concavity of η. The last expression is equal to the Shannon entropy of the POVM $\{|\phi_y\rangle\langle\phi_y|\}$ when performed on the state ρ. $\square$

11.2   Joint Quantum Entropy

The joint quantum entropy $H(AB)_\rho$ of the density operator $\rho_{AB} \in \mathcal{D}(\mathcal{H}_A \otimes \mathcal{H}_B)$ for a bipartite system AB follows naturally from the definition of quantum entropy:

$$H(AB)_\rho \equiv -\operatorname{Tr}\{\rho_{AB} \log \rho_{AB}\}. \qquad (11.21)$$

Now suppose that ρ_{ABC} is a tripartite state, i.e., in $\mathcal{D}(\mathcal{H}_A \otimes \mathcal{H}_B \otimes \mathcal{H}_C)$. Then the entropy $H(AB)_\rho$ in this case is defined as above, where $\rho_{AB} = \operatorname{Tr}_C\{\rho_{ABC}\}$. This is a convention that we take throughout this book. We introduce a few of the properties of joint quantum entropy in the subsections below.

11.2.1   Marginal Entropies of a Pure Bipartite State

The five properties of quantum entropy in the previous section may give you the impression that the nature of quantum information is not too different from that of classical information. We proved all these properties for the classical case, and their proofs for the quantum case seem similar. The first three even resort to the proofs in the classical case!

Theorem 11.2.1 below is where we observe our first radical departure from the classical world. It states that the marginal entropies of a pure bipartite state are equal, while the entropy of the overall state is equal to zero. Recall that the joint entropy $H(X,Y)$ of two random variables X and Y is never less than either of the marginal entropies $H(X)$ or $H(Y)$:

$$H(X,Y) \geq H(X), \qquad H(X,Y) \geq H(Y). \qquad (11.22)$$

The above inequalities follow from the non-negativity of classical conditional entropy. But in the quantum world, these inequalities do not always have to hold, and the following theorem demonstrates that they do not hold for an arbitrary pure bipartite quantum state with Schmidt rank greater than one (see Theorem 3.8.1 for a definition of Schmidt rank). The fact that the joint quantum entropy can be less than the marginal quantum entropy is one of the most fundamental differences between classical and quantum information.

THEOREM 11.2.1   The marginal entropies $H(A)_\phi$ and $H(B)_\phi$ of a pure bipartite state $|\phi\rangle_{AB}$ are equal:

$$H(A)_\phi = H(B)_\phi, \qquad (11.23)$$

while the joint entropy $H(AB)_\phi$ vanishes:

$$H(AB)_\phi = 0. \qquad (11.24)$$

Proof The crucial ingredient for a proof of this theorem is the Schmidt decomposition (Theorem 3.8.1). Recall that any bipartite state $|\phi\rangle_{AB}$ admits a Schmidt decomposition of the following form:

$$|\phi\rangle_{AB} = \sum_i \sqrt{\lambda_i} |i\rangle_A |i\rangle_B, \tag{11.25}$$

where $\lambda_i > 0$ for all i, $\sum_i \lambda_i = 1$, $\{|i\rangle_A\}$ is some orthonormal set of vectors on system A, and $\{|i\rangle_B\}$ is some orthonormal set on system B. Recall that the Schmidt rank is equal to the number of non-zero coefficients λ_i. Then the respective marginal states ρ_A and ρ_B on systems A and B are as follows:

$$\rho_A = \sum_i \lambda_i |i\rangle\langle i|_A, \qquad \rho_B = \sum_i \lambda_i |i\rangle\langle i|_B. \tag{11.26}$$

Thus, the marginal states admit a spectral decomposition with the same eigenvalues. The theorem follows because the quantum entropy depends only on the eigenvalues of a given spectral decomposition. □

The theorem applies not only to two systems A and B, but it also applies to any number of systems if we make a bipartite cut of the systems. For example, if the state is $|\phi\rangle_{ABCDE}$, then the following equalities (and others from different combinations) hold by applying Theorem 11.2.1 and Remark 3.8.1:

$$H(A)_\phi = H(BCDE)_\phi, \tag{11.27}$$
$$H(AB)_\phi = H(CDE)_\phi, \tag{11.28}$$
$$H(ABC)_\phi = H(DE)_\phi, \tag{11.29}$$
$$H(ABCD)_\phi = H(E)_\phi. \tag{11.30}$$

The closest analogy in the classical world to the above property is when we copy a random variable X. That is, suppose that X has a distribution $p_X(x)$ and $\hat{X}$ is some copy of it so that the distribution of the joint random variable $X\hat{X}$ is $p_X(x)\delta_{x,\hat{x}}$. Then the marginal entropies $H(X)$ and $H(\hat{X})$ are both equal. But observe that the joint entropy $H(X\hat{X})$ is also equal to $H(X)$ and this is where the analogy breaks down. That is, there is not a strong classical analogy of the notion of purification.

11.2.2 Additivity

PROPERTY 11.2.1 (Additivity) Let $\rho_A \in \mathcal{D}(\mathcal{H}_A)$ and $\sigma_B \in \mathcal{D}(\mathcal{H}_B)$. The quantum entropy is additive for tensor-product states:

$$H(\rho_A \otimes \sigma_B) = H(\rho_A) + H(\sigma_B). \tag{11.31}$$

One can verify this property simply by diagonalizing both density operators and resorting to the additivity of the joint Shannon entropies of the eigenvalues.

Additivity is an intuitive property that we would like to hold for any measure of information. For example, suppose that Alice generates a large sequence

$|\psi_{x_1}\rangle|\psi_{x_2}\rangle\cdots|\psi_{x_n}\rangle$ of quantum states according to the ensemble $\{p_X(x),|\psi_x\rangle\}$. She may be aware of the classical indices $x_1 x_2\cdots x_n$, but a third party to whom she sends the quantum sequence may not be aware of these values. The description of the state to this third party is then $\rho\otimes\cdots\otimes\rho$, where $\rho\equiv\mathbb{E}_X\{|\psi_X\rangle\langle\psi_X|\}$, and the quantum entropy of this n-fold tensor product state is $H(\rho\otimes\cdots\otimes\rho)=nH(\rho)$, by applying (11.31) inductively.

11.2.3   Joint Quantum Entropy of a Classical–Quantum State

Recall from Definition 4.3.5 that a classical–quantum state is a bipartite state in which a classical system and a quantum system are classically correlated. An example of such a state is as follows:

$$\rho_{XB}\equiv\sum_x p_X(x)|x\rangle\langle x|_X\otimes\rho_B^x. \tag{11.32}$$

The joint quantum entropy of this state takes on a special form that appears similar to entropies in the classical world.

THEOREM 11.2.2   The joint entropy $H(XB)_\rho$ of a classical–quantum state, as given in (11.32), is as follows:

$$H(XB)_\rho=H(X)+\sum_x p_X(x)H(\rho_B^x), \tag{11.33}$$

where $H(X)$ is the entropy of a random variable X with distribution $p_X(x)$.

Proof   Consider that $H(XB)_\rho=-\operatorname{Tr}\{\rho_{XB}\log\rho_{XB}\}$. So we need to evaluate the operator $\log\rho_{XB}$, and we can find a simplified form for it because ρ_{XB} is a classical–quantum state:

$$\log\rho_{XB}=\log\left[\sum_x p_X(x)|x\rangle\langle x|_X\otimes\rho_B^x\right] \tag{11.34}$$

$$=\log\left[\sum_x |x\rangle\langle x|_X\otimes p_X(x)\rho_B^x\right] \tag{11.35}$$

$$=\sum_x |x\rangle\langle x|_X\otimes\log\left[p_X(x)\rho_B^x\right]. \tag{11.36}$$

Then

$$-\operatorname{Tr}\{\rho_{XB}\log\rho_{XB}\}$$

$$=-\operatorname{Tr}\left\{\left[\sum_x p_X(x)|x\rangle\langle x|_X\otimes\rho_B^x\right]\left[\sum_{x'}|x'\rangle\langle x'|_X\otimes\log\left[p_X(x')\rho_B^{x'}\right]\right]\right\} \tag{11.37}$$

$$=-\operatorname{Tr}\left\{\sum_x p_X(x)|x\rangle\langle x|_X\otimes(\rho_B^x\log\left[p_X(x)\rho_B^x\right])\right\} \tag{11.38}$$

$$=-\sum_x p_X(x)\operatorname{Tr}\{\rho_B^x\log\left[p_X(x)\rho_B^x\right]\}. \tag{11.39}$$

Consider that

$$\log \left[p_X(x) \rho_B^x \right] = \log \left(p_X(x) \right) I + \log \rho_B^x, \tag{11.40}$$

which implies that (11.39) is equal to

$$-\sum_x p_X(x) \left[\text{Tr} \left\{ \rho_B^x \log \left[p_X(x) \right] \right\} + \text{Tr} \left\{ \rho_B^x \log \rho_B^x \right\} \right] \tag{11.41}$$

$$= -\sum_x p_X(x) \left[\log \left[p_X(x) \right] + \text{Tr} \left\{ \rho_B^x \log \rho_B^x \right\} \right]. \tag{11.42}$$

This last line is then equivalent to the statement of the theorem. $\qquad\square$

11.3 Potential yet Unsatisfactory Definitions of Conditional Quantum Entropy

The conditional quantum entropy may perhaps seem a bit difficult to define at first because there is no formal notion of conditional probability in the quantum theory. However, there are two senses which are perhaps closest to the notion of conditional probability, but both of them do not lead to satisfactory definitions of conditional quantum entropy. Nevertheless, it is instructive for us to explore both of these notions briefly. The first arises in the noisy quantum theory, and the second arises in the purified quantum theory.

We develop the first notion. Consider an arbitrary bipartite state ρ_{AB}. Suppose that Alice performs a complete projective measurement $\Pi \equiv \{|x\rangle\langle x|\}$ of her system, where $\{|x\rangle\}$ is an orthonormal basis. This procedure leads to an ensemble $\{p_X(x), |x\rangle\langle x|_A \otimes \rho_B^x\}$, where

$$\rho_B^x \equiv \frac{1}{p_X(x)} \text{Tr}_A \left\{ (|x\rangle\langle x|_A \otimes I_B) \rho_{AB} (|x\rangle\langle x|_A \otimes I_B) \right\}, \tag{11.43}$$

$$p_X(x) \equiv \text{Tr} \left\{ (|x\rangle\langle x|_A \otimes I_B) \rho_{AB} \right\}. \tag{11.44}$$

One could then think of the density operators ρ_B^x as being conditioned on the outcome of the measurement, and these density operators describe the state of Bob given knowledge of the outcome of the measurement.

We could potentially define a conditional entropy as follows:

$$H(B|A)_\Pi \equiv \sum_x p_X(x) H(\rho_B^x), \tag{11.45}$$

in analogy with the definition of the classical entropy in (10.17). This approach might seem to lead to a useful definition of conditional quantum entropy, but the problem with it is that the entropy depends on the measurement chosen (the notation $H(B|A)_\Pi$ explicitly indicates this dependence). This problem does not occur in the classical world because the probabilities for the outcomes of measurements do not themselves depend on the measurement selected, unless we apply some coarse graining to the outcomes. However, this dependence on measurement is a fundamental aspect of the quantum theory.

We could then attempt to remove the dependence of the above definition on a particular measurement Π by defining the conditional quantum entropy to be the minimization of $H(B|A)_\Pi$ with respect to all possible measurements. The intuition here is perhaps that entropy should be the minimal amount of conditional uncertainty in a system after employing the best possible measurement on the other. However, the removal of one problem leads to another! This optimized conditional entropy is now difficult to compute as the system grows larger, whereas in the classical world, the computation of conditional entropy is simple if one knows the conditional probabilities. The above idea is useful, but we leave it for now because there is a simpler definition of conditional quantum entropy that plays a fundamental role in quantum information theory.

The second notion of conditional probability is actually similar to the above notion, though we present it in the purified viewpoint. Consider a tripartite state $|\psi\rangle_{ABC}$ and a bipartite cut $A|BC$ of the systems A, B, and C. Theorem 3.8.1 states that every bipartite state admits a Schmidt decomposition, and the state $|\psi\rangle_{ABC}$ is no exception. Thus, we can write a Schmidt decomposition for it as follows:

$$|\psi\rangle_{ABC} = \sum_x \sqrt{p_X(x)}|x\rangle_A|\phi_x\rangle_{BC}, \qquad (11.46)$$

where $p_X(x)$ is some probability density, $\{|x\rangle\}$ is an orthonormal basis for the system A, and $\{|\phi_x\rangle\}$ is an orthonormal basis for the systems BC. Each state $|\phi_x\rangle_{BC}$ is a pure bipartite state, so we can again apply a Schmidt decomposition to each of these states:

$$|\phi_x\rangle_{BC} = \sum_y \sqrt{p_{Y|X}(y|x)}|y_x\rangle_B|y_x\rangle_C, \qquad (11.47)$$

where $p_{Y|X}(y|x)$ is some conditional probability distribution depending on the value of x, and $\{|y_x\rangle_B\}$ and $\{|y_x\rangle_C\}$ are both orthonormal bases with dependence on the value x. Thus, the overall state has the following form:

$$|\psi\rangle_{ABC} = \sum_{x,y} \sqrt{p_{Y|X}(y|x)p_X(x)}|x\rangle_A|y_x\rangle_B|y_x\rangle_C. \qquad (11.48)$$

Suppose that Alice performs a complete projective measurement in the basis $\{|x\rangle\langle x|_A\}$. The state on Bob and Charlie's systems is then $|\psi_x\rangle_{BC}$, and each system on B or C has a marginal entropy of $H(\sigma_x)$ where $\sigma_x \equiv \sum_y p_{Y|X}(y|x)|y_x\rangle\langle y_x|$. We could potentially define the conditional quantum entropy as

$$\sum_x p_X(x)H(\sigma_x). \qquad (11.49)$$

This quantity does not depend on a measurement as before because we simply choose the measurement from the Schmidt decomposition. But there are many problems with the above notion of conditional quantum entropy: it is defined only for pure quantum states, it is not clear how to apply it to a bipartite quantum state, and the conditional entropy of Bob's system given Alice's and that of Charlie's given Alice's is the same (which is perhaps the strangest of all!). Thus this notion of conditional probability is not useful for a definition of conditional quantum entropy.

11.4   Conditional Quantum Entropy

The definition of conditional quantum entropy that has been most useful in quantum information theory is the following simple one, inspired from the relation between joint entropy and marginal entropy in Exercise 10.3.1.

DEFINITION 11.4.1 (Conditional Quantum Entropy)   Let $\rho_{AB} \in \mathcal{D}(\mathcal{H}_A \otimes \mathcal{H}_B)$. The conditional quantum entropy $H(A|B)_\rho$ of ρ_{AB} is equal to the difference of the joint quantum entropy $H(AB)_\rho$ and the marginal entropy $H(B)_\rho$:

$$H(A|B)_\rho \equiv H(AB)_\rho - H(B)_\rho. \tag{11.50}$$

The above definition is the most natural one, both because it is straightforward to compute for any bipartite state and because it obeys many relations that the classical conditional entropy obeys (such as entropy chain rules and conditioning reduces entropy). We explore many of these relations in the forthcoming sections. For now, we state "conditioning cannot increase entropy" as the following theorem and tackle its proof later on after developing a few more tools.

THEOREM 11.4.1 (Conditioning Does Not Increase Entropy)   Consider a bipartite quantum state ρ_{AB}. Then the following inequality applies to the marginal entropy $H(A)_\rho$ and the conditional quantum entropy $H(A|B)_\rho$:

$$H(A)_\rho \geq H(A|B)_\rho. \tag{11.51}$$

We can interpret the above inequality as stating that conditioning cannot increase entropy, even if the conditioning system is quantum.

11.4.1   Conditional Entropy for Classical–Quantum States

A classical–quantum state is an example of a state for which conditional quantum entropy behaves as in the classical world. Suppose that two parties share a classical–quantum state ρ_{XB} of the form in (11.32). The system X is classical and the system B is quantum, and the correlations between these systems are entirely classical, determined by the probability distribution $p_X(x)$. Let us calculate the conditional quantum entropy $H(B|X)_\rho$ for this state:

$$H(B|X)_\rho = H(XB)_\rho - H(X)_\rho \tag{11.52}$$

$$= H(X)_\rho + \sum_x p_X(x) H(\rho_B^x) - H(X)_\rho \tag{11.53}$$

$$= \sum_x p_X(x) H(\rho_B^x). \tag{11.54}$$

The first equality follows from Definition 11.4.1. The second equality follows from Theorem 11.2.2, and the final equality results from algebra.

The above form for conditional entropy is completely analogous with the classical formula in (10.17) and holds whenever the conditioning system is classical.

11.4.2   Negative Conditional Quantum Entropy

One of the properties of the conditional quantum entropy in Definition 11.4.1 that seems counterintuitive at first sight is that it can be negative. This negativity holds for an ebit $|\Phi^+\rangle_{AB}$ shared between Alice and Bob. The marginal state on Bob's system is the maximally mixed state π_B. Thus, the marginal entropy $H(B)$ is equal to one, but the joint entropy vanishes, and so the conditional quantum entropy $H(A|B) = -1$.

What do we make of this result? Well, this is one of the fundamental differences between the classical world and the quantum world, and perhaps is the very essence of the departure from an informational standpoint. The informational statement is that we can sometimes be more certain about the joint state of a quantum system than we can be about any one of its individual parts, and this is the reason that conditional quantum entropy can be negative. This is in fact the same observation that Schrödinger made concerning entangled states (Schrödinger 1935):

"When two systems, of which we know the states by their respective representatives, enter into temporary physical interaction due to known forces between them, and when after a time of mutual influence the systems separate again, then they can no longer be described in the same way as before, viz. by endowing each of them with a representative of its own. I would not call that one but rather the characteristic trait of quantum mechanics, the one that enforces its entire departure from classical lines of thought. By the interaction the two representatives [the quantum states] have become entangled. Another way of expressing the peculiar situation is: the best possible knowledge of a whole does not necessarily include the best possible knowledge of all its parts, even though they may be entirely separate and therefore virtually capable of being 'best possibly known,' i.e., of possessing, each of them, a representative of its own. The lack of knowledge is by no means due to the interaction being insufficiently known – at least not in the way that it could possibly be known more completely – it is due to the interaction itself."

These explanations might aid somewhat in understanding a negative conditional entropy, but the ultimate test for whether we truly understand an information measure is if it is the answer to some operational task. The task which gives an interpretation of the conditional quantum entropy is known as *state merging*. Suppose that Alice and Bob share n copies of a bipartite state ρ_{AB} where n is a large number and A and B are qubit systems. We also allow them free access to a classical side channel, but we count the number of times that they use a noiseless qubit channel. Alice would like to send Bob qubits over a noiseless qubit channel so that he receives her share of the state ρ_{AB}, i.e., so that he possesses all of the A shares. The naive approach would be for Alice simply to send her shares of the state over the noiseless qubit channels, i.e., she would use the channel n times to send all n shares. But the state-merging protocol allows her to do much better, depending on the state ρ_{AB}. If the state ρ_{AB} has positive conditional quantum entropy, she needs to use the noiseless qubit channel only $\approx nH(A|B)$ times (we will prove later that $H(A|B) \leq 1$ for any bipartite state on qubit systems). However, if the conditional quantum entropy is negative, she does not need to use the noiseless qubit channel at all, and at the end of the protocol, Alice and Bob share $\approx nH(A|B)$ noiseless ebits! They can then use these ebits for future communication purposes, such as a teleportation or super-dense coding protocol (see Chapter 6). Thus, a negative conditional quantum entropy implies that Alice and Bob gain the potential for future quantum communication, making clear in an operational sense what a negative conditional quantum entropy means.[2] (We will cover this protocol in Chapter 22).

EXERCISE 11.4.1 Let $\sigma_{ABC} = \rho_{AB} \otimes \tau_C$, where $\rho_{AB} \in \mathcal{D}(\mathcal{H}_A \otimes \mathcal{H}_B)$ and $\tau_C \in \mathcal{D}(\mathcal{H}_C)$. Show that $H(A|B)_\rho = H(A|BC)_\sigma$.

11.5 Coherent Information

Negativity of the conditional quantum entropy is so important in quantum information theory that we even have an information quantity and a special notation to denote the negative of the conditional quantum entropy:

DEFINITION 11.5.1 (Coherent Information) The coherent information $I(A\rangle B)_\rho$ of a bipartite state $\rho_{AB} \in \mathcal{D}(\mathcal{H}_A \otimes \mathcal{H}_B)$ is as follows:

$$I(A\rangle B)_\rho \equiv H(B)_\rho - H(AB)_\rho. \tag{11.55}$$

You should immediately notice that this quantity is the negative of the conditional quantum entropy in Definition 11.4.1, but it is perhaps more useful to

---

[2] After Horodecki, Oppenheim, and Winter published the state-merging protocol (Horodecki et al., 2005), the *Bristol Evening Post* featured a story about Andreas Winter with the amusing title "Scientist Knows Less Than Nothing," as a reference to the potential negativity of conditional quantum entropy. Of course, such a title may seem a bit nonsensical to the layman, but it does grasp the idea that we can know less about a part of a quantum system than we do about its whole.

think of the coherent information not merely as the negative of the conditional quantum entropy, but as an information quantity in its own right. This is why we employ a separate notation for it. The "I" is present because the coherent information is an information quantity that measures quantum correlations, much like the mutual information does in the classical case. For example, we have already seen that the coherent information of an ebit is equal to one. Thus, it is measuring the extent to which we know less about part of a system than we do about its whole. Perhaps surprisingly, the coherent information obeys a quantum data-processing inequality (discussed in Section 11.9.2), which gives further support for it having an "I" present in its notation. The Dirac symbol "$\rangle$" is present to indicate that this quantity is a quantum information quantity, having a good meaning really only in the quantum world. The choice of "$\rangle$" over "$\langle$" also indicates a directionality from Alice to Bob, and this notation will make more sense when we begin to discuss the coherent information of a quantum channel in Chapter 13.

EXERCISE 11.5.1 Calculate the coherent information $I(A\rangle B)_\Phi$ of the maximally entangled state

$$|\Phi\rangle_{AB} \equiv \frac{1}{\sqrt{d}} \sum_{i=1}^{d} |i\rangle_A |i\rangle_B. \tag{11.56}$$

Calculate the coherent information $I(A\rangle B)_{\overline{\Phi}}$ of the maximally correlated state

$$\overline{\Phi}_{AB} \equiv \frac{1}{d} \sum_{i=1}^{d} |i\rangle\langle i|_A \otimes |i\rangle\langle i|_B. \tag{11.57}$$

EXERCISE 11.5.2 Let $\rho_{AB} \in \mathcal{D}(\mathcal{H}_A \otimes \mathcal{H}_B)$. Consider a purification $|\psi\rangle_{ABE}$ of this state to some environment system E. Show that

$$I(A\rangle B)_\rho = H(B)_\psi - H(E)_\psi. \tag{11.58}$$

Thus, there is a sense in which the coherent information measures the difference in the uncertainty of Bob and the uncertainty of the environment.

EXERCISE 11.5.3 (Duality of Conditional Entropy) Show that $-H(A|B)_\rho = I(A\rangle B)_\rho = H(A|E)_\psi$ for the purification in the above exercise.

The coherent information can be both negative or positive depending on the bipartite state for which we evaluate it, but it cannot be arbitrarily large or arbitrarily small. The following theorem places a useful bound on its absolute value.

THEOREM 11.5.1 Let $\rho_{AB} \in \mathcal{D}(\mathcal{H}_A \otimes \mathcal{H}_B)$. The following bound applies to the absolute value of the conditional entropy $H(A|B)_\rho$:

$$|H(A|B)_\rho| \leq \log \dim(\mathcal{H}_A). \tag{11.59}$$

The bounds are saturated for $\rho_{AB} = \pi_A \otimes \sigma_B$, where π_A is the maximally mixed state and $\sigma_B \in \mathcal{D}(\mathcal{H}_B)$, and for $\rho_{AB} = \Phi_{AB}$ (the maximally entangled state).

Proof We first prove the inequality $H(A|B)_\rho \leq \log \dim(\mathcal{H}_A)$:

$$H(A|B)_\rho \leq H(A)_\rho \leq \log \dim(\mathcal{H}_A). \tag{11.60}$$

The first inequality follows because conditioning reduces entropy (Theorem 11.4.1), and the second inequality follows because the maximum value of the entropy $H(A)_\rho$ is $\log \dim(\mathcal{H}_A)$. We now prove the inequality $H(A|B)_\rho \geq -\log \dim(\mathcal{H}_A)$. Consider a purification $|\psi\rangle_{EAB}$ of the state ρ_{AB}. We then have that

$$H(A|B)_\rho = -H(A|E)_\psi \tag{11.61}$$
$$\geq -H(A)_\rho \tag{11.62}$$
$$\geq -\log \dim(\mathcal{H}_A). \tag{11.63}$$

The first equality follows from Exercise 11.5.3. The first and second inequalities follow by the same reasons as the inequalities in the previous paragraph. $\square$

EXERCISE 11.5.4 (Conditional Coherent Information) Consider a tripartite state ρ_{ABC}. Show that

$$I(A\rangle BC)_\rho = I(A\rangle B|C)_\rho, \tag{11.64}$$

where $I(A\rangle B|C)_\rho \equiv H(B|C)_\rho - H(AB|C)_\rho$ is the conditional coherent information.

EXERCISE 11.5.5 (Conditional Coherent Information of a Classical–Quantum State) Suppose we have a classical–quantum state σ_{XAB} where

$$\sigma_{XAB} = \sum_x p_X(x)|x\rangle\langle x|_X \otimes \sigma_{AB}^x, \tag{11.65}$$

p_X is a probability distribution on a finite alphabet $\mathcal{X}$ and $\sigma_{AB}^x \in \mathcal{D}(\mathcal{H}_A \otimes \mathcal{H}_B)$ for all $x \in \mathcal{X}$. Show that

$$I(A\rangle BX)_\sigma = \sum_x p_X(x)I(A\rangle B)_{\sigma^x}. \tag{11.66}$$

11.6 Quantum Mutual Information

The standard informational measure of correlations in the classical world is the mutual information, and such a quantity plays a prominent role in measuring classical and quantum correlations in the quantum world as well.

DEFINITION 11.6.1 (Quantum Mutual Information) The quantum mutual information of a bipartite state $\rho_{AB} \in \mathcal{D}(\mathcal{H}_A \otimes \mathcal{H}_B)$ is defined as follows:

$$I(A;B)_\rho \equiv H(A)_\rho + H(B)_\rho - H(AB)_\rho. \tag{11.67}$$

The following relations hold for quantum mutual information, in analogy with the classical case:

$$I(A;B)_\rho = H(A)_\rho - H(A|B)_\rho \tag{11.68}$$

$$= H(B)_\rho - H(B|A)_\rho. \tag{11.69}$$

These immediately lead to the following relations between quantum mutual information and the coherent information:

$$I(A;B)_\rho = H(A)_\rho + I(A\rangle B)_\rho \tag{11.70}$$

$$= H(B)_\rho + I(B\rangle A)_\rho. \tag{11.71}$$

The theorem below gives a fundamental lower bound on the quantum mutual information—we merely state it for now and give a full proof later.

THEOREM 11.6.1 (Non-Negativity of Quantum Mutual Information) The quantum mutual information $I(A;B)_\rho$ of any bipartite quantum state ρ_{AB} is non-negative:

$$I(A;B)_\rho \geq 0. \tag{11.72}$$

EXERCISE 11.6.1 (Conditioning Does Not Increase Entropy) Show that non-negativity of quantum mutual information implies that conditioning does not increase entropy (Theorem 11.4.1).

EXERCISE 11.6.2 Calculate the quantum mutual information $I(A;B)_\Phi$ of the maximally entangled state Φ_{AB}. Calculate the quantum mutual information $I(A;B)_{\overline{\Phi}}$ of the maximally correlated state $\overline{\Phi}_{AB}$.

EXERCISE 11.6.3 (Bound on Quantum Mutual Information) Let $\rho_{AB} \in \mathcal{D}(\mathcal{H}_A \otimes \mathcal{H}_B)$. Prove that the following bound applies to the quantum mutual information:

$$I(A;B)_\rho \leq 2\log\left[\min\left\{\dim(\mathcal{H}_A), \dim(\mathcal{H}_B)\right\}\right]. \tag{11.73}$$

What is an example of a state that saturates the bound?

EXERCISE 11.6.4 Consider a pure state $|\psi\rangle_{RA} \in \mathcal{H}_R \otimes \mathcal{H}_A$. Suppose that an isometry $U : \mathcal{H}_A \to \mathcal{H}_B \otimes \mathcal{H}_E$ acts on the A system of $|\psi\rangle_{RA}$ to produce the pure state $|\phi\rangle_{RBE} \in \mathcal{H}_R \otimes \mathcal{H}_B \otimes \mathcal{H}_E$. Show that

$$I(R;B)_\phi + I(R;E)_\phi = I(R;A)_\psi. \tag{11.74}$$

EXERCISE 11.6.5 Consider a tripartite pure state $|\psi\rangle_{SRA} \in \mathcal{H}_S \otimes \mathcal{H}_R \otimes \mathcal{H}_A$. Suppose that an isometry $U : \mathcal{H}_A \to \mathcal{H}_B \otimes \mathcal{H}_E$ acts on the A system of $|\psi\rangle_{SRA}$ to produce the state $|\phi\rangle_{SRBE} \in \mathcal{H}_S \otimes \mathcal{H}_R \otimes \mathcal{H}_B \otimes \mathcal{H}_E$. Show that

$$I(R;A)_\psi + I(R;S)_\psi = I(R;B)_\phi + I(R;SE)_\phi. \tag{11.75}$$

EXERCISE 11.6.6 (Entropy, Coherent Information, and Mutual Information) Consider a pure state $|\phi\rangle_{ABE}$ on systems ABE. Using the Schmidt decomposition with respect to the bipartite cut $A \mid BE$, we can write $|\phi\rangle_{ABE}$ as follows:

$$|\phi\rangle_{ABE} = \sum_x \sqrt{p_X(x)}|x\rangle_A \otimes |\phi_x\rangle_{BE}, \tag{11.76}$$

for some orthonormal states $\{|x\rangle_A\}_{x \in \mathcal{X}}$ on system A and some orthonormal states $\{|\phi_x\rangle_{BE}\}$ on the joint system BE. Prove the following relations:

$$I(A\rangle B)_\phi = \frac{1}{2}I(A;B)_\phi - \frac{1}{2}I(A;E)_\phi, \tag{11.77}$$

$$H(A)_\phi = \frac{1}{2}I(A;B)_\phi + \frac{1}{2}I(A;E)_\phi. \tag{11.78}$$

EXERCISE 11.6.7 (Coherent Information and Private Information)   We obtain a decohered version $\overline{\phi}_{ABE}$ of the state in Exercise 11.6.6 by measuring the A system in the basis $\{|x\rangle_A\}_{x \in \mathcal{X}}$. Let us now denote the A system as the X system because it becomes a classical system after the measurement:

$$\overline{\phi}_{XBE} = \sum_x p_X(x)|x\rangle\langle x|_X \otimes \phi_{BE}^x. \tag{11.79}$$

Prove the following relation:

$$I(A\rangle B)_\phi = I(X;B)_{\overline{\phi}} - I(X;E)_{\overline{\phi}}. \tag{11.80}$$

The quantity on the right-hand side is known as the private information, because there is a sense in which it quantifies the classical information in X that is accessible to Bob while being private from Eve.

EXERCISE 11.6.8 (Additivity)   Let $\rho_{A_1 B_1} \in \mathcal{D}(\mathcal{H}_{A_1} \otimes \mathcal{H}_{B_1})$ and $\sigma_{A_2 B_2} \in \mathcal{D}(\mathcal{H}_{A_2} \otimes \mathcal{H}_{B_2})$. Set $\omega_{A_1 B_1 A_2 B_2} \equiv \rho_{A_1 B_1} \otimes \sigma_{A_2 B_2}$. Prove that $I(A_1 A_2; B_1 B_2)_\omega = I(A_1; B_1)_\rho + I(A_2; B_2)_\sigma$.

11.6.1   Holevo Information

Suppose that Alice prepares some classical ensemble $\mathcal{E} \equiv \{p_X(x), \rho_B^x\}$ and then hands this ensemble to Bob without telling him the classical index x. The expected density operator of this ensemble is

$$\rho_B \equiv \mathbb{E}_X\{\rho_B^X\} = \sum_x p_X(x)\rho_B^x, \tag{11.81}$$

and this density operator ρ_B characterizes the state from Bob's perspective because he does not have knowledge of the classical index x. His task is to determine the classical index x by performing some measurement on his system B. Recall from Section 10.9.2 that the accessible information quantifies Bob's information gain after performing some optimal measurement $\{\Lambda_y\}$ on his system B:

$$I_{\text{acc}}(\mathcal{E}) = \max_{\{\Lambda_y\}} I(X;Y), \tag{11.82}$$

where Y is a random variable corresponding to the outcome of the measurement.

What is the accessible information of the ensemble? In general, this quantity is difficult to compute, but another quantity, called the Holevo information, provides a useful upper bound. The Holevo information $\chi(\mathcal{E})$ of the ensemble is

$$\chi(\mathcal{E}) \equiv H(\rho_B) - \sum_x p_X(x) H(\rho_B^x). \tag{11.83}$$

Exercise 11.9.2 asks you to prove this upper bound after we develop the quantum data-processing inequality for quantum mutual information. The Holevo information characterizes the correlations between the classical variable X and the quantum system B.

EXERCISE 11.6.9 (Mutual Information of Classical–Quantum States)   Consider the following classical–quantum state representing the ensemble $\mathcal{E}$:

$$\sigma_{XB} \equiv \sum_x p_X(x) |x\rangle\langle x|_X \otimes \rho_B^x. \tag{11.84}$$

Show that the Holevo information $\chi(\mathcal{E})$ is equal to the mutual information $I(X;B)_\sigma$:

$$\chi(\mathcal{E}) = I(X;B)_\sigma. \tag{11.85}$$

In this sense, the quantum mutual information of a classical–quantum state is most similar to the classical mutual information of Shannon.

EXERCISE 11.6.10 (Concavity of Quantum Entropy)   Prove the concavity of entropy (Property 11.1.4) using Theorem 11.6.1 and the result of Exercise 11.6.9.

EXERCISE 11.6.11 (Dimension Bound)   Let $\sigma_{XB} \in \mathcal{D}(\mathcal{H}_X \otimes \mathcal{H}_B)$ be a classical–quantum state of the form:

$$\sigma_{XB} = \sum_x p_X(x) |x\rangle\langle x|_X \otimes \sigma_B^x. \tag{11.86}$$

Prove that the following bound applies to the Holevo information:

$$I(X;B)_\sigma \leq \log\left[\min\left\{\dim(\mathcal{H}_X), \dim(\mathcal{H}_B)\right\}\right]. \tag{11.87}$$

What is an example of a state that saturates the bound?

11.7   Conditional Quantum Mutual Information

We define the conditional quantum mutual information $I(A;B|C)_\rho$ of any tripartite state $\rho_{ABC} \in \mathcal{D}(\mathcal{H}_A \otimes \mathcal{H}_B \otimes \mathcal{H}_C)$ similarly to how we did in the classical case:

$$I(A;B|C)_\rho \equiv H(A|C)_\rho + H(B|C)_\rho - H(AB|C)_\rho. \tag{11.88}$$

In what follows, we sometimes abbreviate "conditional quantum mutual information" as CQMI.

One can exploit the above definition and the definition of quantum mutual information to prove a chain rule for quantum mutual information.

PROPERTY 11.7.1 (Chain Rule for Quantum Mutual Information)   The quantum mutual information obeys a chain rule:

$$I(A; BC)_\rho = I(A; B)_\rho + I(A; C|B)_\rho. \tag{11.89}$$

The interpretation of the chain rule is that we can build up the correlations between A and BC in two steps: in a first step, we build up the correlations between A and B, and now that B is available (and thus conditioned on), we build up the correlations between A and C.

EXERCISE 11.7.1   Use the chain rule for quantum mutual information to prove that

$$I(A; BC)_\rho = I(AC; B)_\rho + I(A; C)_\rho - I(B; C)_\rho. \tag{11.90}$$

11.7.1   Non-Negativity of CQMI

In the classical world, non-negativity of conditional mutual information follows trivially from non-negativity of mutual information (recall Theorem 10.6.1). The proof of non-negativity of conditional quantum mutual information is far from trivial in the quantum world, unless the conditioning system is classical (see Exercise 11.7.2). It is a foundational result that non-negativity of this quantity holds because so much of quantum information theory rests upon this theorem's shoulders (in fact, we could say that this inequality is one of the "bedrocks" of quantum information theory). The list of its corollaries includes the quantum data-processing inequality, the answers to some additivity questions in quantum Shannon theory, the Holevo bound, and others. The proof of Theorem 11.7.1 follows directly from monotonicity of quantum relative entropy (Theorem 11.8.1), which we prove in Chapter 12. In fact, it is possible to show that monotonicity of quantum relative entropy follows from strong subadditivity as well, so that these two entropy inequalities are essentially equivalent statements.

THEOREM 11.7.1 (Non-Negativity of CQMI)   Let $\rho_{ABC} \in \mathcal{D}(\mathcal{H}_A \otimes \mathcal{H}_B \otimes \mathcal{H}_C)$. Then the conditional quantum mutual information is non-negative:

$$I(A; B|C)_\rho \geq 0. \tag{11.91}$$

This condition is equivalent to the strong subadditivity inequality in Exercise 11.7.7, so we also refer to this entropy inequality as strong subadditivity.

EXERCISE 11.7.2 (CQMI of Classical–Quantum States)   Consider a classical–quantum state σ_{XAB} of the form in (11.65). Prove the following relation:

$$I(A; B|X)_\sigma = \sum_x p_X(x) I(A; B)_{\sigma_x}. \tag{11.92}$$

Conclude that non-negativity of conditional quantum mutual information is trivial in this special case in which the conditioning system is classical, simply by exploiting non-negativity of quantum mutual information (Theorem 11.6.1).

EXERCISE 11.7.3 (Conditioning Does Not Increase Entropy)   Let $\rho_{ABC} \in \mathcal{D}(\mathcal{H}_A \otimes \mathcal{H}_B \otimes \mathcal{H}_C)$. Show that Theorem 11.7.1 is equivalent to the following stronger form of Theorem 11.4.1:

$$H(B|C)_\rho \geq H(B|AC)_\rho. \tag{11.93}$$

EXERCISE 11.7.4 (Conditional Entropy and Recoverability)   Show that $H(B|C)_\rho = H(B|AC)_\rho$ if there exists a recovery channel $\mathcal{R}_{C \to AC}$ such that $\rho_{ABC} = \mathcal{R}_{C \to AC}(\rho_{BC})$ for $\rho_{ABC} \in \mathcal{D}(\mathcal{H}_A \otimes \mathcal{H}_B \otimes \mathcal{H}_C)$. (We will see later that this can be strengthened to "if and only if.")

EXERCISE 11.7.5 (Concavity of Conditional Quantum Entropy)   Show that strong subadditivity implies that conditional entropy is concave. That is, prove that

$$\sum_x p_X(x) H(A|B)_{\rho^x} \leq H(A|B)_\rho, \tag{11.94}$$

where p_X is a probability distribution on a finite alphabet $\mathcal{X}$, $\rho_{AB}^x \in \mathcal{D}(\mathcal{H}_A \otimes \mathcal{H}_B)$ for all $x \in \mathcal{X}$, and $\rho_{AB} \equiv \sum_x p_X(x) \rho_{AB}^x$.

EXERCISE 11.7.6 (Convexity of Coherent Information)   Prove that coherent information is convex:

$$\sum_x p_X(x) I(A\rangle B)_{\rho^x} \geq I(A\rangle B)_\rho, \tag{11.95}$$

by exploiting the result of the above exercise.

EXERCISE 11.7.7 (Strong Subadditivity)   Theorem 11.7.1 also goes by the name of "strong subadditivity" because it is an example of a function ϕ that is strongly subadditive:

$$\phi(E) + \phi(F) \geq \phi(E \cap F) + \phi(E \cup F). \tag{11.96}$$

Let $\rho_{ABC} \in \mathcal{D}(\mathcal{H}_A \otimes \mathcal{H}_B \otimes \mathcal{H}_C)$. Show that non-negativity of conditional quantum mutual information is equivalent to the following strong subadditivity of quantum entropy:

$$H(AC)_\rho + H(BC)_\rho \geq H(C)_\rho + H(ABC)_\rho, \tag{11.97}$$

where we think of ϕ in (11.96) as the entropy function H, the argument E in (11.96) as AC, and the argument F in (11.96) as BC.

EXERCISE 11.7.8 (Duality of CQMI)   Let $|\psi\rangle_{ABCD} \in \mathcal{H}_A \otimes \mathcal{H}_B \otimes \mathcal{H}_C \otimes \mathcal{H}_D$ be a pure state. Prove that

$$I(A; B|C)_\psi = I(A; B|D)_\psi. \tag{11.98}$$

EXERCISE 11.7.9 (Dimension Bound)   Let $\rho_{ABC} \in \mathcal{D}(\mathcal{H}_A \otimes \mathcal{H}_B \otimes \mathcal{H}_C)$. Prove the following dimension bound:

$$I(A; B|C)_\rho \leq 2 \log \left[\min \left\{ \dim(\mathcal{H}_A), \dim(\mathcal{H}_B) \right\} \right]. \tag{11.99}$$

Let $\sigma_{XBC} \in \mathcal{D}(\mathcal{H}_X \otimes \mathcal{H}_B \otimes \mathcal{H}_C)$ be a classical–quantum–quantum state of the form

$$\sum_x p_X(x)|x\rangle\langle x|_X \otimes \sigma_{BC}^x. \tag{11.100}$$

Prove that

$$I(X; B|C)_\sigma \leq \log \dim(\mathcal{H}_X). \tag{11.101}$$

EXERCISE 11.7.10 (Araki–Lieb Triangle Inequality)   Let $\rho_{AB} \in \mathcal{D}(\mathcal{H}_A \otimes \mathcal{H}_B)$. Show that

$$|H(A)_\rho - H(B)_\rho| \leq H(AB)_\rho. \tag{11.102}$$

11.8 Quantum Relative Entropy

The quantum relative entropy is one of the most important entropic quantities in quantum information theory, mainly because we can re-express many of the entropies given in the previous sections in terms of it. This in turn allows us to establish many properties of these quantities from the properties of relative entropies. Its definition is a natural extension of that for the classical relative entropy (see Definition 10.5.2). Before defining it, we need the notion of the support of an operator:

DEFINITION 11.8.1 (Kernel and Support)   The kernel of an operator $A \in \mathcal{L}(\mathcal{H}, \mathcal{H}')$ is defined as

$$\ker(A) \equiv \{|\psi\rangle \in \mathcal{H} : A|\psi\rangle = 0\}. \tag{11.103}$$

The support of A is the subspace of $\mathcal{H}$ orthogonal to its kernel:

$$\operatorname{supp}(A) \equiv \{|\psi\rangle \in \mathcal{H} : A|\psi\rangle \neq 0\}. \tag{11.104}$$

If A is Hermitian and thus has a spectral decomposition as $A = \sum_{i:a_i \neq 0} a_i |i\rangle\langle i|$, then $\operatorname{supp}(A) = \operatorname{span}\{|i\rangle : a_i \neq 0\}$. The projection onto the support of A is denoted by

$$\Pi_A \equiv \sum_{i:a_i \neq 0} |i\rangle\langle i|. \tag{11.105}$$

DEFINITION 11.8.2 (Quantum Relative Entropy)   The quantum relative entropy $D(\rho\|\sigma)$ between a density operator $\rho \in \mathcal{D}(\mathcal{H})$ and a positive semi-definite operator $\sigma \in \mathcal{L}(\mathcal{H})$ is defined as follows:

$$D(\rho\|\sigma) \equiv \operatorname{Tr}\left\{\rho\left[\log\rho - \log\sigma\right]\right\}, \tag{11.106}$$

if the following support condition is satisfied

$$\text{supp}(\rho) \subseteq \text{supp}(\sigma), \tag{11.107}$$

and it is defined to be equal to $+\infty$ otherwise.

This definition is consistent with the classical definition in Definition 10.5.2. However, we should note that there could be several ways to generalize the classical definition to obtain a quantum definition of relative entropy. For example, one could take

$$D'(\rho\|\sigma) = \text{Tr}\left\{\rho \log\left(\rho^{1/2}\sigma^{-1}\rho^{1/2}\right)\right\}, \tag{11.108}$$

as a definition and it reduces to the classical definition in Definition 10.5.2 as well. In fact, it is easy to see that there are an infinite number of quantum generalizations of the classical definition of relative entropy. So how do we single out which definition is the right one to use? The definition given in (11.106) is the answer to a meaningful quantum information-processing task in the context of quantum hypothesis testing (we do not elaborate on this further here but just mention that it is known as the quantum Stein's lemma). Furthermore, this definition generalizes the quantum entropic quantities we have given in this chapter, which all in turn are the answers to meaningful quantum information-processing tasks. For these reasons, we take the definition given in (11.106) as *the* quantum relative entropy. Recall that it was this same line of reasoning that allowed us to single out the entropy and the mutual information as meaningful measures of information in the classical case.

Similar to the classical case, we can intuitively think of the quantum relative entropy as a distance measure between quantum states. But it is not strictly a distance measure in the mathematical sense because it is not symmetric and it does not obey a triangle inequality.

The following proposition justifies why we take the definition of quantum relative entropy to have the particular support conditions as given above:

PROPOSITION 11.8.1 Let $\rho \in \mathcal{D}(\mathcal{H})$ and $\sigma \in \mathcal{L}(\mathcal{H})$ be positive semi-definite. The quantum relative entropy is consistent with the following limit:

$$D(\rho\|\sigma) = \lim_{\varepsilon \searrow 0} D(\rho\|\sigma + \varepsilon I). \tag{11.109}$$

Proof First observe that the operator $\sigma + \varepsilon I$ has support equal to $\mathcal{H}$ for all $\varepsilon > 0$, so that $D(\rho\|\sigma + \varepsilon I)$ is finite for all $\varepsilon > 0$. We will see that the limit is finite and consistent with (11.106) if (11.107) is satisfied, and otherwise the limit blows up to infinity. The idea in proving this proposition is to represent both ρ and σ with respect to the decomposition $\mathcal{H} = \text{supp}(\sigma) \oplus \ker(\sigma)$. Let Π_σ denote the projection onto $\text{supp}(\sigma)$ and let $\Pi_\sigma^\perp$ denote the projection onto $\ker(\sigma)$. So we take

$$\rho = \begin{bmatrix} \rho_{00} & \rho_{01} \\ \rho_{10} & \rho_{11} \end{bmatrix}, \qquad \sigma = \begin{bmatrix} \sigma_0 & 0 \\ 0 & 0 \end{bmatrix}. \tag{11.110}$$

First suppose that the support condition in (11.107) is satisfied. Then this means that $\rho_{01} = \rho_{10}^{\dagger} = 0$ and $\rho_{11} = 0$. Observe that

$$D(\rho \| \sigma + \varepsilon I) = \operatorname{Tr} \{ \rho \log \rho \} - \operatorname{Tr} \{ \rho \log (\sigma + \varepsilon I) \}. \tag{11.111}$$

The first term is finite for any ρ, so we should focus on the second term exclusively, since this is where an issue could arise. Then

$$
\begin{aligned}
\operatorname{Tr} \{ \rho \log (\sigma + \varepsilon I) \} &= \operatorname{Tr} \left\{ \begin{bmatrix} \rho_{00} & 0 \\ 0 & 0 \end{bmatrix} \log \begin{bmatrix} \sigma_0 + \varepsilon \Pi_\sigma & 0 \\ 0 & \varepsilon \Pi_\sigma^\perp \end{bmatrix} \right\} \\
&= \operatorname{Tr} \left\{ \begin{bmatrix} \rho_{00} & 0 \\ 0 & 0 \end{bmatrix} \begin{bmatrix} \log (\sigma_0 + \varepsilon \Pi_\sigma) & 0 \\ 0 & \log (\varepsilon \Pi_\sigma^\perp) \end{bmatrix} \right\} & (11.112) \\
&= \operatorname{Tr} \{ \rho_{00} \log (\sigma_0 + \varepsilon \Pi_\sigma) \} + \operatorname{Tr} \{ 0 \cdot \log (\varepsilon \Pi_\sigma^\perp) \} & (11.113) \\
&= \operatorname{Tr} \{ \rho_{00} \log (\sigma_0 + \varepsilon \Pi_\sigma) \}. & (11.114)
\end{aligned}
$$

Taking the limit $\varepsilon \searrow 0$, we get

$$\lim_{\varepsilon \searrow 0} \operatorname{Tr} \{ \rho_{00} \log (\sigma_0 + \varepsilon \Pi_\sigma) \} = \operatorname{Tr} \{ \rho_{00} \log \sigma_0 \} = \operatorname{Tr} \{ \rho \log \sigma \}. \tag{11.115}$$

So we can conclude that

$$\lim_{\varepsilon \searrow 0} D(\rho \| \sigma + \varepsilon I) = \operatorname{Tr} \{ \rho \log \rho \} - \operatorname{Tr} \{ \rho \log \sigma \}, \tag{11.116}$$

in this case.

Now suppose that the support condition in (11.107) is not satisfied. Then $\rho_{11} \neq 0$, and we find that

$$
\begin{aligned}
\operatorname{Tr} \{ \rho \log (\sigma + \varepsilon I) \} &= \operatorname{Tr} \left\{ \begin{bmatrix} \rho_{00} & \rho_{01} \\ \rho_{10} & \rho_{11} \end{bmatrix} \begin{bmatrix} \log (\sigma_0 + \varepsilon \Pi_\sigma) & 0 \\ 0 & \log (\varepsilon \Pi_\sigma^\perp) \end{bmatrix} \right\} \\
&= \operatorname{Tr} \{ \rho_{00} \log (\sigma_0 + \varepsilon \Pi_\sigma) \} + \operatorname{Tr} \{ \rho_{11} \cdot \log (\varepsilon \Pi_\sigma^\perp) \}, & (11.117)
\end{aligned}
$$

and thus $\lim_{\varepsilon \searrow 0} D(\rho \| \sigma + \varepsilon I) = +\infty$, given that $\lim_{\varepsilon \searrow 0} [-\log \varepsilon] = +\infty$. $\qquad\square$

One of the most fundamental entropy inequalities in quantum information theory is the monotonicity of quantum relative entropy. When the arguments to the quantum relative entropy are quantum states, the physical interpretation of this entropy inequality is that states become less distinguishable when noise acts on them. We defer a proof of this theorem until Chapter 12, where we also establish a strengthening of it.

THEOREM 11.8.1 (Monotonicity of Quantum Relative Entropy) Let $\rho \in \mathcal{D}(\mathcal{H})$, $\sigma \in \mathcal{L}(\mathcal{H})$ be positive semi-definite, and $\mathcal{N} : \mathcal{L}(\mathcal{H}) \to \mathcal{L}(\mathcal{H}')$ be a quantum channel. The quantum relative entropy can only decrease or stay the same if we apply the same quantum channel $\mathcal{N}$ to ρ and σ:

$$D(\rho \| \sigma) \geq D(\mathcal{N}(\rho) \| \mathcal{N}(\sigma)). \tag{11.118}$$

Theorem 11.8.1 then implies non-negativity of quantum relative entropy in certain cases.

THEOREM 11.8.2 (Non-Negativity) Let $\rho \in \mathcal{D}(\mathcal{H})$, and let $\sigma \in \mathcal{L}(\mathcal{H})$ be positive semi-definite and such that $\text{Tr}\{\sigma\} \leq 1$. Then the quantum relative entropy $D(\rho\|\sigma)$ is non-negative:

$$D(\rho\|\sigma) \geq 0, \tag{11.119}$$

and $D(\rho\|\sigma) = 0$ if and only if $\rho = \sigma$.

Proof The first part of the theorem follows from applying Theorem 11.8.1, taking the quantum channel to be the trace-out map. We then have that

$$D(\rho\|\sigma) \geq D(\text{Tr}\{\rho\}\|\,\text{Tr}\{\sigma\}) = \text{Tr}\{\rho\} \log\left(\frac{\text{Tr}\{\rho\}}{\text{Tr}\{\sigma\}}\right) \geq 0. \tag{11.120}$$

If $\rho = \sigma$, then the support condition in (11.107) is satisfied and plugging into (11.106) gives that $D(\rho\|\sigma) = 0$. Now suppose that $D(\rho\|\sigma) = 0$. This means that the inequality above is saturated and thus $\text{Tr}\{\sigma\} = \text{Tr}\{\rho\} = 1$, so that σ is a density operator. Let $\mathcal{M}$ be an arbitrary measurement channel. From the monotonicity of quantum relative entropy (Theorem 11.8.1), we can conclude that $D(\mathcal{M}(\rho)\|\mathcal{M}(\sigma)) = 0$. The equality condition for the non-negativity of the classical relative entropy (Theorem 10.7.1) in turn implies that $\mathcal{M}(\rho) = \mathcal{M}(\sigma)$. Now since this equality holds for any possible measurement channel, we can conclude that $\rho = \sigma$. (For example, we could take $\mathcal{M}$ to be the optimal measurement for the trace distance, which would allow us to conclude that $\max_{\mathcal{M}} \|\mathcal{M}(\rho) - \mathcal{M}(\sigma)\|_1 = \|\rho - \sigma\|_1 = 0$, and hence $\rho = \sigma$.) $\square$

11.8.1 Deriving Other Entropies from Quantum Relative Entropy

There is a sense in which the quantum relative entropy is a "parent quantity" for other entropies in quantum information theory, such as the quantum entropy, the conditional quantum entropy, the quantum mutual information, and the conditional quantum mutual information. The following exercises explore these relations. The main tool needed to solve some of them is the non-negativity of quantum relative entropy.

EXERCISE 11.8.1 (Operator Logarithm) Let $P_A \in \mathcal{L}(\mathcal{H}_A)$ and $Q_B \in \mathcal{L}(\mathcal{H}_B)$ be positive semi-definite operators. Show that the following identity holds:

$$\log(P_A \otimes Q_B) = \log(P_A) \otimes I_B + I_A \otimes \log(Q_B). \tag{11.121}$$

EXERCISE 11.8.2 (Mutual Information and Relative Entropy) Let $\rho_{AB} \in \mathcal{D}(\mathcal{H}_A \otimes \mathcal{H}_B)$. Show that the following identities hold:

$$I(A;B)_\rho = D(\rho_{AB}\|\rho_A \otimes \rho_B) \tag{11.122}$$

$$= \min_{\sigma_B} D(\rho_{AB}\|\rho_A \otimes \sigma_B) \tag{11.123}$$

$$= \min_{\omega_A} D(\rho_{AB}\|\omega_A \otimes \rho_B) \tag{11.124}$$

$$= \min_{\omega_A, \sigma_B} D(\rho_{AB}\|\omega_A \otimes \sigma_B), \tag{11.125}$$

where the optimizations are with respect to $\omega_A \in \mathcal{D}(\mathcal{H}_A)$ and $\sigma_B \in \mathcal{D}(\mathcal{H}_B)$.

EXERCISE 11.8.3 (Conditional and Relative Entropy)   Let $\rho_{AB} \in \mathcal{D}(\mathcal{H}_A \otimes \mathcal{H}_B)$. Show that the following identities hold:

$$I(A\rangle B)_\rho = D(\rho_{AB}\|I_A \otimes \rho_B) \tag{11.126}$$

$$= \min_{\sigma_B \in \mathcal{D}(\mathcal{H}_B)} D(\rho_{AB}\|I_A \otimes \sigma_B). \tag{11.127}$$

Note that these are equivalent to

$$H(A|B)_\rho = -D(\rho_{AB}\|I_A \otimes \rho_B) \tag{11.128}$$

$$= -\min_{\sigma_B \in \mathcal{D}(\mathcal{H}_B)} D(\rho_{AB}\|I_A \otimes \sigma_B). \tag{11.129}$$

EXERCISE 11.8.4 (CQMI and Relative Entropy)   Let $\rho_{ABC} \in \mathcal{D}(\mathcal{H}_A \otimes \mathcal{H}_B \otimes \mathcal{H}_C)$. Let ω_{ABC} be the following positive semi-definite operator:

$$\omega_{ABC} \equiv 2^{[\log \rho_{AC} + \log \rho_{BC} - \log \rho_C]}, \tag{11.130}$$

where identities are implicit if not written (e.g., ρ_{BC} is a shorthand for $I_A \otimes \rho_{BC}$). Show that

$$I(A;B|C)_\rho = D(\rho_{ABC}\|\omega_{ABC}). \tag{11.131}$$

EXERCISE 11.8.5 (Dimension Bound)   Let $\rho_{ABC} \in \mathcal{D}(\mathcal{H}_A \otimes \mathcal{H}_B \otimes \mathcal{H}_C)$. Prove the following dimension bound:

$$I(A\rangle BC)_\rho \leq I(AC\rangle B)_\rho + \log \dim(\mathcal{H}_C). \tag{11.132}$$

(Hint: One way to do this is to use the formula in (11.127). Another way is to use the chain rule and previous dimension bounds.)

COROLLARY 11.8.1 (Subadditivity of Quantum Entropy)   The quantum entropy is subadditive for a bipartite state ρ_{AB}:

$$H(A)_\rho + H(B)_\rho \geq H(AB)_\rho. \tag{11.133}$$

Proof Subadditivity of entropy is equivalent to non-negativity of quantum mutual information. We can prove non-negativity by exploiting the result of Exercise 11.8.2 and non-negativity of quantum relative entropy (Theorem 11.8.2).   □

11.8.2   Mathematical Properties of Quantum Relative Entropy

This section contains several auxiliary mathematical properties of quantum relative entropy, including its isometric invariance, additivity for tensor-product states, its form for classical–quantum states (these are left as exercises). There are two other properties given which are commonly used in relative entropy calculations.

EXERCISE 11.8.6 (Isometric Invariance)   Let $\rho \in \mathcal{D}(\mathcal{H})$ and $\sigma \in \mathcal{L}(\mathcal{H})$ be positive semi-definite. Show that the quantum relative entropy is invariant with respect to an isometry $U : \mathcal{H} \to \mathcal{H}'$:

$$D(\rho\|\sigma) = D(U\rho U^\dagger \| U\sigma U^\dagger). \tag{11.134}$$

EXERCISE 11.8.7 (Additivity of Quantum Relative Entropy)   Let $\rho_1 \in \mathcal{D}(\mathcal{H}_1)$ and $\rho_2 \in \mathcal{D}(\mathcal{H}_1)$ be density operators, and let $\sigma_1 \in \mathcal{L}(\mathcal{H}_1)$ and $\sigma_2 \in \mathcal{L}(\mathcal{H}_2)$ be positive semi-definite operators. Show that the quantum relative entropy is additive in the following sense:

$$D(\rho_1 \otimes \rho_2 \| \sigma_1 \otimes \sigma_2) = D(\rho_1\|\sigma_1) + D(\rho_2\|\sigma_2). \tag{11.135}$$

We can apply the above additivity relation inductively to conclude that

$$D(\rho^{\otimes n} \| \sigma^{\otimes n}) = nD(\rho\|\sigma), \tag{11.136}$$

for $\rho \in \mathcal{D}(\mathcal{H})$ and $\sigma \in \mathcal{L}(\mathcal{H})$ positive semi-definite.

EXERCISE 11.8.8 (Relative Entropy of Classical–Quantum States)   Show that the quantum relative entropy between classical–quantum states ρ_{XB} and σ_{XB} is as follows:

$$D(\rho_{XB}\|\sigma_{XB}) = \sum_x p_X(x) D(\rho_B^x \| \sigma_B^x), \text{ where} \tag{11.137}$$

$$\rho_{XB} \equiv \sum_x p_X(x) |x\rangle\langle x|_X \otimes \rho_B^x, \qquad \sigma_{XB} \equiv \sum_x p_X(x) |x\rangle\langle x|_X \otimes \sigma_B^x, \tag{11.138}$$

with p_X a probability distribution over a finite alphabet $\mathcal{X}$, $\rho_B^x \in \mathcal{D}(\mathcal{H}_B)$ for all $x \in \mathcal{X}$, and $\sigma_B^x \in \mathcal{L}(\mathcal{H}_B)$ positive semi-definite for all $x \in \mathcal{X}$.

EXERCISE 11.8.9   Let $a, b > 0$, $\rho \in \mathcal{D}(\mathcal{H})$, and $\sigma \in \mathcal{L}(\mathcal{H})$ be positive semi-definite. Show that

$$D(a\rho\|b\sigma) = a\left[D(\rho\|\sigma) + \log(a/b)\right]. \tag{11.139}$$

(Note that we only defined quantum relative entropy to have its first argument equal to a density operator, but one could more generally allow for the first argument to be positive semi-definite.)

PROPOSITION 11.8.2   Let $\rho \in \mathcal{D}(\mathcal{H})$ and $\sigma, \sigma' \in \mathcal{L}(\mathcal{H})$ be positive semi-definite. Suppose that $\sigma \leq \sigma'$. Then

$$D(\rho\|\sigma') \leq D(\rho\|\sigma). \tag{11.140}$$

Proof   The assumption that $\sigma \leq \sigma'$ is equivalent to $\sigma' - \sigma$ being positive semi-definite. Then the following operator is positive semi-definite: $\sigma \otimes |0\rangle\langle 0|_X + (\sigma' - \sigma) \otimes |1\rangle\langle 1|_X$, and as a consequence

$$D(\rho\|\sigma) = D(\rho \otimes |0\rangle\langle 0|_X \| [\sigma \otimes |0\rangle\langle 0|_X + (\sigma' - \sigma) \otimes |1\rangle\langle 1|_X]), \tag{11.141}$$

which follows by a direct calculation (essentially the same reasoning as that used to solve Exercise 11.8.8). By monotonicity of quantum relative entropy

(Theorem 11.8.1), the quantum relative entropy does not increase after discarding the system X, so that

$$D(\rho \otimes |0\rangle\langle 0|_X \| [\sigma \otimes |0\rangle\langle 0|_X + (\sigma' - \sigma) \otimes |1\rangle\langle 1|_X])$$
$$\geq D(\rho \| [\sigma + (\sigma' - \sigma)]) = D(\rho\|\sigma'), \quad (11.142)$$

concluding the proof. $\qquad\square$

11.9 Quantum Entropy Inequalities

Monotonicity of quantum relative entropy has as its corollaries many of the important entropy inequalities in quantum information theory (but keep in mind that some of these also imply the monotonicity of quantum relative entropy).

COROLLARY 11.9.1 (Strong Subadditivity) Let $\rho_{ABC} \in \mathcal{D}(\mathcal{H}_A \otimes \mathcal{H}_B \otimes \mathcal{H}_C)$. The quantum entropy is strongly subadditive, in the following sense:

$$H(AC)_\rho + H(BC)_\rho \geq H(ABC)_\rho + H(C)_\rho. \quad (11.143)$$

Proof Consider from Exercise 11.7.7 that

$$I(A;B|C)_\rho = H(AC)_\rho + H(BC)_\rho - H(ABC)_\rho - H(C)_\rho, \quad (11.144)$$

so that

$$I(A;B|C)_\rho = H(B|C)_\rho - H(B|AC)_\rho. \quad (11.145)$$

From Exercise 11.8.3, we know that

$$-H(B|AC)_\rho = D(\rho_{ABC}\|I_B \otimes \rho_{AC}), \quad (11.146)$$
$$H(B|C)_\rho = -D(\rho_{BC}\|I_B \otimes \rho_C). \quad (11.147)$$

Then

$$D(\rho_{ABC}\|I_B \otimes \rho_{AC}) \geq D(\mathrm{Tr}_A\{\rho_{ABC}\}\|\,\mathrm{Tr}_A\{I_B \otimes \rho_{AC}\}) \quad (11.148)$$
$$= D(\rho_{BC}\|I_B \otimes \rho_C). \quad (11.149)$$

The inequality is a consequence of the monotonicity of quantum relative entropy (Theorem 11.8.1), taking $\rho = \rho_{ABC}$, $\sigma = I_B \otimes \rho_{AC}$, and $\mathcal{N} = \mathrm{Tr}_A$. By (11.144)–(11.147), the inequality in (11.148)–(11.149) is equivalent to the inequality in the statement of the corollary. $\qquad\square$

COROLLARY 11.9.2 (Joint Convexity of Quantum Relative Entropy) Let p_X be a probability distribution over a finite alphabet $\mathcal{X}$, $\rho^x \in \mathcal{D}(\mathcal{H})$ for all $x \in \mathcal{X}$, and $\sigma^x \in \mathcal{L}(\mathcal{H})$ be positive semi-definite for all $x \in \mathcal{X}$. Set $\overline{\rho} \equiv \sum_x p_X(x)\rho^x$ and $\overline{\sigma} \equiv \sum_x p_X(x)\sigma^x$. The quantum relative entropy is jointly convex in its arguments:

$$\sum_x p_X(x)D(\rho^x\|\sigma^x) \geq D(\overline{\rho}\|\overline{\sigma}). \quad (11.150)$$

Proof Consider classical–quantum states of the following form:

$$\rho_{XB} \equiv \sum_x p_X(x)|x\rangle\langle x|_X \otimes \rho_B^x, \tag{11.151}$$

$$\sigma_{XB} \equiv \sum_x p_X(x)|x\rangle\langle x|_X \otimes \sigma_B^x. \tag{11.152}$$

Observe that $\overline{\rho} = \rho_B$ and $\overline{\sigma} = \sigma_B$. Then

$$\sum_x p_X(x)D(\rho_B^x\|\sigma_B^x) = D(\rho_{XB}\|\sigma_{XB}) \geq D(\rho_B\|\sigma_B). \tag{11.153}$$

The equality follows from Exercise 11.8.8, and the inequality follows from monotonicity of quantum relative entropy (Theorem 11.8.1), where we take the channel to be the partial trace over the system X. □

COROLLARY 11.9.3 (Unital Channels Increase Entropy)   Let $\rho \in \mathcal{D}(\mathcal{H})$ and let $\mathcal{N} : \mathcal{L}(\mathcal{H}) \to \mathcal{L}(\mathcal{H})$ be a unital quantum channel (see Definition 4.4.7). Then

$$H(\mathcal{N}(\rho)) \geq H(\rho). \tag{11.154}$$

Proof Consider that

$$H(\rho) = -D(\rho\|I), \tag{11.155}$$
$$H(\mathcal{N}(\rho)) = -D(\mathcal{N}(\rho)\|I) = -D(\mathcal{N}(\rho)\|\mathcal{N}(I)), \tag{11.156}$$

where in the last equality, we have used that $\mathcal{N}$ is a unital quantum channel. The inequality in (11.154) is a consequence of the monotonicity of quantum relative entropy (Theorem 11.8.1) because $D(\rho\|I) \geq D(\mathcal{N}(\rho)\|\mathcal{N}(I))$. □

A particular example of a unital channel occurs when we completely dephase a density operator ρ with respect to some dephasing basis $\{|y\rangle\}$. Let ω denote the dephased version of ρ:

$$\omega \equiv \Delta_Y(\rho) = \sum_y |y\rangle\langle y|\rho|y\rangle\langle y|. \tag{11.157}$$

Then the entropy $H(\omega)$ of the completely dephased state is never smaller than the entropy $H(\rho)$ of the original state. More generally, if we have a set of projectors $\{\Pi_x\}$ satisfying $\sum_x \Pi_x = I$, then the channel $\rho \to \sum_x \Pi_x \rho \Pi_x$ is unital, so that

$$H\left(\sum_x \Pi_x \rho \Pi_x\right) \geq H(\rho). \tag{11.158}$$

The quantum relative entropy itself is not a distance measure, but it actually gives a useful upper bound on the trace distance between two quantum states. This result is known as the quantum Pinsker inequality. Thus, in this sense, we can think of the quantum relative entropy as being comparable to a distance measure when it is small—if the quantum relative entropy between two quantum states is small, then their trace distance is small as well. We can view the quantum Pinsker inequality as a refinement of the statement that the quantum relative entropy is non-negative (Theorem 11.8.2).

THEOREM 11.9.1 (Quantum Pinsker Inequality)   Let $\rho \in \mathcal{D}(\mathcal{H})$ and let $\sigma \in$ $\mathcal{L}(\mathcal{H})$ be positive semi-definite such that $\mathrm{Tr}\{\sigma\} \leq 1$. Then

$$D(\rho\|\sigma) \geq \frac{1}{2\ln 2} \|\rho - \sigma\|_1^2. \tag{11.159}$$

Proof This is a direct consequence of the classical Pinsker inequality (Theorem 10.8.1) and the fact that a measurement achieves the trace distance (see Exercise 9.1.10). To get the statement for subnormalized σ, we add an extra dimension to the Hilbert space $\mathcal{H}$. Let $\rho' \equiv \rho \oplus [0]$ and $\sigma' \equiv \sigma \oplus [1 - \mathrm{Tr}\{\sigma\}]$, so that σ' is a density operator. Let $\mathcal{M}$ denote a measurement channel that achieves the trace distance for ρ' and σ' (see Exercise 9.1.10). Then

$$D(\rho\|\sigma) = D(\rho'\|\sigma') \tag{11.160}$$

$$\geq D(\mathcal{M}(\rho')\|\mathcal{M}(\sigma')) \tag{11.161}$$

$$\geq \frac{1}{2\ln 2} \|\mathcal{M}(\rho') - \mathcal{M}(\sigma')\|_1^2 \tag{11.162}$$

$$= \frac{1}{2\ln 2} \|\rho' - \sigma'\|_1^2 \tag{11.163}$$

$$= \frac{1}{2\ln 2} [\|\rho - \sigma\|_1 + (1 - \mathrm{Tr}\{\sigma\})]^2 \tag{11.164}$$

$$\geq \frac{1}{2\ln 2} \|\rho - \sigma\|_1^2. \tag{11.165}$$

The first inequality is a consequence of the monotonicity of quantum relative entropy (Theorem 11.8.1). The second inequality follows from the classical Pinsker inequality (Theorem 10.8.1). The second equality follows because we chose the measurement channel $\mathcal{M}$ to achieve the trace distance.   □

11.9.1   Equivalence of Quantum Entropy Inequalities

We have already seen how the monotonicity of quantum relative entropy (Theorem 11.8.1) implies many of the important entropy inequalities in quantum information theory. However, what is less obvious is that some of these other entropy inequalities also imply the monotonicity of quantum relative entropy. Thus, we can say that together, these entropy inequalities constitute a "law" of quantum information theory, saying either that information, correlations, or distinguishability decrease under the action of a quantum channel or conditional uncertainty increases under the action of a quantum channel on a conditioning system. We formalize this equivalence in the following theorem:

THEOREM 11.9.2   The following statements are equivalent, in the sense that one can prove the other statements as a consequence of one of them:

1. The quantum relative entropy is monotone with respect to quantum channels: $D(\rho\|\sigma) \geq D(\mathcal{N}(\rho)\|\mathcal{N}(\sigma))$, where $\rho, \sigma \in \mathcal{D}(\mathcal{H})$, and $\mathcal{N} : \mathcal{L}(\mathcal{H}) \to \mathcal{L}(\mathcal{H}')$ is a quantum channel.

2. The quantum relative entropy is monotone with respect to partial trace: $D(\rho_{AB}\|\sigma_{AB}) \geq D(\rho_B\|\sigma_B)$, where $\rho_{AB}, \sigma_{AB} \in \mathcal{D}(\mathcal{H}_A \otimes \mathcal{H}_B)$.
3. The quantum relative entropy is jointly convex: $\sum_x p_X(x)D(\rho^x\|\sigma^x) \geq D(\overline{\rho}\|\overline{\sigma})$, where p_X is a probability distribution over a finite alphabet $\mathcal{X}$, $\rho^x, \sigma^x \in \mathcal{D}(\mathcal{H})$ for all $x \in \mathcal{X}$, $\rho \equiv \sum_x p_X(x)\rho^x$, and $\sigma \equiv \sum_x p_X(x)\sigma^x$.
4. The conditional quantum mutual information is non-negative: $I(A; B|C)_\rho \geq 0$, where $\rho_{ABC} \in \mathcal{D}(\mathcal{H}_A \otimes \mathcal{H}_B \otimes \mathcal{H}_C)$.
5. The conditional quantum entropy is concave: $H(A|B)_\rho \geq \sum_x p_X(x)H(A|B)_{\rho^x}$, where p_X is a probability distribution on a finite alphabet $\mathcal{X}$, $\rho_{AB}^x \in \mathcal{D}(\mathcal{H}_A \otimes \mathcal{H}_B)$ for all $x \in \mathcal{X}$, and $\rho_{AB} \equiv \sum_x p_X(x)\rho_{AB}^x$.

Proof We have already proved 2-4 starting from 1, and 5 from 4 as well (some of these are left as exercises), so it remains to work our way back up to 1 from the others. Consider that we can get 1 from 2 by using the Stinespring dilation theorem. That is, let $U : \mathcal{H} \to \mathcal{H}' \otimes \mathcal{H}_E$ be an isometric extension of the channel $\mathcal{N}$. Consider that

$$D(\rho\|\sigma) = D(U\rho U^\dagger\|U\sigma U^\dagger) \tag{11.166}$$
$$\geq D(\mathrm{Tr}_E\{U\rho U^\dagger\}\|\mathrm{Tr}_E\{U\sigma U^\dagger\}) \tag{11.167}$$
$$= D(\mathcal{N}(\rho)\|\mathcal{N}(\sigma)). \tag{11.168}$$

The first equality follows from invariance of quantum relative entropy with respect to isometries (Exercise 11.8.6). The inequality follows from monotonicity with respect to partial trace (by assumption), and the last equality follows from the fact that U is an isometric extension of $\mathcal{N}$.

We can also get 1 from 3 by a related approach. Let $d = \dim(\mathcal{H}_E)$ and $\{V_E^i\}$ be a Heisenberg–Weyl set of unitaries for the environment system E. Consider that

$$D(\mathcal{N}(\rho)\|\mathcal{N}(\sigma)) = D(\mathcal{N}(\rho) \otimes \pi_E\|\mathcal{N}(\sigma) \otimes \pi_E) \tag{11.169}$$
$$= D\left(\frac{1}{d^2}\sum_i V_E^i U\rho U^\dagger \left(V_E^i\right)^\dagger \middle\| \frac{1}{d^2}\sum_i V_E^i U\sigma U^\dagger \left(V_E^i\right)^\dagger\right) \tag{11.170}$$
$$\leq \frac{1}{d^2}\sum_i D(V_E^i U\rho U^\dagger \left(V_E^i\right)^\dagger \|V_E^i U\sigma U^\dagger \left(V_E^i\right)^\dagger) \tag{11.171}$$
$$= D(\rho\|\sigma). \tag{11.172}$$

The first equality follows from additivity of quantum relative entropy (Exercise 11.8.7) and the fact that $D(\pi_E\|\pi_E) = 0$. The second equality follows from the fact that a random application of a Heisenberg–Weyl unitary is equivalent to a channel that traces out system E and replaces it with π_E (see Exercise 4.7.6). The inequality follows from joint convexity (by assumption), and the last equality follows from invariance of quantum relative entropy with respect to isometries (Exercise 11.8.6).

We now show that concavity of conditional entropy implies monotonicity of quantum relative entropy, which has the most involved proof. Before doing so, we need a somewhat advanced theorem from matrix analysis. Suppose that f is a differentiable function on an open neighborhood of the spectrum of some self-adjoint operator A. Then its derivative Df at A is given by

$$Df(A) : K \rightarrow \sum_{\lambda, \eta} f^{[1]}(\lambda, \eta) P_A(\lambda) K P_A(\eta), \tag{11.173}$$

where $A = \sum_\lambda \lambda P_A(\lambda)$ is the spectral decomposition of A, and $f^{[1]}$ is what is known as the first divided difference function. In particular, if $x \longmapsto A(x) \in \mathcal{L}(\mathcal{H})$ (where $A(x)$ is positive semi-definite) is a differentiable function on an open interval in $\mathbb{R}$, with derivative A', then

$$\frac{d}{dx} f(A(x)) = \sum_{\lambda, \eta} f^{[1]}(\lambda, \eta) P_{A(x)}(\lambda) A'(x) P_{A(x)}(\eta), \tag{11.174}$$

so that

$$\frac{d}{dx} \text{Tr} \{f(A(x))\} = \text{Tr} \{f'(A(x)) A'(x)\}. \tag{11.175}$$

Note how (11.175) appears strikingly similar to the usual chain rule. So if $A(x) = A + xB$, then

$$\frac{d}{dx} \text{Tr} \{f(A(x))\} = \text{Tr} \{f'(A(x)) B\}, \tag{11.176}$$

which is the main formula that we need to proceed. In what follows, we will be taking $A(x) = \sigma_{AB} + x\rho_{AB}$, where $\rho_{AB}, \sigma_{AB} \in \mathcal{D}(\mathcal{H}_A \otimes \mathcal{H}_B)$ and $x > 0$. If we do not have that $\text{supp}(\rho_{AB}) \subseteq \text{supp}(\sigma_{AB})$, then we can take $\sigma'_{AB} \equiv (1 - \varepsilon)\sigma_{AB} + \varepsilon\pi_{AB}$ for $\varepsilon \in (0, 1)$ and π_{AB} the maximally mixed state. After doing so, we can take a limit as $\varepsilon \rightarrow 0$ at the end. We also make use of the standard fact that the function $f : X \rightarrow X^{-1}$ is everywhere differentiable on the set of invertible density operators, and at an invertible X, its derivative is $f'(X) : Y \rightarrow -X^{-1}YX^{-1}$. Consider that the conditional entropy is homogeneous, in the sense that

$$H(A|B)_{xG} = xH(A|B)_G, \tag{11.177}$$

where $G_{AB} \in \mathcal{L}(\mathcal{H}_A \otimes \mathcal{H}_B)$ is a positive semi-definite operator. Let

$$\xi_{YAB} \equiv \frac{1}{x+1} |0\rangle\langle 0|_Y \otimes \sigma_{AB} + \frac{x}{x+1} |1\rangle\langle 1|_Y \otimes \rho_{AB}. \tag{11.178}$$

Then it follows from homogeneity and concavity of conditional entropy (taking 5 true by assumption) that

$$H(A|B)_{\sigma+x\rho} = (x+1)H(A|B)_\xi \tag{11.179}$$

$$\geq (x+1) \left[\frac{1}{x+1} H(A|B)_\sigma + \frac{x}{x+1} H(A|B)_\rho \right] \tag{11.180}$$

$$= H(A|B)_\sigma + xH(A|B)_\rho. \tag{11.181}$$

Manipulating the above inequality then gives

$$\frac{H(A|B)_{\sigma+x\rho} - H(A|B)_{\sigma}}{x} \geq H(A|B)_{\rho}, \tag{11.182}$$

and taking the limit as $x \searrow 0$ gives

$$\lim_{x \searrow 0} \frac{H(A|B)_{\sigma+x\rho} - H(A|B)_{\sigma}}{x} = \left. \frac{d}{dx} H(A|B)_{\sigma+x\rho} \right|_{x=0} \geq H(A|B)_{\rho}. \tag{11.183}$$

We now evaluate the limit on the left-hand side. So we consider

$$\frac{d}{dx} H(A|B)_{\sigma+x\rho} = \frac{d}{dx} \left[- \mathrm{Tr} \left\{ (\sigma_{AB} + x\rho_{AB}) \log (\sigma_{AB} + x\rho_{AB}) \right\} \right]$$

$$+ \frac{d}{dx} \mathrm{Tr} \left\{ (\sigma_B + x\rho_B) \log (\sigma_B + x\rho_B) \right\}. \tag{11.184}$$

We evaluate this by using $\frac{d}{dy} [g(y) \log g(y)] = [\log g(y) + 1] g'(y)$ (up to a scale factor of $\ln 2$ from using the binary logarithm) and (11.176) to find that

$$\frac{d}{dx} \mathrm{Tr} \left\{ (\sigma_{AB} + x\rho_{AB}) \log (\sigma_{AB} + x\rho_{AB}) \right\} = \mathrm{Tr} \left\{ [\log (\sigma_{AB} + x\rho_{AB}) + I_{AB}] \rho_{AB} \right\},$$

$$\tag{11.185}$$

so that

$$\frac{d}{dx} H(A|B)_{\sigma+x\rho} = - \mathrm{Tr} \left\{ \rho_{AB} \log (\sigma_{AB} + x\rho_{AB}) \right\} + \mathrm{Tr} \left\{ \rho_B \log (\sigma_B + x\rho_B) \right\},$$

$$\tag{11.186}$$

and thus

$$\left. \frac{d}{dx} H(A|B)_{\sigma+x\rho} \right|_{x=0} = - \mathrm{Tr} \left\{ \rho_{AB} \log \sigma_{AB} \right\} + \mathrm{Tr} \left\{ \rho_B \log \sigma_B \right\}. \tag{11.187}$$

Substituting back into the inequality (11.183), we find that

$$- \mathrm{Tr} \left\{ \rho_{AB} \log \sigma_{AB} \right\} + \mathrm{Tr} \left\{ \rho_B \log \sigma_B \right\} \geq - \mathrm{Tr} \left\{ \rho_{AB} \log \rho_{AB} \right\} + \mathrm{Tr} \left\{ \rho_B \log \rho_B \right\},$$

$$\tag{11.188}$$

which is equivalent to

$$D(\rho_{AB} \| \sigma_{AB}) \geq D(\rho_B \| \sigma_B). \tag{11.189}$$

If the support condition $\mathrm{supp}(\rho_{AB}) \subseteq \mathrm{supp}(\sigma_{AB})$ does not hold, then we can take σ'_{AB} as mentioned above and all of the above development holds. At the end, we can take the limit as $\varepsilon \to 0$ to find that $D(\rho_{AB} \| \sigma_{AB}) = +\infty$, so that the inequality holds trivially in this case. $\qquad \square$

11.9.2   Quantum Data Processing

The quantum data-processing inequalities discussed below are similar in spirit to the classical data-processing inequality. Recall that the classical data-processing inequality states that processing classical data reduces classical correlations. The quantum data-processing inequalities state that processing *quantum* data reduces *quantum* correlations.

One variant applies to the following scenario. Suppose that Alice and Bob share some bipartite state ρ_{AB}. The coherent information $I(A\rangle B)_\rho$ is one measure of the quantum correlations present in this state. Bob then processes his system B according to some quantum channel $\mathcal{N}_{B\to B'}$ to produce some quantum system B' and let $\sigma_{AB'}$ denote the resulting state. The quantum data-processing inequality states that this step of quantum data processing reduces quantum correlations, in the sense that

$$I(A\rangle B)_\rho \geq I(A\rangle B')_\sigma. \tag{11.190}$$

THEOREM 11.9.3 (Data Processing for Coherent Information) Let $\rho_{AB} \in \mathcal{D}(\mathcal{H}_A \otimes \mathcal{H}_B)$ and let $\mathcal{N} : \mathcal{L}(\mathcal{H}_B) \to \mathcal{L}(\mathcal{H}_{B'})$ be a quantum channel. Set $\sigma_{AB'} \equiv \mathcal{N}_{B\to B'}(\rho_{AB})$. Then the following quantum data-processing inequality holds

$$I(A\rangle B)_\rho \geq I(A\rangle B')_\sigma. \tag{11.191}$$

Proof This is a consequence of Exercise 11.8.3 and Theorem 11.8.1. By Exercise 11.8.3, we know that

$$I(A\rangle B)_\rho = D(\rho_{AB}\|I_A \otimes \rho_B), \tag{11.192}$$
$$I(A\rangle B')_\sigma = D(\sigma_{AB'}\|I_A \otimes \sigma_{B'}) \tag{11.193}$$
$$= D(\mathcal{N}_{B\to B'}(\rho_{AB})\|I_A \otimes \mathcal{N}_{B\to B'}(\rho_B)) \tag{11.194}$$
$$= D(\mathcal{N}_{B\to B'}(\rho_{AB})\|\mathcal{N}_{B\to B'}(I_A \otimes \rho_B)). \tag{11.195}$$

The statement then follows from the monotonicity of quantum relative entropy by picking $\rho = \rho_{AB}$, $\sigma = I_A \otimes \rho_B$, and $\mathcal{N} = \mathrm{id}_A \otimes \mathcal{N}_{B\to B'}$ in Theorem 11.8.1. □

THEOREM 11.9.4 (Data Processing for Mutual Information) Let $\rho_{AB} \in \mathcal{D}(\mathcal{H}_A \otimes \mathcal{H}_B)$, $\mathcal{N} : \mathcal{L}(\mathcal{H}_A) \to \mathcal{L}(\mathcal{H}_{A'})$ be a quantum channel, and $\mathcal{M} : \mathcal{L}(\mathcal{H}_B) \to \mathcal{L}(\mathcal{H}_{B'})$ be a quantum channel. Set $\sigma_{A'B'} \equiv (\mathcal{N}_{A\to A'} \otimes \mathcal{M}_{B\to B'})(\rho_{AB})$. Then the following quantum data-processing inequality applies to the quantum mutual information:

$$I(A; B)_\rho \geq I(A'; B')_\sigma. \tag{11.196}$$

Proof From Exercise 11.8.2, we know that

$$I(A; B)_\rho = D(\rho_{AB}\|\rho_A \otimes \rho_B), \tag{11.197}$$
$$I(A'; B')_\sigma = D(\sigma_{A'B'}\|\sigma_{A'} \otimes \sigma_{B'}) \tag{11.198}$$
$$= D((\mathcal{N}_{A\to A'} \otimes \mathcal{M}_{B\to B'})(\rho_{AB})\|\mathcal{N}_{A\to A'}(\rho_A) \otimes \mathcal{M}_{B\to B'}(\rho_B)) \tag{11.199}$$
$$= D((\mathcal{N}_{A\to A'} \otimes \mathcal{M}_{B\to B'})(\rho_{AB})\|(\mathcal{N}_{A\to A'} \otimes \mathcal{M}_{B\to B'})(\rho_A \otimes \rho_B)). \tag{11.200}$$

The statement then follows from the monotonicity of quantum relative entropy by picking $\rho = \rho_{AB}$, $\sigma = \rho_A \otimes \rho_B$, and $\mathcal{N} = \mathcal{N}_{A\to A'} \otimes \mathcal{M}_{B\to B'}$ in Theorem 11.8.1. □

EXERCISE 11.9.1   Let $\rho_{AB} \in \mathcal{D}(\mathcal{H}_A \otimes \mathcal{H}_B)$, $\mathcal{N} : \mathcal{L}(\mathcal{H}_A) \to \mathcal{L}(\mathcal{H}_{A'})$ be a unital quantum channel, and $\mathcal{M} : \mathcal{L}(\mathcal{H}_B) \to \mathcal{L}(\mathcal{H}_{B'})$ be a quantum channel. Set $\sigma_{A'B'} \equiv (\mathcal{N}_{A \to A'} \otimes \mathcal{M}_{B \to B'})(\rho_{AB})$. Prove that

$$I(A\rangle B)_\rho \geq I(A'\rangle B')_\sigma. \tag{11.201}$$

EXERCISE 11.9.2 (Holevo Bound)   Use the quantum data-processing inequality to show that the Holevo information $\chi(\mathcal{E})$ is an upper bound on the accessible information $I_{\mathrm{acc}}(\mathcal{E})$:

$$I_{\mathrm{acc}}(\mathcal{E}) \leq \chi(\mathcal{E}), \tag{11.202}$$

where $\mathcal{E}$ is an ensemble of quantum states. (See Section 10.9.2 for a definition of accessible information.)

EXERCISE 11.9.3 (Shannon Entropy vs. von Neumann Entropy)   Consider an ensemble $\{p_X(x), |\psi_x\rangle\}$. The expected density operator of the ensemble is

$$\rho \equiv \sum_x p_X(x) |\psi_x\rangle\langle\psi_x|. \tag{11.203}$$

Use the quantum data-processing inequality to show that the Shannon entropy $H(X)$ is never less than the quantum entropy of the expected density operator ρ:

$$H(X) \geq H(\rho). \tag{11.204}$$

(Hint: Begin with a classical shared randomness state $\sum_x p_X(x)|x\rangle\langle x|_X \otimes |x\rangle\langle x|_{X'}$ and apply a preparation channel to system X'). Conclude that the Shannon entropy of the ensemble is strictly greater than the quantum entropy whenever the states in the ensemble are non-orthogonal.

EXERCISE 11.9.4   Use the idea in the above exercise to show that the conditional entropy $H(X|B)_\rho$ is always non-negative whenever the state ρ_{XB} is a classical–quantum state:

$$\rho_{XB} \equiv \sum_x p_X(x)|x\rangle\langle x|_X \otimes \rho_B^x. \tag{11.205}$$

Additionally, show that $H(X|B)_\rho \geq 0$ is equivalent to $H(B)_\rho \leq H(X)_\rho + H(B|X)_\rho$ and $I(X; B)_\rho \leq H(X)_\rho$.

EXERCISE 11.9.5 (Separability and Negativity of Coherent Information)   Show that the following inequality holds for any separable state ρ_{AB}:

$$\max\{I(A\rangle B)_\rho, I(B\rangle A)_\rho\} \leq 0. \tag{11.206}$$

EXERCISE 11.9.6 (Quantum Data Processing for CQMI)   Let $\rho_{ABC} \in \mathcal{D}(\mathcal{H}_A \otimes \mathcal{H}_B \otimes \mathcal{H}_C)$, $\mathcal{N} : \mathcal{L}(\mathcal{H}_A) \to \mathcal{L}(\mathcal{H}_{A'})$ be a quantum channel, and $\mathcal{M} : \mathcal{L}(\mathcal{H}_B) \to \mathcal{L}(\mathcal{H}_{B'})$ be a quantum channel. Set $\sigma_{A'B'C} \equiv (\mathcal{N}_{A \to A'} \otimes \mathcal{M}_{B \to B'})(\rho_{ABC})$. Prove that

$$I(A; B|C)_\rho \geq I(A'; B'|C)_\sigma. \tag{11.207}$$

11.9.3 Entropic Uncertainty Principle

The uncertainty principle reviewed in Section 3.4.2 aims to capture a fundamental feature of quantum mechanics, namely, that there is an unavoidable uncertainty in the measurement outcomes of incompatible (non-commuting) observables. This uncertainty principle is a radical departure from classical intuitions, where there it seems as if there should not be any obstacle to measuring incompatible observables such as position and momentum.

However, the uncertainty principle that we reviewed before (the standard version in most textbooks) suffers from a few deficiencies. First, the measure of uncertainty used there is the standard deviation, which is not just a function of the probabilities of measurement outcomes but also of the values of the outcomes. Thus, the values of the outcomes may skew the uncertainty measure (however, one could always relabel the values in order to avoid this difficulty). More importantly however, from an information-theoretic perspective, there is not a clear operational interpretation for the standard deviation as there is for entropy. Second, the lower bound in (3.88) depends not only on the observables but also on the state. In Exercise 3.4.5, we saw how this lower bound can vanish for a state even when the distributions corresponding to the measurement outcomes in fact do have uncertainty. So, it would be ideal to separate this lower bound into two terms: one which depends only on measurement incompatibility and another which depends only on the state.

Additionally, it might seem as if giving two parties access to a maximally entangled state allows them to defy the uncertainty principle (and this is what confounded Einstein, Podolsky, and Rosen after quantum mechanics had been established). Indeed, suppose that Alice and Bob share a Bell state $|\Phi^+\rangle = 2^{-1/2}(|00\rangle + |11\rangle) = 2^{-1/2}(|++\rangle + |--\rangle)$. If Alice measures the Pauli Z observable on her system, then Bob can guess the outcome of her measurement with certainty. Also, if Alice were instead to measure the Pauli X observable on her system, then Bob would also be able to guess the outcome of her measurement with certainty, in spite of the fact that Z and X are incompatible observables. So, a revision of the uncertainty principle is clearly needed to account for this possibility, in the scenario where Bob shares a *quantum memory* correlated with Alice's system.

The *uncertainty principle in the presence of quantum memory* is such a revision that meets all of the desiderata stated above. It quantifies uncertainty in terms of quantum entropy rather than with standard deviation, and it also accounts for the scenario in which an observer has a quantum memory correlated with the system being measured. So, suppose that Alice and Bob share systems A and B, respectively, that are in some state ρ_{AB}. If Alice performs a measurement channel corresponding to a POVM $\{\Lambda_A^x\}$ on her system A, then the post-measurement state is as follows:

$$\sigma_{XB} \equiv \sum_x |x\rangle\langle x|_X \otimes \operatorname{Tr}_A\left\{(\Lambda_A^x \otimes I_B)\rho_{AB}\right\}. \tag{11.208}$$

In the above classical–quantum state, the measurement outcomes x are encoded into orthonormal states $\{|x\rangle\}$ of the classical register X, and the probability for obtaining outcome x is $\mathrm{Tr}\{(\Lambda_A^x \otimes I_B)\rho_{AB}\}$. We would like to quantify the uncertainty that Bob has about the outcome of the measurement, and a natural quantity for doing so is with the conditional quantum entropy $H(X|B)_\sigma$. Similarly, starting from the state ρ_{AB}, Alice could choose to perform some other measurement channel corresponding to POVM $\{\Gamma_A^z\}$ on her system A. In this case, the post-measurement state is as follows:

$$\tau_{ZB} \equiv \sum_z |z\rangle\langle z|_Z \otimes \mathrm{Tr}_A\{(\Gamma_A^z \otimes I_B)\rho_{AB}\}, \qquad (11.209)$$

with a similar interpretation as before. We can quantify Bob's uncertainty about the measurement outcome z in terms of the conditional quantum entropy $H(Z|B)_\tau$. We define Bob's total uncertainty about the measurement outcomes to be the sum of both entropies: $H(X|B)_\sigma + H(Z|B)_\tau$. We will call this the *uncertainty sum*, in analogy with the uncertainty product in (3.88).

We stated above that it would be desirable to have a lower bound on the uncertainty sum consisting of a measurement incompability term and a state-dependent term. One way to quantify the incompatibility of the POVMs $\{\Lambda_A^x\}$ and $\{\Gamma_A^z\}$ is in terms of the following quantity:

$$c \equiv \max_{x,z} \left\| \sqrt{\Lambda_A^x}\sqrt{\Gamma_A^z} \right\|_\infty^2, \qquad (11.210)$$

where $\|\cdot\|_\infty$ is the infinity norm of an operator (for the finite-dimensional case, $\|A\|_\infty$ is just the maximal eigenvalue of $|A|$). To grasp an intuition for this incompatibility measure, suppose that $\{\Lambda_A^x\}$ and $\{\Gamma_A^z\}$ are actually complete projective measurements with one common element. In this case, it follows that $c = 1$, so that the measurements are regarded as maximally compatible. On the other hand, if the measurements are of Pauli observables X and Z, these are maximally incompatible for a two-dimensional Hilbert space and $c = 1/2$. We now state the uncertainty principle in the presence of quantum memory:

THEOREM 11.9.5 (Uncertainty Principle with Quantum Memory) Suppose that Alice and Bob share a state ρ_{AB} and that Alice performs either of the POVMs $\{\Lambda_A^x\}$ or $\{\Gamma_A^z\}$ on her share of the state (with at least one of $\{\Lambda_A^x\}$ or $\{\Gamma_A^z\}$ being a rank-one POVM). Then Bob's total uncertainty about the measurement outcomes has the following lower bound:

$$H(X|B)_\sigma + H(Z|B)_\tau \geq \log(1/c) + H(A|B)_\rho, \qquad (11.211)$$

where the states σ_{XB} and τ_{ZB} are defined in (11.208) and (11.209), respectively, and the measurement incompatibility is defined in (11.210).

Interestingly, the lower bound given in the above theorem consists of both the measurement incompatibility and the state-dependent term $H(A|B)_\rho$. As we know from Exercise 11.9.5, when the conditional quantum entropy $H(A|B)_\rho$ becomes negative, this implies that the state ρ_{AB} is entangled (but not necessarily the converse). Thus, a negative conditional entropy implies that the lower bound on the uncertainty sum can become lower than $\log(1/c)$, and furthermore, that it might be possible to reduce Bob's total uncertainty about the measurement outcomes down to zero. Indeed, this is the case for the example we mentioned before with measurements of Pauli X and Z on the maximally entangled Bell state. One can verify for this case that $\log(1/c) = 1$ and $H(A|B) = -1$, so that this is consistent with the fact that $H(X|B)_\sigma + H(Z|B)_\tau = 0$ for this example. We now give a path to proving the above theorem (leaving the final steps as an exercise).

Proof We actually prove the following uncertainty relation instead:

$$H(X|B)_\sigma + H(Z|E)_\omega \geq \log(1/c), \qquad (11.212)$$

where ω_{ZE} is a classical–quantum state of the following form:

$$\omega_{ZE} \equiv \sum_z |z\rangle\langle z|_Z \otimes \mathrm{Tr}_{AB}\left\{(\Gamma_A^z \otimes I_{BE})\, \phi_{ABE}^\rho\right\}, \qquad (11.213)$$

and ϕ_{ABE}^ρ is a purification of ρ_{AB}. We leave it as an exercise to demonstrate that the above uncertainty relation implies the one in the statement of the theorem whenever Γ_A^z is a rank-one POVM. Consider the following isometric extensions of the measurement channels for $\{\Lambda_A^x\}$ and $\{\Gamma_A^z\}$:

$$U_{A\to XX'A} \equiv \sum_x |x\rangle_X \otimes |x\rangle_{X'} \otimes \sqrt{\Lambda_A^x}, \qquad (11.214)$$

$$V_{A\to ZZ'A} \equiv \sum_z |z\rangle_Z \otimes |z\rangle_{Z'} \otimes \sqrt{\Gamma_A^z}, \qquad (11.215)$$

where $\{|x\rangle\}$ and $\{|z\rangle\}$ are both orthonormal bases. Let $\omega_{ZZ'ABE}$ denote the following state:

$$|\omega\rangle_{ZZ'ABE} \equiv V_{A\to ZZ'A} |\phi^\rho\rangle_{ABE}, \qquad (11.216)$$

so that $\omega_{ZE} = \mathrm{Tr}_{Z'AB}\{\omega_{ZZ'ABE}\}$. Exercise 11.5.3 establishes that

$$H(Z|E)_\omega = -H(Z|Z'AB)_\omega, \qquad (11.217)$$

so that (11.212) is equivalent to

$$-H(Z|Z'AB)_\omega \geq \log(1/c) - H(X|B)_\sigma. \qquad (11.218)$$

Recalling the result of Exercise 11.8.3, we then have that (11.218) is equivalent to

$$D(\omega_{ZZ'AB}\|I_Z \otimes \omega_{Z'AB}) \geq \log(1/c) + D(\sigma_{XB}\|I_X \otimes \sigma_B), \qquad (11.219)$$

where we observe that $\sigma_B = \omega_B$. So we aim to prove (11.219). Consider the following chain of inequalities:

$$D(\omega_{ZZ'AB}\|I_Z \otimes \omega_{Z'AB}) \qquad (11.220)$$
$$\geq D\left(\omega_{ZZ'AB}\|VV^\dagger (I_Z \otimes \omega_{Z'AB})\, VV^\dagger\right) \qquad (11.221)$$

$$= D\left(\rho_{AB}\middle\| V^\dagger\left(I_Z \otimes \omega_{Z'AB}\right)V\right) \tag{11.222}$$

$$= D\left(U\rho_{AB}U^\dagger\middle\| UV^\dagger\left(I_Z \otimes \omega_{Z'AB}\right)VU^\dagger\right). \tag{11.223}$$

The first inequality follows from monotonicity of quantum relative entropy under the channel $\rho \rightarrow \Pi\rho\Pi + (I - \Pi)\rho(I - \Pi)$, where the projector $\Pi \equiv VV^\dagger$, and also from the fact that $(I - \Pi)\omega_{ZZ'AB}(I - \Pi) = 0$. The first equality follows from invariance of quantum relative entropy with respect to isometries (Exercise 11.8.6) and the fact that $\omega_{ZZ'AB} = V\rho_{AB}V^\dagger$. The second equality again follows from invariance of quantum relative entropy with respect to isometries. Let us define $\sigma_{XX'ABE}$ as

$$|\sigma\rangle_{XX'ABE} \equiv U_{A\rightarrow XX'A}|\phi^\rho\rangle_{ABE}. \tag{11.224}$$

We then have that (11.223) is equal to

$$D\left(\sigma_{XX'AB}\middle\| UV^\dagger\left(I_Z \otimes \omega_{Z'AB}\right)VU^\dagger\right), \tag{11.225}$$

and explicitly evaluating $UV^\dagger\left(I_Z \otimes \omega_{Z'AB}\right)VU^\dagger$ as

$$UV^\dagger\left(I_Z \otimes \omega_{Z'AB}\right)VU^\dagger \tag{11.226}$$

$$= U\sum_{z',z}\langle z'|z\rangle_Z\left(\langle z'|_{Z'} \otimes \sqrt{\Gamma_A^{z'}}\right)\omega_{Z'AB}\left(|z\rangle_{Z'} \otimes \sqrt{\Gamma_A^z}\right)U^\dagger \tag{11.227}$$

$$= U\sum_{z}\left(\langle z|_{Z'} \otimes \sqrt{\Gamma_A^z}\right)\omega_{Z'AB}\left(|z\rangle_{Z'} \otimes \sqrt{\Gamma_A^z}\right)U^\dagger, \tag{11.228}$$

gives that (11.225) is equal to

$$D\left(\sigma_{XX'AB}\middle\| U\sum_{z}\left(\langle z|_{Z'} \otimes \sqrt{\Gamma_A^z}\right)\omega_{Z'AB}\left(|z\rangle_{Z'} \otimes \sqrt{\Gamma_A^z}\right)U^\dagger\right). \tag{11.229}$$

We trace out the $X'A$ systems and exploit monotonicity of quantum relative entropy and cyclicity of trace to show that the above is not less than

$$D\left(\sigma_{XB}\middle\| \sum_{z,x}|x\rangle\langle x|_X \otimes \text{Tr}_{Z'A}\left\{\left(|z\rangle\langle z|_{Z'} \otimes \sqrt{\Gamma_A^z}\Lambda_A^x\sqrt{\Gamma_A^z}\right)\omega_{Z'AB}\right\}\right). \tag{11.230}$$

Using the fact that $\sqrt{\Gamma_A^z}\Lambda_A^x\sqrt{\Gamma_A^z} = |\sqrt{\Gamma_A^z}\sqrt{\Lambda_A^x}|^2 \leq cI$, it follows that

$$\sum_{z,x}|x\rangle\langle x|_X \otimes \text{Tr}_{Z'A}\left\{\left(|z\rangle\langle z|_{Z'} \otimes \left[cI_A - \sqrt{\Gamma_A^z}\Lambda_A^x\sqrt{\Gamma_A^z}\right]\right)\omega_{Z'AB}\right\} \tag{11.231}$$

is a positive semi-definite operator, or equivalently, that

$$\sum_{z,x}|x\rangle\langle x|_X \otimes \text{Tr}_{Z'A}\left\{\left(|z\rangle\langle z|_{Z'} \otimes \sqrt{\Gamma_A^z}\Lambda_A^x\sqrt{\Gamma_A^z}\right)\omega_{Z'AB}\right\} \leq c\,I_X \otimes \omega_B. \tag{11.232}$$

Proposition 11.8.2 and Exercise 11.8.9 imply that (11.230) is not less than

$$D(\sigma_{XB}\|c\,I_X \otimes \omega_B) = \log(1/c) + D(\sigma_{XB}\|I_X \otimes \omega_B) \tag{11.233}$$

$$= \log(1/c) + D(\sigma_{XB}\|I_X \otimes \sigma_B), \tag{11.234}$$

which finally proves the inequality in (11.212). We now leave it as an exercise to prove the statement of the theorem starting from the inequality in (11.212). □

EXERCISE 11.9.7   Prove that (11.212) implies Theorem 11.9.5.

EXERCISE 11.9.8   Prove that Theorem 11.9.5 implies the following entropic uncertainty relation for a state ρ_A on a single system:

$$H(X) + H(Z) \geq \log(1/c) + H(A)_\rho, \qquad (11.235)$$

where $H(X)$ and $H(Z)$ are the Shannon entropies of the measurement outcomes.

11.10   Continuity of Quantum Entropy

Suppose that two density operators ρ and σ are close in trace distance. We might then expect several properties to hold: the fidelity between them should be close to one and we would suspect that their entropies should be close. Theorem 9.3.1 states that the fidelity is close to one if the trace distance is small.

An important theorem below, the Fannes–Audenaert inequality, states that quantum entropies are close as well. This theorem usually finds application in a proof of a converse theorem in quantum Shannon theory. Usually, the specification of any good protocol (in the sense of asymptotically vanishing error) involves placing a bound on the trace distance between the actual state resulting from a protocol and the ideal state that it should produce. The Fannes–Audenaert inequality then allows us to translate these statements of error into informational statements that bound the asymptotic rates of communication in any good protocol.

THEOREM 11.10.1 (Fannes–Audenaert Inequality)   Let $\rho, \sigma \in \mathcal{D}(\mathcal{H})$ and suppose that $\frac{1}{2} \|\rho - \sigma\|_1 \leq \varepsilon \in [0, 1]$. Then the following inequality holds

$$|H(\rho) - H(\sigma)| \leq \begin{cases} \varepsilon \log\left[\dim(\mathcal{H}) - 1\right] + h_2(\varepsilon) & \text{if } \varepsilon \in [0, 1 - 1/\dim(\mathcal{H})] \\ \log \dim(\mathcal{H}) & \text{else} \end{cases}.$$

$$(11.236)$$

Putting these together, a universal bound is

$$|H(\rho) - H(\sigma)| \leq \varepsilon \log \dim(\mathcal{H}) + h_2(\varepsilon). \qquad (11.237)$$

Proof   A proof of this theorem follows by applying the classical result in Theorem 10.7.4. We first prove that

$$H(\rho) - H(\sigma) \leq \varepsilon \log\left[\dim(\mathcal{H}) - 1\right] + h_2(\varepsilon) \qquad (11.238)$$

if $\varepsilon \in [0, 1 - 1/\dim(\mathcal{H})]$. First note that the function $f(\varepsilon) \equiv \varepsilon \log\left[\dim(\mathcal{H}) - 1\right] + h_2(\varepsilon)$ is monotone non-decreasing on the interval $[0, 1 - 1/\dim(\mathcal{H})]$ because $f'(\varepsilon) = \log\left[\dim(\mathcal{H}) - 1\right] + \log\left(\frac{1-\varepsilon}{\varepsilon}\right) \geq 0$ for $\varepsilon \in [0, 1 - 1/\dim(\mathcal{H})]$. Let

$\sigma = \sum_y p(y)|y\rangle\langle y|$ be a spectral decomposition of σ. Let $\overline{\Delta}_\sigma$ denote the following completely dephasing channel:

$$\overline{\Delta}_\sigma(\omega) = \sum_y |y\rangle\langle y|\omega|y\rangle\langle y|. \tag{11.239}$$

Then $\overline{\Delta}_\sigma(\sigma) = \sigma$ and Corollary 11.9.3 gives that $H(\rho) \le H(\overline{\Delta}_\sigma(\rho))$, so that

$$H(\rho) - H(\sigma) \le H(\overline{\Delta}_\sigma(\rho)) - H(\overline{\Delta}_\sigma(\sigma)). \tag{11.240}$$

At the same time, we know from the monotonicity of trace distance with respect to channels (Exercise 9.1.9) that

$$\|\rho - \sigma\|_1 \ge \left\|\overline{\Delta}_\sigma(\rho) - \overline{\Delta}_\sigma(\sigma)\right\|_1. \tag{11.241}$$

Putting everything together, we find that

$$H(\rho) - H(\sigma) \le H(\overline{\Delta}_\sigma(\rho)) - H(\overline{\Delta}_\sigma(\sigma)) \tag{11.242}$$

$$\le f\left(\frac{1}{2}\left\|\overline{\Delta}_\sigma(\rho) - \overline{\Delta}_\sigma(\sigma)\right\|_1\right) \tag{11.243}$$

$$\le f\left(\frac{1}{2}\|\rho - \sigma\|_1\right), \tag{11.244}$$

where the second inequality follows from Theorem 10.7.4 and the last inequality follows because f is monotone non-decreasing on the interval $[0, 1 - 1/\dim(\mathcal{H})]$.

The other inequality $H(\sigma) - H(\rho) \le \varepsilon \log[\dim(\mathcal{H}) - 1] + h_2(\varepsilon)$ follows by the same proof method, but instead dephasing with respect to the eigenbasis of ρ. The bound $|H(\rho) - H(\sigma)| \le \log(\dim(\mathcal{H}))$ follows trivially from the fact that the entropy is non-negative and cannot exceed $\log(\dim(\mathcal{H}))$. □

There is another variation of this theorem, which we state below. We do not however give a full proof, but instead just argue for it. The proof sketch makes use of an original insight by Audenaert (2007).

THEOREM 11.10.2 (Fannes–Audenaert Inequality)　Let $\rho, \sigma \in \mathcal{D}(\mathcal{H})$ and let $T \equiv \frac{1}{2}\|\rho - \sigma\|_1$. Then the following inequality holds

$$|H(\rho) - H(\sigma)| \le T\log[\dim(\mathcal{H}) - 1] + h_2(T). \tag{11.245}$$

Furthermore, this bound is optimal because there exists a pair of states that saturates it for all $T \in [0, 1]$ and dimension $\dim(\mathcal{H})$.

Proof　The following inequalities are known from the theory of matrix analysis (Bhatia, 1997, Inequality IV.62):

$$T_0 \equiv \frac{1}{2}\left\|\mathrm{Eig}^\downarrow(\rho) - \mathrm{Eig}^\downarrow(\sigma)\right\|_1 \le T = \frac{1}{2}\|\rho - \sigma\|_1$$

$$\le T_1 \equiv \frac{1}{2}\left\|\mathrm{Eig}^\downarrow(\rho) - \mathrm{Eig}^\uparrow(\sigma)\right\|_1, \tag{11.246}$$

where $\mathrm{Eig}^\downarrow(A)$ is the list of eigenvalues of Hermitian A in non-increasing order and $\mathrm{Eig}^\uparrow(A)$ is the list in non-decreasing order. Then applying the fact that the entropy depends only on the eigenvalues and is invariant with respect to permutations of them, we find that

$$|H(\rho) - H(\sigma)| = \left| H(\text{Eig}^{\downarrow}(\rho)) - H(\text{Eig}^{\downarrow}(\sigma)) \right| \tag{11.247}$$

$$\leq T_0 \log\left[\dim(\mathcal{H}) - 1\right] + h_2(T_0), \tag{11.248}$$

where the inequality follows from Theorem 10.7.4. Similarly, we find that

$$|H(\rho) - H(\sigma)| = \left| H(\text{Eig}^{\downarrow}(\rho)) - H(\text{Eig}^{\uparrow}(\sigma)) \right| \tag{11.249}$$

$$\leq T_1 \log\left[\dim(\mathcal{H}) - 1\right] + h_2(T_1). \tag{11.250}$$

We know from (11.246) that $T = \lambda T_0 + (1 - \lambda)T_1$ for some $\lambda \in [0,1]$. Applying concavity of the binary entropy, we find that

$$\begin{aligned}
|H(\rho) - H(\sigma)| &\leq \lambda \left[T_0 \log\left[\dim(\mathcal{H}) - 1\right] + h_2(T_0)\right] \\
&+ (1 - \lambda) \left[T_1 \log\left[\dim(\mathcal{H}) - 1\right] + h_2(T_1)\right] \\
&\leq T \log\left[\dim(\mathcal{H}) - 1\right] + h_2(T). \quad (11.251)
\end{aligned}$$

The inequality is optimal because choosing $\rho = |0\rangle\langle 0|$ and $\sigma = (1 - \varepsilon)|0\rangle\langle 0| + \varepsilon/(d-1)|1\rangle\langle 1| + \cdots + \varepsilon/(d-1)|d-1\rangle\langle d-1|$ saturates the bound for all $\varepsilon \in [0,1]$ and for all dimensions d. $\qquad\square$

An important theorem below, the Alicki–Fannes–Winter (AFW) inequality, states that conditional quantum entropies are close as well. This statement does follow directly from the Fannes–Audenaert inequality, but the main advantage of the AFW inequality is that the upper bound has a dependence only on the dimension of the first system in the conditional entropy (no dependence on the conditioning system). The AFW inequality also finds application in a proof of a converse theorem in quantum Shannon theory.

THEOREM 11.10.3 (AFW Inequality) Let $\rho_{AB}, \sigma_{AB} \in \mathcal{D}(\mathcal{H}_A \otimes \mathcal{H}_B)$. Suppose that

$$\frac{1}{2}\|\rho_{AB} - \sigma_{AB}\|_1 \leq \varepsilon, \tag{11.252}$$

for $\varepsilon \in [0,1]$. Then

$$|H(A|B)_\rho - H(A|B)_\sigma| \leq 2\varepsilon \log \dim(\mathcal{H}_A) + (1 + \varepsilon)h_2(\varepsilon/[1 + \varepsilon]). \tag{11.253}$$

If ρ_{XB} and σ_{XB} are classical–quantum and have the following form:

$$\rho_{XB} = \sum_x p(x)|x\rangle\langle x|_X \otimes \rho_B^x, \tag{11.254}$$

$$\sigma_{XB} = \sum_x q(x)|x\rangle\langle x|_X \otimes \sigma_B^x, \tag{11.255}$$

where p and q are probability distributions defined over a finite alphabet $\mathcal{X}$, $\{|x\rangle\}$ is an orthonormal basis, and $\rho_B^x, \sigma_B^x \in \mathcal{D}(\mathcal{H}_B)$ for all $x \in \mathcal{X}$, then

$$|H(X|B)_\rho - H(X|B)_\sigma| \leq \varepsilon \log \dim(\mathcal{H}_X) + (1+\varepsilon)h_2\left(\varepsilon/\left[1+\varepsilon\right]\right), \quad (11.256)$$

$$|H(B|X)_\rho - H(B|X)_\sigma| \leq \varepsilon \log \dim(\mathcal{H}_B) + (1+\varepsilon)h_2\left(\varepsilon/\left[1+\varepsilon\right]\right). \quad (11.257)$$

Proof The bounds trivially hold when $\varepsilon = 0$, so henceforth we assume that $\varepsilon \in (0,1]$. All of the upper bounds are monotone non-decreasing with ε, so it suffices to assume that $\frac{1}{2}\|\rho_{AB} - \sigma_{AB}\|_1 = \varepsilon$. Let $\rho_{AB} - \sigma_{AB} = P_{AB} - Q_{AB}$ be a decomposition of $\rho_{AB} - \sigma_{AB}$ into its positive part $P_{AB} \geq 0$ and its negative part $Q_{AB} \geq 0$ (as in the proof of Lemma 9.1.1). Let $\Delta_{AB} \equiv P_{AB}/\varepsilon$. Since $\mathrm{Tr}\{P_{AB}\} = \frac{1}{2}\|\rho_{AB} - \sigma_{AB}\|_1$ (see the proof of Lemma 9.1.1), it follows that Δ_{AB} is a density operator. Now consider that

$$\rho_{AB} = \sigma_{AB} + (\rho_{AB} - \sigma_{AB}) \quad (11.258)$$

$$= \sigma_{AB} + P_{AB} - Q_{AB} \quad (11.259)$$

$$\leq \sigma_{AB} + P_{AB} \quad (11.260)$$

$$= \sigma_{AB} + \varepsilon\Delta_{AB} \quad (11.261)$$

$$= (1+\varepsilon)\left(\frac{1}{1+\varepsilon}\sigma_{AB} + \frac{\varepsilon}{1+\varepsilon}\Delta_{AB}\right) \quad (11.262)$$

$$= (1+\varepsilon)\,\omega_{AB}, \quad (11.263)$$

where we define $\omega_{AB} \equiv \frac{1}{1+\varepsilon}\sigma_{AB} + \frac{\varepsilon}{1+\varepsilon}\Delta_{AB}$. Now let $\Delta'_{AB} \equiv \frac{1}{\varepsilon}\left[(1+\varepsilon)\,\omega_{AB} - \rho_{AB}\right]$. It follows from (11.258)–(11.263) that Δ'_{AB} is positive semi-definite. Furthermore, one can check that $\mathrm{Tr}\{\Delta'_{AB}\} = 1$, so that Δ'_{AB} is a density operator. One can also quickly check that

$$\omega_{AB} = \frac{1}{1+\varepsilon}\rho_{AB} + \frac{\varepsilon}{1+\varepsilon}\Delta'_{AB} = \frac{1}{1+\varepsilon}\sigma_{AB} + \frac{\varepsilon}{1+\varepsilon}\Delta_{AB}. \quad (11.264)$$

Now consider that

$$H(A|B)_\omega = -D(\omega_{AB}\|I_A \otimes \omega_B) \quad (11.265)$$

$$= H(\omega_{AB}) + \mathrm{Tr}\{\omega_{AB}\log\omega_B\} \quad (11.266)$$

$$\leq h_2\left(\frac{\varepsilon}{1+\varepsilon}\right) + \frac{1}{1+\varepsilon}H(\rho_{AB}) + \frac{\varepsilon}{1+\varepsilon}H(\Delta'_{AB})$$

$$\quad + \frac{1}{1+\varepsilon}\mathrm{Tr}\{\rho_{AB}\log\omega_B\} + \frac{\varepsilon}{1+\varepsilon}\mathrm{Tr}\{\Delta'_{AB}\log\omega_B\} \quad (11.267)$$

$$= h_2\left(\frac{\varepsilon}{1+\varepsilon}\right) - \frac{1}{1+\varepsilon}D(\rho_{AB}\|I_A \otimes \omega_B)$$

$$\quad - \frac{\varepsilon}{1+\varepsilon}D(\Delta'_{AB}\|I_A \otimes \omega_B) \quad (11.268)$$

$$\leq h_2\left(\frac{\varepsilon}{1+\varepsilon}\right) + \frac{1}{1+\varepsilon}H(A|B)_\rho + \frac{\varepsilon}{1+\varepsilon}H(A|B)_{\Delta'}. \quad (11.269)$$

The first equality follows from Exercise 11.8.3, and the second equality follows from the definition of quantum relative entropy. The first inequality follows because $H(AB) \leq H(Y) + H(AB|Y)$ for a classical–quantum state on systems

Y and AB (see Exercise 11.9.4), here taking the state as

$$\frac{1}{1+\varepsilon}|0\rangle\langle0|_Y \otimes \rho_{AB} + \frac{\varepsilon}{1+\varepsilon}|1\rangle\langle1|_Y \otimes \Delta'_{AB}. \tag{11.270}$$

The third equality follows from algebra and the definition of quantum relative entropy. The last inequality follows from Exercise 11.8.3. From concavity of the conditional entropy (Exercise 11.7.5), we have that

$$H(A|B)_\omega \geq \frac{1}{1+\varepsilon}H(A|B)_\sigma + \frac{\varepsilon}{1+\varepsilon}H(A|B)_\Delta. \tag{11.271}$$

Putting together the upper and lower bounds on $H(A|B)_\omega$, we find that

$$H(A|B)_\sigma - H(A|B)_\rho \leq (1+\varepsilon)\, h_2\left(\frac{\varepsilon}{1+\varepsilon}\right) + \varepsilon\left[H(A|B)_{\Delta'} - H(A|B)_\Delta\right] \tag{11.272}$$

$$\leq (1+\varepsilon)\, h_2\left(\frac{\varepsilon}{1+\varepsilon}\right) + 2\varepsilon\log\dim(\mathcal{H}_A), \tag{11.273}$$

where the second inequality follows from a dimension bound for the conditional entropy (Theorem 11.5.1).

The statements for classical–quantum states follow because the density operator Δ is classical–quantum in this case and we know that $H(X|B)_\Delta, H(B|X)_\Delta \geq 0$ (see Exercise 11.9.4). $\square$

EXERCISE 11.10.1 (AFW for Coherent Information)   Prove that

$$|I(A\rangle B)_\rho - I(A\rangle B)_\sigma| \leq 2\varepsilon\log\dim(\mathcal{H}_A) + (1+\varepsilon)h_2\left(\varepsilon/\left[1+\varepsilon\right]\right), \tag{11.274}$$

with $\frac{1}{2}\|\rho_{AB} - \sigma_{AB}\|_1 \leq \varepsilon \in [0,1]$.

EXERCISE 11.10.2 (AFW for Quantum Mutual Information)   Prove that

$$|I(A;B)_\rho - I(A;B)_\sigma| \leq 3\varepsilon\log\dim(\mathcal{H}_A) + 2(1+\varepsilon)h_2\left(\varepsilon/\left[1+\varepsilon\right]\right), \tag{11.275}$$

for any ρ_{AB} and σ_{AB} with $\frac{1}{2}\|\rho_{AB} - \sigma_{AB}\|_1 \leq \varepsilon \in [0,1]$.

We can also use these results to get a refinement of the non-negativity of mutual information and the dimension upper bounds on mutual information and conditional mutual information. A refinement of the non-negativity of conditional mutual information (strong subadditivity) will appear in Chapter 12. The refinements of mutual information are quantified in terms of the trace distance between ρ_{AB} and the product of its marginals. The refinement of conditional mutual information is quantified in terms of the trace distance between ρ_{ABC} and a "recovered version" of ρ_{BC}, which represents a quantum generalization of a Markov chain. So these results represent quantum generalizations of the statements in Theorems 10.8.2 and 10.8.3.

THEOREM 11.10.4   Let $\rho_{AB} \in \mathcal{D}(\mathcal{H}_A \otimes \mathcal{H}_B)$ and let $\Delta \equiv \frac{1}{2}\|\rho_{AB} - \rho_A \otimes \rho_B\|_1$. Then

$$I(A;B) \geq \frac{2}{\ln 2}\Delta^2, \tag{11.276}$$

$$I(A;B)_\rho \leq 2\Delta \log\left[\min\left\{\dim(\mathcal{H}_A), \dim(\mathcal{H}_B)\right\}\right] + (1+\Delta)h_2(\Delta/[1+\Delta]).$$
$$\tag{11.277}$$

Proof The first inequality is a direct application of Exercise 11.8.2 and the quantum Pinsker inequality (Theorem 11.9.1). Let $\omega_{AB} \equiv \rho_A \otimes \rho_B$. The next inequality follows because

$$I(A;B)_\rho = |I(A;B)_\rho - I(A;B)_\omega| \tag{11.278}$$
$$= |H(A)_\rho - H(A|B)_\rho - [H(A)_\omega - H(A|B)_\omega]| \tag{11.279}$$
$$= |H(A|B)_\omega - H(A|B)_\rho| \tag{11.280}$$
$$\leq 2\Delta \log \dim(\mathcal{H}_A) + (1+\Delta)h_2(\Delta/[1+\Delta]), \tag{11.281}$$

where in the last line we applied Theorem 11.10.3. The other inequality

$$I(A;B)_\rho \leq 2\Delta \log \dim(\mathcal{H}_B) + (1+\Delta)h_2(\Delta/[1+\Delta]) \tag{11.282}$$

follows by expanding the mutual information in the other way.   □

THEOREM 11.10.5   Let $\rho_{ABC} \in \mathcal{D}(\mathcal{H}_A \otimes \mathcal{H}_B \otimes \mathcal{H}_C)$ and let

$$\Delta \equiv \frac{1}{2}\inf_{\mathcal{R}_{C\to AC}} \|\rho_{ABC} - \mathcal{R}_{C\to AC}(\rho_{BC})\|_1, \tag{11.283}$$

where the optimization is with respect to channels $\mathcal{R} : \mathcal{L}(\mathcal{H}_C) \to \mathcal{L}(\mathcal{H}_A \otimes \mathcal{H}_C)$. Then

$$I(A;B|C)_\rho, \; I(A;B|C)_\sigma \leq 2\Delta \log \dim(\mathcal{H}_B) + (1+\Delta)h_2(\Delta/[1+\Delta]), \quad (11.284)$$

where $\sigma_{ABC} \equiv \mathcal{R}^*_{C\to AC}(\rho_{BC})$ with $\mathcal{R}^*_{C\to AC}$ the optimal recovery channel in (11.283).

Proof Let $\Delta_\mathcal{R} \equiv \frac{1}{2}\|\rho_{ABC} - \mathcal{R}_{C\to AC}(\rho_{BC})\|_1$ for some $\mathcal{R}_{C\to AC}$ and define $\omega_{ABC} \equiv \mathcal{R}_{C\to AC}(\rho_{BC})$. Consider that

$$I(A;B|C)_\rho = H(B|C)_\rho - H(B|AC)_\rho \tag{11.285}$$
$$\leq H(B|AC)_\omega - H(B|AC)_\rho \tag{11.286}$$
$$\leq 2\Delta_\mathcal{R} \log \dim(\mathcal{H}_B) + (1+\Delta_\mathcal{R})h_2(\Delta_\mathcal{R}/[1+\Delta_\mathcal{R}]). \tag{11.287}$$

The first inequality follows from quantum data processing (Theorem 11.9.3) and the second from Theorem 11.10.3. Since the inequality holds for all recovery channels and the upper bound is monotone non-decreasing in $\Delta_\mathcal{R}$, we can conclude the inequality in the statement of the theorem. Now consider that

$$I(A;B|C)_\sigma = H(B|C)_\sigma - H(B|AC)_\sigma \tag{11.288}$$
$$\leq H(B|C)_\sigma - H(B|C)_\rho \tag{11.289}$$
$$\leq 2\Delta \log \dim(\mathcal{H}_B) + (1+\Delta)h_2(\Delta/[1+\Delta]). \tag{11.290}$$

The justifications for these inequalities are the same as those for the above ones (we additionally need to use monotonicity of the trace distance with respect to partial trace).   □

11.11   History and Further Reading

The quantum entropy and its relatives, such as conditional entropy and mutual information, are useful information measures and suffice for our studies in this book. However, the quantum entropy is certainly not the only information measure worthy of study. In recent years, entropic measures such as the min- and max-entropy have emerged (and their smoothed variants), and they are useful in developing a more general theory that applies beyond the i.i.d. setting that we study in this book. In fact, one could view this theory as more fundamental than the theory presented in this book, since the "one-shot" results often imply the i.i.d. results studied in this book. Rather than developing this theory in full, we point to several excellent references on the subject (Renner, 2005; Datta, 2009; Datta & Renner, 2009; Koenig et al., 2009; Tomamichel, 2016).

The fact that the conditional entropy can be negative is discussed in Wehrl (1978), Horodecki & Horodecki (1994), and Cerf & Adami (1997). Holevo (1973a) proved the important bound bearing his name. Only later was it understood that this bound is a consequence of the monotonicity of quantum relative entropy. Lieb & Ruskai (1973b; see also Lieb & Ruskai, 1973a) established the strong subadditivity of quantum entropy and concavity of conditional quantum entropy by invoking an earlier result of Lieb (1973), and Lieb & Ruskai (1973b) also showed that the monotonicity of quantum relative entropy with respect to partial trace is a consequence of the concavity of conditional quantum entropy (the proof of this given in Theorem 11.9.2 is due to them). Araki & Lieb (1970) proved the inequality in Exercise 11.7.10. Umegaki (1962) established the modern definition of the quantum relative entropy. The fact that it is non-negative for states is a result known as Klein's inequality (see Lanford & Robinson, 1968, for attribution to Klein). Lindblad (1975) established the monotonicity of quantum relative entropy for separable Hilbert spaces based on the results of Lieb & Ruskai (1973b), Lieb & Ruskai (1973a), and Uhlmann (1977) extended Lindblad's result to more general settings. Coles, Colbeck, Yu & Zwolak (2012) proved Proposition 11.8.2. Ohya & Petz (1993, Theorem 1.15) proved the quantum Pinsker inequality (stated here as Theorem 11.9.1). The coherent information first appeared in Schumacher & Nielsen (1996), where they proved that it obeys a quantum data-processing inequality (this was the first clue that the coherent information would be an important information quantity for characterizing quantum capacity).

Entropic uncertainty relations have a long and interesting history. We do not review this history here but instead point to the survey article (Coles et al., 2015). There has been much interest in entropic uncertainty relations, with perhaps the most notable advance being the entropic uncertainty relation in the presence of quantum memory (Berta et al., 2010). The proof that we give for Theorem 11.9.5 is the same as that in Coles et al. (2012), which in turn exploits ideas from Tomamichel & Renner (2011).

Fannes (1973) proved his eponymous inequality, and Audenaert (2007) gave a significant improvement of it. Winter (2015a) proved the inequality in Theorem 11.10.3. Earlier, Alicki & Fannes (2004) proved a weaker version of the inequality in Theorem 11.10.3 (which, however, has been extremely useful for many purposes in quantum information theory). Berta, Seshadreesan & Wilde (2015) proved Theorem 11.10.5 (see also Fawzi & Renner, 2015).

12 Quantum Entropy Inequalities and Recoverability

The quantum entropy inequalities discussed in the previous chapter lie at the core of quantum Shannon theory and in fact underlie some important principles of physics such as the uncertainty principle (see Section 11.9.3). In fact, we will use these entropy inequalities to prove the converse parts of every coding theorem appearing in the last two parts of this book. Their prominence in both quantum Shannon theory and other areas of physics motivates us to study them in more detail. We delved into more depth in Chapter 10 regarding many of the classical entropy inequalities and, in the process, we established necessary and sufficient conditions for the saturation of the inequalities (Section 10.7.1) while also understanding the near saturation of the entropy inequalities (Section 10.8). The aim of this chapter is to carry out a similar program for all of the quantum entropy inequalities presented in the previous chapter. The outcome will be a proof for the monotonicity of quantum relative entropy (Theorem 11.8.1), with the added benefit of an understanding of the saturation and near saturation of this quantum entropy inequality.

12.1 Recoverability Theorem

The main theorem in this chapter can be summarized informally as follows: if the decrease in quantum relative entropy between two quantum states after a quantum channel acts is relatively small, then it is possible to perform a recovery channel such that we can perfectly recover one state while approximately recovering the other. This can be interpreted as quantifying how well one can reverse the action of a quantum channel. Throughout, we take ρ, σ, and $\mathcal{N}$ as given in the following definition:

DEFINITION 12.1.1 Let $\rho \in \mathcal{D}(\mathcal{H})$ and let $\sigma \in \mathcal{L}(\mathcal{H})$ be positive semi-definite, such that $\operatorname{supp}(\rho) \subseteq \operatorname{supp}(\sigma)$. Let $\mathcal{N} : \mathcal{L}(\mathcal{H}) \to \mathcal{L}(\mathcal{H}')$ be a quantum channel.

The formal statement of the theorem is as follows:

THEOREM 12.1.1 Given ρ, σ, and $\mathcal{N}$ as in Definition 12.1.1, there exists a recovery channel $\mathcal{R}_{\sigma,\mathcal{N}} : \mathcal{L}(\mathcal{H}') \to \mathcal{L}(\mathcal{H})$, depending only on σ and $\mathcal{N}$, such that

$$D(\rho\|\sigma) - D(\mathcal{N}(\rho)\|\mathcal{N}(\sigma)) \geq -\log F(\rho, (\mathcal{R}_{\sigma,\mathcal{N}} \circ \mathcal{N})(\rho)), \quad \text{and} \qquad (12.1)$$

$$(\mathcal{R}_{\sigma,\mathcal{N}} \circ \mathcal{N})(\sigma) = \sigma. \qquad (12.2)$$

Given that the quantum fidelity F takes values between zero and one, we can immediately conclude that

$$-\log F(\rho, (\mathcal{R}_{\sigma,\mathcal{N}} \circ \mathcal{N})(\rho)) \geq 0, \qquad (12.3)$$

so that the above theorem implies the monotonicity of quantum relative entropy (Theorem 11.8.1) as a consequence. Furthermore, the recovery channel satisfying (12.1) has the property that it perfectly recovers σ from $\mathcal{N}(\sigma)$, satisfying (12.2): a fact which we prove later and which makes the inequality in (12.1) nontrivial.

The proof given here for Theorem 12.1.1 relies on the method of complex interpolation and the notion of a Rényi generalization of a relative entropy difference. We review this background first before going through the proof. One of the consequences of Theorem 12.1.1 is to provide physically meaningful improvements to many quantum entropy inequalities discussed in the previous chapter, such as strong subadditivity, joint convexity of quantum-relative entropy, and concavity of conditional quantum entropy. We explore these consequences in Section 12.6.

12.2   Schatten Norms and Complex Interpolation

The proof of Theorem 12.1.1 given here requires a bit of mathematical background before we can delve into it. So we first begin by defining the Schatten norms and several of their properties. We then review some essential results from complex analysis, that lead to a complex interpolation theorem known as the Stein–Hirschman interpolation theorem.

12.2.1   Schatten Norms and Duality

An important technical tool in the proof given here is the Schatten p-norm of an operator A, defined as

$$\|A\|_p \equiv [\mathrm{Tr}\,\{|A|^p\}]^{1/p}, \qquad (12.4)$$

where $A \in \mathcal{L}(\mathcal{H})$, $|A| \equiv \sqrt{A^\dagger A}$, and $p \geq 1$. We have already studied two special cases of this norm, which are the trace norm when $p = 1$ (Section 9.1.1) and the Hilbert–Schmidt norm when $p = 2$ (Section 9.6). One can show, along the same lines as the proof for Proposition 9.1.1, that $\|A\|_p$ is equal to the p-norm of the singular values of A. That is, if $\sigma_i(A)$ is the vector of singular values of A, then

$$\|A\|_p = \left[\sum_i \sigma_i(A)^p\right]^{1/p}. \qquad (12.5)$$

The convention is for $\|A\|_\infty$ to be defined as the largest singular value of A because $\|A\|_p$ converges to this in the limit as $p \to \infty$. In the proof of

Theorem 12.1.1, we repeatedly use the fact that $\|A\|_p$ is unitarily invariant. That is, $\|A\|_p$ is invariant with respect to linear isometries in the sense that $\|A\|_p = \|UAV^\dagger\|_p$, where $U, V \in \mathcal{L}(\mathcal{H}, \mathcal{H}')$ are linear isometries satisfying $U^\dagger U = I_\mathcal{H}$ and $V^\dagger V = I_\mathcal{H}$. Isometric invariance follows from (12.5) and because these isometries do not change the singular values of A. From these norms, one can define information measures relating quantum states and channels, with the main one used here known as a Rényi generalization of a relative entropy difference.

Extending the Cauchy–Schwarz inequality is an important inequality known as the Hölder inequality:

$$|\langle A, B \rangle| = \left|\text{Tr}\{A^\dagger B\}\right| \leq \|A\|_p \|B\|_q, \tag{12.6}$$

holding for $p, q \in [1, \infty]$ such that $\frac{1}{p} + \frac{1}{q} = 1$ and $A, B \in \mathcal{L}(\mathcal{H})$. When $p, q \in [1, \infty]$ and $\frac{1}{p} + \frac{1}{q} = 1$, p and q are said to be Hölder conjugates of each other. One can see that Cauchy–Schwarz is a special case by picking $p = q = 2$. Observe that equality is achieved in (12.6) if A and B are such that $A^\dagger = a \, |B|^{q/p} \, U^\dagger$ for some constant $a \geq 0$ and where U is a unitary such that $B = U \, |B|$ is a left polar decomposition of B (see Theorem A.0.1). The Hölder inequality along with the sufficient equality condition is enough for us to conclude the following variational expression for the p-norm in terms of its Hölder dual q-norm:

$$\|A\|_p = \max_{\|B\|_q \leq 1} \text{Tr}\{A^\dagger B\}. \tag{12.7}$$

This expression can be very useful in calculations.

EXERCISE 12.2.1 Prove that $\|AB\|_1 \leq \|A\|_p \|B\|_q$ for $p, q \in [1, \infty]$ such that $\frac{1}{p} + \frac{1}{q} = 1$ and $A, B \in \mathcal{L}(\mathcal{H})$.

Throughout we adopt the convention from Definition 3.3.1 and define $f(A)$ for a function f and a positive semi-definite operator A as follows: $f(A) \equiv \sum_{i:\lambda_i \neq 0} f(\lambda_i)|i\rangle\langle i|$, where $A = \sum_i \lambda_i |i\rangle\langle i|$ is a spectral decomposition of A. We denote the support of A by $\text{supp}(A)$, and we let Π_A denote the projection onto the support of A.

12.2.2 Complex Analysis

We now review a few concepts from complex analysis. We will not prove these results in detail, but the purpose instead is to recall them, and the interested reader can follow references to books on complex analysis for details of proofs. The culmination of the development is the Stein–Hirschman complex interpolation theorem (Theorem 12.2.3).

The derivative of a complex-valued function $f : \mathbb{C} \to \mathbb{C}$ at a point $z_0 \in \mathbb{C}$ is defined in the usual way as

$$\left.\frac{df(z)}{dz}\right|_{z=z_0} = \lim_{z \to z_0} \frac{f(z) - f(z_0)}{z - z_0}. \tag{12.8}$$

In order for this limit to exist, it must be the same for all possible directions that one could take in the complex plane to approach z_0, and this requirement demarcates a substantial difference between differentiability of real functions and complex ones. Complex differentiability shares several properties with real differentiability: it is linear and obeys the product rule, the quotient rule, and the chain rule. If f is complex differentiable at every point z_0 in an open set U, then we say that f is *holomorphic* on U.

There is a connection between real differentiability and complex differentiability, given by the Cauchy–Riemann equations. Let $f(x+iy) = u(x,y) + iv(x,y)$ where $x, y \in \mathbb{R}$ and $u, v : \mathbb{R} \to \mathbb{R}$. If f is holomorphic, then u and v have first partial derivatives with respect to x and y and satisfy the Cauchy–Riemann equations:

$$\frac{\partial u}{\partial x} = \frac{\partial v}{\partial y}, \qquad \frac{\partial u}{\partial y} = -\frac{\partial v}{\partial x}. \tag{12.9}$$

The converse is not always true. However, if the first partial derivatives of u and v are continuous and satisfy the Cauchy–Riemann equations, then f is holomorphic. An important holomorphic function for our purposes is given in the following exercise:

EXERCISE 12.2.2   Verify that $f(z) = a^z = e^{[\ln a]z}$, where $a > 0$ and $z \in \mathbb{C}$, is a holomorphic function everywhere in the complex plane. (Hint: Use that $e^z = e^x [\cos(y) + i\sin(y)]$ for $z = x + iy$ and $x, y \in \mathbb{R}$.)

Holomorphic functions have good closure properties. That is, the sums, products, and compositions of holomorphic functions are holomorphic as well, given that complex differentiation is linear and satisfies the product, quotient, and chain rules. Note that the quotient of two holomorphic functions is holomorphic wherever the denominator is not equal to zero.

The *maximum modulus principle* is an important principle that holomorphic functions obey. Formally, it is the following statement: let $f : \mathbb{C} \to \mathbb{C}$ be a function holomorphic on some connected, bounded open subset U of $\mathbb{C}$. If $z_0 \in U$ is such that $|f(z_0)| \geq |f(z)|$ for all z in a neighborhood of z_0, then the function f is constant on U. A consequence of this is that if f is not constant on a bounded, connected, open subset U of $\mathbb{C}$, then it achieves its maximum on the boundary of U.

The maximum modulus principle has an extension to an unbounded strip in $\mathbb{C}$, which we call the *maximum modulus principle on a strip*. Let S denote the standard strip in $\mathbb{C}$, $\overline{S}$ its closure, and $\partial \overline{S}$ its boundary:

$$S \equiv \{z \in \mathbb{C} : 0 < \operatorname{Re}\{z\} < 1\}, \tag{12.10}$$

$$\overline{S} \equiv \{z \in \mathbb{C} : 0 \leq \operatorname{Re}\{z\} \leq 1\}, \tag{12.11}$$

$$\partial \overline{S} \equiv \{z \in \mathbb{C} : \operatorname{Re}\{z\} = 0 \vee \operatorname{Re}\{z\} = 1\}. \tag{12.12}$$

Let $f : \overline{S} \to \mathbb{C}$ be bounded on $\overline{S}$, holomorphic on S, and continuous on $\partial \overline{S}$. Then the supremum of $|f|$ is attained on $\partial \overline{S}$. That is, $\sup_{z \in \overline{S}} |f(z)| = \sup_{z \in \partial \overline{S}} |f(z)|$.

The maximum modulus principle on a strip implies a result known as the Hadamard three-lines theorem:

THEOREM 12.2.1 (Hadamard Three-Lines) Let $f : \overline{S} \to \mathbb{C}$ be a function that is bounded on $\overline{S}$, holomorphic on S, and continuous on the boundary $\partial \overline{S}$. Let $\theta \in (0,1)$ and $M(\theta) \equiv \sup_{t \in \mathbb{R}} |f(\theta + it)|$. Then $\ln M(\theta)$ is a convex function on $[0,1]$, implying that

$$\ln M(\theta) \leq (1 - \theta) \ln M(0) + \theta \ln M(1). \tag{12.13}$$

There is a strengthening of the Hadamard three-lines theorem due to Hirschman, which in fact implies the Hadamard three-lines theorem:

THEOREM 12.2.2 (Hirschman) Let $f(z) : \overline{S} \to \mathbb{C}$ be a function that is bounded on $\overline{S}$, holomorphic on S, and continuous on the boundary $\partial \overline{S}$. Then for $\theta \in (0,1)$, the following bound holds:

$$\ln |f(\theta)| \leq \int_{-\infty}^{\infty} dt \, \left(\alpha_\theta(t) \ln \left[|f(it)|^{1-\theta} \right] + \beta_\theta(t) \ln \left[|f(1 + it)|^{\theta} \right] \right), \tag{12.14}$$

where

$$\alpha_\theta(t) \equiv \frac{\sin(\pi\theta)}{2(1 - \theta)\left[\cosh(\pi t) - \cos(\pi\theta) \right]}, \tag{12.15}$$

$$\beta_\theta(t) \equiv \frac{\sin(\pi\theta)}{2\theta\left[\cosh(\pi t) + \cos(\pi\theta) \right]}. \tag{12.16}$$

For a fixed $\theta \in (0,1)$, we have that $\alpha_\theta(t), \beta_\theta(t) \geq 0$ for all $t \in \mathbb{R}$ and

$$\int_{-\infty}^{\infty} dt \, \alpha_\theta(t) = \int_{-\infty}^{\infty} dt \, \beta_\theta(t) = 1 , \tag{12.17}$$

(see, e.g., Grafakos, 2008, Exercise 1.3.8) so that $\alpha_\theta(t)$ and $\beta_\theta(t)$ can be interpreted as probability density functions. Furthermore, we have that

$$\lim_{\theta \searrow 0} \beta_\theta(t) = \frac{\pi}{2} \left[\cosh(\pi t) + 1 \right]^{-1} \equiv \beta_0(t) , \tag{12.18}$$

where β_0 is also a probability density function on $\mathbb{R}$. With these observations, we can see that Hirschman's theorem implies the Hadamard three-lines theorem, given that an expectation can never exceed a supremum.

12.2.3   Complex Interpolation of Schatten Norms

We can extend much of the development above to operator-valued functions, which is needed to prove Theorem 12.1.1. Let $G : \mathbb{C} \to \mathcal{L}(\mathcal{H})$ be an operator-valued function. We say that $G(z)$ is holomorphic if every function mapping z to a matrix entry is holomorphic. For our purposes in what follows, we are interested in operator-valued functions of the form A^z, where A is a positive semi-definite operator. In this case, we apply the convention from Definition 3.3.1 and take $A^z = \sum_{i : \lambda_i \neq 0} \lambda_i^z |i\rangle\langle i|$, where $A = \sum_i \lambda_i |i\rangle\langle i|$ is an eigendecomposition of A with

$\lambda_i \geq 0$ for all i. Given the result of Exercise 12.2.2 combined with the closure properties of holomorphic functions mentioned above, we can conclude that A^z is holomorphic if A is positive semi-definite.

We can now establish a version of the Hirschman theorem which applies to operator-valued functions and allows for bounding their Schatten norms. This is one of the main technical tools that we need to establish Theorem 12.1.1.

THEOREM 12.2.3 (Stein–Hirschman)   Let $G : \overline{S} \rightarrow L(\mathcal{H})$ be an operator-valued function that is bounded on $\overline{S}$, holomorphic on S, and continuous on the boundary $\partial \overline{S}$. Let $\theta \in (0, 1)$ and define p_θ by

$$\frac{1}{p_\theta} = \frac{1-\theta}{p_0} + \frac{\theta}{p_1} , \tag{12.19}$$

where $p_0, p_1 \in [1, \infty]$. Then the following bound holds:

$$\ln \|G(\theta)\|_{p_\theta} \leq \int_{-\infty}^{\infty} dt \left(\alpha_\theta(t) \ln \left[\|G(it)\|_{p_0}^{1-\theta} \right] + \beta_\theta(t) \ln \left[\|G(1+it)\|_{p_1}^{\theta} \right] \right) , \tag{12.20}$$

where $\alpha_\theta(t)$ and $\beta_\theta(t)$ are defined in (12.15)–(12.16).

Proof   For fixed $\theta \in (0, 1)$, let q_θ be the Hölder conjugate of p_θ, defined by

$$\frac{1}{p_\theta} + \frac{1}{q_\theta} = 1 . \tag{12.21}$$

Similarly, let q_0 and q_1 be Hölder conjugates of p_0 and p_1, respectively. From the sufficient equality condition for the Hölder inequality, we can find an operator X such that $\|X\|_{q_\theta} = 1$ and $\mathrm{Tr}\{XG(\theta)\} = \|G(\theta)\|_{p_\theta}$. We can write the singular value decomposition for X in the form $X = UD^{1/q_\theta}V$ (implying $\mathrm{Tr}\{D\} = 1$). For $z \in S$, define

$$X(z) \equiv UD^{\frac{1-z}{q_0} + \frac{z}{q_1}}V . \tag{12.22}$$

As a consequence, $X(z)$ is bounded on $\overline{S}$, holomorphic on S, and continuous on the boundary $\partial \overline{S}$. Also, observe that $X(\theta) = X$. Then the following function satisfies the requirements needed to apply Theorem 12.2.2:

$$g(z) \equiv \mathrm{Tr}\{X(z)G(z)\} . \tag{12.23}$$

Indeed, we have that

$$\ln \|G(\theta)\|_{p_\theta} = \ln |g(\theta)| \tag{12.24}$$

$$\leq \int_{-\infty}^{\infty} dt \left(\alpha_\theta(t) \ln \left[|g(it)|^{1-\theta} \right] + \beta_\theta(t) \ln \left[|g(1+it)|^{\theta} \right] \right). \tag{12.25}$$

Now, from applying Hölder's inequality and the facts that $\|X(it)\|_{q_0} = 1 = \|X(1+it)\|_{q_1}$, we find that

$$|g(it)| = |\mathrm{Tr}\{X(it)G(it)\}| \leq \|X(it)\|_{q_0} \|G(it)\|_{p_0} = \|G(it)\|_{p_0} , \tag{12.26}$$

and

$$|g(1 + it)| = |\text{Tr}\{X(1 + it)G(1 + it)\}| \tag{12.27}$$

$$\leq \|X(1 + it)\|_{q_1} \|G(1 + it)\|_{p_1} \tag{12.28}$$

$$= \|G(1 + it)\|_{p_1}. \tag{12.29}$$

Bounding (12.25) from above using these inequalities then gives (12.20). $\qquad\square$

The theorem above is known as a complex interpolation theorem because it allows us to obtain estimates on the "intermediate" norm in terms of other norms which might be available. Furthermore, we are interpolating through the holomorphic family of operators given by $G(z)$.

12.3 Petz Recovery Map

The channel appearing in the lower bound of Theorem 12.1.1 has an explicit form and is constructed from a map known as the Petz recovery map, which we define as follows:

DEFINITION 12.3.1 Let $\sigma \in \mathcal{L}(\mathcal{H})$ be positive semi-definite, and let $\mathcal{N} : \mathcal{L}(\mathcal{H}) \to \mathcal{L}(\mathcal{H}')$ be a quantum channel. The Petz recovery map $\mathcal{P}_{\sigma,\mathcal{N}} : \mathcal{L}(\mathcal{H}') \to \mathcal{L}(\mathcal{H})$ is a completely positive, trace-non-increasing linear map defined as follows for $Q \in \mathcal{L}(\mathcal{H}')$:

$$\mathcal{P}_{\sigma,\mathcal{N}}(Q) \equiv \sigma^{1/2} \mathcal{N}^\dagger \left([\mathcal{N}(\sigma)]^{-1/2} Q [\mathcal{N}(\sigma)]^{-1/2} \right) \sigma^{1/2}. \tag{12.30}$$

The Petz recovery map $\mathcal{P}_{\sigma,\mathcal{N}}$ is linear, and it is completely positive because it is equal to a serial concatenation of three completely positive maps: $Q \to [\mathcal{N}(\sigma)]^{-1/2} Q [\mathcal{N}(\sigma)]^{-1/2}$, $Q \to \mathcal{N}^\dagger(Q)$, and $M \to \sigma^{1/2} M \sigma^{1/2}$ for $M \in \mathcal{L}(\mathcal{H})$. It is trace-non-increasing because the following holds for positive semi-definite Q:

$$\text{Tr}\{\mathcal{P}_{\sigma,\mathcal{N}}(Q)\} = \text{Tr}\left\{\sigma \mathcal{N}^\dagger \left([\mathcal{N}(\sigma)]^{-1/2} Q [\mathcal{N}(\sigma)]^{-1/2} \right) \right\} \tag{12.31}$$

$$= \text{Tr}\left\{ \mathcal{N}(\sigma) [\mathcal{N}(\sigma)]^{-1/2} Q [\mathcal{N}(\sigma)]^{-1/2} \right\} \tag{12.32}$$

$$= \text{Tr}\{\Pi_{\mathcal{N}(\sigma)} Q\} \leq \text{Tr}\{Q\}. \tag{12.33}$$

An important special case of the Petz recovery map occurs when σ and $\mathcal{N}$ are effectively classical. That is, suppose that $\mathcal{N}$ is a classical-to-classical channel with Kraus operators $\{\sqrt{N(y|x)}|y\rangle\langle x|\}$ (see Section 4.6.4), where $N(y|x)$ is a conditional probability distribution. Suppose further that $\sigma = \sum_x q(x)|x\rangle\langle x|$, with $q(x) \geq 0$ for all x. In this case, one can check that the Petz recovery map is a classical-to-classical channel with Kraus operators $\{\sqrt{R(x|y)}|x\rangle\langle y|\}$, where $R(x|y)$ is a conditional probability distribution given by the Bayes theorem, satisfying

$$R(x|y)(Nq)(y) = N(y|x)q(x) \tag{12.34}$$

for all x and y, where $(Nq)(y) = \sum_x N(y|x)q(x)$. We leave the details of this calculation as an exercise for the reader and point out that this recovery channel appears in the refinement of the monotonicity of classical relative entropy from Theorem 10.8.4.

We can also define a partial isometric map $\mathcal{U}_{\sigma,t}$ in the following way:

$$\mathcal{U}_{\sigma,t}(M) \equiv \sigma^{it} M \sigma^{-it}. \tag{12.35}$$

Since $\sigma^{it}\sigma^{-it} = \Pi_\sigma$, we can conclude that

$$\mathcal{U}_{\sigma,t}(\sigma) = \sigma, \tag{12.36}$$

so that this isometric map does not have any effect when σ is input. In the case that σ is positive definite, $\mathcal{U}_{\sigma,t}$ is a unitary channel. We can then define a rotated or "swiveled" Petz map, which plays an important role in the construction of a recovery channel satisfying the lower bound in Theorem 12.1.1.

DEFINITION 12.3.2 (Rotated Petz Map)   Let $\sigma \in \mathcal{L}(\mathcal{H})$ be positive semi-definite, and let $\mathcal{N} : \mathcal{L}(\mathcal{H}) \to \mathcal{L}(\mathcal{H}')$ be a quantum channel. A rotated Petz map is defined as follows for $Q \in \mathcal{L}(\mathcal{H}')$:

$$\mathcal{R}^t_{\sigma,\mathcal{N}}(Q) \equiv (\mathcal{U}_{\sigma,-t} \circ \mathcal{P}_{\sigma,\mathcal{N}} \circ \mathcal{U}_{\mathcal{N}(\sigma),t})(Q). \tag{12.37}$$

PROPOSITION 12.3.1 (Perfect Recovery)   Let $\sigma \in \mathcal{L}(\mathcal{H})$ be positive semi-definite, and let $\mathcal{N} : \mathcal{L}(\mathcal{H}) \to \mathcal{L}(\mathcal{H}')$ be a quantum channel. A rotated Petz map $\mathcal{R}^t_{\sigma,\mathcal{N}}$ perfectly recovers σ from $\mathcal{N}(\sigma)$:

$$\mathcal{R}^t_{\sigma,\mathcal{N}}(\mathcal{N}(\sigma)) = \sigma. \tag{12.38}$$

Proof   Consider that

$$\mathcal{P}_{\sigma,\mathcal{N}}(\mathcal{N}(\sigma)) = \sigma^{1/2}\mathcal{N}^\dagger \left([\mathcal{N}(\sigma)]^{-1/2} \, \mathcal{N}(\sigma) \, [\mathcal{N}(\sigma)]^{-1/2} \right) \sigma^{1/2} \tag{12.39}$$

$$= \sigma^{1/2}\mathcal{N}^\dagger (\Pi_{\mathcal{N}(\sigma)})\sigma^{1/2} \tag{12.40}$$

$$\leq \sigma^{1/2}\mathcal{N}^\dagger (I)\sigma^{1/2} = \sigma^{1/2}I\sigma^{1/2} = \sigma. \tag{12.41}$$

The inequality follows because $\Pi_{\mathcal{N}(\sigma)} \leq I$ and $\mathcal{N}^\dagger$ is a completely positive map. The second to last equality follows because the adjoint is unital.

Now we prove the other operator inequality $\mathcal{P}_{\sigma,\mathcal{N}}(\mathcal{N}(\sigma)) \geq \sigma$, which will allow us to conclude that $\mathcal{P}_{\sigma,\mathcal{N}}(\mathcal{N}(\sigma)) = \sigma$. Let $U : \mathcal{H} \to \mathcal{H}' \otimes \mathcal{H}_E$ be an isometric extension of the channel $\mathcal{N}$. From Lemma A.0.4, we know that $\mathrm{supp}(U\sigma U^\dagger) \subseteq \mathrm{supp}(\mathcal{N}(\sigma) \otimes I_E)$, which implies that $\Pi_{U\sigma U^\dagger} \leq \Pi_{\mathcal{N}(\sigma)\otimes I_E} = \Pi_{\mathcal{N}(\sigma)} \otimes I_E$. Then for any vector $|\psi\rangle \in \mathcal{H}$, we have that

$$\langle\psi|\Pi_\sigma|\psi\rangle = \langle\psi|U^\dagger\Pi_{U\sigma U^\dagger} U|\psi\rangle \tag{12.42}$$

$$\leq \langle\psi|U^\dagger \left(\Pi_{\mathcal{N}(\sigma)} \otimes I_E \right) U|\psi\rangle \tag{12.43}$$

$$= \mathrm{Tr}\{U|\psi\rangle\langle\psi|U^\dagger \left(\Pi_{\mathcal{N}(\sigma)} \otimes I_E \right)\} \tag{12.44}$$

$$= \mathrm{Tr}\{\mathcal{N}(|\psi\rangle\langle\psi|)\Pi_{\mathcal{N}(\sigma)}\} \tag{12.45}$$

$$= \mathrm{Tr}\{|\psi\rangle\langle\psi|\mathcal{N}^\dagger(\Pi_{\mathcal{N}(\sigma)})\} \qquad (12.46)$$

$$= \langle\psi|\mathcal{N}^\dagger(\Pi_{\mathcal{N}(\sigma)})|\psi\rangle. \qquad (12.47)$$

Since $|\psi\rangle$ is arbitrary, this establishes that $\Pi_\sigma \leq \mathcal{N}^\dagger(\Pi_{\mathcal{N}(\sigma)})$. We can then use this operator inequality to see that

$$\mathcal{P}_{\sigma,\mathcal{N}}(\mathcal{N}(\sigma)) = \sigma^{1/2}\mathcal{N}^\dagger(\Pi_{\mathcal{N}(\sigma)})\sigma^{1/2} \qquad (12.48)$$

$$\geq \sigma^{1/2}\Pi_\sigma\sigma^{1/2} = \sigma. \qquad (12.49)$$

Finally, we can conclude that

$$\mathcal{R}_{\sigma,\mathcal{N}}^t(\mathcal{N}(\sigma)) = (\mathcal{U}_{\sigma,-t}\circ\mathcal{P}_{\sigma,\mathcal{N}}\circ\mathcal{U}_{\mathcal{N}(\sigma),t})(\mathcal{N}(\sigma)) \qquad (12.50)$$

$$= (\mathcal{U}_{\sigma,-t}\circ\mathcal{P}_{\sigma,\mathcal{N}})(\mathcal{N}(\sigma)) \qquad (12.51)$$

$$= \mathcal{U}_{\sigma,-t}(\sigma) = \sigma, \qquad (12.52)$$

where the second and last equalities follow from (12.36). □

EXERCISE 12.3.1   Verify that a rotated Petz map satisfies the following:

$$\mathrm{Tr}\{\mathcal{R}_{\sigma,\mathcal{N}}^t(Q)\} = \mathrm{Tr}\{\Pi_{\mathcal{N}(\sigma)}Q\} \leq \mathrm{Tr}\{Q\}, \qquad (12.53)$$

for positive semi-definite $Q \in \mathcal{L}(\mathcal{H}')$, which implies that it is trace-non-increasing.

EXERCISE 12.3.2   Let ω be positive semi-definite and let $\langle A, B\rangle_\omega \equiv \mathrm{Tr}\{A^\dagger\omega^{1/2}B\omega^{1/2}\}$. The adjoint of the Petz recovery map (with respect to the Hilbert–Schmidt inner product) is equal to

$$\mathcal{P}_{\sigma,\mathcal{N}}^\dagger(M) = [\mathcal{N}(\sigma)]^{-1/2}\mathcal{N}\left(\sigma^{1/2}M\sigma^{1/2}\right)[\mathcal{N}(\sigma)]^{-1/2}, \qquad (12.54)$$

where $M \in \mathcal{L}(\mathcal{H})$. Show that $\mathcal{P}_{\sigma,\mathcal{N}}^\dagger$ is the unique linear map with domain $\mathrm{supp}(\sigma)$ and range $\mathrm{supp}(\mathcal{N}(\sigma))$, which satisfies the following for all $M \in \mathcal{L}(\mathcal{H})$ and $Q \in \mathcal{L}(\mathcal{H}')$:

$$\langle M, \mathcal{N}^\dagger(Q)\rangle_\sigma = \langle\mathcal{P}_{\sigma,\mathcal{N}}^\dagger(M), Q\rangle_{\mathcal{N}(\sigma)}. \qquad (12.55)$$

(Hint: Consider picking $M = |i\rangle\langle j|$ and $Q = |k\rangle\langle l|$.)

12.4   Rényi Information Measure

Given ρ, σ, and $\mathcal{N}$ as in Definition 12.1.1, we define a Rényi information measure $\widetilde{\Delta}_\alpha$ known as a Rényi generalization of a relative entropy difference:

$$\widetilde{\Delta}_\alpha(\rho,\sigma,\mathcal{N}) \equiv \frac{1}{\alpha-1}\ln\widetilde{Q}_\alpha(\rho,\sigma,\mathcal{N}), \qquad (12.56)$$

$$\widetilde{Q}_\alpha(\rho,\sigma,\mathcal{N}) \equiv \left\|\left([\mathcal{N}(\rho)]^{\frac{1-\alpha}{2\alpha}}[\mathcal{N}(\sigma)]^{\frac{\alpha-1}{2\alpha}}\otimes I_E\right)U\sigma^{\frac{1-\alpha}{2\alpha}}\rho^{1/2}\right\|_{2\alpha}^{2\alpha}, \qquad (12.57)$$

where $\alpha \in (0,1)\cup(1,\infty)$ and $U : \mathcal{H} \to \mathcal{H}'\otimes\mathcal{H}_E$ is an isometric extension of the channel $\mathcal{N}$. That is, U is a linear isometry satisfying $\mathrm{Tr}_E\{U(\cdot)U^\dagger\} = \mathcal{N}(\cdot)$

and $U^\dagger U = I_{\mathcal{H}}$. Recall that all isometric extensions of a channel are related by an isometry acting on the environment system E, so that the definition in (12.56) is invariant under any such choice. Recall from Proposition 5.2.1 that the adjoint $\mathcal{N}^\dagger$ of a channel is given in terms of an isometric extension U as $\mathcal{N}^\dagger(\cdot) = U^\dagger ((\cdot) \otimes I_E) U$.

The following lemma is one of the main reasons that we say that $\tilde{\Delta}_\alpha(\rho, \sigma, \mathcal{N})$ is a Rényi generalization of a relative entropy difference.

LEMMA 12.4.1   The following limit holds for ρ, σ, and $\mathcal{N}$ as given in Definition 12.1.1:

$$\frac{1}{\ln 2} \lim_{\alpha \to 1} \tilde{\Delta}_\alpha(\rho, \sigma, \mathcal{N}) = D(\rho \| \sigma) - D(\mathcal{N}(\rho) \| \mathcal{N}(\sigma)). \tag{12.58}$$

Proof Let Π_ω denote the projection onto the support of ω. From the condition $\operatorname{supp}(\rho) \subseteq \operatorname{supp}(\sigma)$, it follows that $\operatorname{supp}(\mathcal{N}(\rho)) \subseteq \operatorname{supp}(\mathcal{N}(\sigma))$ (see Lemma A.0.5). We can then conclude that

$$\Pi_\sigma \Pi_\rho = \Pi_\rho, \qquad \Pi_{\mathcal{N}(\rho)} \Pi_{\mathcal{N}(\sigma)} = \Pi_{\mathcal{N}(\rho)}. \tag{12.59}$$

We also know that $\operatorname{supp}(U\rho U^\dagger) \subseteq \operatorname{supp}(\mathcal{N}(\rho) \otimes I_E)$ (see Lemma A.0.4), so that

$$\left(\Pi_{\mathcal{N}(\rho)} \otimes I_E \right) \Pi_{U\rho U^\dagger} = \Pi_{U\rho U^\dagger}. \tag{12.60}$$

When $\alpha = 1$, we find from the above facts that

$$\tilde{Q}_1(\rho, \sigma, \mathcal{N}) = \left\| \left(\Pi_{\mathcal{N}(\rho)} \Pi_{\mathcal{N}(\sigma)} \otimes I_E \right) U \Pi_\sigma \rho^{1/2} \right\|_2^2 \tag{12.61}$$

$$= \left\| \left(\Pi_{\mathcal{N}(\rho)} \otimes I_E \right) U \Pi_\rho \rho^{1/2} \right\|_2^2 \tag{12.62}$$

$$= \left\| \left(\Pi_{\mathcal{N}(\rho)} \otimes I_E \right) \Pi_{U\rho U^\dagger} U \rho^{1/2} \right\|_2^2 \tag{12.63}$$

$$= \left\| \Pi_{U\rho U^\dagger} U \rho^{1/2} \right\|_2^2 = \left\| \rho^{1/2} \right\|_2^2 = 1. \tag{12.64}$$

So from the definition of the derivative, this means that

$$\lim_{\alpha \to 1} \tilde{\Delta}_\alpha(\rho, \sigma, \mathcal{N}) = \lim_{\alpha \to 1} \frac{\ln \tilde{Q}_\alpha(\rho, \sigma, \mathcal{N}) - \ln \tilde{Q}_1(\rho, \sigma, \mathcal{N})}{\alpha - 1} \tag{12.65}$$

$$= \frac{d}{d\alpha} \left[\ln \tilde{Q}_\alpha(\rho, \sigma, \mathcal{N}) \right] \Big|_{\alpha=1} \tag{12.66}$$

$$= \frac{1}{\tilde{Q}_1(\rho, \sigma, \mathcal{N})} \frac{d}{d\alpha} \left[\tilde{Q}_\alpha(\rho, \sigma, \mathcal{N}) \right] \Big|_{\alpha=1} \tag{12.67}$$

$$= \frac{d}{d\alpha} \left[\tilde{Q}_\alpha(\rho, \sigma, \mathcal{N}) \right] \Big|_{\alpha=1}. \tag{12.68}$$

Let $\alpha' \equiv \frac{\alpha-1}{\alpha}$. Now consider that

$$\widetilde{Q}_\alpha(\rho,\sigma,\mathcal{N})$$
$$= \text{Tr}\left\{ \left[\rho^{1/2}\sigma^{-\alpha'/2}\mathcal{N}^\dagger\left(\mathcal{N}(\sigma)^{\alpha'/2}\mathcal{N}(\rho)^{-\alpha'}\mathcal{N}(\sigma)^{\alpha'/2}\right)\sigma^{-\alpha'/2}\rho^{1/2}\right]^\alpha \right\}. \quad (12.69)$$

Define the function

$$\widetilde{Q}_{\alpha,\beta}(\rho,\sigma,\mathcal{N})$$
$$\equiv \text{Tr}\left\{ \left[\rho^{1/2}\sigma^{-\alpha'/2}\mathcal{N}^\dagger\left(\mathcal{N}(\sigma)^{\alpha'/2}\mathcal{N}(\rho)^{-\alpha'}\mathcal{N}(\sigma)^{\alpha'/2}\right)\sigma^{-\alpha'/2}\rho^{1/2}\right]^\beta \right\}, \quad (12.70)$$

and consider that

$$\frac{d}{d\alpha}\left[\widetilde{Q}_\alpha(\rho,\sigma,\mathcal{N})\right]\Big|_{\alpha=1} = \frac{d}{d\alpha}\widetilde{Q}_{\alpha,\alpha}(\rho,\sigma,\mathcal{N})\Big|_{\alpha=1} \quad (12.71)$$

$$= \frac{d}{d\alpha}\widetilde{Q}_{\alpha,1}(\rho,\sigma,\mathcal{N})\Big|_{\alpha=1} + \frac{d}{d\beta}\widetilde{Q}_{1,\beta}(\rho,\sigma,\mathcal{N})\Big|_{\beta=1}. \quad (12.72)$$

We first compute $\widetilde{Q}_{1,\beta}(\rho,\sigma,\mathcal{N})$ as follows:

$$\widetilde{Q}_{1,\beta}(\rho,\sigma,\mathcal{N}) = \text{Tr}\left\{ \left[\rho^{1/2}\Pi_\sigma\mathcal{N}^\dagger(\Pi_{\mathcal{N}(\sigma)}\Pi_{\mathcal{N}(\rho)}\Pi_{\mathcal{N}(\sigma)})\Pi_\sigma\rho^{1/2}\right]^\beta \right\} \quad (12.73)$$

$$= \text{Tr}\left\{ \left[\rho^{1/2}\mathcal{N}^\dagger(\Pi_{\mathcal{N}(\rho)})\rho^{1/2}\right]^\beta \right\} \quad (12.74)$$

$$= \text{Tr}\left\{ \left[\rho^{1/2}U^\dagger\left(\Pi_{\mathcal{N}(\rho)}\otimes I_E\right)U\rho^{1/2}\right]^\beta \right\} \quad (12.75)$$

$$= \text{Tr}\left\{ \left[\left(\Pi_{\mathcal{N}(\rho)}\otimes I_E\right)U\rho U^\dagger\left(\Pi_{\mathcal{N}(\rho)}\otimes I_E\right)\right]^\beta \right\} \quad (12.76)$$

$$= \text{Tr}\left\{ \left[U\rho U^\dagger\right]^\beta \right\} = \text{Tr}\left\{\rho^\beta\right\}. \quad (12.77)$$

So then

$$\frac{d}{d\beta}\widetilde{Q}_{1,\beta}(\rho,\sigma,\mathcal{N})\Big|_{\beta=1} = \frac{d}{d\beta}\text{Tr}\left\{\rho^\beta\right\}\Big|_{\beta=1} = \text{Tr}\left\{\rho^\beta\ln\rho\right\}\big|_{\beta=1} \quad (12.78)$$

$$= \text{Tr}\left\{\rho\ln\rho\right\}. \quad (12.79)$$

Now we turn to the other term $\frac{d}{d\alpha}\widetilde{Q}_{\alpha,1}(\rho,\sigma,\mathcal{N})$. First consider that

$$\frac{d}{d\alpha}(-\alpha') = \frac{d}{d\alpha}\left(\frac{1-\alpha}{\alpha}\right) = \frac{d}{d\alpha}\left(\frac{1}{\alpha}-1\right) = -\frac{1}{\alpha^2}, \quad (12.80)$$

$$\widetilde{Q}_{\alpha,1}(\rho,\sigma,\mathcal{N})$$
$$= \text{Tr}\left\{\rho\sigma^{-\alpha'/2}\mathcal{N}^\dagger\left(\mathcal{N}(\sigma)^{\alpha'/2}\mathcal{N}(\rho)^{-\alpha'}\mathcal{N}(\sigma)^{\alpha'/2}\right)\sigma^{-\alpha'/2}\right\}. \quad (12.81)$$

Now we show that $\frac{d}{d\alpha}\widetilde{Q}_{\alpha,1}(\rho,\sigma,\mathcal{N})$ is equal to

$$\frac{d}{d\alpha}\text{Tr}\left\{\rho\sigma^{-\alpha'/2}\mathcal{N}^\dagger\left(\mathcal{N}(\sigma)^{\alpha'/2}\mathcal{N}(\rho)^{-\alpha'}\mathcal{N}(\sigma)^{\alpha'/2}\right)\sigma^{-\alpha'/2}\right\}$$

$$= \text{Tr} \left\{ \rho \left[\frac{d}{d\alpha} \sigma^{-\alpha'/2} \right] \mathcal{N}^\dagger \left(\mathcal{N}(\sigma)^{\alpha'/2} \mathcal{N}(\rho)^{-\alpha'} \mathcal{N}(\sigma)^{\alpha'/2} \right) \sigma^{-\alpha'/2} \right\}$$

$$+ \text{Tr} \left\{ \rho \sigma^{-\alpha'/2} \mathcal{N}^\dagger \left(\left[\frac{d}{d\alpha} \mathcal{N}(\sigma)^{\alpha'/2} \right] \mathcal{N}(\rho)^{-\alpha'} \mathcal{N}(\sigma)^{\alpha'/2} \right) \sigma^{-\alpha'/2} \right\}$$

$$+ \text{Tr} \left\{ \rho \sigma^{-\alpha'/2} \mathcal{N}^\dagger \left(\mathcal{N}(\sigma)^{\alpha'/2} \left[\frac{d}{d\alpha} \mathcal{N}(\rho)^{-\alpha'} \right] \mathcal{N}(\sigma)^{\alpha'/2} \right) \sigma^{-\alpha'/2} \right\}$$

$$+ \text{Tr} \left\{ \rho \sigma^{-\alpha'/2} \mathcal{N}^\dagger \left(\mathcal{N}(\sigma)^{\alpha'/2} \mathcal{N}(\rho)^{-\alpha'} \left[\frac{d}{d\alpha} \mathcal{N}(\sigma)^{\alpha'/2} \right] \right) \sigma^{-\alpha'/2} \right\}$$

$$+ \text{Tr} \left\{ \rho \sigma^{-\alpha'/2} \mathcal{N}^\dagger \left(\mathcal{N}(\sigma)^{\alpha'/2} \mathcal{N}(\rho)^{-\alpha'} \mathcal{N}(\sigma)^{\alpha'/2} \right) \left[\frac{d}{d\alpha} \sigma^{-\alpha'/2} \right] \right\} \tag{12.82}$$

$$= \frac{1}{\alpha^2} \left[-\frac{1}{2} \text{Tr} \left\{ \rho \left[\ln \sigma \right] \sigma^{-\alpha'/2} \mathcal{N}^\dagger \left(\mathcal{N}(\sigma)^{\alpha'/2} \mathcal{N}(\rho)^{-\alpha'} \mathcal{N}(\sigma)^{\alpha'/2} \right) \sigma^{-\alpha'/2} \right\} \right.$$

$$+ \frac{1}{2} \text{Tr} \left\{ \rho \sigma^{-\alpha'/2} \mathcal{N}^\dagger \left(\left[\ln \mathcal{N}(\sigma) \right] \mathcal{N}(\sigma)^{\alpha'/2} \mathcal{N}(\rho)^{-\alpha'} \mathcal{N}(\sigma)^{\alpha'/2} \right) \sigma^{-\alpha'/2} \right\}$$

$$- \text{Tr} \left\{ \rho \sigma^{-\alpha'/2} \mathcal{N}^\dagger \left(\mathcal{N}(\sigma)^{\alpha'/2} \left[\ln \mathcal{N}(\rho) \right] \mathcal{N}(\rho)^{-\alpha'} \mathcal{N}(\sigma)^{\alpha'/2} \right) \sigma^{-\alpha'/2} \right\}$$

$$+ \frac{1}{2} \text{Tr} \left\{ \rho \sigma^{-\alpha'/2} \mathcal{N}^\dagger \left(\mathcal{N}(\sigma)^{\alpha'/2} \mathcal{N}(\rho)^{-\alpha'} \mathcal{N}(\sigma)^{\alpha'/2} \left[\ln \mathcal{N}(\sigma) \right] \right) \sigma^{-\alpha'/2} \right\}$$

$$\left. - \frac{1}{2} \text{Tr} \left\{ \rho \sigma^{-\alpha'/2} \mathcal{N}^\dagger \left(\mathcal{N}(\sigma)^{\alpha'/2} \mathcal{N}(\rho)^{-\alpha'} \mathcal{N}(\sigma)^{\alpha'/2} \right) \sigma^{-\alpha'/2} \left[\ln \sigma \right] \right\} \right]. \tag{12.83}$$

Taking the limit as $\alpha \to 1$ gives

$$\frac{d}{d\alpha} \widetilde{Q}_{\alpha,1}(\rho,\sigma,\mathcal{N}) \bigg|_{\alpha=1} = -\frac{1}{2} \text{Tr} \left\{ \rho \left[\ln \sigma \right] \Pi_\sigma \mathcal{N}^\dagger \left(\Pi_{\mathcal{N}(\sigma)} \Pi_{\mathcal{N}(\rho)} \Pi_{\mathcal{N}(\sigma)} \right) \Pi_\sigma \right\}$$

$$+ \frac{1}{2} \text{Tr} \left\{ \rho \Pi_\sigma \mathcal{N}^\dagger \left(\left[\ln \mathcal{N}(\sigma) \right] \Pi_{\mathcal{N}(\sigma)} \Pi_{\mathcal{N}(\rho)} \Pi_{\mathcal{N}(\sigma)} \right) \Pi_\sigma \right\}$$

$$- \text{Tr} \left\{ \rho \Pi_\sigma \mathcal{N}^\dagger \left(\Pi_{\mathcal{N}(\sigma)} \left[\ln \mathcal{N}(\rho) \right] \Pi_{\mathcal{N}(\rho)} \Pi_{\mathcal{N}(\sigma)} \right) \Pi_\sigma \right\}$$

$$+ \frac{1}{2} \text{Tr} \left\{ \rho \Pi_\sigma \mathcal{N}^\dagger \left(\Pi_{\mathcal{N}(\sigma)} \Pi_{\mathcal{N}(\rho)} \Pi_{\mathcal{N}(\sigma)} \left[\ln \mathcal{N}(\sigma) \right] \right) \Pi_\sigma \right\}$$

$$- \frac{1}{2} \text{Tr} \left\{ \rho \Pi_\sigma \mathcal{N}^\dagger \left(\Pi_{\mathcal{N}(\sigma)} \Pi_{\mathcal{N}(\rho)} \Pi_{\mathcal{N}(\sigma)} \right) \left[\ln \sigma \right] \Pi_\sigma \right\}. \tag{12.84}$$

We now simplify the first three terms and note that the last two are Hermitian conjugates of the first two:

$$\text{Tr} \left\{ \rho \left[\ln \sigma \right] \Pi_\sigma \mathcal{N}^\dagger (\Pi_{\mathcal{N}(\sigma)} \Pi_{\mathcal{N}(\rho)} \Pi_{\mathcal{N}(\sigma)}) \Pi_\sigma \right\}$$

$$= \text{Tr} \left\{ \rho \left[\ln \sigma \right] \mathcal{N}^\dagger (\Pi_{\mathcal{N}(\rho)}) \right\} \tag{12.85}$$

$$= \text{Tr} \left\{ \mathcal{N}(\rho \left[\ln \sigma \right]) (\Pi_{\mathcal{N}(\rho)}) \right\} \tag{12.86}$$

$$= \text{Tr} \left\{ U \rho \left[\ln \sigma \right] U^\dagger (\Pi_{\mathcal{N}(\rho)} \otimes I_E) \right\} \tag{12.87}$$

$$= \text{Tr} \left\{ \Pi_{U \rho U^\dagger} U \rho U^\dagger U \left[\ln \sigma \right] U^\dagger (\Pi_{\mathcal{N}(\rho)} \otimes I_E) \right\} \tag{12.88}$$

$$= \text{Tr} \left\{ U \rho U^\dagger U \left[\ln \sigma \right] U^\dagger \right\} \tag{12.89}$$

$$= \text{Tr} \left\{ \rho \left[\ln \sigma \right] \right\}, \tag{12.90}$$

$$\text{Tr}\left\{\rho\Pi_\sigma\mathcal{N}^\dagger([\ln\mathcal{N}(\sigma)]\,\Pi_{\mathcal{N}(\sigma)}\Pi_{\mathcal{N}(\rho)}\Pi_{\mathcal{N}(\sigma)})\Pi_\sigma\right\}$$
$$=\text{Tr}\left\{\rho\mathcal{N}^\dagger([\ln\mathcal{N}(\sigma)]\,\Pi_{\mathcal{N}(\rho)})\right\} \tag{12.91}$$
$$=\text{Tr}\left\{\mathcal{N}(\rho)\,[\ln\mathcal{N}(\sigma)]\,\Pi_{\mathcal{N}(\rho)}\right\} \tag{12.92}$$
$$=\text{Tr}\left\{\mathcal{N}(\rho)\,[\ln\mathcal{N}(\sigma)]\right\}, \tag{12.93}$$

$$\text{Tr}\left\{\rho\Pi_\sigma\mathcal{N}^\dagger(\Pi_{\mathcal{N}(\sigma)}\,[\ln\mathcal{N}(\rho)]\,\Pi_{\mathcal{N}(\rho)}\Pi_{\mathcal{N}(\sigma)})\Pi_\sigma\right\}$$
$$=\text{Tr}\left\{\rho\mathcal{N}^\dagger([\ln\mathcal{N}(\rho)]\,\Pi_{\mathcal{N}(\rho)})\right\} \tag{12.94}$$
$$=\text{Tr}\left\{\mathcal{N}(\rho)\,([\ln\mathcal{N}(\rho)]\,\Pi_{\mathcal{N}(\rho)})\right\} \tag{12.95}$$
$$=\text{Tr}\left\{\mathcal{N}(\rho)\,[\ln\mathcal{N}(\rho)]\right\}. \tag{12.96}$$

This then implies that the following equality holds:

$$\frac{d}{d\alpha}\widetilde{Q}_{\alpha,1}(\rho,\sigma,\mathcal{N})\bigg|_{\alpha=1}=-\,\text{Tr}\left\{\mathcal{N}\left(\rho\,[\ln\sigma]\right)\right\}$$
$$+\text{Tr}\left\{\mathcal{N}(\rho)\,[\ln\mathcal{N}(\sigma)]\right\}-\text{Tr}\left\{\mathcal{N}(\rho)\,[\ln\mathcal{N}(\rho)]\right\}. \tag{12.97}$$

Putting together (12.68), (12.72), (12.79), and (12.97), we can then conclude the statement of the theorem. $\qquad\square$

For $\alpha=1/2$, observe that

$$\widetilde{\Delta}_{1/2}(\rho,\sigma,\mathcal{N})=-\ln\left\|\left([\mathcal{N}(\rho)]^{1/2}\,[\mathcal{N}(\sigma)]^{-1/2}\otimes I_E\right)U\sigma^{1/2}\rho^{1/2}\right\|_1^2 \tag{12.98}$$
$$=-\ln F(\rho,\mathcal{P}_{\sigma,\mathcal{N}}(\mathcal{N}(\rho))) \tag{12.99}$$

where $F(\rho,\sigma)\equiv\left\|\sqrt{\rho}\sqrt{\sigma}\right\|_1^2$ is the quantum fidelity. Thus, if $\widetilde{\Delta}_\alpha(\rho,\sigma,\mathcal{N})$ were monotone non-decreasing with respect to α, we could combine these observations to conclude that

$$D(\rho\|\sigma)-D(\mathcal{N}(\rho)\|\mathcal{N}(\sigma))=\frac{1}{\ln 2}\widetilde{\Delta}_1(\rho,\sigma,\mathcal{N}) \tag{12.100}$$
$$\overset{?}{\geq}\frac{1}{\ln 2}\widetilde{\Delta}_{1/2}(\rho,\sigma,\mathcal{N}) \tag{12.101}$$
$$=-\log F\left(\rho,\mathcal{P}_{\sigma,\mathcal{N}}(\mathcal{N}(\rho))\right). \tag{12.102}$$

If this were true, then we could conclude that Theorem 12.1.1 would be true with the recovery channel taken to be the Petz recovery map. However, it is not known whether this is true, and we will instead invoke the Stein–Hirschman theorem to conclude that a convex combination of rotated Petz maps satisfies the bound stated in Theorem 12.1.1.

12.5 Proof of the Recoverability Theorem

This section presents the proof of Theorem 12.1.1. In fact, we prove a stronger statement, which implies Theorem 12.1.1 for a particular recovery channel that we discuss below.

THEOREM 12.5.1   Let ρ, σ, and $\mathcal{N}$ be as given in Definition 12.1.1. Then the following inequality holds

$$D(\rho\|\sigma) - D(\mathcal{N}(\rho)\|\mathcal{N}(\sigma)) \geq -\int_{-\infty}^{\infty} dt\ \beta_0(t)\ \log\left[F\left(\rho, (\mathcal{R}_{\sigma,\mathcal{N}}^{t/2} \circ \mathcal{N})(\rho)\right)\right],$$

(12.103)

where $\beta_0(t) = \frac{\pi}{2}\left[\cosh(\pi t) + 1\right]^{-1}$ is a probability density function for $t \in \mathbb{R}$ and $\mathcal{R}_{\sigma,\mathcal{N}}^{t/2}$ is a rotated Petz recovery map from Definition 12.3.2.

Proof   We can prove this result by employing Theorem 12.2.3. We first establish the inequality in (12.103). Let $U : \mathcal{H} \to \mathcal{H}' \otimes \mathcal{H}_E$ be an isometric extension of the channel $\mathcal{N}$. Pick

$$G(z) \equiv \left([\mathcal{N}(\rho)]^{z/2}\,[\mathcal{N}(\sigma)]^{-z/2} \otimes I_E\right) U\sigma^{z/2}\rho^{1/2},$$

(12.104)

for $z \in \overline{S}$, $p_0 = 2$, $p_1 = 1$, and $\theta \in (0,1)$, which fixes $p_\theta = \frac{2}{1+\theta}$. The operator valued-function $G(z)$ satisfies the conditions needed to apply Theorem 12.2.3. For the choices above, we find

$$\|G(\theta)\|_{2/(1+\theta)} = \left\|\left([\mathcal{N}(\rho)]^{\theta/2}\,[\mathcal{N}(\sigma)]^{-\theta/2} \otimes I_E\right) U\sigma^{\theta/2}\rho^{1/2}\right\|_{2/(1+\theta)},$$

(12.105)

$$\|G(it)\|_2 = \left\|\left([\mathcal{N}(\rho)]^{it/2}\,[\mathcal{N}(\sigma)]^{-it/2} \otimes I_E\right) U\sigma^{it}\rho^{1/2}\right\|_2$$

$$\leq \left\|\rho^{1/2}\right\|_2$$

$$= 1,$$

(12.106)

$$\|G(1+it)\|_1 = \left\|\left([\mathcal{N}(\rho)]^{(1+it)/2}\,[\mathcal{N}(\sigma)]^{-(1+it)/2} \otimes I_E\right) U\sigma^{(1+it)/2}\rho^{1/2}\right\|_1$$

$$= \left\|\left([\mathcal{N}(\rho)]^{\frac{it}{2}}\,[\mathcal{N}(\rho)]^{\frac{1}{2}}\,[\mathcal{N}(\sigma)]^{-\frac{it}{2}}\,[\mathcal{N}(\sigma)]^{-\frac{1}{2}} \otimes I_E\right) U\sigma^{\frac{1}{2}}\sigma^{\frac{it}{2}}\rho^{\frac{1}{2}}\right\|_1$$

$$= \left\|\left([\mathcal{N}(\rho)]^{1/2}\,[\mathcal{N}(\sigma)]^{-it/2}\,[\mathcal{N}(\sigma)]^{-1/2} \otimes I_E\right) U\sigma^{1/2}\sigma^{it/2}\rho^{1/2}\right\|_1$$

$$= \sqrt{F}\left(\rho, \left(\mathcal{U}_{\sigma,-t/2} \circ \mathcal{P}_{\sigma,\mathcal{N}} \circ \mathcal{U}_{\mathcal{N}(\sigma),t/2}\right)(\mathcal{N}(\rho))\right)$$

$$= \sqrt{F}(\rho, (\mathcal{R}_{\sigma,\mathcal{N}}^{t/2} \circ \mathcal{N})(\rho)).$$

(12.107)

Then we can apply Theorem 12.2.3 to conclude that

$$\ln\left\|\left([\mathcal{N}(\rho)]^{\theta/2}\,[\mathcal{N}(\sigma)]^{-\theta/2} \otimes I_E\right) U\sigma^{\theta/2}\rho^{1/2}\right\|_{2/(1+\theta)}$$

$$\leq \int_{-\infty}^{\infty} dt\ \beta_\theta(t)\ \ln\left[F\left(\rho, (\mathcal{R}_{\sigma,\mathcal{N}}^{t/2} \circ \mathcal{N})(\rho)\right)^{\theta/2}\right].$$

(12.108)

This implies that

$$-\frac{2}{\theta} \ln\left\|\left([\mathcal{N}(\rho)]^{\theta/2}\,[\mathcal{N}(\sigma)]^{-\theta/2} \otimes I_E\right) U\sigma^{\theta/2}\rho^{1/2}\right\|_{2/(1+\theta)}$$

$$\geq -\int_{-\infty}^{\infty} dt\ \beta_\theta(t)\ \ln\left[F\left(\rho, (\mathcal{R}_{\sigma,\mathcal{N}}^{t/2} \circ \mathcal{N})(\rho)\right)\right].$$

(12.109)

Letting $\theta = (1 - \alpha)/\alpha$, we see that this is the same as

$$\widetilde{\Delta}_\alpha(\rho, \sigma, \mathcal{N}) \geq -\int_{-\infty}^{\infty} dt \; \beta_{(1-\alpha)/\alpha}(t) \; \ln\left[F\left(\rho, (\mathcal{R}_{\sigma,\mathcal{N}}^{t/2} \circ \mathcal{N})(\rho)\right)\right]. \tag{12.110}$$

Since the inequality in (12.109) holds for all $\theta \in (0,1)$, and thus (12.110) holds for all $\alpha \in (1/2, 1)$, we can take the limit as $\alpha \nearrow 1$ and apply (12.58) and the dominated convergence theorem to conclude that (12.103) holds. $\qquad\square$

With the theorem above in hand, Theorem 12.1.1 follows as a consequence by taking $\mathcal{R}_{\sigma,\mathcal{N}}$ to be the following recovery channel:

$$\mathcal{R}_{\sigma,\mathcal{N}}(Q) \equiv \int_{-\infty}^{\infty} dt \; \beta_0(t) \; \mathcal{R}_{\sigma,\mathcal{N}}^{t/2}(Q) + \text{Tr}\{(I - \Pi_{\mathcal{N}(\sigma)})Q\}\omega, \tag{12.111}$$

where $Q \in \mathcal{L}(\mathcal{H}')$ and $\omega \in \mathcal{D}(\mathcal{H})$. This is because

$$-\int_{-\infty}^{\infty} dt \; \beta_0(t) \; \log\left[F\left(\rho, (\mathcal{R}_{\sigma,\mathcal{N}}^{t/2} \circ \mathcal{N})(\rho)\right)\right]$$
$$\geq -\log\left[F\left(\rho, \left(\int_{-\infty}^{\infty} dt \; \beta_0(t)\mathcal{R}_{\sigma,\mathcal{N}}^{t/2} \circ \mathcal{N}\right)(\rho)\right)\right]$$
$$\geq -\log\left[F(\rho, (\mathcal{R}_{\sigma,\mathcal{N}} \circ \mathcal{N})(\rho))\right], \tag{12.112}$$

where the first inequality is due to the concavity of both the logarithm and the fidelity, and the second inequality follows from the assumption that $\text{supp}(\rho) \subseteq \text{supp}(\sigma)$ and a reasoning similar to that in the proof of Proposition 11.8.2 (one can also argue this last step from the operator monotonicity of the square root function).

The extra term $\text{Tr}\{(I - \Pi_{\mathcal{N}(\sigma)})Q\}\omega$ is needed to ensure that $\mathcal{R}_{\sigma,\mathcal{N}}$ is trace-preserving in addition to being completely positive. Trace preservation of $\mathcal{R}_{\sigma,\mathcal{N}}$ follows because

$$\text{Tr}\{\mathcal{R}_{\sigma,\mathcal{N}}(Q)\} = \int_{-\infty}^{\infty} dt \; \beta_0(t) \; \text{Tr}\{\mathcal{R}_{\sigma,\mathcal{N}}^{t/2}(Q)\} + \text{Tr}\{(I - \Pi_{\mathcal{N}(\sigma)})Q\} \tag{12.113}$$

$$= \int_{-\infty}^{\infty} dt \; \beta_0(t) \; \text{Tr}\{\Pi_{\mathcal{N}(\sigma)}Q\} + \text{Tr}\{(I - \Pi_{\mathcal{N}(\sigma)})Q\} \tag{12.114}$$

$$= \text{Tr}\{\Pi_{\mathcal{N}(\sigma)}Q\} + \text{Tr}\{(I - \Pi_{\mathcal{N}(\sigma)})Q\} = \text{Tr}\{Q\}, \tag{12.115}$$

where the second equality follows from Exercise 12.3.1. Observe that this recovery channel has the "perfect recovery of σ" property mentioned in (12.2), which follows from Proposition 12.3.1 and the particular form in (12.111).

As a corollary of Theorem 12.5.1, we obtain equality conditions for the monotonicity of quantum relative entropy:

COROLLARY 12.5.1 (Equality Conditions) Let ρ, σ, and $\mathcal{N}$ be as given in Definition 12.1.1. Then

$$D(\rho\|\sigma) = D(\mathcal{N}(\rho)\|\mathcal{N}(\sigma)) \tag{12.116}$$

if and only if all rotated Petz recovery maps perfectly recover ρ from $\mathcal{N}(\rho)$:

$$\forall t \in \mathbb{R} : (\mathcal{R}_{\sigma,\mathcal{N}}^t \circ \mathcal{N})(\rho) = \rho. \tag{12.117}$$

Proof Recall from Proposition 12.3.1 that, independent of the conditions in the statement of the corollary, we always have that $(\mathcal{R}_{\sigma,\mathcal{N}}^t \circ \mathcal{N})(\sigma) = \sigma$ for all $t \in \mathbb{R}$.

We start by proving the "only if" part. Suppose that $\forall t \in \mathbb{R} : (\mathcal{R}_{\sigma,\mathcal{N}}^t \circ \mathcal{N})(\rho) = \rho$. Then for a particular $t \in \mathbb{R}$, the monotonicity of quantum relative entropy implies that

$$D(\rho\|\sigma) \geq D(\mathcal{N}(\rho)\|\mathcal{N}(\sigma)) \tag{12.118}$$

$$D(\mathcal{N}(\rho)\|\mathcal{N}(\sigma)) \geq D((\mathcal{R}_{\sigma,\mathcal{N}}^t \circ \mathcal{N})(\rho)\|(\mathcal{R}_{\sigma,\mathcal{N}}^t \circ \mathcal{N})(\sigma)) \tag{12.119}$$

$$= D(\rho\|\sigma), \tag{12.120}$$

which in turn imply that $D(\rho\|\sigma) = D(\mathcal{N}(\rho)\|\mathcal{N}(\sigma))$.

We now prove the "if" part of the theorem. Suppose that $D(\rho\|\sigma) = D(\mathcal{N}(\rho)\|\mathcal{N}(\sigma))$. By Theorem 12.5.1, we can conclude that

$$\int_{-\infty}^{\infty} dt \, \beta_0(t) \left[-\log \left[F\left(\rho, (\mathcal{R}_{\sigma,\mathcal{N}}^{t/2} \circ \mathcal{N})(\rho) \right) \right] \right] = 0. \tag{12.121}$$

Since $\beta_0(t)$ is a positive definite function for all $t \in \mathbb{R}$, $-\log F \geq 0$, the recovery maps $\mathcal{R}_{\sigma,\mathcal{N}}^{t/2}$ are continuous in t and so is the fidelity, we can conclude that

$$-\log \left[F\left(\rho, (\mathcal{R}_{\sigma,\mathcal{N}}^{t/2} \circ \mathcal{N})(\rho) \right) \right] = 0 \tag{12.122}$$

for all $t \in \mathbb{R}$, which is the same as $F(\rho, (\mathcal{R}_{\sigma,\mathcal{N}}^{t/2} \circ \mathcal{N})(\rho)) = 1$ for all $t \in \mathbb{R}$. We can then conclude that (12.117) holds because the fidelity between two states is equal to one if and only if the states are the same. $\square$

12.6   Refinements of Quantum Entropy Inequalities

Theorem 12.1.1 leads to a strengthening of many quantum entropy inequalities, including strong subadditivity of quantum entropy, concavity of conditional entropy, joint convexity of relative entropy, nonnegativity of quantum discord, and the Holevo bound. We list these as corollaries and give brief proofs for them in the following subsections.

12.6.1   Strong Subadditivity

Recall the conditional quantum mutual information of a tripartite state ρ_{ABC}:

$$I(A; B|C)_\rho \equiv H(AC)_\rho + H(BC)_\rho - H(C)_\rho - H(ABC)_\rho. \tag{12.123}$$

Strong subadditivity is the statement that $I(A; B|C)_\rho \geq 0$ for all tripartite states ρ_{ABC}.

Corollary 12.6.1 below gives an improvement of strong subadditivity. It is a direct consequence of Theorem 12.1.1 after choosing

$$\rho = \rho_{ABC}, \quad \sigma = \rho_{AC} \otimes I_B, \quad \mathcal{N} = \mathrm{Tr}_A, \tag{12.124}$$

so that

$$\mathcal{N}(\rho) = \rho_{BC}, \quad \mathcal{N}(\sigma) = \rho_C \otimes I_B, \quad \mathcal{N}^\dagger(\cdot) = (\cdot) \otimes I_A, \tag{12.125}$$

and

$$D(\rho\|\sigma) - D(\mathcal{N}(\rho)\|\mathcal{N}(\sigma)) = D(\rho_{ABC}\|\rho_{AC} \otimes I_B) - D(\rho_{BC}\|\rho_C \otimes I_B)$$
$$= I(A; B|C)_\rho, \tag{12.126}$$
$$\mathcal{P}_{\sigma,\mathcal{N}}(\cdot) = \sigma^{1/2} \mathcal{N}^\dagger \left([\mathcal{N}(\sigma)]^{-1/2} (\cdot) [\mathcal{N}(\sigma)]^{-1/2}\right) \sigma^{1/2}$$
$$= \rho_{AC}^{1/2} \left[\rho_C^{-1/2}(\cdot)\rho_C^{-1/2} \otimes I_A\right] \rho_{AC}^{1/2}. \tag{12.127}$$

COROLLARY 12.6.1 Let $\rho_{ABC} \in \mathcal{D}(\mathcal{H}_A \otimes \mathcal{H}_B \otimes \mathcal{H}_C)$. Then the following inequality holds:

$$I(A; B|C)_\rho \geq -\log\left[F(\rho_{ABC}, \mathcal{R}_{C \to AC}(\rho_{BC}))\right], \tag{12.128}$$

where the recovery channel $\mathcal{R}_{C \to AC} = \int_{-\infty}^{\infty} dt\, \beta_0(t)\, \mathcal{R}_{\rho_{AC},\mathrm{Tr}_A}^{t/2}$ perfectly recovers ρ_{AC} from ρ_C.

12.6.2 Concavity of Conditional Quantum Entropy

Let $\mathcal{E} \equiv \{p_X(x), \rho_{AB}^x\}$ be an ensemble of bipartite quantum states with expectation $\overline{\rho}_{AB} \equiv \sum_x p_X(x)\rho_{AB}^x$. Concavity of conditional entropy is the statement that

$$H(A|B)_{\overline{\rho}} \geq \sum_x p_X(x) H(A|B)_{\rho^x}. \tag{12.129}$$

Let ω_{XAB} denote the following classical–quantum state in which we have encoded the ensemble $\mathcal{E}$:

$$\omega_{XAB} \equiv \sum_x p_X(x)|x\rangle\langle x|_X \otimes \rho_{AB}^x. \tag{12.130}$$

We can rewrite

$$H(A|B)_{\overline{\rho}} - \sum_x p_X(x) H(A|B)_{\rho^x}$$

$$= H(A|B)_\omega - H(A|BX)_\omega \tag{12.131}$$
$$= I(A; X|B)_\omega \tag{12.132}$$
$$= H(X|B)_\omega - H(X|AB)_\omega \tag{12.133}$$
$$= D(\omega_{XAB}\|I_X \otimes \omega_{AB}) - D(\omega_{XB}\|I_X \otimes \omega_B). \tag{12.134}$$

We can see the last line above as a relative entropy difference, as defined in the right-hand side of (12.58), by picking $\rho = \omega_{XAB}$, $\sigma = I_X \otimes \omega_{AB}$, and $\mathcal{N} = \mathrm{Tr}_A$.

Applying Theorem 12.1.1 and Exercise 9.2.10, we find the following improvement of concavity of conditional entropy:

COROLLARY 12.6.2   Let an ensemble $\mathcal{E}$ be as given above. Then the following inequality holds

$$H(A|B)_{\overline{\rho}} - \sum_x p_X(x) H(A|B)_{\rho^x}$$

$$\geq -2 \log \sum_x p_X(x) \sqrt{F(\rho_{AB}^x, \mathcal{R}_{B \to AB}(\rho_B^x))}, \quad (12.135)$$

where the recovery map $\mathcal{R}_{B \to AB} \equiv \int_{-\infty}^{\infty} dt\, \beta_0(t)\, \mathcal{R}_{\overline{\rho}_{AB}, \text{Tr}_A}^{t/2}$ perfectly recovers $\overline{\rho}_{AB}$ from $\overline{\rho}_B$.

12.6.3   Joint Convexity of Quantum Relative Entropy

Let $\{p_X(x), \rho_x\}$ be an ensemble of density operators and $\{p_X(x), \sigma_x\}$ be an ensemble of positive semi-definite operators such that $\text{supp}(\rho_x) \subseteq \text{supp}(\sigma_x)$ for all x and with expectations $\overline{\rho} \equiv \sum_x p_X(x)\rho_x$ and $\overline{\sigma} \equiv \sum_x p_X(x)\sigma_x$. Joint convexity of quantum relative entropy is the statement that distinguishability of these ensembles does not increase under the loss of the classical label:

$$\sum_x p_X(x) D(\rho_x \| \sigma_x) \geq D(\overline{\rho} \| \overline{\sigma}). \quad (12.136)$$

By picking

$$\rho = \rho_{XB} \equiv \sum_x p_X(x) |x\rangle\langle x|_X \otimes \rho_x, \quad (12.137)$$

$$\sigma = \sigma_{XB} \equiv \sum_x p_X(x) |x\rangle\langle x|_X \otimes \sigma_x, \quad (12.138)$$

$$\mathcal{N} = \text{Tr}_X, \quad (12.139)$$

and applying Theorem 12.1.1, we arrive at the following improvement of joint convexity of quantum relative entropy:

COROLLARY 12.6.3   Let ensembles be as given above. Then the following inequality holds

$$\sum_x p_X(x) D(\rho_x \| \sigma_x) - D(\overline{\rho} \| \overline{\sigma}) \geq -\log F(\rho_{XB}, \mathcal{R}_{\sigma_{XB}, \text{Tr}_X}(\overline{\rho})), \quad (12.140)$$

where the recovery map $\mathcal{R}_{\sigma_{XB}, \text{Tr}_X} = \int_{-\infty}^{\infty} dt\, \beta_0(t)\, \mathcal{R}_{\sigma_{XB}, \text{Tr}_X}^{t/2}$ perfectly recovers σ_{XB} from σ_B.

12.6.4   Nonnegativity of Quantum Discord

Let ρ_{AB} be a bipartite density operator and let $\{|\varphi_x\rangle\langle\varphi_x|_A\}$ be a rank-one quantum measurement on system A (i.e., the vectors $|\varphi_x\rangle_A$ satisfy

$\sum_x |\varphi_x\rangle\langle\varphi_x|_A = I_A$). It suffices for us to consider rank-one measurements for our discussion here because every quantum measurement can be refined to have a rank-one form, such that it delivers more classical information to the experimentalist observing the apparatus. Then the (unoptimized) quantum discord is defined to be the difference between the following mutual informations:

$$I(A;B)_\rho - I(X;B)_\omega, \quad \text{where} \tag{12.141}$$

$$\omega_{XB} \equiv \mathcal{M}_{A\to X}(\rho_{AB}), \tag{12.142}$$

$$\mathcal{M}_{A\to X}(\cdot) \equiv \sum_x \langle\varphi_x|_A(\cdot)|\varphi_x\rangle_A |x\rangle\langle x|_X. \tag{12.143}$$

The quantum channel $\mathcal{M}_{A\to X}$ is a measurement channel, so that the state ω_{XB} is the classical–quantum state resulting from the measurement. The set $\{|x\rangle_X\}$ is an orthonormal basis so that X is a classical system. The quantum discord is non-negative, and by applying Theorem 12.1.1, we find the following improvement of this entropy inequality:

COROLLARY 12.6.4   Let ρ_{AB} and $\mathcal{M}_{A\to X}$ be as given above. Then the following inequality holds

$$I(A;B)_\rho - I(X;B)_\omega \geq -\log F(\rho_{AB}, \mathcal{E}_A(\rho_{AB})), \tag{12.144}$$

where

$$\mathcal{E}_A \equiv \int_{-\infty}^{\infty} dt\, \beta_0(t)\, (\mathcal{U}_{\rho_A,t} \circ \mathcal{P}_{\rho_A,\mathcal{M}_{A\to X}} \circ \mathcal{M}_{A\to X}) \tag{12.145}$$

is an entanglement-breaking map, $\mathcal{P}_{\rho_A,\mathcal{M}_{A\to X}} \circ \mathcal{M}_{A\to X}$ is an entanglement-breaking map:

$$(\mathcal{P}_{\rho_A,\mathcal{M}_{A\to X}} \circ \mathcal{M}_{A\to X})(\cdot) = \sum_x \langle\varphi_x|_A(\cdot)|\varphi_x\rangle_A \frac{\rho_A^{1/2}|\varphi_x\rangle\langle\varphi_x|_A\rho_A^{1/2}}{\langle\varphi_x|_A\rho_A|\varphi_x\rangle_A}, \tag{12.146}$$

and the map $\mathcal{U}_{\rho_A,t}$ is defined from (12.35). The recovery map $\int_{-\infty}^{\infty} dt\, \beta_0(t)\, (\mathcal{U}_{\rho_A,t} \circ \mathcal{P}_{\rho_A,\mathcal{M}_{A\to X}})$ perfectly recovers ρ_A from $\mathcal{M}_{A\to X}(\rho_A)$.

Proof   We start with the rewriting

$$I(A;B)_\rho - I(X;B)_\omega = D(\rho_{AB}\|\rho_A \otimes I_B) - D(\omega_{XB}\|\omega_X \otimes I_B), \tag{12.147}$$

and follow by picking $\rho = \rho_{AB}$, $\sigma = \rho_A \otimes I_B$, and $\mathcal{N} = \mathcal{M}_{A\to X}$, and applying Theorem 12.1.1. This then shows the corollary with a recovery map of the form $\int_{-\infty}^{\infty} dt\, \beta_0(t)\, \mathcal{R}_{\rho_A,\mathcal{M}_{A\to X}}^{t/2}$.

The channel $\mathcal{R}_{\rho_A,\mathcal{M}_{A\to X}}^t \circ \mathcal{M}_{A\to X}$ is entanglement-breaking because it consists of a measurement channel $\mathcal{M}_{A\to X}$ followed by a preparation. We now work out the form of the recovery map in (12.144). Consider that $\mathcal{M}_{A\to X}(\rho_A) = \sum_x \langle\varphi_x|_A\rho_A|\varphi_x\rangle_A |x\rangle\langle x|_X$, so that

$$\mathcal{U}_{\mathcal{M}_{A \to X}(\rho_A), -t}(\cdot)$$

$$= \left[\sum_x [\langle \varphi_x |_A \rho_A | \varphi_x \rangle_A]^{-it} |x\rangle\langle x|_X \right] (\cdot) \left[\sum_{x'} [\langle \varphi_{x'} |_A \rho_A | \varphi_{x'} \rangle_A]^{it} |x'\rangle\langle x'|_X \right]. \tag{12.148}$$

Thus, when composing $\mathcal{M}_{A \to X}$ with $\mathcal{U}_{\mathcal{M}_{A \to X}(\rho_A), -t}$, the phases cancel out to give the following relation: $\mathcal{U}_{\mathcal{M}_{A \to X}(\rho_A), -t}(\mathcal{M}_{A \to X}(\cdot)) = \mathcal{M}_{A \to X}(\cdot)$. One can then work out that

$$(\mathcal{P}_{\rho_A, \mathcal{M}_{A \to X}} \circ \mathcal{M}_{A \to X})(\cdot)$$

$$= \rho_A^{1/2} \mathcal{M}^\dagger \left([\mathcal{M}_{A \to X}(\rho_A)]^{-1/2} \mathcal{M}_{A \to X}(\cdot) [\mathcal{M}_{A \to X}(\rho_A)]^{-1/2} \right) \rho_A^{1/2} \tag{12.149}$$

$$= \sum_x \langle \varphi_x |_A (\cdot) | \varphi_x \rangle_A \frac{\rho_A^{1/2} | \varphi_x \rangle\langle \varphi_x |_A \rho_A^{1/2}}{\langle \varphi_x |_A \rho_A | \varphi_x \rangle_A}, \tag{12.150}$$

concluding the proof. □

12.6.5　Holevo Bound

The Holevo bound is a special case of the nonnegativity of quantum discord in which ρ_{AB} is a quantum-classical state, which we write explicitly as

$$\rho_{AB} = \sum_y p_Y(y) \rho_A^y \otimes |y\rangle\langle y|_Y, \tag{12.151}$$

where each ρ_A^y is a density operator, so that $\rho_A = \sum_y p_Y(y) \rho_A^y$. The Holevo bound states that the mutual information of the state ρ_{AB} in (12.151) is never smaller than the mutual information after system A is measured. By applying Corollary 12.6.4 and (9.146), we find the following improvement:

COROLLARY 12.6.5 (Holevo Bound)　Let ρ_{AB} be as in (12.151), and let $\mathcal{M}_{A \to X}$ and ω_{XB} be as in Section 12.6.4, respectively. Then the following inequality holds

$$I(A; B)_\rho - I(X; B)_\omega \geq -2 \log \sum_y p_Y(y) \sqrt{F} (\rho_A^y, \mathcal{E}_A(\rho_A^y)), \tag{12.152}$$

where $\mathcal{E}_A$ is an entanglement-breaking map of the form in (12.146) and the partial isometric map $\mathcal{U}_{\rho_A, t}$ is defined from (12.35).

12.7　History and Further Reading

Section 11.11 reviews the history of many quantum entropy inequalities in quantum information. Here, we detail the history of the refinements. Petz (1986; see also Petz, 1988) considered the equality conditions for monotonicity of quantum relative entropy, defined what is now known as the Petz recovery map (there called "transpose channel"), and gave many such equality conditions, one of which is that $D(\rho\|\sigma) = D(\mathcal{N}(\rho)\|\mathcal{N}(\sigma))$ if and only if the Petz recovery map perfectly recovers ρ from $\mathcal{N}(\rho)$: $(\mathcal{P}_{\sigma,\mathcal{N}} \circ \mathcal{N})(\rho) = \rho$. Later, Hayden, Jozsa, Petz & Winter (2004) invoked Petz's result to elucidate the structure of tripartite states that saturate the strong subadditivity of quantum entropy with equality. Mosonyi & Petz (2004) then invoked Petz's result to establish the structure of triples $(\rho, \sigma, \mathcal{N})$ for which the monotonicity of quantum relative entropy is saturated with equality (see also Mosonyi, 2005). The transpose channel was independently discovered many years after Petz's work by Barnum & Knill (2002) in the context of approximate quantum error correction.

The topic of the near saturation of quantum entropy inequalities is a more recent development. Brandao et al. (2011) established a lower bound on conditional mutual information related to how entangled the two unconditioned systems are with respect to the 1-LOCC norm. Interest then turned to obtaining lower bounds in terms of the trace norm. Much of the very recent work was inspired by the posting of Winter & Li (2012) and a presentation of Kim (2013). The main conjecture of Winter & Li (2012) (hitherto unproven) is that

$$D(\rho\|\sigma) - D(\mathcal{N}(\rho)\|\mathcal{N}(\sigma)) \geq D(\rho\|(\mathcal{R}_{\sigma,\mathcal{N}} \circ \mathcal{N})(\rho)), \tag{12.153}$$

for some recovery channel $\mathcal{R}_{\sigma,\mathcal{N}}$, depending only on σ and $\mathcal{N}$ and such that $(\mathcal{R}_{\sigma,\mathcal{N}} \circ \mathcal{N})(\sigma) = \sigma$. Carlen & Lieb (2014) then established an interesting lower bound on the monotonicity of quantum relative entropy with respect to partial trace, which directly leads to a related lower bound on conditional quantum mutual information, as pointed out by Zhang (2014) by making use of the well-known relation $I(A; B|C)_\rho = D(\rho_{ABC}\|I_B \otimes \rho_{AC}) - D(\rho_{BC}\|I_B \otimes \rho_C)$. Motivated by these developments, Berta, Seshadreesan & Wilde (2015) defined a Rényi generalization of the conditional mutual information. This notion and known properties of Rényi entropies led them to conjecture that $I(A; B|C)_\rho \geq -\log F(\rho_{ABC}, \mathcal{P}_{\rho_{AC}, \text{Tr}_A}(\rho_{BC}))$, which hitherto remains unproven. Shortly thereafter, Seshadreesan, Berta & Wilde (2015) put forward the notion of a Rényi generalization of a relative entropy difference, which is one of the main tools used in the proof of Theorem 12.1.1.

Fawzi & Renner (2015) established the following:

$$I(A; B|C)_\rho \geq -\log F(\rho_{ABC}, \mathcal{R}_{C\to AC}(\rho_{BC})), \tag{12.154}$$

where $\mathcal{R}_{C\to AC}$ is a recovery channel consisting of some unitary acting on C, followed by the Petz recovery map $\mathcal{P}_{\rho_{AC}, \text{Tr}_A}$, and then some unitary acting on AC. Since their argument made use of the probabilistic method, they could not give further information about the aforementioned unitaries. Concurrently, Seshadreesan & Wilde (2015) defined the "fidelity of recovery":

$$F(A; B|C)_\rho \equiv \sup_{\mathcal{R}_{C\to AC}} F(\rho_{ABC}, \mathcal{R}_{C\to AC}(\rho_{BC})) \tag{12.155}$$

as an information measure analogous to conditional mutual information, and they proved many of its properties. Li & Winter (2014), based on earlier arguments in Winter & Li (2012), used the result of Fawzi & Renner (2015) to establish a lower bound on an entanglement measure known as squashed entanglement, and further elaborated on the conjecture in (12.153). Brandao et al. (2014) proved the bound $I(A;B|C)_\rho \geq -\log F(A;B|C)_\rho$ by invoking quantum state redistribution, but their method gave less information about the structure of the recovery channel. Wilde (2014) showed how to apply the bound in (12.154) to give lower bounds on multipartite information measures, which had an interpretation in terms of local recoverability. Berta, Lemm & Wilde (2015) used the techniques of Fawzi & Renner (2015) to establish a nontrivial lower bound on a relative entropy difference. Datta & Wilde (2015) proved that $\widetilde{\Delta}_\alpha(\rho,\sigma,\mathcal{N}) \geq 0$ for all $\alpha \in (1/2,1) \cup (1,\infty)$ in addition to other related statements. Berta & Tomamichel (2016) proved that the fidelity of recovery is multiplicative with respect to tensor-product states, which then simplified the proof of the bound $I(A;B|C)_\rho \geq -\log F(A;B|C)_\rho$. Sutter et al. (2016) showed that the recovery map in (12.154) possesses a universal property in the sense that $\mathcal{R}_{C\to AC}$ could be taken to depend only on the marginal state ρ_{AC}. Their argument also led to the conclusion that the unitaries could be taken to commute with ρ_C and ρ_{AC}.

Wilde (2015) invoked the Hadamard three-lines theorem and the notion of a Rényi generalization of a relative entropy difference to establish the following bound:

$$D(\rho\|\sigma) - D(\mathcal{N}(\rho)\|\mathcal{N}(\sigma)) \geq -\log\left[\sup_{t\in\mathbb{R}} F(\rho, (\mathcal{R}^t_{\sigma,\mathcal{N}} \circ \mathcal{N})(\rho))\right], \qquad (12.156)$$

where $(\mathcal{R}^t_{\sigma,\mathcal{N}} \circ \mathcal{N})(\sigma) = \sigma$. Notice that the recovery map above is not universal, because the optimal t could depend on ρ. Wilde (2015) also established an upper bound on $D(\rho\|\sigma) - D(\mathcal{N}(\rho)\|\mathcal{N}(\sigma))$, which in some cases has an interpretation in terms of recoverability. Dupuis & Wilde (2016) subsequently defined "swiveled Rényi entropies" in an attempt to address some of the open questions raised in Berta, Seshadreesan & Wilde (2015) and Seshadreesan, Berta & Wilde (2015). An upshot of this work was to establish further lower and upper bounds on $D(\rho\|\sigma) - D(\mathcal{N}(\rho)\|\mathcal{N}(\sigma))$. Sutter et al. (2015) then showed the following lower bound by a different method of proof, known as "the pinched Petz recovery" approach:

$$D(\rho\|\sigma) - D(\mathcal{N}(\rho)\|\mathcal{N}(\sigma)) \geq D_M(\rho\|(\mathcal{R}_{\rho,\sigma,\mathcal{N}} \circ \mathcal{N})(\rho)), \qquad (12.157)$$

where $(\mathcal{R}_{\rho,\sigma,\mathcal{N}} \circ \mathcal{N})(\sigma) = \sigma$ and $\mathcal{R}_{\rho,\sigma,\mathcal{N}}$ is some convex combination of rotated Petz maps and D_M is the "measured relative entropy", which satisfies $D_M \geq -\log F$. Junge et al. (2015) invoked Hirschman's improvement (Hirschman, 1952) of the Hadamard three-lines theorem and the method of proof from Wilde (2015) to establish Theorem 12.1.1, with the consequence of having an explicit recovery channel $\mathcal{R}_{\sigma,\mathcal{N}}$ which depends only on σ and $\mathcal{N}$ and satisfies $(\mathcal{R}_{\sigma,\mathcal{N}} \circ \mathcal{N})(\sigma) = \sigma$. This approach also directly recovers the equality conditions from Petz (1986) and Petz (1988).

More information about the theory of complex interpolation is available in Bergh & Löfström (1976) and Reed & Simon (1975). Grafakos (2008) provides an excellent review of Hirschman's theorem. Stein (1956) proved the Stein–Hirschman interpolation theorem, which is essential to the proof of Theorem 12.1.1. Zurek (2000) and Ollivier & Zurek (2001) defined the quantum discord. Jencova (2012) proved Proposition 12.3.1 for $t = 0$.

13 The Information of Quantum Channels

We introduced several classical and quantum entropic quantities in Chapters 10 and 11: entropy, conditional entropy, joint entropy, mutual information, relative entropy, and conditional mutual information. Each of these entropic quantities is static, in the sense that each is evaluated with respect to random variables or quantum systems that certain parties possess.

In this chapter, we introduce several dynamic entropic quantities for channels, whether they be classical or quantum. We derive these measures by exploiting the static measures from the two previous chapters. They come about by sending one share of a state through a channel, computing a static measure with respect to the input–output state, and then maximizing the static measure with respect to all possible states that we can transmit through the channel. This process then gives rise to a dynamic measure that quantifies the ability of a channel to preserve correlations. For example, we could send one share of a pure entangled state $|\phi\rangle_{AA'}$ through a quantum channel $\mathcal{N}_{A'\to B}$—this transmission gives rise to some bipartite state $\mathcal{N}_{A'\to B}(\phi_{AA'})$. We would then evaluate the mutual information of the resulting state and maximize the mutual information with respect to all such pure input states:

$$\max_{\phi_{AA'}} I(A;B)_\omega, \tag{13.1}$$

where $\omega_{AB} \equiv \mathcal{N}_{A'\to B}(\phi_{AA'})$. The above quantity is a dynamic information measure of the channel's ability to preserve correlations—Section 13.4 introduces this quantity as the mutual information of the channel $\mathcal{N}$.

For now, we simply think of the quantities in this chapter as measures of a channel's ability to preserve correlations. Later, we show that these quantities have explicit operational interpretations in terms of a channel's ability to perform a certain task, such as the transmission of classical or quantum information.[1] Such an operational interpretation gives meaning to an entropic measure—otherwise, it is difficult to understand a measure in an information-theoretic sense without having a specific operational task to which it corresponds.

---

[1] Giving operational interpretations to information measures is in fact one of the main goals of this book!

Recall that the entropy obeys an additivity property for any two independent random variables X_1 and X_2:

$$H(X_1, X_2) = H(X_1) + H(X_2). \qquad (13.2)$$

The above additivity property extends to a large sequence $X_1, \ldots, X_n$ of independent and identically distributed random variables. That is, applying (13.2) inductively shows that $nH(X)$ is equal to the entropy of the sequence:

$$H(X_1, \ldots, X_n) = \sum_{i=1}^{n} H(X_i) = \sum_{i=1}^{n} H(X) = nH(X), \qquad (13.3)$$

where random variable X has the same distribution as each of $X_1, \ldots, X_n$. Similarly, quantum entropy is additive for any two quantum systems in a product state $\rho \otimes \sigma$:

$$H(\rho \otimes \sigma) = H(\rho) + H(\sigma), \qquad (13.4)$$

and applying (13.4) inductively to a sequence of quantum states gives the following similar simple formula: $H(\rho^{\otimes n}) = nH(\rho)$. Additivity is a desirable property and a natural expectation that we have for any measure of information evaluated on independent systems.

In analogy with the static measures, we would like additivity to hold for the dynamic information measures. Without additivity holding, we cannot really make sense of a given measure because we would have to evaluate the measure on a potentially infinite number of independent channel uses. This evaluation on so many channel uses is generally an impossible optimization problem. Additionally, the requirement to maximize over so many uses of the channel does not identify a given measure as a unique measure of a channel's ability to perform a certain task. There could generally be other measures that are equal to the original one when we take the limit of many channel uses. Thus, a measure does not have much substantive meaning if additivity does not hold.

We devote this chapter to the discussion of several dynamic measures. Additivity holds in the general case for only three of the dynamic measures presented here: the mutual information of a classical channel, the private information of a classical wiretap channel, and the mutual information of a quantum channel. For all other measures, there are known counterexamples of channels for which additivity does not hold. In this chapter, we do not discuss the counterexamples, but instead focus only on classes of channels for which additivity does hold, in an effort to understand it in a technical sense. The proof techniques for additivity exploit many of the ideas introduced in the two previous chapters and give us a chance to practice with what we have learned there on one of the most important problems in quantum Shannon theory.

13.1   Mutual Information of a Classical Channel

Suppose that we would like to determine how much information we can transmit through a classical channel $\mathcal{N}$. Recall our simplified model of a classical channel $\mathcal{N}$ from Chapter 2, in which some conditional probability density $p_{Y|X}(y|x)$ models the effects of noise. That is, we obtain some random variable Y if we input a random variable X to the channel.

What is a good measure of the information throughput of this channel? The mutual information is perhaps the best starting point. Suppose that random variables X and Y are Bernoulli. If the classical channel is noiseless and X is completely random, the input and output random variables X and Y are perfectly correlated, the mutual information $I(X;Y)$ is equal to one bit, and the sender can transmit one bit per transmission as we would expect. If the classical channel is completely noisy (in the sense that it prepares an output that has a constant probability distribution irrespective of the input), the input and output random variables are independent and the mutual information is equal to zero bits. This observation matches our intuition that the sender should not be able to transmit any information through this completely noisy channel.

In the above model for a classical channel, the conditional probability density $p_{Y|X}(y|x)$ remains fixed, but we can "play around" with the input random variable X by modifying its probability density $p_X(x)$.[2] Thus, we still "have room" for optimizing the mutual information of the channel $\mathcal{N}$ by modifying this input density. This gives us the following definition:

DEFINITION 13.1.1 (Mutual Information of a Classical Channel)   The mutual information $I(\mathcal{N})$ of a classical channel $\mathcal{N} \equiv p_{Y|X}$ is defined as follows:

$$I(\mathcal{N}) \equiv \max_{p_X(x)} I(X;Y). \tag{13.5}$$

13.1.1   Regularized Mutual Information of a Classical Channel

We now consider whether exploiting multiple uses of a classical channel $\mathcal{N}$ and allowing for correlations between its inputs can increase its mutual information. That is, suppose that we have two independent uses of a classical channel $\mathcal{N}$ available. Let X_1 and X_2 denote the random variables input to the respective first and second copies of the channel, and let Y_1 and Y_2 denote the output random variables. Each of the two uses of the channel is equivalent to the mapping $p_{Y|X}(y|x)$ so that the channel uses are independent and identically distributed. Let $\mathcal{N} \otimes \mathcal{N}$ denote the *joint channel* that corresponds to the mapping

$$p_{Y_1,Y_2|X_1,X_2}(y_1,y_2|x_1,x_2) = p_{Y_1|X_1}(y_1|x_1)p_{Y_2|X_2}(y_2|x_2), \tag{13.6}$$

---

[2] Recall the idea from Section 2.2.4 where Alice and Bob actually choose a code for the channel randomly according to the density $p_X(x)$.

where both $p_{Y_1|X_1}(y_1|x_1)$ and $p_{Y_2|X_2}(y_2|x_2)$ are equal to the mapping $p_{Y|X}(y|x)$. The mutual information of a classical joint channel is as follows:

$$I(\mathcal{N} \otimes \mathcal{N}) \equiv \max_{p_{X_1,X_2}(x_1,x_2)} I(X_1, X_2; Y_1, Y_2). \tag{13.7}$$

We might think that we could increase the mutual information of this classical channel by allowing for correlations between the inputs to the channels through a correlated distribution $p_{X_1,X_2}(x_1, x_2)$. That is, there could be some superadditive effect if the mutual information of the classical joint channel $\mathcal{N} \otimes \mathcal{N}$ is strictly greater than two individual mutual informations:

$$I(\mathcal{N} \otimes \mathcal{N}) \overset{?}{>} 2I(\mathcal{N}). \tag{13.8}$$

Figure 13.1 displays the scenario corresponding to the above question.

In fact, we can take the above argument to its extreme, by defining the regularized mutual information $I_{\text{reg}}(\mathcal{N})$ of a classical channel as follows:

$$I_{\text{reg}}(\mathcal{N}) \equiv \lim_{n \to \infty} \frac{1}{n} I(\mathcal{N}^{\otimes n}). \tag{13.9}$$

In the above definition, the quantity $I(\mathcal{N}^{\otimes n})$ is defined as follows:

$$I(\mathcal{N}^{\otimes n}) \equiv \max_{p_{X^n}(x^n)} I(X^n; Y^n), \tag{13.10}$$

and $\mathcal{N}^{\otimes n}$ denotes n channels corresponding to the following conditional probability distribution:

$$p_{Y^n|X^n}(y^n|x^n) = \prod_{i=1}^{n} p_{Y_i|X_i}(y_i|x_i), \tag{13.11}$$

where $X^n \equiv X_1, X_2, \ldots, X_n$, $x^n \equiv x_1, x_2, \ldots, x_n$, and $Y^n \equiv Y_1, Y_2, \ldots, Y_n$. The potential superadditive effect would have the following form after bootstrapping the inequality in (13.8) to the regularization:

$$I_{\text{reg}}(\mathcal{N}) \overset{?}{>} I(\mathcal{N}). \tag{13.12}$$

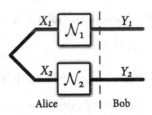

Figure 13.1 This figure displays the scenario for determining whether the mutual information of two classical channels $\mathcal{N}_1$ and $\mathcal{N}_2$ is additive. The question of additivity is equivalent to the possibility of classical correlations being able to enhance the mutual information of two classical channels. The result proved in Theorem 13.1.1 is that the mutual information is additive for any two classical channels, so that classical correlations cannot enhance it.

EXERCISE 13.1.1   Determine a finite upper bound on $I_{\text{reg}}(\mathcal{N})$. Thus, this quantity is always finite.

The next section shows that the above strict inequalities do not hold for a classical channel, implying that no such superadditive effect occurs for its mutual information. In fact, the mutual information of a classical channel obeys an additivity property that represents one of the cornerstones of our understanding of classical information theory. This additivity property is the statement that

$$I(\mathcal{N} \otimes \mathcal{M}) = I(\mathcal{N}) + I(\mathcal{M}) \tag{13.13}$$

for any two classical channels $\mathcal{N}$ and $\mathcal{M}$, and thus

$$I_{\text{reg}}(\mathcal{N}) = I(\mathcal{N}), \tag{13.14}$$

by an inductive argument. Thus, classical correlations between inputs do not increase the mutual information of a classical channel.

We are stressing the importance of additivity in classical information theory because recent research has demonstrated that superadditive effects can occur in quantum Shannon theory (see Section 20.5, for example). These quantum results imply that our understanding of quantum Shannon theory is not complete, but they also demonstrate the fascinating possibility that quantum correlations can increase the information throughput of a quantum channel.

13.1.2   Additivity

The mutual information of classical channels satisfies the important and natural property of additivity. We prove the strongest form of additivity that occurs for the mutual information of two different classical channels. Let $\mathcal{N}_1$ and $\mathcal{N}_2$ denote two *different* classical channels corresponding to the respective mappings $p_{Y_1|X_1}(y_1|x_1)$ and $p_{Y_2|X_2}(y_2|x_2)$, and let $\mathcal{N}_1 \otimes \mathcal{N}_2$ denote the joint channel that corresponds to the mapping

$$p_{Y_1,Y_2|X_1,X_2}(y_1, y_2|x_1, x_2) = p_{Y_1|X_1}(y_1|x_1)p_{Y_2|X_2}(y_2|x_2). \tag{13.15}$$

The mutual information of the joint channel is then as follows:

$$I(\mathcal{N}_1 \otimes \mathcal{N}_2) \equiv \max_{p_{X_1,X_2}(x_1,x_2)} I(X_1, X_2; Y_1, Y_2). \tag{13.16}$$

The following theorem states the additivity property:

THEOREM 13.1.1 (Additivity of Mutual Information of Classical Channels)   The mutual information of the classical joint channel $\mathcal{N}_1 \otimes \mathcal{N}_2$ is the sum of their individual mutual informations:

$$I(\mathcal{N}_1 \otimes \mathcal{N}_2) = I(\mathcal{N}_1) + I(\mathcal{N}_2). \tag{13.17}$$

Proof   We first prove the inequality $I(\mathcal{N}_1 \otimes \mathcal{N}_2) \geq I(\mathcal{N}_1) + I(\mathcal{N}_2)$. This inequality is more trivial to prove than the other direction. Let $p_{X_1}^*(x_1)$ and $p_{X_2}^*(x_2)$ denote distributions that achieve the respective maximums of $I(\mathcal{N}_1)$ and $I(\mathcal{N}_2)$. The joint probability distribution for all input and output random variables is then as follows:

$$p_{X_1,X_2,Y_1,Y_2}(x_1,x_2,y_1,y_2) = p^*_{X_1}(x_1)p^*_{X_2}(x_2)p_{Y_1|X_1}(y_1|x_1)p_{Y_2|X_2}(y_2|x_2).$$
$$(13.18)$$

Observe that X_1 and Y_1 are independent of X_2 and Y_2. Then the following chain of inequalities holds:

$$I(\mathcal{N}_1) + I(\mathcal{N}_2) = I(X_1;Y_1) + I(X_2;Y_2) \qquad (13.19)$$
$$= I(X_1,X_2;Y_1,Y_2) \qquad (13.20)$$
$$\leq I(\mathcal{N}_1 \otimes \mathcal{N}_2). \qquad (13.21)$$

The first equality follows by evaluating the mutual informations $I(\mathcal{N}_1)$ and $I(\mathcal{N}_2)$ with respect to the maximizing distributions $p^*_{X_1}(x_1)$ and $p^*_{X_2}(x_2)$. The second equality follows because the mutual information is additive with respect to the independent joint random variables (X_1,Y_1) and (X_2,Y_2). The final inequality follows because the input distribution $p^*_{X_1}(x_1)p^*_{X_2}(x_2)$ is a particular input distribution of the more general form $p_{X_1,X_2}(x_1,x_2)$ needed in the maximization of the mutual information of the joint channel $\mathcal{N}_1 \otimes \mathcal{N}_2$.

We now prove the non-trivial inequality $I(\mathcal{N}_1 \otimes \mathcal{N}_2) \leq I(\mathcal{N}_1) + I(\mathcal{N}_2)$. Let $p^*_{X_1,X_2}(x_1,x_2)$ denote a distribution that maximizes $I(\mathcal{N}_1 \otimes \mathcal{N}_2)$, and let

$$q_{X_1|X_2}(x_1|x_2) \text{ and } q_{X_2}(x_2) \qquad (13.22)$$

be distributions such that

$$p^*_{X_1,X_2}(x_1,x_2) = q_{X_1|X_2}(x_1|x_2)q_{X_2}(x_2). \qquad (13.23)$$

Recall that the conditional probability distribution for the joint channel $\mathcal{N}_1 \otimes \mathcal{N}_2$ is as follows:

$$p_{Y_1,Y_2|X_1,X_2}(y_1,y_2|x_1,x_2) = p_{Y_1|X_1}(y_1|x_1)p_{Y_2|X_2}(y_2|x_2). \qquad (13.24)$$

By summing over y_2, we observe that Y_1 and X_2 are independent when conditioned on X_1 because

$$p_{Y_1|X_1,X_2}(y_1|x_1,x_2) = p_{Y_1|X_1}(y_1|x_1). \qquad (13.25)$$

Also, the joint distribution $p_{X_1,Y_1,Y_2|X_2}(x_1,y_1,y_2|x_2)$ has the form

$$p_{X_1,Y_1,Y_2|X_2}(x_1,y_1,y_2|x_2) = p_{Y_1|X_1}(y_1|x_1)q_{X_1|X_2}(x_1|x_2)p_{Y_2|X_2}(y_2|x_2). \quad (13.26)$$

Then Y_2 is conditionally independent of X_1 and Y_1 when conditioning on X_2. Consider the following chain of inequalities:

$$I(\mathcal{N}_1 \otimes \mathcal{N}_2) = I(X_1,X_2;Y_1,Y_2) \qquad (13.27)$$
$$= H(Y_1,Y_2) - H(Y_1,Y_2|X_1,X_2) \qquad (13.28)$$
$$= H(Y_1,Y_2) - H(Y_1|X_1,X_2) - H(Y_2|Y_1,X_1,X_2) \qquad (13.29)$$
$$= H(Y_1,Y_2) - H(Y_1|X_1) - H(Y_2|X_2) \qquad (13.30)$$

$$\leq H(Y_1) + H(Y_2) - H(Y_1|X_1) - H(Y_2|X_2) \tag{13.31}$$

$$= I(X_1; Y_1) + I(X_2; Y_2) \tag{13.32}$$

$$\leq I(\mathcal{N}_1) + I(\mathcal{N}_2). \tag{13.33}$$

The first equality follows from the definition of $I(\mathcal{N}_1 \otimes \mathcal{N}_2)$ in (13.16) and by evaluating the mutual information with respect to the distributions $p^*_{X_1,X_2}(x_1, x_2)$, $p_{Y_1|X_1}(y_1|x_1)$, and $p_{Y_2|X_2}(y_2|x_2)$. The second equality follows by expanding the mutual information $I(X_1, X_2; Y_1, Y_2)$. The third equality follows from the entropy chain rule. The fourth equality follows because $H(Y_1|X_1, X_2) = H(Y_1|X_1)$ given that Y_1 is independent of X_2 when conditioned on X_1 as pointed out in (13.24). Also, the equality follows because $H(Y_2|Y_1, X_1, X_2) = H(Y_2|X_2)$ given that Y_2 is conditionally independent of X_1 and Y_1 as pointed out in (13.26). The first inequality follows from subadditivity of entropy (Exercise 10.3.3). The last equality follows from the definition of mutual information, and the final inequality follows because the marginal distributions for X_1 and X_2 can only achieve a mutual information less than or equal to the respective maximizing marginal distributions for $I(\mathcal{N}_1)$ and $I(\mathcal{N}_2)$.   □

A simple corollary of Theorem 13.1.1 is that correlations between input random variables cannot increase the mutual information of a classical channel. The proof follows by a straightforward induction argument. Thus, the *single-letter* expression in (13.5) for the mutual information of a classical channel suffices for understanding the ability of a classical channel to maintain correlations between its input and output.

COROLLARY 13.1.1   The regularized mutual information of a classical channel is equal to its mutual information:

$$I_{\text{reg}}(\mathcal{N}) = I(\mathcal{N}). \tag{13.34}$$

Proof   We prove the result using induction on n, by showing that $I(\mathcal{N}^{\otimes n}) = nI(\mathcal{N})$ for all n, implying that the limit in (13.9) is not necessary. The base case for $n = 1$ is trivial. Suppose the result holds for n: $I(\mathcal{N}^{\otimes n}) = nI(\mathcal{N})$. The following chain of equalities then proves the inductive step:

$$I(\mathcal{N}^{\otimes n+1}) = I(\mathcal{N} \otimes \mathcal{N}^{\otimes n}) \tag{13.35}$$

$$= I(\mathcal{N}) + I(\mathcal{N}^{\otimes n}) \tag{13.36}$$

$$= I(\mathcal{N}) + nI(\mathcal{N}). \tag{13.37}$$

The first equality follows because the channel $\mathcal{N}^{\otimes n+1}$ is equivalent to the parallel concatenation of $\mathcal{N}$ and $\mathcal{N}^{\otimes n}$. The second critical equality follows from the application of Theorem 13.1.1 because the distributions of $\mathcal{N}$ and $\mathcal{N}^{\otimes n}$ factor as in (13.24). The final equality follows from the induction hypothesis.   □

13.1.3   The Problem with Regularization

The main problem with a regularized information quantity is that it does not uniquely characterize the capacity of a channel for a given information-processing task, whether it be a classical or quantum one. This motivates the task of proving additivity of an information quantity.

We illustrate this point now with an example. Let $I_a(\mathcal{N})$ denote the following function of a classical channel $\mathcal{N}$:

$$I_a(\mathcal{N}) = \max_{p_X(x)} [H(X) - aH(X|Y)], \tag{13.38}$$

where $a > 1$. From the definitions we can conclude that

$$I(\mathcal{N}) \geq I_a(\mathcal{N}), \tag{13.39}$$

and in fact that

$$\frac{1}{n} I(\mathcal{N}^{\otimes n}) \geq \frac{1}{n} I_a(\mathcal{N}^n), \tag{13.40}$$

for any fixed positive integer n. However, something interesting happens when we regularize the quantity $I_a(\mathcal{N})$, i.e., when we consider the following limit:

$$\lim_{n \to \infty} \frac{1}{n} I_a(\mathcal{N}^{\otimes n}) = \lim_{n \to \infty} \frac{1}{n} \max_{p_{X^n}(x^n)} [H(X^n) - aH(X^n|Y^n)]. \tag{13.41}$$

Let n be a large fixed integer (large enough so that the law of large numbers comes into play). That is, we can fix constants $\varepsilon \in (0, 1)$ and $\delta > 0$. From Shannon's channel coding theorem, we know that there exists a code $\{x^n(m)\}_{m \in \mathcal{M}}$ of rate $\frac{1}{n} \log |\mathcal{M}| = I(\mathcal{N}) - \delta$ and length n for the channel $\mathcal{N}$, such that the probability of error when decoding is no larger than ε. So we can pick $p_{X^n}(x^n)$ to be the uniform distribution over the codewords for this code, and for this choice, we get

$$H(X^n) = \log |\mathcal{M}| = n [I(\mathcal{N}) - \delta]. \tag{13.42}$$

Furthermore, we can apply Fano's inequality (Theorem 10.7.3) to conclude that

$$H(X^n|Y^n) \leq h_2(\varepsilon) + \varepsilon \log [|\mathcal{M}| - 1] \tag{13.43}$$

$$\leq h_2(\varepsilon) + \varepsilon n [I(\mathcal{N}) - \delta]. \tag{13.44}$$

Putting these inequalities together implies that

$$\frac{1}{n} I_a(\mathcal{N}^{\otimes n}) = \frac{1}{n} \max_{p_{X^n}(x^n)} [H(X^n) - aH(X^n|Y^n)] \tag{13.45}$$

$$\geq \frac{1}{n} (n [I(\mathcal{N}) - \delta] - a [h_2(\varepsilon) + \varepsilon n [I(\mathcal{N}) - \delta]]) \tag{13.46}$$

$$= (1 - a\varepsilon) I(\mathcal{N}) - a\delta\varepsilon - \frac{1}{n} [\delta - ah_2(\varepsilon)]. \tag{13.47}$$

Taking the limit $n \to \infty$ then gives

$$\lim_{n \to \infty} \frac{1}{n} I_a(\mathcal{N}^{\otimes n}) \geq (1 - a\varepsilon) I(\mathcal{N}) - a\delta\varepsilon. \tag{13.48}$$

However, as n gets larger, we can make both ε and δ go to zero (in principle we could write ε and δ as explicit functions of n that go to zero as $n \to \infty$). This establishes that

$$\lim_{n \to \infty} \frac{1}{n} I_a(\mathcal{N}^{\otimes n}) \geq I(\mathcal{N}). \tag{13.49}$$

However, we have for every n that

$$\frac{1}{n}[H(X^n) - aH(X^n|Y^n)] \leq \frac{1}{n}[H(X^n) - H(X^n|Y^n)] \tag{13.50}$$

$$\leq \lim_{n\to\infty} \frac{1}{n}I(\mathcal{N}^{\otimes n}) \tag{13.51}$$

$$= I(\mathcal{N}), \tag{13.52}$$

where the last equality follows from Corollary 13.1.1. These two bounds lead us to the conclusion that

$$\lim_{n\to\infty} \frac{1}{n}I_a(\mathcal{N}^{\otimes n}) = I(\mathcal{N}). \tag{13.53}$$

Thus, even though for a given channel $\mathcal{N}$ we can have a strict inequality between $I_a(\mathcal{N})$ and $I(\mathcal{N})$ on the single-copy level (and even on the multi-copy level for finite n), this difference gets washed away or "blurred" in the limit $n \to \infty$ for any finite $a > 1$. For this reason, we should always be wary of a regularized characterization of capacity, knowing that it is incomplete. It is only when we have additivity of an information quantity that we can conclude that it fully characterizes capacity for a given information-processing task. Unfortunately, regularization is a problem that plagues much of quantum Shannon theory (except for a few tasks, such as entanglement-assisted classical communication, discussed in Chapter 21).

13.1.4   Optimizing the Mutual Information of a Classical Channel

The definition in (13.5) seems like a suitable definition for the mutual information of a classical channel, but how difficult is the maximization problem that it sets out? Theorem 13.1.2 below states an important property of the mutual information $I(X;Y)$ that allows us to answer this question. Suppose that we fix the conditional density $p_{Y|X}(y|x)$, but can vary the input density $p_X(x)$. Theorem 13.1.2 below states that the mutual information $I(X;Y)$ is a concave function of the density $p_X(x)$. In particular, this result implies that the channel mutual information $I(\mathcal{N})$ has a global maximum, and the optimization problem is therefore a straightforward computation that can exploit convex optimization methods.

THEOREM 13.1.2   Suppose that we fix the conditional probability density $p_{Y|X}(y|x)$. Then the mutual information $I(X;Y)$ is concave in the marginal density $p_X(x)$:

$$\lambda I(X_1;Y) + (1 - \lambda) I(X_2;Y) \leq I(Z;Y), \tag{13.54}$$

where random variable X_1 has density $p_{X_1}(x)$, X_2 has density $p_{X_2}(x)$, and Z has density $\lambda p_{X_1}(x) + (1 - \lambda) p_{X_2}(x)$ for $\lambda \in [0, 1]$.

Proof   Let us fix the density $p_{Y|X}(y|x)$. The density $p_Y(y)$ is a linear function of $p_X(x)$ because $p_Y(y) = \sum_x p_{Y|X}(y|x)p_X(x)$. Thus $H(Y)$ is concave in $p_X(x)$.

Recall that the conditional entropy $H(Y|X) = \sum_x p_X(x)H(Y|X = x)$. The entropy $H(Y|X = x)$ is fixed when the conditional probability density $p_{Y|X}(y|x)$ is fixed. Thus, $H(Y|X)$ is a linear function of $p_X(x)$. These two results imply that the mutual information $I(X;Y)$ is concave in the marginal density $p_X(x)$ when the conditional density $p_{Y|X}(y|x)$ is fixed. □

13.2 Private Information of a Wiretap Channel

Suppose now that we extend the above two-user classical communication scenario to a three-user communication scenario, where the parties involved are Alice, Bob, and Eve. Suppose that Alice would like to communicate to Bob while keeping her messages private from Eve. The channel $\mathcal{N}$ corresponding to this setting is called the wiretap channel, which has the following conditional probability density:

$$p_{Y,Z|X}(y,z|x). \tag{13.55}$$

Alice has access to the input random variable X, Bob receives output random variable Y, and Eve receives the random variable Z. Figure 13.2 depicts this setting.

We would like to establish a measure of information throughput for this scenario. It might seem intuitive that it should be the amount of correlations that Alice can establish with Bob, less the correlations that Eve receives: $I(X;Y) - I(X;Z)$. However, a more general procedure would allow Alice to pick an auxiliary random variable U and then to pick X given the value of U, leading to the following information quantity:

$$I(U;Y) - I(U;Z). \tag{13.56}$$

But Alice can maximize over all such input distributions $p_{U,X}(u,x)$ on her end. This leads us to the following definition:

DEFINITION 13.2.1 (Private Information of a Wiretap Channel)   The private information $P(\mathcal{N})$ of a classical wiretap channel $\mathcal{N} \equiv p_{Y,Z|X}$ is defined as follows:

$$P(\mathcal{N}) \equiv \max_{p_{U,X}(u,x)} [I(U;Y) - I(U;Z)]. \tag{13.57}$$

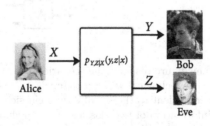

Figure 13.2 The setting for the classical wiretap channel.

It is possible to provide an operational interpretation of the private information, but we do not do that here. We instead focus on the additivity properties
of the private information $P(\mathcal{N})$.

One may wonder if the above quantity is non-negative, given that it is equal
to the difference of two mutual informations. Non-negativity does hold, and a
simple proof demonstrates this fact.

PROPERTY 13.2.1   The private information $P(\mathcal{N})$ of a wiretap channel is non-
negative:

$$P(\mathcal{N}) \geq 0. \tag{13.58}$$

Proof We can choose the joint density $p_{U,X}(u, x)$ in the maximization of $P(\mathcal{N})$
to be the degenerate distribution $p_{U,X}(u, x) = \delta_{u,u_0}\delta_{x,x_0}$ for some values u_0 and
x_0. Then both mutual informations $I(U; Y)$ and $I(U; Z)$ vanish, and their difference vanishes as well. The private information $P(\mathcal{N})$ can then only be greater
than or equal to zero because the above choice is a particular choice of the density
$p_{U,X}(u, x)$ and $P(\mathcal{N})$ requires a maximization over all such distributions.   □

EXERCISE 13.2.1   Show that adding an auxiliary random variable cannot
increase the mutual information of a classical channel. That is, let $\mathcal{N} \equiv p_{Y|X}$
and show that $I(\mathcal{N}) = \max_{p_{U,X}} I(U; Y)$. Explain why it is possible for an auxiliary random variable to increase the private information of a classical wiretap
channel.

13.2.1   Additivity of Private Information

The private information of general classical wiretap channels is additive. This
result follows essentially from an application of the chain rule for mutual information. Figure 13.3 displays the scenario corresponding to the analysis involved
in determining whether the private information is additive.

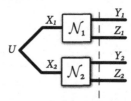

Figure 13.3 This figure displays the scenario for determining whether the private
information of two classical wiretap channels $\mathcal{N}_1$ and $\mathcal{N}_2$ is additive. The question of
additivity is equivalent to the possibility of classical correlations being able to enhance
the private information of two classical wiretap channels. The result stated in
Theorem 13.2.1 is that the private information is additive for two wiretap channels, so
that classical correlations cannot enhance the private information.

THEOREM 13.2.1 (Additivity of Private Information) Let $\mathcal{N}_i$ be a classical wiretap channel with distribution $p_{Y_i, Z_i | X_i}$, for $i \in \{1, 2\}$. The private information of the classical joint channel $\mathcal{N}_1 \otimes \mathcal{N}_2$ is the sum of the individual private informations of the channels:

$$P(\mathcal{N}_1 \otimes \mathcal{N}_2) = P(\mathcal{N}_1) + P(\mathcal{N}_2). \tag{13.59}$$

Proof The inequality $P(\mathcal{N}_1 \otimes \mathcal{N}_2) \geq P(\mathcal{N}_1) + P(\mathcal{N}_2)$ is trivial and we leave it as an exercise for the reader to complete.

We thus prove the following non-trivial inequality: $P(\mathcal{N}_1 \otimes \mathcal{N}_2) \leq P(\mathcal{N}_1) + P(\mathcal{N}_2)$. Let $p_{U, X_1, X_2}(u, x_1, x_2)$ be any probability distribution that we could consider for the quantity $P(\mathcal{N}_1 \otimes \mathcal{N}_2)$, where U is an auxiliary random variable. The joint channel has the following probability distribution:

$$p_{Y_1, Z_1 | X_1}(y_1, z_1 | x_1) p_{Y_2, Z_2 | X_2}(y_2, z_2 | x_2). \tag{13.60}$$

Consider the following chain of equalities:

$$
\begin{aligned}
& I(U; Y_1 Y_2) - I(U; Z_1 Z_2) \\
&= I(U; Y_1) + I(U; Y_2 | Y_1) - I(U; Z_2) - I(U; Z_1 | Z_2) \tag{13.61} \\
&= I(U; Y_1 | Z_2) + I(U; Y_2 | Y_1) - I(U; Z_2 | Y_1) - I(U; Z_1 | Z_2) \tag{13.62} \\
&= I(U; Y_1 | Z_2) - I(U; Z_1 | Z_2) + I(U; Y_2 | Y_1) - I(U; Z_2 | Y_1). \tag{13.63}
\end{aligned}
$$

The first equality follows from an application of the chain rule for mutual information. The second equality follows from the identity

$$I(U; Y_1) - I(U; Z_2) = I(U; Y_1 | Z_2) - I(U; Z_2 | Y_1), \tag{13.64}$$

which can be verified using definitions. The third equality is a simple rearrangement. We now focus on the term $I(U; Y_1 | Z_2) - I(U; Z_1 | Z_2)$. Note that the probability distribution for these random variables can be written as

$$p_{Y_1, Z_1 | X_1}(y_1, z_1 | x_1) p_{X_1 | U}(x_1 | u) p_{U | Z_2}(u | z_2) p_{Z_2}(z_2), \tag{13.65}$$

where $p_{U | Z_2}(u | z_2) = \sum_{x_2} p_{U, X_2 | Z_2}(u, x_2 | z_2)$. (The fact that the distribution factors in this way is where the assumption of independent wiretap channels comes into play.) Consider that

$$
\begin{aligned}
& I(U; Y_1 | Z_2) - I(U; Z_1 | Z_2) \\
&= \sum_{z_2} p_{Z_2}(z_2) \left[I(U; Y_1 | Z_2 = z_2) - I(U; Z_1 | Z_2 = z_2) \right] \tag{13.66} \\
&\leq \max_{z_2} \left[I(U; Y_1 | Z_2 = z_2) - I(U; Z_1 | Z_2 = z_2) \right] \tag{13.67} \\
&\leq P(\mathcal{N}_1). \tag{13.68}
\end{aligned}
$$

The first equality follows because the conditional mutual informations can be expanded as a convex combination of mutual informations. The last inequality follows because $p_{U|Z_2}(u|z_2)$ is a particular distribution for an auxiliary random variable $U|Z_2 = z_2$. By the same kind of reasoning, we find that

$$I(U; Y_2|Y_1) - I(U; Z_2|Y_1) \leq P(\mathcal{N}_2), \tag{13.69}$$

and can then conclude that

$$I(U; Y_1 Y_2) - I(U; Z_1 Z_2) \leq P(\mathcal{N}_1) + P(\mathcal{N}_2). \tag{13.70}$$

Since this inequality holds for any auxiliary random variable U, we can finally conclude that $P(\mathcal{N}_1 \otimes \mathcal{N}_2) \leq P(\mathcal{N}_1) + P(\mathcal{N}_2)$.   □

EXERCISE 13.2.2   Show that the sum of the individual private informations can never be greater than the private information of the classical joint channel:

$$P(\mathcal{N}_1 \otimes \mathcal{N}_2) \geq P(\mathcal{N}_1) + P(\mathcal{N}_2). \tag{13.71}$$

EXERCISE 13.2.3   Show that the regularized private information of a wiretap channel $\mathcal{N}$ is equal to its private information: $\lim_{n\to\infty} \frac{1}{n} P(\mathcal{N}^{\otimes n}) = P(\mathcal{N})$.

13.2.2   Degraded Wiretap Channels

The formula for the private information simplifies for a particular type of wiretap channel, called a physically degraded wiretap channel. A wiretap channel is physically degraded if X, Y, and Z form the following Markov chain: $X \to Y \to Z$. That is, the channel distribution factors as $p_{Y,Z|X}(y, z|x) = p_{Z|Y}(z|y) p_{Y|X}(y|x)$, so that there is some channel $p_{Z|Y}(z|y)$ that Bob can apply to his output to simulate the channel $p_{Z|X}(z|x)$ to Eve:

$$p_{Z|X}(z|x) = \sum_y p_{Z|Y}(z|y) p_{Y|X}(y|x). \tag{13.72}$$

This condition allows us to apply the data-processing inequality to give the following simplified formula for the private information of a degraded wiretap channel, in which there is no need for an auxiliary random variable:

PROPOSITION 13.2.1   The private information $P(\mathcal{N})$ of a degraded classical wiretap channel $\mathcal{N} \equiv p_{Y,Z|X}$ simplifies as follows:

$$P(\mathcal{N}) \equiv \max_{p_X(x)} [I(X; Y) - I(X; Z)]. \tag{13.73}$$

Proof   Consider that we always have

$$\max_{p_{U,X}(u,x)} [I(U; Y) - I(U; Z)] \geq \max_{p_X(x)} [I(X; Y) - I(X; Z)], \tag{13.74}$$

by picking the distribution on the left-hand side as $p_{U,X}(u, x) = p_X(x)\delta_{x,u}$. That is, we set U to be a random variable with the same alphabet size as the channel input and then just send U directly into the channel. To prove the other inequality, we need to use the assumption of degradability, which implies that $U - X - Y - Z$ is a Markov chain. Consider that

$$I(U;Y) = I(X;Y) + I(U;Y|X) - I(X;Y|U) \tag{13.75}$$

$$= I(X;Y) - I(X;Y|U). \tag{13.76}$$

The first equality follows from two applications of the chain rule for mutual information. The second equality follows because $U - X - Y$ is a Markov chain, so that $I(U;Y|X) = 0$. By the same reasoning, we have that $I(U;Z) = I(X;Z) - I(X;Z|U)$. Then

$$I(U;Y) - I(U;Z) = I(X;Y) - I(X;Y|U) - [I(X;Z) - I(X;Z|U)] \tag{13.77}$$

$$= I(X;Y) - I(X;Z) - [I(X;Y|U) - I(X;Z|U)] \tag{13.78}$$

$$\leq I(X;Y) - I(X;Z) \tag{13.79}$$

$$\leq \max_{p_X(x)} [I(X;Y) - I(X;Z)]. \tag{13.80}$$

The inequality follows from the assumption that the wiretap channel is degraded, so that we can apply the data-processing inequality and conclude that $I(X;Y|U) \geq I(X;Z|U)$. Since the inequality holds for any auxiliary random variable U, we can conclude that

$$\max_{p_{U,X}(u,x)} [I(U;Y) - I(U;Z)] \leq \max_{p_X(x)} [I(X;Y) - I(X;Z)], \tag{13.81}$$

which completes the proof. $\square$

An analogous notion of degradability exists in the quantum setting, and Section 13.5 demonstrates that degradable quantum channels have additive coherent information. The coherent information of a quantum channel is a measure of how much quantum information a sender can transmit through that channel to a receiver and thus is an important quantity to consider for quantum data transmission.

EXERCISE 13.2.4 Show that the private information of a degraded wiretap channel can also be written as $\max_{p_X(x)} I(X;Y|Z)$.

13.3 Holevo Information of a Quantum Channel

We now turn our attention to the case of dynamic information measures for quantum channels, and we begin with a measure of classical correlations. Suppose that Alice would like to establish classical correlations with Bob, by means of a quantum channel. Alice can prepare an ensemble $\{p_X(x), \rho^x\}$ in her laboratory, where the states ρ^x are acceptable inputs to the quantum channel. She keeps a copy of the classical index x in some classical register X. The expected density operator of this ensemble is the following classical–quantum state:

$$\rho_{XA} \equiv \sum_x p_X(x)|x\rangle\langle x|_X \otimes \rho_A^x. \tag{13.82}$$

Such a preparation is the most general way that Alice can correlate classical data with a quantum state to input to the channel. Let ρ_{XB} be the state that arises from sending the A system through the quantum channel $\mathcal{N}_{A \to B}$:

$$\rho_{XB} \equiv \sum_x p_X(x) |x\rangle\langle x|_X \otimes \mathcal{N}_{A \to B}(\rho_A^x). \tag{13.83}$$

We would like to determine a measure of the ability of the quantum channel to preserve classical correlations. We can appeal to ideas from the classical case in Section 13.1, while incorporating the static quantum measures from Chapter 11. A good measure of the input–output classical correlations is the Holevo information of the above classical–quantum state: $I(X;B)_\rho$. This measure corresponds to a particular preparation that Alice chooses, but observe that she can prepare the input ensemble in such a way as to achieve the highest possible correlations. Maximizing the Holevo information over all possible preparations gives a dynamic measure called the Holevo information of the channel.

DEFINITION 13.3.1 (Holevo Information of a Quantum Channel) The Holevo information $\chi(\mathcal{N})$ of a channel $\mathcal{N}$ is a measure of the classical correlations that Alice can establish with Bob:

$$\chi(\mathcal{N}) \equiv \max_{\rho_{XA}} I(X;B)_\rho, \tag{13.84}$$

where the maximization is with respect to all input classical–quantum states of the form in (13.82) and $I(X;B)_\rho$ is evaluated with respect to the state in (13.83).

13.3.1   Additivity of the Holevo Information for Specific Channels

The Holevo information of a quantum channel is generally not additive (by no means is this obvious!). The question of additivity for this case is *not* whether classical correlations can enhance the Holevo information, but it is *rather* whether quantum correlations can enhance it. That is, Alice can choose an ensemble of the form $\{p_X(x), \rho_{A_1 A_2}^x\}$ for input to two uses of the quantum channel. The conditional density operators $\rho_{A_1 A_2}^x$ can be entangled and these quantum correlations can potentially increase the Holevo information.

The question of additivity of the Holevo information of a quantum channel was a longstanding open conjecture in quantum information theory—many researchers thought that quantum correlations would not enhance it and that additivity would hold. But recent research has demonstrated a counterexample to the additivity conjecture, and perhaps unsurprisingly in hindsight, this counterexample exploits maximally entangled states to demonstrate superadditivity (see Section 20.5). Figure 13.4 displays the scenario corresponding to the question of additivity of the Holevo information.

Additivity of Holevo information may not hold for all quantum channels, but it is possible to prove its additivity for certain classes of quantum channels. One such class for which additivity holds is the class of entanglement-breaking channels, and the proof of additivity is perhaps the simplest for this case.

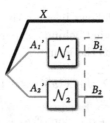

Figure 13.4 The scenario for determining whether the Holevo information of two quantum channels $\mathcal{N}_1$ and $\mathcal{N}_2$ is additive. The question of additivity is equivalent to the possibility of quantum correlations being able to enhance the Holevo information of two quantum channels. The result stated in Theorem 13.3.1 is that the Holevo information is additive for the tensor product of an entanglement-breaking channel and any other quantum channel, so that quantum correlations cannot enhance the Holevo information in this case. This is perhaps intuitive because an entanglement-breaking channel destroys quantum correlations in the form of quantum entanglement.

THEOREM 13.3.1 (Additivity for Entanglement-Breaking Channels) Suppose that a quantum channel $\mathcal{N}^{\mathrm{EB}}$ is entanglement breaking and another channel $\mathcal{M}$ is arbitrary. Then the Holevo information $\chi(\mathcal{N}^{\mathrm{EB}} \otimes \mathcal{M})$ of the tensor-product channel $\mathcal{N}^{\mathrm{EB}} \otimes \mathcal{M}$ is the sum of the individual Holevo informations $\chi(\mathcal{N}^{\mathrm{EB}})$ and $\chi(\mathcal{M})$:

$$\chi(\mathcal{N}^{\mathrm{EB}} \otimes \mathcal{M}) = \chi(\mathcal{N}^{\mathrm{EB}}) + \chi(\mathcal{M}). \tag{13.85}$$

Proof The trivial inequality $\chi(\mathcal{N}^{\mathrm{EB}} \otimes \mathcal{M}) \geq \chi(\mathcal{N}^{\mathrm{EB}}) + \chi(\mathcal{M})$ holds for any two quantum channels $\mathcal{N}^{\mathrm{EB}}$ and $\mathcal{M}$ because we can choose the input ensemble on the left-hand side to be a tensor product of the ones that individually maximize the terms on the right-hand side.

We now prove the non-trivial inequality $\chi(\mathcal{N}^{\mathrm{EB}} \otimes \mathcal{M}) \leq \chi(\mathcal{N}^{\mathrm{EB}}) + \chi(\mathcal{M})$ that holds when $\mathcal{N}^{\mathrm{EB}}$ is entanglement breaking. Let $\rho_{XB_1B_2}$ be a state that maximizes the Holevo information $\chi(\mathcal{N}^{\mathrm{EB}} \otimes \mathcal{M})$, where

$$\rho_{XB_1B_2} \equiv (\mathcal{N}^{\mathrm{EB}}_{A_1 \to B_1} \otimes \mathcal{M})(\rho_{XA_1A_2}), \tag{13.86}$$

$$\rho_{XA_1A_2} \equiv \sum_x p_X(x)|x\rangle\langle x|_X \otimes \rho^x_{A_1A_2}. \tag{13.87}$$

Let $\rho_{XB_1A_2}$ be the state after only the entanglement-breaking channel $\mathcal{N}^{\mathrm{EB}}_{A_1 \to B_1}$ acts. We can write this state as follows:

$$\rho_{XB_1A_2} \equiv \mathcal{N}^{\mathrm{EB}}_{A_1 \to B_1}(\rho_{XA_1A_2}) = \sum_x p_X(x)|x\rangle\langle x|_X \otimes \mathcal{N}^{\mathrm{EB}}_{A_1 \to B_1}(\rho^x_{A_1A_2}) \tag{13.88}$$

$$= \sum_x p_X(x)|x\rangle\langle x|_X \otimes \sum_y p_{Y|X}(y|x)\, \sigma^{x,y}_{B_1} \otimes \theta^{x,y}_{A_2} \tag{13.89}$$

$$= \sum_{x,y} p_{Y|X}(y|x)p_X(x)|x\rangle\langle x|_X \otimes \sigma^{x,y}_{B_1} \otimes \theta^{x,y}_{A_2}. \tag{13.90}$$

The third equality follows because the channel $\mathcal{N}^{EB}$ breaks any entanglement in the state $\rho_{A_1 A_2}^x$, leaving behind a separable state $\sum_y p_{Y|X}(y|x)\, \sigma_{B_1}^{x,y} \otimes \theta_{A_2}^{x,y}$. Then the state $\rho_{X B_1 B_2}$ has the form

$$\rho_{X B_1 B_2} = \sum_{x,y} p_{Y|X}(y|x) p_X(x) |x\rangle\langle x|_X \otimes \sigma_{B_1}^{x,y} \otimes \mathcal{M}(\theta_{A_2}^{x,y}). \tag{13.91}$$

Let $\omega_{X Y B_1 B_2}$ be an extension of $\rho_{X B_1 B_2}$ where

$$\omega_{X Y B_1 B_2} \equiv \sum_{x,y} p_{Y|X}(y|x) p_X(x) |x\rangle\langle x|_X \otimes |y\rangle\langle y|_Y \otimes \sigma_{B_1}^{x,y} \otimes \mathcal{M}(\theta_{A_2}^{x,y}), \tag{13.92}$$

and $\mathrm{Tr}_Y\{\omega_{X Y B_1 B_2}\} = \rho_{X B_1 B_2}$. Then the following chain of inequalities holds

$$\chi(\mathcal{N}^{EB} \otimes \mathcal{M}) = I(X; B_1 B_2)_\rho \tag{13.93}$$

$$= I(X; B_1)_\rho + I(X; B_2|B_1)_\rho \tag{13.94}$$

$$\leq \chi(\mathcal{N}^{EB}) + I(X; B_2|B_1)_\rho \tag{13.95}$$

The first equality follows because we took $\rho_{X B_1 B_2}$ to be a state that maximizes the Holevo information $\chi(\mathcal{N}^{EB} \otimes \mathcal{M})$ of the tensor-product channel $\mathcal{N}^{EB} \otimes \mathcal{M}$. The second equality is an application of the chain rule for conditional mutual information (Property 11.7.1). The inequality follows because the Holevo information $I(X; B_1)_\rho$ is with respect to the following state:

$$\rho_{X B_1} \equiv \sum_x p_X(x) |x\rangle\langle x|_X \otimes \mathcal{N}_{A_1 \to B_1}^{EB}(\rho_{A_1}^x), \tag{13.96}$$

whereas the Holevo information of the channel $\mathcal{N}_{A_1 \to B_1}^{EB}$ is defined to be the maximal Holevo information with respect to all input ensembles. Now let us focus on the term $I(X; B_2|B_1)_\rho$. Consider that

$$I(X; B_2|B_1)_\rho = I(X; B_2|B_1)_\omega \tag{13.97}$$

$$\leq I(X B_1; B_2)_\omega \tag{13.98}$$

$$\leq I(X Y B_1; B_2)_\omega \tag{13.99}$$

$$= I(X Y; B_2)_\omega + I(B_1; B_2|X Y)_\omega \tag{13.100}$$

$$= I(X Y; B_2)_\omega \tag{13.101}$$

$$\leq \chi(\mathcal{M}). \tag{13.102}$$

The first equality follows because the reduced state of $\omega_{X Y B_1 B_2}$ on systems X, B_1, and B_2 is equal to $\rho_{X B_1 B_2}$. The first inequality follows from the chain rule: $I(X; B_2|B_1) = I(X B_1; B_2) - I(B_1; B_2) \leq I(X B_1; B_2)$. The second inequality follows from the quantum data-processing inequality. The second equality is again from the chain rule for conditional mutual information. The third equality is the crucial one that exploits the entanglement-breaking property. It follows by examining (13.92) and observing that the state $\omega_{X Y B_1 B_2}$ on systems B_1 and B_2 is product when conditioned on classical variables X and Y, so that the conditional mutual information between systems B_1 and B_2 given both X and Y is equal to zero. The final inequality follows because ω_{XYB_2} is a particular state of the form needed in the maximization of $\chi(\mathcal{M})$. $\square$

COROLLARY 13.3.1 The regularized Holevo information of an entanglement-breaking quantum channel $\mathcal{N}^{\text{EB}}$ is equal to its Holevo information:

$$\chi_{\text{reg}}(\mathcal{N}^{\text{EB}}) = \chi(\mathcal{N}^{\text{EB}}). \tag{13.103}$$

Proof A proof of this property uses the same induction argument as in Corollary 13.1.1 and exploits the additivity property in Theorem 13.3.1 above. $\square$

13.3.2 Optimizing the Holevo Information

Pure States are Sufficient

The following theorem allows us to simplify the optimization problem that (13.84) sets out—we show that it is sufficient to consider ensembles of pure states at the input.

THEOREM 13.3.2 It is sufficient to maximize the Holevo information with respect to pure states:

$$\chi(\mathcal{N}) = \max_{\rho_{XA}} I(X;B)_\rho = \max_{\tau_{XA}} I(X;B)_\tau, \tag{13.104}$$

where

$$\tau_{XA} \equiv \sum_x p_X(x)|x\rangle\langle x|_X \otimes |\phi_x\rangle\langle\phi_x|_A, \tag{13.105}$$

and ρ_{XB} and τ_{XB} are the states that result from sending the A system of ρ_{XA} and τ_{XA} through the quantum channel $\mathcal{N}_{A\to B}$, respectively.

Proof Suppose that ρ_{XA} is any state of the form in (13.82). Consider a spectral decomposition of the states ρ_A^x:

$$\rho_A^x = \sum_y p_{Y|X}(y|x)\psi_A^{x,y}, \tag{13.106}$$

where the states $\psi_A^{x,y}$ are pure. Then let σ_{XYA} denote the following state:

$$\sigma_{XYA} \equiv \sum_x p_{Y|X}(y|x)p_X(x)|x\rangle\langle x|_X \otimes |y\rangle\langle y|_Y \otimes \psi_A^{x,y}, \tag{13.107}$$

so that $\text{Tr}_Y\{\sigma_{XYA}\} = \rho_{XA}$. Also, observe that σ_{XYA} is a state of the form τ_{XA} with XY as the classical system. Let σ_{XYB} denote the state that results from sending the A system through the quantum channel $\mathcal{N}_{A\to B}$. Then the following relations hold:

$$I(X;B)_\rho = I(X;B)_\sigma \leq I(XY;B)_\sigma. \tag{13.108}$$

The equality follows because $\text{Tr}_Y\{\sigma_{XYB}\} = \rho_{XB}$ and the inequality follows from the quantum data-processing inequality. It then suffices to consider ensembles with only pure states because the state σ_{XYB} is a state of the form τ_{XB} with the combined system XY acting as the classical system. $\square$

Concavity in the Distribution and Convexity in the Signal States

We now show that the Holevo information is concave as a function of the input distribution when the signal states are fixed.

THEOREM 13.3.3 The Holevo information $I(X; B)$ is concave in the input distribution when the signal states are fixed, in the sense that

$$\lambda I(X; B)_\sigma + (1 - \lambda) I(X; B)_\tau \leq I(X; B)_\omega, \tag{13.109}$$

where σ_{XB} and τ_{XB} are of the form

$$\sigma_{XB} \equiv \sum_x p_X(x) |x\rangle\langle x|_X \otimes \mathcal{N}(\rho^x), \tag{13.110}$$

$$\tau_{XB} \equiv \sum_x q_X(x) |x\rangle\langle x|_X \otimes \mathcal{N}(\rho^x), \tag{13.111}$$

and ω_{XB} is a mixture of the states σ_{XB} and τ_{XB} of the form

$$\omega_{XB} \equiv \sum_x [\lambda p_X(x) + (1 - \lambda) q_X(x)] |x\rangle\langle x|_X \otimes \mathcal{N}(\rho^x), \tag{13.112}$$

where $0 \leq \lambda \leq 1$.

Proof Let ω_{XUB} be the state

$$\omega_{XUB} \equiv \sum_x [p_X(x) |x\rangle\langle x|_X \otimes \lambda |0\rangle\langle 0|_U + q_X(x) |x\rangle\langle x|_X \otimes (1 - \lambda) |1\rangle\langle 1|_U] \otimes \mathcal{N}(\rho^x). \tag{13.113}$$

Observe that $\text{Tr}_U \{\omega_{XUB}\} = \omega_{XB}$. Then the statement of concavity is equivalent to $I(X; B|U)_\omega \leq I(X; B)_\omega$. We can rewrite this as $H(B|U)_\omega - H(B|UX)_\omega \leq H(B)_\omega - H(B|X)_\omega$. Observe that $H(B|UX)_\omega = H(B|X)_\omega$, i.e., one can calculate that both of these conditional entropies are equal to

$$\sum_x [\lambda p_X(x) + (1 - \lambda) q_X(x)] H(\mathcal{N}(\rho^x)). \tag{13.114}$$

The statement of concavity then becomes $H(B|U)_\omega \leq H(B)_\omega$, which follows from concavity of quantum entropy. □

The Holevo information is convex as a function of the signal states when the input distribution is fixed.

THEOREM 13.3.4 The Holevo information $I(X; B)$ is convex in the signal states when the input distribution is fixed, in the sense that

$$\lambda I(X; B)_\sigma + (1 - \lambda) I(X; B)_\tau \geq I(X; B)_\omega, \tag{13.115}$$

where σ_{XB} and τ_{XB} are of the form

$$\sigma_{XB} \equiv \sum_x p_X(x) |x\rangle\langle x|_X \otimes \mathcal{N}(\sigma^x), \tag{13.116}$$

$$\tau_{XB} \equiv \sum_x p_X(x) |x\rangle\langle x|_X \otimes \mathcal{N}(\tau^x), \tag{13.117}$$

and ω_{XB} is a mixture of the states σ_{XB} and τ_{XB} of the form

$$\omega_{XB} \equiv \sum_x p_X(x)|x\rangle\langle x|_X \otimes \mathcal{N}(\lambda \sigma^x + (1 - \lambda) \tau^x), \qquad (13.118)$$

where $0 \leq \lambda \leq 1$.

Proof Let ω_{XUB} be the state

$$\omega_{XUB} \equiv \sum_x p_X(x)|x\rangle\langle x|_X \otimes [\lambda|0\rangle\langle 0|_U \otimes \mathcal{N}(\sigma^x) + (1 - \lambda)|1\rangle\langle 1|_U \otimes \mathcal{N}(\tau^x)].$$

$$(13.119)$$

Observe that $\text{Tr}_U\{\omega_{XUB}\} = \omega_{XB}$. Then convexity in the input states is equivalent to the statement $I(X; B|U)_\omega \geq I(X; B)_\omega$. Consider that $I(X; B|U)_\omega = I(X; BU)_\omega - I(X; U)_\omega$, by the chain rule for the quantum mutual information. Since the input distribution $p_X(x)$ is fixed, there are no correlations between X and the convexity variable U, so that $I(X; U)_\omega = 0$. Thus, the above inequality is equivalent to $I(X; BU)_\omega \geq I(X; B)_\omega$, which follows from the quantum data-processing inequality. $\qquad\square$

In the above two theorems, we have shown that the Holevo information is either concave or convex depending on whether the signal states or the input distribution are fixed, respectively. Thus, the computation of the Holevo information of a general quantum channel becomes difficult as the input dimension of the channel grows larger, since a local maximum of the Holevo information is not necessarily a global maximum. However, if the channel has a classical input and a quantum output, the computation of the Holevo information is straightforward because the only input parameter is the input distribution, and we proved that the Holevo information is a concave function of the input distribution.

13.4 Mutual Information of a Quantum Channel

We now consider a measure of the ability of a quantum channel to preserve quantum correlations. The way that we arrive at this measure is similar to what we have seen before. Alice prepares some pure quantum state $\phi_{AA'}$ in her laboratory, and inputs the A' system to a quantum channel $\mathcal{N}_{A' \to B}$—this transmission gives rise to the following bipartite state:

$$\rho_{AB} = \mathcal{N}_{A' \to B}(\phi_{AA'}). \qquad (13.120)$$

The quantum mutual information $I(A; B)_\rho$ is a static measure of correlations present in the state ρ_{AB}. To maximize the correlations that the quantum channel can establish, Alice should maximize the quantum mutual information $I(A; B)_\rho$ with respect to all possible pure states that she can input to the channel $\mathcal{N}_{A' \to B}$. This procedure leads to the definition of the mutual information $I(\mathcal{N})$ of a quantum channel:

$$I(\mathcal{N}) \equiv \max_{\phi_{AA'}} I(A; B)_\rho. \qquad (13.121)$$

The mutual information of a quantum channel corresponds to an important operational task that is not particularly obvious from the above discussion. Suppose that Alice and Bob share unlimited bipartite entanglement in whatever form they wish, and suppose they have access to a large number of independent uses of the channel $\mathcal{N}_{A' \to B}$. Then the mutual information of the channel corresponds to the maximal amount of classical information that they can transmit in such a setting. This setting is the noisy analog of the super-dense coding protocol from Chapter 6 (recall the discussion in Section 6.4). By teleportation, the maximal amount of quantum information that they can transmit is half of the mutual information of the channel. We discuss how to prove these statements rigorously in Chapter 21.

13.4.1   Additivity

There might be little reason to expect that the quantum mutual information of a quantum channel is additive, given that the Holevo information is not. But perhaps surprisingly, additivity does hold for the mutual information of a quantum channel! This result means that we completely understand this measure of information throughput, and it also means that we understand the operational task to which it corresponds (entanglement-assisted classical coding discussed in the previous section).

We might intuitively attempt to explain this phenomenon in terms of this operational task—Alice and Bob already share unlimited entanglement between their terminals and so entangled correlations at the input of the channel do not lead to any superadditive effect as it does for the Holevo information. This explanation is somewhat rough, but perhaps the additivity proof explains best why additivity holds. The crucial tool in the proof is the chain rule for mutual information and one application of subadditivity of entropy (Corollary 11.8.1). Figure 13.5 illustrates the setting corresponding to the analysis for additivity of the mutual information of a quantum channel.

THEOREM 13.4.1 (Additivity of Q. Mutual Information of Q. Channels)   Let $\mathcal{N}$ and $\mathcal{M}$ be any quantum channels. Then the mutual information of the tensor-product channel $\mathcal{N} \otimes \mathcal{M}$ is the sum of their individual mutual informations:

$$I(\mathcal{N} \otimes \mathcal{M}) = I(\mathcal{N}) + I(\mathcal{M}). \tag{13.122}$$

Proof   We first prove the trivial inequality $I(\mathcal{N} \otimes \mathcal{M}) \geq I(\mathcal{N}) + I(\mathcal{M})$. Let $\phi_{A_1 A_1'}$ and $\psi_{A_2 A_2'}$ be states that maximize the respective mutual informations $I(\mathcal{N})$ and $I(\mathcal{M})$. Let

$$\rho_{A_1 A_2 B_1 B_2} \equiv (\mathcal{N}_{A_1' \to B_1} \otimes \mathcal{M}_{A_2' \to B_2})(\phi_{A_1 A_1'} \otimes \psi_{A_2 A_2'}). \tag{13.123}$$

Observe that the state $\rho_{A_1 A_2 B_1 B_2}$ is a particular state of the form required in the maximization of $I(\mathcal{N} \otimes \mathcal{M})$, by taking $A \equiv A_1 A_2$. Then the following holds:

$$I(\mathcal{N}) + I(\mathcal{M}) = I(A_1; B_1)_{\mathcal{N}(\phi)} + I(A_2; B_2)_{\mathcal{M}(\psi)} \tag{13.124}$$

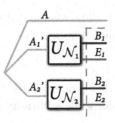

Figure 13.5 This figure displays the scenario for determining whether the mutual information of two quantum channels $\mathcal{N}_1$ and $\mathcal{N}_2$ is additive. The question of additivity is equivalent to the possibility of quantum correlations between channel inputs being able to enhance the mutual information of two quantum channels. The result stated in Theorem 13.4.1 is that the mutual information is additive for any two quantum channels, so that quantum correlations cannot enhance it.

$$= I(A_1 A_2; B_1 B_2)_\rho \tag{13.125}$$
$$\leq I(\mathcal{N} \otimes \mathcal{M}). \tag{13.126}$$

The first equality follows by evaluating the mutual informations $I(\mathcal{N})$ and $I(\mathcal{M})$ with respect to the maximizing states $\phi_{A_1 A_1'}$ and $\psi_{A_2 A_2'}$. The second equality follows from the fact that mutual information is additive with respect to tensor-product states (Exercise 11.6.8). The final inequality follows because the input state $\phi_{A_1 A_1'} \otimes \psi_{A_2 A_2'}$ is a particular input state of the more general form $\phi_{AA_1' A_2'}$ needed in the maximization of the quantum mutual information of the tensor-product channel $\mathcal{N} \otimes \mathcal{M}$.

We now prove the non-trivial inequality $I(\mathcal{N} \otimes \mathcal{M}) \leq I(\mathcal{N}) + I(\mathcal{M})$. Let $\phi_{AA_1' A_2'}$ be a state that maximizes the mutual information $I(\mathcal{N} \otimes \mathcal{M})$ and let

$$\rho_{AB_1 B_2} \equiv (\mathcal{N}_{A_1' \to B_1} \otimes \mathcal{M}_{A_2' \to B_2})(\phi_{AA_1' A_2'}). \tag{13.127}$$

Consider the following chain of inequalities:

$$I(\mathcal{N} \otimes \mathcal{M}) = I(A; B_1 B_2)_\rho \tag{13.128}$$
$$= I(A; B_1)_\rho + I(AB_1; B_2)_\rho - I(B_1; B_2)_\rho \tag{13.129}$$
$$\leq I(A; B_1)_\rho + I(AB_1; B_2)_\rho \tag{13.130}$$
$$\leq I(\mathcal{N}) + I(\mathcal{M}). \tag{13.131}$$

The first equality follows from the definition of $I(\mathcal{N} \otimes \mathcal{M})$ in (13.121) and evaluating $I(A; B_1 B_2)$ with respect to the maximizing state ϕ. The second equality follows by expanding the quantum mutual information, using Exercise 11.7.1. The first inequality follows because $I(B_1; B_2)_\rho \geq 0$. The last inequality follows because $I(A; B_1)_\rho \leq I(\mathcal{N})$ and $I(AB_1; B_2)_\rho \leq I(\mathcal{M})$, where we have applied the result of Exercise 13.4.4 and the fact that the A system extends the A_1 system which is input to the channel $\mathcal{N}$ and the fact that the AB_1 systems extend the A_2 system which is input to the channel $\mathcal{M}$. $\qquad \square$

COROLLARY 13.4.1 The regularized mutual information of a quantum channel $\mathcal{N}$ is equal to its mutual information:

$$I_{\text{reg}}(\mathcal{N}) = I(\mathcal{N}). \tag{13.132}$$

Proof A proof of this property uses the same induction argument as in Corollary 13.1.1 and exploits the additivity property in Theorem 13.4.1 above. □

EXERCISE 13.4.1 (Alternate Mutual Information of a Quantum Channel) Let ρ_{XAB} denote a state of the following form:

$$\rho_{XAB} \equiv \sum_x p_X(x)|x\rangle\langle x|_X \otimes \mathcal{N}_{A'\to B}(\phi_{AA'}^x). \tag{13.133}$$

Consider the following alternate definition of the mutual information of a quantum channel:

$$I_{\text{alt}}(\mathcal{N}) \equiv \max_{\rho_{XAB}} I(AX; B), \tag{13.134}$$

where the maximization is with respect to states of the form ρ_{XAB}. Show that

$$I_{\text{alt}}(\mathcal{N}) = I(\mathcal{N}). \tag{13.135}$$

EXERCISE 13.4.2 Compute the mutual information of a dephasing channel with dephasing parameter p.

EXERCISE 13.4.3 Compute the mutual information of an erasure channel with erasure parameter ε.

EXERCISE 13.4.4 (Pure States are Sufficient) Let $\mathcal{N}_{A'\to B}$ be a quantum channel. Show that it is sufficient to consider pure states $\phi_{AA'}$ for determining the mutual information of a quantum channel. That is, one does not need to consider mixed states $\rho_{AA'}$ in the optimization task because

$$\max_{\phi_{AA'}} I(A; B)_{\mathcal{N}(\phi)} = \max_{\rho_{AA'}} I(A; B)_{\mathcal{N}(\rho)}. \tag{13.136}$$

(Hint: Consider purifying and using the quantum data-processing inequality.)

13.4.2 Optimizing the Mutual Information of a Quantum Channel

We now show that the mutual information of a quantum channel is concave as a function of the input state. This result allows us to compute this quantity with standard convex optimization techniques.

THEOREM 13.4.2 The mutual information $I(A; B)$ is concave in the input state, in the sense that

$$\sum_x p_X(x)I(A; B)_{\rho_x} \le I(A; B)_\sigma, \tag{13.137}$$

where $\rho_{AB}^x \equiv \mathcal{N}_{A'\to B}(\phi_{AA'}^x)$, $\sigma_{A'} \equiv \sum_x p_X(x)\rho_{A'}^x$, $\phi_{AA'}$ is a purification of $\sigma_{A'}$, and $\sigma_{AB} \equiv \mathcal{N}_{A'\to B}(\phi_{AA'})$.

Proof Let ρ_{XABE} be the following classical–quantum state:

$$\rho_{XABE} \equiv \sum_x p_X(x)|x\rangle\langle x|_X \otimes \mathcal{U}^{\mathcal{N}}_{A'\to BE}(\phi^x_{AA'}),\qquad(13.138)$$

where $U^{\mathcal{N}}_{A'\to BE}$ is an isometric extension of the channel. Consider the following chain of inequalities:

$$\sum_x p_X(x)I(A;B)_{\rho_x} = I(A;B|X)_\rho \qquad(13.139)$$

$$= H(A|X)_\rho + H(B|X)_\rho - H(AB|X)_\rho \qquad(13.140)$$

$$= H(BE|X)_\rho + H(B|X)_\rho - H(E|X)_\rho \qquad(13.141)$$

$$= H(B|EX)_\rho + H(B|X)_\rho \qquad(13.142)$$

$$\leq H(B|E)_\rho + H(B)_\rho \qquad(13.143)$$

$$= H(B|E)_\sigma + H(B)_\sigma \qquad(13.144)$$

$$= I(A;B)_\sigma. \qquad(13.145)$$

The first equality follows because the conditioning system X in $I(A;B|X)_\rho$ is classical. The second equality follows by expanding the quantum mutual information. The third equality follows because the state on ABE is pure when conditioned on X. The fourth equality follows from the definition of conditional quantum entropy. The inequality follows from strong subadditivity and concavity of quantum entropy. The equality follows by inspecting the definition of the state σ, and the final equality follows because the state is pure on systems ABE. $\square$

13.5 Coherent Information of a Quantum Channel

This section presents an alternative, important measure of the ability of a quantum channel to preserve quantum correlations: the coherent information of the channel. The way we arrive at this measure is similar to how we did for the mutual information of a quantum channel. Alice prepares a pure state $\phi_{AA'}$ and inputs the A' system to a quantum channel $\mathcal{N}_{A'\to B}$. This transmission leads to a bipartite state ρ_{AB} where

$$\rho_{AB} = \mathcal{N}_{A'\to B}(\phi_{AA'}).\qquad(13.146)$$

The coherent information of the state that arises from the channel is as follows: $I(A\rangle B)_\rho = H(B)_\rho - H(AB)_\rho$, leading to our next definition.

DEFINITION 13.5.1 (Coherent Information of a Quantum Channel) The coherent information $Q(\mathcal{N})$ of a quantum channel is the maximum of the coherent information with respect to all input pure states:

$$Q(\mathcal{N}) \equiv \max_{\phi_{AA'}} I(A\rangle B)_\rho.\qquad(13.147)$$

The coherent information of a quantum channel corresponds to an important operational task (perhaps the most important for quantum information). It is a good lower bound on the capacity for Alice to transmit quantum information to Bob, but it is actually equal to such a quantum communication capacity of a quantum channel in some special cases. We prove these results in Chapter 24.

EXERCISE 13.5.1   Let $I_c(\rho, \mathcal{N})$ denote the coherent information of a channel $\mathcal{N}$ when state ρ is its input:

$$I_c(\rho, \mathcal{N}) \equiv H(\mathcal{N}(\rho)) - H(\mathcal{N}^c(\rho)), \tag{13.148}$$

where $\mathcal{N}^c$ is a channel complementary to the original channel $\mathcal{N}$. Show that

$$Q(\mathcal{N}) = \max_\rho I_c(\rho, \mathcal{N}). \tag{13.149}$$

An equivalent way of writing the above expression on the right-hand side is

$$\max_{\phi_{AA'}} \left[H(B)_\psi - H(E)_\psi \right], \tag{13.150}$$

where $|\psi\rangle_{ABE} \equiv U^{\mathcal{N}}_{A' \to BE} |\phi\rangle_{AA'}$ and $U^{\mathcal{N}}_{A' \to BE}$ is an isometric extension of the channel $\mathcal{N}$.

The following property points out that the coherent information of a channel is always non-negative, even though the coherent information of any given state can sometimes be negative.

PROPERTY 13.5.1 (Non-Negativity of Channel Coherent Information)   The coherent information $Q(\mathcal{N})$ of a quantum channel $\mathcal{N}$ is non-negative:

$$Q(\mathcal{N}) \geq 0. \tag{13.151}$$

Proof We can choose the input state $\phi_{AA'}$ to be a product state of the form $\psi_A \otimes \varphi_{A'}$. The coherent information of this state vanishes:

$$I(A \rangle B)_{\psi \otimes \mathcal{N}(\varphi)} = H(B)_{\mathcal{N}(\varphi)} - H(AB)_{\psi \otimes \mathcal{N}(\varphi)} \tag{13.152}$$

$$= H(B)_{\mathcal{N}(\varphi)} - H(A)_\psi - H(B)_{\mathcal{N}(\varphi)} \tag{13.153}$$

$$= 0. \tag{13.154}$$

The first equality follows by evaluating the coherent information for the product state. The second equality follows because the state on AB is product. The last equality follows because the state on A is pure. Non-negativity then holds because the coherent information of a channel can only be greater than or equal to this amount, given that it involves a maximization over all input states and the above state is a particular input state.   □

13.5.1   Additivity of Coherent Information for Some Channels

The coherent information of a quantum channel is generally not additive for arbitrary quantum channels. One might potentially view this situation as unfortunate, but it implies that quantum Shannon theory is a richer theory than its classical counterpart. Attempts to understand why and how this quantity is not additive have led to many breakthroughs (see Section 24.8).

Degradable quantum channels form a special class of channels for which the coherent information is additive. These channels have a property that is analogous to a property of the degraded wiretap channels from Section 13.2. To understand this property, recall that any quantum channel $\mathcal{N}_{A'\to B}$ has a complementary channel $\mathcal{N}^c_{A'\to E}$, realized by considering an isometric extension of the channel and tracing over Bob's system.

DEFINITION 13.5.2 (Degradable Quantum Channel) A quantum channel $\mathcal{N}_{A'\to B}$ is degradable if there exists a degrading channel $\mathcal{D}_{B\to E}$ such that

$$\mathcal{N}^c_{A'\to E}(\rho_{A'}) = \mathcal{D}_{B\to E}(\mathcal{N}_{A'\to B}(\rho_{A'})), \qquad (13.155)$$

for any input state $\rho_{A'}$ and where $\mathcal{N}^c_{A'\to E}$ is a channel complementary to $\mathcal{N}_{A'\to B}$.

The intuition behind a degradable quantum channel is that the channel from Alice to Eve is noisier than the channel from Alice to Bob, in the sense that Bob can simulate the channel to Eve by applying a degrading channel to his system. The picture to consider for the analysis of additivity is the same as that in Figure 13.5.

There are also antidegradable channels, defined in the opposite way:

DEFINITION 13.5.3 (Antidegradable Quantum Channel) A quantum channel $\mathcal{N}_{A'\to B}$ is antidegradable if there exists a degrading channel $\mathcal{D}_{E\to B}$ such that

$$\mathcal{D}_{E\to B}(\mathcal{N}^c_{A'\to E}(\rho_{A'})) = \mathcal{N}_{A'\to B}(\rho_{A'}), \qquad (13.156)$$

for any input state $\rho_{A'}$ and where $\mathcal{N}^c_{A'\to E}$ is a channel complementary to $\mathcal{N}_{A'\to B}$.

THEOREM 13.5.1 (Additivity for Degradable Quantum Channels) Let $\mathcal{N}$ and $\mathcal{M}$ be any quantum channels that are degradable. Then the coherent information of the tensor-product channel $\mathcal{N}\otimes\mathcal{M}$ is the sum of their individual coherent informations:

$$Q(\mathcal{N}\otimes\mathcal{M}) = Q(\mathcal{N}) + Q(\mathcal{M}). \qquad (13.157)$$

Proof We leave the proof of the inequality $Q(\mathcal{N}\otimes\mathcal{M}) \geq Q(\mathcal{N}) + Q(\mathcal{M})$ as Exercise 13.5.3 below, and we prove the non-trivial inequality $Q(\mathcal{N}\otimes\mathcal{M}) \leq Q(\mathcal{N}) + Q(\mathcal{M})$ that holds when quantum channels $\mathcal{N}$ and $\mathcal{M}$ are degradable. Consider a pure state $\phi_{AA'_1A'_2}$ that serves as the input to the two quantum channels. Let $U^{\mathcal{N}}_{A'_1\to B_1E_1}$ denote an isometric extension of the first channel and let $U^{\mathcal{M}}_{A'_2\to B_2E_2}$ denote an isometric extension of the second channel. Let

$$\sigma_{AB_1E_1A'_2} \equiv U^{\mathcal{N}}\phi(U^{\mathcal{N}})^\dagger, \qquad (13.158)$$

$$\theta_{AA'_1B_2E_2} \equiv U^{\mathcal{M}}\phi(U^{\mathcal{M}})^\dagger, \qquad (13.159)$$

$$\rho_{AB_1E_1B_2E_2} \equiv (U^{\mathcal{N}}\otimes U^{\mathcal{M}})\phi((U^{\mathcal{N}})^\dagger\otimes(U^{\mathcal{M}})^\dagger). \qquad (13.160)$$

We need to show that $Q(\mathcal{N} \otimes \mathcal{M}) = Q(\mathcal{N}) + Q(\mathcal{M})$ when both channels are degradable. Furthermore, let $\rho_{AB_1E_1B_2E_2}$ be a state that maximizes $Q(\mathcal{N} \otimes \mathcal{M})$. Consider the following chain of inequalities:

$$Q(\mathcal{N} \otimes \mathcal{M}) = I(A\rangle B_1 B_2)_\rho \tag{13.161}$$

$$= H(B_1 B_2)_\rho - H(AB_1 B_2)_\rho \tag{13.162}$$

$$= H(B_1 B_2)_\rho - H(E_1 E_2)_\rho \tag{13.163}$$

$$= H(B_1)_\rho - H(E_1)_\rho + H(B_2)_\rho - H(E_2)_\rho$$
$$\quad - [I(B_1; B_2)_\rho - I(E_1; E_2)_\rho] \tag{13.164}$$

$$\leq H(B_1)_\rho - H(E_1)_\rho + H(B_2)_\rho - H(E_2)_\rho \tag{13.165}$$

$$= H(B_1)_\sigma - H(AA_2'B_1)_\sigma + H(B_2)_\theta - H(AA_1'B_2)_\theta \tag{13.166}$$

$$= I(AA_2'\rangle B_1)_\sigma + I(AA_1'\rangle B_2)_\theta \tag{13.167}$$

$$\leq Q(\mathcal{N}) + Q(\mathcal{M}). \tag{13.168}$$

The first equality follows from the definition of $Q(\mathcal{N} \otimes \mathcal{M})$ and because we set ρ to be a state that maximizes the tensor-product channel coherent information. The second equality follows from the definition of coherent information, and the third equality follows because the state ρ is pure on systems $AB_1 E_1 B_2 E_2$. The fourth equality follows by expanding the entropies in the previous line. The first inequality follows because there is a degrading channel from both B_1 to E_1 and B_2 to E_2, allowing us to apply the quantum data-processing inequality to get $I(B_1; B_2)_\rho \geq I(E_1; E_2)_\rho$. The fifth equality follows because the entropies of ρ, σ, and θ on the given reduced systems are equal and because the state σ on systems $AA_2'B_1 E_1$ is pure and the state θ on systems $AA_1'B_2 E_2$ is pure. The last equality follows from the definition of coherent information, and the final inequality follows because the coherent informations are less than their respective maximizations over all possible states. □

COROLLARY 13.5.1   The regularized coherent information of a degradable quantum channel is equal to its coherent information: $Q_{\text{reg}}(\mathcal{N}) = Q(\mathcal{N})$.

Proof   A proof of this property uses the same induction argument as in Corollary 13.1.1 and exploits the additivity property in Theorem 13.5.1 above. □

EXERCISE 13.5.2   Consider the quantum erasure channel where the erasure parameter $\varepsilon \in [0, 1/2]$. Find the channel that degrades this one, reproducing the channel from input to environment.

EXERCISE 13.5.3 (Superadditivity of Coherent Information)   Show that the coherent information of the tensor-product channel $\mathcal{N} \otimes \mathcal{M}$ is never less than the sum of their individual coherent informations: $Q(\mathcal{N} \otimes \mathcal{M}) \geq Q(\mathcal{N}) + Q(\mathcal{M})$.

EXERCISE 13.5.4   Prove using monotonicity of relative entropy that the coherent information is subadditive for a degradable channel: $Q(\mathcal{N}) + Q(\mathcal{M}) \geq Q(\mathcal{N} \otimes \mathcal{M})$.

EXERCISE 13.5.5 Consider a quantity known as the reverse coherent information:

$$Q_{rev}(\mathcal{N}) \equiv \max_{\phi_{AA'}} I(B\rangle A)_\omega, \tag{13.169}$$

where $\omega_{AB} \equiv \mathcal{N}_{A' \to B}(\phi_{AA'})$. Show that the reverse coherent information is additive with respect to any quantum channels $\mathcal{N}$ and $\mathcal{M}$: $Q_{rev}(\mathcal{N} \otimes \mathcal{M}) = Q_{rev}(\mathcal{N}) + Q_{rev}(\mathcal{M})$.

EXERCISE 13.5.6 Prove that the coherent information of an antidegradable channel is equal to zero. (Hint: Consider using the identity from Exercise 11.6.6.)

EXERCISE 13.5.7 Prove that an entanglement-breaking channel is antidegradable.

13.5.2 Optimizing the Coherent Information

We would like to determine how difficult it is to maximize the coherent information of a quantum channel. For general channels, this problem is difficult, but it turns out to be straightforward for the class of degradable quantum channels. Theorem 13.5.2 below states an important property of the coherent information $Q(\mathcal{N})$ of a degradable quantum channel $\mathcal{N}$ that allows us to answer this question. The theorem states that the coherent information $Q(\mathcal{N})$ of a degradable quantum channel is a concave function of the input density operator $\rho_{A'}$ over which we maximize it. In particular, this result implies that a local maximum of the coherent information $Q(\mathcal{N})$ is a global maximum since the set of density operators is convex, and the optimization problem is therefore a straightforward computation that can exploit convex optimization methods. The theorem below exploits the characterization of the channel coherent information from Exercise 13.5.1.

THEOREM 13.5.2 Suppose that a quantum channel $\mathcal{N}$ is degradable. Then the coherent information $I_c(\rho, \mathcal{N})$ is concave in the input density operator:

$$\sum_x p_X(x) I_c(\rho_x, \mathcal{N}) \leq I_c\left(\sum_x p_X(x)\rho_x, \mathcal{N}\right), \tag{13.170}$$

where $p_X(x)$ is a probability density function and each ρ_x is a density operator.

Proof Consider the following states:

$$\sigma_{XB} \equiv \sum_x p_X(x)|x\rangle\langle x|_X \otimes \mathcal{N}(\rho_x), \tag{13.171}$$

$$\theta_{XE} \equiv \sum_x p_X(x)|x\rangle\langle x|_X \otimes (\mathcal{T} \circ \mathcal{N})(\rho_x), \tag{13.172}$$

where $\mathcal{T}$ is a degrading channel for the channel $\mathcal{N}$, so that $\mathcal{T} \circ \mathcal{N} = \mathcal{N}^c$. Then the following statements hold:

$$I(X;B)_\sigma \geq I(X;E)_\theta \tag{13.173}$$

$$\therefore \quad H(B)_\sigma - H(B|X)_\sigma \ge H(E)_\theta - H(E|X)_\theta \tag{13.174}$$

$$\therefore \quad H(B)_\sigma - H(E)_\theta \ge H(B|X)_\sigma - H(E|X)_\theta \tag{13.175}$$

$$\therefore \quad H\left(\mathcal{N}\left(\sum_x p_X(x)\rho_x\right)\right) - H\left(\mathcal{N}^c\left(\sum_x p_X(x)\rho_x\right)\right)$$
$$\ge \sum_x p_X(x)\left[H\left(\mathcal{N}(\rho_x)\right) - H\left(\mathcal{N}^c(\rho_x)\right)\right] \tag{13.176}$$

$$\therefore \quad I_c\left(\sum_x p_X(x)\rho_x, \mathcal{N}\right) \ge \sum_x p_X(x)I_c\left(\rho_x, \mathcal{N}\right). \tag{13.177}$$

The first statement is the crucial one and follows from the quantum data-processing inequality and the fact that the map $\mathcal{T}$ degrades Bob's state to Eve's state. The second and third statements follow from the definition of quantum mutual information and rearranging entropies. The fourth statement follows by plugging in the density operators into the entropies in the previous statement. The final statement follows from the alternate definition of coherent information in Exercise 13.5.1.   □

13.6   Private Information of a Quantum Channel

The private information of a quantum channel is the last information measure that we consider in this chapter. Alice would like to establish classical correlations with Bob, but does not want the environment of the channel to have access to these classical correlations. The ensemble that she prepares is similar to the one we considered for the Holevo information. The expected density operator of the ensemble she prepares is a classical–quantum state of the form

$$\rho_{XA'} \equiv \sum_x p_X(x)|x\rangle\langle x|_X \otimes \rho_{A'}^x. \tag{13.178}$$

Sending the A' system through an isometric extension $U_{A'\to BE}^{\mathcal{N}}$ of a quantum channel $\mathcal{N}$ leads to a state ρ_{XBE}. A good measure of the private classical correlations that she can establish with Bob is the difference of the classical correlations she can establish with Bob, less the classical correlations that Eve can obtain: $I(X;B)_\rho - I(X;E)_\rho$, leading to our next definition (Chapter 23 discusses the operational task corresponding to this information quantity).

DEFINITION 13.6.1 (Private Information of a Quantum Channel)   The private information $P(\mathcal{N})$ of a quantum channel $\mathcal{N}$ is defined as follows:

$$P(\mathcal{N}) \equiv \max_{\rho_{XA'}} I(X;B)_\rho - I(X;E)_\rho, \tag{13.179}$$

where the maximization is with respect to all states of the form in (13.178) and the entropic quantities are evaluated with respect to the state $\mathcal{U}_{A'\to BE}^{\mathcal{N}}(\rho_{XA'})$.

PROPERTY 13.6.1 The private information $P(\mathcal{N})$ of a quantum channel $\mathcal{N}$ is non-negative:

$$P(\mathcal{N}) \geq 0. \tag{13.180}$$

Proof We can choose the input state $\rho_{XA'}$ to be a state of the form $|0\rangle\langle 0|_X \otimes \psi_{A'}$, where $\psi_{A'}$ is pure. The private information of the output state vanishes

$$I(X;B)_{|0\rangle\langle 0| \otimes \mathcal{N}(\psi)} - I(X;E)_{|0\rangle\langle 0| \otimes \mathcal{N}^c(\psi)} = 0. \tag{13.181}$$

The equality follows just by evaluating both mutual informations for the above state. The above property then holds because the private information of a channel can only be greater than or equal to this amount, given that it involves a maximization over all input states and the above state is a particular input state. $\qquad\square$

The regularized private information is as follows:

$$P_{\text{reg}}(\mathcal{N}) = \lim_{n \to \infty} \frac{1}{n} P(\mathcal{N}^{\otimes n}). \tag{13.182}$$

13.6.1 Private Information and Coherent Information

The private information of a quantum channel bears a special relationship to that channel's coherent information. It is always at least as great as the coherent information of the channel and is equal to it for certain channels. The following theorem states the former inequality, and the next theorem states the equivalence for degradable quantum channels.

THEOREM 13.6.1 The private information $P(\mathcal{N})$ of any quantum channel $\mathcal{N}$ is never smaller than its coherent information $Q(\mathcal{N})$:

$$Q(\mathcal{N}) \leq P(\mathcal{N}). \tag{13.183}$$

Proof We can see this relation through a few steps. Consider a pure state $\phi_{AA'}$ that maximizes the coherent information $Q(\mathcal{N})$, and let ϕ_{ABE} denote the state that arises from sending the A' system through an isometric extension $U^{\mathcal{N}}_{A' \to BE}$ of the channel $\mathcal{N}$. Let $\phi_{A'}$ denote the reduction of this state to the A' system. Suppose that it admits the following spectral decomposition:

$$\phi_{A'} = \sum_x p_X(x) |\phi_x\rangle\langle\phi_x|_{A'}. \tag{13.184}$$

We can create an augmented classical–quantum state that correlates a classical variable with the index x:

$$\sigma_{XA'} \equiv \sum_x p_X(x) |x\rangle\langle x|_X \otimes |\phi_x\rangle\langle\phi_x|_{A'}. \tag{13.185}$$

Let σ_{XBE} denote the state that results from sending the A' system through an isometric extension $U^{\mathcal{N}}_{A'\to BE}$ of the channel $\mathcal{N}$. Then the following chain of inequalities holds:

$$Q(\mathcal{N}) = I(A\rangle B)_\phi \tag{13.186}$$

$$= H(B)_\phi - H(E)_\phi \tag{13.187}$$

$$= H(B)_\sigma - H(E)_\sigma \tag{13.188}$$

$$= H(B)_\sigma - H(B|X)_\sigma - H(E)_\sigma + H(B|X)_\sigma \tag{13.189}$$

$$= I(X;B)_\sigma - H(E)_\sigma + H(E|X)_\sigma \tag{13.190}$$

$$= I(X;B)_\sigma - I(X;E)_\sigma \tag{13.191}$$

$$\le P(\mathcal{N}). \tag{13.192}$$

The first equality follows from evaluating the coherent information of the state ϕ_{ABE} that maximizes the coherent information of the channel. The second equality follows because the state ϕ_{ABE} is pure. The third equality follows from the definition of σ_{XBE} in (13.185) and its relation to ϕ_{ABE}. The fourth equality follows by adding and subtracting $H(B|X)_\sigma$, and the next one follows from the definition of the mutual information $I(X;B)_\sigma$ and the fact that the state of σ_{XBE} on systems B and E is pure when conditioned on X. The last equality follows from the definition of the mutual information $I(X;E)_\sigma$. The final inequality follows because the state σ_{XBE} is a particular state of the form in (13.178), and $P(\mathcal{N})$ involves a maximization over all states of that form. $\qquad\square$

THEOREM 13.6.2   Suppose that a quantum channel $\mathcal{N}$ is degradable. Then its private information $P(\mathcal{N})$ is equal to its coherent information $Q(\mathcal{N})$:

$$P(\mathcal{N}) = Q(\mathcal{N}). \tag{13.193}$$

Proof   We prove the inequality $P(\mathcal{N}) \le Q(\mathcal{N})$ for degradable quantum channels because we have already proven that $Q(\mathcal{N}) \le P(\mathcal{N})$ for any quantum channel $\mathcal{N}$. Consider a classical–quantum state ρ_{XBE} that arises from transmitting the A' system of the state in (13.178) through an isometric extension $U^{\mathcal{N}}_{A'\to BE}$ of the channel. Suppose further that this state maximizes $P(\mathcal{N})$. We can take a spectral decomposition of each $\rho^x_{A'}$ in the ensemble to be as follows:

$$\rho^x_{A'} = \sum_y p_{Y|X}(y|x)\psi^{x,y}_{A'}, \tag{13.194}$$

where each state $\psi^{x,y}_{A'}$ is pure. We can construct the following extension of the state ρ_{XBE}:

$$\sigma_{XYBE} \equiv \sum_{x,y} p_{Y|X}(y|x)p_X(x)|x\rangle\langle x|_X \otimes |y\rangle\langle y|_Y \otimes \mathcal{U}^{\mathcal{N}}_{A'\to BE}(\psi^{x,y}_{A'}). \tag{13.195}$$

Then the following chain of inequalities holds:

$$P(\mathcal{N}) = I(X;B)_\rho - I(X;E)_\rho \tag{13.196}$$

$$= I(X;B)_\sigma - I(X;E)_\sigma \tag{13.197}$$

$$= I(XY;B)_\sigma - I(Y;B|X)_\sigma - [I(XY;E)_\sigma - I(Y;E|X)_\sigma] \quad (13.198)$$

$$= I(XY;B)_\sigma - I(XY;E)_\sigma - [I(Y;B|X)_\sigma - I(Y;E|X)_\sigma]. \quad (13.199)$$

The first equality follows from the definition of $P(\mathcal{N})$ and because we set ρ to be the state that maximizes it. The second equality follows because $\rho_{XBE} = \text{Tr}_Y\{\sigma_{XYBE}\}$. The third equality follows from the chain rule for quantum mutual information. The fourth equality follows from a rearrangement of entropies. Continuing,

$$\leq I(XY;B)_\sigma - I(XY;E)_\sigma \quad (13.200)$$

$$= H(B)_\sigma - H(B|XY)_\sigma - H(E)_\sigma + H(E|XY)_\sigma \quad (13.201)$$

$$= H(B)_\sigma - H(B|XY)_\sigma - H(E)_\sigma + H(B|XY)_\sigma \quad (13.202)$$

$$= H(B)_\sigma - H(E)_\sigma \quad (13.203)$$

$$\leq Q(\mathcal{N}). \quad (13.204)$$

The first inequality (the crucial one) follows because there is a degrading channel from B to E, so that the quantum data-processing inequality implies that $I(Y;B|X)_\sigma \geq I(Y;E|X)_\sigma$. The second equality is a rewriting of entropies, the third follows because the state of σ on systems B and E is pure when conditioned on classical systems X and Y, and the fourth follows by canceling entropies. The last inequality follows because the entropy difference $H(B)_\sigma - H(E)_\sigma$ is less than the maximum of that difference over all possible input states. $\square$

13.6.2 Additivity of Private Information of Degradable Channels

The private information of general quantum channels is not additive, but it is so in the case of degradable quantum channels. The method of proof is somewhat similar to that in the proof of Theorem 13.5.1, essentially exploiting the degradability property. Figure 13.6 illustrates the setting to consider for additivity of the private information.

THEOREM 13.6.3 (Additivity for Degradable Quantum Channels) Let $\mathcal{N}$ and $\mathcal{M}$ be any quantum channels that are degradable. Then the private information of the tensor-product channel $\mathcal{N} \otimes \mathcal{M}$ is the sum of their individual private informations:

$$P(\mathcal{N} \otimes \mathcal{M}) = P(\mathcal{N}) + P(\mathcal{M}). \quad (13.205)$$

Furthermore, it holds that

$$P(\mathcal{N} \otimes \mathcal{M}) = Q(\mathcal{N} \otimes \mathcal{M}) = Q(\mathcal{N}) + Q(\mathcal{M}). \quad (13.206)$$

Proof We first prove the more trivial inequality $P(\mathcal{N} \otimes \mathcal{M}) \geq P(\mathcal{N}) + P(\mathcal{M})$. Let $\rho_{X_1 A_1'}$ and $\sigma_{X_2 A_2'}$ be states of the form in (13.178) that maximize the respective private informations $P(\mathcal{N})$ and $P(\mathcal{M})$. Let $\theta_{X_1 X_2 A_1' A_2'}$ be the tensor product of these two states: $\theta = \rho \otimes \sigma$. Let $\rho_{X_1 B_1 E_1}$ and $\sigma_{X_2 B_2 E_2}$ be the states that

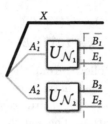

Figure 13.6 This figure displays the scenario for determining whether the private information of two quantum channels $\mathcal{N}_1$ and $\mathcal{N}_2$ is additive. The question of additivity is equivalent to the possibility of quantum correlations between channel inputs being able to enhance the private information of two quantum channels. The result stated in Theorem 13.6.3 is that the private information is additive for any two degradable quantum channels, so that quantum correlations cannot enhance it in this case.

arise from sending $\rho_{X_1 A_1'}$ and $\sigma_{X_2 A_2'}$ through the respective isometric extensions $U_{A_1' \to B_1 E_1}^{\mathcal{N}}$ and $U_{A_2' \to B_2 E_2}^{\mathcal{M}}$. Let $\theta_{X_1 X_2 B_1 B_2 E_1 E_2}$ be the state that arises from sending $\theta_{X_1 X_2 A_1' A_2'}$ through the tensor-product channel $\mathcal{U}_{A_1' \to B_1 E_1}^{\mathcal{N}} \otimes \mathcal{U}_{A_2' \to B_2 E_2}^{\mathcal{M}}$. Then

$$P(\mathcal{N}) + P(\mathcal{M})$$
$$= I(X_1; B_1)_\rho - I(X_1; E_1)_\rho + I(X_2; B_2)_\sigma - I(X_2; E_2)_\sigma \qquad (13.207)$$
$$= I(X_1 X_2; B_1 B_2)_\theta - I(X_1 X_2; E_1 E_2)_\theta \qquad (13.208)$$
$$\leq P(\mathcal{N} \otimes \mathcal{M}). \qquad (13.209)$$

The first equality follows from the definition of the private informations $P(\mathcal{N})$ and $P(\mathcal{M})$ and by evaluating them on the respective states $\rho_{X_1 A_1'}$ and $\sigma_{X_2 A_2'}$ that maximize them. The second equality follows because the mutual information is additive on tensor-product states (see Exercise 11.6.8). The final inequality follows because the state $\theta_{X_1 X_2 B_1 B_2 E_1 E_2}$ is a particular state of the form needed in the maximization of the private information of the tensor-product channel $\mathcal{N} \otimes \mathcal{M}$.

We now prove the inequality $P(\mathcal{N} \otimes \mathcal{M}) \leq P(\mathcal{N}) + P(\mathcal{M})$. Let $\rho_{X A_1' A_2'}$ be a state that maximizes $P(\mathcal{N} \otimes \mathcal{M})$ where

$$\rho_{X A_1' A_2'} \equiv \sum_x p_X(x) |x\rangle\langle x|_X \otimes \rho_{A_1' A_2'}^x, \qquad (13.210)$$

and let $\rho_{X B_1 B_2 E_1 E_2}$ be the state that arises from sending $\rho_{X A_1' A_2'}$ through the tensor-product channel $\mathcal{U}_{A_1' \to B_1 E_1}^{\mathcal{N}} \otimes \mathcal{U}_{A_2' \to B_2 E_2}^{\mathcal{M}}$. Consider a spectral decomposition of each state $\rho_{A_1' A_2'}^x$:

$$\rho_{A_1' A_2'}^x = \sum_y p_{Y|X}(y|x) \psi_{A_1' A_2'}^{x,y}, \qquad (13.211)$$

where each state $\psi^{x,y}_{A'_1 A'_2}$ is pure. Let $\sigma_{XY A'_1 A'_2}$ be an extension of $\rho_{X A'_1 A'_2}$ where

$$\sigma_{XY A'_1 A'_2} \equiv \sum_{x,y} p_{Y|X}(y|x) p_X(x) |x\rangle\langle x|_X \otimes |y\rangle\langle y|_Y \otimes \psi^{x,y}_{A'_1 A'_2}, \tag{13.212}$$

and let $\sigma_{XY B_1 E_1 B_2 E_2}$ be the state that arises from sending $\sigma_{XY A'_1 A'_2}$ through the tensor-product channel $\mathcal{U}^{\mathcal{N}}_{A'_1 \to B_1 E_1} \otimes \mathcal{U}^{\mathcal{M}}_{A'_2 \to B_2 E_2}$. Consider the following chain of inequalities:

$$P(\mathcal{N} \otimes \mathcal{M}) \tag{13.213}$$

$$= I(X; B_1 B_2)_\rho - I(X; E_1 E_2)_\rho \tag{13.214}$$

$$= I(X; B_1 B_2)_\sigma - I(X; E_1 E_2)_\sigma \tag{13.215}$$

$$= I(XY; B_1 B_2)_\sigma - I(XY; E_1 E_2)_\sigma$$
$$\quad - [I(Y; B_1 B_2|X)_\sigma - I(Y; E_1 E_2|X)_\sigma] \tag{13.216}$$

$$\leq I(XY; B_1 B_2)_\sigma - I(XY; E_1 E_2)_\sigma \tag{13.217}$$

$$= H(B_1 B_2)_\sigma - H(B_1 B_2|XY)_\sigma - H(E_1 E_2)_\sigma + H(E_1 E_2|XY)_\sigma \tag{13.218}$$

$$= H(B_1 B_2)_\sigma - H(B_1 B_2|XY)_\sigma - H(E_1 E_2)_\sigma + H(B_1 B_2|XY)_\sigma \tag{13.219}$$

$$= H(B_1 B_2)_\sigma - H(E_1 E_2)_\sigma \tag{13.220}$$

$$= H(B_1)_\sigma - H(E_1)_\sigma + H(B_2)_\sigma - H(E_2)_\sigma$$
$$\quad - [I(B_1; B_2)_\sigma - I(E_1; E_2)_\sigma] \tag{13.221}$$

$$\leq H(B_1)_\sigma - H(E_1)_\sigma + H(B_2)_\sigma - H(E_2)_\sigma \tag{13.222}$$

$$\leq Q(\mathcal{N}) + Q(\mathcal{M}) \tag{13.223}$$

$$= P(\mathcal{N}) + P(\mathcal{M}). \tag{13.224}$$

The first equality follows from the definition of $P(\mathcal{N} \otimes \mathcal{M})$ and from evaluating it on the state ρ that maximizes it. The second equality follows because the state $\sigma_{XY B_1 E_1 B_2 E_2}$ is equal to the state $\rho_{X B_1 E_1 B_2 E_2}$ after tracing out the system Y. The third equality follows from the chain rule for mutual information: $I(XY; B_1 B_2) = I(Y; B_1 B_2|X) + I(X; B_1 B_2)$. It holds that $I(Y; B_1 B_2|X)_\sigma \geq I(Y; E_1 E_2|X)_\sigma$ because there is a degrading channel from B_1 to E_1 and from B_2 to E_2. Then the first inequality follows because $I(Y; B_1 B_2|X)_\sigma - I(Y; E_1 E_2|X)_\sigma \geq 0$. The fourth equality follows by expanding the mutual informations, and the fifth equality follows because the state σ on systems $B_1 B_2 E_1 E_2$ is pure when conditioning on the classical systems X and Y. The sixth equality follows from algebra, and the seventh follows by rewriting the entropies. It holds that $I(B_1; B_2)_\sigma \geq I(E_1; E_2)_\sigma$ because there is a degrading channel from B_1 to E_1 and from B_2 to E_2. Then the inequality follows because $I(B_1; B_2)_\sigma - I(E_1; E_2)_\sigma \geq 0$. The third inequality follows because the entropy difference $H(B_i) - H(E_i)$ is always less than the coherent information of the channel, and the final equality follows because the coherent information of a channel is equal to its private information when the channel is degradable (Theorem 13.6.2). □

COROLLARY 13.6.1   Suppose that a quantum channel $\mathcal{N}$ is degradable. Then the regularized private information $P_{\text{reg}}(\mathcal{N})$ of the channel is equal to its private information $P(\mathcal{N})$:

$$P_{\text{reg}}(\mathcal{N}) = P(\mathcal{N}). \tag{13.225}$$

Proof   A proof follows by the same induction argument as in Corollary 13.1.1 and by exploiting the result of Theorem 13.6.3 and the fact that the tensor power channel $\mathcal{N}^{\otimes n}$ is degradable if the original channel $\mathcal{N}$ is.   □

13.7   Summary

We conclude this chapter with a table that summarizes the main results regarding the mutual information of a classical channel $I(p_{Y|X})$, the private information of a classical wiretap channel $P(p_{Y,Z|X})$, the Holevo information of a quantum channel $\chi(\mathcal{N})$, the mutual information of a quantum channel $I(\mathcal{N})$, the coherent information of a quantum channel $Q(\mathcal{N})$, and the private information of a quantum channel $P(\mathcal{N})$. The table exploits the following definitions:

$$\rho_{XA'} \equiv \sum p_X(x)|x\rangle\langle x|_X \otimes \phi_{A'}^x, \tag{13.226}$$

$$\sigma_{XA'} \equiv \sum p_X(x)|x\rangle\langle x|_X \otimes \rho_{A'}^x. \tag{13.227}$$

Quantity	Input	Output	Formula	Single-letter
$I(p_{Y|X})$	p_X	$p_X p_{Y|X}$	$\max_{p_X} I(X;Y)$	all channels
$P(p_{Y,Z|X})$	p_X	$p_X p_{Y,Z|X}$	$\max_{p_{U,X}} I(U;Y) - I(U;Z)$	all channels
$\chi(\mathcal{N})$	$\rho_{XA'}$	$\mathcal{N}_{A'\to B}(\rho_{XA'})$	$\max_\rho I(X;B)$	some channels
$I(\mathcal{N})$	$\phi_{AA'}$	$\mathcal{N}_{A'\to B}(\phi_{AA'})$	$\max_\phi I(A;B)$	all channels
$Q(\mathcal{N})$	$\phi_{AA'}$	$\mathcal{N}_{A'\to B}(\phi_{AA'})$	$\max_\phi I(A\rangle B)$	degradable
$P(\mathcal{N})$	$\sigma_{XA'}$	$U_{A'\to BE}^{\mathcal{N}}(\sigma_{XA'})$	$\max_\sigma I(X;B) - I(X;E)$	degradable

13.8   History and Further Reading

Boyd & Vandenberghe (2004) is a good reference for the theory and practice of convex optimization, which is helpful for computing capacity formulas. Wyner (1975) introduced the classical wiretap channel and proved that the private information is additive for degraded wiretap channels. Csiszár & Körner (1978) proved that the private information is additive for general wiretap channels. Holevo (1998) and Schumacher & Westmoreland (1997) provided an operational interpretation of the Holevo information of a quantum channel. Shor (2002a) showed the additivity of the Holevo information for entanglement-breaking channels.

Adami & Cerf (1997) introduced the mutual information of a quantum channel, and they proved several of its important properties that appear in this chapter: non-negativity, additivity, and concavity. Bennett et al. (1999) and Bennett et al. (2002) later gave an operational interpretation for this information quantity as the entanglement-assisted classical capacity of a quantum channel. Lloyd (1997), Shor (2002b), and Devetak (2005) gave increasingly rigorous proofs that the coherent information of a quantum channel is an achievable rate for quantum communication. Devetak & Shor (2005) showed that the coherent information of a quantum channel is additive for degradable channels. Yard et al. (2008) proved that the coherent information of a quantum channel is a concave function of the input state whenever the channel is degradable. Devetak et al. (2006) and García-Patrón et al. (2009) discussed the reverse coherent information of a quantum channel and showed that it is additive for all quantum channels. Devetak (2005) and Cai et al. (2004) independently introduced the private classical capacity of a quantum channel, and both papers proved that it is an achievable rate for private classical communication over a quantum channel. Smith (2008) showed that the private classical information is additive and equal to the coherent information for degradable quantum channels.

14 Classical Typicality

This chapter begins our first technical foray into the asymptotic theory of information. We start with the classical setting in an effort to build up our intuition of asymptotic behavior before delving into the asymptotic theory of quantum information.

The central concept of this chapter is the asymptotic equipartition property. The name of this property may sound somewhat technical at first, but it is merely an application of the law of large numbers to a sequence drawn independently and identically from a distribution $p_X(x)$ for some random variable X. The asymptotic equipartition property reveals that we can divide sequences into two classes when their length becomes large: those that are overwhelmingly likely to occur and those that are overwhelmingly likely not to occur. The sequences that are likely to occur are the *typical* sequences, and the ones that are not likely to occur are the *atypical* sequences. Additionally, the size of the set of typical sequences is exponentially smaller than the size of the set of all sequences whenever the random variable generating the sequences is not uniform. These properties are an example of a more general mathematical phenomenon known as "measure concentration," in which a smooth function over a high-dimensional space or over a large number of random variables tends to concentrate around a constant value with high probability.

The asymptotic equipartition property immediately leads to the intuition behind Shannon's scheme for compressing classical information. The scheme first generates a realization of a random sequence and asks the question: Is the produced sequence typical or atypical? If it is typical, compress it. Otherwise, throw it away. The error probability of this compression scheme is non-zero for any fixed length of a sequence, but it vanishes in the asymptotic limit because the probability of the sequence being in the typical set converges to one, while the probability that it is in the atypical set converges to zero. This compression scheme has a straightforward generalization to the quantum setting, in which we wish to compress qubits instead of classical bits.

The bulk of this chapter is here to present the many technical details needed to make rigorous statements in the asymptotic theory of information. We begin with an example, follow with the formal definition of a typical sequence and a typical set, and prove the three important properties of a typical set. We then discuss other forms of typicality such as joint typicality and conditional typicality. These other notions turn out to be useful for proving Shannon's classical capacity theorem as well (recall that Shannon's theorem gives the ultimate rate at which a sender can transmit classical information over a classical channel to a receiver). We also introduce the method of types, which is a powerful technique in classical information theory, and apply this method in order to develop a stronger notion of typicality. The chapter then features a development of the strong notions of joint and conditional typicality and ends with a concise proof of Shannon's channel capacity theorem.

14.1 An Example of Typicality

Suppose that Alice possesses a binary random variable X that takes the value zero with probability 3/4 and the value one with probability 1/4. Such a random source might produce the following sequence:

$$0110001101, \tag{14.1}$$

if we generate ten independent realizations. The probability that such a sequence occurs is

$$\left(\frac{1}{4}\right)^5 \left(\frac{3}{4}\right)^5, \tag{14.2}$$

determined simply by counting the number of ones and zeros in the above sequence and by applying the assumption that the source is i.i.d.

The *information content* of the above sequence is the negative logarithm of its probability divided by its length:

$$-\frac{1}{10}\log\left(\left(\frac{1}{4}\right)^5\left(\frac{3}{4}\right)^5\right) = -\frac{5}{10}\log\left(\frac{1}{4}\right) - \frac{5}{10}\log\left(\frac{3}{4}\right) \approx 1.207. \tag{14.3}$$

We also refer to this quantity as the *sample entropy*. The true entropy of the source is

$$-\frac{1}{4}\log\left(\frac{1}{4}\right) - \frac{3}{4}\log\left(\frac{3}{4}\right) \approx 0.8113. \tag{14.4}$$

We would expect that the sample entropy of a random sequence tends to approach the true entropy as its length increases because the number of zeros should be approximately $n(3/4)$ and the number of ones should be approximately $n(1/4)$ according to the law of large numbers.

Another sequence of length 100 might be as follows:

$$0000000010001000100000000000011001101000000100000$$
$$00000110101001000000010000001000000010000100010000, \tag{14.5}$$

featuring 81 zeros and 19 ones. Its sample entropy is

$$-\frac{1}{100}\log\left(\left(\frac{1}{4}\right)^{19}\left(\frac{3}{4}\right)^{81}\right) = -\frac{19}{100}\log\left(\frac{1}{4}\right) - \frac{81}{100}\log\left(\frac{3}{4}\right) \approx 0.7162. \quad (14.6)$$

The above sample entropy is closer to the true entropy in (14.4) than the sample entropy of the previous sequence, but it still deviates significantly from it.

Figure 14.1 continues this game by generating random sequences according to the distribution $\left(\frac{3}{4}, \frac{1}{4}\right)$, and the result is that a concentration around the true entropy begins to occur around $n \approx 10^6$. That is, it becomes highly likely that the sample entropy of a random sequence is close to the true entropy if we increase the length of the sequence, and this holds for the realizations generated in Figure 14.1.

14.2 Weak Typicality

This first section generalizes the example from the introduction to an arbitrary discrete, finite-cardinality random variable. Our first notion of typicality is the same as discussed in the example—we define a sequence to be typical if its sample

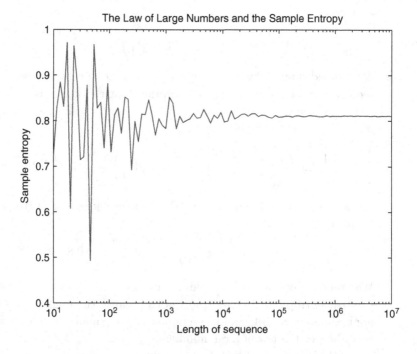

Figure 14.1 This figure depicts the sample entropy of a realization of a random binary sequence as a function of its length. The source is a binary random variable with distribution $\left(\frac{3}{4}, \frac{1}{4}\right)$. For the realizations generated, the sample entropy of the sequences is converging to the true entropy of the source.

entropy is close to the true entropy of the random variable that generates it. This notion of typicality is known as *weak typicality*. Section 14.7 introduces another notion of typicality that implies weak typicality, but the implication does not hold in the other direction. For this reason, we distinguish the two different notions of typicality as weak typicality and strong typicality.

Suppose that a random variable X takes values in an alphabet $\mathcal{X}$ with cardinality $|\mathcal{X}|$. Let us label the symbols in the alphabet as $a_1, a_2, \ldots, a_{|\mathcal{X}|}$. An i.i.d. information source samples *independently* from the distribution of random variable X and emits n realizations $x_1, \ldots, x_n$. Let $X^n \equiv X_1 \cdots X_n$ denote the n random variables that describe the information source, and let $x^n \equiv x_1 \cdots x_n$ denote an emitted realization of X^n. The probability $p_{X^n}(x^n)$ of a particular string x^n is as follows:

$$p_{X^n}(x^n) \equiv p_{X_1,\ldots,X_n}(x_1,\ldots,x_n), \tag{14.7}$$

and $p_{X^n}(x^n)$ factors as follows because the source is i.i.d.:

$$p_{X^n}(x^n) = p_{X_1}(x_1) \cdots p_{X_n}(x_n) = p_X(x_1) \cdots p_X(x_n) = \prod_{i=1}^{n} p_X(x_i). \tag{14.8}$$

Roughly speaking, we expect a long string x^n to contain about $n p_X(a_1)$ occurrences of symbol a_1, $n p_X(a_2)$ occurrences of symbol a_2, etc., when n is large, due to the law of large numbers. If this is occurring, the probability that the source emits a particular string x^n is approximately

$$p_{X^n}(x^n) = p_X(x_1) \cdots p_X(x_n) \approx p_X(a_1)^{n p_X(a_1)} \cdots p_X(a_{|\mathcal{X}|})^{n p_X(a_{|\mathcal{X}|})}, \tag{14.9}$$

and the information content of a given string is thus roughly

$$-\frac{1}{n} \log(p_{X^n}(x^n)) \approx -\sum_{i=1}^{|\mathcal{X}|} p_X(a_i) \log(p_X(a_i)) = H(X). \tag{14.10}$$

The above intuitive argument shows that the information content divided by the length of the sequence is roughly equal to the entropy in the limit of large n. It then makes sense to think of this quantity as the *sample entropy* of the sequence x^n.

DEFINITION 14.2.1 (Sample Entropy)   The sample entropy $\overline{H}(x^n)$ of a sequence x^n with respect to a probability distribution $p_X(x)$ is defined as follows:

$$\overline{H}(x^n) \equiv -\frac{1}{n} \log(p_{X^n}(x^n)), \tag{14.11}$$

where $p_{X^n}(x^n) = \prod_{i=1}^{n} p_X(x_i)$.

This definition of sample entropy leads us to our first important definitions in asymptotic information theory.

DEFINITION 14.2.2 (Typical Sequence)   A sequence x^n is δ-*typical* if its sample entropy $\overline{H}(x^n)$ is δ-close to the entropy $H(X)$ of random variable X, where this random variable is the source of the sequence.

DEFINITION 14.2.3 (Typical Set)   The δ-*typical set* $T_\delta^{X^n}$ is the set of all δ-typical sequences x^n:

$$T_\delta^{X^n} \equiv \left\{ x^n : \left| \overline{H}(x^n) - H(X) \right| \leq \delta \right\}. \tag{14.12}$$

14.3   Properties of the Typical Set

The set of typical sequences enjoys three useful and beautifully surprising properties that occur when we step into the "land of large numbers." We can summarize these properties as follows: the typical set contains almost all the probability, yet it is exponentially smaller than the set of all sequences, and each typical sequence has almost uniform probability. Figure 14.2 attempts to depict the main idea of the typical set.

PROPERTY 14.3.1 (Unit Probability)   The typical set asymptotically has probability one. So as n becomes large, it is highly likely that a source emits a typical sequence. We formally state this property as follows:

$$\Pr\left\{ X^n \in T_\delta^{X^n} \right\} = \sum_{x^n \in T_\delta^{X^n}} p_{X^n}(x^n) \geq 1 - \varepsilon, \tag{14.13}$$

for all $\varepsilon \in (0, 1)$, $\delta > 0$, and sufficiently large n.

PROPERTY 14.3.2 (Exponentially Smaller Cardinality)   The number $\left| T_\delta^{X^n} \right|$ of δ-typical sequences is exponentially smaller than the total number $|\mathcal{X}|^n$ of sequences for every random variable X besides the uniform random variable. We formally state this property as follows:

$$\left| T_\delta^{X^n} \right| \leq 2^{n(H(X)+\delta)}. \tag{14.14}$$

We can also bound the size of the δ-typical set from below:

$$\left| T_\delta^{X^n} \right| \geq (1 - \varepsilon)\, 2^{n(H(X)-\delta)}, \tag{14.15}$$

for all $\varepsilon \in (0, 1)$, $\delta > 0$, and sufficiently large n.

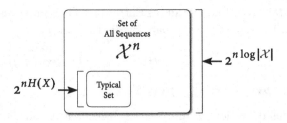

Figure 14.2 This figure depicts the idea that the typical set is exponentially smaller than the set of all sequences because $|\mathcal{X}|^n = 2^{n \log |\mathcal{X}|} > 2^{nH(X)}$ whenever X is not a uniform random variable. Yet, this exponentially smaller set contains nearly all of the probability.

PROPERTY 14.3.3 (Equipartition) The probability of a particular δ-typical sequence x^n is approximately uniform:

$$2^{-n(H(X)+\delta)} \leq p_{X^n}(x^n) \leq 2^{-n(H(X)-\delta)}. \tag{14.16}$$

This last property represents the "equipartition" in "asymptotic equipartition property" because all typical sequences occur with nearly the same probability when n is large.

The size $\left|T_\delta^{X^n}\right|$ of the δ-typical set is approximately equal to the total number $|\mathcal{X}|^n$ of sequences only when random variable X is uniform because $H(X) = \log|\mathcal{X}|$ in such a case and thus

$$\left|T_\delta^{X^n}\right| \leq 2^{n(H(X)+\delta)} = 2^{n(\log|\mathcal{X}|+\delta)} = |\mathcal{X}|^n \cdot 2^{n\delta} \approx |\mathcal{X}|^n. \tag{14.17}$$

14.3.1 Proofs of Typical Set Properties

Proof of the Unit Probability Property (Property 14.3.1) The weak law of large numbers states that the sample mean converges in probability to the expectation. More precisely, consider a sequence of i.i.d. random variables $Z_1, \ldots, Z_n$ that each have expectation μ. The sample average of this sequence is as follows:

$$\overline{Z} = \frac{1}{n} \sum_{i=1}^n Z_i. \tag{14.18}$$

The formal statement of the law of large numbers is that $\forall \varepsilon \in (0,1), \delta > 0 \ \exists n_0 :$ $\forall n > n_0$

$$\Pr\left\{\left|\overline{Z} - \mu\right| \leq \delta\right\} \geq 1 - \varepsilon. \tag{14.19}$$

We can now consider the sequence of random variables $-\log(p_X(X_1)), \ldots, -\log(p_X(X_n))$. The sample average of this sequence is equal to the sample entropy of X^n:

$$-\frac{1}{n} \sum_{i=1}^n \log(p_X(X_i)) = -\frac{1}{n} \log(p_{X^n}(X^n)) \tag{14.20}$$

$$= \overline{H}(X^n). \tag{14.21}$$

Recall from (10.3) that the expectation of the random variable $-\log(p_X(X))$ is equal to the Shannon entropy:

$$\mathbb{E}_X\left\{-\log(p_X(X))\right\} = H(X). \tag{14.22}$$

Then we can apply the law of large numbers and find that $\forall \varepsilon \in (0,1), \delta > 0 \ \exists n_0 :$ $\forall n > n_0$ such that

$$\Pr\left\{\left|\overline{H}(X^n) - H(X)\right| \leq \delta\right\} \geq 1 - \varepsilon. \tag{14.23}$$

The event $\left\{\left|\overline{H}(X^n) - H(X)\right| \leq \delta\right\}$ is precisely the condition for a random sequence X^n to be in the typical set $T_\delta^{X^n}$, and the probability of this event goes to one as n becomes large. $\square$

Proof of the Exponentially Smaller Cardinality Property (Property 14.3.2) Consider the following chain of inequalities:

$$1 = \sum_{x^n \in \mathcal{X}^n} p_{X^n}(x^n) \geq \sum_{x^n \in T_\delta^{X^n}} p_{X^n}(x^n)$$

$$\geq \sum_{x^n \in T_\delta^{X^n}} 2^{-n(H(X)+\delta)} = 2^{-n(H(X)+\delta)} \left| T_\delta^{X^n} \right|. \quad (14.24)$$

The first inequality uses the fact that the probability of the typical set is smaller than the probability of the set of all sequences. The second inequality uses the equipartition property of typical sets (proved below). After rearranging the leftmost side of (14.24) with its rightmost side, we find that

$$\left| T_\delta^{X^n} \right| \leq 2^{n(H(X)+\delta)}. \quad (14.25)$$

The second part of the property follows because the "unit probability" property holds for sufficiently large n. Then the following chain of inequalities holds:

$$1 - \varepsilon \leq \Pr\left\{ X^n \in T_\delta^{X^n} \right\} = \sum_{x^n \in T_\delta^{X^n}} p_{X^n}(x^n)$$

$$\leq \sum_{x^n \in T_\delta^{X^n}} 2^{-n(H(X)-\delta)} = 2^{-n(H(X)-\delta)} \left| T_\delta^{X^n} \right|. \quad (14.26)$$

We can then bound the size of the typical set as follows:

$$\left| T_\delta^{X^n} \right| \geq 2^{n(H(X)-\delta)} (1 - \varepsilon), \quad (14.27)$$

for all $\varepsilon \in (0, 1)$, $\delta > 0$, and sufficiently large n. $\quad\square$

Proof of the Equipartition Property (Property 14.3.3) The property follows immediately by manipulating the definition of a typical set. $\quad\square$

14.4   Application: Data Compression

The above three properties of typical sequences immediately give our first application in asymptotic information theory. It is Shannon's compression protocol, which is a scheme for compressing the output of an i.i.d. information source.

We begin by defining the information-processing task and a corresponding (n, R, ε) source code. It is helpful to recall the picture in Figure 2.1. An information source outputs a sequence x^n drawn independently according to the distribution of some random variable X. A sender Alice encodes this sequence according to some encoding map E where

$$E : \mathcal{X}^n \to \{0, 1\}^{nR}. \quad (14.28)$$

The encoding takes elements from the set $\mathcal{X}^n$ of all sequences to a set $\{0, 1\}^{nR}$ of size 2^{nR}. She then transmits the codewords over nR uses of a noiseless classical bit channel. Bob decodes according to some decoding map $D : \{0, 1\}^{nR} \rightarrow \mathcal{X}^n$. The probability of error for an (n, R, ε) source code is

$$p(e) \equiv \Pr\{(D \circ E)(X^n) \neq X^n\} \leq \varepsilon, \qquad (14.29)$$

where $\varepsilon \in (0, 1)$. The rate of the source code is equal to the number of channel uses divided by the length of the sequence, and it is equal to R for the above scheme. A particular compression rate R is *achievable* for X if there exists an $(n, R + \delta, \varepsilon)$ source code for all $\varepsilon \in (0, 1), \delta > 0$, and sufficiently large n. We can now state Shannon's lossless compression theorem.

THEOREM 14.4.1 (Shannon Compression)   The entropy of an information source specified by a discrete random variable X is the smallest achievable rate for compression:

$$\inf\{R : R \text{ is achievable for } X\} = H(X). \qquad (14.30)$$

A proof of this theorem consists of two parts, traditionally called the direct coding theorem and the converse theorem. The direct coding theorem is the direction LHS $\leq$ RHS—the proof exhibits a coding scheme with an achievable rate and demonstrates that its rate converges to the entropy in the asymptotic limit. The converse theorem is the direction LHS $\geq$ RHS and is a statement of optimality—it establishes that any coding scheme with rate below the entropy is not achievable. The proofs of each part are usually completely different. We employ typical sequences and their properties for proving a direct coding theorem, while the converse part resorts to entropy inequalities from Chapter 10.[1] For now, we prove the direct coding theorem and hold off on the converse part until we reach Schumacher compression for quantum information in Chapter 18. Our main goal here is to illustrate a simple application of typical sequences, and we can wait on the converse part because Shannon compression is in some sense a special case of Schumacher compression.

The idea behind the proof of the direct coding theorem is simple: just keep the typical sequences and throw away the rest. This coding strategy succeeds with asymptotically vanishing probability of error because the typical set asymptotically has all of the probability. Since we are only concerned with error probabilities in communication protocols, it makes sense that we should only be keeping track of a set where all of the probability concentrates. We can formally state a proof as follows. Pick an $\varepsilon \in (0, 1)$, a $\delta > 0$, and a sufficiently large n such that Property 14.3.1 holds. Consider that Property 14.3.2 then holds so that the size of the typical set is no larger than $2^{n[H(X)+\delta]}$. We choose the encoding to be a one-to-one function f that maps a typical sequence to a binary sequence in $\{0, 1\}^{nR}$, where $R = H(X) + \delta$. We define f to map any atypical sequence to 0^n. This scheme gives up on encoding the atypical sequences because

---

[1] The direct part of a quantum coding theorem can employ the properties of typical subspaces (discussed in Chapter 15), and the proof of a converse theorem for quantum information usually employs the quantum entropy inequalities from Chapter 11.

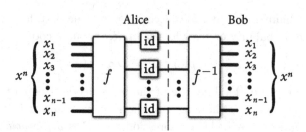

Figure 14.3 Shannon's scheme for the compression of classical data. The encoder f is a map from the typical set to a set of binary sequences of size $\approx 2^{nH(X)}$ where $H(X)$ is the entropy of the information source. The map f is invertible on the typical set but maps an atypical sequence to a constant. Alice then transmits the compressed data over $\approx nH(X)$ uses of a noiseless classical channel. The inverse map f^{-1} (the decoder) is the inverse of f on the typical set and decodes to some error sequence otherwise.

they have vanishingly small probability. We define the decoding operation to be the inverse of f. This scheme has probability of error less than ε, by considering Property 14.3.1. Figure 14.3 depicts this coding scheme.

Shannon's scheme for compression suffers from a problem that plagues all results in classical and quantum information theory. The proof guarantees that there exists a scheme that can compress at the rate of entropy in the asymptotic limit. But the complexity of encoding and decoding is far from practical—without any further specification of the encoding, it could require resources that are prohibitively exponential in the length of the sequence.

The above scheme certainly gives an achievable rate for compression of classical information, but how can we know that it is optimal? The converse theorem addresses this point (recall that a converse theorem gives a sense of optimality for a particular protocol) and completes the operational interpretation of the entropy as the fundamental limit on the compressibility of classical information. For now, we do not prove a converse theorem and instead choose to wait until we cover Schumacher compression because its converse proof applies to Shannon compression as well.

14.5   Weak Joint Typicality

Joint typicality is a concept similar to typicality, but the difference is that it applies to any two random variables X and Y. That is, there are analogous notions of typicality for the joint random variable (X, Y).

DEFINITION 14.5.1 (Joint Sample Entropy)   Consider n independent realizations $x^n = x_1 \cdots x_n$ and $y^n = y_1 \cdots y_n$ of respective random variables X and Y. The sample joint entropy $\overline{H}(x^n, y^n)$ of these two sequences is

$$\overline{H}(x^n, y^n) \equiv -\frac{1}{n} \log \left(p_{X^n, Y^n}(x^n, y^n) \right), \tag{14.31}$$

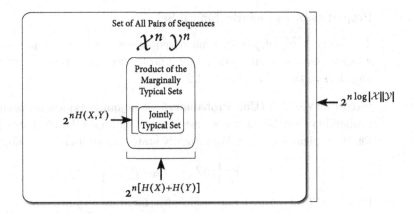

Figure 14.4 A depiction of the jointly typical set. Some sequence pairs (x^n, y^n) are such that x^n is typical or such that y^n is typical, but fewer are such that the pair is jointly typical. The jointly typical set has size roughly equal to $2^{nH(X,Y)}$, which is smaller than the Cartesian product of the marginally typical sets if random variables X and Y are not independent.

where we assume that the joint distribution $p_{X^n, Y^n}(x^n, y^n)$ has the i.i.d. property:

$$p_{X^n, Y^n}(x^n, y^n) \equiv p_{X,Y}(x_1, y_1) \cdots p_{X,Y}(x_n, y_n). \tag{14.32}$$

This notion of joint sample entropy immediately leads to the following definition of joint typicality. Figure 14.4 attempts to depict the notion of joint typicality.

DEFINITION 14.5.2 (Jointly Typical Sequence)   Two sequences x^n, y^n are δ-jointly *typical* if their sample joint entropy $\overline{H}(x^n, y^n)$ is δ-close to the joint entropy $H(X, Y)$ of random variables X and Y and if both x^n and y^n are marginally typical.

DEFINITION 14.5.3 (Jointly Typical Set)   The δ-jointly *typical set* $T_\delta^{X^n Y^n}$ consists of all δ-jointly typical sequences:

$$T_\delta^{X^n Y^n} \equiv \left\{ (x^n, y^n) : \left| \overline{H}(x^n, y^n) - H(X, Y) \right| \leq \delta, \ \ x^n \in T_\delta^{X^n}, \ \ y^n \in T_\delta^{Y^n} \right\}. \tag{14.33}$$

The extra conditions on the marginal sample entropies are necessary to have a sensible definition of joint typicality. That is, it does not necessarily follow that the marginal sample entropies are close to the marginal true entropies if the joint ones are close, but it intuitively makes sense that this condition should hold. Thus, we add these extra conditions to the definition of jointly typical sequences. Later, we find in Section 14.7 that the intuitive implication holds (it is not necessary to include the marginals) when we introduce a different definition of typicality.

14.5.1   Properties of the Jointly Typical Set

The set $T_\delta^{X^n Y^n}$ of jointly typical sequences enjoys three properties similar to what we have seen in Section 14.2, and the proofs of these properties are nearly identical to those in Section 14.2.

PROPERTY 14.5.1 (Unit Probability)   The jointly typical set asymptotically has probability one. So as n becomes large, it is highly likely that a source emits a jointly typical sequence. We formally state this property as follows:

$$\Pr\left\{ (X^n, Y^n) \in T_\delta^{X^n Y^n} \right\} \geq 1 - \varepsilon, \tag{14.34}$$

for all $\varepsilon \in (0, 1)$, $\delta > 0$, and sufficiently large n.

PROPERTY 14.5.2 (Exponentially Smaller Cardinality)   The number $\left| T_\delta^{X^n Y^n} \right|$ of δ-jointly typical sequences is exponentially smaller than the total number $(|\mathcal{X}| |\mathcal{Y}|)^n$ of sequences for any joint random variable (X, Y) that is not uniform. We formally state this property as follows:

$$\left| T_\delta^{X^n Y^n} \right| \leq 2^{n(H(X,Y)+\delta)}. \tag{14.35}$$

We can also bound the size of the δ-jointly typical set from below:

$$\left| T_\delta^{X^n Y^n} \right| \geq (1 - \varepsilon)\, 2^{n(H(X,Y)-\delta)}, \tag{14.36}$$

for all $\varepsilon \in (0, 1)$, $\delta > 0$, and sufficiently large n.

PROPERTY 14.5.3 (Equipartition)   The probability of a particular δ-jointly typical sequence $x^n y^n$ is approximately uniform:

$$2^{-n(H(X,Y)+\delta)} \leq p_{X^n, Y^n}(x^n, y^n) \leq 2^{-n(H(X,Y)-\delta)}. \tag{14.37}$$

EXERCISE 14.5.1   Prove the above three properties of the jointly typical set.

The above three properties may be similar to what we have seen before, but there is another interesting property of jointly typical sequences that we give below. It states that two sequences drawn independently according to the marginal distributions $p_X(x)$ and $p_Y(y)$ are jointly typical according to the joint distribution $p_{X,Y}(x, y)$ with probability $\approx 2^{-nI(X;Y)}$. This property gives a simple interpretation of the mutual information that is related to its most important operational interpretation as the classical channel capacity discussed briefly in Section 2.2.

PROPERTY 14.5.4 (Probability of Joint Typicality)   Consider two independent random variables $\tilde{X}^n$ and $\tilde{Y}^n$ whose respective probability density functions $p_{\tilde{X}^n}(x^n)$ and $p_{\tilde{Y}^n}(y^n)$ are equal to the marginal densities of the joint density $p_{X^n, Y^n}(x^n, y^n)$:

$$(\tilde{X}^n, \tilde{Y}^n) \sim p_{X^n}(x^n) p_{Y^n}(y^n). \tag{14.38}$$

Then we can bound the probability that two random sequences $\tilde{X}^n$ and $\tilde{Y}^n$ are in the jointly typical set $T_\delta^{X^n Y^n}$:

$$\Pr\left\{(\tilde{X}^n, \tilde{Y}^n) \in T_\delta^{X^n Y^n}\right\} \le 2^{-n(I(X;Y)-3\delta)}. \tag{14.39}$$

EXERCISE 14.5.2   Prove Property 14.5.4. (Hint: Consider that

$$\Pr\left\{(\tilde{X}^n, \tilde{Y}^n) \in T_\delta^{X^n Y^n}\right\} = \sum_{x^n, y^n \in T_\delta^{X^n Y^n}} p_{X^n}(x^n) p_{Y^n}(y^n), \tag{14.40}$$

and use the properties of typical and jointly typical sets to bound this probability.)

14.6 Weak Conditional Typicality

Conditional typicality is a property that we expect to hold for any two random sequences—it is also a useful tool in the proofs of coding theorems. Suppose two random variables X and Y have respective alphabets $\mathcal{X}$ and $\mathcal{Y}$ and a joint distribution $p_{X,Y}(x, y)$. We can factor the joint distribution $p_{X,Y}(x, y)$ as the product of a marginal distribution $p_X(x)$ and a conditional distribution $p_{Y|X}(y|x)$, and this factoring leads to a particular way that we can think about generating realizations of the joint random variable. We can consider random variable Y to be a noisy version of X, where we first generate a realization x of the random variable X according to the distribution $p_X(x)$ and follow by generating a realization y of the random variable Y according to the conditional distribution $p_{Y|X}(y|x)$.

Suppose that we generate n independent realizations of random variable X to obtain the sequence $x^n = x_1 \cdots x_n$. We then record these values and use the conditional distribution $p_{Y|X}(y|x)$ n times to generate n independent realizations of random variable Y. Let $y^n = y_1 \cdots y_n$ denote the resulting sequence.

DEFINITION 14.6.1 (Conditional Sample Entropy)   The conditional sample entropy $\overline{H}(y^n|x^n)$ of two sequences x^n and y^n with respect to $p_{X,Y}(x, y) = p_X(x)p_{Y|X}(y|x)$ is

$$\overline{H}(y^n|x^n) = -\frac{1}{n}\log p_{Y^n|X^n}(y^n|x^n), \tag{14.41}$$

where

$$p_{Y^n|X^n}(y^n|x^n) \equiv p_{Y|X}(y_1|x_1) \cdots p_{Y|X}(y_n|x_n). \tag{14.42}$$

DEFINITION 14.6.2 (Conditionally Typical Set)   Let $x^n \in \mathcal{X}^n$. The δ-conditionally typical set $T_\delta^{Y^n|x^n}$ consists of all sequences whose conditional sample entropy is δ-close to the true conditional entropy:

$$T_\delta^{Y^n|x^n} \equiv \left\{y^n : \left|\overline{H}(y^n|x^n) - H(Y|X)\right| \le \delta\right\}. \tag{14.43}$$

Figure 14.5 provides an intuitive picture of the notion of conditional typicality.

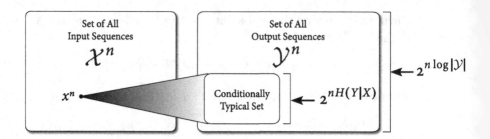

Figure 14.5 The notion of the conditionally typical set. A typical sequence x^n in $T_\delta^{X^n}$ maps stochastically through many instantiations of a conditional distribution $p_{Y|X}(y|x)$ to some sequence y^n. It is overwhelmingly likely that y^n is in a conditionally typical set $T_\delta^{Y^n|x^n}$ when n becomes large. This conditionally typical set has size around $2^{nH(Y|X)}$. It contains nearly all of the probability but is exponentially smaller than the set of all sequences $\mathcal{Y}^n$.

14.6.1 Properties of the Conditionally Typical Set

The set $T_\delta^{Y^n|x^n}$ of conditionally typical sequences enjoys properties similar to what we have seen before, and we list them for completeness.

PROPERTY 14.6.1 (Unit Probability) The set $T_\delta^{Y^n|x^n}$ asymptotically has probability one on average with respect to a random sequence X^n. So as n becomes large, it is highly likely that random sequences Y^n and X^n are such that Y^n is a conditionally typical sequence (on average with respect to X^n). We formally state this property as follows:

$$\mathbb{E}_{X^n}\left\{\Pr_{Y^n|X^n}\left\{Y^n \in T_\delta^{Y^n|X^n}\right\}\right\} \geq 1 - \varepsilon, \tag{14.44}$$

for all $\varepsilon \in (0,1)$, $\delta > 0$, and sufficiently large n.

PROPERTY 14.6.2 (Exponentially Smaller Cardinality) The number $\left|T_\delta^{Y^n|x^n}\right|$ of δ-conditionally typical sequences is exponentially smaller than the total number $|\mathcal{Y}|^n$ of sequences for any conditional random variable $Y|X$ that is not uniform. We formally state this property as follows:

$$\left|T_\delta^{Y^n|x^n}\right| \leq 2^{n(H(Y|X)+\delta)}. \tag{14.45}$$

We can also bound the expected size of the δ-conditionally typical set from below when x^n is a random sequence:

$$\mathbb{E}_{X^n}\left\{\left|T_\delta^{Y^n|X^n}\right|\right\} \geq (1 - \varepsilon)\, 2^{n(H(Y|X)-\delta)}, \tag{14.46}$$

for all $\varepsilon \in (0,1)$, $\delta > 0$, and sufficiently large n.

PROPERTY 14.6.3 (Equipartition) The probability of a given δ-conditionally typical sequence y^n (corresponding to the sequence x^n) is approximately uniform:

$$2^{-n(H(Y|X)+\delta)} \leq p_{Y^n|X^n}(y^n|x^n) \leq 2^{-n(H(Y|X)-\delta)}. \tag{14.47}$$

In summary, averaged over realizations of the random variable X^n, the conditionally typical set $T_\delta^{Y^n|X^n}$ has almost all the probability, and its size is exponentially smaller than the size of the set of all sequences. For each realization of X^n, each δ-conditionally typical sequence has an approximate uniform probability of occurring.

Our last note on the weak conditionally typical set is that there is a subtlety in the statement of Property 14.6.1 that allows for a relatively straightforward proof. This subtlety is that we average over the sequence X^n as well, and this allows one to exploit the extra randomness in order to establish a proof. We do not impose such a constraint later on in Section 14.9 when we introduce the notion of a strong conditionally typical sequence. We instead impose the constraint that the sequence x^n is a strongly typical sequence, and this property is sufficient to prove that similar properties hold for a strong conditionally typical set.

We now prove the first property. This is just again another application of the law of large numbers. Consider that

$$\mathbb{E}_{X^n}\left\{\Pr_{Y^n|X^n}\left\{Y^n \in T_\delta^{Y^n|X^n}\right\}\right\}$$

$$= \mathbb{E}_{X^n}\left\{\mathbb{E}_{Y^n|X^n}\left\{I_{T_\delta^{Y^n|X^n}}(Y^n)\right\}\right\} \tag{14.48}$$

$$= \mathbb{E}_{X^n,Y^n}\left\{I_{T_\delta^{Y^n|X^n}}(Y^n)\right\} \tag{14.49}$$

$$= \sum_{x^n\in\mathcal{X}^n,y^n\in\mathcal{Y}^n} p_{X^n,Y^n}(x^n,y^n)I_{T_\delta^{Y^n|x^n}}(y^n), \tag{14.50}$$

where I denotes an indicator function. Given random variables X and Y, let us define the random variable $g(X,Y) = -\log p_{Y|X}(Y|X)$. The expectation of this random variable is

$$\mathbb{E}_{X,Y}\{g(X,Y)\} = \mathbb{E}_{X,Y}\{[-\log p_{Y|X}(Y|X)]\} \tag{14.51}$$

$$= \sum_{x,y} p_{X,Y}(x,y)[-\log p_{Y|X}(y|x)] \tag{14.52}$$

$$= H(Y|X). \tag{14.53}$$

Consider that the conditional sample entropy $\overline{H}(Y^n|X^n)$ for the random sequences X^n and Y^n factors as follows:

$$\overline{H}(Y^n|X^n) = -\frac{1}{n}\log p_{Y^n|X^n}(Y^n|X^n) \tag{14.54}$$

$$= \frac{1}{n}\sum_{i=1}^n [-\log p_{Y|X}(Y_i|X_i)] \tag{14.55}$$

$$= \frac{1}{n}\sum_{i=1}^n g(X_i,Y_i). \tag{14.56}$$

This is the sample average of the random variables $g(X_i,Y_i)$ for all $i \in \{1,\ldots,n\}$. Given all of the above and the definition of weak conditional typicality, we can rewrite (14.50) as follows:

$$\Pr_{X^n Y^n} \left\{ \left| \frac{1}{n} \sum_{i=1}^{n} g\left(X_i, Y_i\right) - \mathbb{E}_{X,Y}\{g(X,Y)\} \right| \leq \delta \right\}. \qquad (14.57)$$

By applying the law of large numbers, this is $\geq 1 - \varepsilon$ for all $\varepsilon \in (0,1)$, $\delta > 0$, and sufficiently large n.

EXERCISE 14.6.1   Prove Properties 14.6.2 and 14.6.3 for the weak conditionally typical set.

14.7   Strong Typicality

In the development in the previous sections, we showed how the law of large numbers is the underpinning method to prove many of the interesting results regarding typical sequences. These results are satisfactory and provide an intuitive notion of typicality through the idea of the sample entropy approaching the true entropy for sufficiently long sequences.

It is possible to develop a stronger notion of typicality with a different definition. Instead of requiring that the sample entropy of a random sequence is close to the true entropy of a distribution for sufficiently long sequences, strong typicality requires that the empirical distribution or relative frequency of symbols of a random sequence has a small deviation from the true probability distribution for sufficiently large sequence length.

We begin with a simple example to help illustrate this stronger notion of typicality. Suppose that we generate a binary sequence i.i.d. according to the distribution $p(0) = 1/4$ and $p(1) = 3/4$. Such a random generation process could lead to the following sequence:

$$0110111010. \qquad (14.58)$$

Rather than computing the sample entropy of this sequence and comparing it with the true entropy, we can count the number of zeros or ones that appear in the sequence and compare their normalizations with the true distribution of the information source. For the above example, the number of zeros is equal to 4, and the number of ones (the Hamming weight of the sequence) is equal to 6:

$$N(0 \mid 0110111010) = 4, \qquad N(1 \mid 0110111010) = 6. \qquad (14.59)$$

We can compute the empirical distribution of this sequence by normalizing the above numbers by the length of the sequence:

$$\frac{1}{10} N(0 \mid 0110111010) = \frac{2}{5}, \qquad \frac{1}{10} N(1 \mid 0110111010) = \frac{3}{5}. \qquad (14.60)$$

This empirical distribution deviates from the true distribution by the following amount:

$$\max \left\{ \left| \frac{1}{4} - \frac{2}{5} \right|, \left| \frac{3}{4} - \frac{3}{5} \right| \right\} = \frac{3}{20}, \qquad (14.61)$$

which is a fairly significant deviation. However, suppose that the length of the sequence grows large enough so that the law of large numbers comes into play. We would then expect it to be highly likely that the empirical distribution of a random sequence does not deviate much from the true distribution, and the law of large numbers again gives a theoretical underpinning for this intuition. This example gives the essence of strong typicality.

We wish to highlight another important aspect of the above example. The particular sequence in (14.58) has a Hamming weight of six, but this sequence is not the only one with this Hamming weight. By a simple counting argument, there are $\binom{10}{6} - 1 = 209$ other sequences with the same length and Hamming weight. That is, all these other sequences have the same empirical distribution and thus have the same deviation from the true distribution as the original sequence in (14.58). We say that all these sequences are in the same "type class," which simply means that they have the same empirical distribution. The type class is thus an equivalence class on sequences where the equivalence relation is the empirical distribution of the sequence.

We mention a few interesting properties of the type class before giving more formal definitions. We can partition the set of all possible sequences according to type classes. Consider that the set of all binary sequences of length ten has size 2^{10}. There is one sequence with all zeros, $\binom{10}{1}$ sequences with Hamming weight one, $\binom{10}{2}$ sequences with Hamming weight two, etc. The binomial theorem guarantees that the total number of sequences is equal to the number of sequences in all of the type classes:

$$2^{10} = \sum_{i=0}^{10} \binom{10}{i}. \tag{14.62}$$

Suppose now that we generate ten i.i.d. realizations of the Bernoulli distribution $p(0) = 1/4$ and $p(1) = 3/4$. Without knowing anything else, our best description of the distribution of the random sequence is

$$p(x_1, \ldots, x_{10}) = p(x_1) \cdots p(x_{10}), \tag{14.63}$$

where $x_1, \ldots, x_{10}$ are different realizations of the binary random variable. But suppose that a third party tells us the Hamming weight w_0 of the generated sequence. This information allows us to update our knowledge of the distribution of the sequence, and we can say that any sequence with Hamming weight not equal to w_0 has zero probability. All the sequences with the same Hamming weight have the same distribution because we generated the sequence in an i.i.d. way, and each sequence with Hamming weight w_0 has a uniform distribution after renormalizing. Thus, conditioned on the Hamming weight w_0, our best description of the distribution of the random sequence is

$$p(x_1, \ldots, x_{10} | w_0) = \begin{cases} 0 & : \ w(x_1, \ldots, x_{10}) \neq w_0 \\ \binom{10}{w_0}^{-1} & : \ w(x_1, \ldots, x_{10}) = w_0 \end{cases}, \tag{14.64}$$

where w is a function that gives the Hamming weight of a binary sequence. This property has important consequences for asymptotic information processing because it gives us a way to extract uniform randomness from an i.i.d. distribution, and we later see that it has applications in several quantum information-processing protocols as well.

14.7.1   Types and Strong Typicality

We now formally develop the notion of a type and strong typicality. Let x^n denote a sequence $x_1 x_2 \ldots x_n$, where each x_i belongs to the alphabet $\mathcal{X}$. Let $|\mathcal{X}|$ be the cardinality of $\mathcal{X}$. Let $N(x|x^n)$ be the number of occurrences of the symbol $x \in \mathcal{X}$ in the sequence x^n.

DEFINITION 14.7.1 (Type)   The *type* or empirical distribution t_{x^n} of a sequence x^n is a probability mass function whose elements are $t_{x^n}(x)$ where

$$t_{x^n}(x) \equiv \frac{1}{n} N(x|x^n). \tag{14.65}$$

DEFINITION 14.7.2 (Strongly Typical Set)   The δ-strongly typical set $T_\delta^{X^n}$ is the set of all sequences with an empirical distribution $\frac{1}{n} N(x|x^n)$ that has maximum deviation δ from the true distribution $p_X(x)$. Furthermore, the empirical distribution $\frac{1}{n} N(x|x^n)$ of any sequence in $T_\delta^{X^n}$ vanishes for any letter x for which $p_X(x) = 0$:

$$T_\delta^{X^n} \equiv \left\{ x^n : \forall x \in \mathcal{X}, \ \left| \frac{1}{n} N(x|x^n) - p_X(x) \right| \le \delta \right.$$
$$\left. \text{if } p_X(x) > 0, \ \text{else } \frac{1}{n} N(x|x^n) = 0 \right\}. \tag{14.66}$$

The extra condition where $\frac{1}{n} N(x|x^n) = 0$ when $p_X(x) = 0$ is a somewhat technical condition, nevertheless intuitive, that is necessary to prove the three desired properties for the strongly typical set. Also, we are using the same notation $T_\delta^{X^n}$ to indicate both the weakly and strongly typical set, but which one is appropriate should be clear from the context, or we will explicitly indicate which one we are using.

The notion of type class becomes useful for us in our later developments—it is simply a way for grouping together all the sequences with the same empirical distribution. Its most important use is as a way for obtaining a uniform distribution from an arbitrary i.i.d. distribution (recall that we can do this by conditioning on a particular type).

DEFINITION 14.7.3 (Type Class)   Let $T_t^{X^n}$ denote the *type class* of a particular type t. The type class $T_t^{X^n}$ is the set of all sequences with length n and type t:

$$T_t^{X^n} \equiv \{ x^n \in \mathcal{X}^n : t_{x^n} = t \}. \tag{14.67}$$

PROPERTY 14.7.1 (Bound on the Number of Types)   The number of types for a given sequence of length n containing symbols from an alphabet $\mathcal{X}$ is exactly equal to

$$\binom{n + |\mathcal{X}| - 1}{|\mathcal{X}| - 1}. \tag{14.68}$$

A good upper bound on the number of types is $(n+1)^{|\mathcal{X}|}$.

Proof   The number of types is equal to the number of ways that the symbols in a sequence of length n can form $|\mathcal{X}|$ distinct groups. Consider the following visual aid:

$$\bullet\bullet\bullet\bullet\bullet|\bullet\bullet\bullet\bullet\bullet\bullet|\bullet\bullet\bullet\bullet\bullet\bullet\bullet\bullet\bullet\bullet|\bullet\bullet\bullet\bullet\;. \tag{14.69}$$

We can think of the number of types as the number of different ways of arranging $|\mathcal{X}| - 1$ vertical bars to group the n dots into $|\mathcal{X}|$ distinct groups, which gives (14.68). The upper bound follows from a simple argument. The number of types is the number of different ways that $|\mathcal{X}|$ positive numbers can sum to n. Overestimating the count, we can choose the first number in $n + 1$ different ways (it can be any number from 0 to n), and we can choose the $|\mathcal{X}| - 1$ other numbers in $n + 1$ different ways. Multiplying all of these possibilities together gives an upper bound $(n + 1)^{|\mathcal{X}|}$ on the number of types. This bound illustrates that the number of types is only *polynomial* in the length n of the sequence (compare with the total number $|\mathcal{X}|^n$ of sequences of length n being exponential in the length of the sequence).   □

DEFINITION 14.7.4 (Typical Type)   Let $p_X(x)$ denote the true probability distribution of symbols x in the alphabet $\mathcal{X}$. For $\delta > 0$, let τ_δ denote the set of all *typical* types that have maximum deviation δ from the true distribution $p_X(x)$:

$$\tau_\delta \equiv \{t : \forall x \in \mathcal{X},\ |t(x) - p_X(x)| \leq \delta \text{ if } p_X(x) > 0 \text{ else } t(x) = 0\}. \tag{14.70}$$

We can then equivalently define the set of strongly δ-typical sequences of length n as a union over all the type classes of the typical types in τ_δ:

$$T_\delta^{X^n} = \bigcup_{t \in \tau_\delta} T_t^{X^n}. \tag{14.71}$$

14.7.2   Properties of the Strongly Typical Set

The strongly typical set enjoys many useful properties (similar to the weakly typical set).

PROPERTY 14.7.2 (Unit Probability)   The strongly typical set asymptotically has probability one. So as n becomes large, it is highly likely that a source emits a strongly typical sequence. We formally state this property as follows:

$$\Pr\left\{X^n \in T_\delta^{X^n}\right\} \geq 1 - \varepsilon, \tag{14.72}$$

for all $\varepsilon \in (0, 1)$, $\delta > 0$, and sufficiently large n.

PROPERTY 14.7.3 (Exponentially Smaller Cardinality)   The number $\left|T_\delta^{X^n}\right|$ of δ-typical sequences is exponentially smaller than the total number $|\mathcal{X}|^n$ of sequences for most random variables X. We formally state this property as follows:

$$\left|T_\delta^{X^n}\right| \leq 2^{n(H(X)+c\delta)}, \tag{14.73}$$

where c is some positive constant. We can also bound the size of the δ-typical set from below:

$$\left|T_\delta^{X^n}\right| \geq (1-\varepsilon)\, 2^{n(H(X)-c\delta)}, \tag{14.74}$$

for all $\varepsilon \in (0,1)$, $\delta > 0$, and sufficiently large n.

PROPERTY 14.7.4 (Equipartition)   The probability of a given δ-typical sequence x^n occurring is approximately uniform:

$$2^{-n(H(X)+c\delta)} \leq p_{X^n}(x^n) \leq 2^{-n(H(X)-c\delta)}. \tag{14.75}$$

This last property of strong typicality demonstrates that it implies weak typicality up to a constant c.

14.7.3   Proofs of the Properties of the Strongly Typical Set

Proof of the Unit Probability Property (Property 14.7.2)   A proof proceeds similarly to the proof of the unit probability property for the weakly typical set. The law of large numbers states that the sample mean of a random sequence converges in probability to the expectation of the random variable from which we generate the sequence. So consider a sequence of i.i.d. random variables $Z_1, \ldots, Z_n$ where each random variable in the sequence has expectation μ. The sample average of this sequence is as follows:

$$\overline{Z} \equiv \frac{1}{n} \sum_{i=1}^n Z_i. \tag{14.76}$$

The precise statement of the weak law of large numbers is that $\forall \varepsilon \in (0,1), \delta > 0$ $\exists n_0 : \forall n > n_0$ such that

$$\Pr\left\{\left|\overline{Z} - \mu\right| > \delta\right\} < \varepsilon. \tag{14.77}$$

We can now consider the indicator random variables $I(X_1 = a), \ldots, I(X_n = a)$. The sample mean of a random sequence of indicator variables is equal to the empirical distribution $N(a|X^n)/n$:

$$\frac{1}{n} \sum_{i=1}^n I(X_i = a) = \frac{1}{n} N(a|X^n), \tag{14.78}$$

and the expectation of the indicator random variable $I(X = a)$ is equal to the probability of the symbol a:

$$\mathbb{E}_X\left\{I(X = a)\right\} = p_X(a). \tag{14.79}$$

Also, any random sequence X^n has probability zero if one of its symbols x_i is such that $p_X(x_i) = 0$. Thus, the probability that $\frac{1}{n} N(a|X^n) = 0$ is equal to one whenever $p_X(a) = 0$:

$$\Pr\left\{\frac{1}{n} N(a|X^n) = 0 : p_X(a) = 0\right\} = 1, \qquad (14.80)$$

and we can consider the cases when $p_X(a) > 0$. We apply the law of large numbers to find that

$$\forall \varepsilon \in (0,1), \delta > 0 \ \exists n_{0,a} : \forall n > n_{0,a} \quad \Pr\left\{\left|\frac{1}{n} N(a|X^n) - p_X(a)\right| > \delta\right\} < \frac{\varepsilon}{|\mathcal{X}|}. \qquad (14.81)$$

Choosing $n_0 = \max_{a \in \mathcal{X}} \{n_{0,a}\}$, the following condition holds by the union bound of probability theory:

$$\forall \varepsilon \in (0,1), \delta > 0 \ \exists n_0 : \forall n > n_0$$

$$\Pr\left\{\bigcup_{a \in \mathcal{X}} \left|\frac{1}{n} N(a|X^n) - p_X(a)\right| > \delta\right\}$$

$$\leq \sum_{a \in \mathcal{X}} \Pr\left\{\left|\frac{1}{n} N(a|X^n) - p_X(a)\right| > \delta\right\} < \varepsilon. \qquad (14.82)$$

Thus the complement of the above event on the left has high probability. That is, $\forall \varepsilon \in (0,1), \delta > 0 \ \exists n_0 : \forall n > n_0$ such that

$$\Pr\left\{\forall a \in \mathcal{X}, \ \left|\frac{1}{n} N(a|X^n) - p_X(a)\right| \leq \delta\right\} \geq 1 - \varepsilon. \qquad (14.83)$$

The event $\left\{\forall a \in \mathcal{X}, \ \left|\frac{1}{n} N(a|X^n) - p_X(a)\right| \leq \delta\right\}$ is the condition for a random sequence X^n to be in the strongly typical set $T_\delta^{X^n}$, and the probability of this event goes to one as n becomes sufficiently large. $\qquad \square$

Proof of the Exponentially Smaller Cardinality Property (Property 14.7.3) By the proof of Property 14.7.4 (proved below), we know that the following relation holds for any sequence x^n in the strongly typical set:

$$2^{-n(H(X)+c\delta)} \leq p_{X^n}(x^n) \leq 2^{-n(H(X)-c\delta)}, \qquad (14.84)$$

where c is some positive constant that we define when we prove Property 14.7.4. Summing over all sequences in the typical set, we get the following inequalities:

$$\sum_{x^n \in T_\delta^{X^n}} 2^{-n(H(X)+c\delta)} \leq \Pr\left\{X^n \in T_\delta^{X^n}\right\} \leq \sum_{x^n \in T_\delta^{X^n}} 2^{-n(H(X)-c\delta)}, \qquad (14.85)$$

$$\Rightarrow 2^{-n(H(X)+c\delta)} \left|T_\delta^{X^n}\right| \leq \Pr\left\{X^n \in T_\delta^{X^n}\right\} \leq 2^{-n(H(X)-c\delta)} \left|T_\delta^{X^n}\right|. \qquad (14.86)$$

By the unit probability property of the strongly typical set, we know that the following relation holds for sufficiently large n:

$$1 \geq \Pr\left\{X^n \in T_\delta^{X^n}\right\} \geq 1 - \varepsilon. \qquad (14.87)$$

Then the following inequalities result by combining the above inequalities:

$$2^{n(H(X)-c\delta)}(1-\varepsilon) \le \left|T_\delta^{X^n}\right| \le 2^{n(H(X)+c\delta)}, \tag{14.88}$$

concluding the proof. □

Proof of the Equipartition Property (Property 14.7.4) The following relation holds from the i.i.d. property of the distribution $p_{X^n}(x^n)$ and because the sequence x^n is strongly typical:

$$p_{X^n}(x^n) = \prod_{x\in\mathcal{X}^+} p_X(x)^{N(x|x^n)} \tag{14.89}$$

where $\mathcal{X}^+$ denotes all the letters x in $\mathcal{X}$ with $p_X(x) > 0$. (The fact that the sequence x^n is strongly typical according to Definition 14.7.2 allows us to employ this modified alphabet.) Take the logarithm of the above expression:

$$\log(p_{X^n}(x^n)) = \sum_{x\in\mathcal{X}^+} N(x|x^n)\log(p_X(x)). \tag{14.90}$$

Multiply both sides by $-\frac{1}{n}$:

$$-\frac{1}{n}\log(p_{X^n}(x^n)) = -\sum_{x\in\mathcal{X}^+}\frac{1}{n}N(x|x^n)\log(p_X(x)). \tag{14.91}$$

The following relation holds because the sequence x^n is strongly typical:

$$\forall x \in \mathcal{X}^+ : \left|\frac{1}{n}N(x|x^n) - p_X(x)\right| \le \delta, \tag{14.92}$$

and it implies that

$$\Rightarrow \forall x \in \mathcal{X}^+ : -\delta + p_X(x) \le \frac{1}{n}N(x|x^n) \le \delta + p_X(x). \tag{14.93}$$

Now multiply (14.93) by $-\log(p_X(x)) > 0$, sum over all letters in the alphabet $\mathcal{X}^+$, and apply the substitution in (14.91). This procedure gives the following set of inequalities:

$$-\sum_{x\in\mathcal{X}^+}(-\delta + p_X(x))\log(p_X(x)) \le -\frac{1}{n}\log(p_{X^n}(x^n))$$

$$\le -\sum_{x\in\mathcal{X}^+}(\delta + p_X(x))\log(p_X(x)), \tag{14.94}$$

$$\Rightarrow -c\delta + H(X) \le -\frac{1}{n}\log(p_{X^n}(x^n)) \le c\delta + H(X), \tag{14.95}$$

$$\Rightarrow 2^{-n(H(X)+c\delta)} \le p_{X^n}(x^n) \le 2^{-n(H(X)-c\delta)}, \tag{14.96}$$

where

$$c \equiv -\sum_{x\in\mathcal{X}^+}\log(p_X(x)) \ge 0. \tag{14.97}$$

It now becomes apparent why we require the technical condition in the definition of strong typicality (Definition 14.7.2). Were it not there, then the constant c would not be finite, and we would not be able to obtain a reasonable bound on the probability of a strongly typical sequence. $\qquad\square$

14.7.4 Cardinality of a Typical Type Class

Recall that a typical type class is defined to be the set of all sequences with the same empirical distribution, and the empirical distribution happens to have maximum deviation δ from the true distribution. It might seem that the size $\left|T_t^{X^n}\right|$ of a typical type class $T_t^{X^n}$ should be smaller than the size of the strongly typical set. But the following property overrides this intuition and shows that a given typical type class $T_t^{X^n}$ in some sense has almost as many sequences in it as the strongly typical set $T_\delta^{X^n}$ for sufficiently large n.

PROPERTY 14.7.5 (Minimal Cardinality of a Typical Type Class) Let X be a random variable with alphabet $\mathcal{X}$. Fix $\delta \in (0, 2/|\mathcal{X}|]$. For $t \in \tau_\delta$, the size $\left|T_t^{X^n}\right|$ of the typical type class $T_t^{X^n}$ is bounded from below as follows:

$$\left|T_t^{X^n}\right| \geq \frac{1}{(n+1)^{|\mathcal{X}|}} 2^{n[H(X)-\eta(|\mathcal{X}|\delta)]} = 2^{n\left[H(X)-\eta(|\mathcal{X}|\delta)-|\mathcal{X}|\frac{1}{n}\log(n+1)\right]}, \quad (14.98)$$

where $\eta(\delta)$ is some function such that $\eta(\delta) \to 0$ as $\delta \to 0$. Thus, a typical type class is of size roughly $2^{nH(X)}$ when $n \to \infty$ and $\delta \to 0$ (it is about as large as the typical set when n becomes large).

Proof We first show that if $X_1, \ldots, X_n$ are random variables drawn i.i.d. from a distribution $q(x)$, then the probability $q^n(x^n)$ of a particular sequence x^n depends only on its type:

$$q^n(x^n) = 2^{-n(H(t_{x^n})+D(t_{x^n}\|q))}, \quad (14.99)$$

where $D(t_{x^n}\|q)$ is the relative entropy between t_{x^n} and q. To see this, consider the following chain of equalities:

$$q^n(x^n) = \prod_{i=1}^n q(x_i) = \prod_{x\in\mathcal{X}} q(x)^{N(x|x^n)} = \prod_{x\in\mathcal{X}} q(x)^{nt_{x^n}(x)} \quad (14.100)$$

$$= \prod_{x\in\mathcal{X}} 2^{nt_{x^n}(x)\log q(x)} = 2^{n\sum_{x\in\mathcal{X}} t_{x^n}(x)\log q(x)} \quad (14.101)$$

$$= 2^{n\sum_{x\in\mathcal{X}} t_{x^n}(x)\log q(x)-t_{x^n}(x)\log t_{x^n}(x)+t_{x^n}(x)\log t_{x^n}(x)} \quad (14.102)$$

$$= 2^{-n(D(t_{x^n}\|q)+H(t_{x^n}))}. \quad (14.103)$$

It then follows that the probability of the sequence x^n is $2^{-nH(t_{x^n})}$ if the distribution $q(x) = t_{x^n}(x)$. Now consider that each type class $T_t^{X^n}$ has size

$$\binom{n}{nt_{x^n}(x_1), \ldots, nt_{x^n}(x_{|\mathcal{X}|})}, \quad (14.104)$$

where the distribution $t = (t_{x^n}(x_1), \ldots, t_{x^n}(x_{|\mathcal{X}|}))$ and the letters of $\mathcal{X}$ are $x_1, \ldots, x_{|\mathcal{X}|}$. This result follows because the size of a type class is just the number of ways of arranging $n t_{x^n}(x_1), \ldots, n t_{x^n}(x_{|\mathcal{X}|})$ in a sequence of length n. We now prove that the type class $T_t^{X^n}$ has the highest probability among all type classes when the probability distribution is t:

$$t^n(T_t^{X^n}) \geq t^n(T_{t'}^{X^n}) \text{ for all } t' \in \mathcal{P}_n, \tag{14.105}$$

where t^n is the i.i.d. distribution induced by the type t and $\mathcal{P}_n$ is the set of all types. Consider the following equalities:

$$\frac{t^n(T_t^{X^n})}{t^n(T_{t'}^{X^n})} = \frac{\left|T_t^{X^n}\right| \prod_{x \in \mathcal{X}} t_{x^n}(x)^{n t_{x^n}(x)}}{\left|T_{t'}^{X^n}\right| \prod_{x \in \mathcal{X}} t_{x^n}(x)^{n t'_{x^n}(x)}} \tag{14.106}$$

$$= \frac{\binom{n}{n t_{x^n}(x_1), \ldots, n t_{x^n}(x_{|\mathcal{X}|})} \prod_{x \in \mathcal{X}} t_{x^n}(x)^{n t_{x^n}(x)}}{\binom{n}{n t'_{x^n}(x_1), \ldots, n t'_{x^n}(x_{|\mathcal{X}|})} \prod_{x \in \mathcal{X}} t_{x^n}(x)^{n t'_{x^n}(x)}} \tag{14.107}$$

$$= \prod_{x \in \mathcal{X}} \frac{n t'_{x^n}(x)!}{n t_{x^n}(x)!} t_{x^n}(x)^{n(t_{x^n}(x) - t'_{x^n}(x))}. \tag{14.108}$$

Now apply the bound $\frac{m!}{n!} \geq n^{m-n}$ (that holds for any positive integers m and n) to get

$$\frac{t^n(T_t^{X^n})}{t^n(T_{t'}^{X^n})} \geq \prod_{x \in \mathcal{X}} [n t_{x^n}(x)]^{n(t'_{x^n}(x) - t_{x^n}(x))} t_{x^n}(x)^{n(t_{x^n}(x) - t'_{x^n}(x))} \tag{14.109}$$

$$= \prod_{x \in \mathcal{X}} n^{n(t'_{x^n}(x) - t_{x^n}(x))} \tag{14.110}$$

$$= n^{n \sum_{x \in \mathcal{X}} t'_{x^n}(x) - t_{x^n}(x)} \tag{14.111}$$

$$= n^{n(1-1)} \tag{14.112}$$

$$= 1. \tag{14.113}$$

Thus, it holds that $t^n(T_t^{X^n}) \geq t^n(T_{t'}^{X^n})$ for all t'. Now we are close to obtaining the desired bound in Property 14.7.5. Consider the following chain of inequalities:

$$1 = \sum_{t' \in \mathcal{P}_n} t^n(T_{t'}^{X^n}) \leq \sum_{t' \in \mathcal{P}_n} \max_{t'} t^n(T_{t'}^{X^n}) = \sum_{t' \in \mathcal{P}_n} t^n(T_t^{X^n}) \tag{14.114}$$

$$\leq (n+1)^{|\mathcal{X}|} t^n(T_t^{X^n}) = (n+1)^{|\mathcal{X}|} \sum_{x^n \in T_t^{X^n}} t^n(x^n) \tag{14.115}$$

$$= (n+1)^{|\mathcal{X}|} \sum_{x^n \in T_t^{X^n}} 2^{-nH(t)} \tag{14.116}$$

$$= (n+1)^{|\mathcal{X}|} 2^{-nH(t)} \left|T_t^{X^n}\right|. \tag{14.117}$$

Recall that t is a typical type, implying that $|t(x) - p(x)| \leq \delta$ for all x. This then implies that the variational distance between the distributions is small:

$$\sum_x |t(x) - p(x)| \leq |\mathcal{X}| \delta. \tag{14.118}$$

We can apply the continuity of entropy (Theorem 11.10.1) to get a bound on the difference of entropies:

$$|H(t) - H(X)| \leq \frac{1}{2} |\mathcal{X}| \delta \log |\mathcal{X}| + h_2(|\mathcal{X}| \delta/2). \tag{14.119}$$

The desired bound then follows with $\eta(|\mathcal{X}| \delta) \equiv |\mathcal{X}| \delta/2 \log |\mathcal{X}| + h_2(|\mathcal{X}| \delta/2)$. $\quad\square$

EXERCISE 14.7.1   Prove that $2^{nH(t)}$ is an upper bound on the number of sequences x^n of type t:

$$\left| T_t^{X^n} \right| \leq 2^{nH(t)}. \tag{14.120}$$

Use this bound and (14.103) to prove the following upper bound on the probability of a type class where each sequence is generated i.i.d. according to a distribution $q(x)$:

$$\Pr\left\{ T_t^{X^n} \right\} \leq 2^{-nD(t\|q)}. \tag{14.121}$$

14.8 Strong Joint Typicality

It is possible to extend the above notions of strong typicality to jointly typical sequences. In a marked difference with the weakly typical case, we can show that strong joint typicality implies marginal typicality. Thus there is no need to impose this constraint in the definition.

Let $N(x, y | x^n, y^n)$ be the number of occurrences of the symbol $x \in \mathcal{X}, y \in \mathcal{Y}$ in the respective sequences x^n and y^n. The *type* or empirical distribution $t_{x^n y^n}$ of sequences x^n and y^n is a probability mass function whose elements are $t_{x^n y^n}(x, y)$ where

$$t_{x^n y^n}(x, y) \equiv \frac{1}{n} N(x, y | x^n, y^n). \tag{14.122}$$

DEFINITION 14.8.1 (Strong Jointly Typical Sequence)   Two sequences x^n, y^n are δ-strongly jointly *typical* if their empirical distribution has maximum deviation δ from the true distribution and vanishes for any two symbols x and y for which $p_{X,Y}(x, y) = 0$.

DEFINITION 14.8.2 (Strong Jointly Typical Set)   The δ-jointly *typical set* $T_\delta^{X^n Y^n}$ is the set of all δ-jointly typical sequences:

$$T_\delta^{X^n Y^n} \equiv$$

$$\left\{ x^n, y^n : \forall (x, y) \in \mathcal{X} \times \mathcal{Y} \quad \begin{array}{ll} \left| \frac{1}{n} N(x, y | x^n, y^n) - p_{X,Y}(x, y) \right| \leq \delta & \text{if } p_{X,Y}(x, y) > 0 \\ \frac{1}{n} N(x, y | x^n, y^n) = 0 & \text{otherwise} \end{array} \right\}. \tag{14.123}$$

It follows from the above definitions that strong joint typicality implies marginal typicality for both sequences x^n and y^n. We leave justifying this statement as the following exercise.

EXERCISE 14.8.1 Prove that strong joint typicality implies marginal typicality for either the sequence x^n or y^n.

14.8.1 Properties of the Strong Jointly Typical Set

The set $T_\delta^{X^n Y^n}$ of strong jointly typical sequences enjoys properties similar to what we have seen before.

PROPERTY 14.8.1 (Unit Probability) The strong jointly typical set $T_\delta^{X^n Y^n}$ asymptotically has probability one. So as n becomes large, it is highly likely that a source emits a strong jointly typical sequence. We formally state this property as follows:

$$\Pr\left\{X^n Y^n \in T_\delta^{X^n Y^n}\right\} \geq 1 - \varepsilon, \tag{14.124}$$

for all $\varepsilon \in (0,1)$, $\delta > 0$, and sufficiently large n.

PROPERTY 14.8.2 (Exponentially Smaller Cardinality) The number $\left|T_\delta^{X^n Y^n}\right|$ of δ-jointly typical sequences is exponentially smaller than the total number $(|\mathcal{X}| |\mathcal{Y}|)^n$ of sequences for any joint random variable (X, Y) that is not uniform. We formally state this property as follows:

$$\left|T_\delta^{X^n Y^n}\right| \leq 2^{n(H(X,Y)+c\delta)}, \tag{14.125}$$

where c is a positive constant. We can also bound the size of the δ-jointly typical set from below:

$$\left|T_\delta^{X^n Y^n}\right| \geq (1 - \varepsilon) \, 2^{n(H(X,Y)-c\delta)}, \tag{14.126}$$

for all $\varepsilon \in (0,1)$, $\delta > 0$, and sufficiently large n.

PROPERTY 14.8.3 (Equipartition) The probability of a given δ-jointly typical sequence $x^n y^n$ occurring is approximately uniform:

$$2^{-n(H(X,Y)+c\delta)} \leq p_{X^n,Y^n}(x^n, y^n) \leq 2^{-n(H(X,Y)-c\delta)}, \tag{14.127}$$

where c is a positive constant.

PROPERTY 14.8.4 (Probability of Strong Joint Typicality) Consider two independent random variables $\tilde{X}^n$ and $\tilde{Y}^n$ whose respective probability density functions $p_{\tilde{X}^n}(x^n)$ and $p_{\tilde{Y}^n}(y^n)$ are equal to the marginal densities of the joint density $p_{X^n,Y^n}(x^n, y^n)$:

$$(\tilde{X}^n, \tilde{Y}^n) \sim p_{X^n}(x^n) p_{Y^n}(y^n). \tag{14.128}$$

Then we can bound the probability that two random sequences $\tilde{X}^n$ and $\tilde{Y}^n$ are in the jointly typical set $T_\delta^{X^n Y^n}$:

$$\Pr\left\{(\tilde{X}^n, \tilde{Y}^n) \in T_\delta^{X^n Y^n}\right\} \leq 2^{-n(I(X;Y) - 3c\delta)}. \tag{14.129}$$

Proofs of the first three properties are the same as in the previous section, and the proof of the last property is the same as that for the weakly typical case.

14.9   Strong Conditional Typicality

Strong conditional typicality bears some similarities to strong typicality, but it is sufficiently different for us to provide a discussion of it. We first introduce it with a simple example.

Suppose that we draw a sequence from an alphabet $\{0, 1, 2\}$ according to the distribution:

$$p_X(0) = \frac{1}{4}, \qquad p_X(1) = \frac{1}{4}, \qquad p_X(2) = \frac{1}{2}. \tag{14.130}$$

A particular realization sequence could be as follows:

$$20102010201202121222200202222. \tag{14.131}$$

We count up the occurrences of each symbol and find them to be

$$N(0 \mid 20102010201202121222200202222) = 8, \tag{14.132}$$
$$N(1 \mid 20102010201202121222200202222) = 5, \tag{14.133}$$
$$N(2 \mid 20102010201202121222200202222) = 15. \tag{14.134}$$

The maximum deviation of the sequence's empirical distribution from the true distribution of the source is as follows:

$$\max\left\{\left|\frac{1}{4} - \frac{8}{28}\right|, \left|\frac{1}{4} - \frac{5}{28}\right|, \left|\frac{1}{2} - \frac{15}{28}\right|\right\} = \max\left\{\frac{1}{28}, \frac{2}{28}, \frac{1}{28}\right\} = \frac{1}{14}. \tag{14.135}$$

We now consider generating a different sequence from an alphabet $\{a, b, c\}$. However, we generate it according to the following *conditional* probability distribution:

$$\begin{bmatrix} p_{Y|X}(a|0) = \frac{1}{5} & p_{Y|X}(a|1) = \frac{1}{6} & p_{Y|X}(a|2) = \frac{2}{4} \\ p_{Y|X}(b|0) = \frac{2}{5} & p_{Y|X}(b|1) = \frac{3}{6} & p_{Y|X}(b|2) = \frac{1}{4} \\ p_{Y|X}(c|0) = \frac{2}{5} & p_{Y|X}(c|1) = \frac{2}{6} & p_{Y|X}(c|2) = \frac{1}{4} \end{bmatrix}. \tag{14.136}$$

The second generated sequence should thus have correlations with the original sequence. A possible realization of the second sequence could be as follows:

$$abbcbccabcabcabcabcbcbabacba. \tag{14.137}$$

We would now like to analyze how close the empirical conditional distribution is to the true conditional distribution for all input and output sequences. A useful conceptual first step is to apply a permutation to the first sequence so that all of its symbols appear in lexicographic order, and we then apply the same permutation to the second sequence:

$$2\ 0\ 1\ 0\ 2\ 0\ 1\ 0\ 2\ 0\ 1\ 2\ 0\ 2\ 1\ 2\ 1\ 2\ 2\ 2\ 2\ 0\ 2\ 0\ 2\ 2\ 2\ 2$$
$$a\ b\ b\ c\ b\ c\ c\ a\ b\ c\ a\ b\ c\ a\ b\ c\ a\ b\ c\ b\ c\ b\ a\ b\ a\ c\ b\ a$$

$$\xrightarrow{\text{permute}}$$

$$0\ 0\ 0\ 0\ 0\ 0\ 0\ 0\ 1\ 1\ 1\ 1\ 1\ 2\ 2\ 2\ 2\ 2\ 2\ 2\ 2\ 2\ 2\ 2\ 2\ 2\ 2\ 2$$
$$b\ c\ c\ a\ c\ c\ b\ b\ b\ c\ a\ b\ a\ a\ b\ b\ b\ a\ c\ b\ c\ b\ c\ a\ a\ c\ b\ a.$$

$$(14.138)$$

This rearrangement makes it easy to count up the empirical conditional distribution of the second sequence. We first place the joint occurrences of the symbols into the following matrix:

$$\begin{bmatrix} N(0,a)=1 & N(1,a)=2 & N(2,a)=5 \\ N(0,b)=3 & N(1,b)=2 & N(2,b)=6 \\ N(0,c)=4 & N(1,c)=1 & N(2,c)=4 \end{bmatrix}, \qquad (14.139)$$

and we obtain the empirical conditional distribution matrix by dividing these entries by the marginal distribution of the first sequence:

$$\begin{bmatrix} \frac{N(0,a)}{N(0)}=\frac{1}{8} & \frac{N(1,a)}{N(1)}=\frac{2}{5} & \frac{N(2,a)}{N(2)}=\frac{5}{15} \\ \frac{N(0,b)}{N(0)}=\frac{3}{8} & \frac{N(1,b)}{N(1)}=\frac{2}{5} & \frac{N(2,b)}{N(2)}=\frac{6}{15} \\ \frac{N(0,c)}{N(0)}=\frac{4}{8} & \frac{N(1,c)}{N(1)}=\frac{1}{5} & \frac{N(2,c)}{N(2)}=\frac{4}{15} \end{bmatrix}. \qquad (14.140)$$

We then compare the maximal deviation of the elements in this matrix with the elements in the stochastic matrix in (14.136):

$$\max\left\{\left|\frac{1}{5}-\frac{1}{8}\right|, \left|\frac{2}{5}-\frac{3}{8}\right|, \left|\frac{2}{5}-\frac{4}{8}\right|, \left|\frac{1}{6}-\frac{2}{5}\right|, \left|\frac{3}{6}-\frac{2}{5}\right|, \left|\frac{2}{6}-\frac{1}{5}\right|,\right.$$
$$\left.\left|\frac{2}{4}-\frac{5}{15}\right|, \left|\frac{1}{4}-\frac{6}{15}\right|, \left|\frac{1}{4}-\frac{4}{15}\right|\right\}$$
$$=\max\left\{\frac{3}{40}, \frac{1}{40}, \frac{1}{10}, \frac{7}{30}, \frac{1}{10}, \frac{2}{15}, \frac{1}{6}, \frac{3}{20}, \frac{1}{60}\right\} = \frac{7}{30}. \qquad (14.141)$$

The above analysis applies to a finite realization to illustrate the notion of conditional typicality, and there is a large deviation from the true distribution in this case. We would again expect this deviation to vanish for a random sequence in the limit as the length of the sequence becomes large.

14.9.1   Definition of Strong Conditional Typicality

We now give a formal definition of strong conditional typicality.

DEFINITION 14.9.1 (Conditional Empirical Distribution) The conditional empirical distribution $t_{y^n|x^n}(y|x)$ is as follows:

$$t_{y^n|x^n}(y|x) = \frac{t_{x^n y^n}(x,y)}{t_{x^n}(x)}. \qquad (14.142)$$

DEFINITION 14.9.2 (Strong Conditional Typicality)   Suppose that a sequence x^n is a strongly typical sequence in $T_\delta^{X^n}$. Then the δ-strong conditionally typical set $T_\delta^{Y^n|x^n}$ corresponding to the sequence x^n consists of all sequences whose joint empirical distribution $\frac{1}{n}N(x, y|x^n, y^n)$ is δ-close to the product of the true conditional distribution $p_{Y|X}(y|x)$ with the marginal empirical distribution $\frac{1}{n}N(x|x^n)$:

$$T_\delta^{Y^n|x^n} \equiv$$
$$\left\{ y^n : \forall(x,y) \in \mathcal{X} \times \mathcal{Y} \quad \begin{array}{ll} |N(x,y|x^n,y^n) - p(y|x)N(x|x^n)| \le n\delta & \text{if } p(y|x) > 0 \\ N(x,y|x^n,y^n) = 0 & \text{otherwise} \end{array} \right\},$$
$$\tag{14.143}$$

where we abbreviate $p_{Y|X}(y|x)$ as $p(y|x)$.

The above definition of strong conditional typicality implies that the conditional empirical distribution is close to the true conditional distribution, in the sense that

$$\left| \frac{t_{x^n y^n}(x,y)}{t_{x^n}(x)} - p_{Y|X}(y|x) \right| \le \frac{1}{t_{x^n}(x)}\delta. \tag{14.144}$$

Of course, such a relation only makes sense if the marginal empirical distribution $t_{x^n}(x)$ is non-zero.

The extra technical condition ($N(x,y|x^n,y^n) = 0$ if $p_{Y|X}(y|x) = 0$) in Definition 14.9.2 is present again for a reason that we found in the proof of the Equipartition Property for Strong Typicality (Property 14.7.4).

14.9.2   Properties of the Strong Conditionally Typical Set

The set $T_\delta^{Y^n|x^n}$ of conditionally typical sequences enjoys a few useful properties that are similar to what we have for the weak conditionally typical set, but the initial sequence x^n can be deterministic. However, we do impose the constraint that it has to be strongly typical so that we can prove useful properties for the corresponding strong conditionally typical set. So first suppose that a given sequence $x^n \in T_{\delta'}^{X^n}$ for some $\delta' > 0$.

PROPERTY 14.9.1 (Unit Probability)   The set $T_\delta^{Y^n|x^n}$ asymptotically has probability one. So as n becomes large, it is highly likely that a random sequence Y^n corresponding to a given typical sequence x^n is a conditionally typical sequence. We formally state this property as follows:

$$\Pr\left\{ Y^n \in T_\delta^{Y^n|x^n} \right\} \ge 1 - \varepsilon, \tag{14.145}$$

for all $\varepsilon \in (0,1)$, $\delta > 0$, and sufficiently large n.

PROPERTY 14.9.2 (Exponentially Smaller Cardinality)   The number $\left| T_\delta^{Y^n|x^n} \right|$ of δ-conditionally typical sequences is exponentially smaller than the total number

$|\mathcal{Y}|^n$ of sequences for any conditional random variable Y that is not uniform. We formally state this property as follows:

$$\left|T_\delta^{Y^n|x^n}\right| \leq 2^{n\left(H(Y|X)+c(\delta+\delta')\right)}. \tag{14.146}$$

We can also bound the size of the δ-conditionally typical set from below:

$$\left|T_\delta^{Y^n|x^n}\right| \geq (1-\varepsilon)\, 2^{n\left(H(Y|X)-c(\delta+\delta')\right)}, \tag{14.147}$$

for all $\varepsilon \in (0,1)$, $\delta > 0$, and sufficiently large n.

PROPERTY 14.9.3 (Equipartition) The probability of a particular δ-conditionally typical sequence y^n is approximately uniform:

$$2^{-n\left(H(Y|X)+c(\delta+\delta')\right)} \leq p_{Y^n|X^n}(y^n|x^n) \leq 2^{-n\left(H(Y|X)-c(\delta+\delta')\right)}. \tag{14.148}$$

In summary, given a realization x^n of the random variable X^n, the conditionally typical set $T_\delta^{Y^n|x^n}$ has almost all the probability, its size is exponentially smaller than the size of the set of all sequences, and each δ-conditionally typical sequence has an approximately uniform probability of occurring.

14.9.3 Proofs of the Properties of the Strong Conditionally Typical Set

Proof of the Unit Probability Property (Property 14.9.1) A proof of this property is somewhat more complicated for strong conditional typicality. Since we are dealing with an i.i.d. distribution, we can assume that the sequence x^n is lexicographically ordered with an order on the alphabet $\mathcal{X}$. We write the elements of $\mathcal{X}$ as $x_1, \ldots, x_{|\mathcal{X}|}$. Then the lexicographic ordering means that we can write the sequence x^n as follows:

$$x^n = \underbrace{x_1 \cdots x_1}_{N(x_1|x^n)} \underbrace{x_2 \cdots x_2}_{N(x_2|x^n)} \cdots \underbrace{x_{|\mathcal{X}|} \cdots x_{|\mathcal{X}|}}_{N(x_{|\mathcal{X}|}|x^n)}. \tag{14.149}$$

It follows that $N(x|x^n) \geq n\,(p_X(x) - \delta')$ from the typicality of x^n, and the law of large numbers comes into play for each block $x_i \cdots x_i$ with length $N(x_i|x^n)$ when this length is large enough. Let $p_{Y|X=x}(y)$ be the distribution for the conditional random variable $Y|(X=x)$. Then the following is an equivalent way to write the notion of conditional typicality:

$$\left\{y^n \in T_\delta^{Y^n|x^n}\right\} \Leftrightarrow \bigwedge_{x \in \mathcal{X}} \left\{y^{N(x|x^n)} \in T_\delta^{(Y|(X=x))^{N(x|x^n)}}\right\}, \tag{14.150}$$

where the symbol $\wedge$ denotes concatenation (note that the lexicographic ordering of x^n applies to the ordering of the sequence y^n as well). Also, $T_\delta^{(Y|(X=x))^{N(x|x^n)}}$ is the typical set for a sequence of conditional random variables $Y|(X=x)$ with length $N(x|x^n)$:

$$T_\delta^{(Y|(X=x))^{N(x|x^n)}} \equiv \left\{y^{N(x|x^n)} : \forall y \in \mathcal{Y},\ \left|\frac{N(y|y^{N(x|x^n)})}{N(x|x^n)} - p_{Y|X=x}(y)\right| \leq \delta\right\}. \tag{14.151}$$

We can apply the law of large numbers to each of these typical sets $T_\delta^{(Y|(X=x))^{N(x|x^n)}}$ where the length $N(x|x^n)$ becomes large. It then follows that

$$\Pr\left\{Y^n \in T_\delta^{Y^n|x^n}\right\} = \prod_{x \in \mathcal{X}} \Pr\left\{Y^{N(x|x^n)} \in T_\delta^{(Y|(X=x))^{N(x|x^n)}}\right\} \quad (14.152)$$

$$\geq (1-\varepsilon)^{|\mathcal{X}|} \quad (14.153)$$

$$\geq 1 - |\mathcal{X}|\,\varepsilon, \quad (14.154)$$

concluding the proof. $\qquad\square$

Proof of the Equipartition Property (Property 14.9.3) The following relation holds from the i.i.d. property of the conditional distribution $p_{Y^n|X^n}(y^n|x^n)$ and because the sequence y^n is strong conditionally typical according to Definition 14.9.2:

$$p_{Y^n|X^n}(y^n|x^n) = \prod_{(\mathcal{X},\mathcal{Y})^+} p_{Y|X}(y|x)^{N(x,y|x^n,y^n)} \quad (14.155)$$

where $(\mathcal{X},\mathcal{Y})^+$ denotes all the letters x, y in $\mathcal{X}, \mathcal{Y}$ with $p_{Y|X}(y|x) > 0$. Take the logarithm of the above expression:

$$\log\left(p_{Y^n|X^n}(y^n|x^n)\right) = \sum_{x,y \in (\mathcal{X},\mathcal{Y})^+} N(x,y|x^n,y^n)\log\left(p_{Y|X}(y|x)\right). \quad (14.156)$$

Multiply both sides by $-\frac{1}{n}$:

$$-\frac{1}{n}\log\left(p_{Y^n|X^n}(y^n|x^n)\right) = -\sum_{x,y \in (\mathcal{X},\mathcal{Y})^+} \frac{1}{n}N(x,y|x^n,y^n)\log\left(p_{Y|X}(y|x)\right). \quad (14.157)$$

The following relations hold because the sequence x^n is strongly typical and y^n is strong conditionally typical:

$$\forall x \in \mathcal{X}^+ : \left|\frac{1}{n}N(x|x^n) - p_X(x)\right| \leq \delta', \quad (14.158)$$

$$\Rightarrow \forall x \in \mathcal{X}^+ : -\delta' + p_X(x) \leq \frac{1}{n}N(x|x^n) \leq \delta' + p_X(x), \quad (14.159)$$

$$\forall x, y \in (\mathcal{X},\mathcal{Y})^+ : \left|\frac{1}{n}N(x,y|x^n,y^n) - p_{Y|X}(y|x)\frac{1}{n}N(x|x^n)\right| \leq \delta \quad (14.160)$$

$$\Rightarrow \forall x, y \in (\mathcal{X},\mathcal{Y})^+ : -\delta + p_{Y|X}(y|x)\frac{1}{n}N(x|x^n) \leq \frac{1}{n}N(x,y|x^n,y^n)$$

$$\leq \delta + p_{Y|X}(y|x)\frac{1}{n}N(x|x^n). \quad (14.161)$$

Now multiply (14.161) by $-\log\left(p_{Y|X}(y|x)\right) > 0$, sum over all letters in the alphabet $(\mathcal{X},\mathcal{Y})^+$, and apply the substitution in (14.157). This procedure gives the following set of inequalities:

$$- \sum_{x,y \in (\mathcal{X},\mathcal{Y})^+} \left(-\delta + p_{Y|X}(y|x) \frac{1}{n} N(x|x^n) \right) \log \left(p_{Y|X}(y|x) \right)$$

$$\leq -\frac{1}{n} \log \left(p_{Y^n|X^n}(y^n|x^n) \right)$$

$$\leq - \sum_{x,y \in (\mathcal{X},\mathcal{Y})^+} \left(\delta + p_{Y|X}(y|x) \frac{1}{n} N(x|x^n) \right) \log \left(p_{Y|X}(y|x) \right). \quad (14.162)$$

Now apply the inequalities in (14.159) (assuming that $p_X(x) \geq \delta'$ for $x \in \mathcal{X}^+$) to get that

$$\Rightarrow - \sum_{x,y \in (\mathcal{X},\mathcal{Y})^+} \left(-\delta + p_{Y|X}(y|x) \left(-\delta' + p_X(x) \right) \right) \log \left(p_{Y|X}(y|x) \right) \quad (14.163)$$

$$\leq -\frac{1}{n} \log \left(p_{Y^n|X^n}(y^n|x^n) \right) \quad (14.164)$$

$$\leq - \sum_{x,y \in (\mathcal{X},\mathcal{Y})^+} \left(\delta + p_{Y|X}(y|x) \left(\delta' + p_X(x) \right) \right) \log \left(p_{Y|X}(y|x) \right) \quad (14.165)$$

$$\Rightarrow -c(\delta + \delta') + H(Y|X) \leq -\frac{1}{n} \log \left(p_{Y^n|X^n}(y^n|x^n) \right) \leq c(\delta + \delta') + H(Y|X),$$

$$(14.166)$$

$$\Rightarrow 2^{-n \left(H(Y|X) + c(\delta+\delta') \right)} \leq p_{Y^n|X^n}(y^n|x^n) \leq 2^{-n \left(H(Y|X) - c(\delta+\delta') \right)}, \quad (14.167)$$

where

$$c \equiv - \sum_{x,y \in (\mathcal{X},\mathcal{Y})^+} \log \left(p_{Y|X}(y|x) \right) \geq 0. \quad (14.168)$$

It again becomes apparent why we require the technical condition in the definition of strong conditional typicality (Definition 14.9.2). Were it not there, then the constant c would not be finite, and we would not be able to obtain a reasonable bound on the probability of a strong conditionally typical sequence. □

We close this section with a lemma that relates strong conditional, marginal, and joint typicality.

LEMMA 14.9.1   Suppose that y^n is a conditionally typical sequence in $T_\delta^{Y^n|x^n}$ and its conditioning sequence x^n is a typical sequence in $T_{\delta'}^{X^n}$. Then x^n and y^n are jointly typical in the set $T_{\delta+\delta'}^{X^n Y^n}$, and y^n is a typical sequence in $T_{|\mathcal{X}|(\delta+\delta')}^{Y^n}$.

Proof   It follows from the above that $\forall x \in \mathcal{X}, y \in \mathcal{Y}$:

$$p_X(x) - \delta' \leq \frac{1}{n} N(x|x^n) \leq \delta' + p_X(x), \quad (14.169)$$

$$p_{Y|X}(y|x) \frac{1}{n} N(x|x^n) - \delta \leq \frac{1}{n} N(x,y|x^n,y^n) \leq \delta + p_{Y|X}(y|x) \frac{1}{n} N(x|x^n). \quad (14.170)$$

Substituting the upper bound on $\frac{1}{n} N(x|x^n)$ gives

$$\frac{1}{n} N(x,y|x^n,y^n) \leq \delta + p_{Y|X}(y|x) \left(\delta' + p_X(x) \right) \quad (14.171)$$

$$= \delta + p_{Y|X}(y|x)\delta' + p_X(x)p_{Y|X}(y|x) \tag{14.172}$$

$$\leq \delta + \delta' + p_{X,Y}(x,y). \tag{14.173}$$

Similarly, substituting the lower bound on $\frac{1}{n}N(x|x^n)$ gives

$$\frac{1}{n}N(x,y|x^n,y^n) \geq p_{X,Y}(x,y) - \delta - \delta'. \tag{14.174}$$

Putting both of the above bounds together, we get the following bound:

$$\left| \frac{1}{n}N(x,y|x^n,y^n) - p_{X,Y}(x,y) \right| \leq \delta + \delta'. \tag{14.175}$$

This then implies that the sequences x^n and y^n lie in the strong jointly typical set $T_{\delta+\delta'}^{X^nY^n}$. It follows from the result of Exercise 14.8.1 that $y^n \in T_{|\mathcal{X}|(\delta+\delta')}^{Y^n}$. □

14.10 Application: Channel Capacity Theorem

We close the technical content of this chapter with a remarkable application of conditional typicality: Shannon's channel capacity theorem. As discussed in Section 2.2.3, this theorem is one of the central results of classical information theory, appearing in Shannon's seminal paper. The theorem establishes that the highest achievable rate for communication over many independent uses of a classical channel is equal to a simple function of the channel.

We begin by defining the information-processing task and a corresponding (n, R, ε) channel code. It is helpful to recall Figure 2.4 depicting a general protocol for communication over a classical channel $\mathcal{N} \equiv p_{Y|X}(y|x)$. Before communication begins, the sender Alice and receiver Bob have already established a codebook $\{x^n(m)\}_{m\in\mathcal{M}}$, where each codeword $x^n(m)$ corresponds to a message m that Alice might wish to send to Bob. If Alice wishes to send message m, she inputs the codeword $x^n(m)$ to the i.i.d. channel $\mathcal{N}^n \equiv p_{Y^n|X^n}(y^n|x^n)$. More formally, her encoding is some map $E^n : \mathcal{M} \rightarrow \mathcal{X}^n$. She then exploits n uses of the channel to send $x^n(m)$. Bob receives some sequence y^n from the output of the channel, and he performs a decoding $D^n : \mathcal{Y}^n \rightarrow \mathcal{M}$ in order to recover the message m that Alice transmits. The rate R of the code is equal to $[\log|\mathcal{M}|]/n$, measured in bits per channel use. The probability of error p_e for an (n, R, ε) channel code is bounded from above as

$$p_e \equiv \max_m \Pr\{D^n(\mathcal{N}^n(E^n(m))) \neq m\} \leq \varepsilon. \tag{14.176}$$

A communication rate R is *achievable* for $\mathcal{N}$ if there exists an $(n, R - \delta, \varepsilon)$ channel code for all $\varepsilon \in (0,1), \delta > 0$ and sufficiently large n. The channel capacity $C(\mathcal{N})$ of $\mathcal{N}$ is the supremum of all achievable rates for $\mathcal{N}$. We can now state Shannon's channel capacity theorem:

THEOREM 14.10.1 (Shannon Channel Capacity)   The maximum mutual information $I(\mathcal{N})$ is equal to the capacity $C(\mathcal{N})$ of a channel $\mathcal{N} \equiv p_{Y|X}(y|x)$:

$$C(\mathcal{N}) = I(\mathcal{N}) \equiv \max_{p_X(x)} I(X;Y). \tag{14.177}$$

Proof   A proof consists of two parts. The first part, known as the direct coding theorem, demonstrates that the RHS $\leq$ LHS. That is, there is a sequence of channel codes with rate $I(\mathcal{N})$, demonstrating that this rate is achievable. The second part, known as the converse part, demonstrates that the LHS $\leq$ RHS. That is, it demonstrates that the rate on the RHS is optimal, and it is impossible to have achievable rates exceeding it. Here, we prove the direct coding theorem and hold off on proving the converse part until we reach the HSW theorem in Chapter 20 because the converse theorem there suffices as the converse part for this classical theorem. We have already outlined the proof of the direct coding theorem in Section 2.2.4, and it might be helpful at this point to review this section. In particular, the proof breaks down into three parts: random coding to establish the encoding, the decoding algorithm for the receiver, and the error analysis. We now give all of the technical details of the proof because this chapter has established all the tools that we need.

Code Construction. Before communication begins, Alice and Bob agree upon a code by the following random selection procedure. For every message $m \in \mathcal{M}$, generate a codeword $x^n(m)$ i.i.d. according to the product distribution $p_{X^n}(x^n)$, where $p_X(x)$ is a distribution that maximizes $I(\mathcal{N})$. Importantly, this random construction is such that every codeword is generated independently of the other codewords.

Encoding. To send message m, Alice inputs codeword $x^n(m)$ to the channels.

Decoding Algorithm. After receiving the sequence y^n from the channel outputs, Bob tests whether y^n is in the typical set $T_\delta^{Y^n}$ corresponding to the distribution $p_Y(y) \equiv \sum_x p_{Y|X}(y|x)p_X(x)$. If it is not, then he reports an error. He then tests if there is some message m such that the sequence y^n is in the conditionally typical set $T_\delta^{Y^n|x^n(m)}$. If m is the unique message such that $y^n \in T_\delta^{Y^n|x^n(m)}$, then he declares m to be the transmitted message. If there is no message m such that $y^n \in T_\delta^{Y^n|x^n(m)}$ or multiple messages m' such that $y^n \in T_\delta^{Y^n|x^n(m')}$, then he reports an error. Observe that the decoder is a function of the channel, so that we might say that we construct channel codes "from the channel."

Error Analysis. As discussed in the above decoding algorithm, there are three kinds of errors that can occur in this communication scheme when Alice sends the codeword $x^n(m)$ over the channels:

$\mathcal{E}_0(m)$: The event that the channel output y^n is not in the typical set $T_\delta^{Y^n}$.

$\mathcal{E}_1(m)$: The event that the channel output y^n is in $T_\delta^{Y^n}$ but not in the conditionally typical set $T_\delta^{Y^n|x^n(m)}$.

$\mathcal{E}_2(m)$: The event that the channel output y^n is in $T_\delta^{Y^n}$ but it is in the conditionally typical set for some other message:

$$\left\{y^n \in T_\delta^{Y^n}\right\} \text{ and } \left\{\exists m' \neq m : y^n \in T_\delta^{Y^n|x^n(m')}\right\}. \tag{14.178}$$

Recall from Section 2.2.4 that it is helpful to analyze the expectation of the average error probability, where the expectation is with respect to the random selection of the code and the average is with respect to a uniformly random choice of the message m. Let $\mathcal{C} \equiv \{X^n(1), X^n(2), \ldots, X^n(|\mathcal{M}|)\}$ denote the random variable corresponding to the random selection of a code. The expectation of the average error probability of a randomly selected code is as follows:

$$\mathbb{E}_\mathcal{C}\left\{\frac{1}{|\mathcal{M}|}\sum_m \Pr\left\{\mathcal{E}_0(m) \cup \mathcal{E}_1(m) \cup \mathcal{E}_2(m)\right\}\right\}. \tag{14.179}$$

Our first "move" is to exchange the expectation and the sum, following from linearity of the expectation:

$$\frac{1}{|\mathcal{M}|}\sum_m \mathbb{E}_\mathcal{C}\left\{\Pr\left\{\mathcal{E}_0(m) \cup \mathcal{E}_1(m) \cup \mathcal{E}_2(m)\right\}\right\}. \tag{14.180}$$

Since all codewords are selected in the same way (randomly and independently of the message m and according to the same distribution $p_{X^n}(x^n)$), the following equality holds for all $m, m' \in \mathcal{M}$:

$$\mathbb{E}_\mathcal{C}\left\{\Pr\left\{\mathcal{E}_0(m) \cup \mathcal{E}_1(m) \cup \mathcal{E}_2(m)\right\}\right\}$$
$$= \mathbb{E}_\mathcal{C}\left\{\Pr\left\{\mathcal{E}_0(m') \cup \mathcal{E}_1(m') \cup \mathcal{E}_2(m')\right\}\right\}, \tag{14.181}$$

implying that it suffices to analyze $\mathbb{E}_\mathcal{C}\left\{\Pr\left\{\mathcal{E}_0(m) \cup \mathcal{E}_1(m) \cup \mathcal{E}_2(m)\right\}\right\}$ for just a single message m. Without loss of generality, we can pick $m = 1$ (the first message). Using the above, we find that the expectation of the average error probability simplifies as follows:

$$\frac{1}{|\mathcal{M}|}\sum_m \mathbb{E}_\mathcal{C}\left\{\Pr\left\{\mathcal{E}_0(m) \cup \mathcal{E}_1(m) \cup \mathcal{E}_2(m)\right\}\right\}$$
$$= \mathbb{E}_\mathcal{C}\left\{\Pr\left\{\mathcal{E}_0(1) \cup \mathcal{E}_1(1) \cup \mathcal{E}_2(1)\right\}\right\}. \tag{14.182}$$

So we can then apply the union bound:

$$\mathbb{E}_\mathcal{C}\left\{\Pr\left\{\mathcal{E}_0(1) \cup \mathcal{E}_1(1) \cup \mathcal{E}_2(1)\right\}\right\}$$
$$\leq \mathbb{E}_\mathcal{C}\left\{\Pr\left\{\mathcal{E}_0(1)\right\}\right\} + \mathbb{E}_\mathcal{C}\left\{\Pr\left\{\mathcal{E}_1(1)\right\}\right\} + \mathbb{E}_\mathcal{C}\left\{\Pr\left\{\mathcal{E}_2(1)\right\}\right\}. \tag{14.183}$$

We now analyze each error individually. For each of the above events, we can exploit indicator functions in order to simplify the error analysis (we are also doing this to help build a bridge between this classical proof and the packing lemma approach for the quantum case in Chapter 16—projectors in some sense replace indicator functions later on). Recall that an indicator function $I_\mathcal{A}(x)$ is equal to one if $x \in \mathcal{A}$ and equal to zero otherwise. So the following three functions being equal to one or larger then corresponds to error events $\mathcal{E}_0(1)$, $\mathcal{E}_1(1)$, and $\mathcal{E}_2(1)$, respectively:

$$1 - I_{T_\delta^{Y^n}}(y^n), \tag{14.184}$$

$$I_{T_\delta^{Y^n}}(y^n)\left(1 - I_{T_\delta^{Y^n|x^n(1)}}(y^n)\right), \tag{14.185}$$

$$\sum_{m'\neq 1} I_{T_\delta^{Y^n}}(y^n)I_{T_\delta^{Y^n|x^n(m')}}(y^n). \tag{14.186}$$

(The last sum of indicators is a consequence of applying the union bound again to the error $\mathcal{E}_2(1)$, which itself is a union of events.)

By exploiting the indicator function from (14.184), we have that

$$\mathbb{E}_{\mathcal{C}}\left\{\Pr\left\{\mathcal{E}_0(1)\right\}\right\} = \mathbb{E}_{X^n(1)}\left\{\mathbb{E}_{Y^n|X^n(1)}\left\{1 - I_{T_\delta^{Y^n}}(Y^n)\right\}\right\} \tag{14.187}$$

$$= 1 - \mathbb{E}_{X^n(1),Y^n}\left\{I_{T_\delta^{Y^n}}(Y^n)\right\} \tag{14.188}$$

$$= 1 - \mathbb{E}_{Y^n}\left\{I_{T_\delta^{Y^n}}(Y^n)\right\} \tag{14.189}$$

$$= \Pr\left\{Y^n \notin T_\delta^{Y^n}\right\} \leq \varepsilon, \tag{14.190}$$

where the first line follows because Y^n is generated according to the conditional distribution $p_{Y^n|X^n}$ and from $X^n(1)$ (since the first message was transmitted) and all other codewords have no role in the test, so that we marginalize over them. In the last line we have exploited the high probability property of the typical set $T_\delta^{Y^n}$. In the above, we are also exploiting the fact that $\mathbb{E}\{I_{\mathcal{A}}\} = \Pr\{\mathcal{A}\}$. By exploiting the indicator function from (14.185), we have that

$$\mathbb{E}_{\mathcal{C}}\left\{\Pr\left\{\mathcal{E}_1(1)\right\}\right\}$$

$$= \mathbb{E}_{X^n(1)}\left\{\mathbb{E}_{Y^n|X^n(1)}\left\{I_{T_\delta^{Y^n}}(Y^n)\left(1 - I_{T_\delta^{Y^n|X^n(1)}}(Y^n)\right)\right\}\right\} \tag{14.191}$$

$$\leq \mathbb{E}_{X^n(1)}\left\{\mathbb{E}_{Y^n|X^n(1)}\left\{1 - I_{T_\delta^{Y^n|X^n(1)}}(Y^n)\right\}\right\} \tag{14.192}$$

$$= 1 - \mathbb{E}_{X^n(1)}\left\{\mathbb{E}_{Y^n|X^n(1)}\left\{I_{T_\delta^{Y^n|X^n(1)}}(Y^n)\right\}\right\} \tag{14.193}$$

$$= \mathbb{E}_{X^n(1)}\left\{\Pr_{Y^n|X^n(1)}\left\{Y^n \notin T_\delta^{Y^n|X^n(1)}\right\}\right\} \leq \varepsilon, \tag{14.194}$$

where in the last line we have exploited the high probability property of the conditionally typical set $T_\delta^{Y^n|X^n(1)}$. We finally consider the probability of the last kind of error by exploiting the indicator function in (14.186):

$$\mathbb{E}_{\mathcal{C}}\left\{\Pr\left\{\mathcal{E}_2(1)\right\}\right\}$$

$$\leq \mathbb{E}_{\mathcal{C}}\left\{\sum_{m'\neq 1} I_{T_\delta^{Y^n}}(y^n)I_{T_\delta^{Y^n|X^n(m')}}(y^n)\right\} \tag{14.195}$$

$$= \sum_{m'\neq 1} \mathbb{E}_{\mathcal{C}}\left\{I_{T_\delta^{Y^n}}(y^n)I_{T_\delta^{Y^n|X^n(m')}}(y^n)\right\} \tag{14.196}$$

$$= \sum_{m' \neq 1} \mathbb{E}_{X^n(1), X^n(m'), Y^n} \left\{ I_{T_\delta^{Y^n}}(y^n) I_{T_\delta^{Y^n | X^n(m')}}(y^n) \right\} \tag{14.197}$$

$$= \sum_{m' \neq 1} \sum_{x^n(1), x^n(m'), y^n} p_{X^n}(x^n(1)) p_{X^n}(x^n(m'))$$
$$\times p_{Y^n | X^n}(y^n | x^n(1)) I_{T_\delta^{Y^n}}(y^n) I_{T_\delta^{Y^n | x^n(m')}}(y^n) \tag{14.198}$$

$$= \sum_{m' \neq 1} \sum_{x^n(m'), y^n} p_{X^n}(x^n(m')) p_{Y^n}(y^n) I_{T_\delta^{Y^n}}(y^n) I_{T_\delta^{Y^n | x^n(m')}}(y^n). \tag{14.199}$$

The first inequality is from the union bound, and the first equality follows from the way that we select the random code: for every message m, the codewords are selected independently and randomly according to p_{X^n} so that the distribution for the joint random variable $X^n(1) X^n(m') Y^n$ is

$$p_{X^n}(x^n(1)) \, p_{X^n}(x^n(m')) \, p_{Y^n | X^n}(y^n | x^n(1)). \tag{14.200}$$

The second equality follows from marginalizing over $X^n(1)$. Continuing, we have

$$\leq 2^{-n[H(Y) - \delta]} \sum_{m' \neq 1} \sum_{x^n(m'), y^n} p_{X^n}(x^n(m')) I_{T_\delta^{Y^n | x^n(m')}}(y^n) \tag{14.201}$$

$$= 2^{-n[H(Y) - \delta]} \sum_{m' \neq 1} \sum_{x^n(m')} p_{X^n}(x^n(m')) \sum_{y^n} I_{T_\delta^{Y^n | x^n(m')}}(y^n) \tag{14.202}$$

$$\leq 2^{-n[H(Y) - \delta]} 2^{n[H(Y | X) + \delta]} \sum_{m' \neq 1} \sum_{x^n(m')} p_{X^n}(x^n(m')) \tag{14.203}$$

$$\leq |\mathcal{M}| \, 2^{-n[I(X;Y) - 2\delta]}. \tag{14.204}$$

The first inequality follows from the bound $p_{Y^n}(y^n) I_{T_\delta^{Y^n}}(y^n) \leq 2^{-n[H(Y) - \delta]}$ that holds for typical sequences. The second inequality follows from the cardinality bound $\left| T_\delta^{Y^n | x^n(m')} \right| \leq 2^{n[H(Y | X) + \delta]}$ on the conditionally typical set. The last inequality follows because

$$\sum_{x^n(m')} p_{X^n}(x^n(m')) = 1, \tag{14.205}$$

$|\mathcal{M}|$ is an upper bound on $\sum_{m' \neq 1} 1 = |\mathcal{M}| - 1$, and by the identity $I(X;Y) = H(Y) - H(Y|X)$. Thus, we can make this error arbitrarily small by choosing the message set size $|\mathcal{M}| = 2^{n[I(X;Y) - 3\delta]}$. Putting everything together, we have the following bound on (14.179):

$$\varepsilon' \equiv 2\varepsilon + 2^{-n\delta}, \tag{14.206}$$

as long as we choose the message set size as given above. It follows that there exists a particular code with the same error bound on its average error probability. We can then exploit an expurgation argument as discussed in Section 2.2.4 to convert an average error bound into a maximal one (the expurgation step throws away the worse half of the codewords, guaranteeing a bound of $2\varepsilon'$ on the maximum error probability). Thus, we have shown the achievability of an

$(n, C(\mathcal{N}) - \delta', 2\varepsilon')$ channel code for all $\delta' > 0, \varepsilon' \in (0, 1/2)$ and sufficiently large n (where $\delta' = 3\delta + 1/n$). Finally, as a simple observation, our proof above does not rely on whether the definition of conditional typicality employed is weak or strong. $\qquad\square$

14.11 Concluding Remarks

This chapter deals with many different definitions and flavors of typicality in the classical world, but the essential theme is Shannon's central insight—the application of the law of large numbers in information theory. Our main goal in information theory is to analyze the probability of error in the transmission or compression of information. Thus, we deal with probabilities and we do not care much what happens for all sequences, but we instead only care what happens for the likely sequences. This frame of mind immediately leads to the definition of a typical sequence and to a simple scheme for the compression of information—keep only the typical sequences and performance is optimal in the asymptotic limit. Despite the seemingly different nature of quantum information when compared to its classical counterpart, the intuition developed in this chapter carries over to the quantum world in the next chapter where we define several different notions of quantum typicality.

14.12 History and Further Reading

Cover & Thomas (2006) contains a great presentation of typicality in the classical case. The proof of Property 14.7.5 is directly from the Cover and Thomas book. Berger (1977) introduced strong typicality, and Csiszár & Körner (2011) systematically developed it. Other helpful books on information theory are those of Berger (1971) and Yeung (2002). There are other notions of typicality which are useful, including those presented in Gamal & Kim (2012) and Wolfowitz (1978). Our proof of Shannon's channel capacity theorem is similar to that in Savov (2012).

15 Quantum Typicality

This chapter marks the beginning of our study of the asymptotic theory of quantum information, where we develop the technical tools underpinning this theory. The intuition for it is similar to the intuition we developed in the previous chapter on typical sequences, but we will find some important differences between the classical and quantum cases.

So far, there is not a single known information-processing task in quantum Shannon theory where the tools from this chapter are not helpful in proving the achievability part of a coding theorem. For the most part, we can straightforwardly import many of the ideas from the previous chapter about typical sequences for use in the asymptotic theory of quantum information. However, one might initially think that there are some obstacles to doing so. For example, what is the analogy of a quantum information source? Once we have established this notion, how would we determine if a state emitted from a quantum information source is a typical state? In the classical case, a simple way of determining typicality is to inspect all of the bits in the sequence. But there is a problem with this approach in the quantum domain—"looking at quantum bits" is equivalent to performing a measurement and doing so destroys delicate superpositions that we would want to preserve in any subsequent quantum information-processing task.

So how can we get around the aforementioned problem and construct a useful notion of quantum typicality? Well, we should not be so destructive in determining the answer to a question when it has only two possible answers. After all, we are only asking "Is the state typical or not?", and we can be a bit more delicate in the way that we ask this question. As an analogy, suppose Bob is curious to determine whether Alice could join him for dinner at a nice restaurant on the beach. He would likely just phone her and politely ask, "Sweet Alice, are you available for a lovely oceanside dinner?", as opposed to barging into her apartment, probing through all of her belongings in search of her calendar, and demanding that she join him if she is available. This latter infraction would likely disturb her so much that she would never speak to him again (and what would become of quantum Shannon theory without these two communicating!). It is the same with quantum information—we must be gentle when handling quantum states. Otherwise, we will disturb the state so much that it will not be useful in any future quantum information-processing task.

We can gently ask a binary question of a quantum system by constructing an incomplete measurement with only two outcomes. If one outcome has a high probability of occurring, then we do not learn much about the state after learning this outcome, and thus we would expect that this inquiry does not disturb the state very much. For the case above, we can formulate the question, "Is the state typical or not?" as a binary measurement that returns only the answer to this question and no more information. Since it is highly likely that the state is indeed a typical state, we would expect this inquiry not to disturb the state very much, and we could use it for further quantum information-processing tasks. This is the essential content of this chapter, and there are several technicalities necessary to provide a rigorous underpinning.

We structure this chapter as follows. We first discuss the notion of a typical subspace (the quantum analogy of the typical set). We can employ weak or strong notions of typicality in the definition of quantum typicality. Section 15.2 then discusses conditional quantum typicality, a form of quantum typicality that applies to quantum states chosen randomly according to a classical sequence. We end this chapter with a brief discussion of the method of types for quantum systems. All of these developments are important for understanding the asymptotic nature of quantum information and for determining the ultimate limits of storage and transmission with quantum media.

15.1   The Typical Subspace

Our first task is to establish the notion of a quantum information source. It is analogous to the notion of a classical information source, in the sense that the source randomly outputs a quantum state according to some probability distribution, but the states that it outputs do not necessarily have to be distinguishable as in the classical case.

DEFINITION 15.1.1 (Quantum Information Source)   A quantum information source is some device that randomly emits pure qudit states in a Hilbert space $\mathcal{H}_A$ of finite dimension.

We use the symbol A to denote the quantum system for the quantum information source. Suppose that the source outputs states $|\psi_y\rangle$ randomly according to some probability distribution $p_Y(y)$. Note that the states $|\psi_y\rangle$ do not necessarily have to form an orthonormal set. Then the density operator ρ_A of the source is the expected state emitted:

$$\rho_A \equiv \mathbb{E}_Y\left\{|\psi_Y\rangle\langle\psi_Y|_A\right\} = \sum_y p_Y(y)|\psi_y\rangle\langle\psi_y|_A. \tag{15.1}$$

There are many decompositions of a density operator as a convex sum of rank-one projectors (and the above decomposition is one such example), but perhaps the most important such decomposition is a spectral decomposition of the density operator ρ:

$$\rho_A = \sum_{x \in \mathcal{X}} p_X(x) |x\rangle\langle x|_A. \tag{15.2}$$

The above states $|x\rangle_A$ are eigenvectors of ρ_A and form a complete orthonormal basis for Hilbert space $\mathcal{H}_A$, and the non-negative, convex real numbers $p_X(x)$ are the eigenvalues of ρ_A.

We have written the states $|x\rangle_A$ and the eigenvalues $p_X(x)$ in a suggestive notation because it is actually possible to think of our quantum source as a classical information source—the emitted states $\{|x\rangle_A\}_{x \in \mathcal{X}}$ are orthonormal and each corresponding eigenvalue $p_X(x)$ acts as a probability for choosing $|x\rangle_A$. We can say that our source is classical because it is emitting the orthogonal, and thus distinguishable, states $|x\rangle_A$ with probability $p_X(x)$. This description is equivalent to the ensemble $\{p_Y(y), |\psi_y\rangle\}_y$ because the two ensembles lead to the same density operator (recall that two ensembles that have the same density operator are essentially equivalent because they lead to the same probabilities for outcomes of any measurement performed on the system). Our quantum information source then corresponds to the pure-state ensemble:

$$\{p_X(x), |x\rangle_A\}_{x \in \mathcal{X}}. \tag{15.3}$$

Recall that the quantum entropy $H(A)_\rho$ of the density operator ρ_A is as follows (Definition 11.1.1):

$$H(A)_\rho \equiv - \operatorname{Tr}\{\rho_A \log \rho_A\}. \tag{15.4}$$

It is straightforward to show that the quantum entropy $H(A)_\rho$ is equal to the Shannon entropy $H(X)$ of a random variable X with distribution $p_X(x)$ because the basis states $|x\rangle_A$ are orthonormal.

Suppose now that the quantum information source emits a large number n of random quantum states so that the density operator describing the emitted state is as follows:

$$\rho_{A^n} \equiv \underbrace{\rho_{A_1} \otimes \cdots \otimes \rho_{A_n}}_{n} = (\rho_A)^{\otimes n}. \tag{15.5}$$

The labels $A_1, \ldots, A_n$ denote the Hilbert spaces corresponding to the different quantum systems, but the density operator is the same for each quantum system $A_1, \ldots, A_n$ and is equal to ρ_A. The above description of a quantum source is within the i.i.d. setting for the quantum domain. A spectral decomposition of the state in (15.5) is as follows:

$$\rho_{A^n} = \sum_{x_1 \in \mathcal{X}} p_X(x_1)|x_1\rangle\langle x_1|_{A_1} \otimes \cdots \otimes \sum_{x_n \in \mathcal{X}} p_X(x_n)|x_n\rangle\langle x_n|_{A_n} \tag{15.6}$$

$$= \sum_{x_1, \cdots, x_n \in \mathcal{X}} p_X(x_1) \cdots p_X(x_n) \left(|x_1\rangle \cdots |x_n\rangle\right)\left(\langle x_1| \cdots \langle x_n|\right)_{A_1, \ldots, A_n} \tag{15.7}$$

$$= \sum_{x^n \in \mathcal{X}^n} p_{X^n}(x^n)|x^n\rangle\langle x^n|_{A^n}, \tag{15.8}$$

where we employ the shorthand:

$$p_{X^n}(x^n) \equiv p_X(x_1) \cdots p_X(x_n), \qquad |x^n\rangle_{A^n} \equiv |x_1\rangle_{A_1} \cdots |x_n\rangle_{A_n}. \qquad (15.9)$$

The above quantum description of the density operator is essentially equivalent to the classical picture of n realizations of random variable X with each eigenvalue $p_{X_1}(x_1) \cdots p_{X_n}(x_n)$ acting as a probability because the set of states $\{|x_1\rangle \cdots |x_n\rangle_{A_1,\dots,A_n}\}_{x_1,\dots,x_n \in \mathcal{X}}$ is an orthonormal set.

We can now "quantize" or extend the notion of typicality to the quantum information source. The definitions follow directly from the classical definitions in Chapter 14. The quantum definition of typicality can employ either the weak notion as in Definition 14.2.3 or the strong notion as in Definition 14.7.2. We do not distinguish the notation for a typical subspace and a typical set because it should be clear from the context which kind of typicality we are employing.

DEFINITION 15.1.2 (Typical Subspace)   The δ-*typical subspace* $T_{A^n}^{\delta}$ is a subspace of the full Hilbert space $\mathcal{H}_{A^n} = \mathcal{H}_{A_1} \otimes \cdots \otimes \mathcal{H}_{A_n}$, associated with many copies of a density operator, such as the one in (15.2). It is spanned by states $|x^n\rangle_{A^n}$ whose corresponding classical sequences x^n are δ-typical:

$$T_{A^n}^{\delta} \equiv \operatorname{span}\left\{ |x^n\rangle_{A^n} : x^n \in T_{\delta}^{X^n} \right\}, \qquad (15.10)$$

where it is implicit that the typical subspace $T_{A^n}^{\delta}$ on the left-hand side is with respect to a density operator ρ and the typical set $T_{\delta}^{X^n}$ on the right-hand side is with respect to the distribution $p_X(x)$ from the spectral decomposition of ρ in (15.2). We could also denote the typical subspace as $T_{A^n}^{\rho,\delta}$ if we would like to make the dependence of the space on ρ more explicit.

15.1.1   The Typical Subspace Measurement

The definition of the typical subspace (Definition 15.1.2) gives a way to divide up the Hilbert space of n qudits into two subspaces: the typical subspace and the atypical subspace. The properties of the typical subspace are similar to what we found for typical sequences. That is, the typical subspace is exponentially smaller than the full Hilbert space of n qudits, yet it contains nearly all of the probability (in a sense that we show below). The intuition for these properties of the typical subspace is the same as it is classically, as depicted in Figure 14.2, once we have a spectral decomposition of a density operator.

The *typical projector* is a projector onto the typical subspace, and the complementary projector projects onto the atypical subspace. These projectors play an important operational role in quantum Shannon theory because we can construct a quantum measurement from them. That is, this measurement is the best way of asking the question, "Is the state typical or not?" because it minimally disturbs the state while still retrieving this one bit of information.

DEFINITION 15.1.3 (Typical Projector) Let $\Pi_{A^n}^\delta$ denote the typical projector for the typical subspace of a density operator ρ_A with spectral decomposition in (15.2). It is a projector onto the typical subspace:

$$\Pi_{A^n}^\delta \equiv \sum_{x^n \in T_\delta^{X^n}} |x^n\rangle\langle x^n|_{A^n}, \qquad (15.11)$$

where it is implicit that the x^n below the summation is a classical sequence in the typical set $T_\delta^{X^n}$, and the state $|x^n\rangle$ is a quantum state given in (15.9) and associated with the classical sequence x^n via the spectral decomposition of ρ in (15.2). We can also denote the typical projector as $\Pi_{A^n}^{\rho,\delta}$ if we would like to make its dependence on ρ explicit.

The action of multiplying the density operator ρ_{A^n} by the typical projector $\Pi_{A^n}^\delta$ is to select out all the basis states of ρ_{A^n} that are in the typical subspace and form a "sliced" operator $\tilde{\rho}_{A^n}$ that is close to the original density operator ρ_{A^n}:

$$\tilde{\rho}_{A^n} \equiv \Pi_{A^n}^\delta \rho_{A^n} \Pi_{A^n}^\delta = \sum_{x^n \in T_\delta^{X^n}} p_{X^n}(x^n)|x^n\rangle\langle x^n|_{A^n}. \qquad (15.12)$$

That is, the effect of projecting a state onto the typical subspace $T_{A^n}^\delta$ is to "slice" out any component of the state ρ_{A^n} that does not lie in the typical subspace $T_{A^n}^\delta$.

EXERCISE 15.1.1 Show that the typical projector $\Pi_{A^n}^\delta$ commutes with the density operator ρ_{A^n}:

$$\rho_{A^n} \Pi_{A^n}^\delta = \Pi_{A^n}^\delta \rho_{A^n}. \qquad (15.13)$$

The typical projector allows us to formulate an operational method for delicately asking the question: "Is the state typical or not?" We can construct a quantum measurement that consists of two outcomes: the outcome "1" reveals that the state is in the typical subspace, and "0" reveals that it is not. This typical subspace measurement is often one of the first important steps in most protocols in quantum Shannon theory.

DEFINITION 15.1.4 (Typical Subspace Measurement) The following map is a quantum instrument (see Section 4.6.8) that realizes the typical subspace measurement:

$$\sigma \to \left(I - \Pi_{A^n}^\delta\right) \sigma \left(I - \Pi_{A^n}^\delta\right) \otimes |0\rangle\langle0| + \Pi_{A^n}^\delta \sigma \Pi_{A^n}^\delta \otimes |1\rangle\langle1|, \qquad (15.14)$$

where σ is some density operator acting on the Hilbert space $\mathcal{H}_{A^n}$. It associates a classical register with the outcome of the measurement—the value of the classical register is $|0\rangle$ for the support of the state σ that is not in the typical subspace, and it is equal to $|1\rangle$ for the support of the state σ that is in the typical subspace.

The implementation of a typical subspace measurement is currently far from the reality of what is experimentally accessible if we would like to have the measure concentration effects necessary for proving many of the results in quantum Shannon theory. Recall from Figure 14.1 that we required a sequence of about a million bits in order to have the needed measure concentration effects. We would need a similar number of qubits emitted from a quantum information source, and furthermore, we would require the ability to perform noiseless coherent operations over about a million or more qubits in order to implement the typical subspace measurement. Such a daunting requirement firmly places quantum Shannon theory as a "highly theoretical theory," rather than being a theory that can make close connection to current experimental practice.[1]

15.1.2 The Difference between the Typical Set and the Typical Subspace

We now offer a simple example to discuss the difference between the classical viewpoint associated with the typical set and the quantum viewpoint associated with the typical subspace. Suppose that a quantum information source emits the state $|+\rangle$ with probability $1/2$ and it emits the state $|0\rangle$ with probability $1/2$. For the moment, let us ignore the fact that the two states $|+\rangle$ and $|0\rangle$ are not perfectly distinguishable and instead suppose that they are. Then it would turn out that nearly every sequence emitted from this source is a typical sequence because the distribution of the source is uniform. Recall that the typical set has size roughly equal to $2^{nH(X)}$, and in this case, the entropy of the distribution $\left(\frac{1}{2}, \frac{1}{2}\right)$ is equal to one bit. Thus the size of the typical set is roughly the same as the size of the set of all sequences for this distribution because $2^{nH(X)} = 2^n$.

Now let us take into account the fact that the states $|+\rangle$ and $|0\rangle$ are not perfectly distinguishable and use the prescription given in Definition 15.1.2 for the typical subspace. The density operator of the above ensemble is as follows:

$$\frac{1}{2}|+\rangle\langle+| + \frac{1}{2}|0\rangle\langle0| = \begin{bmatrix} \frac{3}{4} & \frac{1}{4} \\ \frac{1}{4} & \frac{1}{4} \end{bmatrix}, \tag{15.15}$$

where its matrix representation is with respect to the computational basis. The spectral decomposition of the density operator is

$$\cos^2(\pi/8)|\psi_0\rangle\langle\psi_0| + \sin^2(\pi/8)|\psi_1\rangle\langle\psi_1|, \tag{15.16}$$

where the states $|\psi_0\rangle$ and $|\psi_1\rangle$ are orthogonal, and thus distinguishable from one another. The quantum information source that outputs $|0\rangle$ and $|+\rangle$ with equal probability is thus equivalent to a source that outputs $|\psi_0\rangle$ with probability $\cos^2(\pi/8)$ and $|\psi_1\rangle$ with probability $\sin^2(\pi/8)$.

We construct the projector onto the typical subspace by taking sums of typical strings of the states $|\psi_0\rangle\langle\psi_0|$ and $|\psi_1\rangle\langle\psi_1|$ rather than the states $|0\rangle\langle0|$ and $|+\rangle\langle+|$, where typicality is with respect to the distribution $\left(\cos^2(\pi/8), \sin^2(\pi/8)\right)$. The dimension of the typical subspace corresponding to the quantum information

---

[1] We should note that this was certainly the case as well for information theory when Claude Shannon developed it in 1948, but in the many years since then, there has been much progress in the development of practical classical codes for achieving the classical capacity of a classical channel.

source is far different from the size of the aforementioned typical set corresponding to the distribution $(1/2, 1/2)$. It is roughly equal to $2^{0.6n}$ because the entropy of the distribution $\left(\cos^2(\pi/8), \sin^2(\pi/8)\right)$ is about 0.6 bits. This stark contrast in the sizes has to do with the non-orthogonality of the states from the original description of the ensemble. That is, non-orthogonality of states in an ensemble implies that the size of the typical subspace can potentially be dramatically smaller than the size of the typical set corresponding to the distribution of the states in the ensemble. This result has implications for the compressibility of quantum information, and we will discuss these ideas in more detail in Chapter 18. For now, we continue with the technical details of typical subspaces.

15.1.3   Properties of the Typical Subspace

The typical subspace $T_{A^n}^\delta$ enjoys several useful properties that are "quantized" versions of the typical sequence properties:

PROPERTY 15.1.1 (Unit Probability)   Suppose that we perform a typical subspace measurement of a state ρ_{A^n}. Then the probability that the quantum state ρ_{A^n} is in the typical subspace $T_{A^n}^\delta$ approaches one as n becomes large. That is,

$$\text{Tr}\left\{\Pi_{A^n}^\delta \rho_{A^n}\right\} \geq 1 - \varepsilon, \tag{15.17}$$

for all $\varepsilon \in (0,1)$, $\delta > 0$, and sufficiently large n, where $\Pi_{A^n}^\delta$ is the typical subspace projector from Definition 15.1.3.

PROPERTY 15.1.2 (Exponentially Smaller Dimension)   The dimension $\dim(T_{A^n}^\delta)$ of the δ-typical subspace is exponentially smaller than the dimension $|A|^n$ of the entire space of quantum states when the output of the quantum information source is not maximally mixed. We formally state this property as follows:

$$\text{Tr}\left\{\Pi_{A^n}^\delta\right\} \leq 2^{n(H(A)+c\delta)}, \tag{15.18}$$

where c is some positive constant that depends on whether we employ the weak or strong notion of typicality. We can also bound the dimension $\dim(T_{A^n}^\delta)$ of the δ-typical subspace from below:

$$\text{Tr}\left\{\Pi_{A^n}^\delta\right\} \geq (1 - \varepsilon)\, 2^{n(H(A)-c\delta)}, \tag{15.19}$$

for all $\varepsilon \in (0,1)$, $\delta > 0$, and sufficiently large n.

PROPERTY 15.1.3 (Equipartition)   The operator $\Pi_{A^n}^\delta \rho_{A^n} \Pi_{A^n}^\delta$ corresponds to a "slicing" of the density operator ρ_{A^n} where we slice out and keep only the part with support in the typical subspace. We can then bound all of the eigenvalues of the sliced operator $\Pi_{A^n}^\delta \rho_{A^n} \Pi_{A^n}^\delta$ as follows:

$$2^{-n(H(A)+c\delta)} \Pi_{A^n}^\delta \leq \Pi_{A^n}^\delta \rho_{A^n} \Pi_{A^n}^\delta \leq 2^{-n(H(A)-c\delta)} \Pi_{A^n}^\delta. \tag{15.20}$$

The above inequality is an operator inequality. It is a statement about the eigenvalues of the operators $\Pi_{A^n}^\delta \rho_{A^n} \Pi_{A^n}^\delta$ and $\Pi_{A^n}^\delta$, and these operators have the same eigenvectors because they commute. Therefore, the above inequality is equivalent to the following inequality that applies in the classical case:

$$\forall x^n \in T_\delta^{X^n} : 2^{-n(H(A)+c\delta)} \leq p_{X^n}(x^n) \leq 2^{-n(H(A)-c\delta)}. \tag{15.21}$$

This equivalence holds because each probability $p_{X^n}(x^n)$ is an eigenvalue of $\Pi_{A^n}^\delta \rho_{A^n} \Pi_{A^n}^\delta$.

The dimension $\dim(T_{A^n}^\delta)$ of the δ-typical subspace is approximately equal to the dimension $|\mathcal{X}|^n$ of the entire space only when the density operator of the quantum information source is maximally mixed because

$$\text{Tr}\left\{\Pi_{A^n}^\delta\right\} \leq |A|^n \cdot 2^{n\delta} \simeq |A|^n. \tag{15.22}$$

Proofs of the above properties are essentially identical to those from the classical case in Sections 14.7.3 and 14.9.3, regardless of whether we employ a weak or strong notion of quantum typicality. We leave the proofs as the three exercises below.

EXERCISE 15.1.2 Prove the unit probability property of the δ-typical subspace (Property 15.1.1). First show that the probability that many copies of a density operator is in the δ-typical subspace is equal to the probability that a random sequence is δ-typical:

$$\text{Tr}\left\{\Pi_{A^n}^\delta \rho_{A^n}\right\} = \text{Pr}\left\{X^n \in T_\delta^{X^n}\right\}. \tag{15.23}$$

EXERCISE 15.1.3 Prove the exponentially smaller dimension property of the δ-typical subspace (Property 15.1.2). First show that the trace of the typical projector $\Pi_{A^n}^\delta$ is equal to the dimension of the typical subspace $T_{A^n}^\delta$:

$$\dim(T_{A^n}^\delta) = \text{Tr}\left\{\Pi_{A^n}^\delta\right\}. \tag{15.24}$$

Then prove the property.

EXERCISE 15.1.4 Prove the equipartition property of the δ-typical subspace (Property 15.1.3). First show that

$$\Pi_{A^n}^\delta \rho_{A^n} \Pi_{A^n}^\delta = \sum_{x^n \in T_\delta^{X^n}} p_{X^n}(x^n)|x^n\rangle\langle x^n|_{A^n}, \tag{15.25}$$

and then argue the proof.

The result of the following exercise shows that the sliced operator $\tilde{\rho}_{A^n} \equiv \Pi_{A^n}^\delta \rho_{A^n} \Pi_{A^n}^\delta$ is a good approximation to the original state ρ_{A^n} in the limit of many copies of the states, and it effectively gives a scheme for quantum data compression (more on this in Chapter 18).

EXERCISE 15.1.5 Use the gentle operator lemma (Lemma 9.4.2) to show that ρ_{A^n} is $2\sqrt{\varepsilon}$-close to the sliced operator $\tilde{\rho}_{A^n}$ when n is large:

$$\|\rho_{A^n} - \tilde{\rho}_{A^n}\|_1 \leq 2\sqrt{\varepsilon}. \tag{15.26}$$

Use the gentle measurement lemma (Lemma 9.4.1) to show that the sliced state

$$\left[\mathrm{Tr}\left\{ \Pi^\delta_{A^n} \rho_{A^n} \right\} \right]^{-1} \tilde{\rho}_{A^n} \tag{15.27}$$

is $2\sqrt{\varepsilon}$-close in trace distance to $\tilde{\rho}_{A^n}$.

EXERCISE 15.1.6   Show that the purity $\mathrm{Tr}\left\{ (\tilde{\rho}_{A^n})^2 \right\}$ of the sliced state $\tilde{\rho}_{A^n}$ satisfies the following bound for sufficiently large n and any $\varepsilon \in (0,1)$ (use weak quantum typicality):

$$(1-\varepsilon)\, 2^{-n(H(A)+\delta)} \leq \mathrm{Tr}\left\{ (\tilde{\rho}_{A^n})^2 \right\} \leq 2^{-n(H(A)-\delta)}. \tag{15.28}$$

EXERCISE 15.1.7   Show that the following bounds hold for the rank and the ∞-norm of the sliced state $\tilde{\rho}_{A^n}$ for any $\varepsilon \in (0,1)$ and sufficiently large n:

$$(1-\varepsilon)\, 2^{n(H(A)-\delta)} \leq \mathrm{rank}(\tilde{\rho}_{A^n}) \leq 2^{n(H(A)+\delta)}, \tag{15.29}$$

$$2^{-n(H(A)+\delta)} \leq \|\tilde{\rho}_{A^n}\|_\infty \leq 2^{-n(H(A)-\delta)}. \tag{15.30}$$

(Recall that the rank of an operator is equal to the size of its support and that the infinity norm is equal to its maximum eigenvalue. Again use weak quantum typicality.)

15.1.4   The Typical Subspace for Bipartite or Multipartite States

Recall from Section 14.5 that two classical sequences x^n and y^n are weak jointly typical if the joint sample entropy of $x^n y^n$ is close to the joint entropy $H(X,Y)$ and if the sample entropies of the individual sequences are close to their respective marginal entropies $H(X)$ and $H(Y)$—where the entropies are with respect to some joint distribution $p_{X,Y}(x,y)$. How would we then actually check that these conditions hold? The most obvious way is simply to look at the sequence $x^n y^n$, compute its joint sample entropy, compare this quantity to the true joint entropy, determine if the difference is under the threshold δ, and do the same for the marginal sequences. These two operations both commute in the sense that we can determine first if the marginals are typical and then if the joint sequence is typical or vice versa without any difference in which one we do first.

But such a commutation does not necessarily hold in the quantum world. The way that we determine whether a quantum state is typical is by performing a typical subspace measurement. If we perform a typical subspace measurement of the whole system followed by such a measurement on the marginals, the resulting state is not necessarily the same as if we performed the marginal measurements followed by the joint measurements. For this reason, the notion of weak joint typicality as given in Definition 14.5.3 does not really exist in general for the quantum case. Nevertheless, we still briefly overview how one would handle such a case and later give an example of a restricted class of states for which weak joint typicality holds.

Suppose that we have a quantum system in the mixed state ρ_{AB} shared between two parties A and B. We can decompose the mixed state with the spectral theorem:

$$\rho_{AB} = \sum_{z \in \mathcal{Z}} p_Z(z) |\psi_z\rangle\langle\psi_z|_{AB}, \tag{15.31}$$

where the states $\{|\psi_z\rangle_{AB}\}_{z \in \mathcal{Z}}$ form an orthonormal basis for the joint quantum system AB and each of the states $|\psi_z\rangle_{AB}$ can be entangled in general.

We can consider the nth extension $\rho_{A^n B^n}$ of the above state and abbreviate its spectral decomposition as follows:

$$\rho_{A^n B^n} \equiv (\rho_{AB})^{\otimes n} = \sum_{z^n \in \mathcal{Z}^n} p_{Z^n}(z^n) |\psi_{z^n}\rangle\langle\psi_{z^n}|_{A^n B^n}, \tag{15.32}$$

where

$$p_{Z^n}(z^n) \equiv p_Z(z_1) \cdots p_Z(z_n), \tag{15.33}$$

$$|\psi_{z^n}\rangle_{A^n B^n} \equiv |\psi_{z_1}\rangle_{A_1 B_1} \cdots |\psi_{z_n}\rangle_{A_n B_n}. \tag{15.34}$$

This development immediately leads to the definition of the typical subspace for a bipartite state.

DEFINITION 15.1.5 (Typical Subspace of a Bipartite State) The δ-*typical subspace* $T^\delta_{A^n B^n}$ of ρ_{AB} is the space spanned by states $|\psi_{z^n}\rangle_{A^n B^n}$ whose corresponding classical sequence z^n is in the typical set $T^{Z^n}_\delta$:

$$T^\delta_{A^n B^n} \equiv \mathrm{span}\left\{ |\psi_{z^n}\rangle_{A^n B^n} : z^n \in T^{Z^n}_\delta \right\}. \tag{15.35}$$

The states $|\psi_{z^n}\rangle_{A^n B^n}$ are from a spectral decomposition of ρ_{AB}, and the distribution to consider for typicality of the classical sequence z^n is $p_Z(z)$ from the spectral decomposition.

DEFINITION 15.1.6 (Typical Projector of a Bipartite State) Let $\Pi^\delta_{A^n B^n}$ denote the projector onto the typical subspace of ρ_{AB}:

$$\Pi^\delta_{A^n B^n} \equiv \sum_{z^n \in T^{Z^n}_\delta} |\psi_{z^n}\rangle\langle\psi_{z^n}|_{A^n B^n}. \tag{15.36}$$

Thus, there is ultimately no difference between the typical subspace for a bipartite state and the typical subspace for a single-party state because the spectral decomposition gives a way for determining the typical subspace and the typical projector in both cases. Perhaps the only difference is a cosmetic one because AB denotes the bipartite system while Z indicates a random variable with a distribution given from a spectral decomposition. Finally, Properties 15.1.1–15.1.3 hold for quantum typicality of a bipartite state.

15.1.5   The Jointly Typical Subspace for Classical States

The notion of weak joint typicality may not hold in the general case, but it does hold for a special class of states that are completely classical. Suppose now that the mixed state ρ_{AB} shared between two parties A and B has the following special form:

$$\rho_{AB} = \sum_{x \in \mathcal{X}} \sum_{y \in \mathcal{Y}} p_{X,Y}(x,y) \left(|x\rangle \otimes |y\rangle \right) \left(\langle x| \otimes \langle y| \right)_{AB} \tag{15.37}$$

$$= \sum_{x \in \mathcal{X}} \sum_{y \in \mathcal{Y}} p_{X,Y}(x,y) |x\rangle\langle x|_A \otimes |y\rangle\langle y|_B, \tag{15.38}$$

where the states $\{|x\rangle_A\}_{x \in \mathcal{X}}$ and $\{|y\rangle_B\}_{y \in \mathcal{Y}}$ form an orthonormal basis for the respective systems $\mathcal{X}$ and $\mathcal{Y}$. This state has only classical correlations because Alice and Bob can prepare it simply by local operations and classical communication. That is, Alice can sample from the distribution $p_{X,Y}(x,y)$ in her laboratory and send Bob the variable y. Furthermore, the states on A and B locally form a distinguishable set.

We can consider the nth extension $\rho_{A^n B^n}$ of the above state:

$$\rho_{A^n B^n} \equiv (\rho_{AB})^{\otimes n} \tag{15.39}$$

$$= \sum_{x^n \in \mathcal{X}^n, y^n \in \mathcal{Y}^n} p_{X^n, Y^n}(x^n, y^n) \left(|x^n\rangle \otimes |y^n\rangle \right) \left(\langle x^n| \otimes \langle y^n| \right)_{A^n B^n} \tag{15.40}$$

$$= \sum_{x^n \in \mathcal{X}^n, y^n \in \mathcal{Y}^n} p_{X^n, Y^n}(x^n, y^n) |x^n\rangle\langle x^n|_{A^n} \otimes |y^n\rangle\langle y^n|_{B^n}. \tag{15.41}$$

This development immediately leads to the definition of the weak jointly typical subspace for this special case.

DEFINITION 15.1.7 (Jointly Typical Subspace) The weak δ-*jointly typical subspace* $T^\delta_{A^n B^n}$ is the space spanned by states $|x^n\rangle|y^n\rangle_{A^n B^n}$ whose corresponding classical sequence $x^n y^n$ is in the *jointly* typical set:

$$T^\delta_{A^n B^n} \equiv \operatorname{span} \left\{ |x^n\rangle_{A^n} |y^n\rangle_{B^n} : x^n y^n \in T^{X^n Y^n}_\delta \right\}. \tag{15.42}$$

DEFINITION 15.1.8 (Jointly Typical Projector) Let $\Pi^\delta_{A^n B^n}$ denote the jointly typical projector. It is the projector onto the jointly typical subspace:

$$\Pi^\delta_{A^n B^n} \equiv \sum_{x^n, y^n \in T^{X^n Y^n}_\delta} |x^n\rangle\langle x^n|_{A^n} \otimes |y^n\rangle\langle y^n|_{B^n}. \tag{15.43}$$

Properties of the Jointly Typical Projector for Classical States
Properties 15.1.1–15.1.3 apply to the jointly typical subspace $T^\delta_{A^n B^n}$ because it is a typical subspace. The following property, analogous to Property 14.5.4 for classical joint typicality, holds whenever the state ρ_{AB} has the special form in (15.37):

PROPERTY 15.1.4 (Probability of Joint Typicality) Let $\rho_{A^n B^n}$ be a classical state as given in (15.39). Consider the following marginal density operators:

$$\rho_{A^n} \equiv \operatorname{Tr}_{B^n} \{\rho_{A^n B^n}\}, \qquad \rho_{B^n} \equiv \operatorname{Tr}_{A^n} \{\rho_{A^n B^n}\}. \tag{15.44}$$

Let us define $\rho_{\tilde{A}^n \tilde{B}^n}$ as the following density operator:

$$\rho_{\tilde{A}^n \tilde{B}^n} \equiv \rho_{A^n} \otimes \rho_{B^n} \neq \rho_{A^n B^n} . \tag{15.45}$$

The marginal density operators of $\rho_{\tilde{A}^n \tilde{B}^n}$ are therefore equivalent to the marginal density operators of $\rho_{A^n B^n}$. Then we can bound the probability that the state $\rho_{\tilde{A}^n \tilde{B}^n}$ lies in the typical subspace $T_{A^n B^n}^\delta$:

$$\text{Tr} \left\{ \Pi_{A^n B^n}^\delta \rho_{\tilde{A}^n \tilde{B}^n} \right\} \leq 2^{-n(I(A;B)-3\delta)} . \tag{15.46}$$

EXERCISE 15.1.8 Prove the bound in Property 15.1.4:

$$\text{Tr} \left\{ \Pi_{A^n B^n}^\delta \rho_{\tilde{A}^n \tilde{B}^n} \right\} \leq 2^{-n(I(A;B)-3\delta)} . \tag{15.47}$$

15.2   Conditional Quantum Typicality

The notion of conditional quantum typicality is somewhat similar to the notion of conditional typicality in the classical domain, but we again quickly notice some departures because different quantum states do not have to be perfectly distinguishable. The technical tools for conditional quantum typicality developed in this section are important for developing schemes that send public or private classical information over a quantum channel (topics discussed in Chapters 20 and 23).

We first develop the notion of a conditional quantum information source. Consider a random variable X with probability distribution $p_X(x)$. Let $\mathcal{X}$ be the alphabet of the random variable, and let $|\mathcal{X}|$ denote its cardinality. We also associate a quantum system X with the random variable X and use an orthonormal set $\{|x\rangle\}_{x \in \mathcal{X}}$ to represent its realizations. We again label the elements of the alphabet $\mathcal{X}$ as $\{x\}_{x \in \mathcal{X}}$.

Suppose we generate a realization x of random variable X according to its distribution $p_X(x)$, and we follow by generating a random quantum state according to some conditional distribution. This procedure then gives us a set of $|\mathcal{X}|$ quantum information sources (each of them are as in Definition 15.1.1). We index them by the classical index x, and the quantum information source has expected density operator ρ_B^x if the emitted classical index is x. Furthermore, we impose the constraint that each ρ_B^x has the same dimension (one could achieve this by embedding the lower dimensional states into a larger Hilbert space). This quantum information source is therefore a "conditional quantum information source." Let $\mathcal{H}_B$ and B denote the respective Hilbert space and system label corresponding to the quantum output of the conditional quantum information source. Let us call the resulting ensemble the "classical–quantum ensemble" and say that a "classical–quantum information source" generates it. The classical–quantum ensemble is as follows:

$$\{p_X(x), |x\rangle\langle x|_X \otimes \rho_B^x\}_{x \in \mathcal{X}} , \tag{15.48}$$

where we correlate the classical state $|x\rangle_X$ with the density operator ρ_B^x of the conditional quantum information source. The expected density operator of the above classical–quantum ensemble is the following classical–quantum state (discussed in Section 4.3.4):

$$\rho_{XB} \equiv \sum_{x \in \mathcal{X}} p_X(x)|x\rangle\langle x|_X \otimes \rho_B^x. \tag{15.49}$$

The conditional quantum entropy $H(B|X)_\rho$ of the classical–quantum state ρ_{XB} is as follows:

$$H(B|X)_\rho = \sum_{x \in \mathcal{X}} p_X(x)H(\rho_B^x). \tag{15.50}$$

We can write a spectral decomposition of each conditional density operator ρ_B^x as follows:

$$\sum_{y \in \mathcal{Y}} p_{Y|X}(y|x)|y_x\rangle\langle y_x|_B, \tag{15.51}$$

where the elements of the set $\{y\}_{y \in \mathcal{Y}}$ label the elements of an alphabet $\mathcal{Y}$, the orthonormal set $\{|y_x\rangle_B\}_{y \in \mathcal{Y}}$ is the set of eigenvectors of ρ_B^x, and the corresponding eigenvalues are $\{p_{Y|X}(y|x)\}_{y \in \mathcal{Y}}$. We need the x label for the orthonormal set $\{|y_x\rangle_B\}_{y \in \mathcal{Y}}$ because the decomposition may be different for different density operators ρ_B^x. The above notation is again suggestive because the eigenvalues $p_{Y|X}(y|x)$ correspond to conditional probabilities, and the set $\{|y_x\rangle_B\}$ of eigenvectors corresponds to an orthonormal set of quantum states conditioned on label x. With this respresentation, the conditional entropy $H(B|X)$ reduces to a formula that looks like that for the classical conditional entropy:

$$H(B|X) = \sum_{x \in \mathcal{X}} p_X(x)H(\rho_B^x) \tag{15.52}$$

$$= \sum_{x \in \mathcal{X}, y \in \mathcal{Y}} p_X(x)p_{Y|X}(y|x) \log \frac{1}{p_{Y|X}(y|x)}. \tag{15.53}$$

We now consider when the classical–quantum information source emits a large number n of states. The density operator for the output state $\rho_{X^n B^n}$ is as follows:

$$\rho_{X^n B^n}$$

$$\equiv (\rho_{XB})^{\otimes n} \tag{15.54}$$

$$= \left(\sum_{x_1 \in \mathcal{X}} p_X(x_1)|x_1\rangle\langle x_1|_{X_1} \otimes \rho_{B_1}^{x_1} \right) \otimes \cdots \otimes \left(\sum_{x_n \in \mathcal{X}} p_X(x_n)|x_n\rangle\langle x_n|_{X_n} \otimes \rho_{B_n}^{x_n} \right) \tag{15.55}$$

$$= \sum_{x_1, \ldots, x_n \in \mathcal{X}} p_X(x_1) \cdots p_X(x_n)|x_1\rangle \cdots |x_n\rangle\langle x_1| \cdots \langle x_n|_{X^n} \otimes \left(\rho_{B_1}^{x_1} \otimes \cdots \otimes \rho_{B_n}^{x_n} \right). \tag{15.56}$$

We can abbreviate the above state as

$$\sum_{x^n \in \mathcal{X}^n} p_{X^n}(x^n) |x^n\rangle\langle x^n|_{X^n} \otimes \rho_{B^n}^{x^n}, \tag{15.57}$$

where

$$p_{X^n}(x^n) \equiv p_X(x_1) \cdots p_X(x_n), \tag{15.58}$$

$$|x^n\rangle_{X^n} \equiv |x_1\rangle_{X_1} \cdots |x_n\rangle_{X_n}, \qquad \rho_{B^n}^{x^n} \equiv \rho_{B_1}^{x_1} \otimes \cdots \otimes \rho_{B_n}^{x_n}, \tag{15.59}$$

and a spectral decomposition for the state $\rho_{B^n}^{x^n}$ is

$$\rho_{B^n}^{x^n} = \sum_{y^n \in \mathcal{Y}^n} p_{Y^n|X^n}(y^n|x^n) |y_{x^n}^n\rangle\langle y_{x^n}^n|_{B^n}, \tag{15.60}$$

where

$$p_{Y^n|X^n}(y^n|x^n) \equiv p_{Y_1|X_1}(y_1|x_1) \cdots p_{Y_n|X_n}(y_n|x_n), \tag{15.61}$$

$$|y_{x^n}^n\rangle_{B^n} \equiv |y_{1\,x_1}\rangle_{B_1} \cdots |y_{n\,x_n}\rangle_{B_n}. \tag{15.62}$$

The above developments are a step along the way for formulating the definitions of weak and strong conditional quantum typicality.

15.2.1 Weak Conditional Quantum Typicality

We can "quantize" the notion of weak classical conditional typicality so that it applies to a classical–quantum information source.

DEFINITION 15.2.1 (Weak Conditionally Typical Subspace)   The conditionally typical subspace $T_{B^n|x^n}^\delta$ corresponds to a particular sequence x^n and an ensemble $\{p_X(x), \rho_B^x\}$. It is the subspace spanned by the states $|y_{x^n}^n\rangle_{B^n}$ whose conditional sample entropy is δ-close to the true conditional quantum entropy:

$$T_{B^n|x^n}^\delta \equiv \text{span}\left\{|y_{x^n}^n\rangle_{B^n} : \left|\overline{H}(y^n|x^n) - H(B|X)\right| \le \delta\right\}, \tag{15.63}$$

where the states $|y_{x^n}^n\rangle_{B^n}$ are formed from the eigenstates of the density operators ρ_B^x (they are of the form in (15.62)) and the sample entropy is with respect to the distribution $p_{Y|X}(y|x)$ from (15.51).

DEFINITION 15.2.2 (Weak Conditionally Typical Projector)   The projector $\Pi_{B^n|x^n}^\delta$ onto the conditionally typical subspace $T_{B^n|x^n}^\delta$ is as follows:

$$\Pi_{B^n|x^n}^\delta \equiv \sum_{y_{x^n}^n \in T_\delta^{Y^n|x^n}} |y_{x^n}^n\rangle\langle y_{x^n}^n|_{B^n}. \tag{15.64}$$

15.2.2 Properties of the Weak Conditionally Typical Subspace

The weak conditionally typical subspace $T_{B^n|x^n}^\delta$ enjoys several useful properties that are "quantized" versions of the properties for weak conditionally typical sequences discussed in Section 14.6. We should point out that we cannot really say much for several of the properties for a particular sequence x^n, but we can do so on average for a random sequence X^n. Thus, several of the properties give expected behavior for a random sequence X^n. This convention for quantum weak conditional typicality is the same as we had for classical weak conditional typicality in Section 14.6.

PROPERTY 15.2.1 (Unit Probability)   The expectation of the probability that we measure a random quantum state $\rho_{B^n}^{X^n}$ to be in the conditionally typical subspace $T_{B^n|X^n}^\delta$ approaches one as n becomes large:

$$\mathbb{E}_{X^n}\left\{\mathrm{Tr}\left\{\Pi_{B^n|X^n}^\delta \rho_{B^n}^{X^n}\right\}\right\} \geq 1 - \varepsilon, \tag{15.65}$$

for all $\varepsilon \in (0,1)$, $\delta > 0$, and sufficiently large n.

PROPERTY 15.2.2 (Exponentially Smaller Dimension)   The dimension $\dim(T_{B^n|x^n}^\delta)$ of the δ-conditionally typical subspace is exponentially smaller than the dimension $|\mathcal{Y}|^n$ of the entire space of quantum states for most classical–quantum sources. We formally state this property as follows:

$$\mathrm{Tr}\left\{\Pi_{B^n|x^n}^\delta\right\} \leq 2^{n(H(B|X)+\delta)}. \tag{15.66}$$

We can also bound the dimension $\dim(T_{B^n|x^n}^\delta)$ of the δ-conditionally typical subspace from below:

$$\mathbb{E}_{X^n}\left\{\mathrm{Tr}\left\{\Pi_{B^n|X^n}^\delta\right\}\right\} \geq (1 - \varepsilon)\, 2^{n(H(B|X)-\delta)}, \tag{15.67}$$

for all $\varepsilon \in (0,1)$, $\delta > 0$, and sufficiently large n.

PROPERTY 15.2.3 (Equipartition)   The density operator $\rho_{B^n}^{x^n}$ looks approximately maximally mixed when projected to the conditionally typical subspace:

$$2^{-n(H(B|X)+\delta)}\Pi_{B^n|x^n}^\delta \leq \Pi_{B^n|x^n}^\delta \rho_{B^n}^{x^n} \Pi_{B^n|x^n}^\delta \leq 2^{-n(H(B|X)-\delta)}\Pi_{B^n|x^n}^\delta. \tag{15.68}$$

EXERCISE 15.2.1   Prove all three of the above properties for weak conditional quantum typicality.

15.2.3   Strong Conditional Quantum Typicality

We now develop the notion of strong conditional quantum typicality. This notion again applies to an ensemble or to a classical–quantum state such as that given in (15.49). However, it differs from weak conditional quantum typicality because we can prove stronger statements about the asymptotic behavior of conditional quantum systems (just as we could for the classical case in Section 14.9). We begin this section with an example to build up our intuition. We then follow with the formal definition of strong conditional quantum typicality, and we end by proving some properties of the strong conditionally typical subspace.

Recall the example from Section 14.7. In a similar way to this example, we can draw a sequence from an alphabet $\{0, 1, 2\}$ according to the following distribution:

$$p_X(0) = \frac{1}{4}, \qquad p_X(1) = \frac{1}{4}, \qquad p_X(2) = \frac{1}{2}. \qquad (15.69)$$

One potential realization sequence is as follows:

$$201020102212. \qquad (15.70)$$

The above sequence has four "zeros," three "ones," and five "twos," so that the empirical distribution of this sequence is $(1/3, 1/4, 5/12)$ and has maximum deviation $1/12$ from the true distribution in (15.69).

For each symbol in the above sequence, we could then draw from one of three quantum information sources based on whether the classical index is 0, 1, or 2. Suppose that the expected density operator of the first quantum information source is ρ^0, that of the second is ρ^1, and that of the third is ρ^2. Then the density operator for the resulting sequence of quantum states is as follows:

$$\rho_{B_1}^2 \otimes \rho_{B_2}^0 \otimes \rho_{B_3}^1 \otimes \rho_{B_4}^0 \otimes \rho_{B_5}^2 \otimes \rho_{B_6}^0 \otimes \rho_{B_7}^1 \otimes \rho_{B_8}^0 \otimes \rho_{B_9}^2 \otimes \rho_{B_{10}}^2 \otimes \rho_{B_{11}}^1 \otimes \rho_{B_{12}}^2, \qquad (15.71)$$

where the subscripts label the systems as usual. So, the state of systems B_1, B_5, B_9, B_{10}, and B_{12} is equal to five copies of ρ^2, the state of systems B_2, B_4, B_6, and B_8 is equal to four copies of ρ^0, and the state of systems B_3, B_7, and B_{11} is equal to three copies of ρ^1. Let I_x be an indicator set for each $x \in \{0, 1, 2\}$, so that I_x consists of all the indices in the sequence for which a symbol is equal to x. For the above example,

$$I_0 = \{2, 4, 6, 8\}, \qquad I_1 = \{3, 7, 11\}, \qquad I_2 = \{1, 5, 9, 10, 12\}. \qquad (15.72)$$

These sets serve as a way of grouping all of the density operators that are the same because they correspond to the same classical symbol, and it is important to do so if we would like to consider concentration of measure effects when we go to the asymptotic setting. As a visual aid, we could permute the sequence of density operators in (15.71) if we would like to see systems with the same density operator grouped together:

$$\rho_{B_2}^0 \otimes \rho_{B_4}^0 \otimes \rho_{B_6}^0 \otimes \rho_{B_8}^0 \otimes \rho_{B_3}^1 \otimes \rho_{B_7}^1 \otimes \rho_{B_{11}}^1 \otimes \rho_{B_1}^2 \otimes \rho_{B_5}^2 \otimes \rho_{B_9}^2 \otimes \rho_{B_{10}}^2 \otimes \rho_{B_{12}}^2. \qquad (15.73)$$

There is then a typical projector for the first four systems with density operator ρ^0, a different typical projector for the next three systems with density operator ρ^1, and an even different typical projector for the last five systems with density operator ρ^2 (however, the length of the above quantum sequence is certainly not large enough to observe any measure concentration effects!). Thus, the indicator sets I_x serve to identify which systems have the same density operator so that we can know upon which systems a particular typical projector should act.

This example helps build our intuition of strong conditional quantum typicality, and we can now begin to state what we would expect in the asymptotic setting. Suppose that the original classical sequence is large and strongly typical, so that it has roughly $n/4$ occurrences of "zero," $n/4$ occurrences of "one," and $n/2$ occurrences of "two." We would then expect the law of large numbers to come into play for $n/4$ and $n/2$ when n is large enough. Thus, we can use the classical sequence to identify which quantum systems have the same density operator, and apply a typical projector to each of these subsets of quantum systems. Then all of the useful asymptotic properties of typical subspaces apply whenever n is large enough.

We can now state the definition of the strong conditionally typical subspace and the strong conditionally typical projector, and we prove some of their asymptotic properties by exploiting the properties of typical subspaces.

DEFINITION 15.2.3 (Strong Conditionally Typical Subspace)   The strong conditionally typical subspace corresponds to a sequence x^n and an ensemble $\{p_X(x), \rho_B^x\}$. Let a spectral decomposition of each state ρ_B^x be as in (15.51) with distribution $p_{Y|X}(y|x)$ and corresponding eigenstates $|y_x\rangle$. The strong conditionally typical subspace $T_{B^n|x^n}^\delta$ is then as follows:

$$T_{B^n|x^n}^\delta \equiv \text{span}\left\{\bigotimes_{x \in \mathcal{X}} |y_x^{I_x}\rangle_{B^{I_x}} : \forall x, \quad y^{I_x} \in T_\delta^{(Y|x)^{|I_x|}}\right\}, \tag{15.74}$$

where $I_x \equiv \{i : x_i = x\}$ is an indicator set that selects the indices i in the sequence x^n for which the ith symbol x_i is equal to $x \in \mathcal{X}$, B^{I_x} selects the systems from B^n where the classical sequence x^n is equal to the symbol x, $|y_x^{I_x}\rangle$ is some string of states from the set $\{|y_x\rangle\}$, y^{I_x} is a classical string corresponding to this string of states, $Y|x$ is a random variable with distribution $p_{Y|X}(y|x)$, and $|I_x|$ is the cardinality of the indicator set I_x.

DEFINITION 15.2.4 (Strong Conditionally Typical Projector)   The strong conditionally typical projector again corresponds to a sequence x^n and an ensemble $\{p_X(x), \rho_B^x\}$. It is a tensor product of typical projectors for each state ρ_B^x in the ensemble:

$$\Pi_{B^n|x^n}^\delta \equiv \bigotimes_{x \in \mathcal{X}} \Pi_{B^{I_x}}^{\rho_x, \delta}, \tag{15.75}$$

where I_x is defined in Definition 15.2.3, and B^{I_x} indicates the systems onto which a particular typical projector for ρ_x projects.[2]

15.2.4   Properties of the Strong Conditionally Typical Subspace

The strong conditionally typical subspace admits several useful asymptotic properties similar to what we have seen before, and the proof strategy for proving all of them is similar to the way that we proved the analogous properties for the strong conditionally typical set in Section 14.9.3. Suppose that we draw a sequence x^n from a probability distribution $p_X(x)$, and we are able to draw as

---

[2] Having the conditional density operators in the subscript breaks somewhat from our convention throughout this chapter, but it is useful here to indicate explicitly which density operator corresponds to a typical projector.

many samples as we wish so that it is very likely that the sequence x^n is strongly typical and the occurrences $N(x|x^n)$ of each symbol x are as large as we wish. Then the following properties hold for x^n strongly typical and each $N(x|x^n)$ large.

PROPERTY 15.2.4 (Unit Probability)   The probability that we measure a quantum state $\rho_{B^n}^{x^n}$ to be in the conditionally typical subspace $T_{B^n|x^n}^{\delta}$ has the following lower bound:

$$\text{Tr}\left\{\Pi_{B^n|x^n}^{\delta}\rho_{B^n}^{x^n}\right\} \geq 1 - \varepsilon, \tag{15.76}$$

for all $\varepsilon \in (0,1)$, $\delta > 0$, and sufficiently large n.

PROPERTY 15.2.5 (Exponentially Smaller Dimension)   The dimension $\dim(T_{B^n|x^n}^{\delta})$ of the δ-conditionally typical subspace is exponentially smaller than the dimension $|B|^n$ of the entire space of quantum states for all classical–quantum information sources besides ones where all their density operators are maximally mixed. We formally state this property as follows:

$$\text{Tr}\left\{\Pi_{B^n|x^n}^{\delta}\right\} \leq 2^{n\left(H(B|X)+\delta''\right)}, \tag{15.77}$$

where δ'' is given in (15.92). We can also bound the dimension $\dim(T_{\delta}^{Y^n|x^n})$ of the δ-conditionally typical subspace from below:

$$\text{Tr}\left\{\Pi_{B^n|x^n}^{\delta}\right\} \geq (1 - \varepsilon)\, 2^{n\left(H(B|X)-\delta''\right)}, \tag{15.78}$$

for all $\varepsilon \in (0,1)$, $\delta > 0$, and sufficiently large n.

PROPERTY 15.2.6 (Equipartition)   The state $\rho_{B^n}^{x^n}$ is approximately maximally mixed when projected onto the strong conditionally typical subspace:

$$2^{-n\left(H(B|X)+\delta''\right)}\Pi_{B^n|x^n}^{\delta} \leq \Pi_{B^n|x^n}^{\delta}\rho_{B^n}^{x^n}\Pi_{B^n|x^n}^{\delta} \leq 2^{-n\left(H(B|X)-\delta''\right)}\Pi_{B^n|x^n}^{\delta}, \tag{15.79}$$

where δ'' is given in (15.92).

15.2.5   Proofs of the Properties of the Strong Conditionally Typical Subspace

Proof of the Unit Probability Property (Property 15.2.4)   A proof of this property is similar to the proof of Property 14.9.1 for the strong conditionally typical set. Since we are dealing with an i.i.d. distribution, we can assume without loss of generality that the sequence x^n is lexicographically ordered with an order on the alphabet $\mathcal{X}$. We write the elements of $\mathcal{X}$ as $a_1, \ldots, a_{|\mathcal{X}|}$. Then the lexicographic ordering means that we can write the sequence of quantum states ρ_{x^n} as follows:

$$\rho_{x^n} = \underbrace{\rho_{a_1} \otimes \cdots \otimes \rho_{a_1}}_{N(a_1|x^n)} \otimes \underbrace{\rho_{a_2} \otimes \cdots \otimes \rho_{a_2}}_{N(a_2|x^n)} \otimes \cdots \otimes \underbrace{\rho_{a_{|\mathcal{X}|}} \otimes \cdots \otimes \rho_{a_{|\mathcal{X}|}}}_{N(a_{|\mathcal{X}|}|x^n)}. \tag{15.80}$$

It follows that $N(a_i|x^n) \geq n\left(p_X(a_i) - \delta'\right)$ from the typicality of x^n, and thus the law of large numbers comes into play for each block $a_i \cdots a_i$ with length

$N(a_i|x^n)$. The strong conditionally typical projector $\Pi^\delta_{B^n|x^n}$ for this system is as follows:

$$\Pi^\delta_{B^n|x^n} \equiv \bigotimes_{x \in \mathcal{X}} \Pi^{\rho_x,\delta}_{B^{N(x|x^n)}}, \tag{15.81}$$

because we assumed the lexicographic ordering of the symbols in the sequence x^n. Each projector $\Pi^{\rho_x,\delta}_{B^{N(x|x^n)}}$ in the above tensor product is a typical projector for the density operator ρ_x when $N(x|x^n) \approx np_X(x)$ becomes very large. Then we can apply the unit probability property (Property 15.1.1) for each of these typical projectors, and it follows that

$$\mathrm{Tr}\left\{ \Pi^\delta_{B^n|x^n} \rho^{x^n}_{B^n} \right\} = \mathrm{Tr}\left\{ \bigotimes_{x \in \mathcal{X}} \Pi^{\rho_x,\delta}_{B^{N(x|x^n)}} \rho^{\otimes N(x|x^n)}_x \right\} \tag{15.82}$$

$$= \prod_{x \in \mathcal{X}} \mathrm{Tr}\left\{ \Pi^{\rho_x,\delta}_{B^{N(x|x^n)}} \rho^{\otimes N(x|x^n)}_x \right\} \tag{15.83}$$

$$\geq (1-\varepsilon)^{|\mathcal{X}|} \tag{15.84}$$

$$\geq 1 - |\mathcal{X}|\varepsilon, \tag{15.85}$$

concluding the proof. $\qquad\square$

Proof of the Equipartition Property (Property 15.2.6) We first assume without loss of generality that we can write the state $\rho^{x^n}_{B^n}$ in lexicographic order as in (15.80). Then the strong conditionally typical projector is again as in (15.81). It follows that

$$\Pi^\delta_{B^n|x^n} \rho_{x^n} \Pi^\delta_{B^n|x^n} = \bigotimes_{x \in \mathcal{X}} \Pi^{\rho_x,\delta}_{B^{N(x|x^n)}} \rho^{\otimes N(x|x^n)}_x \Pi^{\rho_x,\delta}_{B^{N(x|x^n)}}. \tag{15.86}$$

We can apply the equipartition property of the typical subspace for each typical projector $\Pi^{\rho_x,\delta}_{B^{N(x|x^n)}}$ (Property 15.1.3):

$$\bigotimes_{x \in \mathcal{X}} \Pi^{\rho_x,\delta}_{B^{N(x|x^n)}} 2^{-N(x|x^n)(H(\rho_x)+c\delta)} \leq \bigotimes_{x \in \mathcal{X}} \Pi^{\rho_x,\delta}_{B^{N(x|x^n)}} \rho^{\otimes N(x|x^n)}_x \Pi^{\rho_x,\delta}_{B^{N(x|x^n)}}$$

$$\leq \bigotimes_{x \in \mathcal{X}} \Pi^{\rho_x,\delta}_{B^{N(x|x^n)}} 2^{-N(x|x^n)(H(\rho_x)-c\delta)}. \tag{15.87}$$

The following inequalities hold because the sequence x^n is strongly typical as defined in Definition 14.7.2:

$$\bigotimes_{x \in \mathcal{X}} \Pi^{\rho_x,\delta}_{B^{N(x|x^n)}} 2^{-n(p_X(x)+\delta')(H(\rho_x)+c\delta)} \leq \Pi^\delta_{B^n|x^n} \rho_{x^n} \Pi^\delta_{B^n|x^n}$$

$$\leq \bigotimes_{x \in \mathcal{X}} \Pi^{\rho_x,\delta}_{B^{N(x|x^n)}} 2^{-n(p_X(x)-\delta')(H(\rho_x)-c\delta)}. \tag{15.88}$$

We can factor out each term $2^{-n(p_X(x)+\delta')(H(\rho_x)+c\delta)}$ from the tensor products:

$$\prod_{x \in \mathcal{X}} 2^{-n(p_X(x)+\delta')(H(\rho_x)+c\delta)} \bigotimes_{x \in \mathcal{X}} \Pi^{\rho_x,\delta}_{B^{N(x|x^n)}} \le \Pi^{\delta}_{B^n|x^n} \rho_{x^n} \Pi^{\delta}_{B^n|x^n}$$

$$\le \prod_{x \in \mathcal{X}} 2^{-n(p_X(x)-\delta')(H(\rho_x)-c\delta)} \bigotimes_{x \in \mathcal{X}} \Pi^{\rho_x,\delta}_{B^{N(x|x^n)}}. \quad (15.89)$$

We then multiply out the $|\mathcal{X}|$ terms $2^{-n(p_X(x)+\delta')(H(\rho_x)+c\delta)}$:

$$2^{-n\left(H(B|X)+\sum_x (H(\rho_x)\delta'+cp_X(x)\delta+c\delta\delta')\right)} \Pi^{\delta}_{B^n|x^n} \le \Pi^{\delta}_{B^n|x^n} \rho_{x^n} \Pi^{\delta}_{B^n|x^n}$$

$$\le 2^{-n\left(H(B|X)+\sum_x c\delta\delta'-H(\rho_x)\delta'-cp_X(x)\delta\right)} \Pi^{\delta}_{B^n|x^n}. \quad (15.90)$$

The final step below follows because $\sum_x p_X(x) = 1$ and because the bound $\sum H(\rho_x) \le |\mathcal{X}| \log d$ applies where d is the dimension of the density operator ρ_x:

$$2^{-n\left(H(B|X)+\delta''\right)} \Pi^{\delta}_{B^n|x^n} \le \Pi^{\delta}_{B^n|x^n} \rho_{x^n} \Pi^{\delta}_{B^n|x^n} \le 2^{-n\left(H(B|X)-\delta''\right)} \Pi^{\delta}_{B^n|x^n}, \quad (15.91)$$

where

$$\delta'' \equiv \delta' |\mathcal{X}| \log d + c\delta + |\mathcal{X}| c\delta\delta'. \quad (15.92)$$

This concludes the proof. $\qquad\square$

EXERCISE 15.2.2   Prove Property 15.2.5.

15.2.6   Strong Conditional and Marginal Quantum Typicality

We end this section on strong conditional quantum typicality by proving a final property that applies to a state drawn from an ensemble and the typical subspace of the expected density operator of the ensemble.

PROPERTY 15.2.7   Consider an ensemble of the form $\{p_X(x), \rho_x\}$ with expected density operator $\rho \equiv \sum_x p_X(x)\rho_x$. Suppose that x^n is a strongly typical sequence with respect to the distribution $p_X(x)$ and leads to a conditional density operator ρ_{x^n}. Then the probability of measuring ρ_{x^n} in the strongly typical subspace of ρ is high:

$$\text{Tr}\left\{\Pi^n_{\rho,\delta} \, \rho_{x^n}\right\} \ge 1 - \varepsilon, \quad (15.93)$$

for all $\varepsilon \in (0,1)$, $\delta > 0$, and sufficiently large n, where the typical projector $\Pi^n_{\rho,\delta}$ is with respect to the density operator ρ.

Proof   Let the expected density operator have the following spectral decomposition:

$$\rho = \sum_z p_Z(z)|z\rangle\langle z|. \quad (15.94)$$

We define the "pinching" operation as a dephasing with respect to the basis $\{|z\rangle\}$:

$$\sigma \to \Delta(\sigma) \equiv \sum_z |z\rangle\langle z|\sigma|z\rangle\langle z|. \quad (15.95)$$

Let $\bar{\rho}_x$ denote the pinched version of the conditional density operators ρ_x:

$$\bar{\rho}_x \equiv \Delta(\rho_x) = \sum_z |z\rangle\langle z|\rho_x|z\rangle\langle z| = \sum_z p_{Z|X}(z|x)|z\rangle\langle z|, \tag{15.96}$$

where $p_{Z|X}(z|x) \equiv \langle z|\rho_x|z\rangle$. This pinching is the crucial insight for the proof because all of the pinched density operators $\bar{\rho}_x$ have a common eigenbasis and the analysis reduces from a quantum one to a classical one that exploits the properties of strong marginal, conditional, and joint typicality. The following chain of inequalities then holds by exploiting the above definitions:

$$\mathrm{Tr}\left\{\Pi_{\bar{\rho},\delta}^n \rho_{x^n}\right\} = \mathrm{Tr}\left\{\sum_{z^n \in T_\delta^{Z^n}} |z^n\rangle\langle z^n|\rho_{x^n}\right\} \tag{15.97}$$

$$= \mathrm{Tr}\left\{\sum_{z^n \in T_\delta^{Z^n}} |z^n\rangle\langle z^n|z^n\rangle\langle z^n|\rho_{x^n}\right\} \tag{15.98}$$

$$= \mathrm{Tr}\left\{\sum_{z^n \in T_\delta^{Z^n}} |z^n\rangle\langle z^n|\rho_{x^n}|z^n\rangle\langle z^n|\right\} \tag{15.99}$$

$$= \mathrm{Tr}\left\{\sum_{z^n \in T_\delta^{Z^n}} p_{Z^n|X^n}(z^n|x^n)|z^n\rangle\langle z^n|\right\} \tag{15.100}$$

$$= \sum_{z^n \in T_\delta^{Z^n}} p_{Z^n|X^n}(z^n|x^n). \tag{15.101}$$

The first equality follows from the definition of the typical projector $\Pi_{\bar{\rho},\delta}^n$. The second equality follows because $|z^n\rangle\langle z^n|$ is a projector, and the third follows from linearity and cyclicity of the trace. The fourth equality follows because

$$\langle z^n|\rho_{x^n}|z^n\rangle = \prod_{i=1}^n \langle z_i|\rho_{x_i}|z_i\rangle = \prod_{i=1}^n p_{Z|X}(z_i|x_i) \equiv p_{Z^n|X^n}(z^n|x^n). \tag{15.102}$$

Now consider this final expression $\sum_{z^n \in T_\delta^{Z^n}} p_{Z^n|X^n}(z^n|x^n)$. It is equal to the probability that a random conditional sequence $Z^n|x^n$ is in the typical set for $p_Z(z)$:

$$\Pr\left\{Z^n|x^n \in T_\delta^{Z^n}\right\}. \tag{15.103}$$

By taking n large enough, the law of large numbers guarantees that it is highly likely (with probability greater than $1 - \varepsilon$ for any $\varepsilon > 0$) that this random conditional sequence $Z^n|x^n$ is in the conditionally typical set $T_{\delta'}^{Z^n|x^n}$ for some δ'. It then follows that this conditional sequence has a high probability of being in the unconditionally typical set $T_\delta^{Z^n}$ because we assumed that the sequence x^n is strongly typical and Lemma 14.9.1 states that a sequence z^n is unconditionally typical if x^n is strongly typical and z^n is strong conditionally typical. □

15.3   The Method of Types for Quantum Systems

Our final development in this chapter is to establish the method of types in the quantum domain, and the classical tools from Section 14.7 have a straightforward generalization.

We can partition the Hilbert space of n qudits into different type class subspaces, just as we can partition the set of all sequences into different type classes. For example, consider the Hilbert space of three qubits. The computational basis is an orthonormal basis for the entire Hilbert space of three qubits:

$$\{|000\rangle, |001\rangle, |010\rangle, |011\rangle, |100\rangle, |101\rangle, |110\rangle, |111\rangle\}. \tag{15.104}$$

Then the computational basis states with the same Hamming weight form a basis for each type class subspace. So, for the above example, the type class subspaces are as follows:

$$T_0 \equiv \{|000\rangle\}, \tag{15.105}$$
$$T_1 \equiv \{|001\rangle, |010\rangle, |100\rangle\}, \tag{15.106}$$
$$T_2 \equiv \{|011\rangle, |101\rangle, |110\rangle\}, \tag{15.107}$$
$$T_3 \equiv \{|111\rangle\}, \tag{15.108}$$

and the projectors onto the different type class subspaces are as follows:

$$\Pi_0 \equiv |000\rangle\langle000|, \tag{15.109}$$
$$\Pi_1 \equiv |001\rangle\langle001| + |010\rangle\langle010| + |100\rangle\langle100|, \tag{15.110}$$
$$\Pi_2 \equiv |011\rangle\langle011| + |101\rangle\langle101| + |110\rangle\langle110|, \tag{15.111}$$
$$\Pi_3 \equiv |111\rangle\langle111|. \tag{15.112}$$

We can generalize the above example to an n-fold tensor product of qudit systems using the method of types.

DEFINITION 15.3.1 (Type Class Subspace)   The type class subspace is the subspace spanned by all states with the same type:

$$T_{A^n}^t \equiv \operatorname{span}\left\{|x^n\rangle_{A^n} : x^n \in T_t^{X^n}\right\}, \tag{15.113}$$

where the notation $T_{A^n}^t$ on the left-hand side indicates the type class subspace and the notation $T_t^{X^n}$ on the right-hand side indicates the type class of the classical sequence x^n.

DEFINITION 15.3.2 (Type Class Projector)   Let $\Pi_{A^n}^t$ denote the type class subspace projector:

$$\Pi_{A^n}^t \equiv \sum_{x^n \in T_t^{X^n}} |x^n\rangle\langle x^n|_{A^n}. \tag{15.114}$$

PROPERTY 15.3.1 (Resolution of the Identity with Type Class Projectors)   The sum of all type class projectors forms a resolution of the identity on the full Hilbert space $\mathcal{H}_{A^n}$ of n qudits:

$$I_{A^n} = \sum_t \Pi_{A^n}^t, \tag{15.115}$$

where I_{A^n} is the identity operator on $\mathcal{H}_{A^n}$.

DEFINITION 15.3.3 (Maximally Mixed Type Class State)   The maximally mixed density operator proportional to the type class subspace projector is

$$\pi_{A^n}^t \equiv D_t^{-1} \Pi_{A^n}^t, \tag{15.116}$$

where D_t is the dimension of the type class:

$$D_t \equiv \operatorname{Tr}\left\{\Pi_{A^n}^t\right\}. \tag{15.117}$$

Recall from Definition 14.7.4 that a δ-typical type is one for which the empirical distribution has maximum deviation δ from the true distribution, and τ_δ is the set of all δ-typical types. For the quantum case, we determine the maximum deviation δ of a type from the true distribution $p_X(x)$ (this is the distribution from a spectral decomposition of a density operator ρ). This definition allows us to write the strongly δ-typical subspace projector $\Pi_{A^n}^\delta$ of ρ as a sum over all of the δ-typical type class projectors $\Pi_{A^n}^t$:

$$\Pi_{A^n}^\delta = \sum_{t \in \tau_\delta} \Pi_{A^n}^t. \tag{15.118}$$

Some protocols in quantum Shannon theory such as entanglement concentration in Chapter 19 employ the above decomposition of the typical subspace projector into types. The way that such a protocol works is first to perform a typical subspace measurement on many copies of a state, and this measurement succeeds with high probability. One party involved in the protocol then performs a type class measurement $\{\Pi_{A^n}^t\}_t$. We perform this latter measurement in a protocol if we would like the state to have a uniform distribution over states in the type class. One might initially think that the dimension of the remaining state would not be particularly large, but it actually holds that the dimension is large because we can obtain the following useful lower bound on the dimension of any typical type class projector.

PROPERTY 15.3.2 (Minimal Dimension of a Typical Type Class Projector)   Suppose that $p_X(x)$ is the distribution from a spectral decomposition of a density operator ρ, and τ_δ collects all the type class subspaces with maximum deviation δ from the distribution $p_X(x)$. Then for any type $t \in \tau_\delta$ and for sufficiently large n, we can bound the dimension of the type class projector $\Pi_{A^n}^t$ from below as follows:

$$\operatorname{Tr}\left\{\Pi_{A^n}^t\right\} \geq 2^{n[H(\rho)-\eta(d\delta)-d\frac{1}{n}\log(n+1)]}, \tag{15.119}$$

where d is the dimension of the Hilbert space on which ρ acts and the function $\eta(d\delta) \to 0$ as $\delta \to 0$.

Proof   A proof follows directly by exploiting Property 14.7.5 from the previous chapter.   □

15.4   Concluding Remarks

This chapter is about the asymptotic nature of quantum information in the i.i.d. setting. The main technical development is the notion of the typical subspace, and our approach here is simply to "quantize" the definition of the typical set from the previous chapter. The typical subspace enjoys properties similar to those of the typical set—the probability that many copies of a density operator lie in the typical subspace approaches one as the number of copies approaches infinity, the dimension of the typical subspace is exponentially smaller than the dimension of the full Hilbert space, and many copies of a density operator look approximately maximally mixed on the typical subspace. The rest of the content in this chapter involves an extension of these ideas to conditional quantum typicality.

The content in this chapter is here to provide a rigorous underpinning that we can quickly cite later on, and after having mastered the results in this chapter along with the tools in the next two chapters, we will be ready to prove many of the important results in quantum Shannon theory.

15.5   History and Further Reading

Ohya & Petz (1993) devised the notion of a typical subspace, and later Schumacher (1995) independently devised it when he proved the quantum data-compression theorem bearing his name. Holevo (1998) and Schumacher & Westmoreland (1997) introduced the conditionally typical subspace in order to prove the HSW coding theorem. Winter's thesis is a good source for proofs of several properties of quantum typicality (Winter, 1999b). Nielsen & Chuang (2000) use weak conditional quantum typicality to prove the HSW theorem. Bennett et al. (2002) and Holevo (2002b) introduced frequency typical (or strongly typical) subspaces to quantum information theory in order to prove the entanglement-assisted classical capacity theorem. Devetak used strong typicality to prove the HSW coding theorem in Appendix B of Devetak (2005).

16 The Packing Lemma

The packing lemma is a general method for one party to "pack" or encode classical messages into a Hilbert space so that another party can distinguish the encoded messages. The first party can prepare an ensemble of quantum states, and the other party has access to a set of projectors using which he can form a quantum measurement. If the ensemble and the projectors satisfy the conditions of the packing lemma, then it guarantees the existence of a scheme by which the second party can distinguish the classical messages that the first party prepares.

The statement of the packing lemma is quite general, and this approach has a great advantage because we can use it as a primitive for many coding theorems. Examples of coding theorems that we can prove using the packing lemma are the Holevo–Schumacher–Westmoreland (HSW) theorem for the transmission of classical information over a quantum channel and the entanglement-assisted classical capacity theorem for the transmission of classical information over an entanglement-assisted quantum channel (furthermore, Chapter 22 shows that these two protocols are sufficient to generate most known protocols in quantum Shannon theory). Combined with the covering lemma of the next chapter, the packing lemma gives a method for transmitting private classical information over a quantum channel, and this technique in turn gives a way to communicate quantum information over a quantum channel. As long as we can determine an ensemble and a set of projectors satisfying the conditions of the packing lemma, we can apply it in a straightforward way. For example, we prove the HSW coding theorem in Chapter 20 largely by relying on the properties of typical and conditionally typical subspaces that we proved in the previous chapter, and some of these properties are equivalent to the conditions of the packing lemma.

The packing lemma is a "one-shot" lemma because it applies to a general scenario that is not limited only to i.i.d. uses of a quantum channel. This "one-shot" approach is part of the reason that we can apply it to a variety of situations. The technique of proving a "one-shot" result and applying it to the i.i.d. scenario is a common method of attack in quantum Shannon theory (Chapter 17 does this also by establishing a covering lemma, which helps in determining a method for sending private classical information over a quantum channel).

We begin in the next section with a simple example that illustrates the main ideas of the packing lemma. We then generalize this setting and give the statement of the packing lemma. We dissect its proof in several sections that explain the random selection of a code, the construction of a quantum measurement (called the "square-root measurement"), and the error analysis. We then show how to derandomize the packing lemma so that there exists some scheme for packing classical messages into Hilbert space with negligible probability of error for determining each classical message. Finally, we show how a different quantum measurement, called a sequential decoder, can also be used by a receiver to decode the messages transmitted.

16.1   Introductory Example

Suppose that Alice would like to communicate classical information to Bob, and suppose further that she can prepare a message for Bob using the following BB84 ensemble:

$$\{|0\rangle, |1\rangle, |+\rangle, |-\rangle\}, \tag{16.1}$$

where each state occurs with equal probability. Let us label each of the above states by the classical indices a, b, c, and d so that a labels $|0\rangle$, b labels $|1\rangle$, etc. She cannot use all of the states for transmitting classical information because, for example, $|0\rangle$ and $|+\rangle$ are non-orthogonal states and there is no measurement that can distinguish them with high probability.

How can Alice communicate to Bob using this ensemble? She can choose a subset of the states in the BB84 ensemble for transmitting classical information. She can choose the states $|0\rangle$ and $|1\rangle$ for encoding one classical bit of information. Bob can then perform a complete projective measurement in the basis $\{|0\rangle, |1\rangle\}$ to determine the message that Alice encodes. Alternatively, Alice and Bob can use the states $|+\rangle$ and $|-\rangle$ in a similar fashion for encoding one classical bit of information.

In the above example, Alice can send two messages by using the labels a and b only. We say that the labels a and b constitute the *code*. The states $|0\rangle$ and $|1\rangle$ are the *codewords*, the projectors $|0\rangle\langle 0|$ and $|1\rangle\langle 1|$ are each a *codeword projector*, and the projector $|0\rangle\langle 0| + |1\rangle\langle 1|$ is the *code projector* (in this case, the code projector projects onto the whole Hilbert space).

The construction in the above example gives a way to use a certain ensemble for "packing" classical information into Hilbert space, but there is only so much room for packing. For example, it is impossible to encode more than one bit of classical information into a qubit such that someone else can access this classical information reliably—this is the statement of the Holevo bound (Exercise 11.9.2).

16.2   The Setting of the Packing Lemma

We generalize the above example to show how Alice can effectively pack classical information into a Hilbert space such that Bob can retrieve it with high probability. Suppose that Alice's resource for communication is an ensemble

$\{p_X(x), \sigma_x\}_{x \in \mathcal{X}}$ of quantum states that she can prepare for Bob, where the states σ_x are not necessarily perfectly distinguishable. We define the ensemble as follows:

DEFINITION 16.2.1 (Ensemble)   Suppose $\mathcal{X}$ is a set of size $|\mathcal{X}|$ with elements x, and suppose X is a random variable with probability density function $p_X(x)$. Suppose we have an ensemble $\{p_X(x), \sigma_x\}_{x \in \mathcal{X}}$ of quantum states where we encode each realization x into a quantum state $\sigma_x \in \mathcal{D}(\mathcal{H})$. The expected density operator of the ensemble is

$$\sigma \equiv \sum_{x \in \mathcal{X}} p_X(x) \sigma_x. \tag{16.2}$$

How can Alice transmit classical information reliably to Bob by making use of this ensemble? As suggested in the example from the previous section, Alice can select a subset of messages from the set $\mathcal{X}$, and Bob's task is to distinguish this subset of states as best he can. We equip him with certain tools: a *code* subspace projector Π and a set of *codeword* subspace projectors $\{\Pi_x\}_{x \in \mathcal{X}}$ with certain desirable properties (we explain these terms in more detail below). As a rough description, he can use these projectors to construct a quantum measurement that determines the message Alice sends. He would like to be almost certain that the received state lies in the subspace onto which the code subspace projector Π projects. He would also like to use the codeword subspace projectors $\{\Pi_x\}_{x \in \mathcal{X}}$ to determine the classical message that Alice sends. If the ensemble and the projectors satisfy certain conditions, the four conditions of the packing lemma, then it is possible for Bob to build up a measurement such that Alice can communicate reliably with him.

Suppose that Alice chooses some subset $\mathcal{C}$ of $\mathcal{X}$ for encoding classical information. The subset $\mathcal{C}$ that Alice chooses constitutes a *code*. Let us index the code $\mathcal{C}$ by a message set $\mathcal{M}$ with elements labeled by m. The set $\mathcal{M}$ contains messages that Alice would like to transmit to Bob, and we assume that she chooses each message m with equal probability. The subensemble that Alice uses for transmitting classical information is thus as follows:

$$\left\{ \frac{1}{|\mathcal{M}|}, \sigma_{c_m} \right\}, \tag{16.3}$$

where each c_m is a *codeword* that depends on the message m and takes a value in $\mathcal{X}$.

Bob needs a way to determine the classical message that Alice transmits. The most general way that quantum mechanics offers for retrieving classical information is a POVM. Thus, Bob performs some measurement described by a POVM $\{\Lambda_m\}_{m \in \mathcal{M}}$. Bob constructs this POVM by using the codeword subspace projectors $\{\Pi_x\}_{x \in \mathcal{X}}$ and the code subspace projector Π (we give an explicit construction in the proof of the packing lemma, called the "square-root" measurement—later we give a different construction called sequential decoding). If Alice transmits a message m, the probability that Bob correctly retrieves the message m is as follows:

$$\mathrm{Tr}\left\{\Lambda_m \sigma_{c_m}\right\}. \tag{16.4}$$

Thus, the probability of error for a given message m while using the code $\mathcal{C}$ is as follows:

$$p_e(m, \mathcal{C}) \equiv 1 - \mathrm{Tr}\left\{\Lambda_m \sigma_{c_m}\right\} \tag{16.5}$$

$$= \mathrm{Tr}\left\{\left(I - \Lambda_m\right) \sigma_{c_m}\right\}. \tag{16.6}$$

We are interested in the performance of the code $\mathcal{C}$ that Alice and Bob choose, and we consider three different measures of performance.

1. The first and strongest measure of performance is the *maximal probability of error of the code $\mathcal{C}$*. A code $\mathcal{C}$ has maximum probability of error ε if

$$\varepsilon = \max_{m \in \mathcal{M}} p_e(m, \mathcal{C}). \tag{16.7}$$

2. A weaker measure of performance is the *average probability of error $\bar{p}_e(\mathcal{C})$ of the code $\mathcal{C}$*, where

$$\bar{p}_e(\mathcal{C}) \equiv \frac{1}{|\mathcal{M}|} \sum_{m=1}^{|\mathcal{M}|} p_e(m, \mathcal{C}). \tag{16.8}$$

3. The third measure of performance is even weaker than the previous two but turns out to be the most useful in the mathematical proofs. It uses a conceptually different notion of code called a *random code*. Suppose that Alice and Bob choose a code $\mathcal{C}$ randomly from the set of all possible codes according to some probability density $p_{\mathcal{C}}$ (the code $\mathcal{C}$ itself therefore becomes a random variable!). The third measure of performance is the *expectation of the average probability of error of a random code $\mathcal{C}$* where the expectation is with respect to the set of all possible codes, with each code chosen according to some density $p_{\mathcal{C}}$:

$$\mathbb{E}_{\mathcal{C}}\left\{\bar{p}_e(\mathcal{C})\right\} \equiv \mathbb{E}_{\mathcal{C}}\left\{\frac{1}{|\mathcal{M}|} \sum_{m=1}^{|\mathcal{M}|} p_e(m, \mathcal{C})\right\} \tag{16.9}$$

$$= \sum_{\mathcal{C}} p_{\mathcal{C}} \left(\frac{1}{|\mathcal{M}|} \sum_{m=1}^{|\mathcal{M}|} p_e(m, \mathcal{C})\right). \tag{16.10}$$

We will see that considering this performance criterion simplifies the mathematics in the proof of the packing lemma. Then we will employ a series of arguments to strengthen the result from this weakest performance criterion to the first and strongest performance criterion.

16.3 Statement of the Packing Lemma

LEMMA 16.3.1 (Packing Lemma)   Suppose that we have an ensemble as in Definition 16.2.1. Suppose that a code subspace projector Π and codeword subspace projectors $\{\Pi_x\}_{x \in \mathcal{X}}$ exist, they project onto subspaces of $\mathcal{H}$, and these projectors and the ensemble satisfy the following conditions:

$$\text{Tr}\{\Pi \sigma_x\} \geq 1 - \varepsilon, \tag{16.11}$$

$$\text{Tr}\{\Pi_x \sigma_x\} \geq 1 - \varepsilon, \tag{16.12}$$

$$\text{Tr}\{\Pi_x\} \leq d, \tag{16.13}$$

$$\Pi \sigma \Pi \leq \frac{1}{D}\Pi, \tag{16.14}$$

where $\varepsilon \in (0,1)$, $D > 0$, and $d \in (0, D)$. Suppose that $\mathcal{M}$ is a set of size $|\mathcal{M}|$ with elements m. We generate a set $\mathcal{C} = \{C_m\}_{m \in \mathcal{M}}$ of random variables C_m independently at random according to $p_X(x)$, so that each random variable C_m takes a value in $\mathcal{X}$ and corresponds to the message m, but its distribution is independent of the particular message m. The set $\mathcal{C}$ constitutes a random code. Then there exists a corresponding POVM $\{\Lambda_m\}_{m \in \mathcal{M}}$ that reliably distinguishes the states $\{\sigma_{C_m}\}_{m \in \mathcal{M}}$, in the sense that the expectation of the average probability of detecting the correct state is high:

$$\mathbb{E}_{\mathcal{C}}\left\{\frac{1}{|\mathcal{M}|} \sum_{m \in \mathcal{M}} \text{Tr}\{\Lambda_m \sigma_{C_m}\}\right\} \geq 1 - 2\left(\varepsilon + 2\sqrt{\varepsilon}\right) - 4|\mathcal{M}|\frac{d}{D}, \tag{16.15}$$

when D/d is large, $|\mathcal{M}| \ll D/d$, and ε is small.

Condition (16.11) states that the code subspace with projector Π contains each message σ_x with high probability. Condition (16.12) states that each codeword subspace projector Π_x contains its corresponding state σ_x with high probability. Condition (16.13) states that the dimension of each codeword subspace projector Π_x is less than some positive number $d \in (0, D)$. Condition (16.14) states that the expected density operator σ of the ensemble is approximately maximally mixed when projecting it onto the subspace with projector Π. Conditions (16.11) and (16.14) imply that

$$\text{Tr}\{\Pi\} \geq D(1 - \varepsilon), \tag{16.16}$$

so that the dimension of the code subspace projector Π is approximately D if ε is small. We show how to construct a code with messages that Alice wants to send. These four conditions are crucial for constructing a decoding POVM with the desirable property that it can distinguish the encoded messages with high probability.

The main idea of the packing lemma is that we can pack $|\mathcal{M}|$ classical messages into a subspace with corresponding projector Π. There is then a small probability of error when trying to detect the classical messages using codeword subspace projectors Π_x. The intuition is the same as that depicted in Figure 2.6. We are trying to pack as many subspaces of size d into a larger space of size D. In the proof of the HSW coding theorem in Chapter 20, D will be of size $\approx 2^{nH(B)}$ and d will be of size $\approx 2^{nH(B|X)}$, suggesting that we can pack in $\approx 2^{n[H(B)-H(B|X)]} = 2^{nI(X;B)}$ messages while still being able to distinguish them reliably.

16.4   Proof of the Packing Lemma

The proof technique employs a Shannon-like argument in which we generate a code at random. We first show how to construct a POVM, the "pretty good" or "square-root" measurement, that can decode a classical message with high probability. We then prove that the expectation of the average error probability is small (where the expectation is with respect to all random codes). In a corollary in the next section, we finally use standard Shannon-like arguments to show that a code exists whose maximal probability of error for all messages is small.

16.4.1   Code Construction

We present a Shannon-like random coding argument to simplify the mathematics that follow. We construct a code $\mathcal{C}$ at random by independently generating $|\mathcal{M}|$ codewords according to the distribution $p_X(x)$. Let $\mathcal{C} \equiv \{c_m\}_{m \in \mathcal{M}}$ be a collection of the realizations c_m of $|\mathcal{M}|$ independent random variables C_m. Each C_m takes a value c_m in $\mathcal{X}$ with probability $p_X(c_m)$ and represents a classical codeword in the random code $\mathcal{C}$. The probability $p(\mathcal{C})$ of choosing a particular code $\mathcal{C}$ is equal to the following:

$$p(\mathcal{C}) = \prod_{m=1}^{|\mathcal{M}|} p_X(c_m). \tag{16.17}$$

There is a great advantage to choosing the code in this way. The expectation of any product $f(C_m)g(C_{m'})$ of two functions f and g of two different random codewords C_m and $C_{m'}$, where the expectation is with respect to the random choice of code, factors as follows:

$$\mathbb{E}_{\mathcal{C}} \{f(C_m)g(C_{m'})\} = \sum_c p(c)f(c_m)g(c_{m'}) \tag{16.18}$$

$$= \sum_{c_1 \in \mathcal{X}} p_X(c_1) \cdots \sum_{c_{|\mathcal{M}|} \in \mathcal{X}} p_X(c_{|\mathcal{M}|})f(c_m)g(c_{m'}) \tag{16.19}$$

$$= \sum_{c_m \in \mathcal{X}} p_X(c_m)f(c_m) \sum_{c_{m'} \in \mathcal{X}} p_X(c_{m'})g(c_{m'}) \tag{16.20}$$

$$= \mathbb{E}_X \{f(X)\} \mathbb{E}_X \{g(X)\}. \tag{16.21}$$

This factoring happens because of the random way in which we choose the code, and we exploit this fact in the proof of the packing lemma. We employ the following events in sequence:

1. We choose a random code as described above.
2. We reveal the code to the sender and receiver (i.e., they are allowed to meet beforehand to agree on a strategy before communication begins).
3. The sender chooses a message m at random (with uniform probability according to some random variable M) from $\mathcal{M}$ and encodes it in the codeword c_m. The quantum state that the sender transmits is then equal to σ_{c_m}.
4. The receiver performs a POVM $\{\Lambda_m\}_{m \in \mathcal{M}}$ to determine the message that the sender transmits, and each POVM element Λ_m corresponds to a message m in the code. The receiver obtains a classical result from the measurement, and we model it with the random variable M'. The conditional probability $\Pr\{M' = m | M = m\}$ of obtaining the correct result from the measurement is equal to

$$\Pr\{M' = m | M = m\} = \mathrm{Tr}\{\Lambda_m \sigma_{c_m}\}. \tag{16.22}$$

5. The receiver decodes correctly if $M' = M$ and decodes incorrectly if $M' \neq M$.

16.4.2   POVM Construction

We cannot directly use the projectors Π_x in a POVM because they do not satisfy the conditions for being a POVM. Namely, it is not necessarily true that $\sum_{x \in \mathcal{X}} \Pi_x = I$. Furthermore, the codeword subspace projectors Π_x may have support outside that of the code subspace projector Π. It is necessary for us to have the code subspace projector involved in the analysis because we will need to invoke condition (16.14) of the packing lemma.

To remedy these issues, first consider the following set of operators:

$$\forall x \quad \Upsilon_x \equiv \Pi \Pi_x \Pi. \tag{16.23}$$

The operator Υ_x is a positive semi-definite operator, and the effect of "coating" the codeword subspace projector Π_x with the code subspace projector Π is to slice out any part of the support of Π_x that is not in the support of Π. From the conditions (16.11)–(16.12) of the packing lemma, there should be little probability for our states of interest to lie in the part of the support of Π_x outside the support of Π. The operators Υ_x have the desirable property that they only have support inside the subspace corresponding to the code subspace projector Π. So we have remedied the second issue stated above. Exercise 16.5.4 explores an alternative way of resolving this issue.

We now remedy the first problem stated above by constructing a set $\{\Lambda_m\}_{m \in \mathcal{M}}$ with the following elements:

$$\Lambda_m \equiv \left(\sum_{m'=1}^{|\mathcal{M}|} \Upsilon_{c_{m'}}\right)^{-1/2} \Upsilon_{c_m} \left(\sum_{m'=1}^{|\mathcal{M}|} \Upsilon_{c_{m'}}\right)^{-1/2}. \tag{16.24}$$

The elements of the set $\{\Lambda_m\}_{m \in \mathcal{M}}$ constitute the "pretty good" or "square-root" measurement. These elements generally have the property that $\sum_{m=1}^{|\mathcal{M}|} \Lambda_m \leq I$, and we can "complete" the set to be a full POVM by inserting the element $\Lambda_0 \equiv I - \sum_{m=1}^{|\mathcal{M}|} \Lambda_m$ into the set $\{\Lambda_m\}_{m \in \mathcal{M}}$. The extra element Λ_0 corresponds to a failed decoding. Note that the inverse square root $A^{-1/2}$ of a positive semi-definite operator A is defined as the inverse square root operation only on the support of A, per the usual convention from Definition 3.3.1. The idea of the pretty good measurement is that the POVM elements $\{\Lambda_m\}_{m=1}^{|\mathcal{M}|}$ correspond to the messages sent and the element Λ_0 corresponds to an error result (an inability to identify any of the messages).

16.4.3 Error Analysis

Before proceeding with the error analysis, we need the following operator inequality, which will be helpful in analyzing the error probability:

LEMMA 16.4.1 (Hayashi–Nagaoka)   Let $S, T \in \mathcal{L}(\mathcal{H})$ be positive semi-definite operators such that $I - S$ is positive semi-definite also. Then for a strictly positive constant c, the following operator inequality holds:

$$I - (S + T)^{-1/2} S (S + T)^{-1/2} \leq (1 + c)(I - S) + (2 + c + c^{-1}) T. \quad (16.25)$$

Proof For any two operators $A, B \in \mathcal{L}(\mathcal{H})$, the following operator inequality holds

$$(A - cB)^\dagger (A - cB) \geq 0, \quad (16.26)$$

which is equivalent to

$$c^{-1} A^\dagger A + c B^\dagger B \geq A^\dagger B + B^\dagger A. \quad (16.27)$$

Now pick $A = \sqrt{T} R$ and $B = \sqrt{T}(I - R)$, where $R \in \mathcal{L}(\mathcal{H})$, and plug into the above to find that

$$c^{-1} R^\dagger T R + c (I - R)^\dagger T (I - R) \geq R^\dagger T (I - R) + (I - R)^\dagger T R. \quad (16.28)$$

Thus, we find that

$$T = R^\dagger T R + R^\dagger T (I - R) + (I - R)^\dagger T R + (I - R)^\dagger T (I - R) \quad (16.29)$$

$$\leq (1 + c^{-1}) R^\dagger T R + (1 + c)(I - R)^\dagger T (I - R). \quad (16.30)$$

Setting $R = (S + T)^{1/2}$, we find that

$$T \leq (1 + c^{-1})(S + T)^{1/2} T (S + T)^{1/2}$$
$$+ (1 + c)\left(I - (S + T)^{1/2}\right) T \left(I - (S + T)^{1/2}\right). \quad (16.31)$$

Since $T \leq S + T$, we can conclude that

$$T \leq (1 + c^{-1})(S + T)^{1/2} T (S + T)^{1/2}$$
$$+ (1 + c)\left(I - (S + T)^{1/2}\right)(S + T)\left(I - (S + T)^{1/2}\right) \quad (16.32)$$

$$= (S+T)^{1/2} \left[\left(1 + c^{-1} \right) T + \left(1 + c \right) \left(I + S + T - 2 \left(S + T \right)^{1/2} \right) \right] (S+T)^{1/2} \tag{16.33}$$

$$= (S+T)^{1/2} \left[\left(2 + c + c^{-1} \right) T + \left(1 + c \right) \left(I + S - 2 \left(S + T \right)^{1/2} \right) \right] (S+T)^{1/2} \tag{16.34}$$

$$\leq (S+T)^{1/2} \left[\left(2 + c + c^{-1} \right) T + \left(1 + c \right) \left(I + S - 2S \right) \right] (S+T)^{1/2} \tag{16.35}$$

$$= (S+T)^{1/2} \left[\left(2 + c + c^{-1} \right) T + \left(1 + c \right) \left(I - S \right) \right] (S+T)^{1/2} . \tag{16.36}$$

The last inequality follows because $S \leq S^{1/2} \leq (S+T)^{1/2}$. This makes use of the assumption that $S \leq I$ and that fact that the square root function is operator monotone, meaning that if $X \leq Y$ for positive semi-definite X and Y, then $X^{1/2} \leq Y^{1/2}$. Multiplying both sides of this operator inequality by $(S+T)^{-1/2}$, we find that

$$(S+T)^{-1/2} T (S+T)^{-1/2} \leq \left(2 + c + c^{-1} \right) T + \left(1 + c \right) \left(\Pi_{S+T} - S \right), \tag{16.37}$$

where Π_{S+T} denotes the projector onto the support of $S + T$, so that $\Pi_{S+T} T \Pi_{S+T} = T$ and $\Pi_{S+T} S \Pi_{S+T} = S$. Then consider that

$$I - (S+T)^{-1/2} S (S+T)^{-1/2}$$

$$= I - (S+T)^{-1/2} (S+T) (S+T)^{-1/2} + (S+T)^{-1/2} T (S+T)^{-1/2} \tag{16.38}$$

$$= I - \Pi_{S+T} + (S+T)^{-1/2} T (S+T)^{-1/2} \tag{16.39}$$

$$\leq \left(1 + c \right) \left(I - \Pi_{S+T} \right) + \left(2 + c + c^{-1} \right) T + \left(1 + c \right) \left(\Pi_{S+T} - S \right) \tag{16.40}$$

$$= \left(2 + c + c^{-1} \right) T + \left(1 + c \right) \left(I - S \right). \tag{16.41}$$

This concludes the proof. $\qquad\qquad\qquad\qquad\qquad\qquad\qquad\qquad\qquad\qquad\square$

Suppose we have chosen a particular code $\mathcal{C}$. Let $p_e(m, \mathcal{C})$ be the probability of decoding incorrectly given that message m was sent while using the code $\mathcal{C}$:

$$p_e(m, \mathcal{C}) \equiv \text{Tr} \left\{ \left(I - \Lambda_m \right) \sigma_{c_m} \right\}. \tag{16.42}$$

In Lemma 16.4.1, we can set

$$T = \sum_{m' \neq m}^{|\mathcal{M}|} \Upsilon_{c_{m'}}, \qquad S = \Upsilon_{c_m}, \tag{16.43}$$

and pick $c = 1$,[1] so that the bound in (16.25) becomes

$$I - \Lambda_m \leq 2 \left(I - \Upsilon_{c_m} \right) + 4 \sum_{m' \neq m}^{|\mathcal{M}|} \Upsilon_{c_{m'}}. \tag{16.44}$$

---

[1] For our purposes here, it suffices to pick the parameter $c = 1$, but for more fine-tuned error analyses, it is essential to choose the parameter c to vary with other code parameters.

Then using (16.44) and linearity of trace, we obtain the following upper bound on the error probability:

$$p_e(m, \mathcal{C}) \leq 2 \operatorname{Tr} \left\{ (I - \Upsilon_{c_m}) \sigma_{c_m} \right\} + 4 \sum_{m' \neq m}^{|\mathcal{M}|} \operatorname{Tr} \left\{ \Upsilon_{c_{m'}} \sigma_{c_m} \right\}. \tag{16.45}$$

The above bound on the message error probability for code $\mathcal{C}$ has a similar interpretation as that in classical Shannon-like proofs. We bound the error probability by the probability of incorrectly decoding the message m with the message operator Υ_{c_m} (the first term in (16.45)) summed with the probability of confusing the transmitted message with a message $c_{m'}$ different from the transmitted one (the second term in (16.45)).

Consider the first term $\operatorname{Tr} \left\{ (I - \Upsilon_{c_m}) \sigma_{c_m} \right\}$ on the right-hand side of (16.45). We can bound it from above by a small number, simply by applying (16.11)–(16.12) and the gentle operator lemma (Lemma 9.4.2). Consider the following chain of inequalities:

$$\operatorname{Tr} \left\{ \Upsilon_{c_m} \sigma_{c_m} \right\} = \operatorname{Tr} \left\{ \Pi \Pi_{c_m} \Pi \sigma_{c_m} \right\} \tag{16.46}$$

$$= \operatorname{Tr} \left\{ \Pi_{c_m} \Pi \sigma_{c_m} \Pi \right\} \tag{16.47}$$

$$\geq \operatorname{Tr} \left\{ \Pi_{c_m} \sigma_{c_m} \right\} - \left\| \Pi \sigma_{c_m} \Pi - \sigma_{c_m} \right\|_1 \tag{16.48}$$

$$\geq 1 - \varepsilon - 2\sqrt{\varepsilon}. \tag{16.49}$$

The first equality follows from the definition of Υ_{c_m} in (16.23). The second equality follows from cyclicity of the trace. The first inequality follows from applying Exercise 9.1.8. The last inequality follows from applying (16.11) to $\operatorname{Tr} \left\{ \Pi_{c_m} \sigma_{c_m} \right\}$ and from applying (16.12) and the gentle operator lemma (Lemma 9.4.2) to $\left\| \Pi \sigma_{c_m} \Pi - \sigma_{c_m} \right\|_1$. The above bound then implies the following one:

$$\operatorname{Tr} \left\{ (I - \Upsilon_{c_m}) \sigma_{c_m} \right\} = 1 - \operatorname{Tr} \left\{ \Upsilon_{c_m} \sigma_{c_m} \right\} \leq \varepsilon + 2\sqrt{\varepsilon}, \tag{16.50}$$

and by substituting into (16.45), we get the following bound on the probability of error:

$$p_e(m, \mathcal{C}) \leq 2 \left(\varepsilon + 2\sqrt{\varepsilon} \right) + 4 \sum_{m' \neq m}^{|\mathcal{M}|} \operatorname{Tr} \left\{ \Upsilon_{c_{m'}} \sigma_{c_m} \right\}. \tag{16.51}$$

The average error probability $\bar{p}_e(\mathcal{C})$ over all transmitted messages for code $\mathcal{C}$ is

$$\bar{p}_e(\mathcal{C}) = \frac{1}{|\mathcal{M}|} \sum_{m=1}^{|\mathcal{M}|} p_e(m, \mathcal{C}), \tag{16.52}$$

if we assume that Alice chooses the message m according to the uniform distribution. From (16.51), we see that the average error probability $\bar{p}_e(\mathcal{C})$ obeys the following bound:

$$\bar{p}_e(\mathcal{C}) \leq 2 \left(\varepsilon + 2\sqrt{\varepsilon} \right) + \frac{4}{|\mathcal{M}|} \sum_{m=1}^{|\mathcal{M}|} \sum_{m' \neq m}^{|\mathcal{M}|} \operatorname{Tr} \left\{ \Upsilon_{c_{m'}} \sigma_{c_m} \right\}. \tag{16.53}$$

At this point, bounding the average error probability further is a bit difficult, given the sheer number of combinations of terms $\text{Tr}\{\Upsilon_{c_{m'}}\sigma_{c_m}\}$ that we would have to consider to do so. Thus, we now invoke the classic Shannon argument in order to simplify the mathematics. Instead of considering the average probability of error, we consider the expectation of the average error probability $\mathbb{E}_{\mathcal{C}}\{\bar{p}_e(\mathcal{C})\}$ with respect to all possible random codes $\mathcal{C}$. Considering this error quantity significantly simplifies the mathematics because of the way in which we constructed the code. We can use the probability distribution $p_X(x)$ to compute the expectation $\mathbb{E}_{\mathcal{C}}$ because we constructed our code according to this distribution. The bound above becomes as follows, now denoting each codeword as a random variable C_m:

$$\mathbb{E}_{\mathcal{C}}\{\bar{p}_e(\mathcal{C})\} \leq \mathbb{E}_{\mathcal{C}}\left\{2\left(\varepsilon + 2\sqrt{\varepsilon}\right) + \frac{4}{|\mathcal{M}|}\sum_{m=1}^{|\mathcal{M}|}\sum_{m'\neq m}^{|\mathcal{M}|}\text{Tr}\left\{\Upsilon_{C_{m'}}\sigma_{C_m}\right\}\right\} \tag{16.54}$$

$$= 2\left(\varepsilon + 2\sqrt{\varepsilon}\right) + \frac{4}{|\mathcal{M}|}\sum_{m=1}^{|\mathcal{M}|}\sum_{m'\neq m}^{|\mathcal{M}|}\mathbb{E}_{\mathcal{C}}\left\{\text{Tr}\left\{\Upsilon_{C_{m'}}\sigma_{C_m}\right\}\right\}, \tag{16.55}$$

where the equality follows from the linearity of expectation.

We now calculate the expectation of $\text{Tr}\{\Upsilon_{C_{m'}}\sigma_{C_m}\}$ over all random codes $\mathcal{C}$:

$$\mathbb{E}_{\mathcal{C}}\left\{\text{Tr}\left\{\Upsilon_{C_{m'}}\sigma_{C_m}\right\}\right\} = \mathbb{E}_{\mathcal{C}}\left\{\text{Tr}\left\{\Pi\Pi_{C_{m'}}\Pi\sigma_{C_m}\right\}\right\} \tag{16.56}$$

$$= \mathbb{E}_{\mathcal{C}}\left\{\text{Tr}\left\{\Pi_{C_{m'}}\Pi\sigma_{C_m}\Pi\right\}\right\} \tag{16.57}$$

$$= \mathbb{E}_{C_m,C_{m'}}\left\{\text{Tr}\left\{\Pi_{C_{m'}}\Pi\sigma_{C_m}\Pi\right\}\right\}. \tag{16.58}$$

The first equality follows from the definition in (16.23), and the second equality follows from cyclicity of trace. The third equality follows because only the codewords for m and m' are involved. Independence of random variables C_m and $C_{m'}$ (from the code construction) gives that the above expression equals

$$\text{Tr}\left\{\mathbb{E}_{C_{m'}}\{\Pi_{C_{m'}}\}\Pi\mathbb{E}_{C_m}\{\sigma_{C_m}\}\Pi\right\} = \text{Tr}\left\{\mathbb{E}_{C_{m'}}\{\Pi_{C_{m'}}\}\Pi\sigma\Pi\right\} \tag{16.59}$$

$$\leq \text{Tr}\left\{\mathbb{E}_{C_{m'}}\{\Pi_{C_{m'}}\}\frac{1}{D}\Pi\right\} \tag{16.60}$$

$$= \frac{1}{D}\text{Tr}\left\{\mathbb{E}_{C_{m'}}\{\Pi_{C_{m'}}\}\Pi\right\}, \tag{16.61}$$

where the first equality uses the fact that $\mathbb{E}_{C_m}\{\sigma_{C_m}\} = \sum_{x\in\mathcal{X}}p(x)\sigma_x = \sigma$ and Π is a constant with respect to the expectation. The first inequality uses the fourth condition (16.14) of the packing lemma, the fact that $\Pi\sigma\Pi$, Π, and $\Pi_{C_{m'}}$ are all positive semi-definite operators, and $\text{Tr}\{CA\} \geq \text{Tr}\{CB\}$ for $C \geq 0$ and $A \geq B$. Continuing, we have

$$\frac{1}{D} \operatorname{Tr} \left\{ \mathbb{E}_{C_{m'}} \{ \Pi_{C_{m'}} \} \Pi \right\} \leq \frac{1}{D} \operatorname{Tr} \left\{ \mathbb{E}_{C_{m'}} \{ \Pi_{C_{m'}} \} \right\} \tag{16.62}$$

$$= \frac{1}{D} \mathbb{E}_{C_{m'}} \left\{ \operatorname{Tr} \{ \Pi_{C_{m'}} \} \right\} \tag{16.63}$$

$$\leq \frac{d}{D}. \tag{16.64}$$

The first inequality follows from the fact that $\Pi \leq I$ and $\Pi_{C_{m'}}$ is a positive semi-definite operator. The last inequality follows from (16.13). The following inequality then holds by considering the development from (16.56) to (16.64):

$$\mathbb{E}_{\mathcal{C}} \left\{ \operatorname{Tr} \left\{ \Upsilon_{C_{m'}} \sigma_{C_m} \right\} \right\} \leq \frac{d}{D}. \tag{16.65}$$

We substitute into (16.55) to show that the expectation $\mathbb{E}_{\mathcal{C}} \{ \bar{p}_e(\mathcal{C}) \}$ of the average error probability $\bar{p}_e(\mathcal{C})$ over all codes obeys the bound stated in the packing lemma:

$$\mathbb{E}_{\mathcal{C}} \{ \bar{p}_e(\mathcal{C}) \} \leq 2 \left(\varepsilon + 2\sqrt{\varepsilon} \right) + \frac{4}{|\mathcal{M}|} \sum_{m=1}^{|\mathcal{M}|} \sum_{m' \neq m}^{|\mathcal{M}|} \mathbb{E}_{\mathcal{C}} \left\{ \operatorname{Tr} \left\{ \sigma_{c_m} \Upsilon_{c_{m'}} \right\} \right\} \tag{16.66}$$

$$\leq 2 \left(\varepsilon + 2\sqrt{\varepsilon} \right) + \frac{4}{|\mathcal{M}|} \sum_{m=1}^{|\mathcal{M}|} \sum_{m' \neq m}^{|\mathcal{M}|} \frac{d}{D} \tag{16.67}$$

$$\leq 2 \left(\varepsilon + 2\sqrt{\varepsilon} \right) + 4 \left(|\mathcal{M}| - 1 \right) \frac{d}{D} \tag{16.68}$$

$$\leq 2 \left(\varepsilon + 2\sqrt{\varepsilon} \right) + 4 |\mathcal{M}| \frac{d}{D}. \tag{16.69}$$

16.5   Derandomization and Expurgation

The above version of the packing lemma is a randomized version that shows how the expectation of the average probability of error is small. We now prove a derandomized version that guarantees the existence of a code with small maximal error probability for each message. The last two arguments are traditionally called *derandomization* and *expurgation*.

COROLLARY 16.5.1   Suppose we have the ensemble as in Definition 16.2.1. Suppose that a code subspace projector Π and codeword subspace projectors $\{ \Pi_x \}_{x \in \mathcal{X}}$ exist, they project onto subspaces of $\mathcal{H}$, and these projectors and the ensemble have the following properties:

$$\operatorname{Tr} \{ \Pi \sigma_x \} \geq 1 - \varepsilon, \tag{16.70}$$

$$\operatorname{Tr} \{ \Pi_x \sigma_x \} \geq 1 - \varepsilon, \tag{16.71}$$

$$\operatorname{Tr} \{ \Pi_x \} \leq d, \tag{16.72}$$

$$\Pi \sigma \Pi \leq \frac{1}{D} \Pi, \tag{16.73}$$

where $\varepsilon \in (0,1)$ and $d \in (0,D)$. Suppose that $\mathcal{M}$ is a set of size $|\mathcal{M}|$ with elements m. Then there exists a code $\mathcal{C}_0 = \{c_m\}_{m \in \mathcal{M}}$ with codewords c_m depending on the message m and taking values in $\mathcal{X}$, and there exists a corresponding POVM $\{\Lambda_m\}_{m \in \mathcal{M}}$ that reliably distinguishes the states $\{\sigma_{c_m}\}_{m \in \mathcal{M}}$ in the sense that the probability of detecting the correct state is high:

$$\forall m \in \mathcal{M} \qquad \mathrm{Tr}\{\Lambda_m \sigma_{c_m}\} \geq 1 - 4\left(\varepsilon + 2\sqrt{\varepsilon}\right) - 16\left|\mathcal{M}\right| \frac{d}{D}, \tag{16.74}$$

if ε is small and $|\mathcal{M}| \ll D/d$. We can then use the code $\mathcal{C}_0$ and the POVM $\{\Lambda_m\}_{m \in \mathcal{M}}$ to encode and decode, respectively, $|\mathcal{M}|$ classical messages with high success probability.

Proof Generate a random code according to the construction in the previous lemma. The expectation of the average error probability then satisfies the bound in the statement of the packing lemma. We now make a few standard Shannon-like arguments to strengthen the result of the previous lemma.

Derandomization. The expectation of the average error probability $\mathbb{E}_{\mathcal{C}}\{\bar{p}_e(\mathcal{C})\}$ satisfies the following bound:

$$\mathbb{E}_{\mathcal{C}}\{\bar{p}_e(\mathcal{C})\} \leq 2\left(\varepsilon + 2\sqrt{\varepsilon}\right) + 4\left|\mathcal{M}\right| \frac{d}{D}. \tag{16.75}$$

It then follows that the average error probability of at least one code $\mathcal{C}_0 = \{c_m\}_{m \in \mathcal{M}}$ satisfies the same bound:

$$\bar{p}_e(\mathcal{C}_0) \leq 2\left(\varepsilon + 2\sqrt{\varepsilon}\right) + 4\left|\mathcal{M}\right| \frac{d}{D}. \tag{16.76}$$

Choose this code $\mathcal{C}_0$ as the code, and it is possible to find this code $\mathcal{C}_0$ in practice by exhaustive search. This process is known as *derandomization*.

EXERCISE 16.5.1   Use Markov's inequality to prove the following strong statement: if $\varepsilon' \equiv 2\left(\varepsilon + 2\sqrt{\varepsilon}\right) + 4\left|\mathcal{M}\right| \frac{d}{D}$ is small, then the overwhelming fraction $1 - \sqrt{\varepsilon'}$ of codes contructed randomly have average error probability less than $\sqrt{\varepsilon'}$.

Expurgation. We now go from average error probability to maximal error probability instead by employing an expurgation argument. We know from Exercise 2.2.1 that $p_e(m) \leq 2\left[2\left(\varepsilon + 2\sqrt{\varepsilon}\right) + 4\left|\mathcal{M}\right| \frac{d}{D}\right]$ for at least half of the indices (if it were not true, then these indices would contribute more than ε' to the average error probability $\bar{p}_e$). Throw out the half of the codewords with the worst decoding probability and redefine the code according to the new set of indices. If we redefine the message set $\mathcal{M}'$ such that the message size $|\mathcal{M}'| = |\mathcal{M}|/2$, then the error bound becomes $p_e(m) \leq 2\left[2\left(\varepsilon + 2\sqrt{\varepsilon}\right) + 8\left|\mathcal{M}'\right| \frac{d}{D}\right]$. We could then use the decoding POVM from the original code and be guaranteed that every codeword has an error probability no larger than this amount (alternatively, we could also use a modified square-root decoding POVM that is built from the codeword subspace projectors remaining after expurgation). These steps have a negligible effect on the parameters of the code when we later consider a large number of uses of a noisy quantum channel.   □

EXERCISE 16.5.2   Use Markov's inequality to prove an even stronger expurgation argument (following on the result of Exercise 16.5.1). Prove that we can retain a large fraction $1 - \sqrt[4]{\varepsilon'}$ of the codewords (expurgating $\sqrt[4]{\varepsilon'}$ of them) so that each remaining codeword has error probability less than $\sqrt[4]{\varepsilon'}$.

EXERCISE 16.5.3   Prove that the packing lemma and its corollary hold for the same ensemble and a set of projectors for which the following conditions hold:

$$\sum_{x \in \mathcal{X}} p_X(x) \operatorname{Tr}\{\sigma_x \Pi\} \geq 1 - \varepsilon, \tag{16.77}$$

$$\sum_{x \in \mathcal{X}} p_X(x) \operatorname{Tr}\{\sigma_x \Pi_x\} \geq 1 - \varepsilon, \tag{16.78}$$

$$\operatorname{Tr}\{\Pi_x\} \leq d, \tag{16.79}$$

$$\Pi \sigma \Pi \leq \frac{1}{D} \Pi. \tag{16.80}$$

EXERCISE 16.5.4   Prove that a variation of the packing lemma holds in which the POVM is of the following form:

$$\Lambda_m \equiv \left(\sum_{m'=1}^{|\mathcal{M}|} \Pi_{c_{m'}} \right)^{-1/2} \Pi_{c_m} \left(\sum_{m'=1}^{|\mathcal{M}|} \Pi_{c_{m'}} \right)^{-1/2}. \tag{16.81}$$

That is, it is not actually necessary to "coat" each operator in the square-root measurement with the overall message subspace projector.

16.6   Sequential Decoding

We now prove a variation of the packing lemma by making use of a completely different decoding scheme, called *sequential decoding*. This scheme has the receiver perform sequential tests using the codeword subspace projectors to "ask" sequentially, "Was the first codeword sent?", "The second?", "The third?", etc. until the outcome of one of these measurements is "yes."

It is perhaps unintuitive that such a measurement strategy should work. After all, we are well aware by this point that measurements can disturb the state of a quantum system. However, what the packing lemma demonstrates is that if good codeword projectors are available and we do not try to pack in too many messages, then reliable decoding is possible. This also means that the codewords selected are approximately orthogonal. In this sense, it is perhaps less surprising that such a sequential decoding strategy should work if we know that the states to be distinguished are approximately orthogonal. The main tool for analyzing the performance of a sequential decoder is the "non-commutative union bound"

(Lemma 16.6.1) which is a generalization of the union bound from probability theory.

Here we divide up the proof into several parts, and some of the analysis is similar to that presented in the previous section. The parts of the proof consist of codebook generation, POVM construction, and the error analysis. We begin with all of the objects and premises of the Packing Lemma (in Lemma 16.3.1).

Codebook Generation. This part is exactly the same as before, so we instead point to the discussion of this part in Section 16.4.1.

POVM Construction. The method for Bob to decode the state that Alice transmits is as follows: Bob should first ask "Is the received state in the code subspace?" He can do this operationally by performing the measurement $\{\Pi, I - \Pi\}$. Next, he asks in sequential order, "Is the received codeword in the ith codeword subspace?" This is in some sense equivalent to the question, "Is the received codeword the ith transmitted codeword?" He can ask these questions operationally by performing the codeword subspace measurements $\{\Pi_{c_i}, I - \Pi_{c_i}\}$.

Why should this sequential decoding scheme work well? Supposing that Alice transmits message m, one reason is that the encoded state σ_{c_m} lies in the code subspace with high probability, as indicated by (16.11). Also, the projector Π_{c_m} is a "good detector" for the encoded state σ_{c_m}, due to (16.12).

Error Analysis. The probability of detecting the mth codeword correctly under our sequential decoding scheme is equal to

$$\text{Tr}\left\{\Pi_{c_m}\hat{\Pi}_{c_{m-1}}\cdots\hat{\Pi}_{c_1}\Pi\sigma_{c_m}\Pi\hat{\Pi}_{c_1}\cdots\hat{\Pi}_{c_{m-1}}\Pi_{c_m}\right\}, \tag{16.82}$$

where we make the abbreviation $\hat{\Pi}_{c_m} \equiv I - \Pi_{c_m}$. That is, the receiver should get an initial "yes" for projecting into the code subspace, $m - 1$ "no"s, and finally a "yes" for the mth test. Thus, the probability of an incorrect detection for the mth codeword is given by

$$1 - \text{Tr}\left\{\Pi_{c_m}\hat{\Pi}_{c_{m-1}}\cdots\hat{\Pi}_{c_1}\Pi\sigma_{c_m}\Pi\hat{\Pi}_{c_1}\cdots\hat{\Pi}_{c_{m-1}}\Pi_{c_m}\right\}, \tag{16.83}$$

and the average error probability of this scheme is equal to

$$1 - \frac{1}{|\mathcal{M}|}\sum_m \text{Tr}\left\{\Pi_{c_m}\hat{\Pi}_{c_{m-1}}\cdots\hat{\Pi}_{c_1}\Pi\sigma_{c_m}\Pi\hat{\Pi}_{c_1}\cdots\hat{\Pi}_{c_{m-1}}\Pi_{c_m}\right\}. \tag{16.84}$$

Instead of analyzing the average error probability, we analyze the expectation of the average error probability, where the expectation is with respect to the random choice of code:

$$1 - \mathbb{E}_{\mathcal{C}}\left\{\frac{1}{|\mathcal{M}|}\sum_m \text{Tr}\left\{\Pi_{C_m}\hat{\Pi}_{C_{m-1}}\cdots\hat{\Pi}_{C_1}\Pi\sigma_{C_m}\Pi\hat{\Pi}_{C_1}\cdots\hat{\Pi}_{C_{m-1}}\Pi_{C_m}\right\}\right\}. \tag{16.85}$$

We rewrite the above expression just slightly, by observing that

$$1 = \mathbb{E}_{\mathcal{C}}\left\{\frac{1}{|\mathcal{M}|}\sum_m \text{Tr}\left\{\sigma_{C_m}\right\}\right\} \tag{16.86}$$

$$= \mathbb{E}_{\mathcal{C}} \left\{ \frac{1}{|\mathcal{M}|} \sum_m \mathrm{Tr}\left\{ \Pi \sigma_{C_m} \right\} + \mathrm{Tr}\left\{ \hat{\Pi} \sigma_{C_m} \right\} \right\} \tag{16.87}$$

$$\leq \mathbb{E}_{\mathcal{C}} \left\{ \frac{1}{|\mathcal{M}|} \sum_m \mathrm{Tr}\left\{ \Pi \sigma_{C_m} \Pi \right\} \right\} + \varepsilon, \tag{16.88}$$

where we have used (16.11) in the last line. Substituting into (16.85) (and forgetting about the small ε term for now) gives an upper bound of

$$\mathbb{E}_{\mathcal{C}} \left\{ \frac{1}{|\mathcal{M}|} \sum_m \mathrm{Tr}\left\{ \Pi \sigma_{C_m} \Pi \right\} - \mathrm{Tr}\left\{ \Pi_{C_m} \hat{\Pi}_{C_{m-1}} \cdots \hat{\Pi}_{C_1} \Pi \sigma_{C_m} \Pi \hat{\Pi}_{C_1} \cdots \hat{\Pi}_{C_{m-1}} \Pi_{C_m} \right\} \right\}. \tag{16.89}$$

We now need a tool for analyzing this error probability, which is known as the non-commutative union bound:

LEMMA 16.6.1 (Non-Commutative Union Bound)   Let ω be such that $\omega \geq 0$ and $\mathrm{Tr}\{\omega\} \leq 1$. Let $P_1, \ldots, P_L$ be Hermitian projectors. Then

$$\mathrm{Tr}\{\omega\} - \mathrm{Tr}\{P_L \cdots P_1 \omega P_1 \cdots P_L\} \leq 2\sqrt{\sum_{i=1}^L \mathrm{Tr}\{(I - P_i)\omega\}}. \tag{16.90}$$

Proof It suffices to prove the following bound for a vector $|\psi\rangle$ such that $\||\psi\rangle\|_2^2 \leq 1$:

$$\||\psi\rangle\|_2^2 - \|P_L \cdots P_1 |\psi\rangle\|_2^2 \leq 2\sqrt{\sum_{i=1}^L \|(I - P_i)|\psi\rangle\|_2^2}. \tag{16.91}$$

This is because

$$\||\psi\rangle\|_2^2 = \mathrm{Tr}\{|\psi\rangle\langle\psi|\}, \tag{16.92}$$

$$\|P_L \cdots P_1 |\psi\rangle\|_2^2 = \mathrm{Tr}\{P_L \cdots P_1 |\psi\rangle\langle\psi| P_1 \cdots P_L\}, \tag{16.93}$$

$$\|(I - P_i)|\psi\rangle\|_2^2 = \mathrm{Tr}\{(I - P_i)|\psi\rangle\langle\psi|\}, \tag{16.94}$$

and any ω satisfying the conditions given can be written as a convex combination $\omega = \sum_z p(z)|\psi_z\rangle\langle\psi_z|$ where $p(z)$ is a probability distribution and each $|\psi_z\rangle$ satisfies $\||\psi_z\rangle\|_2^2 \leq 1$. Then (16.90) follows from (16.91) by concavity of the square root function. So we now focus on proving (16.91). We begin by showing that

$$\||\psi\rangle - P_L \cdots P_1 |\psi\rangle\|_2^2 \leq \sum_{i=1}^L \|(I - P_i)|\psi\rangle\|_2^2. \tag{16.95}$$

To see this, consider that

$$\||\psi\rangle - P_L \cdots P_1 |\psi\rangle\|_2^2$$
$$= \|(I - P_L)|\psi\rangle\|_2^2 + \|P_L (|\psi\rangle - P_{L-1} \cdots P_1 |\psi\rangle)\|_2^2 \tag{16.96}$$

$$\leq \||(I - P_L)|\psi\rangle\|_2^2 + \||\psi\rangle - P_{L-1}\cdots P_1|\psi\rangle\|_2^2 \tag{16.97}$$

$$\leq \sum_{i=1}^{L} \||(I - P_i)|\psi\rangle\|_2^2. \tag{16.98}$$

The first equality follows from the Pythagorean theorem. The first inequality follows because a projection cannot increase the norm of a vector. The last inequality is by induction. Now we take the square root of (16.95):

$$\||\psi\rangle - P_L \cdots P_1|\psi\rangle\|_2 \leq \sqrt{\sum_{i=1}^{L} \||(I - P_i)|\psi\rangle\|_2^2}, \tag{16.99}$$

from which we can conclude the following by the triangle inequality:

$$\||\psi\rangle\|_2 - \|P_L \cdots P_1|\psi\rangle\|_2 \leq \sqrt{\sum_{i=1}^{L} \||(I - P_i)|\psi\rangle\|_2^2}. \tag{16.100}$$

Then rearrange this as follows:

$$\||\psi\rangle\|_2 - \sqrt{\sum_{i=1}^{L} \||(I - P_i)|\psi\rangle\|_2^2} \leq \|P_L \cdots P_1|\psi\rangle\|_2 \tag{16.101}$$

and square both sides to get

$$\left(\||\psi\rangle\|_2 - \sqrt{\sum_{i=1}^{L} \||(I - P_i)|\psi\rangle\|_2^2} \right)^2$$

$$= \||\psi\rangle\|_2^2 - 2\||\psi\rangle\|_2 \sqrt{\sum_{i=1}^{L} \||(I - P_i)|\psi\rangle\|_2^2} + \sum_{i=1}^{L} \||(I - P_i)|\psi\rangle\|_2^2 \tag{16.102}$$

$$\leq \|P_L \cdots P_1|\psi\rangle\|_2^2. \tag{16.103}$$

This then implies (16.91) by dropping the non-negative term $\sum_{i=1}^{L} \||(I - P_i)|\psi\rangle\|_2^2$. $\square$

REMARK 16.6.1 We can think of the bound in (16.90) as a "non-commutative union bound" because it is analogous to the following union bound from probability theory:

$$\Pr\left\{ (A_1 \cap \cdots \cap A_N)^c \right\} = \Pr\left\{ A_1^c \cup \cdots \cup A_N^c \right\} \leq \sum_{i=1}^{N} \Pr\left\{ A_i^c \right\}, \tag{16.104}$$

where $A_1, \ldots, A_N$ are events. The analogous bound for projector logic would be

$$\mathrm{Tr}\left\{ (I - P_1 \cdots P_N \cdots P_1) \rho \right\} \leq \sum_{i=1}^{N} \mathrm{Tr}\left\{ (I - P_i) \rho \right\}, \tag{16.105}$$

if we think of $P_1 \cdots P_N$ as a projector onto the intersection of subspaces. However, the above bound only holds if the projectors $P_1, \ldots, P_N$ are commuting (choosing $P_1 = |+\rangle\langle+|$, $P_2 = |0\rangle\langle0|$, and $\rho = |0\rangle\langle0|$ gives a counterexample). If the projectors are non-commuting, then the non-commutative union bound seems to be the next best thing and suffices for our purposes here.

Continuing, we then apply the non-commutative union bound to the expression in (16.89) with $\omega = \Pi \sigma_{C_m} \Pi$ and the sequential projectors as Π_{C_m}, $\hat{\Pi}_{C_{m-1}}$, $\dots$, $\hat{\Pi}_{C_1}$. This gives the following upper bound on (16.89):

$$
\mathbb{E}_{\mathcal{C}}\left\{ \frac{1}{|\mathcal{M}|} \sum_m 2 \left[\mathrm{Tr}\left\{(I - \Pi_{C_m})\Pi\sigma_{C_m}\Pi\right\} + \sum_{i=1}^{m-1} \mathrm{Tr}\left\{\Pi_{C_i}\Pi\sigma_{C_m}\Pi\right\} \right]^{1/2} \right\}
$$

$$
\leq 2 \left[\mathbb{E}_{\mathcal{C}}\left\{ \frac{1}{|\mathcal{M}|} \sum_m \mathrm{Tr}\left\{(I - \Pi_{C_m})\Pi\sigma_{C_m}\Pi\right\} + \sum_{i\neq m} \mathrm{Tr}\left\{\Pi_{C_i}\Pi\sigma_{C_m}\Pi\right\} \right\} \right]^{1/2},
$$

$$(16.106)$$

where the inequality follows from concavity of the square root function and by summing over all of the codewords not equal to the mth codeword (these terms can only increase the expression). At this point, we have two error terms to analyze that are essentially the same as those in (16.45). Thus, we can invoke the analysis from before to conclude that

$$
\mathrm{Tr}\left\{(I - \Pi_{c_m})\Pi\sigma_{c_m}\Pi\right\} \leq \varepsilon + 2\sqrt{\varepsilon}, \tag{16.107}
$$

$$
\mathbb{E}_{\mathcal{C}}\left\{ \frac{1}{|\mathcal{M}|} \sum_m \sum_{i\neq m} \mathrm{Tr}\left\{\Pi_{C_i}\Pi\sigma_{C_m}\Pi\right\} \right\} \leq |\mathcal{M}|\frac{d}{D}, \tag{16.108}
$$

which leads to a final bound of

$$
1 - \mathbb{E}_{\mathcal{C}}\left\{ \frac{1}{|\mathcal{M}|} \sum_m \mathrm{Tr}\left\{ \Pi_{C_m}\hat{\Pi}_{C_{m-1}}\cdots\hat{\Pi}_{C_1}\Pi\sigma_{C_m}\Pi\hat{\Pi}_{C_1}\cdots\hat{\Pi}_{C_{m-1}}\Pi_{C_m} \right\} \right\}
$$

$$
\leq 2\sqrt{\varepsilon + 2\sqrt{\varepsilon} + |\mathcal{M}|\frac{d}{D}} + \varepsilon. \tag{16.109}
$$

We can then derandomize and expurgate codewords as before to establish the existence of a code and a sequential decoder with maximum error probability no larger than $4(\varepsilon + 2\sqrt{\varepsilon} + 2|\mathcal{M}|d/D)^{1/2} + 2\varepsilon$.

EXERCISE 16.6.1   Following Exercise 16.5.4, show that a variation of the sequential decoder, in which there is no initial code subspace projection, works well for decoding the messages transmitted.

EXERCISE 16.6.2   Show that the sequential decoding strategy works when assuming only the conditions in Exercise 16.5.3.

16.7   History and Further Reading

Holevo (1998) and Schumacher & Westmoreland (1997) did not prove the classical coding theorem using the packing lemma, but they instead used other arguments to bound the probability of error. The operator inequality in (16.25) is at the heart of the packing lemma. Hayashi & Nagaoka (2003) proved this operator inequality in order to develop the more general setting of the quantum information spectrum method, where there is no i.i.d. constraint and essentially no structure to a channel. Hsieh, Devetak & Winter (2008) later exploited this operator inequality in the context of entanglement-assisted classical coding and followed the approach in Hayashi & Nagaoka (2003) to prove the packing lemma.

Giovannetti et al. (2012) and Lloyd et al. (2011) introduced the method of sequential decoding to quantum information theory. Sen (2011) proved the non-commutative union bound and applied it to various problems in quantum information theory. Wilde (2013) extended the non-commutative union bound to non-projective tests (ones of the form $\{\Lambda, I - \Lambda\}$ for $\Lambda \geq 0$) and established a "one-shot" characterization of sequential decoding for classical communication.

17 The Covering Lemma

The goal of the covering lemma is perhaps opposite to that of the packing lemma because it applies to a setting in which one party wishes to make messages *indistinguishable* to another party (instead of trying to make them distinguishable, as in the packing lemma of the previous chapter). That is, the covering lemma is helpful when one party is trying to simulate a noisy channel to another party, rather than trying to simulate a noiseless channel. One party can accomplish this task by randomly "covering" the Hilbert space of the other party (this viewpoint gives the covering lemma its name).

One can certainly simulate noise by choosing a quantum state uniformly at random from a large set of quantum states and passing along the chosen quantum state to a third party without indicating which state was chosen. But the problem with this approach is that it could potentially be expensive if the set from which we choose a random state is large, and we would really like to use as few resources as possible in order to simulate noise. That is, we would like the set from which we choose a quantum state uniformly at random to be as small as possible when simulating noise. The covering lemma is similar to the packing lemma in the sense that its conditions for application are general (involving bounds on projectors and an ensemble), and it gives an effective scheme for simulating noise when we apply it in an i.i.d. setting.

One application of the covering lemma in quantum Shannon theory is in the construction of a code for transmitting private classical information over a quantum channel (discussed in Chapter 23). The method of proof for private classical transmission involves a clever combination of packing messages so that Bob can distinguish them, while covering Eve's space in such a way that Eve cannot distinguish the messages intended for Bob. A few other applications of the covering lemma are in secret key distillation, determining the amount of noise needed to destroy correlations in a bipartite state, and compressing the outcomes of an i.i.d. measurement on an i.i.d. quantum state.

We begin this chapter with a simple example to explain the main idea behind the covering lemma. Section 17.2 then discusses its general setting and gives its statement. We dissect its proof into several different parts: the construction of a "Chernoff ensemble," the construction of a "Chernoff code," the application of the operator Chernoff bound, and the error analysis.

The main tool that we use to prove the covering lemma is the operator Chernoff bound. This bound is a generalization of the standard Chernoff bound from probability theory, which states that the sample mean of a sequence of i.i.d. random variables converges exponentially fast to its true mean. A proof of the operator version of the Chernoff bound appears in Section 17.3. The exponential convergence in the Chernoff bound is much stronger than the polynomial convergence from Chebyshev's inequality and is helpful for establishing the existence of good private classical codes in Chapter 23.

17.1   Introductory Example

Suppose that Alice is trying to communicate with Bob as before, but now there is an eavesdropper Eve listening in on their communication. Alice wants the messages that she is sending to Bob to be *private* so that Eve does not gain any information about the message that she is sending.

How can Alice make the information that she is sending private? The strongest criterion for security is to ensure that whatever Eve receives is independent of what Alice is sending. Alice may have to sacrifice the amount of information she can communicate to Bob in order to have privacy, but this sacrifice is worth it to her because she really does not want Eve to know anything about the intended message for Bob.

We first give an example to motivate a general method that Alice can use to make her information private. Suppose Alice can transmit one of four messages $\{a, b, c, d\}$ to Bob, and suppose he receives them perfectly as distinguishable quantum states. She chooses from these messages with equal probability. Suppose further that Alice and Eve know that Eve receives one of the following four states corresponding to each of Alice's messages:

$$a \rightarrow |0\rangle, \qquad b \rightarrow |1\rangle, \qquad c \rightarrow |+\rangle, \qquad d \rightarrow |-\rangle. \qquad (17.1)$$

Observe that each of Eve's states lies in the two-dimensional Hilbert space of a qubit. We refer to the quantum states in the above ensemble as "Eve's ensemble."

We are not so much concerned for what Bob receives for the purposes of this example, but we just make the assumption that he can distinguish the four messages that Alice sends. Without loss of generality, let us just assume that he receives the messages unaltered in some preferred orthonormal basis such as $\{|a\rangle, |b\rangle, |c\rangle, |d\rangle\}$ so that he can distinguish the four messages, and let us call this ensemble "Bob's ensemble."

Both Alice and Eve then know that the expected density operator of Eve's ensemble is the maximally mixed state if Eve does not know which message Alice chooses:

$$\frac{1}{4}|0\rangle\langle 0| + \frac{1}{4}|1\rangle\langle 1| + \frac{1}{4}|+\rangle\langle +| + \frac{1}{4}|-\rangle\langle -| = \pi, \qquad (17.2)$$

where $\pi \equiv I/2$ is the maximally mixed state of a qubit. How can Alice ensure that Eve's information is independent of the message Alice is sending? Alice can choose subsets or subensembles of the states in Eve's ensemble to simulate the expected density operator of Eve's ensemble. Let us call these new simulating ensembles the "fake ensembles." Alice chooses the member states of the fake ensembles according to the uniform distribution in order to randomize Eve's knowledge. The density operator for each new fake ensemble is its "fake expected density operator."

Which states work well for being members of the fake ensembles? An equiprobable mixture of the states $|0\rangle$ and $|1\rangle$ suffices to simulate the expected density operator of Eve's ensemble because the fake expected density operator of this new ensemble is as follows: $[|0\rangle\langle 0| + |1\rangle\langle 1|]/2 = \pi$. An equiprobable mixture of the states $|+\rangle$ and $|-\rangle$ also works because the fake expected density operator of this other fake ensemble is as follows: $[|+\rangle\langle + | + |-\rangle\langle -|]/2 = \pi$.

So it is possible for Alice to encode a private bit in this way. She first generates a random bit that selects a particular message within each fake ensemble. So she selects a or b according to the random bit if she wants to transmit a "0" privately to Bob, and she selects c or d according to the random bit if she wants to transmit a "1" privately to Bob. In each of these cases, Eve's resulting expected density operator is the maximally mixed state. Thus, there is no measurement that Eve can perform to distinguish the original message that Alice transmits, in the sense that she cannot do better than a random guessing strategy. Bob, on the other hand, can perform a measurement in the basis $\{|a\rangle, |b\rangle, |c\rangle, |d\rangle\}$ to determine Alice's private bit. In the case in which one private bit is being transmitted, Eve can guess its value correctly with probability $1/2$, but Alice and Bob can make this probability exponentially small if Alice sends more private bits using this technique (the guessing probability is 2^{-n} if n private bits are transmitted in this way).

We can explicitly calculate Eve's information about the private bit. Consider Eve's description of the state if she does not know which message Alice transmits—it is an equal mixture of the following states: $\{|0\rangle, |1\rangle, |+\rangle, |-\rangle\}$ (equal to the maximally mixed state π). Eve's description of the state "improves" to an equal mixture of the states $\{|0\rangle, |1\rangle\}$ or $\{|+\rangle, |-\rangle\}$, each having density operator π, if she does know which message Alice transmits. The following classical–quantum state describes this setting:

$$\rho_{MKE} \equiv \frac{1}{4}|0\rangle\langle 0|_M \otimes |0\rangle\langle 0|_K \otimes |0\rangle\langle 0|_E$$

$$+ \frac{1}{4}|0\rangle\langle 0|_M \otimes |1\rangle\langle 1|_K \otimes |1\rangle\langle 1|_E$$

$$+ \frac{1}{4}|1\rangle\langle 1|_M \otimes |0\rangle\langle 0|_K \otimes |+\rangle\langle +|_E$$

$$+ \frac{1}{4}|1\rangle\langle 1|_M \otimes |1\rangle\langle 1|_K \otimes |-\rangle\langle -|_E, \qquad (17.3)$$

where we suppose that Eve never has access to the K register. Tracing over the register K gives the reduced state ρ_{ME}:

$$\rho_{ME} = \frac{1}{4}|0\rangle\langle 0|_M \otimes |0\rangle\langle 0|_E + \frac{1}{4}|0\rangle\langle 0|_M \otimes |1\rangle\langle 1|_E$$
$$+ \frac{1}{4}|1\rangle\langle 1|_M \otimes |+\rangle\langle +|_E + \frac{1}{4}|1\rangle\langle 1|_M \otimes |-\rangle\langle -|_E \qquad (17.4)$$
$$= \frac{1}{2}|0\rangle\langle 0|_M \otimes \frac{1}{2}\left[|0\rangle\langle 0|_E + |1\rangle\langle 1|_E\right]$$
$$+ \frac{1}{2}|1\rangle\langle 1|_M \otimes \frac{1}{2}\left[|+\rangle\langle +|_E + |-\rangle\langle -|_E\right] \qquad (17.5)$$
$$= \frac{1}{2}|0\rangle\langle 0|_M \otimes \pi_E + \frac{1}{2}|1\rangle\langle 1|_M \otimes \pi_E \qquad (17.6)$$
$$= \pi_M \otimes \pi_E. \qquad (17.7)$$

Then Eve's register is completely independent of the private bit in M and her information about the private bit in M is given by evaluating the mutual information of the reduced state ρ_{ME}: $I(M; E)_\rho = 0$, because the state is product. Thus, using this scheme, Eve has no information about the private bit as we argued before.

We are interested in making this scheme use as little noise as possible because Alice would like to transmit as much information as she can to Bob while still retaining privacy. Therefore, Alice should try to make the fake ensembles use as little randomness as possible. In the above example, Alice cannot make the fake ensembles any smaller because a smaller size would leak information to Eve.

17.2 Setting and Statement of the Covering Lemma

The setting of the covering lemma is a generalization of the setting in the above example. It essentially uses the same strategy for making information private, but the mathematical analysis becomes more involved in the more general setting. In general, we cannot have perfect privacy as in the above example, but instead we ask only for approximate privacy. Approximate privacy then becomes perfect in the asymptotic limit in the i.i.d. setting.

We first define the relevant ensemble for the covering lemma. We call it the "true ensemble" in order to distinguish it from the "fake ensemble."

DEFINITION 17.2.1 (True Ensemble)   Suppose $\mathcal{X}$ is a set of size $|\mathcal{X}|$ with elements x. Suppose we have an ensemble $\{p_X(x), \sigma_x\}_{x \in \mathcal{X}}$ of quantum states where each value x occurs with probability $p_X(x)$ according to some random variable X, and suppose we encode each value x into a quantum state $\sigma_x \in \mathcal{D}(\mathcal{H})$. The expected density operator of the ensemble is $\sigma \equiv \sum_{x \in \mathcal{X}} p_X(x)\sigma_x$.

The definition for a fake ensemble is similar to the way that we constructed the fake ensembles in the example. It is merely a subset of the states in the true ensemble chosen according to a uniform distribution.

DEFINITION 17.2.2 (Fake Ensemble)   Let $\mathcal{S}$ be a set such that $\mathcal{S} \subseteq \mathcal{X}$. The fake ensemble is defined as follows:

$$\{1/|\mathcal{S}|, \sigma_s\}_{s \in \mathcal{S}}. \tag{17.8}$$

Let $\bar{\sigma}$ denote the "fake expected density operator" of the fake ensemble:

$$\bar{\sigma}(\mathcal{S}) \equiv \frac{1}{|\mathcal{S}|} \sum_{s \in \mathcal{S}} \sigma_s. \tag{17.9}$$

In the example, Alice was able to obtain perfect privacy from Eve. We need a good measure of privacy because it is not possible in general to obtain perfect privacy, but Alice can instead obtain only approximate privacy. We call this measure the "obfuscation error" because it determines how well Alice can obfuscate the state that Eve receives.

DEFINITION 17.2.3 (Obfuscation Error)   The obfuscation error $o_e(\mathcal{S})$ of set $\mathcal{S}$ is a measure of how close the fake expected density operator $\bar{\sigma}(\mathcal{S})$ is to the actual expected density operator:

$$o_e(\mathcal{S}) = \|\bar{\sigma}(\mathcal{S}) - \sigma\|_1. \tag{17.10}$$

The goal for Alice is to make the size of her fake ensembles as small as possible while still having privacy from Eve. The covering lemma quantifies this trade-off by determining how small each fake ensemble can be in order to obtain a certain obfuscation error.

The hypotheses of the covering lemma are somewhat similar to those of the packing lemma. But as stated in the introduction to this chapter, the goal of the covering lemma is much different.

LEMMA 17.2.1 (Covering Lemma)   Let $\{p_X(x), \sigma_x\}_{x \in \mathcal{X}}$ be an ensemble as in Definition 17.2.1. Suppose a total subspace projector Π and codeword subspace projectors $\{\Pi_x\}_{x \in \mathcal{X}}$ are given, they project onto subspaces of $\mathcal{H}$, and these projectors and each state σ_x satisfy the following conditions:

$$\text{Tr}\{\sigma_x \Pi\} \geq 1 - \varepsilon, \tag{17.11}$$

$$\text{Tr}\{\sigma_x \Pi_x\} \geq 1 - \varepsilon, \tag{17.12}$$

$$\text{Tr}\{\Pi\} \leq D, \tag{17.13}$$

$$\Pi_x \sigma_x \Pi_x \leq \frac{1}{d} \Pi_x, \tag{17.14}$$

where $\varepsilon \in (0,1)$, $D > 0$, and $d \in (0, D)$. Suppose that $\mathcal{M}$ is a set of size $|\mathcal{M}|$ with elements m. Let a random covering code $\mathcal{C} \equiv \{C_m\}_{m \in \mathcal{M}}$ consist of random codewords C_m where the codewords C_m are chosen independently according to the distribution $p_X(x)$ and give rise to a fake ensemble $\{1/|\mathcal{M}|, \sigma_{C_m}\}_{m \in \mathcal{M}}$. Then there is a high probability that the obfuscation error $o_e(\mathcal{C})$ of the random covering code $\mathcal{C}$ is small:

$$\Pr_{\mathcal{C}}\left\{o_e(\mathcal{C}) \leq \varepsilon + 4\sqrt{\varepsilon} + 24\sqrt[4]{\varepsilon}\right\} \geq 1 - 2D \exp\left(-\frac{\varepsilon^3}{4\ln 2} \frac{|\mathcal{M}| d}{D}\right), \tag{17.15}$$

when ε is small and $|\mathcal{M}| \gg \varepsilon^3 d/D$. Thus, it is highly likely that a given fake ensemble $\{1/|\mathcal{M}|, \sigma_{c_m}\}_{m\in\mathcal{M}}$ has its expected density operator indistinguishable from the expected density operator of the original ensemble $\{p_X(x), \sigma_x\}_{x\in\mathcal{X}}$. It is in this sense that the fake ensemble $\{1/|\mathcal{M}|, \sigma_{c_m}\}_{m\in\mathcal{M}}$ "covers" the original ensemble $\{p_X(x), \sigma_x\}_{x\in\mathcal{X}}$.

17.3 Operator Chernoff Bound

Before giving the proof of the covering lemma, we first state and prove the operator Chernoff bound, which is the most critical tool for establishing the covering lemma. The operator Chernoff bound is a theorem from the theory of large deviations and essentially states that the sample average of a large number of i.i.d. operator-valued random variables is close to their expectation (with some constraints on the operator-valued random variables).

LEMMA 17.3.1 (Operator Chernoff Bound) Let $\xi_1, \ldots, \xi_K \in \mathcal{L}(\mathcal{H})$ be K i.i.d. positive semi-definite operator-valued random variables. Suppose that each ξ_k has all of its eigenvalues between zero and one:

$$\forall k \in [K] : 0 \le \xi_k \le I. \tag{17.16}$$

Let $\bar{\xi}$ denote the sample average of the K operator-valued random variables:

$$\bar{\xi} = \frac{1}{K} \sum_{k=1}^{K} \xi_k. \tag{17.17}$$

Suppose that the expectation $\mathbb{E}_\xi \{\xi_k\} \equiv \mu$ of each operator ξ_k is positive definite, so that μ exceeds the identity operator scaled by a number $a \in (0,1)$: $\mu \ge aI$. Then for every η where $0 < \eta < 1/2$ and $(1+\eta)a \le 1$, we can bound the probability that the sample average $\bar{\xi}$ lies inside the operator interval $[(1 \pm \eta)\mu]$:

$$\Pr_\xi \left\{ (1-\eta)\mu \le \bar{\xi} \le (1+\eta)\mu \right\} \ge 1 - 2\dim(\mathcal{H}) \exp\left(-\frac{K\eta^2 a}{4\ln 2} \right). \tag{17.18}$$

Thus it is highly likely that the sample average operator $\bar{\xi}$ becomes close to the true expected operator μ as K becomes large.

We prove the above lemma by making a progression through the operator Markov inequality all the way to the proof of the operator Chernoff bound. Recall that we write $A \ge B$ if $A - B$ is a positive semi-definite operator, and we write $A \not\ge B$ otherwise. In what follows, we take the convention $\exp\{A\} = \sum_i \exp(a_i)|i\rangle\langle i|$ for a Hermitian operator A with spectral decomposition $A = \sum_i a_i|i\rangle\langle i|$ (this differs from our usual convention $\exp\{A\} = \sum_{i:a_i\neq 0} \exp(a_i)|i\rangle\langle i|$).

LEMMA 17.3.2 (Operator Markov Inequality)   Let $X \in \mathcal{L}(\mathcal{H})$ be a positive semi-definite operator-valued random variable. Let $\mathbb{E}\{X\}$ denote its expectation. Let A be a fixed positive definite operator in $\mathcal{L}(\mathcal{H})$. Then

$$\Pr\{X \nleq A\} \leq \operatorname{Tr}\{\mathbb{E}\{X\}A^{-1}\}. \tag{17.19}$$

Proof   Observe that if $X \nleq A$ then $A^{-1/2}XA^{-1/2} \nleq I$. This then implies that the largest eigenvalue of $A^{-1/2}XA^{-1/2}$ exceeds one: $\|A^{-1/2}XA^{-1/2}\|_{\infty} > 1$. Let $I_{X \nleq A}$ denote an indicator function for the event $X \nleq A$. We then have that

$$I_{X \nleq A} \leq \operatorname{Tr}\{A^{-1/2}XA^{-1/2}\}. \tag{17.20}$$

The above inequality follows because the right-hand side is non-negative if the indicator is zero. If the indicator is one, then the right-hand side exceeds one because its largest eigenvalue is greater than one and the trace exceeds the largest eigenvalue for a positive semi-definite operator. We then have the following inequalities:

$$\Pr\{X \nleq A\} = \mathbb{E}\left\{I_{X \nleq A}\right\} \leq \mathbb{E}\left\{\operatorname{Tr}\left\{A^{-1/2}XA^{-1/2}\right\}\right\} \tag{17.21}$$

$$= \mathbb{E}\{\operatorname{Tr}\{XA^{-1}\}\} = \operatorname{Tr}\{\mathbb{E}\{X\}A^{-1}\}, \tag{17.22}$$

where the inequality follows from (17.20) and the second equality from cyclicity of trace. $\square$

LEMMA 17.3.3 (Bernstein Trick)   Let $X, X_1, \ldots, X_K \in \mathcal{L}(\mathcal{H})$ be i.i.d. Hermitian operator-valued random variables, and let A be a fixed Hermitian operator. Then for any invertible operator T, the following bound holds

$$\Pr\left\{\sum_{k=1}^{K} X_k \nleq KA\right\} \leq \dim(\mathcal{H}) \left\|\mathbb{E}\left\{\exp\left\{T\left(X - A\right)T^{\dagger}\right\}\right\}\right\|_{\infty}^{K}. \tag{17.23}$$

Proof   The proof of this lemma relies on the Golden–Thompson trace inequality from statistical mechanics, which holds for any two Hermitian operators A and B (we state it without proof):

$$\operatorname{Tr}\{\exp\{A + B\}\} \leq \operatorname{Tr}\{\exp\{A\}\exp\{B\}\}. \tag{17.24}$$

Consider the following chain of inequalities:

$$\Pr\left\{\sum_{k=1}^{K} X_k \nleq KA\right\} = \Pr\left\{\sum_{k=1}^{K}(X_k - A) \nleq 0\right\} \tag{17.25}$$

$$= \Pr\left\{\sum_{k=1}^{K} T\left(X_k - A\right)T^{\dagger} \nleq 0\right\} \tag{17.26}$$

$$= \Pr \left\{ \exp \left\{ \sum_{k=1}^{K} T(X_k - A) T^\dagger \right\} \npreceq I \right\} \tag{17.27}$$

$$\leq \mathrm{Tr} \left\{ \mathbb{E} \left\{ \exp \left\{ \sum_{k=1}^{K} T(X_k - A) T^\dagger \right\} \right\} \right\}. \tag{17.28}$$

The first two equalities are straightforward and the third follows because $A \leq B$ is equivalent to $\exp\{A\} \leq \exp\{B\}$ for commuting operators A and B. The inequality follows by applying the operator Markov inequality (Lemma 17.3.2). Continuing, we have

$$= \mathbb{E} \left\{ \mathrm{Tr} \left\{ \exp \left\{ \sum_{k=1}^{K} T(X_k - A) T^\dagger \right\} \right\} \right\} \tag{17.29}$$

$$\leq \mathbb{E} \left\{ \mathrm{Tr} \left\{ \exp \left\{ \sum_{k=1}^{K-1} T(X_k - A) T^\dagger \right\} \exp \left\{ T(X_K - A) T^\dagger \right\} \right\} \right\} \tag{17.30}$$

$$= \mathbb{E}_{X_1, \ldots, X_{K-1}} \left\{ \mathrm{Tr} \left\{ \exp \left\{ \sum_{k=1}^{K-1} T(X_k - A) T^\dagger \right\} \right. \right.$$
$$\left. \left. \mathbb{E}_{X_K} \left\{ \exp \left\{ T(X_K - A) T^\dagger \right\} \right\} \right\} \right\} \tag{17.31}$$

$$= \mathbb{E}_{X_1, \ldots, X_{K-1}} \left\{ \mathrm{Tr} \left\{ \exp \left\{ \sum_{k=1}^{K-1} T(X_k - A) T^\dagger \right\} \mathbb{E}_X \left\{ \exp \left\{ T(X - A) T^\dagger \right\} \right\} \right\} \right\}. \tag{17.32}$$

The first equality follows from exchanging the expectation and the trace. The inequality follows from applying the Golden–Thompson trace inequality. The second and third equalities follow from the i.i.d. assumption. Continuing,

$$\leq \mathbb{E}_{X_1, \ldots, X_{K-1}} \left\{ \mathrm{Tr} \left\{ \exp \left\{ \sum_{k=1}^{K-1} T(X_k - A) T^\dagger \right\} \right\} \right\}$$
$$\left\| \mathbb{E}_X \left\{ \exp \left\{ T(X - A) T^\dagger \right\} \right\} \right\|_\infty \tag{17.33}$$

$$\leq \mathrm{Tr}\{I\} \left\| \mathbb{E}_X \left\{ \exp \left\{ T(X - A) T^\dagger \right\} \right\} \right\|_\infty^K \tag{17.34}$$

$$= \dim(\mathcal{H}) \left\| \mathbb{E}_X \left\{ \exp \left\{ T(X - A) T^\dagger \right\} \right\} \right\|_\infty^K. \tag{17.35}$$

The first inequality follows from $\mathrm{Tr}\{AB\} \leq \mathrm{Tr}\{A\} \|B\|_\infty$ for A positive semi-definite. The second inequality follows from a repeated application of the same steps. The final equality follows because the trace of the identity operator is equal to the dimension of the Hilbert space. This proves the "Bernstein trick" lemma. $\qquad \square$

Proof of the Operator Chernoff Bound (Lemma 17.3.1)   We first prove that the following inequality holds for i.i.d. Hermitian operator-valued random variables $X, X_1, \ldots, X_K$ such that $\mathbb{E}\{X\} \leq mI$, $A \geq aI$, and $1 \geq a > m \geq 0$:

$$\Pr\left\{\sum_{k=1}^{K} X_k \not\leq KA\right\} \leq \dim(\mathcal{H}) \exp\{-KD(a\|m)\}, \qquad (17.36)$$

where $D(a\|m)$ is the binary relative entropy:

$$D(a\|m) = a\ln a - a\ln m + (1-a)\ln(1-a) - (1-a)\ln(1-m). \qquad (17.37)$$

We first apply the Bernstein Trick (Lemma 17.3.3) with $T = \sqrt{t}I$, for $t > 0$:

$$\Pr\left\{\sum_{k=1}^{K} X_k \not\leq KA\right\} \leq \Pr\left\{\sum_{k=1}^{K} X_k \not\leq KaI\right\} \qquad (17.38)$$

$$\leq \dim(\mathcal{H})\, \|\mathbb{E}\{\exp\{tX\}\exp\{-ta\}\}\|_\infty^K. \qquad (17.39)$$

So it is clear that it is best to optimize t in such a way that

$$\|\mathbb{E}\{\exp\{tX\}\exp\{-ta\}\}\|_\infty < 1, \qquad (17.40)$$

so that we have exponential decay with increasing K. Now consider the following inequality:

$$\exp\{tX\} - I \leq X(\exp\{t\} - 1), \qquad (17.41)$$

which holds because a similar one holds for all real $x \in [0,1]$:

$$(\exp\{tx\} - 1) \leq x(\exp\{t\} - 1). \qquad (17.42)$$

Applying this inequality gives

$$\mathbb{E}\{\exp\{tX\}\} \leq \mathbb{E}\{X\}(\exp\{t\} - 1) + I \qquad (17.43)$$

$$\leq mI(\exp\{t\} - 1) + I \qquad (17.44)$$

$$= (m\exp\{t\} + 1 - m)I, \qquad (17.45)$$

which in turn implies

$$\|\mathbb{E}\{\exp\{tX\}\exp\{-ta\}\}\|_\infty \leq (m\exp\{t\} + 1 - m)\exp\{-ta\}. \qquad (17.46)$$

Choosing

$$t = \ln\left(\frac{a}{m} \cdot \frac{1-m}{1-a}\right) > 0, \qquad (17.47)$$

which follows from the assumption that $a > m$, gives

$$(m\exp\{t\} + 1 - m)\exp\{-ta\}$$

$$= \left(m\left(\frac{a}{m} \cdot \frac{1-m}{1-a}\right) + 1 - m\right)\exp\left\{-\ln\left(\frac{a}{m} \cdot \frac{1-m}{1-a}\right)a\right\} \qquad (17.48)$$

$$= \left(a \cdot \frac{1-m}{1-a} + 1 - m\right)\exp\left\{-a\ln\left(\frac{a}{m}\right) - a\ln\left(\frac{1-m}{1-a}\right)\right\} \qquad (17.49)$$

$$= \left(\frac{1-m}{1-a}\right) \exp\left\{-a\ln\left(\frac{a}{m}\right) - a\ln\left(\frac{1-m}{1-a}\right)\right\} \tag{17.50}$$

$$= \exp\left\{-a\ln\left(\frac{a}{m}\right) - (1-a)\ln\left(\frac{1-a}{1-m}\right)\right\} \tag{17.51}$$

$$= \exp\left\{-D(a\|m)\right\}, \tag{17.52}$$

proving the desired bound in (17.36).

By substituting $Y_k = I - X_k$ and $B = I - A$ into (17.36) and having the opposite conditions $\mathbb{E}\{X\} \geq mI$, $A \leq aI$, and $0 \leq a < m \leq 1$, we can show that the following inequality holds for i.i.d. operators $X, X_1, \ldots, X_K$:

$$\Pr\left\{\sum_{k=1}^{K} X_k \not\geq KA\right\} \leq \dim(\mathcal{H})\exp\left\{-KD(a\|m)\right\}. \tag{17.53}$$

To finish off the proof of the operator Chernoff bound, consider the variables $Z_k = L\mu^{-1/2}X_k\mu^{-1/2}$ with $\mu \equiv \mathbb{E}\{X\} \geq LI$. Then $\mathbb{E}\{Z_k\} = LI$ and $0 \leq Z_i \leq I$. The following events are thus equivalent

$$(1-\eta)\mu \leq \frac{1}{K}\sum_{k=1}^{K} X_k \leq (1+\eta)\mu$$

$$\Longleftrightarrow (1-\eta)LI \leq \frac{1}{K}\sum_{k=1}^{K} Z_k \leq (1+\eta)LI, \tag{17.54}$$

and we can apply (17.36), (17.53), and the union bound to obtain

$$\Pr\left\{\left((1-\eta)\mu \not\leq \frac{1}{K}\sum_{k=1}^{K} X_k\right) \cup \left(\frac{1}{K}\sum_{k=1}^{K} X_k \not\leq (1+\eta)\mu\right)\right\}$$

$$\leq \dim(\mathcal{H})\exp\left\{-KD((1-\eta)L\|L)\right\}$$

$$\quad + \dim(\mathcal{H})\exp\left\{-KD((1+\eta)L\|L)\right\} \tag{17.55}$$

$$\leq 2\dim(\mathcal{H})\exp\left\{-K\frac{\eta^2 L}{4\ln 2}\right\}, \tag{17.56}$$

where the last line exploits the following inequality valid for $-1/2 \leq \eta \leq 1/2$ and $(1+\eta)L \leq 1$:

$$D((1+\eta)L\|L) \geq \frac{1}{4\ln 2}\eta^2 L. \tag{17.57}$$

This concludes the proof of Lemma 17.3.1.   □

17.4   Proof of the Covering Lemma

The first step of the proof of the covering lemma is to construct an alternate ensemble that is close to the original ensemble yet satisfies the conditions of the operator Chernoff bound (Lemma 17.3.1). We call this alternate ensemble the

"Chernoff ensemble." We then generate a random code, a set of M i.i.d. random variables, using the Chernoff ensemble. Call this random code the "Chernoff code." We apply the operator Chernoff bound to the Chernoff code to obtain a good bound on the obfuscation error of the Chernoff code. We finally show that the bound holds for a covering code generated by the original ensemble because the original ensemble is close to the Chernoff ensemble in trace distance.

17.4.1 Construction of the Chernoff Ensemble

We first establish a few definitions to construct intermediary ensembles. We then use these intermediary ensembles to construct the Chernoff ensemble. We construct the first "primed" ensemble $\{p_X(x), \sigma'_x\}$ by using the projection operators Π_x to slice out some of the support of the states σ_x:

$$\forall x \quad \sigma'_x \equiv \Pi_x \sigma_x \Pi_x. \tag{17.58}$$

The above "slicing" operation cuts outs any part of the support of σ_x that is not in the support of Π_x. The expected operator σ' for the first primed ensemble is as follows:

$$\sigma' \equiv \sum_{x \in \mathcal{X}} p_X(x) \sigma'_x. \tag{17.59}$$

We then continue slicing with the projector Π and form the second primed ensemble $\{p_X(x), \sigma''_x\}$ as follows:

$$\forall x \quad \sigma''_x \equiv \Pi \sigma'_x \Pi. \tag{17.60}$$

The expected operator for the second primed ensemble is as follows:

$$\sigma'' \equiv \sum_{x \in \mathcal{X}} p_X(x) \sigma''_x. \tag{17.61}$$

Let $\hat{\Pi}$ be the projector onto the subspace spanned by the eigenvectors of σ'' whose corresponding eigenvalues are greater than ε/D. We would expect that this extra slicing does not change the state very much when D is large and ε is small. We construct states ω_x in the Chernoff ensemble by using the projector $\hat{\Pi}$ to slice out some more elements of the support of the original ensemble:

$$\forall x \quad \omega_x \equiv \hat{\Pi} \sigma''_x \hat{\Pi}. \tag{17.62}$$

The expected operator ω for the Chernoff ensemble is then as follows:

$$\omega \equiv \sum_{x \in \mathcal{X}} p_X(x) \omega_x. \tag{17.63}$$

The Chernoff ensemble satisfies the conditions necessary to apply the operator Chernoff bound. We wait to apply the operator Chernoff bound and for now show how to construct a random covering code.

17.4.2 Chernoff Code Construction

We present a Shannon-like random coding argument. We construct a covering code $\mathcal{C}$ at random by independently generating $|\mathcal{M}|$ codewords according to the distribution $p_X(x)$. Let $\mathcal{C} = \{c_m\}_{m \in \mathcal{M}}$ be a collection of the realizations c_m of $|\mathcal{M}|$ independent random variables C_m. Each C_m takes a value c_m in $\mathcal{X}$ with probability $p_X(c_m)$ and represents a codeword in the random code $\mathcal{C}$. This process generates the Chernoff code $\mathcal{C}$ consisting of $|\mathcal{M}|$ quantum states $\{\omega_{c_m}\}_{m \in \mathcal{M}}$. The fake expected operator $\overline{\omega}(\mathcal{C})$ of the states in the Chernoff code is as follows:

$$\overline{\omega}(\mathcal{C}) \equiv \frac{1}{|\mathcal{M}|} \sum_{m=1}^{|\mathcal{M}|} \omega_{c_m}, \tag{17.64}$$

because we assume that Alice randomizes codewords in the Chernoff code according to a uniform distribution (notice that there is a difference in the distribution that we use to choose the code and the distribution that Alice uses to randomize the selected codewords). The expectation $\mathbb{E}_{\mathcal{C}} \{\omega_{C_m}\}$ of each operator ω_{C_m} is equal to the expected operator ω because of the way that we constructed the covering code. We can also define codes with respect to the primed ensembles as follows: $\{\sigma_{c_m}\}_{m \in \mathcal{M}}$, $\{\sigma'_{c_m}\}_{m \in \mathcal{M}}$, $\{\sigma''_{c_m}\}_{m \in \mathcal{M}}$. These codes respectively have fake expected operators of the following form:

$$\overline{\sigma}(\mathcal{C}) \equiv \frac{1}{|\mathcal{M}|} \sum_{m=1}^{|\mathcal{M}|} \sigma_{c_m}, \tag{17.65}$$

$$\overline{\sigma}'(\mathcal{C}) \equiv \frac{1}{|\mathcal{M}|} \sum_{m=1}^{|\mathcal{M}|} \sigma'_{c_m}, \tag{17.66}$$

$$\overline{\sigma}''(\mathcal{C}) \equiv \frac{1}{|\mathcal{M}|} \sum_{m=1}^{|\mathcal{M}|} \sigma''_{c_m}. \tag{17.67}$$

Applying the Operator Chernoff Bound. We make one final modification before applying the operator Chernoff bound. The operators ω_{c_m} are in the operator interval between the zero operator 0 and $\frac{1}{d}\hat{\Pi}$:

$$\forall m \in \mathcal{M} : 0 \leq \omega_{c_m} \leq \frac{1}{d}\hat{\Pi}. \tag{17.68}$$

The above statement holds because the operators σ'_x satisfy $\sigma'_x = \Pi_x \sigma_x \Pi_x \leq \frac{1}{d}\Pi_x$ (the fourth condition of the covering lemma) and this condition implies the following inequalities:

$$\sigma'_x = \Pi_x \sigma_x \Pi_x \leq \frac{1}{d}\Pi_x \tag{17.69}$$

$$\Rightarrow \Pi \sigma'_x \Pi = \sigma''_x \leq \frac{1}{d}\Pi \Pi_x \Pi \leq \frac{1}{d}\Pi \tag{17.70}$$

$$\Rightarrow \omega_x = \hat{\Pi} \sigma''_x \hat{\Pi} \leq \frac{1}{d}\hat{\Pi}\hat{\Pi}\hat{\Pi} \leq \frac{1}{d}\hat{\Pi}. \tag{17.71}$$

Therefore, we consider another set of operators (not necessarily density operators) where we scale each ω_{c_m} by d so that

$$\forall m \in \mathcal{M} : 0 \leq d\omega_{c_m} \leq \hat{\Pi}. \tag{17.72}$$

This code satisfies the conditions of the operator Chernoff bound with $a = \varepsilon d/D$ and with $\hat{\Pi}$ acting as the identity on the subspace onto which it projects. We can now apply the operator Chernoff bound to bound the probability that the sample average $\overline{\omega} \equiv |\mathcal{M}|^{-1} \sum_{m \in \mathcal{M}} \omega_{c_m}$ falls in the operator interval $[(1 \pm \varepsilon)\,\omega]$:

$$\Pr\left\{ (1-\varepsilon)\,\omega \leq \overline{\omega} \leq (1+\varepsilon)\,\omega \right\}$$

$$= \Pr\left\{ d\,(1-\varepsilon)\,\omega \leq d\overline{\omega} \leq d\,(1+\varepsilon)\,\omega \right\} \tag{17.73}$$

$$\geq 1 - 2\,\mathrm{Tr}\left\{ \hat{\Pi} \right\} \exp\left(-\frac{|\mathcal{M}|\,\varepsilon^2\,(\varepsilon d/D)}{4\ln 2} \right) \tag{17.74}$$

$$\geq 1 - 2D \exp\left(-\frac{\varepsilon^3}{4\ln 2} \frac{|\mathcal{M}|\,d}{D} \right). \tag{17.75}$$

17.4.3   Obfuscation Error of the Covering Code

The random covering code is a set of $|\mathcal{M}|$ quantum states $\{\sigma_{C_m}\}_{m \in \mathcal{M}}$ where the quantum states arise from the original ensemble. Recall that our goal is to show that the obfuscation error of the random covering code $\mathcal{C}$,

$$o_e(\mathcal{C}) = \|\overline{\sigma}(\mathcal{C}) - \sigma\|_1, \tag{17.76}$$

has a high probability of being small.

We now show that the obfuscation error of this random covering code is highly likely to be small, by relating it to the Chernoff ensemble. Our method of proof is simply to exploit the triangle inequality, the gentle operator lemma (Lemma 9.4.2), and Exercise 9.1.8 several times. The triangle inequality gives the following bound for the obfuscation error:

$$o_e(\mathcal{C}) = \|\overline{\sigma}(\mathcal{C}) - \sigma\|_1$$

$$= \|\overline{\sigma}(\mathcal{C}) - \overline{\sigma}''(\mathcal{C}) - (\overline{\omega}(\mathcal{C}) - \overline{\sigma}''(\mathcal{C})) + (\overline{\omega}(\mathcal{C}) - \omega) + (\omega - \sigma'') - (\sigma - \sigma'')\|_1 \tag{17.77}$$

$$\leq \|\overline{\sigma}(\mathcal{C}) - \overline{\sigma}''(\mathcal{C})\|_1 + \|\overline{\omega}(\mathcal{C}) - \overline{\sigma}''(\mathcal{C})\|_1$$
$$+ \|\overline{\omega}(\mathcal{C}) - \omega\|_1 + \|\omega - \sigma''\|_1 + \|\sigma - \sigma''\|_1. \tag{17.78}$$

We show how to obtain a good bound for each of the above five terms.

First consider the rightmost term $\|\sigma - \sigma''\|_1$ in (17.78). Consider that the projected state $\sigma'_x = \Pi_x \sigma_x \Pi_x$ is close to the original state σ_x by applying (17.12) and the gentle operator lemma:

$$\|\sigma_x - \sigma'_x\|_1 \leq 2\sqrt{\varepsilon}. \tag{17.79}$$

Consider that

$$\|\sigma'_x - \sigma''_x\|_1 \leq 2\sqrt{\varepsilon + 2\sqrt{\varepsilon}} \tag{17.80}$$

because $\sigma_x'' = \Pi \sigma_x' \Pi$ and from applying the gentle operator lemma to

$$\text{Tr}\left\{\Pi \sigma_x'\right\} \geq \text{Tr}\left\{\Pi \sigma_x\right\} - \left\|\sigma_x - \sigma_x'\right\|_1 \tag{17.81}$$

$$\geq 1 - \varepsilon - 2\sqrt{\varepsilon}, \tag{17.82}$$

where the first inequality follows from Exercise 9.1.8 and the second from (17.11) and (17.79). Then the state σ_x'' is close to the original state σ_x for all x because

$$\left\|\sigma_x - \sigma_x''\right\|_1 \leq \left\|\sigma_x - \sigma_x'\right\|_1 + \left\|\sigma_x' - \sigma_x''\right\|_1 \tag{17.83}$$

$$\leq 2\sqrt{\varepsilon} + 2\sqrt{\varepsilon + 2\sqrt{\varepsilon}}, \tag{17.84}$$

where we first applied the triangle inequality and the bounds from (17.79) and (17.80). Convexity of the trace distance then gives a bound on $\|\sigma - \sigma''\|_1$:

$$\left\|\sigma - \sigma''\right\|_1 = \left\|\sum_{x \in \mathcal{X}} p_X(x)\sigma_x - \sum_{x \in \mathcal{X}} p_X(x)\sigma_x''\right\|_1 \tag{17.85}$$

$$= \left\|\sum_{x \in \mathcal{X}} p_X(x)\left(\sigma_x - \sigma_x''\right)\right\|_1 \tag{17.86}$$

$$\leq \sum_{x \in \mathcal{X}} p_X(x)\left\|\sigma_x - \sigma_x''\right\|_1 \tag{17.87}$$

$$\leq \sum_{x \in \mathcal{X}} p_X(x)\left(2\sqrt{\varepsilon} + 2\sqrt{\varepsilon + 2\sqrt{\varepsilon}}\right) \tag{17.88}$$

$$= 2\sqrt{\varepsilon} + 2\sqrt{\varepsilon + 2\sqrt{\varepsilon}}. \tag{17.89}$$

We now consider the second rightmost term $\|\omega - \sigma''\|_1$ in (17.78). The support of σ'' has dimension less than D by (17.13), the third condition in the covering lemma. Therefore, eigenvalues smaller than ε/D contribute at most ε to $\text{Tr}\left\{\sigma''\right\}$. In particular, if $\sum_i \lambda_i |i\rangle\langle i|$ is a spectral decomposition of σ'', with $\lambda_i \geq 0$ for all i and $\sum_i \lambda_i \leq 1$, we have that

$$\text{Tr}\left\{\sigma''\right\} - \text{Tr}\left\{\omega\right\} = \sum_i \lambda_i - \sum_{i:\lambda_i \geq \varepsilon/D} \lambda_i \tag{17.90}$$

$$= \sum_{i:\lambda_i < \varepsilon/D} \lambda_i \leq \frac{\varepsilon}{D} \cdot D = \varepsilon. \tag{17.91}$$

We can use this to bound the trace of ω as follows:

$$\text{Tr}\left\{\omega\right\} \geq \text{Tr}\left\{\sigma''\right\} - \varepsilon \tag{17.92}$$

$$= \sum_{x \in \mathcal{X}} p_X(x)\,\text{Tr}\left\{\sigma_x''\right\} - \varepsilon \tag{17.93}$$

$$\geq \left(\sum_{x \in \mathcal{X}} p_X(x)\right)\left(1 - \varepsilon - 2\sqrt{\varepsilon}\right) - \varepsilon \tag{17.94}$$

$$= 1 - 2\left(\varepsilon + \sqrt{\varepsilon}\right), \tag{17.95}$$

where the first inequality applies the above "eigenvalue-bounding" argument and the second inequality employs the bound in (17.82). This argument shows that the average operator of the Chernoff ensemble has trace almost equal to one. We can then apply the gentle operator lemma to $\text{Tr}\{\omega\} \geq 1 - 2(\varepsilon + \sqrt{\varepsilon})$ to give

$$\|\omega - \sigma''\|_1 \leq 2\sqrt{2(\varepsilon + \sqrt{\varepsilon})}. \tag{17.96}$$

We now consider the middle term $\|\overline{\omega} - \omega\|_1$ in (17.78). The Chernoff bound gives us a probabilistic estimate and not a deterministic estimate like the other two bounds we have shown above. So we suppose for now that the fake operator $\overline{\omega}$ of the Chernoff code is close to the average operator ω of the Chernoff ensemble:

$$\overline{\omega}(\mathcal{C}) \equiv \frac{1}{|\mathcal{M}|} \sum_{m \in \mathcal{M}} \omega_{cm} \in [(1 \pm \varepsilon)\omega]. \tag{17.97}$$

With this assumption, it holds that

$$\|\overline{\omega}(\mathcal{C}) - \omega\|_1 \leq \varepsilon, \tag{17.98}$$

by employing Lemma A.0.2 from Appendix A and $\text{Tr}\{\omega\} \leq 1$.

We consider the second leftmost term $\|\overline{\omega}(\mathcal{C}) - \overline{\sigma}''(\mathcal{C})\|_1$ in (17.78). The following inequality holds:

$$\text{Tr}\{\overline{\omega}(\mathcal{C})\} \geq 1 - 3\varepsilon - 2\sqrt{\varepsilon}, \tag{17.99}$$

because in (17.95) we showed that $\text{Tr}\{\omega\} \geq 1 - 2(\varepsilon + \sqrt{\varepsilon})$, and the triangle inequality implies that

$$\text{Tr}\{\overline{\omega}(\mathcal{C})\} = \|\overline{\omega}(\mathcal{C})\|_1 \tag{17.100}$$
$$= \|\omega - (\omega - \overline{\omega}(\mathcal{C}))\|_1 \tag{17.101}$$
$$\geq \|\omega\|_1 - \|\omega - \overline{\omega}(\mathcal{C})\|_1 \tag{17.102}$$
$$= \text{Tr}\{\omega\} - \|\omega - \overline{\omega}(\mathcal{C})\|_1 \tag{17.103}$$
$$\geq (1 - 2(\varepsilon + \sqrt{\varepsilon})) - \varepsilon \tag{17.104}$$
$$= 1 - 3\varepsilon - 2\sqrt{\varepsilon}. \tag{17.105}$$

Applying the gentle operator lemma to $\text{Tr}\{\overline{\omega}(\mathcal{C})\} \geq 1 - 3\varepsilon - 2\sqrt{\varepsilon}$ gives that

$$\|\overline{\omega}(\mathcal{C}) - \overline{\sigma}''(\mathcal{C})\|_1 \leq 2\sqrt{3\varepsilon + 2\sqrt{\varepsilon}}. \tag{17.106}$$

We finally bound the leftmost term $\|\overline{\sigma}(\mathcal{C}) - \overline{\sigma}''(\mathcal{C})\|_1$ in (17.78). We can use convexity of trace distance and (17.84) to obtain the following bounds:

$$\|\overline{\sigma}(\mathcal{C}) - \overline{\sigma}''(\mathcal{C})\|_1 \leq \frac{1}{|\mathcal{M}|} \sum_{m \in \mathcal{M}} \|\sigma_{Cm} - \sigma''_{Cm}\|_1 \tag{17.107}$$

$$\leq 2\sqrt{\varepsilon} + 2\sqrt{\varepsilon + 2\sqrt{\varepsilon}}. \tag{17.108}$$

We now combine all of the above bounds with the triangle inequality in order to bound the obfuscation error of the covering code $\mathcal{C}$:

$$o_e(\mathcal{C}) = \|\overline{\sigma}(\mathcal{C}) - \sigma\|_1 \tag{17.109}$$

$$= \|\overline{\sigma}(\mathcal{C}) - \overline{\sigma}''(\mathcal{C}) - (\overline{\omega}(\mathcal{C}) - \overline{\sigma}''(\mathcal{C})) + (\overline{\omega}(\mathcal{C}) - \omega)$$
$$+ (\omega - \sigma'') - (\sigma - \sigma'')\|_1 \tag{17.110}$$

$$\leq \|\overline{\sigma}(\mathcal{C}) - \overline{\sigma}''(\mathcal{C})\|_1 + \|\overline{\omega}(\mathcal{C}) - \overline{\sigma}''(\mathcal{C})\|_1$$
$$+ \|\overline{\omega}(\mathcal{C}) - \omega\|_1 + \|\omega - \sigma''\|_1 + \|\sigma - \sigma''\|_1 \tag{17.111}$$

$$\leq \left(2\sqrt{\varepsilon} + 2\sqrt{\varepsilon + 2\sqrt{\varepsilon}}\right) + \left(2\sqrt{3\varepsilon + 2\sqrt{\varepsilon}}\right) + \varepsilon$$
$$+ \left(2\sqrt{2\left(\varepsilon + \sqrt{\varepsilon}\right)}\right) + \left(2\sqrt{\varepsilon} + 2\sqrt{\varepsilon + 2\sqrt{\varepsilon}}\right) \tag{17.112}$$

$$= \varepsilon + 4\sqrt{\varepsilon} + 4\sqrt{\varepsilon + 2\sqrt{\varepsilon}} + 2\sqrt{3\varepsilon + 2\sqrt{\varepsilon}} + 2\sqrt{2\left(\varepsilon + \sqrt{\varepsilon}\right)} \tag{17.113}$$

$$\leq \varepsilon + 4\sqrt{\varepsilon} + 24\sqrt[4]{\varepsilon}. \tag{17.114}$$

Observe from the above that the event that the quantity ε bounds the obfuscation error $o_e(\mathcal{C})$ of the Chernoff code with states ω_{C_m} implies the event when the quantity $\varepsilon + 4\sqrt{\varepsilon} + 24\sqrt[4]{\varepsilon}$ bounds the obfuscation error $o_e(\mathcal{C})$ of the original code with states σ_{C_m}. Thus, we can bound the probability of obfuscation error of the covering code by applying the Chernoff bound:

$$\Pr\left\{o_e(\mathcal{C}, \{\sigma_{C_m}\}) \leq \varepsilon + 4\sqrt{\varepsilon} + 24\sqrt[4]{\varepsilon}\right\}$$
$$\geq \Pr\left\{o_e(\mathcal{C}, \{\omega_{C_m}\}) \leq \varepsilon\right\} \tag{17.115}$$

$$\geq 1 - 2D\exp\left(-\frac{\varepsilon^3}{4\ln 2}\frac{|\mathcal{M}|\,d}{D}\right). \tag{17.116}$$

This argument shows that it is highly likely that a random covering code is good in the sense that it has a low obfuscation error.

EXERCISE 17.4.1   Prove that the covering lemma holds for the same ensemble and a set of projectors for which the following conditions hold:

$$\sum_{x\in\mathcal{X}} p_X(x) \operatorname{Tr}\left\{\sigma_x \Pi\right\} \geq 1 - \varepsilon, \tag{17.117}$$

$$\sum_{x\in\mathcal{X}} p_X(x) \operatorname{Tr}\left\{\sigma_x \Pi_x\right\} \geq 1 - \varepsilon, \tag{17.118}$$

$$\operatorname{Tr}\left\{\Pi\right\} \leq D, \tag{17.119}$$

$$\Pi_x \sigma_x \Pi_x \leq \frac{1}{d}\Pi_x. \tag{17.120}$$

EXERCISE 17.4.2   Show that there exists a particular covering code with the property that the obfuscation error is small.

17.5   History and Further Reading

Ahlswede & Winter (2002) introduced the operator Chernoff bound in the context of quantum identification. Winter & Massar (2001) and Winter (2004) later applied it to quantum measurement compression. Devetak & Winter (2003) applied the covering lemma to classical compression with quantum side information and to distilling secret key from quantum states (Devetak & Winter, 2005). Devetak (2005) and Cai et al. (2004) applied it to private classical communication over a quantum channel, and Groisman et al. (2005) applied it to study the destruction of correlations in a bipartite state.

Part V

Noiseless Quantum Shannon Theory

18 Schumacher Compression

One of the fundamental tasks in classical information theory is the compression of information. Given access to many uses of a noiseless classical channel, what is the best that a sender and receiver can make of this resource for compressed data transmission? Shannon's compression theorem demonstrates that the Shannon entropy is the fundamental limit for the compression rate in the i.i.d. setting (recall the development in Section 14.4). That is, if one compresses at a rate above the Shannon entropy, then it is possible to recover the compressed data perfectly in the asymptotic limit, and otherwise, it is not possible to do so.[1] This theorem establishes the prominent role of the entropy in Shannon's theory of information.

In the quantum world, it very well could be that one day a sender and a receiver would have many uses of a noiseless quantum channel available,[2] and the sender could use this resource to transmit compressed quantum information. But what exactly does this mean in the quantum setting? A simple model of a quantum information source is an ensemble of quantum states $\{p_X(x), |\psi_x\rangle\}$; i.e., the source outputs the state $|\psi_x\rangle$ with probability $p_X(x)$, and the states $\{|\psi_x\rangle\}$ do not necessarily have to form an orthonormal basis. Let us suppose for the moment that the classical data x is available as well, even though this might not necessarily be the case in practice. A naive strategy for compressing this quantum information source would be to ignore the quantum states coming out, handle the classical data instead, and exploit Shannon's compression protocol from Section 14.4. That is, the sender compresses the sequence x^n emitted from the quantum information source at a rate equal to the Shannon entropy $H(X)$, sends the compressed classical bits over the noiseless quantum channels, the receiver reproduces the classical sequence x^n at his end, and finally reconstructs the sequence $|\psi_{x^n}\rangle$ of quantum states corresponding to the classical sequence x^n.

The above strategy will certainly work, but it makes no use of the fact that the noiseless quantum channels are quantum! It is clear that noiseless quantum channels will be expensive in practice, and the above strategy is wasteful in this sense

---

[1] Technically, we did not prove the converse part of Shannon's data-compression theorem, but the converse of this chapter suffices for Shannon's classical theorem as well.

[2] How we hope so! If working, coherent fault-tolerant quantum computers come along one day, they stand to benefit from quantum compression protocols.

because it could have merely exploited classical channels (channels that cannot preserve superpositions) to achieve the same goals. Schumacher compression is a strategy that makes effective use of noiseless quantum channels to compress a quantum information source down to a rate equal to the quantum entropy. This has a great benefit from a practical standpoint—recall from Exercise 11.9.3 that the quantum entropy of a quantum information source is strictly lower than the source's Shannon entropy if the states in the ensemble are non-orthogonal. In order to execute the protocol, the sender and receiver simply need to know the density operator $\rho \equiv \sum_x p_X(x)|\psi_x\rangle\langle\psi_x|$ of the source. Furthermore, Schumacher compression is provably optimal in the sense that any protocol that compresses a quantum information source of the above form at a rate below the quantum entropy cannot have a vanishing error in the asymptotic limit.

Schumacher compression thus gives an operational interpretation of the quantum entropy as the fundamental limit on the rate of quantum data compression. Also, it sets the term "qubit" on a firm foundation in an information-theoretic sense as a measure of the amount of quantum information "contained" in a quantum information source.

We begin this chapter by giving the details of the general information-processing task corresponding to quantum data compression. We then prove that the quantum entropy is an achievable rate of compression and follow by showing that it is optimal (these two respective parts are the direct coding theorem and the converse theorem for quantum data compression). We illustrate how much savings one can gain in quantum data compression by detailing a specific example. The final section of the chapter closes with a presentation of more general forms of Schumacher compression.

18.1   The Information-Processing Task

We first discuss the general task that any quantum compression protocol attempts to accomplish. Three parameters n, R, and ε, corresponding to the length of the original quantum data sequence, the rate, and the error, respectively, characterize any such protocol. An (n, R, ε) quantum compression code consists of four steps: state preparation, encoding, transmission, and decoding. Figure 18.1 depicts a general protocol for quantum compression.

State Preparation. The quantum information source outputs a sequence $|\psi_{x^n}\rangle_{A^n}$ of quantum states according to the ensemble $\{p_X(x), |\psi_x\rangle\}$ where

$$|\psi_{x^n}\rangle_{A^n} \equiv |\psi_{x_1}\rangle_{A_1} \otimes \cdots \otimes |\psi_{x_n}\rangle_{A_n}. \tag{18.1}$$

The density operator, from the perspective of someone ignorant of the classical sequence x^n, is equal to the tensor power state $\rho^{\otimes n}$ where

$$\rho \equiv \sum_x p_X(x)|\psi_x\rangle\langle\psi_x|. \tag{18.2}$$

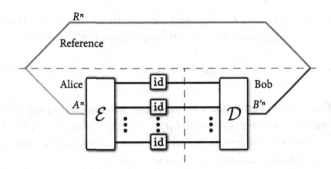

Figure 18.1 The most general protocol for quantum compression. Alice begins with the output of some quantum information source whose density operator is $\rho^{\otimes n}$ on some system A^n. The inaccessible reference system holds the purification of this density operator. She performs some CPTP encoding map $\mathcal{E}$, sends the compressed qubits through nR uses of a noiseless qubit channel, and Bob performs some CPTP decoding map $\mathcal{D}$ to decompress the qubits. The scheme is successful if the initial state and the final state are indistinguishable in the asymptotic limit $n \to \infty$.

Also, we can think about the purification of the above density operator. That is, a related picture is to imagine that the quantum information source produces states of the form

$$|\varphi_\rho\rangle_{RA} \equiv \sum_x \sqrt{p_X(x)}|x\rangle_R|\psi_x\rangle_A, \tag{18.3}$$

where R is the label for an inaccessible reference system (not to be confused with the rate R!). The resulting i.i.d. state produced is $(|\varphi_\rho\rangle_{RA})^{\otimes n}$.

Encoding. Alice encodes the systems A^n according to some compression channel $\mathcal{E}_{A^n \to W}$ where W is a quantum system of size 2^{nR}. Recall that R is the rate of compression:

$$R = \frac{1}{n}\log \dim(\mathcal{H}_W). \tag{18.4}$$

Transmission. Alice transmits the system W to Bob using nR noiseless qubit channels.

Decoding. Bob sends the system W through a decompression channel $\mathcal{D}_{W \to \hat{A}^n}$.

The protocol has $\varepsilon \in [0, 1]$ error if the compressed and decompressed state is ε-close in normalized trace distance to the original state $(|\varphi_\rho\rangle_{RA})^{\otimes n}$:

$$\frac{1}{2}\left\| (\varphi_{RA}^\rho)^{\otimes n} - (\mathcal{D}_{W \to \hat{A}^n} \circ \mathcal{E}_{A^n \to W})((\varphi_{RA}^\rho)^{\otimes n}) \right\|_1 \leq \varepsilon. \tag{18.5}$$

We say that a quantum compression rate R is *achievable* if there exists an $(n, R + \delta, \varepsilon)$ quantum compression code for all $\delta > 0, \varepsilon \in (0, 1)$, and sufficiently large n. The *quantum data compression limit* of ρ is equal to the infimum of all achievable quantum compression rates.

EXERCISE 18.1.1   An alternate figure of merit for the performance of Schumacher compression is the average ensemble trace distance, given by

$$\frac{1}{2} \sum_{x^n} p_{X^n}(x^n) \left\| \psi_{x^n} - (\mathcal{D}_{W \to \hat{A}^n} \circ \mathcal{E}_{A^n \to W})(\psi_{x^n}) \right\|_1. \tag{18.6}$$

Prove that a quantum compression protocol satisfying (18.5) also has an average ensemble trace distance no larger than ε. (Hint: Consider using the monotonicity of trace distance with respect to quantum channels and acting on the reference systems with a particular channel.)

18.2   The Quantum Data Compression Theorem

Schumacher's compression theorem establishes the quantum entropy as the fundamental limit on quantum data compression.

THEOREM 18.2.1 (Quantum Data Compression)   Suppose that ρ_A is the density operator corresponding to a quantum information source. Then the quantum entropy $H(A)_\rho$ is equal to the quantum data compression limit of ρ.

18.2.1   The Direct Coding Theorem

Schumacher's compression protocol demonstrates that the quantum entropy $H(A)_\rho$ is an achievable rate for quantum data compression. It is remarkably similar to Shannon's compression protocol from Section 14.4, but it has some subtle differences that are necessary for the quantum setting. The basic steps of the encoding are to perform a typical subspace measurement and an isometry that compresses the typical subspace. The decoder then performs the inverse of the isometry to decompress the state. The protocol is successful if the typical subspace measurement successfully projects onto the typical subspace, and it fails otherwise. Just like in the classical case, the law of large numbers guarantees that the protocol is successful in the asymptotic limit as $n \to \infty$. Figure 18.2 provides an illustration of the protocol, and we now provide a rigorous argument.

Alice begins with n copies of the state $(\varphi_{RA}^\rho)^{\otimes n}$. Suppose that a spectral decomposition of ρ is as follows:

$$\rho = \sum_z p_Z(z) |z\rangle\langle z|, \tag{18.7}$$

where $p_Z(z)$ is some probability distribution, and $\{|z\rangle\}$ is some orthonormal basis. Her first step is to perform a typical subspace measurement onto the typical subspace of A^n, where the typical projector is with respect to the density operator ρ. Recall from the Shannon compression protocol in Section 14.4 that we exploited a one-to-one function f that mapped from the set of typical sequences to a set of binary sequences $\{0, 1\}^{n[H(\rho)+\delta]}$. Now, we can construct a linear map U_f that

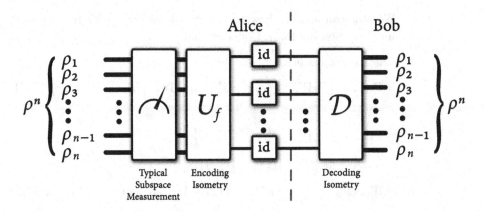

Figure 18.2 Schumacher's compression protocol. Alice begins with many copies of the output of the quantum information source. She performs a measurement onto the typical subspace corresponding to the state ρ and then performs a compression isometry of the typical subspace to a space of dimension $2^{n[H(\rho)+\delta]}$, corresponding to $n\left[H(\rho) + \delta\right]$ qubits. She transmits these compressed qubits over $n\left[H(\rho) + \delta\right]$ uses of a noiseless qubit channel. Bob performs the inverse of the isometry to uncompress the qubits. The protocol is successful in the asymptotic limit due to the properties of typical subspaces.

is a coherent version of this classical function f. It simply maps the orthonormal basis $\{|z^n\rangle_{A^n}\}$ to the basis $\{|f(z^n)\rangle_W\}$:

$$U_f \equiv \sum_{z^n \in T_\delta^{Z^n}} |f(z^n)\rangle_W \langle z^n|_{A^n}, \tag{18.8}$$

where Z is a random variable corresponding to the distribution $p_Z(z)$, so that $T_\delta^{Z^n}$ is its typical set. The inverse of the above operator is an isometry because the input space $\text{span}\{|z^n\rangle_{A^n} : z^n \in T_\delta^{Z^n}\}$ is a subspace of size at most $2^{n[H(\rho)+\delta]}$ (recall Property 15.1.2) embedded in a larger space of size $[\dim(\mathcal{H}_A)]^n$ and the output space is of size at most $2^{n[H(\rho)+\delta]}$. So her next step is to perform the compression conditioned on the typical subspace measurement being successful. We can thus write the encoding as a single quantum channel as follows:

$$\mathcal{E}_{A^n \to W}(X_{A^n}) \equiv U_f \Pi_{A^n}^\delta X_{A^n} \Pi_{A^n}^\delta U_f^\dagger + \text{Tr}\{(I_{A^n} - \Pi_{A^n}^\delta)X_{A^n}\}\sigma_W, \tag{18.9}$$

where $X_{A^n} \in \mathcal{L}(\mathcal{H}_{A^n})$ and σ_W is any density operator with support in $\text{span}\{|f(z^n)\rangle_W : z^n \in T_\delta^{Z^n}\}$. Alice then sends the W system of $\mathcal{E}_{A^n \to W}((\varphi_{RA}^\rho)^{\otimes n})$ (the compressed qubits) over $n\left[H(\rho) + \delta\right]$ uses of the noiseless qubit channel.

Bob's decoding $\mathcal{D}_{W \to A^n}$ essentially performs the inverse of the linear map U_f, implemented as the following quantum channel:

$$\mathcal{D}_{W \to A^n}(Y_W) \equiv U_f^\dagger Y_W U_f + \text{Tr}\{(I - U_f U_f^\dagger)Y_W\}\tau_{A^n}, \tag{18.10}$$

where $Y_W \in \mathcal{L}(\mathcal{H}_W)$ and $\tau_{A^n} \in \mathcal{D}(\mathcal{H}_{A^n})$.

We now can analyze how this protocol performs with respect to our performance criterion in (18.5). Consider that

$$(\mathcal{D}_{W \to A^n} \circ \mathcal{E}_{A^n \to W}) ((\varphi_{RA}^\rho)^{\otimes n})$$

$$= \mathcal{D}_{W \to A^n} \left(U_f \Pi_{A^n}^\delta (\varphi_{RA}^\rho)^{\otimes n} \Pi_{A^n}^\delta U_f^\dagger + \mathrm{Tr}_{A^n} \{ (I_{A^n} - \Pi_{A^n}^\delta) (\varphi_{RA}^\rho)^{\otimes n} \} \otimes \sigma_W \right)$$
(18.11)

$$= \mathcal{D}_{W \to A^n} \left(U_f \Pi_{A^n}^\delta (\varphi_{RA}^\rho)^{\otimes n} \Pi_{A^n}^\delta U_f^\dagger \right)$$
$$+ \mathcal{D}_{W \to A^n} \left(\mathrm{Tr}_{A^n} \{ (I_{A^n} - \Pi_{A^n}^\delta) (\varphi_{RA}^\rho)^{\otimes n} \} \otimes \sigma_W \right)$$
(18.12)

$$= \Pi_{A^n}^\delta (\varphi_{RA}^\rho)^{\otimes n} \Pi_{A^n}^\delta + \mathrm{Tr}_{A^n} \{ (I_{A^n} - \Pi_{A^n}^\delta) (\varphi_{RA}^\rho)^{\otimes n} \} \otimes \mathcal{D}_{W \to A^n} (\sigma_W).$$
(18.13)

Then

$$\left\| (\varphi_{RA}^\rho)^{\otimes n} - (\mathcal{D}_{W \to A^n} \circ \mathcal{E}_{A^n \to W}) ((\varphi_{RA}^\rho)^{\otimes n}) \right\|_1$$

$$\leq \left\| (\varphi_{RA}^\rho)^{\otimes n} - \Pi_{A^n}^\delta (\varphi_{RA}^\rho)^{\otimes n} \Pi_{A^n}^\delta \right\|_1$$
$$+ \left\| \mathrm{Tr}_{A^n} \{ (I_{A^n} - \Pi_{A^n}^\delta) (\varphi_{RA}^\rho)^{\otimes n} \} \otimes \mathcal{D}_{W \to A^n} (\sigma_W) \right\|_1$$
(18.14)

$$\leq 2\sqrt{\varepsilon} + \varepsilon.$$
(18.15)

The first inequality follows from the triangle inequality. The second inequality follows from the first property of typical subspaces:

$$\mathrm{Tr} \left\{ \Pi_{A^n}^\delta (\varphi_{RA}^\rho)^{\otimes n} \right\} = \mathrm{Tr} \left\{ \Pi_{A^n}^\delta \rho^{\otimes n} \right\} \geq 1 - \varepsilon,$$
(18.16)

the gentle operator lemma (Lemma 9.4.2), and the fact that

$$\left\| \mathrm{Tr}_{A^n} \{ (I_{A^n} - \Pi_{A^n}^\delta) (\varphi_{RA}^\rho)^{\otimes n} \} \otimes \mathcal{D}_{W \to A^n} (\sigma_W) \right\|_1$$

$$= \left\| \mathrm{Tr}_{A^n} \{ (I_{A^n} - \Pi_{A^n}^\delta) (\varphi_{RA}^\rho)^{\otimes n} \} \right\|_1 \| \mathcal{D}_{W \to A^n} (\sigma_W) \|_1$$
(18.17)

$$\leq \mathrm{Tr} \{ (I_{A^n} - \Pi_{A^n}^\delta) (\varphi_{RA}^\rho)^{\otimes n} \} \leq \varepsilon.$$
(18.18)

We remark that it is important for the typical subspace measurement in (18.9) to be implemented (as indicated) as a non-destructive quantum measurement. That is, the only information that this measurement should learn is whether the state is typical or not. Otherwise, there would be too much disturbance to the quantum information, and the protocol would fail at the desired task of compression. Such precise control on so many qubits is possible in principle, but it is rather daunting to implement in practice!

18.2.2   The Converse Theorem

We now prove the converse theorem for quantum data compression by considering the most general compression protocol that meets the success criterion in (18.5) and demonstrating that a sequence of such protocols with error approaching zero should have their rate of compression above the quantum entropy of the source. Alice would like to compress a state $\rho^{\otimes n}$ that acts on a Hilbert space A^n. A purification $\phi_{R^n A^n} \equiv (\varphi_{RA}^\rho)^{\otimes n}$ of this state represents the state of the joint systems A^n and R^n where R^n is the purifying system (again, we should not confuse reference system R^n with rate R). If she can compress any system on A^n and recover it faithfully, then she should be able to do so for the purification of the state. An $(n, R + \delta, \varepsilon)$ compression code has the property that it can compress at a rate $R + \delta \equiv [\log \dim(\mathcal{H}_W)]/n$ with only error ε. The quantum data processing is

$$A^n \quad \xrightarrow{\mathcal{E}_{A^n \to W}} \quad W \quad \xrightarrow{\mathcal{D}_{W \to \hat{A}^n}} \quad \hat{A}^n \tag{18.19}$$

and the following inequality holds for a quantum compression protocol with error ε:

$$\frac{1}{2} \left\| \omega_{R^n \hat{A}^n} - (\varphi_{RA}^\rho)^{\otimes n} \right\|_1 \leq \varepsilon, \tag{18.20}$$

where

$$\omega_{R^n \hat{A}^n} \equiv \mathcal{D}_{W \to \hat{A}^n}(\mathcal{E}_{A^n \to W}((\varphi_{RA}^\rho)^{\otimes n})). \tag{18.21}$$

Let $\tau_{R^n W} \equiv \mathcal{E}_{A^n \to W}((\varphi_{RA}^\rho)^{\otimes n})$. Consider the following chain of inequalities:

$$2 \log \dim(\mathcal{H}_W) \geq I(W; R^n)_\tau \tag{18.22}$$
$$\geq I(\hat{A}^n; R^n)_\omega \tag{18.23}$$
$$\geq I(A^n; R^n)_{\varphi^{\otimes n}} - f(n, \varepsilon) \tag{18.24}$$
$$= n I(A; R)_\varphi - f(n, \varepsilon) \tag{18.25}$$
$$= 2n H(A)_\varphi - f(n, \varepsilon). \tag{18.26}$$

The first inequality is a consequence of a dimension bound for the quantum mutual information $I(E; F) \leq 2 \log (\min \{|E|, |F|\})$ (see Exercise 11.6.3). The second inequality follows from the quantum data-processing inequality (Bob processes W using the decoder to get $\hat{A}^n$). The third inequality follows because $H(R^n)_\omega = H(R^n)_{\varphi^{\otimes n}}$, so that

$$\left| I(\hat{A}^n; R^n)_\omega - I(A^n; R^n)_{\varphi^{\otimes n}} \right|$$
$$= \left| H(R^n)_\omega - H(R^n|\hat{A}^n)_\omega - \left[H(A^n)_{\varphi^{\otimes n}} - H(R^n|A^n)_{\varphi^{\otimes n}} \right] \right| \tag{18.27}$$
$$= \left| H(R^n|A^n)_{\varphi^{\otimes n}} - H(R^n|\hat{A}^n)_\omega \right| \tag{18.28}$$
$$\leq f(n, \varepsilon) \equiv 2\varepsilon n \log \dim(\mathcal{H}_R) + (1 + \varepsilon) h_2(\varepsilon/[1 + \varepsilon]). \tag{18.29}$$

The inequality directly above follows from the AFW inequality (Theorem 11.10.3) applied to the success criterion in (18.20). The function $f(n, \varepsilon)$ has the property that $\lim_{\varepsilon \to 0} \lim_{n \to \infty} \frac{1}{n} f(n, \varepsilon) = 0$. The equality in (18.25) follows because the quantum mutual information is additive for tensor-product states. The equality in (18.26) follows because the quantum mutual information of a pure, bipartite state is equal to twice the marginal entropy. Putting everything together, we find that

$$R + \delta = \frac{1}{n} \log \dim(\mathcal{H}_W) \geq H(A)_{\varphi^\rho} - \frac{1}{2n} f(n, \varepsilon). \qquad (18.30)$$

Taking the limit as $n \to \infty$ and $\varepsilon, \delta \to 0$ allows us to conclude that an achievable rate R of quantum data compression necessarily satisfies $R \geq H(A)_{\varphi^\rho}$.

EXERCISE 18.2.1   We proved the converse theorem for Schumacher compression with respect to the error criterion in (18.5). However, it might be the case that if we use the less stringent error criterion in (18.6) that we could achieve a smaller rate of quantum data compression. Show that this is not the case, by establishing that the converse theorem holds with this less stringent error criterion. (Hint: The development is essentially the same as in (18.22)–(18.26), except you should have the reference system be classical, containing a classical label for which state in the i.i.d. ensemble was chosen.)

18.3   Quantum Compression Example

We now highlight a particular example where Schumacher compression gives a big savings in compression rates if noiseless qubit channels are available. Suppose that the ensemble is of the following form:

$$\left\{ \left(\frac{1}{2}, |0\rangle \right), \left(\frac{1}{2}, |+\rangle \right) \right\}. \qquad (18.31)$$

This ensemble is known as the Bennett-92 ensemble because it is useful in Bennett's protocol for quantum key distribution. The naive strategy would be for Alice and Bob to exploit Shannon's compression protocol. That is, Alice would ignore the quantum nature of the states, and supposing that the classical label for them were available, she would encode the classical label. However, the entropy of the uniform distribution on two states is equal to one bit, and she would have to transmit classical messages at a rate of one bit per channel use.

A different strategy is to employ Schumacher compression. The density operator of the above ensemble is

$$\frac{1}{2}|0\rangle\langle 0| + \frac{1}{2}|+\rangle\langle +|, \qquad (18.32)$$

which has the following spectral decomposition:

$$\cos^2(\pi/8) |+'\rangle \langle +'| + \sin^2(\pi/8) |-'\rangle \langle -'|, \qquad (18.33)$$

where

$$|+'\rangle \equiv \cos(\pi/8)|0\rangle + \sin(\pi/8)|1\rangle, \qquad (18.34)$$
$$|-'\rangle \equiv \sin(\pi/8)|0\rangle - \cos(\pi/8)|1\rangle. \qquad (18.35)$$

The binary entropy $h_2(\cos^2(\pi/8))$ of the distribution $[\cos^2(\pi/8), \sin^2(\pi/8)]$ is approximately equal to

$$0.6009 \text{ qubits}, \tag{18.36}$$

and thus they can save a significant amount in terms of compression rate by employing Schumacher compression. This type of savings will always occur whenever the ensemble includes non-orthogonal quantum states.

EXERCISE 18.3.1 In the above example, suppose that Alice associates a classical label with the states, so that the ensemble instead is

$$\left\{ \left(\frac{1}{2}, |0\rangle\langle 0| \otimes |0\rangle\langle 0| \right), \left(\frac{1}{2}, |1\rangle\langle 1| \otimes |+\rangle\langle +| \right) \right\}. \tag{18.37}$$

Does this help in reducing the amount of qubits she has to transmit to Bob?

18.4 Variations on the Schumacher Theme

We can propose several variations on the Schumacher compression theme. For example, suppose that the quantum information source corresponds to the following ensemble instead:

$$\{p_X(x), \rho_A^x\}, \tag{18.38}$$

where each ρ_x is a mixed state. Then the situation is not as "clear-cut" as in the simpler model for a quantum information source, and the entropy of the source does not necessarily serve as a lower bound on the ultimate compressibility rate. This depends on the figure of merit that we choose for mixed-state compression, and there are at least three interesting figures of merit that we could consider. To see these different ones, observe that the following state serves as a purification of the mixed-state source in (18.38):

$$|\phi\rangle_{XX'RA} \equiv \sum_x \sqrt{p_X(x)} |x\rangle_X |x\rangle_{X'} \left| \phi^{\rho^x} \right\rangle_{RA}, \tag{18.39}$$

where $|\phi^{\rho^x}\rangle_{RA}$ is a purification of ρ_A^x, so that the purifying system of A is the joint system $XX'R$. The three figures of merit to consider for any encoding-decoding pair $(\mathcal{E}_{A^n \to W}, \mathcal{D}_{W \to \hat{A}^n})$ are as follows:

$$\frac{1}{2} \left\| \phi_{XX'RA}^{\otimes n} - (\mathcal{D}_{W \to \hat{A}^n} \circ \mathcal{E}_{A^n \to W})(\phi_{XX'RA}^{\otimes n}) \right\|_1, \tag{18.40}$$

$$\frac{1}{2} \sum_{x^n} p_{X^n}(x^n) \left\| \phi_{R^n A^n}^{\rho^{x^n}} - (\mathcal{D}_{W \to \hat{A}^n} \circ \mathcal{E}_{A^n \to W})(\phi_{R^n A^n}^{\rho^{x^n}}) \right\|_1, \tag{18.41}$$

$$\frac{1}{2} \sum_{x^n} p_{X^n}(x^n) \left\| \rho_{A^n}^{x^n} - (\mathcal{D}_{W \to \hat{A}^n} \circ \mathcal{E}_{A^n \to W})(\rho_{A^n}^{x^n}) \right\|_1. \tag{18.42}$$

Consider that satisfying the first error criterion up to some $\varepsilon \in [0, 1]$ implies that second criterion is satisfied as well, which in turn implies that the third is satisfied (this follows from a reasoning similar to that in the hint for Exercise 18.1.1).

How should we handle the mixed source case in general? Let us consider the direct coding theorem and the converse theorem. The direct coding theorem for this case is essentially equivalent to Schumacher's protocol for quantum compression—there does not appear to be a better approach in the general case. The density operator of the source is equal to

$$\rho_A = \sum_x p_X(x)\rho_A^x. \tag{18.43}$$

A compression rate $R \geq H(A)_\rho$ is achievable if we form the typical subspace measurement from the typical subspace projector $\Pi_{A^n}^\delta$ onto the state $(\rho_A)^{\otimes n}$, and the error analysis from before shows that this holds for the error criterion in (18.40), which implies that it holds for the other two error criteria mentioned above.

Although the direct coding theorem stays the same, the converse theorem changes somewhat. If we demand that the converse hold for the error criterion in (18.40), then the method of proof in (18.22)–(18.26) demonstrates that the entropy $H(A)_\rho$ serves as a converse bound. Thus, in this case, we have a statement of optimality. However, if we demand that the converse hold for the error criterion in (18.41), then the same method of proof gives a converse bound of $\frac{1}{2}I(XR;A)_\phi$. If we demand that the converse hold for the error criterion in (18.42), then the method of proof from Exercise 18.2.1 gives a converse bound of $I(X;A)_\phi$. In general, these latter two lower bounds are incomparable, but we can deduce that a sequence of compression schemes each meeting the error criterion in (18.41) should have a compression rate larger than or equal to $\max\{\frac{1}{2}I(XR;A)_\phi, I(X;A)_\phi\}$, given that the error criterion in (18.41) is more stringent than that in (18.42).

Let us consider a special example of the above situation, which allows for comparing the two different error criteria in (18.40) and (18.42) and the optimal rates. Suppose that the mixed states ρ_x act on orthogonal subspaces, and let $\rho_A = \sum_x p_X(x)\rho_x$ denote the expected density operator of the ensemble. The states in $\{\rho_x\}$ are then perfectly distinguishable by a measurement whose projectors project onto the different orthogonal subspaces. As a consequence, Alice could perform this measurement and associate classical labels with each of the states, leading to the following classical–quantum state:

$$\sigma_{XA} \equiv \sum_x p_X(x)|x\rangle\langle x|_X \otimes \rho_A^x. \tag{18.44}$$

Furthermore, she can do this in principle without disturbing the state in any way, and therefore the entropy of the state σ_{XA} is equivalent to the original entropy of the state ρ_A:

$$H(A)_\rho = H(XA)_\sigma. \tag{18.45}$$

Applying Schumacher compression to such a source meets the error criterion in (18.40) at an optimal rate equal to $H(A)_\rho$. This compression rate is equal to

$$H(XA)_\sigma = H(X)_\sigma + H(A|X)_\sigma, \tag{18.46}$$

and in this case, $H(A|X)_\sigma \geq 0$ because the conditioning system is classical. Furthermore, if at least one ρ^x is truly mixed then we have a strict inequality $H(A|X)_\sigma > 0$. However, if we are only interested in a scheme which meets the error criterion in (18.42), then a much better strategy than Schumacher compression is for Alice to measure the classical variable X directly, compress it with Shannon compression, and transmit to Bob so that he can reconstruct the quantum states at his end of the channel. The rate of compression here is equal to the Shannon entropy $H(X)_\sigma$, which is provably lower than $H(XA)_\rho$ for this example. Since $I(X;A)_\sigma = H(X)_\sigma$ (see exercise below), this example has an optimal rate for the error criterion in (18.42) and we see that there can be a strict difference in optimal rates if we consider different error criteria in mixed-state compression.

The next exercise asks you to verify that ensembles of mixed states on orthogonal subspaces saturate the lower bound of $I(X;A)_\phi$.

EXERCISE 18.4.1 Show that the Holevo information of an ensemble of mixed states on orthogonal subspaces has its Shannon information equal to its Holevo information. Thus, this is an example of a class of ensembles that meet the lower bound $I(X;A)_\phi$ on compressibility.

18.5 Concluding Remarks

Schumacher compression was the first quantum Shannon-theoretic result discovered and is the simplest one that we encounter in this book. The proof is remarkably similar to the proof of Shannon's noiseless coding theorem, with the main difference being that we should be more careful in the quantum case not to be learning any more information than necessary when performing measurements. The intuition that we gain for future quantum protocols is that it often suffices to consider only what happens to a high probability subspace rather than the whole space itself if our primary goal is to have a small probability of error in a communication task. In fact, this intuition is the same needed for understanding information-processing tasks such as entanglement concentration, classical communication, private classical communication, and quantum communication.

The problem of characterizing the lower and upper bounds for the quantum compression rate of a mixed state quantum information source still remains open, despite considerable efforts in this direction. It is only in special cases, such as the example mentioned in Section 18.4, that we know of a matching lower and upper bound as in Schumacher's original theorem.

18.6 History and Further Reading

Ohya & Petz (1993) devised the notion of a typical subspace, and Schumacher (1995) independently introduced typical subspaces and additionally proved the quantum data-compression theorem. Jozsa & Schumacher (1994) later generalized this proof, and Lo (1995) further generalized the theorem to mixed state sources. There are other generalizations in Horodecki (1998) and Barnum, Caves, Fuchs, Jozsa & Schumacher (2001). Several schemes for universal quantum data compression exist (Jozsa et al., 1998; Jozsa & Presnell, 2003; Bennett et al., 2006), in which the sender does not need to have a description of the quantum information source in order to compress its output. There are also practical schemes for quantum data compression discussed in work about quantum Huffman codes (Braunstein et al., 2000).

Going beyond the settings considered here, researchers have considered error exponents, strong converses, and second-order characterizations for quantum data compression (we explain what these terms mean in Section 20.7). Winter (1999b) established a strong converse theorem, Hayashi (2002) derived error exponents, and Datta & Leditzky (2015) established second-order characterizations.

19 Entanglement Manipulation

Entanglement is one of the most useful resources in quantum information. If Alice and Bob share noiseless entanglement in the form of maximally entangled states, then they can teleport quantum bits between each other with the help of classical communication, or they can double the capacity of a noiseless qubit channel for transmitting classical information. We will see further applications in Chapter 21 in which they can exploit noiseless entanglement to assist in the transmission of classical or quantum data over a quantum channel.

Given the utility of maximal entanglement, a reasonable question to ask is what two spatially separated parties can accomplish if they share pure entangled states that are not maximally entangled. In the quantum Shannon-theoretic setting, we make the further assumption that the two parties share many copies of the same pure entangled state. We find out in this chapter that they can "concentrate" these non-maximally entangled states to maximally entangled ebits by performing local operations on their systems, and the optimal rate at which they can do so is equal to the "entropy of entanglement" (the quantum entropy of the marginal density operator of the original state). Entanglement concentration is thus another fundamental task in noiseless quantum Shannon theory, and it gives a different operational interpretation to the quantum entropy. Entanglement concentration is perhaps complementary to Schumacher compression in the sense that it gives a firm quantum information-theoretic interpretation of the term "ebit" (just as Schumacher compression did for the term "qubit"), and it plays a part in demonstrating how the entropy of entanglement is the unique measure of entanglement for pure bipartite states.

More generally, Alice and Bob could try to convert a large number of copies of a pure state $|\psi\rangle_{AB}$ into as many copies as possible of another bipartite pure state $|\phi\rangle_{AB}$, by performing only local operations and exchanging classical messages (called "LOCC," an abbreviation for "local operations and classical communication"). It is important to place a constraint on their allowed operations—if they could perform arbitrary global operations on their systems, then the task becomes trivial. We call such a task "entanglement manipulation" as a generalization of the aforementioned entanglement concentration task.

The main result in this chapter is that the optimal rate of conversion for such an entanglement manipulation task is equal to $H(A)_\psi / H(A)_\phi$. That is, if the goal is to convert $|\psi\rangle_{AB}^{\otimes n}$ by LOCC to a state that has very high fidelity with $|\phi\rangle_{AB}^{\otimes nE}$, then this transformation is possible for large n if and only if $E \leq H(A)_\psi / H(A)_\phi$. This conversion rate $H(A)_\psi / H(A)_\phi$ is known as the "entanglement manipulation limit." The achievability part of this theorem follows by breaking the task into two parts. In the first part, Alice and Bob perform entanglement concentration to convert $|\psi\rangle_{AB}^{\otimes n}$ to $\approx nH(A)_\psi$ ebits. The next part makes use of a protocol called "entanglement dilution," which converts $nH(A)_\phi$ ebits to $\approx n$ copies of $|\phi\rangle_{AB}$ by means of LOCC. Scaling the conversion rate appropriately, it follows that $nH(A)_\psi$ ebits can be converted to $\approx n [H(A)_\psi / H(A)_\phi]$ copies of $|\phi\rangle_{AB}$, concluding the direct part. The converse part of this theorem follows by exploiting the properties of an information quantity called the relative entropy of entanglement (the main properties that we need are that it does not increase under the action of an LOCC channel, it is never smaller than the coherent information, and it is equal to the entropy of entanglement for pure states).

The entanglement manipulation theorem mentioned above is one of the most important results in the resource theory of quantum entanglement. It demonstrates that the conversion of pure-state entanglement from one form to another is essentially reversible in the limit of many copies. That is, when n is very large, Alice and Bob could first concentrate $|\psi\rangle_{AB}^{\otimes n}$ to $\approx nH(A)_\psi$ ebits. Then they could execute an entanglement dilution protocol to transform these $\approx nH(A)_\psi$ ebits back to the original state $|\psi\rangle_{AB}^{\otimes n(1-\delta)}$, where $\delta \in (0,1)$ is a small number that can be made to go to zero as n becomes large. Alternatively, they could take the original state to some other "in-between" state besides the ebit at a rate given by the ratio of the entropies of entanglement, but the main advantage of the ebit is that its entropy of entanglement is equal to one, so that we can think of it as a unit resource.

The technique for proving that the quantum entropy is an achievable rate for entanglement concentration exploits the method of types outlined in Sections 14.7 and 15.3 for classical and quantum typicality, respectively (the most important property is Property 14.7.5 which states that the exponentiated entropy is a lower bound on the size of a typical type class). In hindsight, it is perhaps surprising that a typical type class is exponentially large in the large n limit (on the same order as the typical set itself), and we soon discover the quantum Shannon-theoretic consequences of this result. The protocol for entanglement dilution is in some sense just that for entanglement concentration "run backwards," additionally making use of quantum teleportation.

We begin this chapter by discussing a simple example of entanglement concentration for three copies of a state, and then we sketch out how more general entanglement concentration and dilution protocols operate. Section 19.2 gives a formal definition of LOCC and introduces the relative entropy of entanglement (an LOCC monotone). Section 19.3 then details the information-processing task for entanglement manipulation, and Section 19.4 states the entanglement manipulation theorem and proves both the direct coding and converse parts.

19.1   Sketch of Entanglement Manipulation

This section sketches the main ideas underlying entanglement concentration and dilution.

19.1.1   Three-Copy Entanglement Concentration Example

A simple example illustrates the main idea underlying the concentration of entanglement. Consider the following partially entangled state:

$$|\Phi_\theta\rangle_{AB} \equiv \cos(\theta)|00\rangle_{AB} + \sin(\theta)|11\rangle_{AB}, \tag{19.1}$$

where θ is some parameter such that $0 < \theta < \pi/2$. The Schmidt decomposition (Theorem 3.8.1) guarantees that the above state is the most general form to consider for a pure bipartite entangled state on qubits. Now suppose that Alice and Bob share three copies of the above state. We can rewrite the three copies of the above state using simple algebra:

$$|\Phi_\theta\rangle_{A_1 B_1} |\Phi_\theta\rangle_{A_2 B_2} |\Phi_\theta\rangle_{A_3 B_3} = \cos^3(\theta)|000\rangle_A|000\rangle_B + \sin^3(\theta)|111\rangle_A|111\rangle_B$$
$$+ \sqrt{3}\cos(\theta)\sin^2(\theta)\frac{1}{\sqrt{3}}\left(|110\rangle_A|110\rangle_B + |101\rangle_A|101\rangle_B + |011\rangle_A|011\rangle_B\right)$$
$$+ \sqrt{3}\cos^2(\theta)\sin(\theta)\frac{1}{\sqrt{3}}\left(|100\rangle_A|100\rangle_B + |010\rangle_A|010\rangle_B + |001\rangle_A|001\rangle_B\right), \tag{19.2}$$

where we have relabeled all of the systems on Alice and Bob's respective sides as $A \equiv A_1 A_2 A_3$ and $B \equiv B_1 B_2 B_3$. Observe that the subspace with coefficient $\cos^3(\theta)$ whose states have zero "ones" is one-dimensional. The subspace whose states have three "ones" is also one-dimensional. But the subspace with coefficient $\cos(\theta)\sin^2(\theta)$ whose states have two "ones" is three-dimensional, and the same holds for the subspace whose states each have one "one."

A protocol for entanglement concentration in this scenario is then straightforward. Alice performs a projective measurement consisting of the operators Π_0, Π_1, Π_2, Π_3 where

$$\Pi_0 \equiv |000\rangle\langle000|_A, \tag{19.3}$$
$$\Pi_1 \equiv |001\rangle\langle001|_A + |010\rangle\langle010|_A + |100\rangle\langle100|_A, \tag{19.4}$$
$$\Pi_2 \equiv |110\rangle\langle110|_A + |101\rangle\langle101|_A + |011\rangle\langle011|_A, \tag{19.5}$$
$$\Pi_3 \equiv |111\rangle\langle111|_A. \tag{19.6}$$

The subscript i of the projection operator Π_i corresponds to the Hamming weight of the basis states in the corresponding subspace. Bob can perform the same "Hamming weight" measurement on his side. With probability $\cos^6(\theta) + \sin^6(\theta)$, the procedure fails because it results in $|000\rangle_A|000\rangle_B$ or $|111\rangle_A|111\rangle_B$ which are both product states with no entanglement at all. But with probability

$3\cos^2(\theta)\sin^4(\theta)$, the state is in the subspace with Hamming weight two, and it has the following form:

$$\frac{1}{\sqrt{3}}\left(|110\rangle_A|110\rangle_B + |101\rangle_A|101\rangle_B + |011\rangle_A|011\rangle_B\right), \tag{19.7}$$

and with probability $3\cos^4(\theta)\sin^2(\theta)$, the state is in the subspace with Hamming weight one, and it has the following form:

$$\frac{1}{\sqrt{3}}\left(|100\rangle_A|100\rangle_B + |010\rangle_A|010\rangle_B + |001\rangle_A|001\rangle_B\right). \tag{19.8}$$

Alice and Bob can then perform local isometric operations on their respective systems to rotate either of these states to a maximally entangled state with Schmidt rank three:

$$\frac{1}{\sqrt{3}}\left(|0\rangle_A|0\rangle_B + |1\rangle_A|1\rangle_B + |2\rangle_A|2\rangle_B\right). \tag{19.9}$$

19.1.2   Sketch of Entanglement Concentration

The simple protocol outlined above is the basis for the entanglement concentration protocol, but it unfortunately fails with a non-negligible probability in this case. On the other hand, if we allow Alice and Bob to have a large number of copies of a pure bipartite entangled state, the probability of failing becomes negligible in the asymptotic limit due to the properties of typicality, and each type class subspace contains an exponentially large maximally entangled state. The proof of the direct coding theorem in Section 19.4.2 makes this intuition precise.

Generalizing the procedure outlined above to an arbitrary number of copies is straightforward. Suppose Alice and Bob share n copies of the partially entangled state $|\Phi_\theta\rangle$. We can then write the state as follows:

$$|\Phi_\theta\rangle_{A^n B^n} = \sum_{k=0}^{n} \cos^{n-k}(\theta)\sin^k(\theta) \sum_{x:w(x)=k} |x\rangle_{A^n}|x\rangle_{B^n} \tag{19.10}$$

$$= \sum_{k=0}^{n} \sqrt{\binom{n}{k}}\cos^{n-k}(\theta)\sin^k(\theta)\left(\frac{1}{\sqrt{\binom{n}{k}}}\sum_{x:w(x)=k}|x\rangle_{A^n}|x\rangle_{B^n}\right), \tag{19.11}$$

where $w(x)$ is the Hamming weight of the binary vector x. Alice performs a "Hamming weight" measurement whose projective operators are as follows:

$$\Pi_k = \sum_{x:w(x)=k}|x\rangle\langle x|_{A^n}, \tag{19.12}$$

and the Schmidt rank of the maximally entangled state that they then share is $\binom{n}{k}$.

We can give a rough analysis of the performance of the above protocol when n becomes large by exploiting Stirling's approximation (we just need a handle on the term $\binom{n}{k}$ for large n). Recall that Stirling's approximation is $n! \approx \sqrt{2\pi n}\,(n/e)^n$, and this gives

$$\binom{n}{k} = \frac{n!}{k!\,n-k!} \approx \frac{\sqrt{2\pi n}\,(n/e)^n}{\sqrt{2\pi k}\,(k/e)^k \sqrt{2\pi\,(n-k)}\,((n-k)/e)^{n-k}} \tag{19.13}$$

$$= \sqrt{\frac{n}{2\pi k\,(n-k)}} \frac{n^n}{(n-k)^{n-k}\,k^k} \tag{19.14}$$

$$= \text{poly}(n)\left(\frac{n-k}{n}\right)^{-(n-k)}\left(\frac{k}{n}\right)^{-k} \tag{19.15}$$

$$= \text{poly}(n)\,2^{n[-((n-k)/n)\log((n-k)/n)-(k/n)\log(k/n)]} \tag{19.16}$$

$$= \text{poly}(n)\,2^{nh_2(k/n)}, \tag{19.17}$$

where h_2 is the binary entropy function in (1.1) and $\text{poly}(n)$ indicates a term at most polynomial in n. When n is large, the exponential term $2^{nh_2(k/n)}$ dominates the polynomial $\sqrt{n/2\pi k\,(n-k)}$, so that the polynomial term begins to behave merely as a constant. So, the protocol is for Alice to perform a strongly typical subspace measurement with respect to the distribution $(\cos^2(\theta), \sin^2(\theta))$, and the state then reduces to the following one with high probability:

$$\frac{1}{\sqrt{\mathcal{N}}} \sum_{\substack{k=0\,:\\ |k/n-\sin^2(\theta)|\leq\delta,\\ |(n-k)/n-\cos^2(\theta)|\leq\delta}}^{n} \sqrt{\binom{n}{k}}\cos^{n-k}(\theta)\sin^k(\theta)\left(\frac{1}{\sqrt{\binom{n}{k}}}\sum_{x:w(x)=k}|x\rangle_{A^n}|x\rangle_{B^n}\right),$$
$$\tag{19.18}$$

where $\mathcal{N} \geq 1 - \varepsilon$ is an appropriate normalization constant. Alice and Bob then both perform a Hamming weight measurement and the state reduces to a state of the form

$$\frac{1}{\sqrt{\text{poly}(n)2^{nh_2(k/n)}}}\sum_{x:w(x)=k}|x\rangle_{A^n}|x\rangle_{B^n}, \tag{19.19}$$

depending on the outcome k of the measurement. The above state is a maximally entangled state with Schmidt rank $\text{poly}(n)2^{nh_2(k/n)}$, and it follows that

$$h_2(k/n) \geq h_2(\cos^2(\theta)) - \delta, \tag{19.20}$$

from the assumption that the state first projects into the typical subspace. Alice and Bob can then perform local operations to rotate this state to approximately $nh_2(\cos^2(\theta))$ ebits. Thus, this procedure concentrates the original non-maximally entangled state to ebits at a rate equal to the entropy of entanglement of the state $|\Phi_\theta\rangle_{AB}$ in (19.1). The above proof is a bit rough, and it applies only to entangled qubit systems in a pure state. The proof of the direct coding theorem in Section 19.4.2 generalizes this proof to pure entangled states on d-dimensional systems.

19.1.3   Sketch of Entanglement Dilution

Entanglement dilution is easier to sketch out if we are not concerned about the classical communication cost of the protocol. Suppose that the goal is to create n copies of $|\phi\rangle_{AB}$ from $\approx nH(A)_\phi$ ebits. Then Alice can prepare n copies of $|\phi\rangle_{AB}$ in her laboratory. She performs Schumacher compression on the B systems, which compresses these systems to $\approx nH(A)_\phi$ qubits while causing only a small disturbance to the state (when n is large). If she and Bob share $\approx nH(A)_\phi$ ebits, then she can teleport the compressed qubits to Bob (this costs $\approx n2H(A)_\phi$ classical bits). Bob receives the compressed qubits and decompresses them, which is the end of the protocol. So this version of the entanglement dilution protocol is rather straightforward. Later on, we see how the classical communication cost can be much smaller—in fact a modified protocol requires a number of classical bits required which is sublinear in n, so that the rate of classical communication needed vanishes in the large n limit.

19.2   LOCC and Relative Entropy of Entanglement

Before describing the information-processing task for entanglement manipulation, we should formally define what we mean by LOCC, the allowed set of operations. An LOCC channel consists of a finite number of compositions of the following:

1. Alice performs a quantum instrument, which has both a quantum and classical output. She forwards the classical output to Bob, who then performs a quantum channel conditioned on the classical data received. This sequence of actions corresponds to a channel of the following form:

$$\sum_x \mathcal{F}_A^x \otimes \mathcal{G}_B^x, \tag{19.21}$$

where $\{\mathcal{F}_A^x\}$ is a collection of completely positive maps such that $\sum_x \mathcal{F}_A^x$ is a quantum channel and $\{\mathcal{G}_B^x\}$ is a collection of quantum channels.
2. The situation is reversed, with Bob performing the initial instrument, who forwards the classical data to Alice, who then performs a quantum channel conditioned on the classical data. This sequence of actions corresponds to a channel of the form in (19.21), with the A and B labels switched.

An information measure is an *LOCC monotone* if it is non-increasing with respect to an LOCC channel. One such information measure is the relative entropy of entanglement, defined as follows:

DEFINITION 19.2.1 (Relative Entropy of Entanglement)   Let $\rho_{AB} \in \mathcal{D}(\mathcal{H}_A \otimes \mathcal{H}_B)$. The relative entropy of entanglement of ρ_{AB} is equal to the "relative entropy distance" between ρ_{AB} and the closest separable state:

$$E_R(A;B)_\rho \equiv \min_{\sigma_{AB} \in \text{SEP}(A:B)} D(\rho_{AB} \| \sigma_{AB}). \tag{19.22}$$

That $E_R(A;B)_\rho$ is an LOCC monotone follows from the monotonicity of relative entropy with respect to channels (Theorem 11.8.1) and the fact that LOCC channels take separable states to separable states. That is, from the definition of LOCC channels given above, we can see that such operations have Kraus operators of the form $\{F_A^z \otimes G_B^z\}$, so that an LOCC channel Λ_{AB} acts as follows on a separable state $\sigma_{AB} = \sum_y p(y)\omega_A^y \otimes \tau_B^y$:

$$\Lambda_{AB}(\sigma_{AB}) = \sum_z (F_A^z \otimes G_B^z) \left[\sum_y p(y)\omega_A^y \otimes \tau_B^y \right] (F_A^z \otimes G_B^z)^\dagger \qquad (19.23)$$

$$= \sum_{z,y} p(y) F_A^z \omega_A^y (F_A^z)^\dagger \otimes G_B^z \tau_B^y (G_B^z)^\dagger, \qquad (19.24)$$

which is clearly a separable state. So this means that for any separable state σ_{AB} and LOCC channel $\Lambda_{AB \to A'B'}$, we find that

$$D(\rho_{AB}\|\sigma_{AB}) \geq D(\Lambda_{AB \to A'B'}(\rho_{AB})\|\Lambda_{AB \to A'B'}(\sigma_{AB})) \geq E_R(A';B')_{\Lambda(\rho)}, \qquad (19.25)$$

where the first inequality follows from the monotonicity of relative entropy (Theorem 11.8.1). Since the inequality holds for all $\sigma_{AB} \in \text{SEP}(A:B)$, we can conclude that

$$E_R(A;B)_\rho \geq E_R(A';B')_{\Lambda(\rho)}, \qquad (19.26)$$

which is equivalent to the following:

THEOREM 19.2.1 The relative entropy of entanglement is an LOCC monotone.

We need two other properties of the relative entropy of entanglement:

PROPOSITION 19.2.1 Let $\rho_{AB} \in \mathcal{D}(\mathcal{H}_A \otimes \mathcal{H}_B)$. Then the relative entropy of entanglement is never smaller than the coherent information:

$$E_R(A;B)_\rho \geq \max\{I(A\rangle B)_\rho, I(B\rangle A)_\rho\}. \qquad (19.27)$$

Proof Let $\sigma_{AB} \in \text{SEP}(A:B)$. Then

$$\sigma_{AB} = \sum_y p(y)\omega_A^y \otimes \tau_B^y \leq \sum_y p(y) I_A \otimes \tau_B^y = I_A \otimes \sigma_B. \qquad (19.28)$$

The operator inequality follows because $\omega_A^y \leq I_A$, which implies that $\sum_y p(y)(I_A - \omega_A^y) \otimes \tau_B^y$ is positive semi-definite. We can then conclude that

$$D(\rho_{AB}\|\sigma_{AB}) \geq D(\rho_{AB}\|I_A \otimes \sigma_B) \qquad (19.29)$$

$$\geq \min_{\sigma_B} D(\rho_{AB}\|I_A \otimes \sigma_B) \qquad (19.30)$$

$$= I(A\rangle B)_\rho. \qquad (19.31)$$

The first inequality follows from Proposition 11.8.2. The equality follows from Exercise 11.8.3. Since the inequality holds for all $\sigma_{AB} \in \text{SEP}(A:B)$, we can conclude that $E_R(A;B)_\rho \geq I(A\rangle B)_\rho$. The other inequality follows by a symmetric proof. $\qquad \square$

PROPOSITION 19.2.2 Let $|\psi\rangle_{AB} \in \mathcal{H}_A \otimes \mathcal{H}_B$ be a pure bipartite state. Then the relative entropy of entanglement is equal to the entropy of entanglement:

$$H(A)_\psi = E_R(A;B)_\psi. \tag{19.32}$$

Proof From Proposition 19.2.1, we know that $E_R(A;B)_\psi \geq I(A\rangle B)_\psi = H(A)_\psi$. So it remains to prove the other inequality. Suppose that $|\psi\rangle_{AB}$ has a Schmidt decomposition as follows:

$$|\psi\rangle_{AB} = \sum_x \sqrt{p(x)}|x\rangle_A \otimes |x\rangle_B. \tag{19.33}$$

Let Δ denote the following channel:

$$\Delta(X) \equiv PXP + (I-P)X(I-P), \tag{19.34}$$

where $P \equiv \sum_x |x\rangle\langle x|_A \otimes |x\rangle\langle x|_B$. Let

$$\overline{\psi}_{AB} \equiv \sum_x p(x)|x\rangle\langle x|_A \otimes |x\rangle\langle x|_B. \tag{19.35}$$

Note that $\overline{\psi}_{AB}$ is a separable state. Consider that

$$H(A)_\psi = I(A\rangle B)_\psi \tag{19.36}$$
$$= D(\psi_{AB}\|I_A \otimes \psi_B) \tag{19.37}$$
$$\geq D(\Delta(\psi_{AB})\|\Delta(I_A \otimes \psi_B)) \tag{19.38}$$
$$= D(\psi_{AB}\|\overline{\psi}_{AB}) \tag{19.39}$$
$$\geq \min_{\sigma_{AB}\in\text{SEP}(A:B)} D(\psi_{AB}\|\sigma_{AB}) \tag{19.40}$$
$$= E_R(A;B)_\psi. \tag{19.41}$$

The second equality follows from Exercise 11.8.3. The first inequality follows from the monotonicity of quantum relative entropy (Theorem 11.8.1). The third equality follows because $\Delta(\psi_{AB}) = \psi_{AB}$ and

$$\Delta(I_A \otimes \psi_B) = P(I_A \otimes \psi_B)P + (I-P)(I_A \otimes \psi_B)(I-P). \tag{19.42}$$
$$= \overline{\psi}_{AB} + (I-P)(I_A \otimes \psi_B)(I-P). \tag{19.43}$$

Since ψ_{AB} does not have support outside of the subspace onto which P projects, it follows that

$$D(\psi_{AB}\|\overline{\psi}_{AB} + (I-P)(I_A \otimes \psi_B)(I-P)) = D(\psi_{AB}\|\overline{\psi}_{AB}). \tag{19.44}$$

This concludes the proof. □

19.3   Entanglement Manipulation Task

We can now define an $(n, m/n, \varepsilon)$ entanglement manipulation protocol. Alice and Bob begin with n copies of a pure bipartite, entangled state $|\psi\rangle_{AB}$. They then perform an LOCC channel $\Lambda^{(n)}_{A^n B^n \to A^m B^m}$ in an attempt to convert the original state $(|\psi\rangle_{AB})^{\otimes n}$ to m copies of another bipartite pure state $|\phi\rangle_{AB}$. Let $\omega_{A^m B^m}$ denote the state after the LOCC channel:

$$\omega_{A^m B^m} \equiv \Lambda^{(n)}_{A^n B^n \to A^m B^m}(\psi^{\otimes n}_{AB}). \tag{19.45}$$

The protocol has ε error if the final state $\omega_{A^m B^m}$ is ε-close to $\phi^{\otimes m}_{AB}$:

$$\frac{1}{2}\left\|\omega_{A^m B^m} - \phi^{\otimes m}_{AB}\right\|_1 \leq \varepsilon, \tag{19.46}$$

where $\varepsilon \in [0, 1]$ and the rate of entanglement conversion is m/n.

We say that a particular rate E of entanglement manipulation is *achievable* if there exists an $(n, E - \delta, \varepsilon)$ entanglement manipulation protocol for all $\varepsilon \in (0, 1)$, $\delta > 0$, and sufficiently large n. The *entanglement manipulation limit* $E(\psi \to \phi)$ for the conversion $|\psi\rangle_{AB} \to |\phi\rangle_{AB}$ is equal to the supremum of all achievable rates.

19.4 The Entanglement Manipulation Theorem

We first state the entanglement manipulation theorem and then prove it below in two parts (the converse theorem and the direct coding theorem).

THEOREM 19.4.1 (Entanglement Manipulation) Let $|\psi\rangle_{AB}, |\phi\rangle_{AB} \in \mathcal{H}_A \otimes \mathcal{H}_B$ be pure bipartite states. The entanglement manipulation limit for the conversion $|\psi\rangle_{AB} \to |\phi\rangle_{AB}$ is equal to the ratio $H(A)_\psi / H(A)_\phi$:

$$E(\psi \to \phi) = \frac{H(A)_\psi}{H(A)_\phi}. \tag{19.47}$$

REMARK 19.4.1 Theorem 19.4.1 implies that the entanglement concentration and dilution protocols are individually optimal. That is, if the goal is to convert n copies of $|\psi\rangle_{AB}$ to as many ebits as possible, then the maximal rate of ebit generation is equal to $H(A)_\psi$. Furthermore, if the goal is to convert nR ebits to n copies of $|\psi\rangle_{AB}$, then the minimal rate R of ebit consumption is equal to $H(A)_\psi$.

19.4.1 The Converse Theorem

We now prove the converse theorem for entanglement manipulation, i.e., that the entanglement manipulation limit for the conversion $|\psi\rangle_{AB} \to |\phi\rangle_{AB}$ does not exceed $H(A)_\psi / H(A)_\phi$. Suppose that there is a sequence of LOCC transformations $\{\Lambda^{(n)}\}$, each of which takes n copies of a pure state $|\psi\rangle_{AB}$ to m_n approximate copies of a pure state $|\phi\rangle_{AB}$. That is, $\Lambda^{(n)}$ is such that

$$\frac{1}{2}\left\|\Lambda^{(n)}(\psi^{\otimes n}_{AB}) - \phi^{\otimes m_n}_{AB}\right\|_1 \leq \varepsilon, \tag{19.48}$$

where $\varepsilon \in (0,1)$. Let $\omega_{A^{m_n} B^{m_n}} \equiv \Lambda^{(n)}(\psi_{AB}^{\otimes n})$. To bound the rate m_n/n, we use the relative entropy of entanglement. Consider that

$$nH(A)_\psi = H(A^n)_{\psi^{\otimes n}} \tag{19.49}$$
$$= E_R(A^n; B^n)_{\psi^{\otimes n}} \tag{19.50}$$
$$\geq E_R(A^{m_n}; B^{m_n})_\omega \tag{19.51}$$
$$\geq I(A^{m_n} \rangle B^{m_n})_\omega \tag{19.52}$$
$$\geq I(A^{m_n} \rangle B^{m_n})_{\phi^{\otimes m_n}} - f(m_n, \varepsilon) \tag{19.53}$$
$$= H(A^{m_n})_{\phi^{\otimes m_n}} - f(m_n, \varepsilon) \tag{19.54}$$
$$= m_n H(A)_\phi - f(m_n, \varepsilon). \tag{19.55}$$

The first equality follows because the entropy is additive for a tensor-product state. The second equality follows from Proposition 19.2.2. The first inequality follows because the relative entropy of entanglement is an LOCC monotone (Theorem 19.2.1). The second inequality follows from Proposition 19.2.1. The third inequality is a consequence of continuity of conditional entropy (the AFW inequality), with $f(m_n, \varepsilon) \equiv 2\varepsilon m_n \log \dim(\mathcal{H}_A) + (1 + \varepsilon) h_2(\varepsilon/[1 + \varepsilon])$. The third equality follows because the coherent information of a pure state is equal to the marginal entropy. The last equality follows because the entropy of a tensor-product state is additive. Putting everything together, we find that

$$\frac{m_n}{n} (1 - 2\varepsilon \log \dim(\mathcal{H}_A)/H(A)_\phi) \leq \frac{H(A)_\psi}{H(A)_\phi} + \frac{(1 + \varepsilon) h_2(\varepsilon/[1 + \varepsilon])}{nH(A)_\phi}. \tag{19.56}$$

Thus, if we are considering a sequence of $(n, m_n/n, \varepsilon)$ entanglement manipulation protocols with rate $E - \delta_n = m_n/n$, such that $\lim_{n\to\infty} \delta_n = 0$, then the above bound becomes

$$(E - \delta_n)(1 - 2\varepsilon \log \dim(\mathcal{H}_A)/H(A)_\phi) \leq \frac{H(A)_\psi}{H(A)_\phi} + \frac{(1 + \varepsilon) h_2(\varepsilon/[1 + \varepsilon])}{nH(A)_\phi}. \tag{19.57}$$

Taking the limit as $n \to \infty$ and $\varepsilon \to 0$, we find that any achievable rate E of entanglement manipulation for $\psi \to \phi$ necessarily satisfies the following bound:

$$E \leq \frac{H(A)_\psi}{H(A)_\phi}. \tag{19.58}$$

19.4.2   The Direct Coding Theorem

As discussed in the introduction of this chapter, we break the direct coding theorem into two parts: entanglement concentration and entanglement dilution. We begin by discussing entanglement concentration. To do so, it is helpful to discuss a related, exclusively classical task known as randomness concentration (also known as randomness extraction).

Randomness Concentration

In a randomness concentration protocol, the goal is to extract as many approximately uniformly random bits as possible from a given distribution. Since we are operating in a quantum Shannon theoretic regime, let us suppose that a sequence x^n is generated according to an i.i.d. distribution

$$p_{X^n}(x^n) \equiv \prod_{i=1}^{n} p_X(x_i). \tag{19.59}$$

Recall the method of types from Section 14.7.1. Suppose that Alice performs a mapping

$$x^n \rightarrow (t(x^n), f_t(x^n)), \tag{19.60}$$

where $t(x^n)$ is the type (or empirical distribution) of the sequence x^n and the function $f_t(x^n)$ is an index keeping track of the ordering of the symbols in the sequence x^n for a given type class $T_t^{X^n}$. Note that this mapping is reversible (given an output, one can determine the input uniquely).

For example, all three-bit sequences map in this way as follows:

$$000 \rightarrow (0,0), \quad 001 \rightarrow (1,0), \quad 010 \rightarrow (1,1), \tag{19.61}$$

$$011 \rightarrow (2,0), \quad 100 \rightarrow (1,2), \quad 101 \rightarrow (2,1), \tag{19.62}$$

$$110 \rightarrow (2,2), \quad 111 \rightarrow (3,0). \tag{19.63}$$

For binary sequences, the type is the Hamming weight. Thus, 000 has type 0 and is the only sequence in this type class, thus receiving an index 0. Also, 011 has type 2 and we label it as the first sequence in this type class, indexed with 0. The sequence 101 has type 2 and it is the second sequence in this type class, indexed with 1, etc.

What is the use of performing this mapping? First consider that the joint probability of observing a particular type t and index f is equal to

$$p_{t(X^n), f_t(X^n)}(t, f) = p_{X^n}(x^n), \tag{19.64}$$

where $x^n \in T_t^{X^n}$. This is because the mapping $x^n \rightarrow (t(x^n), f_t(x^n))$ is reversible. Consider furthermore that for $x^n \in T_t^{X^n}$, we have that

$$p_{X^n}(x^n) = \prod_{x \in \mathcal{X}} p_X(x)^{N(x|x^n)} = \prod_{x \in \mathcal{X}} p_X(x)^{N(x|x_t^n)} = p_{X^n}(x_t^n), \tag{19.65}$$

where x_t^n is a representative sequence of the type class $T_t^{X^n}$ (having type t as well). Then the probability for observing a particular type t is equal to

$$p_{t(X^n)}(t) = \sum_{x^n \in T_t^{X^n}} p_{X^n}(x^n) = \sum_{x^n \in T_t^{X^n}} p_{X^n}(x_t^n) = \left| T_t^{X^n} \right| \prod_{x \in \mathcal{X}} p_X(x)^{N(x|x_t^n)}. \tag{19.66}$$

That is, $p_{t(X^n)}(t)$ just depends on the size of the type class $\left|T_t^{X^n}\right|$ and the empirical distribution of the type t. These considerations then imply that the conditional probability distribution $p_{f_t(X^n)|t(X^n)}$ is uniform because

$$p_{f_t(X^n)|t(X^n)}(f|t) = \frac{p_{t(X^n),f_t(X^n)}(t,f)}{p_{t(X^n)}(t)} = \frac{1}{\left|T_t^{X^n}\right|}. \tag{19.67}$$

That is, conditioned on observing a particular type t, all of the sequences in the type class $T_t^{X^n}$ are uniformly distributed. Thus, the mapping $x^n \to (t(x^n), f_t(x^n))$ "reshapes" the distribution of x^n in the above way.

This "distribution reshaping" leads to a first idea for a randomness concentration protocol. Given a sequence x^n, send it through the reversible mapping $x^n \to (t(x^n), f_t(x^n))$. Given the type t, the value $f = f_t(x^n)$ is uniformly random on a set of size $\left|T_t^{X^n}\right|$, so that we recover $\log\left|T_t^{X^n}\right|$ uniformly random bits.

There are two main problems with the above method. First, some type classes are very small and lead to little randomness or none at all. Second, the amount of randomness that the above procedure yields is not consistent: it varies from type to type. What we would prefer is to have a method which takes a random sequence X^n and maps it to exactly nR bits, such that the distribution of these nR bits is nearly indistinguishable from a uniform distribution.

How can we accomplish this? To start, we should first have a preprocessing step in which we only proceed with the above method if x^n is a strongly typical sequence and otherwise declare failure. Equivalently, we only proceed if $t(x^n)$ is a strongly typical type, such that the empirical distribution $N(x|x^n)$ satisfies $\max_x |N(x|x^n) - p_X(x)| \le \delta$ for some $\delta > 0$. For sufficiently large n, we are guaranteed that this preprocessing step fails with probability no larger than an arbitrarily small constant $\varepsilon \in (0,1)$, due to the law of large numbers (or the "high probability" property of typicality). By Property 14.7.5, this preprocessing step guarantees that every strongly typical type class has size bounded as follows:

$$\left|T_t^{X^n}\right| \ge 2^{n\left[H(X) - \eta(|\mathcal{X}|\delta) - |\mathcal{X}|\frac{1}{n}\log(n+1)\right]}. \tag{19.68}$$

Note that we also have the following upper bound:

$$\left|T_t^{X^n}\right| \le 2^{n[H(X)+c\delta]}, \tag{19.69}$$

because the size of a typical type class cannot exceed the size of the strongly typical set, for some constant $c > 0$. Thus, the preprocessing step solves the first problem because it guarantees that we will have at least $n[H(X) - \eta(|\mathcal{X}|\delta) - |\mathcal{X}|\frac{1}{n}\log(n+1)]$ uniformly random bits if it is successful.

From here, we can then solve the second problem by performing a hashing function, in order to hash down every typical type class to a set of size $2^{n\left[H(X)-\eta(|\mathcal{X}|\delta)-|\mathcal{X}|\frac{1}{n}\log(n+1)\right]}2^{-n\delta}$, so that we decrease the size of the set by a factor of $2^{n\delta}$. Even though the size drops by an amount that is exponential in n, we only lose δ on the *rate* of randomness concentration, which is the main parameter of interest in the large n limit. That is, at the end of the protocol, we will be left with $n\left[H(X) - \eta(|\mathcal{X}|\,\delta) - |\mathcal{X}|\frac{1}{n}\log(n+1) - \delta\right]$ bits that are nearly indistinguishable from uniformly random bits. As $n \to \infty$, the rate of randomness concentration is equal to $H(X)$ uniformly random bits per source symbol.

To have a complete proof, we need the following hashing lemma, which gives a way for hashing down a uniform random variable on a larger set to one on a much smaller set:

LEMMA 19.4.1 (Hashing)   Let k and l be positive integers such that $k \geq l$ (in fact think of k as being much larger than l). Let W_k be uniformly distributed on the set $\{1,\ldots,k\}$, W_l be uniformly distributed on the set $\{1,\ldots,l\}$, and W_r be uniformly distributed on the set $\{1,\ldots,r = \lceil k/l\rceil\}$. Then there exists a one-to-one function $g : \{1,\ldots,k\} \to \{1,\cdots,l\} \times \{1,\ldots,r\}$ such that

$$\frac{1}{2}\left\|p_{W_l} \times p_{W_r} - p_{g(W_k)}\right\|_1 \leq \frac{l}{k}. \tag{19.70}$$

Proof   Divide the set $\{1,\ldots,k\}$ into l bins, each of which has size no more than $r = \lceil k/l\rceil$. Then take $g(w_k)$ to be the one-to-one mapping which outputs the bin index and the location inside of that bin. The distribution of $g(W_k)$ is uniformly random, equal to $1/k$ for k of the possible $l \cdot \lceil k/l\rceil$ output values and zero for the others (the unfilled locations if k/l is not an integer). The distribution of the joint random variable (W_l, W_r) is uniformly random also, equal to $1/(l \cdot \lceil k/l\rceil)$ for each of the possible $l \cdot \lceil k/l\rceil$ values. The distributions then overlap on exactly k of the possible output values, implying that the trace distance between the two distributions is as follows:

$$\left\|p_{g(W_k)} - p_{W_l} \times p_{W_r}\right\|_1 = k\left|\frac{1}{k} - \frac{1}{l \cdot \lceil k/l\rceil}\right| + (l \cdot \lceil k/l\rceil - k)\left|\frac{1}{l \cdot \lceil k/l\rceil}\right|. \tag{19.71}$$

Consider that

$$k\left|\frac{1}{k} - \frac{1}{l \cdot \lceil k/l\rceil}\right| = k\left|\frac{\lceil k/l\rceil}{k \cdot \lceil k/l\rceil} - \frac{k/l}{k \cdot \lceil k/l\rceil}\right| \tag{19.72}$$

$$= \frac{1}{\lceil k/l\rceil}\left|\lceil k/l\rceil - k/l\right| \leq \frac{1}{\lceil k/l\rceil} \leq \frac{l}{k}. \tag{19.73}$$

Furthermore,

$$(l \cdot \lceil k/l\rceil - k)\left|\frac{1}{l \cdot \lceil k/l\rceil}\right| = (\lceil k/l\rceil - k/l)\left|\frac{1}{\lceil k/l\rceil}\right| \tag{19.74}$$

$$\leq \frac{1}{\lceil k/l\rceil} \leq \frac{l}{k}. \tag{19.75}$$

This concludes the proof. $\square$

We can now specify the complete protocol for randomness concentration. It begins with a sequence x^n being generated at random according to $p_{X^n}(x^n)$. Alice computes whether it is a strongly typical sequence, declaring failure of the protocol in case it is not. Let $\widetilde{X}^n$ be a random variable with the following distribution:

$$p_{\widetilde{X}^n}(x^n) \equiv \begin{cases} p_{X^n}(x^n)/\sum_{x^n \in T_\delta^{X^n}} p_{X^n}(x^n) & \text{if } x^n \in T_\delta^{X^n} \\ 0 & \text{else} \end{cases}, \tag{19.76}$$

where $T_\delta^{X^n}$ is the strongly typical set. This random variable represents the distribution of the sequence conditioned on it being strongly typical. Set the rate

$$R = H(X) - \eta(|\mathcal{X}|\delta) - |\mathcal{X}|\frac{1}{n}\log(n+1) - \delta. \tag{19.77}$$

Let τ_δ denote the set of all strongly typical types for the distribution p_X, for sequences of length n and tolerance δ. Note that $|\tau_\delta| \leq (n+1)^{|\mathcal{X}|}$ (see Property 14.7.1), so that only $|\mathcal{X}|\log(n+1)$ bits are required to record the type. If x^n is strongly typical, then Alice applies the one-to-one mapping

$$x^n \rightarrow (t(x^n), g_t(f_t(x^n))), \tag{19.78}$$

where

$$t: T_\delta^{X^n} \rightarrow \tau_\delta, \tag{19.79}$$

$$g_t: T_t^{X^n} \rightarrow \{0,1\}^{nR} \times \{0,1\}^{n[(1+c)\delta+\eta(|\mathcal{X}|\delta)+|\mathcal{X}|\frac{1}{n}\log(n+1)]}, \tag{19.80}$$

with g_t the one-to-one function guaranteed by Lemma 19.4.1, with $k = |T_t^{X^n}|$ and $l = 2^{nR}$. Let W_{out} denote a uniform random variable over the set $\{0,1\}^{nR}$, and let $W_{\text{rem}}|t(\widetilde{X}^n) = t$ denote a conditional random variable that is uniform over a subset of $\{0,1\}^{n[(1+c)\delta+\eta(|\mathcal{X}|\delta)+|\mathcal{X}|\frac{1}{n}\log(n+1)]}$ of size $\lceil k/l \rceil$. Consider from our discussion around (19.67) that the conditional random variable $f_t(\widetilde{X}^n)|t(\widetilde{X}^n) = t$, for $t \in \tau_\delta$, is a uniform random variable. Thus, we can apply Lemma 19.4.1, taking $k = |T_t^{X^n}|$ and $l = 2^{nR}$, and find that

$$\frac{1}{2}\left\|p_{g_t(f_t(\widetilde{X}^n))|t(\widetilde{X}^n)=t} - p_{W_{\text{out}}} \times p_{W_{\text{rem}}|t(\widetilde{X}^n)=t}\right\|_1 \leq \frac{2^{nR}}{|T_t^{X^n}|}$$

$$\leq \frac{2^{n[H(X)-\eta(|\mathcal{X}|\delta)-|\mathcal{X}|\frac{1}{n}\log(n+1)-\delta]}}{2^{n[H(X)-\eta(|\mathcal{X}|\delta)-|\mathcal{X}|\frac{1}{n}\log(n+1)]}} = 2^{-n\delta}. \tag{19.81}$$

This bound is then sufficient for us to conclude that

$$\frac{1}{2}\left\|p_{t(\widetilde{X}^n),g_t(f_t(\widetilde{X}^n))} - p_{t(\widetilde{X}^n),W_{\text{rem}}} \times p_{W_{\text{out}}}\right\|_1 \leq 2^{-n\delta}, \tag{19.82}$$

because

$$\left\|p_{t(\widetilde{X}^n),g_t(f_t(\widetilde{X}^n))} - p_{t(\widetilde{X}^n),W_{\text{rem}}} \times p_{W_{\text{out}}}\right\|_1$$

$$= \sum_{t \in \tau_\delta} p_{t(\widetilde{X}^n)}(t)\left\|p_{g_t(f_t(\widetilde{X}^n))|t(\widetilde{X}^n)=t} - p_{W_{\text{out}}} \times p_{W_{\text{rem}}|t(\widetilde{X}^n)=t}\right\|_1. \tag{19.83}$$

For all $\varepsilon \in (0,1)$ and sufficiently large n, we know that $P \equiv \sum_{x^n \in T_\delta^{X^n}} p_{X^n}(x^n)$ $\geq 1 - \varepsilon$. Then we can conclude that the distributions $p_{\widetilde{X}^n}$ and p_{X^n} are nearly indistinguishable because

$$\left\| p_{X^n} - p_{\widetilde{X}^n} \right\|_1 = \sum_{x^n \in T_\delta^{X^n}} |p_{X^n}(x^n) - p_{X^n}(x^n)/P| + \sum_{x^n \notin T_\delta^{X^n}} p_{X^n}(x^n) \quad (19.84)$$

$$= \sum_{x^n \in T_\delta^{X^n}} |1 - P| \frac{p_{X^n}(x^n)}{P} + \sum_{x^n \notin T_\delta^{X^n}} p_{X^n}(x^n) \quad (19.85)$$

$$\leq 2\varepsilon. \quad (19.86)$$

We can then finally conclude that

$$\frac{1}{2} \left\| p_{t(X^n), g_t(f_t(X^n))} - p_{t(\widetilde{X}^n), W_{\text{rem}}} \times p_{W_{\text{out}}} \right\|_1 \leq \varepsilon + 2^{-n\delta}, \quad (19.87)$$

by applying the triangle inequality to (19.82) and (19.86), and using the fact that

$$\left\| p_{r(Z)} - p_{r(Y)} \right\|_1 = \left\| p_Z - p_Y \right\|_1 \quad (19.88)$$

for random variables Z and Y and a one-to-one mapping r.

The final step of the randomness concentration protocol consists of discarding the type register containing t and the W_{rem} register. Monotonicity of the trace distance with respect to discardings implies that

$$\frac{1}{2} \left\| \text{Tr}_{W_{\text{rem}}} \{ p_{g_t(f_t(X^n))} \} - p_{W_{\text{out}}} \right\|_1 \leq \varepsilon + 2^{-n\delta}. \quad (19.89)$$

Even though the final step of randomness concentration consists of this discarding, we have developed the protocol using one-to-one functions because it is essential for our development of the entanglement dilution protocol, which follows just after we discuss entanglement concentration next.

Entanglement Concentration

We have actually done the bulk of the "hard work" in the previous section, when developing the method for randomness concentration. We now just need to apply the one-to-one mapping in (19.78) in a coherent way in order to have a method for entanglement concentration. In the setting of entanglement concentration, Alice and Bob begin with n copies of the state $|\psi\rangle_{AB}$. Suppose that $|\psi\rangle_{AB}$ has a Schmidt decomposition of the following form:

$$|\psi\rangle_{AB} = \sum_{x \in \mathcal{X}} \sqrt{p_X(x)} |x\rangle_A |x\rangle_B. \quad (19.90)$$

Then the state $|\psi\rangle_{AB}^{\otimes n}$ has the following form:

$$|\psi\rangle_{AB}^{\otimes n} = \sum_{x^n \in \mathcal{X}^n} \sqrt{p_{X^n}(x^n)} |x^n\rangle_{A^n} |x^n\rangle_{B^n}. \quad (19.91)$$

So we need to figure out local quantum channels that Alice and Bob can each perform in order to convert this state to as many ebits as possible. Before doing so, we state the following lemma, which will allow us to quantify the performance of a coherent version of a classical protocol:

LEMMA 19.4.2   Let p_X and q_X be probability distributions such that

$$\|p_X - q_X\|_1 \le \varepsilon. \tag{19.92}$$

Then the states $|\psi^p\rangle_{AB} \equiv \sum_x \sqrt{p_X(x)}|x\rangle_A|x\rangle_B$ and $|\psi^q\rangle_{AB} \equiv \sum_x \sqrt{q_X(x)}|x\rangle_A|x\rangle_B$ are such that

$$\|\psi^p_{AB} - \psi^q_{AB}\|_1 \le 2\sqrt{\varepsilon}. \tag{19.93}$$

Proof   Consider that the quantum fidelity between $|\psi^p\rangle_{AB}$ and $|\psi^q\rangle_{AB}$ is equal to the classical fidelity of the distributions p_X and q_X:

$$\sqrt{F(\psi^p_{AB}, \psi^q_{AB})} = |\langle\psi^q|\psi^p\rangle_{AB}| = \sum_x \sqrt{q_X(x)p_X(x)}. \tag{19.94}$$

From Corollary 9.3.1, we can conclude that $F(\psi^p_{AB}, \psi^q_{AB}) \ge 1 - \varepsilon$. Corollary 9.3.2 in turn implies (19.93). $\qquad\square$

Let $U_{A^n \to TW_{\mathrm{out}}W_{\mathrm{rem}}}$ denote the following isometric implementation of the one-to-one mapping in (19.78):

$$U_{A^n \to TW_{\mathrm{out}}W_{\mathrm{rem}}} \equiv \sum_{x^n \in T_\delta^{X^n}} |t(x^n), g_t(f_t(x^n))\rangle_{TW_{\mathrm{out}}W_{\mathrm{rem}}}\langle x^n|_{A^n}. \tag{19.95}$$

Then we set Alice's encoding to be the following quantum channel:

$$\mathcal{E}_{A^n \to TW_{\mathrm{out}}W_{\mathrm{rem}}}(Y_{A^n}) \equiv U\Pi^\delta_{A^n} Y_{A^n} \Pi^\delta_{A^n} U^\dagger + \mathrm{Tr}\{(I_{A^n} - \Pi^\delta_{A^n})Y_{A^n}\}\sigma_{TW_{\mathrm{out}}W_{\mathrm{rem}}}, \tag{19.96}$$

where $\Pi^\delta_{A^n}$ is the strongly typical projector for the state $\sum_{x \in \mathcal{X}} p_X(x)|x\rangle\langle x|_A$ and $\sigma_{TW_{\mathrm{out}}W_{\mathrm{rem}}}$ is some state of the registers $TW_{\mathrm{out}}W_{\mathrm{rem}}$. This channel isometrically embeds the typical subspace for Alice's system into the registers $TW_{\mathrm{out}}W_{\mathrm{rem}}$. Let $\mathcal{E}_{B^n \to (TW_{\mathrm{out}}W_{\mathrm{rem}})_B}$ denote the same encoding for Bob, and let $\mathcal{E}_{A^n}$ and $\mathcal{E}_{B^n}$ be a shorthand for Alice and Bob's encodings, respectively.

Let $|\widetilde{\psi}^n\rangle_{A^n B^n}$ denote the following state:

$$|\widetilde{\psi}^n\rangle_{A^n B^n} \equiv \sum_{x^n \in \mathcal{X}^n} \sqrt{p_{\widetilde{X}^n}(x^n)}|x^n\rangle_{A^n}|x^n\rangle_{B^n}, \tag{19.97}$$

where the distribution $p_{\widetilde{X}^n}$ is defined in (19.76). By invoking (19.86) and Lemma 19.4.2, we find that

$$\left\|\psi^{\otimes n}_{AB} - \widetilde{\psi}^n_{A^n B^n}\right\|_1 \le 2\sqrt{2\varepsilon}. \tag{19.98}$$

The monotonicity of trace distance then implies that

$$\left\|(\mathcal{E}_{A^n} \otimes \mathcal{E}_{B^n})(\psi^{\otimes n}_{AB}) - (\mathcal{E}_{A^n} \otimes \mathcal{E}_{B^n})(\widetilde{\psi}^n_{A^n B^n})\right\|_1 \le 2\sqrt{2\varepsilon}. \tag{19.99}$$

Consider that the coherent version of the distribution $p_{t(\widetilde{X}^n), W_{\mathrm{rem}}} \times p_{W_{\mathrm{out}}}$ is the following state:

$$\Upsilon_{T_A W_{A'} T_B W_{B'}} \otimes (\Phi^+_{AB})^{\otimes nR}, \tag{19.100}$$

where $\Upsilon_{T_A W_{A'} T_B W_{B'}}$ is a coherent version of the distribution $p_{t(\widetilde{X}^n), W_{\mathrm{rem}}}$, defined as

$$|\Upsilon\rangle_{T_A W_{A'} T_B W_{B'}} \equiv \sum_{t \in \tau_\delta, w} \sqrt{p_{t(\widetilde{X}^n), W_{\mathrm{rem}}}(t, w)} |t, w\rangle_{T_A W_{A'}} |t, w\rangle_{T_B W_{B'}}, \quad (19.101)$$

and $|\Phi^+\rangle_{AB} \equiv [|00\rangle_{AB} + |11\rangle_{AB}] / \sqrt{2}$. By invoking (19.82) and Lemma 19.4.2, we find that

$$\left\| (\mathcal{E}_{A^n} \otimes \mathcal{E}_{B^n})(\widetilde{\psi}^n_{A^n B^n}) - \Upsilon_{T_A W_{A'} T_B W_{B'}} \otimes \left(\Phi^+_{AB} \right)^{\otimes nR} \right\|_1 \leq 2\sqrt{2 \cdot 2^{-n\delta}}. \quad (19.102)$$

Applying the triangle inequality to (19.99) and (19.102), we find that

$$\left\| (\mathcal{E}_{A^n} \otimes \mathcal{E}_{B^n})(\psi^{\otimes n}_{AB}) - \Upsilon_{T_A W_{A'} T_B W_{B'}} \otimes \left(\Phi^+_{AB} \right)^{\otimes nR} \right\|_1$$
$$\leq 2 \left[\sqrt{2\varepsilon} + \sqrt{2 \cdot 2^{-n\delta}} \right]. \quad (19.103)$$

The final step is for Alice and Bob to discard the registers $T_A T_B W_{A'} W_{B'}$, which implies that

$$\left\| ((\mathrm{Tr}_{T_A W_{A'}} \circ \mathcal{E}_{A^n}) \otimes (\mathrm{Tr}_{T_B W_{B'}} \circ \mathcal{E}_{B^n}))(\psi^{\otimes n}_{AB}) - \left(\Phi^+_{AB} \right)^{\otimes nR} \right\|_1$$
$$\leq 2 \left[\sqrt{2\varepsilon} + \sqrt{2 \cdot 2^{-n\delta}} \right]. \quad (19.104)$$

The rate of ebit generation is equal to $R = H(A)_\psi - \eta(|\mathcal{X}| \delta) - |\mathcal{X}| \frac{1}{n} \log(n + 1) - \delta$. No classical communication is required. This concludes the proof for entanglement concentration.

Entanglement Dilution

We have already outlined an entanglement dilution protocol in Section 19.1.3. However, the protocol sketched there uses far more classical communication than is necessary. Here, we show that entanglement dilution requires a rate of classical communication that vanishes as n becomes large. This result demonstrates that the resource theory of entanglement for pure states is truly a reversible theory, in the sense that the only resource we need to count is the rate of entanglement conversion, given that the classical communication rate is negligible.

We now discuss such an entanglement dilution protocol. The main idea is really just to take the entanglement concentration protocol from the previous section and "run it backwards." So we keep the system labels as they were in the previous section. Let Alice and Bob share the following maximally entangled state at the beginning:

$$\Phi_{T_A W_{A'} T_B W_{B'}} \otimes \left(\Phi^+_{AB} \right)^{\otimes nR}. \quad (19.105)$$

Consider that

$$\log \dim(\mathcal{H}_{T_A}) = |\mathcal{X}| \log n, \quad (19.106)$$
$$\log \dim(\mathcal{H}_{W_{A'}}) = n(1 + c)\delta + n\eta(|\mathcal{X}| \delta) + |\mathcal{X}| \log n, \quad (19.107)$$

implying that the total number of ebits in the state $\Phi_{T_A W_{A'} T_B W_{B'}}$ is equal to $n(1+c)\delta + n\eta(|\mathcal{X}|\delta) + 2|\mathcal{X}|\log n$, and the total number of ebits that they share overall is equal to $nH(A)_\psi + nc\delta + |\mathcal{X}|\log n$. Alice prepares the state $\Upsilon_{T_A W_{A'} T_B W_{B'}}$ locally in her lab and uses the state $\Phi_{T_A W_{A'} T_B W_{B'}}$ to teleport the $T_B W_{B'}$ systems of Υ to Bob. This requires

$$2\left[n(1+c)\delta + n\eta(|\mathcal{X}|\delta) + 2|\mathcal{X}|\log n\right] \tag{19.108}$$

bits of classical communication. At this point, Alice and Bob share the following state:

$$\Upsilon_{T_A W_{A'} T_B W_{B'}} \otimes \left(\Phi_{AB}^+\right)^{\otimes nR}. \tag{19.109}$$

They each then perform the following quantum channel, which is essentially the "inverse" of the encoding in (19.96):

$$\mathcal{E}^{(-1)}(Z) = U^\dagger Z U + \mathrm{Tr}\{(I - UU^\dagger)Z\}\omega, \tag{19.110}$$

where U is the isometry defined in (19.95) and ω is any state having support in $\mathrm{span}\{|x^n\rangle : x^n \in T_\delta^{X^n}\}$. In fact, since $\widetilde{\psi}_{A^n B^n}^n$ exclusively has support in $\mathrm{span}\{|x^n\rangle : x^n \in T_\delta^{X^n}\}$, it follows that

$$(\mathcal{E}_{A^n}^{(-1)} \otimes \mathcal{E}_{B^n}^{(-1)})(\mathcal{E}_{A^n} \otimes \mathcal{E}_{B^n})(\widetilde{\psi}_{A^n B^n}^n) = \widetilde{\psi}_{A^n B^n}^n, \tag{19.111}$$

which along with the monotonicity of trace distance applied to (19.102), implies that

$$\left\| \widetilde{\psi}_{A^n B^n}^n - (\mathcal{E}_{A^n}^{(-1)} \otimes \mathcal{E}_{B^n}^{(-1)}) \left(\Upsilon_{T_A W_{A'} T_B W_{B'}} \otimes \left(\Phi_{AB}^+\right)^{\otimes nR} \right) \right\|_1 \leq 2\sqrt{2 \cdot 2^{-n\delta}}. \tag{19.112}$$

Applying the triangle inequality to (19.98) and (19.112), we find that

$$\left\| \psi_{AB}^{\otimes n} - (\mathcal{E}_{A^n}^{(-1)} \otimes \mathcal{E}_{B^n}^{(-1)}) \left(\Upsilon_{T_A W_{A'} T_B W_{B'}} \otimes \left(\Phi_{AB}^+\right)^{\otimes nR} \right) \right\|_1 \leq 2\left[\sqrt{\varepsilon} + \sqrt{2 \cdot 2^{-n\delta}}\right], \tag{19.113}$$

which concludes the error analysis.

The rate of ebits needed to form $\psi_{AB}^{\otimes n}$ is equal to $H(A)_\psi + c\delta + \frac{|\mathcal{X}|}{n}\log n$ ebits per copy of ψ_{AB}, and the rate of classical communication needed is $2[(1+c)\delta + \eta(|\mathcal{X}|\delta) + 2|\mathcal{X}|\frac{1}{n}\log n]$ cbits per copy of ψ_{AB}. For large n, we can take δ to be order $\sqrt{n}$ and the central limit theorem implies that we can achieve any constant error $\varepsilon \in (0,1)$ (this is a modified version of typicality in which δ changes with n). At the same time, the ebit rate converges to $H(A)_\psi$ and the classical communication rate vanishes.

Entanglement Manipulation

We can now put together entanglement concentration and dilution to give a general achievable strategy for an entanglement manipulation protocol. The goal here is to convert n copies of ψ_{AB} to as many copies of ϕ_{AB} as possible. In order to do so, Alice and Bob first conduct an entanglement concentration protocol, which takes n copies of ψ_{AB} to $\approx nH(A)_\psi$ approximate ebits. Then, using entanglement dilution and a negligible rate of classical communication, they can convert these $\approx nH(A)_\psi$ approximate ebits to $\approx n\left[H(A)_\psi/H(A)_\psi\right]$ approximate copies of ϕ_{AB}. The accuracy of the protocol becomes arbitrarily small and the rate of entanglement conversion approaches $H(A)_\psi/H(A)_\psi$ in the limit as n becomes large.

19.5 Concluding Remarks

Entanglement concentration was one of the earliest discovered protocols in quantum Shannon theory. The protocol exploits one of the fundamental tools of classical information theory (the method of types), but it applies the method in a coherent fashion so that a type class measurement learns only the type and nothing more. The protocol is similar to Schumacher compression in this regard (in that it learns only the necessary information required to execute the protocol and preserves coherent superpositions), and we will continue to see this idea of applying classical techniques in a coherent way in future quantum Shannon-theoretic protocols. For example, the protocol for quantum communication over a quantum channel is a coherent version of a protocol to transmit private classical information over a quantum channel.

19.6 History and Further Reading

Elias (1972) constructed a protocol for randomness concentration in an early paper. Bennett, Bernstein, Popescu & Schumacher (1996) offered two different protocols for entanglement concentration (one of which we developed in this chapter). Nielsen (1999) later connected entanglement concentration protocols to the theory of majorization. Lo & Popescu (1999) and Lo & Popescu (2001) studied entanglement concentration and the classical communication cost of the inverse protocol (entanglement dilution). Hayden & Winter (2003) characterized the classical communication cost of entanglement dilution, as did Harrow & Lo (2004). Kaye & Mosca (2001) developed practical networks for entanglement concentration, and recently, Blume-Kohout et al. (2014) took this line of research a step further by considering streaming protocols for entanglement concentration. Hayashi & Matsumoto (2001) also developed protocols for universal entanglement concentration.

Vedral & Plenio (1998) introduced the relative entropy of entanglement as one of the first LOCC monotones in quantum information theory. Proposition 19.2.1 is due to Plenio et al. (2000).

Going beyond the settings considered here, researchers have considered error exponents, strong converses, and second-order characterizations for entanglement manipulation tasks (we explain what these terms mean in Section 20.7).

Lo & Popescu (2001) established a strong converse theorem for entanglement concentration. Hayashi et al. (2003) derived error exponents and an exact strong converse for entanglement concentration. Kumagai & Hayashi (2013) established exact second-order characterizations of entanglement concentration and dilution.

Part VI

Noisy Quantum Shannon Theory

Introduction

Before quantum information became an established discipline, John R. Pierce issued the following quip at the end of his 1973 retrospective article on the history of information theory (Pierce, 1973):

"I think that I have never met a physicist who understood information theory. I wish that physicists would stop talking about reformulating information theory and would give us a general expression for the capacity of a channel with quantum effects taken into account rather than a number of special cases."

Since the publication of Pierce's article, we have learned much more about quantum mechanics and information theory than he might have imagined at the time, but we have also realized that there is much more to discover. In spite of all that we have learned, we still unfortunately have not been able to address Pierce's concern in the above quote in full generality.

The most basic question that we could ask in quantum Shannon theory (and the one with which Pierce was concerned) is how much classical information a sender can transmit to a receiver by exploiting a quantum channel. We have determined many special cases of quantum channels for which we do know their classical capacities, but we also now know that this most basic question is still wide open in the general case.

What Pierce might not have imagined at the time is that a quantum channel has a much larger variety of capacities than does a classical channel. For example, we might wish to determine the classical capacity of a quantum channel assisted by entanglement shared between the sender and receiver. We have seen that in the simplest of cases, such as the noiseless qubit channel, shared entanglement boosts the classical capacity up to two bits, and we now refer to this phenomenon as the super-dense coding effect (see Chapter 6). Interestingly, the entanglement-assisted capacity of a quantum channel is one of the few scenarios where we can claim to have a complete understanding of the channel's transmission capabilities. From the results regarding the entanglement-assisted capacity, we have learned that shared entanglement is often a "friend" because it tends to simplify results in both quantum Shannon theory and other subfields of quantum information science.

Additionally, we might consider the capacity of a quantum channel for transmitting quantum information. In 1973, it was not even clear what was meant by "quantum information," but we have since been able to formulate what it means, and we have been able to characterize the quantum capacity of a quantum channel. The task of transmitting quantum information over a quantum channel bears some similarities with the task of transmitting private classical information over that channel, where we are concerned with keeping the classical information private from the environment of the channel. This connection has given insight for achieving good rates of quantum communication over a noisy quantum channel, and there is even a certain class of channels for which we already have a good expression for the quantum capacity (the expression being the coherent information of the channel). However, the problem of determining a good expression for the quantum capacity in the general case is still wide open.

The remaining chapters of the book are an attempt to summarize many items the quantum information community has learned in the past few decades, all of which are an attempt to address Pierce's concern in various ways. The most important open problem in quantum Shannon theory is to find better expressions for these capacities so that we can actually compute them for an arbitrary quantum channel.

20 Classical Communication

This chapter begins our exploration of "dynamic" information-processing tasks in quantum Shannon theory, where the term "dynamic" indicates that a quantum channel connects a sender to a receiver and their goal is to exploit this resource for communication. We specifically consider the scenario in which a sender Alice would like to communicate classical information to a receiver Bob, and the capacity theorem that we prove here is one particular generalization of Shannon's noisy channel coding theorem from classical information theory (reviewed in Section 2.2). In later chapters, we will see other generalizations of Shannon's theorem, depending on what resources are available to assist their communication or whether they are trying to communicate classical or quantum information. For this reason and others, quantum Shannon theory is quite a bit richer than classical information theory.

The naive approach to communicate classical information over a quantum channel is for Alice and Bob simply to mimic the approach used in Shannon's noisy channel coding theorem. That is, they randomly select a classical code according to some distribution $p_X(x)$, and Bob performs individual measurements of the outputs of a quantum channel according to some POVM. The POVM at the output induces some conditional probability distribution $p_{Y|X}(y|x)$, which we can in turn think of as an induced classical channel. The classical mutual information $I(X;Y)$ of this channel is an achievable rate for communication, and the best strategy for Alice and Bob is to optimize the mutual information over all of Alice's inputs to the channel and over all measurements that Bob could perform at the output. The resulting quantity is equal to Bob's optimized accessible information, which we previously discussed in Section 10.9.2.

If the aforementioned coding strategy were optimal, then there would not be anything much interesting to say for the information-processing task of classical communication (in fact, there would not be any need for all of the tools we developed in Chapters 15 and 16!). This is perhaps one first clue that the above strategy is not necessarily optimal. Furthermore, we know from Chapter 11 that the Holevo information is an upper bound on the accessible information, and this bound might prompt us to wonder if it is also an achievable rate for classical communication, given that the accessible information is achievable.

The main theorem of this chapter is the classical capacity theorem (also known as the Holevo–Schumacher–Westmoreland theorem), and it states that the Holevo information of a quantum channel is an achievable rate for classical communication. The Holevo information is easier to manipulate mathematically than is the accessible information. The proof of its achievability demonstrates that the aforementioned strategy is not generally optimal, and the proof also shows how performing a collective measurement on all of the channel outputs allows the sender and receiver to achieve the Holevo information as a rate for classical communication. Thus, this strategy fundamentally makes use of quantum-mechanical effects at the decoder and suggests that such an approach is necessary to achieve the Holevo information. Although this strategy exploits a collective measurement at the decoder, it does not make use of entangled states at the encoder. That is, the sender could input quantum states that are entangled across all of the channel inputs, and this encoder entanglement might potentially increase classical communication rates.

One major drawback of the classical capacity theorem (also the case for many other results in quantum Shannon theory) is that it only demonstrates that the Holevo information is an achievable rate for classical communication—the converse theorem is a "multi-letter" converse, meaning that it might be necessary in the general case to evaluate the Holevo information over a potentially infinite number of uses of the channel. The multi-letter nature of the capacity theorem implies that the optimization task for general channels is intractable and thus further implies that we know very little about the actual classical capacity of general quantum channels. Now, there are many natural quantum channels such as the depolarizing channel and the dephasing channel for which the classical capacity is known (the Holevo information becomes "single-letter" for these channels), and these results imply that we have a complete understanding of the classical information-transmission capabilities of these channels. All of these results have to do with the additivity of the Holevo information of a quantum channel, which we studied previously in Chapter 13.

We mentioned that the Holevo–Schumacher–Westmoreland coding strategy does not make use of entangled inputs at the encoder. But a natural question is to wonder whether entanglement at the encoder could boost classical information-transmission rates, given that it is a resource for many quantum protocols. This question was known as the additivity conjecture and went unsolved for many years, but Hastings (2009) offered a proof that entangled inputs can increase communication rates for certain channels. Thus, for these channels, the single-letter Holevo information is not the proper characterization of classical capacity (however, this is not to say that there could be some alternate characterization of the classical capacity other than the Holevo information which would be single-letter). These results demonstrate that we still know little about classical communication in the general case and furthermore that quantum Shannon theory is an active area of research.

We structure this chapter as follows. We first discuss the aforementioned naive strategy in detail, so that we can understand the difference between it and the Holevo–Schumacher–Westmoreland strategy. Section 20.2 describes the steps needed in any protocol for classical communication over a quantum channel. Section 20.3 provides a statement of the classical capacity theorem, and its two subsections prove the corresponding direct coding theorem and the converse theorem. The direct coding theorem exploits two tools: quantum typicality from Chapter 15 and the packing lemma from Chapter 16. The converse theorem exploits two tools from Chapter 11: continuity of entropies (the AFW inequality in Theorem 11.10.3) and the quantum data-processing inequality (Theorem 11.9.4). We then detail how to calculate the classical capacity of several exemplary channels such as entanglement-breaking channels, quantum Hadamard channels, erasure channels, and depolarizing channels—these are channels for which we have a complete understanding of their classical capacity. Finally, we end with a discussion of the proof that the Holevo information can be superadditive (that is, entangled inputs at the encoder can enhance classical communication rates for some channels).

20.1   Naive Approach: Product Measurements

We begin by discussing in more detail the most naive strategy that a sender and receiver can exploit for the transmission of classical information over many uses of a quantum channel. Figure 20.1 depicts this naive approach. This first approach mimics certain features of Shannon's classical approach without making any use of quantum-mechanical effects. Alice and Bob agree on a codebook beforehand, such that each classical codeword $x^n(m)$ in the codebook corresponds to some message m that Alice wishes to transmit. Alice can exploit some set $\{\rho_x\}$ of density operators to act as input to the quantum channel. That is, the quantum codewords are of the form

$$\rho_{x^n}(m) \equiv \rho_{x_1(m)} \otimes \rho_{x_2(m)} \otimes \cdots \otimes \rho_{x_n(m)}. \tag{20.1}$$

Bob then performs individual measurements of the outputs of the quantum channel by exploiting some POVM $\{\Lambda_y\}$. This scheme induces the following conditional probability distribution:

$$
\begin{aligned}
p_{Y_1 \cdots Y_n | X_1 \cdots X_n} &(y_1 \cdots y_n | x_1(m) \cdots x_n(m)) \\
&= \mathrm{Tr}\left\{ \Lambda_{y_1} \otimes \cdots \otimes \Lambda_{y_n} \left(\mathcal{N} \otimes \cdots \otimes \mathcal{N}\right) \left(\rho_{x_1(m)} \otimes \cdots \otimes \rho_{x_n(m)}\right) \right\} \quad (20.2) \\
&= \mathrm{Tr}\left\{ \left(\Lambda_{y_1} \otimes \cdots \otimes \Lambda_{y_n}\right) \left(\mathcal{N}(\rho_{x_1(m)}) \otimes \cdots \otimes \mathcal{N}(\rho_{x_n(m)})\right) \right\} \quad (20.3) \\
&= \prod_{i=1}^{n} \mathrm{Tr}\left\{ \Lambda_{y_i} \mathcal{N}(\rho_{x_i(m)}) \right\}, \quad (20.4)
\end{aligned}
$$

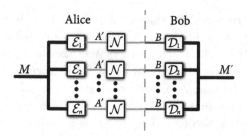

Figure 20.1 The most naive strategy for Alice and Bob to communicate classical information over many independent uses of a quantum channel. Alice wishes to send some message M and selects some tensor product state to input to the channel, conditioned on the message M. She transmits the codeword over the channel, and Bob then receives a noisy version of it. He performs individual measurements of his quantum systems and produces some estimate M' of the original message M. This scheme is effectively a classical scheme because it makes no use of quantum-mechanical features such as entanglement or a collective measurement.

which we immediately realize is equivalent to many i.i.d. instances of the following classical channel:

$$p_{Y|X}(y|x) \equiv \mathrm{Tr}\left\{\Lambda_y \mathcal{N}(\rho_x)\right\}. \tag{20.5}$$

Thus, if they exploit this scheme, the optimal rate at which they can communicate is equal to the following expression:

$$I_{\mathrm{acc}}(\mathcal{N}) \equiv \max_{\{p_X(x), \rho_x, \Lambda\}} I(X;Y), \tag{20.6}$$

where the maximization of the classical mutual information is with respect to all input distributions, all input density operators, and all POVMs that Bob could perform at the output of the channel. This information quantity is known as the accessible information of the channel.

The above strategy is not necessarily an optimal strategy if the channel is truly a quantum channel—it does not make use of any quantum effects such as entanglement or collective measurements (an example of a collective measurement is a Bell measurement, as in quantum teleportation). A first simple modification of the protocol to allow for such effects would be to consider coding for the tensor-product channel $\mathcal{N} \otimes \mathcal{N}$ rather than the original channel. The input states would be entangled across two channel uses, and the output measurements would be over two channel outputs at a time. In this way, they would be exploiting entangled states at the encoder and collective measurements at the decoder. Figure 20.2 illustrates the modified protocol, and the rate of classical communication that they can achieve with such a strategy is $\frac{1}{2}I_{\mathrm{acc}}(\mathcal{N} \otimes \mathcal{N})$. This quantity is always at least as large as $I_{\mathrm{acc}}(\mathcal{N})$ because a special case of the strategy for the tensor-product channel $\mathcal{N} \otimes \mathcal{N}$ is to choose the distribution $p_X(x)$, the states ρ_x, and the POVM Λ to be tensor products of the ones that maximize $I_{\mathrm{acc}}(\mathcal{N})$. We can then extend this construction inductively by forming

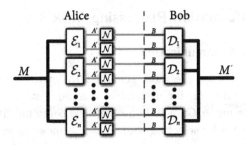

Figure 20.2 A coding strategy that can outperform the previous naive strategy, simply by making use of entanglement at the encoder and decoder.

codes for the tensor-product channel $\mathcal{N}^{\otimes k}$ (where k is a positive integer), and this extended strategy achieves the classical communication rate of $\frac{1}{k} I_{\mathrm{acc}}(\mathcal{N}^{\otimes k})$ for any finite k. These results then suggest that the ultimate classical capacity of the channel is the regularization of the accessible information of the channel:

$$I_{\mathrm{reg}}(\mathcal{N}) \equiv \lim_{k \to \infty} \frac{1}{k} I_{\mathrm{acc}}(\mathcal{N}^{\otimes k}). \tag{20.7}$$

The regularization of the accessible information is intractable for general quantum channels, but the optimization task could simplify immensely if the accessible information is additive (additive in the sense discussed in Chapter 13). In this case, the regularized accessible information $I_{\mathrm{reg}}(\mathcal{N})$ would be equal to the accessible information $I_{\mathrm{acc}}(\mathcal{N})$. However, even if the quantity is additive, the optimization could still be difficult to perform in practice. A simple upper bound on the accessible information is the Holevo information $\chi(\mathcal{N})$ of the channel, defined as

$$\chi(\mathcal{N}) \equiv \max_{\rho} I(X; B), \tag{20.8}$$

where the maximization is with respect to classical–quantum states ρ_{XB} of the following form:

$$\rho_{XB} \equiv \sum_{x} p_X(x) |x\rangle\langle x|_X \otimes \mathcal{N}_{A' \to B}(\psi^x_{A'}). \tag{20.9}$$

The Holevo information is a more desirable quantity to characterize classical communication over a quantum channel because it is always an upper bound on the accessible information and it does not involve an optimization over measurements.

Thus, a natural question to ask is whether Alice and Bob can achieve the Holevo information rate, and the main theorem of this chapter states that it is possible to do so. The resulting coding scheme bears some similarities with the techniques in Shannon's channel coding theorem, but the main difference is that the decoding POVM is a collective measurement over all of the channel outputs.

20.2   The Information-Processing Task

20.2.1   Classical Communication

We now discuss the most general form of the information-processing task and give the criterion for a classical communication rate C to be achievable—i.e., we define an (n, C, ε) code for classical communication over a quantum channel. Alice begins by selecting some classical message m that she would like to transmit to Bob—she selects from a set of messages $\{1, \dots, |\mathcal{M}|\}$. Let M denote the random variable corresponding to Alice's choice of message, and let $|\mathcal{M}|$ denote its cardinality. She then prepares some state $\rho_{A'^n}^m$ as input to the many independent uses of the channel—the input systems are n copies of the channel input system A'. She transmits this state over n independent uses of the channel $\mathcal{N}$, and the state at Bob's receiving end is

$$\mathcal{N}^{\otimes n}(\rho_{A'^n}^m). \tag{20.10}$$

Bob has some decoding POVM $\{\Lambda_m\}$ that he can exploit to determine which message Alice transmits. Figure 20.3 depicts such a general protocol for classical communication over a quantum channel.

Let M' denote the random variable for Bob's estimate of the message. The probability that he determines the correct message m is as follows:

$$\Pr\{M' = m | M = m\} = \mathrm{Tr}\{\Lambda_m \mathcal{N}^{\otimes n}(\rho_{A'^n}^m)\}, \tag{20.11}$$

and thus the probability of error for a particular message m is

$$p_e(m) \equiv 1 - \Pr\{M' = m | M = m\} \tag{20.12}$$
$$= \mathrm{Tr}\{(I - \Lambda_m)\mathcal{N}^{\otimes n}(\rho_{A'^n}^m)\}. \tag{20.13}$$

The maximal probability of error for any coding scheme is then

$$p_e^* \equiv \max_{m \in \mathcal{M}} p_e(m). \tag{20.14}$$

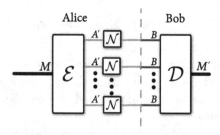

Figure 20.3 The most general protocol for classical communication over a quantum channel. Alice selects some message M and encodes it as a quantum codeword for input to many independent uses of the noisy quantum channel. Bob performs some POVM over all of the channel outputs to determine the message that Alice transmits.

The rate C of communication is

$$C \equiv \frac{1}{n} \log |\mathcal{M}|, \qquad (20.15)$$

and the code has $\varepsilon \in [0,1]$ error if $p_e^* \leq \varepsilon$.

A rate C of classical communication is *achievable* for a channel $\mathcal{N}$ if there exists an $(n, C - \delta, \varepsilon)$ code for all $\delta > 0$, $\varepsilon \in (0,1)$, and sufficiently large n. The classical capacity $C(\mathcal{N})$ of $\mathcal{N}$ is equal to the supremum of all achievable rates for classical communication.

20.2.2 Randomness Distribution

A sender and receiver can exploit a quantum channel for the alternate but related task of *randomness distribution*. Here, Alice prepares a local classical system in a uniformly random state, she makes a copy of it, and the goal is for Bob to have the copy, such that Alice and Bob share a state of the following form at the end of the protocol:

$$\overline{\Phi}_{MM'} \equiv \sum_{m \in \mathcal{M}} \frac{1}{|\mathcal{M}|} |m\rangle\langle m|_M \otimes |m\rangle\langle m|_{M'}. \qquad (20.16)$$

Such shared randomness is not particularly useful as a resource, but this viewpoint is helpful for proving the converse theorem of this chapter and later on when we encounter other information-processing tasks in quantum Shannon theory. The main point to note is that a noiseless classical bit channel can always generate one bit of noiseless shared randomness. Thus, if a quantum channel has a particular capacity for classical communication, it can always achieve the same capacity for randomness distribution. In fact, the capacity for randomness distribution can only be larger than that for classical communication because shared randomness is a weaker resource than classical communication. This relationship gives a simple way to bound the capacity for classical communication from above by the capacity for randomness distribution.

The most general protocol for randomness distribution is as follows. Alice begins by locally preparing a state of the form in (20.16). She then performs an encoding channel that transforms this state to the following one:

$$\sum_{m \in \mathcal{M}} \frac{1}{|\mathcal{M}|} |m\rangle\langle m|_M \otimes \rho_{A'^n}^m, \qquad (20.17)$$

and she transmits the A'^n systems over n independent uses of the quantum channel $\mathcal{N}$, producing the following state:

$$\omega_{MB^n} \equiv \sum_{m \in \mathcal{M}} \frac{1}{|\mathcal{M}|} |m\rangle\langle m|_M \otimes \mathcal{N}^{\otimes n}(\rho_{A'^n}^m). \qquad (20.18)$$

Bob then performs a quantum instrument on the received systems (exploiting some POVM $\{\Lambda_m\}$), and the resulting state is

$$\sum_{m,m'\in\mathcal{M}} \frac{1}{|\mathcal{M}|} |m\rangle\langle m|_M \otimes \sqrt{\Lambda_{m'}}\mathcal{N}^{\otimes n}(\rho_{A'^n}^m)\sqrt{\Lambda_{m'}} \otimes |m'\rangle\langle m'|_{M'}. \qquad (20.19)$$

The state

$$\omega_{MM'} = \sum_{m,m'\in\mathcal{M}} \frac{1}{|\mathcal{M}|} \text{Tr}\left\{\Lambda_{m'}\mathcal{N}^{\otimes n}(\rho_{A'^n}^m)\right\} |m\rangle\langle m|_M \otimes |m'\rangle\langle m'|_{M'} \qquad (20.20)$$

should then be ε-close in trace distance to the original state in (20.16) for an (n, C, ε) protocol for randomness distribution:

$$\frac{1}{2}\left\|\overline{\Phi}_{MM'} - \omega_{MM'}\right\|_1 \leq \varepsilon. \qquad (20.21)$$

A rate C for randomness distribution is achievable if there exists an $(n, C - \delta, \varepsilon)$ randomness distribution code for all $\delta > 0$, $\varepsilon \in (0, 1)$, and sufficiently large n. The capacity for randomness distribution is equal to the supremum of all achievable rates. Clearly, from the definitions, it follows that the classical capacity of a channel can never exceed the capacity for randomness distribution.

20.3   The Classical Capacity Theorem

We now state the main theorem of this chapter, the classical capacity theorem.

THEOREM 20.3.1 (Holevo–Schumacher–Westmoreland)   The classical capacity of a quantum channel is equal to the regularization of the Holevo information of the channel:

$$C(\mathcal{N}) = \chi_{\text{reg}}(\mathcal{N}), \qquad (20.22)$$

where

$$\chi_{\text{reg}}(\mathcal{N}) \equiv \lim_{k\to\infty} \frac{1}{k}\chi(\mathcal{N}^{\otimes k}), \qquad (20.23)$$

and the Holevo information $\chi(\mathcal{N})$ of a channel $\mathcal{N}$ is defined in (20.8).

The regularization in the above characterization is a reflection of our ignorance of a better formula for the classical capacity of a quantum channel. The proof of the above theorem in the next two sections demonstrates that the above quantity is indeed equal to the classical capacity, but the regularization implies that the above characterization is intractable for general quantum channels. However, if the Holevo information of a particular channel is additive (in the sense discussed in Chapter 13), then $\chi_{\text{reg}}(\mathcal{N}) = \chi(\mathcal{N})$, the classical capacity formula simplifies for such a channel, and we can claim to have a complete understanding of the channel's classical transmission capabilities. This "all-or-nothing" situation with capacities is quite common in quantum Shannon theory, and it implies that we still have much remaining to understand regarding classical information transmission over quantum channels.

The next two sections prove the above capacity theorem in two parts: the direct coding theorem and the converse theorem. The proof of the direct coding theorem demonstrates the inequality LHS $\geq$ RHS in (20.22). That is, it shows that the regularized Holevo information is an achievable rate for classical communication, and it exploits typical and conditionally typical subspaces and the packing lemma to do so. The proof of the converse theorem shows the inequality LHS $\leq$ RHS in (20.22). That is, it shows that any sequence of protocols with achievable rate C (with vanishing error in the large n limit) should have this rate below the regularized Holevo information. The proof of the converse theorem exploits the aforementioned idea of randomness distribution, continuity of entropy, and the quantum data-processing inequality.

20.3.1 The Direct Coding Theorem

We first prove the direct coding theorem. Suppose that a quantum channel $\mathcal{N}$ connects Alice to Bob, and they are allowed access to many independent uses of this quantum channel. Alice can choose some ensemble $\{p_X(x), \rho^x\}$ of states which she can exploit to make a random code for this channel. She selects $|\mathcal{M}|$ codewords $\{x^n(m)\}_{m \in \{1,\dots,|\mathcal{M}|\}}$ independently according to the following distribution:

$$
p'_{X'^n}(x^n) = \begin{cases} \left[\sum_{x^n \in T_\delta^{X^n}} p_{X^n}(x^n)\right]^{-1} p_{X^n}(x^n) & : x^n \in T_\delta^{X^n} \\ 0 & : x^n \notin T_\delta^{X^n} \end{cases}, \qquad (20.24)
$$

where X'^n is a random variable with distribution $p'_{X'^n}(x^n)$, $p_{X^n}(x^n) = p_X(x_1)\cdots p_X(x_n)$, and $T_\delta^{X^n}$ denotes the set of strongly typical sequences for the distribution $p_{X^n}(x^n)$ (see Section 14.7). This "pruned" distribution is approximately close to the i.i.d. distribution $p_{X^n}(x^n)$ because the probability mass of the typical set is nearly one. In fact, from (19.86), we have that the following holds if $\Pr\{X^n \in T_\delta^{X^n}\} \geq 1 - \varepsilon$:

$$
\sum_{x^n \in \mathcal{X}^n} |p'_{X'^n}(x^n) - p_{X^n}(x^n)| \leq 2\varepsilon. \qquad (20.25)
$$

Indeed, we know from typicality that $\Pr\{X^n \in T_\delta^{X^n}\} \geq 1 - \varepsilon$ for all $\varepsilon \in (0, 1)$ and sufficiently large n.

These classical codewords $\{x^n(m)\}_{m \in \{1,\dots,|\mathcal{M}|\}}$ lead to quantum codewords of the following form:

$$
\rho^{x^n}(m) \equiv \rho^{x_1(m)} \otimes \cdots \otimes \rho^{x_n(m)}, \qquad (20.26)
$$

by exploiting the quantum states in the ensemble $\{p_X(x), \rho^x\}$. Alice then transmits these codewords through the channel, leading to the following tensor-product density operators:

$$\sigma^{x^n(m)} \equiv \sigma^{x_1(m)} \otimes \cdots \otimes \sigma^{x_n(m)} \tag{20.27}$$

$$\equiv \mathcal{N}(\rho^{x_1(m)}) \otimes \cdots \otimes \mathcal{N}(\rho^{x_n(m)}). \tag{20.28}$$

Bob then detects which codeword Alice transmits by exploiting some detection POVM $\{\Lambda_m\}$ that acts on all of the channel outputs.

At this point, we would like to exploit the packing lemma (Lemma 16.3.1 from Chapter 16). Recall that four objects are needed to apply the packing lemma, and they should satisfy four inequalities. The first object needed is an ensemble from which we can select a code randomly, and the ensemble in our case is $\{p'_{X'^n}(x^n), \sigma^{x^n}\}$. The next object is the expected density operator of this ensemble:

$$\mathbb{E}_{X'^n}\left\{\sigma^{X'^n}\right\} = \sum_{x^n \in \mathcal{X}^n} p'_{X'^n}(x^n)\sigma^{x^n}. \tag{20.29}$$

Finally, we need a message subspace projector and a total subspace projector, and we let these respectively be the conditionally typical projector $\Pi^\delta_{B^n|x^n}$ for the state σ^{x^n} and the typical projector $\Pi^\delta_{B^n}$ for the tensor product state $\sigma^{\otimes n}$ where $\sigma \equiv \sum_x p_X(x)\sigma^x$. Intuitively, the tensor product state $\sigma^{\otimes n}$ should be close to the expected state $\mathbb{E}_{X'^n}\left\{\sigma^{X'^n}\right\}$, and the next exercise asks you to verify this statement.

EXERCISE 20.3.1　Prove that the trace distance between the expected state $\mathbb{E}_{X'^n}\left\{\sigma^{X'^n}\right\}$ and the tensor product state $\sigma^{\otimes n}$ is small for all sufficiently large n:

$$\left\|\mathbb{E}_{X'^n}\left\{\sigma^{X'^n}\right\} - \sigma^{\otimes n}\right\|_1 \leq 2\varepsilon, \tag{20.30}$$

where ε is an arbitrarily small positive number such that $\Pr\left\{X^n \in T^{X^n}_\delta\right\} \geq 1-\varepsilon$.

If the four conditions of the packing lemma are satisfied – see (16.11)–(16.14) – then there exists a coding scheme with a detection POVM that has an arbitrarily low maximal probability of error as long as the number of messages in the code is not too high. We now show how to satisfy these four conditions by exploiting the properties of typical and conditionally typical projectors. The following three conditions follow from the properties of typical subspaces:

$$\mathrm{Tr}\left\{\Pi^\delta_{B^n}\sigma^{x^n}_{B^n}\right\} \geq 1 - \varepsilon, \tag{20.31}$$

$$\mathrm{Tr}\left\{\Pi^\delta_{B^n|x^n}\sigma^{x^n}_{B^n}\right\} \geq 1 - \varepsilon, \tag{20.32}$$

$$\mathrm{Tr}\left\{\Pi^\delta_{B^n|x^n}\right\} \leq 2^{n(H(B|X)+c\delta)}, \tag{20.33}$$

where c is a strictly positive constant. The first inequality follows from Property 15.2.7. The second inequality follows from Property 15.2.4, and the third from Property 15.2.5. We leave the proof of the fourth inequality for the packing lemma as an exercise.

EXERCISE 20.3.2 Prove that the following inequality holds:

$$\Pi^{\delta}_{B^n} \mathbb{E}_{X'^n} \left\{ \sigma^{X'^n}_{B^n} \right\} \Pi^{\delta}_{B^n} \leq [1-\varepsilon]^{-1} 2^{-n\left(H(B)-c'\delta\right)} \Pi^{\delta}_{B^n}, \tag{20.34}$$

where c' is a strictly positive constant. (Hint: First show that $\mathbb{E}_{X'^n} \left\{ \sigma^{X'^n}_{B^n} \right\} \leq [1-\varepsilon]^{-1} \sigma_{B^n}$ and then apply the third property of typical subspaces—Property 15.1.3.)

With these four conditions holding, it follows from Corollary 16.5.1 (the derandomized version of the packing lemma) that there exists a deterministic code and a POVM $\{\Lambda_m\}$ that can detect the transmitted states with arbitrarily low maximal probability of error as long as the size $|\mathcal{M}|$ of the message set is small enough:

$$p^*_e \equiv \max_m \text{Tr} \left\{ (I - \Lambda_m) \mathcal{N}^{\otimes n}(\rho^{x^n(m)}) \right\} \tag{20.35}$$

$$\leq 4\left(\varepsilon + 2\sqrt{\varepsilon}\right) + 16\left[1-\varepsilon\right]^{-1} 2^{-n\left(H(B)-H(B|X)-(c+c')\delta\right)} |\mathcal{M}| \tag{20.36}$$

$$= 4\left(\varepsilon + 2\sqrt{\varepsilon}\right) + 16\left[1-\varepsilon\right]^{-1} 2^{-n\left(I(X;B)-(c+c')\delta\right)} |\mathcal{M}|. \tag{20.37}$$

Thus, we can choose the size of the message set to be $|\mathcal{M}| = 2^{n\left(I(X;B)-(c+c'+1)\delta\right)}$ so that the rate of communication is the Holevo information $I(X;B)$:

$$\frac{1}{n} \log |\mathcal{M}| = I(X;B) - (c+c'+1)\delta, \tag{20.38}$$

and the bound on the maximal probability of error becomes

$$p^*_e \leq 4\left(\varepsilon + 2\sqrt{\varepsilon}\right) + 16\left[1-\varepsilon\right]^{-1} 2^{-n\delta}. \tag{20.39}$$

Let $\varepsilon' \in (0,1)$ and $\delta' > 0$. By picking n large enough, it is clear that we can have both $4\left(\varepsilon + 2\sqrt{\varepsilon}\right) + 16\left[1-\varepsilon\right]^{-1} 2^{-n\delta} \leq \varepsilon'$ and $(c+c'+1)\delta \leq \delta'$. Thus, the Holevo information $I(X;B)_\rho$, with respect to the following classical–quantum state:

$$\rho_{XB} \equiv \sum_{x \in \mathcal{X}} p_X(x)|x\rangle\langle x|_X \otimes \mathcal{N}(\rho^x), \tag{20.40}$$

is an achievable rate for the transmission of classical information over $\mathcal{N}$.

Alice and Bob can achieve the Holevo information $\chi(\mathcal{N})$ of the channel $\mathcal{N}$ simply by selecting a random code according to the ensemble $\{p_X(x), \rho^x\}$ that maximizes $I(X;B)_\rho$. Lastly, they can achieve the rate $\frac{1}{k}\chi(\mathcal{N}^{\otimes k})$ by coding instead for the tensor-product channel $\mathcal{N}^{\otimes k}$, and this last result implies that they can achieve the regularization $\chi_{\text{reg}}(\mathcal{N})$ by making the blocks for which they are coding be arbitrarily large. This concludes the proof of the direct part of the coding theorem.

We comment more on the role of entanglement at the encoder before moving on to the proof of the converse theorem. First, the above coding scheme for the channel $\mathcal{N}$ does not make use of entangled inputs at the encoder because the codeword states $\rho^{x^n(m)}$ are separable across the channel inputs. It is only when we code for the tensor-product channel $\mathcal{N}^{\otimes k}$ that entanglement comes into play. Here, the codeword states are of the form

$$\rho_{x^n(m)} \equiv \rho_{A'^k}^{x_1(m)} \otimes \cdots \otimes \rho_{A'^k}^{x_n(m)}. \tag{20.41}$$

That is, the states $\rho_{A'^k}^{x_i(m)}$ act on the tensor-product Hilbert space of k channel inputs and can be entangled across these k systems. Whether entanglement at the encoder could increase classical communication rates over general quantum channels was the subject of much intense work over the past few years, but it is now known that there exists a channel for which exploiting entanglement at the encoder is strictly better than not exploiting entanglement (see Section 20.5).

It is worth re-examining the proof of the packing lemma (Lemma 16.3.1) in order to understand better the decoding POVM at the receiving end. The particular decoding POVM elements employed in the packing lemma have the following form:

$$\Lambda_m \equiv \left(\sum_{m' \in \mathcal{M}} \Gamma_{m'} \right)^{-\frac{1}{2}} \Gamma_m \left(\sum_{m' \in \mathcal{M}} \Gamma_{m'} \right)^{-\frac{1}{2}}, \tag{20.42}$$

$$\Gamma_m \equiv \Pi_{B^n}^{\delta} \Pi_{B^n|x^n(m)}^{\delta} \Pi_{B^n}^{\delta}. \tag{20.43}$$

(Simply substitute the conditionally typical projector $\Pi_{B^n|x^n(m)}^{\delta}$ and the typical projector $\Pi_{B^n}^{\delta}$ into (16.24).) A POVM with the above elements is known as a "square-root" measurement because of its particular form. We employ such a measurement at the decoder because it has nice analytic properties that allow us to obtain a good bound on the expectation of the average error probability (in particular, we can exploit the operator inequality from Lemma 16.4.1). This measurement is a collective measurement because the conditionally typical projector and the typical projector are both acting on all of the channel outputs, and we construct the square-root measurement from these projectors. Such a decoding POVM is far more exotic than the naive strategy overviewed in Section 20.1 where Bob measures the channel outputs individually—it is for the construction of this decoding POVM and the proof that it is asymptotically good that Holevo, Schumacher, and Westmoreland were given much praise for their work. However, there is no known way to implement this decoding POVM efficiently, and the original efficiency problems with the decoder in the proof of Shannon's noisy classical channel coding theorem plague the decoders in the quantum world as well.

Alternatively, Bob's decoding operation could take the form of a sequential decoder, as discussed in Section 16.6. That is, Bob would perform the measurements $\{\Pi_{B^n|x^n(m)}^{\delta}, I_{B^n} - \Pi_{B^n|x^n(m)}^{\delta}\}$ one after another in an attempt to learn which message was transmitted. This decoding strategy is also a collective measurement strategy because each of the above measurements is a collective measurement acting on all of the channel outputs. This scheme is also inefficient: even if there is an efficient implementation for each of the individual tests, there are an exponential number of them to perform in the worst case since there are an exponential number of messages in a codebook (exponential in n).

EXERCISE 20.3.3 Show that a measurement with POVM elements of the following form is sufficient to achieve the Holevo information of a quantum channel:

$$\Lambda_m \equiv \left(\sum_{m' \in \mathcal{M}} \Pi^\delta_{B^n | x^n (m')} \right)^{-1/2} \Pi^\delta_{B^n | x^n (m)} \left(\sum_{m' \in \mathcal{M}} \Pi^\delta_{B^n | x^n (m')} \right)^{-1/2}. \tag{20.44}$$

Alternate Proofs of the Direct Part

There are at least two alternate proofs of the direct part of the HSW theorem, which can be useful as building blocks for other scenarios. The first is based on weak typicality and the second is called the *constant-composition coding* approach. We discuss these briefly here.

Let $\{p_X(x), \rho^x_{A'}\}$ be an ensemble of states for the input of the channel $\mathcal{N}_{A' \to B}$, which leads to an ensemble $\{p_X(x), \sigma^x_B\}$ at the output, where $\sigma^x_B \equiv \mathcal{N}_{A' \to B}(\rho^x_{A'})$. Let $\sigma_B \equiv \sum_x p_X(x) \sigma^x_B$ be the expected density operator of the output ensemble. In the weak typicality approach, the codewords $\{x^n(m)\}$ are chosen independently at random according to the product distribution $p_{X^n}(x^n) = \prod_{i=1}^n p_X(x_i)$. One then sets the total subspace projector to be the weakly typical projection $\Pi^\delta_{B^n}$ for $\sigma^{\otimes n}_B$ and each message subspace projection (for the codeword $x^n(m)$) to be the weak conditionally typical projection $\Pi^\delta_{B^n | x^n (m)}$. From the properties of weak typicality (see Chapter 15), the following conditions for the average version of the packing lemma (see Exercise 16.5.3) are satisfied:

$$\sum_{x^n \in \mathcal{X}^n} p_{X^n}(x^n) \, \text{Tr} \left\{ \Pi^\delta_{B^n} \sigma^{x^n}_{B^n} \right\} \geq 1 - \varepsilon, \tag{20.45}$$

$$\sum_{x^n \in \mathcal{X}^n} p_{X^n}(x^n) \, \text{Tr} \left\{ \Pi^\delta_{B^n | x^n} \sigma^{x^n}_{B^n} \right\} \geq 1 - \varepsilon, \tag{20.46}$$

$$\text{Tr} \left\{ \Pi^\delta_{B^n | x^n} \right\} \leq 2^{n(H(B|X)+\delta)}, \tag{20.47}$$

$$\Pi^\delta_{B^n} \sigma^{\otimes n}_B \Pi^\delta_{B^n} \leq 2^{-n(H(B)-\delta)} \Pi^\delta_{B^n}. \tag{20.48}$$

We can then conclude that the rate $I(X; B)$ is achievable for classical communication over $\mathcal{N}_{A' \to B}$, by making use of this slightly different scheme. (The Holevo information is with respect to the output ensemble $\{p_X(x), \sigma^x_B\}$.)

The next scheme that we mention is the constant-composition coding scheme. Consider again the output ensemble $\{p_X(x), \sigma^x_B\}$ with expectation $\sigma_B \equiv \sum_x p_X(x) \sigma^x_B$. Now select a typical type class T_t, as discussed in Definition 14.7.4 and Section 14.7.4. This is a set of all the sequences x^n with empirical distribution $t(x)$ that deviates from the true distribution $p_X(x)$ by no more than $\delta > 0$. All the sequences in the same type class are related to one another by a permutation, and all of them are strongly typical. The idea for selecting a code at random is now to pick all of the codewords independently and uniformly at random from the typical type class t. Thus, the ensemble from which we are selecting codewords is now $\{1/|T_t|, \sigma_{B^n}^{x^n}\}_{x^n \in T_t}$ and we would like to show that in doing so, we can still achieve a rate equal to $I(X; B)$. Let

$$\widetilde{\sigma}_{B^n} \equiv |T_t|^{-1} \sum_{x^n \in T_t} \sigma_{B^n}^{x^n}, \qquad \overline{\sigma}_B \equiv \sum_{x \in \mathcal{X}} t(x) \sigma_B^x. \tag{20.49}$$

Observe that $\frac{1}{2} \|\overline{\sigma}_B - \sigma_B\|_1 \leq |\mathcal{X}| \delta/2$, and thus $|H(B)_{\overline{\sigma}} - H(B)_\sigma| \leq \eta(|\mathcal{X}| \delta)$, with $\eta(\cdot)$ defined just after (14.119) and such that $\lim_{\delta \to 0} \eta(|\mathcal{X}| \delta) = 0$. We can take the total subspace projector to be the strongly typical projection $\Pi_{B^n}^\delta$ for $\overline{\sigma}_B^{\otimes n}$, and we take the message subspace projection (for the codeword $x^n(m)$) to be the strong conditionally typical projector $\Pi_{B^n|x^n(m)}^\delta$. We then need to verify that the conditions of the packing lemma (Corollary 16.5.1) hold. Consider that

$$\text{Tr}\left\{\Pi_{B^n}^\delta \sigma_{B^n}^{x^n}\right\} \geq 1 - \varepsilon, \tag{20.50}$$

$$\text{Tr}\left\{\Pi_{B^n|x^n}^\delta \sigma_{B^n}^{x^n}\right\} \geq 1 - \varepsilon, \tag{20.51}$$

$$\text{Tr}\left\{\Pi_{B^n|x^n}^\delta\right\} \leq 2^{n(H(B|X)+c\delta)}. \tag{20.52}$$

The first inequality follows because each $x^n \in T_t$ is strongly typical with respect to $t(x)$, so that we can apply Property 15.2.7. The second two inequalities are properties of strong conditional typicality. So we need to figure out something about the last condition. Let $t^n(x^n) \equiv \prod_{i=1}^n t(x_i)$, i.e., the product distribution realized by $t(x)$. Consider that

$$\widetilde{\sigma}_{B^n} = \frac{1}{|T_t|} \sum_{x^n \in T_t} \sigma_{B^n}^{x^n} = \sum_{x^n \in \mathcal{X}^n} \frac{I(x^n \in T_t)}{|T_t|} \sigma_{B^n}^{x^n} \tag{20.53}$$

$$\leq \sum_{x^n \in \mathcal{X}^n} (n+1)^{|\mathcal{X}|} t^n(x^n) \sigma_{B^n}^{x^n} = (n+1)^{|\mathcal{X}|} \overline{\sigma}_B^{\otimes n}. \tag{20.54}$$

The inequality follows from the development in (14.114)–(14.117). Using this, we find that

$$\Pi_{B^n}^\delta \widetilde{\sigma}_{B^n} \Pi_{B^n}^\delta \leq 2^{-n(H(B)_{\overline{\sigma}} - \frac{1}{n}|\mathcal{X}| \log(n+1))} \Pi_{B^n}^\delta, \tag{20.55}$$

which is the last condition we need for the packing lemma (Corollary 16.5.1). We can then conclude that the rate $H(B)_{\overline{\sigma}} - H(B|X)$ is achievable for classical communication using constant-composition codes. However, since $|H(B)_{\overline{\sigma}} - H(B)_\sigma| \leq \eta(|\mathcal{X}| \delta)$, we can also conclude that the rate $I(X; B)$ is achievable for classical communication using constant-composition codes, where the Holevo information is with respect to the original output ensemble $\{p_X(x), \sigma_B^x\}$.

20.3.2 The Converse Theorem

The second part of the classical capacity theorem is the converse theorem, and we provide a simple proof of it in this section. Suppose that Alice and Bob are trying to accomplish randomness distribution rather than classical communication—the capacity for such a task can only be larger than that for classical communication as we argued before in Section 20.2. Recall that in such a task, Alice first prepares a maximally correlated state $\overline{\Phi}_{MM'}$ so that the rate of randomness distribution is equal to $\frac{1}{n} \log |\mathcal{M}|$. Alice and Bob share a state of the form in (20.19) after encoding, channel transmission, and decoding. We now show that the regularized Holevo information in (20.23) bounds the capacity of randomness distribution. As a result, the regularized Holevo information also bounds the capacity for classical communication from above. Consider the following chain of inequalities:

$$\log |\mathcal{M}| = I(M; M')_{\overline{\Phi}} \tag{20.56}$$
$$\leq I(M; M')_\omega + f(|\mathcal{M}|, \varepsilon) \tag{20.57}$$
$$\leq I(M; B^n)_\omega + f(|\mathcal{M}|, \varepsilon) \tag{20.58}$$
$$\leq \chi(\mathcal{N}^{\otimes n}) + f(|\mathcal{M}|, \varepsilon). \tag{20.59}$$

The first equality follows because the mutual information of the shared randomness state $\overline{\Phi}_{MM'}$ is equal to $\log |\mathcal{M}|$ bits. The first inequality follows from the error criterion in (20.21) and by applying the AFW inequality (Theorem 11.10.3). That is, since $H(M)_{\overline{\Phi}} = H(M)_\omega$, we know that

$$|I(M; M')_{\overline{\Phi}} - I(M; M')_\omega| \tag{20.60}$$
$$= |H(M)_{\overline{\Phi}} - H(M|M')_{\overline{\Phi}} - [H(M)_\omega - H(M|M')_\omega]| \tag{20.61}$$
$$= |H(M|M')_\omega - H(M|M')_{\overline{\Phi}}| \tag{20.62}$$
$$\leq f(|\mathcal{M}|, \varepsilon) \equiv \varepsilon \log |\mathcal{M}| + (1 + \varepsilon) h_2(\varepsilon / [1 + \varepsilon]). \tag{20.63}$$

The second inequality results from the quantum data-processing inequality for quantum mutual information (Theorem 11.9.4)—recall that Bob processes the B^n system with a quantum instrument to get the classical system M'. Also, the quantum mutual information is evaluated on a classical–quantum state of the form in (20.18). The final inequality follows because the classical–quantum state in (20.18) has a particular distribution and choice of states, and this choice always leads to a value of the quantum mutual information that cannot be greater than the Holevo information of the tensor-product channel $\mathcal{N}^{\otimes n}$. Putting everything together, we find that

$$\frac{1}{n} \log |\mathcal{M}| (1 - \varepsilon) \leq \frac{1}{n} \chi(\mathcal{N}^{\otimes n}) + \frac{1}{n} (1 + \varepsilon) h_2(\varepsilon / [1 + \varepsilon]). \tag{20.64}$$

Thus, if we are considering a sequence of $(n, [\log |\mathcal{M}|] / n, \varepsilon_n)$ classical communication protocols with rate $C - \delta_n = \frac{1}{n} \log |\mathcal{M}|$, such that $\lim_{n \to \infty} \varepsilon_n = \lim_{n \to \infty} \delta_n = 0$, then the above bound becomes

$$(C - \delta_n)(1 - \varepsilon_n) \leq \frac{1}{n} \chi(\mathcal{N}^{\otimes n}) + \frac{1}{n} (1 + \varepsilon_n) h_2(\varepsilon_n / [1 + \varepsilon_n]). \tag{20.65}$$

Taking the limit as $n \to \infty$ then establishes that an achievable rate C necessarily satisfies $C \leq \chi_{\text{reg}}(\mathcal{N})$, where $\chi_{\text{reg}}(\mathcal{N})$ is the regularized Holevo formula given in (20.23).

20.4   Examples of Channels

Observe that the final upper bound in (20.59) on the rate C is the multi-letter Holevo information of the channel. It would be more desirable to have $\chi(\mathcal{N})$ as the upper bound on C rather than $\frac{1}{n}\chi(\mathcal{N}^{\otimes n})$ because the former is simpler, and the optimization problem set out in the latter quantity is simply impossible to compute in general using finite computational resources (for large n). However, the upper bound in (20.59) is the best known upper bound if we do not know anything else about the structure of the channel, and for this reason, the best known characterization of the classical capacity is the one given in (20.22).

If we know that the Holevo information of the tensor product of a certain channel with an arbitrary number of copies of itself is additive, then there is no need for the regularization $\chi_{\text{reg}}(\mathcal{N})$, and the characterization in Theorem 20.3.1 reduces to a very good one: the Holevo information $\chi(\mathcal{N})$. There are many examples of channels for which the classical capacity reduces to the Holevo information of the channel, and we detail a few such classes of examples in this section: entanglement-breaking channels, quantum Hadamard channels, erasure channels, and quantum depolarizing channels. The proof that demonstrates additivity of the Holevo information for each of these channels depends explicitly on structural properties of each one, and there is unfortunately not much to learn from these proofs in order to say anything about additivity of the Holevo information of general quantum channels. Nevertheless, it is good to have some natural channels for which we can compute their classical capacity, and it is instructive to examine these proofs in detail to understand what it is about each channel that makes their Holevo information additive.

20.4.1   Classical Capacity of Entanglement-Breaking Channels

We have already seen in Section 13.3.1 that the Holevo information of an entanglement-breaking channel is additive. As a consequence, we can conclude that the capacity of an entanglement-breaking channel $\mathcal{N}$ is given by $\chi(\mathcal{N})$.

We now focus our discussion on cq channels. Recall from Section 4.6.7 that a quantum channel is a particular kind of entanglement-breaking channel (cq channel) if the action of the channel is equivalent to performing first a complete projective measurement of the input and then preparing a quantum state conditioned on the value of the classical variable resulting from the measurement. Additionally, Theorem 13.3.3 states that the Holevo information is a concave function of the input distribution over which we are optimizing for such channels. Thus, computing the classical capacity of cq channels can be performed by optimization techniques because the Holevo information is additive for them.

The Relation to General Channels
We can always exploit the above result regarding cq entanglement-breaking channels to get a reasonable lower bound on the classical capacity of any quantum

channel $\mathcal{N}$. The sender Alice can simulate an entanglement-breaking channel by modifying the processing at the input of an arbitrary quantum channel. She can first measure the input to her simulated channel in the basis $\{|x\rangle\langle x|\}$, prepare a state ρ_x conditioned on the outcome of the measurement, and subsequently feed this state into the channel $\mathcal{N}$. These actions are equivalent to the following channel:

$$\sigma \to \sum_x \langle x|\sigma|x\rangle\mathcal{N}(\rho_x), \qquad (20.66)$$

and the capacity of this simulated channel is equal to

$$I(X;B)_\rho, \qquad (20.67)$$

where

$$\rho_{XB} \equiv \sum_x p_X(x)|x\rangle\langle x|_X \otimes \mathcal{N}(\rho_x), \qquad (20.68)$$

$$p_X(x) \equiv \langle x|\sigma|x\rangle. \qquad (20.69)$$

Of course, Alice has the freedom to prepare whichever state σ she would like to be input to the simulated channel, and she also has the ability to prepare whichever states ρ_x she would like to be conditioned on the outcomes of the first measurement, so we should let her maximize the Holevo information over all these inputs. Thus, the capacity of the entanglement-breaking channel composed with the actual channel is equal to the Holevo information of the original channel:

$$\max_{p_X(x),\rho_x} I(X;B)_\rho. \qquad (20.70)$$

This capacity is also known as the product-state capacity of the channel because it is the capacity achieved by inputting unentangled, separable states at the encoder (Alice can in fact just input product states), and it can be a good lower bound on the true classical capacity of a quantum channel, even if it does not allow for entanglement at the encoder.

20.4.2 Classical Capacity of Quantum Hadamard Channels

Recall from Section 5.2.3 that quantum Hadamard channels are those with a complementary channel that is entanglement breaking, and this property allows us to prove that the Holevo information of the original channel is additive. Several important natural channels are quantum Hadamard channels. A trivial example is the noiseless qubit channel because Bob could perform a projective measurement of his system and send a constant state to Eve. A less trivial example of a quantum Hadamard channel is a generalized dephasing channel (see Section 5.2.3), but this channel trivially has a maximal classical capacity of $\log d$ bits per channel use because this channel transmits a preferred orthonormal basis without error. A quantum Hadamard channel with a more interesting classical capacity is known as a cloning channel, the channel induced by a universal cloning machine (however, we will not discuss this channel in any detail).

THEOREM 20.4.1   The Holevo information of a quantum Hadamard channel $\mathcal{N}_{\mathrm{H}}$ and any other channel $\mathcal{N}$ is additive:

$$\chi(\mathcal{N}_{\mathrm{H}} \otimes \mathcal{N}) = \chi(\mathcal{N}_{\mathrm{H}}) + \chi(\mathcal{N}). \tag{20.71}$$

Proof   First, recall from Theorem 13.3.2 that it is sufficient to consider ensembles of pure states at the input of the channel when maximizing its Holevo information. That is, we only need to consider classical–quantum states of the following form:

$$\sigma_{XA'} \equiv \sum_x p_X(x)|x\rangle\langle x|_X \otimes |\phi_x\rangle\langle\phi_x|_{A'}, \tag{20.72}$$

where A' is the input to some channel $\mathcal{N}_{A' \to B}$. Let $\omega_{XBE} \equiv \mathcal{U}^{\mathcal{N}}_{A' \to BE}(\sigma_{XA'})$ where $U^{\mathcal{N}}_{A' \to BE}$ is an isometric extension of the channel and $\mathcal{U}^{\mathcal{N}}_{A' \to BE}$ denotes the corresponding channel. Thus, the Holevo information of $\mathcal{N}_{A' \to B}$ is equal to a different expression:

$$\chi(\mathcal{N}) \equiv \max_\sigma I(X;B)_\omega \tag{20.73}$$

$$= \max_\sigma \left[H(B)_\omega - H(B|X)_\omega \right] \tag{20.74}$$

$$= \max_\sigma \left[H(B)_\omega - H(E|X)_\omega \right], \tag{20.75}$$

where the second equality follows from the definition of the quantum mutual information, and the third equality follows because, conditioned on X, the input to the channel is pure and the entropies $H(B|X)_\omega$ and $H(E|X)_\omega$ are equal.

EXERCISE 20.4.1   Prove that it is sufficient to consider pure-state inputs when maximizing the following entropy difference over classical–quantum states:

$$\max_\sigma \left[H(B)_\omega - H(E|X)_\omega \right]. \tag{20.76}$$

Suppose now that σ is a state that maximizes the Holevo information of the joint channel $\mathcal{N}_{\mathrm{H}} \otimes \mathcal{N}$, and suppose it has the following form:

$$\sigma_{XA_1'A_2'} \equiv \sum_x p_X(x)|x\rangle\langle x|_X \otimes |\phi_x\rangle\langle\phi_x|_{A_1'A_2'}. \tag{20.77}$$

Let

$$\omega_{XB_1B_2E_1E_2} \equiv (\mathcal{U}^{\mathcal{N}_{\mathrm{H}}}_{A_1' \to B_1E_1} \otimes \mathcal{U}^{\mathcal{N}}_{A_2' \to B_2E_2})(\sigma_{XA_1'A_2'}). \tag{20.78}$$

The Hadamard channel is degradable, and the degrading channel from Bob to Eve takes a particular form: it is a measurement that produces a classical variable Y, followed by the preparation of a state conditioned on the outcome of the measurement. Let $\mathcal{D}^1_{B_1 \to Y}$ be the first part of the degrading channel that produces the classical variable Y, and let $\theta_{XYE_1B_2E_2} \equiv \mathcal{D}^1_{B_1 \to Y}(\omega_{XB_1B_2E_1E_2})$. Let $\mathcal{D}^2_{Y \to E_1'}$ be the second part of the degrading channel that produces the state of E_1 conditioned on the classical variable Y, and let $\tau_{XE_1'E_1B_2E_2} \equiv \mathcal{D}^2_{Y \to E_1'}(\theta_{XYE_1B_2E_2})$.

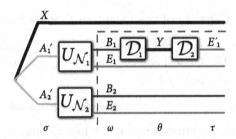

Figure 20.4 A summary of the structural relationships for the additivity question if one channel is a quantum Hadamard channel. Alice first prepares a state of the form in (20.77). She transmits one system A_1' through the quantum Hadamard channel and the other A_2' through the other channel. The first Bob B_1 at the output of the Hadamard channel can simulate the channel to the first Eve E_1 because the first channel is a quantum Hadamard channel. He performs a complete projective measurement of his system, leading to a classical variable Y, followed by the preparation of some state conditioned on the value of the classical variable Y. The bottom of the figure labels the state of the systems at each step.

Figure 20.4 summarizes these structural relationships. Consider the following chain of inequalities:

$$I(X; B_1 B_2)_\omega = H(B_1 B_2)_\omega - H(B_1 B_2 | X)_\omega \tag{20.79}$$
$$= H(B_1 B_2)_\omega - H(E_1 E_2 | X)_\omega \tag{20.80}$$
$$\leq H(B_1)_\omega + H(B_2)_\omega - H(E_1 | X)_\omega - H(E_2 | E_1 X)_\omega \tag{20.81}$$
$$= H(B_1)_\omega - H(E_1 | X)_\omega + H(B_2)_\omega - H(E_2 | E_1' X)_\tau \tag{20.82}$$
$$\leq H(B_1)_\omega - H(E_1 | X)_\omega + H(B_2)_\theta - H(E_2 | Y X)_\theta \tag{20.83}$$
$$\leq \chi(\mathcal{N}_H) + \chi(\mathcal{N}). \tag{20.84}$$

The first equality follows from the definition of the quantum mutual information. The second equality follows because $H(B_1 B_2 | X)_\omega = H(E_1 E_2 | X)_\omega$ when the conditional inputs $|\phi_x\rangle_{A_1' A_2'}$ to the channel are pure states. The next inequality follows from subadditivity of entropy $H(B_1 B_2)_\omega \leq H(B_1)_\omega + H(B_2)_\omega$ and from the chain rule for entropy: $H(E_1 E_2 | X)_\omega = H(E_1 | X)_\omega + H(E_2 | E_1 X)_\omega$. The third equality follows from a rearrangement of terms and realizing that the state of τ on systems $E_1' E_2 X$ is equal to the state of ω on the same systems. The second inequality follows from the quantum data-processing inequality $I(E_2; E_1' | X)_\tau \leq I(E_2; Y | X)_\theta$. The final inequality follows because the state ω is a state of the form in (20.75), because the entropy difference is never greater than the Holevo information of the first channel, and from the result of Exercise 20.4.1. The same reasoning follows for the other entropy difference and by noting that the classical system is the composite system XY. $\square$

20.4.3   Classical Capacity of the Quantum Erasure Channel

The quantum erasure channel is one of the simplest channels for which we can compute the classical capacity. Recall from Section 4.7.6 that the qudit erasure channel is defined as follows:

$$\rho \rightarrow (1 - \varepsilon)\rho + \varepsilon|e\rangle\langle e|, \tag{20.85}$$

where ρ is a d-dimensional qudit input state, $\varepsilon \in [0, 1]$, and $|e\rangle$ is an erasure symbol orthogonal to the input space of the channel.

THEOREM 20.4.2 (Classical Capacity of the Erasure Channel)   The classical capacity of the d-dimensional quantum erasure channel is equal to $(1 - \varepsilon)\log d$.

Proof   The rate $(1 - \varepsilon)\log d$ is achievable by picking the input ensemble to be $\{1/d, |i\rangle\}$ and evaluating the Holevo information. So we need to show that it is not possible to achieve a rate higher than this. Let $\mathcal{M}_{A_1 \rightarrow B_1}$ be some quantum channel and let $\mathcal{N}^{\varepsilon}_{A_2 \rightarrow B_2}$ denote the quantum erasure channel. Let $\rho_{XA_1A_2}$ be the following classical–quantum state

$$\rho_{XA_1A_2} \equiv \sum_x p_X(x)|x\rangle\langle x|_X \otimes \phi^x_{A_1A_2}, \tag{20.86}$$

and suppose that it achieves the Holevo information $\chi(\mathcal{M} \otimes \mathcal{N}^{\varepsilon})$. Consider that

$$\omega_{XB_1B_2}$$
$$\equiv (\mathcal{M}_{A_1 \rightarrow B_1} \otimes \mathcal{N}^{\varepsilon}_{A_2 \rightarrow B_2})(\rho_{XA_1A_2}) \tag{20.87}$$
$$= \sum_x p_X(x)|x\rangle\langle x|_X \otimes \left[(1 - \varepsilon)\mathcal{M}_{A_1 \rightarrow B_1}(\phi^x_{A_1A_2}) + \varepsilon\mathcal{M}_{A_1 \rightarrow B_1}(\phi^x_{A_1}) \otimes |e\rangle\langle e|_{B_2}\right]. \tag{20.88}$$

Consider that the isometry $[|0\rangle\langle 0|_{B_2} + \dots |d-1\rangle\langle d-1|_{B_2}] \otimes |0\rangle_Y + |e\rangle\langle e|_{B_2} \otimes |1\rangle_Y$ takes the above state to the following one:

$$\omega_{XB_1B_2Y} \equiv \sum_x p_X(x)|x\rangle\langle x|_X \otimes \mathcal{M}_{A_1 \rightarrow B_1}(\phi^x_{A_1A_2}) \otimes (1 - \varepsilon)|0\rangle\langle 0|_Y$$
$$+ \sum_x p_X(x)|x\rangle\langle x|_X \otimes \mathcal{M}_{A_1 \rightarrow B_1}(\phi^x_{A_1}) \otimes |e\rangle\langle e|_{B_2} \otimes \varepsilon|1\rangle\langle 1|_Y, \tag{20.89}$$

so that the Y register is a flag indicating whether an erasure occurred. Then

$$\chi(\mathcal{M} \otimes \mathcal{N}^{\varepsilon}) = I(X; B_1B_2)_{\omega} \tag{20.90}$$
$$= I(X; B_1B_2Y)_{\omega} \tag{20.91}$$
$$= I(X; B_1B_2|Y)_{\omega} + I(X; Y)_{\omega} \tag{20.92}$$
$$= I(X; B_1B_2|Y)_{\omega} \tag{20.93}$$
$$= (1 - \varepsilon)I(X; B_1A_2)_{\mathcal{M}(\phi^x)} + \varepsilon I(X; B_1)_{\mathcal{M}(\phi^x)} \tag{20.94}$$
$$\leq (1 - \varepsilon)\chi(\mathcal{M} \otimes \mathrm{id}) + \varepsilon\chi(\mathcal{M}) \tag{20.95}$$

$$= \chi(\mathcal{M}) + (1 - \varepsilon) \chi(\text{id}) \tag{20.96}$$
$$= \chi(\mathcal{M}) + (1 - \varepsilon) \log d. \tag{20.97}$$

The second equality follows because the aforementioned isometry takes $B_1 B_2$ to $B_1 B_2 Y$. The third equality follows from the chain rule for mutual information, and the fourth because $I(X; Y)_\omega = 0$. The fifth equality follows because Y is a classical system, so that we can expand the mutual information as a convex combination of individual mutual informations. The inequality follows by maximizing the Holevo informations with respect to all input ensembles. The second-to-last equality follows because the identity channel is a Hadamard channel, so that Theorem 20.4.1 implies that $\chi(\mathcal{M} \otimes \text{id}) = \chi(\mathcal{M}) + \chi(\text{id})$.

By setting $\mathcal{M} = (\mathcal{N}^\varepsilon)^{\otimes [n-1]}$ and iterating the above, we see that $\chi((\mathcal{N}^\varepsilon)^{\otimes n}) \leq n(1 - \varepsilon) \log d$, so that the regularized Holevo information cannot exceed $(1 - \varepsilon) \log d$. Since this rate is also achievable, this concludes the proof. $\qquad \square$

20.4.4 Classical Capacity of the Depolarizing Channel

The qudit depolarizing channel is another example of a channel for which we can compute its classical capacity. Additionally, we will see that achieving the classical capacity of this channel requires a strategy which is very "classical"—it is sufficient to prepare classical states $\{|x\rangle\langle x|\}$ at the input of the channel and to measure each channel output in the same basis (see Exercise 20.4.3). However, we will later see in Chapter 24 that the depolarizing channel has some rather bizarre, uniquely quantum features when considering its quantum capacity, even though the features of its classical capacity are rather classical.

Recall from Section 4.7.4 that the depolarizing channel is the following map:

$$\mathcal{N}_\mathrm{D}(\rho) = (1 - p)\rho + p\pi, \tag{20.98}$$

where π is the maximally mixed state.

THEOREM 20.4.3 (Classical Capacity of the Depolarizing Channel)   The classical capacity of the qudit depolarizing channel $\mathcal{N}_\mathrm{D}$ is as follows:

$$\chi(\mathcal{N}_\mathrm{D}) = \log d + \left(1 - p + \frac{p}{d}\right) \log \left(1 - p + \frac{p}{d}\right) + (d - 1) \frac{p}{d} \log \left(\frac{p}{d}\right). \tag{20.99}$$

Proof The first part of the proof of this theorem relies on a somewhat technical result, namely, that the Holevo information of the tensor-product channel $\mathcal{N}_\mathrm{D} \otimes \mathcal{N}$ is additive (where the first channel is the depolarizing channel and the other is arbitrary):

$$\chi(\mathcal{N}_\mathrm{D} \otimes \mathcal{N}) = \chi(\mathcal{N}_\mathrm{D}) + \chi(\mathcal{N}). \tag{20.100}$$

This result is due to King (2003), and it exploits a few properties of the depolarizing channel. The result implies that the classical capacity of the depolarizing channel is equal to its Holevo information. We now show how to compute the

Holevo information of the depolarizing channel. To do so, we first determine the minimum output entropy of the channel.

DEFINITION 20.4.1 (Minimum Output Entropy)   The minimum output entropy $H^{\min}(\mathcal{N})$ of a channel $\mathcal{N}$ is the minimum of the entropy at the output of the channel:

$$H^{\min}(\mathcal{N}) \equiv \min_{\rho} H(\mathcal{N}(\rho)), \qquad (20.101)$$

where the minimization is over all states input to the channel.

EXERCISE 20.4.2   Prove that it is sufficient to minimize over only pure-state inputs to the channel when computing the minimum output entropy. That is,

$$H^{\min}(\mathcal{N}) = \min_{|\psi\rangle} H(\mathcal{N}(|\psi\rangle\langle\psi|)). \qquad (20.102)$$

The depolarizing channel is a highly symmetric channel. For example, if we input a pure state $|\psi\rangle$ to the channel, the output is as follows:

$$(1-p)\psi + p\pi = (1-p)\psi + \frac{p}{d}I \qquad (20.103)$$

$$= (1-p)\psi + \frac{p}{d}(\psi + I - \psi) \qquad (20.104)$$

$$= \left(1 - p + \frac{p}{d}\right)\psi + \frac{p}{d}(I - \psi). \qquad (20.105)$$

Observe that the eigenvalues of the output state are the same for any pure state and are equal to $1 - p + \frac{p}{d}$ with multiplicity one and $\frac{p}{d}$ with multiplicity $d-1$. Thus, the minimum output entropy of the depolarizing channel is just

$$H^{\min}(\mathcal{N}_{\mathrm{D}}) = -\left(1 - p + \frac{p}{d}\right)\log\left(1 - p + \frac{p}{d}\right) - (d-1)\frac{p}{d}\log\left(\frac{p}{d}\right). \qquad (20.106)$$

We now compute the Holevo information of the depolarizing channel. Recall from Theorem 13.3.2 that it is sufficient to consider optimizing the Holevo information over a classical–quantum state with conditional states that are pure (a state σ_{XA} of the form in (20.72)). Also, the Holevo information has the following form:

$$\max_{\sigma} I(X;B)_\omega = \max_{\sigma}\left[H(B)_\omega - H(B|X)_\omega\right], \qquad (20.107)$$

where ω_{XB} is the output state. Consider the following augmented input ensemble

$$\rho_{XIJA'} \equiv$$

$$\frac{1}{d^2}\sum_{x}\sum_{i,j=0}^{d-1} p_X(x)|x\rangle\langle x|_X \otimes |i\rangle\langle i|_I \otimes |j\rangle\langle j|_J \otimes X(i)Z(j)\psi_{A'}^x Z^\dagger(j)X^\dagger(i), \qquad (20.108)$$

where $X(i)$ and $Z(j)$ are the generalized Pauli operators from Section 3.7.2. Suppose that we trace over the IJ system. Then the state $\rho_{XA'}$ is as follows:

$$\rho_{XA'} = \sum_{x} p_X(x)|x\rangle\langle x|_X \otimes \pi_{A'}, \qquad (20.109)$$

by recalling the result of Exercise 4.7.6. Also, note that inputting the maximally mixed state to the depolarizing channel results in the maximally mixed state at its output. Consider the following chain of inequalities:

$$I(X;B)_\omega = H(B)_\omega - H(B|X)_\omega \tag{20.110}$$

$$\leq H(B)_\rho - H(B|X)_\omega \tag{20.111}$$

$$= \log d - H(B|XIJ)_\rho \tag{20.112}$$

$$= \log d - \sum_x p_X(x) H(B)_{\mathcal{N}_D(\psi^x)} \tag{20.113}$$

$$\leq \log d - \min_x H(B)_{\mathcal{N}_D(\psi^x)} \tag{20.114}$$

$$\leq \log d - H^{\min}(\mathcal{N}_D). \tag{20.115}$$

The first equality follows by expanding the quantum mutual information. The first inequality follows from concavity of entropy. The second equality follows because the state of ρ on system B is the maximally mixed state π and from the following chain of equalities:

$$H(B|XIJ)_\rho = \frac{1}{d^2} \sum_x \sum_{i,j=0}^{d-1} p_X(x) H(B)_{\mathcal{N}_D(X(i)Z(j)\psi^x Z^\dagger(j)X^\dagger(i))} \tag{20.116}$$

$$= \frac{1}{d^2} \sum_x \sum_{i,j=0}^{d-1} p_X(x) H(B)_{X(i)Z(j)\mathcal{N}_D(\psi^x)Z^\dagger(j)X^\dagger(i)} \tag{20.117}$$

$$= \sum_x p_X(x) H(B)_{\mathcal{N}_D(\psi^x)} \tag{20.118}$$

$$= H(B|X)_\omega. \tag{20.119}$$

The third equality in (20.113) follows from the above chain of equalities. The second inequality in (20.114) follows because the expectation can never be smaller than the minimum (this step is not strictly necessary for the depolarizing channel). The last inequality follows because $\min_x H(B)_{\mathcal{N}_D(\psi^x)} \geq H^{\min}(\mathcal{N}_D)$ (though it is actually an equality for the depolarizing channel).

An ensemble of the following form suffices to achieve the classical capacity of the depolarizing channel:

$$\frac{1}{d} \sum_{i=0}^{d-1} |i\rangle\langle i|_I \otimes |i\rangle\langle i|_{A'}, \tag{20.120}$$

because we only require that the reduced state on A' be equal to the maximally mixed state. The final expression for the classical capacity of the depolarizing channel is as stated in Theorem 20.4.3, which we plot in Figure 20.5 as a function of the dimension d and the depolarizing parameter p. □

EXERCISE 20.4.3 (Achieving the Classical Capacity of the Depolarizing Channel) We actually know that even more is true regarding the method for achieving the

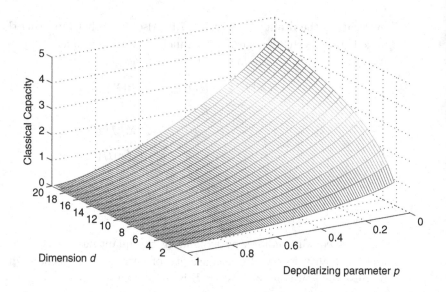

Figure 20.5 The classical capacity of the quantum depolarizing channel as a function of the dimension d of the channel and the depolarizing parameter p. The classical capacity vanishes when $p = 1$ because the channel replaces the input with the maximally mixed state. The classical capacity is maximal at $\log d$ when $p = 0$ because there is no noise. In between these two extremes, the classical capacity is a smooth function of p and d given by the expression in (20.99).

classical capacity of the depolarizing channel. Prove that it is possible to achieve the classical capacity of the depolarizing channel by choosing states from an ensemble $\left\{\frac{1}{d}, |x\rangle\langle x|\right\}$ and performing a complete projective measurement in the same basis at the output of each channel. That is, the naive scheme outlined in Section 20.1 is sufficient to attain the classical capacity of the depolarizing channel. (Hint: First show that the classical channel $p_{Y|X}(y|x)$ induced by inputting a state $|x\rangle$ to the depolarizing channel and measuring $|y\rangle$ at the output is as follows:

$$p_{Y|X}(y|x) = (1-p)\delta_{x,y} + \frac{p}{d}. \tag{20.121}$$

Then show that the distribution $p_Y(y)$ is uniform if $p_X(x)$ is uniform. Finally, show that

$$H(Y|X) = -\left(1 - p + \frac{p}{d}\right)\log\left(1 - p + \frac{p}{d}\right) - (d-1)\left(\frac{p}{d}\right)\log\left(\frac{p}{d}\right). \tag{20.122}$$

Conclude that the classical capacity of the induced channel $p_{Y|X}(y|x)$ is the same as that for the quantum depolarizing channel.)

EXERCISE 20.4.4 A covariant channel $\mathcal{N}_C$ is one for which the state resulting from a unitary U acting on the input state before the channel occurs is equivalent to one where there is a unitary representation R_U of the unitary U acting on the output of the channel:

$$\mathcal{N}_C(U\rho U^\dagger) = R_U \mathcal{N}_C(\rho) R_U^\dagger. \tag{20.123}$$

Show that the Holevo information $\chi(\mathcal{N}_C)$ of a covariant channel is equal to

$$\chi(\mathcal{N}_C) = \log d - H(\mathcal{N}_C(\psi)), \tag{20.124}$$

where ψ is an arbitrary pure state.

20.5 Superadditivity of the Holevo Information

Many researchers thought for some time that the Holevo information would be additive for all quantum channels, implying that it would be a good characterization of the classical capacity in the general case—this conjecture was known as the additivity conjecture. Researchers thought that this conjecture would hold because they discovered a few channels for which it did hold, but without any common theme occurring in the proofs for the different channels, they soon began looking in the other direction for a counterexample to disprove it. After some time, Hastings (2009) found the existence of a counterexample to the additivity conjecture, demonstrating that it cannot hold in the general case. This result demonstrates that even one of the most basic questions in quantum Shannon theory still remains wide open and that entanglement at the encoder can help increase classical communication rates over a quantum channel.

We first review a relation between the Holevo information and the minimum output entropy of a tensor-product channel. Suppose that we have two channels $\mathcal{N}$ and $\mathcal{M}$. The Holevo information of the tensor-product channel is additive if

$$\chi(\mathcal{N} \otimes \mathcal{M}) = \chi(\mathcal{N}) + \chi(\mathcal{M}). \tag{20.125}$$

Since the Holevo information is always superadditive for any two channels:

$$\chi(\mathcal{N} \otimes \mathcal{M}) \geq \chi(\mathcal{N}) + \chi(\mathcal{M}) \tag{20.126}$$

(recall the statement at the beginning of the proof of Theorem 13.3.1), we say that it is non-additive if it is strictly superadditive:

$$\chi(\mathcal{N} \otimes \mathcal{M}) > \chi(\mathcal{N}) + \chi(\mathcal{M}). \tag{20.127}$$

The minimum output entropy $H^{\min}(\mathcal{N} \otimes \mathcal{M})$ of the tensor-product channel is a quantity related to the Holevo information (see Definition 20.4.1). It is additive if

$$H^{\min}(\mathcal{N} \otimes \mathcal{M}) = H^{\min}(\mathcal{N}) + H^{\min}(\mathcal{M}). \tag{20.128}$$

Since the minimum output entropy is always subadditive:

$$H^{\min}(\mathcal{N} \otimes \mathcal{M}) \leq H^{\min}(\mathcal{N}) + H^{\min}(\mathcal{M}), \tag{20.129}$$

we say that it is non-additive if it is strictly subadditive:

$$H^{\min}(\mathcal{N} \otimes \mathcal{M}) < H^{\min}(\mathcal{N}) + H^{\min}(\mathcal{M}). \tag{20.130}$$

Additivity of these two quantities is in fact related—it is possible to show that additivity of the Holevo information implies additivity of the minimum output entropy and vice versa (we leave one of these implications as an exercise). Thus, researchers focused on additivity of minimum output entropy rather than additivity of Holevo information because it is a simpler quantity to manipulate.

EXERCISE 20.5.1   Prove that non-additivity of the minimum output entropy implies non-additivity of the Holevo information:

$$H^{\min}(\mathcal{N}_1 \otimes \mathcal{N}_2) < H^{\min}(\mathcal{N}_1) + H^{\min}(\mathcal{N}_2)$$
$$\Rightarrow \quad \chi(\mathcal{N}_1 \otimes \mathcal{N}_2) > \chi(\mathcal{N}_1) + \chi(\mathcal{N}_2). \quad (20.131)$$

(*Hint*: Consider an augmented version $\mathcal{N}_i'$ of each channel $\mathcal{N}_i$, that has its first input be the same as the input to $\mathcal{N}_i$ and its second input be a control input, and the action of the channel is equivalent to measuring the auxiliary input σ and applying a generalized Pauli operator:

$$\mathcal{N}_i'(\rho \otimes \sigma) \equiv \sum_{k,l} X(k)Z(l)\mathcal{N}_i(\rho)Z^\dagger(l)X^\dagger(k) \, \langle k|\langle l|\sigma|k\rangle |l\rangle. \quad (20.132)$$

What is the Holevo information of the augmented channel $\mathcal{N}_i'$? What is the Holevo information of the tensor product of the augmented channels $\mathcal{N}_1' \otimes \mathcal{N}_2'$?) After proving the above statement, we can also conclude that additivity of the Holevo information implies additivity of the minimum output entropy.

We briefly overview the main ideas behind the construction of a channel for which the Holevo information is not additive. Consider a random-unitary channel of the following form:

$$\mathcal{E}(\rho) \equiv \sum_{i=1}^{D} p_i U_i \rho U_i^\dagger, \quad (20.133)$$

where the dimension of the input state is N and the number of random unitaries is D. This channel is "random unitary" because it applies a particular unitary U_i with probability p_i to the state ρ. The cleverness behind the construction is not actually to provide a deterministic instance of this channel, but rather, to provide a random instance of the channel where both the distribution and the unitaries are chosen at random, and the dimension N and the number D of chosen unitaries satisfy the following relationships:

$$1 \ll D \ll N. \quad (20.134)$$

The other channel to consider to disprove additivity is the conjugated channel

$$\overline{\mathcal{E}}(\rho) \equiv \sum_{i=1}^{D} p_i \overline{U}_i \rho \overline{U}_i^\dagger, \quad (20.135)$$

where p_i and U_i are the same respective probability distribution and unitaries from the channel $\mathcal{E}$, and here $\overline{U}_i$ denotes the complex conjugate of U_i. The goal is then to show that there is a non-zero probability over all channels of these forms that the minimum output entropy is non-additive:

$$H^{\min}(\mathcal{E} \otimes \overline{\mathcal{E}}) < H^{\min}(\mathcal{E}) + H^{\min}(\overline{\mathcal{E}}). \tag{20.136}$$

A good candidate for a state that could saturate the minimum output entropy $H^{\min}(\mathcal{E} \otimes \overline{\mathcal{E}})$ of the tensor-product channel is the maximally entangled state $|\Phi\rangle$, where

$$|\Phi\rangle \equiv \frac{1}{\sqrt{N}} \sum_{i=0}^{N-1} |i\rangle|i\rangle. \tag{20.137}$$

Consider the effect of the tensor-product channel $\mathcal{E} \otimes \overline{\mathcal{E}}$ on the maximally entangled state Φ:

$$(\mathcal{E} \otimes \overline{\mathcal{E}})(\Phi)$$

$$= \sum_{i,j=1}^{D} p_i p_j (U_i \otimes \overline{U}_j) \Phi (U_i^\dagger \otimes \overline{U}_j^\dagger) \tag{20.138}$$

$$= \sum_{i=j} p_i^2 (U_i \otimes \overline{U}_i) \Phi (U_i^\dagger \otimes \overline{U}_i^\dagger) + \sum_{i \neq j} p_i p_j (U_i \otimes \overline{U}_j) \Phi (U_i^\dagger \otimes \overline{U}_i^\dagger) \tag{20.139}$$

$$= \left(\sum_{i=1}^{D} p_i^2 \right) \Phi + \sum_{i \neq j} p_i p_j (U_i \otimes \overline{U}_j) \Phi (U_i^\dagger \otimes \overline{U}_i^\dagger), \tag{20.140}$$

where the last line uses the fact that $(M \otimes I)|\Phi\rangle = (I \otimes M^T)|\Phi\rangle$ for any operator M (this implies that $(U \otimes \overline{U})|\Phi\rangle = |\Phi\rangle$). When comparing the above state to one resulting from inputting a product state to the channel, there is a sense in which the above state is less noisy than the product state because D of the combinations of the random unitaries (the ones which have the same index) have no effect on the maximally entangled state. Using techniques from Hastings (2009), we can make this intuition precise and obtain the following upper bound on the minimum output entropy:

$$H^{\min}(\mathcal{E} \otimes \overline{\mathcal{E}}) \leq H((\mathcal{E} \otimes \overline{\mathcal{E}})(\Phi)) \tag{20.141}$$

$$\leq 2 \ln D - \frac{\ln D}{D}, \tag{20.142}$$

for N and D large enough. However, using techniques in the same paper, we can also show that

$$H^{\min}(\mathcal{E}) \geq \ln D - \delta S^{\max}, \tag{20.143}$$

where

$$\delta S^{\max} \equiv \frac{c}{D} + \text{poly}(D) O\left(\sqrt{\frac{\ln N}{N}} \right), \tag{20.144}$$

c is a constant, and poly(D) indicates a term polynomial in D. Thus, for large enough D and N, it follows that

$$2\delta S^{\text{max}} < \frac{\ln D}{D}, \tag{20.145}$$

and we get the existence of a channel for which a violation of additivity occurs, because

$$H^{\text{min}}(\mathcal{E} \otimes \overline{\mathcal{E}}) \leq 2\ln D - \frac{\ln D}{D} \tag{20.146}$$

$$< 2\ln D - 2\delta S^{\text{max}} \tag{20.147}$$

$$\leq H^{\text{min}}(\mathcal{E}) + H^{\text{min}}(\overline{\mathcal{E}}). \tag{20.148}$$

20.6   Concluding Remarks

The HSW theorem offers a good characterization of the classical capacity of certain classes of channels, but at the same time, it also demonstrates our lack of understanding of classical transmission over general quantum channels. To be more precise, the Holevo information is a useful characterization of the classical capacity of a quantum channel whenever it is additive, but the regularized Holevo information is not particularly useful as a characterization of it because we cannot even compute this quantity. This suggests that there could be some other formula that better characterizes the classical capacity (if such a formula were additive). As of the writing of this book, such a formula is unknown.

Despite the drawbacks of the HSW theorem, it is still interesting because it at least offers a step beyond the most naive characterization of the classical capacity of a quantum channel in terms of the regularized accessible information. The major insight of HSW was the construction of an explicit POVM (corresponding to a random choice of code) that allows the sender and receiver to communicate at a rate equal to the Holevo information of the channel. This theorem is also useful for determining achievable rates in different communication scenarios: for example, when two senders are trying to communicate over a noisy medium to a single receiver or when a single sender is trying to transmit both classical and quantum information to a receiver.

The depolarizing channel is an example of a quantum channel for which there is a simple expression for its classical capacity. Furthermore, the expression reveals that the scheme needed to achieve the capacity of the channel is rather classical— it is only necessary for the sender to select codewords uniformly at random from some orthonormal basis, and it is only necessary for the receiver to perform measurements of the individual channel outputs in the same orthonormal basis. Thus, the coding scheme is classical because entanglement plays no role at the encoder and the decoding measurements act on the individual channel outputs.

Finally, we discussed Hastings' construction of a quantum channel for which the heralded additivity conjecture does not hold. That is, there exists a channel for which entanglement at the encoder can improve communication rates. This superadditive effect is a uniquely quantum phenomenon (recall that Theorem 13.1.1 states that the classical mutual information of a classical channel is additive, and thus correlations at the input cannot increase capacity). This result implies that our best known characterization of the classical capacity of a quantum channel in terms of the channel's Holevo information is far from being a satisfactory characterization of the true capacity, and we still have much more to discover here.

20.7   History and Further Reading

Holevo (1973a) was the first to prove the bound bearing his name, regarding the transmission of classical information using a quantum channel, and Holevo (1998) and Schumacher & Westmoreland (1997) many years later proved that the Holevo information is an achievable rate for classical data transmission. Just prior to these works, Hausladen et al. (1996) proved achievability of the Holevo information for the special case of a channel that accepts a classical input and outputs a pure state conditioned on the input. They also published a preliminary article (Hausladen et al., 1995) in which they answered the catchy question (for the special case of pure states), "How many bits can you fit into a quantum-mechanical it?"

Shor (2002a) established the additivity of the Holevo information for entanglement-breaking channels. Bowen & Nagarajan (2005) proved that the classical capacity of an entanglement-breaking channel is not enhanced by a classical feedback channel from receiver to sender. King (2002) first proved additivity of the Holevo information for unital qubit channels and later showed it for the depolarizing channel (King, 2003). Shor (2004a) later showed the equivalence of several additivity conjectures (that they are either all true or all false). Hayden (2007), Winter (2007), and a joint paper between them (Hayden & Winter, 2008) proved some results leading up to the work of Hastings (2009), who demonstrated a counterexample to the additivity conjecture. Thus, by Shor's aforementioned paper, all of the additivity conjectures are false in general. There has been much follow-up work in an attempt to understand Hastings' result (Brandao & Horodecki, 2010; Fukuda & King, 2010; Fukuda et al., 2010; Aubrun et al., 2011).

In a landmark result, Giovannetti et al. (2015) established the classical capacity of all phase-insensitive quantum Gaussian channels, building on a long series of works starting with that of Holevo & Werner (2001).

Some other papers have tried to understand the HSW coding theorem from the perspective of hypothesis testing. Hayashi & Nagaoka (2003) began much of this work, and Hayashi (2006) covers quite a bit of quantum hypothesis testing in his book. Mosonyi & Datta (2009) followed up with some work along these lines, as did Wang & Renner (2012) and Wilde (2013).

Researchers have invested quite a bit of effort in refining the HSW theorem, with regard to error exponents, strong converse exponents and second-order characterizations. From the proof of the HSW theorem given in this chapter, we see that if we pick the rate R of classical communication to be smaller than the capacity by an additive constant, then it is possible to make the decoding error decay exponentially fast to zero with an increasing number n of channel uses. The optimal exponential decay rate of the error for a given communication rate is known as the error exponent. Burnashev & Holevo (1998) derived a lower bound on the optimal error exponent for pure-state classical–quantum channels, and Holevo (2000) then derived a lower bound on the error exponent for mixed-state classical–quantum channels. Hayashi (2007) later improved upon this result for mixed-state classical–quantum channels. Dalai (2013) derived an upper bound on the optimal error exponent of classical–quantum channels, called the sphere-packing bound.

One can also ask about the behavior of the error probability when the communication rate exceeds the capacity by an additive constant. This regime is known as the strong converse regime, and a channel obeys the strong converse property if the error probability tends to one when the communication rate exceeds the capacity. Winter (1999a) and Ogawa & Nagaoka (1999) proved the strong converse for the classical capacity of classical–quantum channels, Koenig & Wehner (2009) for channels with certain symmetry, Wilde et al. (2014) for entanglement-breaking and Hadamard channels, Bardhan et al. (2015) for phase-insensitive quantum Gaussian channels, and Ding & Wilde (2015) for entanglement-breaking channels assisted by a noiseless classical feedback channel.

A second-order characterization asks how fast the communication rate can converge to capacity if the error probability is fixed to be a constant. One of the main tools here is the Berry–Esseen refinement of the central limit theorem (see, e.g., Feller, 1971 and Tyurin, 2010). Tomamichel & Tan (2015) derived an optimal second-order characterization for classical–quantum channels (even going beyond and establishing it for "image-additive" channels). Wilde et al. (2016) characterized an achievable second-order strategy for the pure-loss bosonic channel (with a converse part remaining open).

21 Entanglement-Assisted Classical Communication

We have learned that shared entanglement is often helpful in quantum communication. This is certainly true for the case of a noiseless qubit channel. Without shared entanglement, the most classical information that a sender can reliably transmit over a noiseless qubit channel is just one classical bit (recall Exercise 4.2.2 and the Holevo bound in Exercise 11.9.2). With shared entanglement, they can achieve the super-dense coding resource inequality from Chapter 7:

$$[q \rightarrow q] + [qq] \geq 2\,[c \rightarrow c]. \tag{21.1}$$

That is, using one noiseless qubit channel and one shared noiseless ebit, the sender can reliably transmit two classical bits.

A natural question then for us to consider is whether shared entanglement could be helpful in transmitting classical information over a noisy quantum channel $\mathcal{N}$. As a first simplifying assumption, we let Alice and Bob have access to an infinite supply of entanglement, in whatever form they wish, and we would like to know how much classical information Alice can reliably transmit to Bob over such an entanglement-assisted quantum channel. That is, we would like to determine the highest achievable rate C of classical communication in the following resource inequality:

$$\langle \mathcal{N} \rangle + \infty\,[qq] \geq C\,[c \rightarrow c]. \tag{21.2}$$

The answer to this question is one of the strongest known results in quantum Shannon theory, and it is given by the entanglement-assisted classical capacity theorem. This theorem states that the mutual information $I(\mathcal{N})$ of a quantum channel $\mathcal{N}$ is equal to its entanglement-assisted classical capacity, where

$$I(\mathcal{N}) \equiv \max_{\varphi_{AA'}} I(A;B)_\rho, \tag{21.3}$$

$\rho_{AB} \equiv \mathcal{N}_{A' \rightarrow B}(\varphi_{AA'})$, and the maximization is with respect to all pure bipartite states of the form $\varphi_{AA'}$. We should stress that there is no need to regularize this formula in order to characterize the capacity (as done in the previous chapter and as is so often needed in quantum Shannon theory). The value of this formula *is equal to* the capacity. Also, the optimization task that the formula in (21.3) sets out is a straightforward convex optimization program. Any local maximum is a global maximum because the quantum mutual information is concave with respect to the input state $\varphi_{A'}$ (recall Theorem 13.4.2 from Chapter 13) and the set of density operators is convex.

From the perspective of an information theorist, we should only say that a capacity theorem has been solved if there is a tractable formula equal to the optimal rate for achieving a particular operational task. The formula should apply to an arbitrary quantum channel, and it should be a function of that channel. Otherwise, the capacity theorem is still unsolved. There are several operative words in the above sentences that we should explain in more detail. The formula should be tractable, meaning that it sets out an optimization task which is efficient to solve in the dimension of the channel's input system. The formula should give the optimal achievable rate for the given information-processing task, meaning that if a rate exceeds the capacity of the channel, then the probability of error for any such protocol should be bounded away from zero as the number of channel uses grows large.[1] Finally, perhaps the most stringent (though related) criterion is that the formula itself (and *not* its regularization) should give the capacity of an arbitrary quantum channel. Despite the success of the HSW coding theorem in demonstrating that the Holevo information of a channel is an achievable rate for classical communication, the classical capacity of a quantum channel is still unsolved because there is an example of a channel for which the Holevo information is not equal to that channel's capacity (see Section 20.5). Thus, it is rather impressive that the formula in (21.3) is equal to the entanglement-assisted classical capacity of an arbitrary channel, given the stringent requirements that we have set out for a formula to give the capacity. In this sense, shared entanglement simplifies quantum Shannon theory.

This chapter presents a comprehensive study of the entanglement-assisted classical capacity theorem. We begin by defining the information-processing task, consisting of all the steps in a general protocol for classical communication over an entanglement-assisted quantum channel. We then present a simple example of a strategy for entanglement-assisted classical coding that is inspired by super-dense coding, and in turn, that inspires a strategy for the general case. Section 21.3 states the entanglement-assisted classical capacity theorem. Section 21.4 gives a proof of the direct coding theorem, making use of strong quantum typicality from Chapter 15 and the packing lemma from Chapter 16. It demonstrates that the rate in (21.3) is an achievable rate for entanglement-assisted classical communication. After taking a step back from the protocol, we can realize that it is merely a glorified super-dense coding applied to noisy quantum channels. Section 21.5 gives a proof of the converse of the entanglement-assisted classical capacity theorem. It exploits familiar tools such as the AFW inequality, the quantum data-processing inequality, and the chain rule for quantum mutual information (all from Chapter 11), and the last part of it exploits additivity of the

---

[1] We could strengthen this requirement even more by demanding that the probability of error increases exponentially to one in the asymptotic limit. Fulfilling such a demand would constitute a proof of a *strong converse theorem*.

mutual information of a quantum channel (from Chapter 13). The converse theorem establishes that the rate in (21.3) is optimal. With the proof of the capacity theorem complete, we then show the interesting result that the classical capacity of a quantum channel assisted by a quantum feedback channel is equal to the entanglement-assisted classical capacity of that channel. We close the chapter by computing the entanglement-assisted classical capacity of both a quantum erasure channel and an amplitude damping channel, and we leave the computation of the entanglement-assisted capacities of two other channels as exercises.

21.1   The Information-Processing Task

We begin by explicitly defining the information-processing task of entanglement-assisted classical communication. That is, we define an (n, C, ε) entanglement-assisted classical code and what it means for a rate C to be achievable. Prior to the start of the protocol, we assume that Alice and Bob share pure-state entanglement in whatever form they wish. Let $\Psi_{T_A T_B}$ denote this state. Alice selects some message m from a set $\mathcal{M}$ of messages. Let M denote the random variable corresponding to Alice's choice of message, and let $|\mathcal{M}|$ be the cardinality of the set $\mathcal{M}$. She applies some encoding channel $\mathcal{E}^m_{T_A \to A'^n}$ to her share of the entangled state $\Psi_{T_A T_B}$ depending on her choice of message m. The global state then becomes

$$\mathcal{E}^m_{T_A \to A'^n}(\Psi_{T_A T_B}). \tag{21.4}$$

Alice transmits the systems A'^n over n independent uses of a noisy channel $\mathcal{N}_{A' \to B}$, leading to the following state:

$$\mathcal{N}_{A'^n \to B^n}(\mathcal{E}^m_{T_A \to A'^n}(\Psi_{T_A T_B})), \tag{21.5}$$

where $\mathcal{N}_{A'^n \to B^n} \equiv (\mathcal{N}_{A' \to B})^{\otimes n}$. Bob receives the systems B^n, combines them with his share T_B of the entanglement, and performs a POVM $\{\Lambda^m_{B^n T_B}\}$ on the channel outputs B^n and his share T_B of the entanglement in order to detect the message m that Alice transmits. Figure 21.1 depicts such a general protocol for entanglement-assisted classical communication.

Let M' denote the random variable corresponding to the output of Bob's decoding POVM (this represents Bob's estimate of the message). The probability of Bob correctly decoding Alice's message is

$$\Pr\{M' = m | M = m\} = \mathrm{Tr}\{\Lambda^m_{B^n T_B} \mathcal{N}_{A'^n \to B^n}(\mathcal{E}^m_{T_A \to A'^n}(\Psi_{T_A T_B}))\}, \tag{21.6}$$

and thus the probability of error $p_e(m)$ for message m is

$$p_e(m) \equiv \mathrm{Tr}\{(I - \Lambda^m_{B^n T_B}) \mathcal{N}_{A'^n \to B^n}(\mathcal{E}^m_{T_A \to A'^n}(\Psi_{T_A T_B}))\}. \tag{21.7}$$

The maximal probability of error p_e^* for the coding scheme is

$$p_e^* \equiv \max_{m \in \mathcal{M}} p_e(m). \tag{21.8}$$

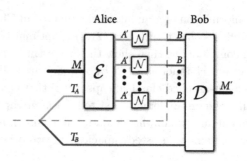

Figure 21.1 The most general protocol for entanglement-assisted classical communication. Alice applies an encoder to her classical message M and her share T_A of the entanglement, and she inputs the encoded systems A'^n to many uses of the channel. Bob receives the outputs of the channels, combines them with his share of the entanglement, and performs some decoding operation to estimate Alice's transmitted message.

The rate C of communication is

$$C \equiv \frac{1}{n} \log |\mathcal{M}|, \tag{21.9}$$

and the code has ε error if $p_e^* \leq \varepsilon$.

A rate C of entanglement-assisted classical communication is *achievable* if there exists an $(n, C - \delta, \varepsilon)$ entanglement-assisted classical code for all $\varepsilon \in (0, 1)$, $\delta > 0$, and sufficiently large n. The entanglement-assisted classical capacity $C_{\mathrm{EA}}(\mathcal{N})$ of a quantum channel $\mathcal{N}$ is equal to the supremum of all achievable rates.

21.2   A Preliminary Example

Let us first recall a few items about qudits. The maximally entangled qudit state is defined as $|\Phi\rangle_{AB} \equiv d^{-1/2} \sum_{i=0}^{d-1} |i\rangle_A |i\rangle_B$. Recall from Section 3.7.2 that the Heisenberg–Weyl operators $X(x)$ and $Z(z)$ are an extension of the Pauli matrices to d dimensions:

$$X(x) \equiv \sum_{x'=0}^{d-1} |x + x'\rangle\langle x'|, \qquad Z(z) \equiv \sum_{z'=0}^{d-1} e^{2\pi i z z'/d} |z'\rangle\langle z'|. \tag{21.10}$$

Let $|\Phi^{x,z}\rangle_{AB}$ denote the state that results when Alice applies the operator $X(x)Z(z)$ to her share of the maximally entangled state $|\Phi\rangle_{AB}$:

$$|\Phi^{x,z}\rangle_{AB} \equiv (X_A(x)Z_A(z) \otimes I_B) |\Phi\rangle_{AB}. \tag{21.11}$$

Recall from Exercise 3.7.11 that the set of states $\{|\Phi^{x,z}\rangle_{AB}\}_{x,z=0}^{d-1}$ forms a complete orthonormal basis:

$$\langle \Phi^{x_1,z_1} | \Phi^{x_2,z_2} \rangle_{AB} = \delta_{x_1,x_2} \delta_{z_1,z_2}, \qquad \sum_{x,z=0}^{d-1} |\Phi^{x,z}\rangle\langle\Phi^{x,z}|_{AB} = I_{AB}. \tag{21.12}$$

Let π_{AB} denote the maximally mixed state on Alice and Bob's system: $\pi_{AB} \equiv I_{AB}/d^2$, and let π_A and π_B denote the respective maximally mixed states on Alice and Bob's systems: $\pi_A \equiv I_A/d$ and $\pi_B \equiv I_B/d$. Observe that $\pi_{AB} = \pi_A \otimes \pi_B$.

We now consider a simple strategy, inspired by super-dense coding and the HSW coding scheme from Theorem 20.3.1, that Alice and Bob can employ for entanglement-assisted classical communication. That is, we show how a strategy similar to super-dense coding induces a particular ensemble at Bob's receiving end, to which we can then apply the HSW coding theorem in order to establish the existence of a good code for entanglement-assisted classical communication. Suppose that Alice and Bob possess a maximally entangled qudit state $|\Phi\rangle_{AB}$. Alice chooses two symbols x and z uniformly at random, each in $\{0, \ldots, d-1\}$. She applies the operators $X(x)Z(z)$ to her share of the maximally entangled state $|\Phi\rangle_{AB}$, and the resulting state is $|\Phi^{x,z}\rangle_{AB}$. She then sends her system A over the noisy channel $\mathcal{N}_{A \to B'}$, and Bob receives the output B' from the channel. The noisy channel on the whole system is $\mathcal{N}_{A \to B'} \otimes \mathrm{id}_B$, and the ensemble that Bob receives is as follows:

$$\left\{ d^{-2}, (\mathcal{N}_{A \to B'} \otimes \mathrm{id}_B)\left(\Phi^{x,z}_{AB}\right) \right\}. \tag{21.13}$$

This constitutes an ensemble that they can prepare with one use of the channel and one shared entangled state (Figure 21.2 depicts all of these steps). But, in general, we allow them to exploit many uses of the channel and however much entanglement that they need. Bob can then perform a collective measurement on both his share of the entanglement and the channel outputs in order to determine a message that Alice is transmitting.

Consider that the above scenario is similar to HSW coding. Theorem 20.3.1 from the previous chapter states that the Holevo information of the above ensemble is an achievable rate for classical communication over this entanglement-assisted quantum channel. Thus, we can already state and prove the following corollary of Theorem 20.3.1, simply by calculating the Holevo information of the ensemble in (21.13).

COROLLARY 21.2.1   The quantum mutual information $I(A; B)_\sigma$ of the state $\sigma_{AB} \equiv \mathcal{N}_{A' \to B}(\Phi_{AA'})$ is an achievable rate for entanglement-assisted classical communication over a quantum channel $\mathcal{N}_{A' \to B}$.

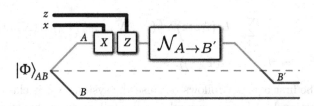

Figure 21.2 A simple scheme, inspired by super-dense coding, for Alice and Bob to exploit shared entanglement and a noisy channel in order to establish an ensemble at Bob's receiving end.

Proof Observe that the ensemble in (21.13) maps to the following classical–quantum state:

$$\rho_{XZB'B} \equiv \sum_{x,z=0}^{d-1} \frac{1}{d^2} |x\rangle\langle x|_X \otimes |z\rangle\langle z|_Z \otimes (\mathcal{N}_{A\rightarrow B'} \otimes \mathrm{id}_B)(\Phi_{AB}^{x,z}). \tag{21.14}$$

The Holevo information of this classical–quantum state is $I(XZ; B'B)_\rho = H(B'B)_\rho - H(B'B|XZ)_\rho$, and it is an achievable rate for entanglement-assisted classical communication over the channel $\mathcal{N}_{A'\rightarrow B}$ by the direct part of Theorem 20.3.1. We now proceed to calculate it. First, we determine the entropy $H(B'B)_\rho$ by tracing over the classical registers XZ:

$$\mathrm{Tr}_{XZ}\{\rho_{XZB'B}\} = \sum_{x,z=0}^{d-1} \frac{1}{d^2}(\mathcal{N}_{A\rightarrow B'} \otimes \mathrm{id}_B)(\Phi_{AB}^{x,z}) \tag{21.15}$$

$$= (\mathcal{N}_{A\rightarrow B'} \otimes \mathrm{id}_B)\left(\sum_{x,z=0}^{d-1} \frac{1}{d^2}\Phi_{AB}^{x,z}\right) \tag{21.16}$$

$$= (\mathcal{N}_{A\rightarrow B'} \otimes \mathrm{id}_B)(\pi_{AB}) \tag{21.17}$$

$$= \mathcal{N}_{A\rightarrow B'}(\pi_A) \otimes \pi_B, \tag{21.18}$$

where the third equality follows from (21.12). Thus, the entropy $H(B'B)$ is as follows:

$$H(B'B) = H(\mathcal{N}_{A\rightarrow B'}(\pi_A)) + H(\pi_B). \tag{21.19}$$

We now determine the conditional quantum entropy $H(B'B|XZ)_\rho$:

$$H(B'B|XZ)_\rho$$

$$= \sum_{x,z=0}^{d-1} \frac{1}{d^2} H((\mathcal{N}_{A\rightarrow B'} \otimes \mathrm{id}_B)(\Phi_{AB}^{x,z})) \tag{21.20}$$

$$= \frac{1}{d^2}\sum_{x,z=0}^{d-1} H\left(\mathcal{N}_{A\rightarrow B'}\left[(X_A(x)Z_A(z))(\Phi_{AB})\left(Z_A^\dagger(z)X_A^\dagger(x)\right)\right]\right) \tag{21.21}$$

$$= \frac{1}{d^2}\sum_{x,z=0}^{d-1} H\left(\mathcal{N}_{A\rightarrow B'}\left[Z_B^T(z)X_B^T(x)(\Phi_{AB})X_B^*(x)Z_B^*(z)\right]\right) \tag{21.22}$$

$$= \frac{1}{d^2}\sum_{x,z=0}^{d-1} H\left(Z_B^T(z)X_B^T(x)\left[(\mathcal{N}_{A\rightarrow B'})(\Phi_{AB})\right](X_B^*(x)Z_B^*(z))\right) \tag{21.23}$$

$$= H(\mathcal{N}_{A\rightarrow B'}(\Phi_{AB})). \tag{21.24}$$

The first equality follows because the system XZ is classical (recall the result in Section 11.4.1). The second equality follows from the definition of the state $\Phi_{AB}^{x,z}$. The third equality follows by exploiting the "transpose trick" in Exercise 3.7.12. The fourth equality follows because the transposed unitaries acting on Bob's system commute with the action of the channel. Finally, the entropy of a state is invariant with respect to unitaries. So the Holevo information $I(XZ; B'B)_\rho$ of the state $\rho_{XZB'B}$ in (21.14) is equal to

$$I(XZ; B'B)_\rho = H(\mathcal{N}(\pi_A)) + H(\pi_B) - H((\mathcal{N}_{A\to B'} \otimes \mathrm{id}_B)(\Phi_{AB})). \quad (21.25)$$

Equivalently, we can write it as the quantum mutual information $I(A; B)_\sigma$, evaluated with respect to the state $\sigma_{AB} \equiv \mathcal{N}_{A'\to B}(\Phi_{AA'})$. $\qquad\square$

For some channels, the quantum mutual information in Corollary 21.2.1 is equal to that channel's entanglement-assisted classical capacity. This occurs for the depolarizing channel, a dephasing channel, and an erasure channel to name a few. But there are examples of channels, such as the amplitude damping channel, where the quantum mutual information in Corollary 21.2.1 is not equal to the entanglement-assisted capacity. In the general case, it might perhaps be intuitive that the quantum mutual information of the channel in (21.3) is equal to the entanglement-assisted capacity of the channel, and it is the goal of the next sections to prove this result.

EXERCISE 21.2.1 Consider the following strategy for transmitting and detecting classical information over an entanglement-assisted depolarizing channel. Alice selects a state $|\Phi^{x_1,z_1}\rangle_{AB}$ uniformly at random and sends the A system over the quantum depolarizing channel $\mathcal{N}^D_{A\to B'}$, where

$$\mathcal{N}^D_{A\to B'}(\rho) \equiv (1-p)\rho + p\pi. \quad (21.26)$$

Bob receives the output B' of the channel and combines it with his share B of the entanglement. He then performs a measurement of these systems in the Bell basis $\{|\Phi^{x_2,z_2}\rangle\langle\Phi^{x_2,z_2}|_{B'B}\}$. Determine a simplified expression for the induced classical channel $p_{Z_2 X_2 | Z_1 X_1}(z_2, x_2 | z_1, x_1)$ where

$$p_{Z_2 X_2 | Z_1 X_1}(z_2, x_2 | z_1, x_1)$$
$$\equiv \langle\Phi^{x_2,z_2}| (\mathcal{N}^D_{A\to B'} \otimes \mathrm{id}_B) (|\Phi^{x_1,z_1}\rangle\langle\Phi^{x_1,z_1}|_{AB}) |\Phi^{x_2,z_2}\rangle. \quad (21.27)$$

Show that the classical capacity of the channel $p_{Z_2 X_2 | Z_1 X_1}(z_2, x_2 | z_1, x_1)$ is equal to the entanglement-assisted classical capacity of the depolarizing channel (you can take it for granted that the entanglement-assisted classical capacity of the depolarizing channel is given by Corollary 21.2.1). Thus, there is no need for the receiver to perform a collective measurement on many channel outputs in order to achieve capacity—it suffices to perform single-channel Bell measurements at the receiving end.

21.3 Entanglement-Assisted Capacity Theorem

We now state the entanglement-assisted classical capacity theorem. Section 21.4 proves the direct part of this theorem, and Section 21.5 proves its converse part.

THEOREM 21.3.1 (Bennett–Shor–Smolin–Thapliyal)   The entanglement-assisted classical capacity of a quantum channel is equal to the channel's mutual information:

$$C_{\mathrm{EA}}(\mathcal{N}) = I(\mathcal{N}), \tag{21.28}$$

where the mutual information $I(\mathcal{N})$ of a channel $\mathcal{N}$ is defined as $I(\mathcal{N}) \equiv \max_{\varphi_{AA'}} I(A; B)_{\rho}$, $\rho_{AB} \equiv \mathcal{N}_{A' \rightarrow B}(\varphi_{AA'})$, and $\varphi_{AA'}$ is a pure bipartite state.

21.4   The Direct Coding Theorem

The direct coding theorem is a statement of achievability:

THEOREM 21.4.1 (Direct Coding)   The following resource inequality corresponds to an achievable protocol for entanglement-assisted classical communication over a quantum channel $\mathcal{N}_{A' \rightarrow B}$:

$$\langle \mathcal{N} \rangle + H(A)_{\rho} \, [qq] \geq I(A; B)_{\rho} \, [c \rightarrow c], \tag{21.29}$$

where $\rho_{AB} \equiv \mathcal{N}_{A' \rightarrow B}(\varphi_{AA'})$.

Proof   We suppose that Alice and Bob share n copies of an arbitrary pure, bipartite entangled state $|\varphi\rangle_{AB}$. This is allowed in the setting of entanglement-assisted communication as discussed in Section 21.1. Alternatively, they could convert $nH(A)$ shared ebits to $\approx n$ copies of $|\varphi\rangle_{AB}$ by making use of the entanglement dilution protocol discussed in Section 19.4.2 (they would need a sublinear amount of classical communication to do so, which has negligible rate). We would like to apply a similar coding technique as outlined in Section 21.2. For example, it would be useful to exploit the transpose trick from Exercise 3.7.12, but we cannot do so directly because this trick only applies to maximally entangled states. However, we can instead exploit the fact that Alice and Bob share many copies of the state $|\varphi\rangle_{AB}$ that decompose into a direct sum of maximally entangled states. First, recall that every pure, bipartite state has a Schmidt decomposition (see Theorem 3.8.1):

$$|\varphi\rangle_{AB} \equiv \sum_{x} \sqrt{p_X(x)} |x\rangle_A |x\rangle_B, \tag{21.30}$$

where $p_X(x) > 0$ for all x, $\sum_x p_X(x) = 1$, and $\{|x\rangle_A\}$ and $\{|x\rangle_B\}$ are orthonormal bases for Alice and Bob's respective systems. Let us take n copies of the above state, giving a state of the following form:

$$|\varphi\rangle_{A^n B^n} \equiv \sum_{x^n} \sqrt{p_{X^n}(x^n)} |x^n\rangle_{A^n} |x^n\rangle_{B^n}, \tag{21.31}$$

where $x^n \equiv x_1 \cdots x_n$, $p_{X^n}(x^n) \equiv p_X(x_1) \cdots p_X(x_n)$, and $|x^n\rangle \equiv |x_1\rangle \cdots |x_n\rangle$. We can write the above state in terms of its type decomposition (see Section 14.7.1):

$$|\varphi\rangle_{A^n B^n} = \sum_{t} \sum_{x^n \in T_t} \sqrt{p_{X^n}(x^n)} |x^n\rangle_{A^n} |x^n\rangle_{B^n} \tag{21.32}$$

$$= \sum_{t} \sqrt{p_{X^n}(x_t^n)} \sum_{x^n \in T_t} |x^n\rangle_{A^n} |x^n\rangle_{B^n} \tag{21.33}$$

$$= \sum_{t} \sqrt{p_{X^n}(x_t^n) d_t} \frac{1}{\sqrt{d_t}} \sum_{x^n \in T_t} |x^n\rangle_{A^n} |x^n\rangle_{B^n} \tag{21.34}$$

$$= \sum_{t} \sqrt{p(t)} |\Phi_t\rangle_{A^n B^n}, \tag{21.35}$$

with the following definitions:

$$p(t) \equiv p_{X^n}(x_t^n) d_t, \tag{21.36}$$

$$|\Phi_t\rangle_{A^n B^n} \equiv \frac{1}{\sqrt{d_t}} \sum_{x^n \in T_t} |x^n\rangle_{A^n} |x^n\rangle_{B^n}. \tag{21.37}$$

The first equality in (21.32) follows by decomposing the state into its different type class subspaces. The next equality follows because $p_{X^n}(x^n)$ is the same for all sequences x^n in the same type class and because the distribution is i.i.d. (let x_t^n be some representative sequence of all sequences in the type class T_t). The third equality follows by introducing d_t as the dimension of a type class subspace T_t, and the final equality in (21.35) follows from the definitions. Observe that the state $|\Phi_t\rangle_{A^n B^n}$ is maximally entangled.

Each state $|\Phi_t\rangle_{A^n B^n}$ is maximally entangled with Schmidt rank d_t, and we can thus apply the transpose trick for operators acting on the type class subspaces. Inspired by the dense-coding-like strategy from Section 21.2, we allow Alice to choose unitary operators from the Heisenberg–Weyl set of d_t^2 operators that act on the A^n share of $|\Phi_t\rangle_{A^n B^n}$. We denote one of these operators as $V(x_t, z_t) \equiv X(x_t)Z(z_t)$ where $x_t, z_t \in \{0, \ldots, d_t - 1\}$. If she does this for every type class subspace and applies a phase $(-1)^{b_t}$ in each subspace, then the resulting unitary operator $U(s)$ acting on all of her A^n systems is a direct sum of all of these unitaries:

$$U(s) \equiv \bigoplus_{t} (-1)^{b_t} V(x_t, z_t), \tag{21.38}$$

where s is a vector containing all of the indices needed to specify the unitary $U(s)$:

$$s \equiv ((x_t, z_t, b_t))_t. \tag{21.39}$$

Let $\mathcal{S}$ denote the set of all possible vectors s. The transpose trick holds for these particular unitary operators:

$$(U_{A^n}(s) \otimes I_{B^n}) |\varphi\rangle_{A^n B^n} = \left(I_{A^n} \otimes U_{B^n}^T(s)\right) |\varphi\rangle_{A^n B^n} \tag{21.40}$$

because it applies in each type class subspace:

$$(U_{A^n}(s) \otimes I_{B^n}) |\varphi\rangle_{A^n B^n}$$

$$= \left(\bigoplus_t (-1)^{b_t} V_{A^n}(x_t, z_t) \right) \sum_t \sqrt{p(t)} |\Phi_t\rangle_{A^n B^n} \qquad (21.41)$$

$$= \sum_t \sqrt{p(t)} (-1)^{b_t} V_{A^n}(x_t, z_t) |\Phi_t\rangle_{A^n B^n} \qquad (21.42)$$

$$= \sum_t \sqrt{p(t)} (-1)^{b_t} V_{B^n}^T(x_t, z_t) |\Phi_t\rangle_{A^n B^n} \qquad (21.43)$$

$$= \left(\bigoplus_t (-1)^{b_t} V_{B^n}^T(x_t, z_t) \right) \sum_t \sqrt{p(t)} |\Phi_t\rangle_{A^n B^n} \qquad (21.44)$$

$$= \left(I_{A^n} \otimes U_{B^n}^T(s) \right) |\varphi\rangle_{A^n B^n}. \qquad (21.45)$$

Now we need to establish a means by which Alice can select a random code. For every message $m \in \mathcal{M}$ that Alice would like to transmit, she chooses the elements of the vector $s \in \mathcal{S}$ uniformly at random, leading to a particular unitary operator $U(s)$. We can write $s(m)$ instead of just s to denote the explicit association of the vector s with the message m—we can think of each chosen vector $s(m)$ as a classical codeword, with the codebook being $\{s(m)\}_{m \in \{1, \dots, |\mathcal{M}|\}}$. This random selection procedure leads to entanglement-assisted quantum codewords of the following form:

$$|\varphi_m\rangle_{A^n B^n} \equiv (U_{A^n}(s(m)) \otimes I_{B^n}) |\varphi\rangle_{A^n B^n}. \qquad (21.46)$$

Alice then transmits her systems A^n through many uses of the quantum channel $\mathcal{N}_{A \to B'}$, leading to the following state that is entirely in Bob's control:

$$\mathcal{N}_{A^n \to B'^n}(|\varphi_m\rangle\langle\varphi_m|_{A^n B^n}). \qquad (21.47)$$

Interestingly, the above state is equal to the state in (21.50) below, by exploiting the transpose trick from (21.40):

$$\mathcal{N}_{A^n \to B'^n}(|\varphi_m\rangle\langle\varphi_m|_{A^n B^n})$$

$$= \mathcal{N}_{A^n \to B'^n}(U_{A^n}(s(m))|\varphi\rangle\langle\varphi|_{A^n B^n} U_{A^n}^\dagger(s(m))) \qquad (21.48)$$

$$= \mathcal{N}_{A^n \to B'^n}(U_{B^n}^T(s(m))|\varphi\rangle\langle\varphi|_{A^n B^n} U_{B^n}^*(s(m))) \qquad (21.49)$$

$$= U_{B^n}^T(s(m))\mathcal{N}_{A^n \to B'^n}(|\varphi\rangle\langle\varphi|_{A^n B^n})U_{B^n}^*(s(m)). \qquad (21.50)$$

Observe that the transpose trick allows us to commute the action of the channel with Alice's encoding unitary $U(s(m))$, just as we did in the example in the proof of Corollary 21.2.1. Let

$$\rho_{B'^n B^n} \equiv \mathcal{N}_{A^n \to B'^n}(|\varphi\rangle\langle\varphi|_{A^n B^n}) \qquad (21.51)$$

so that

$$\mathcal{N}_{A^n \to B'^n}(|\varphi_m\rangle\langle\varphi_m|_{A^n B^n}) = U_{B^n}^T(s(m))\rho_{B'^n B^n}U_{B^n}^*(s(m)). \qquad (21.52)$$

REMARK 21.4.1 (Tensor-Power Channel Output States)   When using the coding scheme given above, the reduced state on the channel output (obtained by ignoring Bob's share of the entanglement in B^n) is the same tensor-power state, independent of the unitary that Alice applies at the channel input:

$$\mathrm{Tr}_{B^n}\left\{\mathcal{N}_{A^n\to B'^n}(|\varphi_m\rangle\langle\varphi_m|_{A^n B^n})\right\} = \rho_{B'^n} \qquad (21.53)$$

$$= \mathcal{N}_{A^n\to B'^n}(\varphi_{A^n}), \qquad (21.54)$$

where $\varphi_{A^n} = (\mathrm{Tr}_B\{\varphi_{AB}\})^{\otimes n}$. This follows directly from (21.52) and taking the partial trace over B^n. We exploit this feature in the next chapter, where we construct codes for transmitting both classical and quantum information with the help of shared entanglement.

After Alice has transmitted her entanglement-assisted quantum codewords over the channel, it becomes Bob's task to determine which message m Alice transmitted, and he should do so with some POVM $\{\Lambda^m\}$ that depends on the random choice of code. Figure 21.3 depicts the protocol.

At this point, we would like to exploit the packing lemma from Chapter 16 in order to establish the existence of a reliable decoding POVM for Bob. Recall that the packing lemma requires four objects, and these four objects should satisfy the four inequalities in (16.11)–(16.14). The first object required is an ensemble from which Alice and Bob can select a code randomly, and in our case, the ensemble is

$$\left\{\frac{1}{|S|}, U_{B^n}^T(s)\rho_{B'^n B^n}U_{B^n}^*(s)\right\}_{s\in S}. \qquad (21.55)$$

The next object required is the expected density operator of this ensemble:

$$\bar{\rho}_{B'^n B^n} \equiv \mathbb{E}_S\left\{U^T(S)_{B^n}\rho_{B'^n B^n}U^*(S)_{B^n}\right\} \qquad (21.56)$$

$$= \frac{1}{|S|}\sum_{s\in S}U_{B^n}^T(s)\rho_{B'^n B^n}U_{B^n}^*(s). \qquad (21.57)$$

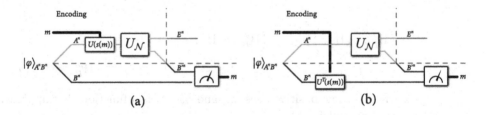

(a)   (b)

Figure 21.3 (a) Alice shares many copies of a pure, bipartite state $|\varphi\rangle^{\otimes n}$ with Bob. She encodes a message m according to some unitary of the form in (21.38). She transmits her share of the entanglement-assisted quantum codeword over many uses of the quantum channel, and it is Bob's task to determine which message she transmits. (b) Alice acting locally with the unitary $U(s(m))$ on her share A^n of the entanglement $|\varphi\rangle^{\otimes n}$ is the same as her acting non-locally with $U^T(s(m))$ on Bob's share B^n of the entanglement. This follows because of the particular structure of the unitaries in (21.38).

We later prove that this expected density operator has the following simpler form:

$$\overline{\rho}_{B'^n B^n} = \sum_t p(t)\, \mathcal{N}_{A^n \to B'^n}(\pi^t_{A^n}) \otimes \pi^t_{B^n}, \tag{21.58}$$

where $p(t)$ is the distribution from (21.36) and $\pi^t_{A^n}$ is the maximally mixed state on a type class subspace: $\pi^t_{A^n} \equiv I_t/d_t$. The final two objects that we require for the packing lemma are the message subspace projectors and the total subspace projector. We assign these respectively as

$$U^T_{B^n}(s)\Pi^{\rho,\delta}_{B'^n B^n} U^*_{B^n}(s), \tag{21.59}$$

$$\Pi^{\rho,\delta}_{B'^n} \otimes \Pi^{\rho,\delta}_{B^n}, \tag{21.60}$$

where $\Pi^{\rho,\delta}_{B'^n B^n}$, $\Pi^{\rho,\delta}_{B'^n}$, and $\Pi^{\rho,\delta}_{B^n}$ are the typical projectors for many copies of the states $\rho_{B'B} \equiv \mathcal{N}_{A \to B'}(\varphi_{AB})$, $\rho_{B'} = \mathrm{Tr}_B\{\rho_{B'B}\}$, and $\rho_B = \mathrm{Tr}_{B'}\{\rho_{B'B}\}$, respectively. Observe that the size of each message subspace projector is $\approx 2^{nH(B'B)}$, and the size of the total subspace projector is $\approx 2^{n[H(B')+H(B)]}$. By dimension counting, this is suggesting that we can pack in $\approx 2^{n[H(B')+H(B)]}/2^{nH(B'B)} = 2^{nI(B';B)}$ messages using this coding technique.

If the four conditions of the packing lemma are satisfied (see (16.11)–(16.14)), then there exists a detection POVM that can reliably decode Alice's transmitted messages as long as the number of messages in the code is not too high. The four conditions in (16.11)–(16.14) translate to the following four conditions for our case:

$$\mathrm{Tr}\left\{ \left(\Pi^{\rho,\delta}_{B'^n} \otimes \Pi^{\rho,\delta}_{B^n}\right)\left(U^T_{B^n}(s)\rho_{B'^n B^n}U^*_{B^n}(s)\right)\right\} \geq 1 - \varepsilon, \tag{21.61}$$

$$\mathrm{Tr}\left\{ \left(U^T_{B^n}(s)\Pi^{\rho,\delta}_{B'^n B^n}U^*_{B^n}(s)\right)\left(U^T_{B^n}(s)\rho_{B'^n B^n}U^*_{B^n}(s)\right)\right\} \geq 1 - \varepsilon, \tag{21.62}$$

$$\mathrm{Tr}\left\{U^T_{B^n}(s)\Pi^{\rho,\delta}_{B'^n B^n}U^*_{B^n}(s)\right\} \leq 2^{n[H(B'B)_\rho + c\delta]}, \tag{21.63}$$

$$\left(\Pi^{\rho,\delta}_{B'^n} \otimes \Pi^{\rho,\delta}_{B^n}\right)\overline{\rho}_{B'^n B^n}\left(\Pi^{\rho,\delta}_{B'^n} \otimes \Pi^{\rho,\delta}_{B^n}\right)$$
$$\leq 2^{-n[H(B')_\rho + H(B)_\rho - \eta(n,\delta) - c\delta]}\left(\Pi^{\rho,\delta}_{B'^n} \otimes \Pi^{\rho,\delta}_{B^n}\right), \tag{21.64}$$

where c is some positive constant and $\eta(n,\delta)$ is a function that approaches zero as $n \to \infty$ and $\delta \to 0$.

We now prove the four inequalities in (21.61)–(21.64), attacking them in the order of increasing difficulty. The condition in (21.62) holds because

$$\mathrm{Tr}\left\{ \left(U^T_{B^n}(s)\Pi^{\rho,\delta}_{B'^n B^n}U^*_{B^n}(s)\right)\left(U^T_{B^n}(s)\rho_{B'^n B^n}U^*_{B^n}(s)\right)\right\}$$
$$= \mathrm{Tr}\left\{\Pi^{\rho,\delta}_{B'^n B^n}\rho_{B'^n B^n}\right\} \tag{21.65}$$
$$\geq 1 - \varepsilon. \tag{21.66}$$

The equality holds by cyclicity of the trace and because $U^* U^T = I$. The inequality holds by exploiting the unit probability property of typical projectors (Property 15.1.1). From this inequality, observe that we choose each message subspace projector so that it is exactly the one that should identify the entanglement-assisted quantum codeword $U_{B^n}^T(s) \rho_{B'^n B^n} U_{B^n}^*(s)$ with high probability.

We next consider the condition in (21.63):

$$\text{Tr}\left\{ U_{B^n}^T(s) \Pi_{B'^n B^n}^{\rho,\delta} U_{B^n}^*(s) \right\} = \text{Tr}\left\{ \Pi_{B'^n B^n}^{\rho,\delta} \right\} \tag{21.67}$$

$$\leq 2^{n\left[H(B'B)_\rho + c\delta \right]}. \tag{21.68}$$

The equality holds again by cyclicity of trace, and the inequality follows from the "exponentially smaller cardinality" property of the typical subspace (Property 15.1.2).

Consider the condition in (21.61). First, define $\hat{P} = I - P$. Then

$$\Pi_{B'^n}^{\rho,\delta} \otimes \Pi_{B^n}^{\rho,\delta} = (I - \hat{\Pi}_{B'^n}^{\rho,\delta}) \otimes (I - \hat{\Pi}_{B^n}^{\rho,\delta}) \tag{21.69}$$

$$= (I_{B'^n} \otimes I_{B^n}) - (\hat{\Pi}_{B'^n}^{\rho,\delta} \otimes I_{B^n})$$
$$- (I_{B'^n} \otimes \hat{\Pi}_{B^n}^{\rho,\delta}) + (\hat{\Pi}_{B'^n}^{\rho,\delta} \otimes \hat{\Pi}_{B^n}^{\rho,\delta}) \tag{21.70}$$

$$\geq (I_{B'^n} \otimes I_{B^n}) - (\hat{\Pi}_{B'^n}^{\rho,\delta} \otimes I_{B^n}) - (I_{B'^n} \otimes \hat{\Pi}_{B^n}^{\rho,\delta}). \tag{21.71}$$

Consider the following chain of inequalities:

$$\text{Tr}\left\{ (\Pi_{B'^n}^{\rho,\delta} \otimes \Pi_{B^n}^{\rho,\delta}) \left(U_{B^n}^T(s) \rho_{B'^n B^n} U_{B^n}^*(s) \right) \right\}$$

$$\geq \text{Tr}\left\{ U_{B^n}^T(s) \rho_{B'^n B^n} U_{B^n}^*(s) \right\}$$

$$- \text{Tr}\left\{ (\hat{\Pi}_{B'^n}^{\rho,\delta} \otimes I_{B^n}) \left(U_{B^n}^T(s) \rho_{B'^n B^n} U_{B^n}^*(s) \right) \right\}$$

$$- \text{Tr}\left\{ (I_{B'^n} \otimes \hat{\Pi}_{B^n}^{\rho,\delta}) \left(U_{B^n}^T(s) \rho_{B'^n B^n} U_{B^n}^*(s) \right) \right\} \tag{21.72}$$

$$= 1 - \text{Tr}\left\{ \hat{\Pi}_{B'^n}^{\rho,\delta} \rho_{B'^n} \right\} - \text{Tr}\left\{ \hat{\Pi}_{B^n}^{\rho,\delta} \rho_{B^n} \right\} \tag{21.73}$$

$$\geq 1 - 2\varepsilon. \tag{21.74}$$

The first inequality follows from the development in (21.69)–(21.71). The first equality follows because $\text{Tr}\left\{ U_{B^n}^T(s) \rho_{B'^n B^n} U_{B^n}^*(s) \right\} = 1$ and from performing a partial trace on B^n and B'^n, respectively (while noting that we can apply the transpose trick for the second one). The final inequality follows from the unit probability property of the typical projectors $\Pi_{B'^n}^{\rho,\delta}$ and $\Pi_{B^n}^{\rho,\delta}$ (Property 15.1.1).

The last inequality in (21.64) requires the most effort to prove. We first need to prove that the expected density operator $\overline{\rho}_{B'^n B^n}$ takes the form given in (21.58). To simplify the development, we evaluate the expectation without the channel applied, and we then apply the channel to the state at the end of the development. Consider that

$$\overline{\rho}_{A^n B^n} = \frac{1}{|\mathcal{S}|} \sum_{s \in \mathcal{S}} U_{B^n}^T(s) |\varphi\rangle\langle\varphi|_{A^n B^n} U_{B^n}^*(s) \tag{21.75}$$

$$= \frac{1}{|\mathcal{S}|} \sum_{s \in \mathcal{S}} U_{B^n}^T(s) \left(\sum_t \sqrt{p(t)} |\Phi_t\rangle_{A^n B^n} \right) \left(\sum_{t'} \langle\Phi_{t'}|_{A^n B^n} \sqrt{p(t')} \right) U_{B^n}^*(s) \tag{21.76}$$

$$= \frac{1}{|\mathcal{S}|} \sum_{s \in \mathcal{S}} \left(\sum_t \sqrt{p(t)} (-1)^{b_t(s)} \left(V_{B^n}^T((z_t, x_t)(s)) \right) |\Phi_t\rangle_{A^n B^n} \right)$$
$$\left(\sum_{t'} \langle\Phi_{t'}|_{A^n B^n} (-1)^{b_{t'}(s)} \left(V_{B^n}^*((z_{t'}, x_{t'})(s)) \right) \sqrt{p(t')} \right). \tag{21.77}$$

Let us first consider the case when $t = t'$. Then the expression in (21.77) becomes

$$\frac{1}{|\mathcal{S}|} \sum_{s \in \mathcal{S}} \sum_t p(t) \left(V_{B^n}^T((z_t, x_t)(s)) \right) |\Phi_t\rangle\langle\Phi_t|_{A^n B^n} \left(V_{B^n}^*((z_t, x_t)(s)) \right)$$

$$= \sum_t p(t) \left[\frac{1}{d_t^2} \sum_{x_t, z_t} V_{B^n}^T(z_t, x_t) |\Phi_t\rangle\langle\Phi_t|_{A^n B^n} V_{B^n}^*(z_t, x_t) \right] \tag{21.78}$$

$$= \sum_t p(t) \pi_{A^n}^t \otimes \pi_{B^n}^t. \tag{21.79}$$

These equalities hold because the sum over all the elements in $\mathcal{S}$ implies that we are uniformly mixing the maximally entangled states $|\Phi_t\rangle_{A^n B^n}$ on the type class subspaces and Exercise 4.7.6 gives us that the resulting state on each type class subspace is equal to $\text{Tr}_{B^n}\{[\Phi_t]_{A^n B^n}\} \otimes \pi_{B^n}^t = \pi_{A^n}^t \otimes \pi_{B^n}^t$. Let us now consider the case when $t \neq t'$. Then the expression in (21.77) becomes

$$\frac{1}{|\mathcal{S}|} \sum_{s \in \mathcal{S}} \sum_{t', t \neq t'} \sqrt{p(t)p(t')} (-1)^{b_t(s) + b_{t'}(s)}$$
$$\times \left(V_{B^n}^T((z_t, x_t)(s)) \right) |\Phi_t\rangle\langle\Phi_{t'}|_{A^n B^n} \left(V_{B^n}^*((z_{t'}, x_{t'})(s)) \right)$$

$$= \sum_{t', t \neq t'} \frac{1}{d_t^2 d_{t'}^2 4} \sum_{b_t, b_{t'}, x_t, z_t, x_{t'}, z_{t'}} \sqrt{p(t)p(t')} (-1)^{b_t + b_{t'}}$$
$$\times V_{B^n}^T(z_t, x_t) |\Phi_t\rangle\langle\Phi_{t'}|_{A^n B^n} V_{B^n}^*(z_{t'}, x_{t'}) \tag{21.80}$$

$$= \sum_{t', t \neq t'} \frac{1}{d_t^2 d_{t'}^2} \sum_{b_t, b_{t'}} \frac{(-1)^{b_t + b_{t'}}}{4}$$

$$\times \left(\sum_{x_t, z_t, x_{t'}, z_{t'}} \sqrt{p(t)p(t')} V_{B^n}^T(z_t, x_t) |\Phi_t\rangle\langle\Phi_{t'}|_{A^n B^n} V_{B^n}^*(z_{t'}, x_{t'}) \right) \tag{21.81}$$

$$= 0. \tag{21.82}$$

It then follows that

$$\frac{1}{|\mathcal{S}|} \sum_{s \in \mathcal{S}} U_{B^n}^T(s) |\varphi\rangle\langle\varphi|_{A^n B^n} U_{B^n}^*(s) = \sum_t p(t) \pi_{A^n}^t \otimes \pi_{B^n}^t, \tag{21.83}$$

and by linearity, that

$$\frac{1}{|\mathcal{S}|} \sum_{s \in \mathcal{S}} U_{B^n}^T(s) \mathcal{N}_{A^n \to B'^n}(|\varphi\rangle\langle\varphi|_{A^n B^n}) U_{B^n}^*(s)$$

$$= \sum_t p(t) \mathcal{N}_{A^n \to B'^n}(\pi_{A^n}^t) \otimes \pi_{B^n}^t. \quad (21.84)$$

We now prove the final condition in (21.64) for the packing lemma. Consider the following chain of inequalities:

$$\left(\Pi_{B'^n}^{\rho,\delta} \otimes \Pi_{B^n}^{\rho,\delta}\right) \overline{\rho}_{B'^n B^n} \left(\Pi_{B'^n}^{\rho,\delta} \otimes \Pi_{B^n}^{\rho,\delta}\right)$$

$$= \left(\Pi_{B'^n}^{\rho,\delta} \otimes \Pi_{B^n}^{\rho,\delta}\right) \left(\sum_t p(t) \mathcal{N}_{A^n \to B'^n}(\pi_{A^n}^t) \otimes \pi_{B^n}^t\right) \left(\Pi_{B'^n}^{\rho,\delta} \otimes \Pi_{B^n}^{\rho,\delta}\right) \quad (21.85)$$

$$= \sum_t p(t) \left(\Pi_{B'^n}^{\rho,\delta} \mathcal{N}_{A^n \to B'^n}(\pi_{A^n}^t) \Pi_{B'^n}^{\rho,\delta} \otimes \Pi_{B^n}^{\rho,\delta} \pi_{B^n}^t \Pi_{B^n}^{\rho,\delta}\right) \quad (21.86)$$

$$= \sum_t p(t) \left(\Pi_{B'^n}^{\rho,\delta} \mathcal{N}_{A^n \to B'^n}(\pi_{A^n}^t) \Pi_{B'^n}^{\rho,\delta} \otimes \Pi_{B^n}^{\rho,\delta} \frac{\Pi_{B^n}^t}{\mathrm{Tr}\{\Pi_{B^n}^t\}} \Pi_{B^n}^{\rho,\delta}\right) \quad (21.87)$$

$$\leq \sum_t p(t) \left(\Pi_{B'^n}^{\rho,\delta} \mathcal{N}_{A^n \to B'^n}(\pi_{A^n}^t) \Pi_{B'^n}^{\rho,\delta} \otimes 2^{-n[H(B)_\rho - \eta(n,\delta)]} \Pi_{B^n}^{\rho,\delta}\right). \quad (21.88)$$

The first equality follows from (21.84). The second equality follows by a simple manipulation. The third equality follows because the maximally mixed state $\pi_{B^n}^t$ is equal to the normalized type class projection operator $\Pi_{B^n}^t$. The inequality follows from Property 15.3.2 and $\Pi_{B^n}^{\rho,\delta} \Pi_{B^n}^t \Pi_{B^n}^{\rho,\delta} \leq \Pi_{B^n}^{\rho,\delta}$ (the support of a typical type projector is always in the support of the typical projector and the intersection of the support of an atypical type with the typical projector is null). Continuing, by linearity, the last line above is equal to

$$\Pi_{B'^n}^{\rho,\delta} \mathcal{N}_{A^n \to B'^n}\left(\sum_t p(t) \pi_{A^n}^t\right) \Pi_{B'^n}^{\rho,\delta} \otimes 2^{-n[H(B)_\rho - \eta(n,\delta)]} \Pi_{B^n}^{\rho,\delta}$$

$$= \Pi_{B'^n}^{\rho,\delta} \mathcal{N}_{A^n \to B'^n}(\varphi_{A^n}) \Pi_{B'^n}^{\rho,\delta} \otimes 2^{-n[H(B)_\rho - \eta(n,\delta)]} \Pi_{B^n}^{\rho,\delta} \quad (21.89)$$

$$\leq 2^{-n[H(B')_\rho - c\delta]} \Pi_{B'^n}^{\rho,\delta} \otimes 2^{-n[H(B)_\rho - \eta(n,\delta)]} \Pi_{B^n}^{\rho,\delta} \quad (21.90)$$

$$= 2^{-n[H(B')_\rho + H(B)_\rho - \eta(n,\delta) - c\delta]} \Pi_{B'^n}^{\rho,\delta} \otimes \Pi_{B^n}^{\rho,\delta}. \quad (21.91)$$

The first equality follows because $\varphi_{A^n} = \sum_t p(t) \pi_{A^n}^t$. The inequality follows from the equipartition property of typical projectors (Property 15.1.3). The final equality follows by rearranging terms.

With the four conditions in (21.61)–(21.64) holding, it follows from Corollary 16.5.1 (the derandomized version of the packing lemma) that there exists a deterministic code and a POVM $\{\Lambda_{B'^n B^n}^m\}$ that can detect the transmitted states with arbitrarily low maximal probability of error as long as the size $|\mathcal{M}|$ of the message set is small enough:

$$p_e^* \equiv \max_m \text{Tr} \left\{ (I - \Lambda_{B'^n B^n}^m) U_{B^n}^T (s(m)) \rho_{B'^n B^n} U_{B^n}^* (s(m)) \right\} \tag{21.92}$$

$$\leq 4 \left(2\varepsilon + 2\sqrt{2\varepsilon} \right) + 16 \cdot 2^{-n[H(B')_\rho + H(B)_\rho - \eta(n,\delta) - c\delta]} 2^{n[H(B'B)_\rho + c\delta]} |\mathcal{M}| \tag{21.93}$$

$$= 4 \left(2\varepsilon + 2\sqrt{2\varepsilon} \right) + 16 \cdot 2^{-n[I(B';B)_\rho - \eta(n,\delta) - 2c\delta]} |\mathcal{M}|. \tag{21.94}$$

We can choose the size of the message set to be $|\mathcal{M}| = 2^{n[I(B';B) - \eta(n,\delta) - 3c\delta]}$ so that the rate of communication is

$$\frac{1}{n} \log |\mathcal{M}| = I(B';B) - \eta(n,\delta) - 3c\delta, \tag{21.95}$$

and the bound on the maximal probability of error becomes

$$p_e^* \leq 4 \left(2\varepsilon + 2\sqrt{2\varepsilon} \right) + 16 \cdot 2^{-nc\delta}. \tag{21.96}$$

Let $\varepsilon' \in (0,1)$ and $\delta' > 0$. It is then clear that by picking n large enough and δ small enough, we can have both $4 \left(2\varepsilon + 2\sqrt{2\varepsilon} \right) + 16 \cdot 2^{-nc\delta} \leq \varepsilon'$ and $\eta(n,\delta) + 3c\delta \leq \delta'$. Thus, the quantum mutual information $I(B';B)_\rho$, with respect to the state $\rho_{B'B} \equiv \mathcal{N}_{A \to B'}(\varphi_{AB})$ is an achievable rate for the entanglement-assisted transmission of classical information over the channel $\mathcal{N}$. To obtain the precise statement in Theorem 21.3.1, we can simply rewrite the quantum mutual information as $I(A;B)_\rho$ with respect to the state $\rho_{AB} \equiv \mathcal{N}_{A' \to B}(\varphi_{AA'})$. Alice and Bob can achieve the maximum rate of communication simply by determining a state $\varphi_{AA'}$ that maximizes the quantum mutual information $I(A;B)_\rho$ and by generating entanglement-assisted classical codes from the state ρ_{AB}. $\qquad\square$

21.5   The Converse Theorem

This section contains a proof of the converse part of the entanglement-assisted classical capacity theorem. Let us begin by supposing that Alice and Bob are trying to use the entanglement-assisted channel many times to accomplish the task of randomness distribution (recall that we took this approach for the converse of the classical capacity theorem in Section 20.3.2). An upper bound on the rate at which Alice can distribute randomness to Bob also serves as an upper bound on the rate at which they can communicate because a noiseless classical channel can distribute randomness. In such a task, Alice and Bob share entanglement in some state $\Psi_{T_A T_B}$. Alice first prepares the maximally correlated state $\overline{\Phi}_{MM'}$, as defined in (20.16), and the rate of randomness in this state is $\frac{1}{n} \log |\mathcal{M}|$. Alice then applies some encoding channel $\mathcal{E}_{M'T_A \to A^n}$ to the classical system M' and her share T_A of $\Psi_{T_A T_B}$. The resulting state is

$$\theta_{MA^n T_B} \equiv \mathcal{E}_{M'T_A \to A^n}(\overline{\Phi}_{MM'} \otimes \Psi_{T_A T_B}). \tag{21.97}$$

She sends her A^n systems through many uses $\mathcal{N}_{A^n \rightarrow B^n}$ of the channel $\mathcal{N}_{A \rightarrow B}$, and Bob receives the systems B^n, producing the state

$$\omega_{MT_B B^n} \equiv \mathcal{N}_{A^n \rightarrow B^n}(\mathcal{E}_{M'T_A \rightarrow A^n}(\overline{\Phi}_{MM'} \otimes \Psi_{T_A T_B})). \qquad (21.98)$$

Finally, Bob performs some decoding channel $\mathcal{D}_{B^n T_B \rightarrow \hat{M}}$ on the above state to give

$$\omega'_{M\hat{M}} \equiv \mathcal{D}_{B^n T_B \rightarrow \hat{M}}(\omega_{MT_B B^n}). \qquad (21.99)$$

An $(n, \lceil \log |\mathcal{M}| \rceil /n, \varepsilon)$ protocol for randomness distribution is such that the actual state $\omega'_{M\hat{M}}$ resulting from the protocol is ε-close in trace distance to the ideal shared randomness state:

$$\frac{1}{2}\left\| \omega'_{M\hat{M}} - \overline{\Phi}_{M\hat{M}} \right\|_1 \leq \varepsilon. \qquad (21.100)$$

We now show that the quantum mutual information of the channel serves as an upper bound on the rate of any reliable protocol for entanglement-assisted randomness distribution—a protocol meeting the error criterion in (21.100). Consider the following:

$$\log |\mathcal{M}| = I(M; \hat{M})_{\overline{\Phi}} \qquad (21.101)$$
$$\leq I(M; \hat{M})_{\omega'} + f(|\mathcal{M}|, \varepsilon) \qquad (21.102)$$
$$\leq I(M; B^n T_B)_{\omega} + f(|\mathcal{M}|, \varepsilon) \qquad (21.103)$$
$$= I(T_B M; B^n)_{\omega} + I(M; T_B)_{\omega} - I(B^n; T_B)_{\omega} + f(|\mathcal{M}|, \varepsilon) \qquad (21.104)$$
$$= I(T_B M; B^n)_{\omega} - I(B^n; T_B)_{\omega} + f(|\mathcal{M}|, \varepsilon) \qquad (21.105)$$
$$\leq I(T_B M; B^n)_{\omega} + f(|\mathcal{M}|, \varepsilon) \qquad (21.106)$$
$$\leq I(\mathcal{N}^{\otimes n}) + f(|\mathcal{M}|, \varepsilon) \qquad (21.107)$$
$$= nI(\mathcal{N}) + f(|\mathcal{M}|, \varepsilon). \qquad (21.108)$$

The first equality follows by evaluating the quantum mutual information of the shared randomness state $\overline{\Phi}_{M\hat{M}}$. The first inequality follows for the exact same reasons as (20.57) does (the first inequality of the converse for the HSW theorem), with $f(|\mathcal{M}|, \varepsilon) \equiv \varepsilon \log |\mathcal{M}| + (1 + \varepsilon) h_2(\varepsilon/ [1 + \varepsilon])$. The second inequality follows from quantum data processing (Theorem 11.9.4)—Bob processes the state $\omega_{MT_B B^n}$ with the decoder $\mathcal{D}_{B^n T_B \rightarrow \hat{M}}$ to get the state $\omega'_{M\hat{M}}$. The second equality follows from the chain rule for quantum mutual information (see Exercise 11.7.1). The third equality follows because the systems M and T_B are in a product state, so that $I(M; T_B)_{\omega} = 0$. The third inequality follows because $I(B^n; T_B)_{\omega} \geq 0$. Observe that the state $\omega_{MT_B B^n} = \mathcal{N}_{A^n \rightarrow B^n}(\theta_{MA^n T_B})$, so that the systems M and T_B extend the A^n system that is input to $\mathcal{N}^{\otimes n}$. Thus, the mutual information between MT_B and B^n can never exceed the maximum mutual information of the channel, where we need to apply the result of Exercise 13.4.4. Finally, the mutual information of a quantum channel is additive (Theorem 13.4.1), and Corollary 13.4.1 implies that $I(\mathcal{N}^{\otimes n}) = nI(\mathcal{N})$. We can then rewrite the above bound as follows:

$$\frac{1}{n} \log |\mathcal{M}| (1 - \varepsilon) \leq I(\mathcal{N}) + \frac{1 + \varepsilon}{n} h_2(\varepsilon / [1 + \varepsilon]). \qquad (21.109)$$

Thus, if we are considering a sequence of $(n, \lfloor \log |\mathcal{M}| \rfloor / n, \varepsilon_n)$ entanglement-assisted classical communication protocols with rate $C - \delta_n = \frac{1}{n} \log |\mathcal{M}|$, such that $\lim_{n \to \infty} \varepsilon_n = \lim_{n \to \infty} \delta_n = 0$, then the above bound becomes

$$(C - \delta_n)(1 - \varepsilon_n) \leq I(\mathcal{N}) + \frac{1 + \varepsilon_n}{n} h_2(\varepsilon_n / [1 + \varepsilon_n]). \qquad (21.110)$$

Taking the limit as $n \to \infty$ then establishes that an achievable rate C necessarily satisfies $C \leq I(\mathcal{N})$. This demonstrates a single-letter upper bound on the entanglement-assisted classical capacity of a quantum channel and completes the proof of Theorem 21.3.1.

21.5.1   Feedback Does Not Increase Capacity

The entanglement-assisted classical capacity formula is the closest formal analogy to Shannon's capacity formula for a classical channel. The mutual information $I(\mathcal{N})$ of a quantum channel $\mathcal{N}$ is the optimum of the quantum mutual information over all bipartite input states:

$$I(\mathcal{N}) = \max_{\phi_{AA'}} I(A; B), \qquad (21.111)$$

and it is equal to the channel's entanglement-assisted classical capacity by Theorem 21.4.1. The mutual information $I(p_{Y|X})$ of a classical channel $p_{Y|X}$ is the optimum of the classical mutual information over all correlated inputs to the channel:

$$I(p_{Y|X}) = \max_{XX'} I(X; Y), \qquad (21.112)$$

where XX' are correlated random variables with the distribution $p_{X,X'}(x, x') = p_X(x)\delta_{x,x'}$. The formula is equal to the classical capacity of a classical channel by Shannon's noisy coding theorem. Both formulas not only appear similar in form, but they also have the important property of being "single-letter," meaning that the above formulas are equal to the capacity (this was not generally the case for the Holevo information from the previous chapter).

We now consider another way in which the entanglement-assisted classical capacity is a good candidate for being the fully quantum generalization of Shannon's formula to the quantum world. Though it might be surprising, it is well known that free access to a classical feedback channel from receiver to sender does not increase the capacity of a classical channel. We state this result as the following theorem.

THEOREM 21.5.1 (Feedback Does Not Increase Classical Capacity) The feedback capacity of a classical channel $p_{Y|X}(y|x)$ is equal to the mutual information of that channel:

$$\sup\left\{C : C \text{ is achievable for } p_{Y|X} \text{ with feedback }\right\} = I(p_{Y|X}), \qquad (21.113)$$

where $I(p_{Y|X})$ is defined in (21.112).

Proof We first define an $(n, C - \delta, \varepsilon)$ classical feedback code as one in which every symbol $x_i(m, Y^{i-1})$ of a codeword $x^n(m)$ is a function of the message $m \in \mathcal{M}$ and all of the previously received values $Y_1, \ldots, Y_{i-1}$ from the receiver. The decoder consists of the decoding function $g : \mathcal{Y}^n \to \{1, 2, \ldots, |\mathcal{M}|\}$ such that

$$\Pr\{M' \neq M\} \leq \varepsilon, \qquad (21.114)$$

where $M' \equiv g(Y^n)$. The lower bound LHS $\geq$ RHS follows because we can always avoid the use of the feedback channel and achieve the mutual information of the classical channel by employing Shannon's noisy coding theorem. The upper bound LHS $\leq$ RHS is less obvious, but it follows from the memoryless structure of the channel and the structure of a feedback code. Consider the following chain of inequalities:

$$\log|\mathcal{M}| = H(M) = I(M; M') + H(M|M') \qquad (21.115)$$
$$\leq I(M; M') + 1 + \varepsilon \log|\mathcal{M}| \qquad (21.116)$$
$$\leq I(M; Y^n) + 1 + \varepsilon \log|\mathcal{M}|. \qquad (21.117)$$

The first equality follows because we assume that the message M is uniformly distributed. The first inequality follows from Fano's inequality (see Theorem 10.7.3) and the assumption in (21.114) that the protocol is good up to error ε. The last inequality follows from classical data processing. Continuing, we can bound $I(M; Y^n)$ from above:

$$I(M; Y^n) = H(Y^n) - H(Y^n|M) = H(Y^n) - \sum_{k=1}^{n} H(Y_k|Y^{k-1}M) \qquad (21.118)$$

$$= H(Y^n) - \sum_{k=1}^{n} H(Y_k|Y^{k-1}MX_k) = H(Y^n) - \sum_{k=1}^{n} H(Y_k|X_k) \qquad (21.119)$$

$$\leq \sum_{k=1}^{n} H(Y_k) - H(Y_k|X_k) = \sum_{k=1}^{n} I(X_k; Y_k) \qquad (21.120)$$

$$\leq n \max_{XX'} I(X; Y). \qquad (21.121)$$

The first equality follows from the definition of mutual information. The second equality follows from the chain rule for entropy (see Exercise 10.3.2). The third equality follows because X_k is a function of Y^{k-1} and M. The fourth equality follows because Y_k is conditionally independent of Y^{k-1} and M through X_k ($Y^{k-1}M \to X_k \to Y_k$ forms a Markov chain). The first inequality follows from subadditivity of entropy. The fifth equality follows by definition, and the final inequality follows because the individual mutual informations in the sum can never exceed the maximum over all inputs. Putting everything together, our final bound on the feedback-assisted capacity of a classical channel is

$$C - \delta \leq I(p_{Y|X}) + \frac{1}{n} + \frac{\varepsilon}{n} \log |\mathcal{M}|, \qquad (21.122)$$

which becomes $C \leq I(p_{Y|X})$ as $n \to \infty$ and $\varepsilon, \delta \to 0$. $\square$

Given the above result, we might wonder if a similar result could hold for the entanglement-assisted classical capacity. Such a result would more firmly place the entanglement-assisted classical capacity as a good generalization of Shannon's coding theorem. Indeed, the following theorem states that this result holds.

THEOREM 21.5.2 (Quantum Feedback Does Not Increase EAC Capacity) The classical capacity of a quantum channel assisted by a quantum feedback channel is equal to that channel's entanglement-assisted classical capacity:

$$\sup \{C \mid C \text{ is achievable for } \mathcal{N} \text{ with quantum feedback}\} = I(\mathcal{N}), \qquad (21.123)$$

where $I(\mathcal{N})$ is defined in (21.111).

Proof We define free access to a quantum feedback channel to mean that there is a noiseless quantum channel of arbitrarily large dimension connecting the receiver Bob to the sender Alice. The bound LHS $\geq$ RHS follows because Bob can use the quantum feedback channel to establish an arbitrarily large amount of entanglement with Alice. They then just execute the protocol from Section 21.4 to achieve the entanglement-assisted classical capacity.

The bound LHS $\leq$ RHS is much less obvious, and it requires a proof that is different from the proof of Theorem 21.5.1. We first need to determine the most general protocol for classical communication with the assistance of a quantum feedback channel. Figure 21.4 depicts such a protocol. The protocol begins with Alice preparing a classical register M with a uniformly random message to be sent, which is correlated with some system A'_0. Bob uses the quantum feedback channel to send a quantum system X_0 to Alice, which is correlated with some quantum system B'_1. Alice performs an encoding $\mathcal{E}^1_{A'_0 X_0 \to A'_1 A_1}$. Alice sends system A_1 through the first use of the channel $\mathcal{N}$. Bob now applies the decoding channel $\mathcal{D}^1_{B_1 B'_1 \to X_1 B'_2}$. The next encoder of Alice occurs, and the procedure repeats. The last decoding channel of Bob outputs a classical system M' which contains Bob's estimate of the message that Alice transmitted. The state of registers $M B_n B'_n$ after the nth channel $\mathcal{N}_{A_n \to B_n}$ has been applied has the following form:

$$\omega^{(n)}_{M B_n B'_n} \equiv \mathcal{N}_{A_n \to B_n}(\rho^{(n)}_{M B'_n A_n}), \qquad (21.124)$$

where $\rho^{(n)}_{M B'_n A_n}$ is the state of registers $M B'_n A_n$ after the nth encoding channel has been applied. Let $\psi^{(n)}_{R^{(n)} M B'_n A_n}$ be a purification of $\rho^{(n)}_{M B'_n A_n}$, and let

$$\omega^{(n)}_{R^{(n)} M B_n B'_n} \equiv \mathcal{N}_{A_n \to B_n}(\psi^{(n)}_{R^{(n)} M B'_n A_n}). \qquad (21.125)$$

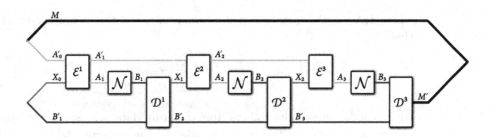

Figure 21.4 Three rounds of the most general protocol for classical communication with a quantum feedback channel.

This protocol is the most general for classical communication with quantum feedback. We can now proceed with proving the upper bound LHS $\leq$ RHS. To do so, we assume that the random variable M modeling Alice's message selection is a uniform random variable, and Bob obtains a random variable M' by measuring all of his systems B_n and B'_n at the end of the protocol. For any ε-good protocol for classical communication, the bound $\Pr\{M' \neq M\} \leq \varepsilon$ applies. Consider the following chain of inequalities (these steps are essentially the same as those in (21.115)–(21.117)):

$$\log|\mathcal{M}| = H(M) = I(M; M') + H(M|M') \tag{21.126}$$
$$\leq I(M; M') + 1 + \varepsilon \log|\mathcal{M}| \tag{21.127}$$
$$\leq I(M; B_n B'_n)_{\omega^{(n)}} + 1 + \varepsilon \log|\mathcal{M}|, \tag{21.128}$$

where the last mutual information is with respect to the state in (21.124). This chain of inequalities follows for the same reason as those in (21.115)–(21.117), with the last step following from quantum data processing. Continuing, we have

$$I(M; B_n B'_n)_{\omega^{(n)}} = I(M; B_n | B'_n)_{\omega^{(n)}} + I(M; B'_n)_{\omega^{(n)}} \tag{21.129}$$
$$\leq I(MB'_n; B_n)_{\omega^{(n)}} + I(M; B'_n)_{\omega^{(n)}} \tag{21.130}$$
$$\leq I(R^{(n)} MB'_n; B_n)_{\omega^{(n)}} + I(M; B'_n)_{\omega^{(n)}}. \tag{21.131}$$

The first equality is the chain rule for mutual information. The first inequality follows because $I(M; B_n | B'_n) = I(MB'_n; B_n) - I(B'_n; B_n) \leq I(MB'_n; B_n)$. The second inequality follows from quantum data processing. Now, given that the mutual information $I(R^{(n)} MB'_n; B_n)$ is with respect to the state in (21.124) and this state has the following form

$$\mathcal{N}_{A_n \to B_n}(\phi_{RA_n}), \tag{21.132}$$

where ϕ_{RA_n} is some pure state and R is some system not going into the channel (here identified with $R^{(n)} MB'_n$), we can optimize over all such inputs to find that

$$I(R^{(n)} MB'_n; B_n)_{\omega^{(n)}} \leq I(\mathcal{N}), \tag{21.133}$$

where $I(\mathcal{N})$ is the quantum mutual information of the channel. So this means that

$$I(M; B_n B'_n)_{\omega^{(n)}} \leq I(\mathcal{N}) + I(M; B'_n)_{\omega^{(n)}} \qquad (21.134)$$

$$\leq I(\mathcal{N}) + I(M; B_{n-1} B'_{n-1})_{\omega^{(n-1)}}, \qquad (21.135)$$

where the last inequality follows from quantum data processing (the system B'_n results from applying the $n-1$ decoder to the systems $B_{n-1} B'_{n-1}$). At this point, we realize that the above chain of steps (21.129)–(21.135) can be applied to $I(M; B_{n-1} B'_{n-1})_{\omega^{(n-1)}}$, so we iterate this sequence until we go all the way back to the beginning of the protocol. Putting everything together, we get the following upper bound on any achievable rate C for classical communication with quantum feedback:

$$C - \delta \leq I(\mathcal{N}) + \frac{1}{n} + \frac{\varepsilon}{n} \log |\mathcal{M}|, \qquad (21.136)$$

which becomes $C \leq I(\mathcal{N})$ as $n \to \infty$ and $\varepsilon, \delta \to 0$. $\qquad \square$

COROLLARY 21.5.1   The capacity of a quantum channel with unlimited entanglement and classical feedback is equal to the entanglement-assisted classical capacity of $\mathcal{N}$.

Proof   This result follows because $I(\mathcal{N})$ is a lower bound on this capacity (simply by avoiding use of the classical feedback channel). Also, $I(\mathcal{N})$ is an upper bound on this capacity because the entanglement and classical feedback channel can simulate an arbitrarily large quantum feedback channel via teleportation, and the above theorem gives an upper bound of $I(\mathcal{N})$ for this setting. $\qquad \square$

21.6   Examples of Channels

This section shows how to compute the entanglement-assisted classical capacity of both the quantum erasure channel and the amplitude damping channel, while leaving the capacity of the quantum depolarizing channel and the dephasing channel as exercises. For three of these channels (erasure, depolarizing, and dephasing), a super-dense coding-like strategy suffices to achieve capacity. This strategy involves Alice locally rotating an ebit shared with Bob, sending one share of it through the noisy channel, and Bob performing measurements in the Bell basis to determine what Alice sent. This process induces a classical channel from Alice to Bob, for which its capacity is equal to the entanglement-assisted capacity of the original quantum channel (in the case of depolarizing, dephasing, and erasure channels). For the amplitude damping channel, this super-dense coding-like strategy does not achieve capacity—in general, it is necessary for Bob to perform a large, collective measurement on all of the channel outputs in order for him to determine Alice's message.

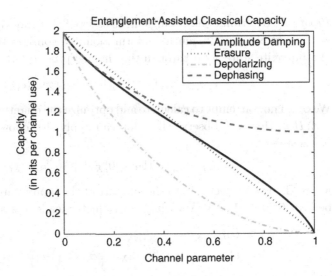

Figure 21.5 The entanglement-assisted classical capacity of the amplitude damping channel, the erasure channel, the depolarizing channel, and the dephasing channel as a function of each channel's noise parameter.

Figure 21.5 plots the entanglement-assisted capacities of these four channels as a function of their noise parameters. As expected, the depolarizing channel has the worst performance because it is a "worst-case scenario" channel—it either sends the state through or replaces it with a completely random state. The erasure channel's capacity is just a line of constant slope down to zero—this is because the receiver can easily determine the fraction of the time that he receives something from the channel. The dephasing channel eventually becomes a completely classical channel, for which entanglement cannot increase capacity beyond one bit per channel use. Finally, perhaps the most interesting curve is for the amplitude damping channel. This channel's capacity is convex when its noise parameter is less than $1/2$ and concave when it is greater than $1/2$.

21.6.1   The Quantum Erasure Channel

Recall that the quantum erasure channel acts as follows on an input density operator $\rho_{A'}$:

$$\rho_{A'} \rightarrow (1-\varepsilon)\,\rho_B + \varepsilon|e\rangle\langle e|_B, \tag{21.137}$$

where $\varepsilon \in [0,1]$ is the erasure probability and $|e\rangle_B$ is an erasure state that is orthogonal to the support of the input state ρ.

PROPOSITION 21.6.1   The entanglement-assisted classical capacity of a quantum erasure channel with erasure probability ε is equal to $2\,(1-\varepsilon)\log d_A$, where d_A is the dimension of the input system.

Proof To determine the entanglement-assisted classical capacity of this channel we need to compute its mutual information. So, consider that sending one share of a bipartite state $\phi_{AA'}$ through the channel produces the output

$$\sigma_{AB} \equiv (1 - \varepsilon)\, \phi_{AB} + \varepsilon\phi_A \otimes |e\rangle\langle e|_B. \tag{21.138}$$

We could now attempt to calculate and optimize the quantum mutual information $I(A; B)_\sigma$. However, observe that Bob can apply the following isometry $U_{B \to BX}$ to his state:

$$U_{B \to BX} \equiv \Pi_B \otimes |0\rangle_X + |e\rangle\langle e|_B \otimes |1\rangle_X, \tag{21.139}$$

where Π_B is a projector onto the support of the input state (for qubits, it would be just $|0\rangle\langle 0| + |1\rangle\langle 1|$). Applying this isometry leads to a state σ_{ABX} where

$$\sigma_{ABX} \equiv U_{B \to BX}\sigma_{AB}U_{B \to BX}^\dagger \tag{21.140}$$

$$= (1 - \varepsilon)\, \phi_{AB} \otimes |0\rangle\langle 0|_X + \varepsilon\phi_A \otimes |e\rangle\langle e|_B \otimes |1\rangle\langle 1|_X. \tag{21.141}$$

The quantum mutual information $I(A; BX)_\sigma$ is equal to $I(A; B)_\sigma$ because entropies do not change under the isometry $U_{B \to BX}$. We now calculate $I(A; BX)_\sigma$:

$$I(A; BX)_\sigma = H(A)_\sigma + H(BX)_\sigma - H(ABX)_\sigma \tag{21.142}$$

$$= H(A)_\phi + H(B|X)_\sigma - H(AB|X)_\sigma \tag{21.143}$$

$$= H(A)_\phi + (1 - \varepsilon)\,[H(B)_\phi - H(AB)_\phi]$$
$$\quad + \varepsilon\,[H(B)_{|e\rangle\langle e|} - H(AB)_{\phi_A \otimes |e\rangle\langle e|}] \tag{21.144}$$

$$= H(A)_\phi + (1 - \varepsilon)\,H(B)_\phi - \varepsilon\,[H(A)_\phi + H(B)_{|e\rangle}] \tag{21.145}$$

$$= (1 - \varepsilon)\,[H(A)_\phi + H(B)_\phi] \tag{21.146}$$

$$= 2\,(1 - \varepsilon)\,H(A)_\phi \tag{21.147}$$

$$\leq 2\,(1 - \varepsilon)\log d_A. \tag{21.148}$$

The first equality follows by the definition of quantum mutual information. The second equality follows from $\phi_A = \mathrm{Tr}_{BX}\{\sigma_{ABX}\}$, from the chain rule of entropy, and by canceling $H(X)$ on both sides. The third equality follows because the X register is a classical register, indicating whether the erasure occurs. The fourth equality follows because $H(AB)_\phi = 0$, $H(B)_{|e\rangle\langle e|} = 0$, and $H(AB)_{\phi_A \otimes |e\rangle\langle e|} = H(A)_\phi + H(B)_{|e\rangle\langle e|}$. The fifth equality follows again because $H(B)_{|e\rangle\langle e|} = 0$ and by collecting terms. The final equality follows because $H(A)_\phi = H(B)_\phi$ (ϕ_{AB} is a pure bipartite state). The final inequality follows because the entropy of a state on system A is never greater than the logarithm of the dimension of A. We can conclude that the maximally entangled state $\Phi_{AA'}$ achieves the entanglement-assisted classical capacity of the quantum erasure channel because $H(A)_\Phi = \log d_A$. $\qquad\square$

The strategy for achieving the entanglement-assisted classical capacity of the quantum erasure channel is straightforward. Alice and Bob simply employ a super-dense coding strategy on all of the channel uses (this means that

Bob performs measurements on each channel output with his share of the entanglement—there is no need for a large, collective measurement on all of the channel outputs). For a good fraction $1 - \varepsilon$ of the time, this strategy works and Alice can communicate $2 \log d_A$ bits to Bob. For the other fraction ε, all is lost to the environment. In order for this to work, Alice and Bob need to make use of a feedback channel from Bob to Alice so that Bob can report which messages come through and which do not, but Corollary 21.5.1 states that this feedback cannot improve the capacity. Thus, the rate of communication they can achieve is equal to the capacity $2(1 - \varepsilon) \log d_A$.

21.6.2 The Amplitude Damping Channel

We now compute the entanglement-assisted classical capacity of the amplitude damping channel $\mathcal{N}_{AD}$. Recall that this channel acts as follows on an input qubit in state ρ:

$$\mathcal{N}_{AD}(\rho) = A_0 \rho A_0^\dagger + A_1 \rho A_1^\dagger, \tag{21.149}$$

where, for $\gamma \in [0, 1]$,

$$A_0 \equiv |0\rangle\langle 0| + \sqrt{1 - \gamma}|1\rangle\langle 1|, \qquad A_1 \equiv \sqrt{\gamma}|0\rangle\langle 1|. \tag{21.150}$$

PROPOSITION 21.6.2 *The entanglement-assisted classical capacity of an amplitude damping channel with damping parameter $\gamma \in [0, 1]$ is equal to*

$$I(\mathcal{N}_{AD}) = \max_{p \in [0,1]} h_2(p) + h_2((1 - \gamma)p) - h_2(\gamma p), \tag{21.151}$$

where $h_2(x) \equiv -x \log x - (1 - x) \log(1 - x)$ is the binary entropy function.

Proof Suppose that a matrix representation of the input qubit density operator ρ in the computational basis is

$$\rho = \begin{bmatrix} 1 - p & \eta^* \\ \eta & p \end{bmatrix}. \tag{21.152}$$

One can readily verify that the density operator for Bob has the following matrix representation:

$$\mathcal{N}_{AD}(\rho) = \begin{bmatrix} 1 - (1 - \gamma)p & \sqrt{1 - \gamma}\eta^* \\ \sqrt{1 - \gamma}\eta & (1 - \gamma)p \end{bmatrix}, \tag{21.153}$$

and by calculating the elements $\mathrm{Tr}\{A_i \rho A_j^\dagger\}|i\rangle\langle j|$, we can obtain a matrix representation for Eve's density operator:

$$\mathcal{N}_{AD}^c(\rho) = \begin{bmatrix} 1 - \gamma p & \sqrt{\gamma}\eta^* \\ \sqrt{\gamma}\eta & \gamma p \end{bmatrix}, \tag{21.154}$$

where $\mathcal{N}_{AD}^c$ is the complementary channel to Eve. By comparing (21.153) and (21.154), we can see that the channel to Eve is an amplitude damping channel with damping parameter $1 - \gamma$. The entanglement-assisted classical capacity of $\mathcal{N}_{\mathrm{AD}}$ is equal to its mutual information:

$$I(\mathcal{N}_{\mathrm{AD}}) = \max_{\phi_{AA'}} I(A; B)_\sigma, \tag{21.155}$$

where $\phi_{AA'}$ is some pure bipartite input state and $\sigma_{AB} = \mathcal{N}_{\mathrm{AD}}(\phi_{AA'})$. We need to determine the input density operator that maximizes the above formula as a function of γ. As it stands now, the optimization depends on three parameters: p, $\mathrm{Re}\{\eta\}$, and $\mathrm{Im}\{\eta\}$. We can show that it is sufficient to consider an optimization over only p with $\eta = 0$. The formula in (21.155) also has the following form:

$$I(\mathcal{N}_{\mathrm{AD}}) = \max_\rho \left[H(\rho) + H(\mathcal{N}_{\mathrm{AD}}(\rho)) - H(\mathcal{N}^c_{\mathrm{AD}}(\rho)) \right], \tag{21.156}$$

because

$$I(A; B)_\sigma = H(A)_\phi + H(B)_\sigma - H(AB)_\sigma \tag{21.157}$$

$$= H(A')_\phi + H(\mathcal{N}_{\mathrm{AD}}(\rho)) - H(E)_\sigma \tag{21.158}$$

$$= H(\rho) + H(\mathcal{N}_{\mathrm{AD}}(\rho)) - H(\mathcal{N}^c_{\mathrm{AD}}(\rho)) \tag{21.159}$$

$$\equiv I_{\mathrm{mut}}(\rho, \mathcal{N}_{\mathrm{AD}}). \tag{21.160}$$

The three entropies in (21.156) depend only on the eigenvalues of the three density operators in (21.152)–(21.154), respectively, which are as follows:

$$\frac{1}{2}\left(1 \pm \sqrt{(1-2p)^2 + 4\,|\eta|^2} \right), \tag{21.161}$$

$$\frac{1}{2}\left(1 \pm \sqrt{(1-2(1-\gamma)\,p)^2 + 4\,|\eta|^2\,(1-\gamma)} \right), \tag{21.162}$$

$$\frac{1}{2}\left(1 \pm \sqrt{(1-2\gamma p)^2 + 4\,|\eta|^2\,\gamma} \right). \tag{21.163}$$

The above eigenvalues are in the order of Alice, Bob, and Eve. All of the above eigenvalues have a similar form, and their dependence on η is only through its magnitude. Thus, it suffices to consider $\eta \in \mathbb{R}$ (this eliminates one parameter). Next, the eigenvalues do not change if we flip the sign of η (this is equivalent to rotating the original state ρ by Z, to $Z\rho Z$), and thus, the mutual information does not change as well:

$$I_{\mathrm{mut}}(\rho, \mathcal{N}_{\mathrm{AD}}) = I_{\mathrm{mut}}(Z\rho Z, \mathcal{N}_{\mathrm{AD}}). \tag{21.164}$$

By the above relation and concavity of quantum mutual information in the input density operator (Theorem 13.4.2), the following inequality holds:

$$I_{\mathrm{mut}}(\rho, \mathcal{N}_{\mathrm{AD}}) = \frac{1}{2}\left[I_{\mathrm{mut}}(\rho, \mathcal{N}_{\mathrm{AD}}) + I_{\mathrm{mut}}(Z\rho Z, \mathcal{N}_{\mathrm{AD}}) \right] \tag{21.165}$$

$$\leq I_{\mathrm{mut}}((\rho + Z\rho Z)/2, \mathcal{N}_{\mathrm{AD}}) \tag{21.166}$$

$$= I_{\mathrm{mut}}(\overline{\Delta}(\rho), \mathcal{N}_{\mathrm{AD}}), \tag{21.167}$$

where $\overline{\Delta}$ is a completely dephasing channel in the computational basis. This demonstrates that it is sufficient to consider diagonal density operators ρ when optimizing the quantum mutual information. Thus, the eigenvalues in (21.161)–(21.163) respectively become

$$\{p, 1-p\}, \tag{21.168}$$

$$\{(1-\gamma)\,p, 1-(1-\gamma)\,p\}, \tag{21.169}$$

$$\{\gamma p, 1-\gamma p\}, \tag{21.170}$$

giving our final expression in the statement of the proposition. $\qquad\square$

EXERCISE 21.6.1 Consider the qubit depolarizing channel: $\rho \to (1-p)\rho + p\pi$. Prove that its entanglement-assisted classical capacity is equal to

$$2 + (1 - 3p/4)\log(1 - 3p/4) + (3p/4)\log(p/4). \tag{21.171}$$

EXERCISE 21.6.2 Consider the dephasing channel: $\rho \to (1-p/2)\,\rho + (p/2)Z\rho Z$. Prove that its entanglement-assisted classical capacity is equal to $2 - h_2(p/2)$, where p is the dephasing parameter.

21.7 Concluding Remarks

Shared entanglement has the desirable property of simplifying quantum Shannon theory. The entanglement-assisted capacity theorem is one of the strongest known results in quantum Shannon theory because it states that the quantum mutual information of a channel is equal to its entanglement-assisted capacity. This function of the channel is concave in the input state and the set of input states is convex, implying that finding a local maximum is equivalent to finding a global one. The converse theorem and additivity of the channel mutual information demonstrates that there is no need to take the regularization of the formula. Furthermore, quantum feedback does not improve this capacity, just as it does not for the classical case of Shannon's setting. In these senses, the entanglement-assisted classical capacity is the most natural generalization of Shannon's capacity formula to the quantum setting.

The direct coding part of the capacity theorem exploits a strategy similar to super-dense coding—effectively the technique is to perform super-dense coding in the type class subspaces of many copies of a shared entangled state. This strategy is *equivalent* to super-dense coding if the initial shared state is a maximally entangled state. The particular protocol that we outlined in this chapter has the appealing feature that we can easily make it coherent, similar to the way that coherent dense coding is a coherent version of the super-dense coding protocol. We take this approach in the next chapter and show that we can produce a whole host of other protocols using this technique, eventually leading to a proof of the direct coding part of the quantum capacity theorem.

This chapter features the calculation of the entanglement-assisted classical capacity of certain channels of practical interest: the depolarizing channel, the dephasing channel, the amplitude damping channel, and the erasure channel.

Each one of these channels has a single parameter that governs its noisiness and the capacity in each case is a straightforward function of this parameter. One could carry out a similar type of analysis to determine the entanglement-assisted capacity of any channel, although it generally will be necessary to employ techniques from convex optimization.

Unfortunately, quantum Shannon theory only gets more complicated from here onward.[2] For the other capacity theorems that we will study, such as the private classical capacity or the quantum capacity, the best expressions that we have for them are good only up to regularization of the formulas. In certain cases, these formulas completely characterize the capabilities of the channel for these particular operational tasks, but these formulas are not particularly useful in the general case. One important goal for future research in quantum Shannon theory would be to improve upon these formulas, in the hopes that we could further our understanding of the best strategy for achieving the information-processing tasks corresponding to these other capacity questions.

21.8   History and Further Reading

Adami & Cerf (1997) figured that the mutual information of a quantum channel would play an important role in quantum Shannon theory, and they proved several of its most important properties. Bennett et al. (1999) and Bennett et al. (2002) later demonstrated that the quantum mutual information of a channel has an operational interpretation as its entanglement-assisted classical capacity. Our proof of the direct part of the entanglement-assisted classical capacity theorem is the same as that in Hsieh, Devetak & Winter (2008). We exploit this approach because it leads to all of the results in the next chapter, implying that this protocol is sufficient to generate all of the known protocols in quantum Shannon theory (with the exception of private classical communication). Giovannetti & Fazio (2005) determined several capacities of the amplitude damping channel, and Wolf & Pérez-García (2007) made some further observations regarding it. Bowen (2004) proved that the classical capacity of a channel assisted by unbounded quantum feedback is equal to its entanglement-assisted classical capacity.

There has also been work on the strong converse and second-order characterization for entanglement-assisted capacity (see Section 20.7 for a discussion of these terms). Bennett et al. (2014) proved the quantum reverse Shannon theorem, which quantifies the rate of classical communication needed to simulate a quantum channel in the presence of unlimited entanglement shared between sender and receiver. Berta et al. (2011) provided an alternate proof of the quantum reverse Shannon theorem. By a simulation argument, the quantum reverse Shannon theorem implies a strong converse for entanglement-assisted capacity

---

[2] We could also view this "unfortunate" situation as being fortunate for conducting open-ended research in quantum Shannon theory.

(Bennett et al., 2014). Gupta & Wilde (2015) gave a direct proof for the strong converse by making use of Rényi entropies. Cooney et al. (2014) later showed that the same strong converse bound still holds in the presence of a quantum feedback channel, strengthening the result of Bowen (2004). Datta et al. (2014) established a second-order achievability result for entanglement-assisted classical communication and proved that this characterization is tight for some channels, by making use of prior results of Matthews & Wehner (2014).

22 Coherent Communication with Noisy Resources

This chapter demonstrates the power of both coherent communication from Chapter 7 and the particular protocol for entanglement-assisted classical coding from the previous chapter. Recall that coherent dense coding is a version of the dense coding protocol in which the sender and receiver perform all of its steps coherently.[1] Since our protocol for entanglement-assisted classical coding from the previous chapter is really just a glorified dense coding protocol, the sender and receiver can perform each of its steps coherently, generating a protocol for entanglement-assisted coherent coding. Then, by exploiting the fact that two coherent bits are equivalent to a qubit and an ebit, we obtain a protocol for entanglement-assisted quantum coding that consumes far less entanglement than a naive strategy would in order to accomplish this task. We next combine this entanglement-assisted quantum coding protocol with entanglement distribution (Section 6.2.1) and obtain a protocol for quantum communication at a rate equal to the channel's coherent information (Section 13.5). This sequence of steps demonstrates an alternate proof of the direct part of the quantum capacity theorem stated in Chapter 24.

Entanglement-assisted classical communication is one generalization of super-dense coding, in which the noiseless qubit channel becomes an arbitrary noisy quantum channel while the noiseless ebits remain noiseless. Another generalization of super-dense coding is a protocol named *noisy super-dense coding*, in which the shared entanglement becomes a shared noisy state ρ_{AB} and the noiseless qubit channels remain noiseless. Interestingly, the protocol that we employ in this chapter for noisy super-dense coding is essentially equivalent to the protocol from the previous chapter for entanglement-assisted classical communication, with some slight modifications to account for the different setting. We can also construct a coherent version of noisy super-dense coding, leading to a protocol that we name *coherent state transfer*. Coherent state transfer accomplishes not only the task of generating coherent communication between Alice and Bob, but it also allows Alice to transfer her share of the state ρ_{AB} to Bob. By combining coherent state transfer with both the coherent communication identity and teleportation, we

---

[1] Performing a protocol coherently means that we replace conditional unitaries with controlled unitaries and measurements with controlled gates (e.g., compare Figures 6.2 and 7.3).

obtain protocols for quantum-assisted state transfer and classical-assisted state transfer, respectively. The latter protocol gives an operational interpretation to the conditional quantum entropy $H(A|B)_\rho$—if it is positive, then the protocol consumes entanglement at the rate $H(A|B)_\rho$, and if it is negative, the protocol generates entanglement at the rate $|H(A|B)_\rho|$.

The final part of this chapter shows that our particular protocol for entanglement-assisted classical communication is even more powerful than suggested in the first paragraph. It allows for a sender to communicate both coherent bits and incoherent classical bits to a receiver, and they can trade off these two resources against one another. The structure of the entanglement-assisted protocol allows for this possibility, by taking advantage of Remark 21.4.1 and by combining it with the HSW classical communication protocol from Chapter 20. Then, by exploiting the coherent communication identity, we obtain a protocol for entanglement-assisted communication of classical and quantum information. Chapter 25 demonstrates that this protocol, teleportation, super-dense coding, and entanglement distribution are sufficient to accomplish any task in dynamic quantum Shannon theory involving the three unit resources of classical bits, qubits, and ebits. These four protocols give a three-dimensional achievable rate region that is the best known characterization for any information-processing task that a sender and receiver would like to accomplish using a quantum channel and the three unit resources. Chapter 25 discusses this triple trade-off scenario in full detail.

22.1 Entanglement-Assisted Quantum Communication

The entanglement-assisted classical capacity theorem states that the quantum mutual information of a channel is equal to its capacity for transmitting classical information with the help of shared entanglement, and the direct coding theorem from Section 21.4 provides a protocol that achieves the capacity. We were not much concerned with the rate at which this protocol consumes entanglement, but a direct calculation reveals that it consumes $H(A)_\varphi$ ebits per channel use, where $|\varphi\rangle_{AB}$ is the bipartite state that they share before the protocol begins. This result follows because they can concentrate n copies of the state $|\varphi\rangle_{AB}$ to $\approx nH(A)_\varphi$ ebits, as we learned in Chapter 19. Also, they can "dilute" $nH(A)_\varphi$ ebits to $\approx n$ copies of $|\varphi\rangle_{AB}$ with the help of a sublinear amount of classical communication that does not factor into the resource count, as also discussed in Chapter 19.

Suppose now that Alice is interested in exploiting the channel and shared entanglement in order to transmit quantum information to Bob. There is a simple (and, as we will see, naive) way that we can convert the protocol in Section 21.4 to one that transmits quantum information: they can just combine it with teleportation. This naive strategy requires consuming ebits at an additional rate of $\frac{1}{2}I(A;B)_\rho$ in order to have enough entanglement to combine with teleporta-tion, where $\rho_{AB} \equiv \mathcal{N}_{A'\to B}(\varphi_{AA'})$. To see this, consider the following resource inequalities:

$$\langle \mathcal{N} \rangle + \left(H(A)_\rho + \frac{1}{2}I(A;B)_\rho \right) [qq] \geq I(A;B)_\rho [c \to c] + \frac{1}{2}I(A;B)_\rho [qq] \quad (22.1)$$

$$\geq \frac{1}{2}I(A;B)_\rho [q \to q]. \quad (22.2)$$

The first inequality follows by having them exploit the channel and the $nH(A)_\rho$ ebits to generate classical communication at a rate $I(A;B)_\rho$ (while doing nothing with the extra $n\frac{1}{2}I(A;B)_\rho$ ebits). Alice then exploits the ebits and the clas-sical communication in a teleportation protocol to send $n\frac{1}{2}I(A;B)_\rho$ qubits to Bob. This rate of quantum communication is provably optimal—were it not so, it would be possible to combine the protocol in (22.1)–(22.2) with super-dense coding and beat the optimal rate for classical communication given by the entanglement-assisted classical capacity theorem.

Although the above protocol achieves the entanglement-assisted quantum capacity, we are left thinking that the entanglement consumption rate of $H(A)_\rho + \frac{1}{2}I(A;B)_\rho$ ebits per channel use might be a bit more than necessary because teleportation and super-dense coding are not dual under resource rever-sal. That is, if we combine the protocol with super-dense coding and teleportation *ad infinitum*, then it consumes an infinite amount of entanglement. In practice, this "back and forth" with teleportation and super-dense coding would be a poor way to consume the precious resource of entanglement.

How might we make more judicious use of shared entanglement? Recall that coherent communication from Chapter 7 was helpful for doing so, at least in the noiseless case. A sender and receiver can combine coherent teleportation and coherent dense coding *ad infinitum* without any net loss in entanglement, essentially because these two protocols are dual under resource reversal. The following theorem shows how we can upgrade the protocol in Section 21.4 to one that generates coherent communication instead of just classical communication. The resulting protocol is one way to have a version of coherent dense coding in which one noiseless resource is replaced by a noisy one.

THEOREM 22.1.1 (Entanglement-Assisted Coherent Communication) The following resource inequality corresponds to an achievable protocol for entanglement-assisted coherent communication over a quantum channel $\mathcal{N}_{A'\to B}$:

$$\langle \mathcal{N} \rangle + H(A)_\rho [qq] \geq I(A;B)_\rho [q \to qq], \quad (22.3)$$

where $\rho_{AB} \equiv \mathcal{N}_{A'\to B}(\varphi_{AA'})$.

Proof Suppose that Alice and Bob share many copies of some pure, bipartite entangled state $|\varphi\rangle_{AB}$. Consider the code from the direct coding theorem in Section 21.4. We can say that it is a set of $D^2 \approx 2^{nI(A;B)_\rho}$ unitaries $U(s(m))$, from which Alice can select, and she applies a particular unitary $U(s(m))$ to her share A^n of the entanglement in order to encode message m. Also, Bob has a detection POVM $\{\Lambda^m_{B'^n B^n}\}$ acting on his share of the entanglement and the channel outputs that he can exploit to detect message m. Just as we were able to construct a coherent super-dense coding protocol in Chapter 7 by performing all the steps in dense coding coherently, we can do so for the entanglement-assisted classical coding protocol in Section 21.4. We track the steps in such a protocol. Suppose Alice shares a state with a reference system R to which she does not have access:

$$|\psi\rangle_{RA_1} \equiv \sum_{l,m=1}^{D^2} \alpha_{l,m} |l\rangle_R |m\rangle_{A_1}, \tag{22.4}$$

where $\{|l\rangle\}$ and $\{|m\rangle\}$ are some orthonormal bases for R and A_1, respectively. We say that Alice and Bob have implemented a coherent channel if they execute the map $|m\rangle_{A_1} \to |m\rangle_{A_1} |m\rangle_{B_1}$, which transforms the above state to

$$\sum_{l,m=1}^{D^2} \alpha_{l,m} |l\rangle_R |m\rangle_{A_1} |m\rangle_{B_1}. \tag{22.5}$$

We say that they have implemented a coherent channel *approximately* if the state resulting from the protocol is ε-close in trace distance to the above state. If we can show that $\varepsilon \in (0,1)$ approaches zero in the limit of many channel uses, then the simulation of an approximate coherent channel becomes perfect in the asymptotic limit. Alice's first step is to append her shares of the entangled state $|\varphi\rangle_{A^n B^n}$ to $|\psi\rangle_{RA_1}$ and apply the following controlled unitary from her system A_1 to her system A^n:

$$\sum_m |m\rangle\langle m|_{A_1} \otimes U_{A^n}(s(m)). \tag{22.6}$$

The resulting global state is as follows:

$$\sum_{l,m} \alpha_{l,m} |l\rangle_R |m\rangle_{A_1} U_{A^n}(s(m))|\varphi\rangle_{A^n B^n}. \tag{22.7}$$

By the structure of the unitaries $U(s(m))$ (see (21.38) and (21.40)), the above state is equivalent to the following one:

$$\sum_{l,m} \alpha_{l,m} |l\rangle_R |m\rangle_{A_1} U^T_{B^n}(s(m))|\varphi\rangle_{A^n B^n}. \tag{22.8}$$

Interestingly, observe that Alice applying the controlled gate in (22.6) is the same as her applying the non-local controlled gate $\sum_m |m\rangle\langle m|_{A_1} \otimes U^T_{B^n}(s(m))$, due to the non-local (and perhaps spooky!) properties of the entangled state $|\varphi\rangle_{A^n B^n}$. Alice then sends her systems A^n through many uses of the quantum channel $\mathcal{N}_{A \to B'}$, whose isometric extension is $U^{\mathcal{N}}_{A \to B'E}$. Let $|\varphi\rangle_{B'^n E^n B^n}$ denote the state resulting from n instances of the isometric extension $U^{\mathcal{N}}_{A \to B'E}$ of the channel acting on the state $|\varphi\rangle_{A^n B^n}$:

$$|\varphi\rangle_{B'^n E^n B^n} \equiv U^{\mathcal{N}}_{A^n \to B'^n E^n} |\varphi\rangle_{A^n B^n}, \tag{22.9}$$

where $U^{\mathcal{N}}_{A^n \to B'^n E^n} \equiv (U^{\mathcal{N}}_{A \to B'E})^{\otimes n}$. After Alice transmits through the isometric extension, the state becomes

$$\sum_{l,m} \alpha_{l,m} |l\rangle_R |m\rangle_{A_1} U^T_{B^n}(s(m))|\varphi\rangle_{B'^n E^n B^n}, \qquad (22.10)$$

where Bob now holds his shares B^n of the entanglement and the channel outputs B'^n. (Observe that the action of the controlled unitary in (22.6) commutes with the action of the channel.) Rather than perform an incoherent measurement with the POVM $\{\Lambda^m_{B'^n B^n}\}$, Bob applies a coherent gentle measurement (see Section 5.4), an isometry of the following form:

$$\sum_m \sqrt{\Lambda^m_{B'^n B^n}} \otimes |m\rangle_{B_1}. \qquad (22.11)$$

Using the result of Exercise 5.4.1, we can readily check that the resulting state is $2\sqrt{2\varepsilon}$-close in trace distance to the following state:

$$\sum_{l,m} \alpha_{l,m} |l\rangle_R |m\rangle_{A_1} U^T_{B^n}(s(m))|\varphi\rangle_{B'^n E^n B^n} |m\rangle_{B_1}. \qquad (22.12)$$

Thus, for the rest of the protocol, we pretend that they are acting on the above state. Alice and Bob would like to coherently remove the coupling of their index m to the environment, so Bob performs the following controlled unitary:

$$\sum_m |m\rangle\langle m|_{B_1} \otimes U^*_{B^n}(s(m)), \qquad (22.13)$$

and the final state is

$$\sum_{l,m=1}^{D^2} \alpha_{l,m} |l\rangle_R |m\rangle_{A_1} |\varphi\rangle_{B'^n E^n B^n} |m\rangle_{B_1}$$

$$= \left(\sum_{l,m=1}^{D^2} \alpha_{l,m} |l\rangle_R |m\rangle_{A_1} |m\rangle_{B_1} \right) \otimes |\varphi\rangle_{B'^n E^n B^n}. \qquad (22.14)$$

Thus, this protocol implements a D^2-dimensional coherent channel up to an arbitrarily small error, which implies that the resource inequality in the statement of the theorem holds. Figure 22.1 depicts the entanglement-assisted coherent coding protocol. □

It is now a straightforward task to convert the protocol from Theorem 22.1.1 into one for entanglement-assisted quantum communication, by exploiting the coherent communication identity from Section 7.5.

COROLLARY 22.1.1 (Entanglement-Assisted Quantum Communication) The following resource inequality corresponds to an achievable protocol for entanglement-assisted quantum communication over a quantum channel $\mathcal{N}_{A' \to B}$:

$$\langle \mathcal{N} \rangle + \frac{1}{2} I(A; E)_\varphi [qq] \geq \frac{1}{2} I(A; B)_\varphi [q \to q], \qquad (22.15)$$

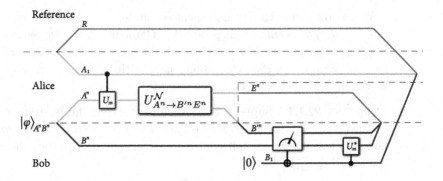

Figure 22.1 The protocol for entanglement-assisted coherent communication. Observe that it is the coherent version of the protocol for entanglement-assisted classical communication, just as coherent dense coding is the coherent version of super-dense coding (compare this figure and Figure 21.3 with Figures 6.2 and 7.3). Instead of applying conditional unitaries, Alice applies a controlled unitary from her system A_1 to her share of the entanglement and sends the encoded state through many uses of the noisy channel. Rather than performing a POVM, Bob performs a coherent gentle measurement from his systems B'^n and B^n to an ancilla B_1. Finally, he applies a similar controlled unitary in order to decouple the environment from the state of his ancilla B_1.

where $|\varphi\rangle_{ABE} \equiv U^{\mathcal{N}}_{A' \to BE}|\varphi\rangle_{AA'}$ and $U^{\mathcal{N}}_{A' \to BE}$ is an isometric extension of the channel $\mathcal{N}_{A' \to B}$.

Proof Consider the coherent communication identity from Section 7.5. This identity states that a D^2-dimensional coherent channel can perfectly simulate a D-dimensional quantum channel and a maximally entangled state $|\Phi\rangle_{AB}$ with Schmidt rank D. In terms of cobits, qubits, and ebits, the coherent communication identity is the following resource equality for D-dimensional systems:

$$2 \log D\, [q \to qq] = \log D\, [q \to q] + \log D\, [qq]. \tag{22.16}$$

Consider the following chain of resource inequalities:

$$\langle \mathcal{N} \rangle + H(A)_\varphi\, [qq] \geq I(A;B)_\varphi\, [q \to qq] \tag{22.17}$$

$$\geq \frac{1}{2} I(A;B)_\varphi\, [q \to q] + \frac{1}{2} I(A;B)_\varphi\, [qq]. \tag{22.18}$$

The first resource inequality is the statement of Theorem 22.1.1, and the second resource inequality follows from an application of coherent teleportation. If we then allow for catalytic protocols, in which we allow for some use of a resource with the demand that it be returned at the end of the protocol, we have a protocol for entanglement-assisted quantum communication:

$$\langle \mathcal{N} \rangle + \frac{1}{2} I(A;E)_\varphi\, [qq] \geq \frac{1}{2} I(A;B)_\varphi\, [q \to q], \tag{22.19}$$

because $H(A)_\varphi - \frac{1}{2} I(A;B)_\varphi = \frac{1}{2} I(A;E)_\varphi$ (see Exercise 11.6.6). $\qquad\square$

When comparing the entanglement consumption rate of the naive protocol in (22.1)–(22.2) with that of the protocol in Corollary 22.1.1, we see that the former requires an additional $I(A;B)_\rho$ ebits per channel use. Also, Corollary 22.1.1 leads to a simple proof of the achievability part of the quantum capacity theorem, as we see in the next section.

EXERCISE 22.1.1   Suppose that Alice can obtain the environment E of the channel $U^{\mathcal{N}}_{A'\to BE}$. Such a channel is known as a *coherent feedback isometry*. Show how they can achieve the following resource inequality with the coherent feedback isometry $U^{\mathcal{N}}_{A'\to BE}$:

$$\langle U^{\mathcal{N}}_{A'\to BE}\rangle \geq \frac{1}{2}I(A;B)_\varphi\,[q\to q] + \frac{1}{2}I(E;B)_\varphi\,[qq]\,, \qquad (22.20)$$

where $|\varphi\rangle_{ABE} = U^{\mathcal{N}}_{A'\to BE}|\varphi\rangle_{AA'}$ and $\rho_{A'} = \text{Tr}_A\{\varphi_{AA'}\}$. This protocol is a generalization of coherent teleportation from Section 7.4 because it reduces to coherent teleportation in the case that $U^{\mathcal{N}}_{A'\to BE}$ is equivalent to two coherent channels.

22.2   Quantum Communication

We can obtain a protocol for quantum communication simply by combining the protocol from Theorem 22.1.1 further with entanglement distribution. The resulting protocol again makes catalytic use of entanglement, in the sense that it exploits some amount of entanglement shared between Alice and Bob at the beginning of the protocol, but it generates the same amount of entanglement at the end, so that the net entanglement consumption rate of the protocol is zero. The resulting rate of quantum communication turns out to be the same as we find for the quantum channel coding theorem in Chapter 24 (though the protocol given there does not make catalytic use of shared entanglement).

COROLLARY 22.2.1 (Quantum Communication)   The coherent information $Q(\mathcal{N})$ is an achievable rate for quantum communication over a quantum channel $\mathcal{N}$. That is, the following resource inequality holds:

$$\langle \mathcal{N}\rangle \geq Q(\mathcal{N})\,[q\to q]\,, \qquad (22.21)$$

where $Q(\mathcal{N}) \equiv \max_\varphi I(A\rangle B)_\rho$ and $\rho_{AB} \equiv \mathcal{N}_{A'\to B}(\varphi_{AA'})$.

Proof   If we further combine the entanglement-assisted quantum communication protocol from Theorem 22.1.1 with entanglement distribution at a rate $\frac{1}{2}I(A;E)_\rho$, we obtain the following resource inequalities:

$$\langle \mathcal{N}\rangle + \frac{1}{2}I(A;E)_\rho\,[qq]$$

$$\geq \frac{1}{2}\left[I(A;B)_\rho - I(A;E)_\rho\right][q\to q] + \frac{1}{2}I(A;E)_\rho\,[q\to q] \qquad (22.22)$$

$$\geq \frac{1}{2}\left[I(A;B)_\rho - I(A;E)_\rho\right][q\to q] + \frac{1}{2}I(A;E)_\rho\,[qq]\,, \qquad (22.23)$$

which after resource cancelation, becomes

$$\langle \mathcal{N} \rangle \geq I(A \rangle B)_\rho \, [q \to q], \tag{22.24}$$

because $I(A \rangle B)_\rho = \frac{1}{2} [I(A; B)_\rho - I(A; E)_\rho]$ (see Exercise 11.6.6). They can achieve the coherent information of the channel simply by generating codes from the state $\varphi_{AA'}$ that maximizes the channel's coherent information. $\quad\square$

22.3 Noisy Super-Dense Coding

Recall that the resource inequality for super-dense coding is

$$[q \to q] + [qq] \geq 2 \, [c \to c]. \tag{22.25}$$

The entanglement-assisted classical communication protocol from the previous chapter is one way to generalize this protocol to a noisy setting, simply by replacing the noiseless qubit channels in (22.25) with many uses of a noisy quantum channel. This replacement leads to the setting of entanglement-assisted classical communication presented in the previous chapter.

Another way to generalize super-dense coding is to let the entanglement be noisy while keeping the quantum channels noiseless. We allow Alice and Bob access to many copies of some shared noisy state ρ_{AB} and to many uses of a noiseless qubit channel with the goal of generating noiseless classical communication. One might expect the resulting protocol to be similar to that for entanglement-assisted classical communication, and this is indeed the case. The resulting protocol is known as *noisy super-dense coding*:

THEOREM 22.3.1 (Noisy Super-Dense Coding) The following resource inequality corresponds to an achievable protocol for quantum-assisted classical communication with a shared quantum state:

$$\langle \rho_{AB} \rangle + H(A)_\rho \, [q \to q] \geq I(A; B)_\rho \, [c \to c], \tag{22.26}$$

where ρ_{AB} is some bipartite state that Alice and Bob share at the beginning of the protocol.

Proof The proof of the existence of a protocol proceeds similarly to the proof of Theorem 21.4.1, with a few modifications to account for our different setting here. We simply need to establish a way for Alice and Bob to select a code randomly, and then we can invoke the packing lemma (Lemma 16.3.1) to establish the existence of a detection POVM that Bob can employ to detect Alice's messages. The method by which they select a random code is exactly the same as they do in the proof of Theorem 21.4.1, and for this reason, we only highlight the key aspects of the proof. First consider the state ρ_{AB}, and suppose that $|\varphi\rangle_{ABR}$ is a purification of this state, with R a reference system to which Alice and Bob do not have access. We can say that the state $|\varphi\rangle_{ABR}$ arises from some isometry $U^{\mathcal{N}}_{A' \to BR}$ acting on system A' of a pure state $|\varphi\rangle_{AA'}$, so that $|\varphi\rangle_{AA'}$ is defined by

$|\varphi\rangle_{ABR} = U^{\mathcal{N}}_{A' \to BR} |\varphi\rangle_{AA'}$. We can also then think that the state ρ_{AB} arises from sending the state $|\varphi\rangle_{AA'}$ through a channel $\mathcal{N}_{A' \to B}$, obtained by tracing out the environment R of $U^{\mathcal{N}}_{A' \to BR}$. Our setting here is becoming closer to the setting in the proof of Theorem 21.4.1, and we now show how it becomes nearly identical. Observe that the state $|\varphi\rangle^{\otimes n}_{AA'}$ admits a type decomposition, similar to the type decomposition in (21.32)–(21.35):

$$|\varphi\rangle^{\otimes n}_{AA'} = \sum_t \sqrt{p(t)} |\Phi_t\rangle_{A^n A'^n}. \tag{22.27}$$

Similarly, we can write $|\varphi\rangle^{\otimes n}_{ABR}$ as

$$|\varphi\rangle^{\otimes n}_{ABR} = \sum_t \sqrt{p(t)} |\Phi_t\rangle_{A^n | B^n R^n}, \tag{22.28}$$

where the vertical line in $A^n | B^n R^n$ indicates the bipartite cut between systems A^n and $B^n R^n$. Alice can select a unitary $U_{A^n}(s)$ of the form in (21.38) uniformly at random, and the expected density operator with respect to this random choice of unitary is

$$\overline{\rho}_{A^n B^n} \equiv \mathbb{E}_S \left\{ U_{A^n}(S) \rho_{A^n B^n} U^{\dagger}_{A^n}(S) \right\} \tag{22.29}$$

$$= \sum_t p(t) \pi^t_{A^n} \otimes \mathcal{N}_{A'^n \to B^n}(\pi^t_{A'^n}), \tag{22.30}$$

by exploiting the development in (21.75)–(21.84). For each message m that Alice would like to send, she selects a vector s of the form in (21.39) uniformly at random, and we can write $s(m)$ to denote the explicit association of the vector s with the message m after Alice makes the assignment. This leads to quantum-assisted codewords[2] of the following form:

$$U_{A^n}(s(m)) \rho_{A^n B^n} U^{\dagger}_{A^n}(s(m)). \tag{22.31}$$

We would now like to exploit the packing lemma (Lemma 16.3.1), and we require message subspace projectors and a total subspace projector in order to do so. We choose them respectively as

$$U_{A^n}(s) \Pi^{\rho,\delta}_{A^n B^n} U^{\dagger}_{A^n}(s), \tag{22.32}$$

$$\Pi^{\rho,\delta}_{A^n} \otimes \Pi^{\rho,\delta}_{B^n}, \tag{22.33}$$

where $\Pi^{\rho,\delta}_{A^n B^n}$, $\Pi^{\rho,\delta}_{A^n}$, and $\Pi^{\rho,\delta}_{B^n}$ are typical projectors for $\rho_{A^n B^n}$, ρ_{A^n}, and ρ_{B^n}, respectively. The following four conditions for the packing lemma hold, for the same reasons that they hold in (21.61)–(21.64):

$$\mathrm{Tr}\left\{ \left(\Pi^{\rho,\delta}_{A^n} \otimes \Pi^{\rho,\delta}_{B^n} \right) \left(U_{A^n}(s) \rho_{A^n B^n} U^{\dagger}_{A^n}(s) \right) \right\} \geq 1 - \varepsilon, \tag{22.34}$$

$$\mathrm{Tr}\left\{ \left(U_{A^n}(s) \Pi^{\rho,\delta}_{A^n B^n} U^{\dagger}_{A^n}(s) \right) \left(U_{A^n}(s) \rho_{A^n B^n} U^{\dagger}_{A^n}(s) \right) \right\} \geq 1 - \varepsilon, \tag{22.35}$$

---

[2] We say that the codewords are "quantum-assisted" because we will allow the assistance of quantum communication in transmitting them to Bob.

$$\text{Tr}\left\{U_{A^n}(s)\Pi^{\rho,\delta}_{A^n B^n}U^\dagger_{A^n}(s)\right\} \le 2^{n[H(AB)_\rho+c\delta]}, \quad (22.36)$$

$$\left(\Pi^{\rho,\delta}_{A^n} \otimes \Pi^{\rho,\delta}_{B^n}\right)\overline{\rho}_{A^n B^n}\left(\Pi^{\rho,\delta}_{A^n} \otimes \Pi^{\rho,\delta}_{B^n}\right)$$
$$\le 2^{-n[H(A)_\rho+H(B)_\rho-\eta(n,\delta)-c\delta]}\left(\Pi^{\rho,\delta}_{A^n} \otimes \Pi^{\rho,\delta}_{B^n}\right), \quad (22.37)$$

where c is some positive constant and $\eta(n,\delta)$ is a function that approaches zero as $n \to \infty$ and $\delta \to 0$. Let us assume for the moment that Alice simply sends her A^n systems to Bob with many uses of a noiseless qubit channel. It then follows from Corollary 16.5.1 (the derandomized version of the packing lemma) that there exists a code and a POVM $\{\Lambda^m_{A^n B^n}\}$ that can detect the transmitted codewords of the form in (22.31) with arbitrarily low maximal probability of error, as long as the size $|\mathcal{M}|$ of Alice's message set is small enough:

$$p^*_e \equiv \max_m \text{Tr}\left\{(I - \Lambda^m_{A^n B^n})\,U(s(m))_{B^n}\rho_{A^n B^n}U^*_{B^n}(s(m))\right\} \quad (22.38)$$

$$\le 4\left(\varepsilon + 2\sqrt{\varepsilon}\right) + 16 \cdot 2^{-n[H(A)_\rho+H(B)_\rho-\eta(n,\delta)-c\delta]}2^{n[H(AB)_\rho+c\delta]}|\mathcal{M}| \quad (22.39)$$

$$= 4\left(\varepsilon + 2\sqrt{\varepsilon}\right) + 16 \cdot 2^{-n[I(A;B)_\rho-\eta(n,\delta)-2c\delta]}|\mathcal{M}|. \quad (22.40)$$

Thus, we can choose the size of the message set to be $|\mathcal{M}| = 2^{n[I(A;B)-\eta(n,\delta)-3c\delta]}$ so that the rate of classical communication is

$$\frac{1}{n}\log|\mathcal{M}| = I(A;B)_\rho - \eta(n,\delta) - 3c\delta, \quad (22.41)$$

and the bound on the maximal probability of error becomes

$$p^*_e \le 4\left(\varepsilon + 2\sqrt{\varepsilon}\right) + 16 \cdot 2^{-nc\delta}. \quad (22.42)$$

Let $\varepsilon' \in (0,1)$ and $\delta' > 0$. By picking n large enough and δ small enough, we can make $4\left(\varepsilon + 2\sqrt{\varepsilon}\right) + 16 \cdot 2^{-nc\delta} \le \varepsilon'$ and $\eta(n,\delta) + 3c\delta \le \delta'$. Thus, the quantum mutual information $I(A;B)_\rho$, with respect to the state ρ_{AB} is an achievable rate for noisy super-dense coding with ρ.

We now summarize the protocol (with a final modification). Alice and Bob begin with the state $\rho_{A^n B^n}$. Alice first performs a typical subspace measurement of her system A^n. This measurement succeeds with high probability and reduces the size of her system A^n to a subspace with size approximately equal to $nH(A)_\rho$ qubits. If Alice wishes to send message m, she applies the unitary $U_{A^n}(s(m))$ to her share of the state. She then performs a compression isometry from her subspace of A^n to $nH(A)_\rho$ qubits. She transmits her qubits over $nH(A)_\rho$ noiseless qubit channels, and Bob receives them. Bob performs the decompression isometry from the space of $nH(A)_\rho$ noiseless qubits to a space isomorphic to Alice's original systems A^n. He then performs the decoding POVM $\{\Lambda^m_{A^n B^n}\}$ and determines Alice's message m with vanishingly small error probability. *Note:* The only modification to the protocol is the typical subspace measurement at the beginning, and one can readily check that this measurement does not affect any of the conditions in (22.34)–(22.37). Figure 22.2 depicts the protocol. $\square$

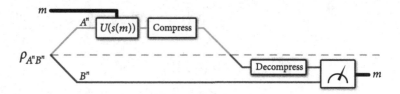

Figure 22.2 The protocol for noisy super-dense coding that corresponds to the resource inequality in Theorem 22.3.1. Alice first projects her share into its typical subspace (not depicted). She then applies a unitary encoding $U(s(m))$, based on her message m, to her share of the state $\rho_{A^n B^n}$. She compresses her state to approximately $nH(A)_\rho$ qubits and transmits these qubits over noiseless qubit channels. Bob decompresses the state and performs a decoding POVM that gives Alice's message m with high probability.

22.4   State Transfer

We can also construct a coherent version of the noisy super-dense coding protocol, in a manner similar to the way in which the proof of Theorem 22.1.1 constructs a coherent version of entanglement-assisted classical communication. However, the coherent version of noisy super-dense coding achieves an additional task: the transfer of Alice's share of the state $\rho_{AB}^{\otimes n}$ to Bob. The resulting protocol is known as coherent state transfer, and from this protocol, we can derive a protocol for quantum-communication-assisted state transfer, or quantum-assisted state transfer[3] for short.

THEOREM 22.4.1 (Coherent State Transfer)   The following resource inequality corresponds to an achievable protocol for coherent state transfer using a state ρ_{AB}:

$$\langle W_{S \to AB} : \rho_S \rangle + H(A)_\rho \, [q \to q] \geq I(A;B)_\rho \, [q \to qq] + \langle \mathrm{id}_{S \to \hat{B}B} : \rho_S \rangle, \quad (22.43)$$

where ρ_{AB} is a bipartite state that Alice and Bob share at the beginning of the protocol.

The resource inequality in (22.43) features some notation that we have not seen yet. The expression $\langle W_{S \to AB} : \rho_S \rangle$ means that a source party S distributes many copies of the state ρ_S to Alice and Bob, by applying some isometry $W_{S \to AB}$ to the state ρ_S. This resource is effectively equivalent to Alice and Bob sharing many copies of the state ρ_{AB}, a resource we expressed in Theorem 22.3.1 as $\langle \rho_{AB} \rangle$. The expression $\langle \mathrm{id}_{S \to \hat{B}B} : \rho_S \rangle$ means that a source party applies the identity map to ρ_S and gives the full state to Bob. We can now state the meaning of the resource inequality in (22.43): Using n copies of the state ρ_{AB} and $nH(A)_\rho$ noiseless qubit channels, Alice can simulate $nI(A;B)_\rho$ noiseless coherent channels to Bob while at the same time transferring her share of the state $\rho_{AB}^{\otimes n}$ to him.

---

[3] This protocol goes by several other names in the quantum Shannon theory literature: state transfer, fully quantum Slepian–Wolf, state merging, and the merging mother.

Proof A proof proceeds similarly to the proof of Theorem 22.1.1. Let $|\varphi\rangle_{ABR}$ be a purification of ρ_{AB}. Alice begins with a state that she shares with a reference system R_1, on which she would like to simulate coherent channels:

$$|\psi\rangle_{R_1 A_1} \equiv \sum_{l,m=1}^{D^2} \alpha_{l,m} |l\rangle_{R_1} |m\rangle_{A_1}, \tag{22.44}$$

where $D^2 \approx 2^{nI(A;B)_\rho}$. She appends $|\psi\rangle_{R_1 A_1}$ to $|\varphi\rangle_{A^n B^n R^n} \equiv |\varphi\rangle_{ABR}^{\otimes n}$ and applies a typical subspace measurement to her system A^n. (In what follows, we use the same notation for the typical projected state because the states are the same up to a vanishingly small error.) She applies the following controlled unitary to her systems $A_1 A^n$:

$$\sum_m |m\rangle\langle m|_{A_1} \otimes U_{A^n}(s(m)), \tag{22.45}$$

resulting in the overall state

$$\sum_{l,m} \alpha_{l,m} |l\rangle_{R_1} |m\rangle_{A_1} U_{A^n}(s(m))|\varphi\rangle_{A^n B^n R^n}. \tag{22.46}$$

Alice compresses her A^n systems, sends them over $nH(A)_\rho$ noiseless qubit channels, and Bob receives them. He decompresses them and places them in systems $\hat{B}^n$ isomorphic to A^n. The resulting state is the same as $|\varphi\rangle_{A^n B^n R^n}$, with the systems A^n replaced by $\hat{B}^n$. Bob performs a coherent gentle measurement of the following form:

$$\sum_m \sqrt{\Lambda_{\hat{B}^n B^n}^m} \otimes |m\rangle_{B_1}, \tag{22.47}$$

resulting in a state that is close in trace distance to

$$\sum_{l,m} \alpha_{l,m} |l\rangle_{R_1} |m\rangle_{A_1} |m\rangle_{B_1} U_{\hat{B}^n}(s(m))|\varphi\rangle_{\hat{B}^n B^n R^n}. \tag{22.48}$$

He finally performs the controlled unitary

$$\sum_m |m\rangle\langle m|_{B_1} \otimes U_{\hat{B}^n}^\dagger(s(m)), \tag{22.49}$$

resulting in the state

$$\left(\sum_{l,m} \alpha_{l,m} |l\rangle_{R_1} |m\rangle_{A_1} |m\rangle_{B_1}\right) \otimes |\varphi\rangle_{\hat{B}^n B^n R^n}. \tag{22.50}$$

Thus, Alice has simulated $nI(A;B)_\rho$ coherent channels to Bob with arbitrarily small error, while also transferring her share of the state $|\varphi\rangle_{A^n B^n R^n}$ to him. Figure 22.3 depicts the protocol. $\quad\square$

We obtain the following resource inequality for quantum-assisted state transfer, by combining the above protocol with the coherent communication identity:

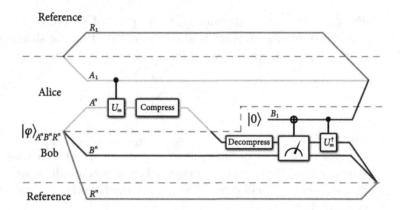

Figure 22.3 The protocol for coherent state transfer, a coherent version of the noisy super-dense coding protocol that accomplishes the task of state transfer in addition to coherent communication.

COROLLARY 22.4.1 (Quantum-Assisted State Transfer)   The following resource inequality corresponds to an achievable protocol for quantum-assisted state transfer using a shared state ρ_{AB}:

$$\langle W_{S \to AB} : \rho_S \rangle + \frac{1}{2} I(A;R)_\varphi \, [q \to q] \geq \frac{1}{2} I(A;B)_\varphi \, [qq] + \langle \mathrm{id}_{S \to \hat{B}B} : \rho_S \rangle, \quad (22.51)$$

where ρ_{AB} is a bipartite state that Alice and Bob share at the beginning of the protocol, and $|\varphi\rangle_{ABR}$ is a purification of it.

Proof   Consider the following chain of resource inequalities:

$$\langle W_{S \to AB} : \rho_S \rangle + H(A)_\varphi \, [q \to q]$$
$$\geq I(A;B)_\varphi \, [q \to qq] + \langle \mathrm{id}_{S \to \hat{B}B} : \rho_S \rangle \quad (22.52)$$
$$\geq \frac{1}{2} I(A;B)_\varphi \, [q \to q] + \frac{1}{2} I(A;B)_\varphi \, [qq] + \langle \mathrm{id}_{S \to \hat{B}B} : \rho_S \rangle, \quad (22.53)$$

where the first follows from coherent state transfer and the second follows from the coherent communication identity. By resource cancelation, we obtain the resource inequality in the statement of the theorem because $\frac{1}{2} I(A;R)_\varphi = H(A)_\rho - \frac{1}{2} I(A;B)_\rho$.   □

COROLLARY 22.4.2 (Classical-Assisted State Transfer)   The following resource inequality corresponds to an achievable protocol for classical-assisted state transfer using a shared state ρ_{AB}:

$$\langle W_{S \to AB} : \rho_S \rangle + I(A;R)_\varphi \, [c \to c] \geq I(A \rangle B)_\varphi \, [qq] + \langle \mathrm{id}_{S \to \hat{B}B} : \rho_S \rangle, \quad (22.54)$$

where ρ_{AB} is a bipartite state that Alice and Bob share at the beginning of the protocol, and $|\varphi\rangle_{ABR}$ is a purification of it.

Proof We simply combine the protocol above with teleportation:

$$\langle W_{S \to AB} : \rho_S \rangle + I(A;R)_\varphi \, [c \to c] + \frac{1}{2} I(A;R)_\varphi \, [qq]$$

$$\geq \langle W_{S \to AB} : \rho_S \rangle + \frac{1}{2} I(A;R)_\varphi \, [q \to q] \qquad (22.55)$$

$$\geq \frac{1}{2} I(A;B)_\varphi \, [qq] + \langle \mathrm{id}_{S \to \hat{B}B} : \rho_S \rangle. \qquad (22.56)$$

Using the fact that $\frac{1}{2} I(A;B)_\varphi - \frac{1}{2} I(A;R)_\varphi = I(A \rangle B)_\varphi$, we obtain the resource inequality in the statement of the corollary. $\qquad \square$

The above protocol gives a wonderful operational interpretation to the coherent information (or negative conditional entropy $-H(A|B)_\rho$). When the coherent information is positive, Alice and Bob share that rate of entanglement at the end of the protocol (and thus the ability to teleport if extra classical communication is available). When the coherent information is negative, they need to consume entanglement at a rate of $H(A|B)_\rho$ ebits per copy in order for the state transfer process to complete.

EXERCISE 22.4.1 Suppose that Alice actually possesses the reference R in the above protocols. Show that Alice and Bob can achieve the following resource inequality:

$$\langle \psi_{ABR} \rangle + \frac{1}{2} I(A;R)_\psi \, [q \to q] \geq \frac{1}{2} \left(H(A)_\psi + H(B)_\psi + H(R)_\psi \right) [qq], \quad (22.57)$$

where $|\psi\rangle_{ABR}$ is some pure state.

22.4.1 The Dual Roles of Quantum Mutual Information

The resource inequality for entanglement-assisted quantum communication in (22.15) and that for quantum-assisted state transfer in (22.51) appear to be strikingly similar. Both contain a noisy resource and both consume a noiseless quantum resource in order to generate another noiseless quantum resource. We say that these two protocols are related by *source–channel duality* because we obtain one protocol from another by changing channels to states and vice versa.

Also, both protocols require the consumed rate of the noiseless quantum resource to be equal to half the quantum mutual information between the system A for which we are trying to preserve quantum coherence and the environment to which we do not have access. In both cases, our goal is to break the correlations between the system A and the environment, and the quantum mutual information is quantifying how much quantum coherence is required to break these correlations. Both protocols in (22.15) and (22.51) have their rates for the generated noiseless quantum resource equal to half the quantum mutual information between the system A and the system B. Thus, the quantum mutual information is also quantifying how much quantum correlations we can establish between two systems—it plays the dual role of quantifying both the destruction and creation of correlations.

22.5   Trade-off Coding

Suppose that you are a communication engineer working at a quantum communication company. Suppose further that your company has made quite a profit from entanglement-assisted classical communication, beating out the communication rates that other companies can achieve simply because your company has been able to generate high-quality noiseless entanglement between several nodes in its network, while the competitors have not been able to do so. But now suppose that your customer base has become so large that there is not enough entanglement to support protocols that achieve the rates given in the entanglement-assisted classical capacity theorem (Theorem 21.3.1). Your boss would like you to make the best of this situation, by determining the optimal rates of classical communication for a fixed entanglement budget. He is hoping that you will be able to design a protocol such that there will only be a slight decrease in communication rates. You tell him that you will do your best.

What should you do in this situation? Your first thought might be that we have already determined unassisted classical codes with a communication rate equal to the channel Holevo information $\chi(\mathcal{N})$ and we have also determined entanglement-assisted codes with a communication rate equal to the channel mutual information $I(\mathcal{N})$. It might seem that a reasonable strategy is to mix these two strategies, using some fraction λ of the channel uses for the unassisted classical code and the other fraction $1-\lambda$ of the channel uses for the entanglement-assisted code. This strategy achieves a rate of

$$\lambda \chi(\mathcal{N}) + (1 - \lambda) I(\mathcal{N}), \tag{22.58}$$

and it has an error no larger than the sum of the errors of the individual codes (thus, this error vanishes asymptotically). Meanwhile, it consumes entanglement at a lower rate of $(1 - \lambda) E$ ebits per channel use, if E is the amount of entanglement that the original protocol for entanglement-assisted classical communication consumes. This simple mixing strategy is known as *time sharing*. You figure this strategy might perform well, and you suggest it to your boss. After your boss reviews your proposal, he sends it back to you, telling you that he already thought of this solution and suggests that you are going to have to be a bit more clever—otherwise, he suspects that the existing customer base will notice the drop in communication rates.

Another strategy for communication is known as *trade-off coding*. We explore this strategy in the forthcoming section and in a broader context in Chapter 25. Trade-off coding beats time sharing for many channels of interest, but for other channels, it just reduces to time sharing. It is not clear *a priori* how to determine which channels benefit from trade-off coding, but it certainly depends on the channel for which Alice and Bob are coding. Chapter 25 follows up on the development here by demonstrating that this trade-off coding strategy is provably optimal for certain channels, and for general channels, it is optimal in the sense of regularized formulas. Trade-off coding is our best known way to deal with the above situation with a fixed entanglement budget, and your boss should be pleased with these results. Furthermore, we can upgrade the protocol outlined below to one that achieves entanglement-assisted communication of both classical and quantum information.

22.5.1 Classical Communication with Limited Entanglement

We first show that the resource inequality given in the following theorem is achievable, and we follow up with an interpretation of it in the context of trade-off coding. We name the protocol *CE trade-off coding* because it captures the trade-off between classical communication and entanglement consumption.

THEOREM 22.5.1 (CE Trade-off Coding) The following resource inequality corresponds to an achievable protocol for entanglement-assisted classical communication over a quantum channel $\mathcal{N}_{A' \to B}$:

$$\langle \mathcal{N} \rangle + H(A|X)_\rho \, [qq] \geq I(AX; B)_\rho \, [c \to c] \, , \qquad (22.59)$$

where ρ_{XAB} is a state of the following form:

$$\rho_{XAB} \equiv \sum_x p_X(x) |x\rangle\langle x|_X \otimes \mathcal{N}_{A' \to B}(\varphi^x_{AA'}), \qquad (22.60)$$

and the states $\varphi^x_{AA'}$ are pure.

Proof The proof of the above trade-off coding theorem exploits the direct parts of both the HSW coding theorem (Theorem 20.3.1) and the entanglement-assisted classical capacity theorem (Theorem 21.4.1). In particular, we exploit the constant-composition coding variant of the HSW theorem, described in Section 20.3.1, and that the entanglement-assisted quantum codewords from Theorem 21.4.1 are tensor-power states after tracing over Bob's shares of the entanglement (this is the observation mentioned in Remark 21.4.1). Suppose that Alice and Bob exploit a constant-composition HSW code for the channel $\mathcal{N}_{A' \to B}$. Such a code consists of a codebook $\{\rho^{x^n(m)}\}_m$ with $\approx 2^{nI(X;B)_\rho}$ quantum codewords. The Holevo information $I(X; B)_\rho$ is with respect to some classical–quantum state ρ_{XB} where

$$\rho_{XB} \equiv \sum_x p_X(x) |x\rangle\langle x|_X \otimes \mathcal{N}_{A' \to B}(\rho^x_{A'}), \qquad (22.61)$$

and each codeword $\rho^{x^n(m)}$ is a tensor-product state of the form

$$\rho_{x^n(m)} = \rho^{x_1(m)} \otimes \rho^{x_2(m)} \otimes \cdots \otimes \rho^{x_n(m)}. \qquad (22.62)$$

Corresponding to the codebook is some decoding POVM $\{\Lambda^m_{B^n}\}$, which Bob can employ to decode each codeword transmitted through the channel with arbitrarily high probability for all $\varepsilon \in (0, 1)$:

$$\forall m \quad \text{Tr}\left\{\Lambda^m_{B^n} \mathcal{N}_{A'^n \to B^n}(\rho^{x^n(m)}_{A'^n})\right\} \geq 1 - \varepsilon. \qquad (22.63)$$

Recall from the constant-composition HSW coding variant described in Section 20.3.1 that we select each codeword $x^n(m)$ from a typical type class, typical with respect to the distribution $p_X(x)$. Let $t(x)$ denote the empirical distribution for the typical type class, and it is such that $\max_x |t(x) - p_X(x)| \leq \delta$ for some $\delta > 0$. This implies that each classical codeword $x^n(m)$ has approximately $np_X(a_1)$ occurrences of the symbol $a_1 \in \mathcal{X}$, $np_X(a_2)$ occurrences of the symbol $a_2 \in \mathcal{X}$, and so on, for all letters in the alphabet $\mathcal{X}$. However, for a typical type class, all sequences have exactly the same empirical distribution, so that there exists some permutation π_m that rearranges each sequence $x^n(m)$ in lexicographical order according to the alphabet $\mathcal{X}$. That is, this permutation π_m arranges the sequence $x^n(m)$ into $|\mathcal{X}|$ blocks, each of length $nt(a_1), \ldots, nt(a_{|\mathcal{X}|})$:

$$\pi_m(x^n(m)) = \underbrace{a_1 \cdots a_1}_{nt(a_1)} \underbrace{a_2 \cdots a_2}_{nt(a_2)} \cdots \underbrace{a_{|\mathcal{X}|} \cdots a_{|\mathcal{X}|}}_{nt(a_{|\mathcal{X}|})}. \tag{22.64}$$

The same holds true for the corresponding permutation operator π_m applied to a quantum state $\rho^{x^n(m)}$ corresponding to the sequence $x^n(m)$:

$$\pi_m(\rho^{x^n(m)}) = \underbrace{\rho^{a_1} \otimes \cdots \otimes \rho^{a_1}}_{nt(a_1)} \otimes \underbrace{\rho^{a_2} \otimes \cdots \otimes \rho^{a_2}}_{nt(a_2)} \otimes \cdots \otimes \underbrace{\rho^{a_{|\mathcal{X}|}} \otimes \cdots \otimes \rho^{a_{|\mathcal{X}|}}}_{nt(a_{|\mathcal{X}|})}. \tag{22.65}$$

Now, we assume that n is quite large, so large that each of $nt(a_1), \ldots, nt(a_{|\mathcal{X}|})$ are large enough for the law of large numbers to come into play for each block in the permuted sequence $\pi_m(x^n(m))$ and tensor-product state $\pi_m(\rho^{x^n(m)})$. Let $\varphi^x_{AA'}$ be a purification of each $\rho^x_{A'}$ in the ensemble $\{p_X(x), \rho^x_{A'}\}$, where we assume that Alice has access to system A' and Bob has access to A. Then, for every HSW quantum codeword $\rho^{x^n(m)}_{A'^n}$, there is some purification $\varphi^{x^n(m)}_{A^n A'^n}$, where

$$\varphi^{x^n(m)}_{A^n A'^n} \equiv \varphi^{x_1(m)}_{A_1 A'_1} \otimes \varphi^{x_2(m)}_{A_2 A'_2} \otimes \cdots \otimes \varphi^{x_n(m)}_{A_n A'_n}, \tag{22.66}$$

Alice has access to the systems $A'^n \equiv A'_1 \cdots A'_n$, and Bob has access to $A^n \equiv A_1 \cdots A_n$. Applying the permutation π_m to any purified tensor-product state φ^{x^n} gives

$$\pi_m(\varphi^{x^n(m)}) = \underbrace{\varphi^{a_1} \otimes \cdots \otimes \varphi^{a_1}}_{nt(a_1)} \otimes \underbrace{\varphi^{a_2} \otimes \cdots \otimes \varphi^{a_2}}_{nt(a_2)} \otimes \cdots \otimes \underbrace{\varphi^{a_{|\mathcal{X}|}} \otimes \cdots \otimes \varphi^{a_{|\mathcal{X}|}}}_{nt(a_{|\mathcal{X}|})}, \tag{22.67}$$

where we have assumed that the permutation applies on both the purification systems A^n and the systems A'^n.

We can now formulate a strategy for trade-off coding. Alice begins with a standard classical sequence $\hat{x}^n$ that is in lexicographical order, of the form in (22.64). According to this sequence, she arranges the states $\{\varphi^{a_i}_{AA'}\}$ to be in $|\mathcal{X}|$ blocks, each of length $n_i \equiv nt(a_i) \approx np_X(a_i)$—the resulting state is of the same form as in (22.67). Since $nt(a_i)$ is large enough for the law of large numbers to come into play, for each block, there exists an entanglement-assisted classical code with $\approx 2^{n_i I(A;B)_{\mathcal{N}(\varphi^{a_i})}}$ entanglement-assisted quantum codewords, where the quantum mutual information $I(A;B)_{\mathcal{N}(\varphi^{a_i})}$ is with respect to the state $\mathcal{N}_{A'\to B}(\varphi^{a_i}_{AA'})$. Then each of these $|\mathcal{X}|$ entanglement-assisted classical codes consumes $\approx n_i H(A)_{\varphi^{a_i}_A}$ ebits (i.e., each state $(\varphi^{a_i})^{\otimes n_i}$ is produced from $\approx n_i H(A)_{\varphi^{a_i}_A}$ ebits via entanglement dilution and a negligible rate of classical communication). The entanglement-assisted quantum codewords for each block are of the form

$$U_{A^{n_i}}(s(l_i))(\varphi^{a_i}_{A^{n_i}A'^{n_i}})U^\dagger_{A^{n_i}}(s(l_i)), \tag{22.68}$$

where l_i is a message in the message set of size $\approx 2^{n_i I(A;B)_{\varphi^{a_i}}}$, the state $\varphi^{a_i}_{A^{n_i}A'^{n_i}} = \varphi^{a_i}_{A_1 A'_1} \otimes \cdots \otimes \varphi^{a_i}_{A_{n_i} A'_{n_i}}$, and the unitaries $U_{A^{n_i}}(s(l_i))$ are of the form in (21.38). Observe that the codewords in (22.68) are all equal to $\rho^{a_i}_{A'^{n_i}}$ after tracing over Bob's systems A^{n_i}, regardless of the particular unitary that Alice applies (this is the content of Remark 21.4.1). Alice then determines the permutation π_m^{-1} needed to permute the standard sequence $\hat{x}^n$ to a codeword sequence $x^n(m)$, and she applies the permutation operator π_m^{-1} to her systems A'^n so that her channel input density operator is the HSW quantum codeword $\rho^{x^n(m)}_{A'^n}$ (we are tracing over Bob's systems A^n and applying Remark 21.4.1 to obtain this result). She transmits her systems A'^n over the channel to Bob. If Bob ignores his share of the entanglement in A^n, the state that he receives from the channel is $\mathcal{N}_{A'^n\to B^n}(\rho^{x^n(m)}_{A'^n})$. He then applies his HSW measurement $\{\Lambda^m_{B^n}\}$ to the systems B^n received from the channel, and he determines the sequence $x^n(m)$, and hence the message m, with nearly unit probability. Also, this measurement has negligible disturbance on the state, so that the post-measurement state is $2\sqrt{\varepsilon}$-close in trace distance to the state that Alice transmitted through the channel (in what follows, we assume that the measurement does not change the state, and we collect error terms at the end of the proof). Now that he knows m, he applies the permutation operator π_m to his systems B^n, and we are assuming that he already has his share A^n of the entanglement arranged in lexicographical order according to the standard sequence $\hat{x}^n$. His state is then as follows:

$$\bigotimes_{i=1}^{|\mathcal{X}|} U_{A^{n_i}}(s(l_i))\left(\varphi^{a_i}_{A^{n_i}A'^{n_i}}\right) U^\dagger_{A^{n_i}}(s(l_i)). \tag{22.69}$$

At this point, he can decode the message l_i in the ith block by performing a collective measurement on the systems $A^{n_i}A'^{n_i}$. He does this for each of the $|\mathcal{X}|$ entanglement-assisted classical codes, and this completes the protocol for trade-off coding. The total error accumulated is no larger than the entanglement dilution error, the sum of ε for the first measurement, $2\sqrt{\varepsilon}$ for the disturbance of the state, and $|\mathcal{X}|\varepsilon$ for the error from the final measurement of the $|\mathcal{X}|$ blocks. Figure 22.4 depicts this protocol for an example.

We now show how the total rate of classical communication adds up to $I(AX;B)_\rho$ where ρ_{XAB} is a state of the form in (22.60). First, we can apply the chain rule for quantum mutual information to observe that the total rate

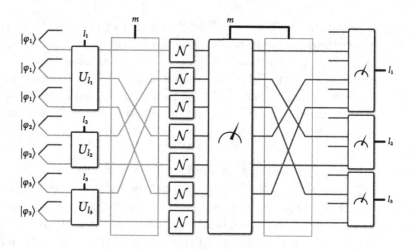

Figure 22.4 A simple protocol for trade-off coding between assisted and unassisted classical communication. Alice wishes to send the classical message m while also sending the messages l_1, l_2, and l_3. Her HSW codebook has the message m map to the sequence 1231213, which in turn gives the HSW quantum codeword $\rho^1 \otimes \rho^2 \otimes \rho^3 \otimes \rho^1 \otimes \rho^2 \otimes \rho^1 \otimes \rho^3$. A purification of these states is the following tensor product of pure states: $\varphi^1 \otimes \varphi^2 \otimes \varphi^3 \otimes \varphi^1 \otimes \varphi^2 \otimes \varphi^1 \otimes \varphi^3$, where Bob possesses the purification of each state in the tensor product. She begins with these states arranged in lexicographic order in three blocks (there are three letters in this alphabet). For each block i, she encodes the message l_i with the local unitaries for an entanglement-assisted classical code. She then permutes her shares of the entangled states according to the permutation associated with the message m. She inputs her systems to many uses of the channel, and Bob receives the outputs. His first action is to ignore his shares of the entanglement and perform a collective HSW measurement on all of the channel outputs. With high probability, he can determine the message m while causing a negligible disturbance to the state of the channel outputs. Based on the message m, he performs the inverse of the permutation that Alice used at the encoder. He combines his shares of the entanglement with the permuted channel outputs. His final three measurements are those given by the three entanglement-assisted codes Alice used at the encoder, and they detect the messages l_1, l_2, and l_3 with high probability.

$I(AX;B)_\rho$ is the sum of a Holevo information $I(X;B)_\rho$ and a conditional quantum mutual information $I(A;B|X)_\rho$:

$$I(AX;B)_\rho = I(X;B)_\rho + I(A;B|X)_\rho. \tag{22.70}$$

They achieve the rate $I(X;B)_\rho$ because Bob first decodes the HSW quantum codeword, of which there can be $\approx 2^{nI(X;B)}$. His next step is to permute and decode the $|\mathcal{X}|$ blocks, each consisting of an entanglement-assisted classical code on $\approx np_X(x)$ channel uses. Each entanglement-assisted classical code communicates $\approx np_X(x)I(A;B)_{\mathcal{N}(\varphi^x)}$ bits and consumes $\approx np_X(x)H(A)_{\varphi^x}$ ebits. Thus, the total rate of classical communication for this last part is

$$\frac{\text{\# of bits generated}}{\text{\# of channel uses}} \approx \frac{\sum_x n\, p_X(x) I(A;B)_{\mathcal{N}(\varphi^x)}}{\sum_x n\, p_X(x)} \tag{22.71}$$

$$= \sum_x p_X(x) I(A;B)_{\mathcal{N}(\varphi^x)} \tag{22.72}$$

$$= I(A;B|X)_\rho, \tag{22.73}$$

and similarly, the total rate of entanglement consumption is

$$\frac{\text{\# of ebit consumed}}{\text{\# of channel uses}} \approx \frac{\sum_x n\, p_X(x) H(A)_{\varphi^x}}{\sum_x n\, p_X(x)} \tag{22.74}$$

$$= \sum_x p_X(x) H(A)_{\varphi^x} \tag{22.75}$$

$$= H(A|X)_\rho. \tag{22.76}$$

This gives the resource inequality in the statement of the theorem. □

22.5.2 Trade-off Coding Subsumes Time Sharing

Before proceeding to other trade-off coding settings, we show how time sharing emerges as a special case of a trade-off coding strategy. Recall from (22.58) that time sharing can achieve the rate $\lambda \chi(\mathcal{N}) + (1-\lambda) I(\mathcal{N})$ for any λ such that $0 \leq \lambda \leq 1$. Suppose that $\phi_{AA'}$ is the pure state that maximizes the channel mutual information $I(\mathcal{N})$, and suppose that $\{p_X(x), \psi_{A'}^x\}$ is an ensemble of pure states that maximizes the channel Holevo information $\chi(\mathcal{N})$ (recall from Theorem 13.3.2 that it is sufficient to consider pure states for maximizing the Holevo information of a channel). Time sharing simply mixes between these two strategies, and we can construct a classical–quantum state of the form in (22.60), for which time sharing turns out to be the strategy executed by the constructed trade-off code:

$$\sigma_{UXAB} \equiv (1-\lambda) |0\rangle\langle 0|_U \otimes |0\rangle\langle 0|_X \otimes \mathcal{N}_{A'\to B}(\phi_{AA'})$$
$$+ \lambda |1\rangle\langle 1|_U \otimes \sum_x p_X(x) |x\rangle\langle x|_X \otimes |0\rangle\langle 0|_A \otimes \mathcal{N}_{A'\to B}(\psi_{A'}^x). \tag{22.77}$$

In the above, the register U is acting as a classical binary flag to indicate whether the code should be an entanglement-assisted classical capacity-achieving code or a code that achieves the channel's Holevo information. The amount of classical bits that Alice can communicate to Bob using a trade-off code is $I(AUX;B)_\sigma$, where we have assumed that U and X together form the classical register. We can then evaluate this mutual information by applying the chain rule:

$$I(AUX;B)_\sigma$$
$$= I(A;B|XU)_\sigma + I(X;B|U)_\sigma + I(U;B)_\sigma \tag{22.78}$$

$$= (1-\lambda) I(A;B)_{\mathcal{N}(\phi)} + \lambda \left[\sum_x p_X(x) I(A;B)_{|0\rangle\langle 0| \otimes \mathcal{N}(\psi^x)} \right]$$
$$+ (1-\lambda) I(X;B)_{|0\rangle\langle 0| \otimes \mathcal{N}(\phi)} + \lambda I(X;B)_{\{p(x),\psi^x\}} + I(U;B)_\sigma \tag{22.79}$$
$$\geq (1-\lambda) I(\mathcal{N}) + \lambda \chi(\mathcal{N}). \tag{22.80}$$

The second equality follows by evaluating the first two conditional mutual informations. The inequality follows from the assumptions that $I(\mathcal{N}) = I(A;B)_{\mathcal{N}(\phi)}$ and $\chi(\mathcal{N}) = I(X;B)_{\{p(x),\psi^x\}}$, the fact that quantum mutual information vanishes on product states, and $I(U;B)_\sigma \geq 0$. Thus, in certain cases, this strategy might do slightly better than time sharing, but for channels for which $\phi_{A'} = \sum_x p(x)\psi_{A'}^x$, this strategy is equivalent to time sharing because $I(U;B)_\sigma = 0$ in this latter case.

Thus, time sharing emerges as a special case of trade-off coding. In general, we can try to see if trade-off coding beats time sharing for certain channels by optimizing the rates in Theorem 22.5.1 over all possible choices of states of the form in (22.60).

22.5.3 Trading between Coherent and Classical Communication

We obtain the following corollary of Theorem 22.5.1, simply by upgrading the $|\mathcal{X}|$ entanglement-assisted classical codes to entanglement-assisted coherent codes. The upgrading is along the same lines as that in the proof of Theorem 22.1.1, and for this reason, we omit the proof.

COROLLARY 22.5.1 The following resource inequality corresponds to an achievable protocol for entanglement-assisted coherent communication over a quantum channel $\mathcal{N}$:

$$\langle \mathcal{N} \rangle + H(A|X)_\rho \,[qq] \geq I(A;B|X)_\rho \,[q \to qq] + I(X;B)_\rho \,[c \to c], \qquad (22.81)$$

where ρ_{XAB} is a state of the following form:

$$\rho_{XAB} \equiv \sum_x p_X(x)|x\rangle\langle x|_X \otimes \mathcal{N}_{A' \to B}(\varphi_{AA'}^x), \qquad (22.82)$$

and the states $\varphi_{AA'}^x$ are pure.

22.5.4 Trading between Classical Communication and Entanglement-Assisted Quantum Communication

We end this section with a protocol that achieves entanglement-assisted communication of both classical and quantum information. It is essential to the trade-off between a quantum channel and the three resources of noiseless classical communication, noiseless quantum communication, and noiseless entanglement. We study this trade-off in full detail in Chapter 25, where we show that combining this protocol with teleportation, super-dense coding, and entanglement distribution is sufficient to achieve any task in dynamic quantum Shannon theory involving the three unit resources.

COROLLARY 22.5.2 (CQE Trade-off Coding) The following resource inequality corresponds to an achievable protocol for entanglement-assisted communication of classical and quantum information over a quantum channel $\mathcal{N}_{A'\to B}$:

$$\langle \mathcal{N} \rangle + \frac{1}{2}I(A;E|X)_\rho \, [qq] \geq \frac{1}{2}I(A;B|X)_\rho \, [q \to q] + I(X;B)_\rho \, [c \to c], \quad (22.83)$$

where ρ_{XABE} is a state of the following form:

$$\rho_{XABE} \equiv \sum_x p_X(x)|x\rangle\langle x|_X \otimes U^{\mathcal{N}}_{A'\to BE}(\varphi^x_{AA'}), \quad (22.84)$$

the states $\varphi^x_{AA'}$ are pure, and $U^{\mathcal{N}}_{A'\to BE}$ is an isometric extension of the channel $\mathcal{N}_{A'\to B}$.

Proof Consider the following chain of resource inequalities:

$$\langle \mathcal{N} \rangle + H(A|X)_\rho \, [qq]$$
$$\geq I(A;B|X)_\rho \, [q \to qq] + I(X;B)_\rho \, [c \to c] \quad (22.85)$$
$$\geq \frac{1}{2}I(A;B|X)_\rho \, [qq] + \frac{1}{2}I(A;B|X)_\rho \, [q \to q] + I(X;B)_\rho \, [c \to c]. \quad (22.86)$$

The first inequality is the statement in Corollary 22.5.1, and the second inequality follows from the coherent communication identity. After resource cancelation and noting that $H(A|X)_\rho - \frac{1}{2}I(A;B|X)_\rho = \frac{1}{2}I(A;E|X)_\rho$, the resulting resource inequality is equivalent to the one in (22.83). $\qquad\square$

22.5.5 Trading between Classical and Quantum Communication

Our final trade-off coding protocol that we consider is that between classical and quantum communication. The proof of the resource inequality below follows by combining the protocol in Corollary 22.5.2 with entanglement distribution, in much the same way as we did in Corollary 22.2.1. Thus, we omit the proof.

COROLLARY 22.5.3 (CQ Trade-off Coding) The following resource inequality corresponds to an achievable protocol for simultaneous classical and quantum communication over a quantum channel $\mathcal{N}_{A'\to B}$:

$$\langle \mathcal{N} \rangle \geq I(A\rangle BX)_\rho \, [q \to q] + I(X;B)_\rho \, [c \to c], \quad (22.87)$$

where ρ_{XAB} is a state of the following form:

$$\rho_{XAB} \equiv \sum_x p_X(x)|x\rangle\langle x|_X \otimes \mathcal{N}_{A'\to B}(\varphi^x_{AA'}), \quad (22.88)$$

and the states $\varphi^x_{AA'}$ are pure.

22.6   Concluding Remarks

The maintainence of quantum coherence is the theme of this chapter. Alice and Bob can execute powerful protocols if they perform encoding and decoding in superposition. In both entanglement-assisted coherent communication and coherent state transfer, Alice performs controlled gates instead of conditional gates and Bob performs coherent measurements that place measurement outcomes in an ancilla register without destroying superpositions. Also, Bob's final action in both of these protocols is to perform a controlled decoupling unitary, ensuring that the state of the environment is independent of Alice and Bob's final state. Thus, the same protocol accomplishes the different tasks of entanglement-assisted coherent communication and coherent state transfer, and these in turn can generate a whole host of other protocols by combining them with entanglement distribution and the coherent and incoherent versions of teleportation and super-dense coding. Among these other generated protocols are entanglement-assisted quantum communication, quantum communication, quantum-assisted state transfer, and classical-assisted state transfer. The exercises in this chapter explore further possibilities if Alice has access to the environments of the different protocols—the most general version of coherent teleportation arises in such a case.

Trade-off coding is the theme of the last part of this chapter. Here, we are addressing the question: Given a fixed amount of a certain resource, how much of another resource can Alice and Bob generate? Noisy quantum channels are the most fundamental description of a medium over which information can propagate, and it is thus important to understand the best ways to make effective use of such a resource for a variety of purposes. We determined a protocol that achieves the task of entanglement-assisted communication of classical and quantum information, simply by combining the protocols we have already found for classical communication and entanglement-assisted coherent communication. Chapter 25 continues this theme of trade-off coding in a much broader context and demonstrates that the protocol given here, when combined with teleportation, super-dense coding, and entanglement distribution, is optimal for some channels of interest and essentially optimal in the general case.

22.7   History and Further Reading

Devetak et al. (2004) and Devetak et al. (2008) showed that it is possible to make the protocols for entanglement-assisted classical communication and noisy super-dense coding coherent, leading to Theorems 22.1.1 and 22.4.1. They called these protocols the "father" and "mother," respectively, because they generated many other protocols in quantum Shannon theory by combining them with entanglement distribution, teleportation, and super-dense coding. Horodecki et al. (2001) formulated a protocol for noisy super-dense coding, but our protocol here makes use of the coding technique in Hsieh, Devetak & Winter (2008). Shor (2004b) first proved a coding theorem for trading between assisted and unassisted classical communication, and Devetak & Shor (2005) followed up on this result by finding a scheme for trade-off coding between classical and quantum communication. Some time later, Hsieh & Wilde (2010a) generalized these two coding schemes to produce the result of Theorem 22.5.2. The proofs given in this chapter for these trade-off results are different from those which appeared in Shor (2004b), Devetak & Shor (2005), and Hsieh & Wilde (2010a).

23 Private Classical Communication

We have now seen in Chapters 20–22 how Alice can communicate classical or quantum information to Bob, perhaps even with the help of shared entanglement. One might argue that these communication tasks are the most fundamental tasks in quantum Shannon theory, given that they have furthered our understanding of the nature of information transmission over quantum channels. However, when discussing the communication of classical information, we made no stipulation as to whether this classical information should be public, so that any third party might have partial or full access to it, or private, so that no third party has access.

This chapter establishes the private classical capacity theorem, which gives the maximum rate at which Alice can communicate classical information privately to Bob without anyone else in the universe knowing what she sent to him. A variation of the information-processing task corresponding to this theorem was one of the earliest studied in quantum information theory, with the Bennett–Brassard-84 quantum key distribution protocol being the first proposed protocol for exploiting quantum mechanics to establish a shared secret key between two parties. The private classical capacity theorem is important for quantum key distribution because it establishes the maximum rate at which two parties can generate a shared secret key.

Another equally important, but less obvious utility of private classical communication is in establishing a protocol for quantum communication at the coherent information rate. Section 22.2 demonstrated a somewhat roundabout way of arriving at the conclusion that it is possible to communicate quantum information reliably at the coherent information rate—recall that we "coherified" the entanglement-assisted classical capacity theorem and then exploited the coherent communication identity and catalytic use of entanglement. Establishing achievability of the coherent information rate via private classical coding is another way of arriving at the same result, with the added benefit that the resulting protocol does not require the catalytic use of entanglement.

The intuition for quantum communication via privacy arises from the no-cloning theorem. Suppose that Alice is able to communicate private classical messages to Bob, so that the channel's environment (Eve) is not able to distinguish which message Alice is transmitting to Bob. That is, Eve's state is completely independent of Alice's message if the transmitted message is private. Then we might expect it to be possible to make a coherent version of this private classical code by exploiting superpositions of the private classical codewords. Since Eve's states are independent of the quantum message that Alice is sending through the quantum channel, she is not able to "steal" any of the coherence in Alice's superposed states. Given that the overall evolution of the channel to Bob and Eve is unitary and the fact that Eve does not receive any quantum information with this scheme, we should expect that the quantum information appears at the receiving end of the channel so that Bob can decode it. Were Eve able to obtain any information about the private classical messages, then Bob would not be able to decode all of the quantum information when they construct a coherent version of this private classical code. Otherwise, they would violate the no-cloning theorem. We discuss this important application of private classical communication in the next chapter.

This chapter follows a similar structure as previous chapters. We first detail the information-processing task for private classical communication. Section 23.2 then states the private classical capacity theorem, with the following two sections proving the achievability part and the converse part. We end with a general discussion of the private classical capacity and a brief overview of the secret-key-assisted private classical capacity.

23.1 The Information-Processing Task

We begin by describing the information-processing task for private classical communication (we define an (n, P, ε) private classical code). Alice selects a message m from a set $\mathcal{M}$ of messages. Alice prepares some state $\rho_{A'^n}^m$ as input to many uses of the quantum channel $\mathcal{N}_{A' \to B}$ and transmits it, producing the following state at Bob's receiving end:

$$\mathcal{N}_{A'^n \to B^n}(\rho_{A'^n}^m),\tag{23.1}$$

where $\mathcal{N}_{A'^n \to B^n} \equiv (\mathcal{N}_{A' \to B})^{\otimes n}$.

Bob employs a decoding POVM $\{\Lambda_m\}$ in order to detect Alice's transmitted message m. The probability of error for a particular message m is as follows:

$$p_e(m) = \mathrm{Tr}\left\{(I - \Lambda_m)\mathcal{N}_{A'^n \to B^n}(\rho_{A'^n}^m)\right\},\tag{23.2}$$

so that the maximal probability of error is

$$p_e^* \equiv \max_{m \in \mathcal{M}} p_e(m),\tag{23.3}$$

where $p_e^* \leq \varepsilon \in [0, 1]$ for an (n, P, ε) code. The rate P of the code is

$$P \equiv \frac{1}{n} \log |\mathcal{M}|.\tag{23.4}$$

So far, the above specification of a private classical code is nearly identical to that for the transmission of classical information outlined in Section 20.2. What distinguishes a private classical code from a public one is the following extra condition for privacy. Let $U_{A'\to BE}^{\mathcal{N}}$ be an isometric extension of the channel $\mathcal{N}_{A'\to B}$, so that the complementary channel $\widehat{\mathcal{N}}_{A'\to E}$ to the environment Eve is as follows:

$$\widehat{\mathcal{N}}_{A'\to E}(\sigma) \equiv \mathrm{Tr}_B\{U_{A'\to BE}^{\mathcal{N}}(\sigma)\}. \tag{23.5}$$

If Alice transmits a message m, then the state for Eve is as follows:

$$\omega_{E^n}^m \equiv \widehat{\mathcal{N}}_{A'^n\to E^n}(\rho_{A'^n}^m). \tag{23.6}$$

Our condition for ε-privacy is that Eve's state is always close to a constant state σ_{E^n}, regardless of which message m Alice transmits through the channel:

$$\forall m \in \mathcal{M}: \frac{1}{2}\|\omega_{E^n}^m - \sigma_{E^n}\|_1 \le \varepsilon. \tag{23.7}$$

This definition is the strongest definition of privacy because it implies that Eve cannot learn anything about the message m that Alice transmits through the channel. Figure 23.1 depicts the information-processing task for private classical communication.

A rate P of private classical communication is achievable for $\mathcal{N}_{A'\to B}$ if there exists an $(n, P-\delta, \varepsilon)$ private classical code for all $\varepsilon \in (0,1)$, $\delta > 0$, and sufficiently large n, where ε characterizes both the reliability and the privacy of the code. The private classical capacity $C_P(\mathcal{N})$ of a channel $\mathcal{N}_{A'\to B}$ is equal to the supremum of all achievable rates for private classical communication.

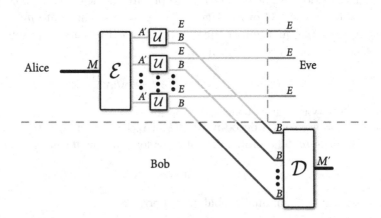

Figure 23.1 The information-processing task for private classical communication. Alice encodes some private message m into a quantum codeword $\rho_{A'^n}^m$ and transmits it over many uses of a quantum channel. The goal of such a protocol is for Bob to be able to reliably distinguish the message, while the channel's environment Eve should not be able to learn anything about it.

23.1.1 Mutual Information of Eve

We comment briefly how the condition in (23.7) implies that Eve has little mutual information about the transmitted message. It follows from (23.7) that

$$\varepsilon \geq \frac{1}{2} \sum_{m \in \mathcal{M}} \frac{1}{|\mathcal{M}|} \left\| \omega_{E^n}^m - \sigma_{E^n} \right\|_1 = \frac{1}{2} \left\| \omega_{ME^n} - \pi_M \otimes \sigma_{E^n} \right\|_1, \tag{23.8}$$

where

$$\omega_{ME^n} \equiv \sum_{m \in \mathcal{M}} \frac{1}{|\mathcal{M}|} |m\rangle\langle m|_M \otimes \omega_{E^n}^m. \tag{23.9}$$

The criterion in (23.8) implies that Eve's Holevo information with M is small:

$$I(M; E^n)_\omega = H(M)_\omega - H(M|E^n)_\omega \tag{23.10}$$

$$= H(M|E^n)_{\pi \otimes \sigma} - H(M|E^n)_\omega \tag{23.11}$$

$$\leq \varepsilon \log |\mathcal{M}| + (1 + \varepsilon) h_2(\varepsilon / [1 + \varepsilon]). \tag{23.12}$$

The inequality follows from applying the AFW inequality (Theorem 11.10.3) to both entropies. Thus, if ε is exponentially small in n (which will be the case for our codes), then it is possible to make Eve's information about the message become arbitrarily small in the asymptotic limit.

23.2 The Private Classical Capacity Theorem

We now state the main theorem of this chapter, the private classical capacity theorem.

THEOREM 23.2.1 (Devetak–Cai–Winter–Yeung) The private classical capacity $C_P(\mathcal{N})$ of a quantum channel $\mathcal{N}_{A' \to B}$ is equal to the regularized private information of the channel:

$$C_P(\mathcal{N}) = P_{\text{reg}}(\mathcal{N}), \tag{23.13}$$

where

$$P_{\text{reg}}(\mathcal{N}) \equiv \lim_{k \to \infty} \frac{1}{k} P(\mathcal{N}^{\otimes k}). \tag{23.14}$$

The private information $P(\mathcal{N})$ is defined as

$$P(\mathcal{N}) \equiv \max_{\rho} \left[I(X; B)_\sigma - I(X; E)_\sigma \right], \tag{23.15}$$

where $\rho_{XA'}$ is a classical–quantum state of the following form:

$$\rho_{XA'} \equiv \sum_x p_X(x) |x\rangle\langle x|_X \otimes \rho_{A'}^x, \tag{23.16}$$

and $\sigma_{XBE} \equiv \mathcal{U}_{A' \to BE}^{\mathcal{N}}(\rho_{XA'})$, with $U_{A' \to BE}^{\mathcal{N}}$ an isometric extension of the channel $\mathcal{N}_{A' \to B}$.

We first prove the achievability part of the coding theorem and follow with the converse proof. Recall that the private information is additive whenever the channel is degradable (Theorem 13.6.3). Thus, for this class of channels, the regularization in (23.14) is not necessary and the private information of the channel is equal to the private classical capacity (in fact, the results from Theorem 13.6.2 and the next chapter demonstrate that the private information of a degradable channel is also equal to its quantum capacity). The regularization of the private information seems to be necessary in general in order to characterize the private capacity because there is an example of a channel for which the private information is superadditive.

23.3   The Direct Coding Theorem

This section gives a proof that the private information in (23.15) is an achievable rate for private classical communication over a quantum channel $\mathcal{N}_{A'\to B}$. We first give the intuition behind the protocol. Alice's goal is to build a doubly indexed codebook $\{x^n(m,k)\}_{m\in\mathcal{M}, k\in\mathcal{K}}$ that satisfies two properties:

1. Bob should be able to detect the message m and the "junk" variable k with high probability. From the classical coding theorem of Chapter 20, our intuition is that he should be able to do so as long as $|\mathcal{M}|\,|\mathcal{K}| \approx 2^{nI(X;B)}$.
2. Randomizing over the "junk" variable k should approximately cover the typical subspace of Eve's system, so that every state of Eve depending on the message m looks like a constant, independent of the message m Alice sends (we would like the code to satisfy (23.7)). Our intuition from the covering lemma (Chapter 17) is that the size of the "junk" variable set $\mathcal{K}$ needs to be at least $|\mathcal{K}| \approx 2^{nI(X;E)}$ in order for Alice to approximately cover Eve's typical subspace.

Our method for generating a code is again random because we can invoke the typicality properties that hold in the asymptotic limit of many channel uses. Thus, if Alice chooses a code that satisfies the above criteria, she can send approximately $|\mathcal{M}| \approx 2^{n[I(X;B)-I(X;E)]}$ distinguishable signals to Bob such that they are indistinguishable to Eve. We devote the remainder of this section to proving that the above intuition is correct. Figure 23.2 displays the anatomy of a private classical code.

23.3.1   Dimensionality Arguments

Before giving the proof of achievability, we confirm the above intuition with some dimensionality arguments and show how to satisfy the conditions of both the packing and covering lemmas. Suppose that Alice has some ensemble $\{p_X(x), \rho_{A'}^x\}$ from which she can generate random codes. Let $U_{A'\to BE}^{\mathcal{N}}$ denote an

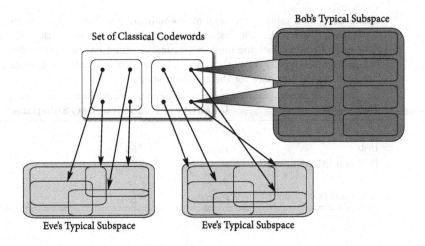

Figure 23.2 The anatomy of a code for private classical communication. In this illustrative example, Alice has eight codewords, with each depicted as a • and indexed by $m \in \{1, 2\}$ and $k \in \{1, 2, 3, 4\}$. Thus, she is interested in sending one of two messages and has the "junk" variable k available for randomizing Eve's state. Each classical codeword $x^n(m, k)$ maps to a distinguishable subspace on Bob's typical subspace (we show two of the mappings in the figure, while displaying eight distinguishable subspaces). From the packing lemma, our intuition is that Alice can reliably send about $2^{nI(X;B)}$ distinguishable signals. The codewords $\{x^n(1, k)\}_{k \in \{1,2,3,4\}}$ and $\{x^n(2, k)\}_{k \in \{1,2,3,4\}}$ are each grouped in a box to indicate that they form a privacy amplification set. When randomizing k, the codewords $\{x^n(1, k)\}_{k \in \{1,2,3,4\}}$ uniformly cover Eve's typical subspace (and so does the set $\{x^n(2, k)\}_{k \in \{1,2,3,4\}}$), so that it becomes nearly impossible in the asymptotic limit for Eve to distinguish whether Alice is sending a codeword in $\{x^n(1, k)\}_{k \in \{1,2,3,4\}}$ or $\{x^n(2, k)\}_{k \in \{1,2,3,4\}}$. In this way, Eve cannot determine which message Alice is transmitting. The minimum size for each privacy amplification set in the asymptotic limit is $\approx 2^{nI(X;E)}$.

isometric extension of the channel $\mathcal{N}_{A' \rightarrow B}$, and let ρ_{BE}^x denote the joint state of Bob and Eve after Alice inputs $\rho_{A'}^x$:

$$\rho_{BE}^x \equiv \mathcal{U}_{A' \rightarrow BE}^{\mathcal{N}}(\rho_{A'}^x). \qquad (23.17)$$

The local respective density operators for Bob and Eve given a letter x are as follows:

$$\rho_B^x \equiv \mathrm{Tr}_E\left\{\rho_{BE}^x\right\}, \qquad \rho_E^x \equiv \mathrm{Tr}_B\left\{\rho_{BE}^x\right\}. \qquad (23.18)$$

The expected respective density operators for Bob and Eve are as follows:

$$\rho_B = \sum_x p_X(x)\rho_B^x, \qquad \rho_E = \sum_x p_X(x)\rho_E^x. \qquad (23.19)$$

Given a particular input sequence x^n, we define the nth extensions of the above states as follows:

Table 23.1 This table lists several mathematical quantities involved in the construction of a random private code. The first column lists the party to whom the quantities belong. The second column lists the random classical or quantum states. The third column gives the appropriate typical set or subspace. The final column lists the appropriate projector onto the typical subspace for the quantum states.

Party	Quantity	Typical Set/Subspace	Projector
Alice	X	$T_\delta^{X^n}$	N/A
Bob	ρ_{B^n}	$T_{B^n}^\delta$	$\Pi_{B^n}^\delta$
Bob conditioned on x^n	$\rho_{B^n}^{x^n}$	$T_{B^n\mid x^n}^\delta$	$\Pi_{B^n\mid x^n}^\delta$
Eve	ρ_{E^n}	$T_{E^n}^\delta$	$\Pi_{E^n}^\delta$
Eve conditioned on x^n	$\rho_{E^n}^{x^n}$	$T_{E^n\mid x^n}^\delta$	$\Pi_{E^n\mid x^n}^\delta$

$$\rho_{B^n}^{x^n} \equiv \mathrm{Tr}_{E^n}\left\{\rho_{B^n E^n}^{x^n}\right\}, \tag{23.20}$$

$$\rho_{E^n}^{x^n} \equiv \mathrm{Tr}_{B^n}\left\{\rho_{B^n E^n}^{x^n}\right\}, \tag{23.21}$$

$$\rho_{B^n} = \sum_{x^n \in \mathcal{X}^n} p_{X^n}(x^n)\rho_{B^n}^{x^n}, \tag{23.22}$$

$$\rho_{E^n} = \sum_{x^n \in \mathcal{X}^n} p_{X^n}(x^n)\rho_{E^n}^{x^n}. \tag{23.23}$$

Table 23.1 organizes these various density operators and their corresponding typical subspaces and projectors.

The following four conditions corresponding to the packing lemma hold for Bob's states $\left\{\rho_{B^n}^{x^n}\right\}$, Bob's average density operator ρ_{B^n}, Bob's typical subspace $T_{B^n}^\delta$, and Bob's conditionally typical subspace $T_{B^n\mid x^n}^\delta$:

$$\mathrm{Tr}\left\{\Pi_{B^n}^\delta \rho_{B^n}^{x^n}\right\} \geq 1 - \varepsilon, \tag{23.24}$$

$$\mathrm{Tr}\left\{\Pi_{B^n\mid x^n}^\delta \rho_{B^n}^{x^n}\right\} \geq 1 - \varepsilon, \tag{23.25}$$

$$\mathrm{Tr}\left\{\Pi_{B^n\mid x^n}^\delta\right\} \leq 2^{n(H(B\mid X)+c\delta)}, \tag{23.26}$$

$$\Pi_{B^n}^\delta \rho_{B^n} \Pi_{B^n}^\delta \leq 2^{-n(H(B)-c\delta)}\Pi_{B^n}^\delta, \tag{23.27}$$

where c is some positive constant (see Properties 15.2.7, 15.1.1, 15.1.2, and 15.1.3).

The following four conditions corresponding to the covering lemma hold for Eve's states $\left\{\rho_{E^n}^{x^n}\right\}$, Eve's typical subspace $T_{E^n}^\delta$, and Eve's conditionally typical subspace $T_{E^n\mid x^n}^\delta$:

$$\mathrm{Tr}\left\{\Pi_{E^n}^\delta \rho_{E^n}^{x^n}\right\} \geq 1 - \varepsilon, \tag{23.28}$$

$$\mathrm{Tr}\left\{\Pi_{E^n\mid x^n}^\delta \rho_{E^n}^{x^n}\right\} \geq 1 - \varepsilon, \tag{23.29}$$

$$\operatorname{Tr}\left\{\Pi_{E^n}^{\delta}\right\} \leq 2^{n(H(E)+c\delta)}, \tag{23.30}$$

$$\Pi_{E^n|x^n}^{\delta} \rho_{E^n}^{x^n} \Pi_{E^n|x^n}^{\delta} \leq 2^{-n(H(E|X)-c\delta)}\Pi_{E^n|x^n}^{\delta}. \tag{23.31}$$

The above properties suggest that we can use the methods of both the packing lemma and the covering lemma for constructing a private code. Consider two sets $\mathcal{M}$ and $\mathcal{K}$ with the following respective sizes:

$$|\mathcal{M}| = 2^{n[I(X;B)-I(X;E)-6c\delta]}, \tag{23.32}$$

$$|\mathcal{K}| = 2^{n[I(X;E)+3c\delta]}, \tag{23.33}$$

so that the product set $\mathcal{M} \times \mathcal{K}$ indexed by the ordered pairs (m, k) is of size

$$|\mathcal{M} \times \mathcal{K}| = |\mathcal{M}||\mathcal{K}| = 2^{n[I(X;B)-3c\delta]}. \tag{23.34}$$

The sizes of these sets suggest that we can use the product set $\mathcal{M} \times \mathcal{K}$ for sending classical information, but we can use $|\mathcal{M}|$ "privacy amplification" sets each of size $|\mathcal{K}|$ for reducing Eve's knowledge of the message m (see Figure 23.2).

23.3.2   Random Code Construction

We now argue for the existence of a good private classical code with rate $P \approx I(X;B) - I(X;E)$ if Alice selects it randomly according to the ensemble

$$\{p'_{X'^n}(x^n), \rho_{A'^n}^{x^n}\}, \tag{23.35}$$

where $p'_{X'^n}(x^n)$ is the pruned distribution (see Section 20.3.1—recall that this distribution is close to the i.i.d. distribution). Let us choose $|\mathcal{M}||\mathcal{K}|$ random variables $X^n(m, k)$ according to the distribution $p'_{X'^n}(x^n)$ where the realizations of the random variables $X^n(m, k)$ take values in $\mathcal{X}^n$. After selecting these codewords randomly, the code $\mathcal{C} = \{x^n(m, k)\}_{m\in\mathcal{M}, k\in\mathcal{K}}$ is then a fixed set of codewords $x^n(m, k)$ depending on the message m and the randomization variable k.

We first consider how well Bob can distinguish the pair (m, k) and argue that the random code is a good code in the sense that the expectation of the average error probability over all codes is low. The packing lemma is the basis of our argument. By applying the packing lemma (Lemma 16.3.1) to (23.24)–(23.27), there exists a POVM $\{\Lambda_{m,k}\}_{(m,k)\in\mathcal{M}\times\mathcal{K}}$ corresponding to the random choice of code that reliably distinguishes the states $\{\rho_{B^n}^{X^n(m,k)}\}_{m\in\mathcal{M}, k\in\mathcal{K}}$ in the following sense:

$$\mathbb{E}_{\mathcal{C}}\left\{\bar{p}_e(\mathcal{C})\right\} = 1 - \mathbb{E}_{\mathcal{C}}\left\{\frac{1}{|\mathcal{M}||\mathcal{K}|}\sum_{m\in\mathcal{M}}\sum_{k\in\mathcal{K}}\operatorname{Tr}\left\{\Lambda_{m,k}\rho_{B^n}^{X^n(m,k)}\right\}\right\} \tag{23.36}$$

$$\leq 2\left(\varepsilon + 2\sqrt{\varepsilon}\right) + 4\left(\frac{2^{n(H(B|X)+c\delta)}|\mathcal{M}\times\mathcal{K}|}{2^{n(H(B)-c\delta)}}\right) \tag{23.37}$$

$$= 2\left(\varepsilon + 2\sqrt{\varepsilon}\right) + 4\left(\frac{2^{n(H(B|X)+c\delta)}2^{n[I(X;B)-3c\delta]}}{2^{n(H(B)-c\delta)}}\right) \tag{23.38}$$

$$= 2\left(\varepsilon + 2\sqrt{\varepsilon}\right) + 4 \cdot 2^{-nc\delta} \equiv \varepsilon', \tag{23.39}$$

where the first equality follows by definition, the first inequality follows by application of the packing lemma to the conditions in (23.24)–(23.27), the second equality follows by substitution of (23.34), and the last equality follows by a straightforward calculation. We can make ε' arbitrarily small by choosing n large enough.

Let us now consider the corresponding density operators $\rho_{E^n}^{X^n(m,k)}$ for Eve. Consider dividing the random code $\mathcal{C}$ into $|\mathcal{M}|$ privacy amplification sets, each of size $|\mathcal{K}|$. Each privacy amplification set $\mathcal{C}_m \equiv \{\rho_{E^n}^{X^n(m,k)}\}_{k \in \mathcal{K}}$ of density operators forms a good covering code according to the covering lemma (Lemma 17.2.1). The fake density operator of each privacy amplification set $\mathcal{C}_m$ is as follows:

$$\hat{\rho}_{E^n}^m \equiv \frac{1}{|\mathcal{K}|} \sum_{k \in \mathcal{K}} \rho_{E^n}^{X^n(m,k)}, \tag{23.40}$$

because Alice chooses the randomizing variable k uniformly at random. The obfuscation error $o_e(\mathcal{C}_m)$ of each privacy amplification set $\mathcal{C}_m$ is as follows:

$$o_e(\mathcal{C}_m) \equiv \|\hat{\rho}_{E^n}^m - \rho_{E^n}\|_1, \tag{23.41}$$

where ρ_{E^n} is defined in (23.23). The covering lemma (Lemma 17.2.1) states that the obfuscation error for each random privacy amplification set $\mathcal{C}_m$ has a high probability of being small if n is sufficiently large and $|\mathcal{K}|$ is chosen as in (23.33):

$$\Pr\left\{o_e(\mathcal{C}_m) \le \varepsilon + 4\sqrt{\varepsilon} + 24\sqrt[4]{\varepsilon}\right\}$$
$$\ge 1 - 2d_E^n \exp\left\{\frac{-\varepsilon^3}{4\ln 2} \frac{|\mathcal{K}| \, 2^{n(H(E|X) - c\delta)}}{2^{n(H(E) + c\delta)}}\right\} \tag{23.42}$$
$$= 1 - 2d_E^n \exp\left\{\frac{-\varepsilon^3}{4\ln 2} \frac{2^{n[I(X;E) + 3c\delta]} 2^{n(H(E|X) - c\delta)}}{2^{n(H(E) + c\delta)}}\right\} \tag{23.43}$$
$$= 1 - 2d_E^n \exp\left\{\frac{-\varepsilon^3}{4\ln 2} 2^{nc\delta}\right\}. \tag{23.44}$$

In particular, let us choose n large enough so that the following bound holds:

$$\Pr\left\{o_e(\mathcal{C}_m) \le \varepsilon + 4\sqrt{\varepsilon} + 24\sqrt[4]{\varepsilon}\right\} \ge 1 - \frac{\varepsilon}{|\mathcal{M}|}. \tag{23.45}$$

That we can do so follows from the important fact that $\exp\left\{-\varepsilon^3 2^{nc\delta}/(4\ln 2)\right\}$ is doubly exponentially decreasing in n. (We also see here why it is necessary to have the "wiggle room" given by an arbitrarily small, yet strictly positive δ.)

This random construction already has some of the desirable features that we are looking for in a private code just by choosing n to be sufficiently large. The expectation of Bob's average error probability for detecting the pair m, k is small, and the obfuscation error of each privacy amplification set has a high probability of being small. Our hope is that there exists some code for which Bob can retrieve the message m with the guarantee that Eve's state is independent of this message m. We argue in the next two sections that such a good private code exists.

23.3.3 Derandomization

We now apply a derandomization argument similar to the one that is needed in the proof of the HSW coding theorem. The argument in this case is more subtle because we would like to find a code that has good classical communication with the guarantee that it also has good privacy. We need to determine the probability over all codes that there exists a good private code. If this probability is non-zero, then we are sure that a good private code exists.

As we have said at the beginning of this section, a good private code has two qualities: the code is ε-good for classical communication and it is ε-private as well. Let E_0 denote the event that the random code $\mathcal{C}$ is ε-good for classical communication:

$$E_0 = \{\bar{p}_e(\mathcal{C}) \le \varepsilon\}, \tag{23.46}$$

where we restrict the performance criterion to the average probability of error for now. Let E_m denote the event that the mth message in the random code is ε-private:

$$E_m = \{o_e(\mathcal{C}_m) \le \varepsilon\}. \tag{23.47}$$

We would like all of the above events to be true, or, equivalently, we would like the intersection of the above events to occur:

$$E_{\text{priv}} \equiv E_0 \cap \bigcap_{m \in \mathcal{M}} E_m. \tag{23.48}$$

If there is a positive probability over all codes that the above event is true, then there exists a particular code that satisfies the above conditions. Let us instead consider the complement of the above event (the event that a good private code does not exist):

$$E_{\text{priv}}^c = E_0^c \cup \bigcup_{m \in \mathcal{M}} E_m^c. \tag{23.49}$$

We can then exploit the union bound from probability theory to bound the probability of the complementary event E_{priv}^c as follows:

$$\Pr\left\{E_0^c \cup \bigcup_{m \in \mathcal{M}} E_m^c\right\} \le \Pr\{E_0^c\} + \sum_{m \in \mathcal{M}} \Pr\{E_m^c\}. \tag{23.50}$$

So if we can make the probability of the event E_{priv}^c small, then the probability of the event E_{priv}, that there exists a good private code, is high.

Let us first bound the probability of the event E_0^c. Markov's inequality states that the following holds for a non-negative random variable Y and strictly positive α:

$$\Pr\{Y \ge \alpha\} \le \frac{\mathbb{E}\{Y\}}{\alpha}. \tag{23.51}$$

We can apply Markov's inequality because the random average error probability $\bar{p}_e(\mathcal{C})$ is always non-negative:

$$\Pr\{E_0^c\} = \Pr\left\{\bar{p}_e(\mathcal{C}) \geq (\varepsilon')^{3/4}\right\} \leq \frac{\mathbb{E}_\mathcal{C}\{\bar{p}_e(\mathcal{C})\}}{(\varepsilon')^{3/4}} \leq \frac{\varepsilon'}{(\varepsilon')^{3/4}} = \sqrt[4]{\varepsilon'}. \tag{23.52}$$

So we now have a good bound on the probability of the complementary event E_0^c.

Let us now bound the probability of the events E_m^c. The bounds in the previous section already give us what we need:

$$\Pr\{E_m^c\} = \Pr\left\{o_e(\mathcal{C}_m) > \varepsilon + 4\sqrt{\varepsilon} + 24\sqrt[4]{\varepsilon}\right\} \tag{23.53}$$

$$< \frac{\varepsilon}{|\mathcal{M}|}, \tag{23.54}$$

implying that

$$\sum_{m \in \mathcal{M}} \Pr\{E_m^c\} < |\mathcal{M}|\frac{\varepsilon}{|\mathcal{M}|} = \varepsilon. \tag{23.55}$$

So it now follows that the probability of the complementary event is small:

$$\Pr\{E_{\text{priv}}^c\} \leq \sqrt[4]{\varepsilon'} + \varepsilon, \tag{23.56}$$

and there is a high probability that there is a good code:

$$\Pr\{E_{\text{priv}}\} \geq 1 - \left(\sqrt[4]{\varepsilon'} + \varepsilon\right). \tag{23.57}$$

Thus, there exists a particular code $\mathcal{C}$ such that its average probability of error is small for decoding the classical information:

$$\bar{p}_e(\mathcal{C}) \leq (\varepsilon')^{3/4}, \tag{23.58}$$

and the obfuscation error of each privacy amplification set is small:

$$\forall m : o_e(\mathcal{C}_m) \leq \varepsilon + 4\sqrt{\varepsilon} + 24\sqrt[4]{\varepsilon}. \tag{23.59}$$

The derandomized code $\mathcal{C}$ is as follows:

$$\mathcal{C} \equiv \{x^n(m,k)\}_{m \in \mathcal{M}, k \in \mathcal{K}}, \tag{23.60}$$

so that each codeword $x^n(m,k)$ is a deterministic variable. Each privacy amplification set for the derandomized code is as follows:

$$\mathcal{C}_m \equiv \{x^n(m,k)\}_{k \in \mathcal{K}}. \tag{23.61}$$

The result in (23.57) is perhaps astonishing in hindsight. By choosing a private code in a random way and choosing the block length n of the private code to be sufficiently large, the overwhelming majority of codes constructed in this fashion are good private codes!

23.3.4 Expurgation

We would like to strengthen the above result even more, so that the code has a low maximal probability of error, not just a low average error probability. We expurgate codewords from the code as before, but we have to be careful with the expurgation argument because we need to make sure that the code still has good privacy after expurgation.

We can apply Markov's inequality for the expurgation in a way similar as in Exercise 2.2.1. It is possible to apply Markov's inequality to the bound on the average error probability in (23.52) to show that at most a fraction $\sqrt{\varepsilon'}$ of the codewords have error probability greater than $\sqrt[4]{\varepsilon'}$. We could merely expurgate the worst $\sqrt{\varepsilon'}$ codewords from the private code. But expurgating in this fashion does not guarantee that each privacy amplification set has the same number of codewords. Therefore, we expurgate the worst fraction $\sqrt{\varepsilon'}$ of the codewords in each privacy amplification set. We then expurgate the worst fraction $\sqrt{\varepsilon'}$ of the privacy amplification sets. The expurgated sets $\mathcal{M}'$ and $\mathcal{K}'$ both become a fraction $1 - \sqrt{\varepsilon'}$ of their original size. We denote the expurgated code as follows:

$$\mathcal{C}' \equiv \{x^n(m,k)\}_{m\in\mathcal{M}',k\in\mathcal{K}'}, \tag{23.62}$$

and the expurgated code has the following privacy amplification sets:

$$\mathcal{C}'_m \equiv \{x^n(m,k)\}_{k\in\mathcal{K}'}. \tag{23.63}$$

The expurgation has a negligible impact on the rate of the private code when n is large.

Does each privacy amplification set still have good privacy properties after performing the above expurgation? The fake density operator for each expurgated privacy amplification set is as follows:

$$\hat{\rho}_{E^n}^{m\prime} \equiv \frac{1}{|\mathcal{C}'_m|} \sum_{k\in\mathcal{K}'} \rho_{E^n}^{x^n(m,k)}. \tag{23.64}$$

It is possible to show that the fake density operators in the derandomized code are $2\sqrt{\varepsilon'}$-close in trace distance to the fake density operators in the expurgated code:

$$\forall m \in \mathcal{M}' \qquad \|\hat{\rho}_{E^n}^{m\prime} - \hat{\rho}_{E^n}^{m}\|_1 \leq 2\sqrt{\varepsilon'}, \tag{23.65}$$

because these operators only lose a small fraction of their mass after expurgation.

We now drop the primed notation to denote the expurgated code. It follows that the expurgated code $\mathcal{C}$ has good privacy:

$$\forall m \in \mathcal{M} \qquad \|\hat{\rho}_{E^n}^{m} - \rho_{E^n}\|_1 \leq \varepsilon + 4\sqrt{\varepsilon} + 24\sqrt[4]{\varepsilon} + 2\sqrt{\varepsilon'}, \tag{23.66}$$

and reliable communication:

$$\forall m \in \mathcal{M}, \ k \in \mathcal{K} \qquad p_e(\mathcal{C}, m, k) \leq \sqrt[4]{\varepsilon'}. \tag{23.67}$$

The first expression follows by application of the triangle inequality to (23.59) and (23.65).

We end the proof by summarizing the operation of the private code. Alice chooses a message m from the message set $\mathcal{M}$ and the randomization variable k uniformly at random from $\mathcal{K}$. She encodes these as $x^n(m,k)$ and inputs the quantum codeword $\rho_{A'^n}^{x^n(m,k)}$ to the channel. Bob receives the state $\rho_{B^n}^{x^n(m,k)}$ and performs a POVM $\{\Lambda_{m,k}\}_{(m,k)\in\mathcal{M}\times\mathcal{K}}$ that determines the pair m and k correctly with probability $1 - \sqrt[4]{\varepsilon'}$. The code guarantees that Eve has almost no knowledge about the message m. The private communication rate P of the private code is equal to the following expression:

$$P \equiv \frac{1}{n}\log|\mathcal{M}| = I(X;B) - I(X;E) - 6c\delta. \tag{23.68}$$

This concludes the proof of the direct coding theorem.

We remark that the above proof applies even in the scenario in which Eve does not get the full purification of the channel. That is, suppose that the channel has one input A' for Alice and two outputs B and E for Bob and Eve, respectively. Then the channel has an isometric extension to some environment F. In this scenario, the private information $I(X;B) - I(X;E)$ is still achievable for some classical–quantum state input such that the Holevo information difference is non-negative. However, one could always give both outputs E and F to an eavesdropper (this is the setting that we proved in the above theorem). Giving the full purification of the channel to the environment ensures that the transmitted information is private from the "rest of the universe" (anyone other than the intended receiver), and it thus yields the highest standard of security in any protocol for private information transmission.

23.4   The Converse Theorem

We now prove the converse part of the private classical capacity theorem, which demonstrates that the regularization of the private information is an upper bound on the private classical capacity. We suppose instead that Alice and Bob are trying to accomplish the task of secret key generation. As we have argued in other converse proofs (see Sections 20.3.2 and 21.5), the capacity for generating this static resource can only be larger than the capacity for private classical communication because Alice and Bob can always use a noiseless private channel to establish a shared secret key. In such a task, Alice first prepares a maximally correlated state $\overline{\Phi}_{MM'}$ and encodes the M' variable as a codeword $\rho_{A'^n}^m$. This encoding leads to a state of the following form, after Alice transmits her systems A'^n over many independent uses of the channel:

$$\omega_{MB^nE^n} \equiv \frac{1}{|\mathcal{M}|}\sum_{m\in\mathcal{M}}|m\rangle\langle m|_M \otimes \mathcal{U}_{A'^n\to B^nE^n}^{\mathcal{N}}(\rho_{A'^n}^m). \tag{23.69}$$

Bob finally applies a decoding channel $\mathcal{D}_{B^n\to M'}$ to recover his share of the secret key:

$$\omega_{MM'E^n} \equiv \mathcal{D}_{B^n\to M'}(\omega_{MB^nE^n}). \tag{23.70}$$

The following condition holds for an $(n, [\log |\mathcal{M}|]/n, \varepsilon)$ protocol for secret key generation:

$$\frac{1}{2} \left\| \omega_{MM'E^n} - \overline{\Phi}_{MM'} \otimes \sigma_{E^n} \right\|_1 \leq \varepsilon, \tag{23.71}$$

so that Eve's state σ_{E^n} is a constant state independent of the secret key $\overline{\Phi}_{MM'}$. In particular, the above condition implies that Eve's information about M is small:

$$I(M; E^n)_\omega \leq f(|\mathcal{M}|, \varepsilon), \tag{23.72}$$

where we apply the reasoning in Section 23.1.1, with $f(|\mathcal{M}|, \varepsilon) \equiv \varepsilon \log |\mathcal{M}| + (1 + \varepsilon) h_2(\varepsilon/[1 + \varepsilon])$. The rate of secret key generation is equal to $\frac{1}{n} \log |\mathcal{M}|$. Consider the following chain of inequalities:

$$\log |\mathcal{M}| = I(M; M')_{\overline{\Phi}} \tag{23.73}$$
$$\leq I(M; M')_\omega + f(|\mathcal{M}|, \varepsilon) \tag{23.74}$$
$$\leq I(M; B^n)_\omega + f(|\mathcal{M}|, \varepsilon) \tag{23.75}$$
$$\leq I(M; B^n)_\omega - I(M; E^n)_\omega + 2f(|\mathcal{M}|, \varepsilon) \tag{23.76}$$
$$\leq P(\mathcal{N}^{\otimes n}) + 2f(|\mathcal{M}|, \varepsilon). \tag{23.77}$$

The first equality follows because the mutual information of the shared randomness state $\overline{\Phi}_{MM'}$ is equal to $\log |\mathcal{M}|$. The first inequality follows from applying the AFW inequality to (23.71). The second inequality follows from quantum data processing. The third inequality follows from (23.72), and the final inequality follows because the classical–quantum state in (23.69) has a particular distribution and choice of states, and this choice always leads to a value of the private information that cannot be larger than the private information of the tensor-product channel $\mathcal{N}^{\otimes n}$. Putting everything together, we find that

$$\frac{1}{n} \log |\mathcal{M}| (1 - 2\varepsilon) \leq \frac{1}{n} P(\mathcal{N}^{\otimes n}) + \frac{2}{n} (1 + \varepsilon) h_2(\varepsilon/[1 + \varepsilon]). \tag{23.78}$$

Thus, if we are considering a sequence of $(n, [\log |\mathcal{M}|]/n, \varepsilon_n)$ private classical communication protocols with rate $P - \delta_n = \frac{1}{n} \log |\mathcal{M}|$, such that $\lim_{n \to \infty} \varepsilon_n = \lim_{n \to \infty} \delta_n = 0$, then the above bound becomes

$$(P - \delta_n)(1 - 2\varepsilon_n) \leq \frac{1}{n} P(\mathcal{N}^{\otimes n}) + \frac{2}{n} (1 + \varepsilon_n) h_2(\varepsilon_n/[1 + \varepsilon_n]). \tag{23.79}$$

Taking the limit as $n \to \infty$ then establishes that an achievable rate P necessarily satisfies $P \leq P_{\text{reg}}(\mathcal{N})$, where $P_{\text{reg}}(\mathcal{N})$ is the regularized private information given in (23.14).

EXERCISE 23.4.1 Prove that free access to a forward public classical channel from Alice to Bob cannot improve the private classical capacity of a quantum channel.

23.5   Discussion of Private Classical Capacity

This last section discusses some important aspects of the private classical capacity. Two of these results have to do with the fact that Theorem 23.2.1 only provides a regularized characterization of the private classical capacity, and the last asks what rates of private classical communication are achievable if the sender and receiver share a secret key before communication begins. For full details, we refer the reader to the original papers in the quantum Shannon theory literature.

23.5.1   Superadditivity of the Private Information

Theorem 23.2.1 states that the private classical capacity of a quantum channel is equal to the regularized private information of the channel. As we have said before (at the beginning of Chapter 21), a regularized formula is not particularly useful from a practical perspective because it is impossible to perform the optimization task that it sets out, and it is not desirable from an information-theoretical perspective because such a regularization does not identify a formula as a unique measure of capacity.

In light of the unsatisfactory nature of a regularized formula, is it really necessary to have the regularization in Theorem 23.2.1 for arbitrary quantum channels? Interestingly, the answer seems to be "yes" in the general case (however, we know it is not necessary if the channel is degradable). The reason is that there exists an example of a channel $\mathcal{N}$ for which the private information is strictly superadditive:

$$mP(\mathcal{N}) < P\left(\mathcal{N}^{\otimes m}\right), \qquad (23.80)$$

for some positive integer m. Specifically, Smith *et al.* showed that the private information of a particular Pauli channel exhibits this superadditivity (Smith et al., 2008). To do so, they calculated the private information $P(\mathcal{N})$ for such a channel. Next, they consider performing an m-qubit "repetition code" before transmitting qubits into the channel. A repetition code is a quantum code that performs the following encoding:

$$\alpha|0\rangle + \beta|1\rangle \rightarrow \alpha|0\rangle^{\otimes m} + \beta|1\rangle^{\otimes m}. \qquad (23.81)$$

Evaluating the private information when sending a particular state through the repetition code and then through m instances of the channel leads to a higher value than $mP(\mathcal{N})$, implying the strict inequality in (23.80). Thus, additivity of the private information formula $P(\mathcal{N})$ cannot hold in the general case.

The implications of this result are that we really do not understand the best way of transmitting information privately over a quantum channel that is not degradable, and it is thus the subject of ongoing research.

23.5.2 Superadditivity of Private Classical Capacity

The private information of a particular channel can be superadditive (as discussed in the previous section), and so the regularized private information is our best characterization of the capacity for this information-processing task. In spite of this, we might hope that some eventual formula for the private classical capacity would be additive (some formula other than the private information $P(\mathcal{N})$). Interestingly, this is also not the case.

To clarify this point, suppose that $P^{?}(\mathcal{N})$ is some formula for the private classical capacity. If it were an additive formula, then it should be additive as a function of channels:

$$P^{?}(\mathcal{N} \otimes \mathcal{M}) = P^{?}(\mathcal{N}) + P^{?}(\mathcal{M}). \tag{23.82}$$

Li *et al.* have shown that this cannot be the case for any proposed private capacity formula, by making a clever argument with a construction of channels (Li et al., 2009). Specifically, they constructed a particular channel $\mathcal{N}$ which has a single-letter *classical* capacity. The fact that the channel's classical capacity is sharply upper bounded implies that its private classical capacity is as well. Let D be the upper bound so that $P^{?}(\mathcal{N}) \leq D$. Also, they considered a 50% erasure channel, one which gives the input state to Bob and an erasure symbol to Eve with probability $1/2$ and gives the input state to Eve and an erasure symbol to Bob with probability $1/2$. Such a channel has zero capacity for sending private classical information essentially because Eve is getting the same amount of information as Bob does on average. Thus, $P^{?}(\mathcal{M}) = 0$. In spite of this, Li *et al.* show that the tensor-product channel $\mathcal{N} \otimes \mathcal{M}$ has a private classical capacity that exceeds D. We can then make the conclusion that these two channels allow for superadditivity of private classical capacity:

$$P^{?}(\mathcal{N} \otimes \mathcal{M}) > P^{?}(\mathcal{N}) + P^{?}(\mathcal{M}), \tag{23.83}$$

and that (23.82) cannot hold in the general case. More profoundly, their results demonstrate that the private classical capacity itself is non-additive, even if a characterization of it is found that is more desirable than that with the formula in Theorem 23.2.1. Thus, it will likely be difficult to obtain a desirable characterization of the private classical capacity for general quantum channels.

23.5.3 Secret-key Assisted Private Classical Communication

The direct coding part of Theorem 23.2.1 demonstrates how to send private classical information over a quantum channel $\mathcal{N}$ at the private information rate $P(\mathcal{N})$. A natural extension to consider is the scenario in which Alice and Bob share a secret key before communication begins. A secret key shared between Alice and Bob and secure from Eve is a tripartite state of the following form:

$$\overline{\Phi}_{AB} \otimes \sigma_{E}, \tag{23.84}$$

where $\overline{\Phi}_{AB}$ is the maximally correlated state and σ_E is a state on Eve's system that is independent of the key shared between Alice and Bob. Like the entanglement-assisted capacity theorem, we assume that they obtain this secret key from some third party, and the third party ensures that the key remains secure.

The resulting capacity theorem is known as the secret-key-assisted private classical capacity theorem, and it characterizes the trade-off between secret key consumption and private classical communication. The main idea for this setting is to show the existence of a protocol that transmits private classical information at a rate of $I(X;B)$ private bits per channel use while consuming secret key at a rate of $I(X;E)$ secret key bits per channel use, where the information quantities are with respect to the state in Theorem 23.2.1. The protocol for achieving these rates is almost identical to the one we gave in the proof of the direct coding theorem, though with one difference. Instead of sacrificing classical bits at a rate of $I(X;E)$ in order to randomize Eve's knowledge of the message (recall that our randomization variable had to be chosen uniformly at random from a set of size $\approx 2^{nI(X;E)}$), the sender exploits the secret key to do so. The converse proof shows that this strategy is optimal (with a multi-letter characterization). Thus, we have the following capacity theorem:

THEOREM 23.5.1 (Secret-Key-Assisted Capacity Theorem)   The secret-key-assisted private classical capacity region $C_{\text{SKA}}(\mathcal{N})$ of a quantum channel $\mathcal{N}$ is given by

$$C_{\text{SKA}}(\mathcal{N}) = \overline{\bigcup_{k=1}^{\infty} \frac{1}{k}\widetilde{C}_{\text{SKA}}^{(1)}(\mathcal{N}^{\otimes k})}, \qquad (23.85)$$

where the overbar indicates the closure of a set. $\widetilde{C}_{\text{SKA}}^{(1)}(\mathcal{N})$ is the set of all $P, S \geq 0$ such that

$$P \leq I(X;B)_{\sigma} - I(X;E)_{\sigma} + S, \qquad (23.86)$$
$$P \leq I(X;B)_{\sigma}. \qquad (23.87)$$

where P is the rate of private classical communication, S is the rate of secret key consumption, the state σ_{XBE} is of the following form:

$$\sigma_{XBE} \equiv \sum_x p_X(x)|x\rangle\langle x|_X \otimes \mathcal{U}_{A'\to BE}^{\mathcal{N}}(\rho_{A'}^x), \qquad (23.88)$$

and $U_{A'\to BE}^{\mathcal{N}}$ is an isometric extension of the channel.

Showing that the above inequalities are achievable follows by time sharing between the protocol from the direct coding part of Theorem 23.2.1 and the aforementioned protocol for secret-key-assisted private classical communication.

23.6 History and Further Reading

Bennett & Brassard (1984) devised the first protocol for sending private classical data over a quantum channel. The protocol given there became known as quantum key distribution, which has now become a thriving field in its own right (Scarani et al., 2009). Devetak (2005) and Cai et al. (2004) proved the characterization of the private classical capacity given in this chapter (both using the techniques that we reviewed in this chapter). Hsieh, Luo & Brun (2008) proved achievability of the secret-key-assisted protocol given in Section 23.5.3, and Wilde (2011) proved the converse and stated the secret-key-assisted capacity theorem. Later work characterized the full trade-off between public classical communication, private classical communication, and secret key (Hsieh & Wilde, 2009; Wilde & Hsieh, 2012a). Smith et al. (2008) showed that the private information can exhibit superadditivity, and Li et al. (2009) showed that the private classical capacity is generally non-additive. Elkouss & Strelchuk (2015) demonstrated a striking superadditivity effect, which suggests that a regularized expression is necessary to determine the private capacity of an arbitrary channel. Smith (2008) later showed that the symmetric-side-channel-assisted private classical capacity is additive. Datta & Hsieh (2010) demonstrated universal private codes for quantum channels.

A different, weaker notion of security is based on the eavesdropper not being able to learn much from any measurement performed on her system. Although this notion might seem similar to the notion of security that we discussed in this chapter, it is in fact much different (König et al., 2007) and is the basis for the information locking effect (DiVincenzo et al., 2004). Impressive information locking schemes exist (Hayden, Leung, Shor & Winter, 2004; Dupuis et al., 2013; Fawzi et al., 2013), and recently, the locking capacity of a channel was introduced and bounded (Guha et al., 2014), calculated for particular channels (Winter, 2015b), and developed further (Lupo & Lloyd, 2014; Lupo & Lloyd, 2015).

24 Quantum Communication

The quantum capacity theorem is one of the most important theorems in quantum Shannon theory. It is a fundamentally "quantum" theorem in that it demonstrates that a fundamentally quantum information quantity, the coherent information, is an achievable rate for quantum communication over a quantum channel. The fact that the coherent information does not have a strong analog in classical Shannon theory truly separates the quantum and classical theories of information.

The no-cloning theorem (Section 3.5.4) provides the intuition behind the quantum capacity theorem. The goal of any quantum communication protocol is for Alice to establish quantum correlations with the receiver Bob. We know well now that every quantum channel has an isometric extension, so that we can think of another receiver, the environment Eve, who is at a second output port of a larger unitary evolution. Were Eve able to learn anything about the quantum information that Alice is attempting to transmit to Bob, then Bob could not be retrieving this information—otherwise, they would violate the no-cloning theorem. Thus, Alice should figure out some subspace of the channel input where she can place her quantum information such that only Bob has access to it, while Eve does not. That the dimensionality of this subspace is exponential in the coherent information is perhaps then unsurprising in light of the above no-cloning reasoning. The coherent information is an entropy difference $H(B) - H(E)$—a measure of the amount of quantum correlations that Alice can establish with Bob less the amount that Eve can gain.[1]

We proved achievability of the coherent information for quantum data transmission in Corollary 22.2.1, but the roundabout path that we followed to prove achievability there perhaps does not give much insight into the structure of a quantum code that achieves the coherent information. Our approach in this chapter is different and should shed more light on this structure. Specifically, we show how to make coherent versions of the private classical codes from the previous chapter. By exploiting the privacy properties of these codes, we can form subspaces where Alice can store her quantum information such that Eve does not

---

[1] Recall from Exercise 11.6.6 that we can also write the coherent information as half the difference of Bob's mutual information with Alice less Eve's:
$$I(A\rangle B) = 1/2 \left[I(A; B) - I(A; E) \right].$$

have access to it. Thus, this approach follows the above "no-cloning intuition" more closely.

The best characterization that we have for the quantum capacity of a general quantum channel is the regularized coherent information. It turns out that the regularization is not necessary for the class of degradable channels, implying that we have a complete understanding of the quantum data transmission capabilities of these channels. However, if a channel is not degradable, there can be some startling consequences, and these results imply that we have an incomplete understanding of quantum data transmission in the general case. First, the coherent information can be strictly superadditive for the depolarizing channel. This means that the best strategy for achieving the quantum capacity is not necessarily the familiar one where we generate random quantum codes from a single instance of a channel. This result is also in marked contrast with the "classical" strategies that achieve the unassisted and entanglement-assisted classical capacities of the depolarizing channel. Second, perhaps the most surprising result in quantum Shannon theory is that it is possible to "superactivate" the quantum capacity. That is, suppose that two channels on their own have zero capacity for transmitting quantum information (for the phenomenon to occur, these channels are specific channels). Then it is possible for the joint channel (the tensor product of the individual channels) to have a non-zero quantum capacity, in spite of them being individually useless for quantum data transmission. This latter result implies that we are rather distant from having a complete quantum theory of information, in spite of the many successes reviewed in this book.

We structure this chapter as follows. We first overview the information-processing task relevant for quantum communication. Next, we discuss the no-cloning intuition for quantum capacity in some more detail, presenting the specific example of a quantum erasure channel. Section 24.3 states the quantum capacity theorem, and the following two sections prove the direct coding and converse theorems corresponding to it. Section 24.7 computes the quantum capacity of two degradable channels: the quantum erasure channel and the amplitude damping channel. We then discuss superadditivity of coherent information and superactivation of quantum capacity in Section 24.8. Finally, we prove the existence of an entanglement distillation protocol, whose proof bears some similarities to the proof of the direct coding part of the quantum capacity theorem.

24.1   The Information-Processing Task

We begin the technical development in this chapter by describing the information-processing task for quantum communication (we define an (n, Q, ε) quantum communication code). First, there are several different tasks that we can consider as quantum communication, but the strongest definition of quantum capacity corresponds to a task known as *entanglement transmission*. Suppose that Alice shares entanglement with a reference system to which she does not have access. Then their goal is to devise a quantum coding scheme such that Alice can transfer this entanglement to Bob. To this end, suppose that Alice and the reference share an arbitrary state $|\varphi\rangle_{RA_1}$, where the systems R and A_1 have the same dimension. Alice then performs some encoder on system A_1 to prepare it for input to many instances of a quantum channel $\mathcal{N}_{A'\rightarrow B}$. The resulting state is as follows: $\mathcal{E}_{A_1\rightarrow A'^n}(\varphi_{RA_1})$. Alice transmits the systems A'^n through many independent uses of the channel $\mathcal{N}_{A'\rightarrow B}$, resulting in the following state: $\mathcal{N}_{A'^n\rightarrow B^n}(\mathcal{E}_{A_1\rightarrow A'^n}(\varphi_{RA_1}))$, where $\mathcal{N}_{A'^n\rightarrow B^n} \equiv (\mathcal{N}_{A'\rightarrow B})^{\otimes n}$. After Bob receives the systems B^n from the channel outputs, he performs some decoding channel $\mathcal{D}_{B^n\rightarrow B_1}$, where B_1 is some system of the same dimension as A_1. The final state after Bob decodes is as follows:

$$\omega_{RB_1} \equiv \mathcal{D}_{B^n\rightarrow B_1}(\mathcal{N}_{A'^n\rightarrow B^n}(\mathcal{E}_{A_1\rightarrow A'^n}(\varphi_{RA_1}))). \tag{24.1}$$

Figure 24.1 depicts all of the above steps. For an (n, Q, ε) protocol, the following condition should hold for all states $|\varphi\rangle_{RA_1}$:

$$\frac{1}{2}\|\varphi_{RA_1} - \omega_{RB_1}\|_1 \le \varepsilon. \tag{24.2}$$

The rate Q of this scheme is equal to the number of qubits transmitted per channel use:

$$Q \equiv \frac{1}{n}\log\dim(\mathcal{H}_{A_1}). \tag{24.3}$$

A rate Q is achievable for $\mathcal{N}$ if there exists an $(n, Q - \delta, \varepsilon)$ quantum communication code for all $\varepsilon \in (0, 1)$, $\delta > 0$, and sufficiently large n. The quantum capacity $C_Q(\mathcal{N})$ is defined as the supremum of all achievable rates for $\mathcal{N}$.

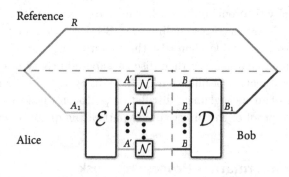

Figure 24.1 The information-processing task for entanglement transmission. Alice is trying to preserve the entanglement with some inaccessible reference system by encoding her system and transmitting the encoded quantum data over many independent uses of a noisy quantum channel. Bob performs a decoding of the systems he receives, and the state at the end of the protocol is close to the original state shared between Alice and the reference if the protocol is any good for entanglement transmission.

The above notion of quantum communication encompasses other quantum information-processing tasks such as mixed-state transmission, pure-state transmission, and entanglement generation. Alice can transmit any mixed or pure state if she can preserve the entanglement with a reference system. Also, she can generate entanglement with Bob if she can preserve entanglement with a reference system—she just needs to create an entangled state locally and apply the above protocol to one system of the entangled state.

EXERCISE 24.1.1   Show that an (n, Q, ε) protocol for quantum communication satisfies the following:

$$\frac{1}{2} \left\| \mathrm{id}_{A_1 \to B_1} - \mathcal{D}_{B^n \to B_1} \circ \mathcal{N}_{A' \to B}^{\otimes n} \circ \mathcal{E}_{A_1 \to A'^n} \right\|_\diamond \le \varepsilon, \tag{24.4}$$

where $\|\cdot\|_\diamond$ denotes the diamond norm, defined in Section 9.1.6.

24.2   No-Cloning and Quantum Communication

We first discuss quantum communication over a quantum erasure channel before stating and proving the quantum capacity theorem. Consider the quantum erasure channel that gives Alice's input state to Bob with probability $1 - \varepsilon$ and an erasure flag to Bob with probability ε:

$$\rho \to (1 - \varepsilon)\,\rho + \varepsilon |e\rangle\langle e|, \tag{24.5}$$

where $\langle e|\rho|e\rangle = 0$ for all inputs ρ. Recall that an isometric extension of this channel is as follows (see Exercise 5.2.6):

$$|\psi\rangle_{RA} \to \sqrt{1-\varepsilon}\,|\psi\rangle_{RB}|e\rangle_E + \sqrt{\varepsilon}\,|\psi\rangle_{RE}|e\rangle_B, \tag{24.6}$$

so that the channel now has the other interpretation that Eve gets the state with probability ε while giving her the erasure flag with probability $1 - \varepsilon$.

Now suppose that the erasure parameter is set to $1/2$. In such a scenario, the channel to Eve is the *same* as the channel to Bob, namely, both have the channel $\rho \to 1/2\,(\rho + |e\rangle\langle e|)$. We can argue that the quantum capacity of such a channel should be equal to zero, by invoking the no-cloning theorem. More specifically, suppose there is a scheme (an encoder and decoder as given in Figure 24.1) for Alice and Bob to communicate quantum information reliably at a non-zero rate over such a channel. If so, Eve could simply use the same decoder that Bob does, and she should also be able to obtain the quantum information that Alice is sending. But the ability for both Bob and Eve to decode the quantum information that Alice is transmitting violates the no-cloning theorem. Thus, the quantum capacity of such a channel should vanish.

EXERCISE 24.2.1   Argue that the quantum capacity of an amplitude damping channel vanishes if its damping parameter is equal to $1/2$.

The no-cloning theorem plays a more general role in the analysis of quantum communication over quantum channels. In the construction of a quantum code we are trying to find a "no-cloning" subspace of the input Hilbert space that is protected from Eve. If Eve is able to obtain any of the quantum information in this subspace, then this information cannot be going to Bob by the same no-cloning argument featured in the previous paragraph. Thus, we might then suspect that the codes from the previous chapter for private classical communication might play a role for quantum communication because we constructed them in such a way that Eve would not be able to obtain any information about the private message that Alice is transmitting to Eve. The main insight needed is to make a coherent version of these private classical codes, so that Alice and Bob conduct every step in superposition (much like we did in Chapter 22).

24.3   The Quantum Capacity Theorem

The main theorem of this chapter is the following quantum capacity theorem.

THEOREM 24.3.1 (Quantum Capacity)   The quantum capacity $C_Q(\mathcal{N})$ of a quantum channel $\mathcal{N}_{A'\to B}$ is equal to the regularized coherent information of the channel:

$$C_Q(\mathcal{N}) = Q_{\mathrm{reg}}(\mathcal{N}), \tag{24.7}$$

where

$$Q_{\mathrm{reg}}(\mathcal{N}) \equiv \lim_{k\to\infty} \frac{1}{k} Q(\mathcal{N}^{\otimes k}). \tag{24.8}$$

The channel coherent information $Q(\mathcal{N})$ is defined as

$$Q(\mathcal{N}) \equiv \max_{\phi} I(A\rangle B)_\sigma, \tag{24.9}$$

where the optimization is with respect to all pure, bipartite states $\phi_{AA'}$ and $\sigma_{AB} \equiv \mathcal{N}_{A'\to B}(\phi_{AA'})$.

We prove this theorem in two parts: the direct coding theorem and the converse theorem. The proof of the direct coding theorem proceeds by exploiting the private classical codes from the previous chapter. The proof of the converse theorem is similar to approaches from previous chapters—we exploit the AFW inequality and quantum data processing in order to obtain an upper bound on the quantum capacity. In general, the regularized coherent information is our best characterization of the quantum capacity, but the regularization is not necessary for the class of degradable channels. Since many channels of interest are degradable (including dephasing, amplitude damping, and erasure channels), we can calculate their quantum capacities.

24.4   The Direct Coding Theorem

The proof of the direct coding part of the quantum capacity theorem follows by taking advantage of the properties of the private classical codes constructed in the previous chapter (see Section 23.3). We briefly recall this construction. Suppose that a classical–quantum–quantum channel connects Alice to Bob and Eve. Specifically, if Alice inputs a classical letter x to the channel, then Bob receives a density operator ρ_B^x and Eve receives a density operator ω_E^x. The direct coding part of Theorem 23.2.1 establishes the existence of a codebook $\{x^n(m,k)\}_{m \in \mathcal{M}, k \in \mathcal{K}}$ selected from a distribution $p_X(x)$ and a corresponding decoding POVM $\{\Lambda_{B^n}^{m,k}\}$ such that Bob can detect Alice's message m and randomizing variable k with high probability:

$$\forall m \in \mathcal{M}, k \in \mathcal{K} : \mathrm{Tr}\left\{\Lambda_{B^n}^{m,k} \rho_{B^n}^{x^n(m,k)}\right\} \geq 1 - \varepsilon, \qquad (24.10)$$

while Eve obtains a negligible amount of information about Alice's message m:

$$\forall m \in \mathcal{M} : \left\| \frac{1}{|\mathcal{K}|} \sum_{k \in \mathcal{K}} \omega_{E^n}^{x^n(m,k)} - \omega^{\otimes n} \right\|_1 \leq \varepsilon, \qquad (24.11)$$

where ω is Eve's expected density operator:

$$\omega \equiv \sum_x p_X(x) \omega_E^x. \qquad (24.12)$$

The above statements hold true for all $\varepsilon \in (0,1)$ and sufficiently large n as long as

$$|\mathcal{M}| \approx 2^{n[I(X;B) - I(X;E)]}, \qquad (24.13)$$

$$|\mathcal{K}| \approx 2^{nI(X;E)}. \qquad (24.14)$$

We can now construct a coherent version of the above code that is good for quantum data transmission. First, suppose that there is some density operator with the following spectral decomposition:

$$\rho_{A'} \equiv \sum_x p_X(x) |\psi_x\rangle\langle\psi_x|_{A'}. \qquad (24.15)$$

Now suppose that the channel $\mathcal{N}_{A' \to B}$ has an isometric extension $U_{A' \to BE}^{\mathcal{N}}$, so that inputting $|\psi_x\rangle_{A'}$ leads to the following state shared between Bob and Eve:

$$|\psi_x\rangle_{BE} \equiv U_{A' \to BE}^{\mathcal{N}} |\psi_x\rangle_{A'}. \qquad (24.16)$$

From the direct coding part of Theorem 23.2.1, we know that there exists a private classical code $\{x^n(m,k)\}_{m \in \mathcal{M}, k \in \mathcal{K}}$ with the properties in (24.10)–(24.11) and with rate

$$I(X;B)_\sigma - I(X;E)_\sigma, \qquad (24.17)$$

where σ_{XBE} is a classical–quantum state of the following form:

$$\sigma_{XBE} \equiv \sum_x p_X(x)|x\rangle\langle x|_X \otimes |\psi_x\rangle\langle\psi_x|_{BE}. \qquad (24.18)$$

The following identity demonstrates that the private information in (24.17) is equal to the coherent information for the particular state σ_{XBE} above:

$$I(X;B)_\sigma - I(X;E)_\sigma = H(B)_\sigma - H(B|X)_\sigma - H(E)_\sigma + H(E|X)_\sigma \qquad (24.19)$$

$$= H(B)_\sigma - H(B|X)_\sigma - H(E)_\sigma + H(B|X)_\sigma \qquad (24.20)$$

$$= H(B)_\sigma - H(E)_\sigma. \qquad (24.21)$$

The first equality follows from the identity $I(C;D) = H(D) - H(D|C)$. The second equality follows because the state on systems BE is pure when conditioned on the classical variable X. Observe that the last expression is a function solely of the density operator ρ in (24.15), and it is also equal to the coherent information of the channel for the particular input state ρ (see Exercise 11.5.2).

Now we show how to construct a quantum code achieving the coherent information rate $H(B)_\sigma - H(E)_\sigma$ by making a coherent version of the above private classical code. Suppose that Alice shares a state $|\varphi\rangle_{RA_1}$ with a reference system R, where

$$|\varphi\rangle_{RA_1} \equiv \sum_{l,m \in \mathcal{M}} \alpha_{l,m} |l\rangle_R |m\rangle_{A_1}, \qquad (24.22)$$

and $\{|l\rangle_R\}$ is some orthonormal basis for R while $\{|m\rangle_{A_1}\}$ is some orthonormal basis for A_1. Also, we set $|\mathcal{M}| \approx 2^{n[H(B)_\sigma - H(E)_\sigma]}$. We would like for Alice and Bob to execute a quantum communication protocol such that Bob can reconstruct Alice's share of the above state on his system with Alice no longer entangled with the reference (we would like for the final state to be close to $|\varphi\rangle_{RA_1}$ where Bob is holding the A_1 system). To this end, Alice creates a quantum codebook $\{|\phi_m\rangle_{A'^n}\}_{m \in \mathcal{M}}$ with quantum codewords:

$$|\phi_m\rangle_{A'^n} \equiv \frac{1}{\sqrt{|\mathcal{K}|}} \sum_{k \in \mathcal{K}} e^{i\gamma_{m,k}} |\psi^{x^n(m,k)}\rangle_{A'^n}, \qquad (24.23)$$

where the states $|\psi^{x^n(m,k)}\rangle_{A'^n}$ are the nth extensions of the states arising from the spectral decomposition in (24.15), the classical sequences $x^n(m,k)$ are from the codebook for private classical communication, and we specify how to choose the phases $\gamma_{m,k}$ later. All the states $|\psi^{x^n(m,k)}\rangle_{A'^n}$ are orthonormal because they are chosen from the spectral decomposition in (24.15) and the expurgation from Section 23.3.4 guarantees that they are distinct (otherwise, they would not be good codewords!). The fact that the states $|\psi^{x^n(m,k)}\rangle_{A'^n}$ are orthonormal implies that the quantum codewords $|\phi_m\rangle_{A'^n}$ are also orthonormal.

Alice's first action is to coherently copy the value of m in the A_1 register to another register A_2, so that the state in (24.22) becomes

$$\sum_{l,m} \alpha_{l,m} |l\rangle_R |m\rangle_{A_1} |m\rangle_{A_2}. \qquad (24.24)$$

Alice then performs some isometric encoding from A_2 to A'^n that takes the above unencoded state to the following encoded state:

$$\sum_{l,m} \alpha_{l,m} |l\rangle_R |m\rangle_{A_1} |\phi_m\rangle_{A'^n} , \qquad (24.25)$$

where each $|\phi_m\rangle_{A'^n}$ is a quantum codeword of the form in (24.23). Alice transmits the systems A'^n through many uses of the quantum channel, leading to the following state shared between the reference, Alice, Bob, and Eve:

$$\sum_{l,m} \alpha_{l,m} |l\rangle_R |m\rangle_{A_1} |\phi_m\rangle_{B^n E^n} , \qquad (24.26)$$

where $|\phi_m\rangle_{B^n E^n}$ is defined from (24.16) and (24.23). Recall from (24.10) that Bob can detect the message m and the variable k in the private classical code with high probability:

$$\forall m, k : \text{Tr}\left\{ \Lambda_{B^n}^{m,k} \psi_{B^n}^{x^n(m,k)} \right\} \geq 1 - \varepsilon. \qquad (24.27)$$

So Bob instead constructs a coherent version of this POVM:

$$\sum_{m \in \mathcal{M}, k \in \mathcal{K}} \sqrt{\Lambda_{B^n}^{m,k}} \otimes |m\rangle_{B_1} |k\rangle_{B_2}. \qquad (24.28)$$

He then performs this coherent POVM, resulting in the state

$$\sum_{\substack{m' \in \mathcal{M}, \, l,m \\ k' \in \mathcal{K}}} \sum_{k \in \mathcal{K}} \frac{1}{\sqrt{|\mathcal{K}|}} \alpha_{l,m} |l\rangle_R |m\rangle_{A_1} \sqrt{\Lambda_{B^n}^{m',k'}} e^{i\gamma_{k,m}} |\psi^{x^n(m,k)}\rangle_{B^n E^n} |m', k'\rangle_{B_1 B_2} . \qquad (24.29)$$

We would like for the above state to be close in trace distance to the following state:

$$\sum_{l,m} \sum_{k \in \mathcal{K}} \frac{1}{\sqrt{|\mathcal{K}|}} \alpha_{l,m} |l\rangle_R |m\rangle_{A_1} e^{i\delta_{m,k}} |\psi^{x^n(m,k)}\rangle_{B^n E^n} |m\rangle_{B_1} |k\rangle_{B_2} , \qquad (24.30)$$

where $\delta_{m,k}$ are some phases that we will specify shortly. To this end, consider that the sets $\{|\chi_{m,k}\rangle_{B^n E^n B_1 B_2}\}_{m,k}$ and $\{|\varphi_{m,k}\rangle_{B^n E^n B_1 B_2}\}_{m,k}$ form orthonormal bases, where

$$|\chi_{m,k}\rangle_{B^n E^n B_1 B_2} \equiv |\psi^{x^n(m,k)}\rangle_{B^n E^n} |m\rangle_{B_1} |k\rangle_{B_2} , \qquad (24.31)$$

$$|\varphi_{m,k}\rangle_{B^n E^n B_1 B_2} \equiv \sum_{m' \in \mathcal{M}, k' \in \mathcal{K}} \sqrt{\Lambda_{B^n}^{m',k'}} |\psi^{x^n(m,k)}\rangle_{B^n E^n} |m'\rangle_{B_1} |k'\rangle_{B_2} . \qquad (24.32)$$

Also, consider that the overlap between corresponding states in the different bases is high:

$$\langle \chi_{m,k} | \varphi_{m,k} \rangle$$

$$= \langle \psi^{x^n(m,k)}|_{B^n E^n} \langle m|_{B_1} \langle k|_{B_2} \sum_{m' \in \mathcal{M}, k' \in \mathcal{K}} \sqrt{\Lambda_{B^n}^{m',k'}} |\psi^{x^n(m,k)}\rangle_{B^n E^n} |m'\rangle_{B_1} |k'\rangle_{B_2}$$

$$(24.33)$$

$$= \sum_{m' \in \mathcal{M}, k' \in \mathcal{K}} \langle \psi^{x^n(m,k)}|_{B^n E^n} \sqrt{\Lambda_{B^n}^{m',k'}} |\psi^{x^n(m,k)}\rangle_{B^n E^n} \langle m|m'\rangle_{B_1} \langle k|k'\rangle_{B_2} \quad (24.34)$$

$$= \langle \psi^{x^n(m,k)}|_{B^n E^n} \sqrt{\Lambda_{B^n}^{m,k}} |\psi^{x^n(m,k)}\rangle_{B^n E^n} \quad (24.35)$$

$$\geq \langle \psi^{x^n(m,k)}|_{B^n E^n} \Lambda_{B^n}^{m,k} |\psi^{x^n(m,k)}\rangle_{B^n E^n} \quad (24.36)$$

$$= \mathrm{Tr}\left\{ \Lambda_{B^n}^{m,k} \psi_{B^n}^{x^n(m,k)} \right\} \quad (24.37)$$

$$\geq 1 - \varepsilon, \quad (24.38)$$

where the first inequality follows from the fact that $\sqrt{\Lambda_{B^n}^{m,k}} \geq \Lambda_{B^n}^{m,k}$ for $\Lambda_{B^n}^{m,k} \leq I$ and the second inequality follows from (24.27). By applying Lemma A.0.3 from Appendix A, we know that there exist phases $\gamma_{m,k}$ and $\delta_{m,k}$ such that

$$\langle \chi_m | \varphi_m \rangle \geq 1 - \varepsilon, \quad (24.39)$$

where

$$|\chi_m\rangle_{B^n E^n B_1 B_2} \equiv \frac{1}{\sqrt{|\mathcal{K}|}} \sum_k e^{i\delta_{m,k}} |\chi_{m,k}\rangle_{B^n E^n B_1 B_2}, \quad (24.40)$$

$$|\varphi_m\rangle_{B^n E^n B_1 B_2} \equiv \frac{1}{\sqrt{|\mathcal{K}|}} \sum_k e^{i\gamma_{m,k}} |\varphi_{m,k}\rangle_{B^n E^n B_1 B_2}. \quad (24.41)$$

So we choose the phases in a way such that the above inequality holds. We can then apply the above result to show that the state in (24.29) has high fidelity with the state in (24.30):

$$\left(\sum_{l,m} \alpha_{l,m}^* \langle l|_R \langle m|_{A_1} \langle \chi_m|_{B^n E^n B_1 B_2} \right) \left(\sum_{l',m'} \alpha_{l',m'} |l'\rangle_R |m'\rangle_{A_1} |\varphi_{m'}\rangle_{B^n E^n B_1 B_2} \right)$$

$$= \sum_{l,m,l',m'} \alpha_{l,m}^* \alpha_{l',m'} \langle l|l'\rangle_R \langle m|m'\rangle_{A_1} \langle \chi_m|\varphi_{m'}\rangle_{B^n E^n B_1 B_2} \quad (24.42)$$

$$= \sum_{l,m} |\alpha_{l,m}|^2 \langle \chi_m|\varphi_m\rangle_{B^n E^n B_1 B_2} \quad (24.43)$$

$$\geq 1 - \varepsilon. \quad (24.44)$$

Thus, the state resulting after Bob performs the coherent POVM is close in trace distance to the following state:

$$\sum_{l,m \in \mathcal{M}} \alpha_{l,m} |l\rangle_R |m\rangle_{A_1} \frac{1}{\sqrt{|\mathcal{K}|}} \sum_{k \in \mathcal{K}} e^{i\delta_{m,k}} |\psi^{x^n(m,k)}\rangle_{B^n E^n} |m\rangle_{B_1} |k\rangle_{B_2}$$

$$= \sum_{l,m \in \mathcal{M}} \alpha_{l,m} |l\rangle_R |m\rangle_{A_1} |\widetilde{\phi}_m\rangle_{B^n E^n B_2} |m\rangle_{B_1}, \quad (24.45)$$

where

$$|\widetilde{\phi}_m\rangle_{B^n E^n B_2} \equiv \frac{1}{\sqrt{|\mathcal{K}|}} \sum_{k \in \mathcal{K}} e^{i\delta_{m,k}} |\psi^{x^n(m,k)}\rangle_{B^n E^n} |k\rangle_{B_2}. \quad (24.46)$$

Consider the state of Eve for a particular value of m:

$$\left[\tilde{\phi}_m\right]_{E^n}$$

$$= \mathrm{Tr}_{B^n B_2}\left\{|\tilde{\phi}_m\rangle\langle\tilde{\phi}_m|_{B^n E^n B_2}\right\} \tag{24.47}$$

$$= \mathrm{Tr}_{B^n B_2}\left\{\sum_{k,k'\in\mathcal{K}}\frac{1}{|\mathcal{K}|}e^{i(\delta_{m,k'}-\delta_{m,k})}|\psi^{x^n(m,k)}\rangle\langle\psi^{x^n(m,k')}|_{B^n E^n}\otimes |k\rangle\langle k'|_{B_2}\right\} \tag{24.48}$$

$$= \frac{1}{|\mathcal{K}|}\sum_{k\in\mathcal{K}}\psi^{x^n(m,k)}_{E^n}. \tag{24.49}$$

We are now in a position to apply the second property of the private classical code. Recall from the privacy condition in (24.11) that Eve's state is guaranteed to be ε-close in trace distance to the tensor-power state $[\mathcal{N}^c_{A'\to E}(\rho)]^{\otimes n}$, where $\mathcal{N}^c_{A'\to E}$ is the complementary channel and ρ is the density operator in (24.15). Let $|\theta_{\mathcal{N}^c(\rho)}\rangle_{E^n B_3}$ be some purification of this tensor-power state. By Uhlmann's theorem and the relation between trace distance and fidelity (see Definition 9.2.3 and Theorem 9.3.1), there is some isometry $U^m_{B^n B_2\to B_3}$ for each value of m such that the following states are $2\sqrt{\varepsilon}$-close in trace distance (see Exercise 9.2.9):

$$U^m_{B^n B_2\to B_3}|\tilde{\phi}_m\rangle_{B^n E^n B_2} \overset{2\sqrt{\varepsilon}}{\approx} |\theta_{\mathcal{N}^c(\rho)}\rangle_{E^n B_3}. \tag{24.50}$$

Bob then performs the following controlled isometry on his systems B^n, B_1, and B_2:

$$\sum_m |m\rangle\langle m|_{B_1}\otimes U^m_{B^n B_2\to B_3}, \tag{24.51}$$

leading to a state that is close in trace distance to the following state:

$$\left(\sum_{l,m\in\mathcal{M}}\alpha_{l,m}|l\rangle_R |m\rangle_{A_1}|m\rangle_{B_1}\right)\otimes |\theta_{\mathcal{N}^c(\rho)}\rangle_{E^n B_3}. \tag{24.52}$$

At this point, the key observation is that the state on $E^n B_3$ is effectively decoupled from the state on systems R, A_1, and B_1, so that Bob can just throw away his system B_3. Thus, they have successfully implemented an approximate coherent channel from system A_1 to $A_1 B_1$.

We now allow for Alice to communicate classical information to Bob in order for them to implement a quantum communication channel rather than just a mere coherent channel (in a moment we argue that this free forward classical communication is not necessary). Alice performs a Fourier transform on the register A_1, leading to the following state:

$$\frac{1}{\sqrt{d_{A_1}}}\sum_{l,m,j\in\mathcal{M}}\alpha_{l,m}\exp\{2\pi i m j/d_{A_1}\}|l\rangle_R |j\rangle_{A_1}|m\rangle_{B_1}, \tag{24.53}$$

where $d_{A_1} \equiv \dim(\mathcal{H}_{A_1})$. She then measures register A_1 in the computationa basis, leading to some outcome j and the following post-measurement state:

$$\left(\sum_{l,m \in \mathcal{M}} \alpha_{l,m} \exp\{2\pi i m j / d_{A_1}\} \, |l\rangle_R \, |m\rangle_{B_1} \right) \otimes |j\rangle_{A_1}. \qquad (24.54)$$

She sends Bob the outcome j of her measurement over a classical channel, and the protocol ends with Bob performing the following unitary:

$$Z^{\dagger}(j)|m\rangle_{B_1} = \exp\{-2\pi i m j / d_{A_1}\} \, |m\rangle_{B_1}, \qquad (24.55)$$

leaving the desired state on the reference and Bob's system B_1:

$$\sum_{l,m \in \mathcal{M}} \alpha_{l,m} \, |l\rangle_R \, |m\rangle_{B_1}. \qquad (24.56)$$

All of the errors accumulated in the above protocol are some finite sum of ε terms, and applying the triangle inequality several times implies that the actual state is close to the desired state in the asymptotic limit of large block length. Figure 24.2 depicts all of the steps in this protocol for quantum communication.

We now argue that the classical communication is not necessary—there exists a scheme that does not require the use of this forward classical channel. After reviewing the above protocol and glancing at Figure 24.2, we realize that Alice's encoder is a quantum instrument of the following form:

$$\mathcal{E}(\rho) \equiv \sum_j \mathcal{E}_j(\rho) \otimes |j\rangle\langle j|. \qquad (24.57)$$

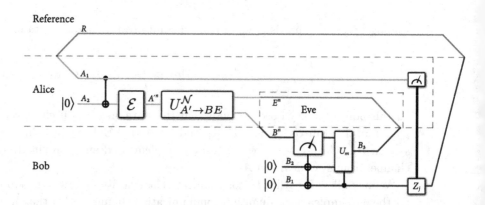

Figure 24.2 All of the steps in the protocol for quantum communication. Alice and Bob's goal is to communicate as much quantum information as they can while making sure that Eve's state is independent of what Alice is trying to communicate to Bob. The figure depicts the series of controlled unitaries that Alice and Bob perform and the final measurement and classical communication that enables quantum communication from Alice to Bob at the coherent information rate.

Each map $\mathcal{E}_j$ is trace-non-increasing and has the following action on a pure-state input $|\varphi\rangle_{RA_1}$:

$$\langle j|_{A_1} F_{A_1} \left(\sum_{m'} |\phi_{m'}\rangle\langle m'|_{A_2} \right) \left(\sum_m |m\rangle\langle m|_{A_1} \otimes |m\rangle_{A_2} \right) |\varphi\rangle_{RA_1}, \qquad (24.58)$$

where $\sum_m |m\rangle\langle m|_{A_1} \otimes |m\rangle_{A_2}$ is Alice's coherent copier in (24.24), $\sum_{m'} |\phi_{m'}\rangle\langle m'|_{A_2}$ is her quantum encoder in (24.25), F_{A_1} is the Fourier transform, and $\langle j|_{A_1}$ represents the projection onto a particular measurement outcome j. We can simplify the above expression as follows:

$$= \langle j|_{A_1} \sum_{m'} |\widetilde{m'}\rangle\langle m'|_{A_1} \left(\sum_m |m\rangle\langle m|_{A_1} \otimes |\phi_m\rangle_{A_2} \right) |\varphi\rangle_{RA_1} \qquad (24.59)$$

$$= \langle j|_{A_1} \sum_m |\widetilde{m}\rangle\langle m|_{A_1} \otimes |\phi_m\rangle_{A_2} |\varphi\rangle_{RA_1} \qquad (24.60)$$

$$= \left(\frac{1}{\sqrt{|\mathcal{M}|}} \sum_m e^{i2\pi mj/|\mathcal{M}|} |\phi_m\rangle_{A_2} \langle m|_{A_1} \right) |\varphi\rangle_{RA_1}. \qquad (24.61)$$

It follows that the trace of each $\mathcal{E}_j$ is uniform and independent of the input state $|\varphi\rangle_{RA_1}$:

$$\text{Tr}\{\mathcal{E}_j(\varphi_{RA_1})\} = \frac{1}{|\mathcal{M}|}. \qquad (24.62)$$

Observe that multiplying the map in (24.61) by $\sqrt{|\mathcal{M}|}$ gives a proper isometry that could suffice as an encoding. Let $\mathcal{E}'_j$ denote the rescaled isometry. Corresponding to each encoder is a decoding map $\mathcal{D}_j$ consisting of Bob's coherent measurement in (24.28), his decoupler in (24.51), and his phase shifter in (24.55). We can thus represent the state output from our classically coordinated protocol as follows:

$$\sum_j \mathcal{D}_j \left(\mathcal{N}^{\otimes n} \left(\mathcal{E}_j \left(\varphi_{RA_1} \right) \right) \right). \qquad (24.63)$$

From the analysis in the preceding paragraphs, we know that the trace distance between the ideal state and the actual state is small for the classically coordinated scheme:

$$\left\| \sum_j \mathcal{D}_j \left(\mathcal{N}^{\otimes n} \left(\mathcal{E}_j \left(\varphi_{RA_1} \right) \right) \right) - \varphi_{RA_1} \right\|_1 \leq \varepsilon', \qquad (24.64)$$

where ε' is some arbitrarily small positive number. Thus, the fidelity between these two states is high:

$$F \left(\sum_j \mathcal{D}_j \left(\mathcal{N}^{\otimes n} \left(\mathcal{E}_j \left(\varphi_{RA_1} \right) \right) \right), \varphi_{RA_1} \right) \geq 1 - \varepsilon'. \qquad (24.65)$$

But we can rewrite the fidelity as follows:

$$F\left(\sum_j \mathcal{D}_j\left(\mathcal{N}^{\otimes n}\left(\mathcal{E}_j\left(\varphi_{RA_1}\right)\right)\right), \varphi_{RA_1}\right)$$

$$= \langle\varphi|_{RA_1} \sum_j \mathcal{D}_j\left(\mathcal{N}^{\otimes n}\left(\mathcal{E}_j\left(\varphi_{RA_1}\right)\right)\right)|\varphi\rangle_{RA_1} \tag{24.66}$$

$$= \sum_j \langle\varphi|_{RA_1}\mathcal{D}_j\left(\mathcal{N}^{\otimes n}\left(\mathcal{E}_j\left(\varphi_{RA_1}\right)\right)\right)|\varphi\rangle_{RA_1} \tag{24.67}$$

$$= \sum_j \frac{1}{|\mathcal{M}|}\left[\langle\varphi|_{RA_1}\mathcal{D}_j\left(\mathcal{N}^{\otimes n}\left(\mathcal{E}_j'\left(\varphi_{RA_1}\right)\right)\right)|\varphi\rangle_{RA_1}\right] \tag{24.68}$$

$$\geq 1 - \varepsilon', \tag{24.69}$$

implying that at least one of the encoder–decoder pairs $(\mathcal{E}_j', \mathcal{D}_j)$ has arbitrarily high fidelity. Thus, Alice and Bob simply agree beforehand to use a scheme $(\mathcal{E}_j', \mathcal{D}_j)$ with high fidelity, obviating the need for the forward classical communication channel.

The protocol given here achieves communication at the coherent information rate. In order to achieve the regularized coherent information rate in the statement of the theorem, Alice and Bob apply the same protocol to the superchannel $(\mathcal{N}_{A'\to B})^{\otimes k}$ instead of the channel $\mathcal{N}_{A'\to B}$.

24.5   Converse Theorem

This section proves the converse part of the quantum capacity theorem, demonstrating that the regularized coherent information is an upper bound on the quantum capacity of any quantum channel. For the class of degradable channels, the coherent information itself is an upper bound on the quantum capacity—this demonstrates that we completely understand the quantum data transmission capabilities of these channels.

For this converse proof, we assume that Alice is trying to generate entanglement with Bob. The capacity for this task is an upper bound on the capacity for quantum data transmission because we can always use a noiseless quantum channel to establish entanglement. We also allow Alice free forward classical communication to Bob, and we demonstrate that this resource cannot increase the quantum capacity (essentially because the coherent information is convex). In a protocol for entanglement generation, Alice begins by preparing the maximally entangled state Φ_{AA_1} of Schmidt rank $|A|$ in her local laboratory, where $\frac{1}{n}\log|A|$ is the rate of this entangled state. She performs some encoding operation $\mathcal{E}_{A_1\to A'^n M}$ that outputs many systems A'^n and a classical register M. She then inputs the systems A'^n to many independent uses of a quantum channel $\mathcal{N}_{A'\to B}$, resulting in the state

$$\omega_{AMB^n} \equiv \mathcal{N}_{A'^n\to B^n}\left(\mathcal{E}_{A_1\to A'^n M}\left(\Phi_{AA_1}\right)\right), \tag{24.70}$$

where $\mathcal{N}_{A'^n \to B^n} \equiv (\mathcal{N}_{A' \to B})^{\otimes n}$. Bob takes the outputs B^n of the channels and the classical register M and performs some decoding operation $\mathcal{D}_{B^n M \to B_1}$, resulting in the state

$$\omega'_{AB_1} \equiv \mathcal{D}_{B^n M \to B_1}(\omega_{AMB^n}). \tag{24.71}$$

The following condition holds for an $(n, \lceil \log|A| \rceil / n, \varepsilon)$ protocol for entanglement generation:

$$\frac{1}{2} \left\| \omega'_{AB_1} - \Phi_{AB_1} \right\|_1 \leq \varepsilon. \tag{24.72}$$

The converse proof then proceeds in the following steps:

$$\log|A| = I(A\rangle B_1)_\Phi \tag{24.73}$$
$$\leq I(A\rangle B_1)_{\omega'} + f(|A|, \varepsilon) \tag{24.74}$$
$$\leq I(A\rangle B^n M)_\omega + f(|A|, \varepsilon). \tag{24.75}$$

The first equality follows because the coherent information of a maximally entangled state is equal to the logarithm of the dimension of one of its systems. The first inequality follows from an application of the AFW inequality to the condition in (24.72), with $f(|A|, \varepsilon) \equiv 2\varepsilon \log|A| + (1 + \varepsilon) h_2 (\varepsilon / [1 + \varepsilon])$. The second inequality follows from quantum data processing. Now consider that the state ω_{MAB^n} is a classical–quantum state of the following form:

$$\omega_{MAB^n} \equiv \sum_m p_M(m)|m\rangle\langle m|_M \otimes \mathcal{N}_{A'^n \to B^n}(\rho^m_{AA'^n}). \tag{24.76}$$

We can then perform a spectral decomposition of each state ρ_m as follows:

$$\rho^m_{AA'^n} = \sum_l p_{L|M}(l|m)|\phi_{l,m}\rangle\langle\phi_{l,m}|_{AA'^n}, \tag{24.77}$$

and augment the above state as follows:

$$\omega_{MLAB^n} \equiv \sum_{m,l} p_M(m)p_{L|M}(l|m)|m\rangle\langle m|_M \otimes |l\rangle\langle l|_L \otimes \mathcal{N}_{A'^n \to B^n}(\phi^{l,m}_{AA'^n}), \tag{24.78}$$

so that $\omega_{MAB^n} = \mathrm{Tr}_L\{\omega_{MLAB^n}\}$. We continue with bounding the relevant term:

$$I(A\rangle B^n M)_\omega \leq I(A\rangle B^n ML)_\omega \tag{24.79}$$
$$= \sum_{m,l} p_M(m)p_{L|M}(l|m)I(A\rangle B^n)_{\mathcal{N}(\phi^{l,m})} \tag{24.80}$$
$$\leq I(A\rangle B^n)_{\mathcal{N}(\phi^*_{l,m})} \tag{24.81}$$
$$\leq Q(\mathcal{N}^{\otimes n}). \tag{24.82}$$

The first inequality follows from the quantum data-processing inequality. The first equality follows because the registers M and L are both classical, and we can apply the result of Exercise 11.5.5. The second inequality follows because the expectation is always less than the maximal value (where we define $\phi^*_{l,m}$ to be the state that achieves this maximum). The final inequality follows from the definition of the channel coherent information as the maximum of the coherent information over all pure, bipartite inputs. Putting everything together, we find that

$$\frac{1}{n} \log |A| (1 - 2\varepsilon) \leq \frac{1}{n} Q(\mathcal{N}^{\otimes n}) + \frac{1 + \varepsilon}{n} h_2 (\varepsilon / [1 + \varepsilon]).$$

Thus, if we are considering a sequence of $(n, [\log |A|] / n, \varepsilon_n)$ quantum communication protocols with rate $Q - \delta_n = \frac{1}{n} \log |A|$, such that $\lim_{n \to \infty} \varepsilon_n = \lim_{n \to \infty} \delta_n = 0$, then the above bound becomes

$$(Q - \delta_n) (1 - 2\varepsilon_n) \leq \frac{1}{n} Q(\mathcal{N}^{\otimes n}) + \frac{1 + \varepsilon_n}{n} h_2(\varepsilon_n / [1 + \varepsilon_n]). \tag{24.83}$$

Taking the limit as $n \to \infty$ then establishes that an achievable rate Q necessarily satisfies $Q \leq Q_{\text{reg}}(\mathcal{N})$, where $Q_{\text{reg}}(\mathcal{N})$ is the regularized coherent information given in (24.8). This concludes the proof of the converse part of the quantum capacity theorem.

There are a few comments we should make regarding the converse theorem. First, we see that classical communication cannot improve quantum capacity because the coherent information is convex. We could obtain the same upper bound on quantum capacity even if there were no classical communication. Second, it is sufficient to consider isometric encoders for quantum communication—that is, it is not necessary to exploit general noisy CPTP maps at the encoder. This makes sense intuitively because it would seem odd if noisy encodings could help in the noiseless transmission of quantum data. Our augmented state in (24.78) and the subsequent development reveals that this is so (again because the coherent information is convex).

We can significantly strengthen the statement of the quantum capacity theorem for the class of degradable quantum channels because the following equality holds for them:

$$Q(\mathcal{N}^{\otimes n}) = nQ(\mathcal{N}). \tag{24.84}$$

This inequality follows from the additivity of coherent information for degradable channels (Theorem 13.5.1). Also, the task of optimizing the coherent information for these channels is straightforward because it is a concave function of the input density operator (Theorem 13.5.2) and the set of density operators is convex.

24.6   An Interlude with Quantum Stabilizer Codes

We now describe a well-known class of quantum error-correcting codes known as the stabilizer codes, and we prove that a randomly chosen stabilizer code achieves a quantum communication rate known as the hashing bound of a Pauli channel (the hashing bound is equal to the coherent information of a Pauli channel when sending one share of a Bell state through it). The proof of this theorem is different from our proof above that the coherent information rate is achievable, and we consider it instructive to see this other approach for the special case of stabilizer codes used for protecting quantum information sent over many independent instances of a Pauli channel. Before delving into the proof, we first briefly introduce the simple repetition code and the more general stabilizer quantum codes.

24.6.1   The Qubit Repetition Code

The simplest quantum error-correction code is the repetition code, which encodes one qubit $|\psi\rangle \equiv \alpha|0\rangle + \beta|1\rangle$ into three physical qubits as follows:

$$\alpha|0\rangle + \beta|1\rangle \rightarrow \alpha|000\rangle + \beta|111\rangle. \tag{24.85}$$

A simple way to perform this encoding is to attach two ancilla qubits in the state $|0\rangle$ to the original qubit and perform a CNOT gate from the first qubit to the second and from the first to the last. This encoding illustrates one of the fundamental principles of quantum error correction: the quantum information is spread across the correlations between the three physical qubits after the encoding takes place. (Of course, this was also the case for the codes we constructed in the direct part of the quantum capacity theorem.)

The above encoding will protect the encoded qubit against an artificial noise where either the first, second, or third qubit is subjected to a bit flip (and no other errors occur). For example, if a bit flip occurs on the second qubit, the encoded state changes as follows:

$$X_2 \left(\alpha|000\rangle + \beta|111\rangle\right) = \alpha|010\rangle + \beta|101\rangle, \tag{24.86}$$

where the notation X_2 indicates that a Pauli operator X acts on the second qubit. The procedure for the receiver to recover from such an error is to perform collective measurements on all three qubits that learn only about the error and nothing about the encoded quantum data. In this case, the receiver can perform a measurement of the operators $Z_1 Z_2$ and $Z_2 Z_3$ to learn only about the error, so that the coherent superposition is preserved. One can easily verify that $Z_1 Z_2$ and $Z_2 Z_3$ are as follows:

$$Z_1 Z_2 \equiv Z \otimes Z \otimes I \tag{24.87}$$

$$= [(|00\rangle\langle00| + |11\rangle\langle11|) - (|01\rangle\langle01| + |10\rangle\langle10|)] \otimes I, \tag{24.88}$$

$$Z_2 Z_3 \equiv I \otimes Z \otimes Z \tag{24.89}$$

$$= I \otimes [(|00\rangle\langle00| + |11\rangle\langle11|) - (|01\rangle\langle01| + |10\rangle\langle10|)], \tag{24.90}$$

revealing that these measurements return a $+1$ if the parity of the basis states is even and -1 if the parity is odd. So, for our example error in (24.86), the syndrome measurements will return -1 for $Z_1 Z_2$ and -1 for $Z_2 Z_3$, which the receiver can use to identify the error that occurs. He can then perform the bit-flip operator X_2 to invert the action of the error. One can verify that the following syndrome table identifies which type of error occurs:

Measurement result	Error
$+1, +1$	I
$+1, -1$	X_3
$-1, +1$	X_1
$-1, -1$	X_2

(24.91)

Thus, if the only errors that occur are either no error or a single-qubit bit-flip error, then it is possible to perfectly correct these. If errors besides these ones occur, then it is not possible to correct them using this code.

24.6.2   Stabilizer Codes

We can generalize the main idea behind the above qubit repetition code to formulate the class of quantum stabilizer codes. These stabilizer codes then generalize the classical theory of linear error correction to the quantum case.

In the repetition code, observe that the encoded state in (24.85) is a $+1$-eigenstate of the operators $Z_1 Z_2$ and $Z_2 Z_3$, i.e., it holds that

$$Z_1 Z_2 \left(\alpha |000\rangle + \beta |111\rangle \right) = \alpha |000\rangle + \beta |111\rangle = Z_2 Z_3 \left(\alpha |000\rangle + \beta |111\rangle \right). \quad (24.92)$$

We say that the operators $Z_1 Z_2$ and $Z_2 Z_3$ stabilize the encoded state. The stabilizing operators form a group under multiplication because we obtain another stabilizing operator if we multiply two of them: one can check that the operator $Z_1 Z_3$ stabilizes the encoded state and that $Z_1 Z_3 = (Z_1 Z_2)(Z_2 Z_3)$. Also, the two operators $Z_1 Z_2$ and $Z_2 Z_3$ commute, implying that the encoded state is in the simultaneous eigenspace of these operators, and that it is possible to measure the operators $Z_1 Z_2$ and $Z_2 Z_3$ in any order, in order to learn about errors that occur.

We now describe the theory of quantum stabilizer codes. Recall that the Pauli matrices for one qubit are I, X, Y, and Z, whose action on the computational basis is as follows:

$$I|0\rangle = |0\rangle, \qquad\qquad\qquad I|1\rangle = |1\rangle, \qquad\qquad (24.93)$$
$$X|0\rangle = |1\rangle, \qquad\qquad\qquad X|1\rangle = |0\rangle, \qquad\qquad (24.94)$$
$$Y|0\rangle = i|1\rangle, \qquad\qquad\qquad Y|1\rangle = -i|0\rangle, \qquad\qquad (24.95)$$
$$Z|0\rangle = |0\rangle, \qquad\qquad\qquad Z|1\rangle = -|1\rangle. \qquad\qquad (24.96)$$

The X operator is known as the "bit-flip" operator, Z as the "phase-flip" operator, and Y as the "bit and phase flip" operator. The Pauli group $\mathcal{G}_n$ acting on n

qubits consists of n-fold tensor products of these operators along with the phase factors ± 1 and $\pm i$:

$$\mathcal{G}_n \equiv \{\pm 1, \pm i\} \otimes \{I, X, Y, Z\}^{\otimes n}. \tag{24.97}$$

The inclusion of the phase factors, along with the relations $Y = iXZ$, $Z = iYX$, and $X = iZY$ and the fact that any one of X, Y, and Z anticommutes with the other two ensures that the set $\mathcal{G}_n$ is closed under multiplication. It is useful in the theory of quantum error correction to consider the Pauli group quotiented out by its center: $\mathcal{G}_n / \{\pm 1, \pm i\}$, essentially because global phases are not physically observable. This reduced version of the Pauli group has 4^n elements.

Let $\mathcal{S}$ be an abelian subgroup of the Pauli group $\mathcal{G}_n$. Any such subgroup $\mathcal{S}$ has size 2^{n-k} for some integer k such that $0 \leq k \leq n$. This subgroup $\mathcal{S}$ can be generated by a set of size $n - k$, so that $\mathcal{S} = \langle S_1, \ldots, S_{n-k} \rangle$. A state $|\psi\rangle$ is stabilized by the subgroup $\mathcal{S}$ if

$$S|\psi\rangle = |\psi\rangle \qquad \forall S \in \mathcal{S}. \tag{24.98}$$

The 2^k-dimensional subspace of the full 2^n-dimensional space for the n qubits that is stabilized by $\mathcal{S}$ is known as the codespace, or equivalently, an $[n, k]$ stabilizer code that encodes k logical qubits into n physical qubits. The decoding operation that the receiver performs is analogous to that for the repetition code—he just measures the $n - k$ operators constituting some generating set of $\mathcal{S}$ and performs a recovery operation based on the results of these measurements.

We can define logical operations on the quantum information encoded inside an $[n, k]$ stabilizer code. These are operations that manipulate the quantum information inside the codespace without taking the encoded information outside the codespace. These logical operations are part of the normalizer of $\mathcal{S}$, defined as

$$N(\mathcal{S}) \equiv \{U \in \mathbb{U}(2^n) : U S U^\dagger = \mathcal{S}\}, \tag{24.99}$$

where $\mathbb{U}(2^n)$ denotes the unitary group for n qubits. We can easily see that any $U \in N(\mathcal{S})$ does not take a state $|\psi\rangle$ in the codespace outside it. First, for all $U \in N(\mathcal{S})$, it follows that $U^\dagger \in N(\mathcal{S})$, so that for all $S \in \mathcal{S}$, we have

$$SU|\psi\rangle = UU^\dagger SU|\psi\rangle = US_U|\psi\rangle = U|\psi\rangle, \tag{24.100}$$

where $S_U = U^\dagger SU$ and $S_U \in \mathcal{S}$ from the definition of the normalizer. From the above, we conclude that the state $U|\psi\rangle$ is in the codespace since it is stabilized by all $S \in \mathcal{S}$: $SU|\psi\rangle = U|\psi\rangle$. It also follows that $\mathcal{S} \subseteq N(\mathcal{S})$ because $\mathcal{S}$ is abelian, implying that

$$S_1 S_2 S_1^\dagger = S_2 S_1 S_1^\dagger = S_2 \qquad \forall S_1, S_2 \in \mathcal{S}. \tag{24.101}$$

In quantum error correction, we are concerned with correcting a fixed set of errors $\mathcal{E} \subseteq \mathcal{G}_n$ such that each element of $\mathcal{E}$ acts on the n physical qubits. In doing so, we might not be able to correct all of the errors in a set $\mathcal{E}$ if there exists a pair $E_1, E_2 \in \mathcal{E}$ such that

$$E_1^\dagger E_2 \in N(\mathcal{S}). \tag{24.102}$$

Consider that for all $S \in \mathcal{S}$, we have

$$E_1^\dagger E_2 S = (-1)^{g(S,E_1)+g(S,E_2)} S E_1^\dagger E_2, \qquad (24.103)$$

where we define $g(P,Q)$ by $PQ = (-1)^{g(P,Q)} QP$ for all $P, Q \in \mathcal{G}_n$. The above relation then implies the following one for all $S \in \mathcal{S}$:

$$E_1^\dagger E_2 S (E_1^\dagger E_2)^\dagger = (-1)^{g(S,E_1)+g(S,E_2)} S. \qquad (24.104)$$

Since we assumed that $E_1^\dagger E_2 \in N(\mathcal{S})$, the only way that the above relation can be true for all $S \in \mathcal{S}$ is if $g(S, E_1) = g(S, E_2)$. Thus, during the error correction procedure, Bob will measure a set $\{S_j\}$ of generators, and since the outcome of a measurement of S_j on $E|\psi\rangle$ is $g(S, E)$, the errors E_1 and E_2 will be assigned the same syndrome. Since they have the same syndrome, the receiver will have to reverse these errors with the same recovery operation, and this is only possible if $E_1|\psi\rangle = E_2|\psi\rangle$ for all states $|\psi\rangle$ in the codespace. This latter condition is only true if $E_1^\dagger E_2 \in \mathcal{S}$, leading us to the error-correcting conditions for quantum stabilizer codes:

THEOREM 24.6.1   It is possible to correct a set of errors $\mathcal{E}$ with a quantum stabilizer code if every pair $E_1, E_2 \in \mathcal{E}$ satisfies

$$E_1^\dagger E_2 \notin N(\mathcal{S}) \backslash \mathcal{S}. \qquad (24.105)$$

A simple way to satisfy the error-correcting conditions is just to demand that every pair of errors in $\mathcal{E}$ be such that $E_1^\dagger E_2 \notin N(\mathcal{S})$. In such a case, each error is assigned a unique syndrome, and codes along with an error set satisfying this property are known as non-degenerate codes. Codes with a corresponding error set not satisfying this are known as degenerate codes.

24.6.3   The Hashing Bound

We now provide a proof that the hashing bound for a Pauli channel (coherent information when sending one share of a Bell state through a Pauli channel) is an achievable rate for quantum communication. Our proof of the direct part of the quantum capacity theorem already suffices as a proof of this statement, but we think it is instructive to provide a proof of this statement using the theory of stabilizer codes. The main idea of the proof is to choose a stabilizer code randomly from the set of all stabilizer codes and show that such a code can correct the typical errors issued by a tensor-product Pauli channel.

THEOREM 24.6.2 (Hashing Bound)   There exists a stabilizer quantum error-correcting code that achieves the hashing bound $R = 1 - H(\mathbf{p})$ for a Pauli channel of the following form:

$$\rho \rightarrow p_I \rho + p_X X \rho X + p_Y Y \rho Y + p_Z Z \rho Z, \qquad (24.106)$$

where $\mathbf{p} = (p_I, p_X, p_Y, p_Z)$ and $H(\mathbf{p})$ is the entropy of this probability vector.

Proof We consider a decoder that corrects only the typical errors. That is, consider defining the typical error set as follows:

$$T_{\delta}^{\mathbf{p}^n} \equiv \left\{ a^n : \left| -\frac{1}{n} \log\left(\Pr\{E_{a^n}\}\right) - H(\mathbf{p}) \right| \leq \delta \right\}, \tag{24.107}$$

where a^n is some sequence consisting of letters corresponding to the Pauli operators $\{I, X, Y, Z\}$ and $\Pr\{E_{a^n}\}$ is the probability that an i.i.d. Pauli channel issues some tensor-product error $E_{a^n} \equiv E_{a_1} \otimes \cdots \otimes E_{a_n}$. This typical set consists of the likely errors in the sense that

$$\sum_{a^n \in T_{\delta}^{\mathbf{p}^n}} \Pr\{E_{a^n}\} \geq 1 - \varepsilon, \tag{24.108}$$

for all $\varepsilon \in (0, 1)$ and sufficiently large n. The error-correcting conditions for a stabilizer code in this case are that $\{E_{a^n} : a^n \in T_{\delta}^{\mathbf{p}^n}\}$ is a correctable set of errors if

$$E_{a^n}^{\dagger} E_{b^n} \notin N(\mathcal{S}) \backslash \mathcal{S}, \tag{24.109}$$

for all error pairs E_{a^n} and E_{b^n} such that $a^n, b^n \in T_{\delta}^{\mathbf{p}^n}$. Also, we consider the expectation of the error probability under a random choice of a stabilizer code. We proceed as follows:

$$\mathbb{E}_{\mathcal{S}}\{p_e\} = \mathbb{E}_{\mathcal{S}}\left\{ \sum_{a^n} \Pr\{E_{a^n}\} I(E_{a^n} \text{ is uncorrectable using } \mathcal{S}) \right\} \tag{24.110}$$

$$\leq \mathbb{E}_{\mathcal{S}}\left\{ \sum_{a^n \in T_{\delta}^{\mathbf{p}^n}} \Pr\{E_{a^n}\} I(E_{a^n} \text{ is uncorrectable using } \mathcal{S}) \right\} + \varepsilon \tag{24.111}$$

$$= \sum_{a^n \in T_{\delta}^{\mathbf{p}^n}} \Pr\{E_{a^n}\} \mathbb{E}_{\mathcal{S}}\{I(E_{a^n} \text{ is uncorrectable using } \mathcal{S})\} + \varepsilon \tag{24.112}$$

$$= \sum_{a^n \in T_{\delta}^{\mathbf{p}^n}} \Pr\{E_{a^n}\} \Pr_{\mathcal{S}}\{E_{a^n} \text{ is uncorrectable using } \mathcal{S}\} + \varepsilon. \tag{24.113}$$

The first equality follows by definition—I is an indicator function equal to one if E_{a^n} is uncorrectable using $\mathcal{S}$ and equal to zero otherwise. The first inequality follows from (24.108)—we correct only the typical errors because the atypical error set has negligible probability mass. The second equality follows by exchanging the expectation and the sum. The third equality follows because the expectation of an indicator function is the probability that the event it selects occurs. Continuing, we now bound the probability $\Pr_{\mathcal{S}}\{E_{a^n} \text{ is uncorrectable using } \mathcal{S}\}$ when $a^n \in T_{\delta}^{\mathbf{p}^n}$:

$$\Pr_{\mathcal{S}}\{E_{a^n} \text{ is uncorrectable using } \mathcal{S}\}$$

$$= \Pr_{\mathcal{S}}\left\{ \exists E_{b^n} : b^n \in T_{\delta}^{\mathbf{p}^n}, \ b^n \neq a^n, \ E_{a^n}^{\dagger} E_{b^n} \in N(\mathcal{S}) \backslash \mathcal{S} \right\} \tag{24.114}$$

$$\leq \Pr_{S}\left\{\exists E_{b^n} : b^n \in T_\delta^{\mathbf{p}^n}, \ b^n \neq a^n, \ E_{a^n}^\dagger E_{b^n} \in N(\mathcal{S})\right\} \tag{24.115}$$

$$= \Pr_{S}\left\{\bigcup_{b^n \in T_\delta^{\mathbf{p}^n}, \ b^n \neq a^n} E_{a^n}^\dagger E_{b^n} \in N(\mathcal{S})\right\} \tag{24.116}$$

$$\leq \sum_{b^n \in T_\delta^{\mathbf{p}^n}, \ b^n \neq a^n} \Pr_{S}\left\{E_{a^n}^\dagger E_{b^n} \in N(\mathcal{S})\right\} \tag{24.117}$$

$$\leq \sum_{b^n \in T_\delta^{\mathbf{p}^n}, \ b^n \neq a^n} 2^{-(n-k)} \tag{24.118}$$

$$\leq 2^{n[H(\mathbf{p})+\delta]} 2^{-(n-k)} \tag{24.119}$$

$$= 2^{-n[1-H(\mathbf{p})-k/n-\delta]}. \tag{24.120}$$

The first equality follows from the error-correcting conditions for a quantum stabilizer code, where $N(\mathcal{S})$ is the normalizer of $\mathcal{S}$. The first inequality follows by ignoring any potential degeneracy in the code—we consider an error uncorrectable if it lies in the normalizer $N(\mathcal{S})$ and the probability can only be larger because $N(\mathcal{S})\backslash\mathcal{S} \subseteq N(\mathcal{S})$. The second equality follows by realizing that the probabilities for the existence criterion and the union of events are equal. The second inequality follows by applying the union bound. The third inequality follows from the fact that the probability for a fixed operator $E_{a^n}^\dagger E_{b^n}$ not equal to the identity commuting with the stabilizer operators of a random stabilizer can be upper bounded as follows:

$$\Pr_{S}\left\{E_{a^n}^\dagger E_{b^n} \in N(\mathcal{S})\right\} = \frac{2^{n+k}-1}{2^{2n}-1} \leq 2^{-(n-k)}. \tag{24.121}$$

The random choice of a stabilizer code is equivalent to fixing operators $Z_1, \ldots,$ Z_{n-k} and performing a uniformly random Clifford unitary U. The probability that a fixed operator commutes with $UZ_1U^\dagger, \ldots, UZ_{n-k}U^\dagger$ is then just the number of non-identity operators in the normalizer $(2^{n+k}-1)$ divided by the total number of non-identity operators $(2^{2n}-1)$. After applying the above bound, we then exploit the typicality bound $|T_\delta^{\mathbf{p}^n}| \leq 2^{n[H(\mathbf{p})+\delta]}$. Plugging back into (24.113), we find that

$$\mathbb{E}_S\left\{p_e\right\} \leq 2^{-n[1-H(\mathbf{p})-k/n-\delta]} + \varepsilon. \tag{24.122}$$

We conclude that as long as the rate $k/n = 1 - H(\mathbf{p}) - 2\delta$, the expectation of the error probability becomes arbitrarily small, so that there exists at least one choice of a stabilizer code with the same bound on the error probability. $\qquad \square$

24.7   Example Channels

We now show how to calculate the quantum capacity for two exemplary channels: the quantum erasure channel and the amplitude damping channel. Both of these channels are degradable for particular channel parameters, simplifying the calculation of their quantum capacities.

24.7.1 The Quantum Erasure Channel

Recall that the quantum erasure channel acts as follows on an input density operator $\rho_{A'}$:

$$\rho_{A'} \to (1 - \varepsilon)\,\rho_B + \varepsilon|e\rangle\langle e|_B, \tag{24.123}$$

where $\varepsilon \in [0, 1]$ is the erasure probability and $|e\rangle_B$ is an erasure state that is orthogonal to the support of any input state ρ.

PROPOSITION 24.7.1 Let d_A be the dimension of the input system for the quantum erasure channel. The quantum capacity of a quantum erasure channel with erasure probability ε is equal to $(1 - 2\varepsilon) \log d_A$ when $\varepsilon \in [0, 1/2]$ and it is equal to zero otherwise.

Proof The quantum erasure channel is antidegradable for $\varepsilon \in [1/2, 1]$. This follows from Exercise 5.2.6 and the fact that the erasure channel is degradable for $\varepsilon \in [0, 1/2]$ (see Exercise 13.5.2). From Exercise 13.5.6 and the fact that $\mathcal{N}^{\otimes n}$ is antidegradable if $\mathcal{N}$ is, we can then conclude that the quantum capacity is equal to zero for $\varepsilon \in [1/2, 1]$.

To determine the quantum capacity for $\varepsilon \in [0, 1/2]$, we know that it is degradable for this range (see Exercise 13.5.2), so it suffices to compute its coherent information. We can do so in a similar way as we did in Proposition 21.6.1. Consider that sending one share of a pure, bipartite state $\phi_{AA'}$ through the channel produces the output

$$\sigma_{AB} \equiv (1 - \varepsilon)\,\phi_{AB} + \varepsilon\phi_A \otimes |e\rangle\langle e|_B. \tag{24.124}$$

Recall that Bob can apply the following isometry $U_{B \to BX}$ to his state:

$$U_{B \to BX} \equiv \Pi_B \otimes |0\rangle_X + |e\rangle\langle e|_B \otimes |1\rangle_X, \tag{24.125}$$

where Π_B is a projector onto the support of the input state (for qubits, it would be just $|0\rangle\langle 0| + |1\rangle\langle 1|$). Applying this isometry leads to a state σ_{ABX} where

$$\sigma_{ABX} \equiv U_{B \to BX}\sigma_{AB}U_{B \to BX}^{\dagger} \tag{24.126}$$

$$= (1 - \varepsilon)\,\phi_{AB} \otimes |0\rangle\langle 0|_X + \varepsilon\phi_A \otimes |e\rangle\langle e|_B \otimes |1\rangle\langle 1|_X. \tag{24.127}$$

The coherent information $I(A\rangle BX)_\sigma$ is equal to $I(A\rangle B)_\sigma$ because entropies do not change under the isometry $U_{B \to BX}$. We now calculate $I(A\rangle BX)_\sigma$:

$$I(A\rangle BX)_\sigma = H(BX)_\sigma - H(ABX)_\sigma \tag{24.128}$$

$$= H(B|X)_\sigma - H(AB|X)_\sigma \tag{24.129}$$

$$= (1 - \varepsilon)\,[H(B)_\phi - H(AB)_\phi]$$

$$\quad + \varepsilon\,[H(B)_{|e\rangle\langle e|} - H(AB)_{\phi_A \otimes |e\rangle\langle e|}] \tag{24.130}$$

$$= (1 - \varepsilon) H(B)_\phi - \varepsilon \left[H(A)_\phi + H(B)_{|e\rangle\langle e|} \right] \tag{24.131}$$

$$= (1 - 2\varepsilon) H(A)_\phi \tag{24.132}$$

$$\leq (1 - 2\varepsilon) \log d_A. \tag{24.133}$$

The first equality follows from the definition of coherent information. The second equality follows from $\phi_A = \mathrm{Tr}_{BX} \{\sigma_{ABX}\}$, from the chain rule of entropy, and by canceling $H(X)$ on both sides. The third equality follows because the X register is a classical register, indicating whether the erasure occurs. The fourth equality follows because $H(AB)_\phi = 0$, $H(B)_{|e\rangle\langle e|} = 0$, and $H(AB)_{\phi_A \otimes |e\rangle\langle e|} = H(A)_\phi + H(B)_{|e\rangle\langle e|}$. The fifth equality follows again because $H(B)_{|e\rangle\langle e|} = 0$, by collecting terms, and because $H(A)_\phi = H(B)_\phi$ (ϕ_{AB} is a pure bipartite state). The final inequality follows because the entropy of a state on system A is never greater than the logarithm of the dimension of A. We can conclude that the maximally entangled state $\Phi_{AA'}$ achieves the quantum capacity of the quantum erasure channel for $\varepsilon \in [0, 1/2]$ because $H(A)_\Phi = \log d_A$. $\square$

24.7.2   The Amplitude Damping Channel

We now compute the quantum capacity of the amplitude damping channel $\mathcal{N}_{\mathrm{AD}}$. Recall that this channel acts as follows on an input qubit in state ρ:

$$\mathcal{N}_{\mathrm{AD}}(\rho) = A_0 \rho A_0^\dagger + A_1 \rho A_1^\dagger, \tag{24.134}$$

where, for $\gamma \in [0, 1]$,

$$A_0 \equiv |0\rangle\langle 0| + \sqrt{1 - \gamma} |1\rangle\langle 1|, \qquad A_1 \equiv \sqrt{\gamma} |0\rangle\langle 1|. \tag{24.135}$$

The development here is similar to the development in the proof of Proposition 21.6.2.

PROPOSITION 24.7.2   The quantum capacity of an amplitude damping channel with damping parameter $\gamma \in [0, 1]$ is equal to the following:

$$\max_{p \in [0,1]} h_2((1 - \gamma)p) - h_2(\gamma p), \tag{24.136}$$

whenever $\gamma \in [0, 1/2]$ (recall that $h_2(x)$ is the binary entropy function). For $\gamma \in [1/2, 1]$, the quantum capacity is equal to zero.

Proof Suppose that a matrix representation of the input qubit density operator ρ in the computational basis is

$$\rho = \begin{bmatrix} 1 - p & \eta^* \\ \eta & p \end{bmatrix}. \tag{24.137}$$

One can readily verify that the density operator for Bob has the following matrix representation:

$$\mathcal{N}_{\mathrm{AD}}(\rho) = \begin{bmatrix} 1 - (1 - \gamma)p & \sqrt{1 - \gamma}\eta^* \\ \sqrt{1 - \gamma}\eta & (1 - \gamma)p \end{bmatrix}, \tag{24.138}$$

and by calculating the elements $\text{Tr}\{A_i \rho A_j^\dagger\}|i\rangle\langle j|$, we can obtain a matrix representation for Eve's density operator:

$$\mathcal{N}_{\text{AD}}^c(\rho) = \begin{bmatrix} 1 - \gamma p & \sqrt{\gamma}\eta^* \\ \sqrt{\gamma}\eta & \gamma p \end{bmatrix}, \tag{24.139}$$

where $\mathcal{N}_{\text{AD}}^c$ is the complementary channel to Eve. By comparing (24.138) and (24.139), we can see that the channel to Eve is an amplitude damping channel with damping parameter $1 - \gamma$. One can verify that the channel is antidegradable for $\gamma \in [1/2, 1]$ and degradable for $\gamma \in [0, 1/2]$ (*Exercise*: find the degrading channel). By the same reasoning in the previous proposition, the quantum capacity is equal to zero for $\gamma \in [1/2, 1]$ and it is equal to the optimized coherent information for $\gamma \in [0, 1/2]$. So we now focus on this latter case. The quantum capacity of $\mathcal{N}_{\text{AD}}$ is equal to its coherent information:

$$Q(\mathcal{N}_{\text{AD}}) = \max_{\phi_{AA'}} I(A\rangle B)_\sigma, \tag{24.140}$$

where $\phi_{AA'}$ is some pure bipartite input state and $\sigma_{AB} = \mathcal{N}_{\text{AD}}(\phi_{AA'})$. We need to determine the input density operator that maximizes the above formula as a function of γ. So far, the optimization depends on three parameters: p, $\text{Re}\{\eta\}$, and $\text{Im}\{\eta\}$. We can show that it is sufficient to consider an optimization over only p with $\eta = 0$. The formula in (24.140) also has the following form:

$$Q(\mathcal{N}_{\text{AD}}) = \max_\rho \left[H(\mathcal{N}_{\text{AD}}(\rho)) - H(\mathcal{N}_{\text{AD}}^c(\rho)) \right], \tag{24.141}$$

because

$$I(A\rangle B)_\sigma = H(B)_\sigma - H(AB)_\sigma \tag{24.142}$$

$$= H(\mathcal{N}_{\text{AD}}(\rho)) - H(E)_\sigma \tag{24.143}$$

$$= H(\mathcal{N}_{\text{AD}}(\rho)) - H(\mathcal{N}_{\text{AD}}^c(\rho)) \tag{24.144}$$

$$\equiv I_{\text{coh}}(\rho, \mathcal{N}_{\text{AD}}). \tag{24.145}$$

The two entropies in (24.141) depend only on the eigenvalues of the two density operators in (24.138)–(24.139), respectively, which are as follows:

$$\frac{1}{2}\left(1 \pm \sqrt{(1 - 2(1-\gamma)p)^2 + 4|\eta|^2(1-\gamma)} \right), \tag{24.146}$$

$$\frac{1}{2}\left(1 \pm \sqrt{(1 - 2\gamma p)^2 + 4|\eta|^2 \gamma} \right). \tag{24.147}$$

The above eigenvalues are in the order of Bob and Eve. All of the above eigenvalues have a similar form, and their dependence on η is only through its magnitude. Thus, it suffices to consider $\eta \in \mathbb{R}$ (this eliminates one parameter). Next, the eigenvalues do not change if we flip the sign of η (this is equivalent to rotating the original state ρ by Z, to $Z\rho Z$), and thus, the coherent information does not change as well:

$$I_{\text{coh}}(\rho, \mathcal{N}_{\text{AD}}) = I_{\text{coh}}(Z\rho Z, \mathcal{N}_{\text{AD}}). \tag{24.148}$$

By the above relation and concavity of coherent information in the input density operator for degradable channels (Theorem 13.5.2), the following inequality holds:

$$I_{\text{coh}}(\rho, \mathcal{N}_{\text{AD}}) = \frac{1}{2}\left[I_{\text{coh}}(\rho, \mathcal{N}_{\text{AD}}) + I_{\text{coh}}(Z\rho Z, \mathcal{N}_{\text{AD}})\right] \qquad (24.149)$$

$$\leq I_{\text{coh}}((\rho + Z\rho Z)/2, \mathcal{N}_{\text{AD}}) \qquad (24.150)$$

$$= I_{\text{coh}}(\overline{\Delta}(\rho), \mathcal{N}_{\text{AD}}), \qquad (24.151)$$

where $\overline{\Delta}$ is a completely dephasing channel in the computational basis. This demonstrates that it is sufficient to consider diagonal density operators ρ when optimizing the coherent information. Thus, the eigenvalues in (24.146)–(24.147) respectively become

$$\{(1-\gamma)p, 1-(1-\gamma)p\}, \qquad (24.152)$$

$$\{\gamma p, 1-\gamma p\}, \qquad (24.153)$$

giving our final expression in the statement of the proposition.   □

EXERCISE 24.7.1   Consider the dephasing channel: $\rho \to (1 - p/2)\rho + (p/2)Z\rho Z$. Prove that its quantum capacity is equal to $1 - h_2(p/2)$, where p is the dephasing parameter.

24.8   Discussion of Quantum Capacity

The quantum capacity is particularly well-behaved and understood for the class of degradable channels. Thus, we should not expect any surprises for this class of channels. If a channel is not degradable, we currently cannot say much about the exact value of its quantum capacity, but the study of non-degradable channels has led to many surprises in quantum Shannon theory and this section discusses two of these surprises. The first is the superadditivity of coherent information for the depolarizing channel, and the second is a striking phenomenon known as *superactivation* of quantum capacity, where two channels that individually have zero quantum capacity can combine to make a channel with non-zero quantum capacity.

24.8.1   Superadditivity of Coherent Information

Recall that the depolarizing channel $\mathcal{N}^{\text{D}}$ transmits its input with probability $1-p$ and replaces it with the maximally mixed state π with probability $p \in [0, 1]$:

$$\mathcal{N}^{\text{D}}(\rho) = (1-p)\rho + p\pi. \qquad (24.154)$$

We focus on the case in which the input and output of this channel is a qubit. The depolarizing channel is an example of a quantum channel that is not degradable.[2]

---

[2] Smith & Smolin (2007) have given an explicit condition for whether a channel is degradable.

As such, we might expect it to exhibit some strange behavior with respect to its quantum capacity. Indeed, it is known that its coherent information is strictly superadditive when the channel becomes very noisy:

$$5Q(\mathcal{N}^D) < Q((\mathcal{N}^D)^{\otimes 5}). \tag{24.155}$$

How can we show that this result is true? First, we can calculate the coherent information of this channel with respect to one channel use. It is possible to show that the maximally entangled state $\Phi_{AA'}$ maximizes the channel coherent information $Q(\mathcal{N}^D)$ for all values of the coherent information for which it is non-negative. To see this, consider that the depolarizing channel is unitarily covariant, so that $\mathcal{N}^D(U\rho U^\dagger) = U\mathcal{N}^D(\rho)U^\dagger$ for any unitary U and any qubit input density operator ρ. Thus, for optimizing the coherent information of $\mathcal{N}^D$, it suffices to consider states of the form $\sqrt{\mu}|00\rangle_{AA'} + \sqrt{1-\mu}|11\rangle_{AA'}$ where $\mu \in [0, 1]$. A numerical optimization over all such states gives the plot in Figure 24.3, which demonstrates that the maximally entangled state ($\mu = 1/2$) is optimal for all values of the depolarizing parameter p for which the coherent information is non-negative, and for all other values, a product state with $\mu = 0$ is optimal. Thus, we can calculate the coherent information as follows:

$$Q(\mathcal{N}^D) = H(B)_\Phi - H(AB)_{\mathcal{N}^D(\Phi)} = 1 - H(AB)_{\mathcal{N}^D(\Phi)}, \tag{24.156}$$

where $H(B)_\Phi = 1$ follows because the output state on Bob's system is the maximally mixed state whenever the input to the channel is one share of a maximally entangled state. In order to calculate $H(AB)_{\mathcal{N}^D(\Phi)}$, observe that the state on AB is

$$(1 - p)\Phi_{AB} + p\pi_A \otimes \pi_B = (1 - p)\Phi_{AB} + \frac{p}{4}I_{AB} \tag{24.157}$$

$$= (1 - p)\Phi_{AB} + \frac{p}{4}([I_{AB} - \Phi_{AB}] + \Phi_{AB}) \tag{24.158}$$

$$= \left(1 - \frac{3p}{4}\right)\Phi_{AB} + \frac{p}{4}(I_{AB} - \Phi_{AB}). \tag{24.159}$$

Since Φ_{AB} and $I_{AB} - \Phi_{AB}$ are orthogonal, the eigenvalues of this state are $1 - 3p/4$ with multiplicity one and $p/4$ with multiplicity three. Thus, the entropy $H(AB)_{\mathcal{N}^D(\Phi)}$ is

$$H(AB)_{\mathcal{N}^D(\phi)} = -\left(1 - \frac{3p}{4}\right)\log\left(1 - \frac{3p}{4}\right) - \frac{3p}{4}\log\left(\frac{p}{4}\right), \tag{24.160}$$

and our final expression for the single-copy coherent information is

$$Q(\mathcal{N}^D) = 1 + \left(1 - \frac{3p}{4}\right)\log\left(1 - \frac{3p}{4}\right) + \frac{3p}{4}\log\left(\frac{p}{4}\right). \tag{24.161}$$

Another strategy for transmitting quantum data is to encode one share of the maximally entangled state with a five-qubit repetition code:

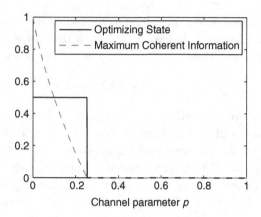

Figure 24.3 This figure plots the maximum coherent information of the depolarizing channel (dashed line) versus the depolarizing parameter $p \in [0, 1]$. It also plots the value $\mu \in [0, 1]$ for the state which optimizes the value of the coherent information (solid line) versus the depolarizing parameter p, considering states of the form $\sqrt{\mu}|00\rangle_{AA'} + \sqrt{1-\mu}|11\rangle_{AA'}$. It demonstrates that the maximum value is achieved for $\mu = 1/2$ (the maximally entangled state) for all values for which the coherent information is larger than zero and for $\mu = 0$ otherwise.

$$\frac{1}{\sqrt{2}}\left(|00\rangle_{AA_1} + |11\rangle_{AA_1}\right)$$

$$\rightarrow \frac{1}{\sqrt{2}}\left(|000000\rangle_{AA_1A_2A_3A_4A_5} + |111111\rangle_{AA_1A_2A_3A_4A_5}\right), \quad (24.162)$$

and calculate the following coherent information with respect to the state resulting from sending the systems $A_1 \cdots A_5$ through the channel:

$$\frac{1}{5}I(A\rangle B_1B_2B_3B_4B_5). \quad (24.163)$$

(We normalize the above coherent information by five in order to make a fair comparison between a code achieving this rate and one achieving the rate in (24.161).) We know that the rate in (24.163) is achievable by applying the direct part of the quantum capacity theorem to the channel $(\mathcal{N}^D)^{\otimes 5}$, and operationally this strategy amounts to concatenating a random quantum code with a five-qubit repetition code. The remarkable result is that this concatenation strategy can beat the single-copy coherent information when the channel becomes very noisy. Figure 24.4 demonstrates that the concatenation strategy has positive coherent information even when the single-copy coherent information in (24.161) vanishes. This demonstrates superadditivity of coherent information.

Why does this phenomenon occur? The simplest (though perhaps not completely satisfying) explanation is that it results from a phenomenon known as *degeneracy*. Consider a qubit $\alpha|0\rangle + \beta|1\rangle$ encoded in a repetition code:

$$\alpha|00000\rangle + \beta|11111\rangle. \quad (24.164)$$

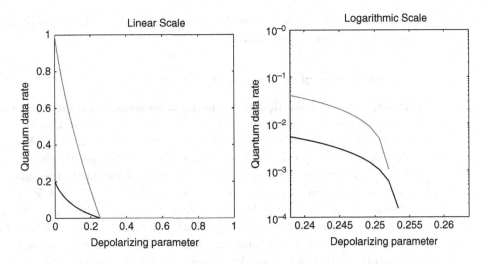

Figure 24.4 The figures plot the coherent information in (24.161) (bottom curves in both figures) and that in (24.163) (top curves in both figures) versus the depolarizing noise parameter p. The figure on the left is on a linear scale, and the one on the right is on a logarithmic scale. The notable features of the figure on the left are that the quantum data rate of the top curve is equal to one and the quantum data rate of the bottom curve is $1/5$ when the channel is noiseless (the latter rate is to be expected for a five-qubit repetition code). Both data rates become small when p is near 0.25, but the figure on the right reveals that the repetition code concatenation strategy still gets positive coherent information even when the rate of the random coding strategy vanishes. This is an example of a channel for which the coherent information can be superadditive.

If the "error" $Z_1 \otimes Z_2$ occurs, then it actually has no effect on this state. The same holds for other two-qubit combinations of Z errors. When the channel noise is low, degeneracy of the code with respect to these errors does not help very much because these two-qubit error combinations are less likely to occur. However, when the channel becomes really noisy, these errors are more likely to occur, and the help from degeneracy of the repetition code offsets the loss in rate.

It is perhaps strange that the coherent information of a depolarizing channel behaves in this way. The channel seems simple enough, and we could say that the strategies for achieving the unassisted and entanglement-assisted classical capacity of this channel are very "classical" strategies. Recall that the best strategy for achieving the unassisted classical capacity is to generate random codes by picking states uniformly at random from some orthonormal basis, and the receiver measures each channel output in this same orthonormal basis. For achieving the entanglement-assisted classical capacity, we choose a random code by picking Bell states uniformly at random and the receiver measures each channel output and his share of each entangled state in the Bell basis. Both of these results follow from the additivity of the respective capacities. In spite of these other results, the best strategy for achieving the quantum capacity of the depolarizing channel remains very poorly understood.

24.8.2 Superactivation of Quantum Capacity

Perhaps the most startling result in quantum communication is a phenomenon known as *superactivation*. Suppose that Alice is connected to Bob by a quantum channel $\mathcal{N}_1$ with zero capacity for transmitting quantum data. Also, suppose that there is some other zero quantum capacity channel $\mathcal{N}_2$ connecting them. Intuitively, we would expect that Alice should not be able to transmit quantum data reliably over the tensor-product channel $\mathcal{N}_1 \otimes \mathcal{N}_2$. That is, using these channels in parallel seems like it should not give any advantage over using the individual channels alone if they are both individually useless for quantum data transmission (this is the intuition that we have whenever a capacity formula is additive). But two examples of zero-capacity channels are known that can *superactivate* each other, such that the joint channel has a non-zero quantum capacity. How is this possible?

First, consider a 50% quantum erasure channel $\mathcal{N}_1$ that transmits its input state with probability $1/2$ and replaces it with an orthogonal erasure state with probability $1/2$. As we have argued before with the no-cloning theorem, such a channel has zero capacity for sending quantum data reliably (see also Proposition 24.7.1). Now consider some other channel $\mathcal{N}_2$. The following theorem states that the coherent information of the joint channel $\mathcal{N}_1 \otimes \mathcal{N}_2$ is at least equal to half the private information of $\mathcal{N}_2$ alone.

THEOREM 24.8.1 Let $\{p_X(x), \rho^x_{A_2}\}$ be an ensemble of inputs for the channel $\mathcal{N}_2$, and let $\mathcal{N}_1$ be a 50% erasure channel. Then there exists a pure state $\varphi_{RA_1A_2}$ such that the coherent information $H(B_1B_2) - H(E_1E_2)$ of the joint channel $\mathcal{N}_1 \otimes \mathcal{N}_2$ is equal to half the private information $I(X; B_2) - I(X; E_2)$ of the second channel:

$$H(B_1B_2)_\omega - H(E_1E_2)_\omega = \frac{1}{2}\left[I(X; B_2)_\rho - I(X; E_2)_\rho\right], \qquad (24.165)$$

where

$$\omega_{RB_1B_2E_1E_2} \equiv \left(\mathcal{U}^{\mathcal{N}_1}_{A_1 \to B_1E_1} \otimes \mathcal{U}^{\mathcal{N}_2}_{A_2 \to B_2E_2}\right)(\varphi_{RA_1A_2}), \qquad (24.166)$$

$$\rho_{XB_2E_2} \equiv \sum_x p_X(x)|x\rangle\langle x|_X \otimes \mathcal{U}^{\mathcal{N}_2}_{A_2 \to B_2E_2}(\rho^x_{A_2}), \qquad (24.167)$$

and $U^{\mathcal{N}_1}_{A_1 \to B_1E_1}$ and $U^{\mathcal{N}_2}_{A_2 \to B_2E_2}$ are respective isometric extensions of $\mathcal{N}_1$ and $\mathcal{N}_2$. This implies that

$$Q(\mathcal{N}_1 \otimes \mathcal{N}_2) \geq P(\mathcal{N}_2)/2. \qquad (24.168)$$

Proof Consider the following classical–quantum state corresponding to the ensemble $\{p_X(x), \rho^x_{A_2}\}$:

$$\rho_{XA_2} \equiv \sum_x p_X(x)|x\rangle\langle x|_X \otimes \rho^x_{A_2}. \qquad (24.169)$$

Let $\rho_{XB_2E_2} \equiv \mathcal{U}^{\mathcal{N}_2}_{A_2 \to B_2 E_2}(\rho_{XA_2})$. A purification of this state is

$$|\varphi\rangle_{XA_1A_2} \equiv \sum_x \sqrt{p_X(x)}|x\rangle_X |x\rangle_{A_1'} |\phi_x\rangle_{A_1''A_2}, \tag{24.170}$$

where we identify $A_1 \equiv A_1'A_1''$ and each $|\phi_x\rangle_{A_1''A_2}$ is a purification of $\rho_{A_2}^x$, so that the state $|\varphi\rangle_{XA_1A_2}$ is a purification of ρ_{XA_2}. Let $|\varphi\rangle_{XB_1E_1B_2E_2}$ be the state resulting from sending A_1 and A_2 through the tensor-product channel $\mathcal{U}^{\mathcal{N}_1}_{A_1 \to B_1 E_1} \otimes \mathcal{U}^{\mathcal{N}_2}_{A_2 \to B_2 E_2}$. Identifying the system $B_1 \equiv B_1'B_1''$ and $E_1 \equiv E_1'E_1''$, we can write this state as follows by recalling the isometric extension of the erasure channel in (24.6):

$$|\varphi\rangle_{XB_1E_1B_2E_2} \equiv \frac{1}{\sqrt{2}} \sum_x \sqrt{p_X(x)}|x\rangle_X |x\rangle_{B_1'} |\phi_x\rangle_{B_1''B_2E_2}|e\rangle_{E_1}$$

$$+ \frac{1}{\sqrt{2}} \sum_x \sqrt{p_X(x)}|x\rangle_X |x\rangle_{E_1'} |\phi_x\rangle_{E_1''B_2E_2}|e\rangle_{B_1}. \tag{24.171}$$

Recall that Bob can perform an isometry on B_1 of the form in (24.125) that identifies whether he receives the state or the erasure symbol, and let Z_B be a flag register indicating the outcome. Eve can do the same, and let Z_E indicate her flag register. The resulting state is as follows:

$$|\psi\rangle_{XB_1E_1B_2E_2Z_BZ_E} \equiv \frac{1}{\sqrt{2}}|\psi^0\rangle_{XB_1E_1B_2E_2}|0\rangle_{Z_B}|1\rangle_{Z_E}$$

$$+ \frac{1}{\sqrt{2}}|\psi^1\rangle_{XB_1E_1B_2E_2}|1\rangle_{Z_B}|0\rangle_{Z_E}, \tag{24.172}$$

where

$$|\psi^0\rangle_{XB_1E_1B_2E_2} \equiv \sum_x \sqrt{p_X(x)}|x\rangle_X |x\rangle_{B_1'} |\phi_x\rangle_{B_1''B_2E_2}|e\rangle_{E_1}, \tag{24.173}$$

$$|\psi^1\rangle_{XB_1E_1B_2E_2} \equiv \sum_x \sqrt{p_X(x)}|x\rangle_X |x\rangle_{E_1'} |\phi_x\rangle_{E_1''B_2E_2}|e\rangle_{B_1}. \tag{24.174}$$

Then we can evaluate the coherent information of the state resulting from sending system A_1 through the erasure channel and A_2 through the other channel $\mathcal{N}_2$:

$$H(B_1B_2)_\varphi - H(E_1E_2)_\varphi$$

$$= H(B_1Z_BB_2)_\psi - H(E_1Z_EE_2)_\psi \tag{24.175}$$

$$= H(B_1B_2|Z_B)_\psi + H(Z_B)_\psi - H(E_1E_2|Z_E)_\psi - H(Z_E)_\psi \tag{24.176}$$

$$= H(B_1B_2|Z_B)_\psi - H(E_1E_2|Z_E)_\psi \tag{24.177}$$

$$= \frac{1}{2}\left[H(B_1B_2)_{\psi^0} + H(B_2)_{\psi^1}\right] - \frac{1}{2}\left[H(E_2)_{\psi^0} + H(E_1E_2)_{\psi^1}\right] \tag{24.178}$$

$$= \frac{1}{2}\left[H(XE_2)_{\psi^0} + H(B_2)_{\psi^1}\right] - \frac{1}{2}\left[H(E_2)_{\psi^0} + H(XB_2)_{\psi^1}\right] \tag{24.179}$$

$$= \frac{1}{2}\left[H(XE_2)_\rho + H(B_2)_\rho\right] - \frac{1}{2}\left[H(E_2)_\rho + H(XB_2)_\rho\right] \tag{24.180}$$

$$= \frac{1}{2}\left[I(X;B_2)_\rho - I(X;E_2)_\rho\right]. \tag{24.181}$$

The first equality follows because Bob and Eve can perform the isometries that identify whether they receive the state or the erasure flag. The second equality follows from the chaining rule for entropy, and the third follows because the entropies of the flag registers Z_B and Z_E are equal for a 50% erasure channel. The fourth equality follows because the registers Z_B and Z_E are classical when tracing over the other Z register, so that we can evaluate the conditional entropies as a uniform convex sum of different possibilities: Bob obtaining the state transmitted or not, and Eve obtaining the state transmitted or not. The fifth equality follows because the states ψ^0 and ψ^1 are pure. The sixth equality follows because $\psi^0_{XE_2} = \rho_{XE_2}$, $\psi^1_{B_2} = \rho_{B_2}$, $\psi^0_{E_2} = \rho_{E_2}$, and $\psi^1_{XB_2} = \rho_{XB_2}$. The final equality follows from the definition of quantum mutual information.   □

Armed with the above theorem, we need to find an example of a quantum channel that has zero quantum capacity, but for which there exists an ensemble that registers a non-zero private information. If such a channel were to exist, we could combine it with a 50% erasure channel in order to achieve a non-zero coherent information (and thus a non-zero quantum capacity) for the joint channel. Indeed, such a channel exists, and it is known as an entanglement-binding channel. It has the ability to generate private classical communication but no ability to transmit quantum information (we point the reader to Horodecki et al. (1996) and Horodecki (1997) for further details on these channels). Thus, the 50% erasure channel and the entanglement-binding channel can superactivate each other.

The startling phenomenon of superactivation has important implications for quantum data transmission. First, it implies that a quantum channel's ability to transmit quantum information depends on the context in which it is used. For example, if other seemingly useless channels are available, it could be possible to transmit more quantum information than would be possible were the channels used alone. Next, and more importantly for quantum Shannon theory, it implies that whatever formula might eventually be found to characterize quantum capacity (some characterization other than the regularized coherent information in Theorem 24.3.1), it should be strongly non-additive in some cases (strongly non-additive in the sense of superactivation). That is, suppose that $Q^?(\mathcal{N})$ is some unknown formula for the quantum capacity of $\mathcal{N}$ and $Q^?(\mathcal{M})$ is the same formula characterizing the quantum capacity of $\mathcal{M}$. Then this formula in general should be strongly non-additive in some cases:

$$Q^?(\mathcal{N} \otimes \mathcal{M}) > Q^?(\mathcal{N}) + Q^?(\mathcal{M}). \tag{24.182}$$

The discovery of superactivation has led us to realize that at present we are much farther than we might have thought from understanding reliable quantum communication rates over quantum channels.

4.9   Entanglement Distillation

We close out this chaper with a final application of the techniques in the direct coding part of Theorem 24.3.1 to the task of entanglement distillation. Entanglement distillation is a protocol where Alice and Bob begin with many copies of some bipartite state ρ_{AB}. They attempt to distill ebits from it at some positive rate by employing local operations and forward classical communication from Alice to Bob. If the state is pure, then Alice and Bob should simply perform the entanglement concentration protocol from Chapter 19, and there is no need for forward classical communication in this case. Otherwise, they can perform the protocol given in the proof of the following theorem.

THEOREM 24.9.1 (Devetak–Winter)   Suppose that Alice and Bob share the state $\rho_{AB}^{\otimes n}$ where n is an arbitrarily large positive integer. Then it is possible for them to distill ebits at the rate $I(A\rangle B)_\rho$ if they are allowed forward classical communication from Alice to Bob.

We should mention that we have already proved the statement in the above theorem with the protocol given in Corollary 22.4.2. Nevertheless, it is still instructive to exploit the techniques from this chapter in proving the existence of an entanglement distillation protocol.

Proof   Suppose that Alice and Bob begin with a general bipartite state ρ_{AB} with purification ψ_{ABE}. We can write the purification in Schmidt form as follows:

$$|\psi\rangle_{ABE} \equiv \sum_{x \in \mathcal{X}} \sqrt{p_X(x)}|x\rangle_A \otimes |\psi_x\rangle_{BE}. \tag{24.183}$$

The nth extension of the above state is

$$|\psi\rangle_{A^n B^n E^n} \equiv \sum_{x^n \in \mathcal{X}^n} \sqrt{p_{X^n}(x^n)}|x^n\rangle_{A^n} \otimes |\psi_{x^n}\rangle_{B^n E^n}. \tag{24.184}$$

The protocol begins with Alice performing a type class measurement given by the type projectors (recall from (15.118) that the typical projector decomposes into a sum of the type class projectors):

$$\Pi_t^n \equiv \sum_{x^n \in T_t^{X^n}} |x^n\rangle\langle x^n|. \tag{24.185}$$

If the type resulting from the measurement is not a typical type, then Alice aborts the protocol (this result happens with arbitrarily small probability). If it is a typical type, they can then consider a code over a particular type class t with the following structure:

$$LMK \approx |T_t| \approx 2^{nH(X)}, \tag{24.186}$$

$$K \approx 2^{nI(X;E)}, \tag{24.187}$$

$$MK \approx 2^{nI(X;B)}, \tag{24.188}$$

where t is the type class and the entropies are with respect to the following dephased state:

$$\sum_{x \in \mathcal{X}} p_X(x)|x\rangle\langle x|_X \otimes |\psi_x\rangle\langle \psi_x|_{BE}. \tag{24.189}$$

It follows that $M \approx 2^{n(I(X;B)-I(X;E))} = 2^{n[H(B)-H(E)]}$ and $L \approx 2^{nH(X|B)}$ We label the codewords as $x^n(l, m, k)$ where $x^n(l, m, k) \in T_t$. Thus, we instead operate on the following state $|\tilde{\psi}_t\rangle_{A^n B^n E^n}$ resulting from the type class measurement:

$$|\tilde{\psi}_t\rangle_{A^n B^n E^n} \equiv \frac{1}{\sqrt{|T_t|}} \sum_{x^n \in T_t} |x^n\rangle_{A^n} \otimes |\psi_{x^n}\rangle_{B^n E^n}. \tag{24.190}$$

The protocol proceeds as follows. Alice first performs an incomplete measurement of the system A^n, with the following measurement operators:

$$\left\{ \Gamma_l \equiv \sum_{m,k} |m, k\rangle\langle x^n(l, m, k)|_{A^n} \right\}_l. \tag{24.191}$$

This measurement collapses the above state as follows:

$$\frac{1}{\sqrt{MK}} \sum_{m,k} |m, k\rangle_{A^n} \otimes |\psi_{x^n(l,m,k)}\rangle_{B^n E^n}. \tag{24.192}$$

Alice transmits the classical information in l to Bob, using $nH(X|B)$ bits of classical information. Bob needs to know l so that he can know in which code they are operating. Bob then constructs the following isometry, a coherent POVM similar to that in (24.28) (constructed from the POVM for a private classical communication code):

$$\sum_{m,k} \sqrt{\Lambda_{B^n}^{m,k}} \otimes |m, k\rangle_B. \tag{24.193}$$

After performing the above coherent POVM, the state is close to the following one:

$$\frac{1}{\sqrt{MK}} \sum_{m,k} |m, k\rangle_{A^n} \otimes |m, k\rangle_B |\psi_{x^n(l,m,k)}\rangle_{B^n E^n}. \tag{24.194}$$

Alice then performs a measurement of the k register in the Fourier-transformed basis:

$$\left\{ |\hat{s}\rangle \equiv \frac{1}{\sqrt{K}} \sum_k e^{i2\pi ks/K} |k\rangle \right\}_{s \in \{1,...,K\}}. \tag{24.195}$$

Alice performs this particular measurement because she would like Bob and Eve to maintain their entanglement in the k variable. The state resulting from this measurement is

$$\frac{1}{\sqrt{MK}} \sum_{m,k} |m\rangle_{A^n} \otimes e^{i2\pi ks/K} |m, k\rangle_B |\psi_{x^n(l,m,k)}\rangle_{B^n E^n}. \tag{24.196}$$

Alice then uses $nI(X;E)$ bits to communicate the s variable to Bob. Bob then applies the phase transformation $Z^\dagger(s)$, where

$$Z^\dagger(s) = \sum_k e^{-i2\pi sk/K} |k\rangle\langle k|, \qquad (24.197)$$

to his k variable in register B. The resulting state is

$$\frac{1}{\sqrt{MK}} \sum_{m,k} |m\rangle_{A^n} \otimes |m,k\rangle_B \left|\psi_{x^n(l,m,k)}\right\rangle_{B^n E^n}. \qquad (24.198)$$

They then proceed as in the final steps (24.45)–(24.52) of the protocol from the direct coding part of Theorem 24.3.1, and they extract a state close to a maximally entangled state of the following form:

$$\frac{1}{\sqrt{M}} \sum_m |m\rangle_{A^n} \otimes |m\rangle_B, \qquad (24.199)$$

with rate equal to $(\log M)/n = H(B) - H(E)$. $\qquad\square$

EXERCISE 24.9.1 Argue that the above protocol cannot perform the task of state transfer as can the protocol in Corollary 22.4.2.

24.10 History and Further Reading

The quantum capacity theorem has a long history that led to many important discoveries in quantum information theory. Shor (1995) first stated the problem of finding the quantum capacity of a quantum channel in his seminal paper on quantum error correction. DiVincenzo et al. (1998) demonstrated that the coherent information of the depolarizing channel is superadditive by concatenating a random code with a repetition code (this result in hindsight was remarkable given that the coherent information was not even known at the time). Smith & Smolin (2007) later extended this result to show that the coherent information is strongly super-additive for several examples of Pauli channels. Schumacher & Nielsen (1996) demonstrated that the coherent information obeys a quantum data-processing inequality, much like the classical data-processing inequality for mutual information. Schumacher & Westmoreland (1998) started making connections between private communication and quantum communication. Bennett, DiVincenzo, Smolin & Wootters (1996) and Barnum et al. (2000) demonstrated that forward classical communication cannot increase the quantum capacity. In the same paper, Bennett, DiVincenzo, Smolin & Wootters (1996) introduced the idea of entanglement distillation, which has connections with the quantum capacity.

Schumacher (1996), Schumacher & Nielsen (1996), Barnum et al. (1998), and Barnum et al. (2000) made important progress on the quantum capacity theorem in a series of papers that established the coherent information upper bound on the quantum capacity. Lloyd (1997), Shor (2002b), and Devetak (2005) are generally credited with proving the coherent information lower bound on the quantum capacity, though an inspection of Lloyd's proof reveals that it is perhaps not as rigorous as the latter two proofs. Shor (2002b) delivered his proof of the lower bound in a lecture, though he never published this proof in a journal. Later, Hayden, Shor & Winter (2008) published a paper detailing a proof of the quantum capacity theorem that they considered to be close in spirit to the proof in Shor (2002b). After Shor's proof, Devetak (2005) provided a detailed proof of the lower bound on the quantum capacity, by analyzing superpositions of the codewords from private classical codes. This is the approach we have taken in this chapter. We should also mention that Hamada (2005) showed how to achieve the coherent information for certain input states by using random stabilizer codes, and Harrington & Preskill (2001) showed how to achieve the coherent information rate for a very specific class of channels.

Gottesman (1997) established the stabilizer formalism for quantum error correction. Our discussion of stabilizer codes in this chapter follows closely the development in the PhD thesis of Smith (2006).

Another approach to proving the quantum capacity theorem is known as the decoupling approach (Hayden, Horodecki, Winter & Yard, 2008). This approach exploits a fundamental concept introduced in Schumacher & Westmoreland (2002). Suppose that the reference, Bob, and Eve share a tripartite pure entangled state $|\psi\rangle_{RBE}$ after Alice transmits her share of the entanglement with the reference through a noisy channel. Then if the reduced state ψ_{RE} on the reference system and Eve's system is approximately decoupled, meaning that

$$\|\psi_{RE} - \psi_R \otimes \sigma_E\|_1 \leq \varepsilon, \qquad (24.200)$$

where σ_E is some arbitrary state, this implies that Bob can decode the quantum information that Alice intended to send to him. Why is this so? Let us suppose that the state is exactly decoupled. Then one purification of the state ψ_{RE} is the state $|\psi\rangle_{RBE}$ that they share after the channel acts. Another purification of $\psi_{RE} = \psi_R \otimes \sigma_E$ is

$$|\psi\rangle_{RB_1} \otimes |\sigma\rangle_{B_2E}, \qquad (24.201)$$

where $|\psi\rangle_{RB_1}$ is the original state that Alice sent through the channel and $|\sigma\rangle_{B_2E}$ is some other state that purifies the state σ_E of the environment. Since all purifications are related by isometries and since Bob possesses the purification of R and E, there exists some unitary $U_{B \to B_1 B_2}$ such that

$$U_{B \to B_1 B_2} |\psi\rangle_{RBE} = |\psi\rangle_{RB_1} \otimes |\sigma\rangle_{B_2E}. \qquad (24.202)$$

This unitary is then Bob's decoder! Thus, the decoupling condition implies the existence of a decoder for Bob, so that it is only necessary to show the existence of an encoder that decouples the reference from the environment. Simply put, the structure of quantum mechanics allows for this way of proving the quantum capacity theorem.

Many researchers have now exploited the decoupling approach in a variety of contexts. This approach is implicit in Devetak's proof of the quantum capacity theorem (Devetak, 2005). Horodecki et al. (2005) and Horodecki et al. (2007) exploited it to prove the existence of a state-merging protocol. Yard & Devetak (2009) and Ye et al. (2008) used it in their proofs of the state redistribution protocol. Dupuis et al. (2010) proved the best known characterization of the entanglement-assisted quantum capacity of the broadcast channel using this approach. The thesis of Dupuis and subsequent work generalized this decoupling approach to settings beyond the traditional i.i.d. setting (Dupuis, 2010; Dupuis et al., 2014). Datta and coworkers have also applied this approach in a variety of contexts (Buscemi & Datta, 2010; Datta & Hsieh, 2011; Datta & Hsieh, 2013), and Wilde & Hsieh (2010) used the approach to study quantum communication using a noisy channel and a noisy state.

Bennett et al. (1997) found the quantum capacity of the erasure channel, and Giovannetti & Fazio (2005) computed the quantum capacity of the amplitude damping channel. Smith & Yard (2008) showed superactivation and later showed superactivation for channels that can be realized more easily in the laboratory (Smith et al., 2011). Devetak & Winter (2005) established that the coherent information is achievable for entanglement distillation. Cubitt et al. (2015) and Elkouss & Strelchuk (2015) demonstrated a striking superadditivity effect, which suggests that a regularized expression is necessary to determine the quantum capacity of an arbitrary channel.

There have also been some results on error exponents, the strong converse, and second-order characterizations of the quantum capacity (see Section 20.7 for a discussion of the meaning of these terms). Berta et al. (2013) proved that a quantity called the entanglement cost of a quantum channel is a strong converse rate for quantum communication. Morgan & Winter (2014) established what they called a "pretty strong converse" for the quantum capacity of degradable channels, meaning that there is a sharp transition in the fidelity from one to $1/2$, when the rate of communication goes from below to above the quantum capacity (this is in the limit of many channel uses). Wilde & Winter (2014) demonstrated that randomly selected codes with a communication rate exceeding the quantum capacity of the quantum erasure channel lead to a fidelity that decreases exponentially fast as the number of channel uses increases (a strong converse would however demonstrate that this behavior occurs for all codes). Tomamichel et al. (2014) proved that a quantity known as the Rains bound (defined in Rains, 2001—see also the later work of Audenaert et al., 2002) is a strong converse rate for quantum communication over any channel, which in turn establishes the strong converse for any dephasing channel.

Beigi et al. (2015) and Tomamichel et al. (2015) established second-order achievability characterizations for quantum capacity. Beigi et al. (2015) did so by making use of a "Petz recovery map" decoder and Tomamichel et al.

(2015) with a version of the decoupling theorem from Morgan & Winter (2014). Tomamichel et al. (2015) also gave a second-order converse for quantum communication by making use of the Rains bound, and they obtained an exact second-order characterization of quantum communication for dephasing channels.

Trading Resources for
Communication

This chapter unifies all of the channel coding theorems that we have studied in this book. One of the most general information-processing tasks that a sender and receiver can accomplish is to transmit classical and quantum information and generate entanglement with many independent uses of a quantum channel and with the assistance of classical communication, quantum communication, and shared entanglement.[1] The resulting rates for communication are *net* rates that give the generation rate of a resource less its consumption rate. Since we have three resources, all achievable rates are rate triples (C, Q, E) that lie in a three-dimensional capacity region, where C is the net rate of classical communication, Q is the net rate of quantum communication, and E is the net rate of entanglement consumption/generation. The capacity theorem for this general scenario is known as the quantum dynamic capacity theorem, and it is the main theorem that we prove in this chapter. All of the rates given in the channel coding theorems of previous chapters are special points in this three-dimensional capacity region.

The proof of the quantum dynamic capacity theorem comes in two parts: the direct coding theorem and the converse theorem. The direct coding theorem demonstrates that the strategy for achieving any point in the three-dimensional capacity region is remarkably simple: we just combine the protocol from Corollary 22.5.2 for entanglement-assisted classical and quantum communication with the three unit protocols of teleportation, super-dense coding, and entanglement distribution. The interpretation of the achievable rate region is that it is the unit resource capacity region from Chapter 8 translated along the points achievable with the protocol from Corollary 22.5.2. In the proof of the converse theorem, we analyze the most general protocol that can consume and generate classical communication, quantum communication, and entanglement along with the consumption of many independent uses of a quantum channel, and we show that the net rates for such a protocol are bounded by the regularization of the achievable rate region. In the general case, our characterization is multi-letter, meaning that

---

[1] Recall that Chapter 8 addressed a special case of this task that applies to the scenario in which the sender and receiver do not have access to many independent uses of a quantum channel.

the computation of the capacity region requires an optimization over a poten tially infinite number of channel uses and is thus intractable. However, both th quantum Hadamard channels from Section 5.2.3 and the quantum erasure chan nel are special classes of channels for which the regularization is not necessary and we can compute their capacity regions with respect to a single instance o the channel. Another important class of channels for which the capacity region is known is the class of pure-loss bosonic channels (though the optimality proo. is only up to a long-standing conjecture which many researchers believe to be true). These pure-loss bosonic channels model free-space communication or loss in a fiber optic cable and thus have an elevated impetus for study because of their importance in practical applications.

One of the most important questions for communication in this three-dimensional setting is whether it is really necessary to exploit the trade-off coding strategy given in Corollary 22.5.2. That is, would it be best simply to use a classical communication code for a fraction of the channel uses, a quantum communication code for another fraction, an entanglement-assisted code for another fraction, etc.? Such a strategy is known as time sharing and allows the sender and receiver to achieve convex combinations of any rate triples in the capacity region. The answer to this question depends on the channel. For example, time sharing is optimal for the quantum erasure channel, but it is not for a dephasing channel or a pure-loss bosonic channel. In fact, trade-off coding for a pure-loss bosonic channel can give tremendous performance gains over time sharing. How can we know which one will perform better in the general case? It is hard to say, but at the very least, we know that time sharing is a special case of trade-off coding as we argued in Section 22.5.2. Thus, from this perspective, it might make sense simply to always use a trade-off strategy.

We organize this chapter as follows. We first review the information-processing task corresponding to the quantum dynamic capacity region. Section 25.2 states the quantum dynamic capacity theorem and shows how many of the capacity theorems we studied previously arise as special cases of it. The next two sections prove the direct coding theorem and the converse theorem. Section 25.4.2 introduces the quantum dynamic capacity formula, which is important for analyzing whether the quantum dynamic capacity region is single-letter. In the final section of this chapter, we compute and plot the quantum dynamic capacity region for the dephasing channels, erasure channels, and the pure-loss bosonic channels.

25.1   The Information-Processing Task

Figure 25.1 depicts the most general protocol for generating classical communication, quantum communication, and entanglement with the consumption of a noisy quantum channel $\mathcal{N}_{A' \to B}$ and the same respective resources. Alice possesses two classical registers (each labeled by M and of dimension $2^{nC_{\text{out}}}$), a quantum register A_1 of dimension $2^{nQ_{\text{out}}}$ entangled with a reference system R,

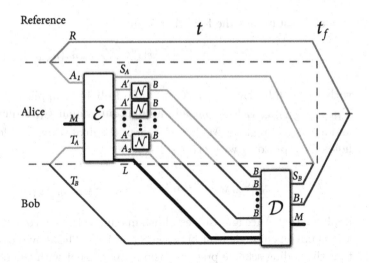

Figure 25.1 The most general protocol for generating classical communication, quantum communication, and entanglement with the help of the same respective resources and many uses of a quantum channel. Alice begins with her classical register M, her quantum register A_1, and her share of the entanglement in register T_A. She encodes according to some encoding channel $\mathcal{E}$ that outputs a quantum register S_A, many registers A'^m, a quantum register A_2, and a classical register L. She inputs A'^m to many uses of the quantum channel $\mathcal{N}$ and transmits A_2 over a noiseless quantum channel and L over a noiseless classical channel. Bob receives the channel outputs B^n, the quantum register A_2, and the classical register L and performs a decoding $\mathcal{D}$ that recovers the quantum information and classical message. The decoding also generates entanglement with system S_A. Many protocols are a special case of the above one. For example, the protocol is entanglement-assisted communication of classical and quantum information if the registers L, S_A, S_B, and A_2 are empty.

and another quantum register T_A of dimension $2^{nE_{\text{in}}}$ that contains her share of the state $\Phi_{T_A T_B}$ maximally entangled with Bob:

$$\omega_{MMRA_1 T_A T_B} \equiv \overline{\Phi}_{MM} \otimes \Psi_{RA_1} \otimes \Phi_{T_A T_B}. \tag{25.1}$$

She passes one of the classical registers and the registers A_1 and T_A into an encoding channel $\mathcal{E}_{MA_1 T_A \to A'^m S_A L A_2}$ that outputs a quantum register S_A of dimension $2^{nE_{\text{out}}}$ and a quantum register A_2 of dimension $2^{nQ_{\text{in}}}$, a classical register L of dimension $2^{nC_{\text{in}}}$, and many quantum systems A'^m. The register S_A is for creating entanglement with Bob. The state after the encoding $\mathcal{E}$ is as follows:

$$\omega_{MA'^m S_A L A_2 RT_B} \equiv \mathcal{E}_{MA_1 T_A \to A'^m S_A L A_2}(\omega_{MMRA_1 T_A T_B}). \tag{25.2}$$

She sends the systems A'^m through many uses $\mathcal{N}_{A'^m \to B^n} \equiv (\mathcal{N}_{A' \to B})^{\otimes n}$ of the quantum channel $\mathcal{N}_{A' \to B}$, transmits L over a noiseless classical channel, and transmits A_2 over a noiseless quantum channel, producing the following state:

$$\omega_{MB^n S_A L A_2 RT_B} \equiv \mathcal{N}_{A'^m \to B^n}(\omega_{MA'^m S_A L A_2 RT_B}). \tag{25.3}$$

The above state has the following form:

$$\sum_x p_X(x)|x\rangle\langle x|_X \otimes \mathcal{N}_{A'^n \to B^n}(\rho^x_{AA'^n}),\qquad(25.4$$

with $A \equiv RT_B A_2 S_A$ and $X \equiv ML$. Bob then applies a decoding channel $\mathcal{D}_{B^n A_2 T_B L \to B_1 S_B \hat{M}}$ that outputs a quantum system B_1, a quantum system S_B and a classical register $\hat{M}$. Let ω' denote the final state. The following condition holds for a protocol with error $\varepsilon \in (0,1)$:

$$\frac{1}{2}\left\| \overline{\Phi}_{M\hat{M}} \otimes \Psi_{RB_1} \otimes \Phi_{S_A S_B} - \omega'_{M B_1 S_B \hat{M} S_A R} \right\|_1 \leq \varepsilon,\qquad(25.5)$$

implying that Alice and Bob establish maximal classical correlations in M and $\hat{M}$ and maximal entanglement between S_A and S_B. The above condition also implies that the coding scheme preserves the entanglement with the reference system R. The net rate triple for the protocol is as follows: $(C_{\text{out}} - C_{\text{in}}, Q_{\text{out}} - Q_{\text{in}}, E_{\text{out}} - E_{\text{in}})$. The protocol generates a resource if its corresponding rate is positive, and it consumes a resource if its corresponding rate is negative. A protocol of the above form is an $(n, C_{\text{out}} - C_{\text{in}}, Q_{\text{out}} - Q_{\text{in}}, E_{\text{out}} - E_{\text{in}}, \varepsilon)$ protocol.

We say that a rate triple (C, Q, E) is achievable for $\mathcal{N}$ if there exists a sequence of $(n, C - \delta, Q - \delta, E - \delta, \varepsilon)$ protocols for all $\delta > 0$, $\varepsilon \in (0,1)$ and sufficiently large n. The quantum dynamic capacity region $\mathcal{C}_{\text{CQE}}(\mathcal{N})$ is equal to the union of all achievable rates.

25.2   The Quantum Dynamic Capacity Theorem

The dynamic capacity theorem gives bounds on the reliable communication rates of a noisy quantum channel when combined with the noiseless resources of classical communication, quantum communication, and shared entanglement. The theorem applies regardless of whether a protocol consumes the noiseless resources or generates them.

THEOREM 25.2.1 (Quantum Dynamic Capacity)   The dynamic capacity region $\mathcal{C}_{\text{CQE}}(\mathcal{N})$ of a quantum channel $\mathcal{N}$ is equal to the following expression:

$$\mathcal{C}_{\text{CQE}}(\mathcal{N}) = \overline{\bigcup_{k=1}^{\infty} \frac{1}{k} \mathcal{C}^{(1)}_{\text{CQE}}(\mathcal{N}^{\otimes k})},\qquad(25.6)$$

where the overbar indicates the closure of a set. The region $\mathcal{C}^{(1)}_{\text{CQE}}(\mathcal{N})$ is equal to the union of the state-dependent regions $\mathcal{C}^{(1)}_{\text{CQE},\sigma}(\mathcal{N})$:

$$\mathcal{C}^{(1)}_{\text{CQE}}(\mathcal{N}) \equiv \bigcup_{\sigma} \mathcal{C}^{(1)}_{\text{CQE},\sigma}(\mathcal{N}).\qquad(25.7)$$

The state-dependent region $C_{\mathrm{CQE},\sigma}^{(1)}(\mathcal{N})$ is the set of all rates C, Q, and E, such that

$$C + 2Q \leq I(AX; B)_\sigma, \tag{25.8}$$

$$Q + E \leq I(A \rangle BX)_\sigma, \tag{25.9}$$

$$C + Q + E \leq I(X; B)_\sigma + I(A \rangle BX)_\sigma. \tag{25.10}$$

The above entropic quantities are with respect to a classical–quantum state σ_{XAB}, where

$$\sigma_{XAB} \equiv \sum_x p_X(x)|x\rangle\langle x|_X \otimes \mathcal{N}_{A' \to B}(\phi_{AA'}^x), \tag{25.11}$$

and the states $\phi_{AA'}^x$ are pure. It is implicit that one should consider states on A'^k instead of A' when taking the regularization in (25.6).

The above theorem is a "multi-letter" capacity theorem due to the regularization in (25.6). However, we show in Section 25.5.1 that the regularization is not necessary for the Hadamard class of channels. We prove the above theorem in two parts:

1. The direct coding theorem in Section 25.3 shows that combining the protocol from Corollary 22.5.2 with teleportation, super-dense coding, and entanglement distribution achieves the above region.
2. The converse theorem in Section 25.4 demonstrates that any coding scheme cannot do better than the regularization in (25.6), in the sense that a sequence of protocols with decreasing error should have the communication rates below the above amounts.

EXERCISE 25.2.1   Show that it suffices to evaluate the following four entropies in order to determine the state-dependent region in Theorem 25.2.1:

$$H(A|X)_\sigma = \sum_x p_X(x) H(A)_{\phi_x}, \tag{25.12}$$

$$H(B)_\sigma = H\left(\sum_x p_X(x)\mathcal{N}_{A' \to B}(\phi_{A'}^x)\right), \tag{25.13}$$

$$H(B|X)_\sigma = \sum_x p_X(x) H(\mathcal{N}_{A' \to B}(\phi_{A'}^x)), \tag{25.14}$$

$$H(E|X)_\sigma = \sum_x p_X(x) H(\mathcal{N}_{A' \to E}^c(\phi_{A'}^x)), \tag{25.15}$$

where the state σ_{XABE} extends the state in (25.11) and is of the form

$$\sigma_{XABE} \equiv \sum_x p_X(x)|x\rangle\langle x|_X \otimes U_{A' \to BE}^{\mathcal{N}}(\phi_{AA'}^x), \tag{25.16}$$

where $U_{A' \to BE}^{\mathcal{N}}$ is an isometric extension of the channel $\mathcal{N}_{A' \to BE}$.

25.2.1   Special Cases of the Quantum Dynamic Capacity Theorem

We first consider five special cases of the above capacity theorem that arise when Q and E both vanish, C and E both vanish, or one of C, Q, or E vanishes. The first two cases correspond respectively to the classical capacity theorem from Chapter 20 and the quantum capacity theorem from Chapter 24. Each of the other special cases traces out a two-dimensional achievable rate region in the three-dimensional capacity region. The five coding scenarios are as follows:

1. Classical communication (C) when there is no entanglement assistance or quantum communication. The achievable rate region lies on the $(C, 0, 0)$ ray extending from the origin.
2. Quantum communication (Q) when there is no entanglement assistance or classical communication. The achievable rate region lies on the $(0, Q, 0)$ ray extending from the origin.
3. Entanglement-assisted quantum communication (QE) when there is no classical communication. The achievable rate region lies in the $(0, Q, -E)$ quarter-plane of the three-dimensional region in Theorem 25.2.1.
4. Classically enhanced quantum communication (CQ) when there is no entanglement assistance. The achievable rate region lies in the $(C, Q, 0)$ quarter-plane of the three-dimensional region in Theorem 25.2.1.
5. Entanglement-assisted classical communication (CE) when there is no quantum communication. The achievable rate region lies in the $(C, 0, -E)$ quarter-plane of the three-dimensional region in Theorem 25.2.1.

Classical Capacity

The following theorem gives the one-dimensional capacity region $\mathcal{C}_C(\mathcal{N})$ of a quantum channel $\mathcal{N}$ for classical communication.

THEOREM 25.2.2 (Holevo–Schumacher–Westmoreland)   The classical capacity region $\mathcal{C}_C(\mathcal{N})$ is given by

$$\mathcal{C}_C(\mathcal{N}) = \overline{\bigcup_{k=1}^{\infty} \frac{1}{k} \mathcal{C}_C^{(1)}(\mathcal{N}^{\otimes k})}. \tag{25.17}$$

The region $\mathcal{C}_C^{(1)}(\mathcal{N})$ is the union of the state-dependent regions $\mathcal{C}_{C,\sigma}^{(1)}(\mathcal{N})$, where $\mathcal{C}_{C,\sigma}^{(1)}(\mathcal{N})$ is the set of all $C \geq 0$, such that

$$C \leq I(X; B)_\sigma + I(A\rangle BX)_\sigma. \tag{25.18}$$

The entropic quantity is with respect to the state σ_{XAB} in (25.11).

The bound in (25.18) is never larger than the bound in (25.10) with $Q = 0$ and $E = 0$, given that $I(X; B)_\sigma + I(A\rangle BX)_\sigma \leq I(AX; B)_\sigma$. The above characterization of the classical capacity region may seem slightly different from the characterization in Chapter 20, until we make a few observations. First, we rewrite the coherent information $I(A\rangle BX)_\sigma$ as $H(B|X)_\sigma - H(E|X)_\sigma$. Then

$I(X;B)_\sigma + I(A\rangle BX)_\sigma = H(B)_\sigma - H(E|X)_\sigma$. Next, pure states of the form $|\varphi^x\rangle_{A'}$ are sufficient to attain the classical capacity of a quantum channel (see Theorem 13.3.2). Then $H(E|X)_\sigma = H(B|X)_\sigma$ so that $I(X;B)_\sigma + I(A\rangle BX)_\sigma = H(B)_\sigma - H(B|X)_\sigma = I(X;B)_\sigma$ for states of this form. Thus, the expression in (25.18) can never exceed the classical capacity and finds its maximum exactly at the Holevo information.

Quantum Capacity

The following theorem gives the one-dimensional quantum capacity region $C_Q(\mathcal{N})$ of a quantum channel $\mathcal{N}$.

THEOREM 25.2.3 (Quantum Capacity) The quantum capacity region $C_Q(\mathcal{N})$ is given by

$$C_Q(\mathcal{N}) = \overline{\bigcup_{k=1}^{\infty} \frac{1}{k} C_Q^{(1)}(\mathcal{N}^{\otimes k})}. \tag{25.19}$$

The region $C_Q^{(1)}(\mathcal{N})$ is the union of the state-dependent regions $C_{Q,\sigma}^{(1)}(\mathcal{N})$, where $C_{Q,\sigma}^{(1)}(\mathcal{N})$ is the set of all $Q \geq 0$, such that

$$Q \leq I(A\rangle BX)_\sigma. \tag{25.20}$$

The entropic quantity is with respect to the state σ_{XAB} in (25.11) with the restriction that the density $p_X(x)$ is degenerate.

The bound in (25.20) is a special case of the bound in (25.9) with $E = 0$. The other bounds in Theorem 25.2.1 are looser than the bound in (25.9) when $C, E = 0$.

Entanglement-Assisted Quantum Capacity

The following theorem gives the two-dimensional entanglement-assisted quantum capacity region $C_{QE}(\mathcal{N})$ of a quantum channel $\mathcal{N}$.

THEOREM 25.2.4 (Devetak–Harrow–Winter) The entanglement-assisted quantum capacity region $C_{QE}(\mathcal{N})$ is given by

$$C_{QE}(\mathcal{N}) = \overline{\bigcup_{k=1}^{\infty} \frac{1}{k} C_{QE}^{(1)}(\mathcal{N}^{\otimes k})}. \tag{25.21}$$

The region $C_{QE}^{(1)}(\mathcal{N})$ is the union of the state-dependent regions $C_{QE,\sigma}^{(1)}(\mathcal{N})$, where $C_{QE,\sigma}^{(1)}(\mathcal{N})$ is the set of all $Q, E \geq 0$, such that

$$2Q \leq I(AX;B)_\sigma, \tag{25.22}$$
$$Q \leq I(A\rangle BX)_\sigma + |E|. \tag{25.23}$$

The entropic quantities are with respect to the state σ_{XAB} in (25.11) with the restriction that the density $p_X(x)$ is degenerate.

The bounds in (25.22) and (25.23) are a special case of the respective bounds in (25.8) and (25.9) with $C = 0$. The other bounds in Theorem 25.2.1 are looser than the bounds in (25.8) and (25.9) when $C = 0$. Observe that the region is a union of general pentagons (see the QE-plane in Figure 25.2 for an example of one of these general pentagons in the union).

Classically-Enhanced Quantum Capacity

The following theorem gives the two-dimensional capacity region $\mathcal{C}_{CQ}(\mathcal{N})$ for classically enhanced quantum communication over a quantum channel $\mathcal{N}$.

THEOREM 25.2.5 (Devetak–Shor)   The classically enhanced quantum capacity region $\mathcal{C}_{CQ}(\mathcal{N})$ is given by

$$\mathcal{C}_{CQ}(\mathcal{N}) = \overline{\bigcup_{k=1}^{\infty} \frac{1}{k} \mathcal{C}_{CQ}^{(1)}(\mathcal{N}^{\otimes k})}. \tag{25.24}$$

The region $\mathcal{C}_{CQ}^{(1)}(\mathcal{N})$ is the union of the state-dependent regions $\mathcal{C}_{CQ,\sigma}^{(1)}(\mathcal{N})$, where $\mathcal{C}_{CQ,\sigma}^{(1)}(\mathcal{N})$ is the set of all $C, Q \geq 0$, such that

$$C + Q \leq I(X; B)_\sigma + I(A\rangle BX)_\sigma, \tag{25.25}$$
$$Q \leq I(A\rangle BX)_\sigma. \tag{25.26}$$

The entropic quantities are with respect to the state σ_{XAB} in (25.11).

The bounds in (25.25) and (25.26) are a special case of the respective bounds in (25.9) and (25.10) with $E = 0$. The first inequality in (25.8) is redundant because $Q \leq I(A\rangle BX)_\sigma = H(A|EX)_\sigma \leq H(A|X)_\sigma$ and combining this with the inequality in (25.25) gives (25.8). Observe that the region is a union of trapezoids (see the CQ-plane in Figure 25.2 for an example of one of these rectangles in the union).

Entanglement-Assisted Classical Capacity with Limited Entanglement

THEOREM 25.2.6 (Shor)   The entanglement-assisted classical capacity region $\mathcal{C}_{CE}(\mathcal{N})$ of a quantum channel $\mathcal{N}$ is

$$\mathcal{C}_{CE}(\mathcal{N}) = \overline{\bigcup_{k=1}^{\infty} \frac{1}{k} \mathcal{C}_{CE}^{(1)}(\mathcal{N}^{\otimes k})}. \tag{25.27}$$

The region $\mathcal{C}_{CE}^{(1)}(\mathcal{N})$ is the union of the state-dependent regions $\mathcal{C}_{CE,\sigma}^{(1)}(\mathcal{N})$, where $\mathcal{C}_{CE,\sigma}^{(1)}(\mathcal{N})$ is the set of all $C, E \geq 0$, such that

$$C \leq I(AX; B)_\sigma, \tag{25.28}$$
$$C \leq I(X; B)_\sigma + I(A\rangle BX)_\sigma + |E|, \tag{25.29}$$

where the entropic quantities are with respect to the state σ_{XAB} in (25.11).

The bounds in (25.28) and (25.29) are a special case of the respective bounds in (25.8) and (25.10) with $Q = 0$. Observe that the region is a union of general polyhedra (see the CE-plane in Figure 25.2 for an example of one of these general polyhedra in the union).

25.3 The Direct Coding Theorem

The unit resource achievable region is what Alice and Bob can achieve using the protocols entanglement distribution, teleportation, and super-dense coding (see Chapter 8). It is the cone of the rate triples corresponding to these protocols:

$$\{\alpha\,(0, -1, 1) + \beta\,(2, -1, -1) + \gamma\,(-2, 1, -1) : \alpha, \beta, \gamma \geq 0\}. \tag{25.30}$$

We can also write any rate triple (C, Q, E) in the unit resource capacity region with a matrix equation:

$$\begin{bmatrix} C \\ Q \\ E \end{bmatrix} = \begin{bmatrix} 0 & 2 & -2 \\ -1 & -1 & 1 \\ 1 & -1 & -1 \end{bmatrix} \begin{bmatrix} \alpha \\ \beta \\ \gamma \end{bmatrix}. \tag{25.31}$$

The inverse of the above matrix is as follows:

$$\begin{bmatrix} -\frac{1}{2} & -1 & 0 \\ 0 & -\frac{1}{2} & -\frac{1}{2} \\ -\frac{1}{2} & -\frac{1}{2} & -\frac{1}{2} \end{bmatrix}, \tag{25.32}$$

and gives the following set of inequalities for the unit resource achievable region:

$$C + 2Q \leq 0, \tag{25.33}$$
$$Q + E \leq 0, \tag{25.34}$$
$$C + Q + E \leq 0, \tag{25.35}$$

by inverting the matrix equation in (25.31) and applying the constraints $\alpha, \beta, \gamma \geq 0$.

Now, let us include the protocol from Corollary 22.5.2 for entanglement-assisted communication of classical and quantum information. Corollary 22.5.2 states that we can achieve the following rate triple by channel coding for $\mathcal{N}_{A' \rightarrow B}$:

$$\left(I(X; B)_\sigma, \frac{1}{2}I(A; B|X)_\sigma, -\frac{1}{2}I(A; E|X)_\sigma \right), \tag{25.36}$$

for any state σ_{XABE} of the form

$$\sigma_{XABE} \equiv \sum_x p_X(x)|x\rangle\langle x|_X \otimes \mathcal{U}^{\mathcal{N}}_{A' \rightarrow BE}(\phi^x_{AA'}), \tag{25.37}$$

where $\mathcal{U}^{\mathcal{N}}_{A' \rightarrow BE}$ is an isometric extension of the quantum channel $\mathcal{N}_{A' \rightarrow B}$. Specifically, we showed in Corollary 22.5.2 that one can achieve the above rates with vanishing error in the limit of large blocklength. Thus the achievable rate region is the following translation of the unit resource achievable region in (25.31):

$$\begin{bmatrix} C \\ Q \\ E \end{bmatrix} = \begin{bmatrix} 0 & 2 & -2 \\ -1 & -1 & 1 \\ 1 & -1 & -1 \end{bmatrix} \begin{bmatrix} \alpha \\ \beta \\ \gamma \end{bmatrix} + \begin{bmatrix} I(X;B)_\sigma \\ \frac{1}{2}I(A;B|X)_\sigma \\ -\frac{1}{2}I(A;E|X)_\sigma \end{bmatrix}. \tag{25.38}$$

We can now determine bounds on an achievable rate region that employs the above coding strategy. We apply the inverse of the matrix in (25.31) to the left-hand side and right-hand side, giving

$$\begin{bmatrix} -\frac{1}{2} & -1 & 0 \\ 0 & -\frac{1}{2} & -\frac{1}{2} \\ -\frac{1}{2} & -\frac{1}{2} & -\frac{1}{2} \end{bmatrix} \begin{bmatrix} C \\ Q \\ E \end{bmatrix} - \begin{bmatrix} -\frac{1}{2} & -1 & 0 \\ 0 & -\frac{1}{2} & -\frac{1}{2} \\ -\frac{1}{2} & -\frac{1}{2} & -\frac{1}{2} \end{bmatrix} \begin{bmatrix} I(X;B)_\sigma \\ \frac{1}{2}I(A;B|X)_\sigma \\ -\frac{1}{2}I(A;E|X)_\sigma \end{bmatrix} = \begin{bmatrix} \alpha \\ \beta \\ \gamma \end{bmatrix}. \tag{25.39}$$

Then using the following identities:

$$I(X;B)_\sigma + I(A;B|X)_\sigma = I(AX;B)_\sigma, \tag{25.40}$$

$$\frac{1}{2}I(A;B|X)_\sigma - \frac{1}{2}I(A;E|X)_\sigma = I(A\rangle BX)_\sigma, \tag{25.41}$$

and the constraints $\alpha, \beta, \gamma \geq 0$, we obtain the inequalities in (25.8)–(25.10), corresponding exactly to the state-dependent region in Theorem 25.2.1. Taking the union over all possible states σ in (25.11) and taking the regularization gives the full dynamic achievable rate region.

Figure 25.2 illustrates an example of the general polyhedron specified by (25.8)–(25.10), where the channel is the qubit dephasing channel $\rho \to (1-p)\rho + pZ\rho Z$ with dephasing parameter $p = 0.2$, and the input state is

$$\sigma_{XAA'} \equiv \frac{1}{2}(|0\rangle\langle0|_X \otimes \phi^0_{AA'} + |1\rangle\langle1|_X \otimes \phi^1_{AA'}), \tag{25.42}$$

where

$$|\phi^0\rangle_{AA'} \equiv \sqrt{1/4}|00\rangle_{AA'} + \sqrt{3/4}|11\rangle_{AA'}, \tag{25.43}$$

$$|\phi^1\rangle_{AA'} \equiv \sqrt{3/4}|00\rangle_{AA'} + \sqrt{1/4}|11\rangle_{AA'}. \tag{25.44}$$

The state σ_{XABE} resulting from the channel is $\mathcal{U}^N_{A'\to BE}(\sigma_{XAA'})$ where $U^N_{A'\to BE}$ is an isometric extension of the qubit dephasing channel. The figure caption provides a detailed explanation of the state-dependent region $C^{(1)}_{\text{CQE},\sigma}$ (note that Figure 25.2 displays the state-dependent region and does not display the full capacity region).

25.4   The Converse Theorem

We provide a catalytic, information-theoretic converse proof of the dynamic capacity region, showing that (25.6) gives a multi-letter characterization of it. The catalytic approach means that we are considering the most general protocol that

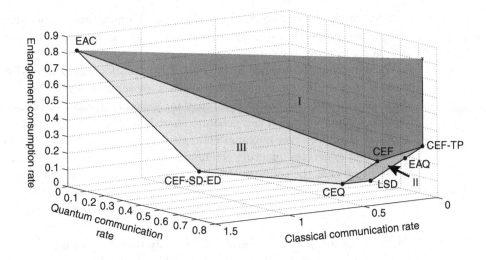

Figure 25.2 An example of the state-dependent achievable region $C_{\text{CQE}\,\sigma}^{(1)}(\mathcal{N})$ corresponding to a state σ_{XABE} that arises from a qubit dephasing channel with dephasing parameter $p = 0.2$. The figure depicts the octant corresponding to the consumption of entanglement and the generation of classical and quantum communication. The state input to the channel $\mathcal{N}$ is $\sigma_{XAA'}$, defined in (25.42). The plot features seven achievable corner points of the state-dependent region. We can achieve the convex hull of these seven points by time sharing any two different coding strategies. We can also achieve any point above an achievable point by consuming more entanglement than necessary. The seven achievable points correspond to entanglement-assisted quantum communication (EAQ), the protocol from Corollary 22.5.3 for classically enhanced quantum communication (CEQ), the protocol from Theorem 22.5.1 for entanglement-assisted classical communication with limited entanglement (EAC), quantum communication (LSD), combining CEF with entanglement distribution and super-dense coding (CEF-SD-ED), the protocol from Corollary 22.5.2 for entanglement-assisted communication of classical and quantum information (CEF), and combining CEF with teleportation (CEF-TP). Observe that we can obtain EAC by combining CEF with super-dense coding, so that the points CEQ, CEF, EAC, and CEF-SD-ED all lie in plane III. Observe that we can obtain CEQ from CEF by entanglement distribution and we can obtain LSD from EAQ and EAQ from CEF-TP, both by entanglement distribution. Thus, the points CEF, CEQ, LSD, EAQ, and CEF-TP all lie in plane II. Finally, observe that we can obtain all corner points by combining CEF with the unit protocols of teleportation, super-dense coding, and entanglement distribution. The bounds in (25.8)–(25.10) uniquely specify the respective planes I-III. We obtain the full achievable region by taking the union over all states σ of the state-dependent regions $C_\sigma^{(1)}(\mathcal{N})$ and taking the regularization, as outlined in Theorem 25.2.1. The above region is a translation of the unit resource capacity region from Chapter 8 to the protocol for entanglement-assisted communication of classical and quantum information.

consumes and generates classical communication, quantum communication, and entanglement in addition to the uses of the noisy quantum channel. This approach has the advantage that we can prove the converse theorem in "one fell swoop."

We employ the AFW inequality, the chain rule for quantum mutual information, elementary properties of quantum entropy, and the quantum data-processing inequality to prove the converse.

We show that the bounds in (25.8)–(25.10) hold for randomness distribution instead of classical communication because a capacity for generating shared randomness can only be better than that for generating classical communication (classical communication can generate shared randomness). We also consider a protocol that preserves maximal entanglement with a reference system instead of one that generates quantum communication.

We prove that the converse theorem holds for a state of the following form:

$$\sigma_{XAB^n} \equiv \sum_x p(x)|x\rangle\langle x|_X \otimes \mathcal{N}_{A'\to B}^{\otimes n}(\rho_{AA'^n}^x), \tag{25.45}$$

where the states $\rho_{AA'^n}^x$ are mixed. We identify this state with ω_{XAB^n} defined in (25.3), setting $A \equiv RS_A A_2 T_B$ and $X \equiv LM$. We do this rather than proving it for a state of the form in (25.11). Then we show in Section 25.4.1 that it is not necessary to consider an ensemble of mixed states—i.e., we can do just as well with an ensemble of pure states, giving the statement of Theorem 25.2.1.

We first prove the bound in (25.8). Consider the following chain of inequalities:

$$n(C_{\text{out}} + 2Q_{\text{out}})$$
$$= I(M;\hat{M})_{\overline{\Phi}} + I(R;B_1)_{\Phi} \tag{25.46}$$
$$= I(RM;B_1\hat{M})_{\Phi\otimes\overline{\Phi}} \tag{25.47}$$
$$\leq I(RM;B_1\hat{M})_{\omega'} + n\delta' \tag{25.48}$$
$$\leq I(RM;B^n A_2 LT_B)_{\omega} + n\delta' \tag{25.49}$$
$$= I(RA_2T_BLM;B^n)_{\omega} + I(RM;A_2T_BL)_{\omega} - I(B^n;A_2T_BL)_{\omega} + n\delta' \tag{25.50}$$
$$\leq I(RS_A A_2 T_B LM;B^n)_{\omega} + I(RM;A_2T_BL)_{\omega} + n\delta' \tag{25.51}$$
$$= I(AX;B^n)_{\omega} + I(RM;T_B)_{\omega} + I(RM;L|T_B)_{\omega}$$
$$\quad + I(RM;A_2|T_BL)_{\omega} + n\delta' \tag{25.52}$$
$$\leq I(AX;B^n)_{\omega} + n(C_{\text{in}} + 2Q_{\text{in}}) + n\delta'. \tag{25.53}$$

The first equality holds by evaluating the quantum mutual informations on the respective states $\overline{\Phi}_{M\hat{M}}$ and Φ_{RB_1}. The second equality follows because the mutual information is additive with respect to tensor-product states (see Exercise 11.6.8). The first inequality follows from the condition in (25.5) and an application of the AFW inequality where δ' is a parameter that vanishes as $n \to \infty$ and $\varepsilon \to 0$. The second inequality follows from quantum data processing. The third equality is a consequence of an identity from Exercise 11.7.1. The third inequality follows from quantum data processing and the fact that $I(B^n;A_2T_BL)_{\omega} \geq 0$. The fourth equality follows by identifying $A \equiv RS_A A_2 T_B$ and $X \equiv LM$, and also from the chain rule, which implies that $I(RM;A_2T_BL)_{\omega} = I(RM;T_B)_{\omega} + I(RM;L|T_B)_{\omega} + I(RM;A_2|T_BL)_{\omega}$.

The final inequality follows because $I(RM; T_B)_\omega = 0$ and from the dimension bounds $I(RM; L|T_B)_\omega \leq \log \dim(\mathcal{H}_L) = nC_{\text{in}}$ and $I(RM; A_2|T_B L)_\omega \leq 2 \log \dim(\mathcal{H}_{A_2}) = n2Q_{\text{in}}$ (see Exercise 11.7.9). Thus, (25.8) holds for the net rates.

We now prove the second bound in (25.9). Consider the following chain of inequalities:

$$n(Q_{\text{out}} + E_{\text{out}}) = I(R\rangle B_1)_\Phi + I(S_A\rangle S_B)_\Phi \tag{25.54}$$

$$= I(RS_A\rangle B_1 S_B)_{\Phi \otimes \Phi} \tag{25.55}$$

$$\leq I(RS_A\rangle B_1 S_B)_{\omega'} + n\delta' \tag{25.56}$$

$$\leq I(RS_A\rangle B^n A_2 T_B LM)_\omega + n\delta' \tag{25.57}$$

$$\leq I(RS_A A_2 T_B\rangle B^n LM)_\omega + \log \dim(\mathcal{H}_{A_2} \otimes \mathcal{H}_{T_B}) + n\delta' \tag{25.58}$$

$$= I(A\rangle B^n X)_\omega + n(Q_{\text{in}} + E_{\text{in}}) + n\delta'. \tag{25.59}$$

The first equality follows by evaluating the coherent informations of the respective states Φ_{RB_1} and $\Phi_{S_A S_B}$. The second equality follows because $\Phi_{RB_1} \otimes \Phi_{S_A S_B}$ is a product state and coherent information is additive with respect to tensor-product states. The first inequality follows from the condition in (25.5) and an application of the AFW inequality with parameter δ' vanishing when $n \to \infty$ and $\varepsilon \to 0$. The second inequality follows from quantum data processing. The third inequality follows from the dimension bound in Exercise 11.8.5. The final equality follows by identifying $A \equiv RS_A A_2 T_B$ and $X \equiv LM$, and noting that $\log \dim(\mathcal{H}_{A_2}) = nQ_{\text{in}}$ and $\log \dim(\mathcal{H}_{T_B}) = nE_{\text{in}}$. Thus, (25.9) holds for the net rates.

We prove the last bound in (25.10). Consider the following chain of inequalities:

$$n(C_{\text{out}} + Q_{\text{out}} + E_{\text{out}})$$

$$= I(M; \hat{M})_{\overline{\Phi}} + I(RS_A\rangle B_1 S_B)_{\Phi \otimes \Phi} \tag{25.60}$$

$$\leq I(M; \hat{M})_{\omega'} + I(RS_A\rangle B_1 S_B)_{\omega'} + n\delta' \tag{25.61}$$

$$\leq I(M; B^n A_2 T_B L)_\omega + I(RS_A\rangle B^n A_2 T_B LM)_\omega + n\delta' \tag{25.62}$$

$$= I(ML; B^n)_\omega + I(RS_A A_2 T_B\rangle B^n LM)_\omega + I(M; L)_\omega$$
$$+ H(A_2 T_B|B^n)_\omega - I(A_2 B^n T_B; L)_\omega + n\delta' \tag{25.63}$$

$$\leq I(X; B^n)_\omega + I(A\rangle B^n X)_\omega + I(M; L)_\omega + H(A_2 T_B|B^n)_\omega + n\delta' \tag{25.64}$$

$$\leq I(X; B^n)_\omega + I(A\rangle B^n X)_\omega + n(C_{\text{in}} + Q_{\text{in}} + E_{\text{in}}) + n\delta'. \tag{25.65}$$

The first equality follows from evaluating the mutual information of the state $\overline{\Phi}_{M\hat{M}}$ and the coherent information of the product state $\Phi_{RB_1} \otimes \Phi_{S_A S_B}$. The first inequality follows from the condition in (25.5) and an application of the AFW inequality with δ' vanishing when $n \to \infty$ and $\varepsilon \to 0$. The second inequality follows from quantum data processing. The second equality is an identity, verified by expanding all quantities as unconditional entropies and seeing that both terms are equal to $H(M)_\omega + H(B^n A_2 T_B L)_\omega - H(RS_A B^n A_2 T_B LM)_\omega$. The third inequality follows by identifying $A \equiv RT_B A_2 S_A$ and $X \equiv ML$, and also because

$I(A_2 B^n T_B; L)_\omega \geq 0$. The last inequality follows from the dimension bound $I(M; L)_\omega \leq \log \dim(\mathcal{H}_L) = nC_{in}$ and $H(A_2 T_B | B^n)_\omega \leq \log \dim(\mathcal{H}_{A_2} \otimes \mathcal{H}_{T_B}) = n(Q_{in} + E_{in})$. Thus, (25.10) applies to the net rates. This concludes the proof of the converse theorem.

25.4.1　Pure-state Ensembles are Sufficient

We prove that it is sufficient to consider an ensemble of pure states as in the statement of Theorem 25.2.1 rather than an ensemble of mixed states as in (25.45) in the proof of our converse theorem. We first determine a spectral decomposition of the mixed-state ensemble, model the index of the pure states in the decomposition as a classical variable Y, and then place this classical variable Y in a classical register. It follows that the communication rates can only improve, and it is sufficient to consider an ensemble of pure states.

Consider that each mixed state in the ensemble in (25.45) admits a spectral decomposition of the following form:

$$\rho_{AA'}^x = \sum_y p(y|x)\psi_{AA'}^{x,y}. \tag{25.66}$$

We can thus represent the ensemble as follows:

$$\rho_{XAB} \equiv \sum_{x,y} p(x)p(y|x)|x\rangle\langle x|_X \otimes \mathcal{N}_{A'\to B}(\psi_{AA'}^{x,y}). \tag{25.67}$$

The inequalities in (25.8)–(25.10) for the dynamic capacity region involve the mutual information $I(AX; B)_\rho$, the Holevo information $I(X; B)_\rho$, and the coherent information $I(A\rangle BX)_\rho$. As we show below, each of these entropic quantities can only improve in each case if we make the variable y be part of the classical variable. This improvement then implies that it is only necessary to consider pure states in the dynamic capacity theorem.

Let θ_{XYAB} denote an augmented state of the following form:

$$\theta_{XYAB} \equiv \sum_x p(x)p(y|x)|x\rangle\langle x|_X \otimes |y\rangle\langle y|_Y \otimes \mathcal{N}_{A'\to B}(\psi_{AA'}^{x,y}). \tag{25.68}$$

This state is actually a state of the form in (25.11) if we subsume the classical variables X and Y into one classical variable. The following three inequalities each follow from an application of the quantum data-processing inequality:

$$I(X; B)_\rho = I(X; B)_\theta \leq I(XY; B)_\theta, \tag{25.69}$$
$$I(AX; B)_\rho = I(AX; B)_\theta \leq I(AXY; B)_\theta \tag{25.70}$$
$$I(A\rangle BX)_\rho = I(A\rangle BX)_\theta \leq I(A\rangle BXY)_\theta. \tag{25.71}$$

Each of these inequalities proves the desired result for the respective Holevo information, mutual information, and coherent information, and it suffices to consider an ensemble of pure states in Theorem 25.2.1. The same argument holds with $\mathcal{N}_{A'\to B}$ replaced by $\mathcal{N}_{A'\to B}^{\otimes n}$.

25.4.2 The Quantum Dynamic Capacity Formula

Here we introduce the quantum dynamic capacity formula and show how its additivity implies that the computation of the Pareto optimal trade-off surface of the capacity region requires an optimization over a single copy of the channel, rather than a potentially infinite number of them. The Pareto optimal trade-off surface consists of all points in the capacity region that are Pareto optimal, in the sense that it is not possible to make improvements in one resource without offsetting another resource (these are essentially the boundary points of the region in our case). We then show how several important capacity formulas discussed previously in this book are special cases of the quantum dynamic capacity formula.

DEFINITION 25.4.1 (Quantum Dynamic Capacity Formula) The quantum dynamic capacity formula of a quantum channel $\mathcal{N}$ is defined as follows:

$$D_{\vec{\lambda}}(\mathcal{N}) \equiv \max_{\sigma} \lambda_1 I(AX;B)_\sigma + \lambda_2 I(A\rangle BX)_\sigma + \lambda_3 \left[I(X;B)_\sigma + I(A\rangle BX)_\sigma \right], \tag{25.72}$$

where σ is a state of the form in (25.11) and $\vec{\lambda} \equiv (\lambda_1, \lambda_2, \lambda_3)$ is a vector of Lagrange multipliers such that $\lambda_1, \lambda_2, \lambda_3 \geq 0$.

DEFINITION 25.4.2 The regularized quantum dynamic capacity formula is defined as follows:

$$D_{\vec{\lambda}}^{\mathrm{reg}}(\mathcal{N}) \equiv \lim_{k \to \infty} \frac{1}{k} D_{\vec{\lambda}}(\mathcal{N}^{\otimes k}). \tag{25.73}$$

LEMMA 25.4.1 Suppose the quantum dynamic capacity formula is additive for a channel $\mathcal{N}$ and any other arbitrary channel $\mathcal{M}$:

$$D_{\vec{\lambda}}(\mathcal{N} \otimes \mathcal{M}) = D_{\vec{\lambda}}(\mathcal{N}) + D_{\vec{\lambda}}(\mathcal{M}). \tag{25.74}$$

Then the regularized quantum dynamic capacity formula for $\mathcal{N}$ is equal to the quantum dynamic capacity formula:

$$D_{\vec{\lambda}}^{\mathrm{reg}}(\mathcal{N}) = D_{\vec{\lambda}}(\mathcal{N}). \tag{25.75}$$

In this sense, the regularized formula "single-letterizes."

Proof We prove the result using induction on n. The base case for $n = 1$ is trivial. Suppose the result holds for n: $D_{\vec{\lambda}}(\mathcal{N}^{\otimes n}) = nD_{\vec{\lambda}}(\mathcal{N})$. Then the following chain of equalities establishes the inductive step:

$$D_{\vec{\lambda}}(\mathcal{N}^{\otimes n+1}) = D_{\vec{\lambda}}(\mathcal{N} \otimes \mathcal{N}^{\otimes n}) = D_{\vec{\lambda}}(\mathcal{N}) + D_{\vec{\lambda}}(\mathcal{N}^{\otimes n}) = D_{\vec{\lambda}}(\mathcal{N}) + nD_{\vec{\lambda}}(\mathcal{N}). \tag{25.76}$$

The first equality follows by expanding the tensor product. The second critical equality follows from the assumption in (25.74), setting $\mathcal{M} = \mathcal{N}^{\otimes n}$. The final equality follows from the induction hypothesis. $\square$

THEOREM 25.4.1 Single-letterization of the quantum dynamic capacity formula implies that the computation of the Pareto optimal trade-off surface of the dynamic capacity region requires an optimization over a single copy of the channel.

Proof We employ ideas from optimization theory for the proof (see Boyd & Vandenberghe, 2004). We would like to characterize all the points in the capacity region that are Pareto optimal. Such a task is a standard vector optimization in the theory of Pareto trade-off analysis (see Section 4.7 of Boyd & Vandenberghe, 2004).

Let $\vec{w} \equiv (w_C, w_Q, w_E) \in \mathbb{R}^3$ be a weight vector, $\vec{R} \equiv (C, Q, E)$ a rate vector and $\mathcal{E} \equiv \{p_X(x), \phi_{AA'}^x\}$ an ensemble. Our main goal here is to show that the computational problem reduces to computing the quantum dynamic capacity formula in (25.72) for all values of $\vec{\lambda}$ such that $\lambda_1, \lambda_2, \lambda_3 \geq 0$. As such, we can focus for now on a single copy of the channel and deduce the statement of the theorem once we are done. We can phrase the task of computing the boundary of the single-copy capacity region as the following optimization problem:

$$P^*(\vec{w}) \equiv \sup_{\vec{R}, \mathcal{E}} \vec{w} \cdot \vec{R} \tag{25.77}$$

$$\text{subject to} \quad C + 2Q \leq I(AX; B)_\sigma, \tag{25.78}$$

$$Q + E \leq I(A\rangle BX)_\sigma, \tag{25.79}$$

$$C + Q + E \leq I(X; B)_\sigma + I(A\rangle BX)_\sigma, \tag{25.80}$$

where the optimization is with respect to all rate vectors $\vec{R} = (C, Q, E)$ and ensembles $\mathcal{E} = \{p_X(x), \phi_{AA'}^x\}$, with σ_{XAB} a state of the form in (25.11).

The geometric interpretation of the optimization task is that we are trying to find a supporting plane of the dynamic capacity region such that the weight vector $\vec{w}$ is the normal vector of the plane and the value of its inner product with $\vec{R}$ characterizes the offset of the plane, so that $P^*(\vec{w})$ for all $\vec{w} \in \mathbb{R}^3$ characterizes the boundary of the region. Note that the optimal value $P^*(\vec{w})$ can sometimes be infinite. For example, if $\vec{w} = (-1, -1, -1)$, then the optimal rates are $\vec{R} = (-\infty, -\infty, -\infty)$, which corresponds to simply consuming all resources (the dynamic capacity theorem does not give any constraint on all resources being consumed at the same time, but rather on the generation of some resources while others are consumed).

For now, let us fix an ensemble $\mathcal{E}$ and let $P^*(\vec{w}, \mathcal{E}) \equiv \sup_{\vec{R}} \vec{w} \cdot \vec{R}$, subject to the constraints in (25.78)–(25.80). The optimization problem then becomes what is known as a linear program, given that the objective function is linear in $\vec{R}$ and the constraints are linear inequalities involving $\vec{R}$. We can then define the following Lagrangian, which introduces Lagrange multipliers $\lambda_1, \lambda_2, \lambda_3$ for the respective constraints in (25.78)–(25.80):

$$\mathcal{L}(\vec{w}, \vec{R}, \mathcal{E}, \vec{\lambda})$$
$$\equiv w_C C + w_Q Q + w_E E + \lambda_1 \left[I(AX; B)_\sigma - (C + 2Q) \right]$$
$$+ \lambda_2 \left[I(A\rangle BX)_\sigma - (Q + E) \right]$$
$$+ \lambda_3 \left[I(X; B)_\sigma + I(A\rangle BX)_\sigma - (C + Q + E) \right] \tag{25.81}$$

$$= (w_C - \lambda_1 - \lambda_3)\, C + (w_Q - 2\lambda_1 - \lambda_2 - \lambda_3)\, Q + (w_E - \lambda_2 - \lambda_3)\, E$$
$$+ \lambda_1 I(AX; B)_\sigma + \lambda_2 I(A \rangle BX)_\sigma + \lambda_3 \left[I(X; B)_\sigma + I(A \rangle BX)_\sigma \right]. \quad (25.82)$$

The Lagrange dual function is defined as

$$g(\vec{w}, \mathcal{E}, \vec{\lambda}) \equiv \sup_{\vec{R}} \mathcal{L}(\vec{w}, \vec{R}, \mathcal{E}, \vec{\lambda}). \quad (25.83)$$

By inspection, $g(\vec{w}, \mathcal{E}, \vec{\lambda})$ is infinite unless $w_C = \lambda_1 + \lambda_3$, $w_Q = 2\lambda_1 + \lambda_2 + \lambda_3$, $w_E = \lambda_2 + \lambda_3$, or equivalently (by inverting these equations), $g(\vec{w}, \mathcal{E}, \vec{\lambda})$ is infinite unless

$$\lambda_1 = \frac{1}{2}(w_Q - w_E), \quad (25.84)$$

$$\lambda_2 = \frac{1}{2}(-2w_C + w_Q + w_E), \quad (25.85)$$

$$\lambda_3 = \frac{1}{2}(2w_C - w_Q + w_E). \quad (25.86)$$

So we see that

$$g(\vec{w}, \mathcal{E}, \vec{\lambda}) = \lambda_1 I(AX; B)_\sigma + \lambda_2 I(A \rangle BX)_\sigma + \lambda_3 \left[I(X; B)_\sigma + I(A \rangle BX)_\sigma \right] \quad (25.87)$$

if (25.84)–(25.86) hold and $g(\vec{w}, \mathcal{E}, \vec{\lambda}) = +\infty$ otherwise. Observe that (25.87) contains the expressions in the quantum dynamic capacity formula in (25.72).

When $\lambda_1, \lambda_2, \lambda_3 \geq 0$, the Lagrange dual function gives upper bounds on $P^*(\vec{w}, \mathcal{E})$. To see this, let $\vec{R}$ be a rate vector satisfying (25.78)–(25.80) for fixed $\mathcal{E}$. Then

$$\vec{w} \cdot \vec{R} \leq \mathcal{L}(\vec{w}, \vec{R}, \mathcal{E}, \vec{\lambda}) \leq g(\vec{w}, \mathcal{E}, \vec{\lambda}). \quad (25.88)$$

We can then obtain the tightest upper bound on $P^*(\vec{w}, \mathcal{E})$ by taking an infimum over all $\vec{\lambda}$ satisfying $\lambda_1, \lambda_2, \lambda_3 \geq 0$:

$$P^*(\vec{w}, \mathcal{E}) \leq D^*(\vec{w}, \mathcal{E}) \equiv \inf_{\lambda_1, \lambda_2, \lambda_3 \geq 0} g(\vec{w}, \mathcal{E}, \vec{\lambda}). \quad (25.89)$$

The optimization problem on the right-hand side is known as the *dual optimization problem* and the inequality $P^*(\vec{w}, \mathcal{E}) \leq D^*(\vec{w}, \mathcal{E})$ is known as *weak duality*, which always holds. Let

$$\lambda_1^* = \frac{1}{2}(w_Q - w_E), \quad (25.90)$$

$$\lambda_2^* = \frac{1}{2}(-2w_C + w_Q + w_E), \quad (25.91)$$

$$\lambda_3^* = \frac{1}{2}(2w_C - w_Q + w_E). \quad (25.92)$$

Then by inspection, observe that

$$D^*(\vec{w}, \mathcal{E}) = \lambda_1^* I(AX; B)_\sigma + \lambda_2^* I(A \rangle BX)_\sigma + \lambda_3^* \left[I(X; B)_\sigma + I(A \rangle BX)_\sigma \right] \quad (25.93)$$

if $\lambda_1^*, \lambda_2^*, \lambda_3^* \geq 0$ and it is equal to $+\infty$ otherwise.

In computing the dual optimal value $D^*(\vec{w}, \mathcal{E})$, we first maximized the Lagrangian $\mathcal{L}(\vec{w}, \vec{R}, \mathcal{E}, \vec{\lambda})$ with respect to the rate vector $\vec{R}$ and then we minimize with respect to the Lagrange multipliers $\vec{\lambda}$, i.e.,

$$D^*(\vec{w}, \mathcal{E}) = \inf_{\lambda_1, \lambda_2, \lambda_3 \geq 0} \sup_{\vec{R}} \mathcal{L}(\vec{w}, \vec{R}, \mathcal{E}, \vec{\lambda}). \tag{25.94}$$

What happens if we conduct the optimizations in the opposite order? By inspection, consider that

$$\inf_{\lambda_1, \lambda_2, \lambda_3 \geq 0} \mathcal{L}(\vec{w}, \vec{R}, \mathcal{E}, \vec{\lambda}) = \begin{cases} \vec{w} \cdot \vec{R} & \text{if (25.78)–(25.80) hold} \\ -\infty & \text{else} \end{cases}. \tag{25.95}$$

As a consequence, we find that

$$\sup_{\vec{R}} \inf_{\lambda_1, \lambda_2, \lambda_3 \geq 0} \mathcal{L}(\vec{w}, \vec{R}, \mathcal{E}, \vec{\lambda}) = P^*(\vec{w}, \mathcal{E}). \tag{25.96}$$

The statement of *strong duality* is that $P^*(\vec{w}, \mathcal{E}) = D^*(\vec{w}, \mathcal{E})$, which we see from the above amounts to an exchange of a minimum and a maximum. Strong duality holds for any linear program (Boyd & Vandenberghe, 2004, Exercise 5.23), provided that at least one of the primal or dual problems is feasible. For our primal problem, this means that there should exist a value $\vec{R}$ meeting the constraints in (25.78)–(25.80). Since this is always the case, we can conclude that strong duality holds:

$$P^*(\vec{w}, \mathcal{E}) = D^*(\vec{w}, \mathcal{E}), \tag{25.97}$$

which in turn implies that the optimal value $P^*(\vec{w})$ in (25.77) can be rewritten as

$$P^*(\vec{w}) = \sup_{\mathcal{E}} P^*(\vec{w}, \mathcal{E}) = \sup_{\mathcal{E}} D^*(\vec{w}, \mathcal{E}). \tag{25.98}$$

By combining with (25.93), we see that the optimal primal value is given by

$$P^*(\vec{w}) = \sup_{\mathcal{E}} D^*(\vec{w}, \mathcal{E}) \tag{25.99}$$

$$= \sup_{\mathcal{E}} \lambda_1^* I(AX; B)_\sigma + \lambda_2^* I(A\rangle BX)_\sigma + \lambda_3^* [I(X; B)_\sigma + I(A\rangle BX)_\sigma], \tag{25.100}$$

if $\lambda_1^*, \lambda_2^*, \lambda_3^* \geq 0$ and it is equal to $+\infty$ otherwise, with $\lambda_1^*, \lambda_2^*, \lambda_3^*$ defined in (25.90)–(25.92). Thus, it is now clear that the quantum dynamic capacity formula in (25.72) plays an essential role in computing the quantum dynamic capacity region. If it is additive, then the computation of the Pareto optimal trade-off surface requires an optimization with respect to a single copy of the channel.　□

Special Cases of the Quantum Dynamic Capacity Formula

We now show how several capacity formulas of a quantum channel, including the entanglement-assisted classical capacity (Theorem 21.3.1), the quantum capacity formula (Theorem 24.3.1), and the classical capacity formula (Theorem 20.3.1) are special cases of the quantum dynamic capacity formula.

We first give a geometric interpretation of these special cases before proceeding to the proofs. Recall that the dynamic capacity region has the simple interpretation as a translation of the three-faced unit resource capacity region along the trade-off curve for entanglement-assisted classical and quantum communication (see Figure 25.4 for an example of the region for the dephasing channel). Any particular weight vector (w_C, w_Q, w_E) in (25.77) gives a set of parallel planes that slice through the (C, Q, E) space, and the goal of the scalar optimization task is to find one of these planes that is a supporting plane, intersecting a point (or a set of points) on the trade-off surface of the dynamic capacity region. We consider three special planes:

1. The first corresponds to the plane containing the vectors of super-dense coding and teleportation. The normal vector of this plane is $(1, 2, 0)$, and suppose that we set the weight vector in (25.77) to be this vector. Then the optimization program finds the set of points on the trade-off surface such that a plane with this normal vector is a supporting plane for the region. The optimization program singles out the constraint in (25.78), and by inspecting (25.90)–(25.92), this is equivalent to setting $\vec{\lambda}^* = (1, 0, 0)$ in the quantum dynamic capacity formula in (25.100). We show below that the optimization program becomes equivalent to finding the entanglement-assisted capacity (Theorem 21.3.1), in the sense that the quantum dynamic capacity formula becomes the entanglement-assisted capacity formula.

2. The next plane contains the vectors of teleportation and entanglement distribution. The normal vector of this plane is $(0, 1, 1)$. Setting the weight vector in (25.77) to be this vector makes the optimization program single out the constraint in (25.79), and and by inspecting (25.90)–(25.92), this is equivalent to setting $\vec{\lambda}^* = (0, 1, 0)$ in the quantum dynamic capacity formula in (25.100). We show below that the optimization program becomes equivalent to finding the quantum capacity (Theorem 24.3.1), in the sense that the quantum dynamic capacity formula becomes the LSD formula for the quantum capacity.

3. A third plane contains the vectors of super-dense coding and entanglement distribution. The normal vector of this plane is $(1, 1, 1)$. Setting the weight vector in (25.77) to be this vector makes the optimization program single out the constraint in (25.80), and by inspecting (25.90)–(25.92), this is equivalent to setting $\vec{\lambda}^* = (0, 0, 1)$ in the quantum dynamic capacity formula in (25.100). We show below that the optimization becomes equivalent to finding the classical capacity (Theorem 20.3.1), in the sense that the quantum dynamic capacity formula becomes the HSW formula for the classical capacity.

COROLLARY 25.4.1   The quantum dynamic capacity formula is equal to the entanglement-assisted classical capacity formula when $\lambda_1 = 1$, $\lambda_2 = 0$, and $\lambda_3 = 0$:

$$\max_{\sigma_{XAA'}} I(AX; B)_\sigma = \max_{\phi_{AA'}} I(A; B)_\rho, \qquad (25.101)$$

where $\sigma_{XAA'} \equiv \sum_x p_X(x)|x\rangle\langle x|_X \otimes |\phi^x\rangle\langle\phi^x|_{AA'}$, $\sigma_{XAB} \equiv \mathcal{N}_{A'\to B}(\sigma_{XAA'})$, an
$\rho_{AB} \equiv \mathcal{N}_{A'\to B}(\phi_{AA'})$.

Proof The inequality $\max_\sigma I(AX;B)_\sigma \geq \max_{\phi_{AA'}} I(A;B)_\rho$ follows because the
state $\sigma_{XAA'}$ is of the form in (25.11) and we can always choose $p_X(x) = \delta_{x,x_0}$
and $\phi_{AA'}^{x_0}$ to be the state that maximizes $I(A;B)$.

We now show the other inequality $\max_\sigma I(AX;B)_\sigma \leq \max_{\phi_{AA'}} I(A;B)_\rho$
Consider that the following state purifies $\sigma_{XAA'}$:

$$|\varphi\rangle_{XRAA'} \equiv \sum_x \sqrt{p_X(x)}|x\rangle_X|x\rangle_R|\phi^x\rangle_{AA'}. \qquad (25.102)$$

Then by quantum data processing, we find that

$$I(AX;B)_\sigma \leq I(RAX;B)_{\mathcal{N}(\varphi)} \leq \max_{\phi_{AA'}} I(A;B)_\rho, \qquad (25.103)$$

where the second inequality follows because systems RAX of $\varphi_{XRAA'}$ purify A'
and the formula on the right involves an optimization over all such purifications.
$\square$

COROLLARY 25.4.2 The quantum dynamic capacity formula is equal to the
LSD quantum capacity formula when $\lambda_1 = 0$, $\lambda_2 = 1$, and $\lambda_3 = 0$:

$$\max_\sigma I(A\rangle BX) = \max_{\phi_{AA'}} I(A\rangle B). \qquad (25.104)$$

Proof The inequality $\max_\sigma I(A\rangle BX) \geq \max_{\phi_{AA'}} I(A\rangle B)$ follows because the
state σ is of the form in (25.11) and we can always choose $p_X(x) = \delta_{x,x_0}$ and
$\phi_{AA'}^{x_0}$ to be the state that maximizes $I(A\rangle B)$. The inequality $\max_\sigma I(A\rangle BX) \leq$
$\max_{\phi_{AA'}} I(A\rangle B)$ follows because $I(A\rangle BX) = \sum_x p_X(x)I(A\rangle B)_{\mathcal{N}(\phi_x)}$ and a
maximum is never smaller than the average.
$\square$

COROLLARY 25.4.3 The quantum dynamic capacity formula is equal to the
HSW classical capacity formula when $\lambda_1 = 0$, $\lambda_2 = 0$, and $\lambda_3 = 1$:

$$\max_\sigma [I(A\rangle BX)_\sigma + I(X;B)_\sigma] = \max_{\{p_X(x),\psi_x\}} I(X;B). \qquad (25.105)$$

Proof The inequality $\max_\sigma I(A\rangle BX)_\sigma + I(X;B)_\sigma \geq \max_{\{p_X(x),\psi_x\}} I(X;B)$ follows by choosing σ to be the pure-state ensemble that maximizes $I(X;B)$ and
noting that $I(A\rangle BX)_\sigma$ vanishes for a pure-state ensemble. We now prove the
inequality $\max_\sigma I(A\rangle BX)_\sigma + I(X;B)_\sigma \leq \max_{\{p_X(x),\psi_x\}} I(X;B)$. Consider a
state ω_{XYBE} obtained by performing a complete projective measurement on
the A system of the state σ_{XABE}. Then

$$I(A\rangle BX)_\sigma + I(X;B)_\sigma = H(B)_\sigma - H(E|X)_\sigma \qquad (25.106)$$

$$= H(B)_\omega - H(E|X)_\omega \qquad (25.107)$$

$$\leq H(B)_\omega - H(E|XY)_\omega \qquad (25.108)$$

$$= H(B)_\omega - H(B|XY)_\omega \qquad (25.109)$$

$$= I(XY;B)_\omega \tag{25.110}$$

$$\leq \max_{\{p_X(x),\psi_x\}} I(X;B). \tag{25.111}$$

The first equality follows by expanding the conditional coherent information and the Holevo information. The second equality follows because the measured A system is not involved in the entropies. The first inequality follows because conditioning does not increase entropy. The third equality follows because the state ω is pure when conditioned on X and Y. The fourth equality follows by definition, and the last inequality follows for clear reasons. □

25.5 Examples of Channels

In this final section, we prove that a broad class of channels, known as the Hadamard channels (see Section 5.2.3), have a single-letter dynamic capacity region. We prove this result by analyzing the quantum dynamic capacity formula for this class of channels. A dephasing channel is a special case of a Hadamard channel, and so we can compute its dynamic capacity region. We also show that the quantum erasure channel has a single-letter dynamic capacity region, and in the process, we see that time-sharing is an optimal coding strategy for this channel. We finally overview the dynamic capacity region of a pure-loss bosonic channel, which is a good model for free-space communication or loss in an optical fiber. However, we only state the main results and do not get into too many details of this channel (doing so requires the theory of quantum optics and infinite-dimensional Hilbert spaces which is beyond the scope of this book). The upshot for this channel is that trade-off coding can give remarkable gains over time sharing.

25.5.1 Quantum Hadamard Channels

Below we show that the regularization in (25.6) is not necessary if the quantum channel is a Hadamard channel. This result holds because a Hadamard channel has a special structure (see Section 5.2.3).

THEOREM 25.5.1 The dynamic capacity region $\mathcal{C}_{\mathrm{CQE}}(\mathcal{N}_H)$ of a quantum Hadamard channel $\mathcal{N}_H$ is equal to its single-letter region $\mathcal{C}_{\mathrm{CQE}}^{(1)}(\mathcal{N}_H)$.

The proof of the above theorem follows in two parts: 1) the lemma below states that the quantum dynamic capacity formula is additive when one of the channels is Hadamard, and 2) the induction argument in Lemma 25.4.1 establishes single-letterization.

LEMMA 25.5.1 The following additivity relation holds for a Hadamard channel $\mathcal{N}_H$, any other channel $\mathcal{N}$, and for all $\vec{\lambda}$ such that $\lambda_1, \lambda_2, \lambda_3 \geq 0$:

$$D_{\vec{\lambda}}(\mathcal{N}_H \otimes \mathcal{N}) = D_{\vec{\lambda}}(\mathcal{N}_H) + D_{\vec{\lambda}}(\mathcal{N}). \tag{25.112}$$

Proof We first note that the inequality $D_{\bar{\chi}}(\mathcal{N}_H \otimes \mathcal{N}) \geq D_{\bar{\chi}}(\mathcal{N}_H) + D_{\bar{\chi}}(\mathcal{N})$ holds for any two channels simply by selecting the state σ in the maximization to be tensor product of the ones that individually maximize $D_{\bar{\chi}}(\mathcal{N}_H)$ and $D_{\bar{\chi}}(\mathcal{N})$.

So we prove that the non-trivial inequality $D_{\bar{\chi}}(\mathcal{N}_H \otimes \mathcal{N}) \leq D_{\bar{\chi}}(\mathcal{N}_H) + D_{\bar{\chi}}(\mathcal{N})$ holds when the first channel is a Hadamard channel. Since the first channel is Hadamard, it is degradable and its degrading channel has a particular structure: there are channels $\mathcal{D}^1_{B_1 \to Y}$ and $\mathcal{D}^2_{Y \to E_1}$ where Y is a classical register and such that the degrading channel is $\mathcal{D}^2_{Y \to E_1} \circ \mathcal{D}^1_{B_1 \to Y}$. Suppose the state we are considering to input to the tensor-product channel is

$$\rho_{XAA_1'A_2'} \equiv \sum_x p_X(x)|x\rangle\langle x|_X \otimes \phi^x_{AA_1'A_2'}, \qquad (25.113)$$

and this state is the one that maximizes $D_{\bar{\chi}}(\mathcal{N}_H \otimes \mathcal{N})$. Suppose that the output of the first channel is

$$\theta_{XAB_1E_1A_2'} \equiv \mathcal{U}^{\mathcal{N}_H}_{A_1' \to B_1E_1}(\rho_{XAA_1'A_2'}), \qquad (25.114)$$

and the output of the second channel is

$$\omega_{XAB_1E_1B_2E_2} \equiv \mathcal{U}^{\mathcal{N}}_{A_2' \to B_2E_2}(\theta_{XAB_1E_1A_2'}). \qquad (25.115)$$

Finally, we define the following state as the result of applying the first part of the degrading channel (a complete projective measurement) to ω:

$$\sigma_{XYAE_1B_2E_2} \equiv \mathcal{D}^1_{B_1 \to Y}(\omega_{XAB_1E_1B_2E_2}). \qquad (25.116)$$

In particular, the state σ on systems $AE_1B_2E_2$ is pure when conditioned on X and Y. Then the following chain of inequalities holds:

$$
\begin{aligned}
&D_{\bar{\chi}}(\mathcal{N}_H \otimes \mathcal{N}) \\
&= \lambda_1 I(AX; B_1B_2)_\omega + \lambda_2 I(A\rangle B_1B_2X)_\omega \\
&\quad + \lambda_3 \left[I(X; B_1B_2)_\omega + I(A\rangle B_1B_2X)_\omega \right] && (25.117) \\
&= \lambda_1 H(B_1B_2E_1E_2|X)_\omega + \lambda_2 H(B_1B_2|X)_\omega + (\lambda_1 + \lambda_3) H(B_1B_2)_\omega \\
&\quad - (\lambda_1 + \lambda_2 + \lambda_3) H(E_1E_2|X)_\omega && (25.118) \\
&= \lambda_1 H(B_1E_1|X)_\omega + \lambda_2 H(B_1|X)_\omega + (\lambda_1 + \lambda_3) H(B_1)_\omega \\
&\quad - (\lambda_1 + \lambda_2 + \lambda_3) H(E_1|X)_\omega + \lambda_1 H(B_2E_2|B_1E_1X)_\omega + \lambda_2 H(B_2|B_1X)_\omega \\
&\quad + (\lambda_1 + \lambda_3) H(B_2|B_1)_\omega - (\lambda_1 + \lambda_2 + \lambda_3) H(E_2|E_1X)_\omega && (25.119) \\
&\leq \lambda_1 H(B_1E_1|X)_\theta + \lambda_2 H(B_1|X)_\theta + (\lambda_1 + \lambda_3) H(B_1)_\theta \\
&\quad - (\lambda_1 + \lambda_2 + \lambda_3) H(E_1|X)_\theta + \lambda_1 H(B_2E_2|YX)_\sigma + \lambda_2 H(B_2|YX)_\sigma \\
&\quad + (\lambda_1 + \lambda_3) H(B_2)_\sigma - (\lambda_1 + \lambda_2 + \lambda_3) H(E_2|YX)_\sigma && (25.120)
\end{aligned}
$$

$$= \lambda_1 I(AA_2'X; B_1)_\theta + \lambda_2 I(AA_2') B_1 X)_\theta + \lambda_3 \left[I(X; B_1)_\theta + I(AA_2') B_1 X)_\theta \right]$$
$$+ \lambda_1 I(AE_1 Y X; B_2)_\sigma + \lambda_2 I(AE_1) B_2 Y X)_\sigma$$
$$+ \lambda_3 \left[I(YX; B_2)_\sigma + I(AE_1) B_2 Y X)_\sigma \right] \tag{25.121}$$
$$\leq D_{\tilde{\lambda}}(\mathcal{N}_H) + D_{\tilde{\lambda}}(\mathcal{N}). \tag{25.122}$$

The first equality follows by evaluating the quantum dynamic capacity formula $D_{\tilde{\lambda}}(\mathcal{N}_H \otimes \mathcal{N})$ on the state ρ. The next two equalities follow by rearranging entropies and because the state ω on systems $AB_1 E_1 B_2 E_2$ is pure when conditioned on X. The inequality in the middle is the crucial one and follows from the Hadamard structure of the channel: we exploit monotonicity of conditional entropy with respect to quantum channels so that

$$H(B_2|B_1 X)_\omega \leq H(B_2|YX)_\sigma, \tag{25.123}$$
$$H(B_2 E_2|B_1 E_1 X)_\omega \leq H(B_2 E_2|YX)_\sigma, \tag{25.124}$$
$$H(E_2|YX)_\sigma \leq H(E_2|E_1 X)_\omega, \tag{25.125}$$
$$H(B_2|B_1)_\omega \leq H(B_2)_\omega. \tag{25.126}$$

The next equality follows by rearranging entropies and the final inequality follows because θ is a state of the form (25.11) for the first channel while σ is a state of the form (25.11) for the second channel. $\qquad\square$

25.5.2 The Dephasing Channel

The theorem below states that the full dynamic capacity region admits a particularly simple form when the noisy quantum channel is a qubit dephasing channel $\overline{\Delta}_p$ where

$$\overline{\Delta}_p(\rho) \equiv (1-p)\rho + p\overline{\Delta}(\rho), \tag{25.127}$$
$$\overline{\Delta}(\rho) \equiv \langle 0|\rho|0\rangle|0\rangle\langle 0| + \langle 1|\rho|1\rangle|1\rangle\langle 1|, \tag{25.128}$$

and $p \in [0,1]$. Figure 25.3 plots this region for the case of a dephasing channel with dephasing parameter $p = 0.2$. Figure 25.4 plots special two-dimensional cases of the full region for various values of the dephasing parameter p. The figure demonstrates that trade-off coding just barely improves upon time sharing.

THEOREM 25.5.2 The dynamic capacity region $\mathcal{C}_{\text{CQE}}(\overline{\Delta}_p)$ of a dephasing channel with dephasing parameter $p \in [0,1]$ is the set of all C, Q, and E such that

$$C + 2Q \leq 1 + h_2(\nu) - h_2(\gamma(\nu, p)), \tag{25.129}$$
$$Q + E \leq h_2(\nu) - h_2(\gamma(\nu, p)), \tag{25.130}$$
$$C + Q + E \leq 1 - h_2(\gamma(\nu, p)), \tag{25.131}$$

where $\nu \in [0, 1/2]$, h_2 is the binary entropy function, and

$$\gamma(\nu, p) \equiv \frac{1}{2} + \frac{1}{2}\sqrt{1 - 16 \cdot \frac{p}{2}\left(1 - \frac{p}{2}\right)\nu(1-\nu)}. \tag{25.132}$$

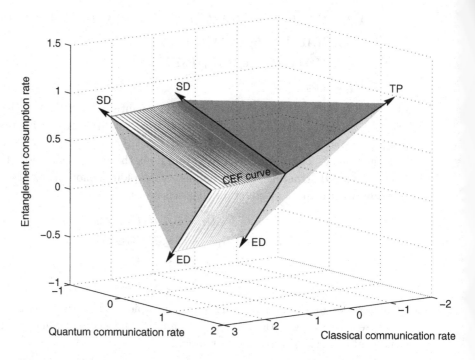

Figure 25.3 A plot of the dynamic capacity region for a qubit dephasing channel with dephasing parameter $p = 0.2$. The plot shows that the CEF trade-off curve (the protocol from Corollary 22.5.2) lies along the boundary of the dynamic capacity region. The rest of the region is simply the combination of the CEF points with the unit protocols teleportation (TP), super-dense coding (SD), and entanglement distribution (ED).

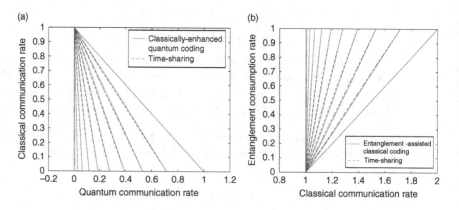

Figure 25.4 Plot of (a) the CQ trade-off curve and (b) the CE trade-off curve for a p-dephasing qubit channel for $p = 0, 0.1, 0.2, \ldots, 0.9, 1$. The trade-off curves for $p = 0$ correspond to those of a noiseless qubit channel and are the rightmost trade-off curves in each plot. The trade-off curves for $p = 1$ correspond to those for a classical channel and are the leftmost trade-off curves in each plot. Each trade-off curve between these two extremes beats a time-sharing strategy, but these two extremes do not beat time-sharing.

Proof The dephasing channel is a Hadamard channel, so that the region single-letterizes and it suffices to simplify the quantum dynamic capacity formula evaluated on a single copy of the channel. We then notice that it suffices to consider an ensemble of pure states whose reductions to A' are diagonal in the dephasing basis (see the following exercise).

EXERCISE 25.5.1   Prove that the following properties hold for a generalized dephasing channel $\mathcal{N}_D$, its complement $\mathcal{N}_D^c$, the completely dephasing channel $\overline{\Delta}$, and all input states ρ:

$$\mathcal{N}_D(\overline{\Delta}(\rho)) = \overline{\Delta}(\mathcal{N}_D(\rho)), \tag{25.133}$$
$$\mathcal{N}_D^c(\overline{\Delta}(\rho)) = \mathcal{N}_D^c(\rho). \tag{25.134}$$

Conclude that

$$H(\rho) \leq H(\overline{\Delta}(\rho)), \tag{25.135}$$
$$H(\mathcal{N}_D(\rho)) \leq H(\overline{\Delta}(\mathcal{N}_D(\rho))) = H(\mathcal{N}_D(\overline{\Delta}(\rho))), \tag{25.136}$$
$$H(\mathcal{N}_D^c(\rho)) = H(\mathcal{N}_D^c(\overline{\Delta}(\rho))), \tag{25.137}$$

so that it suffices to consider diagonal input states for the dephasing channel.

Next we prove below that it is sufficient to consider an ensemble of the following form to characterize the boundary points of the region:

$$\frac{1}{2}|0\rangle\langle 0|_X \otimes \psi_{AA'}^0 + \frac{1}{2}|1\rangle\langle 1|_X \otimes \psi_{AA'}^1, \tag{25.138}$$

where $\psi_{AA'}^0$ and $\psi_{AA'}^1$ are pure states, defined as follows for $\nu \in [0, 1/2]$:

$$\mathrm{Tr}_A\{\psi_{AA'}^0\} = \nu|0\rangle\langle 0|_{A'} + (1-\nu)|1\rangle\langle 1|_{A'}, \tag{25.139}$$
$$\mathrm{Tr}_A\{\psi_{AA'}^1\} = (1-\nu)|0\rangle\langle 0|_{A'} + \nu|1\rangle\langle 1|_{A'}. \tag{25.140}$$

We now prove the above claim. We assume without loss of generality that the dephasing basis is the computational basis. Consider a classical–quantum state with a finite number N of conditional density operators $\phi_{AA'}^x$ whose reduction to A' is diagonal:

$$\rho_{XAA'} \equiv \sum_{x=0}^{N-1} p_X(x)|x\rangle\langle x|_X \otimes \phi_{AA'}^x. \tag{25.141}$$

We can form a new classical–quantum state with double the number of conditional density operators by "bit-flipping" the original conditional density operators:

$$\sigma_{XAA'} \equiv \frac{1}{2}\sum_{x=0}^{N-1} p_X(x)\left(|x\rangle\langle x|_X \otimes \phi_{AA'}^x + |x+N\rangle\langle x+N|_X \otimes X_{A'}\phi_{AA'}^x X_{A'}\right), \tag{25.142}$$

where X is the σ_X "bit-flip" Pauli operator. Consider the following chain of inequalities that holds for all $\lambda_1, \lambda_2, \lambda_3 \geq 0$:

$$\lambda_1 I(AX;B)_\rho + \lambda_2 I(A\rangle BX)_\rho + \lambda_3 \left[I(X;B)_\rho + I(A\rangle BX)_\rho \right]$$
$$= \lambda_1 H(A|X)_\rho + (\lambda_1 + \lambda_3) H(B)_\rho + \lambda_2 H(B|X)_\rho$$
$$\qquad - (\lambda_1 + \lambda_2 + \lambda_3) H(E|X)_\rho \qquad\qquad (25.143)$$
$$\leq (\lambda_1 + \lambda_3) H(B)_\sigma + \lambda_1 H(A|X)_\sigma + \lambda_2 H(B|X)_\sigma$$
$$\qquad - (\lambda_1 + \lambda_2 + \lambda_3) H(E|X)_\sigma \qquad\qquad (25.144)$$
$$= (\lambda_1 + \lambda_3) + \lambda_1 H(A|X)_\sigma + \lambda_2 H(B|X)_\sigma - (\lambda_1 + \lambda_2 + \lambda_3) H(E|X)_\sigma \quad (25.145)$$
$$= (\lambda_1 + \lambda_3)$$
$$\qquad + \sum_x p_X(x) \left[\lambda_1 H(A)_{\phi_x} + \lambda_2 H(B)_{\phi_x} - (\lambda_1 + \lambda_2 + \lambda_3) H(E)_{\phi_x} \right] \quad (25.146)$$
$$\leq (\lambda_1 + \lambda_3) + \max_x \left[\lambda_1 H(A)_{\phi_x} + \lambda_2 H(B)_{\phi_x} - (\lambda_1 + \lambda_2 + \lambda_3) H(E)_{\phi_x} \right]$$
$$\qquad\qquad (25.147)$$
$$= (\lambda_1 + \lambda_3) + \lambda_1 H(A)_{\phi_*^x} + \lambda_2 H(B)_{\phi_*^x} - (\lambda_1 + \lambda_2 + \lambda_3) H(E)_{\phi_*^x}. \quad (25.148)$$

The first equality follows by standard entropic manipulations. The second equality follows because the conditional entropy $H(B|X)$ is invariant under a bit-flipping unitary on the input state that commutes with the channel: $H(B)_{X\rho_B^x X} = H(B)_{\rho_B^x}$. Furthermore, a bit flip on the input state does not change the eigenvalues for the output of the dephasing channel's complementary channel:

$$H(E)_{\mathcal{N}^c(X\rho_{A'}^x X)} = H(E)_{\mathcal{N}^c(\rho_{A'}^x)}. \qquad\qquad (25.149)$$

The first inequality follows because entropy is concave, i.e., the local state σ_B is a mixed version of ρ_B. The third equality follows because

$$H(B)_{\sigma_B} = H\left(\sum_x \frac{1}{2} p_X(x)(\rho_B^x + X\rho_B^x X) \right) = H\left(\frac{1}{2} \sum_x p_X(x) I \right) = 1. \qquad (25.150)$$

The fourth equality follows because the system X is classical. The second inequality follows because the maximum value of a realization of a random variable is not less than its expectation. The final equality simply follows by defining ϕ_*^x to be the conditional density operator on systems A, B, and E that arises from sending through the channel a state whose reduction to A' is of the form $\nu|0\rangle\langle0|_{A'} + (1-\nu)|1\rangle\langle1|_{A'}$. Thus, an ensemble of the kind in (25.138) is sufficient to attain a point on the boundary of the region. Evaluating the entropic quantities in Theorem 25.2.1 on a state of the above form then gives the expression for the region in Theorem 25.5.2. $\qquad\qquad\qquad\qquad\qquad\qquad\qquad\qquad\qquad\square$

25.5.3   The Quantum Erasure Channel

We can also obtain a simple characterization of the quantum dynamic capacity region for a quantum erasure channel for $\varepsilon \in [0, 1/2]$. Recall that the erasure channel is defined as follows:

$$\mathcal{N}^\varepsilon(\rho) = (1 - \varepsilon)\rho + \varepsilon|e\rangle\langle e|, \qquad\qquad (25.151)$$

where ρ is a d-dimensional input state, $|e\rangle$ is an erasure flag state orthogonal to all inputs (so that the output space has dimension $d + 1$), and $\varepsilon \in [0, 1]$ is the erasure probability. Theorem 25.5.3 characterizes the quantum dynamic capacity region for such a channel and establishes that time-sharing is an optimal strategy. Figure 25.5 plots an example of the region for a qubit erasure channel with $\varepsilon = 1/4$.

THEOREM 25.5.3 Let $\mathcal{N}^\varepsilon$ be a quantum erasure channel with $\varepsilon \in [0, 1/2]$. Then the quantum dynamic capacity region $\mathcal{C}_{\mathrm{CQE}}(\mathcal{N}^\varepsilon)$ is equal to the union of the following regions, obtained by varying $\lambda \in [0, 1]$:

$$C + 2Q \leq (1 - \varepsilon)(1 + \lambda) \log d,$$
$$Q + E \leq (1 - 2\varepsilon)\lambda \log d,$$
$$C + Q + E \leq (1 - \varepsilon - \varepsilon\lambda) \log d.$$

The region is achievable for $\varepsilon \in (1/2, 1]$.

Proof We need to show that the above region is achievable and that the regularized quantum dynamic capacity formula simplifies to it as well. For the achievability part, we choose a particular ensemble and show that the above rate region is achievable using it. Let $|\phi\rangle_{AA'} \equiv \sum_x \sqrt{p_X(x)}|x\rangle_A|x\rangle_{A'}$ where $\{|x\rangle_A\}$ and $\{|x\rangle_{A'}\}$ are the standard computational bases for systems A and A', respectively. Observe that $H(p_X) = H(A)_\phi$. We take the input ensemble as $\{1/d, X(x)_{A'}|\phi\rangle_{AA'}\}$, where $X(x)_{A'}$ are the Heisenberg–Weyl shift operators. This ensemble has the property that the expected density operator on system A'

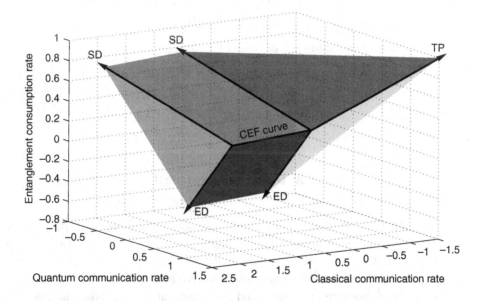

Figure 25.5 The quantum dynamic capacity region for the (qubit) quantum erasure channel with $\varepsilon = 1/4$. The plot demonstrates that time-sharing is optimal.

is the maximally mixed state $\pi_{A'}$. A classical–quantum state for evaluating the rates in Theorem 25.2.1 is as follows:

$$\rho_{XAB} \equiv \sum_x \frac{1}{d}|x\rangle\langle x|_X \otimes \mathcal{N}^\varepsilon_{A' \to B}[X(x)_{A'}|\phi\rangle\langle\phi|_{AA'}X^\dagger(x)_{A'}] \tag{25.152}$$

$$= (1-\varepsilon)\,\rho^0_{XAA'} + \varepsilon\rho^1_{XAB}, \tag{25.153}$$

where

$$\rho^0_{XAA'} \equiv \sum_x \frac{1}{d}|x\rangle\langle x|_X \otimes X(x)_{A'}|\phi\rangle\langle\phi|_{AA'}X^\dagger(x)_{A'}, \tag{25.154}$$

$$\rho^1_{XAB} \equiv \sum_x \frac{1}{d}|x\rangle\langle x|_X \otimes \phi_A \otimes |e\rangle\langle e|_B. \tag{25.155}$$

Then, from Theorem 25.2.1, we see that it suffices to compute the following three information quantities: $I(AX;B)_\rho$, $I(A\rangle BX)_\rho$, and $I(X;B)_\rho$. Consider that we can perform the following isometry on the B system without affecting any of the information quantities:

$$[|0\rangle\langle 0| + \ldots + |d-1\rangle\langle d-1|] \otimes |0\rangle_Y + |e\rangle\langle e| \otimes |1\rangle_Y. \tag{25.156}$$

Let ω_{XABY} denote the resulting state:

$$\omega_{XABY} \equiv (1-\varepsilon)\,\rho^0_{XAA'} \otimes |0\rangle\langle 0|_Y + \varepsilon\rho^1_{XAB} \otimes |1\rangle\langle 1|_Y. \tag{25.157}$$

Then, observing that $\omega_{XAY} = \pi_X \otimes \phi_A \otimes [(1-\varepsilon)|0\rangle\langle 0|_Y + \varepsilon|1\rangle\langle 1|_Y]$, we find that

$$I(AX;B)_\rho = I(AX;BY)_\omega = I(AX;B|Y)_\omega, \tag{25.158}$$
$$I(A\rangle BX)_\rho = I(A\rangle BXY)_\omega = I(A\rangle BX|Y)_\omega, \tag{25.159}$$
$$I(X;B)_\rho = I(X;BY)_\omega = I(X;B|Y)_\omega. \tag{25.160}$$

We now evaluate each of these in turn:

$$I(AX;B|Y)_\omega = (1-\varepsilon)\,I(AX;A')_{\rho^0} + \varepsilon I(AX;B)_{\rho^1}$$
$$= (1-\varepsilon)\,(\log d + H(p_X)), \tag{25.161}$$
$$I(A\rangle BX|Y)_\omega = (1-\varepsilon)\,I(A\rangle A'X)_{\rho^0} + \varepsilon I(A\rangle BX)_{\rho^1}$$
$$= (1-\varepsilon)\,H(p_X) + \varepsilon\,[-H(p_X)]$$
$$= (1-2\varepsilon)\,H(p_X), \tag{25.162}$$
$$I(X;B|Y)_\omega = (1-\varepsilon)\,I(X;A')_{\rho^0} + \varepsilon I(X;B)_{\rho^1}$$
$$= (1-\varepsilon)\,(\log d - H(p_X)). \tag{25.163}$$

Then, by Theorem 25.2.1, we can achieve the rate region in the statement of the theorem. That is, we can pick distributions p_X such that $H(p_X) = \lambda \log d$ for all $\lambda \in [0,1]$.

We now bound the quantum dynamic capacity formula for $(\mathcal{N}^\varepsilon)^{\otimes n}$ from above for all positive integers n, and as a consequence, establish that the region given in the statement of the theorem is optimal for $\varepsilon \in [0, 1/2]$. To begin with, let us consider the quantum dynamic capacity formula for an erasure channel $\mathcal{N}^\varepsilon_{A_1 \to B_1}$.

and an arbitrary degradable channel $\mathcal{M}_{A_2 \to B_2}$. We use the same idea as above, applying the isometry in (25.156) to the output B_1 of the erasure channel. The quantum dynamic capacity formula for $\mathcal{N}^{\varepsilon}_{A_1 \to B_1} \otimes \mathcal{M}_{A_2 \to B_2}$ becomes

$$\lambda_1 I(AX; B_1 Y B_2)_\sigma + \lambda_2 I(A \rangle B_1 Y B_2 X)_\sigma$$
$$+ \lambda_3 \left[I(X; B_1 Y B_2)_\sigma + I(A \rangle B_1 Y B_2 X)_\sigma \right], \quad (25.164)$$

where

$$\sigma_{XAB_1B_2Y} \equiv \sigma^0_{XAA_1B_2} \otimes (1-\varepsilon) |0\rangle\langle 0|_Y + \sigma^1_{XAB_1B_2} \otimes \varepsilon |1\rangle\langle 1|_Y, \quad (25.165)$$

$$\sigma^0_{XAA_1B_2} \equiv \sum_x p_X(x)|x\rangle\langle x|_X \otimes \mathcal{M}_{A_2 \to B_2}(\phi^x_{AA_1A_2}), \quad (25.166)$$

$$\sigma^1_{XAB_1B_2} \equiv \sum_x p_X(x)|x\rangle\langle x|_X \otimes \mathcal{M}_{A_2 \to B_2}(\phi^x_{AA_2}) \otimes |e\rangle\langle e|_{B_1}. \quad (25.167)$$

Observe that $\sigma^0_{XAB_2} = \sigma^1_{XAB_2} = \sigma_{XAB_2}$, so that

$$\sigma_{XAB_2Y} = \sigma_{XAB_2} \otimes \left[(1-\varepsilon) |0\rangle\langle 0|_Y + \varepsilon |1\rangle\langle 1|_Y \right]. \quad (25.168)$$

First we handle the quantum mutual information term:

$$I(AX; B_1 Y B_2)_\sigma = I(AX; B_1 B_2 | Y)_\sigma \quad (25.169)$$
$$= (1-\varepsilon) I(AX; A_1 B_2)_{\sigma^0} + \varepsilon I(AX; B_2)_{\sigma^1} \quad (25.170)$$
$$= (1-\varepsilon) \left[I(AX; B_2)_{\sigma^0} + I(AX; A_1 | B_2)_{\sigma^0} \right]$$
$$+ \varepsilon I(AX; B_2)_{\sigma^1} \quad (25.171)$$
$$= (1-\varepsilon) \left[I(AX; B_2)_\sigma + I(AX; A_1 | B_2)_{\sigma^0} \right]$$
$$+ \varepsilon I(AX; B_2)_\sigma \quad (25.172)$$
$$= (1-\varepsilon) I(AX; A_1 | B_2)_{\sigma^0} + I(AX; B_2)_\sigma. \quad (25.173)$$

We can bound the term $I(AX; A_1 | B_2)_{\sigma^0}$ from above as follows:

$$I(AX; A_1 | B_2)_{\sigma^0} = H(A_1 | B_2)_{\sigma^0} - H(A_1 | B_2 AX)_{\sigma^0} \quad (25.174)$$
$$= H(A_1 | B_2)_{\sigma^0} + H(A_1 | E_2 X)_{\sigma^0} \quad (25.175)$$
$$\leq \log d + H(A_1 | E_2 X)_{\sigma^0}, \quad (25.176)$$

where σ^0 is defined below in (25.184). This then gives the following bound:

$$I(AX; B_1 Y B_2)_\sigma \leq (1-\varepsilon) \left[\log d + H(A_1 | E_2 X)_{\sigma^0} \right] + I(AX; B_2)_\sigma. \quad (25.177)$$

Now we handle the Holevo information term, and the development is similar:

$$I(X; B_1 Y B_2)_\sigma = I(X; B_1 B_2 | Y)_\sigma \quad (25.178)$$
$$= (1-\varepsilon) I(X; A_1 B_2)_{\sigma^0} + \varepsilon I(X; B_2)_{\sigma^1} \quad (25.179)$$
$$= (1-\varepsilon) \left[I(X; B_2)_{\sigma^0} + I(X; A_1 | B_2)_{\sigma^0} \right] + \varepsilon I(X; B_2)_{\sigma^1} \quad (25.180)$$
$$= (1-\varepsilon) \left[I(X; B_2)_\sigma + I(X; A_1 | B_2)_{\sigma^0} \right] + \varepsilon I(X; B_2)_\sigma \quad (25.181)$$
$$= (1-\varepsilon) I(X; A_1 | B_2)_{\sigma^0} + I(X; B_2)_\sigma. \quad (25.182)$$

We finally handle the coherent information term. To this end, note that an iso
metric extension of the erasure channel is as follows: $|\psi\rangle_A \rightarrow \sqrt{1-\varepsilon}|\psi\rangle_B|e\rangle_E$
$\sqrt{\varepsilon}|e\rangle_B|\psi\rangle_E$. Both the receiver and the environment can perform the isometr
in (25.156) on their systems, without affecting the information quantities. Le
$U^M_{A_2 \rightarrow B_2 E_2}$ be an isometric extension of $M_{A_2 \rightarrow B_2}$ and define

$$|\sigma\rangle_{XX'AB_1B_2E_1E_2YZ} \equiv |\sigma^0\rangle_{XX'AA_1B_2E_1E_2} \otimes \sqrt{1-\varepsilon}|0\rangle_Y|1\rangle_Z$$
$$+ |\sigma^1\rangle_{XX'AB_1B_2A_1E_2} \otimes \sqrt{\varepsilon}|1\rangle_Y|0\rangle_Z, \quad (25.183)$$

where

$$|\sigma^0\rangle_{XX'AA_1B_2E_1E_2} \equiv \sum_x \sqrt{p_X(x)}|x\rangle_X|x\rangle_{X'} \otimes U^M_{A_2 \rightarrow B_2 E_2}|\phi^x\rangle_{AA_1A_2}|e\rangle_{E_1},$$

$$(25.184)$$

$$|\sigma^1\rangle_{XX'AB_1B_2A_1E_2} \equiv \sum_x \sqrt{p_X(x)}|x\rangle_X|x\rangle_{X'} \otimes U^M_{A_2 \rightarrow B_2 E_2}|\phi^x\rangle_{AA_1A_2}|e\rangle_{B_1}.$$

$$(25.185)$$

Then

$$I(A\rangle B_1 Y B_2 X)_\sigma = I(A\rangle B_1 B_2 | XY)_\sigma$$
$$= H(B_1 B_2 | YX)_\sigma - H(E_1 E_2 | YX)_\sigma \qquad (25.186)$$
$$= [(1-\varepsilon) H(A_1 B_2 | X)_{\sigma^0} + \varepsilon H(B_2 | X)_{\sigma^1}]$$
$$\quad - [(1-\varepsilon) H(E_2 | X)_{\sigma^0} + \varepsilon H(A_1 E_2 | X)_{\sigma^1}] \qquad (25.187)$$
$$= [(1-\varepsilon) (H(B_2 | X)_{\sigma^0} + H(A_1 | B_2 X)_{\sigma^0}) + \varepsilon H(B_2 | X)_{\sigma^1}]$$
$$\quad - [(1-\varepsilon) H(E_2 | X)_{\sigma^0} + \varepsilon (H(E_2 | X)_{\sigma^1} + H(A_1 | E_2 X)_{\sigma^1})] \qquad (25.188)$$
$$= [(1-\varepsilon) (H(B_2 | X)_\sigma + H(A_1 | B_2 X)_{\sigma^0}) + \varepsilon H(B_2 | X)_\sigma]$$
$$\quad - [(1-\varepsilon) H(E_2 | X)_\sigma + \varepsilon (H(E_2 | X)_\sigma + H(A_1 | E_2 X)_{\sigma^1})] \qquad (25.189)$$
$$= H(B_2 | X)_\sigma - H(E_2 | X)_\sigma + (1-\varepsilon) H(A_1 | B_2 X)_{\sigma^0} - \varepsilon H(A_1 | E_2 X)_{\sigma^1} \quad (25.190)$$
$$= H(B_2 | X)_\sigma - H(E_2 | X)_\sigma + (1-\varepsilon) H(A_1 | B_2 X)_{\sigma^0} - \varepsilon H(A_1 | E_2 X)_{\sigma^0}.$$
$$(25.191)$$

Applying the assumption that the channel M is degradable (so that
$H(A_1 | B_2 X)_{\sigma^0} \leq H(A_1 | E_2 X)_{\sigma^0}$), we find the upper bound

$$\leq H(B_2 | X)_\sigma - H(E_2 | X)_\sigma + (1-\varepsilon) H(A_1 | E_2 X)_{\sigma^0} - \varepsilon H(A_1 | E_2 X)_{\sigma^0} \quad (25.192)$$
$$= H(B_2 | X)_\sigma - H(E_2 | X)_\sigma + (1-2\varepsilon) H(A_1 | E_2 X)_{\sigma^0}. \qquad (25.193)$$

It also follows from (25.182) and (25.191) that

$$I(X; B_1 Y B_2)_\sigma + I(A\rangle B_1 Y B_2 X)_\sigma$$
$$= (1-\varepsilon) I(X; A_1 | B_2)_{\sigma^0} + I(X; B_2)_\sigma + H(B_2 | X)_\sigma - H(E_2 | X)_\sigma$$
$$\quad + (1-\varepsilon) H(A_1 | B_2 X)_{\sigma^0} - \varepsilon H(A_1 | E_2 X)_{\sigma^0} \qquad (25.194)$$
$$= I(X; B_2)_\sigma + H(B_2 | X)_\sigma - H(E_2 | X)_\sigma$$
$$\quad + (1-\varepsilon) H(A_1 | B_2)_{\sigma^0} - (1-\varepsilon) H(A_1 | B_2 X)_{\sigma^0}$$

$$+ (1 - \varepsilon) H(A_1|B_2X)_{\sigma^0} - \varepsilon H(A_1|E_2X)_{\sigma^0} \tag{25.195}$$

$$= I(X; B_2)_\sigma + H(B_2|X)_\sigma - H(E_2|X)_\sigma + (1 - \varepsilon) H(A_1|B_2)_{\sigma^0}$$
$$- \varepsilon H(A_1|E_2X)_{\sigma^0} \tag{25.196}$$

$$\leq I(X; B_2)_\sigma + H(B_2|X)_\sigma - H(E_2|X)_\sigma + (1 - \varepsilon) \log d$$
$$- \varepsilon H(A_1|E_2X)_{\sigma^0}. \tag{25.197}$$

Now putting together (25.177), (25.193), and (25.197), we find the following upper bound on the quantum dynamic capacity formula in (25.164):

$$\lambda_1 I(AX; B_1YB_2)_\sigma + \lambda_2 I(A\rangle B_1YB_2X)_\sigma$$
$$+ \lambda_3 [I(X; B_1YB_2)_\sigma + I(A\rangle B_1YB_2X)_\sigma] \tag{25.198}$$

$$\leq \lambda_1 (1 - \varepsilon) [\log d + H(A_1|E_2X)_{\sigma^0}] + \lambda_2 (1 - 2\varepsilon) H(A_1|E_2X)_{\sigma^0}$$
$$+ \lambda_3 [(1 - \varepsilon) \log d - \varepsilon H(A_1|E_2X)_{\sigma^0}]$$
$$+ \lambda_1 I(AX; B_2)_\sigma + \lambda_2 [H(B_2|X)_\sigma - H(E_2|X)_\sigma]$$
$$+ \lambda_3 [I(X; B_2)_\sigma + H(B_2|X)_\sigma - H(E_2|X)_\sigma] \tag{25.199}$$

$$= (\lambda_1 + \lambda_3) (1 - \varepsilon) \log d + [\lambda_1 (1 - \varepsilon) + \lambda_2 (1 - 2\varepsilon) - \lambda_3\varepsilon] H(A_1|E_2X)_{\sigma^0}$$
$$+ \lambda_1 I(AX; B_2)_\sigma + \lambda_2 [H(B_2|X)_\sigma - H(E_2|X)_\sigma]$$
$$+ \lambda_3 [I(X; B_2)_\sigma + H(B_2|X)_\sigma - H(E_2|X)_\sigma]. \tag{25.200}$$

In the case that $\lambda_1 (1 - \varepsilon) + \lambda_2 (1 - 2\varepsilon) - \lambda_3\varepsilon \geq 0$, we can apply data processing $(H(A_1|E_2X)_{\sigma^0} \leq H(A_1|X)_{\sigma^0})$ to find that the last line is never larger than

$$(\lambda_1 + \lambda_3) (1 - \varepsilon) \log d + [\lambda_1 (1 - \varepsilon) + \lambda_2 (1 - 2\varepsilon) - \lambda_3\varepsilon] H(A_1|X)_{\sigma^0}$$
$$+ \lambda_1 I(AX; B_2)_\sigma + \lambda_2 [H(B_2|X)_\sigma - H(E_2|X)_\sigma]$$
$$+ \lambda_3 [I(X; B_2)_\sigma + H(B_2|X)_\sigma - H(E_2|X)_\sigma]. \tag{25.201}$$

If we now take $\mathcal{M}_{A_2 \to B_2} = (\mathcal{N}^\varepsilon)^{\otimes n-1}$ and iterate this development $n - 1$ more times, we find that

$$\frac{1}{n} D_{\vec{\lambda}}((\mathcal{N}^\varepsilon)^{\otimes n}) \leq (\lambda_1 + \lambda_3) (1 - \varepsilon) \log d$$

$$+ [\lambda_1 (1 - \varepsilon) + \lambda_2 (1 - 2\varepsilon) - \lambda_3\varepsilon] \left[\frac{1}{n} \sum_{i=1}^n H(A_i|X) \right] \tag{25.202}$$

$$\leq (\lambda_1 + \lambda_3) (1 - \varepsilon) \log d$$

$$+ [\lambda_1 (1 - \varepsilon) + \lambda_2 (1 - 2\varepsilon) - \lambda_3\varepsilon] \max_{i,x} H(A_i)_{\phi^x}. \tag{25.203}$$

This establishes the optimality of the region whenever $\lambda_1 (1 - \varepsilon) + \lambda_2 (1 - 2\varepsilon) - \lambda_3\varepsilon \geq 0$. For the case when $\lambda_1 (1 - \varepsilon) + \lambda_2 (1 - 2\varepsilon) - \lambda_3\varepsilon < 0$, we start from (25.200) and use data processing for the channel $\text{Tr}_{B_2}\{\mathcal{U}_{A_2 \to B_2E_2}^{\mathcal{M}}(\cdot)\}$, giving

$$H(A_1|E_2X)_{\sigma^0} \geq H(A_1|A_2X)_{\sigma^0}, \tag{25.204}$$

to find that

$$(\lambda_1 + \lambda_3)(1 - \varepsilon)\log d + [\lambda_1(1 - \varepsilon) + \lambda_2(1 - 2\varepsilon) - \lambda_3\varepsilon]H(A_1|E_2X)_{\sigma^0}$$
$$+ \lambda_1 I(AX; B_2)_\sigma + \lambda_2[H(B_2|X)_\sigma - H(E_2|X)_\sigma]$$
$$+ \lambda_3[I(X; B_2)_\sigma + H(B_2|X)_\sigma - H(E_2|X)_\sigma]$$
$$\leq (\lambda_1 + \lambda_3)(1 - \varepsilon)\log d + [\lambda_1(1 - \varepsilon) + \lambda_2(1 - 2\varepsilon) - \lambda_3\varepsilon]H(A_1|A_2X)_{\sigma^0}$$
$$+ \lambda_1 I(AX; B_2)_\sigma + \lambda_2[H(B_2|X)_\sigma - H(E_2|X)_\sigma]$$
$$+ \lambda_3[I(X; B_2)_\sigma + H(B_2|X)_\sigma - H(E_2|X)_\sigma]. \quad (25.205)$$

If we now take $\mathcal{M}_{A_2 \to B_2} = (\mathcal{N}^\varepsilon)^{\otimes n-1}$ and iterate this development $n - 1$ more times, we find that

$$\frac{1}{n}D_{\vec{\lambda}}((\mathcal{N}^\varepsilon)^{\otimes n}) \leq (\lambda_1 + \lambda_3)(1 - \varepsilon)\log d$$

$$+ [\lambda_1(1 - \varepsilon) + \lambda_2(1 - 2\varepsilon) - \lambda_3\varepsilon]\left[\frac{1}{n}\sum_{i=1}^n H(A_i|A^{i-1}X)\right] \quad (25.206)$$

$$= (\lambda_1 + \lambda_3)(1 - \varepsilon)\log d$$

$$+ [\lambda_1(1 - \varepsilon) + \lambda_2(1 - 2\varepsilon) - \lambda_3\varepsilon]\left[\frac{1}{n}H(A^n|X)\right] \quad (25.207)$$

$$\leq (\lambda_1 + \lambda_3)(1 - \varepsilon)\log d. \quad (25.208)$$

The last line follows because entropy is non-negative. This inequality shows that the inequality $\lambda_1(1 - \varepsilon) + \lambda_2(1 - 2\varepsilon) - \lambda_3\varepsilon < 0$ holding implies that it is optimal to pick $\lambda = 0$ in the statement of the theorem (which just corresponds to the case in which we are maximizing the unassisted classical capacity). This completes the proof. $\qquad\qquad\square$

25.5.4 The Pure-Loss Bosonic Channel

One of the most important practical channels in quantum communication is known as the pure-loss bosonic channel. This channel can model the communication of photons through free space or over a fiber optic cable because the main source of noise in these settings is just the loss of photons. The pure-loss bosonic channel has one parameter $\eta \in [0, 1]$ that characterizes the fraction of photons that make it through the channel to the receiver on average. The environment Eve is able to collect all of the photons that do not make it to the receiver—this fraction is $1 - \eta$. Usually, we also restrict the mean number of photons that the sender is allowed to send through the channel (if we do not do so, then there could be an infinite amount of energy available, which is unphysical from a practical perspective, and furthermore, some of the capacities become infinite, which is less interesting from an information-theoretical perspective). So, we let $N_S \in [0, \infty)$ be the mean number of photons available at the transmitter. Capacities of this channel are then a function of these two parameters η and N_S.

EXERCISE 25.5.2 Prove that the quantum capacity of a pure-loss bosonic channel vanishes when $\eta = 1/2$.

In this section, we show how trade-off coding for this channel can give a remarkable gain over time sharing. Trade-off coding for this channel amounts to a power-sharing strategy, in which the sender dedicates a fraction $\lambda \in [0, 1]$ of the available photons to the quantum part of the code and the other fraction $1 - \lambda$ to the classical part of the code. This power-sharing strategy is provably optimal (up to a long-standing conjecture) and can beat time sharing by significant margins (much more so than the dephasing channel does, for example). Specifically, recall that a trade-off coding strategy has the sender and receiver generate random codes from an ensemble of the following form:

$$\{p_X(x), |\phi_x\rangle_{AA'}\}, \tag{25.209}$$

where $p_X(x)$ is some distribution and the states $|\phi_x\rangle_{AA'}$ are correlated with this distribution, with Alice feeding system A' into the channel. For the pure-loss bosonic channel, it turns out that the best ensemble to choose is of the following form:

$$\{p_{(1-\lambda)N_S}(\alpha), D_{A'}(\alpha)|\psi_{\mathrm{TMS}}(\lambda)\rangle_{AA'}\}, \tag{25.210}$$

where α is a complex variable. The distribution $p_{(1-\lambda)N_S}(\alpha)$ is an isotropic Gaussian distribution with variance $(1 - \lambda) N_S$:

$$p_{(1-\lambda)N_S}(\alpha) \equiv \frac{1}{\pi (1 - \lambda) N_S} \exp\left\{-|\alpha|^2 / [(1 - \lambda) N_S]\right\}, \tag{25.211}$$

where $\lambda \in [0, 1]$ is the power-sharing or photon-number-sharing parameter, indicating how many photons to dedicate to the quantum part of the code, while $1 - \lambda$ indicates how many photons to dedicate to the classical part. In (25.210), $D_{A'}(\alpha)$ is a "displacement" unitary operator acting on system A' (more on this below), and $|\psi_{\mathrm{TMS}}(\lambda)\rangle_{AA'}$ is a "two-mode squeezed" (TMS) state of the following form:

$$|\psi_{\mathrm{TMS}}(\lambda)\rangle_{AA'} \equiv \sum_{n=0}^{\infty} \sqrt{\frac{[\lambda N_S]^n}{[\lambda N_S + 1]^{n+1}}} |n\rangle_A |n\rangle_{A'}, \tag{25.212}$$

where $|n\rangle$ is a state of definite photon number n. Let $\theta(\lambda)$ denote the state resulting from tracing over the mode A:

$$\theta(\lambda) \equiv \mathrm{Tr}_A\{|\psi_{\mathrm{TMS}}(\lambda)\rangle\langle\psi_{\mathrm{TMS}}(\lambda)|_{AA'}\} \tag{25.213}$$

$$= \sum_{n=0}^{\infty} \frac{[\lambda N_S]^n}{[\lambda N_S + 1]^{n+1}} |n\rangle\langle n|_{A'}. \tag{25.214}$$

The reduced state $\theta(\lambda)$ is known as a thermal state with mean photon number λN_S. We can readily check that its mean photon number is λN_S simply by computing the expectation of the photon number n with respect to the geometric distribution $[\lambda N_S]^n / [\lambda N_S + 1]^{n+1}$:

$$\sum_{n=0}^{\infty} n \frac{[\lambda N_S]^n}{[\lambda N_S + 1]^{n+1}} = \lambda N_S. \tag{25.215}$$

The most important property of the displacement operators $D_{A'}(\alpha)$ for our purposes is that averaging over a random choice of them according to the Gaussian distribution $p_{(1-\lambda)N_S}(\alpha)$, where each operator acts on the state θ, gives a thermal state with mean photon number N_S:

$$\bar{\theta} \equiv \int d\alpha \, p_{(1-\lambda)N_S}(\alpha) \, D(\alpha)\theta(\lambda)D^\dagger(\alpha) \qquad (25.216)$$

$$= \sum_{n=0}^{\infty} \frac{[N_S]^n}{[N_S+1]^{n+1}} |n\rangle\langle n|_{A'}. \qquad (25.217)$$

Thus, the choice of ensemble in (25.210) meets the constraint that the average number of photons input to the channel be equal to N_S.

In order to calculate the quantum dynamic capacity region for this pure-loss bosonic channel, it is helpful to observe that the entropy of a thermal state with mean number of photons N_S is equal to

$$g(N_S) \equiv (N_S+1)\log(N_S+1) - N_S\log(N_S), \qquad (25.218)$$

because we will evaluate all of the relevant entropies on thermal states. From Exercise 25.2.1, we know that we should evaluate just the following four entropies:

$$H(A|X)_\sigma = \int d\alpha \, p_{(1-\lambda)N_S}(\alpha) \, H(D(\alpha)\theta(\lambda)D^\dagger(\alpha)), \qquad (25.219)$$

$$H(B)_\sigma = H(\mathcal{N}(\bar{\theta})), \qquad (25.220)$$

$$H(B|X)_\sigma = \int d\alpha \, p_{(1-\lambda)N_S}(\alpha) \, H(\mathcal{N}(D(\alpha)\theta(\lambda)D^\dagger(\alpha))), \qquad (25.221)$$

$$H(E|X)_\sigma = \int d\alpha \, p_{(1-\lambda)N_S}(\alpha) \, H(\mathcal{N}^c(D(\alpha)\theta(\lambda)D^\dagger(\alpha))), \qquad (25.222)$$

where $\mathcal{N}$ is the pure-loss bosonic channel that transmits η of the input photons to the receiver and $\mathcal{N}^c$ is the complementary channel that transmits $1 - \eta$ of the input photons to the environment Eve. We proceed with calculating the above four entropies:

$$\int d\alpha \, p_{(1-\lambda)N_S}(\alpha) \, H(D(\alpha)\theta(\lambda)D^\dagger(\alpha)) = \int d\alpha \, p_{(1-\lambda)N_S}(\alpha) \, H(\theta(\lambda)) \quad (25.223)$$

$$= H(\theta(\lambda)) = g(\lambda N_S). \qquad (25.224)$$

The first equality follows because $D(\alpha)$ is a unitary operator, and the third equality follows because θ is a thermal state with mean photon number N_S. Continuing, we have

$$H(\mathcal{N}(\bar{\theta})) = g(\eta N_S), \qquad (25.225)$$

because $\bar{\theta}$ is a thermal state with mean photon number N_S, but the channel only lets a fraction η of the input photons through on average. The third entropy in (25.221) equals

$$\int d\alpha \, p_{(1-\lambda)N_S}(\alpha) \, H(\mathcal{N}(D(\alpha)\theta(\lambda)D^\dagger(\alpha)))$$

$$= \int d\alpha \, p_{(1-\lambda)N_S}(\alpha) \, H(D(\sqrt{\eta}\alpha)\mathcal{N}(\theta(\lambda))D^\dagger(\sqrt{\eta}\alpha)) \tag{25.226}$$

$$= \int d\alpha \, p_{(1-\lambda)N_S}(\alpha) \, H(\mathcal{N}(\theta(\lambda))) \tag{25.227}$$

$$= H(\mathcal{N}(\theta(\lambda))) = g(\lambda\eta N_S). \tag{25.228}$$

The first equality follows because a displacement operator is covariant with respect to the pure-loss channel (we do not justify this rigorously here). The second equality follows because $D(\alpha)$ is a unitary operator. The final equality follows because $\theta(\lambda)$ is a thermal state with mean photon number λN_S, but the channel only lets a fraction η of the input photons through on average. By the same line of reasoning (except that the complementary channel lets through only a fraction $1 - \eta$ of the input photons), the fourth entropy in (25.222) is equal to

$$\int d\alpha \, p_{(1-\lambda)N_S}(\alpha) \, H(\mathcal{N}^c(D(\alpha)\theta(\lambda)D^\dagger(\alpha)))$$

$$= \int d\alpha \, p_{(1-\lambda)N_S}(\alpha) \, H(D(\sqrt{1-\eta}\alpha)\mathcal{N}^c(\theta(\lambda))D^\dagger(\sqrt{1-\eta}\alpha)) \tag{25.229}$$

$$= \int d\alpha \, p_{(1-\lambda)N_S}(\alpha) \, H(\mathcal{N}^c(\theta(\lambda))) \tag{25.230}$$

$$= H(\mathcal{N}^c(\theta(\lambda))) = g(\lambda(1-\eta)N_S). \tag{25.231}$$

Then, by the result of Exercise 25.2.1 and a matching converse that holds whenever $\eta \geq 1/2$,[2] we have the following characterization of the quantum dynamic capacity region of the pure-loss bosonic channel.

THEOREM 25.5.4 Provided that Strong Conjecture 2 of (Guha 2008) is true, the quantum dynamic capacity region for a pure-loss bosonic channel with transmissivity $\eta \geq 1/2$ is the union of regions of the form:

$$C + 2Q \leq g(\lambda N_S) + g(\eta N_S) - g((1 - \eta)\lambda N_S), \tag{25.232}$$

$$Q + E \leq g(\eta\lambda N_S) - g((1 - \eta)\lambda N_S), \tag{25.233}$$

$$C + Q + E \leq g(\eta N_S) - g((1 - \eta)\lambda N_S), \tag{25.234}$$

where $\lambda \in [0, 1]$ is a photon-number-sharing parameter and $g(N)$ is the entropy defined in (25.218). The region is achievable for all $\eta \in [0, 1]$.

---

[2] We should clarify that the converse holds only if a long-standing minimum-output entropy conjecture is true (researchers have collected much evidence that it should be true).

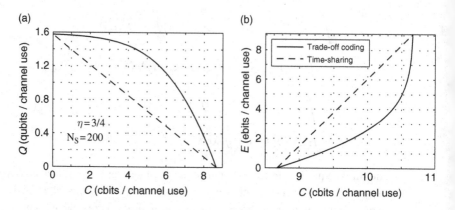

Figure 25.6 (a) Suppose a channel transmits on average 3/4 of the photons to the receiver, while losing the other 1/4 en route. Such a channel can reliably transmit a maximum of $\log(3/4) - \log(1/4) \approx 1.58$ qubits per channel use, and a mean photon budget of about 200 photons per channel use at the transmitter is sufficient to nearly achieve this quantum capacity. A trade-off coding strategy which lowers the quantum data rate to about 1.4 qubits per channel use while retaining the same mean photon budget allows for a sender to reliably transmit an additional 4.5 classical bits per channel use, while time-sharing would only allow for an additional 1 classical bit per channel use with this photon budget. The 6.5 dB increase in the classical data rate that trade-off coding gives over time-sharing for this example is strong enough to demand that quantum communication engineers employ trade-off coding strategies in order to take advantage of such theoretical performance gains. (b) The sender and the receiver share entanglement, and the sender would like to transmit classical information while minimizing the consumption of entanglement. With a mean photon budget of 200 photons per channel use over a channel that propagates only 3/4 of the photons input to it, the sender can reliably transmit a maximum of about 10.7 classical bits per channel use while consuming entanglement at a rate of about 9.1 entangled bits per channel use. With trade-off coding, the sender can significantly reduce the entanglement consumption rate to about 5 entangled bits per channel use while still transmitting about 10.5 classical bits per channel use, only a 0.08 dB decrease in the rate of classical communication for a 2.6 dB decrease in the entanglement consumption rate. The savings in entanglement consumption could be useful for them if they would like to have the extra entanglement for future rounds of assisted communication.

Figure 25.6 depicts two important special cases of the region in the above theorem: (a) the trade-off between classical and quantum communication without entanglement assistance and (b) the trade-off between entanglement-assisted and unassisted classical communication. The figure indicates the remarkable improvement over time sharing that trade-off coding gives.

Other special cases of the above capacity region are the unassisted classical capacity $g(\eta N_S)$ when $\lambda_1, \lambda_2, Q, E = 0$ and $\lambda_3 = 1$, the quantum capacity $g(\eta N_S) - g((1-\eta)N_S)$ when $\lambda_2 = 1$, $\lambda_1, \lambda_3, C, E = 0$, and the entanglement-assisted classical capacity $g(N_S) + g(\eta N_S) - g((1-\eta)N_S)$ when $\lambda_1 = 1$, $\lambda_2, \lambda_3, Q = 0$, and $E = -\infty$.

5.6   History and Further Reading

Shor (2004b) considered the classical capacity of a channel assisted by rate-limited entanglement. He calculated a trade-off curve that determines how a sender can optimally trade the consumption of noiseless entanglement with the generation of noiseless classical communication. This trade-off curve also bounds a rate region consisting of rates of entanglement consumption and generated classical communication. Shor's result then inspired Devetak & Shor (2005) to consider a scenario in which a sender exploits a quantum channel to simultaneously transmit both noiseless classical and quantum information, a scenario later dubbed "classically enhanced quantum coding" in Hsieh & Wilde (2010a), Hsieh & Wilde (2010b) after schemes formulated in the theory of quantum error correction (Kremsky et al., 2008; Wilde & Brun, 2008). Devetak & Shor (2005) provided a multi-letter characterization of the classically enhanced quantum capacity region for general channels, but they were able to show that both generalized dephasing channels and erasure channels admit single-letter capacity regions.

The above scenarios are a part of the dynamic, double-resource quantum Shannon theory, in which a sender can exploit a quantum channel to generate two noiseless resources, or a sender can exploit a quantum channel in addition to a noiseless resource to generate another noiseless resource. This theory culminated with the work of Devetak et al. (2004) and Devetak et al. (2008), that provided a multi-letter characterization for virtually every combination of two resources and a quantum channel which one can consider. Other researchers concurrently considered how noiseless resources might trade off against each other in tasks outside of the dynamic, double-resource quantum Shannon theory, such as quantum compression (Koashi & Imoto, 2001; Barnum, Hayden, Jozsa & Winter, 2001; Hayden et al., 2002), remote state preparation (Abeyesinghe & Hayden, 2003; Bennett et al., 2005), and hybrid quantum memories (Kuperberg, 2003).

Hsieh & Wilde (2010a), Hsieh & Wilde (2010b), and Wilde & Hsieh (2012b) considered the dynamic, triple-resource quantum Shannon theory by providing a multi-letter characterization of an entanglement-assisted quantum channel's ability to transmit both classical and quantum information. Hsieh & Wilde (2010a) also constructed a new protocol, dubbed the "classically enhanced father protocol," that outperforms a time-sharing strategy for transmitting both classical and quantum information over an entanglement-assisted quantum channel. Brádler et al. (2010) showed that the quantum Hadamard channels have a single-letter capacity region. Later studies continued these efforts of exploring information trade-offs (Jochym-O'Connor et al., 2011; Wilde & Hsieh, 2012a).

Wilde, Hayden & Guha (2012a) and Wilde, Hayden & Guha (2012b) found the quantum dynamic capacity region of the pure-loss bosonic channel (up to a long-standing minimum-output entropy conjecture). The results there build on a tremendous body of literature for bosonic channels. Giovannetti, Guha, Lloyd, Maccone, Shapiro & Yuen (2004) found the classical capacity of the pure-loss bosonic channel. Others found the entanglement-assisted classical and quantum capacities of the pure-loss bosonic channel (Bennett et al., 2002; Holevo & Werner, 2001; Giovannetti et al., 2003b; Giovannetti et al., 2003a) and its quantum capacity (Wolf et al., 2007; Guha et al., 2008). The long-standing minimum-output entropy conjecture (different from the one proved by Giovannetti et al., 2015) is detailed in the papers of Giovannetti, Guha, Lloyd, Maccone & Shapiro (2004), Guha et al. (2008), and Giovannetti et al. (2010).

Summary and Outlook

This brief final chapter serves as a compact summary of many results presented in this book, it highlights information-processing tasks that we did not cover, and it discusses new directions. We exploit the resource inequality formalism in our summary.

A resource inequality is a statement of achievability:

$$\sum_k \alpha_k \geq \sum_j \beta_j, \tag{26.1}$$

meaning that the resources $\{\alpha_k\}$ on the left-hand side can simulate the resources $\{\beta_j\}$ on the right-hand side. The simulation can be exact and finite or asymptotically perfect. We can classify resources as follows:

1. Unit, noiseless, or noisy.
2. Dynamic or static. Moreover, dynamic resources can be *relative* (see below).
3. Classical, quantum, or hybrid.

The unit resources are as follows: $[c \rightarrow c]$ represents one noiseless classical bit channel, $[q \rightarrow q]$ represents one noiseless qubit channel, $[qq]$ represents one noiseless ebit, and $[q \rightarrow qq]$ represents one noiseless coherent bit channel. We also have $[c \rightarrow c]_{\text{priv}}$ representing a noiseless private classical bit channel and $[cc]_{\text{priv}}$ representing a noiseless bit of secret key. An example of a noiseless resource is a pure bipartite state $|\phi\rangle_{AB}$ shared between Alice and Bob or an identity channel $\text{id}_{A \rightarrow B}$ from Alice to Bob. An example of a noisy resource could be a mixed bipartite state ρ_{AB} or a noisy channel $\mathcal{N}_{A' \rightarrow B}$. Unit resources are a special case of noiseless resources, which are in turn a special case of noisy resources.

A shared state ρ_{AB} is an example of a noisy static resource, and a channel $\mathcal{N}$ is an example of a noisy dynamic resource. We indicate these by $\langle \rho \rangle$ or $\langle \mathcal{N} \rangle$ in a resource inequality. We can be more precise if necessary and write $\langle \mathcal{N} \rangle$ as a dynamic, relative resource $\langle \mathcal{N}_{A' \rightarrow B} : \sigma_{A'} \rangle$, meaning that the protocol only works as it should if the state input to the channel is $\sigma_{A'}$.

It is obvious when a resource is classical or when it is quantum, and an example of a hybrid resource is a classical–quantum state

$$\rho_{XA} = \sum_x p_X(x) |x\rangle\langle x|_X \otimes \rho_A^x. \tag{26.2}$$

26.1   Unit Protocols

Chapter 6 discussed entanglement distribution

$$[q \to q] \geq [qq], \tag{26.3}$$

teleportation

$$2[c \to c] + [qq] \geq [q \to q], \tag{26.4}$$

and super-dense coding

$$[q \to q] + [qq] \geq 2[c \to c]. \tag{26.5}$$

Chapter 7 introduced coherent dense coding

$$[q \to q] + [qq] \geq 2[q \to qq], \tag{26.6}$$

and coherent teleportation

$$2[q \to qq] \geq [q \to q] + [qq]. \tag{26.7}$$

The fact that these two resource inequalities are dual under resource reversal implies the coherent communication identity:

$$2[q \to qq] = [q \to q] + [qq]. \tag{26.8}$$

We also have the following resource inequalities:

$$[q \to q] \geq [q \to qq] \geq [qq]. \tag{26.9}$$

Other unit protocols not covered in this book are the one-time pad

$$[c \to c]_{\text{pub}} + [cc]_{\text{priv}} \geq [c \to c]_{\text{priv}}, \tag{26.10}$$

secret key distribution

$$[c \to c]_{\text{priv}} \geq [cc]_{\text{priv}}, \tag{26.11}$$

and private-to-public transmission

$$[c \to c]_{\text{priv}} \geq [c \to c]_{\text{pub}}. \tag{26.12}$$

The last protocol assumes a model where the receiver can locally copy information and place it in a register to which Eve has access.

26.2   Noiseless Quantum Shannon Theory

Noiseless quantum Shannon theory consists of resource inequalities involving unit resources and one non-unit, noiseless resource, such as an identity channel or a pure bipartite state.

Schumacher compression from Chapter 18 gives a way to simulate an identity channel $\text{id}_{A \to B}$ acting on a mixed state ρ_A by exploiting noiseless qubit channels at a rate equal to the entropy $H(A)_\rho$:

$$H(A)_\rho [q \to q] \geq \langle \text{id}_{A \to B} : \rho_A \rangle. \tag{26.13}$$

We also know that if n uses of an identity channel are available, then achievability of the coherent information for quantum communication (Chapter 24) implies that we can send quantum data down this channel at a rate equal to $H(B) - H(E)$, where the entropies are with respect to some input density operator ρ_A. But $H(E) = 0$ because the channel is the identity channel (the environment gets no information) and $H(B) = H(A)_\rho$ because Alice's input goes directly to Bob. This gives us the following resource inequality:

$$\langle \text{id}_{A \to B} : \rho_A \rangle \geq H(A)_\rho [q \to q], \tag{26.14}$$

and combining (26.13) and (26.14) gives the following resource equality:

$$\langle \text{id}_{A \to B} : \rho_A \rangle = H(A)_\rho [q \to q]. \tag{26.15}$$

Entanglement concentration from Chapter 19 converts many copies of a pure, bipartite state $|\phi\rangle_{AB}$ into ebits at a rate equal to the entropy of entanglement:

$$\langle \phi_{AB} \rangle \geq H(A)_\phi [qq]. \tag{26.16}$$

Entanglement dilution exploits a sublinear amount of classical communication to dilute ebits into n copies of a pure, bipartite state $|\phi\rangle_{AB}$. Ignoring the sublinear rate of classical communication gives the following resource inequality:

$$H(A)_\phi [qq] \geq \langle \phi_{AB} \rangle. \tag{26.17}$$

Combining entanglement concentration and entanglement dilution gives the following resource equality:

$$\langle \phi_{AB} \rangle = H(A)_\phi [qq]. \tag{26.18}$$

The noiseless quantum Shannon theory is satisfactory in the sense that we can obtain resource *equalities*, illustrating the interconvertibility of noiseless qubit channels with a relative identity channel and pure, bipartite states with ebits.

26.3 Noisy Quantum Shannon Theory

Noisy quantum Shannon theory has resource inequalities with one noisy resource, such as a noisy channel or a noisy state, interacting with other unit resources. We can further classify a resource inequality as dynamic or static, depending on whether the noisy resource involved is dynamic or static.

We first review the dynamic resource inequalities presented in this book. These protocols involve a noisy channel interacting with the other unit resources. Many of the protocols in noisy quantum Shannon theory generate random codes from a state of the following form:

$$\rho_{XABE} \equiv \sum_x p_X(x)|x\rangle\langle x|_X \otimes U^{\mathcal{N}}_{A'\to BE}(\phi^x_{AA'}), \qquad (26.19)$$

where $\phi^x_{AA'}$ is a pure, bipartite state and $U^{\mathcal{N}}_{A'\to BE}$ is an isometric extension of a channel $\mathcal{N}_{A'\to B}$. Also important is a special case of the above form:

$$\sigma_{ABE} \equiv U^{\mathcal{N}}_{A'\to BE}(\phi_{AA'}), \qquad (26.20)$$

where $\phi_{AA'}$ is a pure, bipartite state. Holevo–Schumacher–Westmoreland coding for classical communication over a quantum channel (Chapter 20) is the following resource inequality:

$$\langle \mathcal{N} \rangle \geq I(X;B)_\rho\, [c \to c]. \qquad (26.21)$$

Devetak–Cai–Winter–Yeung coding for private classical communication over a quantum channel (Chapter 23) is as follows:

$$\langle \mathcal{N} \rangle \geq (I(X;B)_\rho - I(X;E)_\rho)\, [c \to c]_{\mathrm{priv}}. \qquad (26.22)$$

Upgrading the private classical code to one that operates coherently gives Devetak's method for coherent communication over a quantum channel (Chapter 24):

$$\langle \mathcal{N} \rangle \geq I(A\rangle B)_\sigma\, [q \to qq], \qquad (26.23)$$

which we showed can be converted asymptotically into a protocol for quantum communication:

$$\langle \mathcal{N} \rangle \geq I(A\rangle B)_\sigma\, [q \to q]. \qquad (26.24)$$

Bennett–Shor–Smolin–Thapliyal coding for entanglement-assisted classical communication over a quantum channel (Chapter 21) is the following resource inequality:

$$\langle \mathcal{N} \rangle + H(A)_\sigma\, [qq] \geq I(A;B)_\sigma\, [c \to c]. \qquad (26.25)$$

We showed how to upgrade this protocol to one for entanglement-assisted coherent communication (Chapter 22):

$$\langle \mathcal{N} \rangle + H(A)_\sigma\, [qq] \geq I(A;B)_\sigma\, [q \to qq], \qquad (26.26)$$

and combining with the coherent communication identity gives the following protocol for entanglement-assisted quantum communication:

$$\langle \mathcal{N} \rangle + \frac{1}{2}I(A;E)_\sigma\, [qq] \geq \frac{1}{2}I(A;B)_\sigma\, [q \to q]. \qquad (26.27)$$

Further combining with entanglement distribution gives the resource inequality in (26.24) for quantum communication. By combining the HSW and BSST protocols together (this needs to be done at the level of coding and not at the level of resource inequalities—see Chapter 22), we recover a protocol for entanglement-assisted communication of classical and quantum information:

$$\langle \mathcal{N} \rangle + \frac{1}{2}I(A; E|X)_\sigma \, [qq] \geq \frac{1}{2}I(A; B|X)_\sigma \, [q \to q] + I(X; B)_\sigma \, [c \to c] . \quad (26.28)$$

This protocol recovers any protocol in dynamic quantum Shannon theory that involves a noisy channel and the three unit resources after combining it with the three unit protocols in (26.3)–(26.5). Important special cases are entanglement-assisted classical communication with limited entanglement:

$$\langle \mathcal{N} \rangle + H(A|X)_\sigma \, [qq] \geq I(AX; B)_\sigma \, [c \to c] , \quad (26.29)$$

and simultaneous classical and quantum communication:

$$\langle \mathcal{N} \rangle \geq I(X; B)_\sigma \, [c \to c] + I(A \rangle BX)_\sigma \, [q \to q] . \quad (26.30)$$

Chapter 22 touched on some important protocols in static quantum Shannon theory. These protocols involve some noisy state ρ_{AB} interacting with the unit resources. The protocol for coherent-assisted state transfer is the static couterpart to the protocol in (26.26):

$$\langle W_{S \to AB} : \rho_S \rangle + H(A)_\rho \, [q \to q] \geq I(A; B)_\rho \, [q \to qq] + \langle \text{id}_{S \to \hat{B}B} : \rho_S \rangle, \quad (26.31)$$

where W is some isometry that distributes the state from a source S to two parties A and B and $\text{id}_{S \to \hat{B}B}$ is the identity. Ignoring the source and state transfer in the above protocol gives a protocol for quantum-assisted coherent communication:

$$\langle \rho \rangle + H(A)_\rho \, [q \to q] \geq I(A; B)_\rho \, [q \to qq] . \quad (26.32)$$

We can also combine (26.31) with the unit protocols to obtain quantum-assisted state transfer:

$$\langle W_{S \to AB} : \rho_S \rangle + \frac{1}{2}I(A; R)_\varphi \, [q \to q] \geq \frac{1}{2}I(A; B)_\varphi \, [qq] + \langle \text{id}_{S \to \hat{B}B} : \rho_S \rangle, \quad (26.33)$$

and classical-assisted state transfer:

$$\langle W_{S \to AB} : \rho_S \rangle + I(A; R)_\varphi \, [c \to c] \geq I(A \rangle B)_\varphi \, [qq] + \langle \text{id}_{S \to \hat{B}B} : \rho_S \rangle, \quad (26.34)$$

where $|\varphi\rangle_{ABR}$ is a purification of ρ_{AB}. We also have noisy super-dense coding

$$\langle \rho \rangle + H(A)_\rho \, [q \to q] \geq I(A; B)_\rho \, [c \to c] , \quad (26.35)$$

and noisy teleportation

$$\langle \rho \rangle + I(A; B)_\rho \, [c \to c] \geq I(A \rangle B)_\rho \, [q \to q] , \quad (26.36)$$

by combining (26.32) with the coherent communication identity and the unit protocols.

26.4   Protocols Not Covered In This Book

There are many important protocols that we have not covered in this boo[k]
because our focus here was mostly on communication over quantum chan[-]
nels. One such example is *quantum state redistribution*. Suppose that Alic[e]
and Bob share many copies of a tripartite state ρ_{ACB} where Alice has th[e]
shares AC and Bob has the share B. The goal of state redistribution is fo[r]
Alice to transfer the C part of the state to Bob using the minimal resource[s]
needed to do so. It is useful to identify a pure state φ_{RACB} as a purificatio[n]
of ρ_{ACB}, where R is the purifying system. Devetak & Yard (2008) and Yar[d]
& Devetak (2009) showed the existence of the following state redistributio[n]
protocol:

$$\langle W_{S \to AC|B} : \rho_S \rangle + \frac{1}{2}I(C;RB)_\varphi \, [q \to q] + \frac{1}{2}I(C;A)_\varphi \, [qq] \geq$$

$$\langle W_{S \to A|CB} : \rho_S \rangle + \frac{1}{2}I(C;B)_\varphi \, [q \to q] + \frac{1}{2}I(C;B)_\varphi \, [qq], \quad (26.37)$$

where $W_{S \to AC|B}$ is some isometry that distributes the system S as AC for
Alice and B for Bob and $W_{S \to A|CB}$ is defined similarly. They also demon-
strated that the above resource inequality gives an optimal cost pair for the
quantum communication rate Q and the entanglement consumption rate E,
with

$$Q = \frac{1}{2}I(C;R|B)_\varphi, \quad (26.38)$$

$$E = \frac{1}{2}\left[I(C;A)_\varphi - I(C;B)_\varphi\right]. \quad (26.39)$$

Thus, their protocol gives a direct operational interpretation to the condi-
tional quantum mutual information $\frac{1}{2}I(C;R|B)_\varphi$ as the net rate of quantum
communication required in quantum state redistribution.

A simple version of the quantum reverse Shannon theorem gives a way to
simulate the action of a channel $\mathcal{N}_{A' \to B}$ on some input state $\rho_{A'}$ by exploiting
classical communication and entanglement (Bennett et al., 2002; Bennett et al.,
2014; Berta et al., 2011):

$$H(B)_\sigma \, [qq] + I(R;B)_\sigma \, [c \to c] \geq \langle \mathcal{N}_{A' \to B} : \rho_{A'} \rangle, \quad (26.40)$$

where $\sigma_{RB} \equiv \mathcal{N}_{A' \to B}(\varphi_{RA'})$, with $\varphi_{RA'}$ a purification of $\rho_{A'}$. One utility of
the quantum reverse Shannon theorem is that it gives an indication of how one
channel might simulate another in the presence of shared entanglement. In the
simulation of the channel $\mathcal{N}_{A' \to B}$, the environment is also simulated and ends
up in Alice's possession. Thus, they end up simulating the quantum feedback
channel $\mathcal{U}_{A' \to AB}^{\mathcal{N}}$, and we can restate (26.40) as follows:

$$H(B)_\sigma \, [qq] + I(R;B)_\sigma \, [c \to c] \geq \langle \mathcal{U}_{A' \to AB}^{\mathcal{N}} : \rho_{A'} \rangle. \quad (26.41)$$

It is possible to upgrade the classical communication to coherent communication (Devetak, 2006), leading to the following coherent, fully-quantum version of the quantum reverse Shannon theorem (Abeyesinghe et al., 2009):

$$\frac{1}{2}I(A;B)_\sigma\,[qq] + \frac{1}{2}I(R;B)_\sigma\,[q \to q] \geq \langle \mathcal{U}_{A' \to AB}^{\mathcal{N}} : \rho_{A'} \rangle. \tag{26.42}$$

Combining this resource inequality with the following one from Exercise 22.1.1

$$\langle \mathcal{U}_{A' \to AB}^{\mathcal{N}} : \rho_{A'} \rangle \geq \frac{1}{2}I(A;B)_\sigma\,[qq] + \frac{1}{2}I(R;B)_\sigma\,[q \to q] \tag{26.43}$$

gives the following satisfying resource equality:

$$\langle \mathcal{U}_{A' \to AB}^{\mathcal{N}} : \rho_{A'} \rangle = \frac{1}{2}I(A;B)_\sigma\,[qq] + \frac{1}{2}I(R;B)_\sigma\,[q \to q]. \tag{26.44}$$

The above resource equality is a generalization of the coherent communication identity. A more general version of the quantum reverse Shannon theorem quantifies the resources needed to simulate many independent instances of a quantum channel on an arbitrary input state, and the proof in this case is more involved (Bennett et al., 2014; Berta et al., 2011).

Other protocols that we did not cover are remote state preparation (Bennett et al., 2001; Bennett et al., 2005; Abeyesinghe & Hayden, 2003), classical compression with quantum side information (Devetak & Winter, 2003), trade-offs between public and private resources and channels (Wilde & Hsieh, 2012a), trade-offs in compression (Hayden et al., 2002), a trade-off for a noisy state with the three unit resources (Hsieh & Wilde, 2010b), measurement compression (Winter, 2004), measurement compression with quantum side information (Wilde, Hayden, Buscemi & Hsieh, 2012), and measurement channel simulation (Berta et al., 2014). The resource inequality formalism is helpful for devising new protocols in quantum Shannon theory by imagining some resources to be unit and others to be noisy.

26.5 Network Quantum Shannon Theory

The field of network quantum Shannon theory has arisen in recent years, motivated by the idea that one day we will be dealing with a quantum Internet in which channels of increasing complexity can connect a number of senders to a number of receivers. A quantum multiple access channel has multiple senders and one receiver. Various authors have considered classical communication over a multiple access channel (Winter, 2001; Fawzi et al., 2012; Wilde & Savov, 2012; Wilde & Guha, 2012; Boche & Notzel, 2014), quantum communication over multiple access channels (Horodecki et al., 2005; Yard et al., 2008), entanglement-assisted protocols (Hsieh, Devetak & Winter, 2008), and nonadditivity effects (Czekaj & Horodecki, 2009; Grudka & Horodecki, 2010). A quantum broadcast channel has one sender and multiple receivers. Various authors have addressed similar scenarios in this setting (Yard et al., 2011; Dupuis et al., 2010; Guha & Shapiro,

2007; Savov & Wilde, 2015; Radhakrishnan et al., 2014; Hirche & Morgan, 201? Seshadreesan, Takeoka & Wilde, 2015). A quantum interference channel has mu? tiple senders and multiple receivers in which certain sender-receiver pairs ar interested in communicating. Recent progress in this direction is in Fawzi et al (2012), Sen (2011), Hirche et al. (2016). One could also consider distributed com pression tasks, and various authors have contributed to this direction (Ahn et al. 2006; Abeyesinghe et al., 2009; Savov, 2008). We could imagine a future text book containing several chapters that summarize all of the progress in networl quantum Shannon theory and the novel techniques needed to handle coding ove: such channels. Savov (2012) highlights much of this direction in his PhD thesi: (at least for classical communication).

26.6   Future Directions

Quantum Shannon theory has evolved from the first and simplest result regarding Schumacher compression to a whole host of protocols that indicate how much data we can transmit over noisy quantum channels or how much we can compress information of varying types—the central question in any task is, "How many unit resources can we extract from a given non-unit resource, perhaps with the help of other non-unit resources?" This book may give the impression that so much has been solved in the area of quantum Shannon theory that little remains for the future, but this is actually far from the truth! There remains much to do to improve our understanding, and this final section briefly outlines just a few of these important questions.

Find a better formula for the classical capacity other than the HSW formula. Our best characterization of the classical capacity is with a regularized version of the HSW formula, and this is unsatisfying in several ways that we have mentioned before. In a similar vein, find a better formula for the private classical capacity, the quantum capacity, and even for the trade-off capacities. All of these formulas are unsatisfying because their regularizations seem to be necessary in the general case. It could be the case that an entropic expression evaluated on some finite tensor power of the channels would be sufficient to characterize the capacity for different tasks, but this is a difficult question to answer. Interestingly, recent work suggests pursuing to find out whether this question is algorithmically undecidable (see Wolf et al., 2011). Effects such as superactivation of quantum capacity (see Section 24.8.2) and non-additivity of private capacity (see Section 23.5.2) have highlighted how little we actually know about the corresponding information-processing tasks in the general case. Also, it is important to understand these effects more fully and to see if there is any way of exploiting them in a practical communication scheme. Finally, a different direction is to expand the number of channels that have additive capacities. For example, finding the quantum capacity of a non-degradable quantum channel would be a great result. Many questions remain open regarding second-order characterizations, error exponents, and strong converses. Results in these directions give much finer characterizations of communication tasks. We have already highlighted progress in these directions at the end of relevant chapters.

Continue to explore network quantum Shannon theory. The single-sender, single-receiver channel setting is a useful model for study and applies to many practical scenarios, but eventually, we will be dealing with channels connecting many inputs to many outputs. Having such an understanding for information transmission in these scenarios could help guide the design of practical communication schemes and might even shed light on the open problems in the preceding paragraph.

Appendix A Supplementary Results

This section collects various useful definitions and lemmas that we use throughout the proofs of certain theorems in this book.

LEMMA A.0.1 Suppose that M and N are positive semi-definite operators. Then the operators $M + N$, MNM, and NMN are positive semi-definite.

LEMMA A.0.2 Suppose that the operators $\hat{\omega}$ and ω have trace less than or equal to one. Suppose $\hat{\omega}$ lies in the operator interval $[(1 - \varepsilon)\omega, (1 + \varepsilon)\omega]$. Then

$$\|\hat{\omega} - \omega\|_1 \leq \varepsilon. \tag{A.1}$$

Proof The statement "$\hat{\omega}$ lies in the operator interval $[(1 - \varepsilon)\omega, (1 + \varepsilon)\omega]$" is equivalent to the following two conditions:

$$(1 + \varepsilon)\omega - \hat{\omega} = \varepsilon\omega - (\hat{\omega} - \omega) \geq 0, \tag{A.2}$$

$$\hat{\omega} - (1 - \varepsilon)\omega = (\hat{\omega} - \omega) + \varepsilon\omega \geq 0. \tag{A.3}$$

Let $\alpha \equiv \hat{\omega} - \omega$. Let us rewrite α in terms of the positive semi-definite operators P and Q:

$$\alpha = P - Q, \tag{A.4}$$

as we did in the proof of Lemma 9.1.1. The above conditions become as follows:

$$\varepsilon\omega - \alpha \geq 0, \tag{A.5}$$

$$\alpha + \varepsilon\omega \geq 0. \tag{A.6}$$

Let the positive projectors Π_P and Π_Q project onto the respective supports of P and Q. We then apply the projector Π_P to the first condition:

$$\Pi_P (\varepsilon\omega - \alpha) \Pi_P \geq 0, \tag{A.7}$$

$$\Rightarrow \varepsilon\Pi_P\omega\Pi_P - \Pi_P\alpha\Pi_P \geq 0, \tag{A.8}$$

$$\Rightarrow \varepsilon\Pi_P\omega\Pi_P - P \geq 0, \tag{A.9}$$

where the first inequality follows from Lemma A.0.1. We apply the projector Π_Q to the second condition:

$$\Pi_Q (\alpha + \varepsilon\omega) \Pi_Q \geq 0, \tag{A.10}$$

$$\Rightarrow \Pi_Q\alpha\Pi_Q + \varepsilon\Pi_Q\omega\Pi_Q \geq 0, \tag{A.11}$$

$$\Rightarrow -Q + \varepsilon\Pi_Q\omega\Pi_Q \geq 0, \tag{A.12}$$

where the first inequality again follows from Lemma A.0.1. Adding the two positive semi-definite operators together gives another positive semi-definite operator by Lemma A.0.1:

$$\varepsilon \Pi_P \omega \Pi_P - P - Q + \varepsilon \Pi_Q \omega \Pi_Q \geq 0, \tag{A.13}$$

$$\Rightarrow \varepsilon \Pi_P \omega \Pi_P - |\hat{\omega} - \omega| + \varepsilon \Pi_Q \omega \Pi_Q \geq 0. \tag{A.14}$$

Apply the trace operation to get the following inequality:

$$\varepsilon \operatorname{Tr}\{\omega\} \geq \operatorname{Tr}\{|\hat{\omega} - \omega|\} = \|\hat{\omega} - \omega\|_1. \tag{A.15}$$

Using the hypothesis that $\operatorname{Tr}\{\omega\} \leq 1$ gives the desired result. □

THEOREM A.0.1 (Polar Decomposition) Any operator A admits a left polar decomposition $A = U\sqrt{A^\dagger A}$, and a right polar decomposition $A = \sqrt{AA^\dagger}V$.

Proof We give a simple proof for just the right polar decomposition by appealing to the singular value decomposition. Any operator A admits a singular value decomposition $A = U_1 \Sigma U_2$, where U_1 and U_2 are unitary operators and Σ is an operator with positive singular values. Then $AA^\dagger = U_1 \Sigma U_2 U_2^\dagger \Sigma U_1^\dagger = U_1 \Sigma^2 U_1^\dagger$, and thus $\sqrt{AA^\dagger} = U_1 \Sigma U_1^\dagger$. We can take $V = U_1 U_2$ and we obtain the right polar decomposition of A as $\sqrt{AA^\dagger}V = U_1 \Sigma U_1^\dagger U_1 U_2 = U_1 \Sigma U_2 = A$. □

LEMMA A.0.3 Consider two collections of orthonormal states $\{|\chi_j\rangle\}_{j\in[N]}$ and $\{|\zeta_j\rangle\}_{j\in[N]}$ such that $\langle\chi_j|\zeta_j\rangle \geq 1 - \varepsilon$ for all j. There exist phases γ_j and δ_j such that

$$\langle\hat{\chi}|\hat{\zeta}\rangle \geq 1 - \varepsilon, \tag{A.16}$$

where

$$|\hat{\chi}\rangle = \frac{1}{\sqrt{N}} \sum_{j=1}^N e^{i\gamma_j} |\chi_j\rangle, \qquad |\hat{\zeta}\rangle = \frac{1}{\sqrt{N}} \sum_{j=1}^N e^{i\delta_j} |\zeta_j\rangle. \tag{A.17}$$

Proof Define the Fourier transformed states

$$|\hat{\chi}_s\rangle \equiv \frac{1}{\sqrt{N}} \sum_{j=1}^N e^{2\pi ijs/N} |\chi_j\rangle, \tag{A.18}$$

and similarly define $|\hat{\zeta}_s\rangle$. By Parseval's relation, it follows that

$$\frac{1}{N} \sum_{s=1}^N \langle\hat{\chi}_s|\hat{\zeta}_s\rangle = \frac{1}{N} \sum_{j=1}^N \langle\chi_j|\zeta_j\rangle \geq 1 - \varepsilon. \tag{A.19}$$

Thus, at least one value of s obeys the following inequality: $e^{i\theta_s}\langle\hat{\chi}_s|\hat{\zeta}_s\rangle \geq 1 - \varepsilon$, for some phase θ_s. Setting $\gamma_j = 2\pi js/N$ and $\delta_j = \gamma_j + \theta_s$ satisfies the statement of the lemma. □

The following "support lemmas" are taken directly from Renner (2005, Appendix B).

LEMMA A.0.4 Let $X_{AB} \in \mathcal{L}(\mathcal{H}_A \otimes \mathcal{H}_B)$ be positive semi-definite, and let $X_A \equiv \mathrm{Tr}_B\{X_{AB}\}$ and $X_B \equiv \mathrm{Tr}_A\{X_{AB}\}$. Then $\mathrm{supp}(X_{AB}) \subseteq \mathrm{supp}(X_A) \otimes \mathrm{supp}(X_B)$.

Proof First suppose that X_{AB} is rank one, so that $X_{AB} = |\Psi\rangle\langle\Psi|_{AB}$ for some vector $|\Psi\rangle_{AB} \in \mathcal{H}_A \otimes \mathcal{H}_B$. Due to the Schmidt decomposition theorem (Theorem 3.8.1), we have that

$$|\Psi\rangle_{AB} = \sum_{z \in \mathcal{Z}} \gamma_z |\theta_z\rangle_A \otimes |\xi_z\rangle_B, \qquad (A.20)$$

where $|\mathcal{Z}| \leq \min\{\dim(\mathcal{H}_A), \dim(\mathcal{H}_B)\}$, $\{\gamma_z\}$ is a set of strictly positive numbers and $\{|\theta_z\rangle_A\}$ and $\{|\xi_z\rangle_B\}$ are orthonormal bases. Then

$$\mathrm{supp}(X_{AB}) = \mathrm{span}\{|\Psi\rangle_{AB}\} \qquad (A.21)$$
$$\subseteq \mathrm{span}\{|\theta_z\rangle_A : z \in \mathcal{Z}\} \otimes \mathrm{span}\{|\xi_z\rangle_B : z \in \mathcal{Z}\}. \qquad (A.22)$$

The statement then follows for this case because $\mathrm{supp}(X_A) = \mathrm{span}\{|\theta_z\rangle_A : z \in \mathcal{Z}\}$ and $\mathrm{supp}(X_B) = \mathrm{span}\{|\xi_z\rangle_B : z \in \mathcal{Z}\}$.

Now suppose that X_{AB} is not rank one. It admits a decomposition into rank-one vectors of the following form:

$$X_{AB} = \sum_{x \in \mathcal{X}} |\Psi^x\rangle\langle\Psi^x|_{AB}, \qquad (A.23)$$

where $|\Psi^x\rangle_{AB} \in \mathcal{H}_A \otimes \mathcal{H}_B$ for all $x \in \mathcal{X}$. Set $\Psi^x_{AB} = |\Psi^x\rangle\langle\Psi^x|_{AB}$, and let $\Psi^x_A \equiv \mathrm{Tr}_B\{\Psi^x_{AB}\}$ and $\Psi^x_B \equiv \mathrm{Tr}_A\{\Psi^x_{AB}\}$. Then

$$\mathrm{supp}(X_{AB}) = \mathrm{span}\{|\Psi^x\rangle_{AB} : x \in \mathcal{X}\} \qquad (A.24)$$

$$\subseteq \mathrm{span}\left[\bigcup_{x \in \mathcal{X}} [\mathrm{supp}(\Psi^x_A) \otimes \mathrm{supp}(\Psi^x_B)] \right] \qquad (A.25)$$

$$\subseteq \mathrm{span}\left[\bigcup_{x \in \mathcal{X}} \mathrm{supp}(\Psi^x_A) \right] \otimes \mathrm{span}\left[\bigcup_{x \in \mathcal{X}} \mathrm{supp}(\Psi^x_B) \right] \qquad (A.26)$$

$$= \mathrm{supp}(X_A) \otimes \mathrm{supp}(X_B), \qquad (A.27)$$

concluding the proof. $\square$

LEMMA A.0.5 Let $X_{AB}, Y_{AB} \in \mathcal{L}(\mathcal{H}_A \otimes \mathcal{H}_B)$ be positive semi-definite, and suppose that $\mathrm{supp}(X_{AB}) \subseteq \mathrm{supp}(Y_{AB})$. Then $\mathrm{supp}(X_A) \subseteq \mathrm{supp}(Y_A)$, where $X_A \equiv \mathrm{Tr}_B\{X_{AB}\}$ and $Y_A \equiv \mathrm{Tr}_B\{Y_{AB}\}$.

Proof First suppose that X_{AB} is rank one, as in the first part of the proof of the previous lemma, and let us use the same notation as given there. Applying the same lemma gives that

$$\mathrm{supp}(X_{AB}) \subseteq \mathrm{supp}(Y_{AB}) \subseteq \mathrm{supp}(Y_A) \otimes \mathrm{supp}(Y_B), \qquad (A.28)$$

which in turn implies that $\mathrm{supp}(X_{AB}) = \mathrm{span}\{|\Psi\rangle_{AB}\} \subseteq \mathrm{supp}(Y_A) \otimes \mathrm{supp}(Y_B)$. This implies that $|\theta_z\rangle_A \in \mathrm{supp}(Y_A)$ for all $z \in \mathcal{Z}$, and thus that

$\mathrm{span}\{|\theta_z\rangle_A\} \in \mathrm{supp}(Y_A)$. We can then conclude the statement in this case because $\mathrm{span}\{|\theta_z\rangle_A\} = \mathrm{supp}(X_A)$.

Now suppose that X_{AB} is not rank one. Then it admits a decomposition as given in the proof of the previous lemma. Using the same notation, we have that $\mathrm{supp}(\Psi^x_{AB}) \subseteq \mathrm{supp}(Y_{AB})$ holds for all $x \in \mathcal{X}$. Since we have proven the lemma for rank-one operators, we can conclude that $\mathrm{supp}(\Psi^x_A) \subseteq \mathrm{supp}(Y_A)$ holds for all $x \in \mathcal{X}$. As a consequence, we find that

$$\mathrm{supp}(X_A) = \mathrm{span}\left[\bigcup_{x \in \mathcal{X}} \mathrm{supp}(\Psi^x_A)\right] \subseteq \mathrm{supp}(Y_A), \qquad (A.29)$$

concluding the proof. $\qquad\qquad\square$

Appendix B Unique Linear Extension of a Quantum Physical Evolution

Recall in Section 4.4.1 that we argued on physical grounds how any quantum physical evolution $\mathcal{N}$ should be convex linear when acting on the space $\mathcal{D}(\mathcal{H}_A)$ of density operators:

$$\mathcal{N}(\lambda \rho_A + (1-\lambda)\sigma_A) = \lambda \mathcal{N}(\rho_A) + (1-\lambda)\mathcal{N}(\sigma_A), \tag{B.1}$$

where $\rho_A, \sigma_A \in \mathcal{D}(\mathcal{H}_A)$ and $\lambda \in [0,1]$. Here we show how to construct a unique linear extension $\widetilde{\mathcal{N}}$ of $\mathcal{N}$, whose action is well defined on the space of all operators $X_A \in \mathcal{L}(\mathcal{H}_A)$. The development follows the approach given in Proposition 2.30 of Heinosaari & Ziman (2012).

We first define $\widetilde{\mathcal{N}}(0) \equiv 0$, where the inputs and outputs are understood to be the zero operator. We next extend the action of $\mathcal{N}$ to all positive semi-definite operators $P_A \neq 0$ as follows:

$$\widetilde{\mathcal{N}}(P_A) \equiv \operatorname{Tr}\{P_A\} \mathcal{N}([\operatorname{Tr}\{P_A\}]^{-1} P_A), \tag{B.2}$$

where it is clear that this is well defined from $\mathcal{N}$ because $[\operatorname{Tr}\{P_A\}]^{-1} P_A$ is a density operator. Now consider for a constant $s > 0$ that we have scale invariance:

$$\widetilde{\mathcal{N}}(sP_A) = \operatorname{Tr}\{sP_A\} \mathcal{N}([\operatorname{Tr}\{sP_A\}]^{-1} sP_A) \tag{B.3}$$

$$= s\operatorname{Tr}\{P_A\} \mathcal{N}([\operatorname{Tr}\{P_A\}]^{-1} P_A) \tag{B.4}$$

$$= s\widetilde{\mathcal{N}}(P_A). \tag{B.5}$$

Furthermore, for two non-zero positive semi-definite operators P_A and Q_A, we have the following additivity relation:

$$\widetilde{\mathcal{N}}(P_A + Q_A) = \widetilde{\mathcal{N}}(P_A) + \widetilde{\mathcal{N}}(Q_A), \tag{B.6}$$

which follows because

$$\widetilde{\mathcal{N}}(P_A + Q_A)$$

$$= \operatorname{Tr}\{P_A + Q_A\} \mathcal{N}([\operatorname{Tr}\{P_A + Q_A\}]^{-1} (P_A + Q_A)) \tag{B.7}$$

$$= \operatorname{Tr}\{P_A + Q_A\} \mathcal{N}\left(\frac{1}{\operatorname{Tr}\{P_A + Q_A\}} P_A + \frac{1}{\operatorname{Tr}\{P_A + Q_A\}} Q_A \right) \tag{B.8}$$

$$= \operatorname{Tr}\{P_A + Q_A\} \mathcal{N}\left(\frac{\operatorname{Tr}\{P_A\}}{\operatorname{Tr}\{P_A + Q_A\}} \frac{P_A}{\operatorname{Tr}\{P_A\}} + \frac{\operatorname{Tr}\{Q_A\}}{\operatorname{Tr}\{P_A + Q_A\}} \frac{Q_A}{\operatorname{Tr}\{Q_A\}} \right) \tag{B.9}$$

$$= \text{Tr}\{P_A\}\mathcal{N}\left(\frac{P_A}{\text{Tr}\{P_A\}}\right) + \text{Tr}\{Q_A\}\mathcal{N}\left(\frac{Q_A}{\text{Tr}\{Q_A\}}\right) \tag{B.10}$$

$$= \tilde{\mathcal{N}}(P_A) + \tilde{\mathcal{N}}(Q_A), \tag{B.11}$$

where in the fourth equality, we exploited convex linearity of the quantum physical evolution $\mathcal{N}$.

For the next step, recall that any Hermitian operator T_A can be written as a linear combination of a positive part and a negative part: $T_A = T_A^+ - T_A^-$, where both T_A^+ and T_A^- are positive semi-definite operators. So we define the action of $\tilde{\mathcal{N}}$ on any Hermitian operator T_A as follows:

$$\tilde{\mathcal{N}}(T_A) \equiv \tilde{\mathcal{N}}(T_A^+) - \tilde{\mathcal{N}}(T_A^-). \tag{B.12}$$

To see that the following additivity relation holds for all Hermitian S_A and T_A

$$\tilde{\mathcal{N}}(S_A + T_A) = \tilde{\mathcal{N}}(S_A) + \tilde{\mathcal{N}}(T_A), \tag{B.13}$$

consider that

$$S_A + T_A = (S_A + T_A)^+ - (S_A + T_A)^-, \tag{B.14}$$

while also

$$S_A + T_A = S_A^+ + T_A^+ - S_A^- - T_A^-. \tag{B.15}$$

Equating both sides, we find that

$$(S_A + T_A)^+ + S_A^- + T_A^- = (S_A + T_A)^- + S_A^+ + T_A^+. \tag{B.16}$$

Now we exploit this equality, (B.6), and the definition in (B.12) to establish (B.13).

The final step is to extend the action of $\tilde{\mathcal{N}}$ to all operators $X_A \in \mathcal{L}(\mathcal{H}_A)$. Here, we recall that any linear operator can be written in terms of a real and imaginary part as follows:

$$X_A^R \equiv \frac{1}{2}\left(X_A + X_A^\dagger\right), \qquad X_A^I \equiv \frac{1}{2i}\left(X_A - X_A^\dagger\right), \tag{B.17}$$

where by inspection, X_A^R and X_A^I are Hermitian operators. So we define

$$\tilde{\mathcal{N}}(X_A) \equiv \tilde{\mathcal{N}}(X_A^R) + i\tilde{\mathcal{N}}(X_A^I). \tag{B.18}$$

This completes the development of a well defined linear extension $\tilde{\mathcal{N}}$ of the quantum physical evolution $\mathcal{N}$.

To show that it is unique, recall that any operator X_A can be expanded as a linear combination of density operators from the basis $\{\rho_A^{x,y}\}$, defined in (4.186), as follows:

$$X_A = \sum_{x,y} \alpha_{x,y} \rho_A^{x,y}, \tag{B.19}$$

where $\alpha_{x,y} \in \mathbb{C}$ for all x and y. It is straightforward to show from the above development that

$$\tilde{\mathcal{N}}(X_A) = \sum_{x,y} \alpha_{x,y} \mathcal{N}(\rho_A^{x,y}). \tag{B.20}$$

Now suppose that $\mathcal{N}'$ is some other linear map for which $\mathcal{N}'(\rho_A) = \mathcal{N}(\rho_A)$ for all $\rho_A \in \mathcal{D}(\mathcal{H}_A)$. Then the following equality holds for all $X_A \in \mathcal{L}(\mathcal{H}_A)$:

$$\mathcal{N}'(X_A) = \sum_{x,y} \alpha_{x,y} \mathcal{N}'(\rho_A^{x,y}) = \sum_{x,y} \alpha_{x,y} \mathcal{N}(\rho_A^{x,y}) = \tilde{\mathcal{N}}(X_A). \tag{B.21}$$

As a result, $\mathcal{N}' = \tilde{\mathcal{N}}$, given that they have the same action on every operator $X_A \in \mathcal{L}(\mathcal{H}_A)$.

References

Abeyesinghe, A. (2006), 'Unification of Quantum Information Theory', PhD thesis, California Institute of Technology.

Abeyesinghe, A., Devetak, I., Hayden, P. & Winter, A. (2009), 'The mother of all protocols: Restructuring quantum information's family tree', *Proceedings of the Royal Society A* **465**(2108), 2537–2563. arXiv:quant-ph/0606225.

Abeyesinghe, A. & Hayden, P. (2003), 'Generalized remote state preparation: Trading cbits, qubits, and ebits in quantum communication', *Physical Review A* **68**(6), 062319. arXiv:quant-ph/0308143.

Adami, C. & Cerf, N. J. (1997), 'von Neumann capacity of noisy quantum channels', *Physical Review A* **56**(5), 3470–3483. arXiv:quant-ph/9609024.

Aharonov, D. & Ben-Or, M. (1997), 'Fault-tolerant quantum computation with constant error', in *STOC '97: Proceedings of the Twenty-Ninth Annual ACM Symposium on Theory of Computing*, ACM, New York, NY, pp. 176–188. arXiv:quant-ph/9906129.

Ahlswede, R. & Winter, A. (2002), 'Strong converse for identification via quantum channels', *IEEE Transactions on Information Theory* **48**(3), 569–579. arXiv:quant-ph/0012127.

Ahn, C., Doherty, A., Hayden, P. & Winter, A. (2006), 'On the distributed compression of quantum information', *IEEE Transactions on Information Theory* **52**(10), 4349–4357. arXiv:quant-ph/0403042.

Alicki, R. & Fannes, M. (2004), 'Continuity of quantum conditional information', *Journal of Physics A: Mathematical and General* **37**(5), L55–L57. arXiv:quant-ph/0312081.

Araki, H. & Lieb, E. H. (1970), 'Entropy inequalities', *Communications in Mathematical Physics* **18**(2), 160–170.

Aspect, A., Grangier, P. & Roger, G. (1981), 'Experimental tests of realistic local theories via Bell's theorem', *Physical Review Letters* **47**(7), 460–463.

Aubrun, G., Szarek, S. & Werner, E. (2011), 'Hastings' additivity counterexample via Dvoretzky's theorem', *Communications in Mathematical Physics* **305**(1), 85–97. arXiv:1003.4925.

Audenaert, K., De Moor, B., Vollbrecht, K. G. H. & Werner, R. F. (2002), 'Asymptotic relative entropy of entanglement for orthogonally invariant states', *Physical Review A* **66**(3), 032310. arXiv:quant-ph/0204143.

Audenaert, K. M. R. (2007), 'A sharp continuity estimate for the von Neumann entropy', *Journal of Physics A: Mathematical and Theoretical* **40**(28), 8127. arXiv:quant-ph/0610146.

Bardhan, B. R., Garcia-Patron, R., Wilde, M. M. & Winter, A. (2015), 'Strong convers
for the classical capacity of all phase-insensitive bosonic Gaussian channels', *IEE.
Transactions on Information Theory* **61**(4), 1842–1850. arXiv:1401.4161.

Barnum, H., Caves, C. M., Fuchs, C. A., Jozsa, R. & Schumacher, B. (2001), 'O.
quantum coding for ensembles of mixed states', *Journal of Physics A: Mathematicc
and General* **34**(35), 6767. arXiv:quant-ph/0008024.

Barnum, H., Hayden, P., Jozsa, R. & Winter, A. (2001), 'On the reversible extractio
of classical information from a quantum source', *Proceedings of the Royal Society*
457(2012), 2019–2039. arXiv:quant-ph/0011072.

Barnum, H. & Knill, E. (2002), 'Reversing quantum dynamics with near-optima
quantum and classical fidelity', *Journal of Mathematical Physics* **43**(5), 2097–2106
arXiv:quant-ph/0004088.

Barnum, H., Knill, E. & Nielsen, M. A. (2000), 'On quantum fidelities and channel capacities', *IEEE Transactions on Information Theory* **46**(4), 1317–1329.
arXiv:quant-ph/9809010.

Barnum, H., Nielsen, M. A. & Schumacher, B. (1998), 'Information transmission
through a noisy quantum channel', *Physical Review A* **57**(6), 4153–4175.

Beigi, S., Datta, N. & Leditzky, F. (2015), 'Decoding quantum information via the Petz
recovery map'. arXiv:1504.04449.

Bell, J. S. (1964), 'On the Einstein–Podolsky–Rosen paradox', *Physics* **1**, 195–200.

Bennett, C. H. (1992), 'Quantum cryptography using any two nonorthogonal states',
Physical Review Letters **68**(21), 3121–3124.

Bennett, C. H. (1995), 'Quantum information and computation', *Physics Today*
48(10), 24–30.

Bennett, C. H. (2004), 'A resource-based view of quantum information', *Quantum
Information and Computation* **4**, 460–466.

Bennett, C. H., Bernstein, H. J., Popescu, S. & Schumacher, B. (1996), 'Concentrating partial entanglement by local operations', *Physical Review A* **53**(4), 2046–2052.
arXiv:quant-ph/9511030.

Bennett, C. H. & Brassard, G. (1984), 'Quantum cryptography: Public key distribution
and coin tossing', in *Proceedings of IEEE International Conference on Computers
Systems and Signal Processing*, Bangalore, India, pp. 175–179.

Bennett, C. H., Brassard, G., Crépeau, C., Jozsa, R., Peres, A. & Wootters, W. K.
(1993), 'Teleporting an unknown quantum state via dual classical and Einstein–
Podolsky–Rosen channels', *Physical Review Letters* **70**(13), 1895–1899.

Bennett, C. H., Brassard, G. & Ekert, A. K. (1992), 'Quantum cryptography', *Scientific
American*, 50–57.

Bennett, C. H., Brassard, G. & Mermin, N. D. (1992), 'Quantum cryptography without
Bell's theorem', *Physical Review Letters* **68**(5), 557–559.

Bennett, C. H., Brassard, G., Popescu, S., Schumacher, B., Smolin, J. A. & Wootters,
W. K. (1996), 'Purification of noisy entanglement and faithful teleportation via noisy
channels', *Physical Review Letters* **76**(5), 722–725. arXiv:quant-ph/9511027.

Bennett, C. H., Devetak, I., Harrow, A. W., Shor, P. W. & Winter, A. (2014),
'The quantum reverse Shannon theorem and resource tradeoffs for simulating
quantum channels', *IEEE Transactions on Information Theory* **60**(5), 2926–2959.
arXiv:0912.5537.

Bennett, C. H., DiVincenzo, D. P., Shor, P. W., Smolin, J. A., Terhal, B. M. & Wootters, W. K. (2001), 'Remote state preparation', *Physical Review Letters* **87**(7), 077902.

Bennett, C. H., DiVincenzo, D. P. & Smolin, J. A. (1997), 'Capacities of quantum erasure channels', *Physical Review Letters* **78**(16), 3217–3220. arXiv:quant-ph/9701015.

Bennett, C. H., DiVincenzo, D. P., Smolin, J. A. & Wootters, W. K. (1996), 'Mixed-state entanglement and quantum error correction', *Physical Review A* **54**(5), 3824–3851. arXiv:quant-ph/9604024.

Bennett, C. H., Harrow, A. W. & Lloyd, S. (2006), 'Universal quantum data compression via nondestructive tomography', *Physical Review A* **73**(3), 032336. arXiv:quant-ph/0403078.

Bennett, C. H., Hayden, P., Leung, D. W., Shor, P. W. & Winter, A. (2005), 'Remote preparation of quantum states', *IEEE Transactions on Information Theory* **51**(1), 56–74. arXiv:quant-ph/0307100.

Bennett, C. H., Shor, P. W., Smolin, J. A. & Thapliyal, A. V. (1999), 'Entanglement-assisted classical capacity of noisy quantum channels', *Physical Review Letters* **83**(15), 3081–3084. arXiv:quant-ph/9904023.

Bennett, C. H., Shor, P. W., Smolin, J. A. & Thapliyal, A. V. (2002), 'Entanglement-assisted capacity of a quantum channel and the reverse Shannon theorem', *IEEE Transactions on Information Theory* **48**(10), 2637–2655. arXiv:quant-ph/0106052.

Bennett, C. H. & Wiesner, S. J. (1992), 'Communication via one- and two-particle operators on Einstein–Podolsky–Rosen states', *Physical Review Letters* **69**(20), 2881–2884.

Berger, T. (1971), *Rate Distortion Theory: A Mathematical Basis for Data Compression*, Prentice-Hall, Englewood Cliffs, NJ.

Berger, T. (1977), 'Multiterminal source coding', *The Information Theory Approach to Communications*, Springer-Verlag, New York, NY.

Bergh, J. & Löfström, J. (1976), *Interpolation Spaces*, Springer-Verlag, Heidelberg.

Berta, M., Brandao, F. G. S. L., Christandl, M. & Wehner, S. (2013), 'Entanglement cost of quantum channels', *IEEE Transactions on Information Theory* **59**(10), 6779–6795. arXiv:1108.5357.

Berta, M., Christandl, M., Colbeck, R., Renes, J. M. & Renner, R. (2010), 'The uncertainty principle in the presence of quantum memory', *Nature Physics* **6**, 659–662. arXiv:0909.0950.

Berta, M., Christandl, M. & Renner, R. (2011), 'The quantum reverse Shannon theorem based on one-shot information theory', *Communications in Mathematical Physics* **306**(3), 579–615. arXiv:0912.3805.

Berta, M., Lemm, M. & Wilde, M. M. (2015), 'Monotonicity of quantum relative entropy and recoverability', *Quantum Information and Computation* **15**(15 & 16), 1333–1354. arXiv:1412.4067.

Berta, M., Renes, J. M. & Wilde, M. M. (2014), 'Identifying the information gain of a quantum measurement', *IEEE Transactions on Information Theory* **60**(12), 7987–8006. arXiv:1301.1594.

Berta, M., Seshadreesan, K. & Wilde, M. M. (2015), 'Rényi generalizations of the conditional quantum mutual information', *Journal of Mathematical Physics* **56**(2), 022205. arXiv:1403.6102.

Berta, M. & Tomamichel, M. (2016), 'The fidelity of recovery is multiplicative', *IEEE Transactions on Information Theory* **62**(4), 1758–1763. arXiv:1502.07973.

Bhatia, R. (1997), *Matrix Analysis*, Springer-Verlag, Heidelberg.

Blume-Kohout, R., Croke, S. & Gottesman, D. (2014), 'Streaming universal distortion-free entanglement concentration', *IEEE Transactions on Information Theory* **60**(1), 334–350. arXiv:0910.5952.

Boche, H. & Notzel, J. (2014), 'The classical–quantum multiple access channel with conferencing encoders and with common messages', *Quantum Information Processing* **13**(12), 2595–2617. arXiv:1310.1970.

Bohm, D. (1989), *Quantum Theory*, Courier Dover Publications.

Bowen, G. (2004), 'Quantum feedback channels', *IEEE Transactions on Information Theory* **50**(10), 2429–2434. arXiv:quant-ph/0209076.

Bowen, G. & Nagarajan, R. (2005), 'On feedback and the classical capacity of a noisy quantum channel', *IEEE Transactions on Information Theory* **51**(1), 320–324. arXiv:quant-ph/0305176.

Boyd, S. & Vandenberghe, L. (2004), *Convex Optimization*, Cambridge University Press, Cambridge, UK.

Brádler, K., Hayden, P., Touchette, D. & Wilde, M. M. (2010), 'Trade-off capacities of the quantum Hadamard channels', *Physical Review A* **81**(6), 062312. arXiv:1001.1732.

Brandao, F. G. S. L., Christandl, M. & Yard, J. (2011), 'Faithful squashed entanglement', *Communications in Mathematical Physics* **306**(3), 805–830. arXiv:1010.1750.

Brandao, F. G. S. L., Harrow, A. W., Oppenheim, J. & Strelchuk, S. (2014), 'Quantum conditional mutual information, reconstructed states, and state redistribution', *Physical Review Letters* **115**(5), 050501. arXiv:1411.4921.

Brandao, F. G. S. L. & Horodecki, M. (2010), 'On Hastings' counterexamples to the minimum output entropy additivity conjecture', *Open Systems & Information Dynamics* **17**(1), 31–52. arXiv:0907.3210.

Braunstein, S. L., Fuchs, C. A., Gottesman, D. & Lo, H.-K. (2000), 'A quantum analog of Huffman coding', *IEEE Transactions on Information Theory* **46**(4), 1644–1649. arXiv:quant-ph/9805080.

Brun, T. A. (n.d.), 'Quantum information processing course lecture slides', http://almaak.usc.edu/~tbrun/Course/.

Burnashev, M. V. & Holevo, A. S. (1998), 'On reliability function of quantum communication channel', *Probl. Peredachi Inform.* **34**(2), 1–13. arXiv:quant-ph/9703013.

Buscemi, F. & Datta, N. (2010), 'The quantum capacity of channels with arbitrarily correlated noise', *IEEE Transactions on Information Theory* **56**(3), 1447–1460. arXiv:0902.0158.

Cai, N., Winter, A. & Yeung, R. W. (2004), 'Quantum privacy and quantum wiretap channels', *Problems of Information Transmission* **40**(4), 318–336.

Calderbank, A. R., Rains, E. M., Shor, P. W. & Sloane, N. J. A. (1997), 'Quantum error correction and orthogonal geometry', *Physical Review Letters* **78**(3), 405–408. arXiv:quant-ph/9605005.

Calderbank, A. R., Rains, E. M., Shor, P. W. & Sloane, N. J. A. (1998), 'Quantum error correction via codes over GF(4)', *IEEE Transactions on Information Theory* **44**(4), 1369–1387. arXiv:quant-ph/9608006.

Calderbank, A. R. & Shor, P. W. (1996), 'Good quantum error-correcting codes exist', *Physical Review A* **54**(2), 1098–1105. arXiv:quant-ph/9512032.

Carlen, E. A. & Lieb, E. H. (2014), 'Remainder terms for some quantum entropy inequalities', *Journal of Mathematical Physics* **55**(4), 042201. arXiv:1402.3840.

Cerf, N. J. & Adami, C. (1997), 'Negative entropy and information in quantum mechanics', *Physical Review Letters* **79**(26), 5194–5197. arXiv:quant-ph/9512022.

Coles, P., Berta, M., Tomamichel, M. & Wehner, S. (2015), 'Entropic uncertainty relations and their applications'. arXiv:1511.04857.

Coles, P. J., Colbeck, R., Yu, L. & Zwolak, M. (2012), 'Uncertainty relations from simple entropic properties', *Physical Review Letters* **108**(21), 210405. arXiv:1112.0543.

Cooney, T., Mosonyi, M. & Wilde, M. M. (2014), 'Strong converse exponents for a quantum channel discrimination problem and quantum-feedback-assisted communication', *Communications in Mathematical Physics* **344**(3), June 2016, 797–829. arXiv:1408.3373.

Cover, T. M. & Thomas, J. A. (2006), *Elements of Information Theory*, 2nd edn, Wiley-Interscience, New York, NY.

Csiszar, I. (1967), 'Information-type measures of difference of probability distributions and indirect observations', *Studia Sci. Math. Hungar.* **2**, 299–318.

Csiszár, I. & Körner, J. (1978), 'Broadcast channels with confidential messages', *IEEE Transactions on Information Theory* **24**(3), 339–348.

Csiszár, I. & Körner, J. (2011), *Information Theory: Coding Theorems for Discrete Memoryless Systems*, Probability and Mathematical Statistics, 2nd edn, Cambridge University Press.

Cubitt, T., Elkouss, D., Matthews, W., Ozols, M., Perez-Garcia, D. & Strelchuk, S. (2015), 'Unbounded number of channel uses may be required to detect quantum capacity', *Nature Communications* **6**, 6739. arXiv:1408.5115.

Czekaj, L. & Horodecki, P. (2009), 'Purely quantum superadditivity of classical capacities of quantum multiple access channels', *Physical Review Letters* **102**(11), 110505. arXiv:0807.3977.

Dalai, M. (2013), 'Lower bounds on the probability of error for classical and classical–quantum channels', *IEEE Transactions on Information Theory* **59**(12), 8027–8056. arXiv:1201.5411.

Datta, N. (2009), 'Min- and max-relative entropies and a new entanglement monotone', *IEEE Transactions on Information Theory* **55**(6), 2816–2826. arXiv:0803.2770.

Datta, N. & Hsieh, M.-H. (2010), 'Universal coding for transmission of private information', *Journal of Mathematical Physics* **51**(12), 122202. arXiv:1007.2629.

Datta, N. & Hsieh, M.-H. (2011), 'The apex of the family tree of protocols: Optimal rates and resource inequalities', *New Journal of Physics* **13**, 093042. arXiv:1103.1135.

Datta, N. & Hsieh, M.-H. (2013), 'One-shot entanglement-assisted quantum and classical communication', *IEEE Transactions on Information Theory* **59**(3), 1929–1939. arXiv:1105.3321.

Datta, N. & Leditzky, F. (2015), 'Second-order asymptotics for source coding, dense coding, and pure-state entanglement conversions', *IEEE Transactions on Information Theory* **61**(1), 582–608. arXiv:1403.2543.

Datta, N. & Renner, R. (2009), 'Smooth entropies and the quantum information spectrum', *IEEE Transactions on Information Theory* **55**(6), 2807–2815. arXiv:0801.0282.

Datta, N., Tomamichel, M. & Wilde, M. M. (2014), 'On the Second-Order Asymptotic for Entanglement-Assisted Communication', *Quantum Information Processing* (15 6, June 2016, 2569–2591. arXiv:1405.1797.

Datta, N. & Wilde, M. M. (2015), 'Quantum Markov chains, sufficiency of quantum channels, and Rényi information measures', *Journal of Physics A* **48**(50), 505301 arXiv:1501.05636.

Davies, E. B. & Lewis, J. T. (1970), 'An operational approach to quantum probability' *Communications in Mathematical Physics* **17**(3), 239–260.

de Broglie, L. (1924), 'Recherches sur la théorie des quanta', PhD thesis, Paris.

Deutsch, D. (1985), 'Quantum theory, the Church–Turing principle and the universal quantum computer', *Proceedings of the Royal Society of London A* **400**(1818) 97–117.

Devetak, I. (2005), 'The private classical capacity and quantum capacity of a quantum channel', *IEEE Transactions on Information Theory* **51**(1), 44–55. arXiv:quant-ph/0304127.

Devetak, I. (2006), 'Triangle of dualities between quantum communication protocols', *Physical Review Letters* **97**(14), 140503.

Devetak, I., Harrow, A. W. & Winter, A. (2004), 'A family of quantum protocols', *Physical Review Letters* **93**(23), 239503. arXiv:quant-ph/0308044.

Devetak, I., Harrow, A. W. & Winter, A. (2008), 'A resource framework for quantum Shannon theory', *IEEE Transactions on Information Theory* **54**(10), 4587–4618. arXiv:quant-ph/0512015.

Devetak, I., Junge, M., King, C. & Ruskai, M. B. (2006), 'Multiplicativity of completely bounded p-norms implies a new additivity result', *Communications in Mathematical Physics* **266**(1), 37–63. arXiv:quant-ph/0506196.

Devetak, I. & Shor, P. W. (2005), 'The capacity of a quantum channel for simultaneous transmission of classical and quantum information', *Communications in Mathematical Physics* **256**(2), 287–303. arXiv:quant-ph/0311131.

Devetak, I. & Winter, A. (2003), 'Classical data compression with quantum side information', *Physical Review A* **68**(4), 042301. arXiv:quant-ph/0209029.

Devetak, I. & Winter, A. (2004), 'Relating quantum privacy and quantum coherence: An operational approach', *Physical Review Letters* **93**(8), 080501. arXiv:quant-ph/0307053.

Devetak, I. & Winter, A. (2005), 'Distillation of secret key and entanglement from quantum states', *Proceedings of the Royal Society A* **461**(2053), 207–235. arXiv:quant-ph/0306078.

Devetak, I. & Yard, J. (2008), 'Exact cost of redistributing multipartite quantum states', *Physical Review Letters* **100**(23), 230501.

Dieks, D. (1982), 'Communication by EPR devices', *Physics Letters A* **92**, 271.

Ding, D. & Wilde, M. M. (2015), 'Strong converse exponents for the feedback-assisted classical capacity of entanglement-breaking channels'. arXiv:1506.02228.

Dirac, P. A. M. (1982), *The Principles of Quantum Mechanics (International Series of Monographs on Physics)*, Oxford University Press, USA.

DiVincenzo, D. P., Horodecki, M., Leung, D. W., Smolin, J. A. & Terhal, B. M. (2004), 'Locking classical correlations in quantum states', *Physical Review Letters* **92**(6), 067902. arXiv:quant-ph/0303088.

DiVincenzo, D. P., Shor, P. W. & Smolin, J. A. (1998), 'Quantum-channel capacity of very noisy channels', *Physical Review A* **57**(2), 830–839. arXiv:quant-ph/9706061.

Dowling, J. P. & Milburn, G. J. (2003), 'Quantum technology: The second quantum revolution', *Philosophical Transactions of The Royal Society of London Series A* **361**(1809), 1655–1674. arXiv:quant-ph/0206091.

Dupuis, F. (2010), 'The decoupling approach to quantum information theory', PhD thesis, University of Montreal. arXiv:1004.1641.

Dupuis, F., Berta, M., Wullschleger, J. & Renner, R. (2014), 'One-shot decoupling', *Communications in Mathematical Physics* **328**(1), 251–284. arXiv:1012.6044.

Dupuis, F., Florjanczyk, J., Hayden, P. & Leung, D. (2013), 'The locking-decoding frontier for generic dynamics', *Proceedings of the Royal Society of London A: Mathematical, Physical and Engineering Sciences* **469**(2159). arXiv:1011.1612.

Dupuis, F., Hayden, P. & Li, K. (2010), 'A father protocol for quantum broadcast channels', *IEEE Transactions on Information Theory* **56**(6), 2946–2956. arXiv:quant-ph/0612155.

Dupuis, F. & Wilde, M. M. (2016), 'Swiveled Rényi entropies', *Quantum Information Processing* **15**(3), 1309–1345. arXiv:1506.00981.

Dutil, N. (2011), 'Multiparty quantum protocols for assisted entanglement distillation', PhD thesis, McGill University. arXiv:1105.4657.

Einstein, A. (1905), 'Über einen die erzeugung und verwandlung des lichtes betreffenden heuristischen gesichtspunkt', *Annalen der Physik* **17**, 132–148.

Einstein, A., Podolsky, B. & Rosen, N. (1935), 'Can quantum-mechanical description of physical reality be considered complete?', *Physical Review* **47**, 777–780.

Ekert, A. K. (1991), 'Quantum cryptography based on Bell's theorem', *Physical Review Letters* **67**(6), 661–663.

Elias, P. (1972), 'The efficient construction of an unbiased random sequence', *Annals of Mathematical Statistics* **43**(3), 865–870.

Elkouss, D. & Strelchuk, S. (2015), 'Superadditivity of private information for any number of uses of the channel', *Physical Review Letters* **115**(4), 040501. arXiv:1502.05326.

Fannes, M. (1973), 'A continuity property of the entropy density for spin lattices', *Communications in Mathematical Physics* **31**, 291.

Fano, R. M. (2008), 'Fano inequality', *Scholarpedia* **3**(10), 6648.

Fawzi, O., Hayden, P., Savov, I., Sen, P. & Wilde, M. M. (2012), 'Classical communication over a quantum interference channel', *IEEE Transactions on Information Theory* **58**(6), 3670–3691. arXiv:1102.2624.

Fawzi, O., Hayden, P. & Sen, P. (2013), 'From low-distortion norm embeddings to explicit uncertainty relations and efficient information locking', *Journal of the ACM* **60**(6), 44:1–44:61. arXiv:1010.3007.

Fawzi, O. & Renner, R. (2015), 'Quantum conditional mutual information and approximate Markov chains', *Communications in Mathematical Physics* **340**(2), 575–611. arXiv:1410.0664.

Feller, W. (1971), *An Introduction to Probability Theory and Its Applications*, 2nd edn, John Wiley and Sons.

Feynman, R. P. (1982), 'Simulating physics with computers', *International Journal of Theoretical Physics* **21**, 467–488.

Feynman, R. P. (1998), *Feynman Lectures On Physics (3 Volume Set)*, Addison Wesley Longman.

Fuchs, C. (1996), 'Distinguishability and Accessible Information in Quantum Theory' PhD thesis, University of New Mexico. arXiv:quant-ph/9601020.

Fuchs, C. A. & Caves, C. M. (1995), 'Mathematical techniques for quantum communication theory', *Open Systems & Information Dynamics* **3**(3), 345–356. arXiv:quant-ph/9604001.

Fuchs, C. A. & van de Graaf, J. (1998), 'Cryptographic distinguishability measures for quantum mechanical states', *IEEE Transactions on Information Theory* **45**(4), 1216–1227. arXiv:quant-ph/9712042.

Fukuda, M. & King, C. (2010), 'Entanglement of random subspaces via the Hastings bound', *Journal of Mathematical Physics* **51**(4), 042201. arXiv:0907.5446.

Fukuda, M., King, C. & Moser, D. K. (2010), 'Comments on Hastings' additivity counterexamples', *Communications in Mathematical Physics* **296**(1), 111–143 arXiv:0905.3697.

Gamal, A. E. & Kim, Y.-H. (2012), *Network Information Theory*, Cambridge University Press. arXiv:1001.3404.

García-Patrón, R., Pirandola, S., Lloyd, S. & Shapiro, J. H. (2009), 'Reverse coherent information', *Physical Review Letters* **102**(21), 210501. arXiv:0808.0210.

Gerlach, W. & Stern, O. (1922), 'Das magnetische moment des silberatoms', *Zeitschrift für Physik* **9**, 353–355.

Giovannetti, V. & Fazio, R. (2005), 'Information-capacity description of spin-chain correlations', *Physical Review A* **71**(3), 032314. arXiv:quant-ph/0405110.

Giovannetti, V., Guha, S., Lloyd, S., Maccone, L. & Shapiro, J. H. (2004), 'Minimum output entropy of bosonic channels: A conjecture', *Physical Review A* **70**(3), 032315. arXiv:quant-ph/0404005.

Giovannetti, V., Guha, S., Lloyd, S., Maccone, L., Shapiro, J. H. & Yuen, H. P. (2004), 'Classical capacity of the lossy bosonic channel: The exact solution', *Physical Review Letters* **92**(2), 027902. arXiv:quant-ph/0308012.

Giovannetti, V., Holevo, A. S. & García-Patrón, R. (2015), 'A solution of Gaussian optimizer conjecture for quantum channels', *Communications in Mathematical Physics* **334**(3), 1553–1571.

Giovannetti, V., Holevo, A. S., Lloyd, S. & Maccone, L. (2010), 'Generalized minimal output entropy conjecture for one-mode Gaussian channels: definitions and some exact results', *Journal of Physics A: Mathematical and Theoretical* **43**(41), 415305. arXiv:1004.4787.

Giovannetti, V., Lloyd, S. & Maccone, L. (2012), 'Achieving the Holevo bound via sequential measurements', *Physical Review A* **85**, 012302. arXiv:1012.0386.

Giovannetti, V., Lloyd, S., Maccone, L. & Shor, P. W. (2003a), 'Broadband channel capacities', *Physical Review A* **68**(6), 062323. arXiv:quant-ph/0307098.

Giovannetti, V., Lloyd, S., Maccone, L. & Shor, P. W. (2003b), 'Entanglement assisted capacity of the broadband lossy channel', *Physical Review Letters* **91**(4), 047901. arXiv:quant-ph/0304020.

Glauber, R. J. (1963a), 'Coherent and incoherent states of the radiation field', *Physical Review* **131**(6), 2766–2788.

Glauber, R. J. (1963b), 'The quantum theory of optical coherence', *Physical Review* **130**(6), 2529–2539.

Glauber, R. J. (2005), 'One hundred years of light quanta', in K. Grandin, ed., *Les Prix Nobel. The Nobel Prizes 2005*, Nobel Foundation, pp. 90–91.

Gordon, J. P. (1964), 'Noise at optical frequencies; information theory', in P. A. Miles, ed., *Quantum Electronics and Coherent Light; Proceedings of the International School of Physics Enrico Fermi, Course XXXI*, Academic Press New York, pp. 156–181.

Gottesman, D. (1996), 'Class of quantum error-correcting codes saturating the quantum Hamming bound', *Physical Review A* **54**(3), 1862–1868. arXiv:quant-ph/9604038.

Gottesman, D. (1997), 'Stabilizer Codes and Quantum Error Correction', PhD thesis, California Institute of Technology. arXiv:quant-ph/9705052.

Grafakos, L. (2008), *Classical Fourier Analysis*, 2nd edn, Springer.

Grassl, M., Beth, T. & Pellizzari, T. (1997), 'Codes for the quantum erasure channel', *Physical Review A* **56**(1), 33–38. arXiv:quant-ph/9610042.

Greene, B. (1999), *The Elegant Universe: Superstrings, Hidden Dimensions, and the Quest for the Ultimate Theory*, W. W. Norton & Company.

Griffiths, D. J. (1995), *Introduction to Quantum Mechanics*, Prentice-Hall, Inc.

Groisman, B., Popescu, S. & Winter, A. (2005), 'Quantum, classical, and total amount of correlations in a quantum state', *Physical Review A* **72**(3), 032317. arXiv:quant-ph/0410091.

Grudka, A. & Horodecki, P. (2010), 'Nonadditivity of quantum and classical capacities for entanglement breaking multiple-access channels and the butterfly network', *Physical Review A* **81**(6), 060305. arXiv:0906.1305.

Guha, S. (2008), 'Multiple-User Quantum Information Theory for Optical Communication Channels', PhD thesis, Massachusetts Institute of Technology.

Guha, S., Hayden, P., Krovi, H., Lloyd, S., Lupo, C., Shapiro, J. H., Takeoka, M. & Wilde, M. M. (2014), 'Quantum enigma machines and the locking capacity of a quantum channel', *Physical Review X* **4**(1), 011016. arXiv:1307.5368.

Guha, S. & Shapiro, J. H. (2007), 'Classical information capacity of the bosonic broadcast channel', in *Proceedings of the IEEE International Symposium on Information Theory*, Nice, France, pp. 1896–1900. arXiv:0704.1901.

Guha, S., Shapiro, J. H. & Erkmen, B. I. (2007), 'Classical capacity of bosonic broadcast communication and a minimum output entropy conjecture', *Physical Review A* **76**(3), 032303. arXiv:0706.3416.

Guha, S., Shapiro, J. H. & Erkmen, B. I. (2008), 'Capacity of the bosonic wiretap channel and the entropy photon-number inequality', in *Proceedings of the IEEE International Symposium on Information Theory*, Toronto, Ontario, Canada, pp. 91–95. arXiv:0801.0841.

Gupta, M. & Wilde, M. M. (2015), 'Multiplicativity of completely bounded *p*-norms implies a strong converse for entanglement-assisted capacity', *Communications in Mathematical Physics* **334**(2), 867–887. arXiv:1310.7028.

Hamada, M. (2005), 'Information rates achievable with algebraic codes on quantum discrete memoryless channels', *IEEE Transactions on Information Theory* **51**(12), 4263–4277. arXiv:quant-ph/0207113.

Harrington, J. & Preskill, J. (2001), 'Achievable rates for the Gaussian quantum channel', *Physical Review A* **64**(6), 062301. arXiv:quant-ph/0105058.

Harrow, A. (2004), 'Coherent communication of classical messages', *Physical Review Letters* **92**(9), 097902. arXiv:quant-ph/0307091.

Harrow, A. W. & Lo, H.-K. (2004), 'A tight lower bound on the classical communication cost of entanglement dilution', *IEEE Transactions on Information Theory* **50**(2), 319–327. arXiv:quant-ph/0204096.

Hastings, M. B. (2009), 'Superadditivity of communication capacity using entangle inputs', *Nature Physics* **5**, 255–257. arXiv:0809.3972.

Hausladen, P., Jozsa, R., Schumacher, B., Westmoreland, M. & Wootters, W. K. (1996), 'Classical information capacity of a quantum channel', *Physical Review A* **54**(3), 1869–1876.

Hausladen, P., Schumacher, B., Westmoreland, M. & Wootters, W. K. (1995), 'Sending classical bits via quantum its', *Annals of the New York Academy of Science* **755**, 698–705.

Hayashi, M. (2002), 'Exponents of quantum fixed-length pure-state source coding', *Physical Review A* **66**(3), 032321. arXiv:quant-ph/0202002.

Hayashi, M. (2006), *Quantum Information: An Introduction*, Springer.

Hayashi, M. (2007), 'Error exponent in asymmetric quantum hypothesis testing and its application to classical–quantum channel coding', *Physical Review A* **76**(6), 062301. arXiv:quant-ph/0611013.

Hayashi, M., Koashi, M., Matsumoto, K., Morikoshi, F. & Winter, A. (2003), 'Error exponents for entanglement concentration', *Journal of Physics A: Mathematical and General* **36**(2), 527. arXiv:quant-ph/0206097.

Hayashi, M. & Matsumoto, K. (2001), 'Variable length universal entanglement concentration by local operations and its application to teleportation and dense coding'. arXiv:quant-ph/0109028.

Hayashi, M. & Nagaoka, H. (2003), 'General formulas for capacity of classical–quantum channels', *IEEE Transactions on Information Theory* **49**(7), 1753–1768. arXiv:quant-ph/0206186.

Hayden, P. (2007), 'The maximal p-norm multiplicativity conjecture is false'. arXiv:0707.3291.

Hayden, P., Horodecki, M., Winter, A. & Yard, J. (2008), 'A decoupling approach to the quantum capacity', *Open Systems & Information Dynamics* **15**(1), 7–19. arXiv:quant-ph/0702005.

Hayden, P., Jozsa, R., Petz, D. & Winter, A. (2004), 'Structure of states which satisfy strong subadditivity of quantum entropy with equality', *Communications in Mathematical Physics* **246**(2), 359–374. arXiv:quant-ph/0304007.

Hayden, P., Jozsa, R. & Winter, A. (2002), 'Trading quantum for classical resources in quantum data compression', *Journal of Mathematical Physics* **43**(9), 4404–4444. arXiv:quant-ph/0204038.

Hayden, P., Leung, D., Shor, P. W. & Winter, A. (2004), 'Randomizing quantum states: Constructions and applications', *Communications in Mathematical Physics* **250**(2), 371–391. arXiv:quant-ph/0307104.

Hayden, P., Shor, P. W. & Winter, A. (2008), 'Random quantum codes from Gaussian ensembles and an uncertainty relation', *Open Systems & Information Dynamics* **15**(1), 71–89. arXiv:0712.0975.

Hayden, P. & Winter, A. (2003), 'Communication cost of entanglement transformations', *Physical Review A* **67**(1), 012326. arXiv:quant-ph/0204092.

Hayden, P. & Winter, A. (2008), 'Counterexamples to the maximal p-norm multiplicativity conjecture for all p > 1', *Communications in Mathematical Physics* **284**(1), 263–280. arXiv:0807.4753.

Heinosaari, T. & Ziman, M. (2012), *The Mathematical Language of Quantum Theory: From Uncertainty to Entanglement*, Cambridge University Press.

Heisenberg, W. (1925), 'Über quantentheoretische umdeutung kinematischer und mechanischer beziehungen', *Zeitschrift für Physik* **33**, 879–893.

Helstrom, C. W. (1969), 'Quantum detection and estimation theory', *Journal of Statistical Physics* **1**, 231–252.

Helstrom, C. W. (1976), *Quantum Detection and Estimation Theory*, Academic, New York, NY.

Herbert, N. (1982), 'Flash—a superluminal communicator based upon a new kind of quantum measurement', *Foundations of Physics* **12**(12), 1171–1179.

Hirche, C. & Morgan, C. (2015), 'An improved rate region for the classical–quantum broadcast channel', *Proceedings of the 2015 IEEE International Symposium on Information Theory* pp. 2782–2786. arXiv:1501.07417.

Hirche, C., Morgan, C. & Wilde, M. M. (2016), 'Polar codes in network quantum information theory', *IEEE Transactions on Information Theory* **62**(2), 915–924. arXiv:1409.7246.

Hirschman, I. I. (1952), 'A convexity theorem for certain groups of transformations', *Journal d'Analyse Mathématique* **2**(2), 209–218.

Holevo, A. S. (1973a), 'Bounds for the quantity of information transmitted by a quantum communication channel', *Problems of Information Transmission* **9**, 177–183.

Holevo, A. S. (1973b), 'Statistical problems in quantum physics', in *Second Japan-USSR Symposium on Probability Theory*, Vol. 330 of *Lecture Notes in Mathematics*, Springer Berlin/Heidelberg, pp. 104–119.

Holevo, A. S. (1998), 'The capacity of the quantum channel with general signal states', *IEEE Transactions on Information Theory* **44**(1), 269–273. arXiv:quant-ph/9611023.

Holevo, A. S. (2000), 'Reliability function of general classical–quantum channel', *IEEE Transactions on Information Theory* **46**(6), 2256–2261. arXiv:quant-ph/9907087.

Holevo, A. S. (2002a), *An Introduction to Quantum Information Theory*, Moscow Center of Continuous Mathematical Education, Moscow. In Russian.

Holevo, A. S. (2002b), 'On entanglement assisted classical capacity', *Journal of Mathematical Physics* **43**(9), 4326–4333. arXiv:quant-ph/0106075.

Holevo, A. S. (2012), *Quantum Systems, Channels, Information*, de Gruyter Studies in Mathematical Physics (Book 16), de Gruyter.

Holevo, A. S. & Werner, R. F. (2001), 'Evaluating capacities of bosonic Gaussian channels', *Physical Review A* **63**(3), 032312. arXiv:quant-ph/9912067.

Horodecki, M. (1998), 'Limits for compression of quantum information carried by ensembles of mixed states', *Physical Review A* **57**(5), 3364–3369. arXiv:quant-ph/9712035.

Horodecki, M., Horodecki, P. & Horodecki, R. (1996), 'Separability of mixed states: necessary and sufficient conditions', *Physics Letters A* **223**(1-2), 1–8. arXiv:quant-ph/9605038.

Horodecki, M., Horodecki, P., Horodecki, R., Leung, D. & Terhal, B. (2001), 'Classical capacity of a noiseless quantum channel assisted by noisy entanglement', *Quantum Information and Computation* **1**(3), 70–78. arXiv:quant-ph/0106080.

Horodecki, M., Oppenheim, J. & Winter, A. (2005), 'Partial quantum information', *Nature* **436**, 673–676.

Horodecki, M., Oppenheim, J. & Winter, A. (2007), 'Quantum state merging and negative information', *Communications in Mathematical Physics* **269**(1), 107–136. arXiv:quant-ph/0512247.

Horodecki, M., Shor, P. W. & Ruskai, M. B. (2003), 'Entanglement breaking channels' *Reviews in Mathematical Physics* **15**(6), 629–641. arXiv:quant-ph/0302031.

Horodecki, P. (1997), 'Separability criterion and inseparable mixed states with positiv partial transposition', *Physics Letters A* **232**(5), 333–339. arXiv:quant-ph/9703004

Horodecki, R. & Horodecki, P. (1994), 'Quantum redundancies and local realism' *Physics Letters A* **194**(3), 147–152.

Horodecki, R., Horodecki, P., Horodecki, M. & Horodecki, K. (2009), 'Quantun entanglement', *Reviews of Modern Physics* **81**(2), 865–942. arXiv:quant-ph/0702225

Hsieh, M.-H., Devetak, I. & Winter, A. (2008), 'Entanglement-assisted capacit of quantum multiple-access channels', *IEEE Transactions on Information Theor* **54**(7), 3078–3090. arXiv:quant-ph/0511228.

Hsieh, M.-H., Luo, Z. & Brun, T. (2008), 'Secret-key-assisted private classical communication capacity over quantum channels', *Physical Review A* **78**(4), 042306 arXiv:0806.3525.

Hsieh, M.-H. & Wilde, M. M. (2009), 'Public and private communication with a quantum channel and a secret key', *Physical Review A* **80**(2), 022306. arXiv:0903. 3920.

Hsieh, M.-H. & Wilde, M. M. (2010a), 'Entanglement-assisted communication of classical and quantum information', *IEEE Transactions on Information Theory* **56**(9), 4682–4704. arXiv:0811.4227.

Hsieh, M.-H. & Wilde, M. M. (2010b), 'Trading classical communication, quantum communication, and entanglement in quantum Shannon theory', *IEEE Transactions on Information Theory* **56**(9), 4705–4730. arXiv:0901.3038.

Jaynes, E. T. (1957a), 'Information theory and statistical mechanics', *Physical Review* **106**, 620.

Jaynes, E. T. (1957b), 'Information theory and statistical mechanics II', *Physical Review* **108**, 171.

Jaynes, E. T. (2003), *Probability Theory: The Logic of Science*, Cambridge University Press.

Jencova, A. (2012), 'Reversibility conditions for quantum operations', *Reviews in Mathematical Physics* **24**(7), 1250016. arXiv:1107.0453.

Jochym-O'Connor, T., Brádler, K. & Wilde, M. M. (2011), 'Trade-off coding for universal qudit cloners motivated by the Unruh effect', *Journal of Physics A: Mathematical and Theoretical* **44**(41), 415306. arXiv:1103.0286.

Jozsa, R. (1994), 'Fidelity for mixed quantum states', *Journal of Modern Optics* **41**(12), 2315–2323.

Jozsa, R., Horodecki, M., Horodecki, P. & Horodecki, R. (1998), 'Universal quantum information compression', *Physical Review Letters* **81**(8), 1714–1717. arXiv:quant-ph/9805017.

Jozsa, R. & Presnell, S. (2003), 'Universal quantum information compression and degrees of prior knowledge', *Proceedings of the Royal Society A: Mathematical, Physical and Engineering Sciences* **459**(2040), 3061–3077. arXiv:quant-ph /0210196.

Jozsa, R. & Schumacher, B. (1994), 'A new proof of the quantum noiseless coding theorem', *Journal of Modern Optics* **41**(12), 2343–2349.

Junge, M., Renner, R., Sutter, D., Wilde, M. M. & Winter, A. (2015), 'Universal recovery from a decrease of quantum relative entropy'. arXiv:1509.07127.

Kaye, P. & Mosca, M. (2001), 'Quantum networks for concentrating entanglement', *Journal of Physics A: Mathematical and General* **34**(35), 6939. arXiv:quant-ph/0101009.

Kelvin, W. T. (1901), 'Nineteenth-century clouds over the dynamical theory of heat and light', *The London, Edinburgh and Dublin Philosophical Magazine and Journal of Science* **2**(6), 1.

Kemperman, J. H. B. (1969), 'On the optimum rate of transmitting information', *Lecture Notes in Mathematics* **89**, 126–169. In Probability and Information Theory.

Kim, I. H. (2013), 'Application of conditional independence to gapped quantum many-body systems', `www.physics.usyd.edu.au/quantum/Coogee2013`. Slide 43.

King, C. (2002), 'Additivity for unital qubit channels', *Journal of Mathematical Physics* **43**(10), 4641–4653. arXiv:quant-ph/0103156.

King, C. (2003), 'The capacity of the quantum depolarizing channel', *IEEE Transactions on Information Theory* **49**(1), 221–229. arXiv:quant-ph/0204172.

King, C., Matsumoto, K., Nathanson, M. & Ruskai, M. B. (2007), 'Properties of conjugate channels with applications to additivity and multiplicativity', *Markov Processes and Related Fields* **13**(2), 391–423. J. T. Lewis memorial issue. arXiv:quant-ph/0509126.

Kitaev, A. Y. (1997), *Uspekhi Mat. Nauk.* **52**(53).

Klesse, R. (2008), 'A random coding based proof for the quantum coding theorem', *Open Systems & Information Dynamics* **15**(1), 21–45. arXiv:0712.2558.

Knill, E. H., Laflamme, R. & Zurek, W. H. (1998), 'Resilient quantum computation', *Science* **279**, 342–345. quant-ph/9610011.

Koashi, M. & Imoto, N. (2001), 'Teleportation cost and hybrid compression of quantum signals'. arXiv:quant-ph/0104001.

Koenig, R., Renner, R. & Schaffner, C. (2009), 'The operational meaning of min- and max-entropy', *IEEE Transactions on Information Theory* **55**(9), 4337–4347. arXiv:0807.1338.

Koenig, R. & Wehner, S. (2009), 'A strong converse for classical channel coding using entangled inputs', *Physical Review Letters* **103**(7), 070504. arXiv:0903.2838.

König, R., Renner, R., Bariska, A. & Maurer, U. (2007), 'Small accessible quantum information does not imply security', *Physical Review Letters* **98**(14), 140502. arXiv:quant-ph/0512021.

Kremsky, I., Hsieh, M.-H. & Brun, T. A. (2008), 'Classical enhancement of quantum-error-correcting codes', *Physical Review A* **78**(1), 012341. arXiv:0802.2414.

Kullback, S. (1967), 'A lower bound for discrimination in terms of variation', *IEEE-IT* **13**, 126–127.

Kumagai, W. & Hayashi, M. (2013), 'Entanglement concentration is irreversible', *Physical Review Letters* **111**(13), 130407. arXiv:1305.6250.

Kuperberg, G. (2003), 'The capacity of hybrid quantum memory', *IEEE Transactions on Information Theory* **49**(6), 1465–1473. arXiv:quant-ph/0203105.

Laflamme, R., Miquel, C., Paz, J. P. & Zurek, W. H. (1996), 'Perfect quantum error correcting code', *Physical Review Letters* **77**(1), 198–201.

Landauer, R. (1995), 'Is quantum mechanics useful?', *Philosophical Transactions of the Royal Society: Physical and Engineering Sciences* **353**(1703), 367–376.

Lanford, O. E. & Robinson, D. W. (1968), 'Mean entropy of states in quantum-statistical mechanics', *Journal of Mathematical Physics* **9**(7), 1120–1125.

Levitin, L. B. (1969), 'On the quantum measure of information', in *Proceedings of the Fourth All-Union Conference on Information and Coding Theory, Sec. II*, Tashkent

Li, K. & Winter, A. (2014), 'Squashed entanglement, k-extendibility, quantum Markov chains, and recovery maps'. arXiv:1410.4184.

Li, K., Winter, A., Zou, X. & Guo, G.-C. (2009), 'Private capacity of quantum channel is not additive', *Physical Review Letters* **103**(12), 120501. arXiv:0903.4308.

Lieb, E. H. (1973), 'Convex trace functions and the Wigner–Yanase–Dyson conjecture' *Advances in Mathematics* **11**, 267–288.

Lieb, E. H. & Ruskai, M. B. (1973a), 'A fundamental property of quantum-mechanical entropy', *Physical Review Letters* **30**(10), 434–436.

Lieb, E. H. & Ruskai, M. B. (1973b), 'Proof of the strong subadditivity of quantum-mechanical entropy', *Journal of Mathematical Physics* **14**, 1938–1941.

Lindblad, G. (1975), 'Completely positive maps and entropy inequalities', *Communications in Mathematical Physics* **40**(2), 147–151.

Lloyd, S. (1997), 'Capacity of the noisy quantum channel', *Physical Review A* **55**(3), 1613–1622. arXiv:quant-ph/9604015.

Lloyd, S., Giovannetti, V. & Maccone, L. (2011), 'Sequential projective measurements for channel decoding', *Physical Review Letters* **106**(25), 250501. arXiv:1012.0106.

Lo, H.-K. (1995), 'Quantum coding theorem for mixed states', *Optics Communications* **119**(5-6), 552–556. arXiv:quant-ph/9504004.

Lo, H.-K. & Popescu, S. (1999), 'Classical communication cost of entanglement manipulation: Is entanglement an interconvertible resource?', *Physical Review Letters* **83**(7), 1459–1462.

Lo, H.-K. & Popescu, S. (2001), 'Concentrating entanglement by local actions: Beyond mean values', *Physical Review A* **63**(2), 022301. arXiv:quant-ph/9707038.

Lupo, C. & Lloyd, S. (2014), 'Quantum-locked key distribution at nearly the classical capacity rate', *Physical Review Letters* **113**(16), 160502. arXiv:1406.4418.

Lupo, C. & Lloyd, S. (2015), 'Quantum data locking for high-rate private communication', *New Journal of Physics* **17**(3), 033022.

MacKay, D. (2003), *Information Theory, Inference, and Learning Algorithms*, Cambridge University Press.

Matthews, W. & Wehner, S. (2014), 'Finite blocklength converse bounds for quantum channels', *IEEE Transactions on Information Theory* **60**(11), 7317–7329. arXiv:1210.4722.

McEvoy, J. P. & Zarate, O. (2004), *Introducing Quantum Theory*, 3rd edn, Totem Books.

Misner, C. W., Thorne, K. S. & Zurek, W. H. (2009), 'John Wheeler, relativity, and quantum information', *Physics Today* .

Morgan, C. & Winter, A. (2014), '"Pretty strong" converse for the quantum capacity of degradable channels', *IEEE Transactions on Information Theory* **60**(1), 317–333. arXiv:1301.4927.

Mosonyi, M. (2005), 'Entropy, Information and Structure of Composite Quantum States', PhD thesis, Katholieke Universiteit Leuven. Available at https://lirias.kuleuven.be/bitstream/1979/41/2/thesisbook9.pdf.

Mosonyi, M. & Datta, N. (2009), 'Generalized relative entropies and the capacity of classical–quantum channels', *Journal of Mathematical Physics* **50**(7), 072104. arXiv:0810.3478.

Mosonyi, M. & Petz, D. (2004), 'Structure of sufficient quantum coarse-grainings', *Letters in Mathematical Physics* **68**(1), 19–30. arXiv:quant-ph/0312221.

Mullins, J. (2001), 'The topsy turvy world of quantum computing', *IEEE Spectrum* **38**(2), 42–49.

Nielsen, M. A. (1998), 'Quantum information theory', PhD thesis, University of New Mexico. arXiv:quant-ph/0011036.

Nielsen, M. A. (1999), 'Conditions for a class of entanglement transformations', *Physical Review Letters* **83**(2), 436–439. arXiv:quant-ph/9811053.

Nielsen, M. A. (2002), 'A simple formula for the average gate fidelity of a quantum dynamical operation', *Physics Letters A* **303**(4), 249 – 252.

Nielsen, M. A. & Chuang, I. L. (2000), *Quantum Computation and Quantum Information*, Cambridge University Press.

Ogawa, T. & Nagaoka, H. (1999), 'Strong converse to the quantum channel coding theorem', *IEEE Transactions on Information Theory* **45**(7), 2486–2489. arXiv:quant-ph/9808063.

Ogawa, T. & Nagaoka, H. (2007), 'Making good codes for classical–quantum channel coding via quantum hypothesis testing', *IEEE Transactions on Information Theory* **53**(6), 2261–2266.

Ohya, M. & Petz, D. (1993), *Quantum Entropy and Its Use*, Springer.

Ollivier, H. & Zurek, W. H. (2001), 'Quantum discord: A measure of the quantumness of correlations', *Physical Review Letters* **88**(1), 017901. arXiv:quant-ph/0105072.

Ozawa, M. (1984), 'Quantum measuring processes of continuous observables', *Journal of Mathematical Physics* **25**(1), 79–87.

Ozawa, M. (2000), 'Entanglement measures and the Hilbert–Schmidt distance', *Physics Letters A* **268**(3), 158–160. arXiv:quant-ph/0002036.

Pati, A. K. & Braunstein, S. L. (2000), 'Impossibility of deleting an unknown quantum state', *Nature* **404**, 164–165. arXiv:quant-ph/9911090.

Peres, A. (2002), 'How the no-cloning theorem got its name'. arXiv:quant-ph/0205076.

Petz, D. (1986), 'Sufficient subalgebras and the relative entropy of states of a von Neumann algebra', *Communications in Mathematical Physics* **105**(1), 123–131.

Petz, D. (1988), 'Sufficiency of channels over von Neumann algebras', *Quarterly Journal of Mathematics* **39**(1), 97–108.

Pierce, J. R. (1973), 'The early days of information theory', *IEEE Transactions on Information Theory* **IT-19**(1), 3–8.

Pinsker, M. S. (1960), 'Information and information stability of random variables and processes', *Problemy Peredaci Informacii* **7**. AN SSSR, Moscow. English translation: Holden-Day, San Francisco, CA, 1964.

Planck, M. (1901), 'Ueber das gesetz der energieverteilung im normalspectrum', *Annalen der Physik* **4**, 553–563.

Plenio, M. B., Virmani, S. & Papadopoulos, P. (2000), 'Operator monotones, the reduction criterion and the relative entropy', *Journal of Physics A: Mathematical and General* **33**(22), L193. arXiv:quant-ph/0002075.

Preskill, J. (1998), 'Reliable quantum computers', *Proceedings of the Royal Society A: Mathematical, Physical and Engineering Sciences* **454**(1969), 385–410. arXiv:quant-ph/9705031.

Radhakrishnan, J., Sen, P. & Warsi, N. (2014), 'One-shot Marton inner bound for classical–quantum broadcast channel'. arXiv:1410.3248.

Rains, E. M. (2001), 'A semidefinite program for distillable entanglement', *IEEE Transactions on Information Theory* **47**(7), 2921–2933. arXiv:quant-ph/0008047.

Reed, M. & Simon, B. (1975), *Methods of Modern Mathematical Physics II: Fourier Analysis, Self-Adjointness*, Academic Press.

Renner, R. (2005), 'Security of Quantum Key Distribution', PhD thesis, ETH Zurich. arXiv:quant-ph/0512258.

Rivest, R., Shamir, A. & Adleman, L. (1978), 'A method for obtaining digital signatures and public-key cryptosystems', *Communications of the ACM* **21**(2), 120–126.

Sakurai, J. J. (1994), *Modern Quantum Mechanics (2nd Edition)*, Addison Wesley.

Sason, I. (2013), 'Entropy bounds for discrete random variables via maximal coupling' *IEEE Transactions on Information Theory* **59**(11), 7118–7131. arXiv:1209.5259.

Savov, I. (2008), 'Distributed compression and squashed entanglement', Master's thesis, McGill University. arXiv:0802.0694.

Savov, I. (2012), 'Network information theory for classical–quantum channels', PhD thesis, McGill University, School of Computer Science. arXiv:1208.4188.

Savov, I. & Wilde, M. M. (2015), 'Classical codes for quantum broadcast channels', *IEEE Transactions on Information Theory* **61**(12), 7017–7028. arXiv:1111.3645.

Scarani, V. (2013), 'The device-independent outlook on quantum physics (lecture notes on the power of Bell's theorem)'. arXiv:1303.3081.

Scarani, V., Bechmann-Pasquinucci, H., Cerf, N. J., Dušek, M., Lütkenhaus, N. & Peev, M. (2009), 'The security of practical quantum key distribution', *Reviews of Modern Physics* **81**(3), 1301–1350. arXiv:0802.4155.

Scarani, V., Iblisdir, S., Gisin, N. & Acín, A. (2005), 'Quantum cloning', *Reviews of Modern Physics* **77**(4), 1225–1256. arXiv:quant-ph/0511088.

Schrödinger, E. (1926), 'Quantisierung als eigenwertproblem', *Annalen der Physik* **79**, 361–376.

Schrödinger, E. (1935), 'Discussion of probability relations between separated systems', *Proceedings of the Cambridge Philosophical Society* **31**, 555–563.

Schumacher, B. (1995), 'Quantum coding', *Physical Review A* **51**(4), 2738–2747.

Schumacher, B. (1996), 'Sending entanglement through noisy quantum channels', *Physical Review A* **54**(4), 2614–2628.

Schumacher, B. & Nielsen, M. A. (1996), 'Quantum data processing and error correction', *Physical Review A* **54**(4), 2629–2635. arXiv:quant-ph/9604022.

Schumacher, B. & Westmoreland, M. D. (1997), 'Sending classical information via noisy quantum channels', *Physical Review A* **56**(1), 131–138.

Schumacher, B. & Westmoreland, M. D. (1998), 'Quantum privacy and quantum coherence', *Physical Review Letters* **80**(25), 5695–5697. arXiv:quant-ph/9709058.

Schumacher, B. & Westmoreland, M. D. (2002), 'Approximate quantum error correction', *Quantum Information Processing* **1**(1/2), 5–12. arXiv:quant-ph/0112106.

Sen, P. (2011), 'Achieving the Han–Kobayashi inner bound for the quantum interference channel by sequential decoding'. arXiv:1109.0802.

Seshadreesan, K. P., Berta, M. & Wilde, M. M. (2015), 'Rényi squashed entanglement, discord, and relative entropy differences', *Journal of Physics A: Mathematical and Theoretical* **48**(39), 395303. arXiv:1410.1443.

Seshadreesan, K. P., Takeoka, M. & Wilde, M. M. (2015), 'Bounds on entanglement distillation and secret key agreement for quantum broadcast channels', *IEEE Transactions on Information Theory* **62**(5), May 2016, 2849–2866. arXiv:1503.08139.

Seshadreesan, K. P. & Wilde, M. M. (2015), 'Fidelity of recovery, squashed entanglement, and measurement recoverability', *Physical Review A* **92**(4), 042321. arXiv:1410.1441.

Shannon, C. E. (1948), 'A mathematical theory of communication', *Bell System Technical Journal* **27**, 379–423.

Shor, P. W. (1994), 'Algorithms for quantum computation: Discrete logarithms and factoring', in *Proceedings of the 35th Annual Symposium on Foundations of Computer Science*, IEEE Computer Society Press, Los Alamitos, California, pp. 124–134.

Shor, P. W. (1995), 'Scheme for reducing decoherence in quantum computer memory', *Physical Review A* **52**(4), R2493–R2496.

Shor, P. W. (1996), 'Fault-tolerant quantum computation', *Annual IEEE Symposium on Foundations of Computer Science* p. 56. arXiv:quant-ph/9605011.

Shor, P. W. (2002a), 'Additivity of the classical capacity of entanglement-breaking quantum channels', *Journal of Mathematical Physics* **43**(9), 4334–4340. arXiv:quant-ph/0201149.

Shor, P. W. (2002b), 'The quantum channel capacity and coherent information', in *Lecture Notes, MSRI Workshop on Quantum Computation*.

Shor, P. W. (2004a), 'Equivalence of additivity questions in quantum information theory', *Communications in Mathematical Physics* **246**(3), 453–472. arXiv:quant-ph/0305035.

Shor, P. W. (2004b), *Quantum Information, Statistics, Probability (Dedicated to A. S. Holevo on the occasion of his 60th Birthday): The classical capacity achievable by a quantum channel assisted by limited entanglement*, Rinton Press, Inc. arXiv:quant-ph/0402129.

Smith, G. (2006), 'Upper and Lower Bounds on Quantum Codes', PhD thesis, California Institute of Technology.

Smith, G. (2008), 'Private classical capacity with a symmetric side channel and its application to quantum cryptography', *Physical Review A* **78**(2), 022306. arXiv:0705.3838.

Smith, G., Renes, J. M. & Smolin, J. A. (2008), 'Structured codes improve the Bennett–Brassard-84 quantum key rate', *Physical Review Letters* **100**(17), 170502. arXiv:quant-ph/0607018.

Smith, G. & Smolin, J. A. (2007), 'Degenerate quantum codes for Pauli channels', *Physical Review Letters* **98**(3), 030501. arXiv:quant-ph/0604107.

Smith, G., Smolin, J. A. & Yard, J. (2011), 'Quantum communication with Gaussian channels of zero quantum capacity', *Nature Photonics* **5**, 624–627. arXiv:1102.4580.

Smith, G. & Yard, J. (2008), 'Quantum communication with zero-capacity channels', *Science* **321**(5897), 1812–1815. arXiv:0807.4935.

Steane, A. M. (1996), 'Error correcting codes in quantum theory', *Physical Review Letters* **77**(5), 793–797.

Stein, E. M. (1956), 'Interpolation of linear operators', *Transactions of the American Mathematical Society* **83**(2), 482–492.

Stinespring, W. F. (1955), 'Positive functions on C*-algebras', *Proceedings of the American Mathematical Society* **6**, 211–216.

Sutter, D., Fawzi, O. & Renner, R. (2016), 'Universal recovery map for approximate markov chains', *Proceedings of the Royal Society A* **472**(2186). arXiv:1504.07251.

Sutter, D., Tomamichel, M. & Harrow, A. W. (2015), 'Strengthened monotonicity of relative entropy via pinched Petz recovery map', *IEEE Transactions on Information Theory* **62**(5), 2016, 2907–2913. arXiv:1507.00303.

Tomamichel, M. (2012), 'A Framework for Non-Asymptotic Quantum Information Theory', PhD thesis, ETH Zurich. arXiv:1203.2142.

Tomamichel, M. (2016), *Quantum Information Processing with Finite Resources — Mathematical Foundations*, Vol. 5 of *SpringerBriefs in Mathematical Physics*. Springer. arXiv:1504.00233.

Tomamichel, M., Berta, M. & Renes, J. M. (2015), 'Quantum coding with finite resources', *Nature Communications* 7:11419 (2016). arXiv:1504.04617.

Tomamichel, M., Colbeck, R. & Renner, R. (2009), 'A fully quantum asymptotic equipartition property', *IEEE Transactions on Information Theory* **55**(12), 5840–5847. arXiv:0811.1221.

Tomamichel, M., Colbeck, R. & Renner, R. (2010), 'Duality between smooth min- and max-entropies', *IEEE Transactions on Information Theory* **56**(9), 4674–4681. arXiv:0907.5238.

Tomamichel, M. & Renner, R. (2011), 'Uncertainty relation for smooth entropies', *Physical Review Letters* **106**(11), 110506. arXiv:1009.2015.

Tomamichel, M. & Tan, V. Y. F. (2015), 'Second-order asymptotics for the classical capacity of image-additive quantum channels', *Communications in Mathematical Physics* **338**(1), 103–137. arXiv:1308.6503.

Tomamichel, M., Wilde, M. M. & Winter, A. (2014), 'Strong converse rates for quantum communication'. arXiv:1406.2946.

Tsirelson, B. S. (1980), 'Quantum generalizations of Bell's inequality', *Letters in Mathematical Physics* **4**(2), 93–100.

Tyurin, I. S. (2010), 'An improvement of upper estimates of the constants in the Lyapunov theorem', *Russian Mathematical Surveys* **65**(3), 201–202.

Uhlmann, A. (1976), 'The "transition probability" in the state space of a *-algebra', *Reports on Mathematical Physics* **9**(2), 273–279.

Uhlmann, A. (1977), 'Relative entropy and the Wigner–Yanase–Dyson–Lieb concavity in an interpolation theory', *Communications in Mathematical Physics* **54**(1), 21–32.

Umegaki, H. (1962), 'Conditional expectations in an operator algebra IV (entropy and information)', *Kodai Mathematical Seminar Reports* **14**(2), 59–85.

Unruh, W. G. (1995), 'Maintaining coherence in quantum computers', *Physical Review A* **51**(2), 992–997. arXiv:hep-th/9406058.

Vedral, V. & Plenio, M. B. (1998), 'Entanglement measures and purification procedures', *Physical Review A* **57**(3), 1619–1633. arXiv:quant-ph/9707035.

von Kretschmann, D. (2007), 'Information Transfer through Quantum Channels', PhD thesis, Technische Universität Braunschweig.

von Neumann, J. (1996), *Mathematical Foundations of Quantum Mechanics*, Princeton University Press.

Wang, L. & Renner, R. (2012), 'One-shot classical–quantum capacity and hypothesis testing', *Physical Review Letters* **108**(20), 200501. arXiv:1007.5456.

Watrous, J. (2015), *Theory of Quantum Information*. Available at https://cs.uwaterloo.ca/~watrous/TQI/.

Wehrl, A. (1978), 'General properties of entropy', *Reviews of Modern Physics* **50**(2), 221–260.

Werner, R. F. (1989), 'Quantum states with Einstein–Podolsky–Rosen correlations admitting a hidden-variable model', *Physical Review A* **40**(8), 4277–4281.

Wiesner, S. (1983), 'Conjugate coding', *SIGACT News* **15**(1), 78–88.

Wilde, M. M. (2011), 'Comment on "Secret-key-assisted private classical communication capacity over quantum channels"', *Physical Review A* **83**(4), 046303.

Wilde, M. M. (2013), 'Sequential decoding of a general classical–quantum channel', *Proceedings of the Royal Society of London A: Mathematical, Physical and Engineering Sciences* **469**(2157). arXiv:1303.0808.

Wilde, M. M. (2014), 'Multipartite quantum correlations and local recoverability', *Proceedings of the Royal Society A* **471**, 20140941. arXiv:1412.0333.

Wilde, M. M. (2015), 'Recoverability in quantum information theory', *Proceedings of the Royal Society A* **471**(2182), 20150338. arXiv:1505.04661.

Wilde, M. M. & Brun, T. A. (2008), 'Unified quantum convolutional coding', in *Proceedings of the IEEE International Symposium on Information Theory*, Toronto, Ontario, Canada, pp. 359–363. arXiv:0801.0821.

Wilde, M. M. & Guha, S. (2012), 'Explicit receivers for pure-interference bosonic multiple access channels', *Proceedings of the 2012 International Symposium on Information Theory and its Applications* pp. 303–307. arXiv:1204.0521.

Wilde, M. M., Hayden, P., Buscemi, F. & Hsieh, M.-H. (2012), 'The information-theoretic costs of simulating quantum measurements', *Journal of Physics A: Mathematical and Theoretical* **45**(45), 453001. arXiv:1206.4121.

Wilde, M. M., Hayden, P. & Guha, S. (2012a), 'Information trade-offs for optical quantum communication', *Physical Review Letters* **108**(14), 140501. arXiv:1105.0119.

Wilde, M. M., Hayden, P. & Guha, S. (2012b), 'Quantum trade-off coding for bosonic communication', *Physical Review A* **86**(6), 062306. arXiv:1105.0119.

Wilde, M. M. & Hsieh, M.-H. (2010), 'Entanglement generation with a quantum channel and a shared state', *Proceedings of the 2010 IEEE International Symposium on Information Theory* pp. 2713–2717. arXiv:0904.1175.

Wilde, M. M. & Hsieh, M.-H. (2012a), 'Public and private resource trade-offs for a quantum channel', *Quantum Information Processing* **11**(6), 1465–1501. arXiv:1005.3818.

Wilde, M. M. & Hsieh, M.-H. (2012b), 'The quantum dynamic capacity formula of a quantum channel', *Quantum Information Processing* **11**(6), 1431–1463. arXiv:1004.0458.

Wilde, M. M., Krovi, H. & Brun, T. A. (2007), 'Coherent communication with continuous quantum variables', *Physical Review A* **75**(6), 060303(R). arXiv:quant-ph/0612170.

Wilde, M. M., Renes, J. M. & Guha, S. (2016), 'Second-order coding rates for pure-loss bosonic channels', *Quantum Information Processing* **15**(3), 1289–1308. arXiv:1408.5328.

Wilde, M. M. & Savov, I. (2012), 'Joint source-channel coding for a quantum multiple access channel', *Journal of Physics A: Mathematical and Theoretical* **45**(43), 435302. arXiv:1202.3467.

Wilde, M. M. & Winter, A. (2014), 'Strong converse for the quantum capacity of the erasure channel for almost all codes', *Proceedings of the 9th Conference on the Theory of Quantum Computation, Communication and Cryptography* . arXiv:1402.3626.

Wilde, M. M., Winter, A. & Yang, D. (2014), 'Strong converse for the classical capacity of entanglement-breaking and Hadamard channels via a sandwiched

Rényi relative entropy', *Communications in Mathematical Physics* **331**(2), 593–62? arXiv:1306.1586.

Winter, A. (1999a), 'Coding theorem and strong converse for quantum channels', *IEE. Transactions on Information Theory* **45**(7), 2481–2485. arXiv:1409.2536.

Winter, A. (1999b), 'Coding Theorems of Quantum Information Theory', PhD thesis Universität Bielefeld. arXiv:quant-ph/9907077.

Winter, A. (2001), 'The capacity of the quantum multiple access channel', *IEEE Transactions on Information Theory* **47**(7), 3059–3065. arXiv:quant-ph/9807019.

Winter, A. (2004), '"Extrinsic" and "intrinsic" data in quantum measurements: asymptotic convex decomposition of positive operator valued measures', *Communication in Mathematical Physics* **244**(1), 157–185. arXiv:quant-ph/0109050.

Winter, A. (2007), 'The maximum output p-norm of quantum channels is not multiplicative for any $p > 2$'. arXiv:0707.0402.

Winter, A. (2015a), 'Tight uniform continuity bounds for quantum entropies: conditional entropy, relative entropy distance and energy constraints'. arXiv:1507.07775.

Winter, A. (2015b), 'Weak locking capacity of quantum channels can be much larger than private capacity', *Journal of Cryptology* pp. 1–21. arXiv:1403.6361.

Winter, A. & Li, K. (2012), 'A stronger subadditivity relation?', `www.maths.bris.ac.uk/$\sim$csajw/stronger$_$subadditivity.pdf`.

Winter, A. & Massar, S. (2001), 'Compression of quantum-measurement operations', *Physical Review A* **64**(1), 012311. arXiv:quant-ph/0012128.

Wolf, M. M., Cubitt, T. S. & Perez-Garcia, D. (2011), 'Are problems in quantum information theory (un)decidable?'. arXiv:1111.5425.

Wolf, M. M. & Pérez-García, D. (2007), 'Quantum capacities of channels with small environment', *Physical Review A* **75**(1), 012303. arXiv:quant-ph/0607070.

Wolf, M. M., Pérez-García, D. & Giedke, G. (2007), 'Quantum capacities of bosonic channels', *Physical Review Letters* **98**(13), 130501. arXiv:quant-ph/0606132.

Wolfowitz, J. (1978), *Coding theorems of information theory*, Springer-Verlag.

Wootters, W. K. & Zurek, W. H. (1982), 'A single quantum cannot be cloned', *Nature* **299**, 802–803.

Wyner, A. D. (1975), 'The wire-tap channel', *Bell System Technical Journal* **54**(8), 1355–1387.

Yard, J. (2005), 'Simultaneous classical–quantum capacities of quantum multiple access channels', PhD thesis, Stanford University, Stanford, CA. arXiv:quant-ph/0506050.

Yard, J. & Devetak, I. (2009), 'Optimal quantum source coding with quantum side information at the encoder and decoder', *IEEE Transactions on Information Theory* **55**(11), 5339–5351. arXiv:0706.2907.

Yard, J., Devetak, I. & Hayden, P. (2005), 'Capacity theorems for quantum multiple access channels', in *Proceedings of the International Symposium on Information Theory*, Adelaide, Australia, pp. 884–888. arXiv:cs/0508031.

Yard, J., Hayden, P. & Devetak, I. (2008), 'Capacity theorems for quantum multiple-access channels: Classical–quantum and quantum–quantum capacity regions', *IEEE Transactions on Information Theory* **54**(7), 3091–3113. arXiv:quant-ph/0501045.

Yard, J., Hayden, P. & Devetak, I. (2011), 'Quantum broadcast channels', *IEEE Transactions on Information Theory* **57**(10), 7147–7162. arXiv:quant-ph/0603098.

Ye, M.-Y., Bai, Y.-K. & Wang, Z. D. (2008), 'Quantum state redistribution based on a generalized decoupling', *Physical Review A* **78**(3), 030302. arXiv:0805.1542.

Yen, B. J. & Shapiro, J. H. (2005), 'Multiple-access bosonic communications', *Physical Review A* **72**(6), 062312. arXiv:quant-ph/0506171.

Yeung, R. W. (2002), *A First Course in Information Theory*, Information Technology: Transmission, Processing, and Storage, Springer (Kluwer Academic/Plenum Publishers), New York, NY.

Zhang, L. (2014), 'A lower bound of quantum conditional mutual information', *J. Phys. A: Math. Theor.* **47** (2014) 415303. arXiv:1403.1424.

Zhang, Z. (2007), 'Estimating mutual information via Kolmogorov distance', *IEEE Transactions on Information Theory* **53**(9), 3280–3282.

Zurek, W. H. (2000), 'Einselection and decoherence from an information theory perspective', *Annalen der Physik* **9**(11–12), 855–864. arXiv:quant-ph/0011039.

Index

Printed in the United States
By Bookmasters